W9-BLM-321

The Holocaust and World War II Almanac

The Holocaust and World War II Almanac

Volume 1

PEGGY SAARI
AARON MAURICE SAARI
Editors

KATHLEEN J. EDGAR
ELLICE ENGDAHL
Coordinating Editors

BOCA RATON PUBLIC LIBRARY
BOCA RATON, FLORIDA

GALE GROUP

Detroit
New York
San Francisco
London
Boston
Woodbridge, CT

Edited by Peggy Saari and Aaron Maurice Saari

Staff

Kathleen J. Edgar, *Senior Coordinating Editor*
Ellice Engdahl, *Coordinating Editor*

Julie Carnagie, Elizabeth Des Chenes, Elizabeth Manar, Christine Slovey, *Contributing Editors*
Barbara C. Bigelow, Susan E. Edgar, George Feldman, Kelly King Howes, Lorie Jenkins McElroy, Mary Kay Rosteck, Linda Schmittroth, Christine Tomassini, *Contributing Writers*
Debra M. Kirby, *Managing Editor*
Thomas Romig, *Program Director*

Rita Wimberley, *Senior Buyer*
Dorothy Maki, *Manufacturing Manager*
Evi Seoud, *Assistant Manager, Composition Purchasing and Electronic Prepress*
Mary Beth Trimper, *Manager, Composition and Electronic Prepress*

Debra J. Freitas, *Permissions Associate*
Cynthia Baldwin, *Art Director*
Barbara J. Yarrow, *Manager, Imaging and Multimedia Content*

Marco Di Vita, Graphix Group, *Typesetting*
Laura Exner, XNR Productions, Inc., *Cartographer*
Katherine Clymer, *Indexer*

Library of Congress Cataloging-in-Publication Data

The Holocaust and World War II Almanac / editors, Peggy Saari, Aaron Maurice
Saari; coordinating editors, Kathleen J. Edgar, Ellice Engdahl
    p. cm.
  Includes bibliographical references and index.
  ISBN 0-7876-5018-8 (set: hardcover)—ISBN 0-7876-5019-6 (v.1)—ISBN 0-7876-5020-X (v.2)—ISBN 0-7876-5063-3 (v.3)
  1. Holocaust, Jewish (1939-1945). 2. World War, 1939-1945. 3. Holocaust, Jewish (1939-1945)—Biography. 4. World War, 1939-1945—Biography. I. Saari, Peggy. II. Saari, Aaron Maurice.

D804.17.H65 2000
940.53'18—dc21

00-046647

Front cover photos reproduced by permission of Corbis Corporation [Bellevue], Hulton Getty/Liaison Agency, and AP/Wide World Photos; others from Main Commission for the Investigation of Nazi War Crimes and National Archives and Records Administration.

While every effort has been made to ensure the reliability of the information presented in this publication, Gale Group, Inc. does not guarantee the accuracy of the data contained herein. Gale Group, Inc. accepts no payment for listing; and inclusion in the publication of any organization, agency, institution, publication, service, or individual does not imply endorsement of the publisher. Errors brought to the attention of the publisher and verified to the satisfaction of the publisher will be corrected in future editions.

This publication is a creative work fully protected by all applicable copyright laws, as well as by misappropriation, trade secret, unfair competition, and other applicable laws. The author and editors of this work have added value to the underlying factual material herein through one or more of the following: unique and original selection, coordination, expression, arrangement, and classification of the information. All rights to this publication will be vigorously defended.

© 2001
Gale Group, Inc., 27500 Drake Road, Farmington Hills, MI 48331-3535

Gale Group and Design is a trademark used herein under license.

All rights reserved, including the right of reproduction in whole or in part in any form.

Printed in the United States of America
10 9 8 7 6 5 4 3 2 1

Table of Contents

Advisory Board

The editors would like to thank the following members of *The Holocaust and World War II Almanac* advisory board for their invaluable assistance.

Armando Delicato majored in history as an undergraduate at the University of Detroit and earned a Masters of Arts in twentieth-century European history at Wayne State University. After teaching history at public schools and at community colleges in Michigan, he earned a degree in library science and is currently a media specialist at North Farmington High School in Michigan.

William J. Munday is a U.S. Navy veteran who has worked or volunteered at various museums and historical sites throughout the country. A military historian, he has studied the subject for more than thirty years. He is a member of several historical and veterans societies, including the Company of Military Historians and the Great Lakes Living History Society. In his spare time, he gives talks and historical demonstrations to students and the public.

Kathy Gillespie Tomajko is Head of Reference Services at the Library and Information Center at Georgia Institute of Technology in Atlanta, Georgia. She was formerly Information Consultant for the School of History, Technology and Society at Georgia Institute of Technology. She is an active member of professional associations, including the American Library Association and Special Libraries Association, and is a past member of publisher advisory committees for the *Internet Reference Services Quarterly* journal, and for the Information Access Company (IAC).

Lynn Whitehouse is Librarian IV at the San Diego Central Library. She supervises the History/Information and Interlibrary Loan sections and is responsible for much of the cultural programming.

Reader's Guide

Between 1939 and 1945, World War II was fought among all the major powers of the world. By the end of the war, more than fifty countries had become involved in the conflict. The scope and brutality of the war greatly impacted the world—more people died during the conflict than in any previous war, and the war changed the political, social, and economic climates of the entire world. *The Holocaust and World War II Almanac* provides a comprehensive range of historical information as well as current studies on World War II and the Holocaust. The three-volume set includes extensive information about the European and Pacific theaters of war as well as the Holocaust. The work also provides biographical profiles of more than 100 men and women who played key or lesser-known roles in the war, whether as civilians or soldiers. Interspersed throughout volumes 1 and 2 are primary sources, which give the reader access to the writings or words of the actual participants in the war or the Holocaust. The primary source documents, complete with introduction and aftermath sections, can be found at the end of the chapter in which that topic is mainly discussed. Each primary source contains enough information for the reader to understand what was happening around the time of the event or topic being described in the source. Information about such events or topics is often restated in the primary source section so that the reader does not have to refer to previous material in the chapter or volume.

Volume 1 begins by exploring the events after World War I (1914–1918) and how certain actions led to the rise of Nazism in Germany, Fascism in Italy, militarism in Japan, and isolationism in the United States. The volume shows how conditions after World War I ultimately led to the Holocaust and World War II. It also details how some world leaders attempted to provoke war while others tried to avoid it; how relationships formed among the Allied countries and among the Axis powers; how Jews, Roma (Gypsies), political prisoners, and others were persecuted by the Nazis and stripped of their rights; how the Nazis were able to conquer so many European countries in a relatively short amount of time; how the war in the Pacific began; how Jews were rounded up for resettlement and sent to ghettos, then labor camps and ultimately death camps; and how the Allies joined forces to thwart the expansion of the German and Japanese empires, which had caused much death among the civilian populations in conquered countries.

Volume 2 continues the story of the war and the Holocaust. The work discusses the Allied invasion of France; life on the home front; spies, secrets, and codes; major turning points in the war, including further fighting in France and the Pacific; the defeat of Nazi Germany and the liberation of the death camps; the use of two atomic bombs and the surrender of Japan; the plight of displaced persons; the Nuremberg Trials; recovery after the war; and memorials for the dead. The volume contains four appendices: A) Jewish Victims of the Holocaust—explains that the number of reported Holocaust victims is different in various sources and discusses some of the reasons why the numbers can never be more precise. B) Nuremberg War Crime Trials—provides detailed information on many of the Nuremberg Trials and includes a chart indicating defendants' names, sentences, and the outcomes. C) Japanese War Crimes—The Tokyo Trials—describes the nature of the trials, the tribunal convened to hear the cases, and the defendants brought to stand trial and why. D) World War II and Holocaust Film Overview—presents a brief look at many of the films devoted to the World War II era, including those produced during the conflict and those being released in recent years, plus many issued in between.

Volume 3 offers the life stories of more than 100 individuals who played a role in World War II and the Holocaust. The biographees were selected in order to present a diversity of wartime experiences, from Axis and Allied leaders to death camp survivors to women on the home front. The subjects include political and military leaders, enlisted men and women, and civilians, including journalists, musicians, and diarists. The volume includes readily recognizable figures, such as U.S. President Franklin D. Roosevelt, British Prime Minister Winston Churchill, Japanese Premier Hideki Tōjō, Soviet leader Joseph Stalin, and Nazi führer Adolf Hitler. The work also features Holocaust survivors, including Renée Roth-Hano, Elie Wiesel, and Simon Wiesenthal; military leaders such as American General Dwight D. Eisenhower, German Army General Erwin Rommel, British Field Marshal Bernard Montgomery, and American Women's Army Corps Director Oveta Culp Hobby; Holocaust victims such as Jewish teenager Anne Frank and Polish photographer Mendel Grossman; journalists/artists, including Edward R. Murrow, Ernie Pyle, Margaret Bourke-White, and Bill Mauldin; Holocaust rescuers such as Miep Gies, Chiune (Sempo) Sugihara, Corrie ten Boom, and Raoul Wallenberg; and Nazi officials Adolf Eichmann, Heinrich Himmler, and others. Also profiled are lesser known people, including American pacifist Jeannette Rankin, Austrian conscientious objector Franz Jaggerstatter, and Hungarian resistance fighter Hannah Senesh (Szenes). In order to include a diversity of experiences, the editors have provided several composite biographies as well on groups of people such as the Comfort Women, Rosie the Riveter, the Navajo Code Talkers, and the Tuskegee Airmen.

Each volume begins with a research and activities section, glossary, and a timeline of events and noteworthy achievements by some of the people profiled in this set. The *Holocaust and World War II Almanac* contains some 800 images, including black-and-white photographs, maps, and illustrations. Due to the nature of this work, some of the photos depict the dead or wounded as well as acts of brutality. Please view them at your own discretion. Chapters and biographies contain sidebars of related information—some focusing on people associated with the war, others taking a closer look at pivotal events. Individual bibliographies appear after each primary source entry and after all biographies. Comprehensive bibliographies appear at the back of each volume as well, followed by a cumulative index for all three volumes.

On occasion, readers might note differences in figures reported in primary sources and the text. This occurs because scholars continue to study the Holocaust and World War II era, seeking to uncover more information about that period. Historians continue to attempt to calculate precisely the total number of losses, in terms of people, resources, and property. As such, the most recent estimates were unknown when the primary sources were written years ago. As noted in Appendix A: Jewish Victims of the Holocaust, historians are unable give an exact figure because of the nature of the war and the way the "Final Solution" was conducted. Records simply do not exist for each individual who was believed to have been killed. The same logic applies to those fighting in Resistance movements and the armed services, as well as those civilians killed while defending their homelands. Plus, not all countries used the same methods for tracking those who died. In some areas, people were buried in mass graves without identification; many of those murdered at death camps were cremated, leaving no trace of their existence. In addition, estimated losses vary significantly between authoritative sources. In this work, the editors have tried to present the most commonly accepted ranges.

Acknowledgements

The editors wish to extend their gratitude to Nancy A. Edgar and Jennifer Keirans for their invaluable assistance during the compilation of this project. Thanks are also extended to the Reader's Advisor team for its support, including Beverly Baer, Dana Ferguson, Nancy Franklin, Robert Franzino, Prindle LaBarge, Charlie Montney, and

Kathy Meek. Special thanks to the Imaging department, including Dean Dauphinais, Senior Editor; Robyn V. Young, Project Manager; Kelly A. Quin, Editor; Leitha Etheridge-Sims, Mary K. Grimes, and David G. Oblender, Image Catalogers; Pam A. Reed, Imaging Coordinator; Randy Bassett, Imaging Supervisor; Robert Duncan, Senior Imaging Specialist; Dan Newell, Imaging Specialist; and Christine O'Bryan, Graphic Specialist. Additional thanks are extended to Larry Baker and Barbara McNeil.

Comments and Suggestions

The Holocaust and World War II Almanac staff welcomes your comments and suggestions for other topics in history to consider for future projects. Please write: Editors, *The Holocaust and World War II Almanac,* Gale Group, 27500 Drake Rd., Farmington Hills, MI 48331-3535; call toll-free: 1-800-347-4253; or send email via http://www.gale group.com.

Timeline

1871 Germany is unified under the domination of the state of Prussia, and the German empire is ruled by a kaiser.

1899 Houston Stewart Chamberlain publishes *The Foundations of the Nineteenth Century,* a book that uses racial theory to explain European history.

1903 Russian anti-Semites circulate *The Protocols of the Elders of Zion,* a forgery that describes the master plan of an alleged Jewish conspiracy to dominate the world.

1914 World War I begins in Europe. At that time, it is known as the Great War.

1916 Jeannette Rankin becomes the first woman elected to the U.S. Congress; she immediately causes controversy by voting against her country's entry into World War I. About 50 other Congressmen vote against war as well, but the focus is on Rankin, the only female member of Congress.

1917 The czar is overthrown in Russia and a Communist government ascends to power after the Bolshevik Revolution. The Russian empire is eventually renamed the Union of Soviet Socialist Republics (USSR), commonly known as the Soviet Union.

1918 The German army is defeated by the Allies in World War I and revolution breaks out in Germany. The kaiser is overthrown and a republic is proclaimed on November 9. The new government agrees to an armistice, ending the war, on November 11.

1919 During the month of June, Adolf Hitler joins the small German Workers' party in Munich. The party soon changes its name to the National Socialist German Workers' party (NSDAP), more commonly known as the Nazi party.

On June 23, Germany signs the Treaty of Versailles. The treaty removes some territory from German control, severely limits the size of the nation's armed forces, and requires Germany to pay reparations and accept guilt for causing World War I. Extreme nationalist groups in Germany blame socialists, communists, and Jews for Germany's defeat.

Communist revolutions in various parts of Germany are put down with much bloodshed.

1920 The League of Nations is formed.

1922 Benito Mussolini and his Fascist party march on Rome. Mussolini is named premier of Italy and eventually establishes a dictatorship that becomes a model for Hitler's Third Reich.

1923 Hyperinflation hits Germany; German currency becomes worthless, causing severe economic distress.

During the year, Alfred Rosenberg reissues an official Nazi party version of *The Protocols of the Elders of Zion*.

In November Adolf Hitler leads a failed attempt to overthrow the German government. Police end the rebellion, called the Munich Beer-Hall Putsch, by arresting Hitler and the other leaders of the party. Sixteen Nazis are killed and others wounded.

1924 At his trial for treason and armed rebellion as a result of the Beer-Hall Putsch, Adolf Hitler gains the attention of extreme nationalists. While serving only eight months of a five-year prison sentence, Hitler dictates his book *Mein Kampf* ("My Struggle"), which outlines his racial beliefs about the superiority of the German people and the inferiority of Jews.

1926 Germany joins the League of Nations.

Anti-Semitic Catholic priest Charles Coughlin broadcasts his first radio sermon in the United States.

Hirohito becomes emperor of Japan, calling his reign "Showa" (meaning "enlightened peace").

1927 Chiang Kai-Shek establishes the Kuomintang (Nationalist) government in Nanking (Nanjing), China.

1928 The Nazi party receives about 800,000 votes—2.6 percent of the total—in national elections.

1929 The Great Depression begins; it will not end until 1939. The worldwide economic depression hits Germany especially hard.

1930 The Nazi party receives almost 6.5 million votes in national elections and becomes the second-largest party in the Reichstag, or German parliament. As part of highly organized campaign tactics, storm troopers (members of the Sturmabteilung or SA) attack opponents, break up meetings, and intimidate Jews and political dissidents.

1931 Vidkun Quisling is one of the cofounders of the Nordic Folk Awakening movement in Norway, which advocates many of the same ideas and principles as Germany's Nazi party.

The Japanese army seizes Manchuria in a short war with China, establishing Manchuria as the "independent" country of Manchukuo, actually controlled by the Japanese.

American journalist Dorothy Thompson interviews Adolf Hitler, a rising German politician, for *Cosmopolitan* magazine.

1932 Although Adolf Hitler receives 11 million votes in July in the first round of elections for German president, and more than 13 million votes (almost 37 percent) in the second round, Paul von Hindenburg, aged military hero of World War I, is reelected president. The SA is briefly banned because of its use of increased violence during the campaign.

1933 Adolf Hitler becomes chancellor of Germany on January 30. Although much of the government at the time is composed of old-line conservatives who believe they can use the Nazis, within a few months Hitler and the Nazi party have taken control of the country.

The Reichstag building is set ablaze on February 27, and Hitler receives emergency powers from President Paul von Hindenburg. Freedoms of speech and of the press are restricted. Acting as police, storm troopers arrest 10,000 opponents of the Nazis, especially Communists.

On March 4, 1933, Franklin D. Roosevelt begins the first of four terms as president of the United States.

Joseph Goebbels is appointed Hitler's minister of enlightenment and propaganda.

Dachau, the first permanent concentration camp, is opened in a suburb of Munich in March. Communists are among the first 10,000 opponents of the Nazis who are arrested and sent to the new camps.

The new Reichstag meets without Communist members, who have been arrested or are in hiding. The Nazis and their allies win support from the Catholic parties and pass the Enabling Act, giving Adolf Hitler dictatorial powers.

In April Nazis organize a national boycott of Jewish-owned businesses. Inge Deutschkron, a young Jewish girl living Berlin, witnesses the boycott. The first anti-Jewish laws are also passed, removing almost all Jews from government jobs, including teaching positions. Further laws follow, and by the end of the year, 53,000 Jews leave Germany.

German labor unions are abolished and replaced by the German Labor Front, run by the Nazis. The Social Democratic party (the largest party before the Nazi rise to power) is outlawed; all other parties follow.

Homosexual researcher Magnus Hirschfeld's Institute for Sexual Science in Berlin is destroyed by the Nazis.

The Nazis conduct public book burnings of works written by Jews and anti-Nazis and impose censorship throughout Germany.

1934 Adolf Hitler orders the murder of SA leader Ernst Röhm and his supporters in what has become known as the Night of the Long Knives, June 30.

Upon the death of German President Paul von Hindenburg, Adolf Hitler combines the offices of chancellor and president, becoming führer, or leader, of the Third Reich, with absolute power. All army officers and soldiers swear allegiance to Hitler.

Adolf Hitler orders American journalist Dorothy Thompson out of Germany, giving her twenty-four hours to leave the country.

Harry S Truman is elected to the U.S. Senate and begins to build a reputation as an effective leader.

1935 On March 16, Germany announces the reintroduction of the military draft and a major expansion of its army, violating the Treaty of Versailles.

German film director Leni Riefenstahl's *Triumph des Willens* (*Triumph of the Will*) premieres. The documentary of a 1934 Nazi party rally at Nuremberg later gains fame as a blatant propaganda film.

Germany passes the Nuremberg Laws, drafted by Wilhelm Frick, which define Jews in racial terms, strip them of German citizenship, and ban marriages and sexual relationships between Jews and non-Jews.

Italy invades Ethiopia on October 3. On May 5, 1936, Ethiopia surrenders.

1936 On March 7, the German army enters the Rhineland, an area of western Germany that had been demilitarized by the Treaty of Versailles.

During the month of March, participation in the Hitler Youth organization becomes mandatory. All ten-year-old boys are required to register at government offices for membership.

The Spanish Civil War begins in July.

Adolf Hitler and the Nazis temporarily ease anti-Jewish actions as the Olympic Games open in Berlin, Germany.

Germany and Italy enter into agreements that develop into a political and military alliance called the Rome-Berlin Axis.

Germany and Japan sign the Anti-Comintern Treaty.

1937 In the first example of aerial bombing against a civilian population, the German air force bombs Guernica, Spain, on April 26, aiding Francisco Franco's fascist troops during the Spanish Civil War.

Neville Chamberlain becomes British prime minister.

Buchenwald concentration camp is established, July 16, 1937.

During the month of July, Japan invades China, capturing Peking (Beijing), Shanghai, Canton, and other major cities. In Nanking (Nanjing), invading Japanese troops rape, torture, and murder tens of thousands of Chinese civilians. This event became known as the "Rape of Nanking."

Karl Koch becomes commandant of the Buchenwald concentration camp, and his wife, Ilse, receives the nickname "the Beast of Buchenwald" as she begins to terrorize prisoners.

1938 Austrians vote in favor of *Anschluss,* an agreement that makes their country part of Nazi Germany. The German army moves into Austria, and crowds cheer Hitler as he enters Vienna. Anti-Semitic laws rapidly go into effect.

Jewish psychotherapist Bruno Bettelheim is arrested by the Nazis and placed in the Dachau concentration camp.

An international conference is held in Évian, France, to discuss the plight of Jewish refugees in Europe. No solutions are found to resolve the crisis.

Europe is at the brink of war as Adolf Hitler makes territorial demands on Czechoslovakia. At a conference in Munich in September, leaders of France and Great Britain agree to grant Germany a section of Czechoslovakia with a large German-speaking population. British Prime Minister Neville Chamberlain signs the Munich Pact with Adolf Hitler, who will soon break his promise not to invade Czechoslovakia.

In Paris, Herschel Grynszpan, a young Jew, shoots and kills Ernst vom Rath, a German embassy official. Grynszpan's actions spark *Kristallnacht* ("Crystal Night" or the "Night of Broken Glass")—a series of organized Nazi attacks throughout Germany in which Jews are beaten, synagogues are burned, Jewish homes and businesses are destroyed, and 30,000 Jewish men are arrested and sent to concentration camps. *New York Times* reporter Otto D. Tolischus alerts the world to Nazi aggression in his account of *Kristallnacht.*

Italian dictator Benito Mussolini adopts the anti-Jewish laws of Adolf Hitler.

First nuclear fission of uranium is produced.

1939 Eugenio Pacelli becomes Pope Pius XII.

Hitler violates the Munich agreement by taking over the remainder of Czechoslovakia by March, and implements anti-Semitic measures there.

The Spanish Civil War ends on March 31.

In accordance with the principles of the Jehovah's Witnesses, young Elisabeth Kusserow refuses to salute the Nazi flag in spring 1939 and is sent to reform school for six years.

Several hundred Jews attempt to emigrate from Germany on board the steamship *St. Louis* in May, but are forced to return to Europe.

During the course of the year, Wilhelmine Haferkamp and other fertile German women receive the Mother's Cross, a medal honoring their Aryan child-bearing accomplishments.

German-born physicist Albert Einstein, at the urging of colleague Leo Szilard, writes a letter to U.S. President Franklin D. Roosevelt, urging American development of an atomic bomb.

On August 23, Germany and the Soviet Union sign the Nazi-Soviet Pact. The two countries promise not to attack each other and secretly agree to divide Poland after it is conquered by Germany.

U.S. General George C. Marshall is sworn in as chief of staff, the highest office in the U.S. Army.

World War II officially begins when Germany invades Poland on September 1; two days later, Great Britain and France declare war on Germany. Poland surrenders to Germany on September 27.

The Nazi euthanasia program begins. In time, 70,000 mentally and physically disabled Germans, including children, are murdered by Nazi doctors and their staffs.

On September 21, Reinhard Heydrich, second in command of the SS, issues a directive to Nazi task forces ordering the "resettlement" of Jewish Poles to urban centers (specifically ghettos) near railroad lines.

In October Adolf Hitler appoints Hans Frank governor-general of certain sections of Poland that later become the "resettlement" areas for Jews and others the Nazis deem unfit for Reich citizenship.

Great Britain begins evacuating children from London to rural towns during the month of November in order to protect them from potential German air raids.

On November 23, Jews in German-occupied Poland are ordered to wear the yellow Star of David on their clothing at all times.

1940 The Lódz ghetto is created in Poland in February, and sealed in April. Jewish photographer Mendel Grossman begins to capture pictures of life there.

On April 10, Germany invades Norway and Denmark. Denmark soon surrenders, but fighting continues in Norway, where Norwegian troops are aided by British and French forces. The Norwegian government flees to Great Britain.

Heinrich Himmler, head of the SS, orders the building of a concentration camp at Auschwitz in occupied Poland.

Winston Churchill becomes prime minister of Great Britain on May 10.

Germany invades the Netherlands, Belgium, Luxembourg, and France on May 10. Luxembourg capitulates shortly after the invasion, the Netherlands surrenders on May 14, and Belgium gives in on May 28.

Italy declares war on France and Great Britain, and invades France on June 10.

French troops evacuate Paris on June 13 and German forces take the city the next day. France signs an armistice with Germany on June 22 and German troops occupy northern France, while a government friendly to Germany (Vichy France) maintains some independence in the south.

Anti-Jewish measures soon begin in western European countries controlled by Germany.

The Germans begin bombing Great Britain in a long air campaign known as the Battle of Britain. American radio journalist Edward R. Murrow broadcasts dramatic reports about the Nazi air raids over London. Defeated by the fighter pilots of the British Royal Air Force (RAF), however, Hitler eventually abandons plans to invade Great Britain.

Field Marshal Philippe Pétain is appointed head of the German-controlled Vichy government in France. He is later convicted of collaborating with the Nazis.

Japanese diplomat Chiune Sugihara, head of the Japanese embassy in Kaunas, Lithuania, disobeys orders and issues transit visas to thousands of refugees.

Italy invades Egypt on September 14.

Germany, Japan, and Italy sign a military alliance called the Tripartite Pact. Within six months, Hungary, Romania, Slovakia, and Bulgaria also join the alliance.

Benjamin O. Davis, Sr., becomes the first African American general in the U.S. Army.

Italy invades Greece.

The Warsaw ghetto in Poland is sealed and nearly 450,000 Jews, including Janina David and her family, are confined within its walls. Chaim A. Kaplan records his observations of the sealing of the ghetto in his diary, later published as *Scroll of Agony*.

American journalist Ernie Pyle arrives in London to report on the war in England.

1941 Germany sends General Erwin Rommel to North Africa in February so that his Afrika Korps can help Italy with its invasion of the area. The seesaw battle for territory will continue until May 1943, when the Germans surrender to the Allies, ending the war in Africa.

A ghetto in Kraków is decreed, established, and sealed, between March 3 and March 20.

The U.S. Congress passes the Lend-Lease Act, signed by President Franklin D. Roosevelt, on March 11. It provides war aid to Great Britain, and later to the Soviet Union and other countries.

The Nazi government orders Franziska Schwarz, a deaf German woman, to appear at a health center for sterilization on March 21. The first attempt (in 1935) had failed.

As German forces attack Yugoslavia, Josip Broz Tito calls for unified resistance to German occupation and begins to organize the Partisans.

On April 13, Japan and the Soviet Union sign a treaty promising that neither will attack the other.

Rudolf Hess makes a flight to Great Britain with the hope of persuading the British to side with Germany in World War II.

Oveta Culp Hobby is named director of the new Women's Auxiliary Army Corps (WAAC), which will eventually be made part of the U.S. Army and renamed the Women's Army Corps (WAC).

The HMS *Hood* is sunk by the German battleship *Bismarck* on May 24. Only three of the 1,400 members of the *Hood* crew survive.

On May 27, the British Royal Navy tracks down the German battleship *Bismarck*. After repeated attacks, the *Bismarck* is sunk, and more than 2,000 German sailors on board die.

American pilot Jackie Cochran flies a Hudson V bomber plane from Canada to Great Britain, becoming the first woman to fly a military aircraft over the Atlantic Ocean.

On June 22, Germany invades the Soviet Union in an offensive called Operation Barbarossa and quickly takes control of much of the country. Special murder squads known as Einsatzgruppen follow the German army into the Soviet Union to eliminate Jews, political dissidents, and others.

In July the United States bans trade with Japan.

Hermann Göring, second to Hitler in Nazi hierarchy, gives Reinhard Heydrich the authority "to carry out all necessary preparations … for a total solution of the Jewish question" throughout Nazi-controlled Europe.

After pressure from the Japanese government, the Vichy French government allows Japan to establish bases in the southern part of French Indochina (Vietnam).

British Prime Minister Winston Churchill and U.S. President Franklin D. Roosevelt meet aboard a warship off the coast of the British colony of Newfoundland (now a province of Canada) in August and issue the Atlantic Charter, in which they agree to promote peace and democracy around the world.

Rudolf Höss, commandant of the Auschwitz concentration camp, oversees the first experiments using poisonous gas for the mass extermination of humans. The first victims of gassing are 600 Soviet prisoners of war and 250 Poles.

Kiev, the capital of the Ukraine, falls to the German army on September 19. More than 33,000 Jews are murdered at Babi Yar outside Kiev on September 29 and 30.

During October, construction begins on Birkenau (Auschwitz II) in Poland.

On October 17, Hideki Tōjō becomes premier of Japan.

Avraham Tory, a Lithuanian Jew, survives an October 28 Nazi-ordered action that removes nearly 10,000 people, about half of whom are children, from the Kovno ghetto.

In Poland, the construction of an extermination camp at Belzec begins on November 1.

Gonda Redlich arrives at the ghetto in Theresienstadt, Czechoslovakia, a Nazi "model Jewish settlement," during December.

Japan bombs the U.S. naval base at Pearl Harbor, Hawaii, on December 7. The United States and Great Britain declare war on Japan the next day. Japan's allies, Germany and Italy, declare war on the United States on December 11, and the United States declares war on them in return.

Jeannette Rankin becomes the only member of the U.S. Congress to vote against American involvement in World War II.

The death camp at Chelmno, in the western part of Poland, begins operation. Jews are gassed in sealed vans.

British troops in Hong Kong surrender to the Japanese on December 25.

1942 Rationing begins in the United States. In January, rationing of rubber is announced, sugar is rationed in May, and by the end of the year, gasoline is also being rationed.

Manila, capital of the Philippines, surrenders to the Japanese on January 2.

Despite having a transit visa, Jewish psychotherapist Viktor E. Frankl remains in Vienna with his parents, who are unable to procure visas, and is sent to a concentration camp in early 1942. Before the war ends, he is transferred to other camps.

Reinhard Heydrich calls the Wannsee Conference, where the "Final Solution," a plan to eliminate all European Jews, is transmitted to various branches of the German government.

In the month of February, the U.S. Marine Corps inducts twenty-nine Navajos to begin training as "Code Talkers"; the men will use the Navajo language to provide secure communications during battles in the Pacific.

Hollywood movie director Frank Capra arrives in Washington, D.C., on February 15, to begin work on *Why We Fight*, a series of documentary films designed to educate soldiers about the causes of World War II and the reasons for American involvement.

Executive Order 9066, signed by U.S. President Franklin D. Roosevelt, directs all Japanese Americans living on the West Coast of the United States into internment camps.

Slovakian Jews become the first Jews from outside Poland to be transported to Auschwitz.

American forces surrender to the Japanese at Bataan on April 9.

American aviator James "Jimmy" Doolittle leads a U.S. Army Air Corps bombing raid on Tokyo and other Japanese cities that is credited with turning the tide of American wartime morale.

During May, some 1,000 British bombers destroy Cologne, Germany's third-largest city.

On May 6, American and Filipino troops on the island of Corregidor in Manila Bay surrender to the Japanese.

On May 7, Allied naval forces ordered to the area by Chester W. Nimitz, commander in chief of the Pacific Fleet, defeat the Japanese fleet in the Battle of the Coral Sea in the Pacific. It is the first great aircraft carrier conflict.

African American sailor Dorie Miller receives the Navy Cross on May 27 for his heroic performance during the Pearl Harbor bombing.

Reinhard Heydrich dies of his wounds on June 4, as a result of an earlier assassination attempt by Czech resistance fighters in Prague.

The U.S. Navy defeats the Japanese fleet at the Battle of Midway, June 4–7, in one of the most decisive naval engagements in history. Rear Admiral Raymond A. Spruance is given tactical responsibilities during the battle.

In June, General Dwight D. Eisenhower takes command of all U.S. forces in Europe.

Erwin Rommel becomes the youngest German officer to be named a field marshal, the highest rank in the German military, in June.

Anne Frank and her family move into a secret annex constructed in the top stories of her father's office building in Amsterdam.

Etty Hillesum secures a job as a typist for the Jewish Council in Amsterdam, the Netherlands, during the month of July, and assists new arrivals at the Westerbork transit camp, where Dutch Jews are held before deportation to death camps in Poland.

During July, British bombers attack Germany's second largest city, Hamburg, on four straight nights, causing a firestorm that kills 30,000 civilians.

The Treblinka death camp begins receiving Jews from Warsaw. It is the last of the three camps, along with Belzec and Sobibór, created to exterminate Polish Jews. The Nazis call this plan "Operation Reinhard," in honor of the assassinated Heydrich.

Judenrat official Adam Czerniaków commits suicide on July 23 after the Nazis order him to hand over 9,000 Jews from the Warsaw ghetto for deportation.

Jewish orphanage director Janusz Korczak and 200 orphans under his care are deported from the Warsaw ghetto in Poland to the Treblinka concentration camp, where they all die in the gas chambers.

On August 7, American troops land on the mid-Pacific island of Guadalcanal in the Solomon Islands in the first American offensive operation of the war in the Pacific.

Edith Stein, a Jew who converted to Catholicism and became a nun, is killed at the Auschwitz concentration camp.

On August 24, Benjamin O. Davis, Jr., officially takes command of the Tuskegee Airmen, trained at the Tuskegee Institute in Alabama, the first African American pilots to enter the U.S. Army Corps.

During the month of September, Brigadier General Leslie Groves, an American civil engineer, is named head of the Manhattan Engineering District (later called the Manhattan Project), which was formed by the U.S. government to develop nuclear weapons.

In September and October, Polish Jews Shimson and Tova Draenger join other Jewish youths in forming the Jewish Fighting Organization to work against the Nazis.

On September 13, Germany begins its attack on the Soviet city of Stalingrad.

Hirsch Grunstein and his brother go into hiding in Belgium to escape the Nazis. The boys stay with a couple that volunteers to give them shelter.

Popular orchestra leader Glenn Miller enlists in the U.S. Army on October 7 with the goal of starting the Glenn Miller Army Air Force Band, which eventually performs for troops in war zones in Europe.

In October 1942 Odette Marie Celine Hallowes, a mother and wife, parachutes into France as a spy for Great Britain; she is later confined to a concentration camp and tortured by the Nazis.

In the Battle of El Alamein in Egypt, Field Marshal Bernard Montgomery leads the British Eighth Army in an important strategic victory against Italian troops and Field Marshal Erwin Rommel's German Afrika Korps.

On November 8 the Allies launch Operation Torch, an invasion of German-occupied North Africa that ends with the Germans being chased from the region. U.S. General George S. Patton takes command of the First Armored Corps (a tank division) and leads it to victory.

Physicist Enrico Fermi achieves the first self-sustaining nuclear fission chain reaction in his laboratory at Columbia University in New York City.

Wladyslaw Bartoszewski, a Catholic Polish resister, helps form a Jewish relief committee called Zegota.

1943 Allied leaders meet at Casablanca, Morocco, in January, and Cairo, Egypt, in November of the same year, to discuss the progress of the war.

German Jewish rabbi Leo Baeck is arrested and sent to the Theresienstadt concentration camp in Czechoslovakia, where he remains until after the camp is liberated by the Soviets at the end of World War II.

On February 2, the Germans surrender to Russian troops at Stalingrad, a major turning point in the war.

Hans and Sophie Scholl are arrested on a Munich university campus for distributing pamphlets for the White Rose resistance group.

Prelude to War, the first film in the *Why We Fight* film series directed by Frank Capra, wins the Oscar for best documentary.

Small groups of Jews in the Warsaw ghetto begin attacking German troops on April 19. They continue fighting for almost one month until the Germans have killed almost all of the Jewish resisters and completely destroyed the ghetto. Jewish resistance leader Mordecai Anielewicz is one of those killed during the Warsaw Ghetto Uprising, on May 8.

U.S. General George S. Patton commands American troops in Sicily, a large island south of the Italian mainland. In July American forces, along with British and Canadian troops, begin the Allied invasion that will continue on the Italian mainland.

Italian dictator Benito Mussolini is removed from office by the Fascist Grand Council on July 25 and tries to establish a separate government in northern Italy, with the help of Adolf Hitler.

During August, Jackie Cochran becomes the director of the Women's Airforce Service Pilots (WASPs).

Austrian farmer Franz Jaggerstatter is executed for refusing to serve in Hitler's army.

The Allies invade the Italian mainland on September 3; the new Italian government surrenders to the Allies on September 8. German troops in Italy continue fighting.

German attempts to deport Danish Jews are defeated when most of the entire Jewish population of Denmark is safely transported to Sweden.

British spy Noor Inayat Khan is captured and tortured by the Nazis in occupied France.

In December U.S. General Dwight D. Eisenhower is put in command of the planned Operation Overlord.

1944 During the course of 1944, Women's Airforce Service Pilots member Ann B. Carl becomes the first woman to test-pilot a jet plane when she conducts an evaluation flight of the turbojet-powered Bell YP-59A.

The Allies land at Anzio, Italy, on January 22.

After abandoning his university studies in order to fight racism, young Italian Jew Primo Levi is sent to Auschwitz in February, having been arrested two months earlier.

Dutch resistance worker Corrie ten Boom, along with several of her family members, is arrested by the Gestapo for hiding Jews in her Amsterdam home. She and her sister are later sent to the Vught concentration camp.

Hannah Senesh (also transliterated as Szenes), a Jew living in Palestine, parachutes behind enemy lines in Yugoslavia as part of a British-sponsored rescue mission to reach Jews and other resisters.

The Germans occupy Hungary on March 19, 1944, and begin large-scale deportations of Hungarian Jews; by July, more than 400,000 Jews have been sent to Auschwitz.

The United States Army enters Rome, the capital of Italy, on June 4.

On June 6, now known as D-Day, Allied forces land in Normandy in northern France during the largest sea invasion in history, called Operation Overlord. After heavy fighting, the Allies break out of Normandy and sweep eastward across France. By the end of August, France is liberated.

The United States passes the "GI Bill" on June 22, making a college education available to almost all veterans of the U.S. armed services.

On the third anniversary of the German invasion of the Soviet Union, June 22, the Soviets launch a massive offensive called Operation Bagration along an 800-mile front in White Russia (Belarus). The Soviets inflict immense losses on the German army and drive them back almost 400 miles within one month.

Young Swedish businessman Raoul Wallenberg arrives in Budapest, Hungary, to help save the surviving Jews trapped in the city.

On July 20, a small group of German army officers, eager to end the war, unsuccessfully attempts to assassinate Adolf Hitler. Many of the conspirators, along with their families, are tortured and executed.

The Soviet army enters Lublin in eastern Poland in late July and liberates the nearby Majdanek death camp. The Soviets confiscate numerous Nazi documents before they can be destroyed.

On August 4, after living undetected for twenty-five months, Anne Frank, her family, and the four others hiding in the secret annex are reported to the Nazis. The annex dwellers are all sent to the Auschwitz concentration camp.

Paris is liberated by Free French and American forces on August 23.

On September 15, U.S. Marines land on Peleliu island, one of the Palau Islands in the western Pacific Ocean.

During the course of October 1944, industrialist Oskar Schindler is granted permission by the Nazis to establish a munitions factory in Czechoslovakia. This allows Schindler to spare Jewish prisoners from death by employing them there.

Concentration camp prisoner Róza Robota participates in the inmates' revolt at Auschwitz, which leads to the destruction of one of the crematoria.

German army commander Erwin Rommel is suspected of being involved in the July 20 failed attempt to assassinate Adolf Hitler and is forced to commit suicide on October 14.

U.S. General Douglas MacArthur returns to liberate the Philippines from Japanese control, just as he had promised three years earlier he would.

The largest naval battle in history, the Battle of Leyte Gulf in the Philippines (October 23–26), ends in almost total destruction of the Japanese fleet.

On October 26, SS chief Heinrich Himmler orders the destruction of the concentration camps and their inmates.

The 761st Battalion, an African American tank unit, arrives in France to take part in the Allied drive toward Germany.

Franklin D. Roosevelt is elected to a fourth term as president of the United States.

The Germans launch a major counteroffensive on December 16 against the Americans in the Ardennes Forest region of Belgium and France. The conflict becomes known as the Battle of the Bulge. After some initial success, the Germans are defeated.

1945 On January 12, the Soviets launch an offensive along the entire Polish front, entering Warsaw on January 17 and Lódz two days later. By February 1, they are within 100 miles of the German capital of Berlin.

As Soviet troops approach, the Nazis begin the evacuation of the Auschwitz death camp on January 18, forcing about 66,000 surviving prisoners on a death march. Soviet troops reach the camp on January 27.

On January 31, U.S. Army Private Eddie Slovik becomes the only American soldier executed for desertion during World War II; in fact, he becomes the only U.S. soldier executed for desertion since 1864.

In February, Allied leaders British Prime Minister Winston Churchill, U.S. President Franklin D. Roosevelt, and Soviet dictator Joseph Stalin meet in Yalta in the Soviet Union to discuss strategies for ending the war and to plan future forms of government for Germany and other parts of Europe. They also schedule the first United Nations conference.

On February 14, Allied raids on Dresden result in firestorms as the city is crammed with German refugees from the fighting farther east.

American marines land on Iwo Jima in the Pacific on February 19.

On March 7, American troops cross the Rhine River in Germany, the last natural obstacle between the Allied forces and Berlin.

American troops land on Okinawa on April 1, beginning the largest land battle of the Pacific war. Japanese forces are defeated by June.

Pastor Christian Reger is freed from Dachau on April 2 after spending five years at the camp for defying the state-sponsored religion known as the German Faith Movement.

On April 4, Kim Malthe-Bruun, a Danish resister, writes a letter to his mother from prison, informing her that he is to be executed by the Nazis.

German Protestant minister Dietrich Bonhoeffer is executed on April 9 for his participation in the plot to assassinate Adolf Hitler.

U.S. General George S. Patton and his Third Army liberate the Buchenwald concentration camp in Germany on April 11, 1945. American photographer Margaret Bourke-White accompanies U.S. forces when they liberate the camp, and her photographs document the deplorable conditions found there. American reporter Edward R. Murrow broadcasts his impressions of the Buchenwald concentration camp a few days after its liberation.

U.S. President Franklin D. Roosevelt dies of a cerebral hemorrhage in Warm Springs, Georgia, on April 12; Vice President Harry S Truman takes the oath of office and becomes president.

British troops liberate the Bergen-Belsen concentration camp. French prisoner Fania Fénelon is among those freed.

While reporting on the Allied invasion of Okinawa, Ernie Pyle is killed by a Japanese sniper on the island of Ie Shima on April 18.

American cartoonist Bill Mauldin wins the Pulitzer Prize during 1945 for his Willie and

Joe cartoons, which realistically portray the experiences of average U.S. infantrymen through the eyes of two scruffy GIs.

On April 20, Soviet troops reach Berlin, Germany.

Swedish diplomat Folke Bernadotte negotiates a deal with Nazi official Heinrich Himmler that allows 10,000 women to be released from the Ravensbrück concentration camp.

On April 28, former Italian dictator Benito Mussolini is captured by resistance fighters and executed. His body is put on public display.

American troops liberate the Dachau concentration camp.

Eva Braun marries Adolf Hitler in his Berlin bunker on April 29.

With the advancement of Soviet troops into Berlin, Adolf Hitler and Eva Braun commit suicide in Hitler's underground bunker on April 30.

On May 8, V-E Day, the new German government officially surrenders unconditionally to the Allies.

Nazi leader Hermann Göring is arrested by American troops during May 1945; a year later, he commits suicide after being condemned to death for war crimes.

Heinrich Himmler, the senior Nazi official responsible for overseeing the mass murder of 6 million European Jews, is captured by the Allies on May 21. Two days later, he commits suicide.

J. Robert Oppenheimer, leader of a group of scientists working to develop an atomic bomb, oversees a successful bomb test on July 16 at the Alamogordo Bombing Range (the Trinity test site) in the New Mexican desert.

The Potsdam Conference begins on July 16. U.S. President Harry S Truman, British Prime Minister Winston Churchill, and Soviet leader Joseph Stalin confirm occupation of Germany by four Allied powers (France, Great Britain, the Soviet Union, and the United States) and issue an ultimatum to Japan demanding unconditional surrender.

The USS *Indianapolis* is sunk by Japanese forces on July 19; search and rescue efforts are delayed and many of the surviving crewmen are consumed by sharks.

On August 6, the United States releases an atomic bomb on Hiroshima, Japan. Some 70,000 people are killed initially during the blast.

The Soviet Union declares war on Japan on August 8; a large Soviet force invades Manchuria the following day.

The United States drops an atomic bomb on Nagasaki, Japan, on August 9.

On August 15, the Allies accept the unconditional surrender of Japan. Japanese leaders sign formal surrender papers aboard the USS *Missouri* in Tokyo Bay on September 2, V-J Day.

U.S. President Harry S Truman and other world leaders sign a charter establishing the United Nations as an international peacekeeping organization.

War crimes trials begin in Nuremberg, Germany, in November. Justice Robert H. Jackson of the U.S. Supreme Court gives the opening address for the United States before the International Military Tribunal at Nuremberg.

1946 The first session of the United Nations General Assembly opens in London, England.

On January 19, the International Military Tribunal for the Far East (IMTFE) is convened to begin prosecution of Japanese war crimes.

Hermann Göring, one of the highest Nazi officials to be accused and convicted of war crimes, testifies in his own defense during the Nuremberg Trials.

U.S. Brigadier General Telford Taylor becomes chief counsel for the remaining Nuremberg Trials after Justice Robert H. Jackson of the U.S. Supreme Court resigns.

1947 During the course of the year, Holocaust survivor Simon Wiesenthal forms the Jewish Historical Documentation Center in Austria to track down Nazi war criminals.

U.S. Secretary of State George C. Marshall proposes the European Recovery Act, or the Marshall Plan, an outline for helping European countries recover from the effects of the war.

India gains its independence from Great Britain.

1948   On May 14, the state of Israel is established.

The Soviets block all overland traffic between Berlin and the Allied-controlled zones of Germany between June 1948 and May 1949. Allies airlift food and fuel to West Berlin during those eleven months in more than 275,000 flights.

U.S. President Harry S Truman issues Executive Order 9981, which calls for the integration of the U.S. armed forces.

On December 23 Japanese Premier Hideki Tōjō is executed for war crimes.

1949   American radio personality Mildred Gillars ("Axis Sally") stands trial for treason in January.

On April 4, the North Atlantic Treaty Organization (NATO) is founded.

The Soviets establish East Germany as a Communist state called the German Democratic Republic (East Germany); France, Great Britain, and the United States combine their power zones into a democratic state called the Federal Republic of Germany (West Germany).

Defeated by the Communists, Chinese leader Chiang Kai-Shek flees his homeland with others loyal to his Nationalist party, taking refuge on the island of Formosa (now Taiwan) on December 10.

1952   Israel and Germany agree on restitution for damages done to Jews by the Nazis.

American General Dwight D. Eisenhower is elected president of the United States.

1953   During 1953, George C. Marshall of the United States wins the Nobel Peace Prize for his efforts to assist Europe's recovery from World War II, becoming the first member of the military to receive the prize.

On August 28, the Israeli parliament passes the Yad Vashem Law, which establishes the Martyrs' and Heroes' Remembrance Authority to commemorate the 6 million Jews killed in the Holocaust, the communities and institutions destroyed, the soldiers and resistance members who fought the Nazis, the dignity of the Jews attacked, and those who risked their lives in order to aid Jews.

1955   The Soviet Union declares an end to war with Germany.

1957   After emigrating to the United States, Gerda Weissmann Klein writes a memoir called *All but My Life.*

1958   Elie Wiesel revises and abridges a previous work, and the result is published in France as *La Nuit,* an autobiographical novel detailing Wiesel's experiences during the Holocaust. The work is published in English in 1960 as *Night.*

1959   German industrialist Alfried Krupp is made to pay reparations to former concentration camp inmates who were forced to work in Krupp's munitions factories.

1960   In May Adolf Eichmann is arrested in Argentina by the Israeli Security Service.

During 1960, former journalist William L. Shirer publishes *The Rise and Fall of the Third Reich: A History of Nazi Germany.*

1961   Jewish journalist Hannah Arendt covers the trial of Adolf Eichmann, a notorious Nazi criminal who escaped to Argentina after the war. Born in Germany, Arendt had fled her homeland during the rise of Nazism. Ultimately, Arendt writes *Eichmann in Jerusalem: A Report on the Banality of Evil.* The views she expresses about the character of Eichmann create considerable controversy.

Communists build the Berlin Wall in order to stop East Germans from fleeing to West Germany.

1962   Former Nazi official Adolf Eichmann is executed after being found guilty of war crimes for his part in the murder of hundreds of thousands of Jews.

1967 Franz Stangl, former commandant of the Sobibór death camp who oversaw the gassing of more than 100,000 people in his first two months there, is taken to Germany to stand trial for war crimes.

1970 After serving twenty years in prison, former Nazi Albert Speer publishes his autobiography, *Inside the Third Reich.*

1971 Beate and Serge Klarsfeld discover former SS officer Klaus Barbie in La Paz, Bolivia. Barbie is not extradited until 1983.

1976 Japanese American activist Michiko Weglyn publishes *Years of Infamy: The Untold Story of America's Concentration Camps,* which exposes the suffering of more than 100,000 Japanese Americans imprisoned in U.S. internment camps during World War II.

1979 A U.S. television miniseries called *Holocaust* is broadcast; it is later credited with breaking the silence about the Holocaust in Germany.

1983 Donald Carroll publishes "Escape from Vichy," an article about American writer Varian Fry, who helped rescue between 1,500 and 4,000 Jews in German-occupied France.

The judgment against Fred Korematsu, who tried in 1944 to claim that internment of Japanese Americans was unconstitutional, is overturned on October 4.

1985 Human remains found in Brazil are confirmed to be those of Nazi doctor Josef Mengele, who performed inhumane medical experiments on prisoners at Auschwitz.

1987 On July 4, former SS officer Klaus Barbie is found guilty of crimes against humanity and is sentenced to life in prison.

1988 The U.S. Congress formally apologizes to Japanese Americans for interning them in camps during World War II. Survivors are offered a one-time payment of $20,000.

1989 The Berlin Wall is destroyed on November 9. The Brandenburg Gate connecting East and West Germany opens on December 22.

1990 Gypsy Holocaust survivor and artist Karl Stojka opens an exhibit titled *The Story of Karl Stojka: A Childhood in Birkenau,* which displays more than 100 paintings depicting his life in a concentration camp.

East Germany and West Germany are reunited on October 3, 1990.

1992 Holocaust survivor Isabella (Katz) Leitner publishes *Isabella: From Auschwitz to Freedom* and *The Big Lie,* both of which describe her experiences during the Holocaust.

1993 The United States Holocaust Memorial Museum in Washington, D.C., is dedicated on April 27.

The Israeli Supreme Court overturns the death sentence of alleged former Nazi John Demjanjuk and acquits him.

1997 Riva Shefer, a seventy-five-year-old Latvian Jew who survived a Nazi labor camp, becomes the first recipient of money from a $200 million Swiss fund established to aid Holocaust survivors.

1998 Fred Korematsu is awarded the Presidential Medal of Freedom, the highest civilian honor in the United States, in January 1998.

The Vatican issues a document stating that Pope Pius XII, leader of the Catholic church during the Holocaust, did all he could to save Jews. Many historians disagree.

Maurice Papon, a former official of the French Vichy government, is sentenced to ten years in prison for helping the Germans illegally arrest and deport French Jews.

In July, German automaker Volkswagen agrees to pay reparations to slave laborers who worked in its factories during the war.

On October 11, Edith Stein becomes the first Jewish person in modern times to be declared a saint by the Roman Catholic church.

1999 Dinko Sakic, the last known living commandant of a World War II concentration camp, is tried for war crimes.

2000 During the year 2000, Germany sets aside $5 billion to provide compensation to slave laborers forced to work for the Nazis during World War II. The money is contributed equally by the German government and German industry

Pope John Paul II makes a historic visit to Israel in March and tours the Israeli Holocaust memorial Yad Vashem.

On August 9, Simon Wiesenthal is awarded the U.S. Presidential Medal of Freedom.

Glossary

Abwehr The intelligence service of the German armed forces' high command.

Afrika Korps Highly effective German troops who fought under General Erwin Rommel in the North African desert.

air raid An attack by aircraft on a target on the ground, often forcing people to take cover in air raid shelters.

Aktion **(plural,** *Aktionen***)** Raid against Jews, often in ghettos, primarily to gather victims for extermination.

Allies Countries that fought against the Axis powers (Germany, Italy, and Japan) during World War II. The makeup of the Allies changed over the course of the war; the first major Allied countries were Great Britain and France. Germany defeated France in 1940, but some Free French forces continued to fight with the Allies until the end of the war. The Soviet Union and the United States joined the Allies in 1941.

Anschluss The annexation of Austria by Nazi Germany on March 13, 1938.

Anti-Comintern Pact Agreement signed in Berlin on November 25, 1936, by Germany and Japan. They were joined in 1937 by Italy, and later by Bulgaria, Hungary, Romania, Spain, and other states. The signers agreed to fight the Commu-

nist International organization (Comintern), that is, the Soviet Union.

anti-Semitism The hatred of or discrimination toward Jews.

appeasement The policy adopted by some European leaders, notably British Prime Minister Neville Chamberlain, toward Adolf Hitler prior to World War II. These leaders attempted to appease Hitler with political and economic concessions.

Ardennes Large forested area in southeastern Belgium; site of the 1944–1945 campaign known as the Battle of the Bulge.

Arrow Cross party A Fascist party in Hungary.

Aryan The name, used by the Nazis and others, of the "race" of people speaking languages thought to be derived from Sanskrit. Aryans were viewed by the Nazis as a superior race.

Aryanization The confiscation of Jewish businesses by the German authorities.

Atlantic Charter Agreement signed in 1941 by U.S. President Franklin D. Roosevelt and British Prime Minister Winston Churchill in which the two countries stated their commitment to worldwide peace and democracy.

Axis Coalition formed by Germany, Italy, and Japan to fight against the Allies during World

War II; during the course of the war, Hungary, Romania, Croatia, Slovakia, Finland, and Bulgaria also joined the Axis.

Beer Hall Putsch A failed attempt by Adolf Hitler and the Nazis to overthrow the Bavarian government on November 9, 1923. Also known as the Hitler Putsch or the Munich Putsch.

blackout Mandatory measure requiring citizens to turn off all lights in homes, businesses, and other facilities, as well as cars and other vehicles; the practice was intended to discourage enemy air raids as pilots would be unable to locate targets in the darkness.

blackshirts Fascists in Italy under the dictatorship of Benito Mussolini.

blitzkrieg "Lightning war"; the military strategy of sending troops in land vehicles to make quick, surprise strikes against the enemy while airplanes provide support from the air. This worked effectively for German troops in Poland and France.

brownshirts See **Sturmabteilung.**

Bund Jewish socialist, non-Zionist resistance group, active mainly in Poland between World War I and World War II.

Bund Deutscher Mädel (BDM) "German Girls' League"; the Nazi organization for girls; the female equivalent of the Hitlerjugend (Hitler Youth).

cavalry Originally referred to horse-mounted troops; in more recent times, refers to troops using armored vehicles, such as tanks.

Code Talkers A group of Native Americans who used the Navajo language as an effective American code in the Pacific theater during World War II.

collaboration Cooperation between citizens of a country and its occupiers.

commissar A Communist party official or Soviet government official.

communism An ideology and/or political philosophy that advocates the abolition of private property, and in which the state controls the means of production.

concentration camp *Konzentrationslager*; a place where people are held against their will without regard to the accepted forms of arrest and

detention. During World War II, the Nazis used concentration camps to hold Jews, Roma (Gypsies), political dissidents, religious figures, homosexuals, and others they considered enemies of the state.

conscientious objector One who refuses to fight in a war for moral, religious, or philosophical reasons.

crematorium (plural, crematoria) An oven designed to incinerate human corpses.

D-Day Usually refers to June 6, 1944, the day Allied forces launched Operation Overlord, an invasion of German-occupied France on the beaches of Normandy; also a military term designating the date and time of an attack.

death marches Forced marches of concentration camp inmates (usually Jews) during the German retreat near the end of World War II; also refers to forced marches of Allied prisoners of war (POWs) in the Pacific (i.e., the Bataan Death March).

deportation Banishment; being sent out of a country.

displaced persons (DPs) Persons forced out of their countries of origin during war. After World War II, DPs had a difficult time finding refuge.

draft System by which a country requires a certain segment of its population to perform a term of military service; also called military conscription or selective service.

Einsatzgruppen "Special action groups"; mobile units of the Schutzstaffel (SS) and Sicherheitsdienst (SD), the military wing of the Nazi party, that followed the German army into Poland in September 1939, and into the Soviet Union in June 1941. Their official duties included the elimination of political opponents and the seizure of state documents. In the Soviet Union, in particular, they carried out mass murders, primarily of the Jewish population.

Endlösung See "Final Solution."

euthanasia Generally refers to mercy killing; the Nazis used the term to refer to the murder of those they deemed unfit to live, including the mentally or physically challenged.

Executive Order 9066 Order issued by U.S. President Franklin D. Roosevelt on February 19, 1942, directing all Japanese Americans on the West Coast to be sent to internment camps.

fascism Political system in which power rests not with citizens but with the central government, which is often run by the military and/or a dictator.

"Final Solution" In full, "Endlösung der Judenfrage in Europa," or "final solution of the Jewish problem in Europe"; Nazi code name for the physical extermination of all European Jews.

Free French Movement headed from outside France by General Charles de Gaulle that tried to organize and encourage French people to resist the German occupation.

Freikorps "Free Corps"; volunteer units consisting mostly of former members in the German army; much of the Sturmabteilung (SA), or storm troopers, was made up of Free Corps members.

führer "Leader"; Adolf Hitler's title as the head of Nazi Germany.

gas chamber A room in which people are killed by means of poisonous gas.

Geheime Staatspolizei (Gestapo) Secret state police in Nazi Germany.

Generalgouvernement General Government; the Germans' name for the administrative unit comprising those parts of occupied Poland that were not incorporated into the Reich. It included five districts: Galicia, Kraków, Lublin, Radom, and Warsaw.

gentiles Non-Jews, especially Christian non-Jews.

Gestapo See Geheime Staatspolizei.

ghettos Crowded, walled sections of cities where Jews were forced to live in substandard conditions; conditions often led to disease and/or starvation.

GI An abbreviation of "government issue"; a term for members of the U.S. armed forces.

Gyspies See Roma.

Hitlerjugend "Hitler Youth"; organization founded in 1922 that trained German boys to idolize and obey German leader Adolf Hitler, to follow Hitler's policies precisely, and to become Nazi soldiers.

Holocaust Period between 1933 and 1945 when Nazi Germany engaged in the systematic persecution and elimination of Jews and other people deemed inferior by the Nazis, such as citizens of eastern Europe and the Soviet Union, Roma (Gypsies), homosexuals, and Jehovah's Witnesses. Also called sho'ah in Hebrew.

Home Army Secret military resistance organization in Poland.

internment camps Guarded facilities usually used to hold citizens of an enemy country during wartime.

island hopping Allied strategy in the Pacific for taking islands one after another, skipping those that were deemed of little military value.

isolationism A country's policy of remaining out of other countries' affairs. Isolationism was a strong force in American politics before World War I (1914–1918) and continued to be an important factor until Japan attacked the United States in December 1941.

Judenrat (plural, Judenräte) "Jewish Council"; a committee of Jewish leaders formed in ghettos under German orders.

Junker A landed Prussian noble; Junkers controlled the German military until the end of World War I (1914–1918).

Kapo Probably from the Italian word capo, or "chief"; supervisor of inmate laborers in a concentration camp.

Kristallnacht "Night of the Broken Glass"; organized pogrom against Jews in Germany and Austria on November 9–10, 1938.

Lebensraum "Room to live"; Nazi idea that the German people, or Aryan race, needed expanded living space to survive and increase in size.

Lend-Lease Program U.S. legislation passed in 1941 (prior to the United States entering the war) that allowed the United States to send supplies needed for the war effort to countries fighting Germany, such as Great Britain and the Soviet Union. Payment was to be made after the war.

liquidation The Nazi process of destroying ghettos by sending prisoners to death camps and burning the buildings.

Luftwaffe German air force.

Maginot Line Defensive fortifications built to protect France's eastern border.

Manhattan Project Project funded by the U.S. government that secretly gathered scientists at facilities in New York City; Chicago, Illinois; Los Alamos, New Mexico; and other locations to work on the development of an atomic bomb.

Mein Kampf "*My Struggle*"; Adolf Hitler's book expounding his ideology, published in two volumes (July 1925 and December 1926).

Munich Pact Agreement signed by the leaders of France, Great Britain, Nazi Germany, and Italy in September 1938, allowing the Nazis to take over the Sudetenland, an area between Austria and Germany. The accord became famous as a symbol of the British and French policy of appeasement of Germany.

Nacht und Nebel "Night and Fog"; code name for rounding up suspected members of the anti-Nazi resistance in occupied western Europe; people were said to disappear in the "night and fog."

Nazi Abbreviated name for the Nationalsozialistische Deutsche Arbeiterpartei, or the National Socialist German Workers' party, the political organization led by Adolf Hitler, who became dictator of Germany. The Nazis controlled Germany from 1933 to 1945, promoting racist and anti-Semitic ideas and enforcing total obedience to Hitler and the party.

Nazi-Soviet Pact Mutual non-aggression treaty signed by Nazi Germany and the Communist Soviet Union in 1939, despite Adolf Hitler's hatred of communism; allowed Hitler to avoid a two-front war in Poland. Also called the Molotov-Ribbentrop Pact.

Night of the Long Knives *Nacht der langen Messer*; Nazi purge of the Sturmabteilung (SA), or storm troopers, June 30–July 1, 1934.

Nuremberg Laws Laws issued in 1935 to further the exclusion of Jews from German life. The first removed Jews' citizenship; the second defined Jews racially and prohibited them from engaging in marital and other relations with Germans. The laws were proclaimed at the annual Nazi party rally in Nuremberg on September 15, 1935, and were expanded on November 14, 1935.

Nuremberg Trial Trial of twenty-two major Nazi figures in Nuremberg in 1945 and 1946 by the International Military Tribunal. Other World War II war crimes trials are also sometimes referred to as the Nuremberg Trials.

occupation Control of a country by a foreign military power.

Operation Overlord Code name for the Normandy invasion, a massive Allied attack on German-occupied France. Also called D-Day.

Operation Reinhard Nazi plan to eliminate European Jews; named in honor of Reinhard Heydrich, chief architect of the "Final Solution."

Operation Torch British and American invasion of North Africa in November 1942.

pacifism A belief opposing war and violence as problem-solving techniques; sometimes is expressed as passivism or a refusal to bear arms.

Palestine Region in the Middle East captured by the British from the Ottoman Turks. In exchange for Jewish help capturing the region, the British promised the establishment of a Jewish national homeland in Palestine.

partisans Guerilla fighters.

Pearl Harbor Inlet on the southern coast of the island of Oahu, Hawaii, and the site of the Japanese attack on a U.S. naval base on December 7, 1941. The attack prompted the United States to enter World War II officially.

pogrom An organized massacre of or violence against a specific group of people, often Jews.

Potsdam Declaration Statement released by British Prime Minister Winston Churchill, U.S. President Harry S Truman, and Soviet leader Joseph Stalin on July 26, 1945, demanding the unconditional surrender of Japan.

prisoner of war (POW) Person captured during a war, especially by enemy forces during combat.

Prussia The largest state in the German empire from 1871 to 1918.

radar Technology using radio waves to detect objects or topographical features. Initial development of radar began in 1935; it allowed combatants in World War II to detect incoming planes. Later, the technology advanced so that radar devices could be fitted into planes, allowing pilots to locate potential bombing targets more easily.

RAF See Royal Air Force.

ration To make something available in fixed amounts; to limit access to scarce goods; the allotted amount of something.

Red Army An abbreviation for Rabochya Krestyanskaya Krasnaya Armiya, or "Workers' and Peasants' Red Army," the official name of the Soviet army until June 1945, when it was changed to Soviet Army.

Reich "Empire"; Adolf Hitler's regime as dictator of Germany was called the Third Reich. The First Reich was the Holy Roman Empire; the second was proclaimed by Otto von Bismarck.

Reichstag German parliament.

reparations Compensation required from a defeated nation for damage or injury during war.

resettlement The Nazi term for forcing Jews into ghettos and concentration camps.

resistance An organized movement in a conquered country designed to attack and subvert occupying troops and, often, native collaborators.

"Righteous among the Nations" Title given by Yad Vashem (Holocaust memorial and museum) to non-Jews who risked their lives to save Jews in Nazi-occupied Europe.

Roma (Gypsies) Dark-haired and dark-skinned, nomadic people who are believed to have originated in India.

"Rosie the Riveter" A nickname for more than 6 million women who entered the American workforce as factory workers during World War II, filling job vacancies left by men heading off to war.

Royal Air Force (RAF) The British aerial armed force.

SA See Sturmabteilung.

Schutzstaffel (SS) "Security squad"; unit that provided Adolf Hitler's personal bodyguards and concentration camp guards.

SD See Sicherheitsdienst.

segregation The forced separation of races. During World War II, African Americans and whites in the United States were segregated in many public places, including schools, and the military.

Selektion **(plural,** *Selektionen***)** "Selection"; the process of selecting, from among Jewish deportees arriving at a Nazi camp, those who were to be used for forced labor and those who were to be killed immediately. The term also refers to the selecting, in ghettos, of Jews to be deported.

sho'ah The Hebrew term for "holocaust"; the mass destruction of Jews by the Nazis.

Sicherheitsdienst (SD) "Security police"; special unit that served as the intelligence service of the Schutzstaffel (SS).

Sonderkommando "Special squad"; SS or Einsatzgruppen detachment. Also refers to the Jewish units in extermination camps who removed the bodies of those gassed for cremation or burial.

SS See Schutzstaffel.

Star of David Jewish religious symbol; the Nazis forced Jews to wear a badge shaped like the Star of David for identification purposes.

Sturmabteilung (SA) "Storm troopers" (also known as Braunhemd, or brownshirts); members of a special armed and uniformed branch of the Nazi party.

swastika Ancient symbol originating in South Asia; appropriated by the Nazis as their emblem.

synagogue Jewish house of worship.

theater From a military standpoint, an area of operations during a war. The two main areas of operations during World War II were the European and Pacific theaters.

Third Reich The official name of the regime that Adolf Hitler headed as führer of Germany; means Third Empire. See also Reich.

Treaty of Versailles Restrictive agreement that Germany was forced to sign in 1919 after World War I (1914–1918). Germany was required to claim responsibility for the war and pay damages to other countries.

Tripartite Pact Agreement that established a military alliance between Germany, Italy, and Japan in 1940. Also known as the Axis or Three-Power Pact.

Tuskegee Airmen Group of African Americans who became the first black Army Air Corps pilots.

U-boat A contraction of *Unterseeboot*; a German submarine.

V-E Day Victory in Europe Day, the day on which German forces officially surrendered, May 8, 1945.

Vichy Regime set up in France in 1940, after the Germans invaded the country. Headed by Field Marshal Philippe Pétain, it was actually under German control. Its name comes from the French town where it was headquartered.

V-J Day Victory over Japan Day, the day on which Japanese forces officially surrendered, September 2, 1945.

Volksdeutsche "Ethnic Germans"; Germans living outside Germany.

WAC See Women's Army Corps.

Waffen-SS Military unit of the Schutzstaffel (SS), the Nazi security squad.

Wannsee Conference Meeting called by Reinhard Heydrich in 1941 to inform the German government of the "Final Solution," a plan to eliminate European Jews.

war crimes Violations of the laws or customs of war; the basis for trials held by the Allies after World War II.

Wartheland (Warthegau) Western Polish district annexed to the Reich after September 1939.

WASPs See Women's Airforce Service Pilots.

Weimar Republic Democratic German government in existence from 1919 to 1933, imposed upon Germany at the end of World War I (1914–1918).

Women's Airforce Service Pilots (WASPs) Organization that recruited and trained women pilots to perform non-combat flying duties.

Women's Army Corps (WAC) Organization that allowed American women to serve a variety of non-combat roles.

World War I A conflict that raged throughout Europe from 1914 to 1918. Austria-Hungary, Germany, Turkey, and Bulgaria fought against Serbia, Russia, France, Great Britain, Japan, Italy, and, later, the United States, along with twenty-one other nations.

Yad Vashem Holocaust memorial in Jerusalem.

Yiddish Language spoken by eastern European Jews.

Zionism Movement that advocated the formation of a Jewish nation in Palestine.

Zydowsk Organizacja Bojowa (ZOB) Military wing of the Jewish underground in the Warsaw ghetto.

Zyklon B Hydrogen cyanide; the brand name of a pesticide used by the Nazis in their euthanasia program and later, especially in the gas chambers of Auschwitz.

Research Ideas

The following research ideas are intended to offer suggestions for complementing social studies and history curricula, to trigger additional ideas for enhancing learning, and to suggest cross-disciplinary projects for library and classroom use.

Ration Recipes

Look in cookbooks published during the 1940s or women's magazines published during World War II and note how recipes account for rationing. What kinds of ingredient substitutions do they specify? Make one of the recipes and invite others to rate the flavor, or adapt a recipe from a modern cookbook to account for rationing.

Personal History

Interview a veteran of World War II or someone who lived during the war. Create a list of questions before the interview. Perhaps ask the interviewee where he or she was during the war, how the war changed his or her life, and what was his or her impression of the war's importance both at the time and in retrospect.

Design a Holocaust Memorial

Create a sketch or a paper model for a historic marker, public display, or building commemorating a person, place, or event in Holocaust history.

Explain how and why you made your design choices, and why you felt your chosen person, place, or event was worthy of commemoration.

Atom Bomb Debate

Study the decision to drop atom bombs on Hiroshima and Nagasaki. Taking into consideration only what was known at the time about the bombs, form two teams, one in favor of dropping the bomb and the other against, and debate the issues. Then repeat the debate, taking into consideration what is currently known about the effects of atomic bombs. Discuss how the first and second debates differed.

Turning Points

On a large map of the world, use pushpins to mark the sites of battles that were important turning points during the war. For each site, create a note card explaining who fought there, who won, and why that battle was significant.

Modern Opinions from Historical Figures

Form a group of four to six people and choose a current event in world politics as the basis for a panel discussion. One person will serve as moderator for the discussion; the remaining group members should each choose a prominent individual involved in World War II. After researching both the issue and the prominent individuals, students will present the positions they think their selected historical figures would have taken on the subject.

War-Inspired Artwork

Choose a creative work related to World War II; this can be anything from a piece of architecture (like the memorial to the USS *Arizona* in Pearl Harbor, Hawaii) to a painting, song, or poem inspired by the war (such as Randall Jarrell's poem "The Death of the Ball Turret Gunner"). Explain the work's relationship to the war: is it about a battle, or an individual's experience of the war? What emotions does the piece evoke: bravery, fear, loneliness, anger?

Create a Board Game Based on Nazi Confiscation of Jewish Property

Trace the history of a painting that was taken from its original owner and ended up in a foreign museum by making a Monopoly-type game.

War Journal

Imagine that you were alive during World War II. You can choose to have lived in any country involved. Write a journal of your activities over the course of one week.

Propaganda

Rent a video of a movie created during World War II that is about the war. Some examples of films available on videocassette include Frank Capra's *Why We Fight* documentary series, *Casablanca*, and *Mrs. Miniver*. Write an essay discussing whether the film has a particular political message and what that message is.

Battlefield Tour

Create an itinerary for a World War II battlefield tour. You could choose to focus the tour on sites in the Pacific, sites throughout Europe or North Africa, or on one specific country. List the sites you'll be visiting on the tour, giving the name of the battles fought, codenames for the operations (if any), key events of the battles, the commanders involved, the victors, and why the battles were important.

D-Day Newspaper Article

Write an article about the June 6, 1944, invasion of France from the viewpoint of either an American or a German war correspondent.

Rescuers

Research individuals who saved or helped save Jewish lives during the Holocaust. Be sure to include less well-known people as well as more famous figures. Write their names and a brief description of the rescue(s) they made on slips of paper that can be pinned to a map in the appropriate places.

Trials

Imagine that you were a guard at a Nazi concentration camp. After the war, you are tried at Nuremberg for war crimes. Explain the reasons for your actions. Or, imagine that you are one of the prosecutors at the Nuremberg trials. Explain the types of questions you would ask and what criteria you would use to determine guilt or innocence.

Prelude to War

World War II began in 1939 with the German invasion of Poland and the subsequent declaration of war on Germany by Great Britain and France. Six years later, when the conflict was officially resolved, fighting had occurred on every continent except South America and Antarctica. Armies had battled on jungle islands in the Pacific Ocean and in the deserts of Africa. Planes had bombed Australia and Hawaii, Britain and Russia, Norway and Egypt, leaving large parts of Europe and eastern Asia in ruins. Two cities in Japan, Hiroshima and Nagasaki, had been utterly destroyed by atomic bombs. Almost 6 million European Jews, including 1.5 million children, had been murdered in Nazi racial cleansing programs. The first international conflict of its kind, World War II completely changed the nature of modern warfare. To trace the evolution of World War II from the discontent of a fragmented political party led by an artist drifter into the largest conflict in human history, one must first understand the political and social situation in Germany prior to the 1930s.

The Jews of Germany

Although Jews had experienced anti-Semitism, or anti-Jewish prejudice, over the centuries in German territories and other areas of Europe, there was little indication during the nineteenth century that the new nation of Germany would later be led by a political party whose foremost goal was to rid the world of the Jewish race. Jews had first arrived in Germany during the period of the Roman Empire (31 B.C–A.D. 476) and lived in the country continuously since the Middle Ages (A.D. 500–1500). Germany became one of the major centers of Jewish learning and culture, though many of the Jews of Germany later settled in eastern Europe. Most European and American Jews are Ashkenazic, which comes from the Hebrew word for "Germany." (Jews whose ancestors lived in Spain are called Sephardic Jews.) Yiddish, based on the Germanic language that was spoken in the Middle Ages but written in the Hebrew alphabet, eventually became the language of Jews throughout central and eastern Europe. Until the nineteenth century, the countries that were later united as Germany all had special laws that kept most Jews from being considered citizens. They could not own land, work for the government, or teach in schools. Many Jewish people were severely impoverished, segregated in ghettos, and subjected to curfews. These German laws against the Jews were gradually abolished during the nineteenth century and, in some places, Jews became legally equal to non-Jews. By 1918 the majority of German Jews had been assimilated into society. They could not be distinguished from other Germans, and they thought of themselves as Germans.

An illustration of "Jewstreet" in the Frankfurt ghetto, 1800s. Until the early nineteenth century, European Jews were required to live in special sections of their towns and usually had to return there by nightfall. The Nazis resurrected this practice in the 1930s. *(Reproduced by permission of Bildarchiv Preussischer Kulturbesitz)*

The Origins of Anti-Semitism

The term anti-Semitism has its roots in linguistics, the study of language. Almost all European and Indian languages, such as English, German, Russian, French, Greek, Iranian, and Armenian, are members of a family of languages called Indo-European. In the past, the word "Aryan" was sometimes used instead of "Indo-European" to describe this language family. Experts believe these languages all derive from one single language spoken thousands of years ago. Another major language family, not connected to the Indo-European line, is Semitic, which includes Hebrew and Arabic. In the nineteenth century, some political writers argued that modern people who spoke Indo-European languages belonged to the Aryan race.

Modern Jews, whose original Hebrew language is not Indo-European, were perceived as being of a separate race, called the Semites. Anti-Semitic writers further argued that people who spoke Indo-European languages were members of a superior race. This "racial anti-Semitism" had a tremendous impact, especially in Germany, where it produced the belief that Jews were not merely members of a separate religion, but a completely separate race.

The gradual disappearance of legal discrimination against Jews allowed their assimilation into German society. As a result, the Jewish community produced some of the most important figures of nineteenth-century German culture, including poet and critic Heinrich Heine and composer Felix Mendelssohn-Bartholdy. Karl Marx, the father of modern socialism and one of the most influential writers of the century, was the grandson of a rabbi, though he himself was baptized as a Christian. During the nineteenth century, large portions of the Jewish community became more prosperous. Some Jews had always been merchants and moneylenders, two of the jobs they were allowed to have under German law. Historically, Jews had not been admitted into the workman's guilds and so were not represented in many trades. As increasing numbers of merchants became owners of large companies and moneylenders became bankers, many German Jews entered the growing middle class. While a high percentage of the Jewish population was still poor, they were generally better off than they had been earlier in the nineteenth century.

Economic prosperity resulted in the Jewish people being able to move out of ghettos and into non-Jewish neighborhoods. They dressed like other Germans of their social class and many became less observant of their religious practices. They went to synagogue only on special holidays rather than every Sabbath, spending less time in prayer and strict religious study; some converted to Christianity, while others chose not to practice any religion. Jews also began to marry outside their religion, and by 1927 about 54 percent of German Jews who got married chose a partner who was not Jewish.

In 1925 Germany contained approximately 564,000 Jews, less than 1 percent of the population. More than two-thirds of German Jews lived in six large cities: Berlin, Frankfurt, Hamburg, Breslau, Leipzig, and Cologne. About 90,000, or 16 percent of the total, lived in smaller cities, with another 97,000 living in towns or villages. The German capital of Berlin was home to 180,000 Jews. Although the pattern differed from place to place, approximately half of the working population was self-employed; of the remainder, about 80 percent held office jobs, 18 percent were manual workers, and 2 percent were domestic servants. In Hamburg, the great port city of northern Germany and a center of the Reform movement in Judaism, the Jewish community was among the most assimilated, with a high rate of intermarriage. Jews there were also more prosperous because they held jobs in banking and shipping as well as prestigious university positions.

German Anti-Semitism

Like most European countries, Germany had a history of anti-Semitism dating back to the Middle Ages. Initially, anti-Semitic beliefs stemmed from a

The German *Volk*

Strictly translated, the German word *volk* means "people" or "nation," but when used by extreme nationalists in the period before World War II, the term took on a different connotation. Used in reference to Germans as a special race of people with a common ancestry, *volk* was meant to conjure up images of the religion and mythology of ancient, pre-Christian Germanic tribes. The *volk* supposedly had a special, almost magical, connection to forests, streams, and mountains.

The idea of the *volk* was different from the modern idea of a nation: A member of the German *volk* was a German regardless of geographical location or citizenship, yet people could not be considered truly German if they were not members of the *volk*—even if they could trace their German ancestry back hundreds of years, spoke only German, and thought of themselves as German. According to extreme nationalists, Jews were not Germans: They were outsiders who posed a threat to true Germans, whom they wished to weaken and enslave.

Christian perception that practicing Jews were actively rejecting Christianity. As time passed, some Christians began to believe that Jews were working in league with the Devil, and the established church contended that ancient Jews had been responsible for killing Jesus. Jews were even accused of murdering Christian children and using their blood in religious ceremonies. In the Middle Ages and early modern times, Jews were attacked and killed by mobs who then burned their homes; a wave of killings swept the towns of western Germany in 1196. Jews were repeatedly driven out of European countries: In 1290 they were ordered to leave England; in 1306 they were expelled from France; and in 1492 they were forcibly ejected from Spain. In the late 1500s Martin Luther, the German religious reformer who founded Protestantism, preached violent hatred of the Jews. Intense anti-Jewish sentiment continued to exist into the twentieth century in Germany and throughout Europe.

The History of the German Nation

At the outset of World War II, Germany had existed as a nation for less than seventy years. Prior to 1871, German territory was divided into numerous individual states, most of which were led by separate monarchies. The regions differed in size, power, laws, resources, and customs. For seventy years after Germany was united as a single nation in 1871, the establishment of a stable system of government was prevented by regional, social, and religious division, as well as world war,

revolution, and economic crises. In 1871 the king of Prussia was named emperor, or kaiser, of Germany, though many German states (such as Saxony and Bavaria) retained their kings until 1918. A majority of citizens, especially in the southern state of Bavaria, which was heavily agricultural and Catholic, wanted to reclaim their independence.

The Kingdom of Prussia was the core of the German empire and, in some respects, the unification of Germany resembled a Prussian takeover of the other German kingdoms. The Prussian military dominated the army of united Germany and was controlled by families of the Prussian nobility. These nobles, called Junkers, lived on estates in the old lands of Prussia in eastern Germany. Though their properties often did not yield enough income to support the lifestyle of wealthy landowners, they maintained an overwhelming presence in the military, which secured their position in society. Contemptuous of businesspeople and workers, the Junkers felt the military was the only suitable occupation for nobility, and generation after generation of Junker sons were trained to be military officers. Politically, economically, and socially conservative, Junkers believed in loyalty to the kaiser and obedience to authority. They resisted the formation of a democracy, believing in the glory of Germany and the power of the army they dominated. Intensely devout Lutherans, they were fiercely anti-Semitic and anti-Catholic. Junkers advocated a government that maintained high crop prices and pro-

Germany before the
Treaty of Versailles

——— Boundary of German
Empire, 1871

A map showing the German states.

tected their estates from being broken up into smaller farms. Until the 1930s Junkers continued to have a greater influence on Germany than their numbers or their wealth merited, due to their domination within the German army.

Large-scale manufacturing and factories arrived in Germany well after the Industrial Revolution had made England and France into great economic powers. After Germany became a united country in 1871, it experienced rapid economic growth, and by the outbreak of World War I in 1914, German industries produced steel, coal, textiles and clothing, electrical equipment, and chemicals. In other industrialized countries, the power of the old nobility was significantly reduced or even eliminated. In Germany, however, the Junkers retained control of the army, the Prussian government, and Germany itself until 1918.

Modern Anti-Semitism

During this period of prosperity, Jews who had once been relegated to secondary positions within society began to emerge as economic leaders. In response, an international form of anti-Semitism surfaced. Jews were accused of controlling businesses and banks that were growing in Europe. For instance, the Rothschilds, a German Jewish family based in Frankfurt, had built a great banking empire that operated from London, England, and Paris, France, as well as from Germany. Jewish businessman Emil Rathenau founded the company that dominated the German electrical industry. Although most big business in Germany was run by non-Jewish Germans, many people thought the German economy was controlled by Jews. Prussian Junkers, along with other conservatives, continued to advocate nationalism through a strong military. An extreme faction of these nationalists believed that any criticism of Germany was a form of treason. They cited Jews' multinational ties as evidence that they were loyal to fellow Jews in other countries and not to Germany. (This attitude toward foreign connections was also behind the Junkers' opposition to the Catholic church.) Some believed that Jews were responsible for bringing modern European ideas, particularly democracy and social-

The Industrial Revolution in Germany

Between 1871 and 1914 there were dramatic changes in German lifestyle and employment. The population rapidly increased and greater numbers of Germans lived in cities. In 1870 approximately 750,000 people lived in Berlin; by 1910 the population had risen to more than 2 million. Cities such as Hamburg, Cologne, Frankfurt, and Leipzig tripled in size during that period. These great changes in Germany's demographics were caused by the phenomenal growth in industry. Germany's progress can be seen in this chart, which compares production and transportation statistics during the industrial revolution in Germany.

	1870	1913
Railroads (approximate miles of track)	11,000 (1910)	37,000
Coal (in millions of metric tons)	29.4 (1871)	191.5
Pig iron (crude iron for steel, in millions of metric tons)	1.6 (1871)	14.8 (1910)
Merchant marine (number of ships)	147	2,100
Merchant marine (loaded weight of all ships, in tons)	9,000	4,300,000

ism, into Germany. The most extreme anti-Semites came to believe that the Jews were behind both big business and socialism, claiming the existence of a conspiracy to undermine German traditions. According to these extremists, Socialists and Jewish industrialists and bankers were only pretending to be enemies as part of a plot to control Germany and the whole world. While most Germans did not accept these extremist ideas, as changes in society seemed to spiral out of control, increasing numbers of citizens began accepting anti-Semitic views to explain emerging problems. Anti-Semitic literature began to proliferate. One significant document was the *Protocols of the Elders of Zion* (see primary source entry), a pamphlet supposedly written by Jewish leaders in preparation for a secret plan to take over the world, but in actuality composed by Russian secret police as a propaganda tool.

World War I

World War I, or the Great War, as it was known at the time, ushered in a period of drastic and overwhelming changes in German society. Fought from 1914 to 1918, the conflict grew out of a struggle for power and territory in Europe. Germany's efforts to expand its empire split the nations of Europe into

two camps: Austria-Hungary, Germany, Turkey, and Bulgaria fought against the combined powers (called the Allies) of Serbia, Russia, France, Britain, Japan, Italy, and, later, the United States, along with twenty-one other nations. Like most other Europeans involved in World War I, the Germans went to battle in 1914 believing that the conflict would be short, that soldiers would soon return home, and that Germany would be victorious. Four years later, in fall 1918, German armies were still fighting; almost 2 million German soldiers had been killed and another 4 million wounded. In the eastern theater, Germany had defeated its enemy, Russia (where a revolution had overthrown the czar and a Communist government had seized power). On the western front, German armies in France were losing their fight against British and French forces. For almost the entire war, the two sides faced each other across fields of barbed wire. Each army dug hundreds of miles of trenches, where soldiers ate, slept, and fought for months on end. The battles settled into a rhythmic pattern of attrition: The attacking army would gain some territory—perhaps a few miles—advancing across the open ground against machine-gun fire and artillery shells, only to be driven back by the opposition. At the end of a week or a month, the two sides had

A wounded soldier is carried off a World War I battlefield. *(Reproduced by permission of Foto Marburg/Art Resource)*

returned to their original position, having lost thousands of soldiers' lives.

The United States joined the Allies, mainly Britain and France, in the war against Germany in 1917. With hundreds of thousands of fresh American troops arriving on the western front, it was clear that the Germans would run out of soldiers before the Allies. Like most of their countrymen, German Jews were strong supporters of Germany in World War I. In 1918 there were approximately 600,000 Jews in Germany; about 100,000 served in the German army and 12,000 lost their lives. Many Jews played vital roles during the war. Among them was Walter Rathenau, the son of a Jewish industrialist, who organized the German War Raw Materials Department, a crucial part of the German war effort.

By 1917, food was becoming scarce in Germany. The British fleet prevented all ships, including those carrying food, from reaching German ports. Ger-

many's allies, the Austrian Empire and Turkey, were collapsing. German generals realized the war was lost and told Kaiser Wilhelm II to surrender. The Allies wanted the kaiser to abdicate his throne before they would end the war; when he refused, the war and the deaths continued. At the end of October 1918, German admirals decided to send their ships out to fight the British navy. Except for submarines, the German fleet had spent most of the war in port because the more powerful British fleet was impossible to defeat. Although they knew the war was lost, German naval commanders forged ahead with plans to pit their entire naval arsenal against the British. When German sailors refused to obey orders, knowing they would be far outgunned by the British, their mutiny soon spread to soldiers stationed in the ports and a revolution began to brew in Germany.

Forming councils, workers and soldiers seized local governments. On November 9, 1918, the

A military cemetery in Verdun, France, where French and German World War I soldiers were laid to rest. *(Reproduced by permission of Foto Marburg/Art Resource)*

Spartacus League, a small communist group, declared Germany a socialist republic. Insisting that the new councils of workers and soldiers should run the country, they called for an immediate end to the war. On the same day, one of the leaders of the larger German Social Democratic party announced a "free German republic." Although the Social Democrats considered themselves a socialist party, they were more moderate than the Spartacus League. They promoted a gradual, peaceful change in Germany as opposed to revolution. Fearing a loss of supporters (especially factory workers and soldiers) to the Spartacus League, the Social Democrats felt they had no choice but to call for the end of the monarchy as well.

On November 10, as disorder spread throughout Germany, the kaiser renounced his throne and left the country. The next day, Germany signed an armistice in France, ending the Great War. Because the war ended while Germany was in a state of revolution, and because the Allies did not require any of Germany's top generals to sign the armistice, some Germans claimed that their armies had never been defeated. Germany had lost the war, they reasoned, because the army had been stabbed in the back, betrayed by Communists, Social Democrats, and politicians in general. Some Germans claimed that Jews were chiefly responsible for this treason.

Years of Disorder

From the end of World War I until 1925, Germany faced one crisis after another. The war left millions dead and millions of others permanently disabled. The loss of soldiers was made even worse by the nation's defeat and the feeling that the deaths had served no purpose. Some historians believe that in the wake of four years of slaughter in Europe, the world became less sensitive to suffering; the unbelievable butchery that occurred during World War I seemed to leave people feeling cold, detached, and indifferent. According to this theory, a deep-seated sense of indifference made possible the killing of millions during the Holocaust. After the war, the citizens of many countries tried to return to their normal prewar lives. In Germany the end of the war was accompanied by revolution and, just as the new German government was born, the collapse of the German army. Over the next few years, repeated attempts were made by various factions in different parts of Germany to overthrow the government.

At the end of World War I, the leader of the Social Democratic party, Friedrich Ebert, was chancellor of Germany. Intent upon restoring order, Ebert was willing to eliminate the rebellious councils of workers and soldiers by force if necessary. Throughout the first half of 1919, his government acted to abolish the

Freikorps members posing with their weapons in 1919. *(Reproduced by permission of Bildarchiv Preussischer Kulturbesitz)*

councils, disarm workers' organizations, and return striking laborers to work throughout the country. In January 1919, a series of strikes occurred in Berlin. Calling on workers to overthrow the government, the Communist party seized several buildings. The attempted revolution was immediately put down but resulted in great bloodshed due to the army's use of artillery and the extremely aggressive units of the Freikorps, or Free Corps, volunteer units (see box on page 10). The same story of rebellion and defeat was played out in other areas of Germany. When workers participated in strikes and building takeovers, they often proclaimed a Soviet Republic in the area, meaning that the government would be composed of a council of workers and soldiers. Then troops, usually the Freikorps, were sent in by the central government in Berlin. The result was typically a bloody defeat of the revolutionaries, followed by shootings and beatings of those suspected of sympathizing with the "reds," or German revolutionaries.

The most important of these uprisings occurred in Munich, the capital of the large state of Bavaria in southern Germany, where the Soviet Republic lasted a little more than three weeks. When the Freikorps entered the city on May 1, 1919, they killed more than 1,000 people and continued the executions after the protesters had surrendered. Many of the victims had nothing to do with the revolution. The result of the Munich uprising was a crackdown on Communism. In an effort to keep the Communists down, the new government of the state of Bavaria welcomed and protected opponents of the "reds." Like members of the Freikorps, they opposed democracy and wanted the reins of government to be held by a single ruler. Munich became a center for extreme nationalists who wanted a powerful German army and expressed an intense hatred for the new republic. They blamed the Jews for the revolution, Germany's defeat in the war, and social problems. Military officers in Munich wanted to aid the nationalists, so the army sent a soldier to investigate one of these groups, the German Workers' party. The soldier was Adolf Hitler.

In January 1919 Germany held its first elections since before the Great War. Even though voting was held during a period of turmoil, the elections were fair and legal; for the first time, everyone over the age of twenty, including women, could vote. More than 80 percent of all eligible voters cast a ballot. The Social Democrats won the

Freikorps

The Freikorps (Free Corps) were volunteer units comprised mainly of former officers and professional soldiers. They were organized by the army soon after the World War I armistice. At the height of its popularity, the Freikorps included about 200 units with 400,000 soldiers—four times the official size of the regular German army. Freikorps members were extremely hostile not only to Communists but also to Social Democrats and to democracy itself. They adamantly opposed unions, were fiercely anti-Semitic, and glorified war and Germany's military past. While the official duties of the Freikorps were to guard Germany's borders and maintain order, they were actually utilized in the bloodiest work and illegal actions.

Many protesters who were killed in the Berlin uprising of 1919, for example, were shot by the Freikorps after they had surrendered. Karl Liebknecht and Rosa Luxemburg, the two most important Communist party leaders, were brutally murdered three days after the end of the uprising. The Freikorps became a perfect tool for crushing the government's enemies, and most of the first Nazi storm troopers were members of the Freikorps.

most votes, approximately 38 percent, but did not gain a majority. The Center party, supported by the Catholic church, received about 20 percent of the vote, and the Democratic party, a moderate group, did almost as well. Although they differed about specific political issues, these three parties supported the new government, referred to as the Weimar Republic after Weimar, the city where the National Assembly met and where the new constitution was being written. More than 75 percent of voters backed parties in favor of the Weimar Republic. Anti-democratic groups, such as the Nationalists and the German People's party, who wanted either a return of the monarchy or some form of dictatorship, received about 16 percent of the vote. The remaining voters supported the Independent Social Democrats, a group whose philosophy fell somewhere between the regular Social Democrats and the Communists, who did not run in the election. The three parties that had garnered a majority of the votes—the Social Democrats, the Center, and the Democrats—became known as the Weimar Coalition.

The Treaty of Versailles and the Great Depression

The Weimar Coalition was faced with the task of negotiating a permanent peace treaty with the Allies. The terms of the agreement, named the Treaty of Versailles after the French city where the Peace Conference was held, were considered harsh by the Germans: (1) The size and power of the German armed forces were strictly limited. The army would have only 100,000 men; the navy would have 15,000 men and no planes, tanks, or submarines. (2) Germany would lose all of its colonies, which would be taken over mainly by France and Britain. (3) Finally, Germany would also lose some of its own territory. Alsace and Lorraine, two regions the Germans had taken from France after a war in 1870, were returned to France. A section of western Germany near France, called the Rhineland, would be controlled by Allied troops for a number of years.

Large sections of eastern Germany went to the newly independent country of Poland. These areas had been under German rule since before 1800, when Poland had been divided among Russia, the Austrian Empire, and Prussia, the country that later became the modern nation of Germany. The easternmost part of Germany, called East Prussia, was cut off from the rest of the country by a section of Poland that became known as the "Polish Corridor." Under the terms of the Treaty of Versailles, Germany lost about one-eighth of its territory.

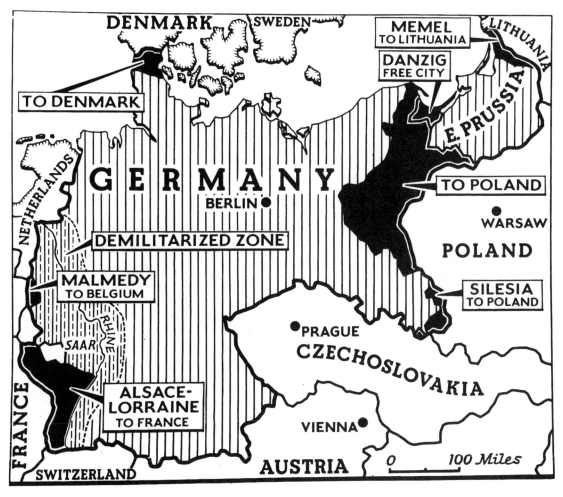

Shaded areas show Germany's territorial losses after World War I. *(Reproduced by permission of AP/Wide World Photos)*

The Allies made two other demands that especially angered German citizens: Germany was to admit that it was responsible for starting the war, and was to make reparations over many years to the Allies, especially to France, for the enormous destruction it caused. When the Allies revealed how much money, coal, lumber, and other products they wanted, Germans found the amount staggering. The terms of the Treaty of Versailles seemed intended to make Germany permanently poor and weak. No one in Germany approved of the treaty. Many representatives in the National Assembly wanted to reject the agreement, but Allied armies were positioned at Germany's borders, ready to continue fighting, and Germany had no hope of defeating them. German prisoners of war were also still waiting to be released. Perhaps most significantly, the British fleet was prepared to blockade German ports once again, an action that would lead to food shortages throughout the country. On

June 23, 1919, the German National Assembly agreed to the Allied terms by a vote of 237 to 138— a vote that did not indicate acceptance of the treaty but resignation to a dictated peace instead.

The German economy had been drastically weakened by war and disorder. A German government short of funds simply printed more paper money, but with no financial resources to support the value of this new tender, the result was dramatic inflation. In July 1919 fourteen German marks were equivalent to one American dollar; by July 1922 the ratio had ballooned to 490 to one. With the rapid loss of currency values, consumers rushed to spend their wages as soon as they were paid in order to buy what they needed before prices increased. As prices rose, so did wages, resulting in yet another change of cost structure. By the middle of August 1923, one American dollar was worth almost 3 million German marks. Two weeks later, it was worth 13 million, then 98 million, then 345 million. By

The League of Nations

The Treaty of Versailles resulted in the creation of the League of Nations, a coalition of countries committed to solving international problems peacefully, similar to today's United Nations. The League achieved some minor successes, such as allowing residents of disputed areas to choose the country in which they wanted to live. However, its real mission, to prevent war by "collective security," was a complete failure. All member states were supposed to provide mutual protection either by utilizing their economic power to punish attackers or by using force to defend weak nations. One reason the League of Nations failed, according to historians, was that the United States refused to join, despite the fact that the League was the idea of Woodrow Wilson, U.S. president during and after World War I. The U.S. Senate rejected membership in the League, reasoning that the United States had no business involving itself in European affairs. This view was echoed by many Americans, who felt U.S. citizens had died in World War I over disputes that had nothing to do with their country. The call for isolationism was a strong force in American politics until Japan attacked the United States in December 1941. America's absence from the League made it seem a

Woodrow Wilson (Library of Congress)

less neutral body than was originally intended. According to some critics, without U.S. participation, the League became a way for Britain and France to protect their own interests and enforce their will on the rest of Europe. Although the League of Nations continued to meet and vote on important issues, the world paid less and less attention to its decisions.

November 15, one American dollar was worth 2.5 trillion German marks. Pensions and bank accounts were wiped out. Savings that once would have paid for a house would not buy a loaf of bread. Most middle-class people fell from positions of comfort into poverty, becoming fearful about the future and distrustful of the government.

For a short time, in the mid- to late-1920s, Germany was once again prosperous. From 1925 to 1929 the economy expanded rapidly, inflation was brought under control, and industry produced at pre-war

capacity. In fact, many factories managed to double their production between 1923 and 1928. In 1923 Germany produced approximately 8 percent of all the world's industrial goods; in 1928 it produced 12 percent. Output of steel increased 255 percent in only six years. Much of Germany's new prosperity depended on exporting manufactured goods to other countries. As unemployment decreased, housing and other conditions improved for many people. Germany also underwent a burst of creative energy in the mid-1920s as Berlin became a great center for writers and artists from all over Europe. During this time the

German film industry created many classic films; architecture and furniture design also flourished.

In fall 1929 the United States plummeted into the Great Depression. Companies could not sell their products and resorted to massive labor cutbacks and factory closings. As unemployment rates increased, the consumer market declined even further. Although this economic crisis began in the United States, it soon spread to the industrial countries of Europe with which the United States had trade relations. Germany was more severely hit by the Depression than any other major European country, partly because German companies were dependent on exports. During the brief economic prosperity of the late 1920s, one-third of German products were exported. Countries that relied on German exports, also affected by the Depression, could not import so many products. German banks closed, industrial production fell rapidly, and by early 1933, 6 million Germans—approximately one-third of the labor force—were unemployed. The unemployed and their families were becoming desperate, as the government seemed unable or unwilling to solve the country's economic problems. Many Germans had no faith in the political parties loyal to the new German government to solve this economic crisis, and supported the newly founded Nazi party instead.

Passive Resistance Against France

Meanwhile, in the early 1920s, Germany had fallen behind on its scheduled reparation shipments of coal and lumber to France. In January 1923 the French government used this as an excuse to send troops to take over the Ruhr region, the most important industrial center in Germany, home to huge steel mills and coal mines. The official purpose of the occupation was to ensure that Germany met its reparation duties, but many Germans believed that France wanted to weaken their country further by permanently separating the Ruhr from Germany. By summer 1923, some 100,000 French troops were controlling the Ruhr. The size of the occupation force equaled the size of the entire German army, eliminating any attempt at military resistance. The German government advocated a policy of passive resistance and, consequently, the people of the Ruhr would not cooperate with the French. Workers refused to load coal bound for France and railroad crews would not transport it. Local officials ignored French instructions. The French retaliated by jailing

Unemployment in Germany

The unemployment figures below are probably much lower than the actual number of people who were out of work in Germany from 1929 to 1933. The numbers include only those unemployed individuals who were registered with the government. In addition, they do not count people who were employed in part-time positions but were looking for full-time work.

September 1929	1,320,000
September 1930	3,000,000
September 1931	4,350,000
September 1932	5,102,000
January/February 1933	6,000,000+

some German workers for refusing to obey their orders; they expelled many others. Some of the expelled people were welcomed in other areas of Germany, but with no jobs, they had to be supported by an already strained German economy.

All Ruhr residents were not passive in resisting the French troops. Despite the real possibility of execution if caught by the French, some Germans dynamited railroad lines and bridges. During a strike at the massive Krupp factories in the city of Essen, French troops fired on the workers, killing thirteen and wounding thirty. When the French assumed control of coal mines, the laborers refused to work and the mines were shut down. Tens of thousands of unemployed miners depended on money sent by the German government. When the French banned the transport of coal from the Ruhr to the rest of Germany, the German government severed all railroad traffic to the Ruhr. At that time most goods were shipped by rail. With the richest area of the country cut off, another economic disaster erupted. Approximately 180,000 Germans had been expelled from the Ruhr, 100 had been killed, and more were imprisoned. Hundreds of millions of gold marks (as opposed to the worthless paper marks) were being spent by the gov-

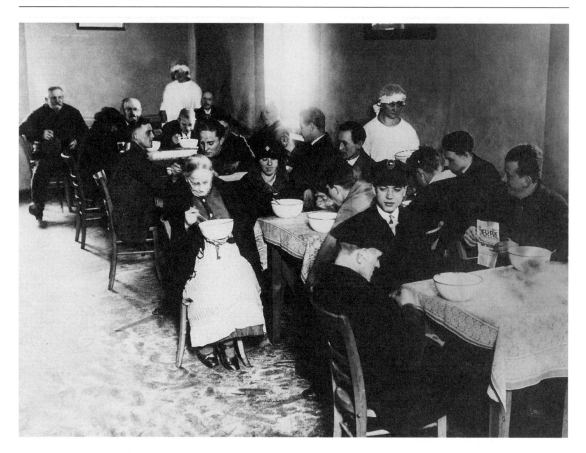

Many unemployed workers had to turn to soup kitchens for free meals during Germany's depression. *(Reproduced by permission of Bildarchiv Preussischer Kulturbesitz)*

ernment every week to support people who had lost their homes or their jobs.

In September 1923 the German government asked the people of the Ruhr to end passive resistance and return to work. Although the government probably had little choice, its decision angered nationalist Germans. To them, the failure to drive the French out of the Ruhr signified another betrayal of Germany by the same traitors who had agreed to the Treaty of Versailles. This brand of nationalism was also encouraged by the rise of communism in Europe. After the Russian Revolution of 1917, in which Communist forces took over the government to form the Union of Soviet Socialist Republics (U.S.S.R.), Communists made frequent attempts to seize power in other parts of Europe, especially in Germany, Italy, and Hungary. For people who opposed communism, particularly wealthy landowners

and industrialists, there was strong appeal in the idea of a powerful government that would stamp out the forces of change that were sweeping Europe in the forms of both democracy and communism.

Five years after the end of the fighting in World War I, Germany was still experiencing deep social divisions. Conservatives and industrialists vied for power against workers' groups; hostilities continued among Catholics and Protestants; and different states within Germany fought against the rule of the national government. High inflation had severely shaken many Germans. Even worse, losing the war and then submitting to France's military intervention had been deeply humiliating. Angry and distrustful of their government, people were looking for scapegoats. German extremist groups found the time ripe for taking action. One such group was the Nazi party.

Introduction to *Protocols of the Elders of Zion*

First published in the Russian newspaper Znamya
August 26–September 7, 1903

The founders of the Nazi party devoutly believed in the idea of a superior race. According to Nazi philosophy, the history of civilization reveals a struggle between the supreme Aryan race and the corrupting influences of other inferior races. Party members felt that Jewish people represented the most dangerous threat to the survival of the German nation, a negative force destined to disrupt and destroy Aryan progress. In the mid-1850s French writer Arthur Comte Gobineau published an influential book, the four-volume *Essays on the Inequality of Human Races,* containing controversial theories of race superiority and the importance of racial purity. Many Germans used Gobineau's ideas to give credibility to anti-Jewish views. In 1879 German racial theorist Wilhelm Marr, coining the term anti-Semitism, established the Anti-Semitic League as the first political organization devoted to the promotion of hatred toward Jews. Houston Stewart Chamberlain, an Englishman who became a German citizen, wrote *Foundation of the Nineteenth Century,* another popular theory of racial doctrine. Published in Munich, Germany, in 1899, the work attempted to trace European history according to race ideology. Chamberlain called the Teutons, an ancient Germanic tribe, a creative, regenerative force; conversely, he labeled the Jews an alien, disruptive influence.

By the early 1930s, Germans were seized by a nationalist spirit that made them susceptible to these theories of race. Defeat in World War I had devastated the morale of German citizens. Mourning the end of imperial rule, they resented the democratic Weimar Republic that had accepted the terms of the Treaty of Versailles. The newly formed republic faced serious challenges from two opposing political movements within Germany: (1) communist influences; (2) a zealous nationalistic movement called *voelkisch,* meaning "of the people." Economic problems further complicated the political turmoil in postwar Germany, as the punitive reparations and naval blockades imposed by the Allies drastically disrupted commerce. Severe inflation and the 1929 New York stock market crash brought further trouble to an already struggling economy. Rampant unemployment, economic insecurity, and the chaotic political situation combined to create a climate in which many Germans felt they were victims of negative outside forces. Increasingly violent nationalist groups believed that the introduction of foreign ideas such as democracy from the West and communism from the East had contaminated their country. Angry nationalists blamed Jewish people in particular for the troubles and instability facing Germany in the 1920s and 1930s.

The first signs of anti-Semitism had surfaced throughout Europe during the Middle Ages. The wave of anti-Semitism that intensified in Germany after World War I originated in eastern and central Europe, which had large Jewish communities. In Russia, anti-Semitism took a deadly turn between 1881 and 1920, when organized mobs began attacking Jews in violent riots and massacres called pogroms. As early as 1903, Russian anti-Semites circulated a forged document entitled *Protocols of the Elders of Zion* to justify the pogroms. The *Protocols* pamphlet reads like a factual firsthand report of a secret meeting of Jewish elders of the twelve tribes of Israel, who are planning to take over the world. While the document is clearly a forgery created by the secret police of the Russian czar in the 1890s, the instigators of the pogroms relied upon the *Protocols* to legitimize the escalating violence that resulted in the brutal killings of 100,000 Jews in Russia between 1918 and 1920. When anti-Semitic army officers fled to Germany after the Russian Revolution, they took the controversial *Protocols* with them.

Members of the nationalistic movement in Germany quickly moved to use the *Protocols* in the anti-Semitic campaign that was raging within their own country. Advocating anti-Semitism, many nationalistic groups retold history as a struggle between the Aryan race and Jews. Although Jews represented less than 1 percent of the German population, many people blamed them for the nation's defeat in World War I and the failing economy that followed. In truth, thousands of Jewish

In Kiev, Ukraine, Alfred Rosenberg walks past a line of Hitler Youth members. *(Reproduced by permission of © Hulton Getty/Liaison Agency)*

wealthy and benefitted financially at the expense of non-Jews. *Protocols* provided the type of evidence that many Germans needed to become convinced of the supposedly evil nature and influence of Jews. The sense of mysticism and secrecy surrounding *Protocols* only contributed to the impression of the pamphlet's authenticity.

The *voelkisch* provided the ideological roots of the Nazi party, which formed in 1920. The Nazis exploited *Protocols* throughout their regime. While the infamous forgery first appeared in Germany in 1918, an influential Nazi leader, Alfred Rosenberg, reissued an official party version, along with commentaries, in 1923. *Protocols* is written in twenty-four sections that outline the master plan of an alleged Jewish conspiracy to take control of the world. The following excerpts describe some methods Jews would allegedly use to destroy existing governments. In 1921 an English newspaper pronounced the *Protocols* a forgery, as did a Swiss court in 1935. The anonymous author plagiarized most of *Protocols* from a French political essay directed against Napoleon III and published in 1864. The forger adapted the original philosophical discussions about despotism to appear as the opinions and plans of Jewish leaders. The Nazis consistently relied on *Protocols* as proof of a vast Jewish conspiracy to dominate the world. The Twelfth Protocol, for example, describes how the Jews are planning to take control of the press as a means to mislead and ultimately rule society. But in 1933 the Nazis themselves applied this technique of controlling public opinion by outlawing all nonparty publications. Historians note that in many ways the *Protocols* served as a guidebook for the way the Nazis eventually tried to conquer and rule the world.

men had served in the German army during the war and many had received military honors. German Jews tended to live in cities such as Hamburg and Berlin and were concentrated in certain professions and occupations associated with urban society. As economic difficulties persisted in Germany, the perception arose that all Jews were

Protocols of the Elders of Zion

First Protocol

People with corrupt instincts are more numerous than those of noble instinct. Therefore in governing the world, the best results are obtained by means of violence and intimidation, and not by academic discussion. Every man aims at power; everyone would like to become a dictator if he could do so, and rare indeed are the men who would not be dis-

posed to sacrifice the welfare of others in order to attain their own personal aims. What restrained the wild beasts of prey we call men? What has ruled them up to now? In the first stages of social life they submitted to brute and blind force, then to law, which in reality is the same force, only masked. From this I am led to deduct that by the law of nature, right lies in might. Political freedom is not a fact, but an idea.

Third Protocol

Today I can assure you that we are ... within a few strides of our goal. There remains only a short distance and the cycle of the Symbolic Serpent—the badge of our people—will be complete. When this circle is locked, all the States of Europe will be enclosed in it, as it were, by unbreakable chains....

Under our auspices the populace exterminated the aristocracy which had supported and guarded the people for its own benefit, which benefit is inseparable from the welfare of the populace. Nowadays, having destroyed the privileges of the aristocracy, the people fall under the yoke of cunning profiteers and upstarts.

We intend to appear as though we were the liberators of the labouring man, come to free him from this oppression, when we shall suggest to him to join the ranks of our armies of Socialists, Anarchists, and Communists. The latter we always patronize, pretending to help them out of fraternal principle and the general interest of humanity evoked by our socialistic masonry. The aristocracy, who ... shared the [fruits of the] labour of the working classes, [wanted the workers to be] well-fed, healthy and strong. We are interested in the opposite, i.e. in the degeneration of the Gentiles. Our strength lies in keeping the working man in perpetual want and impotence; because, by so doing, we retain him subject to our will and, in his own surroundings, he will never find either power or energy to stand up against us....

The Gentiles are no longer capable of thinking without our aid in matters of science. That is why they do not realize the vital necessity of certain things, which we will make a point of keeping against the moment when our hour arrives.... In schools the only true and most important of all sciences must be taught, that is, the science of the life of man and social conditions, both of which require a division of labour and therefore the classification of people in castes and classes....

We persuaded the Gentiles that liberalism would bring them to a kingdom of reason. Our despotism will be of this nature, for it will be in a position to put down all rebellions and by just severity to exterminate every liberal idea from all institutions.

When the populace noticed that it was being given all sorts of rights in the name of liberty, it imagined itself to be the master, and tried to assume power. Of course, like every other blind man, the mass came up against innumerable obstacles. Then, as it did not wish to return to the former régime, it laid its power at our feet.... We have led the nations

Eugenics

The ideas of Arthur Comte Gobineau and English racial theorist Houston Stewart Chamberlain led to the development of eugenics, a scientific practice devoted to controlled race breeding. Although many believe the Nazis attempted to practice eugenics, the genocidal efforts of the Nazi party passed beyond governmental control of breeding. True eugenics surveys the population of a country, giving benefits and support to those elements that produce the most productive offspring. The systematic elimination of a racial group was never established as a postulate of eugenics. True eugenics has never been successful in any civilization.

from one disappointment to another, so that they should even renounce us in favour of the King-Despot of the blood of Zion, whom we are preparing for the world....

Sixth Protocol

Soon we will start organizing great monopolies—reservoirs of colossal wealth, in which even the large fortunes of the Gentiles will be involved to such an extent that they will sink together with the credit of their government the day after a political crisis takes place....

We must use every possible kind of means to develop the popularity of our Supergovernment, holding it up as a protection and recompenser of all who willingly submit to us.

The aristocracy of the Gentiles, as a political power, is no more—therefore we need not consider it any more from that point of view. But as landowners, they are still dangerous to us, because their independent existence is ensured through their resources. Therefore, it is essential for us, at all costs, to deprive the aristocracy of their lands. To this purpose the best method is to force up rates and taxes.... At the same time we must give all possible protection to trade and commerce, and especially to speculation, the principle role of which is to act as a counterpoise to indus-

Automobile magnate Henry Ford published the *Protocols of the Elders of Zion* in his newspaper the *Dearborn Independent*.

try. Without speculation industry will enlarge private capitals....

Twelfth Protocol

Literature and journalism are the two most important educational powers; for this reason our government will buy up the greater number of periodicals. By these means we shall neutralize the bad influence of the private press and obtain an enormous influence over the human mind. If we were to allow ten private periodicals we should ourselves start thirty, and so forth.

But the public must not have the slightest suspicion of these measures, therefore all periodicals published by us will seem to be of contradictory views and opinions, thus inspiring confidence and presenting an attractive appearance to our unsuspecting enemies, who will thus fall into our trap and will be disarmed.... These newspapers, like the Indian god Vishnu, will be possessed of hundreds of hands, each of which will be feeling the pulse of varying public opinion....

If any chatterers are going to imagine that they are repeating the opinion of their party newspaper, they will in reality be repeating our own opinion, or the opinion which we desire. Thinking that they are

following the organ of this party, they will in reality be following the flag which we will fly for them....

Already there exists in French journalism a system of masonic understanding for giving countersigns. All organs of the press are tied by mutual professional secrets in the manner of the ancient oracles. Not one of its members will betray his knowledge of the secret, if such a secret has not been ordered to be made public. No single publisher will have the courage to betray the secret entrusted to him, the reason being that not one of them is admitted into the literary world without bearing the marks of some shady act in his past life. He would only have to show the least sign of disobedience and the mark would be immediately revealed. Whilst these marks remain known only to a few, the prestige of the journalist attracts public opinion throughout the country. The people follow and admire him.

Our plans must extend chiefly to the provinces. It is essential for us to create such ideas and inspire such opinions there....

Epilogue

According to the records of secret Jewish Zionism, Solomon and other Jewish learned men already, in 929 B.C., thought out a scheme in theory for a peaceful conquest of the whole universe by Zion.

As history developed, this scheme was worked out in detail and completed by men, who were subsequently initiated in this question. These learned men decided by peaceful means to conquer the world for Zion with the slyness of the symbolic serpent, whose head was to represent the initiated into the plans of the Jewish administration, and the body of the serpent to represent the Jewish people—the administration was always kept secret, even from the Jewish nation itself. As this serpent penetrated into the hearts of the nations which it encountered, it got under and devoured all the non-Jewish power of these states. It is foretold that the snake has to finish its work, strictly adhering to the designed path, until the course which it has to run is closed by the return of its head to Zion and until by this means, the snake has completed its round of Europe and has encircled it—and until, by dint of enchaining Europe, it has encompassed the whole world. This it is to accomplish by using every endeavor to subdue the other countries by an economical conquest.

The return of the head of the serpent to Zion can only be accomplished after the power of all the Sovereigns of Europe has been laid low, that is to say, when by means of economic crises and wholesale destruction effected everywhere there shall have been brought about a spiritual demoralization and a moral corruption, chiefly with the assistance of Jewish women masquerading as French, Italians, etc. These are the surest spreaders of licentiousness into the lives of the leading men at the heads of nations....

A sketch of the symbolic serpent is shown as follows: Its first stage in Europe was in 429 B.C. in Greece, where, in the time of Pericles, the serpent first started eating into the power of that country. The second stage was in Rome in the time of Augustus about 69 B.C. [more likely 29 B.C.] The third in Madrid in the time of Charles V, A.D. 1552. The fourth in Paris about 1700, in the time of Louis XVI. [This should be Louis XIV.] The fifth in London from 1814 onwards (after the downfall of Napoléon). The sixth in Berlin in 1871 after the Franco-Prussian war. The seventh in St. Petersburg, over which is drawn the head of the serpent under the date of 1881.

All these states which the serpent traversed have had the foundations of their constitutions shaken, Germany, with its apparent power, forming no exception to the rule. In economic conditions England and Germany are spared, but only till the conquest of Russia is accomplished by the serpent, on which at present all its efforts are concentrated. The further course of the serpent is not shown on this map, but arrows indicate its next movement towards Moscow, Kieff, and Odessa.

It is now well known to us to what extent the latter cities form the centres of the militant Jewish race. Constantinople is shown as the last stage of the serpent's course before it reaches Jerusalem.

Only a short distance still remains before the serpent will be able to complete its course by uniting its head to its tail...

Signed by the representatives of Zion,
of the 33rd degree. (Cohn, pp. 285–297)

Aftermath

Adolf Hitler and the Nazi party made anti-Semitism the central tenet of their philosophy and official government policy. As the Nazis grew more powerful, their newspapers continually referred to the *Protocols,* and Hitler claimed it had greatly influenced him. The *Protocols* helped the Nazis exploit the myth of a Jewish world conspiracy to first gain power and then institute a reign of terror against non-Jews. Anyone who challenged Nazi policy or defended the Jewish cause risked being labeled a part of this alleged conspiracy. The literary hoax of the *Protocols* profoundly influenced twentieth-century history by ultimately helping the Nazis justify the genocide of the Jewish people. Six million Jewish men, women, and children—two-thirds of all European Jews—died at the hands of the Nazis during the Holocaust.

Various anti-Semitic individuals and groups around the world translated and published the *Protocols of the Elders of Zion.* After World War I, the *Protocols* were available in every European language plus Japanese, Chinese, and Arabic. In 1920, American automaker and founder of Ford Motor Company, Henry Ford, published the *Protocols* both in his newspaper, the *Dearborn Independent,* and in a book titled *The International Jew.* The prestige of Ford's name gave tremendous credibility to the *Protocols* within the United States and around the world. *The International Jew* sold over half a million copies in the United States, was translated into sixteen languages, and became an official part of Nazi propaganda. Due to a lawsuit and mounting criticism, Ford publicly retracted his accusations of a Jewish conspiracy. In 1927 he denied responsibility for what had been published in *The International Jew* and attempted to withdraw the book from circulation. The damage had already occurred, however, for Ford's book did more to make the *Protocols* famous than any other publication.

Sources

Books

Bachrach, Susan D., *Tell Them We Remember: The Story of the Holocaust,* Little, Brown (Boston), 1994.

Cohn, Norman, *Warrant for Genocide: The Myth of the Jewish Conspiracy and the Protocols of the Elders of Zion,* Serif (London), 1967; reprinted, 1996.

Patterson, Charles, *Anti-Semitism: The Road to the Holocaust and Beyond,* Walker (New York), 1989.

Evolution of the Nazi Party

Adolf Hitler, the man who would ultimately lead the Nazi party, was born in the town of Braunau in Austria-Hungary in 1889, the son of a low-level customs official. A poor student from an early age, Hitler had conflicts with his father, who wanted him to train for a career as a minor government official. Hitler was fourteen when his father died, and he convinced his mother to let him drop out of school two years later. After leaving school, he spent the next three years wandering around Linz attending the theater and spending time in the library. When Hitler was eighteen, he went to Vienna, the capital of Austria-Hungary, where he applied to the painting school at the Academy of Fine Arts. After being rejected once, he applied a second time, only to be turned away again and advised to try the architectural school. Embittered by this experience, Hitler continued to live in Vienna, sometimes in great poverty and often in men's hotels that were nothing more than dormitories for people who would otherwise be homeless. He supported himself by begging and taking odd jobs, such as painting picture postcards that he sold on the streets.

Prior to World War I, Vienna was one of the great capitals of Europe. It was also a center of anti-Semitic sentiments and political movements. The longtime mayor of Vienna, Karl Lüger, had built his career by denouncing Jews. This political climate, accompanied by his inability to find employment or schooling as an artist, contributed to Hitler's intense hatred of Jews. Developing a keen interest in politics, he realized he could become a successful politician by publicly espousing anti-Semitism.

Hitler moved to Munich, Germany, in 1913. When World War I broke out the following year, he avoided induction into the Austrian army and instead joined a Bavarian unit of the German Imperial Army. Serving throughout the war, he was promoted to the rank of corporal after being wounded, and received several medals. Hitler's role in the war provided him a newfound sense of belonging and accomplishment. After the controversial armistice imposed by the Treaty of Versailles, the German army sent him back to Munich. The terms of the treaty and the seeming betrayal of the German people by the government enraged Hitler, who began blaming the Jews for Germany's humiliation. His hatred of Jews and Communists, who he thought were synonymous, became even more intense during the short-lived Soviet Republic in Munich in 1919. He rejoiced at the bloody defeat of the "reds." Soon Hitler came to the attention of officials in charge of hunting down supporters of the Soviet Republic. The officials discovered that he had charisma and a talent for transmitting his extreme nationalist views to crowds of dissatisfied Germans. They appointed Hitler as an education officer to help spread their shared ideals,

Some historians wonder if Adolf Hitler had found success with his art (pictured here), would the world have been spared the Holocaust and World War II?*(Reproduced by permission of AP/Wide World Photos)*

sending him to investigate the Deutsche Arbeiterpartei, or German Workers' party.

When Adolf Hitler joined the German Workers' party in June 1919, it had only forty members under the leadership of Anton Drexler, a locksmith. Despite the party's name, it had hardly any actual support from workers. Soon distinguishing himself in the party, Hitler threatened to leave if he was not appointed leader. Realizing their success was contingent upon Hitler's involvement, party members acquiesced to his demands and gave him control as the führer, or leader. The name of the group was changed to the Nationalsozialistische Deutsche Arbeiterpartei (Nazi party), which translates as the National Socialist German Workers' party. Hitler began reshaping the organization. He established a military wing called the Sturmabteilung (SA), or storm troopers, most of whom were former Free Corps members and brutal fighters. Often referred to as brownshirts because of their uniforms, the storm troopers guarded Nazi meetings, protected party leaders, and intimidated political opponents and the general public with displays of violence. By 1923 the Nazi party had 15,000 members and more than 5,000 storm troopers, who paraded through the towns of Bavaria breaking up meetings of Socialists and

Communists. Although still relatively small, the Nazi party had some powerful allies. The Bavarian government, including important police officials, protected party members, and Hitler retained strong connections with the army. One of the Nazis' most important supporters was Erich Ludendorff, a general who had virtually run Germany in the last years of World War I.

In fall 1923, as Germany yielded to the control of French soldiers in the industrial Ruhr region and the economic situation went into further decline, the Nazis in Munich saw the perfect opportunity to overthrow the Weimar Republic. On November 8, 1923, the eve of the fifth anniversary of the revolution that had overthrown the kaiser, the leader of the Bavarian state government was making a speech in a Munich beer hall. He was a Nazi sympathizer, as were the local army commander and the Munich chief of police, who were present at the meeting. Nazi storm troopers surrounded the hall and Hitler rushed onto the stage, proclaiming a national revolution. When Bavarian leaders refused to join the Nazis in a march on Berlin, Hitler threatened them with a gun. Ludendorff soon arrived and tried to convince the leaders to join the cause. After the Nazis released the hostages, the Bavarian government ordered the

Hitler delivering a speech at the time of the establishment of the Nazi party in 1923. *(Reproduced by permission of Snark/Art Resource)*

army and the police to stop the rebels. The next day, the Nazis, led by Hitler and Ludendorff, marched to the center of town, where a special unit of police blocked the thoroughfare. Gunfire erupted, killing sixteen storm troopers and three police officers and wounding many others, including high-ranking Nazis. Hitler and other Nazi leaders escaped from the scene and went into hiding; Hitler was captured a few days later. The unsuccessful coup became known as the Beer Hall Putsch. (*Putsch* is the German word for an unsuccessful rebellion.)

Hitler was put on trial along with Ludendorff in February 1924. Despite their obvious attempt at armed rebellion and treason, the two men were treated with respect by the judges, who were especially deferential to Ludendorff. The judges even allowed Hitler to make repeated speeches in court, where he openly admitted that he wanted to overthrow the government by force. It was a high-profile case because Ludendorff was a well-known German general; however, Hitler's speaking ability also impressed the people watching the trial. The same

courts that had handed death penalty sentences to Communist agitators in 1919 acquitted Ludendorff. Hitler was convicted of high treason and given the minimum sentence of five years, but only served about eight months in a comfortable prison cell, where he dictated his autobiography, *Mein Kampf* ("My Struggle"; see box on page 26 and primary source entry), to a private secretary. When Hitler was released from prison, he resumed his efforts to establish the party. According to German law, he should have been expelled from the country because he was not a German citizen. Yet he had gained a considerable following and was therefore permitted to remain in Munich. By this time hate groups throughout Germany had heard about Hitler and the Nazis as a result of the Beer Hall Putsch trial.

Defining the Party Platform

The failure of the revolution in Munich convinced Hitler that he could never take over Germany with just a few thousand followers. Even if his storm troopers were armed, they could not

Pernet   Weber   Frick   Kriebel   Ludendorff   Hitler   Brückner   Wagner
Röhm

Defendants at the trial of the Munich Beer Hall Putsch. Adolf Hitler is fourth from the right. *(Reproduced by permission of Snark/Art Resource)*

successfully fight the German army. Hitler therefore devoted his efforts to increasing the influence of the Nazi party. The first step would be to run in elections to gain publicity for Nazi ideas: When Nazi party candidates were elected to state or national parliaments, they would use their positions as platforms to reiterate the party message, just as Hitler had done at his trial. The Nazis began organizing large street rallies and publishing newspapers that emphasized recurring themes. They realized they could draw in the masses by holding demonstrations and parades, with marchers carrying flags, shouting slogans, and displaying intense loyalty to the party.

While numerous other extreme nationalist groups held views similar to those of the Nazis, they were primarily military organizations. They preferred wearing uniforms and carrying weapons to running in elections, and were more like street gangs than political parties, with a general contempt for ordinary Germans. Hitler embraced the military aspect of the evolving Nazi regime but also realized that to win the support of the people, he had to build a party for the masses. He faced a major challenge in forming such an organization because most German workers had no use for the Nazis' goals and showed no interest in ruling others as members of the superior race. Although he

believed Germany should rule over other nations, Hitler found most Germans generally lacking in the greatness he idealized in *Mein Kampf*.

Hitler resolved the conflict between his vision of a superior German race and his disdain for the actual German masses by theorizing that the leaders of the Social Democratic party were purposely poisoning the minds of workers. He claimed that the Social Democrats used the problems of workers, such as low pay and poor living conditions, to advance their own goals. Most importantly, he concluded, the ideas of the Social Democrats really came from the Jews. According to Hitler, German workers were hostile to his extreme nationalist ideas because they had been fooled by the Jews. Behind every problem, behind every opponent of the Nazis, there were the Jews, Hitler told his audiences. He believed that skill in focusing people's attention upon various opponents as if they were a single opponent was the mark of a true leader. Hitler's targeted opponent was the Jewish people.

The Nazis combined their emphasis on military strength with appeals to lower-middle-class Germans who were frightened and confused by recent events in the country. To reach the disillusioned populace, they had to use tactics that differed from those of other extreme nationalists. The Nazis there-

The Swastika and the Red Flag

The swastika, a hooked or twisted cross that became the symbol of the Nazi party, existed long before the Nazis chose to use it. Common in India, the symbol was used by early Christians, and was often featured in the art of Native Americans. Extreme nationalists in Germany believed the swastika was connected with ancient Aryans or Indo-Europeans, and some groups put the symbol on their newspapers or on the helmets of their uniforms. Recognizing the popularity and connotations of the swastika, the Nazis took a design created by Adolf Hitler as their party emblem: a black swastika inside a white circle with a solid red backdrop. Red symbolized the workers' parties and a workers' revolution. The color was already associated with the German Social Democratic party and the Communist party. Thus, by using the red flag, the Nazis were trying to depict themselves as a revolutionary party. Always referring to their goal of a "national revolution," they reiterated their platform through the party symbol, a flag that showed they were both socialists and nationalists.

The flag of the Third Reich incorporated a swastika—an ancient religious symbol that dates back to the bronze age. (*Reproduced by permission of AP/Wide World Photos*)

fore called for citizens to view the party as revolutionary—a force that would change Germany, rather than merely revert it to pre-World War I conditions that were no better than the present situation. This strategy was the socialist aspect of the Nazi platform. While establishing themselves as a political force that could assuage the fears of ordinary people, the Nazis also wanted to distance themselves from conventional political organizations by adopting the tactics of extremist groups. They wore uniforms, had military-style ranks, marched in the streets under the banner of the swastika (see box on this page), and

Mein Kampf

In *Mein Kampf* (see primary source entry), Adolf Hitler tells his life story and explains his ideas about Germany, the world, Jews, and the Nazi party. Portraying himself as a political genius whose ideas are entirely original, he writes that he will become the savior of Germany because he is the only person who can alleviate national problems. Contemporary readers of *Mein Kampf* are often surprised that people exposed to the text at the time could have taken Hitler seriously, as it is rambling, abrupt, and repetitive.

Hitler uses *Mein Kampf* as a platform to rant about the injustice of the Treaty of Versailles. He blames Germany's defeat in World War I on the Jews, whom he accuses of controlling Great Britain and France, the two main powers that forced Germany to agree to the treaty. Hitler also denounces democracy, socialism, and communism as inventions of the Jews. Outlining his goal for German rearmament, he envisions a revitalized country that will seize control of more land and regain its colonies—goals that he believes the Jews are preventing.

Hitler expresses contempt for the people who later became his supporters. Although he elevates Germans as a superior "race," it is clear that he does not think highly of individual members of this race. The "masses," he writes, lack the ability to grasp ideas, and "their understanding is feeble. On the other hand, they quickly forget." Most people are unable to conceptual-

ize solutions to political problems, Hitler goes on to write, noting that their opinions are based on emotion, so people must be told what to think—how to feel. The average citizen does not want to make his or her own decisions. Hitler maintains it is therefore the responsibility of the government to terrorize the populace into submission while continually repeating simple ideas. He writes that people do not realize that sacrificing their right to think for themselves allows "their freedom as human beings" to be taken away. Physical intimidation, along with verbal threats, are also useful in convincing people of the righteousness of a cause, Hitler continues in *Mein Kampf,* for violence or the threat of violence makes a victim believe that further resistance is useless.

Hitler suggests that the way to win people over to the Nazi cause is to tell big lies, a strategy that has already been used effectively by the Jews. People are more willing to believe big lies, he reasons, because "they themselves often tell little lies in little matters, but would be ashamed to resort to large-scale falsehoods." The "primitive simplicity" of the average mind therefore enables the government to tell phenomenal lies on important matters without the threat of challenge. In order to convince people, Hitler writes, every argument should be completely one-sided: No statement should be partly true or mostly true; it must be absolutely true. Opponents or enemies cannot be given the benefit of a doubt; they must be absolutely wrong. The more extreme one's position, the better, because the "masses always respond" to a speaker's "absolute faith in the ideas put forward." The people cannot be given "free choice."

threatened political opponents with violence. Demanding a stronger German army, the Nazis also advocated canceling the terms of the Treaty of Versailles. They wanted Germany to regain the territory it had lost in World War I and to conquer new land in eastern Europe. This was the nationalist aspect of the Nazi party platform.

Anti-Semitism was the connection between socialism and nationalism in the Nazi party and the principal element in Hitler's strategy to expand the Nazi movement and eventually take over Germany. Although Hitler had devoted himself to building up the party since his release from prison in 1924, he realized the success of this plan

A group of SA men (storm troopers) in 1923. *(Reproduced by permission of Bildarchiv Preussicher Kulturbesitz)*

depended on events beyond the Nazis' control. He knew that economic improvement would return people to work and restore national pride, but would not benefit the party. Only a frightened, angry nation would look to Hitler for solutions to their problems.

This theory was borne out in the late 1920s, when Germany experienced a brief period of prosperity. Pleased with the economic and cultural strength of their country, Germans supported traditional political parties that were loyal to the Weimar Republic. The Nazi party did continue to grow (by 1928 its membership stood at 175,000), but had some difficulty winning voters. In the elections of 1928, the party received about 809,000 votes—about 2.6 percent of the total—and won twelve seats out of 491 in the Reichstag, the national legislature. By contrast, Germany's largest political party, the Social Democrats, received more than 9 million votes and won 152 seats. It seemed for a time that the Weimar government might be successful.

Nazi Popularity Grows

After the Great Depression began in the United States in 1929, its effects were felt abroad as well. In Germany unemployment was rapidly increasing

and Germans turned to political parties, including the Nazi party, that rejected the current system of government. Seizing the opportunity to prey on mass fears, Hitler made sweeping promises to strengthen Germany and restore prosperity, but gave no explanation of how he would achieve these goals. Instead, he created a scapegoat for Germany's economic and political problems: the Jews. Many middle-class Germans listened to Hitler and thought he and the Nazis were Germany's last hope. While Hitler made his speeches, the Nazis continued to intimidate political opponents, and the storm troopers became even more powerful. In 1931 there were 170,000 storm troopers; a year later their ranks had swelled to more than 400,000, four times the size of the official German army. Often referred to as fascists, or supporters of an autocratic or dictatorial government ruled by force, the Nazis openly expressed contempt for democracy, which they described as weak and outdated, in contrast to their own political movement, which they promoted as being young and vital.

Political parties that supported the German government could not agree on how to deal with the economic depression that was ravaging the country. The conservatives, who were supported by big business and the middle class, wanted to cut benefits to the unemployed, reduce the pay of government

Paul von Hindenburg

Conservative candidate Paul von Hindenburg was elected president of Germany in 1925 after the death of the nation's first president, Friedrich Ebert. Hindenburg had been commander of the German armies in World War I and was a highly respected national hero. In 1932, when he ran for reelection, he was eighty-five years old. Steadfast in his ideas and opposed to change, he was essentially a monarchist who believed in supporting the kaiser—a political philosophy that was rooted in the nineteenth century. As a Junker, or member of the German landed nobility, Hindenburg was distrustful of the Communist belief in communal ownership of land. As a Lutheran, he also stood firmly against Social Democrats and Catholics. Hindenburg was not pro-Nazi, either. He disliked Hitler, considering him crude and low-born; reportedly Hindenburg once called Hitler a gutter snipe. The Nazi leader had been a mere corporal in the army, whereas Hindenburg had been a field marshal in command of the entire German military. Hindenburg had taken an oath of loyalty to the Weimar Republic, even though he was a monarchist, and believed his personal honor required him to defend the republic against its enemies. Hitler knew that in the event of a Nazi coup, army officers would obey Hindenburg and fight the storm troopers.

German president of the Weimar Republic, Paul von Hindenburg, poses for a photo in his army uniform. Hindenburg, who was part of the German aristocracy, disliked Nazi leader Adolf Hitler, who he believed was low-born. *(Reproduced by permission of Foto Marburg/Art Resource)*

employees, and raise taxes on people who still had jobs. At the other extreme, the Social Democrats, the largest Socialist party in Germany, wanted to continue high unemployment benefits and raise taxes on the rich. Neither side could win a majority of votes in the Reichstag, so the legislature remained deadlocked. The conservative chancellor called new elections for September 1930, hoping voters would break the deadlock by electing enough representatives who agreed with him. The results of the election stunned everyone: The Nazis received almost 6.5 million votes and won 107 seats in the Reichstag. This victory was a stark contrast to the election two years earlier, when Nazis had procured only 809,000 votes and twelve seats. By1930 they were the second-largest party in Germany. The Communist party also did better than it ever had before in the election, winning 4.6 million votes and 77 seats, and becoming Germany's third largest party. It was clear from the results that many voters opposed the Weimar Republic—almost one-third had supported parties that openly wanted to destroy it.

The Elections of 1924 and 1928

Party	Seats Won (1924)	Seats Won (1928)
Social Democratic Party (moderate socialist)	131	152
Nationalist Party	103	78
Center Party (Catholic)	69	61
Communist Party	45	54
German People's Party (moderate nationalists)	51	45
Democratic Party (middle class)	32	25
Economic Party (conservatives)	17	23
Bavarian People's Party (Catholic)	19	17
Nazi Party	14	12

The new Reichstag still had difficulty reaching consensus because the conservatives could not form a majority without including the Nazis. In normal times the German president was essentially a symbolic figurehead similar to the British monarch, yet during states of emergency under the constitution he held the power of rule by decree, a measure in which he could issue laws himself without the approval of the Reichstag. The president, Paul von Hindenburg (see box on page 28), appointed a conservative chancellor, but he, too, was unable to achieve a majority of votes in the Reichstag. Hindenburg therefore ruled Germany by issuing decrees to carry out the chancellor's policies.

Hindenburg's term as president expired early in 1932. At the age of eighty-five, he ran for reelection, not as a conservative but supported instead by the Social Democrats and the Catholic Center party. The Communists ran their own candidate, as did the Nationalist party. The fourth candidate was Hitler who, with the backing of the Nazis, mounted a crusade by making speeches in dozens of cities. He crisscrossed Germany by plane—becoming the first political candidate to use this mode of transportation. In every town where he spoke, Nazi posters were plastered on walls, uniformed storm troopers stood guard, and torchlight parades filled the streets. The storm troopers attacked opponents of the Nazis, inciting physical confrontations between Nazis and Communists. Repeating themes he had been espousing for years, Hitler drew upon *Mein Kampf* in his speeches. He claimed that other parties had failed to make Germany strong, and although he failed to offer a clear plan for dealing with the depression, he hailed his party as the country's last hope. He promised to restore Germany to its former strength, to stand up to other countries across the world, and to end internal strife and division. In every forum he blamed the Jews for the misery of the German people. As the depression grew increasingly worse and internal discontent reached a zenith, more people were willing to listen to Hitler.

When the votes were tallied, Hindenburg came in first, but more than 11 million Germans had

The Vote for President of Germany, 1932

Candidate	First Round	Second Round
Hindenburg	18,650,730 (49.6%)	19,359,635 (53%)
Hitler	11,339,285 (30.1%)	13,418,051 (36.8%)
Thälmann (Communists)	4,983,197 (13%)	3,706,655 (10.2%)
Dürsterberg (Nationalists)	2,558,000 (6.8%)	did not run

Goebbels and Nazi Propaganda

The man principally responsible for Hitler's election campaign strategies was (Paul) Joseph Goebbels, head of Nazi propaganda. Goebbels capitalized on Hitler's contention, outlined in *Mein Kampf,* that the best public-relations policy was to formulate a "big lie," repeating the same accusations until people believed them. Goebbels was the organizer who ensured that Nazi parades, banners, posters, speeches, and songs all coalesced into one powerful effect. Later, when the Nazis had seized power in Germany, he controlled radio broadcasts, films, and theatrical productions. In the initial days of the Nazi government, Goebbels, as Minister of Public Enlightenment and Propaganda, organized the burning of books written by Nazi opponents, Jews, and rival political organizations.

Nazi officials Wilhelm Frick and Gregor Strasser arrive at the Reichstag building in Berlin, wearing storm trooper uniforms, after the Nazis won 107 Reichstag seats. (*Reproduced by permission of AP/Wide World Photos*)

voted for Hitler as president. Nearly 5 million had voted for the Communist candidate, Ernst Thälmann. This meant Hindenburg received just under 50 percent of the total vote. As a result, a run-off election was held between Hindenburg, Hitler, and Thälmann. The Nazis continued their aggressive campaigning, and the storm troopers' violent attacks on opponents became so outrageous that several state governments demanded that the SA be banned. A few days after the second round in the election, the national government outlawed both the SA and the SS. The Nazis publicly disbanded the storm troopers, but the group remained covertly active by discarding their uniforms and discontinuing open threats against opponents. Hindenburg won the second election, but Hitler received almost 37 percent of the vote. Four years earlier the Nazis had won less than 3 percent. Hitler and the Nazis had demonstrated their power.

Goverment Deadlock and Hitler's Ascent to Power

Shortly after reelection, Hindenburg decided to appoint a new chancellor, Franz von Papen, who had minimal support in the Reichstag and needed backing from the Nazis to stay in power. In return, Hindenburg agreed to two Nazi demands: first, new elections to the Reichstag would be scheduled for July 1932, and second, the government would lift the ban on the SA. The storm troopers quickly went back into action for the election campaign. During the month of June and the first three weeks of July, some 461 reported political riots erupted in Prussia, which resulted in the death of more than eighty people and the serious injury of hundreds more. Late in July the Nazis marched through a suburb of Hamburg, a large seaport in northern Germany and a well-known Communist stronghold. In an ensuing gun battle, nineteen people were killed and 300 more were wounded. German legislative elections were held in this atmosphere. The Nazis received almost 14 million votes and won 230 seats in the Reichstag, more than double their totals from 1930 and approximately 37 percent of the total vote, close to the same proportion that Hitler had received for president a few months earlier. By this time the Nazis had become the largest party in Germany, leaving the Social Democrats less than 8 million votes and 133 seats. This was the highest number of votes the Nazis would receive in a fair election.

Meanwhile, the political, economic, and social situation in Germany continued to worsen. In November 1932 yet another Reichstag election was held, the second in four months. The Nazi party won fewer than 12 million votes and 196 seats in the Reichstag. While this would have been considered a tremendous Nazi victory a year earlier, it was a serious setback compared to the election held in July. The Nazis had lost nearly 2 million votes and thirty-four seats in the Reichstag. For the first time since the beginning of the Great Depression, the Nazis'

The Schutzstaffel

In addition to the storm troopers of the Sturmabteilung (SA), Hitler created a second Nazi military organization called the Schutzstaffel (SS), or defense corps, in 1925. SS members wore black uniforms and were considered the elite of the Nazi party. They required all members to prove they were "pure Germans" with no Jewish ancestors. From the outset, the SS showed contempt for the SA. While the SS eventually became directly responsible for carrying out the Holocaust, in the mid-1920s the group was much smaller than the SA and not so well known to outsiders.

popularity had gone into decline. In addition, with the near-constant election campaigns and the funding of the enormous Nazi organization as well as the SA, the Nazis were running out of money. When the Nazis realized they might have missed a chance to take over Germany legally, the opinion of party leaders was split: Some wanted to stick with Hitler's efforts to gain power legally and some wanted the SA to take over the country by force. The latter group believed the army would refuse to fight the storm troopers, and contended that even if the army did fight, the SA could defeat them.

Hitler did not believe that the Nazis could come to power by force. The SA was large, but the storm troopers were no match for highly trained and well-equipped army troops. While numerous army officers were friendly with the Nazis, an attempted coup would result in Hindenburg ordering the army to quell the rebellion. Although Hindenburg was only a figurehead president, he was nevertheless a respected war hero whose orders would be obeyed. Other Nazi leaders attacked Hitler for refusing to compromise with leaders of the conservative parties, who were willing to let Hitler join the government as vice-chancellor but not as chancellor. These conservatives felt the Nazis would be useful as political allies if they could tame the aspirations of Hitler and manipulate the resulting legislative consensus

Benito Mussolini and Fascism in Italy

The term "fascist" was introduced by Italian dictator Benito Mussolini, whose Fascist party ran Italy during World War II. Fascist governments use military-style organizations to help them gain power. Once in control, they continue repressing political opponents and independent organizations (such as labor unions) through violence. Hitler modeled his paramilitary group of storm troopers, often called brownshirts, after Mussolini's blackshirts, who suppressed political opposition in Italy. Like Germany, Italy had undergone a period of turmoil immediately after World War I. Unlike Germany, however, Italy was on the winning side in the war, yet Italians still felt their country had not received sufficient territory or respect in the peace settlement. Italy was much poorer than Great Britain, France, or Germany, and the disruptions of the war had been difficult for the Italian people. Dissatisfied workers staged strikes and took over factories throughout the country.

Mussolini and his Fascist party promised a return to order and discipline, as well as glory and prosperity in Italy. In events that would be mirrored in Germany a decade later, powerful Italian politicians decided that the Fascists were the best hope for maintaining control. They appointed Mussolini head of the government in 1922. Mussolini made the Fascists the only legal party, forcibly destroying all opposition. Building up the Italian armed forces, he also erected massive buildings as part of his promise to return Italy to the preeminence it had enjoyed during the period of the ancient Roman Empire. To mark Italy's new beginning, in 1935 Italy invaded Ethiopia, one of the only countries in Africa that was not a colony of a European nation.

After Adolf Hitler and the Nazis took over Germany, Italy and Germany became close allies. While the two regimes differed on the concept of racial superiority (Mussolini was not especially anti-Semitic until he aligned with Hitler), they shared some common goals. Both countries were interested in change, as exemplified by Italy's African invasion, which challenged British and French colonial control. Both Italy and Germany wanted to cultivate good relations with other European governments. To this end, Italy sent troops to assist General Francisco Franco's pro-Fascist rebels in the Spanish Civil War, while Germany sent airmen and planes. Soon it became clear that Germany, with its much greater economic and military power, was the senior partner, and that Hitler, not Mussolini, was the leader of the Fascist movement in Europe.

General Francisco Franco (pictured above) received help from Mussolini's Fascists during the Spanish Civil War.

From his window in the Reichschancellory, Adolf Hitler addresses the public during a parade to celebrate his appointment as Chancellor of Germany on January 30, 1933. *(Reproduced by permission of Bundesarchiv)*

The Nazi Party Program

Along with adopting *Mein Kampf* as a major statement of their ideals, the Nazis wanted another document that would outline party philosophy. The result was the Nazi party program, which Hitler had helped write in 1920, and which outlined the political beliefs and goals of the organization. Unlike *Mein Kampf,* the Nazi program is brief, consisting of twenty-five clear points. The program does not reflect the way the Nazis actually behaved once they seized power, nor does it accurately represent Hitler's views; instead it shows how the Nazis wanted to be perceived by the general public.

Many of the twenty-five points in the Nazi party program cover the usual ideas of extreme nationalism. The program advocates invalidating the Treaty of Versailles and uniting Germans into a single country that would include Austrians and the German minority living in the new country of Czechoslovakia. The program is strongly anti-Semitic, allowing only pure-blooded Germans to be çitizens of the new Germany or to hold political office. Other people, including Jews, would be relegated to the position of "guests," and Jews who had immigrated to Germany after the beginning of World War I would be expelled from the country.

In contrast to *Mein Kampf,* sections of the program reflect socialist aspects of Nazi politics, such as an emphasis on the party's desire to gain the support of the middle class and small business. The program calls for the government to absorb monopolies, acquire a share of profits from other large industries, and seize all war profits. The Nazis further propose the elimination of unearned income such as interest, and government seizure of land needed by the nation without compensation to owners. Since some of the largest department stores in Germany were owned by Jews, the stores would be dismantled and rented to small shopkeepers. These actions, the program maintains, would threaten industrialists, bankers, and landowners while benefiting small business owners and farmers. The program also contains two demands meant to appeal specifically to factory workers: employee profit-sharing and the abolition of child labor. Although these demands would not gain substantial support from workers, the goal, again, was to threaten owners of large industries.

In 1926 the Nazis declared that their program was not subject to change. Even before issuing this statement, however, Hitler explained that the socialist aspect of the program did not really mean what it seemed to say: The Nazis had no intention of taking over monopolies, he assured the industrialists, they merely aimed to ruin Jewish international bankers. Similarly, Hitler asserted two years later that seizure of land without payment was also directed mainly against Jewish companies. While the Nazi program promised advantages to the lower middle class at the expense of big business, Hitler assured the non-Jewish, big business elite that they should not feel threatened.

however they saw fit. Hitler refused, insisting on being named chancellor. The conservative politicians finally convinced Hindenburg to name Hitler chancellor, a move they did not view as dangerous because the conservatives retained control of the cabinet, the army, and the national police. Hitler, they were certain, would be under their control.

On January 30, 1933, Hitler became chancellor and head of the German government. As a result of the agreement with the conservatives, he took power legally, though without ever winning a majority of the vote. He decided to hold one more election in March 1933, the third in less than a year. Due to the increased power of Hitler and the storm

German policemen view the remains of the Reichstag building after it was destroyed by fire. *(Reproduced by permission of Bildarchiv Preussischer Kulturbesitz)*

troopers, government control of radio stations, and the full coffers of the Nazi party, Hitler was sure that the Nazis would win a majority in the Reichstag. On February 27, 1933, after Hitler had been chancellor less than a month, the Reichstag building was set on fire, an incident that the Nazis claimed was part of a communist plan to start a revolution.

The next day Hitler issued an emergency decree, signed by Hindenburg, which granted Hitler special powers to protect the nation against the threat of Communist violence. Ignoring almost all rights granted in the constitution, the decree allowed Hitler to restrict freedom of speech and of the press, ban meetings, and outlaw political organizations. His police could tap telephones, open private mail, and search homes without a warrant. The government could seize the property of political opponents, and Hitler could take over the governments of German states, thereby ending both the Weimar Republic and any hope for democracy in the country. Realizing they needed to move quickly, the Nazis arrested more than 10,000 people the night after the Reichstag fire. All

Communist party leaders who could be found, including members of the Reichstag, were jailed; remaining party members were forced into hiding. The arrested Communists, the first victims of the Nazi police state, were soon sent to concentration camps where they were kept under guard by Nazi storm troopers. The Nazi government charged several people with setting the Reichstag fire. One, Martinus van der Lubbe, was an ex-Communist from Holland. He was arrested at the scene and admitted to setting the fire, claiming he had acted alone. Many people thought van der Lubbe was mentally unstable, and they did not believe his confession. The other people arrested were leading Communists who denied having anything to do with the fire. There was no evidence to support the involvement of anyone but van der Lubbe, who was convicted and executed.

At the time and in years since, many people have concluded that the Nazis set the fire themselves so Hitler could use emergency powers to become dictator. Historians base this view on two main facts: (1) Hitler and the Nazis reacted so quickly to the fire that they must have made their plans in advance; and (2) several witnesses later claimed that Hermann Göring boasted about being involved in the plot. A leading Nazi and chairman of the Reichstag, Göring had an office connected to the building, so he would have had the opportunity to carry out the plan. No one knows for certain if van der Lubbe actually set the fire or if he acted alone. Regardless of who set the fire, the Nazis were able to use the incident to destroy the Weimar Republic.

Spreading terror throughout the city, 40,000 Nazi storm troopers beat and kidnapped their opponents under direct orders from Chancellor Hitler. They had been specially commissioned as police officers and could not be stopped by the ordinary police force. As the election campaign continued, only Nazi supporters were allowed to hold political meetings. The offices of anti-Nazi newspapers were smashed, and the speeches of

Hitler and other top Nazis dominated radio broadcasts. A final election was held on March 5, 1933, in which almost 90 percent of voters cast ballots. Although Nazi control of the government and storm trooper repression meant that the election was only partly free, voters were still able to choose other parties. The Nazis received more than 17 million votes, approximately 44 percent of the total. The Nationalist party, which had been an ally of the Nazis in the election, took 3 million. The Social Democrats received 7 million votes, and the Communists, even though they were in jail or in hiding, still obtained almost 5 million votes. A large minority of voters, more than 30 percent, had therefore voted for the two parties the Nazis hated most, the Social Democrats and the Communists. Although this was a serious disappointment for Hitler and his followers, the votes did not matter anymore because the Nazis had enough power to control the government.

PRIMARY SOURCE

Adolf Hitler
Excerpt from *Mein Kampf* ("My Struggle")
Published in 1925

Mein Kampf ("My Struggle"), a semi-autobiographical work by Adolf Hitler, reveals the philosophy of the Nazi dictator who took control of Germany, started World War II, and engineered the Holocaust. Written in 1924 during the early stages of Hitler's political career, *Mein Kampf* became the bible of the growing Nazi party. In this rambling book, Hitler presents himself as a political savior to the German people, who were still recovering from their disastrous defeat in World War I. The following passage from *Mein Kampf* shows that Hitler felt it was his destiny, and that of all Germans, to defend Aryan racial purity. The text contains numerous grammatical errors, disjointed thoughts, and awkward expressions, reflecting his limited education. Hitler had great talents as an orator, however, and the content of *Mein Kampf* is better understood if imagined as a speech.

According to the ideology embraced by Hitler and the Nazis, race played a central role in every aspect of human existence. The Nazi party believed

that Germans, as members of the Aryan race, were destined to rule all other races. The Germans had grown weaker over the centuries due to the mixing of their superior blood with the blood of inferior races; Jewish people were said to pose the most sinister threat to the purity and strength of the Aryan race. According to Hitler, Jews were members of a separate race and not simply followers of a different religion. The social, political, and economic resurrection of Germany could be achieved only by understanding and solving "the racial problem and hence the Jewish problem." The divinely inspired task of the German people, Hitler wrote, was to preserve "the most valuable stocks" (the strongest and the brightest Germans) and to remove corrupting influences, such as the despised Jews.

Anti-Semitism intensified in Germany as Hitler and many others blamed the Jews for German losses after the war. They held Jews responsible for spreading Marxism, democracy, and other liberal political ideologies that helped topple

Adolf Hitler walks to his car after addressing a rally in Berlin that celebrated the third year of his chancellorship. *(USHMM Photo Archives)*

imperial rule in Germany. Hitler thought Jews were attempting to gain dominance through the Weimar Republic, the democratic government that was formed in Germany after the signing of the Treaty of Versailles. Like other anti-Semites of his time, Hitler also believed in the myth of a Jewish conspiracy to dominate the world, as described in a widely circulated pamphlet, *Proto-*

cols of the *Elders of Zion* (see primary source entry in Chapter 1).

Hitler entered politics after World War I in opposition to the Weimar regime. In 1920 he helped establish the National Socialist German Workers' (Nazi) party under the banner of fervent anti-Semitism, nationalism, and the belief in Aryan supremacy. Under Hitler's leadership, the Nazis unsuccessfully attempted to overthrow the government on November 8, 1923, in a failed coup known as the Beer Hall Putsch. ("Putsch" is German for "unsuccessful rebellion.") Hitler was jailed for nearly a year, during which time he dictated *Mein Kampf* to a fellow Nazi. For several years, the German government banned the Nazi party and forbade Hitler from speaking publicly, but the Nazis started to regain strength in the late 1920s. As their popularity spread, people throughout Germany and the world began to read *Mein Kampf.* While many of Hitler's followers took his ideas seriously, opponents dismissed them as being too wild and preposterous to cause serious concern. Few foreign leaders believed *Mein Kampf* to be an actual plan for the destruction of the Jews. After Hitler declared himself the führer, or leader, of Germany in 1934, *Mein Kampf* became required reading in schools throughout the Third Reich (Third German Empire). The Nazis also required couples to own a copy of Hitler's book in order to get married. The publication of *Mein Kampf* proved an enormous

financial success for Hitler. The book was translated into eleven languages and sold more than 5.2 million copies by 1939, making him a millionaire.

Mein Kampf serves as Hitler's account of how he developed his racial philosophy. He attributes his transformation into a devout anti-Semite to events that occurred while he was living in Vienna, Austria. One day, while strolling through the city, he noticed an eastern European Jew wearing a black caftan. Hitler asked himself if this man could be a German, and thus began his self-guided study of race and history. He became convinced that Jews are members of an inferior race conspiring to dominate the world. In the passage that follows, Hitler uses the term the "Jewish question" to refer to the problem he believes is presented by the presence of Jews in society. As the supreme leader of Germany, he initiated numerous anti-Jewish measures that eliminated the rights of Jews as citizens. After Germany invaded several countries and became enmeshed in World War II, the Nazis planned for the complete elimination of European Jews through mass extermination, in a plan called *Endlösung,* or the "Final Solution." To preserve the racial purity of Germany, Hitler recommends that the government enact laws regulating human reproductive rights. He contends that physically or mentally disabled people should be sterilized to prevent them from passing on their inferior genes to future generations.

Mein Kampf ("My Struggle")

I gradually became aware that the Social Democratic press was directed predominantly by Jews; yet I did not attribute any special significance to this circumstance, since conditions were exactly the same in the other papers. Yet one fact seemed conspicuous: there was not one paper with Jews working on it which could have been regarded as truly national, according to my education and way of thinking.

I swallowed my disgust and tried to read this type of Marxist press production, but my revulsion became so unlimited in so doing that I endeavored to become more closely acquainted with the men who manufactured these compendiums of knavery.

From the publisher down, they were all Jews.

I took all the Social Democratic pamphlets I could lay hands on and sought the names of their authors: Jews. I noted the names of the leaders; by far the greatest part were likewise members of the 'chosen people,' whether they were representatives in the Reichsrat or trade-union secretaries, the heads of organizations or street agitators. It was always the same gruesome picture. The names of the Austerlitzes, Davids, Adlers, Ellenbogens, etc., will remain forever graven in my memory. One thing had grown clear to me: the party with whose petty representatives I had been carrying on the most violent struggle for months was, as to leadership, almost exclusively in the hands of a foreign people; for, to my deep and joyful satisfaction, I had at last come to the conclusion that the Jew was no German.

Only now did I become thoroughly acquainted with the seducer of our people.

A single year of my sojourn in Vienna has sufficed to imbue me with the conviction that no worker could be so stubborn that he would not in the end succumb to better knowledge and better explanations. Slowly I had become an expert in their own doctrine and used it as a weapon in the struggle for my own profound conviction.

Success almost always favored my side.

The great masses could be saved, if only with the gravest sacrifice in time and patience.

But a Jew could never be parted from his opinions.

At that time I was still childish enough to try to make the madness of their doctrine clear to them; in my little circle I talked my tongue sore and my throat hoarse, thinking I would inevitably succeed in convincing them how ruinous their Marxist madness was; but what I accomplished was often the opposite. It seemed as though their increased understanding of the destructive effects of Social Democratic theories and their results only reinforced their determination.

The more I argued with them, the better I came to know their dialectic. First they counted on the stupidity of their adversary, and then, when there was no other way out, they themselves simply played stupid. If all this didn't help, they pretended not to understand, or, if challenged, they changed the subject in a hurry, quoted platitudes which, if you accepted them, they immediately related to entirely different matters, and then, if again attacked, gave ground and pretended not to know exactly what you were talking about. Whenever you tried to attack one of these apostles, your hand closed on a jelly-like slime which divided up and poured through your fingers, but in the next moment collected again. But if you really struck one of these fellows so telling a blow that, observed by the audience, he couldn't help but agree, and if you believed that this had taken you at least one step forward, your amazement was great the next day. The Jew had not the slightest recollection of the day before, he rattled off his same old nonsense as though nothing at all had happened, and, if indignantly challenged, affected amazement; he couldn't remember a thing, except that he had proved the correctness of his assertions the previous day.

Sometimes I stood there thunderstruck.

I didn't know what to be more amazed at: the agility of their tongues or their virtuosity at lying.

Gradually I began to hate them.

All this had but one good side: that in proportion as the real leaders or at least the disseminators of Social Democracy came within my vision, my love for my people inevitably grew. For who, in view of the diabolical craftiness of these seducers, could damn the luckless victims? How hard it was, even for me, to get the better of this race of dialectical liars! And how futile was such success in dealing with people who twist the truth in your mouth, who without so much as a blush disavow the word they have just spoken, and in the very next minute take credit for it after all.

No. The better acquainted I became with the Jew, the more forgiving I inevitably became toward the worker....

Inspired by the experience of daily life, I now began to track down the sources of the Marxist doctrine. Its effects had become clear to me in individual cases; each day its success was apparent to my attentive eyes, and, with some exercise of my imagination, I was able to picture the consequences. The only remaining question was whether the result of their action in its ultimate form had existed in the mind's eye of the creators, or whether they themselves were the victims of an error.

I felt that both were possible.

In the one case it was the duty of every thinking man to force himself to the forefront of the ill-starred movement, thus perhaps averting catastrophe; in the other, however, the original founders of this plague of the nations must have been veritable devils; for only in the brain of a monster—not that of a man—could the plan of an organization assume form and meaning, whose activity must ultimately result in the collapse of human civilization and the consequent devastation of the world.

In this case the only remaining hope was struggle, struggle with all the weapons which the human spirit, reason, and will can devise, regardless on which side of the scale Fate should lay its blessing.

Thus I began to make myself familiar with the founders of this doctrine, in order to study the foundations of the movement. If I reached my goal more quickly than at first I had perhaps ventured to believe, it was thanks to my newly acquired, though at that time not very profound, knowledge of the Jewish question. This alone enabled me to draw a practical comparison between the reality and the theoretical flim-flam of the founding fathers of Social

Hitler's cell in Landsberg prison, where he was treated more like a guest than a prisoner. In prison, Hitler dictated *Mein Kampf* to a fellow Nazi. *(Reproduced by permission of Bildarchiv Preussischer Kulturbesitz)*

Democracy, since it taught me to understand the language of the Jewish people, who speak in order to conceal or at least to veil their thoughts; their real aim is not therefore to be found in the lines themselves, but slumbers well concealed between them.

For me this was the time of the greatest spiritual upheaval I have ever had to go through.

I had ceased to be a weak-kneed cosmopolitan and become an anti-Semite....

When over long periods of human history I scrutinized the activity of the Jewish people, suddenly there rose up in me the fearful question whether inscrutable Destiny, perhaps for reasons unknown to us poor mortals, did not with eternal and immutable resolve, desire the final victory of this little nation.

Was it possible that the earth had been promised as a reward to this people which lives only for this earth?

Have we an objective right to struggle for our self-preservation...?

As I delved more deeply into the teachings of Marxism and thus in tranquil clarity submitted the

deeds of the Jewish people to contemplation, Fate itself gave me its answer.

The Jewish doctrine of Marxism rejects the aristocratic principle of Nature and replaces the eternal privilege of power and strength by the mass of numbers and their dead weight. Thus it denies the value of personality in man, contests the significance of nationality and race, and thereby withdraws from humanity the premise of its existence and its culture. As a foundation of the universe, this doctrine would bring about the end of any order intellectually conceivable to man. And as, in this greatest of all recognizable organisms, the result of an application of such a law could only be chaos, on earth it could only be destruction for the inhabitants of this planet.

If, with the help of his Marxist creed, the Jew is victorious over the other peoples of the world, his crown will be the funeral wreath of humanity and this planet will, as it did thousands of years ago, move through the ether devoid of men.

Eternal Nature inexorably avenges the infringement of her commands.

Hence today I believe that I am acting in accordance with the will of the Almighty Creator: by defending myself against the Jew, I am fighting for the work of the Lord.... There is only one holiest human right, and this right is at the same time the holiest obligation ... to see to it that the blood is preserved pure and, by preserving the best humanity, to create the possibility of a nobler development of these beings....

The folkish state must make up for what everyone else today has neglected in this field. It must set race in the center of all life. It must take care to keep it pure. It must declare the child to be the most precious treasure of the people. It must see to it that only the healthy beget children; that there is only one disgrace: despite one's own sickness and deficiencies, to bring children into the world, and one highest honor: to renounce doing so. And conversely it must be considered reprehensible: to withhold healthy children from the nation. Here the state must act as the guardian of a millennial future in the face of which the wishes and the selfishness of the individual must appear as nothing and submit. It must put the most modern medical means in the service of this knowledge. It must declare unfit for propagation all who are in any way visibly sick or who have inherited a disease and can therefore pass it on, and put this into actual practice. Conversely, it must take care that the fertility of the healthy woman is not limited by the financial irresponsibility of a state regime which turns the blessing of children into a curse for the parents....

Those who are physically and mentally unhealthy and unworthy must not perpetuate their suffering in the body of their children. In this the folkish state must perform the most gigantic educational task. And some day this will seem to be a greater deed than the most victorious wars of our present bourgeois era....

A prevention of the faculty and opportunity to procreate on the part of the physically degenerate and mentally sick, over a period of only six hundred years, would not only free humanity from an immeasurable misfortune, but would lead to a recovery which today seems scarcely conceivable. If the fertility of the healthiest bearers of the nationality is thus consciously and systematically promoted, the result will be a race which at least will have eliminated the germs of our present physical and hence spiritual decay.

For once a people and a state have started on this path, attention will automatically be directed on increasing the racially most valuable nucleus of the people and its fertility, in order ultimately to let the entire nationality partake of the blessing of a highly bred racial stock. (Hitler, pp. 61–65, 402–405)

Aftermath

Basing their ideology on intense racism, anti-Semitism, and German nationalism, the Nazis came to power in 1933, promising the revival of a broken country. Hitler was fanatically devoted to the principles of Aryan supremacy, which led him to initiate devastating anti-Jewish measures. Through a process that evolved from exclusion to expulsion to annihilation, the Nazi government eliminated Jews from public life in Germany. Hitler's determination to achieve Aryan domination sparked a war that engulfed the entire world. In his quest to gain *Lebensraum*, or living space, he launched the invasion of numerous surrounding countries in Europe and brutally murdered millions of people who belonged to supposedly inferior races.

By 1941, the Nazis had several million Jews incarcerated in Polish ghettos. The party's main goal was to remove Jews from all German-occupied countries through the complete evacuation and extermination of European Jewry in a plan code-named the *Endlösung,* or "Final Solution." Nearly 6 million Jews eventually died in the Holocaust. Hitler's campaign for Aryan world domination resulted in a death toll of more than 35 million people. The brutal manner in which Nazis treated Jews reflects Hitler's quest for racial superiority and purity, as revealed in *Mein Kampf.*

Sources

Books

Hitler, Adolf, *Mein Kampf,* translated by Ralph Manheim, Sentry Edition, Houghton Mifflin (Boston), 1943.

Orgel, Doris, *The Devil in Vienna,* Dial Books for Young Readers (New York), 1978.

Shirer, William, *The Rise and Fall of Adolf Hitler,* Random House (New York), 1984.

3

The Institutionalization of Anti-Semitism

The new Reichstag met on March 24, 1933, to vote on a Nazi-proposed law called the Enabling Act. This act would allow Adolf Hitler, as chancellor, to issue laws (including those that might violate the constitution) for four years without the approval of the Reichstag. Unlike the emergency decree, laws could also be mandated without the consent of the president, Paul von Hindenburg. The Enabling Act required a two-thirds majority vote in the Reichstag. Even with their Nationalist allies, the Nazis did not have this winning majority, a problem they rectified by eliminating their opposition. Of the eighty-one Communists who had been elected to the Reichstag, most were in jail and the remainder knew they would be arrested if they showed up to vote. Two dozen Social Democrats, several of whom were also in jail, were prevented from attending the Reichstag session. Hitler eventually convinced the two major Catholic political groups, the Catholic Center party and the Bavarian People's party, to vote for the Enabling Act by promising that he would not interfere with the activities of the Catholic church. The Reichstag building was surrounded by uniformed SS guards, and inside the crowd was dominated by the SA. During their speeches, the Nazis threatened that there would be violence throughout Germany if the Enabling Act was defeated. The final vote was 441 in favor of the act and 94 against; only Social Democrats cast dissenting votes.

Otto Wels, a leader of the Social Democrats, spoke against the Enabling Act even though he knew his life was in danger and the act would pass. *(Reproduced by permission of Bildarchiv Preussischer Kulturbesitz)*

Events in Germany sent shock waves throughout the world. Daily newspaper stories and radio reports in Europe and the United

Reichminister Joseph Goebbels, responsible for the spread of Nazi propaganda, speaks at a large rally in Berlin, 1933. *(USHMM Photo Archives)*

States detailed the Nazis' actions, especially their policies pertaining to Jews. In several major cities, religious and political groups talked of boycotting German products. In the United States, the Jewish War Veterans of America announced that its members would boycott German goods and urged others to do the same. The Nazis accused German Jews of fabricating stories to denigrate the Nazi party. But the reports being sent across the world were not from Jewish citizens or reporters in Germany—they were issued by reliable newspaper and radio reporters who were witnessing events themselves. On March 26, 1933, Hermann Göring, Nazi economic minister, called leaders of German Jewish organizations to his office for a meeting at which he ordered them to stop spreading stories about Nazi atrocities. He demanded that they tell Jewish organizations in other countries to cancel plans for a boycott, threatening violent retaliation if they did not comply. The leaders sent telegrams to their international counterparts, warning that anti-Nazi stories were harming German Jews. They urged Jewish groups not to boycott German products.

A majority of the recipients realized the messages were sent under extreme duress, but they also understood the Nazi party's threats were real. For this reason, boycotts of German products were never fully effective.

The threat of anti-German boycotts in other countries gave the Nazis an excuse to step up their attacks on Jews. Hitler instructed Nazi propaganda minister Joseph Goebbels to organize a large-scale boycott of all Jewish businesses in Germany, which would be explained to the public as a "defense" against the anti-German stories Jews were supposedly spreading. For years, the Nazis had attempted to convince German citizens not to shop at Jewish-owned stores, and Hitler had planned an anti-Jewish boycott committee even before he knew about the threat of similar measures against the Nazis. The boycott was set for April 1, 1933, and Goebbels began manipulating the Nazi-controlled media to rally supporters. On March 29 the official Nazi party paper used its entire front page to publish detailed orders on how to organize the event. Every local branch of the party was instructed to

SA pickets distribute boycott pamphlets to German pedestrians. The sign held by one of the SA members reads "Attention Germans. These Jewish owners of stores are the parasites and gravediggers of German craftsmen. They pay starvation wages to German workers." *(USHMM Photo Archives)*

create an action committee. City committees were supposed to visit factories to convince workers to support the boycott, while rural committees were instructed to spread the propaganda to villages. Göring was put in charge of Prussia where he publicly declared that he would not protect any Jewish stores; that Jewish judges and prosecutors in Prussia were required to "retire" by April 1, 1933; and that Jews were barred from serving on juries.

The Nazis held mass meetings across the country in support of the boycott, demanding that the government limit the number of Jews in all professions. Though the demands were carefully worded to seem like a spontaneous reaction to public opinion, the Nazi government had already decided to set this limit. The day of the boycott, uniformed storm troopers were stationed at the entrances to Jewish-owned stores. Some held printed posters announcing the boycott, while others painted anti-Jewish slogans and Stars of David (Jewish symbols) on shop windows, as well as on offices of Jewish doctors and lawyers. Bowing to negative world

reaction, the Nazis ceased the boycott after three days and announced that it had been a success.

The First Anti-Jewish Laws and the Concentration Camps

The boycott of Jewish businesses and Nazi-led mass meetings was intended to show that German citizens were outraged at the Jews and had demanded that the government take action. Almost immediately after the boycott, the Nazis began passing a series of laws and official orders targeting Jews. On April 7, 1933, a law removed most Jews from government jobs, including teaching in public schools or universities, and required the termination of any Jew hired after 1913. On objections from Hindenburg, Hitler made an exception for those who had fought in the German army during World War I (1914-1918) and their survivors. Yet Hindenburg did not protest the treatment of Jews in general. The storm troopers were given complete freedom to escalate their campaign of terror: Jews

An SA member stands in front of a Jewish-owned department store. The sign next to him reads "Germans! Defend yourselves! Don't buy from Jews!" *(USHMM Photo Archives)*

A view of Dachau, the first permanent concentration camp. *(USHMM Photo Archives)*

were beaten up on the streets; Jewish lawyers and judges were dragged from courthouses; and Jewish-owned stores were vandalized.

In late April, laws removed Jewish doctors from the National Health Service and limited the number of Jewish students in any school to 1.5 percent of the total enrollment. Other laws and official orders prevented Jews from working as pharmacists or newspaper editors and strictly limited Jewish access to jobs in the theater and film industries. Although the legislation did not apply to most private companies, Jews were soon being fired from these jobs as well. Many Jewish people were unable to earn a decent living, and some moved from smaller towns to larger cities, especially Berlin, in search of work. Other German Jews decided that it was no longer possible to live in their own country. In 1933, some 53,000 Jews, or 10 percent of Germany's Jewish population, left Germany. Roughly 16,000 of them returned later, mainly because of the difficult conditions they faced as refugees.

At the same time Jews were facing unemployment, many Germans were also facing arrest and permanent detainment. So many people were arrested that German prisons could not hold them, and the Nazis therefore opened concentration camps—temporary prison camps that were run not by the government but by the party's military units. Initially headed by the SA, the camps eventually fell under the jurisdiction of the SS, led by Heinrich Himmler, and became a permanent feature of the German war effort. When the Dachau camp opened in March 1933 in a suburb of Munich, its first prisoners were leaders of labor unions and officials of the Communist party. The last prisoners were not freed until the American army reached Dachau at the end of World War II, more than twelve years later. The reputation of the concentration camps soon spread fear among Germans who might oppose the Nazis. The camps became infamous for the brutal acts committed there by the Nazis with no regard to law—prisoners were underfed, forced to perform hard physical labor, and regularly beaten. The Geheime Staatspolizei or Gestapo, the secret police, tortured prisoners who might have information about opponents of the Third Reich. People were routinely executed without trial, their deaths explained by the Nazis as "shot while trying to

Hitler Youth salute the swastika during a 1935 rally. (Reproduced by permission of Snark/Art Resource)

escape." By 1934 the chaos of the lawless concentration camps gave way to the "Dachau System" established by Theodore Eicke, the new commandant of Dachau, and Himmler. Instead of imposing the random violence for which the SA was known, the camps were subject to the strict discipline of the SS and became the sites of highly organized terror.

On May 2, 1933, storm troopers took over the offices of German labor unions, beat union leaders, and sent them to concentration camps. The unions were then replaced by the Nazi-run German Labor Front, and all workers were forced to become members. Later that month, workers' rights to bargain with their employers and to strike were abolished. On May 10 the Nazis took over the Social Democrats' buildings and newspapers and seized the party's money. On May 26 the money and property of the Communist party was absorbed by the Nazis. In June the Social Democratic party was officially banned as "an enemy of the people." The Nationalist party, an ally of the Nazis in the last election, was no longer needed. The SA took over many of the

party's offices in June, an action that neither the Nationalist leader, who was still a member of the government, nor Hindenburg could stop. Soon Nationalist leaders announced that the party had dissolved, knowing that it would soon be eliminated anyway.

As the Nazis either eliminated or gained control over their opposition, they became increasingly determined to hold on to their power in Germany forever. One method for guaranteeing the continuation of their regime was to establish the Hitlerjugend or Hitler Youth movement, an organization that taught Nazi philosophy to German children. Hitler Youth began as a voluntary group for boys only, but in 1932, the Bund Deutscher Mädel (BDM), or League of German Girls, was established for female children. The Nazis constantly pressured parents to enroll their children in these programs, and by 1936 all other youth groups were made illegal. Membership in the Hitler Youth was required by law. This enabled Hitler, under the guise of organizing a social group, to indoctrinate German youth with Nazi ideals and military policy. Hitler Youth

The Boycott: A Rehearsal for the Nazis

A woman reads a boycott sign posted in the window of a Jewish-owned department store. The boycott was intended to hurt the Jews financially and gain support for the Nazis. (*USHMM Photo Archives*)

The anti-Jewish boycott was the first major action taken by the new Nazi government to test their methods. In this early phase of their rule, the Nazis needed to demonstrate to the German public that they were firmly in control. Despite having received less than half the popular vote in the national elections, they had a secure grip on the government. The purpose of the boycott, besides its primary objective of financially crippling the Jewish community, was to attract people who did not generally support the Nazis, such as Catholics, farmers, and factory workers whose labor unions had not yet been destroyed. The Nazis later used the same methods whenever they needed to accomplish a goal, not just when they were attacking Jews. For instance, when Hitler made demands for territory from foreign countries, German newspapers and radio would continually repeat the official version of events and the Nazi party would stage mass meetings. In addition to waging a propaganda campaign, the Nazis threatened violence, thus frightening average citizens into complying with the party line.

members marched at every Nazi rally in full uniform and waved party banners. Even if their parents were anti-Nazi, German children were taught to hate Jews. They were told that Hitler was the savior of their country and that they must always obey him.

The Nazis and the Churches

The Nazis encountered a problem in the German Catholic church. Until March 1933 the church had officially banned membership in the Nazi party because many Nazi ideas conflicted with basic tenets of the Christian faith. Alfred Rosenberg, a leading Nazi philosopher, wanted Germans to return to the pre-Christian practice of worshiping ancient gods and myths, contending that love and forgiveness were forms of weakness that had no place in the new Germany. Christians felt that anyone who accepted Christian beliefs was an equal member of their nation, while German citizenship according to the Nazis was determined by race and blood. In March 1933 Germany's bishops lifted the ban on Nazi party membership when Hitler promised to respect the rights of the churches. As soon as the Nazis achieved this support, they set out to destroy the political parties that had formerly protected the interests of Catholics, especially the freedom to provide a Catholic education for their children. In late June the Nazis took over the offices of the Bavarian People's party in the southern state of Bavaria and

Alfred Rosenberg

Alfred Rosenberg was born in Reval, Estonia, then part of the Russian Empire, where many people of German ancestry lived at the time. He was trained as an engineer and architect and attended school in Moscow. After participating in the 1917 Russian Revolution, he fled to Paris, France, and then Munich, Germany; his hatred of Jews and communists allied him immediately with Hitler. Rosenberg became the main philosopher of the Nazi party, maintaining that racial difference was the central force in history. The Germans, according to this theory, were the superior race meant to reign supreme over the lower races, such as the Jews. Rosenberg also stressed anti-Christian themes, believing the Jews had used Christianity to gain control of Europe because they viewed it as a religion of weakness. Rosenberg wanted Germans to return to the ancient myths and gods they had worshiped before Germany became Christian.

Beginning in 1921, Rosenberg served as publisher of the Nazi party's monthly magazine, *The World Struggle.* When the Nazis took control of the German government in 1933, Hitler appointed Rosenberg to head the Party Foreign Affairs Department. In 1934 Rosenberg became responsible for training all Nazi members in party doctrine. Besides reissuing the German version of the *Protocols of the Elders of Zion* (see primary source entry in Chapter 1), Rosenberg himself wrote a famous anti-Semitic book, *The Myth of the Twentieth Century,* which quickly became a bestseller when it was published in 1930. Rosenberg's book gave pseudo-scientific support to the Nazi idea of "blood purity."

This goal of a pure Aryan race was to be achieved by avoiding the contamination of having children with members of "lesser" races, notably the Jews. Rosenberg's influence helped brand Jews as political opponents of the Germans and established anti-Semitism as an essential part of Nazi ideology. Sales of *The Myth of the Twentieth Century* reached more than 1 million copies by 1944, second in circulation only to Hitler's *Mein Kampf.* Both books were required reading in schools during the Nazi regime.

Rosenberg became the Nazi "expert" on Jews and was instrumental in the mass murder of Jews in eastern Europe during World War II. He was tried, sentenced to death, and hanged after the end of the war.

Alfred Rosenberg, the leading philosopher of the Nazi party. *(William Gallagher Collection/USHMM Photo Archives)*

A page from an anti-Semitic German children's book called *Der Giftpilz* ("The Poisonous Mushroom"). *(USHMM Photo Archives)*

arrested its leaders. The Bavarian People's party was dissolved in July and its ally, the Center party, which had long held the loyalty of millions of Catholic supporters, disbanded the next day.

Immediately after lifting the ban on Nazi party membership, the church signed a concordat with the Nazi government. Many historians believe this concordat was fueled by the church's belief that Communists posed a greater threat to the future of their religion than the Nazis. Like many other groups, Catholics thought the Nazis' anti-communist stand outweighed their brutality and their persecution of Jews. The concordat seemed to imply the Nazis had the support of the church—a validation vital to Hitler's attempts to

Martin Niemöller

As a young man, Martin Niemöller had been a famous World War I submarine commander, and later became a clergyman. Like many Protestant pastors, he had supported the Nazis prior to their rise to power, but he eventually took a public stand against Hitler's policies. Niemöller never abandoned his outspoken opposition to the Nazis and was sent to a concentration camp on Hitler's personal orders. He spent many years in solitary confinement and was not freed until 1945. Niemöller described how Hitler destroyed his opponents one at a time while most Germans watched in silence: "First they came for the communists. I did not speak out because I was not a communist. Then they came for the labor unionists. I did not speak out because I was not a labor unionist. Then they came for the Jews. I did not speak out because I was not a Jew. Then they came for me, and there was no one left to speak for me."

(Reproduced by permission of © Hulton Getty/Liaison Agency)

assuage worldwide anger at his recent actions. Important to Nazi domestic policy was the church's assertion that it was possible to support the Nazis and remain a good German Catholic. In return for the support of German Catholics, the Nazis allowed the church to operate without interference from the Nazi party, and also to run its own schools. The Nazis quickly violated the terms of the concordat, but by the time church leader Pope Pius XII publicly protested in 1937, the Nazis had an iron grip on Germany. Despite the agreement, however, some important clergymen continued to protest the Nazis' treatment of

Jews. Among them was Father Bernard Lichtenberg of St. Hedwig's Cathedral in Berlin, who preached that it was a Christian duty to help the Jews, even though such an act was declared treasonous by the Nazis. Lichtenberg was eventually arrested and died in custody.

Despite the success of the Nazis in gaining support from German Catholics, the majority of Germans were Protestants who had a long tradition of obedience to the government. A significant minority of Protestant pastors led by Martin Niemöller (see box) formed a group called the Confessing (or Confessional) church. In March 1935 they read a protest to their congregations, attacking the Nazi philosophy of race and blood as a violation of Christianity. The Nazis arrested 700 pastors. Hitler proposed the appointment of a Reich bishop to head all German Protestant churches. A majority of pastors agreed to the plan, and in 1938 they swore an oath of obedience to Hitler, just as the army did in 1934. Despite the agreement and the arrests, a few leaders of the Confessing church continued to oppose the Nazis, maintaining that Christian morality required them to organize active resistance. One of the best-known of these pastors was Dietrich Bonhoeffer, a religious writer and philosopher who was arrested for smuggling Jews out of Germany. Later involved in a plot to assassinate Hitler, he was executed near the end of World War II.

Establishing Control Through the Night of the Long Knives

On July 14, 1933, Germany officially became a one-party country. Those who attempted to maintain, or create, another party would be sent to prison. Although opposing political parties and labor unions had been destroyed, however, the Nazis did not control the army, big business executives, and bankers. While Hitler attempted to control these groups through threats of arrest or death, he also engineered deals. One of his most important deals involved the German national army, which was dominated by Junker officers. Most of these officers agreed with Hitler's goal of restoring Germany's military strength through an enlarged army and navy, a modern air force, and the latest tanks and planes. Many officers also wanted to regain the territory Germany had lost after World War I, but they were nervous about Nazi control, as they preferred to run the army themselves. They feared that Hitler would combine

The Third Reich

The Nazis referred to their government as the Third Reich, or third German empire. The First Reich was the continuation of the Holy Roman Empire, which was founded in the ninth century by the emperor Charlemagne and lasted, in a weakened form, until the early 1800s. The Second Reich, the German empire under the kaiser, was created when Germany was unified under the leadership of Prussia in 1871 and lasted until the conclusion of World War I in 1918. The Third Reich ended with the Nazi defeat in 1945.

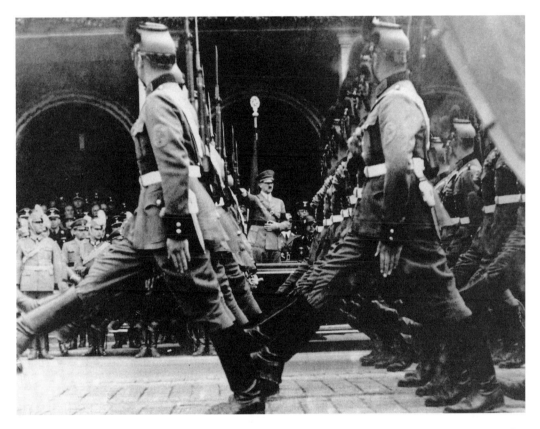

Goose-stepping Nazis soldiers pass by Adolf Hitler as they parade down the streets in Nuremberg during the Third Reich. *(Reproduced by permission of © Hulton Getty/Liaison Agency)*

the army with the SA, which was actually much larger than the army, and that Ernst Röhm, the head of the storm troopers and one of Hitler's closest friends in the Nazi party, would become the new commander of the army.

Although Röhm was a former army officer, he and old-guard officers shared an intense dislike for one another. These officers thought Röhm was a gangster who had no respect for their honor or their traditions, and Röhm opposed Germany's established leaders, including Junker army officers. Röhm wanted the Nazis to lead a second revolution that would change German society as drastically as the first—Hitler's ascent to power. The conflict between Röhm's storm troopers and army officers continued through the first year of Hitler's rule. Röhm continually pushed Hitler to launch the second revolution, but Hitler did not want to risk a showdown with the army. He finally ended the

Ernst Röhm

One of the most important early Nazis was Ernst Röhm, who became an officer in the German army during World War I. After the war, he stayed in the army for several years and served as a political adviser to a general. After leaving the army, Röhm retained contacts with army officers and ex-officers—people who would not normally associate with someone like Hitler, who had only been a corporal. Röhm had joined the Nazi party before Hitler became a member and was integral to the success of the party because of his contacts. As a former member of the Free Corps, he was a key connection between various Free Corps units in Bavaria and between the Free Corps and the army. Röhm was the leader of the SA and brought many Free Corps veterans into the organization. In later years, as the SA grew dramatically, Röhm continued to show that he was a highly effective organizer.

As a result of Röhm's long membership in the Nazi party, his leadership of the storm troopers, and his contact with powerful army officers, he was at one time a possible rival for Hitler as leader of the Nazis. Despite this fact, though, and also despite Röhm's homosexuality (a trait despised by Hitler), Röhm became one of Hitler's most important associates and probably his closest friend in the party.

Röhm regarded the socialist aspect of the Nazi program more seriously than did most of the other early Nazi leaders, including Hitler. He wanted the Nazis to lead a real revolution and completely transform German society. Like other Nazis, he hated the Jews, but he also hated the traditional leaders of Germany. This view would later create a problem for Hitler. Many powerful people, including owners of big businesses and army generals, were willing to support Hitler, but were afraid of Röhm's influence. Not long after the Nazis came to power, Hitler had Röhm killed.

Ernst Röhm, leader of the SA, became Hitler's main target during the Night of the Long Knives.
(Reproduced by permission of AP/World Wide Photos)

Hitler's Method: A Calm Between Storms

While initial anti-Jewish actions perpetrated by the Nazis created a variety of problems for German Jews, few people believed these anti-Semitic measures would later lead to genocide. It was common knowledge that the Nazi party had an extreme hatred of the Jews, yet Jews and non-Jews alike thought the physical and economic intimidation would eventually stop. Over the course of the first few years of the Nazi regime, this is often what happened. For every severe action against the Jewish population, a period of relative calm would follow. People were continually fooled into believing the most severe policies had been implemented and that conditions for Jews would stabilize. These periods of calm were part of Hitler's method of preventing opposition to his acts.

Nazi leader Adolf Hitler waves to the crowd from his motorcade as he heads to the opening ceremonies of the Olympics in Berlin. Hitler halted his attacks on the Jews while the world's eyes were on Germany for the Olympics. *(National Archives/USHMM Photo Archives)*

conflict by force on June 30, 1934, with an event known as the Night of the Long Knives, or the Great Blood Purge, when the SS began rounding up leaders of the SA and their allies. In the early morning hours, the SS seized Röhm and took him to a prison in Munich. On Hitler's orders, they left a gun in Röhm's cell so he could kill himself. Röhm refused, claiming that if Hitler wanted him dead, he should do the deed himself. Two SS men then emptied their pistols into Röhm. Executions continued over the course of two days; at least 100 people were killed, including numerous top SA leaders.

The Nazis and Big Business

The connection between the Nazi party and big business has always been a subject of dispute. Many industrialists did not lend their support to the Nazis, preferring old-fashioned conservative parties such as the Nationalists. They feared that the Nazis were committed to the socialist aspect of their platform and that a Nazi-led government might interfere with the way they ran their companies, or would even absorb them in compliance with the Nazi party program. Yet some business leaders, such as Fritz Thyssen, who controlled much of the German steel industry, had supported the Nazis for many years. In January 1932 Thyssen arranged for Hitler to speak to a group of German industrial leaders in Düsseldorf, the center of the German steel industry. Hitler told them that the Nazi party was totally committed to private ownership of companies and that a Nazi government would not interfere with their business dealings. The Nazis would, in fact, destroy the enemies of private property, the Communists and Social Democrats. At the conclusion of the speech, the businesspeople cheered Hitler. Financial support for the Nazis soon increased and, like many other groups in Germany, the big industrialists decided that the Nazis could be useful allies, and felt both groups were committed to a common goal.

The Night of the Long Knives allowed Hitler to assuage the fears and concerns not only of the army, but of industrialists and bankers as well. The army officers were satisfied when Hitler swore that the SA would never again threaten the independence of the army. The officers, primarily concerned with protecting their own positions, pledged unwavering support for the Nazi government. They also ignored the murder of two army generals during the Night of the Long Knives in exchange for command of the German army. Industrialists were pleased because Röhm had led an extremist faction within the SA that wanted to dismantle their power, and the businessmen had feared the Nazi party would absorb their businesses into the government, as their party platform said they would. The executions of SA leaders were taken as a sign that Hitler was truthful in his assertions that the only businesses subject to government control were those owned by Jews; as long as the industrialists and bankers supported the Nazis, the Nazis would not interfere with them.

Hitler publicly defended the SA murders by claiming that Röhm and the others had been plotting against the government. Advocating swift execution, rather than a criminal trial, Hitler stated that he was the supreme judge of Germany, and that anyone who tried to oppose him by force would die. The Nazi revolution had already been accomplished, he said, and now there was a need for legality and legitimacy, law and order. The Jewish community was somewhat relieved by the cleansing, as the guards at Jewish shops during the boycott had been SA members, and many Jews had feared Röhm' second revolution. After this great wave of violence within the Nazi party, many Germans thought that Germany would settle down and become a country united under a system of law and order, not chaos.

By the time Hindenburg died in August 1934, Hitler had already acquired the support of the army, eliminated any opposing political presence, and reduced the economic and social power of the Jewish population. The death of Hindenburg, who was elderly and had been sick for quite a while, came as no surprise to the German public. Hitler shattered any remaining semblance of the democratic Germany by consolidating the offices of president and chancellor and declaring himself führer, or leader, of the German Reich (empire), and commander in chief of the German army. On the day Hindenburg died, every officer and soldier of the army swore a new oath of allegiance: "I swear by God this holy oath: I will give unconditional obedience to the Führer of the German Reich and People, Adolf Hitler, the Supreme Commander of the Armed Forces, and will be ready, as a brave sol-

German citizens salute Adolf Hitler at the opening of the 1936 Olympic Games in Berlin. *(National Archives/ USHMM Photo Archives)*

dier, to lay down my life at any time for this oath." The German army did not pledge loyalty to the German people, the law, or the German government, but to Adolf Hitler.

The Nuremberg Laws and the Olympic Games

In 1935 Hitler unleashed a new onslaught against the Jewish population of Germany. Nazi newspapers increased their attacks against the Jews and in May, Jews were officially banned from the German armed forces. In July gangs of Nazis began to attack Jews in Berlin's main shopping district and to destroy Jewish-owned shops. In September a special session of the Reichstag, by now composed of only faithful members of the Nazi party, met in the southern city of Nuremberg. Two laws, called the Nuremberg Laws (see primary source entry in this chapter), were passed at that meeting, both written at Hitler's direct order. The first law, called the Reich Citizenship Law, stated that only a person of "German or related blood" could be a citizen of Germany, and that only a citizen could have political rights or hold office. The second law, the Law for the Protection of German Blood and German Honor, made it illegal for Jews and non-Jews to marry or to engage in sexual relations together. Jews were not allowed to have a non-Jewish female servant under forty-five years of age, and were forbidden to fly the German flag. Two months later, the Nazis issued a decree to enforce these laws that stated that anyone with three Jewish grandparents was a Jew; anyone with two Jewish grandparents was a Jew if he or she "belonged to the Jewish religious community" or if he or she were married to a Jew. The Nuremberg Laws also defined a person of mixed Jewish blood as "one who descended from one or two grandparents who were racially full Jews." The Nuremberg Laws accomplished several things. They placed Jews in a special legal category that deprived them of basic rights, stated that Jews were not Germans, and made "blood" a legal standard for determining one's race as German or Jewish.

Hitler halted his attack on the Jews for the opening of the 1936 Olympic Games in Berlin. Anticipating thousands of visitors from around the world, the Nazis wanted to improve their image and so erased anti-Jewish slogans from the windows of Jewish-owned stores. Huge processions and ceremonies occurred with thousands of uniformed Nazis in attendance. The Nazis wanted to demonstrate their might in both the games and in Germany.

German crowds roared their approval and gave the stiff-armed Nazi salute each time Hitler

1333

Reichsgesetzblatt

Teil 1

Erste Verordnung zum Reichsbürgergesetz.
Vom 14. November 1935.

Auf Grund des § 3 des Reichsbürgergesetzes vom 15. September 1935 (Reichsgesetzbl. I S. 1146) wird folgendes verordnet:

§ 1

(1) Bis zum Erlaß weiterer Vorschriften über den Reichsbürgerbrief gelten vorläufig als Reichsbürger die Staatsangehörigen deutschen oder artverwandten Blutes, die beim Inkrafttreten des Reichsbürgergesetzes das Reichstagswahlrecht besessen haben, oder denen der Reichsminister des Innern im Einvernehmen mit dem Stellvertreter des Führers das vorläufige Reichsbürgerrecht verleiht.

(2) Der Reichsminister des Innern kann im Einvernehmen mit dem Stellvertreter des Führers das vorläufige Reichsbürgerrecht entziehen.

§ 2

(1) Die Vorschriften des § 1 gelten auch für die staatsangehörigen jüdischen Mischlinge.

(2) Jüdischer Mischling ist, wer von einem oder zwei der Rasse nach volljüdischen Großelternteilen abstammt, sofern er nicht nach § 5 Abs. 2 als Jude gilt. Als volljüdisch gilt ein Großelternteil ohne weiteres, wenn er der jüdischen Religionsgemeinschaft angehört hat.

§ 3

Nur der Reichsbürger kann als Träger der vollen politischen Rechte das Stimmrecht in politischen Angelegenheiten ausüben und ein öffentliches Amt bekleiden. Der Reichsminister des Innern oder die von ihm ermächtigte Stelle kann für die Übergangszeit Ausnahmen für die Zulassung zu öffentlichen Ämtern gestatten. Die Angelegenheiten der Religionsgesellschaften werden nicht berührt.

§ 4

(1) Ein Jude kann nicht Reichsbürger sein. Ihm steht ein Stimmrecht in politischen Angelegenheiten nicht zu; er kann ein öffentliches Amt nicht bekleiden.

(2) Jüdische Beamte treten mit Ablauf des 31. Dezember 1935 in den Ruhestand. Wenn diese Beamten im Weltkrieg an der Front für das Deutsche Reich oder für seine Verbündeten gekämpft haben, erhalten sie bis zur Erreichung der Altersgrenze als Ruhegehalt die vollen zuletzt bezogenen ruhegehaltsfähigen Dienstbezüge; sie steigen jedoch nicht in Dienstaltersstufen auf. Nach Erreichung der Altersgrenze wird ihr Ruhegehalt nach den letzten ruhegehaltsfähigen Dienstbezügen neu berechnet.

(3) Die Angelegenheiten der Religionsgesellschaften werden nicht berührt.

Reichsgesetzbl. 1935 I

344

A reproduction of the first page of an addendum to the Reich Citizenship Law of 1935, the first of the Nuremberg Laws. *(USHMM Photo Archives)*

Jesse Owens runs in the 200-meter race at the 1936 Olympic Games in Berlin. *(Library of Congress/USHMM Photo Archives)*

appeared at the newly built Olympic Stadium. The Nazis wanted to use the Olympics to prove the superior strength of the Aryan race and expected their athletes to dominate competitors from racially inferior, weak, democratic countries. Jesse Owens, a sprinter who as an African American was a member of a Nazi-defined racially inferior group, dominated the track and field competition. Owens won four Olympic gold medals, including one for the 100-meter run that established Owens as the fastest man in the world. Hitler's fierce racism had another effect on the American team. Two of the four Amer-

icans scheduled to run in the 400-meter relay, Marty Glickman and Sam Stoller, were Jewish. The president of the American Olympic committee, Avery Brundage, removed them from the race; his motives have been debated ever since. Germany went on to win more medals than any other country.

While attempts to display the athletic dominance of the Aryan race were thwarted by Owens, the Nazis had used the Olympics to enhance their image. The countries of the world did not boycott the games, despite the Nuremberg Laws, and

The Nazis used Herschel Grynszpan's shooting of a low-level official as an excuse to wreak terror during *Kristallnacht. (Morris Rosen/USHMM Photo Archives)*

Domestic Events of 1938

The domestic events of 1938 demonstrated to European Jews, and the world, the intentions of Hitler and the Third Reich. The campaign against the Jews increased in legislative intensity and caused unprecedented racial violence and conditions no longer conducive to comfortable living. A law that took effect in March 1938 stripped Jewish organizations, such as synagogues, of the right to own property and enter into contracts. In April all Jewish businesses except the very smallest were required to register with the government. A vague portion of this law, which stated that registered property could be utilized to serve the needs of the German economy, was used by the Nazis to confiscate the possessions of Jews. Early in June 1938, the Great Synagogue of Munich was burned down. Later that month, the police arrested all German Jews with police records, which in many cases con-

sisted of parking tickets. Some 1,500 Jews were sent to concentration camps. The Nazis also expanded their efforts to the Jews of Austria, which had been recently annexed by Germany, and by September, some 4,000 Austrian Jews were in concentration camps, set free only if they agreed to leave the country. A law passed on July 23 required every Jew to obtain an identity card from the police. The Law Regarding Changes of Family Names and Given Names, passed the following month, stipulated that all male Jews take the name Israel and all female Jews take the name Sarah. In August the synagogue in Nuremberg was destroyed. On November 5, 1938, at the request of the Swiss government, Jewish people with passports authorizing foreign travel were required to relinquish their passports and have them marked with a red letter "J."

In October 1938 the Gestapo began rounding up some of the more than 50,000 Jewish Poles living in Germany to deport them to Poland, despite the fact that many of them had been living in Germany for years. The Gestapo arrested 18,000 Jews of Polish origin, including whole families. On the night of October 28, 1938, they were put on special trains and sent to the Polish border, where the Polish government refused to allow them into their native country. Approximately 5,000 people were held in a camp on the Polish side of the border. Among the detainees were members of the Grynszpan family, who had lived in Germany since 1914. Zindel Grynszpan wrote a letter describing their situation to his son, who was living illegally in Paris, France. When seventeen-year-old Herschel Grynszpan read his father's letter, he decided to seek revenge. Armed with a gun, Grynszpan went to the German embassy in Paris on November 7, intent on killing the German ambassador. Failing to gain access to the ambassador's office, Grynszpan shot and fatally wounded a lower-level official, Ernst vom Rath. Upon hearing of the shooting, Hitler promoted vom Rath in an attempt to increase public outcry over the shooting of a "major" German official. Although the Nazis had been planning an attack against the Jews, they used the shooting as an excuse to implement their plan.

Goebbels used the shooting to arouse public outrage. The Nazis declared that Jews were responsible for the attack and called the shooting a crime against all Germans. In countrywide party meetings, local officials gave fiery speeches, which then gave way to mobs determined to destroy Jewish property, beat up Jews, and burn local synagogues. On the night of November 9, 1938, word reached Germany

foreign visitors were presented with the impression of an orderly country whose citizens were intensely supportive of their government and its leader. The elimination of opposition and the temporary halt to anti-Jewish violence had provided a veneer of German political and social content.

Hermann Göring

Unlike other early Nazis, Hermann Göring belonged to the German aristocracy. His father had been the governor of a German colony in Africa. Like many nobles, Göring became a military officer, and was one of Germany's most famous fighter pilots during World War I. When the war ended, Göring could not adjust to peacetime Germany. For a while he lived in Sweden,

Hermann Göring, who was responsible for the German economy, took advantage of the destruction of *Kristallnacht* to seize any insurance money paid to Jews. *(Reproduced by permission of AP/Wide World Photos)*

where he married a wealthy Swedish woman, but upon returning to Germany, he was dazzled by a speech Hitler gave at a nationalist demonstration. Göring joined the Nazi party and was put in charge of training and drilling the storm troopers. He was badly wounded in the Beer Hall Putsch but managed to escape to Austria. Due to his noble background and his fame as a war hero, Göring had access to many wealthy and prominent people. He also had more refined social skills than most of the early Nazis. He seemed much less intense and obsessed than Hitler, who could never talk about anything but politics. Göring used his social connections to advance the Nazi cause and to introduce Hitler to prominent people in Bavaria.

Göring became one of the most powerful men in the Nazi party and in Germany, serving as the commander of the Luftwaffe, or German air force. At various times, Göring was the head of Prussia, the first chief of the Gestapo, or secret police, and the key organizer of Hitler's economic plans for Germany. Despite his supposedly easy-going nature, he used his power ruthlessly and did not hesitate to murder opponents. Göring never lost his taste for good living and became immensely wealthy by robbing great works of art from European countries during the war. Göring committed suicide in his jail cell before he could be hanged as a war criminal.

that vom Rath had died of his wounds. Goebbels, with Hitler's knowledge, launched a nationwide campaign of anti-Jewish mob violence. In every German city, storm troopers wearing civilian clothing attacked Jewish homes, stores, synagogues, and orphanages. While buildings were burned and furniture was thrown into the street, German police were ordered to prevent fires from spreading to non-Jewish property, to prevent looting, and to protect for-

eigners (even if they were Jewish). One thousand synagogues and 7,000 businesses were destroyed, resulting in German streets filled with shattered glass. The sparkling illusion on the streets provided the night with the name *Kristallnacht*—literally, "Crystal Night," or the "Night of Broken Glass."

About 100 Jews were killed during *Kristallnacht*, most of them beaten to death, and

Germans pass by the broken shop window of a Jewish-owned business destroyed during *Kristallnacht*. *(National Archives/USHMM Photo Archives)*

thousands of others were injured. An American diplomat in the city of Leipzig wrote that storm troopers threw terrified Jews into a stream after destroying their homes, then ordered frightened spectators, ordinary Germans, to spit at the Jews and throw mud at them. Goebbels had wanted the violence to look like the spontaneous anger of the German people, not an organized attack perpetrated by the Nazi government, but few were fooled. The attacks were planned by Nazi officials and carried out by storm troopers. Very few German civilians participated and a majority were shocked and disturbed by the violence, but few did anything to stop it.

Certain Nazi leaders had not been informed of Goebbels's plan and were angered by the events. Himmler, now the head of the SS and the Gestapo (secret police), wanted to control anti-Jewish policies himself and was strongly opposed to mob action, even when organized by the Nazis. Himmler preferred that party actions be performed out-

side the view of the general public. Although Himmler disapproved of *Kristallnacht*, he took advantage of it by arresting 30,000 Jewish men and deporting them to concentration camps. Himmler's plan was to force these men and their families to buy their freedom and then force them to leave Germany.

Göring, who was in charge of Hitler's economic plan, was also unaware of Goebbels's intentions for *Kristallnacht*. Göring was furious at the economic destruction caused by the mob actions, but, like Himmler, he used *Kristallnacht* against the Jewish people. He decided that the German government would seize any insurance money paid to Jewish property owners, and mandated that Jews were responsible for repairing the damage caused by the storm troopers. Jewish-owned businesses that had been forced to close because of the destruction would not be allowed to reopen unless they had non-Jewish owners. Göring also announced a "fine" against the Jewish

The Nazi mistreatment of the Jews began with attempts at humiliation. In Austria in spring 1938, Jews were made to get on their knees and scrub the pavement while Nazis and other citizens watched. *(National Archives/USHMM Photo Archives)*

community for the death of vom Rath totaling 1 billion marks.

Forced Deportation of the Jews

On November 12, 1938, Göring issued the Decree on Eliminating the Jews from German Economic Life. It prohibited Jews from selling goods or services, being independent craftsmen, and holding management positions within companies. Three days later, all remaining Jewish children were expelled from the nation's schools. In December, Jews were barred from many public places, including movie theaters and beaches. The Jews could no longer earn a living in Germany, their children could not attend schools, and their property was seized and sold by the government to non-Jews through a process called "Aryanization." After thousands of Jewish people had been arrested and placed in concentration camps, the Nazis shifted their efforts to forcing Jews out of Germany. The Nazis established the Reich Central Office for Jewish Emigration to force Jews to leave Germany by any means possible. The head of the operation was

Reinhard Heydrich, Himmler's deputy, who would later be directly in charge of the Holocaust.

Heydrich had a model to follow in attempting to rid Germany of the Jews. Since March 1938, when Germany had taken over Austria, the Nazis had forced thousands of Austrian Jews to leave the country. Emigration was their only escape from nonstop violence and threats. Heydrich made it difficult for German Jews to leave, requiring the Jews to make exorbitant payments as exit fees. Even wealthy German Jews were left with few resources to take with them as they started a new life in another country, and those who were already impoverished had extreme difficulty. By this time, there were 30,000 Jewish men in concentration camps, who would be released on the condition that they and their families left Germany within thirty days. This was the policy Heydrich followed until September 1939, when World War II began. After that, emigration became almost impossible.

The refugees faced a series of problems when trying to arrange flight from Germany. With so many people required to leave the country, the principal difficulty was locating a country willing

A group of Nazi brownshirts hold hands in an attempt to prevent Jews from entering the University of Vienna in 1938. *(National Archives/USHMM Photo Archives)*

to harbor immigrants. For a few, this was not a problem. Scientists such as physicist Albert Einstein and musicians like conductor Bruno Walter went to the United States. Refugee scientists, many of them Jewish, later played a vital part in the American military effort in World War II, including the building of the atomic bomb. Some actors, screenwriters, and directors, including non-Jewish anti-Nazis, went to Hollywood, where they contributed greatly to the American film industry. (Ironically, the German actors who escaped Hitler often played Nazis in American films.)

Most German Jews, though, were ordinary people, not great scientists or famous actors. Until the early 1920s, the United States had accepted almost any healthy immigrant from Europe who could pay for boat passage. Between 1889 and 1924, more than 2.5 million European Jews, mostly poor eastern Europeans, journeyed to the United States. After a new American immigration law limiting the number of immigrants from each for-

eign country was passed, the number of arrivals fell drastically. Foreigners had to receive permission from an American official stationed in their country, and these officials were often stricter than the law required in issuing permits. Even after Hitler came to power in 1933, far fewer permits were given than the law allowed. In 1933 and 1934 American immigration law would have permitted more than 25,000 Germans to enter the country, but only slightly more than 4,000 actually arrived. In the first three years after the Nazi takeover, only about 13,000 German Jews came to the United States. In the next three years, the Nazi campaign against the Jews worsened. Many Americans pressured President Franklin D. Roosevelt to admit more refugees, and during that period about 50,000 more were allowed to enter the United States. In total, one-fifth of the 300,000 Jews who left Germany went to the United States, but 200,000 others were unable to escape from Germany. At that time, the population of the United States was 130 million; the number of German

American Attitudes

Famed American aviator Charles Lindbergh was outspoken in his isolationist views. Isolationists believed that the United States should steer clear of Europe's problems and wars, maintaining a position of neutrality. *(USHMM Photo Archives)*

Many of the countries that appealed to German Jewish refugees, including the United States, suffered from serious unemployment in the 1930s, and this was sometimes used as a justification for turning away refugees. Some people felt the United States could not handle an influx of immigrants, especially poor immigrants. Part of the reason for refusing refugees, however, was probably anti-Semitism, which existed in the United States as in most other parts of the world. Some well-known Americans of the time made public statements attacking Jews. Henry Ford, the founder of the Ford Motor Company, published the *Protocols of the Elders of Zion* (see primary source entry in Chapter 1) in *The International Jew,* a document meant to prove that Jews were intent on taking over the world. Charles Lindbergh, who became a national hero for making the first nonstop flight across the Atlantic, accepted a medal from Hitler and made some statements defending the Nazi government. Roman Catholic priest Charles Coughlin, who broadcast to more than 3.5 million listeners every Sunday, blamed unemployment in America on banks he said were controlled by Jewish Communists.

Jews allowed into the United States was less than one-twentieth of one percent of that number.

As the Nazi threat to European Jews increased during the 1930s, a refugee crisis developed. Not a single country was willing to accept unlimited numbers of Jews escaping from Germany. In July 1938 delegates from thirty-two countries met in Évian, France, at the invitation of Roosevelt, to discuss the Jewish refugee issue. Instead of sending a high-level official to the conference, however, Roosevelt sent businessman Myron C. Taylor as the U.S. representative. Numerous delegates offered sympathy for the Jews' situation, but they were unwilling to allow Jewish immigration. The United States declared the discussion of its own immigration laws off-limits, the British refused to allow discussion of Palestine, and none of the other major countries were willing to deal seriously with the problem.

One example of the refugee crisis was the German ocean liner SS *St. Louis,* which contained more than 900 Jewish refugees when it set sail from Hamburg, Germany, in 1939, destined for Cuba. Government officials in Cuba had agreed to accept these refugees in return for huge bribes, but the Jewish organization that had made the arrangements was unable to come up with the money upon the ship's arrival in Havana on May 27. The Cuban authorities forced the ship back out to sea, and appeals were made to other countries to accept

A view of the Hotel Royal in Évian, France, the location of the Evian Conference. Nothing was done to resolve the Jewish refugee crisis at the high-level meeting. *(USHMM Photo Archives)*

Not all refugees were turned away from entry into the United States, like those on the *St. Louis*. Here young Jewish refugees wave at the symbol of freedom, New York's Statue of Liberty, as they reach safety on American shores in 1939. *(Reproduced by permission of Associated Press/Library of Congress)*

the passengers. The German government made it clear that if the Jews returned to Germany, they would be sent to concentration camps. The ship sailed slowly along the coast of the United States, shadowed by a U.S. Coast Guard ship ordered to prevent the refugees from landing in the United States. The whole world followed the story in news-

papers and on radio as the ship headed back to Europe on June 6. Due to the efforts of the *St. Louis*'s German captain, Gustav Schroeder, the Jews were not returned to Hamburg. In defiance of orders, he kept the ship at sea for thirty-five days, allowing enough time for harboring arrangements to be made with Great Britain, Belgium, France,

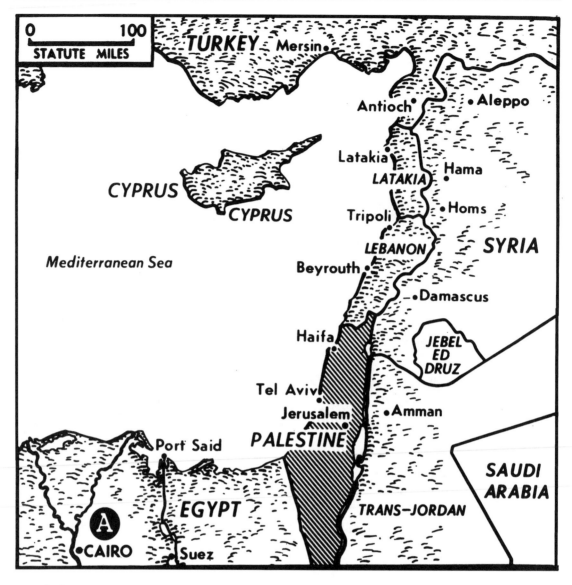

Map of Palestine c. 1945. *(Reproduced by permission of AP/Wide World Photos)*

and the Netherlands. Most of the Jews who found refuge in these countries, however, later fell prey to the Nazis. The Nazis interpreted the event as an indication of international attitudes toward the plight of Jews: They claimed that the same democratic governments that condemned the Nazis for their open persecution of Jews circumspectly shared the same feelings, as they were unwilling to admit Jews into their countries.

Palestine and Zionism

In 1917 and 1918 the British captured Palestine, a region in the Middle East bordered by the Mediterranean and Dead Seas, from the Ottoman Turks. As compensation for the Jews' help in

defeating the Turks, the British government promised the establishment of a Jewish national homeland in Palestine. This declaration was emphatically embraced by members of the Zionist movement, which had developed in the 1890s. They believed that Jews should return to Palestine and build a modern Jewish country in their ancestral homeland. Zionism gained some support among European Jews early in the twentieth century, resulting in a substantial number settling in Palestine, but most Jews wanted to stay in their home countries. Those who did decide to leave often selected other countries. More than 2 million Jews migrated to America, for example, and numerous other eastern European Jews moved to Britain, France, and other wealthy and democratic countries in western Europe, though these Jews later suffered under the ever-spreading Nazi regime. Thousands of Jews in France, for example, were deported and murdered by the Nazis.

For the increasing numbers of Jewish refugees fleeing the escalation of anti-Semitic attitudes and violence, Palestine seemed a suitable harbor. Jewish settlement in Palestine caused anger among the majority Arab population. Great Britain therefore began to limit the number of refugees permitted in the area. In addition to Palestine, Great Britain controlled several other Arabic countries and wanted to stay on good terms with them in case of war with Germany. Approximately 50,000 German Jews entered Palestine legally between 1933 and 1938, with many others coming from other parts of Europe. In 1935 more than 60,000 Jews from various countries settled in Palestine, but as the Nazi threat to the Jews increased, the British kept lowering the number of Jews allowed into Palestine. In 1936 the number was fewer than 30,000; by 1937 it had fallen below 11,000.

Zionist groups tried to smuggle Jewish refugees into Palestine during the 1930s. From the early part of 1938 until the outbreak of World War II in September 1939, approximately forty ships containing 16,000 illegal immigrants arrived in Palestinian waters. Most of these came from Poland and Germany, where the Gestapo released Jewish prisoners from concentration camps on the condition that they leave Germany immediately. The Nazis used the situation as an opportunity to rid themselves of Jews, embarrass the British, and reap financial rewards by taking a percentage of the transportation fees paid to ship owners by the refugees.

The British navy and air force patrolled sea routes to Palestine to stop the refugees. In a two-month period in summer 1939, more than 3,500 illegal immigrants were captured. British agents in Europe were assigned to determine from which ports the ships had sailed. Despite increasing pressure from both British and foreign public opinion, the British government never opened Palestine to refugees from the Nazis. In late summer of 1939 the British government imprisoned 1,400 Jewish refugees when their ship, the *Tiger Hill,* reached Palestine. Their journey had begun one month earlier by train in Poland, and had been delayed in Romania due to British pressure on the Romanian government. Having run completely out of food and almost out of water while

David Ben-Gurion, one of the founders of the Zionist movement, would become the first prime minister of the newly created Jewish nation of Israel in 1948. *(Photograph by Henry Grossman)*

at sea, the *Tiger Hill* was fired upon by a British ship off the coast of Palestine, killing two men. Finally the ship ran aground on a sandbar in the hope that the refugees could reach shore in small boats or by swimming.

Switzerland

Another potential destination for Jewish refugees was Switzerland, which was known for its policy of neutrality. Historically, the country had been a harbor for political refugees. The Swiss initially accepted substantial numbers of people fleeing Nazi Germany, most of whom moved on to other countries. This open-door policy, however, did not apply to Jews. After the German annexation of Austria in March 1938, thousands of Austrian Jews attempted to enter Switzerland. Austrians and Germans were able to enter Switzerland as tourists by showing their passports, but the Swiss government asked Germany to put a special mark on the passports of German and Austrian Jews. On November 5, 1938, the Germans forced all Jewish passports to be stamped with an identifying red "J" for *Jude,* the German word for Jew. After the outbreak of World War II, Swiss police usually tried to stop Jews at the border and force them back into the country from which they were fleeing. The Swiss did, however, make many exceptions, especially for children and the elderly, that resulted in thousands of Jewish refugees finding safety. During the course of the war, the Swiss frequently interned refugees, something they had never before done.

PRIMARY SOURCE

Inge Deutschkron
Excerpt from *Outcast: A Jewish Girl in Wartime Berlin*
First published in 1978
English translation published in 1989

As soon as Hitler became German chancellor on January 30, 1933, he moved quickly to dismantle democratic processes in Germany. Days after being sworn in, he banned public meetings and assemblies that were deemed "dangerous" to national security, a move that allowed the Nazis to control upcoming elections. By enforcing this decree, they silenced their political opponents, including Communists, Social Democrats, and Catholics. A fire destroyed the Reichstag building less than a month later, and the Nazis immediately blamed the incident on Communists (though disagreement still exists today about Nazi involvement in the fire). Fear of violent uprisings paralyzed Germany, and the Nazis seized the opportunity to tighten their hold on the country.

On February 28, 1933, Hitler issued an emergency decree that suspended freedom of speech and the press. These actions effectively eliminated non-Nazi access to newspapers and radio. The results of the last free election, held on March 5, enabled the Nazis to control government power by forming a coalition with other nationalist parties. The Nazis then escalated their suppression of political opposition. On March 24, 1933, the party passed the Enabling Act, which ended the powers of the Reichstag and created a dictatorship by transferring all legislative power to Hitler. Within months, all non-Nazi political parties, trade unions, and organizations were banned. Using the terrorist tactics of the storm troopers, the Nazis arrested political opponents, held them without trial, and sent them to be among the first occupants of concentration camps.

Next, the Nazis turned their attention to other people they considered enemies of the state—German Jews. According to Nazi racial doctrine, Jews threatened the purity of the German or "Aryan" race. The government announced a nationwide boycott of Jewish businesses on April 1—the Nazis' first planned anti-Jewish action. Nazi storm troopers painted graffiti on Jewish shops in cities throughout Germany and pasted signs on windows that read "Don't Buy from Jews" and "The Jews Are Our Misfortune." Members of the SA and the SS stood at the doors of Jewish-owned shops to keep patrons from entering. Violence erupted in many cities, and, according to Nazi instructions, the police made no attempt to control it.

Inge Deutschkron was a ten-year-old Jewish child living in Berlin when Hitler came to power in 1933. In the following document, Deutschkron describes her observations of the days of terror and confusion as the Nazis took over Germany. Her descriptions reveal the feelings of denial and disbelief common among Jewish Germans at that time. Assuming that Nazi rule would be short-lived, many people underestimated the brutality and power of the regime. During the Nazi era, political events such as rallies and marches were frequently marked by violence. Deutschkron witnessed such violence firsthand when she saw a parade marcher mortally wounded and watched as protesters threw stones at her family's home. Deutschkron's family first experienced persecution because of their political activities rather than their religion. As a leader in the Social Democratic party, her father was in danger of being arrested and sent to a concentration camp.

Outcast: A Jewish Girl in Wartime Berlin

"You're Jewish," my mother said to me. "You must let the world know that that doesn't mean you're not every bit as good as they."

What did it mean, being Jewish? I didn't ask. What interested me was what was going on outside in our corner of Berlin, on our quiet street. I liked looking out of the window of our apartment on Hufelandstrasse. It may have been nothing more than a sleepy little corner, yet for a ten-year-old there was much to see. I could watch the other children play. I was not allowed to play outside; my parents thought it wasn't safe. I, of course, didn't agree. I knew all the children by name, but I wasn't allowed to play with them. All I could do was watch. It hurt....

I knew that my parents were Socialists, and like most children growing up in a loving family I identified with my parents. My father held some sort of office in the Social Democratic party, and devoted much of his free time—as a teacher he had more than most—to party work. I took it for granted that all aspects of life were supposed to constitute a conscious, uncompromising affirmation of socialism, whether by being active in the People's Welfare Organization or shopping at the co-op.

Not only did I share my parents' belief, but it also filled me with self-confidence and pride. It may seem odd, but my fondest childhood memories are not of vacations or other childish pleasures but of sitting with adults in some smoke-filled backroom of a Berlin pub helping fold leaflets. And I was also proud to have my parents take me along on one of their "symbolic" walks, at which Social Democrats "accidentally"

Nazi students and SA members unload materials for a book burning. The banner on the back of the truck reads "German students march against the un-German spirit." The Nazis burned materials that conflicted with their ideology. (*Photograph by Abraham Pisarek, courtesy of USHMM Photo Archives*)

bumped into each other and greeted each other loudly with the slogan "Freedom." The May Day demonstrations gave me a taste of the shared feeling of commitment and unity of politically engaged people.

Of course I was not completely unaware of the gathering political storm clouds; no one involved in the political battles of the early thirties could fail to notice them. In my mind's eye I can still see all those different demonstrators: the Communists with their red flags and their bands; the men of the Social Democratic defense organization, with whom I identified; the militarily precise brown columns of the SA, which frightened me. There are indelible memories—of a Communist, mortally wounded in a clash with Nazis, struggling to get back on his feet, of accounts of pitched street battles between political adversaries, including between Communists and Socialists.

Who the Nazis were, what they were doing and what they wanted, I learned from my father. Hitler means terror, dictatorship, war, he used to tell me. He campaigned tirelessly in the last free election before Hitler's takeover. "Berlin will stay Red," he proclaimed in meeting after meeting, indoors and out. He did not let up even when our next-door neighbor was wounded by a bullet meant for him.

Even though I was not familiar with all the details and did not quite understand everything, I sensed the general tension. When stones were thrown at an electioneering banner we had strung along our balcony, I knew intuitively that I too was involved in the battle.

On that evening, March 31, 1933, I looked out the window, but not at the children at play. I had trouble concentrating. I felt apprehensive; an indefinable sense of danger was in the air. I knew that the Nazis, as their first public anti-Jewish measure, were planning a boycott of Jewish businesses on April 1. I kept looking in the direction of the corner pub, which I couldn't see from my window. It was a known Nazi hangout. I listened for my father's footsteps; he should have been home long ago. Mother too was uneasy. She kept going to the door to peer down the staircase. She came into my room, pushed me away from the window, and, more harshly than she probably meant to, told me to go and play dominoes with Lotte, our helper, while she herself remained at the window staring out into the dark.

I sat down with Lotte and listlessly began our game. Suddenly the bell rang. My mother appeared in the doorway. Lotte didn't move. At that moment our fear took concrete shape, filling the room. With great

self-control, my mother asked Lotte to answer the door. As soon as my mother heard the familiar voice of one of our political friends she ran to the door and pulled him into one of the other rooms. All I was able to hear before they disappeared were the words: "Your husband must get out of town immediately."

Our visitor left, and my mother also got ready to go out. I was terrified, but I didn't say a word. I felt she wasn't even aware of my presence. Outwardly calm, she told me she was going out to look for Father, who probably was still tied up with exams at school, and that she'd be back soon. Without another word she was out the door. Lotte nodded silently. She wasn't much older than I, probably around eighteen, and I don't know which of us was more scared. We tried to resume our game, but it was no use. We kept listening for familiar steps that didn't come.

I don't remember how long we sat like that, only that Mother didn't return until quite late. Again, she appeared very calm as she told us that Father would spend the night with friends. She didn't tell us why, and I knew that it was better not to ask. Without further protest I went to bed, but from my room I could hear her telling Lotte that Dr. Ostrowski had been arrested and also Mr. Weber, that no one knew what was going to happen next, that it might be a good idea for us to pack some bags and spend the next night somewhere else.

Two men who were friends of the family had been arrested, and apparently my father was also in danger. "The Nazis keep pointing at your apartment," our visitor had told Mother. Everybody in the neighborhood knew our politics.

"Arrests"—it was a word I had begun to see and hear a lot, but until that evening it had been an abstraction. Now it became frightening reality. At that time the Nazi actions still were directed primarily against their political opponents. The Jews had not yet become prime targets. The overwhelming majority of Berlin Jews was not politically involved. My father's few Jewish friends from his college days neither understood nor sympathized with his politics; some even said that Hitler was the only one who would be able to bring order into the political chaos of the Weimar Republic. As for the arrests of those days, they were simply "excesses."

The night passed without incident. The next day my father came back. There was nothing unusual about him; he appeared to be in good spirits. Apparently the father of one of his students, out of gratitude that his daughter had passed her baccalaureate, offered to put him up for the night when he heard of

The cover of *Der Giftpilz* ("The Poisonous Mushroom"), an anti-Semitic children's book. *(USHMM Photo Archives)*

In the Third Reich, brutality often manifested itself in different ways. Here, a German policeman kicks a man as he tries to climb into a truck. *(Main Commission for the Investigation of Nazi War Crimes/USHMM Photo Archives)*

his predicament. His host was a nonpolitical Jewish doctor, and Father made us laugh with his story of sleeping in the doctor's office amid the medical instruments and a skeleton that cast weird shadows. It was all still strange, unreal. None of us could dream that the day would come when we'd be deeply grateful for such a shelter.

Outside they were marching with the "steady firm steps" of the Horst Wessel song [a popular Nazi tune]. They tore the black, red, and gold banner of the Weimar Republic in shreds and carried placards with slogans like "Germans, don't buy from Jews. World Jewry wants to destroy Germany. Germans, defend yourselves." All this I could see from the window of our apartment. We didn't go out that day....

We left our home on the evening of April 1 as unobtrusively as possible, practically stealing away. After the noise of that day, all those drums, fifes, and marches, the quiet of the evening was almost tangible. Not many people were out on the street. A few Jewish shops bore the traces of what had happened: a Star of David painted on one store front, broken windows in another. That was all. It is not unlikely that in view of the now peaceful atmosphere my parents were asking themselves whether they might not have been able to stay in our apartment, whether what we had been

witnessing was nothing more than a bad dream that would pass as suddenly as it had come.

What we heard in Spandau also sounded reassuring. True, SA guards had posted themselves in front of Uncles Hannes' shop. One of them even excused himself: "It's just one of those measures..." Customers were not molested. The mood that evening was very strange. Hope resurfaced that in the end everything would turn out all right.

We stayed in Spandau for a few days, and then returned to our apartment. But it no longer seemed like our old home to me; it had lost its reassuring aura of security. I kept listening for strange footsteps presaging imminent danger. My parents did not seem quite as worried. Some of our friends who'd been arrested by the Gestapo were released. I overheard only fragments of their accounts: "I had to run along a long corridor, and when I didn't follow their commands fast enough, they beat me until I lost consciousness...." Others refused to talk about their experience, and still others never came back. They were sent to concentration camps; very few of them survived. The initials "KZ" [Konzentrationslager] had not yet acquired their ominous overtone. Names were whispered: "Oranienburg," "Dachau." (Deutschkron, pp. 1–12)

Aftermath

One week after the boycott, the Reich passed the first anti-Jewish law of the Nazi regime. Enacted on April 7, 1933, the Law for the Restoration of the Professional Civil Service forced Jews and other "non-Aryans" out of civil service positions. Additional decrees forbade non-Aryan lawyers from practicing law, and eventually non-Aryan professors, judges, and doctors were also unable to practice their professions. Throughout the 1930s, the Nazis continued to pass legislation designed to strip Jews of their rights and force them onto the fringes of society. Like many other Jewish professionals and civil servants living in Germany, Deutschkron's father was fired from his job as a teacher. He managed to escape to England after realizing that he would soon be arrested, leaving Deutschkron and her mother behind in Berlin. At that time, the Deutschkron family, like countless other Jewish families, hoped that Hitler's rule would not last long.

Together mother and daughter endured the anti-Semitic laws, including being forced to wear yellow cloth stars sewn to their garments at all times. Once World War II began in 1939, escape became impossible for Inge and her mother. The Gestapo rounded up all Jews living in Berlin to prepare them for deportation. In order to escape the concentration camps, the Deutschkrons pretended to be non-Jewish Germans. Living in constant danger and fear, they were dependent on the kindness of others who risked their lives to help protect them. At the close of the war, they managed to secure refugee status, and Deutschkron then traveled to England with her mother to be reunited with her father.

Sources

Books

Deutschkron, Inge, *Outcast: A Jewish Girl in Wartime Berlin,* originally published in German, 1978, reprinted, Fromm International Publishing Corporation (New York), 1989.

Forman, James, *Nazism,* Franklin Watts (New York), 1978.

Richter, Hans P., *Friedrich,* translated by E. Kroll, Holt, Rinehart and Winston (New York), 1970, reprinted, Puffin (New York), 1987.

PRIMARY SOURCE

Nuremberg Laws on Citizenship and Race Issued by the Reichstag Party Congress

September 15 and November 14, 1935

Adolf Hitler was obsessed with ideas about race when he became German chancellor on January 30, 1933. For years he had written articles and given speeches that expressed his belief in racial purity and the superiority of Germany and its people as members of an Aryan "master race." The history of civilization, he believed, reflected the struggle between creative Aryan forces and substandard non-Aryan influences. In the view of Hitler and the Nazis, Jews were members of a completely different, non-Aryan race, not simply members of a distinct religion and culture. Once the Nazis took control of the German government, their racial beliefs became a part of official policy.

Hitler assumed dictatorial control over the German government and people within two months of becoming chancellor. In addition to outlawing political opposition, the Nazis also instituted government-sanctioned violence to silence their critics. On March 20, 1933, the Nazis opened the first concentration camp, Dachau, to hold communists, socialists, trade unionists, and other political dissidents. By seizing control of the press and radio, the Nazis were able to spread racial and nationalist propaganda throughout Germany with few real challenges. As they continued strengthening their power, the Nazis simultaneously escalated anti-Jewish measures, carefully testing reactions within Germany and abroad.

Prisoners of Dachau, one of the first German concentration camps, sit on the steps of a barrack. *(USHMM Photo Archives)*

Hitler relied on the SA to frighten and terrorize Jews living in Germany. During the first few months of his rule as chancellor, violence and administrative actions forced hundreds of Jews from positions as judges, lawyers, journalists, and professors. Roving bands of storm troopers randomly vandalized synagogues and broke windows of Jewish-owned stores and businesses. After months of informally organized and frequently violent anti-Jewish attacks, the Nazi government officially ordered a day-long national boycott of Jewish businesses to begin the morning of April 1, 1933. Angered at international protest against the Nazi government's anti-Jewish activities, Hitler is believed to have ordered the boycott as revenge. He accused international Jewry of spreading lies about Germans. The official boycott was his way of silencing further criticism, both domestic and foreign.

Less than a week after the boycott, the Reich government enacted its first anti-Jewish legislation. It called for the dismissal of Jews and other non-Aryans from civil service jobs. In order to minimize objections, and at the request of President Hindenburg, Hitler allowed exemptions for Jewish civil servants who had fought in World War I and those who had lost fathers or sons in the war. Still, thousands of Jewish workers, including schoolteachers, were fired from their jobs. Other decrees sought to reduce what many Germans perceived as an unfair proportion of Jews in certain professions and positions. Laws prohibited non-Aryan lawyers and doctors from practicing their professions in Germany. In addition, only a limited number of Jewish students were admitted to colleges and universities. Jews were also banned from participating in cultural activities and from owning land.

On March 25, 1933, in New York City, thousands of communists listened as one of their leaders condemned the Hitler regime. *(USHMM Photo Archives)*

After the death of Hindenburg on August 2, 1934, Hitler declared himself führer, or leader, ensuring his complete control over Germany. He established two principles for all Germans to follow: rule by the führer and devotion to achieving race domination. Having mandated the sterilization of people with hereditary diseases to preserve German racial purity, Hitler felt it was time to address the "blood and race" problem created by the presence of Jews. In fall 1935 he requested that Wilhelm Frick, minister of the interior, draft measures concerning Jewish citizenship and blood relationships that would protect Germans from Jewish "impurity." Frick ordered members of his staff to gather in Nuremberg, and there they worked frantically to draft the laws. According to historians, the decision to create these laws occurred so hastily that Frick's assistants forgot to bring enough paper with them, and were forced to jot down their ideas on menu cards instead. The laws were presented on September 15, 1935, at the annual Nazi party rally in Nuremberg, and are therefore known as the Nuremberg Laws. These decrees merely formal-

ized the unofficial discriminatory measures that had existed prior to 1935.

The first Nuremberg Law denied German citizenship to people of non-German blood. The Reich Citizenship Law stripped Jews of their German citizenship and created a distinction between "citizens" and "subjects." According to these new definitions, a citizen of the German Reich was someone of German blood. Since Jews were considered a separate race, they could be only subjects and never citizens.

The second Nuremberg Law, the Law for the Protection of German Blood and German Honor, prohibited marriages and sexual relationships between Germans and Jews. Though the Aryan theory of racial domination saw all non-Aryan races as inferior, the word Jew is used specifically in this law, and designates its true target. Section 3 of the Law for the Protection of German Blood prohibits the employment of German females under age forty-five in Jewish households. The Nazis objected to the use of Aryans as servants to supposedly inferior non-Aryans such as Jews.

According to Section 4, Jews were prohibited from hoisting the newly recognized flag of the German Reich but were allowed to honor "Jewish" colors.

Since the Nuremberg Laws did not define a Jew as a person with certain religious beliefs, considerable confusion arose over how to classify Jews, especially people of mixed Jewish blood (called *Mischlinge*). A supplemental decree, called the First Regulation to the Reich Citizenship Law, passed on November 14, 1935, and defined a Jew as anyone who had three or four Jewish grandparents. The decree also stipulated that a person would be considered a Jew if he had two Jewish parents and either belonged to the Jewish community or was married to a Jewish person. The law classified someone of mixed Jewish blood as "one who descended from one or two grandparents who were racially full Jews." To separate full-blooded Jews from *Mischlinge*, the Nazi administration employed "family researchers." Many families lacked sufficient records and evidence of their full ancestral background. As a result, final decisions about race classifications were frequently based on random, biased court rulings.

Nuremberg Laws on Citizenship and Race

The Reich Citizenship Law of 15 Sept 1935

The Reichstag has adopted unanimously, the following law, which is herewith promulgated:

Article 1

(1) A subject of the State is a person, who belongs to the protective union of the German Reich, and who, therefore, has particular obligations towards the Reich.

(2) The status of the subject is acquired in accordance with the provisions of the Reich- and State Law of Citizenship.

Article 2

(1) A citizen of the Reich is only that subject, who is of German or kindred blood and who, through his conduct, shows that he is both desirous and fit to serve faithfully the German people and Reich.

(2) The right to citizenship is acquired by the granting of Reich citizenship papers.

(3) Only the citizen of the Reich enjoys full political rights in accordance with the provisions of the Laws.

Article 3

The Reich Minister of the Interior in conjunction with the Deputy of the Fuehrer will issue the necessary legal and administrative decrees for the carrying out and supplementing of this law.

[Nuremberg], 15 Sept 1935 at the Reichsparteitag of Liberty

*The Fuehrer and Reichs Chancellor
Adolf Hitler
The Reichs Minister of the Interior
Frick*

Law for the Protection of German Blood and German Honor of 15 September 1935

Thoroughly convinced by the knowledge that the purity of German blood is essential for the further existence of the German people and inturned by the inflexible will to safe-guard the German nation for the entire future, the Reich Parliament (Reichstag) has resolved upon the following law unanimously which is promulgated herewith:

Section 1

(1) Marriages between Jews and nationals of German or kindred blood are forbidden. Marriages concluded in defiance of this law are void, even if, for the purpose of evading this law, they are concluded abroad.

(2) Proceedings for annulment may be initiated only by the Public Prosecutor.

Section 2

Relations outside marriage between Jews and nationals of German or kindred blood are forbidden.

Nazi members display their patriotism during Nazi Party Day in Nuremberg, Germany, in the early 1930s. *(Library of Congress)*

Section 3

Jews will not be permitted to employ female nationals of German or kindred blood in their household.

Section 4

(1) Jews are forbidden to hoist the Reichs and national flag and to present the colors of the Reich.

(2) On the other hand they are permitted to present the Jewish colors. The exercise of this authority is protected by the State.

Section 5

(1) Who acts contrary to the prohibition of section 1 will be punished with hard labor.

(2) The man who acts contrary to the prohibition of section 2 will be punished with imprisonment or with hard labor.

(3) Who acts contrary to the provisions of sections 3 or 4 will be punished with imprisonment up to a year and with a fine or with one of these penalties.

Section 6

The Reich Minister of the Interior in agreement with the Deputy of the Fuehrer and the Reich Minister of Justice will issue the legal and administrative regulations which are required for the implementation and supplementation of this law.

Section 7

The law will become effective on the day after the promulgation, section 3 however only on … 1 January 1936.

[Nuremberg], the 15 September 1935 at the Reich Party Rally of freedom.

The Fuehrer and Reich Chancellor
Adolf Hitler
The Reich Minister of Interior
Frick
The Reich Minister of Justice
Dr. Gurtner
The Deputy of the Fuehrer
R. Hess
Reich Minister without portfolio

First Regulation to the Reich Citizenship Law of 14 Nov. 1935

Article 1

(1) Until further issue of regulations regarding citizenship papers, all subjects of German or kindred blood, who possessed the right to vote in the Reichstag elections, at the time the Citizenship Law came into effect, shall, for the time being, possess the rights of Reich citizens. The same shall be true of those whom the Reich Minister of the Interior, in conjunction with the Deputy of the Fuehrer, has given the preliminary citizenship.

(2) The Reich Minister of the Interior, in conjunction with the Deputy of the Fuehrer, can withdraw the preliminary citizenship.

Article 2

(1) The regulations in Article 1 are also valid for Reichs subjects of mixed, Jewish blood.

(2) An individual of mixed Jewish blood, is one who descended from one or two grandparents who were racially full Jews, insofar as does not count as a Jew according to Article 5, paragraph 2. One grandparent shall be considered a full-blooded Jew if he or she belonged to the Jewish religious community.

Article 3

Only the Reich citizen, as bearer of full political rights, exercises the right to vote in political affairs, and can hold a public office. The Reich Minister of the Interior, or any agency empowered by him, can make exceptions during the transition period, with regard to occupying public offices. The affairs of religious organizations will not be touched upon.

Article 4

(1) A Jew cannot be a citizen of the Reich. He has no right to vote in political affairs; he cannot occupy a public office.

(2) Jewish officials will retire as of 31 December 1935. If these officials served at the front in the World War, either for Germany or her allies, they will receive in full, until they reach the age limit, the pension to which they were entitled according to last received wages; they will, however, not advance in seniority....

(3) The affairs of religious organizations will not be touched upon.

(4) The conditions of service of teachers in Jewish public schools remain unchanged, until new regulations of the Jewish school systems are issued.

Article 5

(1) A Jew is anyone who descended from at least three grandparents who were racially full Jews. Article 2, par. 2, second sentence will apply.

(2) A Jew is also one who descended from two full Jewish parents, if:

(a) he belonged to the Jewish religious community at the time this law was issued or who joined the community later.

(b) he was married to a Jewish person, at the time the law was issued, or married one subsequently.

(c) he is the offspring from a marriage with a Jew, in the sense of Section 1, which was contracted after the Law for the Protection of German Blood and German Honor became effective....

(d) he is the offspring of an extramarital relationship, with a Jew, according to Section 1, and will be born out of wedlock after July 31, 1936.

Article 6

(1) As far as demands are concerned for the pureness of the blood as laid down in Reichs law or in orders of the N.S.D.A.P. and its echelons—not covered in Article 5—they will not be touched upon.

(2) Any other demands on pureness of blood, not covered in Article 5, can only be made with permission from the Reich Minister of the Interior and the Deputy of the Fuehrer....

Article 7

The Fuehrer and Reichs Chancellor can grant exemptions from the regulations laid down in the law.

Berlin, 14 November 1935

*The Fuehrer and Reichs Chancellor
Adolf Hitler*

A photo montage that includes the front page of the *Badische Presse* with the headline "The Nuremberg Laws." The accompanying identification card belongs to a German Jewish woman. *(Reproduced by permission of Landesbildstelle Baden/USHMM Photo Archives)*

The Reich Minister of the Interior
Frick
The Deputy of the Fuehrer
R. Hess
—Reich Minister without Portfolio

(As translated from the Reichsgesetzblatt by the Office of U.S. Chief of Council for the Prosecution of Axis Criminality in Mendelsohn, pp. 22–32)

Aftermath

Some Jews believed that the Nuremberg Laws would help reestablish a degree of stability in Germany. Even though they had lost their political rights, Jews hoped that the official decrees would reduce violent and random attacks against their synagogues, businesses, and homes. In fact, many Jews who had emigrated to other countries during 1933 and 1934 returned to Germany after 1935. Fearing international criticism, Hitler relaxed his anti-Semitic measures in preparation for the 1936 Olympic Games in Berlin. To create a false impression for foreign visitors, the Nazis removed anti-Semitic placards throughout the city, though German Jewish athletes were not allowed to participate in the Olympics. At the games, Hitler had to contend with the outstanding performance of ten African American athletes, including track sensation Jesse Owens, who won four gold medals. Hitler considered blacks to be an inferior race and demonstrated his disapproval by removing himself from the Olympic stadium prior to one of Owens's medal ceremonies. At the conclusion of the Olympic Games, Hitler resumed his anti-Semitic policies.

Under the Nuremberg Laws, for the first time in modern history, race became the legal basis for defining national citizenship. The laws also paved the way for subsequent anti-Jewish legislation. Over the course of the twelve-year Nazi regime, about 400 laws and decrees were enacted regarding Jews living within the jurisdiction of the Third Reich. The Nazis published thirteen supplementary orders to the Reich Citizenship Law (the last passed on July 1, l943). In 1938 the Nazis instituted the "Aryanization" of Jewish businesses, forcing Jews to sell stores to Germans at fractions of the market value. The complex web of anti-Semitic decrees isolated Jews from other Germans and set them outside the protection of the police or the government. They were subjected to political, legal, and social persecution.

Nuremberg, meanwhile, became the Nazis' favorite city in which to stage elaborate rallies. After the Nazis entered World War II, the city was subjected to repeated bombardment by the Allied powers, and suffered severe damage. After the defeat of the Axis powers in 1945, the Allies chose Nuremberg as the site for the public trial of twenty-two Nazi leaders.

SOURCES

Books

Bachrach, Susan D., *Tell Them We Remember: The Story of the Holocaust,* Little, Brown (Boston), 1994.

Chaikin, Miriam, *Nightmare in History: The Holocaust, 1933–1945,* Clarion Books (New York), 1987.

Mendelsohn, John, editor, *The Holocaust: Selected Documents in 18 Volumes,* Garland Publishing (New York), 1982.

Koehn, Ilse, *Mischlinge, Second Degree,* Greenwillow Books (New York), 1977.

Frau Wilhelmine Haferkamp
Interview in *Frauen: German Women Recall the Third Reich*

Conducted by Allison Owings, 1987

Wilhelmine Haferkamp was born in 1911 in Oberhausen, Germany, where her father and two brothers were train conductors. Drastically affected by the crippled German economy after World War I, Haferkamp's family sent her to live with relatives in Holland who owned a restaurant. After a year with her Dutch family, Haferkamp returned to Germany. As a teenager she fell in love with Heinrich Haferkamp, a neighborhood boy who worked in the nearby stone mines. Her Catholic parents opposed the marriage because Heinrich was a Protestant; despite objections, she converted to the Protestant faith and married Heinrich when she was nineteen.

The roles for women in Nazi Germany, like most countries at the time, were extremely limited. Hitler's racial ideals relegated women to the traditional roles of homemaker and child bearer. To achieve his goal of establishing an Aryan master race, Hitler banned birth control and abortion and offered financial aid to worthy, racially-pure Aryan families. Frau (the German equivalent of "Mrs.") Wilhelmine Haferkamp was twenty-two years old and pregnant with her fourth child in 1933 when her husband joined the Nazi party. Consistent with Nazi aspirations, the Haferkamps had many more children during the twelve years of the Third

Reich. Haferkamp received a bronze, silver, and gold Mother's Cross for her childbearing contributions. With each successive child she received money, called *kindergeld*, from the government. By 1945, shortly after the end of World War II, she had given birth to her tenth child.

In the following interview, Haferkamp tells how she risked her own safety and that of her family by giving food to non-Jewish prisoners of the Nazis, but she implies in the following interview that the risks were too high for her to help the Jews. While she and her husband received several stern warnings concerning her kindness toward prison laborers, it is unlikely that such leniency would have been extended if she had been assisting Jews. Those found in violation of Nazis law were subject to arrest, imprisonment without trial, internment in concentration camps, torture, and even death. Haferkamp acknowledges the privileges she and her family enjoyed and relates her efforts to share what she could with those who were cast off as enemies by the Nazis.

This interview was conducted in German, and the following selection is a literal translation. It includes the German words *ja*, meaning "yes," and *nicht*, a typical sentence ending. The interviewer's questions appear in bold.

Frauen: German Women Recall the Third Reich
"Motherhood Times Ten, and Food to Spare"

"But then all at once it happened. When one had ten children, well not ten, but a pile of them, one should join the [Nazi] party; '33 it was, nicht? I already had three children and the fourth on the way. When 'child rich' (kinderreiche) people were in the Party, the children had a great chance to advance. Stake claims and everything. Ja, what else

could my husband do? They joined the Party, nicht? There was nothing else we could do. I got thirty marks per child from the Hitler government, came every month, and twenty marks' child aid from the city of Oberhausen. Was fifty marks per child. That was a lot of money. I sometimes got more 'child money' (Kindergeld) than my husband earned...."

The Nazis had various programs aimed at indoctrinating German youth in the ideology of the Third Reich. Here, a group of Nazi youth marches at the University of Berlin. *(Reproduced by permission of Archive Photos)*

What did she think when Hitler came to power?

"I didn't know him. I had a lot to do with the children. I always said, I had no time. To think about it, nicht? Ja, I often complained. There were meetings there and meetings there and there meetings.... Our 'Dicke,' one of the older children, when she was in school, had to be in the BdM [Bund Deutscher Mädel, or League for German Girls, the girl's division of the Hitler Youth]. Otherwise she couldn't go to school.... You had to be in the BdM. I still see ours running with the little shirts and the little blue skirts and the black scarves." Asked what she thought about the organization itself, she said she thought it was like the Girl Scouts, or a gymnastics or singing club. *"They got their uniforms, nicht? And marched through the streets. They didn't learn anything harmful...."*

Because Herr Haferkamp was a Party member, his children also got more schooling than they would have otherwise. *"If you went to high school, the parents had to pay. And if you were in the NSDAP [the Nazi party], everything was paid."*

Did she join the Party, too?

"Never. My mother wasn't in it either. To the contrary, a couple times I got a warning." With those words, Frau Haferkamp launched into stories that have become lore in her family.

Most of the stories involved slave laborers, prisoners of war or the human booty of Nazi expansionism, who did hard manual work in Germany, got meager rations, and lived an altogether miserable existence. To help insure their misery, the Nazi regime included them in the category of the "enemy" and forbade the German citizenry from having family relations with them. Some slave laborers worked on construction projects right outside the Haferkamp home, and especially caught the eye of Frau Haferkamp and her oldest boy. He had the chore of going to the baker's every morning for fresh breakfast rolls.

"I can still see him running with the net bag on his back, with rolls in it, and [past] the ditches in the streets where a new drainage system was being put in. And our boy always had pity. He always threw rolls [to the laborers] in the ditches." She said laughing, *"He just went by the row like a farmer sowing his*

The Nazis forced many people into slave labor, where they worked in sweat-shop conditions. Here, women work in a German armament factory, set up in a railway tunnel. The makeshift factory was later liberated by U.S. Army troops. *(Library of Congress)*

crop." One of her sisters, at the house on a visit, was so distressed to see the freezing prisoners with "icicles in their beards" that she threw them the Christmas cookies she had brought. The gesture brought a rebuke from the Nazis—rather, another rebuke.

By then, Frau Wilhelmine Haferkamp had also committed the crime of "füttern den Feind" [feeding the enemy].... "Now what really happened, [it] was cold outside. And everyday I cooked a big pot of milk soup for the children, nicht? Nice and hot. Got a lot of milk on the children's ration cards. And then I put a whole cube of butter in it, the pot was full, and a lot of sugar, because sugar nourishes, nicht? And I lived upstairs. My mother-in-law lived downstairs.... I looked out the window and pointed to 'the bandolios' [what she called the laborers] that I was putting something in the hallway. They were afraid to get out of the ditches and they wanted to eat it. Then I went to the watchman and I said, 'Listen, you too are married.' I said, 'I have many children.... And I cooked a big pot of milk soup.' I say, 'Can I not give it to the poor men? You wouldn't want me to throw it down the toilet....'

"He looked at me, he said... 'You are an obstinate dame.... Go ahead and do what you have to, but I have seen nothing.' Then I made the soup so hot, put it down in the hallway and with a ladling spoon, not with individual bowls, and then I pointed to it. One by one, they jumped out of the ditches and took the big soup spoon ... until it was empty. One day, my husband got a card from the Party. They would like him to appear in the Party office.

"And they said, 'Listen, your wife is sure doing fine things. How can she fodder our enemies?' 'Ja, well, I can't do anything about it, I'm not always home, I don't see it.' Then when my husband came home, he really yelled at me ... he said, 'You will land me in the devil's kitchen if you keep doing that. And I am a Party member.... And what do you think will happen when they catch me? They will take me somewhere else....'"

Once, the enemy did something in return. Several of her children were playing near a construction site "canal" when a young daughter, trying to catch up with the older children, fell head-first into a deep hole. "The whole street cried, 'The best-looking

Hitler Youth

The Nazis began sponsoring youth groups as early as 1922. Shortly after seizing power in 1933, they initiated a "coordinating" program that essentially disbanded most non-Nazi youth organizations, though Catholic youth groups were allowed to exist until 1937. The most significant Nazi youth organization, Hitlerjugend, or Hitler Youth, groomed boys to be soldiers and defenders of Nazism. Their activities included camping, sporting competitions, and evening social programs, all conducted with military discipline. Membership required boys to wear uniforms fashioned after those of the military. The Nazis also created a group for girls called Bund Deutscher Mädel, or League for German Girls. The League instructed young girls about the importance of being loyal Nazis and mothers of racially pure Germans. Much like the boys in the Hitler Youth, girls wore standard uniforms and participated in parades, rallies, and other weekly group functions.

A law passed in 1936 made membership in the Hitler Youth compulsory, and more than 7 million boys were enrolled by 1939. German youths had to register with the Reich Youth Headquarters at the age of ten—a process that included extensive investigation of family background to assure racial purity. The Hitler Youth was organized into two age groups, ten to fourteen and fourteen to eighteen. At age eighteen, young men graduated from the Hitler Youth and joined the Nazi party. The next year, they enrolled in the Reichsarbeitsdienst, or State Labor Service, which involved demanding physical labor and more strict discipline. After completing the mandatory six-month term in the State Labor Service, young Nazis then enrolled in the Wehrmacht, or armed forces, for two years of military service.

As the war progressed in Europe, German forces needed additional manpower to replace their losses. Pressure grew to send members of the Hitler Youth to work in military support functions at younger and younger ages. When Allied troops captured areas of Germany in spring 1945, they found eight-year-old boys in uniform armed with weapons and fighting as adults.

For more information on the Hitler Youth, see *Children of the Swastika* by Eileen Heyes, published by Millbrook Press (Brookfield, CT), 1993.

Haferkamp child is dead.'" An "enemy" laborer whom Frau Haferkamp had been "foddering" jumped down after the girl and rescued her.

No matter how humanistic and brave Frau Haferkamp was, the people she had spoken thus far of feeding were "Aryans," a "safer enemy" to help than Jews. But by then, were there any Jews in Oberhausen? For the first time since she began her story, her voice became soft. "Ja. There were Jews. There were even a lot of Jews. We even knew a Jew we did not know was a Jew. Eichherz was their name. Bought furniture [from their store] when we first married. And my husband went to the doctor. Dr. Floss was his name and [he] was also a Nazi.... And my husband laid his jacket over the chair. The [receipt] book fell out of his pocket,

that you bought furniture you couldn't pay for all at once.... And the doctor saw that. Then he said ... 'What? You as a member of the Party, you buy from a Jew?' And he didn't know at all it was a Jew." She implied that her husband continued the payments.

She also implied that she had defied the quasi-order not to shop at Jewish stores. "You shopped where you liked something. They really made you crazy afterward. 'What? [they said.] You shopped at a Jew's store?' How did you know who was a Jew? Now, one knew what one was. What I always thought earlier, it's a difference like Catholic, Protestant. He's a Jew. Nicht?"

[Frau Haferkamp went on:] "We had a ... Dr. Stein. We did not know that [he] was a Jew. [Stein is

Nazi doctrine was taught in schools as evidenced by these Hitler Youth who learn how to give the "Heil Hitler" salute. Membership in the Hitler Youth became mandatory in 1936. Many who grew up as members of the Hitler Youth went directly into the Schutzstaffel (SS), the Nazi police force that operated the concentration camps. *(NSDAP Standarten Kalender)*

usually, but not always, a Jewish name.] My God, I was <u>furious</u>, was I ever furious, when I once went to Market Street and, because he was a Jew … [he had been stripped] naked, and he had a sign hanging around his neck, 'I am the Jew Dr. Stein.'"

She began to shout. "Stark naked, down the middle of the street they chased him, and behind him with the whip. I <u>saw</u> it.… And that was our family doctor.… He had not done anything at all. They just found out who was a Jew.… That's what the Nazi swine did, really.…"

When asked what happened to Dr. Stein, Frau Haferkamp looked distraught. "Ja, they took him away. They took him away. That was terrible." **Was it difficult not to be able to help him?** *"They would have beat us dead.… You can believe it.… Do not get*

involved. Na, that's how we got through, as a little person.…"

Frau Haferkamp knew of many more sad fates, including an example of the Nazis' early use of euthanasia.

"In the house where I lived, my brother-in-law's sister also lived and she had a sick child. Looked fifteen, but she was already nineteen. And she was in Essen, near Oberhausen. It was called the Franz Hals [?] House.… She got her sickness though a festering in the middle ear. Anni von Thiel. And she came first to the Franz Hals House. And then in the Hitler time, if you inherited something or had something, nicht? I was standing below with my milk jug, the milkman came by at the door, and got milk with

Frau von Thiel. And she got a letter from Essen. Anni has been ... transferred, let us say, to Krefeld, nicht? She had an inflammation of her lungs. And [Frau von Thiel] was bawling. She said, 'My God, look, she's been away a whole week. Couldn't they have told me earlier?...' I said, 'Wait, give me the letter and I'll show it to my husband....' [When shown the letter, he] said, 'What?' Looked at it again. 'She's not coming back. They're gassing them all....'

"That was that. When they said she was transferred, the child was already dead. And a couple days later she got another letter. When the burial is going to be.... They gassed her.... Only because she had a disease."

[Frau Haferkamp] knew of nonlethal inhumanities, too. One classmate "also had a child every year" and "did not get a penny from Hitler, that is, from Hitler's side, because they all [all of the children] had inherited diseases. You had to be healthy, the children had to be healthy, so that you can propagate your heirs and no sick ones. I got all that child money and she got nothing at all."

What did such a nice family man, and Party member [Herr Haferkamp], think of Jews?

"I will honestly say, my husband actually had Jews as friends.... Well, we did not really think about what a Jew is. 'Zo vot [so what]?' we always said...."

Did she ever think she should have done something earlier against the Nazis?...

"You could not say a lot. Back then in the Nazi time, you were not even allowed to <u>have</u> your own opinion, nicht? If it already somehow was known that he or he complained against the Party, nicht? We knew one.... They always said to him, Communist, but he was not a Communist. The parents were <u>so</u> nice.... And one day the word was, they beat [him] up. Nobody knew where. Nobody knew how. He was in the hospital...." [He later died in the hospital.] (Owings, pp. 19–26)

Aftermath

When the bombing raids worsened across Germany, Haferkamp and her children were evacuated to a farm in the rural area of southwestern Germany. Even on a remote farm, she continued to help prisoners in the area. Herr Haferkamp spent the war in the army, performing clerical services. When World War II ended in 1945, he rejoined his wife, arriving shortly after the birth of their last child. He died of lung disease soon after the end of the war. With the collapse of the German economy, bank accounts holding *kindergeld* were dissolved. Years later, during a trip to Stuttgart, Germany, Haferkamp ran into the man who had saved her daughter. The man remembered Haferkamp as the only woman who had defied Nazi guards and helped feed starving prisoners.

SOURCES

Books

Friedman, Ina R., *The Other Victims: First Person Stories of Non-Jews Persecuted by the Nazis*, Houghton Mifflin (Boston), 1990.

Gehrts, Barbara, *Don't Say a Word*, M. K. McElderry Books (New York), 1986.

Owings, Alison, *Frauen: German Women Recall the Third Reich*, Rutgers University Press (New Brunswick, NJ), 1993.

Pastor Christian Reger
"Barracks 26"
From *The Other Victims*
Compiled by Ina R. Friedman
Published in 1990

Hitler's *Gleichschaltung* ("coordination") effort, launched shortly after he became chancellor of Germany in 1933, was an attempt to infuse every aspect of German life with Nazi philosophy. Only by creating a blindly devoted populace could Hitler ensure his ultimate goal of German world domination. Within months of taking power, the Nazis seized control of the media, banned opposing political organizations, and regulated cultural events, the arts, and education. Hitler also realized the importance of controlling religion, and envisioned a single Reich church that reflected and supported his ideas on race and German nationalism. Initially, a majority of German clergy eagerly embraced Nazism, and the nationalistic fervor provided hope and jobs to downtrodden and impoverished Germans. Hitler promised to protect Christian religions, and in 1933 signed a concordat with the Vatican—the headquarters of the Roman Catholic church—that ensured German Catholics complete autonomy to practice their religion. Days after signing the treaty, however, Hitler banned the Catholic Youth League and pressured parents to enroll their children in the Hitler Youth. In 1936 Hitler attempted to require Catholic school buildings to remove crucifixes, but the decree was rescinded due to public protest. In 1938 Hitler eliminated all Catholic newspapers, and the following year he prohibited all religious processions.

In attempts to seize control of the Protestant churches, the Nazis created the *Deutsche Glaubensbewegung,* or "German Faith Movement," which denounced the teachings of the Old Testament and advocated rewriting the New Testament in accor-

dance with Nazi ideology. Proponents planned to replace references to Jesus with mentions of Hitler and the German Fatherland. Nazi leaders banned nativity plays and Christmas carols from schools, and attempted to convert Christmas into a pagan solstice festival. Civil servants and teachers, who were most dependent on the Nazi government for employment, were expected to join the German Faith Movement.

While some 3,000 Protestant ministers joined the German Faith Movement, an equal number joined an opposition group called the *Bekenntniskirche,* or the Confessional church. Confessional church leaders declared Christianity to be incompatible with Nazi principles. Members of this organization were targeted by the Nazis, and a number of clergy members were sent to the Dachau concentration camp. As Germany continued to invade and conquer other countries, foreign religious leaders who opposed Nazism were also sent to concentration camps. The Nazis sent more than 2,250 priests and pastors from nineteen different occupied countries to Dachau.

Christian Reger was a pastor who spoke out against the Nazis from his pulpit in a small church in the eastern German town of Stegelitz. In his story that follows, he explains his initial embrace, and ultimate rejection, of Nazism. Reger began using his weekly sermons to preach his message of faith. After repeated warnings, harassment, and arrests, local officials finally sent Reger to Dachau in 1940. The concentration camp at Dachau had a special barracks, Barracks 26, established for clergymen. As a political prisoner, Reger was required to wear a red triangle.

Newly arrived prisoners—including a clergyman (second from left)—stand during roll call at Buchenwald.
(USHMM Photo Archives)

Pastor Christian Reger: "Barracks 26"

For my first sermon in Stegelitz, I wore my Brown Shirt uniform.... The congregation burst into applause. Mina, my wife beamed. Only a few years before, as a young seminary student, I had heard Adolf Hitler speak. Although I did not like his ranting and raving, I saw how much hope he gave the hungry, threadbare men and women in the audience. The huge swastika flags flying from the rafters, the splendidly uniformed soldiers, and the brass band, inspired everyone to stand up and cheer, "Germany, awake!"

I was proud to be a part of this new nationalistic spirit. In 1932, I wore my uniform to show I was one with the people. Hitler had not yet been elected chancellor, but he promised Germany prosperity and power. A few months after his election in 1933, however, Mina and I were walking in the woods. As we strolled toward our favorite glade, we heard voices. We stopped. A young father, in a Brown Shirt uniform, placed a flag with a swastika across a tree stump. Then, holding up his newborn son, he proclaimed, "I baptize thee, Wilhelm Smit, in the name of the Fatherland and to the glory of Germany."

I was shocked. Baptism was the rite of the church. Christians could only be consecrated to Jesus Christ. There were tears in Mina's blue eyes as we turned back. When we came home, she packed away my uniform. The next Sunday, I preached about the sacredness of baptism. That night, a terrible banging awakened us. Lights flooded the bedroom window. "Traitors of Germany, traitors of Germany!" voices shouted in the darkness. "We'll smash you."

Petrified, Mina huddled beneath the covers. I crept over to the window and cautiously peeped outside. Young storm troopers, their faces filled with hate, beat their clubs and sticks against the metal truck over and over, rousing the sleeping village. Then it stopped. "This is a warning, Pastor Reger," shouted a voice that had a familiar sound. I heard the motor start and drive off.

"What should we do, Mina?" I asked. "Leave? Stop protesting the teachings of Hitler?"

"What do you want to do, Christian Reger? Keep quiet?"

"Mina, I have to speak up. I can't be silent in the face of evil."

"Then we stay and fight."

It was not easy. There was constant pressure by the Nazis to join the German Christian Faith Movement. The movement had been established by the Nazis to wipe out Christian beliefs. The Old Testament was to be abolished, the New Testament was to be rewritten to praise Hitler instead of Christ. Blasphemy!

Pastor Martin Niemöller, who had been a submarine captain in World War I, organized the Confessional Church. Three thousand Protestant clergy joined the Confessional Church and three thousand joined the German Christian Faith Movement. Eleven thousand Protestant clergymen remained silent.

The years 1933, 1934, 1935 passed. I continued to preach against the Nazis. As the people became more and more enthusiastic about the jobs the Nazis brought them, the membership in my church grew smaller. Marching bands and huge rallies made the people ignore the persecution of the Jews. After the disgrace of losing World War I, everyone wanted to believe that Germans were superior to other people. One Sunday morning, I stood at the pulpit and pleaded for sanity. "Christianity teaches, 'Thou shalt not kill, thou shalt not steal.' The Nazis preach otherwise. What is the Lord's should remain the Lord's."

With seven hundred other clergymen, I was imprisoned. Suddenly, from all over Germany, people protested our arrests. In a rare instance of responding to public indignation, the Nazis released most of the pastors, including me, but twenty-seven were sent to Dachau.

I could not keep quiet. Every Sunday there was a new outrage. After Crystal Night, the night when synagogues were burned and twenty thousand Jewish men sent to concentration camps, I again protested. "All men are equal in the sight of the Lord." For a second time, I was arrested. After a brief imprisonment, I was released....

Sometimes I wondered how I, a small-town pastor, a man who had never been a leader, could stand up against Hitler. The only thing I excelled in, in all my life, was gymnastics. Was I being foolish to go against the tide? But how could I be a soldier of Christ and not fight against the Nazis? Mina agreed.

Vatican Issues Holocaust Declaration

On March 16, 1998, the Vatican issued a document titled "We Remember: A Reflection on the Shoah." The result of more than a decade of work by the Commission for Religious Relations with the Jews, the text was described as an "act of repentance" for the failure of Roman Catholics (including Pope Pius XII) to prevent the Holocaust. Edward Idris Cardinal Cassidy, head of the commission, told a news conference that all members of the Church shared responsibility for the sins of other Catholics. Many people were not pleased with the document, including Chief Rabbi Meir Lau of Israel. They felt that "We Remember" was too general in addressing the Church's attitude toward Jewish persecution during World War II. Rabbi Lau was also disappointed that there was not an apology for the beliefs and behavior of the Pope during that period. The previous Vatican document relating to Jews, called "In Our Times," was issued in 1965 under the auspices of the Second Vatican Council and Pope Paul VI.

In 1940, the Gestapo arrested me for a third time. For weeks, I paced up and down the narrow prison cell wondering if I would ever see Mina again. I wasn't allowed to receive any mail. The isolation was frightening and I worried about Mina. Was she all right, or had the Nazis imprisoned her? I grew more and more depressed. One morning, a letter fluttered through the prison peephole. I opened the envelope. Mina had copied, in tiny letters, Acts 4:26-30, " … grant unto Thy servants to speak Thy Word with all boldness…." The passage renewed my courage. I would have need of courage, for a few days later, I was sentenced to Dachau.…

How does one describe Dachau? The barking dogs and striking guards, being forced to run through the gates? The photographing, the turning of a man into a number? No longer Pastor Christian Reger, I became 26 661. Even a dog has a name. The shaving of the hair, the beating, standing there naked while a prisoner in charge of clothing threw out a pair of pants, a shirt, and a hat.

"Number 26 661, what is your crime?"…

"Crime? I'm a clergyman. I am Pastor Christian Reger."

"Political prisoner!" the guard shouted, handing me a red triangle. "Answer only to your number."…

It was 1940, in the year of our Lord. I walked down the main road towards the Pastors' Barracks, Barracks 26. A moat, filled with water, surrounded the camp. Electrified barbed wire encircled the area around the moat. Guard towers, with armed sentries, overlooked each corner of the camp. A terrible stench, as though someone were burning putrid meat, assaulted my nose. I started to choke.…

"Welcome to the Pastors' Barracks. I'm Werner Sylten." A small slim man offered me his hand.

"I'm Christian Reger from Stegelitz." As I stood in the "living" area, I saw another room filled with tiers of wooden boards.

The prisoners crowded around me asking for news. They knew that Germany had invaded Poland because there were Polish priests in the barracks.

"Is Germany losing the war?" they asked.

I shook my head, "No, we've taken Norway, Holland, France, Belgium, and Denmark."

Their faces fell. How thin and emaciated they all looked. I turned to Werner. "Why are you here?"

"I had a Jewish grandmother."

Another man came over. "I am Father Fritz Seitz. I was arrested for hearing the confession of a Pole. Hitler declared Poles subhuman. We're not allowed to give them any rites of the church."…

"There are Catholics in the Pastors' Barracks?"

"Yes, and Greek Orthodox. Hatred knows no discrimination. We come from many countries," Fritz Seitz said.

Everyone went out of their way to warn me: "In the Pastors' Barracks, you can trust your fellow man. Outside, trust no one.…"

That night, I lay on the top tier of the wooden boards, unable to turn over because so many were crowded together. I thought of Mina.…

The next morning, the guards marched the German priests out of the camp.... The wind blew dust into my face, intensifying the terrible smell hanging over the camp. "What is that awful odor? Is there a chemical plant nearby?" I asked Werner Sylten. "It chokes my lungs."

"Humanity," he said, looking straight ahead.

"I'm sorry, I didn't understand you." I walked slowly, my hoe over my shoulder. I was starving. I had had only a piece of bread since I arrived.

"Faster, faster," the guards called, lifting their clubs. "You think this is a resort. On the double."

"Those who die of disease or malnutrition or hangings or beatings or from experiments, the Nazis have a long list ... those who die are burned in the crematoriums."

"People are dying?" I was careful not to stop. "But it's uncivilized to kill prisoners. This is a civilized country."...

"This is the Third Reich. The Germany that we knew, or thought we knew, is dead. The barbarians are in command."...

On Christmas Eve, 1942, we knelt, Catholic and Protestant, on the wooden floor and prayed for our families and our parishes. I thought of Mina, I tried to radiate a special message of love to her. It was the only Christmas present I could send. The loneliness of the years overwhelmed me. I began to cry. I prayed, how I prayed that evil would be no more. I even prayed for our Lord to forgive our oppressors. As I stood up, I felt a great peace. I was a man of God. I would not let my oppressors make me hate. (Reger in Friedman, pp. 34–46)

Aftermath

Unlike Reger, the majority of Protestant pastors in Germany remained neutral during the Nazi regime by joining neither the German Faith Movement nor the Confessional church. Their silence, in all probability, saved their lives. The Vatican also remained silent, issuing only one public objection to the actions and racial policies of the Nazis, condemning them for not honoring the concordat. Pope Pius XII never spoke out against Nazi persecution of Jews.

During the course of World War II, the barracks at Dachau became even more crowded. As the Third Reich suffered defeats on the battlefields, its territorial holdings began to decrease. Prisoners from the Russian front, as well as from Italy and France, were shipped to Dachau rather than released to the advancing Allied forces. Reger survived Dachau for five years, much longer than the average prisoner, and he was freed on April 2, 1945, shortly before the collapse of the Nazi government. Following his release, he was reunited with Mina in Stegelitz, which became part of Communist-controlled East Germany after the war. Communist officials felt Reger could be trusted because of his concentration camp experiences. He served a congregation in East Berlin until 1985, and he died at the age of eighty. Mina died in 1970.

SOURCES

Books

Friedman, Ina R., *The Other Victims*, Houghton Mifflin (Boston), 1990.

Rossel, Seymour, *The Holocaust*, Franklin Watts (New York), 1981.

PRIMARY SOURCE

Elisabeth Kusserow
"Elisabeth's Family: Twelve Jehovah's Witnesses Faithful unto Death" From *The Other Victims*
Compiled by Ina R. Friedman

Published in 1990

Adolf Hitler labeled Jehovah's Witnesses a "degenerate race," despite the fact they were German descendants. Jehovah's Witnesses are members of a small Christian denomination whose fundamental beliefs included recognizing only Jehovah God as the supreme sovereign, as well as remaining politically neutral. Jehovah's Witnesses also believed God would resurrect those who had proved faithful to him until death. These religious beliefs put Jehovah's Witnesses at odds with the Nazis. In the fervently nationalist environment of Germany at the time, Jehovah's Witnesses refused political affiliation, would not salute the swastika flag of the Nazi state, and would not raise their arms in the "Heil Hitler" salute. By law, this Nazi greeting, meaning "Hail Hitler," took the place of most ordinary greetings used throughout the day. The beliefs of Jehovah's Witnesses also prohibited them from serving in the military—a position the Nazis considered traitorous. According to the teachings of the Bible, Jehovah's Witnesses believed they must "love thy neighbor as thyself" and only engage in the battle between good and evil on Judgment Day.

Shortly after Hitler rose to power, the Nazis began their persecution of Jehovah's Witnesses. As early as 1933, Jehovah's Witnesses were banned from practicing their faith. They were prohibited from assembling in their churches, called Kingdom Halls. In time, the Nazis sent some Jehovah's Witnesses to concentration camps, while others lost their jobs, civil rights, and welfare benefits.

Like many Jehovah's Witnesses, the Kusserow family practiced the teachings of the Bible. Franz and Hilda Kusserow and their eleven children lived on a farm in Paderborn, Germany, where they studied the Bible, took turns with chores, and played musical instruments. By continuing to practice their religion, they incurred the wrath and hatred of Nazi Germans. The following excerpt is an account given by Elisabeth, one of the Kusserow children who survived the persecution. Elisabeth Kusserow refers to herself and her family as belonging to the International Society of Bible Students. This denomination officially changed its name to Jehovah's Witnesses in 1931.

"Elisabeth's Family: Twelve Jehovah's Witnesses Faithful unto Death"

"Quick, Elisabeth," Annemarie shouted, "the Gestapo!" In Paderborn, very few people besides the Gestapo had cars. The clouds of dust raised by a car coming down the road signaled danger.

Before the Mercedes stopped, I scooped up the <u>Watchtower</u> pamphlets [religious booklets published and distributed by Jehovah's Witnesses] and put

them in my knapsack. Magdalena stuffed the books into hers. We ran outside and hid the literature behind the bushes. At eight, I knew to walk over to the coops and feed the chickens. Magdalena, who was nine, picked up a bottle to feed the baby lamb.

We were Jehovah's Witnesses. Our parents, Franz and Hilda Kusserow, had taught their eleven chil-

dren to hide the books and pamphlets of the International Society of Bible Students if anyone spotted the men from the Gestapo coming toward the house. Anyone found with literature from our Watchtower Society could be arrested.

What a happy family we were before Hitler. Our parents had been sent by the Watchtower Society from Bochum, Germany, to Paderborn to set up a congregation of Jehovah's Witnesses. The house sat on three acres of land. Father organized our daily chores. One week the boys took care of the chickens and ducks and lamb. That week, the girls worked in the garden. Then the following week we switched chores. When the apple and pear trees were ripe, everyone helped to pick the fruit.

But it wasn't all work. Before we went to school in the morning, and in the evening, we sat around the table talking about the Bible and what the passages meant. Mother had graduated from teachers' school, and Father made time for her to teach us music and painting. The house was filled with musical instruments: five violins, a piano, a reed organ, two accordions, a guitar, and several flutes. What joyful music we made as we played from the book Hymns to Jehovah's Praise.…

In 1936, the Nazis tried to get Jehovah's Witnesses to renounce their faith. When the Gestapo knocked on our door, one of them waved a piece of paper in Father's face and shouted, "Franz Kusserow, you must sign this document promising never to have anything to do with the International Society of Bible Students. If you don't, you will be sent to prison."

The whole family stood, dumbfounded. Promise not to be Jehovah's Witnesses? Hitler was truly Satan.

Father read aloud the first paragraph. "'I have recognized that the International Society of Bible Students spreads a false doctrine and pursues goals entirely hostile to the state under the cover of religious activity.'" Father shook his head. "This is ridiculous, I can't sign."

The S.S. man, who was about the same age as my oldest brother, became angry. "Stubborn fool!"

I was shocked; no one ever talked to Father that way. He was one of the most respected people in Paderborn.

The S.S. man turned to Mother. "And you? If you don't, your children will be without parents."

Mother removed her apron and placed it over the chair. "No, I cannot sign. Annemarie"—Mother turned to my oldest sister—"take care of the children."

The agent shoved my parents outside and into the car.

Paul-Gerhard, who was five, began to cry. Hans-Werner, who was six, put his arms around his little brother. Fifi, our dachshund, began to growl. I bent down to calm her and to hide my tears.

After a few days the Nazis released Mother from prison. They kept Father. Why was it a crime to be a Jehovah's Witness? Mother couldn't understand why they released her, because she still refused to sign the paper. Mother and my oldest brother, Wilhelm, made sure we followed Father's schedule and always did our chores. But how we missed Father and his talks about the Bible! What a joyful reunion we had when he was released a year later. All thirteen of us took up our instruments, and the house resounded with hymns of praise.…

As the years passed, the situation in school became more and more painful. Every day, the teacher reprimanded me for not saluting the Nazi flag. The big black swastika on the red banner flew over the schoolhouse and hung on a pole in every classroom. My stomach churned as I tried to think of how I could avoid saluting it or saying "Heil Hitler." My parents had taught me to salute only Jehovah God. To salute a flag or a person was the same as worshiping idols. I wouldn't sing the horrible Nazi songs, either. I kept my lips together.

The teacher always watched me. "So, Elisabeth, you do not want to join in praise of our leader. Come to the front of the classroom." She turned to the others. "Children, Elisabeth thinks it is all right to insult our leader. Tell us why, Elisabeth."

"Acts 4:12 of the New Testament says, 'There is no salvation in anyone else except Jesus Christ.'"

"Imagine, Elisabeth Kusserow believes in that ridiculous New Testament."

The children laughed. I couldn't understand why. All of them went to church. On the way home from school, they pushed me and threw my books to the ground. It got worse when Hans-Werner and then Paul-Gerhard were old enough to go to school. Now I had to worry about the children tormenting them.

Our troubles grew. It wasn't just the terror of going to school. The Nazis cut off Father's pension from World War I because he still refused to say "Heil Hitler." It was hard doing without the money, even though my older

Sachsenhausen prisoners wearing identifying triangles. Jehovah's Witnesses wore purple triangles, political prisoners wore red, "asocials" wore black, homosexuals wore pink, habitual prisoners wore green, and Jews wore yellow. *(USHMM Photo Archives)*

brothers and sisters had jobs. We planted more vegetables and canned as much as we could. In 1938, the Gestapo arrested Father for a second time. What could be wrong in obeying Jehovah God?

In spring 1939, the principal came into my class. "Elisabeth, since you refuse to salute our flag and say 'Heil Hitler,' it is obvious that your parents are neglecting your spiritual and moral development. I have taken it upon myself to obtain a court order to remove you and your two younger brothers from your home. The three of you will be sent to a place where you will get proper instruction." He pulled me into his office. Paul-Gerhard, who was then eight, and Hans-Werner, who was nine, stood there trembling.

At thirteen, the words made no sense to me. "Our parents raised us according to the teachings of Jehovah God," I protested.

"Quiet! This policeman will take you to your new home."

I was so upset, I hadn't noticed the policeman standing next to the window.

"Please, please, let me call my mother." I begged. "She'll be frantic when we don't come home."

"Traitors are not to know what happens to their children."

For several months Mother tried to find out where we were. She went to the police, called orphanages, hospitals, and prisons. Finally, she reached the clerk at the reform school in Dorsten who admitted we were there. Secretly, Mother sent us letters. "Always know that we love you. Be steadfast in your faith to Jehovah God. One day we will be together in heaven or on earth."

The director of the reform school couldn't understand why we were there. "You are the best behaved children I have ever seen. It's ridiculous to have you here with these delinquents." He sent a letter to Mother, "Your children will be arriving in Paderborn on Friday at two p.m."

As we started to climb the steps of the train, two men stopped us. "The director was guilty of misconduct. You are coming with us." They drove us to Nettelstadt, a Nazi training school.

"Don't cry," I told the boys. "Jehovah God will one day rule the earth. We will see our family, either here or in heaven." I didn't feel as brave as I sounded.

At the training school, the teachers became furious when we still refused to salute the flag or say "Heil Hitler." In punishment, the three of us were sent to different places. I kept worrying about Paul-Gerhard and Hans-Werner. They were just little boys.

For six years I remained in the custody of the Nazis, praying that all of my family would survive the war....

One sunny spring morning, I was awakened by songbirds. I ran downstairs. The doors were unlocked. The matron had fled. The war was over! There was nothing to stop me from going home! I said a prayer of thanksgiving and ran to the railway station. The station was jammed with people trying to board the trains. Somehow I squeezed onto the platform between the cars. As the train chugged into the station at Paderborn, I began to have fears. What would I find? Had the boys been forced to go into the army? Was the house still standing?

Would my family recognize me? I had left an awkward teenager. Now I was nineteen. The train stopped. Slowly, I climbed down the steps onto the station platform. I looked at the men and women and children searching the faces of those stepping off the train.

"Elisabeth," three voices shouted.

"Praise Jehovah God," I said aloud as Hans-Werner and my sisters Waltraud and Hildegard ran toward me.

"We've been meeting every train," Hildegard said, her voice breaking, "praying some of us would be on it." She hugged me so hard, I thought my bones would break.

I had so many questions, I didn't know where to begin. Hans-Werner looked so much like [our older brother] Siegfried [who had died in an accident at the age of twenty-one], my heart ached. We walked hand in hand toward the house.

I could scarcely recognize my sisters. Waltraud had been in prison for two years. Hildegard was so thin she looked older than Mother had looked when I last saw her. Hildegard had been at the Ravensbruck concentration camp with Mother and Annemarie.

"Somehow we were separated when we were ordered to march out of the camp," Hildegard said. "I don't know where they are...."

"Tell me everything that happened while I was away. For six years, I've had no news."

Hildegard and Waltraud began to cry. Hans-Werner brushed his tears away with his sleeve. "It was terrible," Hildegard said. "In 1940, Wilhelm was shot for refusing to serve in the army. Mother asked the authorities to permit Father to attend the funeral. By some miracle, he was released. Even in our sadness, we couldn't help noticing how thin and worn he looked. It was such a comfort to have him, if only for the hour of the funeral."

Waltraud nodded. "It was a beautiful funeral. Karl-Heinz read from the Scriptures. But when the Gestapo shouted 'Heil Hitler' at the end of the service, Karl-Heinz refused to return the salute. The Gestapo beat Karl-Heinz and left him on the ground. A few weeks later, they went to the factory where he was working and took him away. We've heard nothing since then...."

"Everyone else was taken away, because we would not renounce our faith. We don't know if the others are dead or alive, except for Wolfgang."

I looked from one face to another.

"When he refused to serve in the army, he was beheaded. It happened on March 28, 1942," Waltraud said softly.

"He was only twenty years old." I couldn't stop trembling.

Hildegard held me in her arms. "Come into the garden, Elisabeth. Mother hid Wilhelm's and Wolfgang's letters so whoever came back would have them. They have been a great comfort to us."

In the garden where I had once played with the baby lamb, I read aloud Wilhelm's letter. "My dear parents and brothers and sisters, ... You know already how much you mean to me.... I have been faithful until the death as it is stated in the scripture.... It is true that it is difficult to follow this course.... But we must still love God above all as our leader Jesus Christ taught. When we stand steadfastly for him, he will reward us...." I put the letter down and began to sob. Wilhelm was only twenty-six.

Among Wolfgang's letters, I found a copy of the defense he had given for refusing to serve in the army. "I was brought up as one of Jehovah's Witnesses according to God's Word contained in the Holy Scriptures.... The greatest and most holy law he gave mankind is, 'You shall love God above all else and your neighbor as yourself....'

"We are living in a time ... that has been predicted in the Bible. People today are unbelievers; they

do not respect the Bible.... They ridicule Jehovah's name and say He is a God of the Jews and persecute those who keep God's laws and apply them.

"If Jehovah's Witnesses refuse military service for the reasons above, because God's laws forbid it, they are sentenced to death by the military court, only because they remain faithful to Jehovah and obey Him first....

"For it is better to suffer because you are doing good, if the will of God wishes it, than because you are being evil."

I hugged the letter to my chest. My brothers had left us a great treasure. (Kusserow in Friedman, pp. 49–57)

Aftermath

The Nazis scattered members of the Kusserow family across Germany during the war. Two of the Kusserow sons were executed for refusing to serve in the German army. After the war, Elisabeth and her brother Hans-Werner returned home safely from state-run reform schools. Their father, Franz Kusserow, came back from prison with a broken leg and in poor health. Another brother, Karl-Heinz, spent the war in Dachau, where he contracted tuberculosis. Although he did make it home, he died a year later from his illness. Elisabeth's mother and her sisters Annemarie and Magdalena also returned from their imprisonment shortly after the war.

Though Jehovah's Witnesses always had the option to end their own persecution by renouncing their beliefs, few did so. Nazi brutality only strengthened the faith of the Jehovah's Witnesses. While succeeding in breaking the will of millions of people across Europe, Nazi terror could not crack the resolve of thousands of Jehovah's Witnesses. Of the 25,000 Jehovah's Witnesses in Germany, very few renounced their faith to earn freedom. (Most of those who did were acting in the interest of their children; they felt it was the only way to keep them from being raised in state-run Nazi homes.) SS leader Heinrich Himmler even used Jehovah's Witnesses as an example of unshakable faith, stating that when all SS officers possessed that same depth of conviction in National Socialism, Nazism would be permanently secure. The Nazis imprisoned up to 10,000 Jehovah's Witnesses, many in concentration camps. Witnesses did not attempt to escape or resist guards in prison, for which they were often selected as domestic servants by Nazi camp officials and officers. After followers of Judaism, Jehovah's Witnesses were the most persecuted of religious groups. However, unlike the Jews, Jehovah's Witnesses were never targeted for systematic murder. Today there are an estimated 5 million Jehovah's Witnesses worldwide in nearly 70,000 congregations from 229 countries.

Sources

Books

Bachrach, Susan D., *Tell Them We Remember*, Little, Brown, and Company (Boston), 1994.

Friedman, Ina R., *The Other Victims*, Houghton Mifflin (Boston), 1990.

Rogasky, Barbara, *Smoke and Ashes: The Story of the Holocaust*, Holiday House (New York), 1988.

Otto D. Tolischus
Newspaper account of *Kristallnacht*

First published in the New York Times, *November 11, 1938*

As soon as he became German chancellor on January 30, 1933, Adolf Hitler began a campaign to rid Germany of Jews. As part of this campaign, the Nazis expelled about 17,000 Jews who had immigrated to Germany from Poland. On October 28, 1938, the party began rounding up Polish Jews by force, then transported them to the border of Poland. When the Polish government refused to readmit these Jews, the refugees were forced to live in sub-standard settlements. A seventeen-year-old Polish Jewish student named Herschel Grynszpan had fled to Paris, France, before the expulsion. Once in France, Grynszpan received a letter from his father that described the freezing and destitute conditions in the no-man's-land where the refugees were being detained. Upset and overwhelmed by his family's ordeal at the hands of the Nazi government, Grynszpan went to the German embassy in Paris on November 7, 1938, to voice his outrage. When he was refused access to the ambassador, he shot another embassy official, Ernst vom Rath. Two days later vom Rath died of his wounds.

Vom Rath's death ignited a violent rampage against Jewish-owned businesses throughout Germany, Austria, and the Sudetenland, a German-speaking area adjacent to Germany. The violence was orchestrated by the Nazis themselves, who viewed the assassination of vom Rath as an ideal opportunity for stirring up anti-Jewish sentiment. The murder of a German diplomat by a Jew was exactly the type of incident Joseph Goebbels, Reich Minister for Public Enlightenment and Propaganda, could use to win public support for an all-out attack on Jewish people. Under the terms of a highly-organized secret plan, the Nazis vandalized and terrorized Jews over the course of two days, launching the first night of assaults on November 9, 1938, shortly after vom Rath died of his injuries. According to the strict orders of Nazi leaders, attacks on stores and businesses were to appear spontaneous. Over the course of two days, roving groups of organized and supervised men burned more than 1,000 synagogues, wrecked at least 7,000 Jewish stores, and killed nearly 100 Jewish people. The pogroms of November 9-10 became known as *Kristallnacht,* or the "Night of Broken Glass," a reference to the shattered glass from broken store windows that littered the sidewalks of German cities and towns. The cost of the ruined plate glass windows alone was 10 million German marks, approximately 4 million U.S. dollars. The following excerpt contains firsthand observations of the destruction from Otto D. Tolischus, a German-born reporter on the staff of the *New York Times.*

The *New York Times* Account of *Kristallnacht*

New York Times
November 11, 1938

NAZIS SMASH, LOOT AND BURN JEWISH SHOPS AND TEMPLES UNTIL GOEBBELS CALLS HALT

Bands Rove Cities

Thousands Arrested for "Protection" as Gangs Avenge Paris Death

EXPULSIONS ARE IN VIEW

Plunderers Trail Wreckers in Berlin— Police Stand Idle–Two Deaths Reported

Reported by Otto D. Tolischus
Wireless to the New York Times

BERLIN, Nov. 10.—A wave of destruction, looting and incendiarism unparalleled in Germany since the Thirty Years War and in Europe generally since the Bolshevist Revolution, swept over Great Germany today as National Socialist cohorts took vengeance on Jewish shops, offices and synagogues for the murder by a young Polish Jew of Ernst vom Rath, third secretary of the German Embassy in Paris.

Beginning systematically in the early morning hours in almost every town and city in the country, the wrecking, looting and burning continued all day. Huge but mostly silent crowds looked on and the police confined themselves to regulating traffic and making wholesale arrests of Jews "for their own protection."

All day the main shopping districts as well as the side streets of Berlin and innumerable other places resounded to the shattering of shop windows falling to the pavement; the dull thuds of furniture and fittings being pounded to pieces and the clamor of fire brigades rushing to burning shops and synagogues. Although shop fires were quickly extinguished, synagogue fires were merely kept from spreading to adjoining buildings.

Two Deaths Reported

As far as could be ascertained the violence was mainly confined to property. Although individuals were beaten, reports so far tell of the deaths of only two persons—a Jew in Polzin, Pomerania, and another in Bunzdorf.

In extent, intensity and total damage, however, the day's outbreaks exceeded even those of the 1918 revolution and by nightfall there was scarcely a Jewish shop, café, office or synagogue in the country that was not either wrecked, burned severely or damaged.

Thereupon Propaganda Minister Joseph Goebbels issued the following proclamation:

The justified and understandable anger of the German people over the cowardly Jewish murder of a German diplomat in Paris found extensive expression during last night. In numerous cities and towns of the Reich retaliatory action has been undertaken against Jewish buildings and businesses.

Now a strict request is issued to the entire population to cease immediately all further

During *Kristallnacht,* the synagogue in Ober Ramstadt burned to the ground after the local fire department made no attempt to stop the blaze. *(Trudy Isenberg/USHMM Photo Archives)*

Jewish Migration from Germany

In order for Jewish people to emigrate from Nazi-controlled Germany, other countries had to agree to accept them as refugees. Some Jews who had the financial resources to cover their travel expenses, passports, and visas were able to escape Germany and move to another country. Nearly 150,000 German Jews—30 percent of all German Jews—managed to emigrate by the end of 1938. Most countries had quotas that limited the number of immigrants allowed to enter each year, and the 1938 annexation of Austria by the Third

Reich overwhelmed the international immigration system. U.S. President Franklin D. Roosevelt organized an international conference to discuss how countries could best deal with the growing flood of refugees. In July 1938 delegates from thirty-two nations met in Évian, France, to examine the situation. The conference was a failure for Jews and their advocates, but it allowed the Nazis to boast that the rest of the world did little to support the Jews.

Following *Kristallnacht*, German Jews knew they could no longer remain safe in their native country. The German government took away their financial assets and prevented them from earning a living. Jews were also prohibited from leaving the country with more than ten German marks (about four U.S. dollars), which closed foreign doors, since most countries would not accept destitute immigrants. Some Jews tried to escape to Cuba, a country that had a liberal immigration policy. Cuba agreed to accept German Jews who could afford passage. However, when the SS *St. Louis* left Hamburg in May of 1939 for Cuba, it was not welcomed in Cuba even though its passengers had obtained visas from a Cuban official in Germany. Forced to return to Europe, the Jewish refugees eventually were allowed to resettle in Great Britain, Belgium, France, and the Netherlands. Most of the Jews who found refuge in these countries, however, later fell prey to the Nazis.

Jewish refugees aboard the *St. Louis* await their fate in the port of Havana, Cuba. *(USHMM Photo Archives)*

---

demonstrations and actions against Jewry, no matter what kind. A final answer to the Jewish assassination in Paris will be given to Jewry by way of legislation and ordinance.

What this legal action is going to be remains to be seen. It is known, however, that measures for the extensive expulsion of foreign Jews are already being

prepared in the Interior Ministry, and some towns, like Munich, have ordered all Jews to leave within forty-eight hours. All Jewish organizational, cultural and publishing activity has been suspended. It is assumed that the Jews, who have now lost most of their possessions and livelihood, will either be thrown into the streets or put into ghettos and concentration camps, or impressed into labor brigades

---

and put to work for the Third Reich, as the children of Israel were once before for the Pharaohs.

Thousands Are Arrested

In any case, all day in Berlin, as throughout the country, thousands of Jews, mostly men, were being taken from their homes and arrested—in particular prominent Jewish leaders, who in some cases, it is understood, were told they were being held as hostages for the good behavior of Jewry outside Germany.

In Breslau, they were hunted out even in the homes of non-Jews where they might have been hiding.

Foreign embassies in Berlin and consulates throughout the country were besieged by frantic telephone calls and by persons, particularly weeping women and children, begging help that could not be given them. Incidentally, in Breslau the United States Consulate had to shut down for some time during the day because of fumes coming from a burning synagogue near by.

All pretense … to the effect that the day's deeds had been the work of irresponsible, even Communist, elements was dropped this time and the official German News Bureau … said specifically:

> Continued anti-Jewish demonstrations occurred in numerous places. In most cities the synagogue was fired by the population. The fire department in many cases was able merely to save adjoining buildings. In addition, in many cities the windows of Jewish shops were smashed.

> Occasionally fires occurred and because of the population's extraordinary excitement the contents of shops were partly destroyed. Jewish shop owners were taken into custody by the police for their own protection.

Excesses in Many Cities

Berlin papers also mention many cities and towns in which anti-Jewish excesses occurred, including Potsdam, Stettin, Frankfort on the Main, Leipzig, Luebeck, Cologne, Nuremberg, Essen, Duesseldorf, Konstanz, Landsberg, Kottbus and Eberswalde. In most of them, it is reported, synagogues were raided and burned and shops were demolished. But in general the press follows a system of reporting only local excesses so as to disguise the national extent of the outbreak, the full spread of which probably never will be known.

On the other had, the German press already warns the world that if the day's events lead to another agitation campaign against Germany "the improvised and spontaneous outbreaks of today will be replaced with even more drastic authoritative action." No doubt is left that the contemplated "authoritative action" would have a retaliatory character.

Says the Angriff, Dr. Goebbel's organ:

> For every suffering, every crime and every injury that this criminal [the Jewish community] inflicts on a German anywhere, every individual Jew will be held responsible. All Judah wants is war with us and it can have this war according to its own moral law: an eye for an eye and a tooth for a tooth.

Possession of Weapons Barred

One of the first legal measures issued was an order by Heinrich Himmler, commander of all German police, forbidding Jews to possess any weapons whatever and imposing a penalty of twenty years' confinement in a concentration camp upon every Jew found in possession of a weapon hereafter.

The dropping of all pretense in the outbreak is also illustrated by the fact that although shops and synagogues were wrecked or burned by so-called Rollkommandos, or wrecking crews, dressed in what the Nazis themselves call "Raeuberzivil," or "bandit mufti," consisting of leather coats or raincoats over uniform boots or trousers, these squads often performed their work in the presence and under the protection of uniformed Nazis or police.

The wrecking work was thoroughly organized, sometimes proceeding under the direct orders of a controlling person in the street at whose command the wreckers ceased, lined up and proceeded to another place.

In the fashionable Tauenzienstrasse the writer [Tolischus] saw a wrecking crew at work in one shop while the police stood outside telling a vast crowd watching the proceeding to keep moving.

"Move on," said the policemen, "there are young Volksgenossen [racial comrades] inside who have some work to do."

At other shops during the wrecking process uniformed Storm Troopers and Elite Guards were seen entering and emerging while soldiers passed by outside.

Joseph Goebbels (1897-1945)

Joseph Goebbels was one of Hitler's most intimate and influential advisers. Born into a strict Catholic working-class family from the Rhineland area of Germany, Goebbels was an intellectual. He attended Roman Catholic schools and earned a doctorate in literature and history at the University of Heidelberg. During World War I he was rejected for army service due to physical disabilities—a crippled foot and a permanent limp. These physical deformities haunted Goebbels throughout his life. Goebbels first attempted a career in literature and the arts before focusing exclusively on Nazi party activities. He helped spread Nazi ideology through an extensive propaganda campaign involving posters, pamphlets, parades, and organized street battles. From 1927 to 1935, he edited his own weekly newspaper, *Der Angriff* ("The Assault"), to promote Nazi beliefs.

When Hitler became German chancellor in 1933, he appointed Goebbels as Reich Minister for Public Enlightenment and Propaganda. In this powerful role, Goebbels controlled all aspects of German press and culture, including newspapers, radio, films, theater, and sports. He was the chief architect of the May 10, 1933 book burning and *Kristallnacht* five years later. After Hitler committed suicide at the close of the war, Goebbels decided he could not bear to live in a defeated Germany either. On May 1, 1945, he arranged to have members of the SS kill himself, his six children, and his wife. Some accounts say Goebbels performed the murders himself.

Joseph Goebbels (pictured here with his daughter Hedda) launched an all-out attack on the Jewish people. *(Reproduced by permission of Archive Photos, Inc.)*

Crowds Mostly Silent

Generally the crowds were silent and the majority seemed gravely disturbed by the proceedings. Only members of the wrecking squads shouted occasionally, "Perish Jewry!" and "Kill the Jews!" and in one case a person in the crowd shouted, "Why not hang the owner in the window?"

In one case on the Kurfuerstendamm actual violence was observed by an American girl who saw one Jew with his face bandaged dragged from a shop, beaten and chased by a crowd while a second Jew was dragged from the same shop by a single man who beat him as the crowd looked on.

One Jewish shopowner, arriving at this wrecked store, exclaimed, "Terrible," and was arrested on the spot.

In some cases on the other hand crowds were observed making passages for Jews to leave their stores unmolested.

Some persons in the crowds—peculiarly enough, mostly women—expressed the view that it was only right that the Jews should suffer what the Germans suffered in 1918. But there were also men and women who expressed protests. Most of them said something about Bolshevism. One man—obviously a worker—watching the burning of a synagogue in Fasanenstrasse exclaimed, "Arson remains arson." The protesters, however, were quickly silenced by the wrecking crews with threats of violence.

Warned Against Looting

To some extent—at least during the day—efforts were made to prevent looting. Crowds were warned they might destroy but must not plunder, and in individual cases looters either were beaten up on the spot by uniformed Nazis or arrested. But for the most part, looting was general, particularly during the night and in the poorer quarters. And in at least one case the wreckers themselves tossed goods out to the crowd with the shout "Here are some cheap Christmas presents."

Children were observed with their mouths smeared with candy from wrecked candy shops or flaunting toys from wrecked toy shops until one elderly women watching the spectacle exclaimed, "So that is how they teach our children to steal."

Foreign Jewish shops, it appears, were not at first marked for destruction and were passed over by the first wrecking crews. But in their destructive enthusiasm others took them on as well and even wrecked some "Aryan" shops by mistake.…

No photographing of the wreckage was permitted and Anton Cellar, American tourist, of Hamden, Conn., was arrested while trying to take such pictures, although he was soon released. Members of a South American diplomat mission likewise got into trouble on that account.

Grave doubt prevails whether insurance companies will honor their policies. Some are reported to have flatly refused to reimburse for the damage because of its extent, and, considering the standing the Jew enjoys in German courts today, there is little likelihood of his collecting by suing. But there still remains to be settled the damage done to "Aryan" houses and other property. (Tolischus, pp.1, 4)

Aftermath

As part of the terror of *Kristallnacht,* more than 30,000 Jewish men were arrested and sent to the concentration camps at Dachau, Buchenwald, and Sachsenhausen. In compliance with official instructions, the Nazis arrested able-bodied Jewish males (particularly focusing on those who were wealthy) under the guise of protection. The prisoners were only released when they had arranged passage out of Germany. The leaders of the Nazi government who had orchestrated *Kristallnacht* gathered on November 12, 1938, to discuss their future course of action regarding the "Jewish question." The group decided that the government would seize all insurance payments for damage to Jewish shops and businesses, valued at 25 million marks (about 10 million U.S. dollars). Jewish owners were also required to repair their stores themselves and were not allowed to reopen their businesses unless they hired non-Jews as managers. Lastly, a 1 billion mark fine was imposed upon German Jews. In addition to financial penalties, the Nazis also imposed numerous legislative measures that removed Jews from social life. Decrees were passed that barred Jewish children from public schools and prohibited all Jews from certain public places, such as movie theaters, beaches, parks, general hospitals, resorts, and sleeping cars on trains. The Nazis also imposed curfews on Jews, thereby strictly controlling their movement. As a result of the worsening conditions for German Jews, many lost hope and committed suicide.

SOURCES

Books

Dawidowicz, Lucy S., *The War against the Jews, 1933–1945,* Behrman House (New York), 1978.

Periodicals

Tolischus, Otto D., "Nazis Smash, Loot and Burn Jewish Shops and Temples until Goebbels Calls Halt," *New York Times,* November 11, 1938, pp. 1,4.

World War II Begins

When Adolf Hitler became chancellor of Germany in 1933, he focused on three immediate goals: (1) elimination of all political opposition; (2) establishment of Germany as a world economic, political, and military power; and (3) elimination of Jews in Germany and eventually in all of Europe. By 1938 Hitler had outlawed all political parties except the Nazis and had issued numerous decrees that severely curtailed the civil rights of Jews. Any attempt to build a strong German military would be in direct violation of the Treaty of Versailles, which not only limited the number of soldiers permissible in the standing army, but also prohibited any military draft, air force, or armored vehicles, and restricted the size of the navy. Hitler's efforts to strengthen the military, however, were supported by German military officers who, prior to his ascension to power, had been making secret plans to circumvent the treaty by training pilots on glider planes and experimenting with designs for modern tanks. Although Hitler initially began rearmament of Germany in secret, he was also determined to take a public stand against the Treaty of Versailles.

Hitler's goal of a strong military was closely entwined with his desire to regain territory Germany had lost in World War I (1914–1918). He was determined to win back regions that had become part of Poland and to reunite Germany with Austria, where most of the people spoke German. These goals were readily supported by German nationalists, including most army officers. Hitler also believed that Germany needed to conquer vast new territory in order to provide *Lebensraum,* or room to live. His first goal was to annex land from eastern Europe through the invasion of western Poland and the conquest of areas like White Russia (now Belarus) and the Ukraine, which had long been part of the Russian empire and were then the western part of the Soviet Union. Motivated by Nazi racial theories and hatred of Communists, Hitler believed that the "inferior" people of eastern Europe were meant to be ruled by Germans. According to his plan, Poles, Russians, Ukrainians, and Belorussians could become cheap sources of labor for German overlords. Poland and the western areas of the Soviet Union were home to the largest Jewish communities in Europe, and Hitler believed that the Communist government of the Soviet Union was part of a Jewish plot to rule the world. When it came, the war for new German territory, therefore, would also be a war to destroy the Jews.

Hitler had achieved success through political maneuvering; the timing of his rise also contributed to his success. Many Germans approved of Hitler and the Nazis during the first few years of the Third Reich, crediting them with eradicating

The Factory Workers

During the years of Nazi rule, German laborers received lower wages than they had been earning before the onset of the Great Depression, but this was still an improvement over the salaries they earned in the early 1930s. Most were relieved to have jobs at all, even if their pay and working conditions were less than ideal. Traditional supporters of the Social Democrats and Communists, laborers at first opposed Nazism and battled storm troopers in the streets. However, improved economic conditions, coupled with the elimination of labor unions and opposition political parties, gave factory workers less reason to oppose the new government in an active way. As fear of Nazi terror combined with better economic conditions, the majority of laborers stayed out of politics.

Production lines at the Krupp steel mills. Some historians claim that Hitler helped the German economy; others believe that he reaped the benefits of programs instituted before he seized power. *(Reproduced by permission of Foto Marburg/Art Resource)*

the rampant unemployment that had devastated Germany in the Great Depression of the early 1930s. A number of the programs that had lowered unemployment, though, had actually been enacted before Hitler came to power. Because the programs needed time to affect the economy, Hitler was in power by the time they did; he received the praise for having sparked a German economic renewal.

Hitler continued to expand economic programs similar to those that President Franklin D. Roosevelt was implementing in the United States.

A German machine gun crew marches into the Rhineland in 1935. *(Reproduced by permission of AP/Wide World Photos)*

Like Roosevelt, Hitler was willing to try bold new policies to create jobs, but he also pushed economic recovery programs in order to maintain support for the Nazi party. In an effort to put people to work, the German government started huge projects, such as autobahns (modern highways) that replaced old country roads. These domestic projects and economic improvements in other countries increased demand for German products, creating more jobs in Germany. A drastic decrease in unemployment came in 1935, when Hitler announced that Germany would begin drafting men into the military. The decree both produced new jobs for men who entered the armed forces and resulted in a tremendous increase in the production of weapons such as cannons, tanks, warships, and fighter planes. Steel mills were busy supplying material for these arms; coal mines produced the fuel for making steel; the chemical industry made explosives; and clothing factories made uniforms.

Although a German military draft was a direct violation of the Treaty of Versailles, Great Britain and France did not respond to Hitler's decree. Within weeks, he went on to announce the creation of a German air force and, on March 16, 1935, Germany officially declared that it would no longer respect the treaty's limitations on the armed forces. The next year, Hitler sent the German army into the Rhineland, a region that was part of Germany but in which a German military presence was prohibited by the treaty. This move was a gamble for Hitler, whose army was still too weak to defend itself if France attempted to mobilize against it. Army generals tried to talk Hitler out of occupying the Rhineland, but he correctly predicted that France and Britain would do nothing more than issue a protest.

Europe's Policy of Appeasement

From 1936 to 1939 a civil war raged in Spain, where Fascist general Francisco Franco, who was friendly to the Nazis, led a rebellion against the elected government. Hitler sent German planes and pilots to support Franco's troops, using the

Adolf Hitler honors Condor Legion veterans after their return from Spain. These German volunteers fought on the Fascist side in the Spanish Civil War. *(Reproduced by permission of Bildarchiv Preussischer Kulturbesitz)*

Viennese police attempt to hold back the crowd cheering the conquering Adolf Hitler entering Vienna. *(Reproduced by permission of AP/Wide World Photos)*

combat opportunity to develop Germany's modern air warfare tactics, which included purposely bombing civilian populations. The German bombing of the town of Guernica shocked the world and inspired Pablo Picasso's famous painting *Guernica.*

In March 1938 the German army moved into Austria and absorbed its territory into Germany, a move called the *Anschluss* ("union"). Hitler worked in conjunction with Austrian Nazis to bring about the *Anschluss,* which was welcomed by many, if not most, Austrians, and which was achieved without Germany ever firing a shot. Intent on acquiring more territory, Hitler demanded that a part of western Czechoslovakia, called the Sudetenland, become part of Germany. Claiming that the Czechoslovakian government was mistreating the German-speaking population of the Sudetenland, Hitler told his generals that he planned to destroy Czechoslovakia through military force. While the crisis over the Sudetenland came close to starting a war, Czechoslovakia's allies, Britain and France, were not willing to defend the country, and it could not stand alone against Germany.

In September 1938 the leaders of France, Britain, and Italy met with Hitler in Munich;

Adolf Hitler addresses a huge enthusiastic crowd in Vienna after the *Anschluss. (Reproduced by permission of AP/Wide World Photos)*

Attendees at the Munich Conference, September 1938: British Prime Minister Neville Chamberlain, French Prime Minister Edouard Daladier, Hitler, and Italian leader Benito Mussolini. A year before Hitler invaded Poland, beginning World War II, Chamberlain assured the world there would be peace. *(Reproduced by permission of AP/Wide World Photos)*

Czechoslovakian officials were not allowed to attend the conference. When Hitler assured British Prime Minister Neville Chamberlain that Germany would not make any other territorial demands in Europe, Chamberlain took him at his word. Britain and France agreed to let Hitler take over the Sudetenland. Upon his return to London, Chamberlain waved a copy of the Munich agreement at the airport and said that he had brought home a lasting peace. The Munich Conference has since become famous as the symbol of the British and French policy of German appeasement.

Opponents of appeasement attacked Chamberlain and Prime Minister Edouard Daladier of France for giving in to Hitler's threats. The prime ministers were so afraid of war, critics argued, that they were willing to go back on their promises and sacrifice the citizens of a democratic country, Czechoslovakia, to the Nazis. In fact, they added, this policy would make war more likely by encouraging further demands by Hitler. At the time, though, the desire to avoid war was so strong in Europe that appeasement was favored by most Europeans, including Germans. According to both German and foreign observers, people in Germany did not respond well to Nazi propaganda about the Czechoslovakian crisis. They did not want to go to war over the Sudetenland, and, like most people in France and Britain, they were relieved that the issue had been settled. Hitler became more popular, even among some anti-Nazi Germans, because he had shown that he could win gains for Germany without war. Another factor contributing to the policy of appeasement was that Chamberlain, Daladier, and their military advisers did not think their armed forces were ready for war. Both Britain and France were rapidly building more weapons and planes, and they welcomed a delay that would help their rearmament efforts. Germany, however, was also building new weapons and in hindsight, many military experts assert that Britain and France would have been better off fighting Germany in fall 1938.

The Asian Front

As a new war in Europe became imminent, intense conflict was already taking place in Asia between Japan and China. This war had spread into eastern Asia and the Pacific region, and would eventually become part of the world war. The causes of World War II in Asia are closely connected with the history of Japan. When ships from Portugal and Spain began arriving in Japan in the early 1600s, the Japanese initially welcomed their visitors but soon closed the country to Europeans. For the next two centuries, Japan was almost completely isolated from the outside world, including its Asian neighbors. Japanese citizens were not allowed to leave the country, and foreigners, whether merchants or missionaries, were not welcome. Beginning in the 1850s, however, Western influence was forced on the Japanese. In 1853 a fleet of American warships commanded by Commodore Matthew Perry entered Tokyo Bay without the permission of the Japanese government. Massive armaments on the ships could have easily destroyed the city of Tokyo, and after a year of pressure, Japan signed a treaty with the United States that allowed the entry of American ships into Japanese ports. Soon thereafter Japan also signed treaties with Russia, Britain, and the Netherlands, establishing forced economic ties with the Western world. Humiliated and angered by pressure from the Western powers, the Japanese feared that their outdated military and technological resources would allow Japan to be made into a European colony. Western nations were drastically expanding their territories, taking over foreign countries and established governments, particularly in Asia and Africa, without regard to the wishes of the people in those nations. The Japanese believed that allowing Western merchants into the country was the first step in this process.

In the late 1860s Japanese leaders began taking measures to avoid colonization. The emperor had already lost his real power, and the true ruler was the shogun, the head of a powerful family who acted as a military dictator. While the shogun ran the central government, local lords held large areas of land and operated their domains virtually as separate countries. With no national army or tax system in Japan, the word of the lords was the law of the land. In 1868, after years of conflict, a group of powerful local leaders was able to seize power from the shogun. Central rule was officially returned to the emperor Meiji in an event known as the Meiji Restoration. Although Meiji was controlled by the leaders of the rebellion and did not actually run the country, he continued to enjoy extraordinary prestige among the people, who regarded the emperor as a godlike symbol of Japan. During Meiji's rule (1868–1912), the government was able to abolish the old feudal system in which lords had almost

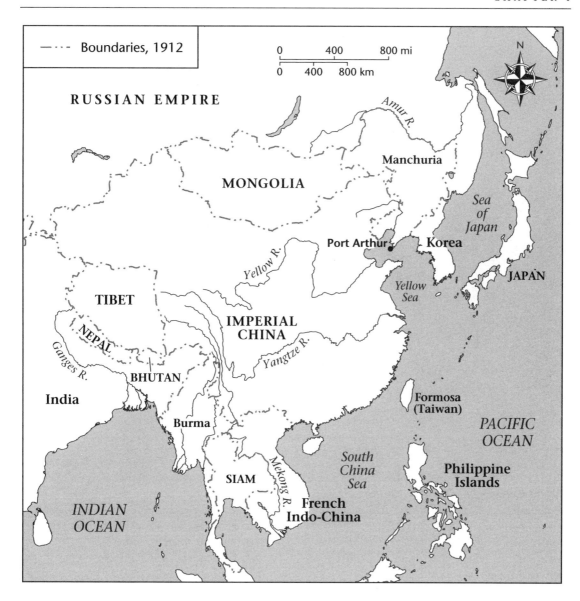

East Asia, 1912.

absolute power over their own lands. Many lords remained wealthy and influential, but Japan now had a single government that ruled the entire country in the emperor's name as well as a written constitution and a legal system. In conjunction with these socio-political changes, Japan began modernizing its economic structure. The Japanese built factories like those in Europe and the United States; introduced widespread use of steam power, electricity, and railroads; and established a telephone network and a modern educational system. Central to the new plan was modernization of the army and navy, which then had new weapons, new Western-style ships, and the latest military training. These rapid changes,

made in just a few decades, resulted in a Japan that resembled the United States and Europe more than its Asian neighbors.

Since Japan had few natural resources, its factories had to import most of their raw materials from foreign countries. Many of the finished products had to be sold in other countries. Japan was faced with a dilemma that Germany, France, and Britain had encountered years earlier. As an expanding nation forced to turn elsewhere for resources, Japan considered an imperialistic approach—colonizing territory that contained the needed resources. The logical place for Japan to both acquire raw materials and sell finished Japan-

Japan's new warships were a vital part of its plan to modernize the country. *(Reproduced by permission of AP/Wide World Photos)*

ese products was the Asian mainland. Large areas of Asia had come under the direct control of Western countries at the end of the nineteenth century during their imperialistic struggles. In order to acquire new territories in Asia, Japan therefore would have to be willing to go to war with the Western powers that were already there, as well as the Asian nations themselves.

In the final decades of the nineteenth century, tensions increased between Japan and China. The two powers fought over control of Korea, a semi-independent country that for centuries had owed allegiance to China. Meanwhile, China was too weak to control its own outlying areas, and Japan began stationing troops in Korea despite Chinese protests. A conflict erupted between China and Japan in 1894 and 1895, resulting in an easy victory for the newly modernized Japanese army. Japan forced China to give up the island of Formosa (Taiwan) and to cease interference in Korea, which was placed under the "protection" of Japan. Essentially a Japanese colony, Korea officially became part of Japan in 1910. Japan also demanded control over part of Manchuria, in northeast China, which was rich in coal and iron and offered vast

farmlands. The Chinese agreed to give up part of Manchuria, but European powers (especially Russia, France, and Germany) did not want Japan to dominate the region. Russia threatened war if Japan attempted to exert control in Manchuria. Though Manchuria officially remained part of China, the Japanese continued to exercise a growing influence in the region.

Meanwhile, Russia was also expanding its empire in eastern Asia. Russian czars had extended their territory to the Pacific Ocean, and Russia's influence, like Japan's, was growing in Manchuria. Conflict between Russia and Japan over Manchuria continued to escalate. In 1905 the two countries went to war when the Japanese navy staged a surprise attack against the Russian fleet anchored in Port Arthur (or Lü-shun, on the southern tip of the Liaotung Peninsula, which juts into the Yellow Sea). The Japanese army won the war, defeating Russian troops in Manchuria and winning another sea battle, almost completely destroying a second Russian fleet. This victory gave Japan freedom to increase its influence and economic power in Manchuria. It also changed national and international views of Japan. For the first time in modern history, an Asian country had defeated a European power, thus proving Japan a major military and naval presence. During World War I, Japan fought alongside France, Britain, and the United States and took over several German-controlled islands in the Pacific Ocean.

The Rise of Militarism in Japan

Japan's power and influence continued to grow. Japanese companies owned railroads and coal mines in Manchuria and controlled the area's economic policies. In 1931 Japanese troops, officially stationed in the country to protect these interests, seized Manchuria without the permission of the Japanese government. A short war with China ensued in which Japanese troops burned villages, shot Chinese civilians, and raped Chinese women. The Japanese army established a new country named Manchukuo as an "independent" nation with a Chinese emperor and its own government, which was actually under the control of the commander of the Japanese troops stationed in the country. The attack on Manchuria was evidence of the increasing power of military figures in the Japanese government. Younger military officers were playing a significant role in Japanese politics by helping organize secret patriotic societies, some of which boasted tens of thousands of members. These organizations, which opposed a democratic political system, encouraged Japan to increase its military and naval forces and to seize a larger empire. Sometimes they assassinated dissenting civilian politicians. By the 1930s, the government of Japan was promoting policies similar to those of the Fascist regimes in Italy and Nazi Germany.

Japan was under the influence of the army and its traditions; the ancestors of many Japanese military officers were samurai—Japanese warriors of the Middle Ages (approximately A.D. 500 to 1500). Traditional Japanese worship of the emperor as a descendant of the gods became more prominent. School children were taught that dying for the emperor was the greatest honor a Japanese person could achieve, and that obedience to the emperor's wishes was both a religious and patriotic duty. Nevertheless, the emperor's decrees were actually made by the military and its political allies, who censored newspapers and magazines, abolished the power of labor unions, and subjected college students to rote memorization rather than allowing

them free thought. Women were discouraged from playing any part in society outside their traditional roles of wives and mothers. The entire country was being organized to support the ideas and goals of the militarists, who wanted all of Japanese society organized on military principles. Any disagreement with the government's policies was considered unpatriotic and could be a crime. The secret police became a powerful body that spied on the general population. Politicians who did not support the army strongly enough, and even some generals who were considered too moderate by younger army officers, were in constant fear of being murdered by secret societies. In February 1936 hundreds of armed junior military officers took over the center of Tokyo. They apprehended and killed several leading antimilitarist politicians. This further increased the militarists' influence in the government.

The militarists openly expressed their dislike of foreigners and promoted the idea that the Japanese were a superior race. Influences from Europe and the United States, such as Western-style ballroom dancing and English-language street signs, were attacked. Japanese leaders began calling for the removal of Western powers from Asia, using the slogan "Asia for the Asians." The treatment of Manchukuo and Korea, however, made it clear that the militarists did not support Asian independence, but instead sought Japanese control over the continent. Even so, the idea of ridding Asia of Western imperial powers initially appealed to a large number of Asian people.

The creation of Manchukuo created conflict between Japan and other countries, especially the United States, which refused to recognize Manchukuo as an independent country and demanded it be returned to China. In an effort to strengthen the Chinese government, the United States provided bank loans to China and began selling planes to the Chinese air force. Tensions continued to grow between the United States and Japan, and would eventually lead to war.

In November 1936 Japan signed the Anti-Comintern treaty with Nazi Germany, in which the two countries pledged to oppose the spread of the world communist movement. The treaty reflected changes in Japan as well as Japanese militarists' admiration of Nazi Germany, but was principally directed against the Soviet Union. Soviet leaders now had to worry about a possible attack on two fronts, thousands of miles apart,

The Rape of Nanking

Nanking (also called Nanjing) had become the capital of China in 1928, and was home, in the 1930s, to about 1 million people, including many refugees fleeing from Japanese invasion troops. On December 12, 1937, Japanese troops reached the city and had occupied it by the following day. During the next six weeks, the Japanese began a series of atrocities that has been called the "Forgotten Holocaust." Japanese troops looted and stole anything of value, then burned homes and other buildings, leaving a shortage of shelter. Thousands of unarmed men, even those too old, too young, or too ill to fight, were taken into the streets and shot. Stories told by survivors and foreign missionaries, eyewitnesses to the atrocities who were spared only by their status as foreigners, were documented by pictures taken by both the missionaries and the Japanese themselves. Atrocities included severe beatings and mutilations; beheadings; bayonetting Chinese civilians during target practice; live burials and cremations; releasing wild dogs onto bound prisoners; and forced marches into icy waters to freeze and drown victims. The women of Nanking were victimized as well as the men and some suffered the additional torture of gang rape and sexual slavery before death. Women were raped indiscriminately; women ranging in age from young children to elderly women were raped, tortured, mutilated, and killed. The Japanese were under orders not to rape, but this merely meant that many of them covered their actions by killing their victims. Others were proud enough to force their victims to pose for souvenir pictures.

Though the Japanese later sought to cover up the severity of the war crimes committed in Nanking, Japanese newspapers of the day featured stories of "killing competitions" by the officers. Two of the most notorious competitors were sub-lieutenants Mukai Toshiaki and Noda Takeshi, who began a competition to decide who had the most "samurai spirit" by killing 100 Chinese with swords before entering the city. By the time they reached the city, one had killed eighty-nine people and the other only seventy-eight, so the men announced they would continue the competition in the city. The numbers reached 105 and 106, but it could not be determined who reached the figure first, so the bar was raised to 150 and later to 1000. This contest was documented in several Japanese newspapers and also in the American-owned English-language paper *The Japan Advertiser*. This was not an isolated incident, and along with other similar episodes, it was used as a tool by the Japanese government to help foster a sense of superiority and pride that encouraged Japanese soldiers to forget their "scores" were humans.

A lone Chinese baby cries in the street as the Japanese attack Chinese cities in 1937. *(Reproduced by permission of © Hulton Getty/Liaison Agency)*

In 1937 Japanese aggression against the Chinese takes the form of using captured prisoners in Nanking as targets in bayonet practice. *(Reproduced by permission of © Hulton Getty/Liaison Agency)*

Estimates for the number of civilians killed in Nanking range from 140,000 to 300,000, and the number of rape victims between 20,000 and 80,000. The Japanese have been reluctant to admit what happened, despite documentation including photographs, film, diaries of foreign observers, personal testimony from survivors, and even the testimony of former Japanese soldiers. Though some of those involved in the Rape of Nanking were put on trial for war crimes beginning in 1946, many of the actions went unpunished. Though the Germans were forced by the world community to deal with the consequences of their actions almost immediately following the war, the

rest of the world was slow to recognize the atrocities committed by the Japanese in China. As recently as the 1990s, a Japanese official called the Rape of Nanking a "fabrication." It has been speculated that reasons for the lack of discussion about the horrors of Nanking are the Cold War attitude that Europe and America had toward Communist China and the position of Japan as a world economic power.

For more information on the Rape of Nanking, consult Iris Chang's *The Rape of Nanking: The Forgotten Holocaust of World War II,* BasicBooks (New York), 1997.

China: Chaos and Civil War

A chief factor in Japan's relatively easy defeat of China was the ongoing Chinese civil war. In 1912 the Chinese empire was overthrown and a republic was established. The old system of government had become increasingly weak and corrupt and its authority severely limited. Much of China was ruled by powerful warlords, whose private armies terrorized impoverished peasants by taking their crops, demanding high taxes, and forcing young men into their armies. The new government of the republic, known as the Kuomintang (Nationalists), was still embroiled in conflict with the warlords when Japan invaded China in 1937.

The new Nationalist government was also corrupt, sometimes allying itself with warlords and favoring the minority of rich Chinese at the expense of millions of poor, starving peasants. Opponents of the Nationalists formed a Chinese Communist party that gained support among the poor by promising land seizure and a communal economic system. Communist soldiers would occasionally perform public shootings of landlords to demonstrate that the Communists were the enemies of the rich. For a brief period, the Nationalists and Communists were allies, but the tentative partnership soon dissolved, and the Nationalist army tried to destroy the Communists. When the Japanese attacked China, the Communists proposed an allegiance against the invaders, but many Nationalists regarded this as a public-

relations ploy to garner more support for the Communists. Throughout the war with Japan, Chiang Kai-Shek, the leader of the Nationalists, was more concerned about defeating the Communists than fighting the Japanese. He deployed his best troops to isolate the Communist armies. During the eight years that China fought Japan, the civil war between the Nationalists and Communists was sometimes pushed into the background with limited cooperation between the two sides. After the defeat of Japan in 1945, a full-scale war was resumed until the Communists won complete control of China in 1949.

Generalissimo Chiang Kai-Shek, leader of the Chinese Nationalists. *(Reproduced by permission of AP/Wide World Photos)*

from Germany and Japan. Japan did not attack the Soviet Union, but instead launched a full-scale invasion of China in July 1937. Japanese troops attacked and conquered large areas of the country, including the great cities of Peking (now Beijing),

Shanghai, and Canton. Repeating the actions of 1931, Japanese soldiers were allowed to burn villages, to steal property, and to rape and murder Chinese civilians. Excessively violent actions occurred in the city of Nanking. After conquering

Westerners Help the Chinese in Nanking

Few foreigners remained in Nanking when the Japanese began their assault in December 1937, and many of them were horrified at the brutality of the Japanese and attempted to assist the Chinese. John Rabe, a German businessman and a member of the Nazi party, organized the Nanking Safety Zone to protect unarmed Chinese citizens. The zone was a two and one-half square mile area from which the Japanese were not allowed to take civilians. Rabe and other Westerners were estimated to have helped save the lives of many of the 250,000 people who fled to the zone, and also may have saved thousands of women from rape. Rabe was able to accomplish this by using his status as a member of the Nazi party and the alliance between Germany and Japan as tools of coercion. Rabe was called home after six months, and was arrested by the Gestapo after attempting to report Japanese atrocities to German authorities. He was later released at the request of his company, but his career was ruined. All of the evidence he turned over to the government, including a videotape of some of the horrors, disappeared. He suffered through the war in Germany, and later he was accused of being a Nazi by the Allies. Rabe was not exonerated until 1946. He faced poverty and starvation for several years, but when Chinese authorities heard of his plight, they sent him money and supplies. The people of Nanking honored him

with the title "The Living Buddha of Nanking." He died in 1950. For more information about John Rabe's experiences in Nanking, see *The Good Man of Nanking: The Diaries of John Rabe*, translated by John E. Woods, Knopf (New York), 1998.

Another of the Westerners in the city was Wilhelmina "Minnie" Vautrin, a 51-year-old American missionary teaching at the Ginling Girls' School. Vautrin stayed and worked with Rabe and the others to help innocent civilians in the city. The diary that Vautrin kept is an important source of information about the atrocities committed in Nanking and shows Vautrin's dedication to the Chinese and her heroism in dealing with the Japanese military. Usually, Vautrin was able to coax the Japanese to remain outside her school, but in at least one case, the Japanese kidnaped several of the girls from the school and took them away to rape them. Although Vautrin was able to help many people in Nanking, and is still recognized as a heroine there today, she was never able to recover from the sights of those weeks. After a mental breakdown in China in 1940, she returned home to Illinois, where she committed suicide in 1941.

---

the city on December 13, 1937, Japanese troops went on a rampage, later called the "Rape of Nanking" (see box on pages 114-115). They dragged thousands of people out of their homes, either shooting, bayonetting, or beheading them. Others were burned or boiled alive, and women were sexually assaulted repeatedly.

China was unable to stop the Japanese from conquering large areas of the country, including important seaports. Although the invaders also controlled most railroads and important farming and industrial areas, they did not have enough

troops to advance into the great interior spaces of China. Sometimes protected by mountains, Chinese armies continued to launch sporadic guerilla raids on the Japanese. By the end of 1938, after a year and a half of heavy fighting, the war between Japan and China had settled into a holding pattern. The Japanese did not try to stage major operations against the remaining Chinese armies, who in turn were unable to counterattack and win back territories conquered by Japan. Although many soldiers and civilians continued to die and Chinese people in Japanese-controlled areas suffered tremendous hardships, no other large-scale battles

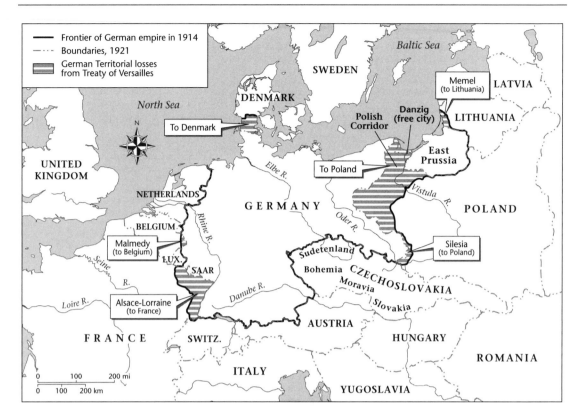

Within six months of the Munich agreement, Germany had completely dismantled Czechoslovakia, taking Bohemia and Moravia for itself and turning the rest into the puppet state of Slovakia.

took place for many years. This was the situation in eastern Asia when Europe went to war in September 1939. The Japanese war against China was still separate from the hostilities in Europe; however, the two conflicts would become a single world war in late 1941.

The Nazi-Soviet Pact

Back in Europe, the Munich settlement did not bring the anticipated peace, and by March 1939 Hitler's army had taken over Czechoslovakia. The provinces of Bohemia and Moravia (most of the territory that is now the Czech Republic) became part of Germany; the Nazis established the "independent" country of Slovakia, a German puppet territory. The destruction of Czechoslovakia violated the Munich agreement, demonstrating that appeasement of the Nazis would not work. Even Chamberlain was now determined to stop Hitler, by force if necessary.

Hitler's next target was Poland. The port city of Danzig (now Gdansk) had been made a "free city" after World War I, which meant it was not part of Germany or Poland. Poland had the right

to use the port for its exports and imports, but the city's residents were almost exclusively German, and the city was run by local Nazis who followed Hitler's orders. Germany demanded that Danzig be returned to Germany, and most citizens of Danzig supported this demand. Hitler also wanted the right to build a thoroughfare across and annex the Polish Corridor, the region that separated the German province of East Prussia from the rest of Germany.

Although the Polish government considered an appeasement policy similar to that promulgated by Britain and France, they believed the German government would make further demands. By this time, the British and French governments also shared this opinion, and they publicly declared their allegiance to Poland. Determined to destroy Poland as an independent country, Hitler believed Britain and France would once again back down. The power struggle resulted in a flurry of preparations for possible conflict. Britain and France began to negotiate with the Soviet Union, Poland's eastern neighbor, in attempts to forge an agreement to defend Poland. The Polish government was suspicious of the

Adolf Hitler's early demands for territory concerned the port city of Danzig and the Polish Corridor, land that Germany lost after World War I.

Soviets, who wanted regions of eastern Poland. Suspicion was intensified by a deeply anti-Communist Polish government, which refused to allow Soviet troops to enter Polish territory in the event of a German attack. The Poles were afraid that Soviet troops, once in the region, would refuse to withdraw after defending Poland. The British and French continued negotiations with the Soviet government but made little real progress.

The Soviet Union, wary of the 1936 agreement between Japan and Germany, began covert discussions with the Nazis. The Soviets were already embroiled in a conflict with the Japanese along the far eastern border of the Soviet Union, and feared the possibility of a two-front war. On August 23, 1939, Germany and the Soviet Union signed the Nazi-Soviet Pact (also called the Molotov-Ribbentrop Pact), a treaty that shocked countries throughout the world. Nazi Germany, whose agreement with Japan was a stipulated joint effort to eradicate Communism, had signed a pact with the most powerful Communist government in the world. The Soviet Union claimed to be the defender of the working class, yet allied itself with

a government known for its harsh treatment of the common laborer. Hitler regarded the treaty as insurance against a dual-front war after his planned Polish invasion; he still believed the British and French would not intervene, and he now had assurance that the Soviets would not interfere. Soviet leader Joseph Stalin also doubted that Britain and France would fight Germany, suspecting instead that the Allies actually wanted Hitler to attack the Soviet Union. The Nazi-Soviet Pact temporarily ended that threat. Soviet officials later claimed that the agreement was intended to buy time to prepare for war with Germany. However, the Soviets provided relatively frequent assistance to Nazi Germany in the twenty-two months after the signing of the treaty. Such action did not seem like a defensive measure. Territorial gains played a part in the Nazi-Soviet Pact. In the pact, Germany secretly agreed to relinquish a large section of eastern Poland to the Soviet Union and to allow the Soviets to take over Lithuania, Latvia, and Estonia. Stalin was able to wait for the Nazis to decimate the Polish army before deploying his own troops and conquering eastern Poland.

Joachim von Ribbentrop, foreign minister of Germany, and Vyacheslav Mikhaylovich Molotov, prime minister of the Soviet Union, sign the Nazi-Soviet nonaggression pact. *(Reproduced by permission of Bildarchiv Preussischer Kulturbesitz)*

The British and French governments were disconcerted by the Nazi-Soviet Pact but felt the alliance did not significantly alter the situation. Their generals did not regard the Soviet army as a powerful force, and were not sure it would have an impact on the outcome of potential conflicts. On the other hand, the British and French both greatly overestimated the strength of the Polish army; though they did not believe Poland would defeat Germany, they thought the Poles could repel an attack long enough to allow an aerial assault from the west by the British and French. Polish leaders were also depending on a strong offensive by the French army into western Germany. Hitler believed his armies could defeat Poland, however, before France and Britain were ready to fight. The Nazis stationed only about forty divisions on the border of France. The French army had about 100 divisions, but most of these were primarily comprised of reserve soldiers, who had been leading civilian lives and had not yet been mobilized. This minimal force on the border left most German divisions free to attack Poland.

The Invasion of Poland

The German army deployed more than sixty divisions, including six armored divisions (called Panzer divisions, after the name of the German tanks included in these divisions) and ten mechanized divisions (which were equipped with trucks and other motorized transportation). This type of warfare combined new technology with traditional styles of transportation. In regular infantry divisions, troops were transported to the front by train, and then proceeded on foot. Their food and ammunition were usually carried in horse-drawn wagons; wheeled artillery pieces were also pulled by horses. Unlike tanks, which could cross open fields, units depending on horse-drawn transport had to travel on roads, which could be easily defended by the enemy. Even the German army, which was considered highly modern and mechanized, still depended on horses for most of its transportation needs in battle during World War II. Although the tank units were not the principal arsenal of the German army, they made the difference in the first year of World

In 1939 Germany was positioned to attack Poland on three sides: from Germany in the west, from the German province of East Prussia in the north, and from German-friendly Slovakia in the south.

War II. Armored and mechanized divisions moved more rapidly than regular infantry units and were very difficult to stop. The Nazis planned to cut through defensive positions manned by infantry, then advance deep into Polish territory, circle behind, and cut off the Poles from supplies and reinforcements. Polish forces would then be stranded and eventually destroyed by the German infantry divisions that followed the Panzer divisions. The Germans had more than 1,300 modern planes, including fighters and dive-bombers, that would attack Polish ground troops resisting the tanks and eliminate antitank artillery and the few Polish tanks. These cooperative efforts—utilizing synchronized aerial and ground attacks based on speed, mobility, and concentrated tank units—were part of a new type of warfare proposed by military strategists in the years after World War I. While British military strategists had originated some of the theories, German generals were the first to implement them. The German attack became known as a *blitzkrieg,* or "lightning war," a term coined by Western newspapers after the Polish invasion.

The Polish army had forty divisions, none of which were armored. Their few tanks were outdat-

ed and more lightly armored than Germany's, and the most mobile units in the Polish army were old-fashioned cavalry. The Polish air force included more than 900 planes, but only half of them were modern; the rest were no match for German aircraft. The outmatched Polish military also faced a geographical problem: Germany directly faced Poland in the west, the German province of East Prussia positioned troops north of central Poland, and the territory of Slovakia, under German control, cut deeply along Poland's southern border. The Poles thus faced a three-front war.

In the late evening hours of August 31, 1939, Nazi soldiers removed prisoners from a concentration camp. They promised to release the prisoners if they performed a final patriotic duty to their country, and then they shot them. The soldiers then clothed the bodies in Polish army uniforms, placed them on the German side of the Poland-Germany border, and claimed the men had attempted an attack on German soil. This excuse, which was not believed by anyone, was used as justification for the pre-dawn invasion of Poland on September 1, 1939. The German Luftwaffe, or air force, nearly annihilated the Polish air force on the

Continuing the Battle

After the Germans invaded Poland in September 1939, about 100,000 Polish troops managed to escape to neighboring countries and eventually reached France or Britain. Many of them continued to fight against Germany in special Polish units for the remainder of the war.

Polish pilots flew in Britain's Royal Air Force and participated in the Battle of Britain, and Polish troops fought at Monte Casino in Italy and in Normandy in France. The Polish government also escaped to Britain. Throughout the war, most of the countries that fought against Germany regarded the displaced Polish officials as the legal government of Poland.

The outdated Polish cavalry was at a strong disadvantage against Germany's army of modern armored tanks and planes. *(Reproduced by permission of AP/Wide World Photos)*

first day of fighting. Many Polish planes were destroyed before they even got off the ground. German tanks pushed quickly into Polish territory, and within two days German troops moving south from East Prussia reached those moving east from the main part of Germany. In less than a week, one German army had fought through southwestern Poland to within forty miles of Warsaw, the Polish capital. Another army, which had moved south from East Prussia, was even closer. By September 17, Warsaw was surrounded and subjected to a barrage of Luftwaffe bombardment, which caused massive civilian casualties until the city surren-

dered on September 27. By mid-September, the Polish army began to retreat to the east in an attempt to establish a defensive position near the Soviet border. On September 17, the Soviet army invaded Poland from the east in accordance with a secret provision of the Nazi-Soviet Pact. More than 200,000 retreating Polish troops had no choice but to surrender to the Soviet army. Farther to the west, some Polish units continued to fight the Germans, but by early October the battle for Poland was over. More than 100,000 Polish soldiers had died, and the Germans captured approximately 700,000 more. Losing comparatively less men

Mobilization

Mobilization is the system under which a country calls up its reserves—soldiers who have been trained during army duty but are no longer on active service. In most European countries at the beginning of World War II, every healthy young man was drafted into the armed forces. After serving one or two years as a full-time soldier, the men were then required to remain in the reserves for many years. Some reserves went on active duty for a week or two each year for further training. This system allowed the army to grow tremendously when the country went to war. Mobilization seriously disrupted the economy of a country, however, by taking millions of men away from their jobs. In summer 1939, fearing damage to its already weak economy, Poland delayed mobilization, and the process was still incomplete at the time of the German invasion in September.

German tanks roll into Warsaw, Poland, in fall 1939. The German invasion of Poland began World War II. *(Reproduced by permission of AP/Wide World Photos)*

(14,000), with 30,000 more injured, Germany proclaimed a resounding victory.

Hitler was surprised when Britain and France declared war on Germany two days after the Polish invasion. He had thought they would do nothing, as they had when he took over Czechoslovakia. Knowing Britain and France could not assist the Polish militarily, Hitler regarded the declaration simply as a scare tactic. During the fighting in Poland, the French launched only a minor attack into Germany, not the major offensive Poland needed and the German generals feared. With Poland defeated so quickly, Germany was in a position to transfer its army to the French-German border. However, Hitler did not want to launch an attack on France yet. He believed he could immediately end the war by

Race and Conquest

Although Germany's decision to attack Norway and Denmark was originally based on military and naval considerations, it coincided with Nazi ideas regarding race. Norwegians and Danes are descended from the same ancient tribes as Germans, and their languages share a common origin. The Nazis felt their Nordic neighbors were entitled to be part of the Germanic empire. The Norwegians and Danes, with very few exceptions, wanted no part of Hitler, the Nazis, or Germany. Their democratic traditions, dislike of war, and belief in tolerance were contrary to Nazi philosophy.

promising that he would never attack another country if Britain and France would accept Germany's conquest of Poland. British and French officials declared, both publicly and in private discussions with various unofficial German representatives, that there could be peace only if Germany withdrew from Poland and restored Czechoslovakia's independence. They also said that peace was not possible with Germany under the leadership of Adolf Hitler.

In the months following the defeat of Poland, almost no fighting occurred on the border between France and Germany. Although weather conditions in late fall and winter discouraged warfare, the inactivity was primarily the result of Britain and France needing time to manufacture weapons and purchase war goods from the United States. The British had a small army and had only recently begun drafting men into service. They needed to build up their forces. The British air force and navy, however, were among the most powerful in the world. Germany used this time to prepare as well, shifting its armored divisions from Poland and building tanks and planes. Hitler hoped the delay would encourage his enemies to end the war, believing public opinion in France and Britain would conclude that defense of a conquered Poland was fruitless. The conflict was questioned publicly,

and this period was referred to by the British as the "phony war"; in France it was known as the *drôle de guerre* (literally, "a funny kind of war").

Despite the temporary halt to ground conflicts, fighting continued at sea. Arms and equipment that Britain and France bought from the United States had to be sent across the Atlantic Ocean on merchant ships. Although it had not yet joined the war, the United States was openly friendly to Britain and France and hostile to Nazi Germany. German submarines, known as *unterseeboots* or U-boats, began to attack and sink ships, while Allied naval vessels protected them and tried to destroy the U-boats. This struggle, which continued for years, became known as the Battle of the Atlantic. The German navy had a greater reliance on submarines than other countries, and their few surface warships were targeted by the British navy. During the months of the phony war, British naval victories encouraged the people at home, who were relieved that despite what happened in Poland, Germany could be defeated.

The Invasion of Norway and Denmark

A principal reason for the resumption of the land war was the German navy's desire for seaports from which its ships could easily reach the Atlantic. Germany had difficulty launching craft from its own ports on the Baltic and North Seas without being seen, and subsequently attacked, by the British navy. To acquire these ports, the commander of the navy argued for an invasion of Norway. Another reason for Germany to conquer Norway was the acquisition of iron ore, which Germany had been purchasing from Sweden. During the winter, Swedish ports were frozen over, preventing ships from sailing to Germany. The Norwegian port of Narvik remained free of ice year-round, which would allow Swedish ore to be shipped by train to Narvik and then by boat to Germany. Hitler and his generals decided to conquer both Norway and Denmark, reasoning that taking Denmark would facilitate gaining control of Norway. Germany invaded both neutral nations on April 9, 1940. The tiny Danish army offered almost no resistance and after the Germans threatened to bomb the capital city of Copenhagen, Denmark quickly surrendered.

The Germans faced a more difficult task when they reached Norway. This was partly due to more difficult terrain: Norway is largely mountainous, while Denmark is flat farmland. Although the Ger-

	Germany, September 1, 1939
	Other boundaries, Sept. 1, 1939

N

0   100   200 mi
0   100 200 km

Narvik

FINLAND

SWEDEN

NORWAY

Oslo

Baltic Sea

Lake Ladoga

ESTONIA   Lake Peipus

U.S.S.R.

North Sea

DENMARK

LATVIA

Copenhagen

LITHUANIA

East Prussia

NETH.

Elbe R.

Vistula R.

GERMANY

POLAND

BELGIUM

Rhine R.

Oder R.

LUX.

FRANCE

The need for ocean ports led Germany to attack Norway. Their primary goal was the port of Narvik in the north. The Germans also attacked Denmark to make taking control of Norway easier.

mans were able to mount a surprise attack on Norwegian ports, which they seized along with the main airfields, they were greeted by an old cannon defending the capital of Oslo, which sunk the *Blücher*, one of the few battleships in the German navy. The Allies deployed a force of 12,000 men to assist the Norwegian army. The British navy sank all ten German destroyers sent to the port of Narvik, leaving the entire German navy with only ten modern destroyers. The only two remaining German battleships in the fleet were heavily damaged by British submarines and were out of action for the rest of the year. Despite these setbacks, the Germans did conquer Norway. British and French troops, outmatched by the Luftwaffe, pulled out. These troops were desperately needed elsewhere: The "phony war" had ended and German tanks were sweeping through France.

The Road to France

Seven months after conquering Poland, German armed forces launched an attack in western Europe. On May 10, 1940, Germany invaded the neutral nations of the Netherlands, Belgium, and Luxembourg. The Nazis employed a two-pronged attack against the Netherlands. Parachute troops and glider-carried units landed behind the Dutch

The *Graf Spee*

Perhaps the most spectacular example of a British victory against the German navy during the phony war was the chase of the *Graf Spee,* a German "pocket battleship" that carried the same arsenal as a regulation battleship but was smaller in size. The *Graf Spee* was one of the showpieces of the German navy and terrorized Allied ships. After a series of naval battles, three British warships finally cornered the *Graf Spee* in the harbor of Montevideo, Uruguay, on the Atlantic coast of South America. Uruguay was a neutral country, and according to the rules of warfare, was required to intern any ship that stayed in its port too long in order to prevent favoring one warring nation over another. The crew of the *Graf Spee,* faced with either a battle with British warships or permanent harbor in Montevideo, destroyed their ship as it sailed out of the harbor on December 13, 1939.

British fliers provided this picture of the German naval vessel, the *Graf Spee.* German sailors are seen on deck as they watch the British plane. *(Reproduced by permission of AP/Wide World Photos)*

army's defensive lines, and German armored forces rolled in from the east. The small Dutch army was soon overwhelmed, and the Netherlands were already negotiating surrender when the Luftwaffe bombed and destroyed the center of the Dutch port of Rotterdam on May 14, killing many civilians. The Dutch army surrendered, and the queen and the government fled to England.

The German attack in Belgium included 600 tanks manned by veterans of the war in Poland. The Belgian army attempted to consolidate its forces and protect the eastern section of the country, which the Allies believed would be the preferred strategic position for a German invasion of France. A large French force consisting of the First and Seventh Armies, some of France's best troops and a few mechanized divisions, along with the small British force in France, the British Expeditionary Force or BEF, moved into Belgium to meet the Germans. Although the Allied forces in Belgium outnumbered the German forces, the Germans had the advantages of armor and speed.

The Germans used the Allied advance into Belgium as a trap. The principal German offensive

The Maginot Line

Named in honor of André Maginot, a former cabinet member in charge of national defense, the Maginot Line became the symbol of flawed French military thinking after France was defeated by Germany at the beginning of World War II. France spent a large part of its defense budget to build the fortification rather than manufacture planes and tanks. The Maginot Line, designed for the type of battles typical of World War I, placed the French exclusively on the defensive. Though the troops who manned the fortifications were safe, they also had no way of leaving their positions and attacking the enemy, except on foot. In 1940 the Germans knew they could not attack the Maginot Line directly, so they circumvented the area. When France surrendered, the 400,000 troops assigned to the line had not played any real part in defending the country. The powerful cannons pointing toward Germany had been useless.

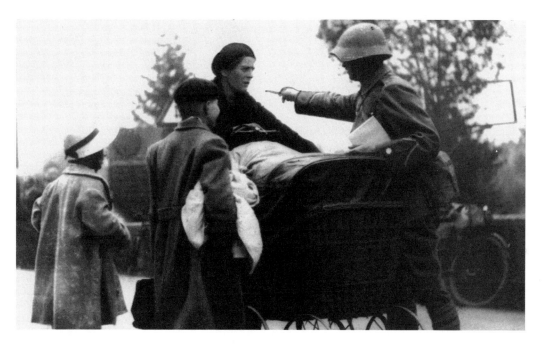

A French refugee arrives at the Swiss border with her children after seven days on the road. The family has been without food for 36 hours. Her husband had been one of the defenders of the Maginot Line. *(Reproduced by permission of AP/Wide World Photos)*

would come farther south and cut off Allied troops. This attack was directed through the Ardennes Forest, along the southern portion of the French-Belgian border. To the north of the Ardennes is the flat plain of Flanders, where the French forces and the BEF had advanced into Belgium. To the south was the Maginot Line (see box above), an immense system of powerful fortifications that the French had built to stop any German attacks. The line was armed with machine guns and cannons inside concrete blockhouses connected by a vast system of tunnels. French troops who manned the Maginot Line could live for months in underground shelters, safe from enemy bullets, shells, or bombs. The Maginot Line stopped at the Ardennes, which was heavily forested with steep

With the German army approaching on all sides, the British Expeditionary Force retreated to Dunkirk and prepared for evacuation. *(Reproduced by permission of the Corbis Corporation [Bellevue])*

hills and extremely narrow roads. French military experts did not believe that large numbers of tanks could pass through this territory, so it was defended only with a few divisions.

The Fight for France

The Germans sent seven armored divisions with 1,800 tanks through the Ardennes and into France. They crossed the Meuse River, an important natural obstacle, against strong French resistance. When large numbers of German tanks reached the other side of the river, French troops began panicking and their defensive positions crumbled. Constant German air attacks, especially from dive-bombers, played a major role in destroying the confidence of the French troops. Pouring through a narrow gap in the French defenses, the German armored divisions began driving west along the Somme River and north toward the English Channel on the coast of France. French troops were unable to stop them, and the French military command failed to organize any plan that might have saved the army. There was also poor coordination between different parts of the French army and air force and among the

French, the British, and the Belgians. The well-planned German attack convinced everyone that Germany had more troops, tanks, and planes than the Allies. Actually, despite some important advantages in weaponry, the success of the German army was due instead to strategy. The Allies, in many categories, were equipped with as many, and sometimes higher quality, weapons than the Germans, but they did not utilize these weapons well. They rarely used tanks together, instead dividing them into small groups to support infantry divisions, and did not use the air force to back up armored and infantry attacks.

When German armored divisions reached the coast, they divided the French army into two separate groups. Retreating units south of the Somme River had taken heavy casualties and needed to be reorganized. On the opposite side of the German tank corridor in Belgium, French troops, the BEF, and the Belgian army were being pushed south. They had become trapped between the two German forces, unable to connect with the remainder of the French units. On May 20, the same day the German tanks reached the sea, the British government began plans to evacuate

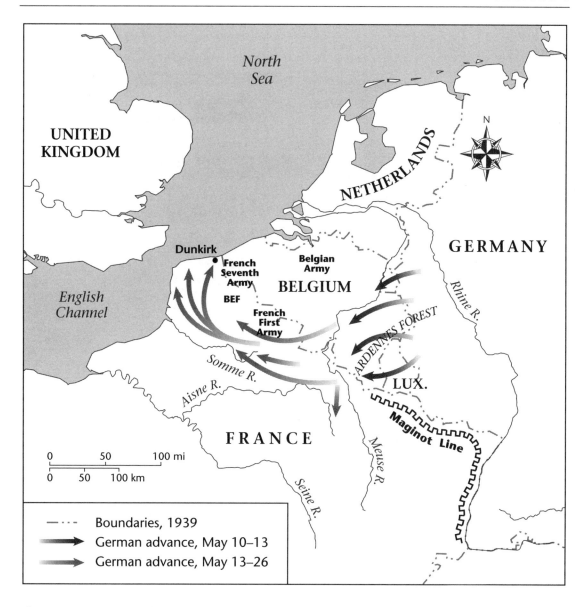

The German army surprised the Allies by driving their tanks through the Ardennes Forest and past France's Maginot Line.

the BEF to England. The BEF, along with the French First Army, began to retreat toward the coast near the English Channel port of Dunkirk, a few miles inside France from the Belgian border. On May 26 some of the British troops boarded boats for the trip back to England. The following day the Belgian army, now northeast of Dunkirk, surrendered. In the next few days a large number of boats—including navy ships, merchant vessels, small fishing boats, and even pleasure boats brought across the Channel by their owners—reached Dunkirk from England. Each day, troops boarded the boats, which took them to England and then returned for more forces.

During this evacuation, the German army continually tried to fight its way into the Dunkirk pocket, the area defended by Allied troops. The British and French held them back long enough for a majority of the troops to escape across the English Channel. The Luftwaffe bombed and machine-gunned Allied troops and boats, but the planes of the British Royal Air Force (RAF), flying from bases in England, offered some protection. The evacuation lasted until June 4, at which time more than 300,000 Allied troops, about two-thirds of them British, had been transported safely to England, having left behind almost all their equipment. Most of the 110,000 French soldiers then returned to

After the Allied evacuation from Dunkirk, British Prime Minister Winston Churchill noted that while many lives had been saved, evacuating did not win wars. *(Reproduced by permission of the Corbis Corporation [Bellevue])*

ports in western France to join fellow troops still fighting the Germans. Many people in Britain hailed Dunkirk as a great victory, as 200,000 British soldiers had been prevented from becoming German prisoners. New British Prime Minister Winston Churchill, however, publicly declared that evacuation was not the way to win a war.

There remained sixty divisions of French troops, although the three armored divisions had lost many of their tanks. The Germans had 104 divisions, including ten armored and five mechanized. The Luftwaffe now far outnumbered the remaining Allied planes. Although defeat appeared certain, French troops fought with greater determination. Extreme feats of French bravery were recognized even by the German generals, but French generals formulated sensible defensive plans too late. On June 10, 1940, Italian dictator Benito Mussolini declared war on France and Britain, sending troops into the southern part of France. Although significantly outnumbered, the four French divisions that met this new invasion easily stopped the Italians. Even so, France was faced with another large army entering its territory.

On the same day that Italy entered the war, the French government left Paris and declared it an open city. Paris would not be defended, and therefore would not be bombed or destroyed in ground fighting. Four days later, the German army entered the city unopposed. Hundreds of thousands of people had already left Paris in an attempt to escape the advancing Germans. Throughout France, roads were jammed with millions of refugees, making transportation for French troops even more difficult. Luftwaffe planes often machine-gunned the columns of refugees, adding to the panic and confusion. The French government moved to the city of Vichy

Adolf Hitler laughs and dances a jig after the French signed the armistice ending their involvement in the war.
(Reproduced by permission of AP/Wide World Photos)

and named Marshal Philippe Pétain as the new prime minister. Pétain was a World War I hero who had helped defeat the Germans in 1918, but in 1940 was eighty-four years old. He immediately requested an armistice as the Germans continued to advance farther into France. On June 22, 1940, the French agreed to an armistice effective on June 25. Hitler arranged for it to be signed in the same railroad car in the same forest clearing in which Germany had signed the armistice ending World War I almost twenty-two years earlier. This was Hitler's special revenge on France. Once the French representatives had signed the armistice, Hitler danced a jig outside the railroad car.

The terms of the armistice divided France into three sections. The German army controlled the northern region and the Atlantic coast; Italy occupied the southeastern section; and Pétain's French government retained the remainder of southern France. France was required to pay the cost of the German occupation—millions of dollars per day.

Germany refused to release 2 million French soldiers taken prisoner in battle, approximately one-quarter of all young Frenchmen. From the beginning of the invasion on May 10 to the end of the fighting on June 25, France lost 90,000 people, an average of about 2,000 each day. Twenty-seven thousand Germans had been killed. The French army, which had been considered the strongest in the world, had been shattered in six weeks. A complete victory of Hitler's Germany in Europe seemed certain.

The Battle of Britain

With the defeat of the French, the British remained the only nation that continued to fight the Germans. Hitler hoped that Britain would make peace by accepting German domination of Europe in return for a promise that Germany would not interfere with Britain and its great overseas empire. The British government never seriously considered this possibility, instead preparing

Leaving Marseilles, France, to seek safety in New York, this refugee brings all the belongings he can carry to begin a new life in America. Many refugees succumbed to sickness—and death— aboard ships bringing them out of Nazi-occupied areas. *(Reproduced by permission of AP/Wide World Photos)*

itself to defend against a German invasion. Invading Britain required sending troops across the English Channel on boats, an impossibility if the British navy controlled the sea. Hitler hoped that the Luftwaffe could destroy the British navy from the air, but this was also impossible as long as the RAF could fight the German planes. The Battle of Britain became an air battle. German air attacks were meant to destroy the RAF and so make possible a ground invasion, and also to terrify the

Germany's nighttime raids over London were not aimed at military targets but were meant to terrorize the civilian population. *(Reproduced by permission of Corbis-Bettman)*

British population into forcing the government to make peace without an invasion. Starting on July 10, 1940, fleets of German bombers, under the protection of fighter planes, launched an attack on the ports of southern England that lasted for nearly a month. The RAF and land-based antiaircraft guns shot down about 100 German bombers and another eighty fighters, losing around seventy of their own fighter planes in the process. The raids left the British navy virtually unaffected. The Luftwaffe then shifted to attacks on factories and military installations throughout England. Although they heavily damaged their targets, the Luftwaffe lost too many planes to continue.

The Germans changed their focus again and began concentrating the power of the Luftwaffe on RAF airfields and nearby ground control stations. From late August to September 7, they knocked out some of the RAF's bases and destroyed nearly 300 British fighters. Had the Germans continued the assault, the RAF would have been crippled. Yet the Nazis once again shifted their focus, inadvertently giving the RAF time to repair its damaged airfields. The Germans knew that winter was coming and the weather over the English Channel would subsequently turn stormy. A German invasion of Britain would therefore have to come soon or be postponed until at least

The Royal Air Force's Advantages

Although German and British fighter planes were nearly equal in quality, with similar top speeds and weaponry, the British RAF had several advantages. Flying near home, the British pilots were able to stay in the air much longer than the Germans, who quickly ran out of fuel after arriving over England. The British also had an effective early warning system, which included thousands of observers along the coast and a chain of radar stations on the ground that warned of the number, direction, speed, and altitude of the Luftwaffe. (Neither side had yet developed radar that could be fitted into planes.) The system allowed the British to send planes from other areas to defend specific targets. Another British advantage, which the Germans greatly underestimated, was that Britain was producing more planes than Germany and it was therefore easier for the British to replace planes that were shot down. When RAF planes were brought down, pilots also had a greater chance of parachuting to safety and being able to return to flight the next day. German pilots who parachuted or crash-landed wound up either in English custody or in the English Channel, where they were likely to drown. This last advantage helped make up for Britain's one great disadvantage, a shortage of trained fighter pilots. Training fighter pilots is a long process, and Germany started with many more experienced airmen than did Britain. During the worst days of the Battle of Britain, the RAF sometimes had more planes ready to fly than they had pilots to fly them.

Royal Air Force Spitfire fighter planes patrolling the English coast. The RAF was able to fight off the German Luftwaffe, keeping British shores safe from a German invasion. At times the RAF had more planes than trained pilots. *(Reproduced by permission of the Corbis Corporation [Bellevue])*

Luftwaffe (German airforce) planes fly in formation over a city in Europe. *(Reproduced by permission of © Hulton Getty/Liaison Agency)*

The Hurricane and the Spitfire were two of the types of planes used in Great Britain's Royal Air Force. *(Reproduced by permission of © Hulton Getty/Liaison Agency)*

In response to the German Blitz on Great Britain, this poster urges the Fire Guard to remain ready to keep the country safe from "Firebomb Fritz." *(Reproduced by permission of AP/Wide World Photos)*

These children sit in front of their house in London, bombed by the German Luftwaffe. *(National Archives and Records Administration)*

the following spring. Hitler decided to send bombers against London, Britain's capital, which had a population of 7 million people. His purpose was to destroy the British people's will to fight by terrorizing them and forcing the RAF into a massive battle.

On September 7, 1940, large formations of German bombers with escorts of fighter planes attacked London, raining bombs on the docks along the Thames River, as well as other military targets, homes, schools, and hospitals. The fighters of the RAF tried to shoot down the German planes before they reached London, and 2,000 antiaircraft guns in the heavily defended city blasted them as they arrived. The largest raid, on September 15, included 200 bombers. Every RAF fighter within flying range was in the air, ultimately shooting down sixty German bombers. German attacks on London continued until the end of the month, but by September 17, Hitler had decided to postpone the ground invasion of Britain. He would never reschedule it. The pilots of the RAF had saved Britain; Churchill said that

never before had so many people owed so much to so few.

Despite their lack of success against the RAF, the Luftwaffe actually escalated attempts to terrorize the British people. Throughout October and November—the period the English called "the Blitz"—the Germans shifted to nighttime raids over London and other cities. (All the previous action in the Battle of Britain had taken place during the day.) Since night bombing was completely inaccurate at that time, the massive bombardment was meant to cause as much damage and loss of life as possible. Although sirens warned of the nightly attacks, allowing people to hide in underground shelters such as cellars and subway stations, 40,000 Londoners died in the air raids. Large parts of London and other English cities were destroyed. English parents sent thousands of children from their homes in large cities to live with strangers in the countryside who had volunteered to take them in. Still, despite the terror of the raids, the British had resisted a German invasion. The German armed forces had been defeated for the first time.

Winston Churchill
"Blood, Toil, Tears, and Sweat"
"Be Ye Men of Valour"
"Their Finest Hour"

Excerpts from selected speeches delivered in spring 1940
Printed in Blood, Toil, Tears and Sweat: The Speeches of Winston Churchill
Published in 1990

World War II grew out of a quest for power and territory in both Europe and Asia. On the European front, the war was sparked by the land-grabbing maneuvers of German dictator Adolf Hitler and the Nazi party. Germany had been in a state of political and economic turmoil since its devastating loss to opposing forces in World War I (1914–1918). In an attempt to restore the nation's former glory and expand German influence across Europe, Hitler began to take over Europe. In an attempt to avoid war, Prime Minister Neville Chamberlain of Britain gave in to German demands for the annexation of German-speaking sections of Czechoslovakia. The acceptance of this territorial absorption did not satisfy Hitler, and by March 1939, Germany claimed the rest of Czechoslovakia. Hitler then went on to launch an invasion of neighboring Poland on September 1, 1939. Great Britain and France responded with a show of solidarity, declaring war on Germany two days later.

The Germans followed up with an attack on Belgium, the Netherlands, and Luxembourg on May 10, 1940. According to a special British press cable published in the *New York Times*, it was "generally believed" that the German "objective [was] to take the Netherlands and Belgium, solidify their positions there and then concentrate their entire attack against Britain." Germany conquered France in another *blitzkrieg*, or lightning war. The first bombing in France occurred in May at Bron Airdrom, an airport near the city of Lyon. German troops entered the capital city of Paris on June 14, 1940. Shortly thereafter, all of northern and western France was occupied by Germany. By this time, Hitler had proven that his word could not be trusted and that he was out to conquer all of Europe. It

Winston Churchill took over as British prime minister in 1940. *(Reproduced by permission of the Bettmann Archive)*

was becoming impossible for European countries to remain neutral.

With the failure of his appeasement policy, British Prime Minister Neville Chamberlain resigned his post to Winston Churchill on May 10, 1940. Churchill's first job was to form a coalition government between the tradition-minded Conservatives, the reform-seeking Liberals, and the workers' Labour party. Churchill also had the difficult job of uniting British civilians against Hitler

Part of the Nazi invasion force, complete with cars, cavalry, and foot soldiers, advances farther into Poland, September 1939. In response, Great Britain and France declared war on Germany. *(Reproduced by permission of the Corbis/Hulton-Deutsch Collection)*

and encouraging them in the face of a full-scale war. Churchill was known for his fiery temper, caustic wit, and astounding sense of self-confidence. He used all of these qualities to his advantage as England's prime minister, denouncing Hitler as a "crocodile" and motivating crowds with his rousing speeches and two-fingered "V-for-victory" sign. Three speeches he wrote and presented in spring 1940 embody his nation's fierce determination to fight Hitler to the very end. These speeches—"Blood, Toil, Tears and Sweat," "Be Ye Men of Valour," and "Their Finest Hour"— were delivered in a five-week period between May 13 and June 18, 1940. Together they chronicle England's early role in the war, document the escalation of the conflict, and reflect the spirit of pride, purpose, and confidence that Churchill inspired in the British people.

"Blood, Toil, Tears and Sweat," given just three days after Churchill was appointed prime minister, is considered a classic example of his gift for public speaking and characteristic of his tireless pursuit of victory. A few days before Churchill gave this speech, Germany invaded the Netherlands, Bel-

gium, France, and Luxembourg. Churchill was working to shape a unified Parliament that would best lead his nation through this perilous time. He wanted to prepare British citizens for the long ordeal ahead and used "Blood, Toil, Tears and Sweat" to convey a message of urgency and commitment to the war effort.

"Be Ye Men of Valour" was Churchill's first speech broadcast to the whole nation after his appointment as prime minister. In it, he calls on the British people to rally around the cause of freedom. He assures them that Germany will be conquered.

"Their Finest Hour" is set against the realization that France had been devastated by the Germans' violent and forceful attack. After France surrendered to the Germans in late June 1940, England was Hitler's next target in his larger scheme to dominate all of Europe. Recognizing England's need for support in the war, Churchill would forge close ties with U.S. President Franklin D. Roosevelt and with Soviet leader Joseph Stalin. "Their Finest Hour" is one of Churchill's best-remembered wartime speeches.

European borders before World War II.

"Blood, Toil, Tears and Sweat"
Delivered to the House of Commons, May 13, 1940

...It must be remembered that we are in the preliminary stage of one of the greatest battles in history, that we are in action at many points in Norway and in Holland, that we have to be prepared in the Mediterranean, that the air battle is continuous and that many preparations have to be made here at home.... I would say to the House, as I said to those [ministers] *who have joined the Government: 'I have nothing to offer but blood, toil, tears and sweat.*

We have before us an ordeal of the most grievous kind. We have before us many, many long months of struggle and of suffering. You ask, what is our policy? I will say: It is to wage war, by sea, land and air, with all our might and with all the strength that God can give us: to wage war against a monstrous tyranny, never surpassed in the dark, lamentable catalogue of human crime. That is our policy. You ask, What is our aim? I can answer in one word: Victory—victory at all costs, victory in spite of all terror, victory, however long and hard the road may be, for without victory, there is no survival....

"Be Ye Men of Valour"
[Broadcast by the British Broadcasting Corporation (BBC), London] May 19, 1940

I speak to you for the first time as Prime Minister in a solemn hour for the life of our country, of our Empire, of our Allies, and, above all, of the cause of Freedom. A tremendous battle is raging in France and Flanders. The Germans, by a remarkable combination of air bombing and heavily armoured tanks, have broken through the French defences north of the Maginot Line, and strong columns of their armoured vehicles are ravaging the open country, which for the first day or two was without defenders.... The regroupment of the French armies to make head against, and also to strike at, this intruding wedge has been proceeding for several days, largely assisted by the magnificent efforts of the Royal Air Force.

We must not allow ourselves to be intimidated by the presence of these armoured vehicles in unexpected places behind our lines....

It would be foolish, however, to disguise the gravity of the hour. It would be still more foolish to lose heart and courage or to suppose that well-trained, well-equipped armies numbering three or four millions of men can be overcome in the space of a few weeks, or even months....

In the air—often at serious odds—often at odds hitherto thought overwhelming—we have been clawing down three or four to one of our enemies; and the relative balance of the British and German Air Forces is now considerably more favourable to us than at the beginning of the battle. In cutting down the German bombers, we are fighting our own battle as well as that of France....

We must expect that as soon as stability is reached on the Western Front, the bulk of that hideous apparatus of aggression which gashed Holland into ruin and slavery in a few days, will be turned upon us. I am sure I speak for all when I say we are ready to face it; to endure it; and to retaliate against it—to any extent that the unwritten laws of war permit.... If the battle is to be won, we must provide our men with ever-increasing quantities of the weapons and ammunition they need....

Our task is not only to win the battle—but to win the War. After this battle in France abates its force, there will come the battle for our island—for all that Britain is, and all that Britain means. That will be the struggle.... The interests of property, the hours of labour, are nothing compared with the struggle for life and honour, for right and freedom, to which we have vowed ourselves.

I have received from the Chiefs of the French Republic, and in particular from its indomitable Prime Minister M. Reynaud, the most sacred pledges that whatever happens they will fight to the end, be it bitter or be it glorious. Nay, if we fight to the end, it can only be glorious.

Having received his Majesty's commission, I have found an administration of men and women of every party and of almost every point of view. We have differed and quarrelled in the past; but now one bond unites us all—to wage war until victory is won, and never to surrender ourselves to servitude and shame, whatever the cost and the agony may be. This is one of the most awe-striking periods in the long history of France and Britain. It is also beyond doubt the most sublime. Side by side,... the British and French peoples have advanced to rescue not only Europe but mankind from the foulest and most soul-destroying tyranny which has ever darkened and stained the pages of history. Behind them—behind us—behind the armies and fleets of Britain and France—gather a group of shattered States and bludgeoned races: the Czechs, the Poles, the Norwegians, the Danes, the Dutch, the Belgians—upon all of whom the long night of barbarism will descend, unbroken even by a star of hope, unless we conquer, as conquer we must; as conquer we shall.

Winston Churchill

Winston Spencer Churchill was born in 1874 in Blenheim Palace near London, England. His parents, Lord Randolph Churchill and American Jennie Jerome (Lady Randolph) lived the extravagant existence of the upper-class and had little time for their son. Young Churchill felt alienated from his mother and father but developed a special bond with the doting nanny who loved and raised him as her own. Churchill showed a gift for writing as a child, but his general lack of ambition and inability to pass Latin and mathematics courses almost ruined his chances for admission to the Royal Military College at Sandhurst. With the help of a tutor he finally passed the entrance exams on his third attempt. After graduating from Sandhurst in 1894, he became a second lieutenant in the Fourth Hussars, a horseback unit. Churchill distinguished himself as a courageous soldier and a keen-eyed war correspondent. He served in the British army in India and Egypt and covered the Boer War (a war fought from 1899 to 1902 between the British and the Dutch for control of South Africa) for England's *Morning Post*. While in South Africa, Churchill was taken prisoner by the Boers, then escaped and made his way back to England.

After an unsuccessful bid for a seat in Parliament in 1899, Churchill won election the following year as the Conservative party candidate from Oldham. He held a number of important government positions over the next decade, married Clementine Hozier in 1908, and became First Lord of the Admiralty, commander of the British navy, in 1911. World War I erupted in Europe in 1914, and England joined the war effort in August, following Germany's assault on Belgium. When a risky British naval attack against Turkish forces ended in defeat, Churchill was held largely responsible. He was demoted from his post as First Lord of the Admiralty in 1915, and he resigned from the government later that year. To cope with his career troubles, Churchill began painting, which developed into a lifelong love. The war ended in 1918, and over the next two decades, Churchill held various political offices. He acted as head of the war department, then the treasury, and switched political parties several times while Britain tried to recover politically and economically from four years of fighting. Except for one election lost in the early 1920s, Churchill maintained a seat in Parliament until the late 1930s.

Churchill's fiery personality led to frequent opposition in Parliament. He was spirited, brash, and quarrelsome, and, as a result, was rather unpopular with his colleagues. Churchill quickly recognized Hitler as a threat to European peace and cautioned against the German program of arms buildup throughout the 1930s. His demands for British rearmament were largely ignored until Germany invaded Poland in 1939. On the eve of World War II, Churchill was again named First Lord of the Admiralty, serving this time under Prime Minister Neville Chamberlain. The failure of his appeasement strategy prompted Chamberlain to resign his post in 1940. Churchill, who took over just as the fighting intensified, inspired the British nation with his strength and fearlessness throughout the war. He was nicknamed the "defiant lion."

Churchill's Conservative party was soundly defeated in the British general elections of 1945. By this time, the British people were tired of war and were more interested in domestic issues. Shortly before the close of World War II, Churchill announced his resignation, but he served another term from 1951 to 1955. He died on January 24, 1965.

Today is Trinity Sunday. Centuries ago words were written to be a call and a spur to the faithful servants of Truth and Justice: 'Arm yourselves, and be ye men of valour, and be in readiness for the con- *flict; for it is better for us to perish in battle than to look upon the outrage of our nation and our altar. As the Will of God is in Heaven, even so let it be.'*

"Their Finest Hour"
Delivered to the House of Commons
June 18, 1940

.... I made it perfectly clear [a fortnight ago] that whatever happened in France would make no difference to the resolve of Britain and the British Empire to fight on, 'if necessary for years, if necessary alone.'...

During the great battle in France, we gave very powerful and continuous aid to the French Army, both by fighters and bombers; but in spite of every kind of pressure we never would allow the entire metropolitan fighter strength of the Air Force to be consumed. This decision was painful, but it was also right, because the fortunes of the battle in France could not have been decisively affected even if we had thrown in our entire fighter force. That battle was lost by the unfortunate strategical opening, by the extraordinary and unforeseen power of the armoured columns and by the great preponderance of the German Army in numbers. Our fighter Air Force might easily have been exhausted as a mere accident in that great struggle, and then we should have found ourselves at the present time in a very serious plight. But as it is ... our fighter strength is stronger at the present time relatively to the Germans, who have suffered terrible losses, than it has ever been; and consequently we believe ourselves possessed of the capacity to continue the war in the air under better conditions than we have ever experienced before....

There remains, of course, the danger of bombing attacks, which will certainly be made very soon upon us by the bomber forces of the enemy. It is true that the German bomber force is superior in numbers to ours; but we have a very large bomber force also, which we shall use to strike at military targets in Germany without intermission. I do not at all underrate the severity of the ordeal which lies before us; but I believe our countrymen will show themselves capable of standing up to it....

In what way has our position worsened since the beginning of the war? It has worsened by the fact that

Winston Churchill giving the two-fingered V-for-victory sign. *(Reproduced by permission of AP/Wide World Photos, Inc.)*

the Germans have conquered a large part of the coastline of Western Europe, and many small countries have been overrun by them. This aggravates the possibilities of air attack and adds to our naval preoccupations. It in no way diminishes, but on the contrary definitely increases, the power of our long-distance blockade.... If [Germany's] invasion [of Great Britain] has become more imminent, as no doubt it has, we, being relieved from the task of maintaining a large army in France, have far larger and more efficient forces to meet it.

If Hitler can bring under his despotic control the industries of the countries he has conquered, this will

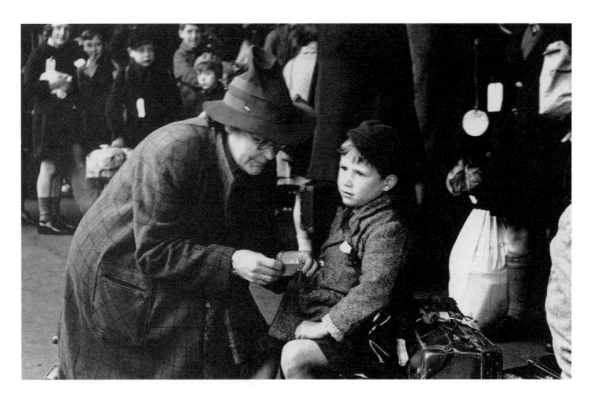

A British woman prepares a young boy for evacuation from London. *(Reproduced by permission of the Corbis/Hulton-Deutsch Collection)*

This mobile canteen wagon supplied British residents, bombed out by German forces, with food and drink. The food wagon was sponsored by the American Allied Relief Fund. *(Reproduced by permission of © Hulton Getty/Liaison Agency)*

add greatly to his already vast armament output. On the other hand, this will not happen immediately, and we are now assured of immense, continuous and increasing support in supplies and munitions of all kinds from the United States; and especially of airplanes and pilots from the Dominions and across the oceans, coming from regions which are beyond the reach of enemy bombers....

What General Weygand called the Battle of France is over. I expect that the Battle of Britain is about to begin. Upon this battle depends the survival of Christian civilization. Upon it depends our own British life, and the long continuity of our institutions and our Empire. The whole fury and might of the enemy must very soon be turned on us. Hitler knows that he will have to break us in this island or lose the war. If we can stand up to him, all Europe may be free.... But if we fail, then the whole world, including the United States, including all that we have known and cared for, will sink into the abyss of a new Dark Age.... Let us therefore brace ourselves to our duties and so bear ourselves that, if the British Empire and its Commonwealth last for a thousand years, men will still say, 'This was their finest hour.' (Churchill, pp. 149, 151–154, 168, 172–178)

Aftermath

The German Luftwaffe and the British Royal Air Force (RAF) engaged in a series of air battles during the summer and fall of 1940, a period known as the Battle of Britain. The Germans tried to conquer England with waves of heavy bombing over the English Channel, but British forces held firm. Germany's efforts to gain control of the air were foiled.

On September 27, 1940, the governments of Germany, Italy, and Japan signed the Tripartite Pact, also known as the Axis or Three-Power Pact. Each nation pledged full cooperation and support to the others in case of attack by another power (namely, the United States) that might enter the war. The terms of the pact were to remain in effect for ten years. Tensions continued to mount between Germany and the Soviet Union. Hitler could not possibly achieve his goal of creating a vast European empire unless Stalin and the Soviet Union were defeated. It was inevitable that the nonaggression pact between the two countries would be broken. The Soviets joined the Allied forces in 1941 after Germany invaded Russia. The United States entered the war that same year after Japan's surprise attack on the U.S. naval base at Pearl Harbor, Hawaii.

Preparing sturdy air raid shelters was a necessity to beat out the German Blitz of Great Britain. Some citizens got fancy and decorated their shelters, like this couple who placed plants and flowers on top. *(Reproduced by permission of © Hulton Getty/Liaison Agency)*

SOURCES

Books

Churchill, Winston, *Blood, Toil, Tears and Sweat: The Speeches of Winston Churchill,* edited with an introduction by David Cannadine, Houghton Mifflin (Boston), 1990.

Kimball, Warren F., *Forged in War: Roosevelt, Churchill, and the Second World War,* Morrow (New York), 1998.

Severance, John B., *Winston Churchill: Soldier, Statesman, Artist,* Clarion Books (New York), 1996.

Periodicals

"Nazis Invade Holland, Belgium, Luxembourg by Land and Air," *New York Times,* May 10, 1940, p. 1.

Other

Churchill and the Generals (video), BBC/LeVien International, 1981.

The Nazi Strike (video), Fusion Video, 1984.

The Churchill Center, *The Winston Churchill Home Page,* http://www.winstonchurchill.org (May 16, 2000).

Churchill College: Churchill Archives Centre, http://www.chu.cam.ac.uk/archives/home.shtml (May 16, 2000).

Life in Occupied Poland

As the Nazis continued their rapid territorial expansion across Europe, Adolf Hitler began implementing steps to eliminate "racially impure" elements in conquered countries. The first group he targeted was not Polish Jews, but Germans with mental or physical disabilities and incurable hereditary diseases. In his book *Mein Kampf*, Hitler had explained his view that the government was responsible for preventing the reproduction of "all those who are in any way visibly sick or who inherited a disease and can therefore pass it on." According to the Nazis, the mentally ill and physically disabled were a burden on society. They were below the standards the Nazis had set for Germany, and therefore were not fit to live. In 1933, just after the Nazis came to power, the government passed a law that allowed for the involuntary sterilization of mentally challenged people; later laws restricted their right to marry. As Germany began preparations for war, Hitler went one step further and declared that killing unfit people was the first step necessary to purify the German race. Deemed "mercy killing" by the Nazis, the policy was implemented without the knowledge or consent of patients or their families.

Nazi Germany's Euthanasia Program

Hitler created the Committee for Scientific Research of Hereditary and Severe Constitutional Diseases to head up the euthanasia program. The group first focused its attention on children. To provide the committee with information about mentally challenged and physically deformed children, forms were sent to local health departments, children's hospitals and clinics, and doctors and midwives who delivered babies. Based on the information compiled from the forms, the committee decided which children would be subjected to mercy killing. Those chosen were transferred to special wards set up in designated hospitals. An estimated 5,000 children were killed through this system, usually by lethal injection. Soon expanded to include adults, the euthanasia program was code-named T-4 after the location of its headquarters at 4 Tiergarten Street, Berlin. Hitler was involved in the development of the program, which was headed by Karl Brandt, Hitler's personal physician, and Philip Bouhler, Hitler's chancellery chief.

The T-4 program was more elaborate than earlier Nazi operations involving children. Most of the T-4 staff were medically trained SS personnel who later went on to staff the death camps. T-4 set up five "observation institutions" around Germany that actually served as transfer stations for the victims. From these stations, people targeted for euthanasia were sent to one of six killing centers disguised as hospitals or nursing homes. The Nazis had difficulty formulating an execution

The T-4 Departments

The T-4 euthanasia program included three separate departments, each with a name designed to disguise its purpose. The first was the Working Team of Asylums and Nursing Homes, which sent out questionnaires to obtain information about potential victims and selected those who would die. The second, the Public-Benefit Patient Transportation Society, was in charge of transporting victims to the killing centers. The third was the General Foundation for Affairs of Insane Asylums, and was comprised of the staff who ran the killing centers.

The work of the T-4 Departments was supposed to be kept secret. But when citizens learned that groups of mentally and physically challenged people were allegedly dying of the same causes at the same six T-4 centers, the public became suspicious. When Hitler finally called a halt to the euthanasia, it was too late. Some doctors were out of control and continued the murders.

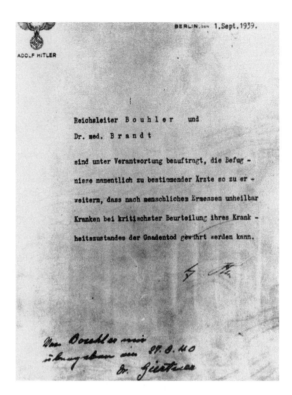

Reproduction of a letter signed by Hitler authorizing Karl Brandt to develop the T-4 program. (*Stadtarchive Nuerenberg/USHMM Photo Archives*)

method because they wanted the victims and their family members to remain unaware of what was going to happen. A committee of T-4 doctors and medical experts studied possible solutions to this problem, formulating procedures they would utilize on a much larger scale when they began the mass extermination of European Jews. Each of the six T-4 killing institutions contained an airtight chamber disguised as a large shower room. Twenty or thirty victims would be brought in at a time, under the pretense of bathing. When the nozzles were turned on, they emitted carbon monoxide gas instead of water. After the victims were dead, the bodies were burned in crematoria attached to the centers. The victims' families were told that the bodies had been burned to prevent the spread of disease. In some cases, T-4 doctors removed and preserved victims' brains so they could study the causes of mental diseases.

Although the existence of T-4 was supposed to be kept secret, German citizens eventually became suspicious. Victims' families received documents informing them of the sudden death of their relatives, usually from pneumonia, and the locations listed on death certificates were always the same six hospitals. Death notices printed in newspapers revealed an overwhelming number of mentally challenged and disabled people dying from pneumonia at the same time and at the same sites. In the small towns where the six killing centers were located, people began to understand the significance of the black SS vans that continually brought people to the "hospital," and the smoke that constantly poured from the nearby crematorium. In one town, Hadamar, children reportedly referred to the SS transports as "murder vans." People began refusing to let their relatives be taken to mental hospitals. Protestant and Catholic leaders wrote letters of

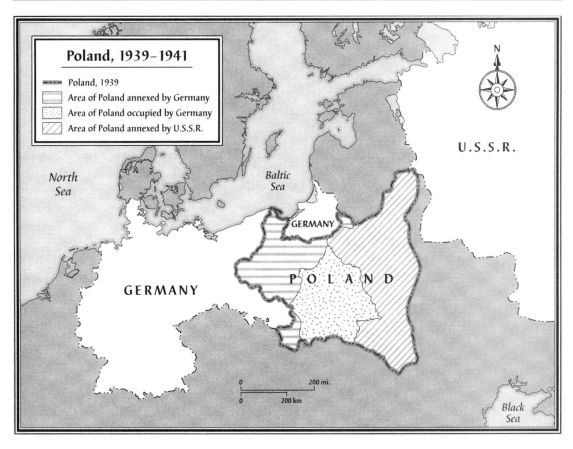

This map of Poland shows its division between Germany and the Soviet Union as a result of the Nazi-Soviet Pact.

protest, and some pastors publicly attacked the program. Despite arrests, the protests continued. In August 1941 Hitler ordered that the T-4 program be terminated officially. By that time, approximately 70,000 people had been killed. During the next few years, another 20,000 died "unofficially," many of them children who were starved to death.

In addition to eliminating mental patients and people with illnesses, the T-4 program was expanded to include concentration camp inmates. Although T-4 doctors were supposed to inspect prisoners and select those who were mentally ill, they instead began choosing Jews who were simply too sick or weak to work. When a new code called "14 f 13" was added to an inmate's file, the victim was subject to "special treatment," transferred to one of the mercy-killing centers, and murdered. Gas chambers were later installed in the concentration camps for this purpose. The men who ran T-4 and 14 f 13 were soon transferred to new duties. Designated as "experts" on death camp design, they were placed in charge of the concentration camps.

Hitler's Plans for Poland

The population of Poland prior to the war was approximately 35 million people, about 3.3 million of whom were Jews—almost 10 percent of Poland's citizenry. It was the largest and most important Jewish community in Europe, with a long and rich cultural tradition. The Germans had split Polish territory with the Soviet Union as a result of the Nazi-Soviet Pact, and about 22 million Polish citizens, including more than 2 million Jews, were subsequently ruled by the Nazis. Approximately 350,000 Jews escaped from the German-occupied part of Poland to the Soviet area. During the next several months, however, about 100,000 returned to be with their families or to escape harsh treatment by the Soviet government. In the initial months after the German victory, the Poles, not the Jews, appeared to be the Nazis' main targets.

Immediately after the German victory in Poland, a large section of western Poland was absorbed into Germany. The Germans called most of this area Wartheland, after the Warthe River. A

The Lublin "Reservation" and the Madagascar Plan

The vast number of Jews sent to Lublin, coupled with reports that 400,000 more would arrive, prompted public speculation about the Nazis' intentions for the area. The Nazis began to circulate rumors that Lublin and the surrounding territory would be converted into a "reservation" for Jews. The U.S. government's establishment of reservations for Native Americans may have inspired the Nazis to produce their own version. Jews would be allowed to run their own affairs under the protection of the Nazis, who would by then have rid German territories of the Jewish presence.

Similar stories were later spread about Madagascar, a large island off the southeast coast of Africa that was controlled by France. The Nazis supposedly intended to ship all European Jews to Madagascar. A few Nazis, including some fairly high-level officials, believed this story to be true. Some of them spent months figuring out transportation requirements and wrestling with the legal entanglements of acquiring the island from France. Reportedly, work on the Madagascar plan was supposed to start after Germany won the war. In actuality, neither the Lublin reservation plan nor the Madagascar plan was ever seriously considered as party policy. The Nazis would soon decide that the "Final Solution" to their "Jewish problem" was extermination.

Hans Frank was governor-general of the section of German-controlled Poland called the General Government. Frank initially joined the Nazi Party in 1923, becoming one of Hitler's early supporters. At one time, Frank worked as a lawyer, defending Nazis in court. *(Lena Fagen/USHMM Photo Archives)*

preponderance of Poland's factories and coal mines were situated in Wartheland and in the other areas that became part of Germany. The second-largest Polish city, Lódz, which the Germans renamed Litzmannstadt, was also located in Wartheland. The rest of German-controlled Poland became the General Government, leaving no remains of the once-independent country. The Nazis intended to force all Poles, including approximately 600,000 Jewish residents, to leave the Wartheland, and replace them with Germans and *Volksdeutsche,* ethnic Germans living outside of Germany. The German plan required the displacement of millions of Poles, usually against their will. The Germans acted quickly, allowing people little time to pack even small amounts of food to take with them. Once the Nazis removed the Poles they confiscated their personal property. Within a year of the defeat of Poland, 300,000 Jews and 1.2 million other Poles were forced to move east into the General Government, and approximately 500,000 ethnic Germans were moved into the Wartheland to replace them. Many of the Jews remaining in Poland were concentrated in Lódz. The Nazis continued relocating both Jews from western Poland and German Jews to the General Government. A number of Jews from both groups were moved to the city of Lublin. By February 1940, almost 80,000 Jews had been forced to move into the Lublin area.

The Nazis had no plans to assimilate the General Government into Germany; rather, they sought to dismantle Poland and run it for the benefit of Germany. Hitler picked Hans Frank, his former attorney, to be governor-general. He instructed Frank to destroy Poland's economic, cultural, and political structure. On October 3, less than a week after Warsaw surrendered to the Germans, Frank explained his plan for Poland to German army officers. He would seize raw materials, industries, and other property that would be useful in the German war effort. He would reduce the Polish economy to the minimum necessary for the basic survival of Poles, who would be slaves of their German masters. A few months later Heinrich Himmler, head of German security forces, sent Hitler a memo on the situation in the General Government and Frank's plan for the area. According to Himmler, Hitler was pleased with the plan, but he ordered that only a few copies be made so the report would remain secret. Among the measures proposed by Frank was limiting the education of Poles to the fourth grade. All the education they would need, according to Frank, was basic arithmetic skills, how to write one's name, and to work hard for the glory of the divinely ordained German state.

The Germans realized it would take time, however, to reduce the Poles to slave laborers who believed that the German presence was divinely ordained. Their first step was to remove anyone who might lead the Poles to resist Nazi policies, and almost every Pole with a university education became a target. As soon as the German army arrived in September 1939, the Nazis murdered 10,000 Poles. Most of the killings were committed by the Einsatzgruppen ("special-action groups" or "special-duty groups"), specially trained strike forces that acted as a combination of army troops and secret police officers. The Einsatzgruppen were units of the Sicherheitsdienst ("security service"), or SD, the intelligence service of the SS. The SD was headed by Reinhard Heydrich, chief assistant to Himmler. The entire SS and the Geheime Staatspolizei, or Gestapo, the secret police, was headed by Himmler. In Poland the Einsatzgruppen supported the regulation German army, arriving in a town immediately after soldiers occupied it. They sought out and killed all the Polish political leaders they could find, even those who shared some of the Nazis' own ideals. They also killed members of the Polish nobility, professors, high school teachers, people with technical training, and priests. The priests were considered important leaders of the largely Catholic community in Poland.

Heinrich Himmler oversaw all the German security forces, including the Gestapo, the SS, the SD, and the Einsatzgruppen, the specially trained strike forces attached to the SD. (*Library of Congress*)

The Nazis arrested thousands of other Poles and sent them to concentration camps. Throughout Poland, the Germans closed down schools. In the city of Vilna in 1943, for example, there was one primary school for a Polish population of 104,000. In response, the Poles created secret schools, including a university with 2,500 students.

A massive anti-Nazi underground was developed, with a network of Polish organizations working secretly to undermine the Germans' efforts. This was probably the largest underground group in any country conquered by the Nazis. The underground published more than 1,000 newspapers and magazines, 300 of which were issued regularly during the occupation. They also published books, including scholarly works unrelated to the war. Despite Hitler's orders to decimate Poland, the Poles were determined to retain their culture and traditions.

An estimated 120,000 Jews were killed during and immediately after the German invasion of Poland. Jews in the Polish army, like all Polish soldiers, suffered heavy losses, and many Jewish civilians died in German air raids. Other Polish citizens were killed simply because they were Jewish. Nazi brutality toward the Jews began as soon as the

German soldiers amuse themselves while they force Jews to dig ditches in an empty lot in Kraków, Poland. *(Main Commission for the Investigation of Nazi War Crimes/USHMM Photo Archives)*

German military stationed troops in the defeated nation. Many of the most severe acts of violence were committed by the *Waffen-SS* ("armed SS"), military units of the SS that fought as part of the regular army. Though the main job of the Einsatzgruppen was to kill and arrest educated Poles, they also attacked and killed Jews at random.

The Nazis did more than simply kill Polish Jews, however—they also tried to humiliate and torture them whenever possible. When the Nazis reached the town of Bielsko on September 3, for instance, they beat and tortured 2,000 Jews that they forced into the courtyard of a Jewish school. Some had boiling water poured on them while they hung by their hands, and others died when water from a hose was forced into their mouths until their stomachs burst. In the town of Mielec, thirty-five Jews were closed inside a slaughterhouse, which was then set on fire, the people within burning alive. In Wloclawek, the Nazis interrupted prayers in a private home during Yom Kippur (the Day of Atonement, a sacred Jewish holiday) and ordered the people to go outside and run.

After a brief time, the Nazis ordered the people to halt. When five or six of them apparently did not hear the order, or simply did not halt quickly enough, they were shot dead. The next day the Nazis burned down the town's two synagogues, a practice that became common throughout Poland. Within the first six months of the German occupation, most Jewish synagogues in Poland were burned to the ground.

The Nazis often forced Jews to watch as their synagogues were destroyed. In one town, a young man reportedly ran into a burning synagogue to save the Torah scrolls, the holiest objects in Judaism. The Germans shot him as he came out, and both the man and the Torah burned along with the synagogue. German soldiers routinely grabbed Jews on the streets and beat them. They cut off the beards of Jewish men who wore the beards as a symbol of their faith, and they forced Jews to crawl through the mud, to pull Germans around in carts, and to give the stiff-armed Hitler salute. The *Waffen-SS* units and the Einsatzgruppen were so brutal that even some German army generals were shocked by their actions. The generals considered the murder and torture of civilians to be crimes that violated miliary war codes, particularly when regular army troops began participating. Rather than demanding a complete end to these actions, though, the generals simply tightened disciplinary reins on their own soldiers. Some historians speculate that military officers were protecting themselves, as they did not want the army to be held responsible for the actions of the Einsatzgruppen. Army leaders requested that these "clearing" actions be delayed until after the military handed over control of a newly captured area to German civilian authorities, thus allowing the Einsatzgruppen to commit murder without involving the German army. On September 19, while the fighting in Poland was still going on, the army's request was denied by Heydrich, who only agreed to keep the military abreast of the Einsatzgruppen's future plans.

Heydrich's Plan: Ghettos, Jewish Councils, Aryanization, and Forced Labor

On September 21, Heydrich sent a secret message to Einsatzgruppen commanders about actions to be taken against the Jews in Poland. Although members of the SS, especially the Einsatzgruppen, were directly in charge of carrying out Heydrich's plan, numerous German authorities also had vary-

Reinhard Heydrich (left) talks with Werner von Blomberg at a party. The execution of the Holocaust fell under Heydrich's direction. *(Library of Congress)*

ing roles in the occupation. Heydrich sent copies of his main goals to the army, to the General Government, and to government departments in charge of the German economy, food supplies, and security. Heydrich's memo stressed that the "final aim" of the Nazi actions was to be kept secret, and that while that aim would take time to achieve, immediate action had to be taken to fulfill this goal. This was the only time the "final aim" was mentioned in Heydrich's message. Experts on the Holocaust strongly disagree about what Heydrich meant in his directive. Some believe the message proves the Nazis had already decided to murder all Polish Jews. Proponents of this theory suggest that his "final aim" later came to be called the *Endlösung*, or the "Final Solution," which was the systematic plan to murder all Jews in Europe. Others maintain that the Nazis wanted to force the Jews into a special "reservation," then perhaps send them into Soviet-held territory. Advocates of this position argue that the decision to kill the Jews came later. Although there is evidence to support both sides of the argument, no clear proof exists for either theory.

The first step in Heydrich's scheme was to remove as many Jews as possible from the sections of Poland that had become part of Germany. The Jews would be transferred into the General

An undated photo of Jews in a Polish ghetto. Heydrich's plan of restricting Jews to one designated area of a city harkened back to the Middle Ages. *(Reproduced by permission of Snark/Art Resource)*

Government and consolidated in as few areas as possible; any Jews remaining outside the General Government were also to be concentrated in a few cities. To facilitate what Heydrich called "later actions," the concentration points were to be located at key railroad stops or along railroad lines. While the "later actions" were not described, it is clear that the concentration points were not intended as final destinations. For towns with fewer than 500 Jewish residents, Heydrich ordered Jews to be forced into the nearest "city of concentration." He supplied Einsatzgruppen commanders with an excuse for this policy: They had to isolate Jews who plundered or were involved in guerrilla attacks on Germans. This declaration marked the beginning of the ghetto system. While many European Jews during the Middle Ages (c. 550–1500) had been required to live in specific sections of their towns and were subject to curfews, at the time that Heydrich developed his plan, there had not been a ghetto in Europe for many decades. Heydrich's message predicted that Jews would end up being barred from certain sections of town or confined to the ghetto.

The second section of Heydrich's message ordered the creation of a council of Jewish elders in each area. Composed of rabbis and other prominent leaders, each council would have either twelve or twenty-four members, depending on the size of the town or city. Only men were allowed to be members of these councils. In most ghettos, the group became known as the *Judenrat* (plural: *Judenräte*), or "Jewish council." Heydrich emphasized that the *Judenräte* would be responsible for ensuring that all German orders were followed precisely and quickly. The events of the next few months made Heydrich's command clear: Members of the councils would pay with their lives, and the lives of their families, if Jews in their area did not cooperate with the Germans. The *Judenräte* in small towns were to provide a census of the Jews in the area, listing such information as their sex, their age, and their occupation. The Germans would inform the *Judenräte* of departure dates, methods, and routes for the transfer of Jews from their areas. The councils then had to make sure the German mandates were followed, and also had to provide food and

View of the gate at the ghetto in Kraków, Poland, c. 1940. *(Main Commission for the Investigation of Nazi War Crimes/USHMM Photo Archives)*

other necessities for the trip to the ghetto. In the cities where ghettos were to be created, the *Judenräte* were also responsible for housing Jews brought in from elsewhere.

Heydrich's message then addressed "Aryanization," or the seizing of Jewish-owned property, which was then sold to non-Jews. He ordered Einsatzgruppen commanders to report continuously on the number of Jews in their areas, how many were being evacuated from the countryside, and how many were already in the cities. Heydrich requested a survey of Jewish-owned businesses, particularly those important to the German economy and the war effort, and an estimate of how quickly and easily they could be "Aryanized."

Although Heydrich's message did not divulge his plans directly, it appears the Nazis wanted to utilize Jewish labor temporarily for the benefit of the German economy, especially for military needs. This would explain why Heydrich wanted to know the sex, ages, and occupations of the Jews, and also why he left a loophole in his plan that would allow Jews to leave the ghetto for "economic" reasons.

The use of Polish Jews as forced labor began at the outset of the German occupation. Jews were seized off the streets and ordered to clear rubble from recent battles and fill in anti-tank ditches dug by the Poles. On October 26, 1939, five weeks after Heydrich issued his message, an official decree gave authority over Jewish forced labor to the top SS leader in each occupied area. Whenever any German agency needed emergency work done, the SS formed a "labor column" from randomly arrested Jews. Within a few months, the Germans had established more permanent labor camps, and 30,000 Jews were soon digging a long anti-tank ditch near the new border with the Soviet Union. The Nazis put 45,000 others from forty separate camps to work building a canal near Lublin, and 25,000 more were sent to work on a project near Warsaw.

Before long, Polish Jews (along with non-Jewish Poles) were forced into factory work. Many German companies, including some owned by the SS, constructed factories next to the work camps to utilize this labor pool; some Nazi officials became rich by making deals with private companies. While certain Jews were paid approximately forty cents per day, most received no pay and labored under terrible conditions. The prisoners were underfed, and the death rate was astronomical. Eventually the work camps developed into a slave labor system.

Slave Labor and Mass Murder

Historians agree that the slave labor system was not the Nazis' long-term goal for the Jews. Slave labor, in fact, began almost by accident and evolved as it made certain Nazi officials wealthier and more influential. The army was interested in using laborers for military production, but there were insufficient plans made to accomplish this goal, and the Germans made few attempts to use workers according to their skills and physical abilities. The forced removal of Jews from western Poland to the General Government and from the countryside to city ghettos hindered production efforts. While these facts support the argument that slave labor was not the Nazis' real goal for the Jews, the clearest proof is provided by what happened next. Within two years, the Nazis began the systematic elimination of the Jews. From the beginning, the victims included many who could have worked. People who were not killed immediately were forced to work themselves to death in a program the Nazis called "destruction through work." Soon, the Nazis were murdering as many Jews as they could, whether or not they were able to work.

Jewish women forced to pull carts of quarried stones at the Plaszów labor camp in Poland. *(Photograph by Raimund Tisch; courtesy of USHMM Photo Archives)*

While the forced-labor columns were being organized, the Nazis moved ahead with Heydrich's plan to establish ghettos. They collected lists of Jews from each *Judenrat* and required Jews to wear a yellow six-pointed Star of David at all times. Confinement to the ghettos prevented Jews from traveling freely.

The Lódz Ghetto and the Role of the Judenrat

In late October 1939, less than two months after the German army had crossed the Polish border, the first experimental ghetto was created in a town near Lódz. Several months later, the

The Jewish Police

The Jewish police force was originally created by the Germans to carry out normal police work inside the ghetto. The officers were responsible for controlling traffic, preventing crime, and keeping people without permits from leaving. Unlike Lódz, most ghettos allowed some restricted travel outside the ghetto walls. Armed German police watched the Jewish officers carefully, making sure they followed German orders and enforced the orders of the *Judenrat*. Before long, the Jewish police were expected to hunt down food smugglers and arrest people who had not reported for forced labor. Ghetto residents came to view the Jewish police as turncoats who used billy clubs and rubber hoses to help the Nazis in exchange for personal gain.

A Jewish policeman and a German soldier direct pedestrian traffic across the main street of the Lódz ghetto before a wooden footbridge is built. The footbridge was used to get Jews from one side of the ghetto to the other while allowing the road below to remain open to traffic. *(Photograph by Paul Mix; courtesy of USHMM Photo Archives)*

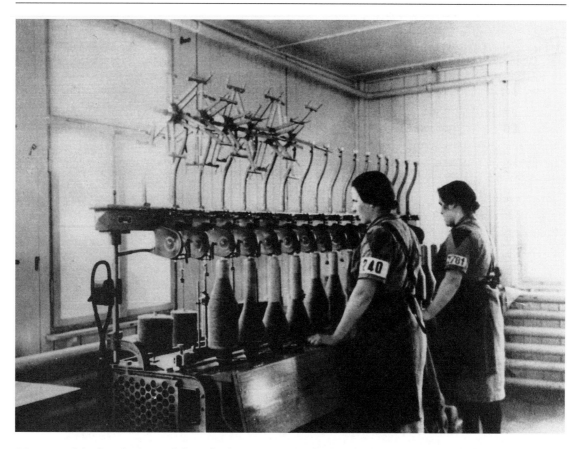

Women work in the spinning workshop of a ghetto. *(USHMM Photo Archives)*

second ghetto was established in Lódz proper. Lódz was located in the Wartheland, an area that was supposed to be free of any Jewish presence, though hundreds of thousands of Jews were still living there. It took nearly a year for the Germans to establish ghettos in the rest of Poland. By April 1941 almost all Jews in both the General Government and areas that had become part of Germany were confined in ghettos. After the German invasion of Russia in June 1941, an area called Galicia was added to the General Government, and its Jewish population was transferred to ghettos as well.

Lódz was in many ways different from ghettos that were established later. It was larger, more industry-based, and completely cut off from the outside world. Unlike residents of other ghettos, Lódz inmates were almost unable to smuggle food and weapons into the ghetto, and they could not maintain contact with the Polish underground. Although these differences were significant, the overall features of Lódz reflected the ghetto system throughout Poland. The Nazis decided to situate the Lódz ghetto in a slum neighborhood

where more than 60,000 Jews, mostly impoverished, already resided. Early in February 1940, the 100,000 Jews who lived in other parts of Lódz were ordered to move into the ghetto. By the end of the month, all Poles and ethnic Germans were forced to evacuate the area, and the ghetto was completely surrounded by barbed wire and guarded by armed police. On March 6, several Jews found outside the ghetto were shot and killed. By May, all non-Jews, except for special police units, were barred from entering.

Inside the ghetto, Jews were not allowed outdoors between 7 p.m. and 7 a.m. The ghetto buildings were run-down, poorly heated throughout the cold Polish winter, and had virtually no indoor bathrooms or running water. The ghetto contained about 32,000 apartments, most of them consisting of only one room. Approximately four people lived in every room, and more than 160,000 people were jammed into an area measuring 1.5 square miles, or approximately thirty city blocks. All food in the ghetto was to be supplied by the Germans, who never provided enough, and many inhabitants were so poor they could not purchase the little the Germans allowed.

Jüdische Soziale Selbsthilfe
KIELCE
Żydowska Samopomoc Społeczna

Dział dożyw. dzieci.

Leg. Nr _____

upoważnia do korzystania
z kuchni Ż. S. S.
ŚNIADANIA

Nazwisko i imię _____ *
1600 śniadań
dziennie

Adres _____

Miesiąc maj 1941 r.

| 31 | 30 | 29 |

A child's identification card that entitles him to receive rations from the soup kitchen in the Kielce ghetto. Similar cards were issued to inhabitants of the Lódz ghetto by its *Judenrat*. *(Rafal Imbro Collection/USHMM Photo Archives)*

The combination of intense cold, poor sanitation, overcrowding, and inadequate diet led to disease and death for many of the Jews of Lódz.

Prior to the outbreak of World War II, Lódz was the most important industrial city in Poland because of its textile mills. Since a large part of the city's workforce was Jewish, the head of the Lódz *Judenrat,* Mordecai Rumkowski, proposed that the ghetto could produce goods for the Germans if they provided the necessary raw materials. Rumkowski believed that making the Jews valuable to the Germans would protect them, and he also realized there was no other way for the people to get work. The Nazis agreed to the proposal, and in addition to producing textiles, the ghetto became the largest armaments center in the area. At a time when Germany needed every available laborer, 80,000 Jews worked in 117 factories and workshops in the Lódz ghetto. Since wages were extremely low, however, and Germans did not pay market value for the goods they got from the Jews, a series of strikes and demonstrations erupted in January 1941, with workers

demanding higher pay and more food. Rumkowski squelched the rebellion by refusing to discuss the workers's demands and ordering them to return to their jobs. He wanted nothing to interfere with the production of goods for the Germans because he believed the survival of the Lódz ghetto Jews depended on it.

In many ways, the Lódz *Judenrat* became the government of the ghetto, collecting taxes, distributing food, making housing assignments, organizing street cleaning, establishing a fire department, and running a statistics office. They even controlled the Jewish police force, which was used to enforce *Judenrat* decisions. The sphere of the *Judenrat's* influence, however, did not extend outside the realm of performing clerical duties for the Nazis. In many places, council leaders were arrested and shot if the Germans did not think they were cooperating fully. In most ghettos, the *Judenrat* became unpopular, and though there were a few important exceptions, heads of the councils were often hated. Some officials, like Rumkowski in Lódz, were viewed as dictators and traitors because

Favoritism and Corruption

One reason *Judenrat* officials were not popular was that they often gave jobs and granted favors to their relatives, friends, and supporters. A person who had contacts inside the *Judenrat* had "protection" or "Vitamin P," which could be achieved through family connections or bribes. At one point, almost 13,000 people worked for the various departments of the Lódz *Judenrat*; the entire population of the ghetto was around 100,000. The number of *Judenrat* employees was proportionally smaller in other ghettos, but still represented a fair percentage of the population. In Warsaw, which was much larger than Lódz, there were 6,000 employees of the *Judenrat*; in Lwów (Lvov), 4,000; in Bialystok, 2,200; and in Vilna, 1,500. Besides appointing people to special jobs, the *Judenrat* could supply extra food rations or even spare certain residents from heavy labor details—both of which often made the difference between life and death.

they went along with the Germans' demands. Historians speculate that in some ghettos, the *Judenrat* was comprised of people trying to protect their own lives and the lives of their families, no matter what the cost to others. In many cases, however, they were simply trying to help their community.

While hoping that all, or at least some, of the Jews could be saved, *Judenrat* members continued to face extremely difficult choices. Protecting Jews required cooperation with the Germans, which often meant handing over people for deportation to concentration camps, sending them to their deaths. In some ghettos, the *Judenräte* attempted to establish a balance, cooperating with the Germans on matters such as the daily running of the ghetto, but refusing to assist with deportation procedures. In some cities, the *Judenräte* had contacts with anti-Nazi underground organizations outside

the ghetto. This was especially true after Germany invaded the Soviet Union. In the area of Poland that had originally been taken over by the Soviet Union, guerrilla units connected to the Russian army battled the Germans in forests, and in some ghettos, the *Judenräte* helped young Jews escape to join the partisans.

In a number of ghettos, though, organized resistance efforts were impossible to coordinate because the *Judenräte* opposed armed rebellion against the Germans. The *Judenräte* and the Jewish underground constantly clashed over the prospect of an uprising. The councils thought members of the underground, typically young people, were recklessly placing the entire community in danger. They believed any attempt at armed resistance would result in massacre, a belief probably shared by a majority of ghetto inhabitants, and based on the fact that the Nazis had historically responded to attacks with mass killings. As people began to realize that the Nazis intended to kill all Jews even if they did cooperate, the underground gradually gained support.

The Deportation of Lódz Jews

Rumkowski continued to have faith that Lódz Jews would be protected by cooperating with and working for the Germans. In some ways his plan seemed to work: The economic importance of the ghetto and the financial gains it provided for SS members resulted in Lódz being the last ghetto to be liquidated. Nevertheless, inmates were being murdered prior to liquidation. In December 1941 Rumkowski was told by the Nazis that 20,000 people had to be deported. He was able to reduce that number to 10,000, and convinced the Germans that the *Judenrat*, not the Germans, should choose them. Rumkowski decided that 2,000 people who had recently arrived in Lódz from nearby towns in Wartheland would be among the deportees. The remainder would be people with police records and their families. Most were not hardened criminals, but ordinary people who had been caught stealing food or firewood. Those chosen for deportation were the poorest families in the ghetto. It took almost two weeks for the 10,000 people to be transported from Lódz, and no one knew where, or why, the Nazis were sending the deportation trains. Their final destination was in fact the Chelmno death camp, about thirty-five miles away, where upon their arrival the deportees were immediately murdered.

Dates of Destruction

In most major towns, as in Lódz, deportations to death camps began long before the final liquidation of the ghetto. As the Germans intended, neither the *Judenräte* nor the rest of the Jews could be sure of their fates until the very end. In late 1941 the Germans began deporting people from the smaller ghettos of Wartheland to Chelmno. Essential workers remained until the next summer, when the ghettos were completely liquidated. Deportations to the Belzec death camp from the ghetto at Kraków, the third-largest city in Poland, began in March 1942, but the ghetto was not liquidated until a year later. More than 300,000 people from the Warsaw ghetto, the largest and most important of the ghettos, were sent to Treblinka and murdered between July and September 1942. However, the final liquidation of the Warsaw ghetto did not begin until April 1943. In Lwów (Lvov), which held the third-largest number of Jews (after Warsaw and Lódz), the first deportations occurred in March 1942, when 15,000 people were sent to Belzec. Five months later, 50,000 were deported, and by January 1943 Lwów had become a labor camp. Deportation from Vilna, one of the great centers of Jewish culture, began almost as soon as the ghetto was established in September 1941. Vilna was liquidated in September 1943. Lódz lasted almost a year longer, until August 1944.

Jewish deportees from the Lódz ghetto being taken to the Chelmno death camp in 1941. *(Sidney Harcsztark Collection/USHMM Photo Archives)*

The Roma, or Gypsies

The Roma, or Gypsies, are a nomadic people originally from India. By the 1930s, some had lived in Europe for centuries. Some had settled in one community, though many continued to wander. Negative Nazi attitudes toward the Roma were puzzling, since the Roma were actually Aryans. Himmler and concentration camp leaders decided that "pure" Roma were examples of original Aryan tribes, who still lived like the ancestors of the Germans. They believed those Roma whose ancestors had intermarried with other ethnic groups, as a majority had, were an example of the racial mixing that led to the collapse of civilizations. Nazi policy, at times, was to kill all mixed-race Roma, including people who were part Roma and part German, while the "pure" Roma were to be protected. Sometimes the Nazis persecuted Roma who had no permanent homes, while tolerating others who had settled down in one location. In some Nazi-dominated countries, Roma were hunted down and sent to death camps. Out of approximately 1 million Roma in Nazi-controlled Europe, an estimated 200,000 were murdered. The Roma were also the victims of forced sterilization and inhumane medical experiments.

The only non-Jews in the Lódz ghetto were a group of 5,000 Roma the Germans had transported into the city. A special section of the ghetto was set aside for Roma, though it is not clear why the Nazis decided to send them to Lódz. All 5,000 were deported to Chelmno and killed in the first half of 1942.

Deportations from the Lódz ghetto were then halted for more than three weeks, but starting February 22, 1942, the Nazis began transporting almost 1,000 people each day. Since no more criminals were left, on March 2 Rumkowski announced that he was forced to select innocent people, especially those who could not find work. The deportations continued until early April, at which time almost 35,000 more people had been sent to their deaths. In early May, another 10,000 were shipped out of the ghetto; this time the deportees were Jews from Germany, Austria, and Czechoslovakia who had been sent to Lódz earlier. In summer 1942 the smaller ghettos of Wartheland were liquidated, and most of the inhabitants were sent to Chelmno to be killed. Approximately 10,000 of them, however, who were young and relatively healthy, were taken to Lódz, which was becoming a massive labor camp.

According to historical records, one of the new arrivals to the Lódz ghetto reported that Lódz Jews were being sent to Chelmno and killed by carbon monoxide gas in trucks. When Rumkowski was told, he reportedly claimed he already knew about the fate of the Chelmno inmates, but felt it was necessary to sacrifice a few people in order to save the majority. In September the Nazis ordered another deportation, this time mainly the elderly, the sick, and 10,000 children under the age of ten. The Germans threatened to deport the whole ghetto if the *Judenrat* did not supply the children, but most parents refused to hand over their offspring. On September 5, 1942, a roundup was conducted by the Jewish police, who had been promised that their own children and families would not be deported if they carried out the order. When the Jewish police were unable to catch enough people to satisfy the Nazis, German police units entered the ghetto. They continued searches until September 12, when 20,000 people, including the requisite number of children, were deported.

The Lódz ghetto produced cloth and arms for the Germans until mid-1944, when fewer than 90,000 people were left in captivity there. There were more deportations and continued hunger and misery, assuaged only by the hope of a German defeat. At this point in the war Germany was fighting the Soviet Union, the United States, and Great Britain. The Lódz Jews followed news of the war closely, aware that the Russian army was pushing the Germans out of the Soviet Union and back into Poland. Celebrations were held throughout the ghetto on June 6, 1944, D-Day, when American and British armies landed on the beaches of Normandy on the coast of France. In August 1944, with the Russian army only seventy-five miles away, the Germans announced that the entire Lódz ghetto, including factories and workshops, was being moved. Rumkowski still urged the Jews to cooperate with the Nazis. Workers from each factory were ordered to report together at a railroad siding, but almost everyone went into hiding instead. For weeks they were hunted down, first by the Jewish police and later by the Germans. Nearly 80,000 people, including Rumkowski, were captured and sent to Auschwitz, where most died in the gas chambers. When the Russian army reached Lódz in January 1945, only 870 Jews were left in the city; more than 170,000 had been killed during the Nazi occupation. When Germany surrendered four months later, about 250,000 Polish Jews, most of whom had been in Soviet territory, were still alive. Three million Polish Jews had died.

PRIMARY SOURCE

Franziska Schwarz
"A Silent Protest against Sterilization"
From *The Other Victims*
Compiled by Ina R. Friedman

Published in 1990

As Adolf Hitler rose to power in the early 1930s, the beliefs he had presented in *Mein Kampf* quickly became institutionalized Nazi ideology. Hitler felt the Germans were part of a superior race, the Aryan race, that had grown weak through years of intermixing with lesser races. The Nazi government therefore enlisted scientists and medical professionals to identify inferior non-Germans, such as Jews, Slavs, and Roma (Gypsies), who were regarded as contaminants of German purity. Nazi leaders and race specialists declared these groups must be prohibited from interbreeding with Aryans. Proponents of racial doctrine established "scientific" criteria to classify true Aryans. In an effort to determine inferiority, teachers were required to measure and record physical attributes, such as skull size, hair, and eye color, of all children in their classrooms. The Nuremberg Laws, passed in 1935, prohibited marriages and sexual relationships between Jews and non-Jews in an effort to prevent the "defilement" of the Aryan race.

In July 1933 the Nazis enacted the Law for the Prevention of Offspring with Hereditary Defects.

The decree required the sterilization of people who had inherited blindness, deafness, physical or mental disabilities, or alcoholism. Government officials and medical specialists reviewed individual cases to determine how best to treat each patient while preserving the racial purity of Germany. Nazi authorities required teachers in schools for the deaf to turn over rosters of their pupils. Reports of physical disabilities required students, and often parents as well, to undergo sterilization. Some Nazi doctors were reportedly sympathetic to the plight of disabled people, who usually did not have lawyers to defend their cases at the hearings before health tribunals. From 1934 to 1939, between 350,000 and 400,000 persons were sterilized involuntarily.

Franziska Schwarz was fourteen years old when Hitler came to power in 1933. Born deaf, she grew up in a loving family and attended a school for the hearing impaired. In the following account, Schwarz tells how she and her mother received a summons in 1935 to appear at a health center and arrange for their own sterilization. At the age of sixteen, Schwarz tried to oppose Nazi policy and protect her reproductive rights.

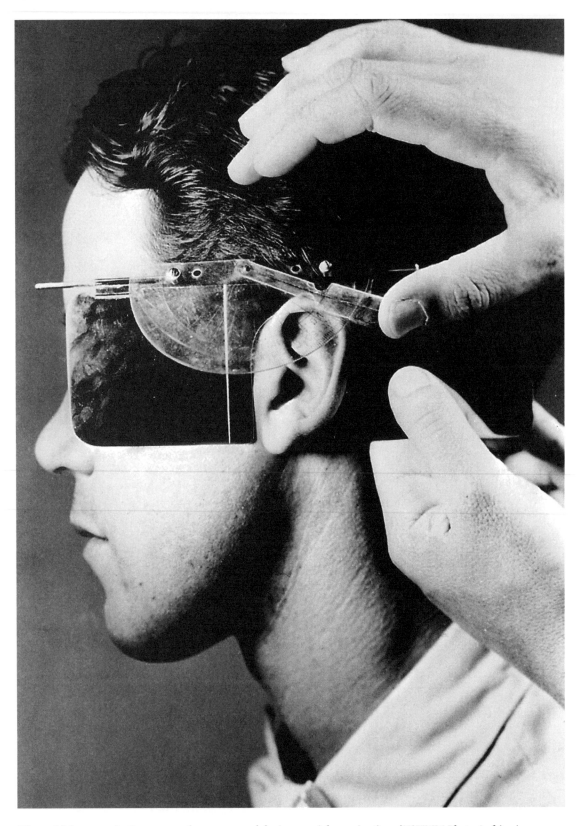

The racial features of a German youth are measured during a racial examination. *(USHMM Photo Archives)*

Franziska: "A Silent Protest against Sterilization"

I never saw anything wrong with being deaf. My younger sister, Theresa, and most of my friends were deaf. Though my parents were hard of hearing, my younger brother, Theo, had normal hearing. My father was one of six brothers. Four of them were hearing. When they came to visit, every hand was busy sharing news of the deaf community or giving advice. Our eyes were glued to the hands and faces of signers. Everyone had so much to say.

In deaf school, the teachers got mad if I signed. They wanted me to read lips and to use my voice. I got so tired of watching the teacher's lips. I couldn't look away for a minute. It was even harder when she tried to teach me to say the letters correctly. The teacher would put a strip of paper in front of my lips. "To make the 'B' sound, purse your lips and blow just enough to make the paper quiver. To make a 'P,' blow a little harder and make the paper shake." Day after day, the teacher drilled me.

I felt like a bellows. I liked it better after school when the teachers weren't around. My friends and I would make signs and chat with our fingers.

When I was fourteen, Hitler took over Germany. Theo, my eleven-year-old hearing brother, liked to go to Munich Stadium to the rallies. Once Theo came home all excited because he had shaken Hitler's hand. My favorite uncle, Karl, who could hear, got mad.

He shouted at my brother and signed at the same time. "Hitler is a disgrace to Germany. Don't waste your time and hearing listening to him."

My father put his fingers on my brother's lips. "Don't ever repeat what you have just heard. Swear by the Holy Father!"

Theo looked scared. "But in school, they tell us to report anything bad [that] people say about Hitler."

"If you don't repeat it, no one will know your uncle said it."…

For me, the trouble started in 1935. I came home from the convent and found my Mother crying. "What's the matter?" I signed.

She handed me a letter that read, "Frau Schwarz and her daughter Franziska are to come to the health office to arrange for their sterilizations. Heil Hitler." I couldn't make out the signature at the bottom.…

The day of the hearing, my mother, my father, and all my uncles accompanied me to the court. "She's only sixteen years." Uncle Karl talked and signed at the same time so I could understand. "Deafness is not always inherited. I'm her uncle, and I can hear perfectly well. As for her mother, she is going through the menopause. Though she is a good Catholic, she promises not to have any more children."

The two men on the judges's bench whispered to each other. They frowned and shook their heads. After a few minutes, the one with the big nose and bald head stood up. "Petition denied for the minor, Franziska Schwarz. Since the mother promises not to have any more children, she will not have to be sterilized."

I started to cry. The previous year, I had met a boy I liked, Christian Mikus. As a child, he had scarlet fever and lost his hearing in one ear. Christian and I liked to walk in the park. We'd sign for hours. Whenever he saw children playing, he'd smile and sign, "One day, we will have children, too." Of course, we couldn't get married then. He didn't make enough money working in a clothing factory.… If I were sterilized, I didn't think Christian would want me anymore.…

A letter came from the department of health. "Franziska Schwarz is to report to the Women's Hospital in Munich for the sterilization."

"I won't go," I cried. "I want to be able to have babies."

Father looked sad. "If you don't go, the police will drag you to the hospital."

I screamed all the way to the hospital. The nurse locked me in a room with two other deaf teenagers. The three of us cried all night. When the nurse came to give us tranquilizers, I tried to fight her off. She held me down and gave me the injection. In the morning, I woke up in a room full of beds. My stomach hurt. I touched the bandages and started to cry. The nurse who brought me water was crying, too. "I'm sorry, there's nothing I could do to help you. With Hitler, you have to be quiet." Her finger pointed to the portrait of

Hitler hanging over the bed. She tapped her temple with her finger, to indicate, "He's crazy."

I had so much pain, I couldn't go to the convent. I asked the public health insurance office for the standard sick pay.

"Why should you get sick pay?" The social worker sneered. "You can have all the fun you want. You don't have to worry about getting pregnant."

When Christian came to the house, I started to cry. "The doctors sterilized me. I guess you won't want to be my boyfriend anymore."

Christian made the sign for love. "Whatever happens, we'll be together. As soon as you're twenty-one, we'll get married."

In 1938, in spite of being sterilized, I missed my period. Christian became excited. "Now we can get married." He began to look for an apartment.

My mother was out of town helping a sick relative. When she returned, a few months later, she saw my swollen stomach. "How could you do this?"

I blushed. "Please, please, don't be angry. We want a baby so much. I was afraid I'd never have one. Now Christian and I can get married."

"All right, but I want to be sure you have proper care. I want you to go to a gynecologist."

The gynecologist who examined me was very jolly. "Congratulations. The Fuehrer wants every young girl to have a baby."

Then I saw my mother say, "I'm surprised Franziska got pregnant. She's been sterilized."

"Sterilized!" The doctor jumped up and opened the door. "You'll have to leave at once."

Within a few days, I had a letter from the health office. "Fraulein Schwarz is to come to the Women's Hospital for an examination."

I took off my clothes and went into the examining room. The doctor felt my stomach. "Yes, you're pregnant. The pregnancy appears normal. Go into the other room."

In the dressing room, I couldn't find my clothes. I looked in all the drawers and under the seats. They were gone.

I banged on the doctor's door. "Clothes, clothes."

The doctor shook his head. He wrote on a pad. "You stay here. We have to check your urine for three days."

I wrote back. "I don't believe you. I want to go home. I can have my urine checked at home."

The doctor pushed me inside the changing room and locked the door. I looked out the window. I was on the fifth floor, too far to jump. I hid behind the door. When the nurse brought lunch, I escaped and ran towards the stairs. All the nurses ran after me. They caught me and locked me in the room.

For three days, I lay there, biting my nails and screaming. No one came to check my urine or examine me. Then the doctor came in. He pointed to my stomach. His lips moved, saying, "Out."

"What do you mean?"

"Out." He left.

I ran to the window. Even though it was on the fifth floor, I was going to jump. The nurse caught me. She dragged me by the hair into the hall and put me in a room with barred windows. I saw a piece of paper and a pencil on the desk. I wrote a note and then tried the door. It was unlocked. I ran into the hallway. A friend was coming up the steps to see me. I handed her the note. "Please, take it to my mother."

A nurse snatched the note. "You'd better leave," she told my friend. "She's acting a little crazy." I had no time to sign and tell my friend that the doctor was going to take my baby.

All night long I banged on the wall so they would let me out. The nurse shoved me into bed and gave me an injection. I woke up just as the stretcher was being wheeled into the operating room. There was a big tray next to the operating table. My baby is going to be on that tray, I thought, instead of inside me. "No, no," I tried to shout. "Christian, stop them."

When I woke up, I had terrible pains. "Christian, Christian," I moaned. "My uterus feels as though it's burning...."

When I woke up from a nap, I saw Christian standing next to the bed. My face was so white he dropped the flowers he had brought me. "Franziska, I'm sorry they took the baby. But we'll still get married. We can't stop Hitler, but he can't stop us from loving each other."

The nurse handed me a notice when I left the hospital. "You are to return to this hospital within 10 weeks to be sterilized." I crumpled the paper and threw it in the trash can. (Schwarz in Friedman, pp. 67–74)

Aftermath

At the outset of World War II in 1939, the Nazis escalated their attempts to eliminate the mentally retarded, mentally ill, or physically disabled. They organized a euthanasia program to provide the "mercy killing" of these groups, which they considered useless burdens on society. The National Coordinating Agency for Therapeutic and Medical Establishments organized this program, which was code-named T-4 after its Berlin address, 4 Tiergarten Street. Between 1940 and 1945, the T-4 program murdered more than 200,000 people. Techniques used to kill these people, such as gas chambers, later served as models for the mass execution methods used at the death camps.

Franziska Schwarz and her boyfriend Christian Mikus ignored her sterilization order and decided to get married. They were unable to obtain a marriage license because of Schwarz's existing file with Nazi authorities. Her uncle Karl obtained yet another hearing regarding sterilization, but her appeal was again denied. When the judges pronounced the sterilization order final,

Schwarz's uncle became enraged and shouted, "God damn Hitler! How can he do this to a young girl?" The judges immediately charged him with slander and ordered him arrested. After he was beheaded, the Schwarz family was billed for the execution. Schwarz underwent the sterilization procedure for the second time on March 21, 1941. Shortly after the surgery, she married Mikus. The couple survived the war, and Schwarz dedicated herself to the education of the deaf, serving as secretary to three organizations for the hearing-impaired. Mikus became a well-known soccer coach for the deaf. His death in the late 1980s was mourned by hearing impaired people throughout Germany and Europe.

Sources

Books

Bachrach, Susan D., *Tell Them We Remember: The Story of the Holocaust,* Little, Brown (Boston), 1994.

Friedman, Ina R., *The Other Victims,* Houghton Mifflin (Boston), 1990.

6

The Warsaw Ghetto

In the 1930s, Warsaw, the capital of Poland, had the second-largest population of Jews in the world (after New York City). At the beginning of World War II, approximately 375,000 Jews were living in Warsaw, nearly 30 percent of the city's population of 1.29 million. Prior to the German invasion of Poland, thousands of Jews and non-Jews fled from Warsaw, but during the next several months, thousands of other refugees moved in, mainly from areas of western Poland that had been made part of Germany. As they were forced to move into the General Government, about 90,000 Jews from other parts of Poland, most of them with virtually no possessions or money, crowded into Warsaw between fall 1939 and November 1940.

Within only a few months, the Nazis had applied all the anti-Jewish measures in Poland that had taken several years to implement in Germany. By November 1939, all Jews in Poland were required to wear a Star of David on their clothing at all times and were forbidden to change their address without permission. In December they were ordered to register their property with the Germans. In January 1940 an order barred Jews from traveling on railroads without special permits, forbade them to enter restaurants and parks, and excluded them from numerous professions.

By March 1940, the Nazis had erected street signs around the main Jewish neighborhood of Warsaw declaring it to be an "infected area." A typhus epidemic in the city served as an excuse for the Nazis to implement their plans. Eleven miles of high brick walls, more than 10 feet high, were built around the "infected area," and the Nazis made the Warsaw *Judenrat* finance this construction with money collected from Jews. The walls had many gaps, and for a time people were allowed to pass from one part of Warsaw to another.

In August 1940 the Germans announced the formation of a ghetto in Warsaw and began forcing Jews to leave apartments in the "Polish" area. On October 12, 1940, loudspeakers throughout the city announced that all Jews must be living in the ghetto by the end of the month. For the next few weeks, the city was in turmoil, as thousands of Warsaw Jews searched for apartments inside the ghetto's boundaries and non-Jewish Poles moved out. Jews moved into the ghettos carrying their belongings on hand carts or on their backs. The boundaries of the ghetto at that point were still unclear, but Jewish property from outside the ghetto was confiscated by the Nazis. By October 31, many Jewish people still had no place to live, so the Nazis extended the deadline to November 15. According to a German report written a year later, a quarter of a million people (113,000 non-Jewish

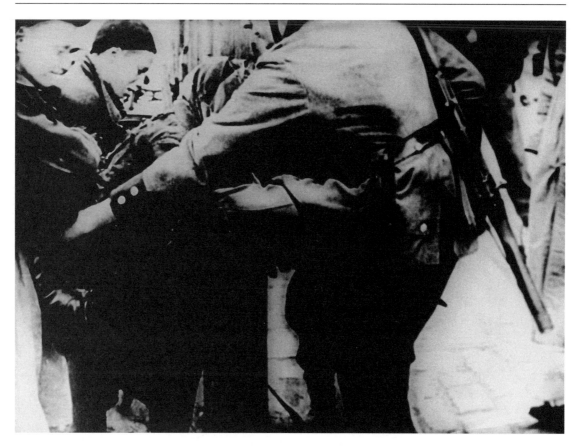

German soldiers search suspected smugglers at an entrance to the Warsaw ghetto. *(USHMM Photo Archives)*

Poles and 138,000 Jews) were required to move when the ghetto was created. Poles were forced out of more than 11,000 apartments in the ghetto, and Jews had to leave nearly 14,000 apartments in other parts of the city.

At first, Jews were unsure if they would be allowed to leave the ghetto. Uncertainty surrounding ghetto life was answered on November 16, 1940, when Jews were informed that the area was sealed. They were not allowed to leave the ghetto unless authorized by the Nazis. Police were stationed at each of the twenty-two surrounding gates, and Jews who were still employed outside the ghetto lost their jobs. (Most Jews had already been fired, on German orders.) By the end of 1940, around 450,000 people lived inside the ghetto walls—about 200,000 people per square mile, almost triple the statistic for the remainder of Warsaw. In the ghetto, an average of nine people lived in every room.

The city of Warsaw was divided into two separate sections, with the portion outside the ghetto designated the "Aryan" side. Connections between

the ghetto and the Aryan side were supposed to be controlled by the Germans, but an elaborate tunnel system dug beneath the wall allowed numerous secret contacts. Now trapped inside the ghetto, residents used the tunnels to sneak out, trading or selling whatever possessions they had (especially clothing) for food and then smuggling the food back into the ghetto. Children were especially adept at smuggling, as it was easier for them to slip in and out without being caught. Polish smugglers also went into the ghetto to buy and sell goods. While a majority of Jewish smugglers were ordinary people who needed the food to feed their families, some were professionals who reaped large profits and lived comfortable lives inside the ghetto. Some had been petty criminals, such as thieves and burglars, before the war. Within a short period of time, people were making products such as hair brushes, woolen socks, pots, and spoons from materials or scrap metal found in the ghetto or from materials brought in by smugglers. In October 1941 the Germans officially made smuggling an offense punishable by death, and a Jew caught outside the ghetto might be shot on sight.

A section of the more than ten-foot-high, eleven-mile-long brick wall that enclosed the Warsaw ghetto. *(Reproduced by permission of Bildarchiv Preussischer Kulturbesitz)*

Hunger

Hunger was generally the main problem plaguing Warsaw ghetto inhabitants. Food in German-controlled Poland was rationed, so even people with money could legally buy only what the Germans allowed. Each person had ration coupons for different categories of food. Jews were not allowed to buy meat, poultry, fish, fruit, vegetables, eggs, or white flour. Their diet mainly consisted of potatoes and bread. The official ration of food in the ghetto is estimated to have amounted to 800 calories a day per person, which was half the ration for non-Jewish Poles and one-third the ration for Germans in Poland. As the Nazis were well aware, humans cannot subsist on 800 calories a day for a prolonged period of time, and hunger and malnutrition became a bleak reality. Anyone merely walking down a ghetto street with a package that might contain food risked his or her safety, because packages were often grabbed from people's hands by others desperate for something to eat. For those who could not steal extra food or buy it from smugglers, death by starvation was certain. More than 43,000 people, almost one-tenth of the population, starved to death in 1941. At a funeral for some children from a ghetto orphanage, a wreath was placed on the graves by the surviving children. It read: "To the Children Who Have Died from Hunger—From the Children Who Are Hungry."

Jews selling off some of their possessions on the streets of the Kraków ghetto in order to obtain money for food, 1940. (*National Archives in Kraków/USHMM Photo Archives*)

The Polish and Jewish Undergrounds

Some Jews continued to live on the Aryan side of Warsaw by obtaining false documents that presented them as non-Jewish Poles. Some of them acted as links between the ghetto and the Polish underground, a massive anti-Nazi network that was equipped with weapons and maintained secret radio contact with the displaced Polish government stationed in London. Via the underground, ghetto inhabitants could also contact Jewish organizations outside Poland.

The long history of anti-Semitism in Poland prevented certain members of the Polish underground from cooperating with the Jews. Some were openly hostile, and relations between Jews and the Polish underground, especially the main underground military organization, the Home Army (known as the AK, from its Polish initials), became tempestuous. Certain members of the Home Army, however, did attempt to assist the Jews. The official newspaper of the Home Army carried regular reports on Nazi actions toward the Jews, and its editor later helped establish contact between the

A group portrait of the members of a Zionist youth organization in Kolbuszowa, Poland, in 1940. Jewish groups were forced to act in secret during the German occupation of Poland. *(Amalia Petranker Salsitz Collection/USHMM Photo Archives)*

Warsaw military command of the Home Army and the Jewish underground inside the ghetto. Some non-Jewish Poles acted as couriers, delivering messages back and forth between the Warsaw ghetto and Jews in the rest of Poland. Many Jews, especially young people who could more easily pass as non-Jewish Poles, also acted as couriers.

People inside the ghetto began to form underground organizations as well. The political parties the Jews belonged to before the war attempted to continue operations, such as publishing newspapers and journals, in secret. They printed reports about events inside the ghetto in hopes of convincing readers that something should be done in protest. Two of the parties, the Communists and the General Jewish Workers Union (known as the Bund), had direct connections with the non-Jewish organizations of the Polish underground. The Bund, which had ties to the Polish Socialist party, was much larger than the Communist party in the ghetto. There were also several different parties of Zionists—people who wanted to establish a Jewish

homeland in the country of Palestine—who kept in contact with Jewish organizations in other countries. All of these parties had youth groups that were active in the underground and were especially important in maintaining connections with Jews in the rest of Poland. The activities conducted by the Jewish underground were covert and fraught with danger. Constant tensions brewed between the underground and the *Judenrat.* Underground leaders were convinced that the *Judenrat* aided the Nazi cause, and the *Judenrat,* in turn, felt the underground endangered the people of the ghetto.

The underground's secret contacts kept Jews informed about events occurring throughout the country. In December 1941, for instance, the Nazis began murdering thousands of Jews from western Poland by gassing them in sealed trucks at Chelmno, the first Nazi death camp. Two of the Jews who had been forced to bury the bodies of the victims at Chelmno escaped and reached Warsaw in January 1942. Through the Polish underground, their reports were passed on to London. Information on

The Secret Archives of the Warsaw Ghetto

Knowledge about life in the Warsaw ghetto can largely be traced to the diaries of underground members. At the outset of the German occupation of Poland, a Jewish historian named Emmanuel Ringelblum began keeping meticulous notes on every aspect of Jewish life. Wanting future generations to understand the ghetto experience, he eventually recruited dozens of people to help him create a detailed written account of political and economic conditions, religious and cultural life, and even jokes people told. They recorded statistics, made copies of official announcements, wrote diaries and articles, and collected posters and photographs. Ringelblum called the project *Oneg Shabbat* (Hebrew for "Sabbath Pleasures"), the name given to Saturday afternoon gatherings following synagogue services. This written record was even more dangerous than other underground activities because there was so much material to hide. Eventually, the *Oneg Shabbat* archives were buried in crates in two separate locations in the ghetto. One of the two locations was found after the war, but the other is still unknown. Ringelblum and his family were shot in Warsaw in March 1944.

A Jewish family in the Lublin ghetto. The killing of the Jews of Lublin was part of a secret Nazi plan. *(Reproduced by permission of AP/Wide World Photos)*

the events at Chelmno were not widely known in the Warsaw ghetto, but within three months the residents were informed that Jews from the eastern Polish city of Lublin had been deported to an unknown destination. There were reports they had been taken to the Belzec death camp and killed. In Warsaw the secret newspapers of the Jewish underground published warnings that the Nazis eventually intended to exterminate all Jews. Most people in the ghetto did not believe this news, regarding the stories as exaggerations. Even with eyewitness reports, Jews in the Warsaw ghetto thought these must be isolated events—the actions of particular Nazi officials or SS soldiers gone on rampages. In fact, the killing of the Jews of Lublin was part of an official and secret Nazi policy to kill all the Jews in Europe that had begun with the German invasion of Russia in June 1941. By January 1942 Nazi officials had developed plans to carry out the *Endlösung*, or the "Final Solution" to the "Jewish problem."

The Bloody Night and Deportations

In early 1942 the Jews of Warsaw became victims of a massacre they called the "Bloody Night." Thousands had already died of hunger and disease, and others had been shot while trying to get out of the ghetto. Yet it was not until the Bloody Night that Warsaw Jews realized cooperation with the Germans would have little or no effect on their

Police escort Jews walking to the deportation trains for "resettlement." *(USHMM Photo Archives)*

chances of survival. On the evening of Friday, April 18, 1942, truckloads of SS men and German soldiers rolled into the ghetto. They stormed apartments, dragged out about sixty men, shot them, and left them lying in the street. Fifty-two were dead, the rest injured. Announcing that the shootings were punishment for the secret publications that had appeared in the ghetto, the Nazis warned they would take even harsher measures the next time. Conflicts intensified after the Bloody Night between the underground and the *Judenrat,* who felt the Nazi retaliation proved that underground activity risked the lives of all ghetto inhabitants. Members of the underground viewed the events in a completely different light, as indicative of future German plans. The Jews who had been hunted down and shot by the Germans were not necessarily involved in printing and distributing secret publications; rather, the Nazis had chosen men of influence, from a variety of fields, who were respected leaders of the ghetto. The underground leaders believed the Nazis had wanted to eliminate these leaders to prevent them from playing a role in future ghetto opposition to German actions. The underground members felt this meant the

Germans were planning major new actions against the Jews, and they were correct.

On July 19, 1942, Heinrich Himmler, head of Nazi security forces, ordered the "resettlement" of all Polish Jews by the end of the year. The Nazis began using broad terms, such as "Final Solution" and "resettlement," to disguise their real intentions. Jews were told they were being relocated to an undisclosed location "in the east," where they would be allowed to start new lives. This method was employed to ensure Jewish cooperation and prevent panic or resistance in the transportation of Jews to the locations where, ultimately, they would be murdered. The Nazis had built four death camps to eliminate the Jews of Poland. Chelmno had been operating since December 1941, Belzec since February 1942, and Sobibór since May 1942. The fourth camp, Treblinka, about fifty miles from Warsaw, was ready to begin the extermination of the Jews of Warsaw.

On July 22, 1942, the Nazis informed the Warsaw *Judenrat* that effective immediately, 6,000 people a day would be deported from the ghetto. Some *Judenrat* members were taken hostage, and posters

The Death of a Leader

On July 23, 1942, Adam Czerniaków, head of the Warsaw *Judenrat,* committed suicide. In a letter to his wife, he wrote that he could find no solution other than death when met with the Nazi demand that he murder children. Like other *Judenrat* leaders, Czerniaków had been faced with an impossible situation. The *Judenräte* were unable to carry out German orders while still protecting their people. Historian Yehuda Bauer notes that although Czerniaków was courageous, he headed a corrupt administration. A large number of *Judenrat* members throughout the Polish ghettos were involved in illegal or exploitative activities. Although many people thought Czerniaków's suicide was an honorable act, the Jewish underground blamed him for failing, even at the end, to call on the people of the ghetto to resist the Nazis.

appeared on the streets of the ghetto stating that "All Jewish persons living in Warsaw, regardless of age and sex, will be resettled in the East." The posters outlined specific categories of people who would be allowed to remain behind: *Judenrat* officials, the Jewish police, hospital and sanitary workers, and the families of these groups. People who worked for the private German companies that had been established in the ghetto would also remain. After accounting for the people who would be left behind, some ghetto residents estimated that 60,000 to 70,000 people were scheduled for deportation. Much like Lódz, it appeared that the Nazis intended to turn the Warsaw ghetto into a slave-labor camp only consisting of workers and their families. Thousands of Jews immediately attempted to get jobs that were included in the special categories, especially jobs with the German companies. Some even supplied their own sewing machines. Thousands were hired as everyone scrambled to procure a stamped work permit that guaranteed they would not be deported.

On the first day of the deportations, most of the arrests were made by the Jewish police, who became the most hated people in the ghetto. A few dozen SS men, German police, and Ukrainian and Latvian auxiliary troops of the SS also participated in rounding up deportees. The initial targets were people from poorhouses, starving and homeless people, and beggars from the poorest section of the ghetto. Jews from Germany, who had been shipped to the ghetto two months earlier, were also among the first group of deportees. They were taken to the *Umschlagplatz* ("transfer place"), a large square located near the ghetto railroad station, and were loaded into sealed freight cars, destined for Treblinka and death.

The Germans, dissatisfied with the rate of deportations in the initial few days, ordered German police to surround whole apartment houses and remove everyone inside. They checked the residents' papers, taking anyone without a work permit to the *Umschlagplatz* for deportation, and conducted exhaustive searches of each building to make sure no one was hiding. If they were unable to find enough people to meet their deportation quotas, the Nazis simply added people who had work permits. Soon they began to surround whole streets in the ghetto instead of searching one building at a time, and by the middle of August, they were ignoring the permits entirely and taking people out of their workplaces instead of their homes. Some people began to report to the *Umschlagplatz* on their own, drawn by German promises of three kilograms (about 6.5 pounds) of bread and one kilogram (2.2 pounds) of jam to those who voluntarily surrendered. Many starving people could not resist this offer.

The deportations began on July 22, 1942, and continued daily until September 9. The entire operation involved around 50 SS men, 400 from the Ukrainian and Latvian SS auxiliaries, and the Jewish police. Although large numbers of SS and German army troops were stationed nearby, very few were needed. Among the last to be deported were members of the Jewish police and their families, despite Nazi promises of protection. Approximately 265,000 people were sent to Treblinka, where almost all were immediately murdered in the gas chambers. An estimated 12,000 people were sent to forced labor camps and 10,000 others were murdered in the streets of Warsaw. Eight thousand people managed to escape to the Aryan side of Warsaw, many of these hidden by non-Jewish Poles who risked their lives working with the underground. At the same time, these Jews were in constant danger of being turned over to the Germans by anti-Semitic Poles.

Of the 350,000 people who had been living in the ghetto on July 22, fewer than 60,000 remained by early September. Around 35,000, only a tenth of the original number, were allowed to stay behind; the rest were there illegally, hiding from the Germans. The ghetto, which had been so overcrowded, was now mostly empty, and the Germans divided it into four areas separated by forbidden zones. No contact between the areas was allowed, and people were forbidden from venturing outdoors except between 5–7:30 a.m. in the morning and again from 4–8 p.m. A majority of the elderly, the sick, and children had been removed from the ghetto, and many of the remaining people had lost their entire families. Those who remained were mostly younger adults who, by ghetto standards, were relatively healthy. They had an easier time obtaining food because they could barter or sell the possessions of those who had been deported, and the death rate consequently dropped. The survivors of the ghetto understood that the Nazis would not stop their plans until all European Jews were eliminated. Many of them, feeling guilty and angry with themselves for not trying to stop the deportations, began resisting the Nazis.

The Jewish Fighting Organization

On the second day of the deportations, leaders of various organizations within the Jewish underground met secretly to plan their next move. Some members of political parties and youth groups advocated armed resistance against the Germans, but several of the most respected leaders strongly opposed the move. They believed that fighting the German army was suicide because the Jews had no weapons and little military training, and the ghetto itself was an isolated unit cut off from outside help. Many Jewish leaders warned that the Germans would react to the actions of a few rebels by killing thousands of people, and they called for passive resistance, feeling this policy was the best strategy for survival. On July 28, 1942, however, several youth groups disregarded the advice of the elders and formed a military wing of the underground called the *Zydowsk Organizacja Bojowa* (ZOB), or the Jewish Fighting Organization. In its early stages, the group's membership was approximately 200 people, all of whom came from youth groups connected to different political parties.

The Orphans' March

On August 6, 1942, the Nazis removed children from every children's institution in the Warsaw ghetto. One was an orphanage run by Janusz Korczak, a famous educator. The actions of Korczak and his orphans are described by historian Israel Gutman as follows:

"Korczak lined his children up in rows of four. The orphans were clutching flasks of water and their favorite books and toys. They were in their best clothes. Korczak stood at the head of his 192 children, holding a child with each hand…. They marched through the ghetto to the *Umschlagplatz* where they joined thousands of people waiting without shade, water, or shelter, in the hot August sun. The children did not cry out. They walked quietly in forty-eight rows of four."

One eyewitness, according to Gutman, viewed the children's procession as a silent protest against the murderous Nazis. Korczak and all the orphans were murdered at Treblinka.

The ZOB was organized under extreme secrecy, and each member knew the identities of only a few others. Only select people knew the overall structure of the ZOB, which safeguarded confidentiality and made it difficult for any one informer to destroy the organization. In addition to the threat of informers, there was also the constant danger that a ZOB member would be arrested and tortured by the Nazis to reveal the organization's secrets. The ZOB was formed without any armaments, but by early August the organization managed to obtain five pistols and half a dozen hand grenades from the military wing of the Polish Communist underground. Realizing that conflict with the SS was impossible without more ammunition, the ZOB decided to take action where it could. A member of the ZOB shot, and seriously wounded, the commander of the Jewish police. Many people in the ghetto believed

Jewish youth peer over the wall overlooking Mirowski Plac (Square) that divided the Warsaw ghetto into the small and large ghettos, 1941. *(Irving Milchberg/USHMM Photo Archives)*

that members of the Polish underground, not the ZOB, were responsible. The Jews had accepted the idea that their people, like non-Jewish Poles, would not fight.

The ZOB suffered a major setback in early September 1942. Eighteen young people traveling with false identity papers were able to get out of Warsaw and attempted to reach a forest in eastern Poland, where a Jewish partisan group was being formed. Only one eluded capture by the Germans. The rest were tortured and executed. Their capture led to the arrest of a ZOB leader in Warsaw who had prepared their false papers. He was shot by the Germans, and another ZOB member was killed trying to rescue him. A third ZOB member was killed while trying to move the ZOB's weapons to a safer location. When the arms were captured by the Germans, the ZOB had to begin acquiring new weapons.

The ZOB found it difficult to get weapons from Poland's Home Army for several reasons. Arms were valuable to the underground, and Home Army leaders did not want them "wasted"

on Jews. They believed that Jews had no intentions of using force against the Germans. The military situation in the ghetto was perceived as being hopeless. Messages sent by some Home Army leaders to London indicate that they thought the Jews were not capable of fighting. Their own prejudices against Jews made them believe that supplying weapons to the ghetto would be a waste. The Home Army was also suspicious of the Polish Communists, who were loyal to the Communist government of the Soviet Union but not to the Polish government in London. The Home Army wanted to preserve its strength and plan for a massive battle against the Germans when the Russian army arrived in Poland. The Communists, on the other hand, wanted to move sooner to help the Russians, who were losing millions of soldiers and civilians (far more than any other country) in the war with the Germans. To the Russians, the Home Army's desire to save its forces showed how unimportant the Soviets were in the Home Army's eyes.

The ZOB mirrored Communist sentiments, claiming that full-scale resistance should be

Ukrainian SS auxiliary soldiers search for Jews in the Warsaw ghetto. *(National Archives/USHMM Photo Archives)*

launched as soon as possible. To save as many Jewish lives as possible—or to preserve Jewish honor, if the lives would be lost anyway—the underground needed to mount an armed attack immediately. The Polish underground hoped that a great uprising would restore pride to the Poles and establish them as a powerful military force independent of the Russian army. A successful rebellion would also allow them to safeguard Poland's interests against Russia, who wanted to claim the eastern parts of pre-war Poland as its own.

When the Warsaw ghetto deportations ended in September, several leaders of the Jewish underground, who had been outside the ghetto, returned to Warsaw. One of them was Mordecai Anielewicz, who had been in southwestern Poland organizing an armed resistance movement. Only twenty-two years old but widely respected for his bravery, he worked to strengthen the ZOB and became its commander. Most of the influential political groups in the underground—including the Bund, most Zionist groups, and the Communists—soon joined the ZOB. The political parties that represented religious Jews did not join; neither did a youth group called Betar, a faction of the Zionist movement that established its own military orga-

nization, the Jewish Fighting Union. On October 29, 1942, the ZOB killed the deputy commander of the Jewish police, announcing its responsibility for the action the next day in small printed notices posted in the ghetto. Soon after, ZOB members executed an official of the *Judenrat* who was known to have cooperated with the Nazis.

Informing the World

The underground wanted the rest of the world to know what was happening to the Jews in Poland, especially those in Warsaw. In fall 1942, two leaders representing the Jewish underground met with Jan Karski, an officer in the Polish underground who was about to be smuggled to London to report on events in Poland. One of the Jewish leaders at the meeting was Leon Feiner, who belonged to the Bund, and the other was a Zionist leader whose identity remains unknown. At the time, Karski did not know the real names of the people he met, and they did not know his. The name "Karski," which he kept after the war, was originally one of the false names he used to disguise himself from the Nazis.

The Jewish leaders described the hunger and death in the ghetto, pacing the floor as they spoke.

Resistance in the Polish Ghettos

The ZOB was the best-known armed resistance movement in the Polish ghettos, and the Warsaw ghetto uprising was by far the largest battle. Armed resistance groups, however, operated in at least twenty-three other ghettos in western and central Poland, and sixty more were established in eastern Poland. These groups faced many of the same problems that plagued the ZOB in Warsaw. It was extremely difficult to get weapons and there were overwhelming German forces nearby. The underground was usually comprised of people from various political groups, each with their own ideas about how to oppose the Nazis. The *Judenräte* usually opposed armed resistance, and the majority of the Jewish population believed that their best chance at survival was to continue to work hard and wait for the Russian army to arrive.

Most of the uprisings occurred when all hope was gone, but there are numerous examples of poorly armed Jewish fighters battling the Germans. Among the most famous ghetto revolts are those that took place in Bialystok in August 1943 and in Vilna the next month. Many thousands of Jews were also able to escape from the ghettos and join partisan units. An estimated 20,000 Jews escaped the Warsaw ghetto in the last few months of its existence. Approximately 4,000 found refuge through Zegota, a relief organization created by underground political parties. The work of the resisters helped save lives even after the failed uprising, as some Jews were able to hide in the abandoned bunkers undetected by the Nazis.

Afraid the Polish government in England would not believe Karski's reports unless he had witnessed the Jews' plight firsthand, Karski was twice smuggled into the ghetto to view the situation for himself. On the first trip, Feiner and Karski crawled through a tunnel connecting the Aryan side to the ghetto. The streets were littered with the naked bodies of people who had starved to death. Feiner explained that the families of the dead had removed their clothing and thrown them into the street to avoid paying burial taxes to the Nazis. People could not pay the tax, and they needed the clothing. Karski witnessed people in rags huddled against buildings, staring into space, barely breathing as they waited to die. He saw two young Germans firing shots at Jews as a game, a "Jew hunt."

Later, disguised as a Ukrainian SS auxiliary policeman, Karski traveled to a camp that the Nazis used as a stopover point for some of the Jews being sent to the Belzec death camp. He saw thousands of people, half-starved, and seemingly in a state of shock, sitting and lying in an open area. The Jews were eventually forced into boxcars, with guards beating, bayonetting, and shooting those who moved too slowly. The dead and wounded were thrown into the cars on top of the others, who were screaming. Finally, the doors of the boxcars were sealed shut.

When Karski reached London after a dangerous trip across Nazi-controlled Europe, he reported to the Polish government on domestic events and delivered a message sent by the Jewish leaders. The Jewish underground sought help from the Allies, especially the United States and Great Britain, and wanted the Jewish communities of those countries to put pressure on their governments. Feiner had told Karski that unless something was done immediately, 3 million Polish Jews would die. The Jewish and Polish undergrounds were not strong enough to fight the Nazis on their own, Feiner said, and only the Allies could save the Polish Jews. Feiner did not want a single leader of the Allied countries to be unaware of the slaughter in Poland. He told Karski that the Jewish underground was mounting a defense of the Warsaw ghetto in order to draw the attention of the world to their hopeless plight.

The two underground leaders proposed a series of actions for the Allies. First, they would ask the Allies to announce publicly that ending the murder

SS general Jürgen Stroop stands among his troops in the Warsaw ghetto in 1943. *(Reproduced by permission of Snark/Art Resource)*

of the Jews was one of the goals of the war against Germany. Second, they wanted the Allies to inform the German populace about Nazi-organized killings, using radio broadcasts and also leaflets dropped from airplanes. Third, they wanted the Allies to use the German people to pressure the Nazi government into stopping the killings. According to Feiner, the German people as a group should be held responsible for the actions of Hitler's government. If nothing else worked, the Jewish leaders said, then selected German cities of special historical or cultural importance should be bombed in retaliation. Finally, German prisoners who remained loyal to Hitler after being told of the mass killings of the Jews should be executed.

Karski delivered this message first to leaders of the British government, and later to leaders of the American government, including President Franklin D. Roosevelt, and the American Jewish community. Unable to return to Poland and rejoin the underground, Karski spoke at meetings in cities throughout the United States, telling the world about Poland and the murder of the Jews. He wrote a book, *Story of a Secret State,* that became a bestseller in America, but he was never sure his message made a real difference.

Karski knew that some of the Jewish underground's ideas would not be implemented. Although the Allies did warn that the Germans would be held responsible after the war for crimes they committed, they would never execute German prisoners during the war, feeling it would only lead to the execution of British and American prisoners. In addition, the idea of "collective responsibility," or punishing people for crimes committed by others, went against the Allies' beliefs. It is unclear why the other ideas were rejected, particularly the provision that requested an Allied announcement be made noting that saving the Jews from mass murder was one of the goals of the war. Some historians believe that Allied leaders feared such a statement might make the war less popular with their own people, who might not want to fight and die for the Jews. Also, an appeal to the German public to stop the mass murders never occurred, and no one knows whether this would have had any effect. Nazi Germany was a violent dictatorship where opposition was squashed. However, less than two years earlier, German public opinion had forced Hitler to stop killing mentally and physically disabled citizens. Historians are deeply divided over the question of whether the Allies could have done more to save the Jews. In general, the Allied leaders believed that the best way to help the Jews was to win the war against Germany as quickly as possible. They opposed any action that might interfere with this goal.

The January Aktion

As Jan Karski informed the British and Americans about the desperate situation in the Warsaw ghetto, the ZOB began formulating its next course of action. The organization decided to hold a public demonstration in the ghetto to build popular support. Members posted notices around the ghetto, urging Jews to resist the Nazis by refusing to board deportation trains or by going into hiding. The demonstration was scheduled for January 22, 1943, but at 6 a.m. on January 18, armed German police and Ukrainian auxiliaries entered the ghetto to begin a new deportation *aktion* ("operation"). Caught by surprise, the ZOB had few weapons and little public support. Although they had not prepared a full-scale military plan, they were still determined to resist deportation.

News of the total destruction of ghettos throughout Poland had already reached Warsaw, and Jews refused to obey Nazi orders to leave buildings and enter courtyards. Most people went to prepared hiding places. One of them, Mordecai Lensky, the ghetto's chief doctor, described what happened in the hospital. Thirty people crowded into a special room hidden behind a closet and listened fearfully while Ukrainian SS auxiliaries entered. The patients and some of the hospital staff had already been arrested, and only a thin wall separated the thirty hiding Jews from the Ukrainians. The Ukrainians, seeing no one about, quickly looted the room, taking everything of value they could find. The people in the closet, who included young children and elderly people, waited nervously, fearing that the slightest movement or sound could give them away.

Although most of the Jews targeted for deportation tried to hide, the Germans were still able to find many, especially in workplaces. When the Germans began to march a line of hundreds of people toward the *Umschlagplatz*, a dozen members of the ZOB, hiding pistols, joined the line. When a signal was given, each ZOB member attacked the nearest guard, disarming and killing several. Other guards fled out of fear, but German reinforcements arrived quickly. Most of the ZOB members died in the ensuing gun battle, their pistols and few rounds of ammunition no match for the heavily armed Germans. In the confusion, the people being brought to the *Umschlagplatz* scat-

tered and hid in the ghetto. Two other gun battles between the ZOB and the Germans took place a short while later. In one case, a group of soldiers searching for Jews entered an apartment where the ZOB was waiting to open fire. One ZOB member was killed in the fight, but most were able to escape to another building.

As the roundup continued over the next few days, 200 German police and 800 SS auxiliaries were sent in. This was a much larger force than was needed during the first deportation, and it was considerably more difficult for the Nazis to find the Jews they wanted to deport. The Germans intensified careful searches of cellars and attics for four days. On the last day, as revenge against ZOB actions, the Nazis shot 1,000 people on the streets of the Warsaw ghetto. In the end, an estimated 6,000 people were killed or deported.

Although most people in Warsaw, both Jews and other Poles (including the Home Army), believed that the armed resistance of the Jews had stopped the Nazis from deporting everyone in the ghetto, this was not necessarily the case. The Nazis had not planned to deport everyone at once, and the best available evidence indicates that they wanted to deport only 8,000 people at that time, leaving the rest for later. The resistance probably caused them to end the operation sooner and to deport about 2,000 fewer people than they had intended. German officers in Warsaw tried to keep the news of the resistance from spreading, as they did not want their superiors in Berlin to know what had happened. Still, the Warsaw ghetto battle enhanced public perception of the ZOB. The Polish underground praised the Jewish action as an extraordinary victory, thus enabling the ZOB to acquire more arms. Many historians assert that the most important impact of this resistance was improved morale in the ghetto. The Jewish underground, especially the ZOB, was accepted as the real leader; the authority of the *Judenrat* became weaker and eventually it was often ignored.

The Warsaw Jews focused on preparations for the next German attack. Throughout the ghetto, cellars were dug and turned into bunkers with carefully hidden entrances. Food and water were stockpiled. A network of tunnels connected the bunkers, and other tunnels were dug underneath the ghetto wall to connect to the Aryan side of Warsaw. Ladders were placed between roofs, thus allowing people an additional way to travel from one building to the next besides the tunnels. The

During the Warsaw ghetto uprising, SS troops find resistance fighters hiding in makeshift bunkers. *(National Archives/USHMM Photo Archives)*

ZOB organized twenty-two fighting squads, with a total of around 500 members. Each member was armed with a pistol, about a dozen rounds of ammunition, and four or five hand grenades, mostly homemade. The ZOB was also equipped with around ten rifles, one or two submachine guns, and about 2,000 Molotov cocktails (gasoline-filled bottles with rag fuses). When lit and thrown, the Molotov cocktails exploded on impact, making them the only weapon the ZOB could use effectively against tanks or armored cars. The other Jewish military group, the Jewish Fighting Union, had about 250 fighters, who may have been somewhat better armed than the ZOB forces.

The Warsaw Ghetto Uprising

April 19, 1943 was the eve of Passover, the Jewish holiday celebrating the Jews' escape to freedom from slavery in Egypt. At 3 a.m., German troops surrounded the Warsaw ghetto. The Polish underground had learned that the Germans were planning another operation against the ghetto, and this time the ZOB was ready. People were hiding in the bunkers and the streets were empty; ZOB fighters were hiding in nearby buildings and on roofs. As the Germans moved into the ghetto, they were met with

bullets, grenades, and Molotov cocktails. The Germans were completely surprised by the attack, and a number were killed or wounded. Battles raged in several sections of the ghetto and, for the first time, the Germans were forced to turn back. When news of these events was telephoned to SS chief Himmler in Berlin, he was furious at his troops for having disgraced themselves. In addition, the Germans were afraid that this example might spread to the rest of Warsaw, causing rebellion among the Home Army as well. Himmler fired the commander of the operation and replaced him with SS General Jürgen Stroop, who was known for his ruthless treatment of civilians during the invasion of Russia.

Three hours after their retreat, German troops ventured back into the ghetto, this time utilizing different tactics. They remained under cover and at a distance, relying on marksmanship to kill Jewish fighters in doorways and windows and on the roofs. The ZOB's pistols were useless in this kind of fighting, and they had few rifles. The underground fighters had to get close enough to their targets to hit them with hand grenades. The Germans attacked one building at a time, forcing their way inside under heavy fire, while the Jews defended themselves in each building as long as possible and

Jews captured during the Warsaw ghetto uprising of April and May 1943 are led by the SS to the *Umschlagplatz* for deportation. *(National Archives/USHMM Photo Archives)*

Survivors of the Warsaw ghetto uprising are rounded up at gunpoint. *(Reproduced by permission of AP/Wide World Photos)*

A section of the Warsaw ghetto burns during the Warsaw ghetto uprising of April and May 1943. *(Reproduced by permission of Bildarchiv Preussischer Kulturbesitz)*

then escaped through the tunnels or attics. The first day of the Warsaw ghetto uprising ended with the roundup of about 580 Jews, a relatively small number. Those who were caught were not taken to the *Umschlagplatz* but were shot on the spot. The Jewish fighters had some casualties but probably not so many as the Germans. At nightfall, the Germans again left the ghetto. The fighters came out on the street, and were joined by the rest of the ghetto residents. For one day at least, they had fought the Germans to a standstill.

The next morning, April 20, 1943, the Germans entered the ghetto with artillery, tanks, and armored cars. Amidst heavy fighting, at least one German armored car was destroyed by Molotov cocktails. The Germans, with greater numbers and much heavier firepower, were able to push the Jewish fighters back continuously and capture buildings, but the fighting simply continued on the next street.

During the Warsaw ghetto uprising, the Germans sent an average of 2,100 soldiers, equipped with unlimited ammunition, into the ghetto each day. In addition to rifles and dozens of submachine guns, the soldiers were supplied with more than

eighty machine guns, a cannon, flamethrowers, and armored cars. By the third day of the uprising, the Germans who entered the ghetto fought in smaller formations, moving carefully under cover of heavy fire. They were no longer deporting helpless Jews, but were fighting a house-to-house battle. The conflict then shifted to the underground bunkers, which the Germans pummeled with explosives, smoke rockets, and poisonous gas. They also burned down buildings above the bunkers; the intense heat from the burned bricks and the lack of air forced many people outside, where the Germans were waiting.

When many bunkers became useless, the ZOB shifted people to other hiding places through the network of tunnels. Sometimes, when the heat or smoke made it impossible to stay underground, they came out shooting. Block after block was burned down, and the Jews hiding inside were forced out. Whole families jumped or climbed down from upper-story windows. The German troops immediately shot both those who climbed down and those who survived the jump.

German troops continued their daily search for hidden entrances to the bunkers. Finding an opening, they attempted entry but were often met by small-arms fire, which they returned with explosives and smoke rockets. The ZOB sometimes traveled through the tunnels to return to an area the Germans had cleared the day before. According to Stroop's estimate, by April 26, after one week of fighting, almost 30,000 Jews had been killed. The ZOB fighters hid, came out briefly to attack Germans whenever they could, and then disappeared until they saw another opportunity to attack. On May 8, almost three weeks after the Germans entered the ghetto, the ZOB's command bunker at 18 Mila Street was destroyed. Most of the ZOB fighters inside committed suicide rather than surrender.

On May 16, 1943, after twenty-eight days of fighting, Stroop blew up the Great Synagogue of Warsaw to show that the battle was over. He reported that the ghetto had been cleared and that 56,000 Jews had been killed or captured during the operation. Some fighting actually continued for at least two more weeks, and a few ZOB fighters succeeded in hiding even longer. Armed clashes in the ruins of the ghetto reportedly took place as late as July. The German army awarded General Stroop the Iron Cross First Class for commanding the operation. (Stroop was hanged as a war criminal after the war.) The largest and most important Jewish community in Europe had been wiped out, but the Warsaw Jews had resisted the Nazis until the very end.

P R I M A R Y   S O U R C E

Chaim A. Kaplan
Excerpt from *Scroll of Agony: The Warsaw Diary of Chaim A. Kaplan*, written September 1, 1939 to August 4, 1942
Translated and edited by Abraham I. Katsh

Published in 1965

German forces attacked Poland on September 1, 1939, starting World War II. While Britain and France declared war on Germany, they failed to provide Poland with the military support it needed to resist Nazi forces. The Germans had several advantages, including a larger army and more modern equipment, and by surrounding Poland on three sides, the Germans conquered the country within a month. Mobile killing units known as Einsatzgruppen accompanied the German army throughout Poland and targeted Jews, aristocrats, intellectuals, and members of the clergy. The Einsatzgruppen murdered 16,000 Polish and Jewish civilians in more than 700 mass executions.

Germany annexed the western and northern parts of Poland and called this newly acquired territory Wartheland. In the southeastern portion of Poland, the Germans formed a civil administration called the Generalgouvernement, or the General Government. Of the 22 million people in German-occupied Poland, several million were Jews. About 600,000 Jews lived in the Wartheland area and 1.5 million lived within the General Government. More than 10 million Poles lived in Warthegau and 12 million lived in the General Government. Hitler ordered the expulsion of all non-Germans from Warthegau so that Germans could take over the vacated areas. The Nazis also instituted a racial reclamation project to screen Polish people and determine if they could undergo "re-Germanization." Certain Poles who fit the German ideal—especially those who were blond and tall—were allowed to remain in segregated areas.

A directive called "The Jewish Question in Occupied Territory" was issued on September 21, 1939, by Reinhard Heydrich, the chief of security police, and contained instructions to Einsatzgruppen chiefs regarding racial policy in Poland. Heydrich ordered that Jews from the countryside be concentrated at once into the larger cities. He also ordered the creation of *Judenräte*, or Councils of Jewish Elders, in each Jewish community, which would assure German orders were followed.

A Jewish businessman is made to wear the Star of David. *(USHMM Photo Archives)*

Reinhard Heydrich (1902-1942)

Reinhard Heydrich was born in Halle, Germany. His father was a famous musician and founder of the Halle Conservatory of Music. Heydrich served as an officer in the German navy but was dismissed upon being found guilty of misconduct. After joining the Nazis in 1931, Heydrich befriended Heinrich Himmler, leader of the SS, and eventually rose to the inner circle of Nazi power, becoming the executive director of the Gestapo. He played a key role in *Kristallnacht*, in which the Gestapo placed thousands of Jews in "protective custody." In the following months, the Nazis established the Central Office for Jewish Emigration under Heydrich to coordinate and implement Jewish policy.

When Germany invaded Poland, Heydrich commanded the process of interning Polish Jews in ghettos. He was one of the main authors of a plan for mass deportation of all European Jews to the island of Madagascar, off the African coast. His ruthless proposal for immediate extermination, rather than capture and imprisonment, of all Jews during the Russian invasion resulted in the deaths of many thousands of Russian Jews. On January 20, 1942, Nazi leaders met in Wannsee, Germany, to coordinate the mass movement of all Jews under Nazi control to labor camps, and ultimately to death camps. Following this conference, Heydrich issued the protocol which ordered the *Endlösung,* or "Final Solution" to the "Jewish problem." Heydrich's enthusiasm and fanaticism resulted in his appointment as acting governor of Bohemia and Moravia, where he continued his policy of brutal repression and mass execution of Jewish communities. On May 27, 1942, two Czech resistance fighters bombed his car near Prague. He died of his wounds on June 4, 1942.

Immediately after Poland surrendered, German forces subjected Jewish Poles to violence and discrimination. Jews were driven away from food lines and randomly seized off the streets for forced labor. The Nazis also humiliated and assaulted Jews wearing traditional religious garb. Many Jews lost their jobs without receiving compensation and were left without any prospect of securing new positions. The Nazis issued numerous anti-Jewish decrees, including the requirement that Jews wear the Star of David on their clothing. The Nazis also banned Jews from owning radios and traveling by train. The most damaging of these orders restricted the economic rights and privileges of Jews and mandated the confiscation of Jewish property. Throughout the General Government in 1940 and 1941, local authorities began the process of confining Jewish people to ghettos—designated areas within certain cities.

Before the outbreak of World War II, Warsaw boasted the largest Jewish community in Europe, about 375,000 people. The Warsaw ghetto, when it was established, was also the largest in Europe, enclosing between 400,000 and 600,000 people, approximately 30 percent of Warsaw's total population. The ghetto was extremely crowded, containing only seventy-three of the city's 1800 streets to support this large percentage of the populace. It was surrounded by a wall more than 10 feet high and 10 inches thick, topped with barbed wire. Guards were posted at each gate and patrolled the wall twenty-four hours a day. Inside the ghetto, hunger was rampant. During the worst period, about 500 people starved to death each week.

Chaim A. Kaplan was principal of a Hebrew school in Warsaw, Poland, in the 1930s. He had started writing a diary in 1933 to record his private thoughts. When World War II broke out, he deliberately changed the style of his writing to serve more as a chronicle. He no longer focused on his personal feelings and problems; instead, he devoted his efforts to reporting the mounting tragedy occurring around him. Cautious and fearful of detection, Kaplan never mentioned his own name in the diary entries and kept them a secret from his family. *Scroll of Agony: The Warsaw Diary of Chaim A. Kaplan* contains a revealing firsthand account of Jewish life within the Warsaw ghetto. The following excerpt describes the confusion concerning the decree of October 12, 1940 that ordered the formation of the ghetto in the heart of the Jewish section of Warsaw. While the Nazi government in Germany had issued a directive to concentrate Jews within Polish cities, it did not explicitly order the organization of ghettos. Local officials had to make that decision themselves. Also recorded is the fact that Jews continued to practice their religion even amidst the oppressive conditions of occupied Warsaw. Although they were barred from using synagogues, they formed small groups within the Warsaw ghetto to pray.

Scroll of Agony: The Warsaw Diary of Chaim A. Kaplan

October 2, 1940
The Eve of the New Year, 5701

We have no public worship, even on the high holy days. There is darkness in our synagogues, for there are no worshipers—silence and desolation within, and sorrow looking on from without. Even for the high holy days, there was no permission for communal worship. I don't know whether the Judenrat made any attempt to obtain it, but if it didn't try it was only because everyone knew in advance that the request would be turned down. Even in the darkest days of our exile we were not tested with this trial. Never before was there a government so evil that it would forbid an entire people to pray. But never before in our history, drenched in tears and blood, did we have so cruel and barbaric an enemy.

Everything is forbidden to us. The wonder is that we are still alive, and that we do everything. And this is true of public prayer, too. Secret minyanim ["number;" refers to the number ten, which is the number of men required for congregational worship] by the hundreds throughout Warsaw organize services, and do not skip over even the most difficult hymns in the liturgy. There is not even a shortage of sermons. Everything is in accordance with the ancient customs of Israel. When there is no informer at work, the enemy doesn't know what is going on, and we can assume that no Jewish man, even if he is a Jew born in Poland, would inform on Jews standing before their Maker in prayer.

They pick some inside room whose windows look out onto the courtyard, and pour out their supplications before the God of Israel in whispers. This time there are no cantors and choirs, only whispered prayers. But the prayers are heartfelt; it is possible to weep in secret, too, and the gates of tears are not locked.

And so we give praise to the God of Israel "who kept us alive and supported us and brought us unto this season." During the year many individuals drank the cup of hemlock; many have gone to their graves. The community has been debased and impoverished. But it still exists.

October 12, 1940
End of Yom Kippur, 5701

…To our great sorrow, as the day drew to a close, at a time when the gates of tears were still open, we learned that a new edict has been issued for us, a barbaric edict which by its weight and results is greater than all the other edicts made against us up to now, to which we have become accustomed.

At last the ghetto edict has gone into effect. For the time being it will be an open ghetto, but there is no doubt that in short order it will be closed. In Lódz the ghetto edict was not carried out all at once, but rather step by step, and many signs indicate that it will be the same in Warsaw. After the ghetto plan was postponed two weeks ago, we were almost tranquil. But the enemy of Israel neither sleeps nor slumbers.

This new edict was issued in a somewhat humane form—perhaps for the sake of world opinion—but we know that in its new form it is still the last link in the chain of troubles and misfortunes.

Before the thirty-first of October the Jews who live in the streets outside the walls must move lock, stock, and barrel to the streets within the walls; and all the Aryans (read Poles) living in the streets within the walls must move to the Aryan quarter. To a certain extent the edict has hurt the Poles more than the Jews, for the Poles are ordered to move not only from the ghetto, but from the German quarter as well. Nazism wants to separate everyone—the lords by themselves, the underlings by themselves, the slaves by themselves. The blessed and the accursed must not mingle.

A hundred and twenty thousand people will be driven out of their homes and will have to find sanctuary and shelter within the walls. Where will we put this great mass of people? Most of them are wealthy, accustomed to beautiful apartments and lives of comfort, and they will be totally impoverished from now on. Their businesses and livelihoods were directly connected with the areas where they lived. In leaving their homes they are also leaving their incomes.

The Gentiles too are in mourning. Not one tradesman or storekeeper wants to move to a strange section, even if it be to an Aryan section. It is hard for any man, whether Jewish of Aryan, to start making his life over. And so the panic in captured Warsaw, occupied by harsh masters, is great. As I have said, for the time being we are in an open ghetto; but we will end by being in a real ghetto, within closed walls.

Hundreds of Germans are coming in, refugees from the English bombs, half-mad women with their children. They complain angrily to their fat, comfortable relatives who are enjoying the spoils of a strange land out of all danger. An eyewitness reports that a German soldier dared to write these words on the wall of one of the trolley cars: 'We ride back and forth. We have no more homeland!'...

October 24, 1940
The night of Simhat Torah, 5701

The Warsaw ghetto is making its full appearance. Everyone is vacating his forbidden apartment in advance of the deadline, and taking some new apartment in the Jewish area. So long as poverty can be locked in the innermost places, people forget it exists; but when it is brought outside it awakens disgust and loathing. Now we see the used furniture and household utensils of the poor as they search through the streets for a new refuge. There is no sense to this. For what reason are these miserable and oppressed creatures made to roam around like shadows, these who have nothing to keep themselves alive with, even under their own roofs?

The naïve among the Jews and Poles ask: Can the world sit silent? Will the evil and the corrupt always have the upper hand? Will the ax fall upon the entire world? O Leader of the city, where are you?

But He Who sits in Heaven laughs.

The torments of the creation of the ghetto are harder, perhaps, than the ghetto itself. At every hour new changes are made regarding one area or another. Thus Zelazna Street, a place of refuge for 60,000 Poles and 26,000 Jews, has been in limbo for several days, and no one knows what its fate will be. Is it ours, or our competitor's? There is a rumor that two delegations, one Jewish (Wielikowski and Sztolcman) and one Polish, went to Cracow, but neither managed to see the ruler, and both returned empty-handed. There are also various rumors about extension of the period of evacuation. Some say it was extended until November 15; others say the original date still stands. Yesterday the radio announced that the time stated before, October 31, remains in effect. Today people in Judenrat circles announce that on the twenty-eighth a notice will be published extending the time until November 15.

And an additional doubt is gnawing at us:

Will it be a closed ghetto? There are signs in both directions, and we hoped for a miracle—which doesn't always happen in time of need. A closed ghetto means gradual death. An open ghetto is only a halfway catastrophe.

October 27, 1940

As long as the ghetto is open and there is still a gap, no larger than the eye of a needle, through which we may come in contact with the outside world, the Judenrat has jurisdiction only over internal affairs; from the time when the ghetto is closed, we will become a foreign national organism, separated from the civil life of the nation. We will stop paying taxes to the government, and be exempt from paying rent. "Sinners and criminals" are not obligated to bear the burdens of debt and taxes, because they have been doomed to elimination, and all the arteries of life are stopped up before them. Thus it is that the Judenrat will be the representative of the Jewish people both within and without....

The Judenrat is not the same as our traditional Jewish Community Council, which wrote such brilliant chapters in our history. Strangers in our midst, foreign to our spirit, ... the president of the Judenrat and his advisors are musclemen who were put on our backs by strangers. Most of them are nincompoops whom no one knew in normal times. They were never elected, and would not have dared dream of being elected, as Jewish representatives; had they dared, they would have been defeated. All their lives until now

A Warsaw ghetto *Judenrat* official at work in his office. *(National Museum of American Jewish History/USHMM Photo Archives)*

they were outside the Jewish fold; they did not rejoice in our happiness nor mourn our misfortunes....

November 4, 1940

The face of Warsaw has changed so that no one who knows it would recognize it. People from the outside do not enter now, but if a miracle were to take place and one of its inhabitants who fled returned to the city, he would say, "Can this be Warsaw?"

Not even the Poles are in a hurry to rebuild their ruins. The holes and cracks in the burned and destroyed buildings have been patched up with bricks and lime; the rubble of destruction has been cleared; the broken sidewalks shine. The conquerors boast of the order they have instituted. Yes, the order of a graveyard....

Since the Jewish quarter was established, Jewish Warsaw has become a city unto itself, with characteristics quite different from those of Aryan Warsaw....

Jewish Warsaw has changed for the worse, in the direction of ugliness, tastelessness, and lack of beauty. Here too is a graveyard, only here the skeletons of the dead walk about the streets. They have gathered from all the parts of the country and come to Warsaw. They came empty-handed, broken and crushed, without a penny, without food for a single meal or clothes to cover their nakedness.

November 28, 1940

The ghetto is empty of all Gentiles and has turned into a Jewish kingdom. The police are leaving and the Jewish police will inherit their place. The same applies to the post office; Jews working for the Judenrat will head it and all the jobs will be filled by Jews. An exceptional concession will apparently be made in the case of the tax bureau, and for the public utility departments—if the cruel conquerors do not forbid us to use gas and electricity. In short, [this is] a Jewish state complete in every detail, but a closed, cramped one, imprisoned, mummified within its narrow borders.

December 2, 1940

Life in the ghetto is becoming "normal." The chaos lasted no more than a week. When half a million people are locked in a small cage, faced with hunger, privation, epidemics, atrocities, naturally it causes a stir. Even the conquerors were confused. This is a unique political experiment. The intention was to starve and impoverish us in body and in spirit, to segregate us from the outside world; to undermine our very existence. A great project of this sort demands extraordinary exertions and cannot be brought into effect by words alone. But to our sorrow,

it must be admitted that the tyrants succeeded....
(Kaplan, pp. 202–229)

Aftermath

Chaim A. Kaplan continued writing entries in his diary, faithfully reporting and reflecting on the events of ghetto existence. His last entry was dated August 4, 1942, one of the days the Nazis conducted a mass deportation from the Warsaw ghetto to the extermination camps. The last sentence reads: "When my end comes—what will happen to the diary?" A day or two later, Kaplan and his wife were deported to the death camp at Treblinka. Historians believe Kaplan perished at the camp in December 1942 or January 1943. After the war ended in 1945, Kaplan's diary was discovered inside a kerosene can on a farm outside Warsaw. Kaplan had managed to smuggle out his diary through a Jewish friend, who worked daily at forced labor outside the ghetto. The diary, which resembles the small notebooks used by grade-school children, is one of the few original works of its kind to have survived the Holocaust.

Sources

Books

Kaplan, Chaim A., *Scroll of Agony: The Warsaw Diary of Chaim A. Kaplan,* translated and edited by Abraham I. Katsh, Collier (New York), 1973.

Treseder, Terry Walton, *Hear O Israel: A Story of the Warsaw Ghetto,* Atheneum (New York), 1990.

Zar, Rose, *In the Mouth of the Wolf,* Jewish Publishing Society of America (Philadelphia), 1983.

P R I M A R Y   S O U R C E

Janina David
Excerpt from *A Square of Sky*

Published in 1964

Janina David grew up enjoying all the comforts and pleasures of a middle-class Jewish home with her parents in western Poland, near the German border. With the threat of a German invasion looming in 1939, nine-year-old Janina and her family moved to Warsaw. The family survived devastating German air raids only to find themselves in the grip of the Nazis with the defeat of Poland. Germany annexed the western and northern parts of Poland and called this territory Wartheland. In the southeastern portion of Poland, the Germans formed a civil administration called Generalgouvernement, or General Government. Under the supervision of Governor-General Hans Frank, this area became the designated repository for Jews and all others deemed unfit for Reich citizenship.

Polish Jews had little or no opportunity for escape from the quickly implemented anti-Semitic measures imposed by the Nazi regime. Less than a year after the German invasion of Poland, the Nazis prohibited Jews from leaving the country. Shortly after German occupation, Polish Jews were forced to give up their jobs. The German administration imposed numerous anti-Jewish decrees that robbed both Poles and Jews of their property and assets.

Several million more Jews fell under Nazi rule when Germany invaded the Soviet Union in 1941. The Germans forced the Jews in occupied territories to move into certain sections of towns and cities, creating more than 400 areas known as ghettos or "Jewish residential quarters," located mainly in Poland, but also in the Baltic states (Lithuania,

The "backyards" of the Warsaw ghetto. *(USHMM Photo Archives)*

Latvia, and Estonia) and in the occupied parts of the Soviet Union. Most ghettos were created around existing Jewish neighborhoods, usually those that were run-down. Non-Jewish residents were forcibly evicted before the Jews moved in. The Nazis relied on *Judenräte*, Nazi-sanctioned Jewish councils, to organize the mass moves into the ghettos according to imposed deadlines. Streams of Jews were forced from their homes into miserable, life-threatening conditions in densely crowded buildings and neighborhoods. The Warsaw ghetto, the largest ghetto in occupied Poland, held between 400,000 and 600,000 people, including 100,000 children. An average room in the ghetto had to accommodate eight to fourteen people.

Life in the ghettos meant a daily fight for survival against hunger, contagious diseases, poor sanitation, and other threats. The daily food rations allotted to Jews, less than a third of the quota granted to Germans, were hardly enough to keep them alive, and thousands died. Jews, including children, were forced to find ways to smuggle food into the ghetto in order to survive. It is estimated that during some periods 500 people per week starved to death in the Warsaw ghetto. In addition to hunger, prisoners sometimes froze to death in winter months. Jews living in the Warsaw ghetto are said to have called coal "black pearls." Illness also took its toll. In 1941 16,000 Warsaw ghetto inhabitants died of typhus, a serious disease marked by high fever and a rash. The Nazis rounded up infected persons and killed them or left them to die untreated.

In her personal account *A Square of Sky,* Janina David writes of the unforgettable horror and terror of living in the Nazi-controlled Jewish ghetto of Warsaw. In the following excerpt, David describes her experiences in fall 1940, when the Warsaw ghetto was sealed off from surrounding neighborhoods.

A Square of Sky

November [1940] came, and the gates of the ghetto closed. The trap was sprung. During the last weeks some 140,000 Jews moved into it and the crowding was indescribable. Refugee centres [centers] were set up. Despite the cold weather typhus was spreading, and we wondered what would happen in the spring. But the dominant feeling of those days was fear and depression. There was defeat on the faces of adults, and when I met my friends we avoided the subject. It was too painful and too frightening to admit that our parents and other all-powerful grown-ups were helpless and afraid. It was inadmissable, and yet it was obvious. We did not know how to reconcile the two aspects of the situation.

Privately we assured each other that our parents were staying in the ghettos because at the moment it was the most convenient place for us to be. They could leave when they chose, of course, and no amount of German orders could stop them. And then the look on our parents' faces as they discussed the situation would raise doubts in our minds, doubts which we tried to suppress as soon as they arose, because they threatened our whole universe.

Late in November Father returned home one evening with an unmistakable 'surprise' look on his face. It was the look he had when he was planning a special treat or brought an unexpected present. Standing in the centre [center] of the room, he slowly drew out of his pocket three small packages and dropped them in our laps. We unwrapped the tissue paper. Inside were two cakes of Yardley lavender soap and a bottle of Lavender Water.

We threw ourselves on Father, begging for explanations. We had not seen such luxuries since the war started, and they brought a flood of memories. Scented bathrooms and warm nursery evenings swam in my mind as I pressed my nose to the little cake of soap and sniffed rapturously. Father, enjoying his success, would not at first answer any questions. We had to let him undress and eat his dinner. Then, stretching his legs and lighting a cigarette, he finally condescended to let us into the secret.

'Do you remember Lydia?' he asked, turning to Mother.

She looked puzzled: 'Lydia? No, I don't think so....'

'Oh surely,' Father insisted, 'the wife of your hairdresser, a very tall blond....'

A little light shone in Mother's eyes, and suddenly her face was tense. Lydia did not evoke pleasant memories.

'I met her today,' continued Father, 'here, in the ghetto. You can imagine my surprise. She saw me first, screamed, and threw herself into my arms. Created quite a stir, too. Everybody was staring at us. Me, in my shabby coat and that beautiful woman in her sables, diamonds flashing all over, weeping on my shoulder.'

Father obviously enjoyed the memory and the impression it was having on us.

'What was she doing here?' Mother wanted to know. Her voice was hard. There was no doubt she remembered Lydia well and did not like her at all.

'Oh, visiting someone, I suppose. Anyway, she was very surprised to hear we were here. She said she was sure we were abroad. And she wants to come and see us.'

'What—here?' Mother looked with dismay around her. 'I could never receive her here.'

Father leaned forward, suddenly grave:

'I know how you feel, Celia, but this is important. Lydia's husband is very prosperous. They have one of the biggest hairdressing salons in Warsaw and a Beauty Institute—whatever that may be. Lydia certainly looks like a successful film star. She told me she may be able to help us if we ever wanted to get out of here, and she was certain we shall have to leave quite soon. I have a feeling she knows quite a lot of things which may be useful. It may be a very important contact.'

'Isn't her husband a German? I seem to remember—'

'He was naturalized years ago, and refused to take German nationality when the war started, which speaks for itself.'

'But what will she think of us when she sees this room?'

'She will think the rich Davids have come down in life, which is precisely what has happened. And she may feel quite at home here. She started life in just such a room, only it was in the basement. Her mother ran an agency procuring domestics and such like.... She gave me the soap and lavender water for you and asked to see me tomorrow. Shall I tell her to come here on Sunday?'

Mother sighed, nodding.

On Sunday afternoon Father brought Lydia home, and at first sight of her I ran and buried my face in her coat.

'Love at first sight,' they all laughed as Mother, embarrassed, apologized for my behaviour [behavior] and assured Lydia that I was always very shy with visitors and she didn't know what had got into me.

Lydia was as tall as Father. She stood there in the centre [center] of the room smiling slowly at him as he took her coat. She had a radiant smile, large blue eyes and hair of a most extraordinary honey shade. It was very long and she wore it pinned in intricate coils on the top of her head, like a shining crown. In our dark cavern of a room she glowed like a being from a different world.

'Is this what they all look like, those from the "Outside"?' I wondered, forgetting that only two years ago we too had lived outside and that whatever differences existed between us they were of the spiritual order rather than of the physical.

Waves of scent spread through the room. There were different ones flowing from her hair, her dress and her coat with it silver fox trimming. I buried my nose furtively in the long hair of the animal and remembered immediately when I did just that the last time. There was my parents' bedroom back home, and a black coat trimmed with a silver fox lay in readiness on a chair. Mother was dressing before the long mirror. I was sitting on the floor, stroking the fox and playing with his paws. It gave off a sharp, unfamiliar smell and I couldn't decide whether I liked it or not. The room was filled with Mother's favourite [favorite] scent; it was French and was called 'Mitsouko.' I was given the empty box, brown and gold, to play with and I sat flushed with happiness and admiration as Mother finished her dressing, smoothed the new black dress over her hips and began putting on her jewellrey [jewelry]. One of the rings, a sapphire set in a circle of diamonds, was for me. Mother promised to give it to me when I matriculated. In the meantime she wore it herself, while I contented myself with a tiny sapphire in a gold flower. Originally I had asked for a tin ring with the picture of [popular American child actress] Shirley Temple which all my friends wore. Father would not hear of it, and Mother bought me a gold one instead. I still wanted a ring with Shirley but realized that ... it was not for me.

Hans Frank (1900-1945)

Hans Frank was born in Karlsruhe, a city in southwestern Germany. He served briefly in the German army during World War I (1914–1918), and joined the Nazi storm troopers in 1923. When Frank began practicing law in Munich in 1926, he quickly earned a reputation as the top defense counsel of the Nazi party. He successfully defended Hitler in several hundred legal actions and became Hitler's personal lawyer. After the Nazis took control of the German government in 1933, Hitler rewarded Frank with several prestigious and powerful positions.

Following the invasion of Poland in 1939, Hitler appointed Frank as governor-general of those sections of Poland not incorporated into Germany. In this capacity, Frank destroyed Poland and exploited its people and resources for the German war effort. He confiscated Polish properties and businesses and demolished Polish cultural and scientific institutions. While the citizens of Poland suffered severe food shortages, Frank hosted lavish feasts in the governor's palace in Kraków. He also took valuable art, adding works by Italian master Leonardo da Vinci and Dutch painter Rembrandt van Rijn to his personal collection. Frank ruthlessly terrorized the Poles, and regarded them as slaves for Germany. He especially despised Jews, and vowed to destroy them. By December 1942 more than 85 percent of the Jews in Poland had been sent to death camps.

After the fall of the Third Reich, Frank was arrested and charged with war crimes. He confessed his guilt but also announced his conversion to Catholicism and begged for forgiveness. Found guilty of war crimes and crimes against humanity, he was subsequently hanged at Nuremberg, Germany, on October 16, 1946.

Lydia opened a large box she had brought with her, and waves of Guerlain retreated before the scent of poppy-seed cake. I came back to reality and approached the table.

Mother served 'tea.' I watched our guest politely sipping the hot water coloured [colored] with a few drops of carmelized sugar. This, together with ersatz coffee, was all we could offer.

Conversation was difficult. Lydia could not avoid looking around her and Mother watched her, tight-lipped, resenting every glance.

Father struggled manfully—asking questions, trying to remember old times, but the memories seemed embarrassing to them all. Lydia began talking of recent events, and the tension gradually vanished. She left our town, with her husband and two sons, two years before the war. They established themselves in Warsaw and, from modest beginnings, reached their present success. They lived in a fashionable part of town. Business was expanding. The hairdressing shop now included a beauty salon and a cosmetic store where all foreign makes were still obtainable.

'How?' Mother asked.

'Oh, a trade secret,' laughed Lydia. 'I can't tell you, but if you need anything I can get it for you— French perfume, make-up, soap, everything.'

Mother smiled and shook her head. At the moment she had everything she needed. I thought of the gritty, greyish-green soap and felt disappointed. So we were going to be 'poor but proud.' Good. I buried my face in Lydia's lap and she patted my hair.

'Would you like to come home with me and meet my boys?'

I nodded, speechless.

'Can I have her for Christmas?' Asked Lydia. Mother looked uneasy, thanked her and promised to think it over. It could be dangerous. She wouldn't wish to cause trouble.

'No trouble at all. She will be quite safe with me.'

*Curfew approached, but Lydia appeared uncon-
cerned. She began to talk in earnest now. Why did we
stay in the ghetto? Why did we allow ourselves to be
trapped? How could we live in these conditions?*

*'I don't mean this room,' she added quickly, see-
ing Mother blush. 'I mean the whole thing—the
overcrowding, the epidemics, the walls. And the danger. Don't you know that you are here like rats in a
trap? The Germans have a definite plan. They won't
let you stay here to die peacefully of typhus. They will
put an end to the whole thing, and pretty soon. You
must get out!'*

Father shook his head:

*'Dear Lydia, you are quite right and we agree. But
we can't get out. To do this we would need a fortune.
False papers cost a lot. And then one must live. And if
we were caught or recognized we should need another
fortune to pay off blackmailers. You don't seem to
understand that we have no money at all. If we had a
little more we wouldn't be living in this hovel!'*

*Lydia looked incredulous. 'But you—why, Mark,
you were millionaires, you couldn't have lost it all?'*

*Father shrugged his shoulders. 'We weren't as
rich as you think, and anyway most of our wealth*

*was in real estate. All that is German now. Other
things were lost in bombing here in Warsaw, and in
requisitions back home. Lots of smaller things, jew-
ellery [jewelry] and such, Sophie lost at the frontier
when she tried to smuggle it through. And we are living on the remainder. I am not earning enough to
keep us, even here.'*

Lydia shook her head, her eyes wide with disbelief.

*'We shall have to do something about you,' she
decided, putting her coat on. It was long past curfew
and Father expressed his concern.*

*She smiled and patted his shoulder. 'Don't you
worry. I have a pass. I shall be quite safe.'*

*She allowed him to take her to the gate, where
she waved something at the gendarme and crossed to
the 'other side.'*

*We were too excited to sleep much that night.
The room was full of wonderful, expensive scents, the
poppy-seed cake was still on the table and I thought,
as my eyes slowly closed, that fairy godmothers really
existed and the world was not so hopelessly bad after
all. (David, pp. 121–125)*

Aftermath

As the liquidation of the ghettos began in spring 1942, prisoners were transported by freight trains and trucks to six main extermination camps in Poland: Chelmno, Treblinka, Sobibór, Belzec, Auschwitz, and Majdanek-Lublin. Once the deportees arrived at the camps, most were killed on the spot with poisonous gas. This killing process soon spread to other Nazi-occupied countries, such as the Netherlands, Greece, Czechoslovakia, Romania, and Hungary. Most of the Jewish people living in Denmark and Bulgaria, however, managed to survive under the protection of the local population.

As rumors and reports of deportations from other ghettos reached Warsaw, tension and fear grew among the hopelessly trapped Jews. In a night raid in the Warsaw ghetto on April 18, 1942, police broke into apartments, hauled off victims according to a prepared list, and shot them nearby. Fifty-two people were killed that night, which came to be known as "Bloody Night." According to

underground Jewish leaders, the purpose of these raids was to instill terror among the ghetto population and eliminate the people most likely to lead organized resistance.

From July to September 1942, during the first wave of deportations from the Warsaw ghetto, more than 265,000 Jews were sent to the extermination camp Treblinka. When the second wave of deportations began, on January 18, 1943, the Germans met resistance. Refusing to assemble as ordered, some Jewish people went into hiding while others engaged in hand-to-hand fighting with the Germans. On April 19, the eve of Passover (a Jewish holiday commemorating the liberation of the Hebrews from slavery in Egypt), German military forces assembled to attempt the final liquidation of the ghetto. The remaining Jews organized an extensive operation involving a network of bunkers beneath the buildings. Members of underground organizations managed to obtain limited weapons and were prepared to fight. The

Jews of the Warsaw ghetto held out for a month of fighting but finally yielded to the raging fires set by Nazi forces. By mid-May 1943, the Warsaw ghetto was liquidated. The Warsaw ghetto revolt became a legend throughout Poland and Europe, inspiring Jews and non-Jews alike.

Janina David's parents managed to smuggle her out of the ghetto on January 18, 1943, the day the second wave of deportations began. As thirteen-year-old David was leaving in the early morning hours, her mother gave her a gold medallion engraved with the Hebrew name for God, *Shadai*. She rode with her father in a truck transporting laborers to their jobs outside the camp. When the truck arrived in a residential section of Warsaw, David's father lifted her over the side rail and placed her on the sidewalk. Paralyzed with sorrow and shock, she watched as the truck pulled away. A family friend then escorted her to Lydia's home, where she met Lydia's two sons and struggled to pretend everything was normal. In 1946, after the

deaths of her parents in the Holocaust, she left Poland to spend two years in an international orphanage in Paris. She then emigrated to Australia, where she obtained citizenship just before her eighteenth birthday. Working in factories to support herself, David won a state scholarship and graduated from Melbourne University. In 1958 she settled in London, where she worked as a social worker in a hospital.

SOURCES

Books

David, Janina, *A Square of Sky,* Norton (New York), 1964.

Eisner, Jack, *The Survivor,* William Morrow (New York), 1980.

Orlev, Uri, *The Island on Bird Street,* translated from Hebrew by Hillel Halkin, Houghton Mifflin (Boston), 1984.

P R I M A R Y   S O U R C E

Wladyslaw Bartoszewski
Excerpt from *The Warsaw Ghetto: A Christian's Testimony*
Translated by Stephen G. Cappellari
Published in 1987

Several million Jews lived in Poland at the outbreak of World War II, about 10 percent of the total population. After the German invasion and occupation in 1939, Polish Jews were expelled from Wartheland, the area of Poland incorporated into Germany. In the remaining portion, called the Generalgouvernement, or General Government, the Nazis concentrated Jews in ghettos. By the end of 1941, the Nazis began constructing a series of extermination camps in Poland built specifically for systematic mass murder. As these camps became operational, Jewish prisoners were deported by train from the ghettos and told they were participating in "resettlement" programs. In reality, the Nazis were transporting Jewish Poles— and eventually Jews from other countries—to specially designed gas chambers for extermination.

Many factors made it difficult for non-Jewish Poles to help Jews. Separated by walls and Nazi guards, inhabitants of the Jewish ghettos could not easily interact with those Poles living in "Aryan" sections. Since anti-Semitism was widespread in Polish society, Jews could not automatically trust their fellow compatriots. In addition, the Nazis killed not only those people who hid Jews, but also all others found in the house. As the Nazis intensified their efforts to eliminate Polish Jews, however, many non-Jewish Poles attempted to help Jews by offering refuge in private homes. Historians estimate that as much as 2.5 percent of the Aryan population, 160,000 to 360,000 people, gave assistance to Jews in eastern Poland. Relief efforts took place in two main areas: Kraków and Warsaw, where 20,000 to 30,000 Jews were in hiding. As the Ger-

A view of the Warsaw ghetto in summer 1941. *(Photograph by Willy Georg, courtesy of USHMM Photo Archives)*

man occupation expanded and violence toward the Jews escalated, underground organizations were formed to provide aid throughout Poland. These organizations, which included trade unions, religious groups, and political parties, coordinated aid through a central group called Zegota, the code name for the Council for Aid to Jews.

In operation from December 1942 to January 1945, Zegota was the only relief organization that was run jointly by Jews and non-Jews. Its board included members of five Polish and two Jewish political movements, from a widely varied political spectrum. Members of Zegota used various methods to obtain or manufacture tens of thousands of forged Aryan documents, including birth and marriage certificates and employment papers, which they gave free of charge to Jews remaining in Poland. Zegota also placed some 2,500 Jewish children in special public orphanages, frequently run by convents, and helped connect Jews who needed medical care with a secret network of trusted doctors. After repeated attempts, Zegota successfully convinced the Polish government-in-exile to issue formal appeals to the Polish population at large, urging them to give aid to the Jews.

Wladyslaw Bartoszewski was one of many Catholic Poles who assisted Jews during the Holocaust. Along with several hundred other people, he had been arrested by the Nazis in 1940 during a large-scale operation against members of Polish intellectual circles. After spending nearly a year in Auschwitz as a political prisoner, Bartoszewski returned to the city of Warsaw to find a newly created Jewish ghetto enclosed by a wall about ten feet (three meters) high. His stay at Auschwitz convinced him of the importance of aiding victims of Nazi terror.

Bartoszewski started assisting Jews living in hiding in winter 1941–1942. He obtained false documents for Jews in the Warsaw area that provided them with "Aryan" identities. He worked closely with many people in the resistance movement, including Zofia Kossak-Szatkowska and Wanda Krahelska-Filipowicz—two women who helped create the Provisional Committee for Aid to Jews in September 1942. In December 1942 this committee became the Council for Aid to Jews, also known as Zegota. As a member of the Zegota board, Bartoszewski represented an underground group of young Catholics called *Front Odrodzenia Polski,* or Front for Poland's Renewal.

In his book *The Warsaw Ghetto: A Christian's Testimony,* Bartoszewski wrote about his experiences as a Christian Pole who dared to help Jews. The following excerpt begins with a description of his early attempts to provide aid and ends with an account of the Warsaw ghetto uprising, which began on April 19, 1943, on the eve of Passover, and was the first urban uprising in German-occupied Europe.

Wladyslaw Bartoszewski:
The Warsaw Ghetto: A Christian's Testimony

Early in the summer of 1941 I returned to Warsaw with several hundred other men who had been released from Auschwitz. I had been arrested in 1940 during the course of a large-scale operation directed against the intelligentsia of Warsaw and taken to the camp where I was detained as a political prisoner, with the "protective custody inmate" number 4427. At the time I was just nineteen years old. But I was soon to gather experiences bitter beyond any that I had known, even though this was a time when there were as yet no gas chambers and mass executions— only "normal" deaths from exhaustion brought about by excessive work, unimaginable hunger, and brutal beatings. Before my arrest I was an employee

of the Polish Red Cross in occupied Warsaw. The problems of charity work and of aiding people who had suffered the ravages of war were thus not unknown to me. In the camp, where I saw and experienced the deepest human misery, I developed the conviction that helping the victims of Nazi terror was of the utmost importance.

Prior to my internment in Auschwitz there was no ghetto in my home town. The encirclement of a section of Warsaw with a wall three meters high and the forced resettlement of a half a million people behind it were the most significant changes I encountered there upon my return. In the Christian Polish community, on the "Aryan" side of the wall, several thousand Jews, perhaps more than ten thousand, lived illegally. They needed birth certificates and certificates of baptism issued in "Aryan" names, forged work permits and identification papers, a roof over their heads, and often financial support as well. My first attempt to help those living underground (this was during the winter months of 1941/42) involved obtaining documents for people I did not know personally, but only from a photograph attached to the documents. At the time, my most important source of free documents was my friend Zbigniew Karnibad, a medical student my own age, who worked in an illegal cell involved in manufacturing forged documents for a section of the Home Army. At the time many members of the various underground organizations as well as Catholic priests were involved in aiding Jews hidden in and around Warsaw and in forging documents. In mid 1942 I established contact with two people, both respected in prewar Poland, who were active in completely different ideological-political areas. One of them, Zofia Kossak-Szatkowska, a Catholic author well known throughout Europe, had been living in Warsaw illegally since the beginning of the Nazi occupation and was wanted by the Gestapo for her anti-Nazi views, which she held before the war; the other, Wanda Krahelska-Filipowicz, was close to socialist circles during her student years and, as a young student before World War I, was responsible for the famous bomb attack on the Russian governor of Warsaw, General Skallon. For many months the two had been heading a secret rescue operation of refugees from the ghetto, mainly for women and children, in which they provided material goods, documents, and shelter. Their large circle of friends and their social standing helped them greatly in this endeavor. They devoted themselves to the underground whole-heartedly and gladly welcomed anyone who was willing to risk participation in their undertaking. I began working with Zofia Kossak immediately, and from that point on I frequently played the role of intermediary between her and various persons, Polish Christians as well as Jews, with whom she cooperated. It was my responsibility to deliver documents and money and, if necessary, warnings.

At the beginning of 1943 those of us in Warsaw did not have the slightest idea that we would soon be witnesses to the hitherto most heroic and stunning event in the history of the resistance to the occupying forces in Poland: the armed April revolt of the Warsaw ghetto.

On 13 March shots were once again fired in the streets of the Warsaw ghetto: a Jewish combat group was offering armed resistance to the police and to members of the German Industrial Protection Unit engaged in looting. In retribution, the SS mowed down several dozen people on the street. The command of the Jewish Combat Organization in the ghetto posted flyers during the night of 14/15 March informing the population of a new "action" being planned.

We soon found out that the tragic fate of the Jewish community in Krakow had been sealed on 13 March. There were still about 10,000 people living in the ghetto there who had survived the June and October 1942 "resettlements" to the extermination camps. Now some of them—those who had been declared able-bodied—were killed on the spot or sent to their deaths in Auschwitz; some were taken to the camp in Plaszow near Krakow, where they were forced into slave labor that ultimately proved fatal. Only a few individuals were saved. These survivors had been sheltered by Christian Poles in Krakow and its surroundings with the help of Christian friends or by establishing contacts with the Council of Aid to Jews in Krakow. Dr. Julian Aleksandrowicz, an outstanding hematologist, was one of those who managed to escape from the Krakow ghetto during those critical days in March. He later participated in the fight against the Germans as a member of the Home Army. He is now an academic known throughout Europe and professor emeritus at the hospital for Internal Medicine at the Krakow Medical Academy.

The alarming news from Krakow increased the anxiety of those of us in Warsaw. In view of our experiences during the past few years we were well aware of the fact that Berlin's centrally coordinated extermination campaigns were guided by an ulterior criminal purpose and that the Warsaw ghetto, which still had 70,000 inhabitants, would soon be a target. But the members of the two Jewish combat groups, the Jewish Combat Organization and the Jewish Military Association, were not wasting any time: the network of bunkers and fortifications was expanded systematically; considerable numbers of Molotov cocktails and hand grenades were manufactured according to the guidelines supplied by the Polish Home Army.

The spring of 1943 came early. April was mild and generally warm, and there was relatively heavy traffic on the streets of Warsaw. The Easter holidays were imminent, as was Passover. On Palm Sunday, 18 April 1943, rumors spread through Warsaw that a large police action was to take place in the ghetto during the next few hours. The rumors were underscored by, among other things, a considerable

The bodies of Jewish resistance fighters, shot by the SS during the Warsaw Ghetto Uprising, are left in a pile of rubble. *(National Archives/USHMM Photo Archives)*

concentration of the collaborating Ukrainian-Latvian support units in the city. In the evening, shortly before the curfew for Christian Poles, I went to the vicinity of the ghetto wall and noted an increased number of police patrols, which were also immediately noticed by the vigilant reconnaissance troops of the Jewish Combat Organization in the ghetto. They alarmed the combat groups, who took up their positions during the same night; the majority of the civilian population hid in their cellars.

"No one got any sleep during the night from Sunday to Monday," a participant in the events, an official of the Jewish National Committee, recalls in a report published in June of 1943 in the underground Catholic monthly Prawda:

"The combat groups posted sentries. The civilian population retreated into shelters, cellars, or upper floors. The apartments were empty. The first reports of the observers came in: the walls of the ghetto were surrounded by German troops. So it was *an action."*

Several hours later, at daybreak of 19 April ... 850 SS troops and sixteen officers of the Waffen-SS marched into the ghetto protected by tanks and two armored cars. They moved along Nalewki Street—the main artery of the Jewish residential area—in the

direction of the center of the ghetto. After they had gone a few hundred meters they had already encountered unexpected resistance: young members of the Jewish Combat Organization threw hand grenades and Molotov cocktails out of the windows of the adjoining houses. One of the tanks was hit and went up in flames; twelve Nazis were killed on the street, and the SS column hurriedly retreated from the ghetto. The Germans resumed the fight again after two hours, this time with greater caution and larger forces, SS brigade commander [Jürgen Stroop], the major general of the police, took over the command....

United by a common and deeply felt sorrow, every piece of bad news from the other side of the wall touched us profoundly. Discussions of various unrealistic possibilities to save the combatants filled us with new illusions. The conditions under which we ourselves lived precluded any possibility of aid— to help was not in our power. Accordingly, we thought our most important task was to transmit news to the West regularly to keep it informed about the events in Warsaw. In addition, we attempted systematically to influence Christian Polish public opinion to win over as many people as possible who might assume the great risk of offering help and shelter to refugees. We tried to exert influence through personal contacts as well as through the underground press. We stressed the important historical and moral meaning of the ghetto uprising: this was, after all, the first rebellion of a city in the history of the European resistance movement, the first mutinous battle in the center of a major city where there was a contingent of several tens of thousands of German troops. And finally, this uprising was also a turning point in the history of the Jewish people under the occupation, a phenomenon that even surpassed the goals and expectations of the organizers and leaders of the fight themselves. I can still clearly remember the impression that [Mordecai] Anielewicz's letter made on us. It was written on 23 April 1943, the fifth day of the fighting in the ghetto, and was addressed to his representative and friend Jitzchak Cukierman, then in the "Aryan" sector. Berman translated the letter into Polish for us:

"What we are experiencing surpasses our most daring hopes. The Germans fled from the ghetto

twice.... The most important thing is this: the dream of my life has been fulfilled—I am experiencing Jewish self-defense in the Warsaw ghetto in all its pride and glory."

The underground newspapers somberly directed the attention of the Christian Polish population to the heroism of the fighting Jews and appealed for its support. On 5 May 1943, while the fighting in Warsaw was still going on, the then prime minister of the Polish government in exile, General Sikorski, gave a speech on London radio and emphasized:

"We are witnesses to the greatest crime in human history. We know that you are giving all the help you can to the tortured Jews. For that, my countrymen, I thank you in my own name and in that of the government of Poland. I ask you to continue to grant them any conceivable help and at the same time to put a stop to this inhuman cruelty." (Bartoszewski, pp. 42–80)

Aftermath

Mass deportations of Jews from the Warsaw ghetto began on July 22, 1942. By September, 300,000 Jews had been rounded up, 265,000 of those going directly to the Treblinka death camp. Some 60,000 Jews remained in the ghetto, anxiously anticipating another transport. In January 1943, when the Germans started the next wave of deportations, they met with armed resistance for the first time. Since the Nazis captured only 5,000 to 6,000 Jews, the ghetto inmates saw their display of armed resistance as a victory that prevented the complete liquidation of the entire population. However, historians in the postwar era have determined that the Nazis only intended a partial deportation in the second wave. Nonetheless, the remaining Jews began to gather arms for the next and final wave of deportations, determined to fight until death.

After the success of this initial display of force, many Jews who had previously refrained from any violent action began to support resistance groups within the ghetto. On April 19, 1943, on the eve of Passover, the Nazis entered the ghetto intending to round up all remaining Jews for a final deportation. This time they met with considerable resistance, which led to the month-long Warsaw ghetto uprising. The total fighting force within the ghetto

numbered about 750, including young men armed with pistols, home-made fire bombs, and hand grenades supplied by non-Jewish resisters from outside the ghetto.

Despite being heavily outmatched, the Jewish resistance fighters managed to push back the Nazi forces. On the first day of the uprising, German losses totaled twelve soldiers, one tank, and two armored vehicles. Following several days of street fighting, the Germans resorted to burning the ghetto one building at a time to flush out their quarry. After nearly four weeks of fighting, resistance forces fell and the ghetto itself was burned. Nazi reports indicated that 56,065 Jews had been "destroyed." As the first urban rebellion against the Nazis, the Warsaw ghetto uprising provided inspiration to Jews and non-Jews alike throughout German-occupied Europe.

Thereafter, Christian Poles and other resisters escalated their fight against the Nazis. The Zegota organization continued to operate, sheltering Jews who managed to escape the ghetto as well as those who had been in hiding since the German invasion. The Polish Home Army continued to resist the Nazis at every opportunity, and in 1944 led an armed uprising that raged for several months in Warsaw. After the Germans overcame the resistance fighters, they burned and razed the city. Warsaw was completely destroyed. Some 170,000 Poles perished during the uprising, and 165,000 surviving residents were sent to concentration camps or drafted for slave labor.

Bartoszewski remained active in the resistance movement throughout the war, acting as a "Delegatura," or underground representative for the Polish government-in-exile in England, keeping officials informed about events in Warsaw and Poland. Following the war, he became a scholar and prolific author and served for many years on the faculty of the Catholic University of Lublin in eastern Poland. His studies and writings on the Nazi occupation of Poland, particularly the Warsaw uprisings, are now considered among the most accurate accounts available. In 1963 Bartoszewski was honored by Yad Vashem in Jerusalem as "Righteous Among the Nations"

for his efforts to save Jews in Poland during World War II.

SOURCES

Books

Bartoszewski, Wladyslaw, *The Warsaw Ghetto: A Christian's Testimony,* originally published in 1983, English translation by Stephen G. Cappellari, Beacon Press (Boston), 1987.

Fluek, Toby Knobel, *Memories of My Life in a Polish Village, 1930–1949,* Random House (New York), 1990.

Gelman, Charles, *Do Not Go Gentle: A Memoir of Jewish Resistance in Poland, 1941–1945,* Archon (Hamden, CT), 1989.

Pretzel, M. M., *Portrait of a Young Forger: An Incredible True Story of Triumph over the Third Reich,* Knightsbridge Publishing Co. (New York), 1990.

7

The Expansion of War

After the fall of France in June 1940, Great Britain remained the only major power fighting Germany until the Nazis invaded the Soviet Union on June 22, 1941. Great Britain was not, however, completely alone: Canada, Australia, New Zealand, and South Africa, all former colonies of Britain, declared war on Germany in summer 1940 and became part of the Allied forces. These nations contributed soldiers who fought in their own units throughout the war, as well as money, food, and industrial products. Troops from current British colonies, especially India, also played a major role in the fighting and were included in British regiments. The United States also contributed much assistance to the British war effort. Though the United States was still neutral, a majority of Americans had favored the Allies from the beginning of the war, a sentiment that only intensified after the defeat of France, when a German victory seemed imminent. In autumn 1940 a public opinion poll found that 75 percent of the American people wanted to provide assistance to Britain; 83 percent, however, did not want the United States to enter the conflict.

Isolationism and the Atlantic Charter

Isolationism had been the traditional American policy from the United States' declaration of independence from Great Britain in the late eigh-

teenth century. An overwhelming majority of Americans believed the United States should stay out of Europe's quarrels, a policy violated in 1917 when the United States joined Britain and France to fight against Germany in World War I (1914–1918). Many Americans came to believe that entry into that conflict had been a mistake that cost the United States thousands of lives and millions of dollars, but did nothing to alleviate the problems that generated the conflict. Proponents of isolationism claimed that America, protected by two great oceans, should stay out of Europe's troubles. Isolationist sentiments were popular during the 1920s and early 1930s, but Adolf Hitler's rise in Germany altered American public opinion. The Nazi ban on other political parties and labor unions, along with their brutal methods and campaign against the Jews, disturbed many Americans. As Nazism and similar political systems came to power and destroyed democracy in one European country after another, more Americans began to feel these developments threatened their own freedom. Still, despite trepidation about events in Europe, isolationism remained an important political force in the United States. The isolationist "America First" organization, founded in September 1940, had 850,000 members. Isolationists included respected figures like Charles Lindbergh, who had become a national hero after completing the first solo nonstop flight across the Atlantic. Some isolationists admired Nazi Germany and

Indian Troops Help Great Britain

Great Britain's colonies helped the nation after it declared war on the Axis Powers. One of the regiments that participated in the African campaign was the Royal Bombay Sappers and Miners from India. The job of the sappers and miners was to locate and disarm land mines.

Second Lieutenant Premindra Singh Bhagat commanded a unit of the sappers and miners in 1941. Bhagat's unit moved in advance of the Allies, clearing 15 mine-fields over a 44-mile stretch. The sappers used large, mobile carriers to move carefully across the minefields placed in the shifting sands of the Ethiopian desert. Often times, the sappers crawled on the ground, probing the sands with bayonets. One false move could mean a man's life. When a mine was located, it was disarmed. The sappers worked for four days, from daybreak until nightfall, clearing the way for the advancing Allied troops. For his efforts, Bhagat received Britain's Victoria Cross.

Troops from countries that were once British colonies, like Canada and Australia, as well as troops from countries still ruled by Britain, like these Indian soldiers fighting in Italy in 1943, played a major role in the war. *(Reproduced by permission of AP/Wide World Photos)*

opposed American involvement for this reason. However, pro-Nazi sentiments were never a major force in the United States.

U.S. President Franklin D. Roosevelt understood the conflicting sentiments of the American public.

He declared that the United States would be "the Arsenal of Democracy," and use its industrial power to provide arms, but not troops, to the Allies. The fall of France left Britain in a tenuous situation, and the need for American assistance became increasingly urgent. Britain had no petroleum or rubber and only

Selective Service officers in Washington twirl a glass cage as they prepare a draft lottery in Washington. Once the 7,000 capsules are thoroughly mixed up, some of them will be pulled to see who will be conscripted into military service. *(Reproduced by permission of AP/Wide World Photos)*

a few metals besides iron. It was able to grow only half the food needed by its people, and American shipments of wheat, meat, and other food were as important as tanks and cannons—by 1941 almost 30 percent of Britain's food came from the United States. These factors made Britain more dependent on imports than almost any other country.

American aid to Britain went beyond food, however. In September 1940 the United States gave Britain fifty outdated American destroyers—warships often used to escort and defend merchant ships in convoy missions. In return, Britain gave the United States the right to station American naval bases on various British-controlled islands near the United States. By providing these naval stations, the British secured the safety of areas that were previously unprotected because British naval forces were fully engaged in the conflict with Germany elsewhere. The agreement also helped connect the British and American defense efforts in the minds of many Americans, as did a North American defense agreement between the United States and Canada, Britain's ally. By signing these agreements with Britain and Canada, the United States committed itself to the Allies in the event the Germans carried the war across the Atlantic.

In summer 1940 Congress voted to increase the budget for construction of American warships, which when built would double the size of the U.S. Navy. In September, the United States began drafting men into the army—the first peacetime draft of troops in American history—and supplied this enlarged standing army with modern weapons. In March 1941 Congress passed the Lend-Lease agreement, which was a complicated document allowing the British to buy American goods and weapons on credit, to be repaid after the conclusion of the war. The law did not specifically name the countries that were to benefit from it, which allowed Roosevelt later to extend Lend-Lease to other countries. Within a year, substantial amounts of aid were also being sent to the Soviet Union. The agreement was of great assistance to the British, whose financial resources had been stripped by the war. Within weeks of the agreement, Congress voted that the first installment of Lend-Lease would be 7 billion dollars. Knowing that Britain would be unable to repay the debt if it lost the war, the United States was essentially wagering billions of dollars on a British victory.

Only a few weeks after Congress passed the Lend-Lease law, Roosevelt expanded the "American Security Zone" to include much of the Atlantic

Did President Roosevelt Want War?

Historians debate the motives behind some of President Franklin D. Roosevelt's decisions regarding U.S. involvement in World War II prior to the Japanese attack on Pearl Harbor. Many of his opponents, and even some of his supporters, believed he secretly wanted the United States to go to war against Germany but knew the American people and Congress would oppose involvement. Some proponents of this argument claim Roosevelt did everything possible to force Germany to attack the United States. For example, in spring 1941, he ordered the American navy to protect British ships. In September 1941, three months before the United States officially entered the war, he ordered American warships to fire on any German submarine seen in the United States' "Atlantic Security Zone." If, as a result of these actions, U.S. ships were sunk and American sailors killed, the American people might be much more willing to declare war on Germany. Other historians point to evidence, including conversations not made public at the time, that Roosevelt would do everything possible, including risking war with Germany, to prevent the Nazis from winning. However, thinking he might yet be able to keep the country out of war, Roosevelt did not ask Congress to declare war when German submarines sank American warships while the United States was still neutral. Even after the Japanese bombed Pearl Harbor on December 7, 1941, the United States did not initiate war against Germany; instead, Germany released a declaration of war against the United States.

Ocean. Within this zone, the U.S. Navy would protect American merchant ships, including those carrying weapons for Britain, and would report the presence of all German ships to the British navy. By May, American warships were escorting convoys of U.S. ships to Britain. Beginning in June 1941, British merchant ships were allowed to sail in American convoys, thus placing them under the protection of the U.S. Navy.

In August 1941 Roosevelt and British Prime Minister Winston Churchill met aboard a warship off the coast of Newfoundland (then a British colony; now part of Canada) in the North Atlantic, the first in a series of personal meetings that would continue until Roosevelt's death almost four years later. In private, Roosevelt reaffirmed his "Germany first" strategy, encouraging the concentration of Allied military forces against the Germans before moving on to defeat other Axis powers. But the public result of the meeting was a joint British-American declaration known as the Atlantic Charter. The document committed Britain and the United States to oppose territorial change unless it was the "freely expressed" desire of the people involved. The statement represented a promise to restore the European

borders altered by Germany, but also appeared to support independence for the Asian and African colonies of European powers such as Britain, France, and the Netherlands, if the natives of the colonies desired it. The issue of colonialism was a basic disagreement between Britain, a major colonial power, and the United States, where the president and a majority of the population were hostile to the colonial system their country had fought against in the American Revolution (1775–1783). Critics have often argued that the United States opposed colonies because it could influence and dominate other countries through its economic power, rendering colonies unnecessary, and they cite U.S. influence in Latin America as an example. Whether this was the reasoning behind American policy or not, public opinion supported colonized countries' efforts to achieve independence. At the time, India, the largest and most important British colony, had an organized and influential independence movement, and, of all British political leaders, Churchill was the most strongly opposed to Indian independence.

In April 1941 the United States signed an agreement with the Danish ambassador in Washington, D.C., that called for the two countries to

South African soldiers served with British Imperial Forces during World War II. *(Reproduced by permission of AP/Wide World Photos)*

defend the large island of Greenland, a Danish possession off the northeast coast of Canada. As Denmark was under military occupation by Germany, the agreement actually meant the United States would defend Greenland in the event of a German attempt to use it as a base to attack British ships. Soon afterward, a unit of U.S. Marines replaced British forces in Iceland, an island country in the North Atlantic, for the same purpose.

These measures were all part of the Battle of the Atlantic. As vital food and weapons were shipped from the United States to Britain, German submarines known as U-boats (because of the German word for submarine, *Unterseeboot*) lay in wait in the Atlantic. The German navy relied on submarines because it had relatively few warships, and these were hunted down and destroyed by the British. In the last eight months of 1941, U-boats sank 328 British merchant ships, approximately one and one-half times the number of ships that Britain could build in a year. If the U-boats had

continued at this rate, the Germans would have won the Battle of the Atlantic and the British people would have starved. The British and Canadian navies (and, increasingly, the American navy) took measures to protect the ships, only to be met with U-boat countermeasures. While the Allies utilized the convoy system to protect their ships, for example, the Germans began attacking with large groups of U-boats, known as wolf packs. The advantage shifted back and forth as both sides added technical improvements, such as being able to intercept and decode radio messages sent by the enemy. Perhaps the most important factor in the battle was the ability of American industry to produce more ships than anyone had imagined possible. A prime example was a standard freighter called the Liberty ship, which took an average of only three months to build. In October 1942 three completed Liberty ships left American shipyards every day. Although U-boats sank dozens of Allied freighters in a month, the number of ships successfully crossing to Britain continued to rise.

Rows of Liberty ships in a California shipyard. *(National Archives and Records Administration)*

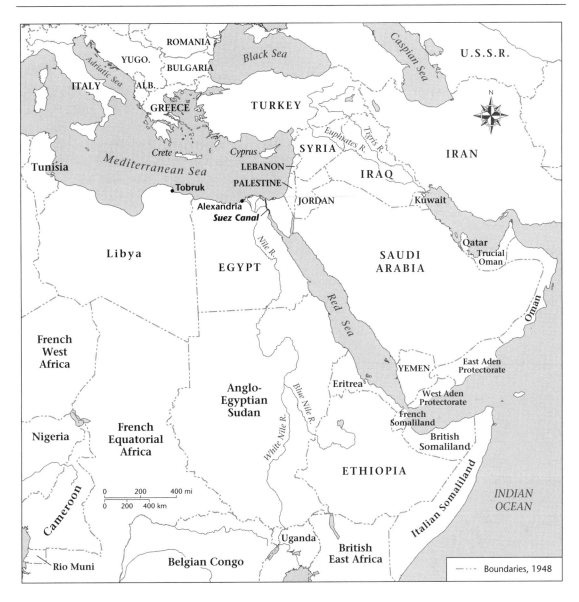

A successful Italian invasion of Egypt threatened the Suez Canal, an important shortcut for British ships traveling to and from the Indian Ocean.

The German submarines had a strategic edge when they attacked underwater, being able to fire torpedos from below the surface. Warships protecting the convoys were equipped with electronic devices to find submarines, but were unable to measure how far below the surface they were, so the depth charges, or underwater bombs, deployed by the warships often exploded too far above or below the U-boat to inflict serious damage. The primary difficulty faced by the German navy was the lengthy span of time required to recharge a vessel's batteries, which had to be done on the surface. Surfacing left U-boats susceptible to attack by airplanes, a vulnerability the Germans attempted to remedy by surfac-

ing at night. The British, and the Americans, after they entered the war, used radar and improved searchlights on long-range bombers to find and destroy an increasing number of U-boats. As American production of these bombers increased, the U-boats began to lose the battle. By May 1943 Germany was losing submarines twice as fast as it could build new ones, forcing the German navy to stop sending U-boats into the Atlantic. Almost 2,500 Allied merchant ships and 175 warships were sunk during the Battle of the Atlantic, and approximately 700 of 830 U-boats were destroyed. Of the 40,000 men in German U-boat crews, more than 25,000 were killed and another 5,000 were taken prisoner.

The Italian Failure in East Africa

In August 1940, an Italian army captured the undefended British colony of Somaliland (part of present-day Somalia). The Italians already controlled part of Somaliland as an Italian colony and all of Ethiopia, which they had invaded and conquered in 1935. While Mussolini's dream of an African empire at first appeared to be a realistic goal, Italian success in Africa was short-lived. In February 1941, a British force consisting mostly of Indian troops moved south from the Sudan, and another force (mainly South Africans but also including Kenyans and Nigerians) moved north from Kenya. (The British controlled Sudan, Kenya, and far-off Nigeria.) A third group, landing from the sea, recaptured British Somaliland. The Allied forces quickly captured Italian Somaliland and moved into Ethiopia as large numbers of Ethiopians, who opposed Italy, began a campaign of guerrilla warfare. Although there was some heavy fighting, the Italians were poorly equipped and had no way to get supplies from home. By May, the entire Italian army in East Africa, more than 70,000 men, had surrendered to the Allies.

During the fighting in Africa, British soldiers patrol the sands of the Libyan desert in tanks. (*Library of Congress*)

The War in the Desert

As the U-boats attempted to intercept American shipments of supplies to Britain, land battles began to intensify. The North African country of Libya had been a colony of Italy, Germany's most important ally, since 1912, and 200,000 Italian soldiers were stationed there. In September 1940 Italian dictator Benito Mussolini ordered this army to cross the border eastward into British-controlled

Axis Distrust

Italy's decision to invade Greece without informing Germany was not atypical for the Axis partners. Italian leadership, including Benito Mussolini, believed Germany treated Italy as a conquered territory rather than as an ally. The Germans rarely divulged their plans to the Italians, and German generals openly held a low opinion of the Italian military. The Italian army was almost always ill-equipped, and had faulty leadership. Italian soldiers had little confidence in their leaders. For these reasons, a minor setback often caused the troops to lose their willingness to fight, and could turn a battle into a major defeat. An increasing number of Italians, including soldiers, opposed Italy's participation in the war, which seemed beneficial only to the Germans. As more Italians died or were captured, Mussolini's popularity faded. Insufficient joint planning among the Axis powers (including Japan, later) differed greatly from the close cooperation that developed between the British and Americans.

General Erwin Rommel, the "Desert Fox," in North Africa. (*National Archives and Records Administration*)

Egypt. Although the Italians stopped after sixty miles and prepared defensive positions, the invasion greatly worried the British. A successful Italian invasion of Egypt would threaten access to the Suez Canal in the northeast region of the country. Loss of the canal would require ships launched from the Indian Ocean, and destined for Britain via the Mediterranean Sea, to travel around Africa, increasing both travel time and fuel consumption. Even more important than the canal were the oil fields of Iraq and Arabia, located beyond Egypt.

One of the Axis powers' greatest weaknesses was that they had few safe supplies of oil—Libyan oil not yet having been discovered.

In December 1940 the greatly outnumbered British surprised the Italians by launching an attack. The Italians retreated and were chased by the British 400 miles into Libya. By the time the retreat ended in February 1941, the British had captured 130,000 Italian troops. Fighting in this area presented strategical concerns, with the nar-

A German anti-aircraft gun on the lower slopes of the Acropolis in Athens, with the ancient Greek temple, the Parthenon, seen in the background. *(Reproduced by permission of AP/Wide World Photos)*

row strip of land between the Mediterranean Sea to the north and an almost impassable desert to the south offering only one real road. Supplies and reinforcements for both armies came by sea, which actually provided the retreating side with the tactical advantage of being closer to the ports where it received supplies. Each success increased the danger that the other side would be able to launch a successful counterattack, a pattern that was repeated from December 1940 until October 1942.

Mussolini was reluctant to admit he needed help after the disastrous defeat of the Italian army, but he finally agreed to allow a German force to land in Libya in a bid to salvage the situation. The Germans were led by General Erwin Rommel, one of the most successful German Panzer commanders during the conquest of France. Although the force was mainly composed of Italians, Rommel's German troops (known as the Afrika Korps) were soon popular heroes in Germany. Known as the "Desert Fox," Rommel became the German general most admired at home and most feared by the Allies. In March 1941 he attacked the British and, within a few weeks, forced them back to where they had been

in December. A British counterattack failed, but a second major assault, launched in November, forced the Germans and Italians back to their original position. In January 1942 it was Rommel's turn to again press the British back into Egypt. In this series of attacks, retreats, and counterattacks, each side lost fuel, tanks, planes, and troops. Despite the repeated advances and retreats, the desert war remained a standoff until Rommel was forced to fight both the British to his east and an invading American army, which entered the war in December of 1941, to his west.

Greece under Attack

Even before his African schemes ended in disaster, Mussolini was turning his attention to Europe. He wanted Italy to return to glory comparable to that of the ancient Roman Empire. Most historians maintain that jealousy of Hitler also played a major part in Mussolini's decisions. In April 1939 Italy had sent an army to take over Albania, a small, poor country across the Adriatic Sea from Italy. Deciding to use his base in Albania to invade Greece, Mussolini launched an attack on

Countries allied with the Axis powers, countries occupied by the Axis powers, and neutral countries, in June 1942.

October 28. He apparently ordered the invasion of Greece without informing the Germans, who might have pressured him to give up the idea, since Hitler was anxious to avoid any military actions in Europe that could interfere with his secret plan to invade the Soviet Union, scheduled for the following spring.

Though they vastly outnumbered the Greeks, the poorly equipped Italian army launched its invasion with insufficient planning. After some early successes, the Italian offensive stalled, and in the middle of November the Greek army counterattacked, quickly driving the Italians back into Albania and crossing the border in pursuit. By Jan-

uary 1941 the Italians were in danger of being forced to evacuate Albania. As in Africa, Mussolini was required to ask Germany for assistance. The Italian defeat in Greece set off a complicated chain reaction in which one country in the region after another was impacted. The Greeks had requested help from the British, who sent troops from North Africa. British forces in Greece would eventually number 68,000 men. Hitler did not want to do anything that might delay his invasion of the Soviet Union, but Italy's attack on Greece had once again brought British troops to Europe. The Germans did not want a threat to their south while they fought in Russia. Among other dangers, British planes could take off from Greece and

A German soldier gets some realistic training before he heads off to the front. *(Reproduced by permission of © Hulton Getty/Liaison Agency)*

bomb the oil fields in Romania, the main source of petroleum for Germany. Also, Hitler felt he needed to help Mussolini because an Italian defeat might encourage other countries to resist the Axis.

Deploying German troops into Greece required access to other countries, and after intense pressure, Bulgaria, which borders Greece, signed an alliance with Germany in March 1941. The agreement allowed German troops to invade Greece from Bulgarian territory. Germany also wanted to attack Greece through Yugoslavia, and on March 25 Prince Paul, the regent of Yugoslavia, agreed to join the Axis. Two days later, a group of Yugoslav army officers who opposed the alliance with Germany overthrew Prince Paul and withdrew the agreement, under the encouragement of British (and probably American) secret agents. An enraged Hitler ordered the German army to invade Yugoslavia as well, and the Germans attacked both Yugoslavia and Greece on April 6. Although the Yugoslav army had 1 million soldiers, the Germans easily broke through. The Luftwaffe heavily bombed the Yugoslav capital of Belgrade and other targets, and Germans entered the

city on April 12. Five days later, Yugoslavia surrendered. Only 151 German soldiers were killed in the invasion. Germany, Italy, Hungary, and Bulgaria all took parts of Yugoslav territory. Serbia, one of the main areas of Yugoslavia, was put under German military administration. A new "independent" country of Croatia was created in western Yugoslavia and ruled by a pro-Nazi government that was violently anti-Serb. Although this victory had been easy, the Germans would face much greater resistance in Yugoslavia in the following years.

The German invasion of Greece, launched from Bulgaria, was almost as easy. The Greek army was still concentrated against the Italians in Albania, and the British force was not large enough to stop the Germans. The Germans entered Athens, the Greek capital, on April 27, forcing the British to evacuate their troops by sea and leave most of their equipment behind. A number of British troops relocated to the large Greek island of Crete in the Mediterranean Sea. A few weeks later, German parachute troops landed on the island and, with strong Luftwaffe support, defeated the British

Armored half-tracks, part of a Panzer group, and German troops move deep into Russia, summer 1941. *(Reproduced by permission of AP/Wide World Photos)*

and Greek defenders, who heavily outnumbered them. The British again evacuated some of their forces by sea. Germany's spectacular victory devastated British morale, acting as a terrible reminder that less than a year before, Britain had evacuated troops from Dunkirk in France. Britain was not strong enough to maintain a foothold in Europe. Germany, Italy, and their Axis partners now controlled almost the entire continent, up to the border of Soviet Russia. Beyond that border, however, lay the land Hitler had always wanted.

The Invasion of the Soviet Union

Hitler believed the remainder of the *Lebensraum,* or room to live, needed by Germany would come from eastern Europe. Germany would conquer White Russia (now Belarus) and the Ukraine, both of which had been longtime holdings of the Russian Empire. These areas were then the western part of the Soviet Union, the Communist country established by the overthrow of the Russian Empire. In addition to occupying the eastern half of Poland

in 1939, the Soviets had also taken over the three small countries of Lithuania, Latvia, and Estonia, on the shores of the Baltic Sea. Since all these territories were part of the communist Soviet Union, conquering them would satisfy both Hitler's hatred of communists and his desire to conquer territory. Germany would take over the land and populate it with Germans, thus satisfying Nazi racial policy; Poles, Russians, Ukrainians, White Russians, and others would be used as sources of cheap labor for superior "Aryans." The western Soviet Union, including eastern Poland, was also home to 5 million Jews. This provided Hitler with yet another reason to invade Soviet territory. For Hitler and the Nazis, the invasion of the Soviet Union would be a war to conquer land for the German race, to destroy communism, and to eliminate the Jews. This combination of motives made the German invasion of the Soviet Union especially brutal.

On June 22, 1941, Germany launched its surprise attack on the Soviet Union, giving it the code name Operation Barbarossa ("Red Beard"), after the nickname of a German emperor in the Middle Ages.

A German soldier rides past a burning Russian tank during Germany's invasion of Russia, 1941. *(Reproduced by permission of AP/Wide World Photos)*

The Soviet army and government were completely unprepared as German forces, led by tanks, pushed into Soviet territory with tremendous speed. Whole Soviet divisions, and even whole armies, were frequently trapped behind the advancing German Panzer divisions. Then the German infantry, moving much more slowly than the tanks, would destroy these pockets of surrounded Soviet troops. Although the trapped Soviet soldiers usually fought fiercely, tens of thousands surrendered when they ran out of food and ammunition. The remainder of the Soviet army retreated toward the east in an attempt to prevent a total collapse. The German air force attacked roads, railroads, cities, and towns, and this German blitzkrieg caused chaos and panic just as similar actions had in Poland and France. After less than three weeks, the Germans (joined by Hungarian, Romanian, and Italian units) had advanced 280 miles and taken 300,000 prisoners. During the battle, the Germans had destroyed or captured 1,500 Soviet tanks, 2,000 planes, and 3,000 cannons.

The devastation increased as the Germans continued their advance into the Soviet Union. In September, in a great battle around the Ukrainian capital, Kiev, the Germans trapped fifty Soviet divisions. Pounded by the Luftwaffe and attacked by Panzers and German infantry, more than 650,000 Soviet troops were taken prisoner in this single battle. In total, the Germans had succeeded in capturing almost 3 million Russian soldiers. In the first months of the Soviet invasion, the Germans were even more successful than they had been in Poland and France. Unlike the previous invasions, however, German territorial gains did not prevent the Soviets from retreating deeper into their own large country. Although millions of Soviet soldiers had been killed or captured, there were still millions more fighting or ready for battle. The Germans had destroyed thousands of tanks, cannons, and planes, and captured many of the factories where they were manufactured, and yet the Soviets were transferring whole factories, building new ones, and relying on extant ones in the east, far from the reach of the Germans. By the end of August 1941, the Soviets had moved more than 1,500 factories east by railroad, and many more would follow in the next few months.

The Soviet Union had vast interior spaces, a large population that could provide men to replace lost troops, and great industrial potential. These

Poland and the western Soviet Union, 1939–1941. Shaded areas show German-occupied Poland and areas of Poland taken by the Soviet Union. The arrows indicate the direction of Germany's invading armies.

factors meant that the German invasion, though astounding in military terms, was not enough to defeat the Soviet Union. After the first few weeks of confusion, the Soviet army fought hard, and, although it continued to take heavy losses, began inflicting heavy losses on the Germans as well. As the Russians retreated, they attempted to destroy every bridge, railroad line, dam, warehouse, and barn, in a "scorched earth" policy that left little or nothing that could be used by the invaders. The three invading German Army Groups were spread over a battlefront hundreds of miles wide from north to south. As they advanced eastward, the front kept growing, and every mile they advanced

increased the distance required to send supplies over the primitive Russian road system. Few roads were paved, and dirt roads turned to mud during rain. Although tracked vehicles, like tanks, could sometimes travel over these roads and through fields, wheeled vehicles had to wait until the roads dried out. Tanks were delayed, waiting for food, ammunition, and, most importantly, fuel to arrive in trucks or horse-drawn wagons.

By August 30, German Army Group North had reached Leningrad, the Soviet Union's second-largest city, which had a population of 3 million people. Leningrad also held great symbolic impor-

When Leningrad was besieged by German forces, most of the city's supply routes were cut off. Many Russians relied on the Ladoga Trail, which was a makeshift road over the Ladoga Lake. Truck drivers often traveled with doors open in case they had to bail out when their rigs sank. *(Reproduced by permission of © Hulton Getty/Liaison Agency)*

tance, as it had been the capital of imperial Russia before the Communist revolution. Then known as Saint Petersburg, the city had been renamed in honor of the founder of the communist government, Vladimir Lenin. (Today, the city is again called Saint Petersburg.) German troops surrounded nearly the entire city, preventing the Russians from bringing supplies into Leningrad except across Lake Ladoga, a huge lake northeast of the city. The people remaining in the city dug almost 400 miles of antitank ditches and built thousands of blockhouses to stop the Germans. Under its new commander, Marshal Georgy Zhukov, the Soviet army made a stand and stopped the German advance. For the next two and one-half years, the people of Leningrad lived under the German guns and bombs. The few supplies they received had to be brought 125 miles through deep arctic forests and then across Lake Ladoga in boats; in the winter, trucks crossed the frozen water. Death from starvation and freezing became common, and in December 1941, some 50,000 people died in the city. By the time the Germans were finally driven out of Russia in spring 1944, 1 million citizens of Leningrad had died—yet the Germans never captured the city.

As Army Group North engaged the Russians at Leningrad, Army Group Center drove east toward the Soviet capital of Moscow, the headquarters and symbol of the world communist movement. Leading German troops were supposedly so close they could see the reflection of the sun off the golden domes of the churches in the Kremlin, the ancient walled district that housed the Soviet government. Like their comrades in Leningrad, civilians in Moscow dug trenches while the Soviet army made a stand. As autumn rains turned roads and fields into sticky mud that even tanks could not cross, the German advance halted. When the rains turned into snow and German tanks could cross the frozen ground, it was the Russians who launched an attack.

Winter in Russia

German troops were not outfitted with winter gear, partly because equipping them with winter clothes and special boots would have meant admitting that the war would be lengthy, and German leaders feared this would discourage the troops and hinder their ability to fight. As the German invasion of the Soviet Union continued into winter, thousands of German soldiers developed frostbitten feet and were unable to walk. The engines of German tanks and trucks would not work, gasoline froze, and rubber tires turned as

Unprepared for the cold Soviet winters, German soldiers bundle up in whatever clothes they can find. *(Reproduced by permission of AP/Wide World Photos)*

During the siege of Leningrad, Soviet women helped construct anti-tank ditches using picks and shovels. *(Library of Congress)*

hard as metal. The horses, hungry and cold like the men, were too weak to pull artillery through the deep snowdrifts. Every German officer—and every Soviet officer—knew how Napoleon, French general and emperor, had led a great army to Moscow in 1812, winning battle after battle. The Russians had burned everything as they retreated, leaving no sources of food for the invaders. The Russian winter and the Russian soldiers had destroyed the seemingly unbeatable French enemy. These events seemed to be repeating themselves more than a century later. As the temperature kept dropping (at times it reached 40 degrees below zero) amid howling winds and blowing snow, the Soviet counteroffensive, commanded by Zhukov, forced the Germans back from Moscow. At times, it appeared that Army Group Center might be surrounded and destroyed. For the first time, signs of panic appeared among some German soldiers.

The German generals managed to save most of their forces by retreating, forming defensive positions, and waiting for spring. Though they were back where they had been in October, they were still deep inside Russia. The German army had suffered its first major defeat of the war, but was not yet beaten. The German soldiers had experienced the power of "General Winter" and seen the tenacity with which the Russians would defend their country. Hundreds of thousands more Russian and German soldiers would die before the defeated Germans would leave Russia forever.

PRIMARY SOURCE

Winston Churchill and Franklin D. Roosevelt
The Atlantic Charter

Issued August 14, 1941. Printed by United Press in the New York Times, *August 15, 1941, p. 1.*

After participating in World War I (1914-1918), the United States adopted a policy of isolationism, vowing to remain neutral in conflicts between foreign countries. The rise of Adolf Hitler and Benito Mussolini in the 1930s, however, signaled the vulnerability of other world nations in the path of their territorial and political acquisitions. Mussolini's invasion of Abyssinia (the eastern African kingdom of Ethiopia) in 1935, Japan's invasion of China two years later, and the outbreak of war in Europe all conjoined to demonstrate the necessity for active preparation against potential conflict. In September 1940, the U.S. Congress authorized a peacetime draft that required men between the ages of twenty and thirty-five to enroll for military training. American industries began preparations for increased production of war supplies. In January 1941 President Franklin D. Roosevelt told Congress that America would provide support. In March the Lend-Lease Act allowed the United States to provide supplies to Britain on loan, to be repaid after the war. On May 27, 1941, Roosevelt proclaimed a national emergency and encouraged military readiness for possible aggression. By mid-1941 Germany controlled virtually all European territo-

ry west of the Soviet Union. Despite the signing of the Nazi-Soviet Pact in 1939, which prohibited the two nations from attacking each other, the Germans launched Operation Barbarossa and attacked the Soviet Union on June 22, 1941. The Soviets, completely unprepared for the surprise invasion, lost battle after battle in the first few months as the Germans pushed deep into Soviet territory. The attack revealed to world leaders Hitler's intention to conquer all of Europe.

Meanwhile, tensions mounted between the United States and Japan. The Japanese attempted to expand their empire in Asia and the Pacific by taking over Asian and Pacific territories controlled by Britain, France, and the Netherlands—all nations unable to defend their outlying areas because of domestic attacks by the Germans. Both Britain and the United States regarded the movement of Japanese troops into French-controlled southern Indochina (modern-day Vietnam) as a sign of Japanese aggression. A Japanese agreement with the Vichy government on July 24, 1941, allowed Japan to station troops in northern Vietnam, which worried British leaders about possible attacks against Indonesia, British Malaya, and the Philippines.

President Franklin D. Roosevelt led efforts by the United States to help Britain fight Germany. *(Library of Congress)*

In August 1941 Roosevelt and British Prime Minister Winston Churchill met (for the first time face-to-face) secretly, aboard a warship anchored in the coastal waters of Newfoundland, to discuss defensive measures and war goals. Confidentially, they discussed what the Allied strategy would be if the United States entered the war. Publicly, their meetings yielded a joint declaration known as the Atlantic Charter, which stressed the supreme importance of human rights and outlined steps for achieving peace. First made public on August 14, 1941, this "recipe for peace" set forth principles that would guide the actions of the Allies in the escalating global conflict. The charter also served as a foundation for the creation of the United Nations, an international peace organization formally established on October 24, 1945.

The Atlantic Charter

The President of the United States of America and the Prime Minister, Mr. Churchill, representing His Majesty's Government in the United Kingdom, being met together, deem it right to make known certain common principles in the national policies of their respective countries on which they base their hopes for a better future for the world.

FIRST, their countries seek no aggrandizement, territorial or other;

SECOND, they desire to see no territorial changes that do not accord with the freely expressed wishes of the peoples concerned;

THIRD, they respect the right of all peoples to

Franklin D. Roosevelt (seated, left) and Winston Churchill (seated, right) at the Atlantic Charter meeting. *(Reproduced by permission of AP/Wide World Photos, Inc.)*

choose the form of government under which they will live; and they wish to see sovereign rights and self-government restored to those who have been forcibly deprived of them;

FOURTH, they will endeavor, with due respect for their existing obligations, to further the enjoyment by all States, great or small, victor or vanquished, of access, on equal terms, to the trade and to the raw materials of the world which are needed for their economic prosperity;

FIFTH, they desire to bring about the fullest collaboration between all nations in the economic field with the object of securing, for all, improved labor standards, economic adjustment, and social security;

SIXTH, after the final destruction of the Nazi tyranny, they hope to see established a peace which will afford to all nations the means of dwelling in safety within their own boundaries, and which will afford assurance that all the men in all the lands may live out their lives in freedom from fear and want;

SEVENTH, such a peace should enable all men to traverse the high seas and oceans without hindrance;

EIGHTH, they believe that all of the nations of the world, for realistic as well as spiritual reasons, must come to the abandonment of the use of force. Since no future peace can be maintained if land, sea or air armaments continue to be employed by nations which threaten, or may threaten, aggression outside of their frontiers, they believe ... that the disarmament of such nations is essential. They will likewise aid and encourage all other practicable measures which will lighten for peace-loving peoples the crushing burden of armaments.

Franklin D. Roosevelt
Winston S. Churchill

Franklin D. Roosevelt

Franklin Delano Roosevelt was born January 30, 1882, on his family's estate near Hyde Park, New York. He came from a wealthy, and prominent family—President Theodore Roosevelt was his cousin. Roosevelt received his early education at home from his mother, father, and private tutors. He went on to excel at the prestigious Groton School in Massachusetts, Harvard University, and Columbia Law School. In 1905 he married social crusader Eleanor Roosevelt, a distant cousin. Franklin Roosevelt first entered the political spotlight in 1910, winning election to the New York state senate as a Democrat. A close political adviser to President Woodrow Wilson, he also served as assistant secretary of the navy from 1913 to 1920. Following an unsuccessful bid for the vice presidency of the United States, Roosevelt decided to put his political career on hold. In 1921 Roosevelt contracted poliomyelitis (also known as polio, or infantile paralysis) and lost the use of both his legs at age thirty-nine. Roosevelt was forced to use either a wheelchair or steel leg braces and crutches for the remainder of his life. According to family members, friends, and other observers, Roosevelt's illness altered his outlook on life; he gained a greater understanding of people's problems and a newfound sense of compassion for others. Roosevelt did not want to be seen as disabled and focused on developing his upper body muscles—he even had special hand controls installed in his Ford convertible so he could drive.

Roosevelt reemerged on the political scene in the late 1920s, and in 1928 he narrowly won election to the first of two terms as governor of New York. His commitment to helping impoverished Americans brought him national prominence and, in time, fueled his political rise. Roosevelt defeated Herbert Hoover in the presidential election of 1932, in the midst of the Great Depression. By 1932 approximately 12 million Americans were unemployed, and more and more found themselves homeless and hungry. Roosevelt took the oath of the office of president on March 4, 1933, and delivered a memorable speech that captured the hearts of the American people with soon-famous lines like "The only thing we have to fear is fear itself." Roosevelt set out to use the powers of the government to spark social and economic reform, and instituted the "New Deal," which created a number of agencies to assist and employ millions of Americans. Roosevelt's critics charged that government involvement in everyday American life had transformed the nation into a huge welfare state and created an enormous national debt. His advocates maintained that his actions helped restore the nation's faith in its government.

With his easy charm and winning ways, Roosevelt revolutionized the way the president communicated with the American people. He informally updated the American public on government business in his "Fireside Chats," broadcast by radio to millions of homes. By the late 1930s, Roosevelt was forced to focus primarily on foreign affairs as the United States moved closer and closer to direct involvement in World War II. Roosevelt was elected to his fourth and final term as president in November 1944. On April 12, 1945, during a vacation in Warm Springs, Georgia, Roosevelt suffered a cerebral hemorrhage while posing for a painting by artist Elizabeth Shoumatoff; he never regained consciousness. Some historians maintain that the stress of the war contributed greatly to his death just five months after the election.

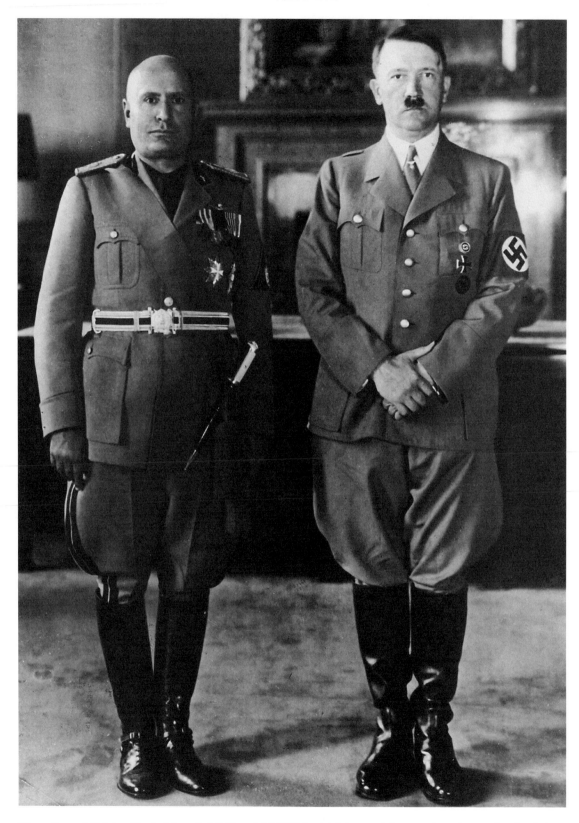

The actions of dictators Benito Mussolini (left) and Adolf Hitler (right) caused democratic nations to fear for their safety. *(Reproduced by permission of Snark/Art Resource)*

Aftermath

On September 27, 1940, the governments of Germany, Italy, and Japan signed the Tripartite Pact, also known as the Axis or Three-Power Pact. Each nation pledged full cooperation and support—political, economic, and military—in the event of attack by another power; the terms of the pact were to remain in effect for ten years. The United States officially joined the war when the Japanese bombed the American naval base at Pearl Harbor, Hawaii, in December 1941, nearly four months after Roosevelt and Churchill signed the Atlantic Charter. The United States and Britain declared war on Japan, and a few days later Germany and Italy declared war on the United States. By the end of December, Japan controlled most of the Pacific region, including the Philippines, Guam, the Gilbert Islands, Malaya, and Singapore.

SOURCES

Books

Freedman, Russell, *Franklin Delano Roosevelt*, Clarion Books (New York), 1990.

Kimball, Warren F., *Forged in War: Roosevelt, Churchill and the Second World War*, Morrow (New York), 1998.

Severance, John B., *Winston Churchill: Soldier, Statesman, Artist*, Clarion Books (New York), 1996.

Ward, Geoffrey C., *Before the Trumpet: Young Franklin Roosevelt, 1882–1905*, originally published in 1985, reprinted, Smithmark (New York), 1994.

Periodicals

New York Times, May 7, 1941, p. 1; June 23, 1941, p. 1; July 3, 1941, p. 1; August 14, 1941, p. 1; October 4, 1941; October 10, 1941, p. 2.

Other

The American Experience: The Presidents, http://www.pbs.org/wgbh/pages/amex/presidents/ (May 16, 2000).

FDR, "The American Experience," WGBH Educational Foundation and David Grubin Productions, Inc., 1994.

Franklin D. Roosevelt Library and Digital Archives, http://www.academic.marist.edu/fdr/ (May 16, 2000).

P R I M A R Y   S O U R C E

Adolf Hitler
Excerpt from "Hitler's Order of the Day to the German Troops on the Eastern Front"

Issued October 2, 1941
Excerpt taken from Associated Press release reprinted in the
New York Times, *October 10, 1941, p. 2*

After Adolf Hitler was named chancellor of Germany in 1933, the German government stepped up efforts to expand its territory in Europe. In March 1938 the German army moved into Austria and united it with Germany. Soon, Hitler began demanding the return of land that Germany had lost after World War I (1914–1918). His first target was the Sudetenland, a German-speaking section of Czechoslovakia. The Czechoslovakian military could not stand alone against Germany, and its allies, Britain and France, did not want to go to war over that territory. So Hitler took the Sudetenland for Germany. Though Hitler claimed this would be his last territorial demand in Europe, in reality, he already had plans for conquering all of Europe.

By March 1939, Hitler's army had taken over all of Czechoslovakia. Soon after, Hitler turned to the port city of Danzig. Before World War I, Danzig had been a German city, but after the war, it became a "free city," belonging neither to Germany nor to Poland, though it fell within Poland's borders. Poland had a right to use the port for its exports and imports, but the people of the city were almost all German. Hitler wanted Danzig returned to Germany, and also wanted to build a road through Polish territory connecting Danzig and Germany. European leaders, however, were no longer willing to give in to Hitler's demands: Poland refused to give up its right to use Danzig, and England and France swore to defend Poland if Germany attacked.

In August 1939 Germany and the Soviet Union signed the Nazi-Soviet Pact, in which the two countries agreed not to attack each other. On September 1, 1939, Hitler launched a German attack on Poland. Under the terms of the pact, the Soviet Union did not interfere with Germany's actions in Poland, but Britain and France declared war on Germany two days later. By late September, Germany had conquered Poland in a stunning blitzkrieg, or "lightning war."

In May and June, 1940, Germany conquered Norway, Denmark, the Netherlands, Belgium, Luxembourg, and France. By mid-1941, Germany controlled virtually all European territory west of the Soviet Union. This quest for territory seemed unquenchable, and tensions mounted between Hitler and Soviet leader Joseph Stalin. Hitler was infuriated by Stalin's moves to expand Soviet territory farther into central Europe. On June 22, 1941, more than 3 million German troops invaded the Soviet Union, launching an assault that Hitler named Operation Barbarossa. In a July 3 radio address, Stalin warned his nation of the seriousness of Germany's aggression, and predicted that the fight for Soviet freedom would have the same goal as the Allies' fight: to promote freedom and end threats of enslavement by Hitler. On July 12, the British and Soviet governments signed an agreement pledging mutual assistance in the war against Germany. Italy sided with Germany, declaring war on the Soviet Union and setting the stage for a long conflict with the Soviets, the British, and the Americans.

Hitler's order to the German troops on the eastern front was issued on October 2, 1941, about three and one-half months after Germany invaded the Soviet Union. At that time, Hitler felt confident that Germany had won the war against the Soviets. He played upon his soldiers' deepest emotions and instincts of loyalty, courage, and survival by telling them that Stalin had long planned a devastating invasion of Germany. He also called on a higher power—God—to lead the German forces to victory in their war against the Soviet "beasts."

Hitler's Order of the Day to the German Troops on the Eastern Front
Issued October 2, 1941

Filled with the greatest concern for the existence and future of our people, I decided on June 22 to appeal to you to anticipate in the nick of time threatening aggression by one opponent [the Soviet Union].

It was the intention of the Kremlin powers—as we know today—to destroy not only Germany but all Europe....

God's mercy on our people and the entire European world if this barbaric enemy had been able to move his tens of thousands of tanks before we moved ours!

All Europe would have been lost. For this enemy does not consist of soldiers, but a majority of beasts....

Soldiers, when I called on you on June 22 to ward off the terrible danger menacing our homeland you faced the biggest military power of all times....

Within a few weeks his three most important industrial regions will be completely in our hands. Your names, soldiers of the German armed forces, and the names of our brave allies, the names of your divisions and regiments, and your tank forces and air squadrons, will be associated for all time with the most tremendous victories in history.

You have taken more than 2,400,000 prisoners, destroyed or captured more than 17,500 tanks and more than 21,600 pieces of artillery. Fourteen thou-

Dressed to face the harsh winter weather in Leningrad, Russian snipers look for their targets. *(Reproduced by permission of © Hulton Getty/Liaison Agency)*

During the siege of Leningrad, many Russians died of starvation as the Germans blocked most supply routes to the city. Here, a woman moves a corpse via sled through the snow-covered streets. *(Reproduced by permission of © Hulton Getty/Liaison Agency)*

A German tank rolls through Soviet territory during Operation Barbarossa. *(Reproduced by permission of the Corbis Corporation [Bellevue])*

sand two hundred planes were brought down or destroyed on the ground.

The world hitherto never has experienced similar events....

Since June 22 the strongest fortifications have been penetrated, tremendous streams have been crossed, innumerable localities have been stormed and fortresses and casemate systems have been crushed or smoked out.

From far in the north, where our superbly brave Finnish allies gave evidence of their courage a second time, down to Crimea you stand today together with Slovak, Hungarian, Italian and Rumanian divisions roughly 1,000 kilometers deep in the enemy's country.

Spanish, Croat and Belgian units now join you and others will follow. This fight—perhaps for the first time—is recognized by all European nations as a common action to safeguard the future of this most cultural continent....

This outstanding achievement of one struggle was obtained with sacrifices that, however painful in individual cases, in the total amount to not yet five percent of those of the World War[I]....

During these three and a half months, my soldiers, the precondition, at least, has been created for a last mighty blow that shall crush this opponent before Winter sets in.

All preparations ... have been made.... We can now strike a deadly blow.

Today begins the last great, decisive battle of this year. It will hit this enemy destructively and with it the instigator of the entire war, England herself. For if we crush this opponent, we also remove the last English ally on the [European] Continent.

Thus we will free the German Reich and entire Europe from a menace greater than any since the time of the Huns and later of the Mongol tribes.

The German people, therefore, will be with you more than ever before during the few ensuing weeks. What you and allied soldiers have achieved already merits our deepest thanks.

With bated breath, the blessing of the entire German homeland accompanies you during the hard days ahead. With the Lord's aid you not only will bring victory but also the most essential condition for peace.

The Fuehrer's Headquarters: Oct. 2, 1941.

Adolf Hitler, Fuerher and Supreme Commander of the Armed Forces.

Aftermath

Although German forces captured the Soviet city of Kiev in September 1941, their December advance on Moscow failed. Stalin used the unbearably cold Russian winters to his advantage, launching a counterattack just as temperatures plunged to a bitter 40 degrees below zero Fahrenheit. The Germans retreated, but fierce fighting in the cities of Leningrad and Stalingrad broke out in 1942. Food was scarce, and once-thriving towns were reduced to rubble. Thousands of Soviet citizens died of starvation; others fell into the hands of the Nazis and became prisoners of war. By December, however, Soviet forces surround-

German leader Adolf Hitler reviewing German cavalry troops as they prepare to join the fighting. *(Reproduced by permission of the Corbis Corporation [Bellevue])*

ed the German troops occupying Stalingrad, isolating them in the heart of the city. The German campaign in the Soviet Union ended on January 31, 1943, with the surrender of German forces. The Soviets' triumphant defense of Stalingrad was a staggering blow to Hitler and his supposedly unbeatable army.

In December 1941 the United States officially joined the war after Japanese forces attacked the U.S. naval base at Pearl Harbor, Hawaii. The United States declared war on Japan; in turn, Japan's allies, Germany and Italy, declared war on the United States. Britain, the Soviet Union, and the United States established a unified strategy for defeating Germany, and the United States and Britain almost immediately launched an offensive against the Germans in North Africa. Britain and the United States also planned to launch an assault in western Europe (the western front) as soon as possible, while the Soviets kept fighting in the east (the eastern front). Forcing Hitler to fight on numerous fronts, the Allies hoped the German army would be spread too thin, leaving them susceptible to attack. The plan was to advance from three directions— the east, west, and south—and squeeze the Germans between the advancing Allied armies.

After the death of Bolshevik leader Vladimir Lenin, Stalin eliminated all of his political oppo-

nents and managed to establish himself as the premier of the Soviet Union. He held this position until his death in 1953. Stalin's brand of Marxism was particularly harsh, leaving no room for economic freedom or political dissent. He transformed the Soviet Union's economy by implementing a program of rapid industrialization and collectivizing agriculture. As restrictions on freedom were tightened, feelings of discontent and conflict spread among the Soviet people, who were shot or imprisoned in labor camps if they resisted. At the outset of World War II, Stalin allied himself with Hitler in hopes of gaining more European territory for the Soviet Union. In time, however, Hitler came to view Stalin as an obstacle to German world dominance, and ordered an invasion of the Soviet Union in June 1941. After numerous long and bloody conflicts, Soviet forces finally defeated the Germans in 1943 in the Battle of Stalingrad.

In the years following World War II, Stalin's efforts to expand Soviet influence throughout Eastern Europe weakened his relationship with Great Britain and the United States. The Soviet Union's apparent quest for European, and even world, domination led to intense anti-Soviet and anticommunist sentiment in the United States from the 1950s through the 1980s, a period known as the Cold War.

Joseph Stalin

Soviet political leader Joseph Stalin was born December 21, 1879, in Gori, Georgia, a southwest Asian territory then part of the Russian Empire. When he was a child, he survived smallpox and cruel beatings by his father. An enthusiastic student of Georgian history, Stalin displayed a revolutionary spirit. His philosophies clashed with those of the theological seminary he attended in the Georgian capital of Tbilisi in the mid-1890s. Stalin joined a Marxist political group in 1898 and was eventually expelled from the seminary, going on to pursue a path of political rebellion against Russia's czarist system of government. By the turn of the century, Stalin had joined Russia's Social Democratic party, and when a more aggressive, radical, and militant wing of the party was developed, Stalin became an active member, known as a Bolshevik. The Bolsheviks led the Russian Revolution of 1917, which resulted in the overthrow of the czar and the formation of the communist Soviet Union.

During Stalin's leadership of the Soviet Union, millions of people died as he introduced a new form of government. *(Reproduced by permission of Corbis/Bettmann)*

SOURCES

Books

Fuchs, Thomas, *The Hitler Fact Book,* Fountain Books (Los Angeles), 1990.

Marrin, Albert, *Hitler,* Viking Kestrel (New York), 1987.

Skipper, G. C., *The Battle of Stalingrad,* Children's Press (Chicago), 1981.

Stein, R. Conrad, *Invasion of Russia,* Children's Press (Chicago), 1985.

Stein, R. Conrad, *Siege of Leningrad,* Children's Press (Chicago), 1983.

Whitelaw, Nancy, *Josef Stalin: From Peasant to Premier,* Macmillan (New York), 1992.

Periodicals

New York Times, May 7, 1941, p. 1; June 23, 1941, p. 1; July 3, 1941, p. 1; August 14, 1941, p. 1; October 4, 1941; October 10, 1941, p. 2.

Other

Stalin (movie), HBO, 1992.

A rescuer assists survivors of the German attack on the passenger ship *Athenia. (Reproduced by permission of the Corbis/Hulton-Deutsch Collection)*

Herbert A. Werner
Excerpt from *Iron Coffins: A Personal Account of the German U-Boat Battles of World War II*

First published in 1969; reprinted in 1998

Great Britain and France, having promised to protect Poland in the event of a German attack, declared war on Germany two days after its invasion of Poland. On that same day, September 3, 1939, the British passenger ship *Athenia,* traveling westward across the Atlantic Ocean toward Canada, was attacked without warning and sunk by a German submarine. More than 100 of the ocean liner's 1,300 passengers perished, marking the beginning of the six-year-long Battle of the Atlantic. Great Britain, surrounded by water on all sides (the Atlantic Ocean to the west and north, the North Sea to the east, and the English Channel

to the south) relied on Atlantic waterways as routes through which to receive food, fuel, manpower, military supplies, and equipment to fight the Germans. Hitler's forces sought to cut off these supply lines. Submarines called U-boats were key to Germany's early dominance in the Battle of the Atlantic, and allowed them to launch both surface and underwater attacks. British Prime Minister Winston Churchill asserted that in the end, all aspects of the war would be determined by the Battle of the Atlantic. The convoy system was used to keep war supplies flowing into the British Isles from the United States. It was the job of the sub-

Hood and *Bismarck* Sinkings

The *Bismarck* was a massive German battleship, the most powerful ship in the German naval fleet. In May 1941 it was paired with the German cruiser *Prinz Eugen* to search the North Atlantic for British convoys. On May 23 the ships found two patrolling British cruisers, whose calls for assistance were received by the British battleships HMS *Hood* and HMS *Prince of Wales*. A short but fierce battle followed between the *Bismarck* and the *Hood,* which exploded after being hit by enemy fire in the early morning hours of May 24, 1941. The ship broke into pieces and sank, with only three of 1,400 crew members surviving. The incident was a major defeat for Britain's Royal Navy. In response, the British deployed battleships, cruisers, destroyers, torpedo planes, aircraft carriers, and flying boats to find the *Bismarck*. After searching for two days through foggy, dark, wet skies, the Royal Navy finally located the German battleship. On May 27, 1941, after repeated attacks, the *Bismarck* sank, killing more than 2,000 German sailors.

The HMS *Hood* was sunk by the German battleship *Bismarck* in May 1941. Only three of 1,400 crew members survived. *(Reproduced by permission of AP/Wide World Photos, Inc.)*

Launching of the *Bismarck,* Germany's largest battleship. *(Reproduced by permission of AP/Wide World Photos, Inc.)*

marines and battleships of the *Kriegsmarine,* the German navy, to destroy the convoys before they reached Great Britain.

The Battle of the Atlantic was intense, even very early in the war. While patrolling the Atlantic for submarines in September 1939, for example, the British aircraft carrier *Courageous* was torpedoed by a German U-boat. The *Courageous* exploded and sank, killing hundreds of British sailors. The next month, the German U-boat *U-47,* commanded by ace Günther Prien, slipped into a Scottish harbor under the cloak of darkness and sank the HMS *Royal Oak,* a massive British battleship, killing more than 800 British sailors. In addition to its submarines and standard battleships, the *Kriegsmarine* had two lightweight, high-speed "pocket battleships" in its arsenal. One of these, the *Graf Spee,* was sent into the South Atlantic and sank nine merchant ships in fall 1939. A punishing encounter with three British cruisers (the *Exeter,* the *Ajax,* and the *Achilles*) proved to be the *Graf Spee*'s undoing. After taking shelter in a harbor in Uruguay, South America, and assessing his chances

for a successful escape, *Graf Spee* Captain Hans Langsdorff destroyed his own ship with explosives to avoid capture by the British. The next night he committed suicide.

Around this time, Admiral Karl Dönitz, commander of the German U-boat force, formulated a plan to assure German victory in the Atlantic. He believed the fighting power of the submarines would be unbeatable if the boats traveled in clusters, or "wolf packs," of five or six U-boats. Traveling together in summer 1940, the wolf packs proved highly effective against Allied convoys. U-boats also worked in cooperation with German bomber aircraft, which scouted for enemy ships. The Allied powers also utilized air power for protection: A U-boat that was above water typically dived for cover whenever an aircraft approached, and once submerged was far less capable of detecting and tracking enemy ships.

German battleships continued to play a key role in the Battle of the Atlantic throughout 1940. The British merchant cruiser *Jervis Bay* was escorting more than three dozen ships through the North Atlantic in November 1940 when it encountered the German pocket battleship *Admiral Scheer.* The *Jervis Bay* took on the much larger and more heavily armed *Admiral Scheer,* giving the ships in the British convoy a chance to scatter and reach safety. The *Jervis Bay* was sunk, but the heroic action of her captain and crew saved thirty-two of the thirty-seven ships in the convoy from a similar fate. By the end of 1940, the Germans had destroyed approximately 1,000 British ships.

The German navy dominated the Battle of the Atlantic in 1941. The sinking of the HMS *Hood* (see box on page 234) in May 1941, for example, was a stunning blow to the British. By midsummer 1941, American ships had joined in efforts to convoy merchant ships bound for Britain, even though the United States had not officially entered the war. The United States had previously allowed its navy only to patrol neutral waters, but in September, President Franklin D. Roosevelt declared that American naval convoys could and would attack German war vessels. On October 30, 1941, a German submarine sank the American destroyer *Reuben James,* America's first real loss in the Battle of the Atlantic.

Dominance in the Battle of the Atlantic switched from one side to the other. After conquering Norway and France in spring 1940, the Germans were able to use the Atlantic coastal waters of these nations as U-boat bases. The bases gave the German navy a distinct advantage over the Allies on the high seas throughout 1941 and 1942. In 1942 alone, U-boats sank more than 1,200 Allied ships, and, in the first half of the year, 200 merchant ships in the western Atlantic. The U-boats had started to come closer to American shores than ever before. In the early phases of the battle, it was next to impossible to detect German submarines lurking in the Atlantic Ocean. Allied forces realized that the war against the U-boats could be won only with advanced tracking methods. Technological breakthroughs such as radar and sonar, which made use of reflected radio and sound waves, respectively, to pinpoint the location of enemy submarines, gave the Allies the upper hand in the later stages of the battle.

Herbert A. Werner took part in his first U-boat battle in May 1941, when he was just twenty-one years old. Between 1941 and 1945, Werner served on five different German submarines. He used his wartime notes and letters to compose *Iron Coffins.* In its introduction, he wrote: "Because I was one of the few U-boat commanders who fought through most of the war and who managed to survive, I felt it was my duty to my fallen comrades to set the record straight.... This book belongs to my dead comrades, stricken down wholesale in the prime of youth. I hope it pays them the honor they deserve. If I have succeeded in handing down to the reader the ancient lesson that each generation seems to forget—that war is evil ... then I consider this my most constructive deed."

The following excerpt from *Iron Coffins* describes a grueling two-day clash that occurred in May 1943, after the Allies had gained superiority in the Battle of the Atlantic. Werner was then the executive officer of *U-230,* second in command to the captain. The four-digit numbers in the paragraphs below indicate the twenty-four-hour scale of military time—the first two digits represent hours and the last two represent minutes.

Excerpt from *Iron Coffins*

May 12. 0716:... Before we could risk resurfacing to race into a new attack position, we had to put distance between us and the convoy.... For almost two hours we traveled diagonally away from the giants of steel.

0915: U-230 surfaced. Mounting the bridge while the deck was still awash, I took a hurried look in a circle. Far to the northeast, mastheads and funnels moved along the sharp line which divided the ocean from the sky. U-230 forged through the sea, parallel to the convoy's track, in an attempt to reach a forward position before dusk....

0955:... I saw a twin-engined plane dropping out of the sun. The moment of surprise was total.

"Alarrrmmm!" We plunged head over heels into the conning tower. The boat reacted at once and shot below the surface....

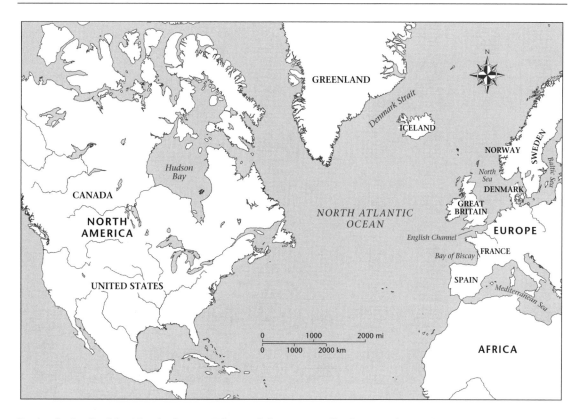

During the Battle of the Atlantic, German U-boats tried to stop supplies from North America en route to Great Britain.

Four short, ferocious explosions shattered the water above and around us. The boat trembled and fell at a 60-degree angle. Water splashed, steel shrieked, ribs moaned, valves blew, deck-plates jumped, and the boat was thrown into darkness. As the lights flickered on, I saw astonishment in the ... eyes of the men. They had every right to be astounded: the attack out of the sun was a complete mystery. Where had the small plane come from? It did not have the range to fly a round-trip between the nearest point of land and the middle of the Atlantic. The conclusion was inescapable that the convoy launched its own airplanes.... The idea of a convoy with its own air defense smashed our basic concept of U-boat warfare. No longer could we mount a surprise attack or escape without meeting savage counterattacks....

1035: U-230 came up to periscope depth. A careful check with our "sky scope," an instrument similar to the periscope, revealed no aircraft. We surfaced at high speed.

The hunt went on. We pressed forward obstinately.... I glanced only occasionally at the ... horizon and concentrated on the sky....

1110: I detected a glint of metal between the clouds. It was a small aircraft, and it was diving into the attack.

"Alarrrmmm!"

Fifty seconds later, four explosions nearby taught us that the pilot was a well-trained bombardier....

1125: U-230 surfaced. We drove forward and clung to the fringes of the convoy with grim determination....

1217: "Aircraft dead astern, alarrrmmm!"

U-230 dived once more and descended rapidly. I bit my lip and waited for the final blast. At forty-five seconds, four booms whipped the boat with violent force. Every second we were able to snatch from the pursuing aircraft brought us closer to the convoy and success. But if we dived a second too late, bombs would end our hunt with sudden death....

1323: Our radio mate delivered an urgent message to the Captain: ATTACKED BY AIRCRAFT. UNABLE TO DIVE. SINKING.... HELP. U-456.

"Have Prager [U-230's navigator] check position," Siegmann [U-230's captain] shouted back. "Maybe we can save the crew."

A German submarine sinking after a combined attack by several aircraft. *(Reproduced by permission of the Corbis Corporation [Bellevue])*

The captain's impulse to rescue our comrades might well result in suicide. We were closer to death than to life ourselves. But help was imperative—we would have expected the same. Moments later, Prager reported that U-456 was only twelve miles ahead.... Immediately, the Captain changed course.

1350: We spotted a plane circling four miles ahead. Then my glasses picked up the bow of U-456 poking out of the rough sea. The men clung to the slippery deck and to the steel cable strung from bow to bridge. Most of them stood in the water up to their chests. The aircraft kept circling above the sinking boat, making it foolhardy for us to approach. Another danger prevented rescue: astern, a corvette [a small, fast escort ship that is well armed with machine guns and explosive depth charges] crept over the horizon, evidently summoned by the plane. Now our own lives were in jeopardy. We turned away from the aircraft, the escort, and U-456, and fled in the direction of the convoy.

1422: "Aircraft astern!"

... It was too late to dive. The single-engined plane came in low in a straight line [over us]. I fingered the trigger of my gun.... [It] was jammed. I kicked its magazine, clearing the jam. Then I emptied the gun at the menace. The mate's automatic bellowed. Our boat veered to starboard, spoiling the plane's bomb run. The pilot revved up his engine, circled, then roared toward us from dead ahead. As the plane dived very low, its engine sputtered, then stopped. Wing first, the plane crashed into the surging ocean, smashing its other wing on our superstructure as we raced by. The pilot, thrown out of his cockpit, lifted his arm and waved for help, but then I saw him disintegrate in the explosion of the four bombs which were meant to destroy us. Four violent shocks kicked into our starboard side astern, but we left the horrible scene unharmed....

1545: A report from the radio room put our small victory into proper perspective: DEPTH

CHARGES BY THREE DESTROYERS. SINKING. U-186. This new loss was the 11th we had heard of since our patrol began....

1600: U-230 cut into the projected path of the convoy. I saw four columns of ships creep over the sharp horizon in the southwest, headed in our direction. We had to halt them....

1638:... Siegmann ... cried, "Down with the boat, Chief, take her down for God's sake, destroyer in ramming position...."

.... As the boat swiftly descended, the harrowing sound of the destroyer's engines and propellers hit the steel of our hull. It grew so fast, and echoed so deafeningly, that we were all unable to move. Only our boat was moving, and she went downward much too slowly to escape the blow.

An earshattering boom ruptured the sea. A spread of six depth charges lifted the boat, tossed her out of the water, and left her on the surface at the mercy of four British destroyers. The screws of U-230 rotated in highest revolutions, driving us ahead. For seconds there was silence. For seconds the British were baffled and stunned. After a whole eternity, our bow dipped and the boat sank—and sank.

A new series of exploding charges lifted our stern with a mighty force. Our boat, entirely out of control, was catapulted toward the bottom five miles

Three U-boat Aces

Among the leading names in U-boat warfare were Otto Kretschmer, Günther Prien, and Erich Topp. Together these German commanders sank 106 ships during the Battle of the Atlantic. Admiral Topp's *Odyssey of a U-Boat Commander* is considered a classic wartime memoir.

below.... U-230 tumbled to 250 meters before [we were] able to reverse her fall....

1716: A new spread deafened us and took our breath away.... The steel knocked and shrieked and valves were thrown into open position.... Water everywhere. Its weight forced the boat deeper into the depths. In the meantime, the convoy crawled in a thunderous procession over our boat.

1740: The uproar was at its peak. A sudden splash told us that we had 10 or 15 seconds to brace

Smoke and flames billow from a tanker torpedoed by Axis forces. *(Reproduced by permission of Corbis/Bettmann)*

Winston Churchill (center) with officers of the Royal Canadian Air Force. The American and Royal Canadian air forces helped Britain defend its ships in the Battle of the Atlantic. *(Reproduced by permission of AP/Wide World Photos, Inc.)*

against another barrage. The charges went off just beyond lethal range.... Perhaps we should risk going deeper. I did not know where our limit was, where the hull would finally crack. No one knew. Those who had found out took their knowledge into the depths. For hours we suffered the punishment and sank gradually deeper. In a constant pattern, spreads of twenty-four charges battered our boat every twenty minutes....

2000: [A] new group [of escorts] launched its first attack, then another, and another. We sat helpless 265 meters below.... Our bodies were stiff from cold, stress, and fear.... The bilges were flooded with water, oil, and urine. Our washrooms were under lock and key; to use them then could have meant instant death, for the tremendous outside pressure would have acted in reverse.... Added to the stench of waste, sweat, and oil was the stink of the battery gases. The increasing humidity condensed on the cold steel, dropped into the bilges, dripped from pipes, and soaked our clothes. By midnight, the Cap-

tain realized that the British would not let up in their bombardment, and he ordered the distribution of potash cartridges [devices that deliver potassium compounds] to supplement breathing. Soon every man was equipped with a large metal box attached to his chest, a rubber hose leading to his mouth, and a clamp on his nose....

May 13.... [As of] 0400 ... we had been under assault for 12 hours and there was no sign of relief. This day was my birthday and I wondered whether it would be my last....

May 14. By midnight, we had approached the limit for boat and crew. We had reached a depth of 280 meters and the boat was still sinking. I dragged myself through the aisle, pushing and tossing men around, forcing them to stay awake. Whoever fell asleep might never be awakened.

0310: A thunderous spread rattled down, but without effect. We were closer to being crushed by the mounting pressure than by the exploding canis-

ters. As the echo of the last blast slowly subsided, something else attracted our attention. It was the thrashing of retreating propellers. For a long time we listened to the fading sound, unable to believe that the Tommies [British soldiers] had given up the hunt.

0430:… U-230 broke through to air and life. We pushed ourselves up to the bridge. Around us spread the infinite beauty of night, sky, and ocean…. We could not believe that death had kept his finger on us for thirty-five gruesome hours.

Abruptly I felt the impact of the oxygen-rich air upon my system. Almost losing consciousness, I sagged to my knees and slumped over the rim of the bridge….

The diesels coughed to life. Since the convoy had disappeared long ago, we traveled south, toward our last position. The engines muttered reassuringly…. The bilges were emptied, the foul air expelled, and the accumulated refuse thrown overboard. When the darkness dissolved and a new day dawned, U-230 was again ready for combat. (Werner, pp. 119–126)

Aftermath

Werner was promoted to commander in December 1943 and began his training in January 1944. By that time, the Germans were losing the Battle of the Atlantic, as British, American, and Canadian bombers worked together to provide air cover over the Atlantic from North America to Europe. In April 1944 Werner took command of his own U-boat, *U-415*. He and his crew successfully evaded heavy bombing raids that spring, but the vessel sank in July while docked at Brest Harbor, a seaport off the northwestern coast of France, having activated a mine laid by the British. In August, Werner assumed command of *U-953*, a dilapidated boat with an inexperienced crew, who nonetheless managed to survive until the end of the war.

When hostilities finally ceased in May 1945, Werner writes, "the ocean floor was littered with the wreckage of the U-boat war." About 800 U-boats had been destroyed, and some 28,000 of the 39,000 men in Germany's U-boat force had died in battle. Of all the submarines that had seen battle duty, in fact, only three remained afloat when Germany surrendered in 1945; one of them was *U-953*, under Werner's command. Werner attributes his survival, in large part, to luck. Werner immigrated to the United States in 1957 and later became an American citizen.

Sources

Books

Ballard, Robert D., *Exploring the Bismarck*, Madison Press (Toronto), 1991.

Black, Wallace B., and Jean F. Blashfield, *Battle of the Atlantic*, "World War II 50th Anniversary" series, Crestwood House (New York), 1991.

Buchheim, Lothart-Günther, *Das Boot*, originally published in 1975, published in English translation as *The Boat*, Dell (New York), 1988.

Burn, A., *Fighting Captain: The Story of Frederic John Walker and the Battle of the Atlantic*, Trans-Atlantic Publications (Philadelphia), 1993, reprinted, 1998.

Werner, Herbert A., *Iron Coffins: A Personal Account of the German U-Boat Battles of World War II*, H. Holt (New York), 1969, reprinted, Da Capo Press (New York), 1998.

Other

The Boat (movie), from the book *Das Boot* by Lothart-Günther Buchheim, Radiant Film, 1982.

HMS Hood Association—Battle Cruiser Hood, http://hmshood.com/ (May 16, 2000).

Uboat.net: The U-boat War 1939–1945, http://uboat.net (May 16, 2000).

Nazi Policy in the Soviet Union

In December 1940 Adolf Hitler ordered his generals to prepare a plan for the invasion of the Soviet Union. In March 1941 Field Marshal Wilhelm Keitel, chief of the high command of the armed forces, issued secret "orders for special areas" to the top German generals. A portion of the order defined the role of Heinrich Himmler, who commanded most of the security forces of the Nazi police state: the Gestapo, the regulation police, the SS, and the SD (a subsidiary branch of the SS). The SS ran the concentration camps and the SD spied on both Germans and Nazi party members to identify opponents of the Nazi government and to ensure loyalty. Many historians describe the SS as a "state within a state," an organization so powerful that it was like a government of its own. By the early 1940s, the SS, and especially the SD, had become the main organization in charge of the anti-Jewish policies of Nazi Germany.

Field Marshal Wilhelm Keitel, as chief of the high command of the German armed forces, was ultimately responsible for planning the invasion of the Soviet Union, and the deaths of Soviet Jews. *(Photograph by Heinrich Hoffman, courtesy of the USHMM Photo Archives)*

Keitel's Order Regarding Soviet Citizens and Jews

According to Keitel's order, Himmler and the SS would be in charge of carrying out "special tasks" in the territory captured from the Soviet Union. The order stated that the "special tasks" were necessary because the conflict represented "the final struggle" between Nazism and Com-

A map showing the countries conquered by Adolf Hitler and his German forces during World War II. (*AP/Wide World Photos*)

munism. Himmler would have the authority to issue orders to the SS without permission from the army. Like that of other Nazi plans put into writing, the language used in Keitel's portion of the order was meant to disguise its meaning to outsiders. It soon became clear that the "special tasks" included killing Soviet Jews. Historians have found evidence suggesting that the "special tasks" portion of Keitel's order was written by Hitler himself.

Though German Jews had been persecuted for years, and many Jews in Poland had been murdered, the Nazis had not yet planned the mass killing of all Jews in any particular country. Keitel's order proved that the Nazis were formulating a policy of genocide, although experts are unsure whether this policy (at the time of Keitel's order) applied only to the Jews of the Soviet Union or to all Jews in Nazi-controlled Europe. Some scholars have argued that there must have been a later

Hitler salutes a group of German officers. He expected complete obedience from his soldiers. *(Reproduced by permission of Bildarchiv Preussischer Kulturbesitz)*

order, never found, to extend the genocide to the remainder of Europe. Despite disagreements about the existence and timing of the order, historians generally assert that by March 1941, the Nazis had decided to destroy at least the Jews of the Soviet Union. By December, at the latest, they had decided to kill all European Jews.

On March 30, Hitler secretly gathered the top commanders assigned to the Soviet invasion and presented a speech, which lasted two and one-half hours and essentially served as an explanation of Keitel's order. Hitler told the officers that in fight-

ing the Russians, they had to forget their normal code of military honor. The conflict would be a clash of ideas and races, "a war of destruction." Captured Communist officials, civilian or military, were not to be treated as prisoners of war: They were criminals, Hitler said, and should be either shot immediately or handed over to the SD. This directive was not only a violation of military honor, but also a military crime. Anticipating opposition from the commanders, Hitler promised: "German soldiers guilty of breaking international law … will be excused." The generals, according to Keitel, sat silently, shocked through

Field Marshal Walter von Reichenau, commander of the German Sixth Army, issued harsh orders that violated international laws of war. *(Reproduced by permission of Bildarchiv Preussischer Kulturbesitz)*

Hitler's speech. Hitler said he did not expect the officers to understand his orders, but did expect them to obey.

On May 13, 1941, Hitler issued a directive that made the key points of his speech became official Nazi policy. It authorized members of the armed forces to shoot enemy civilians who resisted the Germans in any way, allowed the army to exact punishment from a whole community if specific resisters could not be located, and stated that members of the armed forces would not be prosecuted for carrying out these actions, even the ones deemed crimes by military law. Approximately three weeks later, on June 4, 1941, German army headquarters issued a paper titled "Guidelines for the Conduct of the Troops in Russia" to serve as an educational manual for soldiers. According to that document, the German struggle against Bolshevism required "ruthless and energetic measures."

On June 6, the army high command issued the Commissar Order (*Kommissarbefehl*), which was later used as evidence in post-war Nazi trials. (Commissar, meaning "commissioner" in Russian, referred to Communist government officials and also applied to the officer in each Soviet army unit

charged with communicating and enforcing the official Communist party position on each issue.) Copies of the Commissar Order were passed via word of mouth by Germany's top field commanders. The order declared that German officers were required to assure that their troops understood it was wrong to abide by international law in the case of commissars. All commissars, including soldiers captured in battle, should be shot.

Once the invasion of the Soviet Union began, the officers of the German army issued orders to their troops that made it clear the German army was expected to participate in the murder of civilians, including women and children. They emphasized that Jews were as dangerous an enemy as the Soviet army. On September 12, 1941, Keitel issued another order, this one linking Jews and communists, and again demanding "ruthless" measures against the Jews.

On October 10 Field Marshal Walter von Reichenau, the commander of the German Sixth Army operating in the Ukraine, issued an order that met with Hitler's approval. The führer held the directive in such high esteem that it was soon used by other generals:

> The most essential goal of the war against the Jewish-Bolshevist system is the complete destruction of its means of power and the extermination of Asiatic [Soviet] influence from Europe. This creates tasks for the troops that are beyond the one-dimensional pattern of ordinary soldiering. In the Eastern region, the soldier is not just a fighter according to the rules of war.... The soldier must fully understand the necessity of a severe but just revenge against Jewish subhumanity.

In addition, Reichenau said, the army needed to prevent any revolts in the countryside they had conquered: revolts that "experience proves, [have] always been stirred up by Jews" (though at that time there had been almost no resistance to the Nazis by the local people, Jewish or otherwise). The order was intended to deliver the message that the killing of Jews was not only permissable, but actually necessary to accomplish German goals in the war and to ensure German safety.

The Einsatzgruppen

The forces assigned to perform a majority of the killings were the Einsatzgruppen, who had played a central role during the invasion of Poland

Educated Men

Otto Ohlendorf, head of Einsatzgruppe D, testifying at the Nuremberg trial. Ohlendorf held a doctorate in economics. *(Reproduced by permission of AP/Wide World Photos)*

Of the four men chosen to command the Einsatzgruppen, three had earned Ph.D. degrees, thus placing them among the most educated people in pre-war Europe. The Einsatzgruppen commander who became the most notorious, Otto Ohlendorf, was both a lawyer and a research economist. Before and after the time he commanded Einsatzgruppe D in the Soviet Union, Ohlendorf worked on economic studies. In the interim, however, he was directly responsible for the deaths of 90,000 people. He stood trial after the war and was hanged in 1951.

At his trial, Ohlendorf detailed how the Einsatzgruppen performed their duty. First, the Einsatzgruppen would ask Jewish leaders to call together Jews for resettlement. They would then assemble the Jews in a central location, confiscate their valuables, and take them to a nearby forest. The Jews would be shot and then thrown in a ditch.

in 1939. Similar strike forces had also been used by the SD to hunt down opponents of the Nazis when Germany took over Austria in March 1938. Following closely behind the regulation army, the Einsatzgruppen had arrived in each town to eliminate anyone who might lead opposition to the Nazis' plan to enslave the Poles. The Einsatzgruppen killed Polish political leaders, members of the Polish nobility, professors, high school teachers, people with technical training, and many priests. They also arrested thousands of other Poles and sent them to concentration camps. Each of the four Einsatzgruppen, formed by Reinhard Heydrich, had between 500 and 900 members and all four totaled approximately 3,000 men. The groups were assigned to specific geographic areas during the Russian invasion. The Einsatzgruppen were then divided into smaller, special-duty units of about 100 to 150 men apiece, which were in turn subdivided.

The officers of the Einsatzgruppen came mainly from the *Waffen-SS*, the SD, and the security police, with a few coming from the Gestapo. Later, Ukrainians and men from the three Baltic states would be used as auxiliaries to increase the size of the Einsatzgruppen when needed. By selecting members from these organizations, Heydrich was able to ensure that both the officers and men of the new Einsatzgruppen were dedicated Nazis. They already believed that Jews and communists were synonymous, and regarded both as dangerous enemies that had to be eliminated. Still, during their special training for the Soviet campaign, the men were bombarded with lectures on Nazi ideas, including the need to exterminate subhumans such as Jews. Members of the Einsatzgruppen were also given operational training in the collection and execution of large segments of civilian populations. (Each Ein-

Jewish men digging their own graves before being executed by *Waffen-SS* troops in the Soviet Union, 1942. The officers of the Einsatzgruppen were selected from the *Waffen-SS*. *(Russian Federation/USHMM Photo Archives)*

satzgruppe utilized the same procedures from the outset of the invasion, though they operated many hundreds of miles apart.) By the time their training was completed, Einsatzgruppen officers and their men had a thorough understanding of their responsibilities. Since it was possible to transfer out of the Einsatzgruppen, anyone who stayed in the units had decided he was willing to participate in mass murder.

While the Einsatzgruppen were being trained in Germany, Heydrich and the army formulated an agreement. Heydrich's Main Office for Reich Security, or RSHA, would have complete control over the Einsatzgruppen, allowing them to perform their "special tasks" not only in the rear of the combat zone, but also in areas where military operations were ongoing. They would be supplied with vehicular transportation, not forced to travel on foot like infantrymen, and would not be fighting the Soviet army. The Einsatzgruppen were also charged with quickly capturing and eliminating all unarmed civilians before they could escape.

On June 22, 1941, Germany launched its surprise attack on the Soviet Union, which was caught completely unprepared. With no evacuation plan, 2.5 million Jews remained in areas that would soon be reached by the German army. Historians note that some people in the Soviet Union, especially citizens of the Ukraine and the Baltic states, independent countries that had been taken over by the Soviet Union a year earlier, actually welcomed the Germans. Many of the people in the Baltic states thought the Germans would free them from harsh Russian domination. The Soviets had arrested opponents of the Communists and sent them to Siberia. In the Ukraine, thousands of farmers had been executed by Joseph Stalin's secret police during the 1930s. Hundreds of thousands (some estimate the number to be in the millions) of people had died in famines that resulted from Soviet economic policies. Many of the people who welcomed the German advance also agreed with Nazi policies regarding Jews, having convinced themselves that the hated communist regime was headed by Jews and only benefitted other Jews. (In fact, although the Soviet government officially gave Jews rights equal to those of other citizens, Stalin's government banned all Jewish cultural organizations, persecuted people who tried to practice their religion, and was ruthlessly hostile to anyone who tried to maintain a Jewish identity.)

A long history of anti-Semitism existed among the people in the Baltic states and the Ukraine, and the arrival of the Germans only intensified the hatred of Jews. Despite having lived in these countries for hundreds of years, Jews were considered foreigners. Pogroms—organized acts of violence against Jews that were often supported by authorities—were especially common in the Ukraine in the late nineteenth and early twentieth centuries, and were frequently orchestrated by the government of the Russian czar. In 1919, during the war between communists and Ukrainian nationalists, Ukrainian forces massacred tens of thousands of Jews.

It seemed likely that the people of these countries would be natural allies for the Germans due to their desire to establish independent countries free from Russian domination, their hatred of the communist dictatorship, and their anti-Semitism. They were, however, completely unprepared for Nazi policies regarding their own countries. The Nazis encouraged local anti-Semitic sentiment as a means to destroy Jews, and citizens in the Ukraine and the Baltic states joined SS auxiliary units and other groups that aided the Germans. The Germans also tried to stir up new pogroms whenever they could. The Nazi belief in the superiority of the German race was so deeply ingrained, however, that they never made a concerted effort to organize the local people into a permanent, cohesive force against the Soviet army. The Germans never established separate countries in the conquered area; rather they relegated each region to the rule of Nazi officials who treated the local population with contempt. The Germans seized valuable items, which they sent back to Germany, and treated the population as semi-slaves. Before long, large partisan movements, often in cooperation with the Soviet army, arose to oppose the Germans.

The attitude of many Soviet Jews toward the German invasion was even more surprising than that of non-Jews. Apparently, most Jews in towns and smaller cities had no idea that the Nazis wanted to harm them, thus making it easier for German troops to kill a great number of Jews in the initial days of the invasion. In July 1941, one German offi-

The RSHA: The Bureaucracy of Death

At the beginning of World War II, the various branches of the SS and the government police were assimilated into one central organization, called the Main Office for Reich Security, or RSHA (the initials of its German name). The head of the RSHA was Reinhard Heydrich, leader of the SD and second in command to Heinrich Himmler, who headed most of the Nazi security forces. The RSHA was comprised of seven bureaus. Bureau IV was the Gestapo and IVB was the branch of the Gestapo responsible for watching and controlling various religious groups. Section 4 of Bureau IVB, known as IVB-4, was the "Jewish Affairs Section," headed by Adolf Eichmann. Before the war, Eichmann was in charge of forcing Jews to leave Austria and Germany; later his job would be to consolidate Jews throughout Europe and send them to their deaths. Himmler, Heydrich, and Eichmann became the three men who, more than any other individuals, directed the Holocaust.

cer reported that Soviet Jews were unaware of the treatment of Jews in Germany and Poland. Although they did not expect to have equal rights with other Russians, he said, they thought the Germans would leave them alone. The Soviet Jews' passiveness was understandable in light of their isolation: Small-town Jews in Russia were impoverished and largely unaware of world events, including recent developments in neighboring Poland. The Soviet government, which had been on friendly terms with Germany since the signing of the Nazi-Soviet Pact, manipulated newspapers and radio broadcasts in the country, and Stalin had banned any news regarding Nazi atrocities against Polish Jews.

Between 1933 and 1939, prior to the ill-fated agreement between the nations, the Soviet govern-

German soldiers look on as a member of Einsatzgruppe D prepares to shoot a Ukrainian Jew kneeling on the edge of a mass grave filled with corpses. *(Library of Congress/USHMM Photo Archives)*

ment often publicized and denounced the Nazis' actions. A number of factors led many Jews to ignore these reports or question their truthfulness. The Soviet government tended to spread stories about poor conditions in other countries in order to present their own government as a decent alternative. Many Jews also had favorable memories of the Germans from World War I, when Germany had invaded and occupied parts of Russia. At that time, German troops had been friendly and courteous to the Jewish population, who largely remembered the Germans as protectors who stopped the pogroms of the hated Russian czar. The Jews and the Germans were also united by similarities in their languages: German is closely related to Yiddish, the language of eastern European Jews. More than twenty years after the end of World War I, many Russian Jews still thought that Germans were not as anti-Jewish as their own neighbors in the Soviet Union.

The Shootings

Aided by the Jewish population's lack of knowledge about world events, by the chaos of the Soviet army's retreat, and often by the anti-Semitism of the local population, the Nazis were able to murder hundreds of thousands of Jews within the first few months of the Russian invasion. A subunit of an Einsatzgruppe, an Einsatzkommando, swept into one town and village after another and crushed the Jewish population. In his post-World War II testimony, Otto Ohlendorf, commander of Einsatzgruppe D, described events in Russia. The Germans would ask prominent Jewish leaders to call together Jews for "resettlement." They then gathered the Jews in a central location (such as a school or the grounds of a factory), seized their valuables, and marched everyone—men, women, and children— away, usually to a nearby forest. The Einsatzkommando lined up the Jews beside a ditch, ordered them to remove their outer clothing (in many cases, all clothing), and shot them. The corpses were then thrown into the ditch. Ohlendorf testified that he never allowed one individual man to shoot, but rather ordered several troops to shoot at the same time, so that no one man was directly responsible. The Einsatzkommando officer would climb into the ditch full of dead bodies and shoot people who were still moving.

In other Einsatzgruppen operations, victims were forced to lie down on their stomachs at the edge of a ditch. A German armed with a rifle would stand over them, shoot them in the back of the neck, push the body into the ditch, and repeat the process. Blood and brain fragments would often splatter onto the Germans' uniforms. Ohlendorf testified that he disapproved of this method because the psychological burden was too great, both for the victim and the man who did the shooting.

Kovno

In December 1941 an SS colonel in Einsatzgruppe A, attempting to impress upon his superiors the difficulties of fulfilling execution orders, described the methods and procedures followed by his unit. Each operation required considerable knowledge about local conditions, he said. The colonel's men had to travel from their base in the Lithuanian city of Kovno (Kaunas) to their *aktions,* a round trip of between 90 and 120 miles. They had to plan carefully in order to carry out as many as five execution operations each week and still have time to keep up with their duties in Kovno. Things were easier in Kovno itself, the colonel admitted, because there were enough Lithuanian auxiliaries available. Many Jews in

Kovno were already dead when the SS colonel wrote this report; the murders began as soon as the Soviet army retreated from the city. Gangs of Lithuanian anti-Semites attacked and robbed Jews on June 23 and June 24, 1941. On June 25, they conducted a vicious pogrom, marching from house to house in the Jewish slum district and killing every Jew they could find. As they did in many places, the Germans encouraged these actions and secretly helped organize the mobs. It was important, the commander of Einsatzgruppe A wrote, to make it seem that the local population had attacked the Jews on their own initiative and not under the direction of the Nazis.

During the pogrom, 10,000 Jews were arrested and taken to Fort Number Seven, one of several old military posts surrounding Kovno. For days, the Lithuanians killed large groups of Jews, sometimes raping the women first. The bodies, numbering almost 7,000, were buried in large pits. The 30,000 surviving Jews in the area were forced to move into a ghetto established in the slum district where the murder march had occurred. Throughout the summer of 1941, the Germans forced hundreds of people out of the ghetto and executed them. In October 9,000-10,000 people, including thousands of children, were taken to Fort Number Nine and shot. The Germans referred to Fort Number Nine as the *Schlachtfeld,* or "slaughter ground." During the time the Germans held Kovno, 100,000 people (70,000 of whom were Jews) were killed in the forts surrounding the city.

Minsk

The German army captured Minsk, the capital of White Russia (Belarus), on June 30, 1941, only eight days after the invasion began, and placed most of the city's adult men in a guarded camp. When Einsatzgruppe B arrived, its members picked out Jews, Communist officials, and "Asiatics [Soviet people]," took them away, and shot them. By late July, the 80,000 to 100,000 remaining Jews in the Minsk area were confined to a ghetto. Following the protocol established in Poland, the Germans ordered the creation of a *Judenrat.* Unlike most of the Jewish councils in Poland, however, the Minsk *Judenrat* immediately began to help organize resistance to the Nazis. Some Jews from the Minsk ghetto were able to escape to join partisan units in nearby forests, and others formed their own units.

Explaining the Murder of Children

When Otto Ohlendorf, the commander of Einsatzgruppe D, testified in the Nuremberg trials after the war, he was asked why the lives of Jewish children were not spared. Ohlendorf responded that he was simply following orders to exterminate all Jews. He defended the killings by saying that Jews were a threat to the security of the German forces. His orders included Jewish children in that security risk. When asked if genocide and racial policies were the true reasons for the killing of children, Ohlendorf said they were not: If children were allowed to grow up, he rationalized, they would surely become the enemies of the Nazis, who had killed their parents. The only way to prevent this was to eliminate everyone.

On November 7 and November 20, a total of nearly 20,000 people were taken from the Minsk ghetto, forced to dig pits for their own graves in the forest, and were shot. In March 1942 the Germans murdered 5,000 people in retaliation for the *Judenrat's* failure to cooperate. Among the victims were the children of the ghetto orphanage, who were burned alive. After this, thousands of Jews tried to escape the ghetto to hide in the forests, but in July 1942 another 30,000 people were shot. The last inhabitants of the ghetto were killed in October 1943.

Babi Yar

The worst massacre was perpetrated at the Ukranian capital of Kiev, which the German army captured on September 19 after forty-five-days of battle. Within a few days, all Jews were ordered to report for "resettlement." They gathered together, carrying small bundles, and were led out of town past the Jewish cemetery to Babi Yar, an area of sand dunes with a large ravine. As each small group reached Babi Yar they were ordered to strip,

Jewish Partisans

Tens of thousands of Jews participated in partisan movements organized to fight the Germans in the countryside. Initial attempts at organization were plagued by anti-Semitism, however, as some partisan groups refused to allow Jews to join or killed them. While this was less true of groups controlled by the Soviet army, the partisan organizations usually only accepted people who could supply their own weapons, and Jews often could not. Some Jewish units became famous for their resistance, and were often known by the names of their commanders, such as "Uncle Mischa" in western White Russia and "Abba Kovner" in Lithuania. Kovner had been a commander of the armed resistance group in the Vilna ghetto (the FPO, the initials for United Partisan Organization in the Yiddish language). He escaped into the forest after the Germans put down a revolt in the Vilna ghetto in September 1943.

In addition to ordinary partisan groups, some Jews who escaped from the Einsatzgruppen or from the ghettos hid in the forests with their families, establishing "family camps" that combined offensive partisan activities with defensive protection measures. Probably the largest of these was the 1,200-person camp commanded by the Belski brothers in western White Russia. It was difficult to protect such a large number of people, including children, from German patrols. There were also at least sixty armed resistance movements active in ghettos located in the westernmost sections of the Soviet Union (those areas that had been part of Poland until 1939).

A thirteen-year-old Russian partisan, one of a large number of children who fought against the German army. *(Reproduced by permission of AP/Wide World Photos)*

hand over their bundles, and march to the edge of the ravine, where they were shot with machine guns. Working for two days, the machine gunners filled the ravine with 33,000 bodies.

The "Final Solution"

With stunning speed, German tanks rolled through the Baltic states, White Russia, and the Ukraine, then penetrated into Russia itself. The Einsatzgruppen followed closely behind, killing Jews in each town: 7,000 in Zhitomir, 4,000 in Vitebsk, 4,900 in Mogilev, 4,000 in Gomel. This pattern was repeated in each part of the Soviet Union that was captured by the Germans: The Einsatzgruppen would enter an area, round up as many Jews as they could, march them to an isolated area in the woods outside the town, and shoot

A Memorial to the Jews

At least 21 million Soviet citizens died in World War II, far more than in any other country. During and after the war, the Soviet government underscored the suffering of the Soviet people at the hands of the Nazis and praised their heroism in defeating Germany. The government particularly tried to downplay the fact that Jews were the main targets of the Nazis, a claim that many observers consider an example of Soviet anti-Semitism. Fifteen years after the war, popular young Russian poet Yevgeny Yevtushenko wrote "Babi Yar," a poem confronting the issues of the Holocaust, Soviet silence, and anti-Semitism:

> There is no gravestone at Baby Yar,
> Only coarse earth piled roughly over the gash.
> I am afraid. Today I feel old,
> As old as the Jews....
> O my own people, my own Russian folk,
> Believers in the brotherhood of man!
> But dirty hands too often dare to raise
> The banner of your pure and lofty name....

> No drop of Jewish blood flows in my veins,
> But every anti-Semite, with a bitter, hard hate
> Hates me like a Jew.
> O know me truly Russian through their hate!

Soviet authorities attacked Yevtushenko for his poem, which gained worldwide attention. The government claimed he had smeared the Russian people and concentrated too much on the suffering of the Jews. In 1966 memorial plaques were placed at Babi Yar; in 1974, more than thirty years after the massacre, a monument was built at the site. There was no mention that the preponderance of people buried there were Jewish victims. A new memorial has since been added, describing the fate of the Jews.

German police look through the clothing of people killed during a shooting action at Babi Yar. *(Hessiches Hauptstaatsarchiv/USHMM Photo Archives)*

Adolf Eichmann, head of the RSHA's Jewish Affairs Section, researched the fastest, most efficient and least bloody ways to kill millions of Jews. When tried in Israel after the war, he said he was only doing his job. He was found guilty and executed for his crimes. *(Library of Congress)*

them. Then the Einsatzgruppen would move farther east, following the advance of the German army. According to German statistics, 250,000 Jews were killed in the Baltic states and White Russia in the first three months of invasion. Within five months, 500,000 Soviet Jews were dead. In January 1942 the commander of Einsatzgruppe A reported that Lithuania was clear of Jews, and that more than 136,000 people had been killed. Despite the sheer number of people executed in some of the operations, the Nazis were unable to kill all the Jews. Two million were still alive in conquered Soviet territory, and millions more lived in other European countries under German control. The Nazis were nonetheless undeterred in their efforts to eliminate all European Jews.

On July 31, 1941, a little over a month after the invasion of the Soviet Union began, Reinhard Heydrich received an order from Hermann Göring, the officer in charge of Nazi policy toward the Jews and second in command to Hitler. (Soon Himmler, the head of the SS, would take over Göring's job and become the second most powerful man in Germany.) In 1939 Göring put Heydrich in charge

of the initial solution to the "Jewish question," which was forced emigration of the Jews, as was carried out in Germany and Austria. Germany now controlled a majority of Europe. Requiring Jews from so many countries to move, especially during wartime, was impossible. A new plan was needed. After giving Heydrich the authority to involve all necessary agencies of the German government, Göring ordered him to submit a plan for the *Endlösung*, or "Final Solution" to the Jewish question. The ambiguity of the language does not disguise the true meaning of the "Final Solution": the systematic physical destruction of European Jews. The decision was not Göring's alone and had already been discussed at the top levels of the Nazi party and government. Victor Brack, one of Hitler's closest assistants, admitted after the war that several months before Göring's order to Heydrich was issued, many high-ranking Nazis were aware of the extermination policy. Although no written record of such an order survived the war, historians agree that the decision must have been made by Hitler.

As head of the Main Office for Reich Security or RSHA, Heydrich was charged with carrying out the "Final Solution." Playing a central role in the Russian invasion as head of the Einsatzgruppen, supervising the "emigration" of Jews from Germany, and playing an important role in the relocation and murder of Jews in Poland all qualified Heydrich to execute the large-scale murder proposed by the Nazi government. He had issued an order in 1939 that situated Jewish ghettos along railroad lines to ease subsequent efforts in fulfilling the "final aim." He wrote that achieving this elusive goal would take a long time and would require absolute secrecy.

Heydrich met with Adolf Eichmann, the head of the Jewish Affairs Section of the RSHA who had been directly responsible for enforcing much of the "emigration" policy in Poland. (At his trial in Israel in 1961, Eichmann testified that Heydrich claimed Hitler had ordered the mass extermination of Jews.) Heydrich sent Eichmann to the Polish city of Lublin to learn more about the methods being used to kill the Jews there. According to Eichmann's testimony, Nazi officials at Lublin's Majdanek concentration camp showed him airtight chambers disguised as farmers' cottages. They could pump in carbon monoxide fumes from the exhaust of a captured Russian submarine's motor to kill everyone inside the chamber. Eichmann later delivered a message from Hey-

The First Massacres

The first wave of shootings by the Einsatzgruppen resulted in the deaths of hundreds of thousands of people, totals that only account for some of the towns and cities invaded by the Germans. In many of these places, especially larger cities, the first massacres did not kill all

Jews. In these cases, a ghetto was usually established to house the Jews until the remainder could be killed, bringing the total number of deaths much higher than shown here. Like many statistics of wartime deaths, numbers vary depending on the source.

Bakchiserai	1,099	Mariupol	9,000
Berdichev	35,000	Melitopol	2,000
Bobruisk	6,179	Minsk	21,000
Borisov	8,200	Mogilev	4,844
Chernigov	10,000	Piatigorsk	1,500
Dniepropetrovsk	31,000	Polotsk	8,000
Essentuki	1,500	Poltava	12,000
Gomel	4,000	Rostov	18,000
Kerch	7,000	Smolensk	3,000
Kharkov	20,000	Uman	30,000
Kiev	50,000	Vitebsk	4,090
Kislovodsk	2,000	Zhitimir	7,000

drich to the SS commander in Lublin, General Odilo Globocnik, ordering him to start killing 250,000 Polish Jews. Eichmann then went to Auschwitz, a concentration camp in southeastern Poland. Himmler had ordered that Auschwitz be changed into a death camp. Eichmann and the commander of Auschwitz discussed plans to make the camp into the main killing center for European Jews. Sometime later, probably in November 1941, Eichmann traveled to Minsk under orders from Heinrich Müller, head of the Gestapo. Sent to investigate the most efficient, quickest, and least bloody methods of execution, Eichmann watched as a group of Jews were forced to jump into a pit and were shot. At his trial, Eichmann claimed he was terribly upset at witnessing the execution of a woman and her small child because he had children of his own.

In winter 1941, Heydrich called a conference at Wannsee, a lakeside suburb of Berlin. The conference was originally scheduled for December but was postponed, probably due to the Japanese bombing

of the U.S naval base in Pearl Harbor, Hawaii, and attack on British-controlled areas in Asia. Surprising almost everyone in Germany, Hitler declared war on the United States, thus placing the Nazis at war with Great Britain, the Soviet Union, and the United States—all of them powerful enemies. Despite these military entanglements, the Nazis continued to apply their resources to killing the Jews, and Heydrich's conference was delayed only until January 20, 1942. By this time, half a million Soviet Jews had already been killed, and the Nazis had opened a death camp at Chelmno in western Poland, and were using gas vans to kill the Jews of that area. Himmler had also issued orders to convert Auschwitz into a massive death camp.

The purpose of the Wannsee Conference was not to decide what to do about the Jews, but to inform the various branches of the German government about the decision and ensure they complied with its execution. A total of fifteen men attended the meeting, including Heydrich, Eichmann, and Müller. High officials of the German foreign min-

The Wannsee Villa, where details for the "Final Solution" were ironed out. *(Reproduced by permission of Bildarchiv Preussischer Kulturbesitz),*

istry and the ministries of the interior, justice, and economic planning also attended, as did a representative of the German governor-general of occupied Poland, two people from the ministry for the occupied eastern territories, top officials from the head office of the Nazi party, and administrators from the office of the Reich chancellor.

Heydrich reported that his previous attempts at solving the "Jewish problem" by forced emigration were now disrupted by the expansion of the war. Himmler had banned the emigration of Jews, and Heydrich informed his listeners that "evacuation of the Jews to the east" was the current policy of Nazi Germany. Applied knowledge was being gathered, Heydrich added, which would assist in the execution of the "Final Solution." This referred to the Einsatzgruppen operations in Russia and the experiments with gas vans at Chelmno. The "Final Solution" meant sending Jews to the east "for labor utilization," said Heydrich. They would be separated by sex; those able to work would be put into large labor columns to build roads. Heydrich did not explain what would happen to those who were

too old, too young, or too sick to work, but made it clear that those who could not work would not live for long. Those who did not die from overwork, malnourishment, and disease were the toughest Jews, according to Heydrich. If they were ever freed, they would be a seed from which the Jews might develop again, and would therefore "have to be dealt with appropriately." Heydrich estimated the number of Jews in each European country, placing the total at nearly 11 million, a figure that included Jewish populations in Great Britain, Spain, Switzerland, and even Ireland—countries outside the German sphere of influence. Every European Jew was a target.

The fifteen men at the conference discussed the problems involved in arresting and deporting the Jews of each country under German control. The representative of the Foreign Ministry worried that the deportation of Jews in some German-occupied countries like Denmark might lead to opposition in those countries. (In fact, the Danish people succeeded in saving almost all Danish Jews.) In other countries, such as Romania (which was an ally of

Heydrich's Report to the Wannsee Conference

This table shows the number of Jews still alive in each country, according to Reinhard Heydrich's report to the Wannsee Conference. The total given is 10,803,500, but some of the figures Heydrich used were inaccurate;

for example, his estimate of 3 million Jews in the Ukraine was almost double the actual number, and many had already been killed. Similarly, there were less than half as many Jews in France as Heydrich thought.

Albania	200	Latvia	3,500
Austria	43,700	Lithuania	34,000
Belgium	43,000	Netherlands	160,800
Bulgaria	48,000	Norway	1,300
Croatia	40,000	Poland (Bialystok District)	400,000
Czech lands	74,200	Poland (Main Part)	2,284,000
(Bohemia and Moravia)		Romania	342,000
Denmark	5,600	Serbia	10,000
Estonia	"Free of Jews"	Slovakia	88,000
France	865,000	Spain	6,000
Germany	131,800	Switzerland	18,000
Great Britain	330,000	USSR (total)	5,000,000
Greece	69,600	"Eastern Territories"	420,000
Hungary	742,800	Ukraine	2,994,684
Ireland	4,000	White Russia	446,484
Italy	58,000		

Germany and under strong German influence), the Nazis were afraid the government might protect Jews who could bribe government officials.

Conference members also discussed the treatment of people who were one-half or one-quarter Jewish, or who were married to non-Jews. They talked about certain exceptions, including Jews who had won medals or had been seriously wounded fighting in the German army in World War I (1914–1918). These Jews would be sent to a special camp at Theresienstadt in Czechoslovakia, Heydrich said, rather than being "resettled." (In fact, most Jews sent to Theresienstadt were later sent to Auschwitz and killed.) Jews working at jobs necessary to the German war effort were not supposed to be deported until they could be replaced, a special concern of the army and Hermann Göring, who was in charge of economic planning. This exception was usually ignored in practice—Nazi leaders

were often willing to damage their chances of winning the war in favor of eliminating Jews.

Although the written record of the conference prepared by Eichmann does not reflect this, he testified at his trial that the conference ended with discussions of exactly how to kill the Jews. The technical problems of mass shooting and poison gas were described and debated, and every person at the conference understood that "evacuation" meant genocide. Eichmann would soon begin work on technical details regarding the consolidation and transportation of Jews in each country, and the death camps in Poland were being equipped to receive their first victims. The men in charge of the "Final Solution" celebrated. When the Wannsee Conference ended and the others left, Heydrich, Müller, and Eichmann reportedly stayed behind, sitting around the fireplace, drinking brandy, and singing songs.

Soviet POWs are forced to conceal the bodies of an Einsatzgruppe action in the Ukraine, 1943. *(Hessiches Hauptstaatsarchiv/USHMM Photo Archives)*

A German Eyewitness to Genocide

The decision to eliminate the Jews of Europe was already being implemented in the Soviet Union. As the army and the Einsatzgruppen moved out of an area, it was handed over to German civilian administrators, who established ghettos for the remaining Jews forced to work for the Germans. Large groups of people, usually beginning with those too old, too young, or too sick to work, were periodically removed from the ghettos and massacred. In the summer and fall of 1942, a second massive wave of killings swept through the occupied Soviet Union as most ghettos were eliminated completely. In October, a German construction engineer named Hermann Friedrich Graebe was in Dubno, Ukraine, working as a civilian under contract to the army. He heard reports that the Jews of the Dubno ghetto were being killed in large pits near the construction project he was supervising, and decided to investigate for himself. Truckloads of Jews were being unloaded near mounds of earth six feet high and thirty yards long. From behind the mounds, Graebe heard rifle shots. SS men and Ukrainian auxiliaries guarded Jews, who undressed and placed their clothes in piles. Graebe estimated that there were already 800 to 1,000 pairs of shoes.

Groups of about twenty people at a time were ordered to go behind the mound, where Graebe saw a huge mass grave. Graebe estimated 1,000 people were shoved into the grave: many dead, some still moving, almost all of them covered in blood. People were forced to climb over the dead and dying into the pit, and were then shot.

In the winter of 1942–1943 the Soviet army began a series of successful counteroffensives against the Germans. In huge battles that destroyed entire army groups, the Germans were forced back, and the Soviets recaptured cities and towns the German army had taken in 1941. It took almost two years to drive the Germans completely out of Soviet territory. Ninety percent of the Jews, or about 228,000 people, in the three Baltic countries of Lithuania, Latvia, and Estonia had been killed; two-thirds of Ukrainian Jews (900,000 people) and about 60 percent (245,000 people) of those in White Russia (Belarus) were dead. Some 90 percent of Russian Jews survived, but only because the German army never reached them.

Most Russian Jews were shot to death, but some were driven into the sea or rivers and drowned, and yet others had been burned alive. In addition, on the orders of Himmler, the Nazis experimented with another method. Specially constructed trucks were brought to Russia from Germany. Women and children (who were targeted for this method of killing because Himmler felt shooting them was too hard on SS men) were forced into the trucks and told they were being transport-ed elsewhere. The motor was turned on, and the exhaust fumes were piped into the sealed truck. Those inside died in about ten or fifteen minutes. This was the first time gassing had been used to kill Jews. It would not be the last, however—gassing would become the Nazis' preferred method of exterminating European Jews.

PRIMARY SOURCE

Avraham Tory
Excerpt from *Surviving the Holocaust: The Kovno Ghetto Diary*
Published in 1990

When Adolf Hitler prepared to invade Poland, he first made an agreement with Premier Joseph Stalin of the Soviet Union that made the two countries allies. A secret protocol divided eastern Europe into German and Soviet spheres, and allocated specific sections of Poland to each of the two nations before any shots were even fired. Hitler gave Stalin control over Lithuania, a small country located on the southeastern shore of the Baltic Sea, bordering both Poland and modern-day Belarus. Shortly after the German invasion of Poland, the Soviets established military bases throughout Lithuania. By summer 1940, Lithuania was officially annexed to the Soviet Union as the Lithuanian SSR (Soviet Socialist Republic).

Under Soviet rule, the situation for Lithuanian Jews changed dramatically. The Soviets abolished the esteemed Hebrew educational system, closed down cultural organizations, and eliminated most Yiddish daily newspapers. During a massive deportation, some 7,000 Jews were exiled to Siberia and other areas of Soviet Asia; among those sent away were business leaders, Zionist activists, merchants, and public figures.

Then Germany invaded Lithuania, spreading anti-Semitic destruction and terror in the process. Anti-Semitic sentiment raged in the country after the Nazis took over in 1941. Many anti-Jewish nationals thought the Germans were heros for rescuing the country from the Soviets. Shortly after the German invasion, many Jews made a desperate attempt to flee Lithuania, but while 15,000 Jews managed to escape to the Soviet Union, some 220,000 more remained in Lithuania. The Nazis quickly implemented an organized program for the complete elimination of Lithuania's Jews. Within the first two months of German occupation, an estimated 10,000 Jews were murdered by rioting Lithuanian anti-Semites and Nazis. Much of the violence occurred in the city of Kovno (now Kaunas) at the Seventh Fort (one of the forts circling the city that dated back to czarist rule). On June 24, 1941, the Nazis established two ghettos in Kovno. The "large ghetto" and "small ghetto" were located in the district of Slobodka, just outside the city, and imprisoned about 30,000 people.

Avraham Tory was born Avraham Golub in Lazdijai, Lithuania, in 1909. He attended religious schools, graduating in 1927, and then studied law in Kovno and in the United States at the University of Pittsburgh. Tory completed his law studies in 1933. He was active in promoting sports activities and local Zionist movements. His activities led him to travel throughout Europe representing Lithuanian Jews. Tory was attending a Zionist conference in Geneva when the German army invaded Poland in September of 1939. Delegates from eastern European countries debated on whether to return home or to remain in neutral Switzerland. Tory decided to return to Kovno, and Lithuania soon fell to the Soviets, who established military bases and installed communist rule over the country. With the German invasion of Lithuania in June 1941, Nazi repression replaced Soviet repression.

The Nazis immediately moved all Jews into ghettos in segments of major cities, and Tory became a member of the *Judenrat* in the Kovno ghetto. It was in this capacity that he wrote a diary and collected whatever photographs, paintings, and sketches he could obtain, in order to document the events he witnessed accurately and objectively. The following excerpt describes an action on October 28, 1941, that effectively reduced the size of the ghetto by 9,000-10,000 people, nearly half of whom were children. Only those who could work were not killed in the mass executions.

Surviving the Holocaust: The Kovno Ghetto Diary

October 28, 1941
MEMOIR

On Friday afternoon, October 24, 1941, a Gestapo car entered the Ghetto. It carried the Gestapo chief, Captain Schmitz, and Master Sergeant Rauca. Their appearance filled all onlookers with fear. The Council was worried and ordered the Jewish Ghetto police to follow all their movements. These movements were rather unusual. The two Ghetto rulers turned neither to the Council offices nor to the Jewish police, nor to the German labor office, nor even to the German commandant, as they used to in their visits to the ghetto. Instead, they toured various places as if looking for something, tarried awhile in Demokratu Square, looked it over, and left through the gate, leaving in their wake an ominously large question mark: what were they scheming to do?

The next day, Saturday afternoon, an urgent message was relayed from the Ghetto gate to the Council: Rauca, accompanied by a high-ranking Gestapo officer, was coming....

The two Germans entered the offices of the Council. Rauca did not waste time. He opened with a major pronouncement: it is imperative to increase the size of the Jewish labor force in view of its importance for the German war effort—an allusion to the indispensability of Jewish labor to the Germans. Furthermore, he continued, the Gestapo is aware that food rations allotted to the ghetto inmates do not provide proper nourishment to heavy-labor workers and, therefore, he intends to increase rations for both the workers and their families so that they will be able to achieve greater output for the Reich. The remaining ghetto inmates, those not included in the Jewish labor force, would have to make do with the existing rations. To forestall competition and envy between them and the Jewish labor force, they would be separated from them and

transferred to the small Ghetto [a smaller, separate, and secure section of the Kovno Ghetto]. In this fashion, those contributing to the war effort would obtain more spacious and comfortable living quarters. To carry out this operation a roll call would take place. The Council was to issue an order in which all the Ghetto inmates, without exception, and irrespective of sex and age, were called to report to Demokratu Square on October 28, at 6 A.M. on the dot. In the square they should line up by families and by the workplace of the family head. When leaving for the roll call they were to leave their apartments, closets, and drawers open. Anybody found after 6 A.M. in his home would be shot on the spot.

The members of the Council were shaken and overcome by fear. This order boded very ill for the future of the Ghetto. But what did it mean? Dr. Elkes attempted to get Rauca to divulge some information about the intention behind this roll call, but his efforts bore no fruit. Rauca refused to add another word to his communication and, accompanied by his associate, left the Council office and the Ghetto.

The members of the Council remained in a state of shock. What lay in wait for the Ghetto? What was the true purpose of the roll call? Why did Rauca order the Council to publish the order, rather than publish it himself? Was he planning to abuse the trust the Ghetto population had in the Jewish leadership? And if so, had the Council the right to comply with Rauca's order and publish it, thereby becoming an accomplice in an act which might spell disaster?

Some Council members proposed to disobey the Gestapo and not publish the order, even if this would mean putting the lives of the Council members at risk. Others feared that in the case of disobedience the arch-henchmen would not be contented with punishing the Council alone, but would vent their wrath also on the Ghetto inmates, and that thou-

sands of Jews were liable to pay with their lives for the impudence of their leaders. After all, no one could fathom the intentions of Rauca and his men; why, then, stir the beasts of prey into anger? Was the Council entitled to take responsibility for the outcome of not publishing the order? On the other hand, was the Council entitled to take upon itself the heavy burden of moral responsibility and go ahead with publishing the order?...

Immediately after their visit to the chief rabbi, members of the Council convened for a special meeting and decided to publish the decree. So it was that on October 27, 1941, announcements in Yiddish and German were posted by the Council throughout the Ghetto. Their text was as follows:

The Council has been ordered by the authorities to publish the following official decree to Ghetto inmates:

All inmates of the Ghetto, without exception, including children and the sick, are to leave their homes on Tuesday, October 28, 1941, at 6 A.M. and to assemble in the square between the big blocks and the Demokratu Street, and to line up in accordance with police instructions.

The Ghetto inmates are required to report by families, each family being headed by the worker who is the head of the family.

It is forbidden to lock apartments, wardrobes, cupboards, desks, etc....

After 6 A.M. nobody may remain in his apartment.

Anyone found in the apartments after 6 A.M. will be shot on sight.

The wording was chosen by the Council so that everyone would understand that it concerned a Gestapo order; that the Council had no part in it.

The Ghetto was agog. Until the publication of this order everyone had carried his fears in his own heart. Now those fears and forebodings broke out.... The Ghetto remembered well the way the previous "actions" had been prepared, in which some 2,800 people had met their deaths. An additional sign of the impending disaster was that on the very same day workers in various places were furnished with special papers issued by their German employers— military and paramilitary—certifying that their holders were employed on a permanent basis at such-and-such a German factory or workplace....

Tuesday morning, October 28, was rainy. A heavy mist covered the sky and the whole Ghetto was shrouded in darkness. A fine sleet filled the air and covered the ground in a thin layer. From all directions, dragging themselves heavily and falteringly, groups of men, women, and children, elderly and sick who leaned on the arms of their relatives or neighbors, babies carried in their mothers' arms, proceeded in long lines. They were all wrapped in winter coats, shawls, or blankets, so as to protect themselves from the cold and the damp. Many carried in their hands lanterns or candles, which cast a faint light, illuminating their way in the darkness.

Many families stepped along slowly, holding hands. They all made their way in the same direction—to Demokratu Square. It was a procession of mourners grieving over themselves. Some thirty thousand people proceeded that morning into the unknown, toward a fate that could already have been sealed for them by the bloodthirsty rulers.

A deathlike silence pervaded this procession tens of thousands strong. Every person dragged himself along, absorbed in his own thoughts, pondering his own fate and the fate of his family whose lives hung by a thread. Thirty thousand lonely people, forgotten by God and by man, delivered to the whim of tyrants whose hands had already spilled the blood of many Jews....

The Ghetto inmates were lined up in columns according to the workplace of the family heads. The first column consisted of Council members, followed by the column of the Jewish policemen and their families. On both sides and behind stood the workers in the Ghetto institutions, and many columns of the various Jewish labor brigades together with their families, since on that day the Ghetto was sealed off. No one was allowed to go out to work....

Three hours went by. The cold and the damp penetrated their bones. The endless waiting for the sentence had driven many people out of their minds. Religious Jews mumbled prayers and Psalms. The old and the sick whimpered. Babies cried aloud. In every eye the same horrible question stood out: "When will it begin?! When will it begin?!"

At 9 A.M. a Gestapo entourage appeared at the square: the deputy Gestapo-chief, Captain Schmitz, Master Sergeant Rauca, Captain Jordan, and Captain Tornbaum, accompanied by a squad of the German policemen and Lithuanian partisans.

The square was surrounded by machine-gun emplacements. Rauca positioned himself on top of a *little mound from which he could watch the great crowd that waited in the square in tense and anxious anticipation. His glance ranged briefly over the column of the Council members and the Jewish Ghetto police, and by a movement of his hand he motioned them to the left, which, as it became clear later, was the "good" side. Then he signaled with the baton he held in his hand and ordered the remaining columns: "Forward!" The selection had begun.*

The columns of employees of the Ghetto institutions and their families passed before Rauca, followed by other columns, one after another. The Gestapo man fixed his gaze on each pair of eyes and with a flick of the finger on his right hand passed sentence on individuals, families, or even whole groups. Elderly and sick persons, families with children, single women, and persons whose physique did not impress him in terms of labor power, were directed to the right. There, they immediately fell into the hands of the German policemen and the Lithuanian partisans, who showered them with shouts and blows and pushed them toward an opening especially made in the fence, where two Germans counted them and then reassembled them in a different place.

At first, nobody knew which was the "good" side. Many therefore rejoiced at finding themselves on the right. They began thanking Rauca, saying "Thank you kindly," or even "Thank you for your mercy." There were many men and women who, having been directed to the left, asked permission to move over to the right and join their relatives from whom they had been separated. Smiling sarcastically, Rauca gave his consent....

The selection process was completed only after nightfall, but not before Rauca made sure that the quota had been fulfilled and that some 10,000 people had been transferred to the small Ghetto. Only then were those who had passed through the selection, and had remained standing in the square, allowed to return to their homes.

About 17,000 out of some 27,000 people slowly left the vast square where they had been standing for more than twelve hours. Hungry, thirsty, crushed, and dejected, they returned home, most of them bereaved or orphaned, having been separated from a father, a mother, children, a brother or a sister, a grandfather or grandmother, an uncle or an aunt. A deep mourning descended on the Ghetto. In every

house there were now empty rooms, unoccupied beds, and the belongings of those who had not returned from the selection. One-third of the Ghetto population had been cut down....

[The next morning, there] was an autumnal, foggy, and gloomy dawn.... German policemen and drunken Lithuanian partisans broke into the small Ghetto, like so many ferocious beasts, and began driving the Jews out of their homes. The assault was so unexpected and brutal that the wretched inmates did not have a single moment to grasp what was going on. The partisans barked out their orders to leave the houses and to line up in rows and columns. Each column was immediately surrounded by partisans, shouting "Forward march, you scum, forward march," and driving the people by rifle butts out of the small Ghetto toward the road leading to the Ninth Fort. It was in the same direction that the Jews had been led away in the "action" ... on September 26, 1941, and in the "action" of the liquidation of the small Ghetto on October 4, 1941. The same uphill road led Jews in one direction alone—to a place from which no one returned.

It was a death procession. The cries of despair issuing from thousands of mouths were hovering above them. Bitter weeping could be heard from far off. Column after column, family after family, those sentenced to death passed by the fence of the large Ghetto. Some men, even a number of women, tried to break through the chain of guards and flee to the large Ghetto, but were shot dead on the spot. One woman threw her child over the fence, but missed her aim and the child remained hanging on the barbed wire. Its screams were quickly silenced by bullets....

In the fort, the wretched people were immediately set upon by the Lithuanian killers, who stripped them of every valuable article—gold rings, earrings, bracelets. They forced them to strip naked, pushed them into pits which had been prepared in advance, and fired into each pit with machine guns which had been positioned there in advance. The murderers did not have time to shoot everybody in one batch before the next batch of Jews arrived. They were accorded the same treatment as those who had preceded them. They were pushed into the pit on top of the dead, the dying, and those still alive from the previous group. So it continued, batch after batch, until the 10,000 men, women, and children had been butchered. (Tory, pp. 43–58)

Aftermath

Following the action of October 28, 1941, the Kovno ghetto inmates experienced a period of relative calm, with fewer murders, beatings, and indignities suffered at the hands of their Nazi captors. This calm did not last long, however. In February 1942 Nazi leaders banned books, manuscripts, and all other printed material in the Kovno ghetto. Later that year, the party closed the synagogues and outlawed public prayer. The Kovno ghetto, as well as that of Riga, the capital of Latvia, became the destination for many German Jews deported from Germany during late 1941. As a greater number of people continued to arrive, the German military objected to the use of ammunition for mass executions. They argued that bullets, grenades, and other munitions were needed for the war effort and should not be wasted on the Jews. Their objections influenced the later mass extermination of Jews in gas chambers.

The Kovno ghetto was liquidated in July 1944, just before the Soviet army recaptured the city. Those prisoners still able to work were sent to German concentration camps. Ghetto buildings were burned, and many inmates were killed. When the German concentration camps were finally liberated, approximately 2,000 Kovno Jews remained.

The Soviets, who recaptured Lithuania in summer 1944, estimated that 22,000 out of 220,000 Lithuanian Jews survived the war.

Tory chronicled life in the Kovno ghetto with almost daily entries in his diary from July 1941 until his escape on March 23, 1944. Due to Tory's access to the *Judenrat*, his accuracy and objectivity, and his law background, his diary is considered among the most authentic and complete documentaries of ghetto life, but most of the evidence he collected, aside from the diary, was lost during the liquidation of the ghetto. The diary itself has been used as a reference in several war-crimes trials. Following the war, Tory emigrated to Israel, where he abandoned his Russian name, Golub ("dove"), and adopted its Hebrew translation, Tory. He continued to practice law in Tel Aviv, Israel, and his diary was published in 1990.

SOURCES

Books

Suhl, Yuri, *On the Other Side of the Gate: A Novel,* Franklin Watts (New York), 1975.

Tory, Abraham, *Surviving the Holocaust: The Kovno Ghetto,* translated by Jerzy Michalowicz, Harvard University Press (Cambridge, MA), 1990.

9

The United States Enters the War

As the war in Europe raged, tensions between Japan and the United States began to become heated. Japan had aligned itself with the Axis powers after signing the Anti-Comintern Treaty with Germany in 1936. The pact was signed by Italy in 1937. The term "Comintern," which referred to the "Communist International" organization of world Communist parties run by the Soviet Union, was used to make the treaty sound like a defensive agreement. The three countries that signed the agreement were similar in many ways—each was anti-democratic, glorified military strength, and wanted to conquer new territory.

In Japan, for example, the militarists who dominated the government believed the country had a sacred mission to conquer new territory and provide the natural resources lacking in their own nation. Japan had been expanding its empire in Asia throughout the 1930s and had been engaged in an ongoing conflict with China since 1937. The Japanese had conquered the great cities on China's coast and other key locations, but a complete victory proved more difficult than Japan had expected. Despite the presence of 1 million Japanese soldiers in China, Chinese armies were protected by the mountainous geography of China's interior, and the war had been deadlocked for several years. The Japanese government believed it could finally defeat China by cutting off military supplies shipped from countries

such as France, Britain, and especially the United States. Cut off from ports, the Chinese armies had only a few supply routes. The Burma Road, a motorway that cut through the high mountains of the British colony of Burma (present-day Myanmar), was important. However, the most important was a railroad that ran from northern Vietnam, then part of the French colony of Indochina, to China.

Japan Sets New Goals

Events in Europe in spring 1940 provided Japan with the opportunity to close these supply routes. When France surrendered to Germany in June, the Vichy government maintained control of most French colonies overseas. Japan demanded the right to station troops and establish airfields in northern Vietnam. After Japanese troops in the area briefly attacked the French in September 1940, the Vichy government acquiesced to their demands. Japan also demanded that Britain close the Burma Road. The British, under threat of German invasion and in no position to risk another war with Japan, agreed in July 1940 to a three-month closing of the Burma Road.

German victories in Europe may have aided in Japan's attempts to conquer China, but they also directly influenced the ability of Britain and France to defend their vast colonial empires in Asia. Germany had also conquered and occupied the Nether-

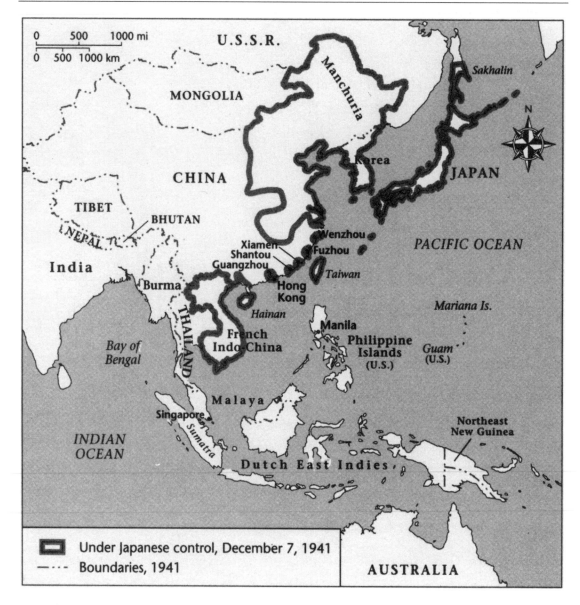

Areas of eastern Asia under Japanese control in 1941.

lands, and the Dutch government had fled to Britain, where it established a government-in-exile that was recognized by the Allies as the rightful government of the Netherlands. This government controlled the Dutch East Indies (today's Indonesia), a large group of islands between Southeast Asia and Australia that contained a vast oil supply, one resource that Japan lacked entirely. Dutch and Indonesian troops stationed in the Dutch East Indies could not expect help from the Dutch government-in-exile in the event of a Japanese attack.

Taking over the British, French, and Dutch colonies in Asia would enlarge the Japanese empire and supply large quantities of oil, rubber, and metals such as tin. Japanese companies would be able to sell their products in their own empire without competition from other countries. By autumn 1940, Japanese military leaders were confident they could defeat the British and Dutch colonial forces, and the French were not a threat due to the Nazi-controlled Vichy government. The only other major power in the Pacific was the United States. American aid to China was already a major concern to Japan. Japanese expansion in Southeast Asia and the Dutch East Indies would threaten the U.S.-controlled Philippines, seized from Spain during the Spanish-American War in 1898. The islands were scheduled

Japanese, German, and Italian officials signing the Tripartite Pact, September 1940. *(Reproduced by permission of AP/Wide World Photos)*

to become independent in 1944, with remaining U.S. military forces evacuating two years later. But in the meantime, the Philippines was essentially a U.S. colony. Japan also knew that the United States would not accept total Japanese control of Southeast Asia and the western Pacific, as this would isolate the United States from economically important areas and set a precedent for future Japanese expansion.

By summer 1940, some Japanese leaders were convinced that their plan of conquest would require war with the United States. Timing and speed, they felt, were essential as the United States had a major program to produce warships and the British and Dutch were preoccupied with European conflict. The longer Japan waited, the stronger the American navy would become. In September 1940, Japan, Germany, and Italy signed a new agreement known as the Tripartite Pact. The treaty gave Japan a promise of German support for its plans in Asia and the Pacific. In this way, the pact was a warning to the United States that interference with Japanese affairs could result in war with Germany and Italy as well.

Within a few months, Japan furthered its preparations for war by signing a treaty with the Soviet Union. The two nations had been brought into conflict by Japanese conquests in northern China, and had engaged in vicious border battles in 1939, resulting in heavy losses for Japan. The unexpected strength of the Soviet army contributed to a Japanese focus on the Pacific rather than the Soviet Union. The treaty, signed in April 1941, guaranteed each nation's neutrality if the other entered into war, allowing Japanese southward expansion without worry of Soviet interference from the north. When Germany invaded the Soviet Union in June, the danger of the Soviet army interfering with the Japanese in China became even less likely.

In May 1941 the United States extended its Lend-Lease program to China, confirming that it would continue to support China in China's war against Japan. Though talks began at the same time between Japan and the United States in Washington, D.C., and continued for months, most historians agree that the negotiations were futile

General Hideki Tōjō, already minister of war, also became the premier of Japan in October 1941. *(Reproduced by permission of AP/Wide World Photos)*

three years in normal circumstances, or about eighteen months in wartime, but the Japanese army estimated it would take three years to defeat China. This was yet another reason for the Japanese government to either settle its differences with the United States or go to war. In October 1941 the Japanese government finally decided to go to war with the United States.

Pearl Harbor

On November 26, 1941, a great Japanese fleet that included four battleships, two heavy cruisers, ten destroyers, and two dozen long-range submarines began a 2,800-mile voyage across the Pacific. The warships were meant to protect the six large aircraft carriers, which were transporting 360 planes, including dive-bombers and planes equipped to drop torpedoes designed to operate in shallow water. Operation orders had been delivered via courier to prevent interception of radio messages, and the Japanese fleet maintained absolute radio silence throughout its long voyage. The ships started out in the northern Pacific, far from the usual routes of commercial ships or air patrols, to avoid being seen. The extra length of the trip required accompanying tankers to refuel the ships at sea. Their destination was the base of the American Pacific Fleet in Pearl Harbor, Hawaii, a few miles from Honolulu on the island of Oahu. Japanese spies had ascertained the usual location of every anchored American ship, and each group of Japanese pilots had targeted a specific ship. They had practiced their attack on a carefully designed model of Pearl Harbor. From spies, the Japanese knew that a majority of the anti-aircraft guns on the ships and nearby shore installations would not be manned on a Sunday morning. They knew that most of the ships' officers would spend Saturday night onshore, and that crews would sleep late. Although the threat of war was growing, the United States was still at peace, and security around the base was lax. Anyone could climb the hills above the harbor and observe, through binoculars, the American navy's routine.

The Japanese fleet stopped approximately 200 miles from Hawaii and launched its planes on the morning of Sunday, December 7, 1941. Just before eight in the morning, Hawaii time, the first wave of Japanese planes attacked the anchored American fleet and nearby military barracks and airfields. They dive-bombed their primary targets, the eight battleships in the harbor. A second wave of Japanese

because each nation insisted on stipulations to which the other would never agree. The United States wanted to prevent Japan from controlling China and Southeast Asia. The Japanese felt this would keep their country at the economic mercy of other nations. The United States, Britain, and the other Western powers would never accept such a situation for themselves, and the Japanese interpreted it as an American effort to treat Japan as a second-rate power.

As the negotiations continued, the Asian situation became increasingly heated. On July 24, Vichy France agreed to allow Japanese troops into southern Indochina. This move did not seem related to Japan's war with China, and the United States, Britain, and the Netherlands felt Japan planned to invade Indonesia, British Malaya, and perhaps the Philippines. The United States issued a demand that Japan withdraw from Indochina and froze all Japanese assets in the United States two days later, preventing Japan from purchasing goods from America, particularly oil. Britain and the Dutch government-in-exile also banned the export of oil to Japan, which now had almost no sources of petroleum and faced serious shortages of other products. Japan, expecting the American petroleum embargo, had stockpiled enough oil to last

Did President Roosevelt Know about Pearl Harbor?

After the bombing of Pearl Harbor, the United States attempted to pinpoint the causes of that disaster. Some people accused President Franklin D. Roosevelt of having foreknowledge of the attack and purposely doing nothing because he wished the United States to join Britain in the war against Germany. Those who made these accusations cited several pieces of evidence. First, the United States had broken the code used by Japanese diplomats and therefore knew a great deal about Japanese plans. However, military and naval forces did not utilize this code. American officials believed Japan was preparing for war, but were uncertain of when or where. Second, the navy had aligned battleships anchored in Pearl Harbor like perfect targets, with no protection against torpedoes and little protection of any kind. Defensive preparations were completely inadequate, and the Japanese were able to destroy a number of American planes on the ground. Third, the American military ignored radar warnings and other signs of the approaching Japanese.

While all these factors are indicative of poor military preparations, errors in judgment, and carelessness, they do not reveal a deliberate plan to allow a Japanese attack. Most historians doubt Roosevelt would have allowed Japan to destroy the American fleet if his purpose was to get the United States into war against Germany itself. Such a strategy could have resulted in popular demand for all resources to be used against Japan, and opposition to assistance in the British campaign against Germany. Roosevelt never had to face this problem because of the German and Italian declarations of war against the United States. Historians generally reject the idea that Roosevelt, or any other American officials, knew about Pearl Harbor beforehand.

The USS *West Virginia* is hit by Japanese bombers during the attack on the U.S. Naval base in Pearl Harbor, Hawaii, on December 7, 1941. Some of the sailors make their escape via a small rescue boat. *(Reproduced by permission of © Hulton Getty/Liaison Agency)*

The USS *Shaw* explodes during the Japanese raid on Pearl Harbor. *(National Archives and Records Administration)*

Japanese Navy Commander Mitsuo Fuchida led the bombing raid on Pearl Harbor on December 7, 1941. *(Reproduced by permission of AP/Wide World Photos)*

planes attacked at around 9 a.m. and continued the destruction. By the end of the attack, many ships were heavily damaged. The *Arizona, California,* and *West Virginia* were among those that were sunk, while the *Oklahoma* had capsized. Another dozen warships were also hit. Of nearly 400 American planes based on Oahu, almost 200 were destroyed and less than fifty survived undamaged. Two thousand, four hundred and one American sailors and soldiers were killed, and more than 1,100 others were injured.

The Japanese attack seemed to have accomplished its purpose by destroying the American Pacific Fleet, the only naval force that could interfere with Japan's plans. Although Pearl Harbor was a military disaster for the United States, it was not as great a success for the Japanese as it appeared. The shallow water in Pearl Harbor allowed the Americans to raise all the sunken battleships (except the *Arizona*) from the bottom, placing the repaired and modernized American battleships back in service much earlier than anyone expected. The aircraft carriers of the American Pacific Fleet were not at Pearl Harbor at the time of the bombing; two were at sea, one was in California, and

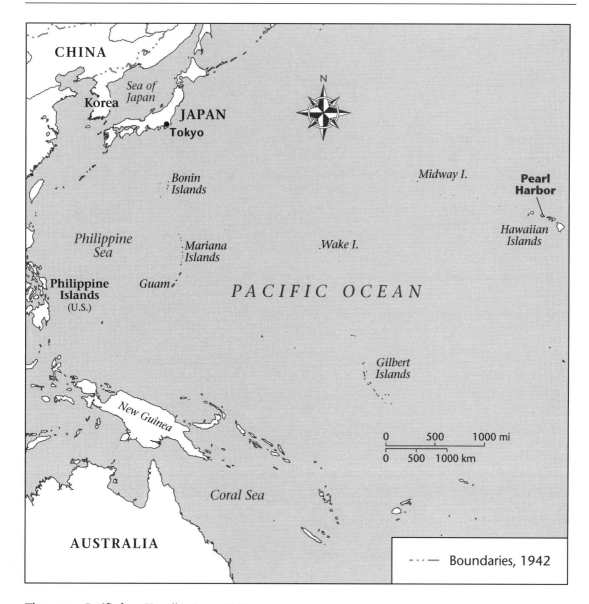

The western Pacific from Hawaii to Japan, 1942.

three others were in the Atlantic. Within a few months, the aircraft carriers would inflict a major defeat on the Japanese navy. In the long run, the attack on Pearl Harbor had an opposite effect than what Japan desired. The Japanese strategy for winning the war depended on reaching peace with the United States eventually, and Pearl Harbor made that impossible.

Japan's plan was to conquer new territory in Southeast Asia, including Indonesia, the Philippines, and a string of small Pacific islands and island groups, some uninhabited. Japan already controlled some of these islands and could use them as bases from which to launch attacks on the others. Japan wanted to conquer most of these small islands not because they contained valuable natural resources or because they were potential trade partners, but because they could be used as sites for military, naval, and air bases. The Japanese believed the United States would have to rebuild its navy after Pearl Harbor and attack these islands one by one. They also speculated that the American people would not support a war for unfamiliar territory in which thousands of Americans would die, particularly to reinstate British and Dutch control over colonies whose inhabitants, in all probability, did not want to remain under British or Dutch domination. Japanese strategy would be to resist American forces in the Pacific long

The "Sneak Attack"

The attack on Pearl Harbor was executed without an official declaration of war, a fact that infuriated Americans. The Japanese government had not wanted to launch a surprise attack, and sent a lengthy coded message, a declaration of war, to its Washington, D.C., embassy, to be delivered to the U.S. government half an hour before the attack. When it took longer than expected to decode the message, translate it into English, and deliver it, the attack had already begun.

enough to force the United States to make peace rather than risk too many American lives. By then, Japan would have completed its conquest of Southeast Asia and China. The Japanese could bargain from a position of strength that would require the United States to accept Japan as the dominant power in eastern Asia.

U.S. President Franklin D. Roosevelt signs the declaration of war against Japan, December 8, 1941. *(National Archives and Records Administration)*

The bombing at Pearl Harbor, however, ensured that these Japanese plans would never come to fruition. The American public responded with outrage to a domestic attack during a time of peace. President Roosevelt addressed Congress on the morning of December 8, 1941, referring to Pearl Harbor as "a date which will live in infamy" (see primary source entry), and asked Congress to issue a declaration of war against Japan. Two and one-half hours later, Roosevelt signed that declaration, officially entering the United States into war with the Japanese. A negotiated peace with Japan was virtually impossible, as American public opinion called for the total defeat of the Japanese. The military and civilian leaders of Japan, however, never thought they could win a full-scale war, knowing American industrial strength far outweighed their own.

There are several reasons why most Americans supported war against Japan: the attack against Pearl Harbor, opposition to the Japanese invasion of China and the subsequent murder of hundreds of thousands of Chinese civilians, and the Japanese government's open hostility toward democracy. Historians generally agree that anti-Japanese feeling in the United States was fomented also by strong appeals to racism. American propaganda depicted the Japanese as savages, exaggerating their facial features in cartoons to make them look like monkeys. Propaganda described the Japanese as sneaky and treacherous people of low intelligence. Even U.S. government officials referred to the Japanese as "Japs," and American citizens of Japanese ancestry soon found themselves attacked as they tried to go about their business. Japanese Americans on the West Coast were soon forced from their homes and sent to guarded detention camps, yet German Americans and Italian Americans were not treated in the same fashion, although some were questioned and detained. The U.S. government continually emphasized that America was fighting Adolf Hitler's Nazis and Benito Mussolini's Fascists, not the German or Italian people. But with Japan, the United States declaration of war seemed to be a war against the Japanese people. The difference in terms could be attributed to the fact that the Japanese had declared war on the United States and attacked American installations, pulling the United States into World War II officially.

Japan Sweeps Forward

Japan's stunning attack on the Pacific Fleet was followed by an even more impressive series of

At the Santa Anita Assembly Center in California, one of the detention camps, young Japanese Americans are encouraged to show their patriotism as they go through an Americanization program. *(Library of Congress)*

victories. Many of these successes followed a pattern that utilized surprise, great skill, and command of air power to ensure Japanese forces always outnumbered defenders in any particular area, even if those defenders had more troops overall. Japanese soldiers were well-trained and fought with bravery, and they, along with their generals, were regularly underestimated by their opponents. The Allies were constantly amazed by the daring, speed, and planning of the Japanese attacks. They acknowledged that Japanese military equipment was advanced, that Japanese planes were better than those of the Western powers, and that Japanese pilots flew skillfully.

In the western Pacific, Japan moved against two islands under United States control. The day after Pearl Harbor, they attacked the 500 American troops stationed on Guam, who surrendered the following day, and on December 9, they took the British-held Gilbert Islands. On tiny Wake Island, a small detachment of U.S. Marines held out until

December 23, when their food and water supplies were depleted. Thousands of miles farther west, the Japanese used troops based in China to attack the British colony of Hong Kong on December 8. Soon the defenders, including many Canadians, retreated to Hong Kong Island. On December 18, Japanese troops landed on the island and 12,000 remaining Allied troops surrendered on Christmas Day.

Japan landed troops in the north of the British colony of Malaya (now part of Malaysia) early on the morning of December 8 (local time), an hour before the attack on Pearl Harbor. Although the Japanese were outnumbered, their force was comprised of better-trained troops, 200 tanks, and 560 planes. The British, Australian, Indian, and Malay defenders were equipped with no tanks and approximately 160 planes, mostly outdated. On December 10, the battleship *Prince of Wales,* one of the newest and best ships in the British navy, along with the powerful cruiser *Repulse,* tried to intercept Japanese troop transports. Attacked by eighty-five

Filipino soldiers prepare to blow up a bridge in order to stop the advancing Japanese army in the Philippines. *(Reproduced by permission of AP/Wide World Photos)*

Japanese dive-bombers and torpedo planes, the two ships sank. Despite the ships' powerful antiaircraft guns, the Japanese lost only three planes. The Allied forces began a general retreat southward down the long Malay peninsula. The Japanese pursued, advancing 400 miles through mountains and jungles in only five weeks. By the end of January, they were at the southern end of the peninsula, and Allied troops were evacuated across the mile-wide strait to the island of Singapore.

Crossing the strait in small boats, the Japanese landed troops on the island on February 8. Although they still outnumbered the Japanese, Allied troops were demoralized by the long retreat and could not stop them. Fearing for the safety of the 1 million civilians crowded into the city of Singapore, the British commander surrendered on February 15, 1942. The Japanese took 130,000 troops prisoner in the worst defeat in Britain's long military history. Though the British naval base in Singapore was one of the greatest in the world, its guns were designed to defend the island against ships and were not effective against land troops. Singapore was the symbol of the British Empire's power in Asia, and many historians believe that the capture of Singapore sent a powerful message to

the people of Asia. Even if Britain won the war, the myth that European technology made it impossible for Asians to defeat European colonial powers was gone forever.

Combat in the Philippines

The Japanese attacked the Philippines ten hours after Pearl Harbor (although it was December 8, local time). They destroyed eighty to ninety planes, including eighteen B-17 bombers, on the American air force base on the island of Luzon. (The Japanese army only lost an estimated five to seven planes in that attack, protected by the high altitude at which they flew.) The Philippines was a tempting target due to its location between Japan and other Southeast Asian territories. Control of the area would allow Japan to keep an eye on previously conquered territories and to launch attacks on other targets. American warships, lacking planes to protect them from air attack, were ordered to leave the Philippines to help defend the Dutch East Indies.

Within days, Japanese forces began landing in several key areas in the Philippines, including northern Luzon, the bay of Lamon (to the south of

Manila), the Lingayen Gulf (to the north of Manila), and the southern Mindanao Islands. Their plan was to move inward to take over the capital. U.S. General Douglas MacArthur was in control of the Filipino and American troops in the region. He ordered them to head off Japanese forces at their landing points, despite the plan created prior to the war that called for all forces to retreat into the Bataan Peninsula and Corregidor in case of attack. Though the troops held out for several weeks, the success of this plan was hindered by many factors. Though some American troops and American-trained Philippine scouts were prepared for combat, many members of those forces were not seasoned combat veterans and were pitted against Japanese forces who were. American pilots were unaccustomed to ground combat and were forced into new roles. Most of the Filipino enlisted men were untrained reservists who, to add to the confusion, spoke different dialects than the Filipino officers and a completely different language than the American forces. In addition, supplies in the area were extremely limited due to a severe lack of funds from both the Philippine and American governments. Though the American government had taken steps in 1941 to begin updating defense of the area, most of the troops' weaponry was outdated (some left over from World War I), and the United States was focused on Hitler's movements in Europe. Even the uniforms of the men were inadequate to keep them warm during cool nights on the island. Due to the unexpected nature of the attack, the Allied forces had limited water, food, and medical supplies, even at the beginning of the resistance.

By the beginning of January, MacArthur had ordered a withdrawal of forces into the Bataan Peninsula. His plan was to stall the Japanese and force them to use more weapons, time, and men than they had planned. The hasty retreat, however, forced the Filipino and American men to leave many of their supplies behind. Since the troops had previously spread out to try to contain the Japanese at many different locations, rather than just in Bataan and Corregidor as planned, the supplies were now located in inaccessible areas. Roads had been captured; the Japanese had gained control of the majority of the island; and Bataan was now isolated. This meant there was no simple means of getting more supplies into the Bataan area. As the men continued to hold their ground in Bataan, less than thirty miles long and about twenty miles wide, conditions began to get worse. All personnel were

General Douglas MacArthur

The American commander in the Philippines at the time of the Japanese attack was General Douglas MacArthur, who had led the army in the 1930s and was probably America's most experienced military officer. A colorful and controversial figure, he wore dark glasses and often smoked a corncob pipe. MacArthur's critics regarded him as an overly ambitious publicity seeker. Prior to the United States' entry into the war, the American military "loaned" MacArthur to the government of the Philippines, which was preparing to become independent, in an attempt to strengthen its army. In July 1941, as war threatened the United States, the Filipino troops and MacArthur again became part of the U.S. Army. In March of 1942, President Franklin D. Roosevelt, not wanting MacArthur to be captured by the Japanese, ordered the general to leave the Philippines and fly to Australia to take command of the Allied forces in the southwest Pacific. As he left, MacArthur promised his troops, "I shall return." In America, where the only war news had been of one defeat after another, MacArthur's words became a symbol of America's determination to win the war no matter how long it took.

forced to go on half rations. Diseases like malaria, beriberi, and dysentery began to affect the malnourished and exhausted men. On March 11, 1942, MacArthur was ordered to leave the Philippines to take command of forces in Australia. But he promised: "I shall return." Major General Jonathan M. Wainwright, previously in charge of the north Luzon forces, took MacArthur's place.

Major General Edward King took control of the forces in Bataan. At the end of March, he deter-

An aerial view of Ft. Mills on Corregidor Island shows the area where more than 11,500 Allied sailors, marines, and civilians were forced to surrender to Japanese forces in 1942. *(Reproduced by permission of AP/Wide World Photos)*

mined that his men were fighting at only 20 to 30 percent of their capacity due to a lack of weaponry, cut rations (one-fourth regulation), and general fatigue. His assessment was made in preparation for a planned offensive by the Japanese to take Bataan, which began on April 3 (local time) with aerial and artillery bombardment. The troops held out for several days, but King believed surrender was necessary due to the state of his forces. Wainwright disagreed. King surrendered his forces to Major General Kameichiro Nagano on April 9, 1942, after extracting a promise they would be treated humanely. The Japanese, though, had not agreed to the terms at the Geneva Convention in 1929, which described how prisoners of war were to be treated. Many Japanese soldiers held the conviction that it was better to die than surrender. King's men would soon learn that the Japanese promise of humane treatment would not be honored.

After the surrender of Bataan, General Wainwright attempted to resist the Japanese for as long as possible with the limited supplies and men left on the islands. Yet once the Japanese succeeded in capturing Bataan and moving the troops from this area to Camp O'Donnell, they were in an excellent position to start bombarding one of the last areas of Philippine/American resistance—the rocky island of Corregidor, only two miles from Bataan. The base of operations in Corregidor was located in the Malinta Tunnel—a main tunnel and several underground passages providing bombproof shelter, a communications area, a makeshift hospital, and room for ammunition and supplies. Approximately 13,000 Filipino and American troops at Corregidor were submitted to a constant barrage of artillery fire from all directions.

During the weeks following the surrender of Bataan, Corregidor was targeted by Japanese amphibious, air, tank, and infantry battalions. Antiaircraft defenses were quickly demolished, which allowed the Japanese to cut off access to drinking water and communications. The island was bombed and burned, and the defenders became exhausted from lack of food and water and the continual stress of fighting the enemy and disease, while witnessing death. On May 1, 1942,

American and Filipino troops could not repel the Japanese attack on Corregidor in 1942. *(Reproduced by permission of the Corbis Corporation [Bellevue])*

the Japanese began an increasingly intense bombardment and their troops began closing in on Malinta Hill and the Tunnel. By May 5, the Japanese were dangerously close to Malinta Hill. On May 6, General Wainwright attempted to surrender the forces of Corregidor to General Homma Masaharu without surrendering the remainder of the forces in the Philippines. But Homma, knowing that Wainwright was in a position to surrender all forces in the Philippines, demanded that this be done. Wainwright surrendered the forces of Corregidor that day (including ninety-nine female army and navy nurses who became prisoners of war) and ordered the surrender of other forces on May 8, though some troops held out as long as possible. All of the forces in the Philippines had surrendered by June 9, 1942.

After the surrender, the men of Corregidor were subjected to a "sun treatment," in which they were left exposed to the elements for two weeks, and then were transferred to Manila. At that point, some of the Philippine scouts and men were moved to Camp O'Donnell, while the remainder, including the majority of the American prisoners, were moved by train to several prison camps at Cabanatuan. In June, a few weeks after this removal, the American men captured at Bataan were transferred from Camp O'Donnell to Cabanatuan. Though the men from Corregidor were in relatively better condition than those from Bataan when they were captured, the conditions and brutality of the guards at Cabanatuan soon began to take their toll on all prisoners. Lice, malaria-carrying mosquitoes, dysentery, beriberi,

The Bataan Death March

When the Japanese arrived at the city of Mariveles in the Philippines, they had some 10,000 American and 60,000 Filipino captives. Since the Japanese wanted them out of the area, they began moving the men to a centralized location at Camp O'Donnell, via a forced march now known as the "Bataan Death March." Depending on where a Filipino or American soldier had been stationed, he could be marched fifty to sixty miles to San Fernando in five to nine days. These men were already in horrible condition: sick, hungry, and mentally exhausted from three months of inadequate rations, few medical supplies, a mosquito-infested jungle environment, and a constant barrage of enemy fire.

The Japanese were unsympathetic to the plight of their conquered prisoners of war. Some prisoners were systematically executed. The wounded were killed if they were unable to complete the march, and the sick and weak were pushed to march in sweltering heat without water or food. If the captives showed signs of weakness, they were shot, beheaded, bayoneted, or beaten with rifles by the Japanese guards and left to die. If they fell from exhaustion on the road, drivers of Japanese tanks would go out of their way to run them over. Prisoners who tried to help their comrades were also killed. Some of the survivors reported that when their comrades heard water and tried to get to it, they were killed for their efforts. Others made it to shallow puddles in which caraboa (water buffalo) rolled to coat themselves in mud. Eventually this would kill some in a less direct fashion, since drinking this non-potable water resulted in dysentery, which led to diarrhea and further dehydration.

From San Fernando, the prisoners were loaded into railroad boxcars, meant for shipping supplies, that would take them about six miles outside of the camp. A car could reasonably hold about forty men, but at least 100 were crammed into each one, making it impossible to sit or lie down. The men were forced to stand, though some were beyond the point of exhaustion. Many were violently ill with dysentery, but there were no accommodations for human waste. After four hours, some of the men were dead from the crush and the heat of the cars. The remaining men were then forced to march the remaining six miles to Camp O'Donnell. Estimates of how many men survived the march vary: Some sources say 600 to 1,000 Americans died on the march, while others go as high as 2,300. The figures for Filipinos killed during the march range from 5,000 to 15,000. It is generally agreed that only about 54,000 men reached Camp O'Donnell.

Due to starvation, the physical brutality of their Japanese captors, the diseases from which prisoners suffered without medical aid, and the use of prisoners as work slaves, it is estimated that 37 to 40 percent of all prisoners of war held by the Japanese during the war died. This is in stark contrast to the percentage of prisoners of war who died while held by German and Italian forces which was far lower.

During the fighting in Bataan and its aftermath, American forces became known as "The Bat-

FAREWELL, AMERICAN SOLDIERS!

You are still alive! What a miracle! And marching, too. But WHERE? To the Philippines? To Tokyo? But do you know what awaits you in the Philippines? Let me tell you. It is the Japanese forces with the combined support, both moral and material, of all the awakened Asiatics—the Manchukuoans, Chinese, Filipinos, Annamese, Thailanders, Burmese, Indians, Malayans and Indonesians. And the Japanese are there to pound you incessantly and relentlessly as you should have known. Perhaps they may retreat temporarily, but only to attack you again with double fierceness after your reinforcements have arrived. Day in and day out the Japanese troops are also pushing to the front in ever-increasing numbers. And remember, entire Asia is behind them! As long as you persist in marching west, the attacks will continue. Innumerable strongholds are all set to give you hearty welcome from the land, air and sea. The reverberation of their rousing welcome must even now be in your ears.

But this is not all. There is still another thing in store for you along the Philippines front. What is this thing? I will again answer you. It is a grave, YOUR GRAVE! Nobody can say where it exactly is, but it is certain that it does exist somewhere in the Philippines, and you are bound to find it sooner or later, far or near. Today? Tomorrow? Who knows? But one thing is positive. You are heading west for your grave—as positive as the sun sets in the west. Officers and men, you still insist on marching west? If so, I shall have to carve an epitaph for you.

There are only two definite things on earth. LIFE and DEATH. The difference between LIFE and DEATH is absolute. One cannot rely upon the dead; no one can make friends with the dead; the dead can neither speak nor mingle with the living. If you insist on marching west, we (by we I mean all living things) must bid you goodbye and stop bothering with you, because we, the living, are too busy to have anything to do with the dead.

Your politicians are among those who survive and are enjoying life comfortably at home. General Marshall and General MacArthur can enjoy their reputation as heroes only because they are alive. But you... you continue to march westwards to sure death, to keep your rendezvous with the grave. The same holds true for your comrades-in-arms who are pathetically struggling to escape their ultimate fate. The graves await you, and you, and ALL OF YOU! So, officers and men, I bid you a pitiful goodbye. Today, you are with the living—tomorrow, with the dead. So again goodbye, American soldiers!...... Farewell!...... Farewell!......

This propaganda cartoon was distributed in an effort to intimidate American troops from fighting in the Philippines. Most likely this was created by the Japanese military. (*Library of Congress*)

tling Bastards of Bataan." Those soldiers who survived the Bataan Death March struggled against disease, Japanese mistreatment, and the harsh realities of living in internment camps. The following rhyme, describing the men's state, is recorded at the Museum of the Pacific War (Chester Nimitz Museum), in Fredericksburg, Texas.

"We're the Battling Bastards of Bataan,

No mama, no papa, no Uncle Sam;

No aunts, no uncles, no cousins, no nieces;

No rifles, no planes, no artillery pieces;

And nobody gives a damn."

In April 2000, a memorial was dedicated to the American forces who died at Camp O'Donnell. The memorial, which lists the names of the men who died, was erected in the Philippines.

The Angels of Bataan and Corregidor

In November 1941, eighty-seven army nurses and twelve navy nurses from the United States were on duty in and around Manila, the Philippines. Many of these women saw their assignment in the Philippines as an opportunity to enjoy an adventure in a tropical location: The United States had not yet declared war, and the nurses were able to spend time on the beaches and at officers' dances. This idyllic existence came to an end on December 8, 1941, when Japanese forces attacked the U.S. base in Manila. As a land battle ensued, these ninety-nine nurses became the first American women ever placed in a combat situation.

The nurses remained in the heart of the action, caring for the wounded soldiers. When American forces retreated to Bataan in late December, many of the nurses were ordered there as well. In addition to the American women, there were approximately twenty-five Filipino nurses. They helped erect two makeshift hospitals on the island, and promptly began administering to patients. Conditions at Bataan were harsh—the nurses had to battle jungle diseases such as dengue fever and malaria, and treat their patients on open-air cots. The island was overrun with jungle creatures, including enormous rats.

Shortly before the surrender in Bataan in early April 1942, the nurses were ordered to Corregidor. This island was believed to be relatively protected from bombing, but the nurses were distraught at leaving their patients behind to suffer at the hands of the Japanese. Still, there were patients to care for on Corregidor, and the nurses set up a hospital in the Malinta Tunnel, where military operations were centered. Conditions there were no better than in Bataan, and the hos-

As U.S. and Filipino forces defended the Bataan Peninsula, nurses were on hand to treat the sick and wounded. *(Reproduced by permission of © Bettmann/Corbis Corporation)*

Before the fall of Bataan, nurses washed their clothes in a stream. *(Reproduced by permission of AP/Wide World Photos)*

pital was bombed relentlessly. By early May, American forces surrendered to the Japanese, and the nurses were captured. They were forced to remain in the Malinta Tunnel until late June, when they were marched to another section of Corregidor to be transported to the Santo Tomas Internment Camp in Manila.

The nurses remained in Manila as prisoners of war until February 1945. Inside the internment camp, they set up facilities to care for injured soldiers. During the nearly three years the nurses spent as prisoners, their food rations dwindled. Many of their patients, who otherwise would have survived, died of malnutrition, which was frustrating for the nurses. Still, the nurses worked relentlessly, even though they themselves were hungry and exhausted. They had no opportunity for leisure activities to escape from the horrors of tending to war vic-

tims. Despite these conditions, all of the nurses managed to survive the ordeal.

When the nurses returned to the United States, they were greeted as heroes. The media had dubbed them "the Angels of Bataan and Corregidor." For the most part, the women avoided the spotlight and focused on adjusting to life in civilian society.

For further information on the Angels of Bataan and Corregidor, please consult *We Band of Angels: The Untold Story of American Nurses Trapped on Bataan by the Japanese* by Elizabeth M. Norman (New York: Random House, 1999), or the Internet site *We Band of Angels Official Page*, located at http://www.webandofangels. com (July 20, 2000).

American troops surrender after the siege of Corregidor. *(National Archives and Records Administration)*

starvation, and lack of water continued to be standard for those in the camps. After several weeks at Cabanatuan, an estimated 2,000 to 3,000 more men, mainly those from Bataan, were dead. Men were sent from Cabanatuan to other slave labor camps in the Philippines, and also to China, Japan, and Korea, in unmarked vessels called "Hell Ships" because of the miserable conditions on board. Some of these ships were sunk by the U.S. military, which was unaware that the ships were carrying American prisoners of war. Of those who survived the voyages, most were used for slave labor until all of the Japanese prisoner of war camps were liberated in 1945.

A total of 95,000 American and Filipino troops had been taken as Japanese prisoners on Bataan and Corregidor. Many of these prisoners were forced on a long, brutal march to prison camps, resulting in the deaths of some 7,000-10,000 men (estimates vary) from disease, wounds, and mistreatment by Japanese guards. The "Bataan Death March," as it came to be called, became for many Americans a symbol of Japanese cruelty.

Burma and the Dutch East Indies

The Japanese invasion of the British colony of Burma (present-day Myanmar) began in mid-December. Although China sent troops into northern Burma to aid the British, the Japanese continued to advance. By late April 1942, the Chinese had

Composed of Filipino Americans, the 1st Filipino Infantry Regiment became part of the U.S. Army in 1942. *(Photograph courtesy of the U.S. Army Military History Institute)*

retreated north back into China, and the British, chased by the Japanese, had crossed into India, the largest and most important British colony. The Japanese began their invasion of the Dutch East Indies with troop landings on some of the outlying islands, capturing or building airfields to use as bases to continue their advance. As the Japanese threatened the most important island, Java, an Allied naval force attempted to stop them. Under the command of a Dutch admiral, the fleet included American, British, Dutch, and Australian ships. Beginning on February 27, this fleet engaged a Japanese force of comparable size in the Battle of the Java Sea, resulting in another decisive victory for the Japanese navy. The last important Allied naval force for thousands of miles was almost destroyed. The Japanese could now land forces on Java, and Dutch and East Indian troops could not stop them. On March 12, faced with a Japanese threat to bomb the main cities, the Dutch surrendered. In addition to taking military prisoners, the Japanese placed many Dutch civilians, including women and children, in guarded detention camps for the remainder of the war.

Japan now controlled Southeast Asia and all the islands of the western Pacific north of the equator. They had lost approximately 15,000 men in the process. The whole Japanese fleet was still afloat, while Allied navies had lost most of their ships. Between Hawaii and Australia, the Japanese controlled the entire ocean, except for the small American-held island of Midway, 1,100 miles west of Hawaii. Sailing past Midway in April 1942, the American aircraft carrier *Hornet* came to within about 800 miles of Japan before a Japanese patrol boat spotted it and turned it back. However, the *Hornet* had launched sixteen B-25 bombers from its decks. Though the B-25 was a land-based plane, really too big and heavy to take off from an aircraft carrier, it could fly much farther than normal carrier-based bombers.

The American planes were ordered to launch an aerial attack on Tokyo and other Japanese cities, under the leadership of Colonel James Doolittle. The B-25s would not have enough fuel to return to the *Hornet,* so the plan called for them to fly to Japan, drop their bombs, and then land in China if possible. However, since they were detected before they reached their target area (which was to be about 400 miles from Japan), the crews were prepared to bail out if they ran out of fuel before reaching China. On April 18 Doolittle's men bombed three Japanese cities. Most of the planes crashed when they ran out of fuel, but the majority of the crews were able to parachute out. Some men were captured, while others were escorted to safety

On April 18, 1942, sixteen bombers left the deck of the USS *Hornet* aircraft carrier on their way to bomb Tokyo, Japan. The surprise attack by the Americans, four months after the Japanese bombed the U.S. Naval Base in Pearl Harbor, Hawaii, dealt a psychological blow to the Japanese. *(National Archives and Records Administration)*

through dangerous territory. While the Doolittle Raid caused little physical damage to Japan, it showed that American bombers could reach Japanese soil. Until that point, the Japanese thought they were safe from attack. Also, Roosevelt wanted a symbolic action to demonstrate to the American people that the United States was striking back. The Doolittle Raid greatly improved American morale. Though most ordinary citizens in Japan were unaware that the attack had occurred, the raid had a great effect on Japanese military leaders. They were determined to prevent any future strikes against the Japanese homeland by destroying the American aircraft carriers they had failed to find at Pearl Harbor.

The Japanese soon had a chance to target some American aircraft carriers after the U.S. military learned of Japanese plans to land troops in the southern part of the vast island of New Guinea, further threatening Australia. After decoding secret Japanese messages, the United States sent the carriers *Lexington* and *Yorktown* to thwart the invasion, which was protected by three Japanese carriers. On May 7 and 8, planes from each country's carriers

attacked the other's ships, though the watercraft themselves were nearly 200 miles apart. This fight, called the Battle of the Coral Sea, was the first naval battle in which none of the ships were within sight of the others. At the conclusion of the battle, the *Lexington* had been set ablaze and destroyed, and one Japanese carrier had been sunk and another heavily damaged. Although neither side won a clear-cut victory, the Japanese threat against northern Australia was greatly reduced.

The Japanese navy was now more determined than ever to force an all-out battle with the remaining American carriers. On June 4, 1942, a Japanese invasion fleet that included four large carriers as well as battleships and cruisers approached the island of Midway. Against them stood the last three American carriers in the Pacific, the *Yorktown, Hornet,* and *Enterprise,* and American planes based on Midway. For several hours, the planes dueled while trying to attack enemy carriers. Eventually, and partly by luck, a group of American dive-bombers caught the Japanese carriers while their decks were full of planes being refueled and rearmed, with fuel hoses

American sailors abandon the aircraft carrier USS *Lexington*, which burns during the Battle of the Coral Sea, May 8, 1942. *(Reproduced by permission of the Corbis Corporation [Bellevue])*

and bombs lying everywhere. The American bombs triggered devastating fires. Two Japanese carriers burned and sank, and a third was left helpless with no power (an American submarine sank it a short while later). The fourth Japanese carrier tried to escape, but American planes found and destroyed it several hours later. Military historians consider this, the Battle of Midway, one of the most important naval battles in history and one of the turning points of World War II. Japan had conquered a great empire and could still defend it, but were unable to expand except on land. It could not invade Australia or threaten Hawaii or North America, and it would be difficult for Japan to protect ships bringing oil and other resources from its new empire. After Midway, the U.S. government could safely turn its attention to the defeat of Germany for a time.

The United States and Britain

Four days after Pearl Harbor, on December 11, 1941, Germany and Italy declared war on the Unit-

ed States. The Axis powers signed a treaty in which each promised not to make peace with Britain or the United States without the compliance of the others. The most important issue facing the American government was whether to concentrate on the Pacific conflict with Japan, or on the European front against Germany. As early as November 1940, American and British military officials agreed that in a war against the Axis, they would try to defeat Germany first. While meeting with British Prime Minister Winston Churchill during the signing of the Atlantic Charter in August 1941, Roosevelt had privately confirmed the "Germany first" decision. Soon after Pearl Harbor, Churchill and top British military leaders flew to Washington, D.C., for a series of meetings, code-named the Arcadia Conference, from December 22, 1941 to January 14, 1942. The two countries agreed that the "Germany first" policy was official. They also decided to make cooperative decisions on utilization of all economic and military resources.

The Arcadia Conference created a Combined Chiefs of Staff made up of the commanders of the

During the Battle of Midway, U.S. pilots prepare to take off from the deck of the USS *Enterprise.* The squadron consisted of "Devastator" torpedo bombers. *(Reproduced by permission of © Hulton Getty/Liaison Agency)*

army, navy, and air force of each country. The committee would meet in Washington, so the British commanders each named a permanent substitute to represent them when they were unable to attend. This system remained in place for the remainder of the war. The British representatives, who were in constant contact with Great Britain, met to decide their position, while the Americans did the same. Then the Combined Chiefs of Staff met (a total of 200 times during the course of the war) to deliberate on all British-American war operations. While they often disagreed on the details, compromise was usually reached. In major disagreements, Roosevelt and Churchill intervened to settle the differences. The Arcadia Conference occurred while the Japanese army was conquering the Philippines, and American public opinion was directed against Japan (only weeks after Pearl Harbor). While the "Germany first" strategy made sense for the United States, it involved serious military risks in the Pacific (at least until the American victory at Midway) and domestic political risks for Roosevelt. The American president was willing to assume these consequences due to the needs of his major allies, Britain and the Soviet Union.

In addition to personal meetings, Roosevelt and Churchill constantly exchanged opinions, information, and arguments by coded radio messages. Churchill claimed he sent 950 messages to Roosevelt during the war and received 800 messages in return. Through these messages and face-to-face meetings, Roosevelt and Churchill developed respect and affection for each other.

Although some writers have probably exaggerated the importance of this personal relationship, historians generally accept that it played a significant role in promoting British-American cooperation. Though his position made him commander in chief of all American armed forces, Roosevelt had little interest in military strategy and did not pretend to be an expert. On the purely military aspects of war, he listened to and trusted his advisers, the most important of whom was the army chief of staff, General George C. Marshall. The final decision on how America would fight the war, however, such as the "Germany first" policy, was made by Roosevelt himself. In contrast to Roosevelt, Churchill had been an army officer as a young man and had been in charge of the British navy during World War I. He not only expressed opinions about military matters but also attempted to convince Roosevelt (and everyone else) about strategy, tactics, and personnel. One British naval writer claimed there was not a single British admiral from 1939 to 1943 that Churchill did not try to fire, and this was also true for many British generals. Hitler told his own generals they were lucky—compared with Churchill, he essentially left them alone.

Allied Policy and the Free French

One disagreement between Churchill and Roosevelt involved their policy toward General Charles de Gaulle and his Free French movement. De Gaulle had been a little-known one-star French general who refused to surrender to the Germans in 1940, retreating to England instead. From there he had used British radio to call on the French to keep fighting alongside the British, and had organized the Free French (later called Fighting France) troops, which became part of the Allied armies. Due to political maneuvers over the course of several years, the many resistance organizations within German-occupied France accepted de Gaulle as their overall leader and his organization as the rightful government of their country. The Allies, however, had not.

Churchill was the most favorable to de Gaulle, partly because de Gaulle had urged France to continue fighting alongside Britain when it looked as if Britain would lose the war. Still, despite these gracious feelings, Churchill had concluded that the United States would play the key role in the war because of its superior economic strength. He would always side with the Americans on issues important to them, and they did not support de Gaulle, partially because Roosevelt personally disliked de Gaulle. It is generally agreed that de Gaulle had a difficult nature and showed little gratitude for any support he was given. De Gaulle was regarded by Roosevelt as an old-fashioned military man who did not believe in democracy. Roosevelt did not want the Allies to impose de Gaulle and his movement on the French people, and called for the installation of another military man to replace him. They agreed on General Henri Giraud, who had commanded an army in 1940, been captured by the Germans, and escaped. Giraud, however, provided problems of his own: He was not nearly as skilled in politics as de Gaulle, was distrusted by the French resistance, and was adamantly antidemocratic.

In January 1943 Roosevelt and Churchill held a series of talks near Casablanca, Morocco. Both de Gaulle and Giraud were invited to attend, and Roosevelt and Churchill forced the two generals to accept a compromise in which they shared power. Before long, however, Giraud began to fade out of the picture, and de Gaulle's movement was eventually accepted by the Soviet Union, Britain, and the United States as the provisional government of France.

The Western Allies and the Soviet Union

The most serious Allied differences of opinion were between the Soviet Union and the Western Allies (Britain and the United States), and arose out of basic mistrust. The British and Americans were afraid that the Soviets were planning to

The Greater East Asia Coprosperity Sphere

Japan claimed that its purpose in conquering Southeast Asia was to create a "Greater East Asia Coprosperity Sphere." This phrase implied that under Japanese leadership, an association of the people of eastern Asia would be beneficial and prosperous to all. Like the Japanese slogan "Asia for the Asians," it also implied that Japan would lead the Asian people to freedom from European colonial powers. Removing the Europeans was a very popular goal in Asia, especially among highly educated people living in cities. Independence movements had existed throughout the area before the war. The European powers, determined to hold on to their colonies, often made these movements illegal and imprisoned a number of their leaders. In many places, Japan's defeat of the European powers was welcomed, and in some cases the prewar independence movements cooperated with Japanese authorities. Japan later declared a few of the countries officially "independent," though the Japanese essentially assumed the roles formerly fulfilled by the Europeans: Citizens were still unable to make their own decisions, and the countries' natural resources were now used for Japan's benefit, not for Europe's. The Japanese authorities (mainly army officers) acted like conquerors and treated the local population as inferior. Japanese rule was considered despotic and exceptionally harsh.

impose communism in areas their army conquered, while the Soviets feared that the Western Allies still wanted to strangle the communist system, as they had attempted to do before World War II. Both sides felt continually wary that the other would seek to make peace with Germany without their consent. The Nazi-Soviet Pact between Russia and Germany concerned the Western Allies; the

"Unconditional Surrender"

At the Casablanca conference, U.S. President Franklin D. Roosevelt publicly announced that the goal of the war was easy to summarize: "the unconditional surrender of Germany, Italy, and Japan." Roosevelt emphasized that the Allies did not want to destroy the people of the Axis countries or the countries themselves, but did want to destroy the "philosophy based on the conquest and subjugation of other peoples" on which the Axis countries were based. The demand for unconditional surrender is quite unusual in war, where countries usually fight for limited goals, such as control of a particular region. One purpose of Roosevelt's declaration was to reassure the Soviet Union that the Western Allies would not make peace with Germany without including the Soviets. The declaration was also intended to influence American and British public opinion, while reassuring people in German-occupied European countries. It promised that the Allies would not make deals with the Nazis. The demand for unconditional surrender was also a symbolic demonstration that the war was being fought between two ways of life that could not coexist. Some historians believe that Roosevelt was influenced by the example of President Abraham Lincoln dealing with the slave-holding Confederacy during the American Civil War. Roosevelt's declaration has since been strongly criticized on the grounds that it encouraged Germany and Japan to continue fighting, and ultimately prolonged the war. British military writer B. H. Liddell Hart called it the "biggest blunder of the war," but other historians disagree, arguing that Germany and Japan would never have negotiated any terms that the Allies could have accepted.

Henri Giraud, Franklin D. Roosevelt, Charles de Gaulle, and Winston Churchill at the Casablanca conference, January 1943. (*Reproduced by permission of AP/Wide World Photos*)

Soviets felt the Western Allies had appeased Hitler for years in an attempt to use him as an insurance policy against communism, hoping to encourage him to invade Soviet Russia. While these disputes were significant, they should not be exaggerated. Germany always hoped and predicted that suspicion would destroy the Allies, but that was never a real possibility. Even in the most serious arguments, both sides recognized the importance of maintaining their alliance until Germany was defeated. After the fall of the Third Reich, the alliance quickly disintegrated.

The Soviet Union was at the root of the most important disagreement between the British and Americans, the timing and location of a second front in Europe. After the Germans invaded their country in June 1941, the Soviets immediately began pressing the British to open a second front in western Europe, and wanted British troops to engage the Nazis in close proximity to Germany proper to take pressure off the Soviet armies. At that time, the British did not have the troops, landing ships, tanks, artillery, or planes to mount a successful invasion. When the United States entered the war, the Soviets again pressured both countries for a second front.

While the Allies all agreed on the "Germany first" strategy, they had differing opinions regarding how to implement that strategy. American and Soviet military leaders felt "Germany first" meant a full-scale invasion of western Europe, to be conducted as soon as possible, and probably in France. After crossing France, the British and Americans would be able to attack Germany from the west as the Soviets closed in from the east. They thought this was the fastest—and probably the only—way to defeat Germany. Churchill and his military advisers disagreed, feeling a rushed invasion would lead to disaster. They remembered their defeat by the German army in France in 1940 and the bloodshed that occurred during World War I when armies attacked built-up defensive positions. Rather than an invasion of western Europe, the British advocated fighting around the edges of German-controlled Europe. One example of this type of strategy was the campaign in Egypt and Libya, fought mainly against the Italians, and another was Churchill's ongoing interest in sending British troops to fight the Germans in Greece.

The British-American invasion of North Africa in November 1942, code-named Operation Torch, was yet another part of this strategy. The British

American master spy Allen Dulles. His secret contacts with German officials raised Soviet fears that the United States might make a separate peace with Germany. *(Reproduced by permission of AP/Wide World Photos)*

convinced the Americans that while it was impossible to invade France in 1942, Operation Torch would be a good way to engage American troops in fighting with the Germans, something Roosevelt, Marshall, and the American people favored. It took until May 1943 to clear Axis forces out of North Africa, at which point Churchill argued for an invasion of Sicily, a large Italian island off the coast of Italy. The invasion of Sicily began in July 1943 and moved into mainland Italy in September. These operations were designed to eliminate Italy from the war, and did, but were accepted by the United States only on the condition that they did not cause the delay of the second front against Germany. It soon became clear, however, that an invasion of France would not be possible in 1943, partly due to the military personnel and equipment tied up in the Italian campaign.

General Marshall and other American leaders regarded the North African and Italian campaigns as secondary concerns that did little to advance the war against Germany. They came to believe these operations actually hurt the overall goal by diverting scarce resources. At the beginning of 1944, with the invasion of France scheduled for spring, Churchill was still trying to postpone it in favor of other strategies. He wanted to send the Allied

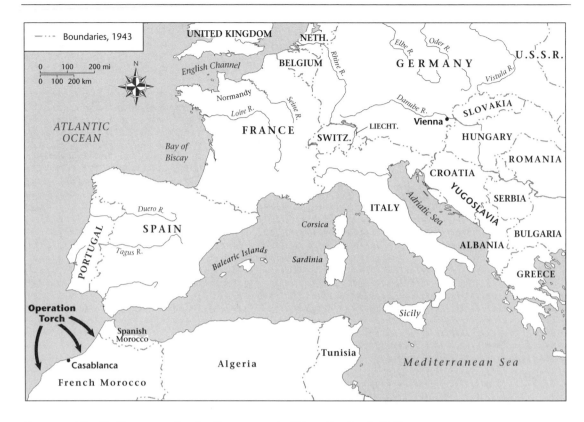

Europe and the Mediterranean, showing the movement of Operation Torch, 1943.

armies from Italy into Yugoslavia toward the Austrian capital of Vienna. This plan could take years, as the Allied armies were still bogged down in southern Italy. Roosevelt and his advisers suspected that Churchill wanted to maintain British economic and political influence in Greece, southeastern Europe, and the Mediterranean via his plan. Many historians also believe Churchill was afraid the Soviets would otherwise control these areas after the war. Western military historians generally agree with the British that an invasion of western Europe in 1942 would have resulted in disaster, and many also believe that the British were right not to invade in 1943, either.

Soviet historians, while admitting that an earlier invasion probably would have cost the lives of many more British and American soldiers, point out that in the meantime their soldiers were dying instead. Soviet leaders always suspected during the war that their allies wanted the Soviet Union to emerge from the war in a weakened condition. They believed the British agreed to an invasion of western Europe only after the Soviets spent years fighting and weakening the German army. The Soviets suffered far more severe losses than the remainder of the Allies, with the deaths of 7 mil-

lion Soviet soldiers and at least 13 million Soviet civilians. Comparatively, the British sustained the loss of approximately 250,000 troops and 60,000 civilians, while the United States lost about 300,000 soldiers and almost no civilians.

The Western Allies, the Soviet Union, and Poland

Another source of disagreement between the Western Allies and the Soviet Union concerned Poland. These concerns went back to the beginning of the war. The Soviets had acquired the eastern half of Poland under the Nazi-Soviet Pact. This was regarded by many as an underhanded attempt to grab neighboring land. The Soviets believed they were entitled to the land, which had been taken from the new Soviet government by Poland in 1920 as a result of the Polish-Soviet War. They pointed to the borders defined by British Foreign Minister Lord Curzon in 1919. The boundary he drew between Poland and the Soviet state, known as the Curzon Line, put most of the territory that the Soviets annexed in 1939 on the USSR's side of the map.

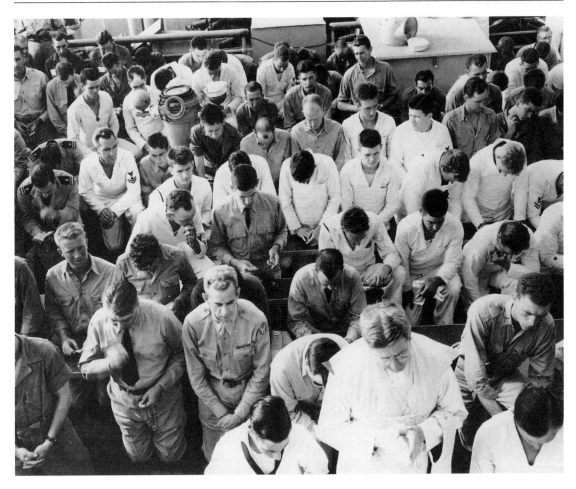

U.S. Navy officers and enlisted men take time out to pray before an invasion. *(Library of Congress)*

Less than two years later, in June 1941, the Germans had invaded the Soviet Union and conquered eastern Poland in the process, placing the whole of Poland under German control. By the end of 1943, however, the Soviet Red Army had pushed the Germans far back toward the west. As the Soviet military approached eastern Poland, Soviet leaders made it clear to the British and Americans that they considered this area part of the Soviet Union, and had no intentions of restoring Poland's 1939 borders. Although the Soviets had not consulted the people who lived there, violating the principles of the Atlantic Charter, the British and Americans realized there was not much they could do. The Red Army physically controlled the area: Only a serious threat to break up the alliance against Germany could possibly have changed the Soviet leaders' minds, and this was too high a price for the British and Americans to pay.

At the first meeting of Roosevelt, Churchill, and Stalin, held in Teheran, Iran, in November 1943, the two Western leaders generally agreed to the Soviets' demand regarding Poland's eastern border. To make up for the loss of territory on its east, the British and Americans suggested, Poland should be given land on its west that would be taken from Germany after its defeat, essentially moving Poland westward. The Soviets agreed with this suggestion, partly because it might permanently weaken Germany, and partly because it would mean that Poland would never side with Germany against the Soviets. In 1939 the Polish government had escaped from the Germans and established residency in London. Britain and the United States considered this government-in-exile the legal representative of the Polish people. The London Poles, as the government-in-exile was often called, absolutely refused to give up the eastern half of Poland to the Soviets.

The territorial dispute was worsened by a stunning accusation from the Germans. In spring 1943 the Germans announced they had discovered a

Western Aid to the Soviets

Although there is no question that the Soviet Union suffered greatly in World War II, the West provided important aid to the Soviet effort. For years, convoys of Allied ships carried vast amounts of supplies across the North Atlantic and Arctic waters to the Soviet port of Murmansk. German submarines attacked these convoys at every opportunity, causing heavy losses; in one particular convoy, only eleven of thirty-six ships reached Murmansk safely. Sometimes the submarine attacks were so heavy that the convoys had to be canceled. Though Soviet leaders constantly complained about the amount of supplies getting through, the total value of American aid to the Soviet Union was 11 billion dollars. In November 1943 Soviet dictator Joseph Stalin told U.S. President Franklin D. Roosevelt that without the American supplies his country received in the first two years of the German invasion, the Soviet Union would have lost the war.

1940, possibly to eliminate Poles who could have been potential leaders in regaining their country's independence. Some historians believe the killings may have been caused by a misunderstanding of orders sent by Soviet leaders.

The argument over Polish borders became closely connected to the question of Poland's postwar government. The Western Allies were concerned that the Soviets would impose communist governments in the areas they liberated. These fears increased in July 1944 when the Soviets created the Polish Committee of National Liberation, dominated by Polish communists. The Soviets soon recognized this committee as the legitimate Polish government instead of the government-in-exile located in London. Almost simultaneously, the underground Polish Home Army, which was loyal to the London Poles, led a major uprising against the Germans in Warsaw, the Polish capital. The Red Army, which was very close to Warsaw, did not assist in the uprising, and did not even enter the capital until months later, after the Germans had already crushed the Home Army. The Soviets claimed their army had been unable to

mass grave in the Katyn forest region of eastern Poland that contained 1,700 bodies (this number was later adjusted upward, eventually reaching 4,000) of Polish army officers, each with a bullet in his head. The Germans claimed these deaths were the responsibility of the Soviets, who had controlled the area between September 1939 and June 1941. The Soviets strongly denied the German accusation, claiming the Germans themselves had committed the murders. At first most people in the West believed the Soviets, as an accusation of mass murder coming from the Nazis could not be trusted. The Polish government-in-exile, however, refused to accept the Soviet explanation and demanded an investigation by the International Red Cross. The Soviets considered this an insult, maintained that the London Poles were siding with the Nazis, and soon broke off all relations with the London Poles. Today it is known that the Soviet secret police murdered the Polish officers in spring

General Wladyslaw Sikorski, head of the Polish government-in-exile in London, who later died in a plane crash. His death removed the most respected and capable leader of the London Poles. *(Reproduced by permission of AP/Wide World Photos)*

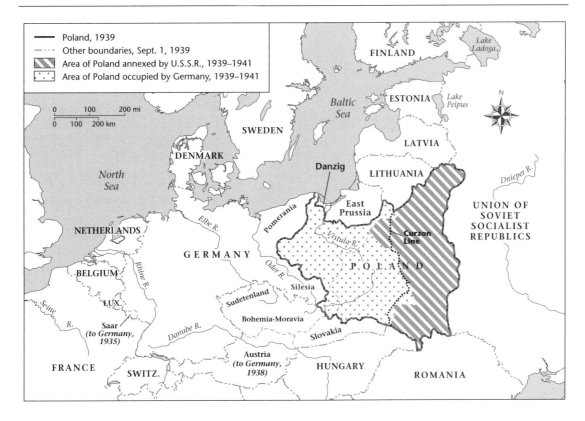

Poland's 1939 and 1941 borders.

advance for military reasons, but most Poles believed the Soviets had purposely allowed the Germans to destroy the Home Army. In any case, relations between the Soviet Union and the London Poles worsened.

By the last year of the war, it was becoming evident that the Soviet Union was determined to install a communist government in Poland, though historians have strongly disputed Soviet motivations for this. Some believe the Soviets intended to implement communist governments throughout eastern Europe, either to spread communism or to gain control over those countries. Other historians believe the Soviets acted defensively, in response to British and American actions elsewhere, such as Italy. In summer 1943 Stalin requested that the Soviet Union be allowed to take part in governing newly liberated territory in southern Italy. In October the Allies created an Advisory Council for Italy, which included the Soviet Union and France but had no real power. The Anglo-American Control Commission, made up of the British and Americans, truly governed Italy. Some historians maintain that the Soviet response to this situation in Italy was to eliminate

any British or American participation in the Polish government. The Soviets contended that only the formulation of communist governments would produce nations friendly to the Soviet Union and would prevent countries such as Romania and Hungary from ever attacking the Soviet Union again. Arguments about these actions became embittered in the years following World War II, spiraling disputes between the Western Allies and the Soviet Union into a worldwide struggle known as the Cold War.

The Western Allies, the Soviet Union, and Japan

Yet more disagreement arose between the Western Allies and the Soviet Union over the war against Japan, a nation with which the Soviets had signed a neutrality agreement in April 1941. When Germany invaded the Soviet Union two months later, Japan stood by its agreement and did not launch an attack against the Soviets. When Japan attacked the United States in December 1941, Germany quickly declared war on America in support of its Japanese ally, which still did not enter the war against the Soviet Union. Hitler believed that Germany could achieve victory over the Soviets without assistance from Japan, and, at least at first, did not desire its aid. For most of the war, the United States, Britain, and the Soviet Union were at war with Germany, but only the United States and Britain were at war with Japan. In the first years after Germany invaded the Soviet Union, the Soviet army could have lent little or no assistance to the war against Japan, a fact well understood and appreciated by the Western Allies. Even then, the United States wanted to use air bases in the far eastern Soviet Union to deploy American bombers against Japan, but the Soviets refused, afraid the action would prompt Japan to attack Soviet territory. Both Japan and the Soviet Union were reluctant to go to war with each other, despite pressures from their respective allies to do so.

By 1944, it became clear that the Allies would soon defeat Germany while Japan would continue fighting. American military leaders believed that the United States would have to invade Japan and that vast numbers of American and Japanese soldiers would be killed. The United States pressured the Soviets to agree to join the war against Japan after Germany surrendered, and wanted the Soviet army to invade Manchuria, in northern China, to engage the large Japanese army stationed there. This would prevent the Japanese from using these troops to defend Japan itself and could potentially convince Japanese leaders that continuation of the war was futile, rendering an American invasion unnecessary. Convincing the Soviet Union to declare war on Japan was so vital to the United States that the American government was willing to agree to numerous Soviet demands in exchange for the declaration. The Americans promised the Soviets special economic privileges in Manchuria (a promise they made without asking the Chinese government) and control of some islands belonging to Japan, and also agreed to some Soviet demands regarding the war in Europe.

The Soviets eventually promised to collaborate in the war against Japan as soon as possible after Germany's defeat, usually saying that it would take approximately three months to mobilize their efforts. Following Germany's surrender, the Soviets shifted some of their most experienced and well-equipped troops from Europe to the Far East. On August 8, 1945, exactly three months after Germany's surrender, the Soviet Union declared war on Japan, and a huge Soviet army invaded Manchuria the next day. Despite a hard fight against the Soviet offensive, Japan's defenses were

soon infiltrated and the Soviets took many Japanese prisoners of war. In less than two weeks, the Soviets drove the remainder of the Japanese army back into northern Korea.

By that time, however, the Americans were no longer certain they wanted the Soviets in the war against Japan. On July 16, 1945, the United States had successfully tested the first atomic bomb in the desert of New Mexico. American leaders believed atomic weapons could force Japan to surrender without an American invasion and without help from the Soviet Union. In that case, a Soviet invasion of Manchuria would increase Soviet influence in China without any benefit for the United States. It was too late, however, to change the plan for a Soviet invasion, and no one knew for sure if the bomb would end the war with Japan. On August 6, 1945, two days before the Soviet declaration of war, an American plane dropped an atomic bomb on the Japanese city of Hiroshima, completely destroying it. On August 9 a second atomic bomb was dropped on Nagasaki. On August 15 Emperor Hirohito of Japan informed the Japanese populace in a radio broadcast that the war was lost. Although the threat of further atomic attacks was probably the most important reason for the admission of defeat, many historians believe that the Soviet invasion of Manchuria was also a key factor.

Axis Relationships

Compared with the complicated relationships between the three major Allied powers, the connection between Germany and Japan, the two most important Axis powers, was much simpler. While Germany and Japan shared some information, they never coordinated any military operations. Their top military and naval officers never met, never discussed strategy, and never timed campaigns to take advantage of what the other was doing. Germany and Japan were fighting parallel wars: Each was fighting Britain and the United States, and each hoped the other would succeed. Allied propaganda during the war implied that Germany and Japan had formulated a plan to divide the world between them. This plan only amounted to vague ideas about the Japanese conquering India and moving west while the German army moved south from the Caucasus region of the Soviet Union. The two armies would then meet somewhere around Iran. Neither side actually planned any operations to launch this offensive,

Secrets and Spying among Allies

The atomic bomb project illustrates the suspicion between the Western Allies and the Soviet Union. The atomic bomb was secretly developed in the United States by scientists working for the army. Though scientists and engineers from around the world were involved, no Soviet scientists were asked to participate. Although there were some disputes, the United States generally kept the British government informed about the development, construction, and testing of the new weapon. The agreement of British Prime Minister Winston Churchill was officially required before the United States could use the bomb (though the decision was actually made by Harry S Truman, who became president of the United States after Franklin D. Roosevelt's death in April 1945). Meanwhile, the Western Allies kept the existence of the project secret from the Soviets. It was only after they had successfully

tested the bomb, in July 1945, that Truman told Soviet leader Joseph Stalin of its existence, using very general terms and referring to the bomb only as a powerful new weapon. He offered no specific details, and Stalin did not request any.

It is now known that spies kept the Soviet government informed of the progress of the atom bomb project, although it is unclear whether the Soviet leaders appreciated its immense power. The atom bomb project is an excellent example of the rampant distrust between the Western Allies and the Soviet Union: The Americans attempted to keep the most vital military secret of the war from one of their most important allies, while the Soviets used every possible method to spy on the United States.

Winston Churchill, Franklin D. Roosevelt, and Joseph Stalin at Yalta on the Crimean Peninsula, February 1945. At this final meeting of the "Big Three," Roosevelt pressed the Soviet Union for a commitment to join the war against Japan. Roosevelt's health was quickly deteriorating; he died two months after this picture was taken. *(Library of Congress)*

and the two armies were never within 3,000 miles of each other.

The third major Axis power was Italy, which had served in many ways as an example for Hitler as he gained control of Germany. Hitler and Italian dictator Benito Mussolini began to work together: For example, Italy sent troops to support General Francisco Franco's rebels in the Spanish Civil War, while Germany sent airmen and planes. It soon became clear, however, that Germany's greater economic and military power made it the senior partner. This was even more true once Italy entered the war in June 1940. Both in the North African desert and in Greece, the Germans had to help save Italian armies from defeat. German generals had a very low opinion of the Italian army and did not attempt to hide it. The alliance with Germany was never popular among the Italian people, who increasingly wanted Italy to get out of the war. By the time the Allies invaded Italy in summer 1943 and Mussolini was overthrown, Germany was treating Italy more like a conquered country than an ally.

In November 1940, Romania and Hungary declared allegiance to the Axis by signing the Tripartite Pact, which had been forged by the original Axis powers two months before. Germany wanted the two countries, which bordered the Soviet Union, to join its planned Soviet invasion. Though both countries had antidemocratic governments sympathetic to Nazi Germany, these alliances were always complicated. Romania and Hungary, while strongly influenced by Germany, were still independent countries that were traditional enemies of each other. Under pressure from the Germans in August 1940, Romania gave up large sections of its country to Hungary but neither side was satisfied. Both suffered tremendous losses in the Soviet

Union and by summer 1943, both were secretly and separately attempting to contact the Western Allies to establish peace. The British and Americans essentially told them they would have to deal directly with the Soviet Union. In March 1944, afraid that Hungary was secretly planning to get out of the war, the Germans took over the country and installed an extreme pro-Nazi government—soon Germany controlled every aspect of Hungarian life. As the Red Army crossed into Romania in August 1944, on the other hand, Romania surrendered, declared war on Germany, and joined the Soviet attack on Hungary.

Of the three remaining German allies, two did not fully cooperate with the Axis. While Bulgaria signed the Tripartite Pact and joined in the German invasion of Yugoslavia in 1941, it refused to declare war on the Soviet Union (though it did declare war on the United States and Britain). Soon after the Soviet Union declared war on Bulgaria in September 1944, Bulgaria declared war on Germany and sent 150,000 troops to fight its former allies. Finland also fought with Germany against the Soviet Union, mainly because it wanted to regain territory it had lost to the Soviets in the winter of 1939–1940, but never declared war on Britain or the United States, and was influenced very little by Germany. Slovakia, which the Germans had recently established as an independent country, was a puppet regime under the control of Hitler. It signed the Tripartite Pact in November 1940 and provided troops to invade the Soviet Union. Despite the pressure Hitler placed on various nations, Germany's reluctance to include its allies in military plans and efforts prevented a cohesive Axis alliance. Historians generally assert that this was a primary factor in Germany's loss in the war.

The USS *Arizona* after Japan's attack on Pearl Harbor. *(Reproduced by permission of UPI/Corbis-Bettmann)*

PRIMARY SOURCE

Franklin D. Roosevelt
"A Date Which Will Live in Infamy"

War message delivered to U.S. Congress
December 8, 1941

Japanese forces had been fighting in China since July 1937, and by 1940, they had taken over much of Southeast Asia. Japan's next targets were island groups in the southwest Pacific Ocean. Alarmed by the Japanese government's quest to dominate Asia, the United States took steps to restrict (but not totally ban) trade with Japan, and demanded the nation withdraw its troops from China and French Indochina (now Vietnam). Although the trade restrictions interfered with the manufacture of war materials, the Japanese did not buckle under the economic pressure, and Japan's military steadfastly refused to remove troops from

occupied areas. As a result, U.S. President Franklin D. Roosevelt took more definitive action in summer 1941, cutting off all U.S. trade with Japan, including the sale of oil, which was vital to the Japanese war effort. Shortly thereafter, the governments of Great Britain and the Netherlands did the same.

In December 1941 the United States had been on the brink of war with the Axis Powers for months, but events that occurred on Sunday, December 7, propelled the nation into the very heart of the growing global conflict. During the early morning hours, a Japanese fleet launched a surprise attack on the U.S. naval base at Pearl Harbor, Hawaii, on the southern coast of Oahu. While U.S. officials had expected Japan to attack in the Pacific, many had suspected that the Philippines would be the target—not Pearl Harbor. The raid lasted less than two hours, with Japanese torpedo planes and bombers launched from aircraft carriers (stationed about 200 miles north of Oahu) hitting eighteen American warships. The USS *Arizona* was destroyed in a fiery explosion; the *Oklahoma* capsized; the *California, West Virginia,* and several others were sunk; and still others were heavily damaged. Approximately 200 planes, a majority of which were on the ground, were destroyed, and another 150 were damaged. The Pearl Harbor attack left more than 2,400 Americans dead and 1,100 wounded. Roosevelt's "A Date Which Will Live in Infamy" speech, delivered to the U.S. Congress on December 8, 1941, called for a declaration of war against Japan in retaliation for the bombing. Congress agreed with Roosevelt's request, and the president signed the declaration two and one-half hours after giving his speech. In a radio address to the nation on December 9, 1941, President Roosevelt declared: "We are now in this war. We are all in it—all the way."

"A Date Which Will Live in Infamy"

Yesterday, December 7, 1941—a date which will live in infamy—the United States of America was suddenly and deliberately attacked by naval and air forces of the Empire of Japan.

The United States was at peace with that nation and, at the solicitation of Japan, was still in conversation with its government and its Emperor looking toward the maintenance of peace in the Pacific. Indeed, one hour after Japanese air squadrons had commenced bombing in Oahu, the Japanese ambassador to the United States and his colleague delivered to the Secretary of State [Cordell Hull] a formal reply to a recent American message. While this reply stated that it seemed useless to continue the existing diplomatic negotiations, it contained no threat or hint of war or armed attack.

It will be recorded that the distance of Hawaii from Japan makes it obvious that the attack was deliberately planned many days or even weeks ago. During the intervening time the Japanese Government has deliberately sought to deceive the United States by false statements and expressions of hope for continued peace.

The attack yesterday on the Hawaiian Islands has caused severe damage to American naval and military forces. Very many American lives have been lost. In addition American ships have been reported torpedoed on the high seas between San Francisco and Honolulu.

Yesterday the Japanese government also launched an attack against Malaya.

The memorial to the 1,177 sailors who died aboard the USS *Arizona* at Pearl Harbor is visited by 1.5 million people per year. The ship, with the remains of most of the sailors still inside it, lies beneath the memorial. *(Reproduced by permission of the Corbis Corporation [Bellevue])*

Last night Japanese forces attacked Hong Kong.

Last night Japanese forces attacked Guam.

Last night Japanese forces attacked the Philippine Islands.

Last night the Japanese attacked Wake Island.

The Attack on Pearl Harbor: A Sequence of Events

1. The Japanese fleet set out from a harbor in the North Pacific at 6 a.m. on November 26, 1941 (Japanese local time).

2. Twelve days later (having crossed the international date line in the Pacific, adding one day), the aircraft carriers reached their launching point, a little more than 200 miles north of Oahu.

3. Government officials in Washington, D.C., sent a war-alert message to Hawaii on December 6. The United States was bracing for war with Japan, but an attack on the American naval base at Pearl Harbor was hardly considered.

4. Two representatives of the Japanese government were in Washington, D.C., carrying on talks with Secretary of State Cordell Hull of the United States on Sunday, December 7, 1941. Peace talks were still going on after the attack on Pearl Harbor had begun.

5. Japanese bombers began their infamous December 7 run on Pearl Harbor at 7:50 a.m., Hawaii time. Prior to the raid, Japan had not declared war on the United States.

6. The attack, which lasted 110 minutes, paralyzed the U.S. Pacific Fleet.

7. President Roosevelt delivered a message to Congress on the morning of December 8.

8. Two and one-half hours after completing his message, Roosevelt signed a formal declaration of war against Japan.

The USS *West Virginia* in flames during the Japanese attack on Pearl Harbor. *(National Archives and Records Administration)*

The scene at Pearl Harbor, Hawaii, taken by a Japanese pilot. Note the cluster of American ships. During the attack, the Japanese sank and heavily damaged many American ships. *(Reproduced by permission of AP/Wide World Photos)*

This morning the Japanese attacked Midway Island.

Japan has, therefore, undertaken a surprise offensive extending throughout the Pacific area. The facts of yesterday speak for themselves. The people of the United States have already formed their opinions and well understand the implications to the very life and safety of our nation.

As Commander-in-Chief of the Army and Navy, I have directed that all measures be taken for our defense.

Always will we remember the character of the onslaught against us.

No matter how long it may take us to overcome this premeditated invasion, the American people in their righteous might will win through to absolute victory.

I believe I interpret the will of the Congress and of the people when I assert that we will not only defend ourselves to the uttermost but will make very certain that this form of treachery shall never endanger us again.

Hostilities exist. There is no blinking at the fact that our people, our territory and our interests are in grave danger.

With confidence in our armed forces—with the unbounding determination of our people—we will gain the inevitable triumph—so help us God.

I ask that the Congress declare that since the unprovoked and dastardly attack by Japan on Sunday, December 7th, a state of war has existed between the United States and the Japanese Empire. (Roosevelt, pp. 302–303)

Hideki Tōjō

Hideki Tōjō, prime minister of Japan from October 1941 through July 1944. *(Reproduced by permission of AP/Wide World Photos, Inc.)*

General Hideki Tōjō (1884–1948) was the dominant figure in the Japanese government during World War II. Always aggressive and militant, he earned the nickname "Kamisori," meaning the "Razor," for his keen mind. As chief of staff of the Japanese army (1937), minister of war (beginning in 1940), and prime minister of Japan (from October 1941 through July 1944), Tōjō pushed hard for the expansion of Japanese influence throughout Asia. He authorized the Japanese attack on the American naval base at Pearl Harbor in 1941. Four years later, following Japan's surrender to Allied forces at the war's end, Tōjō attempted to commit suicide. He was arrested later in 1945, tried by the Allies as a war criminal, and hanged in Tokyo on December 23, 1948.

At the end of his trial, Tōjō apologized for the atrocities that Japan had committed against the Allies. However, he believed that the United States should apologize, in turn, for the bombings levied on Japanese cities, including Hiroshima and Nagasaki.

Aftermath

On December 11, 1941, Germany and Italy declared war on the United States. Admiral Isoroku Yamamoto, commander in chief of Japan's navy, had suggested the Pearl Harbor attack to cripple the U.S. Pacific Fleet and thereby clear the way for Japanese expansion in the western and southern Pacific. In accordance with this strategy, while America was scrambling to recover from the raid on Pearl Harbor, the Japanese staged a series of invasions in the Pacific. U.S. military bases on Guam (a U.S. territory in the western Pacific) and Wake Island (located northeast of Guam) were attacked the same day as Pearl Harbor. Japanese forces captured Guam several days later and Wake Island on December 23, 1941. On December 25, following a week of steady bombing, Hong Kong

fell to Japan. Manila, the capital city of the Philippine Islands, surrendered to the Japanese eight days later, and the southeast Asian island of Singapore, located at the southern tip of the Malay Peninsula, followed suit in February 1942. The American fight against Japanese forces in the Philippines reached a fever pitch in March 1942. U.S. troops surrendered to Japan at Bataan (a key peninsula in the northern part of the Philippines) on April 9, 1942, and a nightmarish "Death March" of American and Filipino prisoners of war ensued. The captured soldiers were forced to hike fifty to sixty miles across the rocky, dusty terrain to their prison camp. By the time it was over, 7,000-10,000 of the 70,000 POWs on the march had died.

The naval battle at Midway, which took place during the first week of June 1942, marked a turn-

During the war, soldiers had to contend with all types of weather. In Guadalcanal in the Solomon Islands, rain turned this dirt road to mud, making it impassable. *(Library of Congress)*

ing point in the war in the Pacific. On June 4, 1942, 100 Japanese warships staged what was supposed to be a surprise attack on Midway Island, located in the northern Pacific Ocean between Hawaii and Japan. Two factors gave American forces the upper hand in the Battle of Midway: (1) Japanese military codes had been deciphered by the United States, revealing Japan's battle plan, and (2) American aircraft carriers (called "flattops") had not been at Pearl Harbor at the time of the attack. Two were at sea, three were in the Atlantic, and one was in a California harbor. As such, U.S. aircraft carriers and bombers were well prepared for the Japanese assault on Midway. After losing four of their own carriers in the battle against American forces, the Japanese retreated. The American victory at Midway was considered revenge for the attack on Pearl Harbor, and any threat of a Japanese invasion of the continental United States was eradicated.

In the first half of 1942 the Japanese also captured the Solomon Islands, located north of Australia, and used them as bases to launch further attacks in the Pacific. U.S. Marines landed on

Guadalcanal, one of the Solomon Islands, on August 7, 1942. For six months Americans fought on the ground, in the air, and in the shark-infested waters to win control of the Japanese-held island. By January 1943, the Japanese had lost Guadalcanal.

SOURCES

Books

Dunnahoo, Terry, *Pearl Harbor: America Enters the War,* F. Watts (New York), 1991.

Prange, Gordon W., *At Dawn We Slept: The Untold Story of Pearl Harbor,* Viking Penguin (New York), 1982.

Prange, Gordon W., with Donald M. Goldstein and Katherine V. Dillon, *God's Samurai: Lead Pilot at Pearl Harbor,* Brassey's (Washington, DC), 1990.

Roosevelt, Franklin Delano, *Nothing to Fear: The Selected Addresses of Franklin Delano Roosevelt, 1932–1945,* edited by B. D. Zevin, Houghton (New York), 1946.

Periodicals

Newsweek, March 8, 1999, pp. 42–44, 49.

New York Times, December 8, 1941, pp. 1, 8.

Other

The History Place, *December 7, 1941-Japanese Bomb Pearl Harbor* http://www.historyplace.com/worldwar2/timeline/pearl.htm (May 16, 2000).

Pearl Harbor: 50 Years Later, Turner Entertainment, 1991.

Pearl Harbor Remembered, http://www.execpc.com/~dschaaf/mainmenu.html (May 16, 2000).

Pearl Harbor: Two Hours That Changed the World, MPI Home Video, 1991.

10

The Allies Alter the Course of the War

From fall 1942 to summer 1943, the course of World War II was changed by a series of Allied victories. In May 1943 German submarines were forced to abandon their attempts to prevent shipments of North American supplies from reaching Britain. Other key victories occurred on the shores of the Mediterranean Sea and in Russia. At the beginning of this period, the possibility of an Axis victory was still very real; by the end, Germany, though far from defeated, had little chance of winning the war.

Montgomery Confronts Rommel in Africa

The British Eighth Army had been fighting in the deserts of Egypt and Libya in North Africa since September 1940. The British were mainly engaged with Italian forces, who were reinforced by the Afrika Korps, German armored and mechanized troops. All the Axis forces in North Africa were under the direction of Erwin Rommel, the "Desert Fox." Rommel's lightning attacks had made him a national hero in Germany and a respected adversary of the Allies. In August 1942 the British appointed a new commander of the Eighth Army, General Bernard Montgomery. Within two weeks, Rommel attacked the British, but the Eighth Army held its position and forced Rommel to break off his attack. Montgomery

painstakingly prepared the Eighth Army's next move. The British had more troops, planes, fuel, and shells than the Axis. Montgomery's forces were also armed with six times as many tanks, including the recently arrived, American-built Sherman tanks, which were superior to Rommel's.

Montgomery wanted to end the ceaseless see-saw battle for territory in North Africa. The British had chased the Axis forces from Egypt into Libya twice, and in turn were chased back again each time. Determined to destroy the Axis forces, the British general attacked on October 23, 1942, and began the Battle of El Alamein. Rommel had been resting at home in Germany, recovering from an illness, when he learned of the attack. He rushed back to Africa by plane to join his troops. Yet despite his efforts, he was unable to alter the outcome of the battle, which lasted for ten days. After suffering heavy losses, Rommel began a long retreat westward along the single coast road. By the end of the year, he had retreated 1,000 miles, deep into Libyan territory. The retreat had cost him 40,000 prisoners. Rommel was left with only 60,000 troops and fewer than 100 tanks.

On November 8, 1942, while Rommel was retreating, American and British forces landed in three locations much farther west and opened up a new battlefront. Under the overall command of U.S. General Dwight D. Eisenhower, this strategy, called Operation Torch, began with one landing

The End of Unoccupied France

Since June 1940, the German army had held direct control of the northern half of France and the entire Atlantic coast. Italy occupied the southeast corner of the country. The rest of France was under the authority of the Vichy government. When the Allies landed in French-controlled North Africa in November 1942, the German army immediately poured troops into most of the unoccupied zone, while the Italians took over the rest, effectively eliminating unoccupied France and placing the Vichy government under even greater German scrutiny.

The Germans also wanted to gain control of the French fleet, anchored in the port of Toulon on the Mediterranean coast of southern France. The Allies urged the commander of the fleet to sail his warships to North Africa and join them, but he hesitated, and when the Germans attacked the Toulon naval base, it was too late for the ships to sail away. Determined not to hand over their warships to the Germans, French naval officers and sailors blew them up instead.

near Casablanca, on the Atlantic coast of Morocco, and two on the Mediterranean Sea, near Algiers and Oran, the two largest cities of Algeria. Morocco and Algeria, as well as neighboring Tunisia, were French colonies still under the control of the Vichy government, which in turn was dominated by the Nazis.

In November 1942, approximately 100,000 French troops were stationed in North Africa, but the Allies hoped these forces would not oppose their landings. The Allied command, in fact, wanted the French to join them, and American representatives had secretly contacted Vichy military and civilian officials, as well as opponents of the Vichy government, both in France and in North

Africa. Many Vichy supporters were beginning to believe that Germany would lose the war and wanted to ally themselves with the victorious side.

There was considerable confusion among French officials when the Allies landed. Some pro-Allied French officers arrested those who wanted to resist the Allies, but then they themselves were, in turn, arrested. In Casablanca and Oran, the landings were resisted, but the landings in Algiers saw minimal conflict, partly because pro-Allied residents had taken over the city prior to the landings. French troops stopped fighting altogether when the Allies made a deal with Admiral Jean François Darlan, the second-highest official of the Vichy government and the commander in chief of French military forces. In a lucky break for the Allies, Darlan happened, purely by chance, to be in Algiers when the Allies landed in November 1942, visiting his critically ill son.

In return for Darlan's cooperation, the Allies put him in charge of North Africa, a deal that resulted in a major political controversy because of Darlan's two years of close cooperation with the Nazi government. The French resistance and Charles de Gaulle's London-based Free French movement both disliked Darlan. His appointment also caused unexpected outrage in Britain and the United States, where many people believed that placing a former Nazi collaborator in a position of power betrayed the Allies' principles. Many also feared that this would set a precedent for dealing with pro-Nazi officials in other countries, or possibly even with Nazis in Germany who wanted to remain in power in the event of a German defeat. On Christmas Eve, 1942, Darlan was assassinated, and though the Allies were not involved, his death came as a political relief. After the war Winston Churchill wrote that the Allies had already reaped the benefit of the deal with Darlan, and his death ended their embarrassment of having to work with him.

Although they no longer faced any resistance, Allied troops moved slowly toward Tunisia (located between Algeria and Libya), where they planned to trap Rommel's forces between themselves and Montgomery's Eighth Army, advancing westward. Their hesitation provided Germany and Italy with an opportunity to rush troops into Tunisia, first by air, and then by sea. French authorities in Tunisia followed Vichy orders, rather than Admiral Darlan's, and allowed the Axis troops to enter the country unopposed. At the time, it seemed like the Allies had committed a costly tactical error, as they could

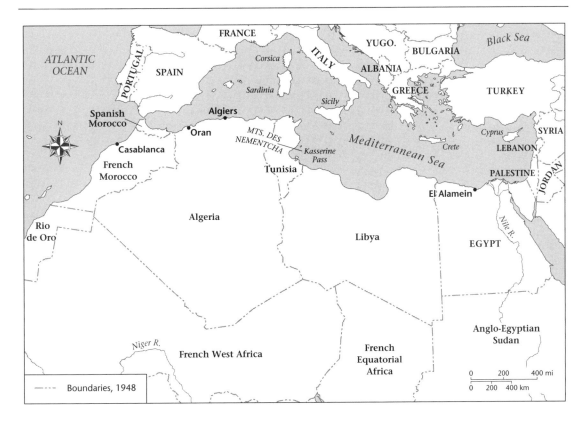

North Africa, 1948.

The flag-draped coffin of Admiral Jean François Darlan after his assassination in December 1942. *(Reproduced by permission of AP/Wide World Photos)*

American soldiers landing on a beach in Sicily. *(Reproduced by permission of AP/Wide World Photos)*

have taken Tunisia before the Axis deployed reenforcements. It later became clear that Germany and Italy had made a mistake by sending additional troops: Eventually all Axis forces in North Africa, including Rommel's army and the new troops in Tunisia, would be destroyed or captured.

When Allied forces reached Tunisia, they faced determined German resistance in the mountainous countryside, where Rommel's forces had established defensive positions against Montgomery's troops coming from the east. Rommel also launched several counterattacks against the Allied forces to his west, some quite successful. At the Kasserine Pass, a narrow pass through the mountains, for example, Rommel took an American force by surprise and inflicted serious casualties, capturing some prisoners, and forcing them to abandon a great deal of equipment. Like almost all American troops, these soldiers had never been in serious combat before. Their generals were also inexperienced, and Rommel recognized and used these facts to his advantage.

Still, the Axis forces did not have the manpower or equipment to convert these small victories into bigger successes. Their supplies, coming across the Mediterranean by ship and plane, were not reaching them in sufficient quantities. As the fighting continued through the winter months, the Allied forces, which now included French troops, grew stronger. The Americans, now under the command of General George S. Patton, had acquired more experience in fighting the Germans. Adolf Hitler assessed the situation as futile, and ordered Rommel to abandon his army and return to Germany on March 6. In late March 1943, Montgomery's troops broke through the Axis defensive positions and attacked from the rear. As the Germans and Italians retreated, they continued to fight defensive battles until early May, when, low on supplies and ammunition, large numbers of troops began to surrender, the last of whom gave up on May 13. Although estimates vary, the Axis had probably lost more than 200,000 men, and the war in Africa was over.

The Allies Enter Italy

On July 9, 1943, less than two months after the end of the fighting in Africa, the Allies invaded the large Italian island of Sicily. Ten Allied divisions (about 150,000 men), including two parachute divisions, were to invade the island, which was protected by twelve Axis divisions, only two of them German. Some Italian troops treated the Allies as liberators rather than invaders, and in some cases assisted in the unloading of their landing boats. Large numbers of Italian troops imme-

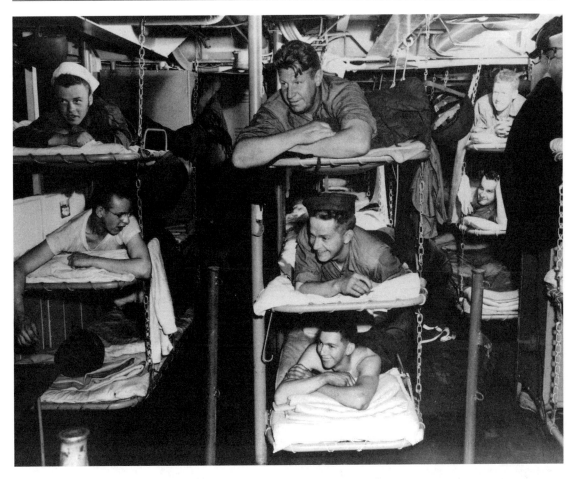

Sailors rest in their bunks on the way to invade Sicily. These cramped quarters are typical of life aboard ship. *(Library of Congress)*

diately surrendered when Allied troops reached them. American forces commanded by General Patton raced up the western side of the island, while the British, led by General Montgomery, went up the eastern side. The British met strong resistance from first-rate German units, including two additional German divisions sent as reinforcements. Even so, the Italians began evacuating their troops to the Italian mainland on August 3, and the Germans began to do the same a week later. Most of the Germans successfully evaded capture, but by the middle of August, Allied troops controlled all of Sicily.

While the series of Axis defeats in Africa had hurt Germany, they had been a disaster for Italy, which lost the empire that Benito Mussolini had dreamed would resurrect the glory of ancient Rome. Sicily had now been invaded, more than 300,000 Italian soldiers were prisoners of war in Africa, and another Italian army, with more than 200,000 men, had been wiped out in Russia. In both Russia and Africa, the Allies had captured vast quantities of arms and equipment. This was a much greater loss for Italy than for the other major powers, whose economies were far stronger. Most Italians were more impoverished than they had been before the war, and there were increasing shortages of most supplies. Allied planes constantly bombed Italian cities, and the Italian and German air forces seemed unable to protect them. Few Italians had ever been enthusiastic about the conflict, especially after Italy declared war on the United States—a large number of Italians had relatives in America, and most admired the country. The alliance with Hitler's Germany had never been popular with the Italian people, and it became even more unpopular as Italians came to believe that Germany did not treat Italy as an equal. As dissatisfaction grew, many of the country's most powerful leaders, including King Victor Emmanuel III and top military officers, decided Italy should withdraw from the war. Although the king and the army had sup-

After Italian dictator Benito Mussolini was ousted from power, he and his mistress, Clara Petacci, were killed. Their bodies were hung up at a gas station for public display. *(Reproduced by permission of © Hulton Getty/Liaison Agency)*

ported Mussolini for more than twenty years, they now plotted to oust him.

On July 25, 1943, with fighting in Sicily still going on, the king and his men removed Mussolini from his position as prime minister and placed him under arrest. After his arrest, Mussolini was held in a series of different locations before finally being incarcerated in a mountaintop house. On September 16, 1943, a small force of German commandos, under the leadership of Otto Skorzeny, launched a glider rescue mission and removed Mussolini from custody. The Germans then set him up in northern Italy, where he declared himself head of the Italian Socialist Republic. This new government assisted the Germans in fighting the

Italian anti-Nazi resistance movement in German-held areas. Near the end of the war, the resistance captured and executed Mussolini.

The new leader of the Italian government was Marshal Pietro Badoglio, the senior general in the Italian army; the king took over direct command of the armed forces. Although the new government promised Germany that Italians would continue to fight alongside German soldiers, Italy began covert negotiations with the Allies about an Italian surrender. The Italians secretly signed the surrender on September 3, 1943, the same day that General Montgomery led a force across the narrow strait from Sicily and landed at the toe of Italy. Designed as a decoy

Map of Italy showing the Gustav Line and Gothic Line, 1943.

rather than the main Allied invasion of Italy, the landing was a diversionary tactic meant to draw German troops into the area. The mission failed, mainly because the region was mountainous and Montgomery's troops were only able to move forward on a few roads along the coastline, which could be defended by a relatively small number of German troops.

On September 8, 1943, British radio announced the Italian surrender, and the next morning, the main Allied invasion force landed near

Hitler and His Generals

The German generals had to deal with increasing interference from Hitler, who was insisting on much more direct control of army operations, partly because he distrusted his generals. Top German officers usually came from old, noble families that looked down on Hitler as half-educated and ill-mannered. Although they cooperated with the Nazis, many officers considered them street thugs. In return, many Nazis hated the reactionary politics of the old-line officers. To add to this background tension, Hitler believed a majority of his generals were too cautious and did not understand the finer points of politics. Hitler appreciated the fact that military policy and political issues were closely connected. For example, Hitler's generals tried to dissuade him from sending troops into the Rhineland in 1936 because they knew Germany could not fight France, but Hitler himself correctly theorized that France would not use force to oppose that move.

Especially in the early years, Hitler was often right—and the generals wrong—about these types of issues, and Hitler came to see himself as a military genius. While he had a good memory and understood military details, such as specific types of weapons and where each army division was located, he frequently became so involved in these finer points that he lost sight of larger issues. Hitler's distrust of his generals also led him to divide authority among them without establishing clear lines of command. Disputes between generals had to be settled by Hitler himself. The entire Nazi government operated on this principle, which, for the army, meant that commanders in the field often did not have the authority to make immediate decisions, even though delay could result in defeat.

Hitler's belief that only he understood the big picture led to disastrous mistakes. He was always reluctant to order a retreat, even when it was the only way to save his army. The best example of this is the battle of Stalingrad, in which Hitler became obsessed with capturing the city, even if it did not make military sense, and refused to heed any military advice that contradicted his goal. As a result of this fixation, he sent an army into a Soviet trap and ordered it to stay there, even when it became clear the troops would be destroyed.

As military events began to turn against Germany, Hitler blamed his generals and constantly replaced them. By the end of the war he was increasingly unrealistic, unwilling to believe negative reports, and giving orders impossible to

---

Salerno, south of Naples, the largest city of southern Italy. The Allies had hoped the announcement of Italy's surrender would prevent them from facing any serious opposition, but Hitler had anticipated Italy's surrender and had formulated plans to counter it. German troops moved quickly to take over all important cities, roads, and bridges. They disarmed Italian soldiers, who generally did not resist. Many of them became prisoners and were sent to Germany to work in arms factories, while others were allowed to go home. The Germans also overtook areas outside Italy that had been con-

trolled by Italian forces. In southeastern France and Croatia (the western part of Yugoslavia), as in Italy itself, Italian troops usually did not put up resistance. On several Greek islands, however, heavy fighting took place between the Italians and the Germans. In revenge, the Germans executed every Italian officer captured on these islands. The new Italian government's declaration of war against Germany had little practical effect.

The Germans rushed troops to Salerno, nearly forcing the American and British invasion force to

Adolf Hitler (center right), Benito Mussolini (center left), and German generals study battle maps. *(Reproduced by permission of AP/Wide World Photos)*

implement (such as vast increases in tank production). Hitler put more and more faith in the introduction of new weapons, which he believed would change the course of the war—even when it was clear that Germany would be defeated.

return to its ships. Allied planes, artillery, and massive armaments on nearby warships prevented this eventuality, and by September 18, the Germans began to withdraw from the invasion area in a planned retreat. The Germans intended to prepare a defensive position stretching across Italy, called the Gustav Line. Most of the Gustav Line was in rugged terrain in the mountains, making it virtually impossible for the Allies to stage a direct attack on the Germans there. The Allies would have to advance along the two narrow plains between the mountains and each coast—plains that were crisscrossed by a series of rapidly flowing and easily defendable rivers running down from the mountains to the sea.

British troops entered Naples on October 1, 1943, and began what would prove to be a slow advance up the Italian peninsula. The Gustav Line soon became known as the Winter Line, as the Allied armies attacked it throughout the winter of 1943–1944. Unable to get past it, the Allies finally decided to go around it, and in January 1944 a large Allied force landed on the beaches around the town of Anzio, north of the Gustav

Three American soldiers in foxhole near the Anzio Nettuno Beachhead in Italy. *(Reproduced by permission of AP/Wide World Photos)*

Line and only thirty miles south of Rome, Italy's capital. Again rushing reinforcements to the area, the Germans were able to keep the invasion force from moving away from the beaches. In mid-February the Germans counterattacked at Anzio and nearly succeeded in pushing the Allies back into the sea. After heavy fighting and numerous casualties on both sides, the Allies managed to stop the Germans, but were still penned-in near the beaches. The Anzio landings had not freed Rome and had not forced the Germans to abandon the Gustav Line.

On its western end, the Gustav Line was dominated by the mountaintop abbey of Monte Cassino, and, as it became clear that the Allied troops at Anzio could not reach the Gustav Line from the rear, the Allies repeatedly attacked Cassino. The Monte Cassino monastery had great historical significance, as it had been founded by Saint Benedict in the sixth century and had survived fourteen centuries of war and turmoil. German troops around Cassino apparently did not take defensive positions inside the historic buildings, though they may have stored ammunition in them. It is unclear whether the Allies knew this. Four separate attacks

were carried out on the abbey, with Allied troops from all over the world participating. The first attack, launched in early February 1944, was conducted by American troops. On February 15, 1944, massive Allied bombing destroyed the monastery buildings, the wreckage of which was used by the Germans to establish defensive positions and create even more obstacles for the attacking Allied troops. Military historians agree for these reasons that this bombing of Cassino only helped the Germans. The second and third attacks were made by soldiers from New Zealand, India, and Britain. These two assaults, like the first, were defeated, with heavy Allied casualties. In the final battle, launched in May, French and Moroccan troops broke through near Cassino, allowing Polish troops to reach the ruins of the monastery. British and American armored divisions could now move past the Gustav Line, forcing the Germans to abandon it and retreat north.

At the same time, the Allies finally broke through the German encirclement at Anzio. The Americans entered Rome on June 4, 1944, but the Germans retreated to another position in the mountains farther north, called the Gothic Line.

The abbey of Monte Cassino before the Allied bombing. *(Reproduced by permission of AP/Wide World Photos)*

The ruins of the abbey of Monte Cassino after the Allied bombing. *(Reproduced by permission of AP/Wide World Photos)*

As a Russian village burns in the background, German Panzers continue on their journey. *(Reproduced by permission of © Hulton Getty/Liaison Agency)*

The Allies did not reach the great cities of the north, where most of Italy's industries were located, until spring 1945. By that time, British and American troops that had invaded France were fighting deep in Germany, and the Soviet army was at the gates of Berlin.

The War in Soviet Russia

While the fighting in Africa was still ongoing, much larger battles were being waged in the Soviet Union, where the main part of the German army had deployed most of its best troops, tanks, and air force. The German invasion of the Soviet Union in June 1941 had driven the Soviet army back hundreds of miles, killed 1 million Soviet soldiers, and taken 3 million prisoners. The Soviets had managed to stop the German advance in the fall, and Soviet counteroffensives in the winter of 1941–1942 had pushed the Germans back from Moscow. Although it seemed like a large part of the German army might be overwhelmed by the Soviet attack and the terrible winter conditions, it pulled back and established defensive positions. At the end of the winter, the Germans prepared to attack again. The battlefront now stretched 2,100 miles from north to south, and the Germans were too weak to launch the all-encompassing attacks they had staged the previous year. The Nazis had lost too many men and tanks, in addition to 250,000 horses needed to pull cannons and supply wagons. The German Luftwaffe was weaker than it had been the previous summer because more planes were needed to defend German cities from British bombing raids. The Luftwaffe was met by a much stronger Soviet air force. The Soviets were producing more tanks than the Germans, and supplies from the United States, especially trucks, were beginning to arrive in large quantities. The Red Army was being reinforced to make up for the huge losses of the past year. It had many new generals, often younger men who had succeeded in earlier fighting. Having learned the strategy and tactics of modern warfare, they were beginning to equal the German generals in skill.

In spring 1942 Hitler decided that the German armies should capture the Caucasus, the region of the Soviet Union between the Black Sea and the Caspian Sea, north of Iran. The Caucasus was a major producer of petroleum, and Germany was beginning to experience serious oil shortages. In early May the Germans began an offensive to remove Soviet troops from the Crimean Peninsula, out of fear that the Soviets could utilize Crimea, which jutted into the Black Sea, as a base to attack the Germans in their offensive on the Caucasus. In a week, the Germans had taken another 170,000

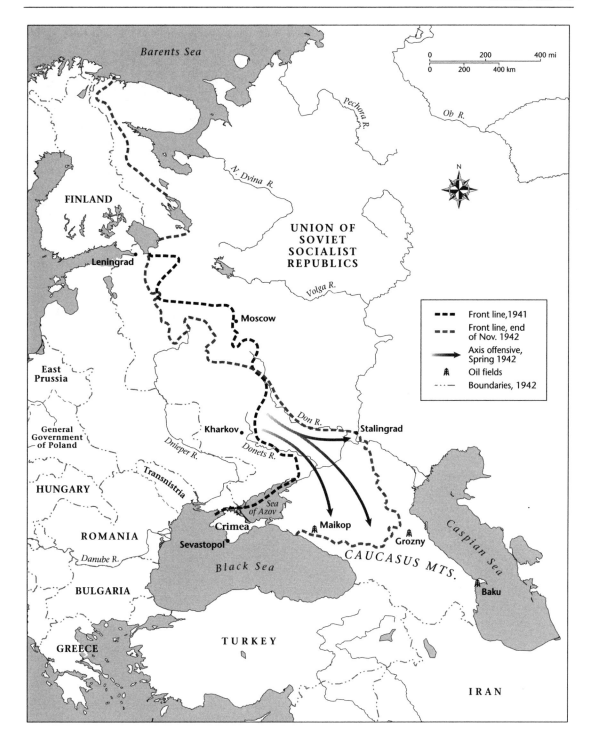

The eastern front, 1941 and 1942.

prisoners and controlled the entire peninsula except for the fortress city of Sevastopol. Surrounded by the Germans since the previous October, Sevastopol did not surrender until July 2. About the same time, the Soviet army launched its own offensive around the city of Kharkov, north of

Crimea. Although this attack initially threatened to disrupt German plans, it ultimately played into the Germans' hands. German forces north and south of the city moved forward and encircled the Soviet troops. The Russians lost another 250,000 troops taken prisoner and more than 1,000 tanks.

Fighting in the streets of suburban Stalingrad, German soldiers use a machine gun from their entrenched position. *(Reproduced by permission of AP/Wide World Photos)*

On June 28 the main German attack began when four German armies, with strong tank support, swept south from the Kharkov area onto the grassy plain that stretched between the Donets and Don Rivers. They drove down into the Caucasus, forcing the Soviet troops back but taking far fewer prisoners than in previous advances. The Soviets retreated rather than allow themselves to be encircled by the attacking German tanks. The German advance was slowed by Soviet resistance, intense summer heat, and the ever-greater distance that supplies had to be shipped to reach the German troops. As the flat terrain began to change to the foothills of the Caucasus mountains, the Germans ground to a halt.

Stalingrad

As the Germans moved south into the Caucasus, they also sent a strong force eastward across the river Don toward the city of Stalingrad, located on the river Volga. Their purpose was to block the route to the Caucasus from Soviet reinforcements and supplies. Stalingrad, a city of 600,000

people, was not originally an essential military target, but soon became important, and was the site of one of the most significant battles of World War II. The battle for Stalingrad was important for symbolic as well as military reasons: The capture of Stalingrad, named in honor of Soviet leader Joseph Stalin, would represent a symbolic capture of its namesake.

In mid-August the German Sixth Army reached the outskirts of Stalingrad from the west as the Fourth Panzer Army approached from the southwest. The Soviets rushed reinforcements to the city, dug defensive ditches, and ordered troops not to retreat. The attack turned into a battle for every street and every building. The entire city was destroyed as German troops slowly pushed the Russians back toward the banks of the mile-wide Volga. One German officer described fighting for more than two weeks to capture one house. Stalingrad, he said, was like a vast, glowing furnace. General Vasili Chuikov, the Russian commander, said that it was impossible to hear separate shots or explosions. Everything was one single, continuous roar. By the middle of October, the Russians controlled only a few pockets of the city. Although German radio announced that Stalingrad had been captured, fighting continued inside the city. The Germans were exhausted by two months of the worst fighting of the entire war. Neither side made any progress.

On November 19, 1942, the Soviet armies finally sprang their trap. They had carefully prepared two forces with vast quantities of artillery and tanks. One, which was many miles west of Stalingrad on the river Don, struck southward through an area defended by troops from Hungary, Italy, and Romania (due to a German shortage of troops). None of these Axis troops were so well-equipped as the Germans and the Soviets smashed through them, as well as through every German unit they encountered. The following day, the second Soviet force attacked from southeast of Stalingrad, heading west. When the two armies met on November 23, they had the German Sixth Army trapped in Stalingrad. Although there was still time for the Germans to retreat westward and possibly break through the trap, Hitler personally prohibited a retreat. He wanted the troops supplied by air while tank forces attempted to break through the Soviet ring into Stalingrad. The winter weather, the Soviet air force, and antiaircraft guns prevented the Luftwaffe from supplying anywhere near enough food and ammunition to German forces. Freezing, starving, and short of ammunition, the Sixth Army stayed in Stalingrad as the Russians began to retake the city.

The German force sent to break through the trap was far too small and did not have enough tanks. Needing to travel a distance of sixty miles, the division advanced only thirty before being driven back. The Germans in Stalingrad, on Hitler's orders, did not attempt to break out and retreat with the advancing column. Meanwhile, on December 16, 1942, the Soviets attacked again, even farther west. In a blinding snowstorm, they destroyed the Italian Eighth Army and retook much of the area between the Don and Donets Rivers, which meant the German troops in the Caucasus were nearly trapped too. Even Hitler agreed there was no choice but to retreat. In January the German troops managed to escape from the Caucasus before the Soviet army could block the way.

Hitler, however, refused to order a retreat from Stalingrad, where the temperature was twenty degrees below zero. On January 10, 1943, as the

Unaccustomed to the bitter cold on the Eastern Front, a German soldier shows the signs of fighting a war in the winter. *(Reproduced by permission of © Hulton Getty/Liaison Agency)*

Russians began their final attack to retake Stalingrad, 7,000 cannons blasted the Germans in the largest artillery bombardment in history. The German-held area was split in two and then divided into smaller pockets. The Russians captured the German headquarters and the German commander finally surrendered on January 31. In the final three weeks of the battle, a total of 100,000 German soldiers died. Another 100,000 (including twenty-four German generals) were taken prisoner. The entire Sixth Army, with its twenty-two divisions, was destroyed. In Germany, all regular radio programming was stopped for three days, and only somber music was played.

The Red Army Advances

The main battle lines were already far west of Stalingrad, and in the next weeks the Soviet army pushed the exhausted Germans back, but the Germans regrouped and counterattacked. The city of Kharkov, already captured and recaptured, changed hands twice more in bitter fighting. By March 1943, the spring thaw again flooded the dirt roads and turned the countryside into marsh that tanks could not cross. Both sides paused to try to

Von Manstein on Hitler as Supreme Commander

Field Marshal Erich von Manstein commanded German Army Group B during the siege on Stalingrad in the Soviet Union from 1942 until the Germans withdrew in defeat.

Von Manstein was born in Berlin, Germany, on November 21, 1887, the tenth child of an artillery general. He entered the military in 1905 as an ensign. During World War I, von Manstein served on both the western and Russian fronts. In 1933, the year Hitler rose to power, von Manstein was promoted to colonel, and in 1935 he was posted to the general staff of the Wehrmacht. In 1939 he was appointed chief of staff to Field Marshal Karl Rudolph Gerd von Rundstedt, who directed the Ardennes offensive in the Polish campaign. The following year, von Manstein planned the assault against France, which resulted in Nazi occupation of a major portion of the country. In 1941 he was transferred to the Russian front, and in 1942 was promoted to field marshal. He continued to serve on the eastern front until March 30, 1944,

when he was dismissed by Hitler. In May 1945 von Manstein was captured by the British. Four years later, he was tried as a war criminal and found guilty, though he was not convicted on charges that he had been involved in carrying out massacres on Jews. He was released from prison in 1953 and died in June 1973.

In von Manstein's memoir *Lost Victories* (first published in English in 1958), he evaluates Hitler's abilities as a supreme commander. As a commander of Army Group B, von Manstein had been under Hitler's direct command. The following excerpt is cited in *The War, 1939–1945*, edited by Desmond Flower and James Reeves (New York: Da Capo Press, 1997).

"Now that I had come immediately under Hitler in my capacity as an army group commander, however, I was to get my first real experience of him in his exercise of the supreme command.

"When considering Hitler in the role of a military leader, one should certainly not dismiss him with such clichés as 'the lance-corporal of World War I'.

"He undoubtedly had a certain eye for operational openings, as had been shown by the way he opted for Army Group A's plan in the west.

replace men and equipment lost in the battles. Many top German generals wanted to withdraw their forces to an area much farther west and prepare a defensive line that was shorter and closer to its sources of supply—in essence admitting the German military no longer believed it could destroy the Soviet armies. Their new plan was a defensive war against Russia, in which they would try to hold on to some of the vast territory they had conquered in summer 1941. Still believing in the possibility of a total German victory, Hitler ordered the German army to attack again. Its goal this time was to encircle and destroy large Soviet forces, as it had done in 1941.

The winter battles had left the two armies facing each other for hundreds of miles, but the line

between them was not straight. In some places, German positions jutted out toward the east, while in others, Soviet forces were positioned farther west. These bulges, or salients, were classic military targets. The idea was to attack the two sides of the bulge at its base, cutting off the main enemy forces inside the bulge from supplies and reinforcements. The attack would disrupt the ability of each unit's headquarters to communicate with its troops and control their movements. The largest Soviet bulge centered on the city of Kursk. Known as the Kursk salient, the bulge extended 150 miles west on its northern side, fifty miles west on its southern side, and was almost 100 miles wide; inside the salient were sixty Soviet divisions. On July 5, 1943, the Germans attacked both sides of the salient with a force that included 2,700 tanks—almost all the

Indeed, this is often to be found in military amateurs—otherwise history would not have recorded so many dukes and princes as successful military commanders. In addition, though, Hitler possessed an astoundingly retentive memory and an imagination that made him quick to grasp all technical matters and problems of armaments. He was amazingly familiar with the effect of the very latest enemy weapons and could reel off whole columns of figures on both our own and the enemy's war production. Indeed, this was his favourite way of sidetracking any topic that was not to his liking. There can be no question that his insight and unusual energy were responsible for many achievements in the sphere of armaments. Yet his belief in his own superiority in this respect ultimately had disastrous consequences. His interference prevented the smooth and timely development of the Luftwaffe, and it was undoubtedly he who hampered the development of rocket propulsion and atomic weapons.

"Moreover, Hitler's interest in everything technical led him to over-estimate the importance of his technical resources. As a result, he would count on a mere handful of assault-gun detachments or the new Tiger tanks to restore situations where only large bodies of troops could have any prospect of success.

"What he lacked, broadly speaking, was simply *military ability based on experience*—something for which his 'intuition' was no substitute.

"….Hitler had a masterly knack of psychologically adapting himself to the individual whom he wished to bring round to his point of view. In addition, of course, he always knew anyone's motive for coming to see him, and could thus have all his counter-arguments ready beforehand. His faculty for inspiring others with his own confidence—whether feigned or genuine—was quite remarkable. This particularly applied when officers who did not know him well came to see him from the front. In such cases a man who had set out to 'tell Hitler the truth about things out there' came back converted and bursting with confidence."

Field-Marshal von Manstein

Germans had stationed in the entire Soviet Union. Despite this powerful force, they made relatively slow progress. Soviet military leaders had expected the attack and had issued large numbers of anti-tank weapons to their troops. They had laid 5,000 mines on every mile of the front line, and in addition, troops and civilians in the area had built a series of strongly fortified positions so that if the Germans overran one, Soviet troops could withdraw to the next and escape capture. Soviet tanks fought it out with the advancing Germans, and the two German forces were unable to reach each other to cut off the salient.

On July 12 the Red Army began a counterattack. In one particular engagement, each side deployed 900 tanks against the other. At the conclusion of the day-long battle, the Germans had lost 300 tanks, and the Russians suffered even greater losses, but managed to stop the German advance. In other battles throughout the area, the result was the same: The Soviets pushed the Germans back, but both armies suffered heavy losses. On July 13 Hitler ordered an end to the German offensive.

For the next two months, the Soviets followed up their victory at Kursk by pushing the Germans eastward. By September they were in the Ukraine and White Russia (Belarus), and had driven the Germans from all of southern Russia. On November 3 the Red Army entered Kiev, capital of the Ukraine, which the Germans had captured more than two years earlier.

Soldiers of the German Sixth Army after their surrender at Stalingrad. Few of them survived the war. *(Reproduced by permission of the Corbis Corporation [Bellevue])*

Although both sides had suffered heavily at Kursk and during subsequent battles, the Soviets could replace their lost troops and equipment while the Germans could not. Russia had more citizens and therefore more soldiers than the Germans, and the Red Army's supply of tanks was replenished each month by Soviet factories. The same was true for planes, cannons, and bullets. As a result of aid from the United States, the Soviets had greater surpluses in every category of military supplies. The Germans were also fighting the British and Americans in Italy, and soon would be fighting them in France. The losses at Kursk meant that the German army would never again be able to launch a major offensive in the Soviet Union: Until the end of the war, two years later, the Germans would retreat. The Germans fought hard, occasionally inflicting heavy losses on the Soviets, and even periodically stopping the Red Army, especially while it was being resupplied, but the German army's counteroffensives were never major threats.

PRIMARY SOURCE

Erwin Rommel
Excerpts from *The War, 1939-1945*
Edited by Desmond Flower and James Reeves
Published in 1997

In September 1940 Italian dictator Benito Mussolini pursued his vision of establishing an African empire and ordered his army to cross into Egypt, then controlled by the British. Although the Italians halted after only sixty miles, the invasion made the British nervous. The Italian

During the fighting in North Africa, the crew of a German Panzer surrenders to British soldiers, who charge the tank with bayonets fixed. *(Reproduced by permission of © Hulton Getty/Liaison Agency)*

forces greatly outnumbered the British, and Italian occupation of Egypt would give the Axis powers control of the Suez Canal as well as potential access to oil fields in nearby Iraq and Arabia. In December 1940 the British Eighth Army attacked the Italians, who, surprised, retreated 400 miles into Libya. By February 1941, when the retreat ended, the British had captured 130,000 Italian troops. Fighting in the area presented strategic problems for both sides, however, as the narrow strip of land between nearly impassable desert to the south and the Mediterranean Sea to the north offered only one functional road. Sea transport provided supplies and reinforcements for both armies, which meant the retreating side was closer to the ports, and hence, to its supply lines. Each successive push increased the danger that the other side would be able to stage a successful counterattack.

Although Mussolini had suffered a terrible rout, he was reluctant to admit he needed assistance, but finally, he agreed to allow the Afrika Korps, an elite German division, to land in Libya. The Germans were led by General Erwin Rommel, a top Panzer commander who had participated in the conquest of France and would become known as the "Desert Fox." Rommel moved against the British in March 1941, forcing them back to their original position within a few weeks. The combined Axis force was mainly Italians, but Rommel's German Afrika Korps troops became popular heroes at home in Germany. Although a British

counterattack failed, a second strike, launched in November, returned the Germans and Italians to their original encampment. In January 1942 Rommel pressed the British once again into Egypt. In this series of attacks, retreats, and counterattacks, each side lost supplies and men.

The desert war remained a standoff until Rommel was forced to fight the British to the east and an invading American army to the west. In August 1942 the British appointed a new Eighth Army commander, General Bernard Montgomery, who wanted to end the seesaw battle for territory. The Afrika Korps attacked within two weeks, but broke off the attack when the British held their position. On October 23, 1942, Montgomery launched the Battle of El Alamein. Rommel had been recovering from an illness at home in Germany, but rushed back to Africa by plane to join his troops. Still, the ten-day battle resulted in a victory for the British. The Allies forced the Germans and Italians to begin retreating from North Africa.

Only days before the retreat, Adolf Hitler had ordered Rommel to continue the fighting. At that point, the Afrika Korps and the Twentieth Italian Motorized Corps were outnumbered and outclassed by British tank and artillery units. Rommel was also severely hampered by the inept interference of Hitler, who had conducted German military strategy for most of the war. In the following excerpts from Rommel's papers, which reveal the tense relationship between the general and the führer, Rommel is critical of Hitler's directive to hold fast in the face of insurmountable odds. The first excerpt is a letter Rommel wrote to his wife, in which he describes the deteriorating situation around Kidney Ridge during the Battle of El Alamein on November 2, 1942. He also reproduces a memo from Hitler that advises him to "throw every gun and every man into the battle." The second excerpt, dated November 3, demonstrates

Rommel's internal conflict between fulfilling his duty and launching reckless operations that ensure the deaths of his men. Rommel reveals that he and his officers repeatedly had to ignore the meddling of Hitler, and even Mussolini, in an effort to save German and Italian soldiers. In the third excerpt, Rommel describes how the British overwhelmed the Afrika Korps and completely destroyed the Twentieth Corps, leaving the general powerless to stop them.

Excerpts from *The War, 1939-1945*

2 November

Dearest Lu,

Very heavy fighting again, not going well for us. The enemy, with his superior strength, is slowly levering us out of our position. That will mean the end. You can imagine how I feel. Air raid after air raid after air raid!

Rommel

At about midday [3 November] I returned to my command post, only just escaping by some frantic driving a carpet of bombs laid by eighteen British aircraft. At 13.30 hours an order arrived from the Führer. It read in roughly the following words:

To Field-Marshal Rommel:

In the situation in which you find yourself there can be no other thought but to stand fast and throw every gun and every man into the battle. The utmost efforts are being made to help you. Your enemy, despite his superiority, must also be at the end of his strength. It would not be the first time in history that a strong will has triumphed over the bigger battalions. As to your troops, you can show them no other road than that to victory or death.

Adolf Hitler

This order demanded the impossible. Even the most devoted soldier can be killed by a bomb. In spite of our unvarnished situation reports, it was apparently still not realized at the Führer's H.Q. how matters really stood in Africa. Arms, petrol and aircraft could have helped us, but not orders. We were completely stunned, and for the first time during the African campaign I did not know what to do. A kind

of apathy took hold of us as we issued orders for all existing positions to be held on instructions from the highest authority. I forced myself to this action, as I had always demanded unconditional obedience from others and, consequently, wished to apply the same principle to myself. Had I known what was to come I should have acted differently, because from that time on we had continually to circumvent orders from the Führer or Duce [Mussolini] in order to save the army from destruction. But this first instance of interference by higher authority in the tactical conduct of the African war came as a considerable shock.

Rommel

Enormous dust-clouds could be seen south and south-east of headquarters, where the desperate struggle of the small and inefficient Italian tanks of XX Corps was being played out against the hundred or so British heavy tanks which had come round their open right flank. I was later told by Major von Luck, whose battalion I had sent to close the gap between the Italians and the Afrika Korps, that the Italians, who at the time represented our strongest motorized force, fought with exemplary courage. Von Luck gave what assistance he could with his guns, but was unable to avert the fate of the Italian armoured corps. Tank after tank split asunder or burned out, while all the time a tremendous British barrage lay over the Italian infantry and artillery positions. The last signal came from the Ariete at about 15.30 hours:

'Enemy tanks penetrated south of Ariete. Ariete now encircled. Location five kilometers north-west Bir el Abd. Ariete's tanks in action.'

By evening XX Italian Corps had been completely destroyed after a very gallant action. In the Ariete we lost our oldest Italian comrades, from whom we had probably always demanded more than they, with their poor armament, had been capable of performing.

A view over the battlefield from Corps H.Q. showed that strong British tank formations had also broken through the Afrika Korps and were pressing on to the west.

Thus the picture in the early afternoon was as follows: on the right of the Afrika Korps, powerful enemy armoured forces had destroyed the XX Italian Motorized Corps, and thus burst a twelve-mile hole

in our front, through which strong bodies of tanks were moving to the west. As a result of this, our forces in the north were threatened with encirclement by enemy formations twenty times their superior in tanks. 90 Light Division had defended their line magnificently against all British attacks, but the Afrika Korps' line had been penetrated after a very gallant resistance by their troops. There were no reserves, as every available man and gun had had to be put into the line.

Rommel

Aftermath

Having sustained heavy losses, Rommel retreated 1,000 miles westward along the single coast road, moving deep into Libyan territory by the end of December. He had only 60,000 troops left, and fewer than 100 tanks. On November 8, 1942, the Allies had opened up a new battlefront by landing forces in three locations in North Africa in a strategy called Operation Torch. Under the overall command of U.S. General Dwight D. Eisenhower, the campaign forced the Germans to give up. On March 6 Hitler ordered Rommel to abandon his army and return to Germany. In late March 1943 Montgomery's troops assaulted Axis positions from the rear. The retreating Germans and Italians continued to defend themselves until early May, when they began surrendering in large numbers. The final surrenders took place on May 13, ending the war in Africa.

Sources

Books

Barnett, Correlli, *The Battle of El Alamein: Decision in the Desert,* Macmillan (New York), 1964.

Flower, Desmond, and James Reeves, editors, *The War, 1939–1945,* Da Capo Press (New York), 1997.

Fraser, David, *Knight's Cross: A Life of Field Marshal Erwin Rommel,* HarperCollins (New York), 1994.

Hamilton, Nigel, *Monty: The Battles of Field Marshal Bernard Montgomery,* Random House (New York), 1994.

Other

Battle of El Alamein—Simon Wiesenthal Center, http://motlc.wiesenthal.org/text/x18/xm1853.html (July 15, 2000).

Bernard Law Montgomery: The Soldier's General (video), A & E Home Video, 1997.

El Alamein, 1942—Sands of Death and Valor, http://www.geocities.com/Pentagon/6813/ (July 15, 2000).

Prelude to El Alamein—Britain in World War II, http://britaininworldwar2.future.easyspace.com/Campaigns/Africa1942.html (July 15, 2000).

Rommel, the Desert Fox (video), MPI Home Video, 1989.

11

The Death Camps

The organized murder of the Jews of Europe began in spring 1941. Hundreds of thousands of Jews had died in mass shootings carried out by the Einsatzgruppen that followed the German army through Russia. With 11 million Jews in Europe, however, even these mass shootings were not efficient enough for the Nazis. The mass shootings had also drained the resources and morale of the German military. Some of the men conducting the shootings had mental breakdowns, as the personal contact between the executioner and his victims took a psychological toll. The shootings were also time-consuming and difficult to conceal. Outsiders could hear shots and see the bodies of the dead. In order to prevent resistance or escape efforts by Jews, the Germans decided the Jews would be taken away for "resettlement" in the east, and then would be killed in secret. Secrecy would also prevent non-Jews from coming to the aid of the Jews. Although many eastern Europeans had anti-Semitic leanings, the Nazis knew that the systematic murder of Jews would be viewed in a different light than "relocation."

The Nazis decided that the first region to be "cleansed" of Jews would be the General Government section of Poland, where, according to German calculations, 2,284,000 Jews still lived. In addition, Jews from the remainder of conquered Europe were being moved into the General Gov-

ernment every day. As in other parts of Poland, the Jews of the General Government were concentrated in ghettos. From the ghettos, Jews were told they were being resettled. They were then packed into train cars and shipped away to their deaths. The liquidation of smaller ghettos might take only a day or two, but larger ghettos often required that shipments of thousands of Jews be conducted over the course of several months before an area was emptied. The Germans called their plan Aktion Reinhard (Operation Reinhard), in honor of Reinhard Heydrich, who had coordinated the Wannsee Conference, where the "Final Solution" had been officially decided. He was attacked by resistance fighters in Czechoslovakia in May 1942, and died from his wounds in June.

The Death Camps Are Established

The Jews of Poland were sent to camps, but these camps were different from the older concentration camps in Germany. While conditions in those camps were terrible—prisoners were mistreated, underfed, and forced to work long, hard hours—the new Polish camps were worse. In the new camps, death was not just a possibility—it was a certainty. Six camps were set up as killing centers. Majdanek and Auschwitz housed Jews, but also many non-Jewish victims, especially Poles and captured Russian soldiers. Prisoners at these two camps worked in on-site factories,

Prisoners from Buchenwald concentration camp await execution in a forest. The Nazis soon determined that mass shooting was not an efficient way to kill Jews. *(USHMM Photo Archives)*

Jews of the Lódz ghetto on their way to the train station, where they will be herded into cars and sent to the Auschwitz death camp. *(USHMM Photo Archives)*

In retaliation of the assassination of Nazi SS officer Reinhard Heydrich, Adolf Hitler ordered that the inhabitants of Lidice, Czechoslovakia be massacred. His orders were carried out immediately. *(Library of Congress)*

making items needed for the German war effort, but those who did not die of maltreatment were killed as soon as they became too weak to work. Some 1.5 million people were executed in Majdanek and Auschwitz. Chelmno, Belzec, Sobibór, and Treblinka, the other four camps, were built for the sole purpose of killing Jews and were not meant to serve any other function. Prisoners were not put to work—except to assist in the extermination process. Each trainload of Jews was killed as soon as possible, eliminating the need to house large numbers of people. Combined, the four camps resulted in deaths of more than 2 million Jews.

In December 1941 Chelmno (Kulmhof in German) began operation thirty-five miles from the city of Lódz in the region of Poland annexed by Germany. The Nazis used a method of execution they had devised during their Russian invasion. Prisoners were sent by train to designated railroad stations where trucks shipped them to Chelmno. There, Nazis forced as many prisoners as possible into the back of a truck that looked like a furniture van. The back was sealed so that no air could enter. The truck engine was then turned on and the exhaust was directed into the back through a

hose until all the people inside were dead from carbon monoxide poisoning. The truck was driven to the nearby forest and the bodies were dumped into mass graves. The Nazis repeated this process over and over throughout the early war. An estimated 340,000 people died at Chelmno, including approximately 5,000 Roma (Gypsies) and hundreds of Poles. It was also at Chelmno that the Germans murdered many of the children of the village of Lidice, Czechoslovakia. The Nazis had completely destroyed all the buildings in Lidice in a two-day period in June 1942 to avenge the assassination of Reinhard Heydrich. Only three people who were sent to Chelmno are known to have survived.

Although Chelmno was considered an advancement, surpassing mass shootings in ease and efficiency of execution, this new method was not entirely satisfactory. While each truck was loaded as tightly as possible, the killings could not keep pace with the great numbers of intended victims. Aktion Reinhard officials therefore ordered the building of three new camps, each located near a large Jewish population center but far enough away, and hidden well enough in the forests, that their activities could be kept secret. Strategically

After a mass execution of Jewish women from the Mizocz ghetto, a Nazi continues to shoot until he is sure that all are dead. *(Reproduced by permission of Instytut Pamieci Narodowej/Institute of National Memory, courtesy of USHMM Photo Archives)*

located on railroad lines, the camps received trains first from Poland, and then from all over Europe—Holland, Greece, France, Russia, and Germany. The camps were staffed by relatively few people: twenty or thirty SS men, almost all of whom were men who orchestrated the Nazis' euthanasia program. In addition, each camp had ninety to 120 armed Ukrainian guards, formerly soldiers in the Soviet army, who had been captured by the Germans and had volunteered to help the Nazis.

The first of the three new camps was Belzec, which was built between the cities of Lublin and Lwów (Lvov) and remained operational from February to December 1942. Approximately 600,000 people, almost all of whom were Jewish, died at Belzec; only two people survived. Sobibór was situated east of Lublin and operated from May 1942 through October 1943. An estimated 250,000 people died at Sobibór, almost all of them Jewish, and only sixty-four people survived. The last of the three camps to begin its work, Treblinka, was located near Warsaw, Poland's capital and the city with the most Jews. The Nazis incorporated

knowledge acquired from the other camps to improve processes at Treblinka to make it the most efficient of the killing centers. Treblinka operated from July 1942 to August 1943. In the first five weeks it was open, more than 312,000 people were killed there; in total, approximately 870,000 people were murdered at Treblinka, almost all of them Jewish, with between forty and seventy people surviving. Seventy-eight hundred railroad cars had passed through Treblinka in a little over a year of operation. In less than two years, a total of 1.75 million people were killed at Belzec, Sobibór, and Treblinka by fewer than 450 men working at the death camps, thus achieving the maximum efficiency envisioned by the Nazis. In Treblinka alone, 70,000 people per month were murdered with fewer than thirty SS men in charge. Organizing each step of the prisoners' journey from ghetto to grave as a technical problem, the Nazis planned out every detail, including how to transport the Jews to the camps, how to deal with them upon their arrival, how to kill them, and how to get rid of prisoners' clothing, possessions, and bodies.

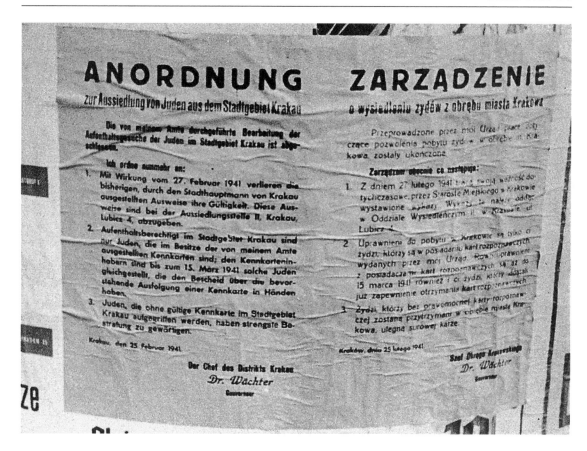

A close-up of an announcement ordering the "resettlement" of Jews from the Polish city of Kraków in 1941. *(USHMM Photo Archives)*

Ukrainian guards march at a concentration camp. The Ukrainian guards were Soviet soldiers who volunteered to help their captors, the Germans, at the camps. *(Photograph by Raimund Tisch; Professor Leopold Pfefferberg-Page Collection/USHMM Photo Archives)*

Nazi Priorities: Killing before Winning

The Nazi campaign to eliminate Jews at all costs is exemplified by problems that arose with the use of German trains for Jewish transports. Records indicate that there was sometimes a serious shortage of trains to take German soldiers and equipment to fight in the Soviet Union, while hundreds of locomotives and cars were being used to transport Jews to the death camps. The army actually tried to suspend the death trains temporarily but their attempts were stopped by Heinrich Himmler, the head of the SS and the second most powerful man in Germany. Some historians assert that this development greatly impacted Germany's chance of victory.

A majority of skilled construction workers in Latvia and Lithuania were Jewish, a labor force that German administrators knew could not be replaced by non-Jews. The Nazi government made it clear that the killing of Jews must take precedence over everything else, even if it hurt the army. By autumn 1942, more than 1 million laborers in Poland were working in German war industries. Among them more than 300,000 Jews, 100,000 of whom were skilled workers.

The military commander of the General Government argued that it was impossible to replace these workers and claimed that removing them would have a severe impact on the German army's ability to win the war. Himmler sent a memo to top SS leaders, with copies to army officers, informing them that Jews employed in war industries would be sent to concentration camps regardless of the effect on the war. The army followed his instructions.

The small number of Nazis and Ukrainian guards at Belzec, Sobibór, and Treblinka were able to control thousands of victims at a time, partially because the Jews who arrived at the camps had already suffered harsh conditions on the transport trains. Exhausted, starving, and desperate for water, they had watched fellow passengers die during the trip. When the survivors were finally allowed off the trains, they were informed they had reached a transit camp, a temporary stop along the way to resettlement.

One Transport to Belzec

Several descriptions of transports were written by officers of the German reserve police who guarded many of the trains. In *Ordinary Men: Reserve Police Battalion 101 and the Final Solution in Poland* (1992), historian Christopher R. Browning collected some of these accounts, including the reports of a Lieutenant Westermann, German reserve police officer, on two separate transports made a few days apart in 1942, from the town of Kolomyja, in Galicia, the southeastern part of Poland. Mass shootings of Jews had taken place in Galicia the previous year, so Jews in the area most likely concluded that they were also going to be killed. Although the Jews were informed that they were being transported for resettlement, the Nazis suspected that these Jews might take great risks to escape. The Jews were ordered to report for "registration" at 5:30 on the morning of September 7, 1942; approximately 5,300 people complied with the mandate. Westermann wrote that his company surrounded the ghetto "and searched thoroughly, whereby some 600 additional Jews were hunted down." It took until 7 p.m. that evening to complete the loading of the train. "Each car of the transport was loaded with 100 Jews. The great heat prevailing that day made the entire operation very difficult," Westermann reported.

The cars were sealed and the doors nailed shut, as usual, but because of the great heat that day, and because it was dark by the time the train left at 9 p.m., "many Jews escaped by squeezing through the air holes after removing the barbed wire [that covered them]. While the guard was

A German soldier oversees Jews being deported in 1942. The Nazis carefully planned the transportation of Jews to the camps; strategies to deal with them upon arrival; and ways to kill them. *(USHMM Photo Archives)*

Jewish police give assistance to Jews boarding a deportation train. *(Trudi Gidan Collection/USHMM Photo Archives)*

Loaded transport trains arrive at one of the death camps in May 1944. Conditions in the boxcars were unbearable. *(Photograph by Bernhard Walter, courtesy of Yad Vashem Photo Archives/USHMM Photo Archives)*

able to shoot many of them immediately, most of the escaping Jews were eliminated that night or the next day by the railroad guard or other police units." Although the train reached Belzec without further incident, Westermann complained that the guard unit of one officer and nine men was not enough. The day after the transport left Kolomyja he wrote, "some 300 Jews—old and weak, ill, frail, and no longer transportable—were executed." Demonstrating the minute detail with which the Nazis planned the efficient and cost-effective extermination of the Jews, Westermann explained that he had obeyed a recent order concerning ammunition: "90% of those executed were shot with carbines and rifles. Only in exceptional cases were pistols used."

As soon as most of the Jews of Kolomyja had been sent to their deaths, Jews from the surrounding area were brought to the vacated town. Some were marched more than thirty miles on foot and many were shot by German guards while waiting overnight in the town. The survivors were loaded into thirty freight cars, the conditions of which Westermann described in his report: "Given the great heat prevailing on those days and the strain on the Jews from the long foot marches or from waiting for days without being given any provisions worth noting, the excessively great overload-

ing of the cars with 180 to 200 Jews was catastrophic in a way that had tremendously adverse effects on the transport." The cars loaded in Kolomyja were attached to twenty other cars that already carried passengers from two nearby towns, bringing the total number of people on the train to 8,205. The heat was stifling and everyone in the cars removed their clothing. Night fell as the cars were nailed shut and the small air holes were covered with barbed wire "in the usual regulation manner."

Jews repeatedly tried to escape from the train as it stood still. "Breakout attempts from the parked train could not be prevented in the darkness, nor could the escaping Jews be shot in flight," reported Westermann. When the train finally moved out of the town, the prisoners continued to try to flee by breaking through the sides and the roofs of the cars. The train stopped at several stations along the way so that the escape holes could be boarded up. Only ten German guards were on the train, five at each end, but they shot as many escapees as possible. Before the train reached Belzec, the guards had used all their ammunition, as well as extra ammunition they had acquired from soldiers along the way. They used bayonets on Jews who attempted to escape when the train was stopped,

Two young boys display the Star of David patches that the Nazis required Jews to wear. *(USHMM Photo Archives)*

"You are in a transit camp, from which you will be sent to a labor camp. In order to avoid epidemics, you must present your clothing and belongings for immediate disinfection. Gold, money, foreign currency, and jewelry should be deposited with the cashiers in return for a receipt. They will be returned to you later when you present the receipt. Bodily cleanliness requires that everyone bathe before continuing the journey."

The first building encountered by the Jews at Treblinka was disguised as a small-town railroad station. Signs pointed to the waiting room, the ticket office, and the trains for various destinations. In actuality there was no waiting room or ticket office, and there were no other tracks. A clock hung on the wall, but the hands were painted on.

but could only throw rocks at those who were able to jump off the train while it was moving. "Because of the special circumstances described," Westermann wrote, "the number of Jews who escaped from this transport cannot be specified. Nonetheless, it can be assumed that at least two-thirds of the escaping Jews were shot or rendered harmless in some other way." When the train reached Belzec, 2,000 Jews were dead from suffocation or heat prostration.

Arrival at the Death Camps

When transport trains reached the death camps, the first twenty freight cars were brought to the unloading area while others waited farther away. Belzec, Sobibór, and Treblinka were disguised as transit camps so victims would not realize this was their final destination. They were told that these were only stops along the route, and that their journey would proceed after they were processed. After the war, one SS man said Jews arriving at Sobibór had no idea what was happening to them until they were actually inside the gas chamber. At Treblinka, where the Jews of Warsaw were sent, a large sign warned:

"Jews of Warsaw, Attention!"

Camp inmates were often subjected to delousing. Such disinfection continued after the camps were liberated as evidenced in this photo. Here, a Russian is deloused after the Dachau concentration camp is liberated. *(Reproduced by permission of United States Holocaust Memorial Museum)*

Concentration camp inmates walk near a large pile of shoes of those prisoners who were "processed." *(USHMM Photo Archives)*

The rear side of a gas chamber. The engine to the right was used to create carbon monoxide for gassing prisoners. *(National Museum in Majdanek/USHMM Photo Archives)*

Prisoners working on a rifle production line in the SS-owned munitions factory at Dachau, the first concentration camp. *(USHMM Photo Archives)*

The camps were not very large: Treblinka and Sobibór were rectangles of about 400 by 600 yards, and a walking trip around the perimeter would have taken only twenty or twenty-five minutes. Belzec was even smaller, a square fewer than 300 yards long on each side. The camps were surrounded by barbed-wire fences with high watchtowers at the corners; tree branches and leaves had been placed in the fencing to shield the interior from view. When the first twenty cars stopped at the unloading area, the doors were opened by a group of prisoners and the Jews were ordered out. The prisoners who opened the doors were men, usually young and relatively healthy, who had arrived on earlier transports and had not been killed. The SS men and the Ukrainian guards marched the new arrivals into the camp as quickly as possible. Those who lagged behind were beaten with a rifle butt or were whipped. Meanwhile, the prisoners who had opened the cars removed the bodies of the dead and cleansed the cars of blood, vomit, and human waste. They swept out bits of clothing or personal possessions left

behind, within a few minutes erasing all evidence of what had happened on the train.

When people got off the train and entered the camp, they were told to leave all their belongings behind; suitcases were taken from them. While the new arrivals were being processed, the permanent prisoners sorted through their belongings. All valuables, such as money and jewels, were collected. All identification had to be removed, the Jewish stars that the Nazis had ordered the Jews to wear were ripped off clothing, and names were taken off suitcases. The Nazis were sending the belongings of the dead to Germany, and no one was to know their origins. Huge mounds of clothing and shoes were gathered in a large open area. Identification papers, passports, and birth certificates were burned, as were photographs and letters—the Nazis wanted no trace of their victims to survive.

SS officers separated men from women and children. The women and children were then marched to a long barrack where they were told they were to submit to disinfection/delousing in the shower houses, ordered to undress, and

The Nazis would later use ovens, like this one from the Buchenwald camp, to burn the bodies of their victims. (*National Archives/USHMM Photo Archives*)

directed to tie their shoes together with the piece of string provided to them. The women's hair was then cut off by prisoners who told them it was an effort to prevent the spread of disease, through in fact the hair was used to make products such as water-resistant rope for the German navy. After the hair removal, the guards beat and whipped the still-naked women and children, forcing them to run a narrow, 100-yard path between two barbed-wire fences. Like the fence outside the camp, these were camouflaged with tree branches to prevent anyone from seeing through. Called the "tube" or "the road to heaven" by the Nazis, the path led to the part of the camp hidden from arriving passengers and was marked by a sign that read: "To the showers." It led to the gas chambers. While women were being processed, the men waited. After perhaps half an hour or more, also naked like the women, they were forced to run the same path.

Many Jews were too weak from hunger and disease to walk to the gas chambers, even under the threat of beatings. At Treblinka, these people were carried on stretchers by other prisoners to a small building identified by a red cross as a field hospital or infirmary. On the other side of the building was a wall of earth fifteen feet high behind which, hid-

den from the sorting area and the barracks where people undressed, was a large open pit. The back of the infirmary building was near the edge of this pit. One by one, the sick were taken out of the "infirmary" through the back and shot by one of the Ukrainian guards, who then pushed the dead body into the pit.

The Gas Chambers

In each of the camps, the building that housed the gas chambers was disguised as a public bathhouse, a familiar sight in Europe during this period. When prisoners emerged from the path, they were forced to enter the building through the main door. Inside were doors to smaller rooms where shower heads hung from the ceiling; these rooms also had doors leading to the outside of the building, but they were sealed. Treblinka originally held three of these rooms, each only thirteen square feet. Jews were packed into these rooms as tightly as possible, 200 at a time, and then the rooms were sealed. The engine of a captured Russian tank was turned on and carbon monoxide gas from the engine was pumped through the shower heads into the sealed rooms. The gas would continue to pump for half an hour as the people inside gasped, coughed, choked, and tried desperately to escape. Their bodies were drenched with sweat, blood, and their own waste. Since they did not have room to fall down, they died pressed against each other.

After everyone inside the gas chambers was dead, the outside doors were opened by a special group of the permanent prisoners. They had to separate and remove the bodies, and other prisoners washed out the chamber in preparation for the next victims. Yet other prisoners, known as the "dentists," searched the mouths of the dead for gold teeth and fillings, which they removed with pliers. Then the bodies were carried to several giant pits located about 150 to 200 yards from the chambers, thrown into the pits, and buried. After all these procedures had been completed, the next twenty cars of the train, which had been parked farther away, were brought to the camp and the process was repeated. When Treblinka was operating at its peak, the entire process—from the arrival of a train to the entrance into the gas chamber—took less than two hours. In October 1942 ten new gas chambers were added at Treblinka. Instead of 600 people, they could now hold 3,800 people at once. Up to 15,000 people per day could be murdered.

The Nazis hid gold taken from Holocaust victims for later use. Some 100 tons of gold were hidden by the Nazis near Merkers, Germany. As the Allies began to liberate Nazi-occupied areas, U.S. General George S. Patton's Third Army troops discovered the large sacks of gold bullion hidden along with art treasures and money. *(Reproduced by permission of AP/Wide World Photos)*

Women inmates sort through a pile of shoes from those who were gassed. The Nazis sent their victims' belongings to Germany. *(Photograph by Bernhard Walter, courtesy of Yad Vashem Photo Archives/USHMM Photo Archives)*

Saving a Friend's Life

Samuel Willenberg was a prisoner at Treblinka. His boyhood friend, Alfred Boehm, became ill when a typhus epidemic raged through the camp. More than half of the "permanent" prisoners died, most of them shot when they became too weak to work. Willenberg dragged his friend to roll calls and supported him as necessary. After roll calls, he hid Boehm in a bed made up to look empty. For five days, Willenberg dragged Boehm to the roll calls and hid him during the day. During one roll call, when he was afraid an SS man would notice how sick Boehm looked, Willenberg and another prisoner staged a fight. Willenberg grabbed Boehm's head, and the other prisoner held him from behind. The SS man walked away. Alfred Boehm recovered from typhus, but was killed in the Treblinka uprising on August 2, 1943. Samuel Willenberg survived Treblinka.

In March 1943 Heinrich Himmler, head of the SS, visited Treblinka. He was worried that hundreds of thousands of bodies had been buried in the Aktion Reinhard death camps. By that time, the German armies were beginning to lose the war against the Soviet Union, and the Nazis knew the bodies were evidence of their actions. Although the Soviet army was still remote, it was possible that Russian soldiers would eventually reach the death camps in Poland. Himmler therefore ordered that the buried bodies be dug up and burned. Prisoners unearthed the corpses and placed them on steel rails laid on top of concrete pillars. The Nazis brought a large crane to Treblinka to expedite the exhumations, and prisoners arranged the dead on the rails. Corpses were piled in layers, 2,000 on the pile at one time, with dry wood underneath. Work continued throughout the day, and the pile was set on fire. The blaze burned all night, and the next morning the ashes were mixed with sand and buried in deep ditches. Body parts that had not burned completely had to be placed on the pile again. Eventually six of these facilities were built at Treblinka, and about 12,000 bodies could be burned at one time. Seven hundred thousand people had already been killed, so it took several months for the corpses to be burned. During that time, the flames could be seen for many miles around Treblinka and the odor of burning flesh filled the air. Later, some death camp survivors would describe how they were forced to be part of the crew that had to dig up and burn the bodies. A few have described their horror at finding their loved ones' bodies in the pile, which marked the first time they knew for sure what had become of their families.

"Permanent" Prisoners

At first, the Nazis killed everyone who arrived on a train before the next one arrived. Some of the Jewish men from each transport were forced to clean the cars and sort the prisoners' possessions before being sent to the gas chambers themselves. After a while, however, the Nazis realized this was inefficient, and they decided to keep some Jews alive to help in the killing process. This would allow prisoners to be trained to do a particular job as each transport arrived and, with practice, accomplish the tasks more quickly. As many as 1,300 of these prisoners worked at Treblinka, approximately 1,000 in the main part of the camp. They were divided into work groups. One group, for example, had to open and clean out the train cars, and the largest group sorted the clothing and possessions of the new arrivals. Other prisoners worked as barbers, and yet others were sent into the woods, under heavy guard, to cut the branches put into the barbed wire to keep the interior of the camp hidden from view. Some were used as servants for the SS men.

A special group of 200 or 300 lived and worked in the separate area of the camp where the killing took place. These prisoners separated the dead bodies and took them to the burial pits. All permanent prisoners understood that they had been spared only temporarily from death, and if they became too sick or weak to work efficiently, they would be killed immediately and replaced by men from the next transport. Their work was exhausting, and guards constantly screamed at the prisoners to work faster, whipping them for loafing. Two or three times a day, at each roll call, the Nazis selected prisoners to die; the men whose names were called were taken to the "infirmary" and shot.

The permanent prisoners of Treblinka, Belzec, and Sobibór suffered not only physical agonies—beatings, disease, and the constant threat of death—but also had to contend with psychological stress. They had arrived on the trains with their parents, wives, children, friends, and/or neighbors, all of whom were now dead. In many cases they had seen their loved ones marched off to be killed but were helpless to stop it. Perhaps even worse, their own survival depended on how well they did their job—helping the Nazis kill more Jews. The Nazis had set up a system in which the survival of these few Jews depended on the deaths of thousands of others. As long as the trains kept coming, the permanent prisoners were needed and might be allowed to live a while longer.

The death transports also provided another means of survival for permanent prisoners. New arrivals often brought food with them, for their trip "to the east," and the prisoners who sorted through their clothing took this food for themselves and their fellow prisoners. This meant these prisoners often had more and higher quality food than they had available in the ghettos. In addition, they could have warm clothes and boots for the winter. Some prisoners even found money hidden in the clothing of new arrivals and the brave ones, risking punishment of death, took the money and used it to bribe Ukrainian guards for food. Permanent prisoners knew their survival was tenuous; however, they tried to stay alive, hoping the Russian army would arrive before the Nazis could kill them all, or that they could escape.

Some permanent prisoners did manage to escape by hiding in the trains that left the camps loaded with piles of clothing taken from the dead. Others made plans to overpower their guards, take their weapons, and fight their way to freedom. In early 1943, for example, a small group of Treblinka prisoners began to plan an uprising. One of the

prisoners was able to make a copy of the key to the storeroom where the guards kept their weapons. On the day of the uprising, the prisoners secured about a dozen rifles, hand grenades, and some pistols without being noticed. Gasoline was sprayed on the camp's wooden buildings by a prisoner who pretended to be disinfecting them, and wire cutters were hidden. The uprising did not go according to plan, however. The reasons remain unclear, but according to one version of events, a prisoner was searched by an SS guard shortly before the attack. He had money hidden on him that he planned to use after escaping. The other prisoners feared the man would be tortured and reveal the plan. Somewhat unprepared, because all of the weapons had not been distributed, they managed to shoot the SS man and set off the uprising. Setting nearly the entire camp ablaze, the prisoners fought the Nazis and Ukrainian guards, who fired on them from the watchtower. Approximately 400 Jews were killed and another 100 were captured inside the camp, but 300 or 400 were able to escape. Some of them were quickly killed or captured by patrols, but about 150 to 200 succeeded in getting away. Many were killed fighting German troops before the war finally ended. Between forty and seventy prisoners survived.

By the time of the Treblinka uprising (and a similar rebellion in Sobibór in October 1943), the work of the three camps of Aktion Reinhard was almost completed. Belzec had already been shut down. There were no more transports; the Jews of Poland were now dead, and those who remained were in hiding. Jews from other parts of Europe were being sent to Auschwitz. The burned ruins of Treblinka were dismantled in fall 1943. At each camp, the fences and watchtowers were taken down, the ground was plowed over, and crops were planted. The Nazis wanted the camps, like their victims, to disappear without a trace.

Egon "Gonda" Redlich
Excerpt from *The Terezin Diary of Gonda Redlich,* written from 1942-1944
Edited by Saul S. Friedman

Published in 1992

The Nazis wanted to remove Jews not only from Germany, but from all of Europe. After 1939, they replaced their original emigration tactics with deportations to ghettos and camps. Beginning in 1941, Jews were deported into eastern Europe in preparation for their physical extermination at death camps specifically designed for mass murder. To disguise the murderous intentions of this *Endlösung,* or "Final Solution," from the world, the Nazis funneled Jews through a series of ghettos into the various death camps. In November 1941 the city of Theresienstadt, Czechoslovakia, became a ghetto for Jews, originally intended by the Nazis to be presented as a "model Jewish settlement." It housed prominent Jewish artists, intellectuals, and others who warranted special treatment, such as World War I veterans and clergymen. The Nazis even created currency for Theresienstadt as part of their attempt to fool the world into believing that the ghetto existed as an autonomous Jewish community. Any hope that Theresienstadt would somehow be a refuge was dashed when mass deportations to death camps began in January 1942.

Egon "Gonda" Redlich arrived in the ghetto in December 1941. A Jewish Czech, Redlich had been born in 1916 in Olmutz, Moravia. The youngest of five children, he grew up in a working-class family. While Redlich did not have a strongly religious upbringing, he was prompted to join a Zionist Youth movement by anti-Semitic incidents that occurred in school. Following the Nazi takeover of Czechoslovakia in March 1939, Redlich abandoned legal study and prepared to emigrate to Palestine, but his deportation to Theresienstadt interfered

with his plans. At the time, he had been working as an assistant school director in Prague, teaching Hebrew and Jewish history, coaching soccer, and counseling students. Due to his reputation as an educator, he was appointed head of the *Jugendfursorge,* or Youth Welfare Department, within the ghetto. In this role, Redlich oversaw the housing, care, and education of 15,000 children who passed through Theresienstadt. He began keeping a diary in January 1942 and started a second diary dedicated to his son, Dan, who was born in the ghetto on March 16, 1944. He wrote his diary on sheets of office calendars and used a notebook for his *Diary of Dan.* Redlich's diary to his son gives a day-by-day account of his impressions of life in the ghetto amidst the deportations "to the east."

Life in the ghetto was hard, particularly for married couples and those with children. While religious marriages did take place, they were not officially recognized by the Nazi government. For this reason Redlich refers to his child as a *mamzer,* or bastard. Gestapo officials also outlawed births within the ghetto. This may be what Redlich means when he claims his son was born twice: the first time being the mother's decision not to have an abortion, and the second time referring to the actual birth. Redlich and his wife feared the prospect of their captors murdering their infant.

Redlich also mentions having a portrait done by a Jewish artist who was arrested and taken "to an unknown place." When the Nazis discovered that Jewish artists were painting realistic depictions of ghetto life in July 1944, the artists were taken to a nearby fortress and tortured.

At the "model" concentration camp Theresienstadt, women prepare food. *(Reproduced by permission of the YIVO Institute for Jewish Research)*

The Terezin Diary of Gonda Redlich
"Diary of Dan"

March 16, 1944.

This is the fate of our people. That in every generation a new Pharaoh arises and brings disaster—destruction to the Jews, fear and dread. Even in our generation a great enemy arose, hated and terrible, an even greater foe than Pharaoh in Egypt. The ancient pharaoh only wanted to kill male infants, but the new pharaoh did not even show compassion for the girls.

It was forbidden for Jews to be born, for women to give birth. We were forced to hide your mother's pregnancy.

Even Jews themselves asked us to slaughter you, the fruit of our womb, because the enemy threatened to levy punishment on the community for every Jewish birth in the ghetto.

I hope that you will never have to encounter these degradations and insults, the weakness of a people on foreign soil, a people without a homeland.

I admit that your mother was stronger than I. Remember this, my son, and honor your mother, the heroine, among all women. Without her, you would not be alive today. You would not play or be happy. You would not cry or laugh. You would not drink or eat. You would return to the nothingness that was before your birth.

For the light of the world, twice you should give thanks to her. Twice she gave birth to you....

They say that in our generation miracles do not occur. They occur, my son, for by a miracle were you saved, along with her.

Why did they cancel the order forbidding births when you and others were born? Do you know of the plagues that God sent upon Egypt? The last plague also came on our enemies. The wife of an enemy officer gave birth before her time to a stillborn child. Jewish doctors saved the woman. Our enemies felt for the bereaved mother and allowed your mother and other mothers to give birth.

An occurrence or a miracle? I believe that a miracle occurred.

March 20, 1944.

Your mother had no peace and quiet during her pregnancy. In the outer world, a war raged fiercely, the fourth and fifth year. Men killed each other, without pity or compassion. Our enemies declared that Jews are responsible for the war. A heavy burden oppresses us like a dark and heavy cloud. [One] lightning bolt, and we, a Jewish community among tens of thousands of Germans, would burn to ashes.

You were born on a spring day. There was mud in the streets and the sun was reflected in puddles. Even your birth wasn't easy, as if you did not want to come out from the secure enclosure into this godforsaken world.

March 22, 1944.

Every day, the Judenältester (head of the Jewish community and its spokesman vis-a-vis the Germans) [parenthetical note added to Redlich's diary by editor Saul S. Friedman] informs the Dienststelle (the German office that supervises the ghetto) of births, number of deaths, and new incidents of dangerous and contagious diseases. After you were born, he [Eppstein] announced your name: Dan Peter Beck, along with thirty dead and another outbreak of typhus. You carried your mother's family name because our marriage was performed in the ghetto and such marriages were not legal according to the law of the land.

I must acknowledge that you are my son and I your father. Formally, you are a mamzer [bastard]. Please note that the public formality never was and never will be crucial. What counts is what's inside, the real, inner feelings and not outward appearances, even if they seem important.

April 13, 1944.

You are beginning to see, to see this world which is draping itself slowly in the green and warmth of spring. The world is casting off winter a little by little. The weather is still cold and there isn't enough coal.

We live a proletarian life. We have a small kitchen where we live, sleep and eat. In the hospital, we found bedbugs on you. All the surroundings are proletarian. But even here, there are great social

Sick prisoners rest on pallets in the women's camp at Theresienstadt. *(Reproduced by permission of YIVO Institute for Jewish Research Archives*

differences. We have a small kitchen and live with your mother. Most of the families do not live together, a husband with his wife. There are separate barracks for men and women. There isn't enough food for everyone. We have a lot of advantages. There is no justification for this. Sometimes I am ashamed. But for you, they are very important.

A child died from among those whom the Germans permitted to be born. Just think of a mother's sorrow, who by a miracle gained a child only to lose it. It is true that: "The Lord giveth and the Lord taketh away." A great truth—but truth doesn't console.

April 13, 1944 [continued].

A strong bond exists among women with the same fate, similar to people who have endured a common experience.... Out of ten women, three children have died. One woman still has not given birth, but will do so shortly.

The mothers go for walks together. They talk to each other, sharing concerns, whether their children are drinking, growing, etc.

[From] a conversation: one mother, a gardener, boasts: "I'm already giving spinach to my son." (The child is three months old.)

Another mother asks: "How much do you give him?"

The mother answers: "A little—but if he wants, he could have a few kilos."

The modesty is hilarious. It is legally impossible to get vegetables into the ghetto. Spinach is stolen, taken surreptitiously because if the spinach is handed over to our enemy, it isn't "stolen." "A thief of thieves is innocent...." The boastfulness is ridiculous.

Yesterday, you reached the weight of three kilos. Your mother was as happy as a small child. She wanted the doctor to come in order to announce the happy news. I went to the doctor and humbly requested that he visit us. Everyone thought it funny to call a doctor for a healthy child. But the mother—who understands a mother's soul? I went humbly because I was a little embarrassed. Your mother was proud—so very proud.

A woman cleans clothing in a Theresienstadt barrack. *(Reproduced by permission of YIVO Institute for Jewish Research/USHMM Photo Archives)*

April 13, 1944 [continued].

Today we went out with you for the first time. We have a nice baby carriage, a product of the ghetto. Usually the craftsmanship in the ghetto is second-rate, but this baby carriage is very pretty. It was made by two young men, relatives of your mother. It's made of wood, light as a feather, with springs.

Bright afternoons. In the city square, the Jewish orchestra played. A Jewish orchestra, as if a hard war full of blood was not being fought, a war of survival. Our enemies have new tactics—eyecatching, building a "Potemkin Village" [an impressive facade designed to hide an undesirable fact or condition]. So the Jewish orchestra played in the ghetto when people were permitted to stroll. But the melody never blocked out the memory of the terrible sacrifice, the pogroms, the danger still ahead of us, the danger that only now has a new face.

June 2, 1944.

One week: for you it means you have grown in weight a few grams. One week: seventy-five hundred Jews left the ghetto and went somewhere unknown, to greet an uncertain future. They went in order to make space. Now the [International Red Cross] Commission will come, inspect the city and express its opinion: everything is fine, the city is beautiful, full of children's houses, coffee houses, beautiful halls and gardens, Jews living in spacious quarters.

They ordered us to vacate the ground floor of these houses. The first floors won't be seen by members of the commission at all. In the houses they shall visit everything will be ready and prepared. There won't be any reason to object.

Our enemies are merciful, full of compassion. They will send the sick, the weak, orphans, old people eastward in boxcars. But they have commanded that we change a picture on a wall of a tiger with a small tiger in its mouth, lest it frighten small children. The orchestra is to perform only light music. They want us to be cheerful. They want to show that the Jewish city is happy. They are the merciful ones.

Yesterday, I was at the chicken house. There is a small chicken house. The fowl are raised for the Germans. For the first time in my life I saw a hen turkey, sitting with its young. It reminded me of your mother.

Children in Theresienstadt. *(State Museum of Auschwitz-Birkenau/USHMM Photo Archives)*

Your baby carriage disappeared. Maybe someone took it and will bring it back later.

Yes, after a few hours the "thief" returned the carriage.

June 23, 1944.

The first movement that you have made with your hands. You already play with your hands and feel everything around you. The first sounds are also heard from your mouth.

Meanwhile, many things have occurred in the great world. The invasion has started. [This is a reference to the 1944 Allied invasion of Normandy, France, a massive campaign led by American general Dwight D. Eisenhower that led to the liberation of Western Europe from German control.] German armies have retreated on all fronts, and here in the ghetto (it is forbidden to use "ghetto"), we play a big game. They built a Potemkin Village. The Red Cross Committee inspected it. They visited us and saw the wonderful children, houses, post office, hospitals, and nice schools. The ban on teaching has not been lifted, but we have schools.... It's enough if there is a sign "school" and magically, overnight, one appears. Jews are laughing, content with their fate.... Thus the committee has looked around and then they left.... The only question is: did they really believe what they were shown?

July 20, 1944.

Your eyes are as blue as heaven. This is no poetic exaggeration. Your eyes stand out the most. Everyone praises them.

Your mother fears that you will have long, drooping ears. Why? Don't ask. Every mother must have the most beautiful, the smartest, the healthiest child.

I wanted to give your mother a gift on her birthday: a picture of you. I asked an artist to draw your picture. Today they arrested the artist and took him to an unknown place. What was his crime? Along with others, he sketched realistic drawings of the ghetto (funerals, hospitals), drawings that served no purpose in the beautification of the city. These drawings were found in the possession of a collector.

October 6, 1944.

... One of your games! I lift your body and you flutter with your legs like a fish on dry land. Afterwards, I bring my face to yours and you look at me with such surprise. Learn, my son, to read the face of a man, because everything is written in the countenance of a man: his wisdom and his folly, his anger and his calmness, his happiness and his sadness, his honesty and his falsehood—everything, everything.

They are making a movie of the ghetto, a nice movie. They ordered the evacuation of two

Aerial view of the Theresienstadt concentration camp in Czechoslovakia. Conditions in this camp were better than at other camps as the Nazis kept it tidy for inspection by the International Red Cross. *(Reproduced by permission of AP/Wide World Photos)*

beautified youth homes. But before they did it, they filmed the "happy" children's houses. A movie on ghetto life which will show the happy life of the Jews, without worry, "with praises and celebrations." (Indeed, they filmed Jews dancing parlor dances.) They wanted to film you, in order to show a happy family. Luckily, it did not work out. This film would have been a nice reminder of your infancy in place of a photo. In spite of this, it was depressing and degrading. Even the kings of Egypt did not film the children they wanted to kill.

We bought a new baby carriage for you. The seller was one of my clerks and wanted to bribe me by giving me the carriage free. We paid one kilo of sugar, one kilo of margarine, and two cans of sardines.

What is going to happen? Tomorrow, we travel, my son. We will travel on a transport like thousands before us. As usual, we did not register for the trans-

port. They put us in without a reason. But never mind, my son, it is nothing. All of our family already left in the last weeks. Your uncle went, your aunt, and also your beloved grandmother. Your grandmother who worked from morning to evening for you and us. Parting with her was especially difficult. We hope to see her there.

It seems they want to eliminate the ghetto and leave only the elderly and people of mixed origin. In our generation, the enemy is not only cruel but also full of cunning and malice. They promise [something] but do not fulfill their promise. They send small children, and their prams are left here. Separated families. On one transport a father goes. On another, a son. An on a third, the mother.

Tomorrow we go, too, my son. Hopefully, the time of our redemption is near. (Redlich, pp. 151–161)

Aftermath

Redlich mentions preparations for a visit from representatives of the International Red Cross in June 1944. The Nazis allowed the Red Cross to visit Theresienstadt only after they erected dummy stores, a café, a school, and flower gardens. Before the arrival of these visitors, deportations to death camps were accelerated to relieve overcrowding. Shortly after the inspection by the Red Cross, the Nazis deported most of the residents of Theresienstadt to Auschwitz. There is no evidence that the inspection of Theresienstadt by the Red Cross aided the masses of Jews in Nazi custody across Europe—in fact, some historians suggest deportations were accelerated due to their intervention.

In his diary, Redlich mentions that Nazis are filming within the ghetto for propaganda purposes. Twenty minutes of *Aktion Z,* the film about Theresienstadt that was made as part of the Nazi propaganda campaign, survived the war and is part of the Yad Vashem archive in Jerusalem. The majority of the film's "cast" was sent to Auschwitz for extermination after the film was made.

Although the Nazis established Theresienstadt as a model Jewish settlement, it eventually became the principal transit camp for Jews from central Europe. Records show that 140,000 Jews were deported to Theresienstadt. Of these, 33,000 died in the ghetto and 88,000 were sent to extermination camps. A total of 19,000 survived the Holocaust. Of the 15,000 children who passed through Theresienstadt, a mere 100 survived.

Records indicate the Redlich family (Gonda Redlich, his wife, Gerta Beck, and their son, Dan) went directly to Auschwitz in October 1944 and were executed. In preparation for his own deportation, Redlich left the manuscripts of his diaries behind at Theresienstadt, hidden inside a woman's purse. Redlich's writings remained undiscovered until 1967, when workers clearing an attic found the documents and turned them over to the State Museum in Prague. The communist Czech government eventually gave copies to Theresienstadt survivors living in Israel.

SOURCES

Books

Volavkova, Hana, editor, *I Never Saw Another Butterfly: Children's Drawings and Poems from Terezin Concentration Camp, 1942–1944,* Schocken Books (New York), 1978.

Redlich, Gonda, *The Terezin Diary of Gonda Redlich,* edited by Saul S. Friedman, translated by Laurence Kutler, University of Kentucky Press (Lexington, KY), 1992.

Auschwitz

uschwitz is the German name for the small town of Oświęcim in southwest-ern Poland, which was the location of the largest slave-labor and death camp in the Nazi regime. More than 10,000 Russian pris-oners of war, some 15,000-16,500 Roma (Gypsies), over 1 million Jews, and an unknown number of Poles (in the tens of thousands) were killed within the camp. Estimates greatly vary. In the years since World War II, Auschwitz has become a symbol of the darkest side of humanity.

The Camp's Beginnings

Annexed after Germany conquered Poland in 1939, the area around Auschwitz was damp, swampy, and mosquito-infested, with few sources of fresh water. Winters were especially harsh, but the location offered certain tactical advantages to the Nazis. It was far from public view, had good railroad connections, and provided housing for inmates in barracks at an abandoned Polish army base. In spring 1940, the Nazis opened a concentra-tion camp at the site. Its first inmates were Polish political prisoners. During 1940, a large area of countryside around Auschwitz was taken over by the camp, and seven small villages were emptied of inhabitants, making the total territory of the camp about fifteen and one-half square miles. In May 1940 Rudolph Höss, an SS man who had earlier

SS guards sometimes used attack dogs to keep prisoners in line. *(Main Commission for the Investigation of Nazi War Crimes/USHMM Photo Archives)*

headed the German Sachsenhausen camp, was appointed commandant of Auschwitz.

A group of Sachsenhausen prisoners was also sent to Auschwitz. They were common criminals, but had been detained in concentration camps instead of prison. These men were utilized to take control of other Auschwitz inmates. Referred to as

Rudolf Höss

Rudolf Höss grew up in a strict religious environment and his parents wanted him to enter the Catholic priesthood. At fifteen, he lied about his age in order to join the German army and fight in World War I (1914–1918); he received an Iron Cross for bravery and became an officer by the time he was eighteen. Like many soldiers returning from the war, Höss could not adjust to life in the defeated nation, and joined a paramilitary nationalist organization called the Freikorps (Free Corps), which put down the workers' uprisings sweeping Germany after World War I. Freikorps members were violently opposed to Jews, democracy, and the philosophies of socialism and communism. After hearing Adolf Hitler speak in Munich in 1922, Höss joined the Nazi party when it was still a small organization, and he gave up his affiliation with the Catholic church. The next year, he and some other Freikorps men beat one of their former comrades to death because they thought he was a police informant. Höss was sentenced to ten years in prison for his part in the crime but was released after serving half his time. When Hitler came to power in 1933, Höss joined the SS and served at Dachau, the first concentration camp. He then worked at the German concentration camp Sachsenhausen before being chosen as commandant of Auschwitz.

After World War II, Höss was a witness at the trial of the main Nazi leaders. His testimony then, and later at his own trial, was different from that of almost any other Nazi. He did not try to avoid answering questions and openly admitted what had happened at Auschwitz, explaining both those actions and the roles played by other Nazis. At the same time, however, he did not appear to understand the horror of his crimes. Historians note that he appeared neither remorseful nor apologetic, nor did he seem like a fanatical Nazi who had committed these crimes because he hated Jews. He simply felt that he had carried out the duties assigned to him to the best of his abilities. While he awaited execution, Höss wrote an autobiography. Its first English translation, published in 1959, was *Commandant of Auschwitz,* and it was later published as *Death Dealer: The Memoirs of the SS Kommandant at Auschwitz* (see primary source entry) in 1992 and 1996. In this autobiography, Höss fondly recalled his life at Auschwitz and the beautiful rose garden his wife had planted there. Only a few hundred yards from the house where his wife gardened and his children played was Block 11, where the Gestapo tortured prisoners, and Block 10, where SS doctors performed horrible "medical" experiments on them. A few hundred yards in another direction was a gas chamber and crematorium I. Höss was hanged at Auschwitz in 1947.

Kapos, the men were granted special privileges, such as greater quantity and quality of food and a private room in the barracks. Supervising the barracks and the workgangs, the *Kapos* also served as spies for the SS and informed on the political prisoners. They were often as cruel as the SS officers, punishing other prisoners with beatings, dividing food unfairly to reward their friends, and assigning the hardest labor to those who opposed them. This system, with the most brutal and criminal prisoners put in charge of others, continued in Auschwitz even after the camp had expanded to many times its original size. Eventually other types of prisoners, including Jews, became *Kapos.* Although most *Kapos* were hated, some attempted to protect other prisoners and became leaders. Despite having more power than other inmates, the *Kapos* were still prisoners at the mercy of the Nazis.

By the beginning of March 1941, 11,000 prisoners had been through Auschwitz, but many were already dead. Prisoners never received enough to

Heinrich Himmler (second from the left), head of the SS and the Gestapo, on an inspection of Auschwitz in 1942. *(Main Commission for the Investigation of Nazi War Crimes/USHMM Photo Archives)*

eat (especially men doing heavy physical labor). The barracks were unheated, and prisoners were not given warm clothing. Primitive sanitation conditions and filthy drinking water contributed to the spread of disease among the inmates. These conditions resulted in poor health, exhaustion, and death for some of the prisoners. Many others were executed by the Nazis. Some died in the building called Block 11, where the Gestapo questioned inmates suspected of planning their escape or of organizing resistance to the Nazi party. The German secret police tortured these prisoners to make them reveal the names of other prisoners helping them. A prisoner was beaten if he did not talk when questioned by the Gestapo, and he was tortured if he still did not reveal the information sought. Prisoners had their fingernails slowly pulled out with pliers, or were tied to a metal bar by the wrists and ankles and swung around while being beaten with a club. When the prisoners were taken out of this torture contraption on a stretcher, their faces and bodies were so badly damaged that they could not be recognized. Prisoners knew that if they still did not talk, they might be placed

in "standing cells," small boxes that provided only enough room to stand up. The prisoner was left to stand in one of these boxes without being fed, sometimes for two or three weeks, until starving to death. Still other prisoners were shot at the "wall of death," a wall of black cork with sand in front of it to soak up the blood of the bullet-riddled bodies.

On March 1, 1941, Auschwitz was inspected by Heinrich Himmler, head of the SS and the Gestapo, along with high officials of I. G. Farben, the giant German chemical company. As one of the most powerful men in the German empire, Himmler ordered a vast expansion of Auschwitz that would allow the camp to hold 30,000 prisoners. This section became known as Auschwitz I. Himmler also ordered the building of a second camp about two miles away that was to hold 100,000 prisoners, a number that soon expanded to 200,000. This immense camp was Auschwitz II, also known as Birkenau, from the German word for birch trees. An additional camp, Auschwitz III, would be built in the nearby village of Monowitz, and there I. G. Farben would build an artificial rubber factory to

Canisters of Zyklon B, a powerful disinfectant usually used to kill lice, and a gas mask found after the liberation of one of the concentration camps. *(Archiwum Akt Nowych/USHMM Photo Archives)*

Brick and wooden bunks at the Auschwitz concentration camp, covered in straw, were used by four or five people at a time. *(Reproduced by permission of © Hulton Getty/Liaison Agency)*

supply tires for German army trucks. A plant would be constructed to convert coal into oil, and Himmler would supply the company with 10,000 prisoners to work in the factory.

Himmler's plan was not just to make Auschwitz a much larger concentration camp, but to establish it as the key location for the destruction of Jews. At the time of Himmler's visit, the German armies had conquered most of Europe up to the Soviet border, territory Hitler intended Germany to dominate forever. As Himmler knew, Hitler was planning to invade the Soviet Union in an attempt to gain control of its entire western section, while also laying claim to Soviet-ruled countries, such as the Ukraine and Belarussia (White Russia). If Hitler could succeed in this goal, almost all European Jews would be in areas controlled by Nazi Germany. Three months after Himmler's visit to Auschwitz, German armies invaded the Soviet Union and began to execute their plans for the mass murder of the Jewish people.

As the Germans launched the Soviet invasion, Nazi officials began conducting an experiment at

Auschwitz. In September 1941 they took 250 Polish prisoners from the camp hospital to the Gestapo's Block 11, then rounded up 600 Russian prisoners of war, all either Jews or Communists. In a cellar of Block 11, these prisoners were gassed to death using Zyklon B, a brand name for the powerful disinfectant hydrogen cyanide, which was used to kill lice. Anyone who handled the compound had to wear a gas mask, and anyone who breathed it for any length of time would die. Höss would later brag about the efficiency of both Auschwitz and Zyklon B, which was faster-acting and therefore far more effective than carbon monoxide, the gas used at the other death camps that soon began operation in Poland.

Soon a room in the crematorium was converted into a gas chamber. The crematorium had originally been built to burn the bodies of prisoners who were executed or who died from "natural" causes—the terrible conditions at Auschwitz almost ensured that a significant number of prisoners would die every day without being gassed. The Nazis used their new gas chamber to kill

A door to a gas chamber in Auschwitz. The note reads: "Harmful gas! Entering endangers your life." *(Photograph by Stanislaw Luczko courtesy of the Main Commission for the Investigation of Nazi War Crimes/USHMM Photo Archives)*

An aerial photograph of the Auschwitz area taken by Allied reconnaissance units sometime between April 4, 1944, and January 14, 1945. *(USHMM Photo Archives)*

hundreds of Russian prisoners of war. Later, when transport trains filled with Jews began to arrive at Auschwitz, sometimes every person on a train was taken immediately to the gas chamber and killed. This first gas chamber at Auschwitz was not large enough to suit the Nazis' needs, and the crematorium continually broke down. The chamber was also situated in the main camp, which made it difficult to conceal what was happening within its walls. The killing would have to be moved to the new camp, Birkenau.

In October 1941, a month after the gassing of 850 men in Block 11, prisoners began to build Auschwitz II, or Birkenau. Much larger than any other concentration camp, it had row after row of

wooden barracks to hold inmates. Prisoners were crammed into these buildings and forced to sleep on narrow planks, or bunks, arranged three tiers high. Three men slept on each plank, and there was so little space that if one of them died during the night, it was impossible to move his body until the morning. Sanitary facilities were completely inadequate for so many prisoners, and a horrible stench from human waste, filth, and death was a permanent feature of the camp. On the grounds of Birkenau were two small cottages, originally the homes of Polish farmers, surrounded by woods and located far enough from the barracks to ensure privacy. One of these cottages was made of red brick with a tile roof, and was called Bunker 1 by the Nazis; the prisoners referred to it as "the little red house." The

The Jews of Europe

Auschwitz was the main killing center for much of Nazi-occupied Europe. A study by Franciszek Piper, the chief historian at the Auschwitz-Birkenau State Museum in Oświęcim, Poland, attempts to trace the home countries of the Jews deported to Auschwitz. Although Piper's numbers are estimates, most experts agree that they are probably close to the actual numbers:

Hungary	438,000
Poland	300,000
France	69,000
Holland	60,000
Greece	55,000
Bohemia and Moravia (the Czech Republic today)	46,000
Slovakia	27,000
Belgium	25,000
Germany and Austria	23,000
Yugoslavia	10,000
Italy	7,500
Norway	690

Piper was unable to trace the original home of about 34,000 Jews because in most cases they were sent to Auschwitz from other concentration camps.

Not all Jews were sent to Auschwitz. Jews living in the Soviet territory captured by the Germans were usually killed by the Einsatzgruppen without being sent to camps. Although Jews living in the part of Romania taken over by Hungary during World War II went to Auschwitz, other Romanian Jews did not. In other countries, only a minority of the Jews who were killed met their deaths at Auschwitz. Almost 200,000 German and Austrian Jews were killed by the Nazis, but only 23,000 were sent to Auschwitz. While about 300,000 Polish Jews died in Auschwitz, the Nazis killed ten times that number, most of them in other camps.

---

other cottage, which had plastered walls and a thatched roof, was known officially as Bunker 2 but nicknamed "the little white house" by the prisoners.

At the beginning of 1942, the Nazis bricked up the windows of the houses and sealed the doors so no air could get in or out. These were the new gas chambers, where scores of people eventually died. Still, like crematorium I at Auschwitz I, the structures could not accommodate the enormous number of intended victims. The two cottages had no ventilation equipment, so after people were gassed in the evening, it was necessary to leave the doors open until morning for the rooms to be cleared of Zyklon B fumes before the bodies could be removed. This prevented the gas chambers from being used continuously. The bodies then had to be moved to large pits where they were buried. Thus, the two cottages proved to be temporary killing centers, but the Germans had already decided on a more efficient means of extermination.

In October 1941, when construction began on Birkenau, the SS ordered the erection of four special buildings on the site. German engineering and construction companies were hired to design and build the structures, but the actual labor was performed by prisoners. Work went on around the clock, but it took until spring 1943 to complete the work. The buildings were crematoria, each one holding furnaces designed to burn bodies. The buildings called crematoria IV and V were over 100 yards long and about forty feet wide. Crematoria II and III were smaller because they also had underground rooms. A tall brick chimney rose high above each structure. Unlike crematorium I, the four new buildings were not designed to burn the bodies of prisoners who had died from malnutrition, exhaustion, or the diseases that swept through the camp. Instead, they were conceived as a crucial mechanism in the "Final Solution." Part of each building housed a large gas chamber, which had been carefully planned by experts. In

An aerial photograph of the Auschwitz area, showing the Birkenau camp, taken by the Allies in 1944. *(USHMM Photo Archives)*

each crematorium building, 2,000 people could be gassed at one time, and the furnaces then burned the bodies. In crematoria II and III, the gas chambers were located in the basement, with a freight elevator connecting them to the furnaces on the ground floor. The doors to the elevator were designed to open automatically. In contrast to Treblinka and the other death camps, there was no need to take bodies from the gas chambers to open pits where they would be buried.

Arrival Procedures

The first new prisoners for Auschwitz were Jews from the surrounding area. In March 1942 transports of Jews began from Slovakia, and by summer, trains were carrying Jews across Europe to Auschwitz from France, Belgium, and Holland. In late summer 1942, the Jews of Croatia were sent there, then more Jews from Holland. Half the small Jewish population of Norway reached Auschwitz in November. In February 1943 the transports brought the last Jews of Berlin, and the next month the Jews of Greece arrived. In fall and winter, Italian Jews were funneled in and, in spring 1944, the Nazis sent hundreds of thousands of Hungarian Jews to the camp. Finally, by August, 70,000 Jews from Lódz, the last Polish ghetto, along with the final transport of French Jews, were loaded up and sent to their deaths at Auschwitz, even while the American and British armies were driving the Germans from France.

Luck and Survival

Sometimes survival at Auschwitz depended on luck. Historian Otto Friedrich tells the story of how one man, Sim Kessel, lived through the ordeal. A French boxer, Kessel had been sent to Auschwitz for participating in the French resistance movement against the Nazis. He was told to undress, and stood naked, with others, waiting in the snow. When SS men arrived on motorcycles, Kessel saw that one of them, a corporal or sergeant, had scar tissue over his eyes and a broken nose, just like Kessel himself.

Knowing he had nothing to lose, he asked the SS man whether he had been a boxer. "Yes," said the SS man, who looked at Kessel's face and recognized a fellow prizefighter. The SS man asked Kessel where he had fought, and Kessel told him. Then the SS man told Kessel, still naked, to hop onto the back of his motorcycle. They drove through the camp, and Kessel was taken to the hospital instead of the gas chambers.

The railroad tracks leading to Birkenau carried already exhausted prisoners, many of whom had been held in transit camps in their home countries after being arrested. They had then traveled packed in locked freight cars, usually with no food or water for many days and nights. In the summer the heat and thirst were indescribable, and in the winter the prisoners froze in the unheated railroad cars. In every transport, many people died long before they reached Auschwitz.

When the trains stopped at Birkenau, the doors were opened and the Jews were ordered out by SS men with whips. The freight cars were littered with the bodies of those who had not endured the trip, some of them children. The surviving prisoners were hungry, frightened, drained, and horrified at the atrocities they had witnessed thus far. They were instructed to leave their suitcases or bundles on the platform, stand in line, and to walk past two men, SS doctors, sitting at a table. As each prisoner passed the table, one of the doctors waved his hand either to the left or to the right, indicating which way the prisoner should go. Usually about 90 percent—including children and the elderly, most women, and anyone who appeared sick or weak—were sent to the left. Adult men under the age of forty who appeared healthy had the best chance of being sent to the right, as they were considered strong enough to work. Those sent to the right did not know it, but they had been chosen to live, if only for a short time. Those sent to the left would die in the gas chambers. Life or death might depend on how exhausted someone looked, or on the mood of the SS doctors that day.

Those who were sent to the left were marched through the camp, and told that before going to their barracks, they would be bathed and disinfected to prevent disease. SS men forced the prisoners forward with whips and attack dogs. People who were too weak or sick to walk were loaded into trucks. The exact details of the following events tend to vary. Some procedures changed during the years Auschwitz was in operation. Additional factors might also depend on the number of people in a particular transport, and whether the train arrived during the day or at night. Still, the following is by most accounts what happened to those sent to crematoria II and III.

Both buildings were situated outside the fence surrounding the barracks at Birkenau. Each was enclosed by its own barbed-wire fence and numerous bushes and trees to prevent anyone from seeing events occurring inside. Prisoners were led down a flight of stairs to the basement, where they were met by signs reading "To the Baths" and "To Disinfection." The permanent signs were in German but the Nazis also posted temporary signs in the language of that day's victims. Prisoners entered a windowless room lined with wooden benches and were told to undress. The room was fifty yards long and eight yards wide, and above the benches were wooden hooks on which they hung their clothes. Each hook was numbered, and the

Zyklon B

After the Nazis decided to use Zyklon B for mass killings of European Jews, the profits of the firm that manufactured the product increased significantly. I. G. Farben, the parent company of DEGESCH (Deutsche Gesellschaft für Schädlingsbekämpfung mbH, or German Vermin-Combating Corporation), one of the companies that produced Zyklon B, earned twice the amount on its DEGESCH dividends from 1942 to 1944 that it had earned on them in 1940 and 1941. The company's management was probably aware of the use of their product because the SS ordered the gas to be made without the standard warning odor, or "indicator." By removing the warning odor, the Nazis stopped victims from being alerted to their fate in the camp gas chambers.

After the war, in March 1946, a trial was held before a British tribunal in Hamburg. The defendants were owners and executives of Tesch and Stabenow Company, the other company that produced Zyklon B. The trial established that the production of gas for killing prisoners was a war crime. Two men, the owner and executive manager of the factory, were sentenced to death. One employee of the factory was acquitted.

victims were told to remember their number so that they could reclaim their clothes later. When they had undressed, they were led through a narrow hall to another room; women and children usually went first. Sometimes they were given soap and a towel by the SS men. Like the signs that pointed to the "baths," this was a way of keeping victims from realizing what was going to happen to them.

The Gas Chambers

The next room was the gas chamber, which was smaller than the dressing room—about thirty yards by seven yards—with white-washed plaster walls and metal plates on the ceiling that looked like shower heads. SS men forced 2,000 people into this room, cramming about nine people into every square yard; the SS men then left and bolted the airtight door behind them. In the door was a round peephole made of thick glass protected on the inside by a metal grill. At the command of an SS doctor, Zyklon B pellets were poured down specially made vents into the gas chamber. They turned to gas when they came in contact with the air. People nearest the vents died almost immediately, while others, according to Rudolf Höss in *Commandant of Auschwitz*, "staggered about and began to scream and struggle for air. The screaming, however, soon changed to the death rattle and in a few minutes all lay still." Other witnesses tell an even more horrible story. The pellets of Zyklon B first turned into deadly gas near the floor, then the gas rose upward. Therefore, the children, who were shorter, died first. Sometimes, according to witnesses, the bodies were found in a pyramid with those who had been the strongest lying on top. They had climbed onto the dead and dying in a desperate attempt to breathe a few minutes longer. About thirty minutes after the gas had been released, ventilation fans were turned on and the door was opened. A special squad of prisoners, wearing gas masks, dragged the bodies out. Called the Sonderkommando, or "special commando," these prisoners were among those from earlier transports who had been selected to live. They removed glasses and artificial limbs from bodies, cut off women's hair, and loaded bodies onto the elevator platform to be sent up to the ground floor. There, other members of the Sonderkommando removed jewelry from the corpses, and opened the mouths of the dead to pull out gold teeth. The gold would be melted down and used to help finance the German war effort. If a Sonderkommando worker was found to have left a gold tooth in the mouth of a victim, he was severely punished—sometimes even thrown into the furnace alive.

It took the Sonderkommando four hours to empty the gas chamber, and it took approximately

Hungarian Jewish women, separated from the men, await selection on a ramp at Auschwitz in May 1944. *(Photograph by Bernhard Walter, courtesy of Yad Vashem Photo Archives/USHMM Photo Archives)*

twenty minutes for the furnace to burn the two or three corpses that had been loaded into each compartment. Sometimes the Sonderkommando loaded four or five bodies into one compartment and burned the bodies longer. Crematoria II and III could each cremate about 2,500 bodies in twenty-four hours, while crematoria IV and V could each burn as many as 1,500 bodies in the same period. Ashes and incompletely burned bones fell through a grill at the bottom of the furnace into a pit, where they were ground up by members of the Sonderkommando and mixed with the ashes. Ashes were usually dumped into the river or ponds, or used as fertilizer.

This procedure allowed the gas chambers to kill, and the crematoria to burn, as many as 8,000 people in twenty-four hours. Sometimes, though, even this was not enough. When large transports of Hungarian Jews were sent to Auschwitz, for instance, the crematoria could not handle the huge volume of victims and the corpses had to be burned in open pits. Records dating back to summer 1944 indicate that the crematoria and pits together could burn 20,000 dead bodies in a single

day. The men of the Sonderkommando who disposed of the bodies had no hope of surviving the war. They knew the Nazis would never let them live to reveal what they had seen, but some of them secretly wrote down their stories, sealing them in bottles or cans and burying them among the ashes of the dead near the crematoria. Six of these hidden reports or diaries, by three different authors, were found in the first fifteen years after Auschwitz was liberated. Each writer tells the story of how the Jewish community in his town was rounded up, transported to Auschwitz, and processed through the camp. Other eyewitness accounts are believed to have existed but are lost.

The Registered Prisoners

While Auschwitz was in operation, the Nazis sent about 1,500,500 people to the camp, killing the majority of them almost immediately. Despite this rapid rate of execution, about 400,000 people, half of them Jewish and the rest primarily non-Jewish Poles, were officially registered as prisoners and given numbers. People who resided in the

The remains of a crematorium at the Bergen-Belsen concentration camp. Crematoria were also used at Auschwitz. *(Hadassah Rosensaft Collection/USHMM Photo Archives)*

camps had been selected by the SS doctors for work details and were mostly healthy adult men. While their families and friends were being marched to the gas chambers, those who had survived the selection were processed by the Nazis. The procedure usually took all day or all night, during which time the prisoners remained unfed. They were brought to a yard between two barracks, and told to undress. They waited while each prisoner's hair was shaved off. They were then forced to run naked to take cold showers, while the SS men used whips and dogs to hurry them. After the showers, they ran to another yard and received camp uniforms, which were pajama-like garments with blue and white stripes. They were also given caps that they were required to wear at all times, and wooden clogs instead of shoes. A colored triangle was attached to each uniform: Common criminals wore uniforms with green triangles, political prisoners wore red, homosexuals wore pink, Jehovah's Witnesses wore purple, and Jews wore either yellow triangles or two triangles that together formed a Jewish Star of David. The next step was the tattooing of a prisoner number on the left arm, between the wrist and the elbow.

Prisoners were then sent to the quarantine barracks, where they were kept for a month or two to ensure they were not harboring dangerous diseases that could spread to other prisoners or to camp personnel. SS guards also used the quarantine time to "train" the prisoners in the routine of the concentration camp. Every day, inmates had to stand at roll call, which began at 4:30 in the morning and often lasted several hours (and sometimes much longer). Prisoners were instructed in the Nazi method of "physical training," which involved running in place, dropping down and hopping like a frog, then getting up and running in place again, all on command. This process, also, could continue for hours. In addition, prisoners were forced to dig ditches and perform other physically demanding work in the quarantine area. They were ordered to line up "correctly," to remove their caps upon command, and to sing anti-Jewish songs. At the end of each long day came the evening roll call, which began at 6:30 p.m.

During these activities, the SS and the *Kapos* scrutinized every move the prisoners made to make sure there were no "mistakes." If a prisoner did not

"Kanada"

Money stolen from Auschwitz victims was deposited in special SS bank accounts, and any gold or silver they might have possessed was melted down into bars and sent to the German Central Bank. Clothing and household goods Jews took with them for "resettlement" were confiscated by the Nazis and sent to warehouses, where the items were sorted and prepared to be either used in the camp or shipped out for distribution to German citizens. Eventually dozens of buildings, including large barracks, were needed to hold all the stolen goods. Several thousand prisoners worked in these buildings, as part of a work detachment called "Kanada," or "Canada," because that country was a symbol of wealth to the prisoners. Even though many trainloads of these items were sent out of the camp, huge quantities of goods were still found at the end of the war. As they retreated from the Soviet army, the Nazis tried to burn the warehouses, successfully destroying twenty-nine of them and leaving only six buildings standing. In these, however, the Soviets found 350,000 men's suits, over 800,000 women's outfits, more than 40,000 pairs of shoes, and almost 14,000 rugs.

line up according to orders, took an excessive amount of time to remove a cap, or could no longer keep up when ordered to hop, the punishment was a violent beating. Rules varied from day to day: An action, movement, or maneuver that was correct one day might be considered a mistake the next. Inconsistency in policies was inconsequential, as prisoners were not supposed to think for themselves, but only to obey their captors. During the quarantine period, the Nazis did everything they could to dehumanize the prisoners and to crush their spirit. They were reminded in every way that they were in a place where death was normal and expected. The Germans wanted the prisoners to believe that the only way they might prolong their own lives, even a little, was by caring about no one but themselves. While the stress of imprisonment broke the spirit of many, who sometimes stole food from their fellow captives, some inmates also risked their own lives to assist others. Prisoners were also kept in filthy conditions to break their spirit. If they were dirty, they would begin to feel inferior, according to the Nazis. If they felt inferior, they would not revolt. Plus, it was easier for the guards to think of their prisoners as dirty, inferior people. Then the guards would be less inclined to feel sympathy or compassion for their captives.

Life Inside the Camps

Prisoners who survived the weeks in the quarantine barracks were transferred to the regular barracks in Auschwitz I or Birkenau, and subjected to intolerable conditions and scarcity of food. Although there were official regulations regarding how much the prisoners were supposed to be fed, the Nazis usually ignored their own rules. SS men often stole money budgeted for food, and guards and *Kapos* took much of the food that was delivered to the camp. On average, Auschwitz prisoners probably received 1,500 calories a day, but many were given far less. An average adult male needs more than twice that to maintain his weight, and men working at heavy labor, as the Auschwitz prisoners did, require more than three times that many calories to produce enough energy.

Despite the quarantine of new prisoners, the lack of sanitation in the camps meant that there were often major outbreaks of disease. As a result of poor diets and generally weakened states, the prisoners usually did not have enough resistance to fight off these diseases. Any germs, even the common cold, could be life-threatening. One of the most feared illnesses was typhus, a serious bacterial disease usually transmitted through body lice. In summer 1942, typhus killed 4,000 Auschwitz prisoners each month. There were also major outbreaks of typhoid fever that resulted from drinking untreated water. (SS men and employees of the German companies that were building Birkenau were given free bottled water to drink.)

View of the entrance to the main camp of Auschwitz, with the motto *"Arbeit Macht Frei"* ("Work makes you free").
(Main Commission for the Investigation of Nazi War Crimes/USHMM Photo Archives)

The high death rate from the combination of disease, malnutrition, and exhaustion was not an accident but a goal. As part of the "Final Solution," the Nazis had decided that a small number of Jews would not be killed immediately in the gas chambers, but would be made to work until they died. This process was called "destruction through work" and its ramifications were secretly discussed by the top Nazis. In September 1942, Joseph Goebbels told meeting participants in Berlin that "destruction through work" should apply to all Jews and Roma in concentration camps, to Poles who were sentenced to more than three years, and to Germans and Czechs sentenced to life in prison. Individuals outside these categories could also be included, depending on the specific case. On the gate at Auschwitz, as at other concentration camps, was the deceptive slogan *"Arbeit Macht Frei"*— "Work makes you free."

Many prisoners were needed to keep the concentration camps running. Some worked on the construction of new buildings as Birkenau expanded, while others worked in "Kanada." Some worked on farms inside the camp, where the Nazis experimented with ways to grow new crops, and some served as barbers. Prisoners assigned to kitchen duty had desirable jobs because it was possible to steal extra food. Others were assigned to the Sonderkommando and forced to empty the gas chambers and dispose of the bodies. Many prisoners worked outside the electrified fences of Auschwitz and Birkenau but returned each night. They were marched under heavy guard to their workplaces, sometimes several miles away, regardless of the weather, before beginning an eleven- or twelve-hour work shift. Among these workers were members of the "shoe commando," women prisoners who worked in a hut outside the camp separating parts of shoes so the leather or the soles could be re-used. Yet another "commando" consisted of women who made thread from the hair of female prisoners whose heads had been shaved.

In all these jobs, the half-starved prisoners were expected to work at full speed without ever taking a break, except for a lunch that usually consisted of watery soup. They were subjected to long

An Auschwitz warehouse filled with sacks of human hair used to make thread. *(Main Commission for the Investigation of Nazi War Crimes/USHMM Photo Archives)*

roll calls each morning and night, and were never given enough time to sleep. Sunday was supposed to be a rest day, but they were often forced to do "physical training," or "sport," as the Nazis called it. Sometimes, Sundays were used for special jobs like moving bricks from one part of the camp to another. If prisoners did not work fast enough, they were beaten. If they broke a camp rule, they were punished by whipping; serious violations were punishable by death. Inmates who became too sick or too tired to work were selected for the gas chambers.

Medical Experiments

Some of the people who were selected by the SS doctors to live at Auschwitz were chosen to be the subjects of medical experiments. These experiments were done without the consent of the inmate and therefore violated accepted standards within the medical profession. Many of the experiments caused extreme pain, and they were almost always conducted without anesthesia. Many of the experi-

ment subjects were killed so that autopsies could be performed on the bodies to evaluate the success of the experiment. Most of these medical experiments had no serious scientific basis and were merely attempts to prove Nazi ideas about race.

While Auschwitz was the most famous site of medical experiments, it was not the only place where they were conducted. There were so many experimental subjects in Auschwitz that test prisoners were sometimes sent elsewhere for evaluation. For example, children were often transferred to Germany to be used in testing resistance to tuberculosis. The main location of medical experiments at Auschwitz was Block 10, which housed only Jewish prisoners and was situated across a courtyard from Block 11, where the Gestapo tortured prisoners. In the courtyard was the "wall of death," the black cork wall where prisoners were shot.

Many of the experiments involved ways to sterilize people, similar to experiments conducted during the German euthanasia program in the beginning of the Nazi reign. The Nazis had long been interested in

Interior view of one of the barracks in a subcamp of Auschwitz. *(Main Commission for the Investigation of Nazi War Crimes/USHMM Photo Archives)*

prohibiting "inferior" or "imperfect" people from reproducing. Hitler had even argued for this a full twenty years earlier in *Mein Kampf*. At Auschwitz, Dr. Horst Schumann subjected about 1,000 young women and men of childbearing age to massive doses of X rays, causing great pain and the deaths of many. Approximately 200 of these victims also had their sex organs surgically removed. Professor Carl Clauberg, a fertility expert before the war, had personally discussed his ideas with Himmler. At Auschwitz, Clauberg injected chemicals into women's reproductive systems to find out which drugs would sterilize them, a practice that caused agonizing pain, sometimes lasting for weeks. Often, the women's sex organs were surgically removed and sent to Berlin for further study. Doctor Johann Kremer had been a professor of anatomy who was interested in the effects of starvation on different organs. To further his studies, a test prisoner was placed on a dissection table, the prisoner's weight-loss history was recorded, and then he or she was killed with an injection directly into the heart. Kremer immediately removed the victim's organs for study.

Josef Mengele, the most notorious of the Nazi doctors, gained a reputation as the "Angel of Death." Mengele, chief of selections, is said to have worn white gloves and hummed opera to himself while he chose who would live and who would die.

On some of those prisoners selected to live, Mengele conducted numerous experiments. He used dwarfs as test subjects, and also subjected Roma to assorted procedures. His best-known experiments were conducted on identical twins, many of whom were children. He wanted to see, for example, if each twin reacted the same way to pain. He carefully measured every part of each sibling: the shape and size of their ears, the lengths of their legs, the coloring of their skin. He dripped chemicals into prisoners' eyes, apparently trying to change their eye color. He even tried transferring blood between them. All the while, Mengele kept meticulous records. After the observations and studies were complete, the twins were usually killed—by an injection into the heart, sometimes performed by Mengele himself—and then dissected. Although no one is certain what motivated Mengele, experts speculate that his goal was to figure out how twins were produced so that more Aryans could be born. Despite the fact that he had both a medical degree and a Ph.D., Mengele seemed to perform experiments that made little or no scientific sense.

The Family Camps

Almost all registered prisoners in Auschwitz and Birkenau were segregated by gender; no

Nazi Doctors

Robert Jay Lifton, author of *The Nazi Doctors,* has pointed out that experiments were only a small part of what medical doctors did at Auschwitz. Physicians were in charge of the initial "selections" of who would live and who would die. They supervised the procedures in the gas chambers by deciding when to release Zyklon B and when the victims were all dead. Doctors were also consulted on methods for burning bodies more quickly.

At Dachau, this young man was forced to endure low air pressure tests as the Nazis conducted experiments on humans. The Nazis hoped this test would provide useful information to the Luftwaffe (German airforce). *(KZ Gedenkstatte Dachau/USHMM Photo Archives)*

contact between men and women was allowed. A special women's camp was set up in Birkenau with SS women in charge. Hardly any children lived in the Auschwitz camps because children were usually selected for death when a transport arrived. A few young people survived by convincing SS doctors that they were older than they looked. Other children, especially twins, were spared immediate death in the gas chambers because Mengele had chosen them for his medical experiments. For a while, however, there were two "family camps" set up inside Auschwitz, where whole families were allowed to live together.

The first family camp was established in September 1943 for prisoners from the Theresienstadt "model ghetto" in what is now the Czech Republic. Theresienstadt was created for German Jews who were well-known in society—for example, famous artists or writers or leaders of the Jewish community. Conditions at Theresienstadt were among the best in the concentration camp system, and the Nazis used it as a model to convince outsiders that they treated the Jews well. They even made films featuring Theresienstadt, and it was the only camp to be inspected by the International Red Cross. The Nazis deceived the International Red Cross into believing that they were treating Jews humanely.

The Red Cross inspection of Theresienstadt led to the establishment of an Auschwitz family camp. As rumors that Jews were being murdered in Auschwitz and Birkenau spread, the Red Cross wanted to inspect Birkenau. The Nazis sent a transport of 5,000 people from Theresienstadt to Auschwitz, but did not subject them to the selection process upon their arrival. Families instead remained together in barracks in a special section of the camp. They were not given prison uniforms, and their heads were not shaved. This was not really a "model ghetto" like Theresienstadt, however, because dietary and sanitary conditions were similar to those in the rest of Auschwitz. Approximately one out of every five prisoners in the family camp died within six months. A second transport of 5,000 more people arrived from Theresienstadt three months later, in December 1943. On March 7, 1944, the family camp prisoners were given postcards, which they were told to address to relatives, including those in Theresienstadt. They were instructed to write that they were in good health and being treated well, and to postdate the postcards March 25, more than two weeks in the future. The same night the postcards were written, every survivor of the first transport was taken out

Adelaide Hautval Protests Nazi Experiments

A French Protestant physician who was imprisoned in Nazi concentration camps, Adelaide Hautval was born in 1906 and studied medicine in Strasbourg, France, before working at psychiatric clinics in France and Switzerland. While traveling to her mother's funeral in April 1942, she was arrested by Nazi border guards who charged her with trying to cross between the occupied and unoccupied zones of France without a permit. Taken to a Bourges prison to await trial, Hautval was alarmed to witness the harsh treatment of Jewish prisoners by the Gestapo. When she protested to Nazi officials, she was transferred to a prison for political detainees at Romainville; in January 1943 she was sent to Auschwitz with a group of Jewish women.

When Eduard Wirths, a physician at Auschwitz, learned that Hautval was a doctor, he asked her to work as a gynecologist in Block 10. Hautval had heard reports of the sterilization experiments that the Nazis were conducting on Jewish women in that section of the camp, so she took the opportunity to see for herself. She learned that Wirths and three other doctors—Horst Schumann, Carl Clauberg, and Wladyslaw Dering—were sterilizing women with X rays and ovariectomies (removal of the ovaries). This was the preliminary stage of a massive program planned by the Nazis in which sterilizations would be performed on all surviving part-Jewish women once Germany had won the war. Expressing her outrage at the brutality of such procedures, Hautval told Wirths she would not participate in the experiments. She was sent to the Birkenau camp, where she gave medical treatment to inmates; in August 1944 she was transferred to the women's camp at Ravensbrück and finally liberated in April 1945.

In 1964 Hautval testified at a trial in London involving libel charges brought by Wladyslaw Dering, one of the doctors who performed the Auschwitz experiments, against Leon Uris, author of *QB VII*. Claiming that Uris had slandered him in the book, Dering said that he had only been following orders at Auschwitz and that he would have endangered his own life by not carrying out the sterilizations. In her testimony, Hautval rejected Dering's excuse, pointing out that he could have secretly circumvented orders without risking punishment. She was honored in 1965 by Yad Vashem as "Righteous among the Nations" for her assistance to Jews during the Holocaust.

---

of the family camp and sent to the gas chambers. There was no selection process—even those who were healthy enough to work were killed. They had been in Auschwitz exactly six months.

Two more transports arrived from Theresienstadt. A special code was written by their names—SB6, which stood for the German words for "special handling" or "special treatment." The number "6" meant six months; SB6 therefore meant that the prisoners were to be killed six months after their arrival. Meanwhile, representatives of the International Red Cross inspected Theresienstadt on June 23, 1944, with Birkenau scheduled as their next stop. The Nazis were able to convince them that a second stop was unnecessary, and some speculate that the Red Cross inspectors were shown the postcards from the people in the family camp. By July, the people who had arrived at Auschwitz in the December transport were taken from the family camp and sent to the gas chambers—their six months were up. At the same time, those who had come in the later transports went through the selection process. Prisoners able to work were sent to other barracks in Auschwitz or Birkenau, while the rest, including children, were gassed. It was the end of the Jewish family camp.

The other family camp at Auschwitz was set up for the Roma, or Gypsies. Nazi policy toward the

---

Polish children imprisoned in Auschwitz, the Nazis' largest slave-labor and murder camp, look out from behind the barbed-wire fence. *(Main Commission for the Investigation of Nazi War Crimes/USHMM Photo Archives*

Roma was highly inconsistent: Sometimes they were treated as poorly as the Jews, while at other times, and in some parts of Nazi-controlled Europe, they were left alone. The Nazis ordered German Roma to Auschwitz in early 1943, and the first transport reached the camp on February 26. During the next few months, more transports of Roma arrived from various areas of Europe, and by the end of 1943, almost 19,000 Roma had reached Auschwitz. As early as March, 1,700 Roma who were ill with typhoid fever were sent to the gas chambers. Another 1,000 sick people were murdered at the end of May.

Although some Roma were transferred to the regular labor camps at Auschwitz and to other concentration camps, most lived in family units in the special camp. This preferential treatment remains a mystery, as do the events of May 17, 1944. On that day, the SS surrounded the Roma camp and prepared to lead all of its occupants to the gas chambers. However, they had been warned, apparently by the German commander of the Roma camp. Subsequently, the Roma were waiting with iron pipes and knives. The SS men, who could easily have shot all of them, were ordered to retreat instead. A week later, about 1,500 of the Roma were transferred from the family camp to the main camps, where they were assigned to work details.

In August another 1,400 were selected for work and the rest of the people in the camp, including children, were killed in the gas chambers. Approximately 6,500 Roma died in the gas chambers at Auschwitz; another 10,000 died from disease and hunger.

Auschwitz III: The Slave-Labor System

One of the reasons for Himmler's decision to expand Auschwitz was to enable chemical company I. G. Farben to build a factory there using slave labor. Located at Monowitz and called Auschwitz III, the factory was built by Auschwitz prisoners forced to labor without any safety equipment. It is estimated that 25,000 prisoners died while working on the factory. Monowitz was only one of the twenty-five to fifty sub-camps of Auschwitz, some of them located as far as fifty miles away from the main camp. (The total number of sub-camps depends on whether certain camps are counted separately or as parts of the same sub-camp.) Prisoners were sent to work in steel factories, a cement plant, a shoe factory, and coal mines. In one plant, opened by the Krupp steel company, prisoners made fuses for bombs.

The Nazis maintained their philosophy of "destruction through work" throughout the

A close-up of a Roma (Gypsy) couple sitting in an open area in a concentration camp. *(Photograph by Jerzy Ficowski, courtesy of the USHMM Photo Archives)*

remainder of the war, so conditions at the Auschwitz work camps were horrendous. Some jobs, however, were worse than others. For example, being stationed in the coal mine at Jaworzno was like getting a death sentence. Very few prisoners had experience as miners, so they were given jobs that required intense physical labor and no skill. They loaded coal onto carts and hauled it around, often on their hands and knees, in sweltering heat without adequate ventilation inside the mine. Desperate for water, they sometimes drank their own urine. Miners were not equipped with hard hats, boots, or other safety equipment. Such dangerous work conditions, combined with the workers' inexperience at the job, guaranteed serious injuries on a daily basis. Auschwitz prisoners on mining duty were required to produce as much coal as regular miners, but none of the prisoners received nearly enough food to do this kind of work. Jewish prisoners were only allowed half as much food as German prisoners, though Jews comprised a great majority of inmates in the sub-camps. At Jaworzno, for example, about 80 percent of the slave laborers were Jews, and in some sub-camps the percentage was higher. Those who could not keep up were sent back to Auschwitz to be gassed. SS doctors from Auschwitz made inspections of the sub-camps and selected the workers who would die.

The SS, not the workers, received pay for this slave labor. I. G. Farben reportedly paid the SS one dollar per day for each skilled worker, seventy-five cents per day for unskilled workers, and around forty cents per day for children. The Nazis spent less than thirty-five cents per day to maintain each prisoner. By 1944, 37,000 prisoners (out of a total of 105,000 registered prisoners) worked for private companies as slave laborers; 11,000 of these worked for I. G. Farben. Other prisoners worked for companies owned by the SS itself, including one company that was among the largest brick producers in Germany. The SS often based the location of new concentration camps on their proximity to deposits of clay that could be used for making bricks. This ensured that the SS-owned company would always have enough workers who did not have to be paid, who could not quit, and who could be forced to work under subhuman conditions.

Uprising

Prisoners assigned to duty with the Sonderkommando had the most gruesome jobs, as they had to witness the daily results of gassings and then dispose of the bodies. As summer 1944 ended, the Nazis were almost finished with the mass killing of the Hungarian Jews. The Sonderkommando knew

Escape from Auschwitz

Prisoners tried to escape from Auschwitz, yet it was a very difficult task. The camp was surrounded by a high-voltage electrified fence. Anyone who approached the area near the fence was shot without warning by SS guards sitting above in tall watchtowers. Outside the fence was a large security area, about fifteen square miles, that was patrolled by the SS and closed to civilians. As soon as an escape was discovered, the SS searched every likely hiding place in the security zone around the camp, and men were sent into the watchtowers scattered in this large area. Dogs were used to hunt down the prisoners.

A successful escape usually required careful preparation and assistance from the secret Polish underground outside the camp, which supplied escaped prisoners with civilian clothes, wigs to hide their shaved heads, and false identification papers. They could be hidden and fed until they were strong enough to travel. Several times, Auschwitz prisoners escaped by wearing stolen SS uniforms and walking through the gate. The Nazis, though, continued to hunt for escapees, even if they were far from the camp. The guards sent escapees' names and tattooed serial numbers to every police station and border patrol. Prisoners who were captured after escaping were brought back to Auschwitz, tortured by the Gestapo to reveal who had helped them, and then hanged in front of the assembled inmates. Many times, the Nazis also executed other prisoners in the same barracks or work squad as a warning against trying to escape.

A double, electrified fence made escape from Auschwitz an impossible task. *(USHMM Photo Archives)*

Róza Robota, a prisoner who worked in an Auschwitz factory, managed to smuggle explosives to the Sonderkommando, aiding in their uprising. She was arrested and hanged. *(Yad Vashem Photo Archives/USHMM Photo Archives)*

Ala Gertner participated in the Sonderkommando uprising at Auschwitz-Birkenau along with Róza Robota. During the rebellion, resistance fighters blew up one of the camp's crematoria. Gertner was executed in January of 1945. *(USHMM Photo Archives)*

that when their work was done, they would be killed as well. There was no chance that the Nazis would allow them to leave Auschwitz alive with so much intimate knowledge of Nazi mass killings.

The Sonderkommando men managed to have explosive powder smuggled to them from one of the slave-labor factories where Auschwitz prisoners worked. A few of the women in the factory, led by Róza Robota, were able to bring explosives into the camp a little at a time. Although accounts of the uprising vary, some historians note that on October 7, 1944, the Sonderkommando blew up crematorium IV and attempted to escape. Then the Sonderkommando in crematorium II overwhelmed the German *Kapo* and an SS officer and threw them into the furnace alive. They too tried to break out of the camp.

The Nazis sent hundreds of SS guards after the escaped Sonderkommando members. Many of them were trapped inside a barn within the camp. The SS set it on fire, and shot the prisoners as they attempted to escape the blaze. Approximately 250 Sonderkommando were killed and another 200 were executed soon after; three SS men were killed and a dozen were wounded. The Nazis were able to

determine how the prisoners had obtained the explosives, and several young women who worked at the factory, including Robota, were arrested by the Gestapo and tortured for several weeks. They were hanged in front of the assembled prisoners on January 6, 1945, just three weeks before the Russian army reached Auschwitz.

The Auschwitz Death March

For months, Auschwitz prisoners could hear the thunder of cannon fire as the Soviet army approached the camp. Beginning in August 1944, when there were about 105,000 prisoners left in the camp, thousands were relocated by train to concentration camps in Germany. On November 25, 1944, the order came from Berlin: Himmler wanted the Auschwitz gas chambers and crematoria destroyed. Inmates, mostly women, were put to work erasing the evidence of the Holocaust. The burned wreck of crematorium IV, which the Sonderkommando had destroyed in their revolt, was demolished. Furnaces, chimneys, and roofs were dismantled in the other crematoria; piping and ventilation were removed from the gas chambers. The Nazis also tried to burn

Primo Levi

One of the prisoners still left in Auschwitz when the first Russian soldiers arrived was Primo Levi, an Italian Jew and chemist. Levi reported later that the Russian soldiers did not talk or acknowledge the prisoners, but simply stared in disbelief at the scene before them. Levi believes this was because they felt guilt that such inhumane treatment of one group of human beings could have been promulgated by other human beings. The prisoners, he theorized, had felt the same sort of shame when witnessing Nazi atrocities toward fellow prisoners committed in the camps.

Prisoners of Auschwitz greet their Russian liberators in January 1945. *(Central State Archive of Film, Photo and Phonographic Documents/USHMM Photo Archives)*

all documents relating to what had happened at Auschwitz, afraid evidence of their crimes would be captured by the Russians, as had been the case at the Majdanek death camp in July 1944.

On January 18, 1945, the evacuation of the camp began. At that time, around 65,000 prisoners remained, including some 16,000 women. About 58,000 were lined up and went through their last roll call at Auschwitz. Then they were marched out of the camp with most of the SS men guarding them. Approximately 7,000 prisoners were left behind because they were too weak to walk. The Nazis had planned to kill the surviving prisoners before the evacuation, but the process would have taken a long time without the gas chambers, and SS personnel were more interested in escaping from the Soviets than in killing half-dead inmates. The shells of cre-

A column of prisoners on a death march from the Dachau concentration camp in April 1945. As they struggled on, prisoners who fell down from exhaustion were shot. *(Photograph by Fritz Melbach, courtesy of USHMM Photo Archives)*

matoria II and III were blown up with dynamite on January 20, 1945; crematorium V was destroyed later. On January 24, the last SS men left. Three days later, the first Russian soldiers reached the camp.

For those 58,000 prisoners marched out of Auschwitz by the Germans, the temperature was below zero and the cold winter wind was blowing heavily when the march began. Few had overcoats. They were divided into different columns of several thousand prisoners under SS guard. The SS pushed prisoners to hurry, sometimes in complete darkness. Prisoners who fell down from exhaustion were shot. As each column of prisoners moved forward, they could see the bloody bodies from previous columns lying in the ditch alongside the road. A prisoner in a later column saw a body every 40 or 50 yards for many miles. The columns were supposed to be headed for the Gross-Rosen concentration camp. Rudolf Höss, the former Auschwitz commander who at this time was supervising concentration camps from his office in Berlin, saw the death march from his car. He wrote in his memoir: "I now met columns of prisoners, struggling through the deep snow. They had no food. Most of the non-commissioned officers in charge of these stumbling columns of corpses had no idea where they were supposed to be going. They only knew that

their final destination was Gross-Rosen. But how to get there was a mystery."

Some of the prisoners were able to use the confusion to escape. Twenty-one-year-old Sara Erenhalt and a group of other women had marched for twenty-four hours through the snow with no shoes and no food. The SS guards stopped the column in a village and told the prisoners to find a place to sleep. There was no place to lock up the prisoners, and the SS men were probably too tired themselves to guard them all night. Erenhalt and six others went into a house and asked the old man there if they could sleep in his barn. He turned out to be a priest, and he agreed to hide them, even though SS men were using his house for the night. In the morning, the seven women stayed in the barn instead of rejoining the column. They hid in the priest's barn for three and one-half weeks, until Russian soldiers reached the village. Most of the guards were more careful, however.

Each column of prisoners struggled forward on different routes through the cold with little food. They rarely slept. One group reached a railroad line after a week. The prisoners were loaded onto open freight cars, with the SS shooting to make them keep their heads down. They lay in the cars for five days, many of them freezing to death, before reaching the Mauthausen concentration camp in Aus-

Captured SS troops are forced to load trucks with the dead from the Bergen-Belsen concentration camp, 1945. *(Reproduced by permission of AP/Wide World Photos)*

tria, not far from Hitler's hometown. Eight thousand Auschwitz prisoners arrived at the camp alive.

Ten thousand others, including many women, eventually reached the Bergen-Belsen camp in northwestern Germany. Bergen-Belsen had been receiving similar transports of prisoners from the east for some time. It was completely overcrowded and lacking in food, even by concentration camp standards. Epidemics swept through the camp, killing thousands. British troops who liberated Bergen-Belsen in April 1945 found 10,000 bodies lying on the ground. For five days before the British arrived, the people had been without food or water, and 14,000 prisoners were so sick or weak that they died even after the camp was liberated.

Some 58,000 prisoners had been marched out of Auschwitz on January 18, 1945. Between 15,000-17,000 died on the march. Many of the others died in places like Mauthausen and Bergen-Belsen. The Auschwitz death march was the largest of many such marches. During winter 1944–1945, as Russian troops closed in from the east, the SS drove prison-

ers westward to the concentration camps in Germany. In spring 1945, during the last months of World War II, the American and British armies approached these camps from the west. The Nazis waited until the last minute to try to evacuate these final camps. Many prisoners—including most of the same people who had only recently arrived from the east—were marched out. At that point, though, there was no place left for the SS to go. Between 15,000 and 20,000 prisoners from Dachau, the first concentration camp, were marched aimlessly around the countryside in groups of different sizes. Many died before the American army reached them. There is no way to know the number of people who died during the dozens of death marches staged by the Nazis, but historian Martin Gilbert estimates that several hundred thousand people perished during the marches themselves.

The Numbers at Auschwitz

Researchers are still unsure how many people were sent to Auschwitz and how many people died

American generals Dwight D. Eisenhower, Omar Bradley, and George S. Patton examine the corpses of prisoners found at the Buchenwald concentration camp in April 1945. *(Photograph by William Newhouse, courtesy of USHMM Photo Archives)*

at the camp. Hundreds of thousands of people, never registered as "official" prisoners, were sent directly from transport trains to be killed in the gas chambers. At first, the Nazis kept detailed records of the registered prisoners, but as enemy armies approached, they did everything possible to destroy these documents. Höss, the commandant of Auschwitz for much of its existence, first said that "at least 2.5 million people were put to death, gassed, and subsequently burned there; in addition, 500,000 people died of exhaustion and illness, which gives a total of 3 million victims." Later, Höss said that these numbers were too high and that the real number was 1.13 million people. The first Allied attempt to estimate the number of victims of the camp was commissioned by the Soviet government. It was based on the testimony of eyewitnesses and the capacity of the gas chambers and crematoria. It concluded that at least 4 million people had died at Auschwitz. A Polish commission investigating Auschwitz produced a similar estimate.

Decades after the Holocaust, scholars tried once again to determine an accurate number of Auschwitz victims. Although they all agree that the exact number will never be known, they have found ways to make their estimates as reliable as possible. Historians have examined the records of the transports to Auschwitz, the number of people deported from the different countries of Europe, and the number of people who survived. Franciszek Piper, the chief historian at the Auschwitz-Birkenau State Museum in Poland, conducted one of the most careful studies, in which he concluded that at least 1.1 million people died at Auschwitz, about 1 million of them Jews. The highest total estimate that he considers possible is 1.5 million, including 1.35 million Jews. In addition, many more thousands of people transferred from Auschwitz during the evacuation died in the death marches or after resettlement in other concentration camps.

Auschwitz and Holocaust Denial

In the years since World War II, historians of the Holocaust have given many wide-ranging figures for the number of people killed at Auschwitz and other concentration camps. Some skeptics use these wide variations in mortality rates to argue that the Holocaust never really occurred—or that the total number of victims has been greatly exaggerated. The testimony of many survivors, though, as well as that of Rudolf Höss, Adolf Eichmann and other Nazis, along with surviving records, all indicate that the Holocaust was very real indeed. Regardless of how many Jews and others were killed at Auschwitz, its existence and function are beyond question, despite claims otherwise.

Two boys who survived Auschwitz display their prisoner numbers tattooed on their arms. *(USHMM Photo Archives)*

Ruth Minsky Sender
Excerpt from *The Cage*

Published in 1986

More than 100 concentration camps were established by the Nazis during World War II. Jewish prisoners of the concentration camps were starved, overworked, beaten, humiliated, and exposed to filth and disease. Prisoners who became ill or weak were killed. In 1942 the Nazis began implementing the "Final Solution" to the "Jewish problem," calling for the extermination of Jews in German-occupied territories in Europe. To achieve this objective, the Nazis set up six special death camps, different from the other concentration camps because their sole purpose was mass murder.

The six camps were Auschwitz-Birkenau, Belzec, Chelmno, Majdanek, Sobibór, and Treblinka. Jews in the ghettos were rounded up and transported by rail to the death camps, which were equipped with gas chambers and crematoria—designed specifically to murder all European Jews. An estimated 3 million adults and children were killed at these six extermination centers; about 1.25 to 1.5 million died at Auschwitz alone.

Ruth Minsky Sender was born Riva Minska on May 3, 1926, in Lódz, Poland. She came from a tightly knit family, headed by a strong, loving, and deeply devoted mother. While living out the nightmare of the Holocaust in the Lódz ghetto, at Auschwitz, and later at German work camps, Sender never forgot her mother's words of inspiration: "As long as there is life, there is hope."

Sender's wartime memoir, *The Cage*, is so-named because of the Nazi practice of housing Jews behind barbed-wire fencing. *The Cage* recounts the author's memories of the Holocaust, and is filled with a host of characters. Riva Minska is the author; Motele and Moishele are her brothers; Mrs. Boruchowich is the mother of Sender's friends Laibish and Rifkele; Mrs. Mikita is the mother of Sender's friends Karola and Berl; and Tola is another friend of Sender's.

Excerpt from *The Cage*

The railroad station is packed with people. Bundles, sacks, cartons, neatly tied packages all around us. A whole city is leaving on a mass pilgrimage. "Where to? Where are we all going? What is the name of the place? Does anyone know?"

"Please stay together," Motele urges us. "Let's not lose one another in this crowd."

"Children, my dear children, hold on to one another," pleads Mrs. Boruchowich. "We must stay together, children. We must."

On the tracks, freight trains are waiting. They are cattle cars.

"Why cattle cars?" someone asks, full of panic. "We will suffocate in there from the heat. It is mid-August. The heat will kill us."

"What did you expect?" I hear another voice. "You thought they would send us first class?"

"To them we are animals," one voice cuts in sarcastically. "Besides, they want to make sure that these animals cannot escape. They need our hands to make them uniforms. They need our skilled labor...."

"Keep still! Keep quiet! Do not push! You will all get into the wagons! We have plenty of trains for you!" call the guards.

I look around me, search for familiar faces. We wave good-bye to people we know. They wave back. Eyes meet, petrified, aghast.

"What choice do we have? What can we do other than go into the cattle cars? We have no way out, no choice."

People all around me, desperately trying to find an answer. Clinging to tiny sparks of hope. Optimistically spreading rumors: "They stopped the deportation. The Russian front is too close. They are sending us back home. They need us. They will not hurt us as long as they need our labor."

But the trains keep filling up with people. Each wagon is locked. One train pulls away, and another pulls up, ready to be loaded. We wait our turn, holding on to one another.

"Next. Hurry up! Get your bundles! Move! Move! Get into the wagons! You there, hurry, you stupid Jews."

They are calling our group. Panic seizes me. This is it. We are going into the cattle cars for a journey to the unknown. The guards are getting very impatient. They are already bored with the game of loading Jews into the wagons. They are angrier and louder now: "Jew, make it faster!"

Laibish is helping his mother up into the wagon. She slips. He pulls her quickly into the wagon before the whip of the angry Nazi can touch her body. "You cursed old Jew," the Nazi guard shouts, swinging his whip in all directions.

We move fast, trying to duck the whip. So many families are being separated. We must try to stay together. We must try. We are at the end of the line. The train is almost full.

Whatever happens, please let us stay together, I pray silently. Just let us be together.

Someone reaches out to help me up into the cattle car. Motele and Moishele are behind me, lifting me up. They jump in after me.

"Are we all here?" I call out to Laibish.

"Yes. Yes. We all made it into the same wagon. There is Karola, Berl, Mrs. Mikita, my mother, and my sister." He points to the corner of the car. "Let's try to make our way toward them."

We squeeze through the crowded wagon. We sit down on the floor, worn out from the horrible ordeal but relieved to be all together again. We can hardly move our arms. We are just like one big mass of tired

flesh, hot and steaming. The doors are about to close. I hear someone scream: "I am part of a family. Don't leave me behind!"

"Here, stay with your family!" I hear a sarcastic remark in German, and someone is pushed into the wagon. The doors close. We are all in total darkness. Some cry out hysterically; others pray aloud.

Slowly my eyes penetrate the darkness. From some cracks in the walls rays of light break through, throwing ghastly shadows on our terrified faces.

"Is this what a grave feels like?" someone wonders aloud.

"In a grave you have more room than this," a sobbing voice answers.

"We must have hope. We must not give up hope."…

I cannot see any faces. They are all covered in darkness. I see only shadows around me. But the voices are clear, painfully clear.

"So, where is God? Why does he not answer us? Have we not suffered enough? What is he waiting for?"

"You are sinning with that kind of talk. We must pray, pray."

"Maybe I have sinned, but what about my little children? What sins can little children commit? They were only babies. Why did they take them from us? Why did God allow this to happen?"

Bitter voices, angry, heartbroken, wailing.

We sit huddled together, listening to the voices around us. Mrs. Boruchowich puts her head on her daughter's lap, mumbling something to herself. Rifkele caresses her mother's head, whispering, "It's all right, Mama."

"Riva." Motele turns toward me, taking my hands in his. His voice sounds so strange. "Riva, they may separate us. They may separate the men from the women. Remember, if this happens, stay with Karola and Rifkele. You must look out for one another. You must be strong. We must live. We must survive. I'll take care of Moishele, I promise. Laibish, Berl, and I are the older boys. We'll keep Moishele between us so he'll look older than thirteen. We'll take care of Moishele. I promise you."

I pull them both close to me. We cry silently together.

Mrs. Boruchowich raises her head from her daughter's lap. "I will watch over my children. I will

A victim of a Nazi gas chamber still in the position in which he died. *(National Archives and Records Administration)*

Jewish women and children, carrying clothes and belongings, wait outside a train for deportation. (*Copyright Archive Photos, Inc. Reproduced by permission*)

watch over my children," she says with sudden determination. "Don't worry, my children. Don't worry."

Moishele turns suddenly toward Rifkele. He puts his hand on Rifkele's shoulder. "Rifkele, please take care of my sister," he says. "You are the oldest of the girls here. You are their big sister. Riva is not very strong. She always had us to watch over her. We are leaving her in your hands. Please, look after her."

"I will, Moishele. I will," she whispers softly.

Days turn to nights and nights into days again. The cracks in the walls let in some rays of sunlight to tell us it is a new day. The rays of moonlight coming through the cracks let us know it is night again. We doze, resting our heads on one another's shoulders, awaken startled by nightmares to find that the nightmares are real.

The stench of human secretion mixed with the sweltering heat makes it hard to breathe. The buckets used as toilets are overflowing. People faint from the smell, from the heat, from exhaustion. The trains stop several times, but no doors are opened.

"How much longer? How much more can we endure?"

"Hold on. Do not give up. We will survive." Voices of strangers, trying to comfort one another. Searching for the courage to stay alive.

It has been three long, horrible days and three terrifying nights. "Where are we going? Where are we going?"

The train stops. The doors finally open. The sudden sunlight is blinding, but our ears are filled with music. Music all around us.

"Where are we? What is this place?"

"Welcome to Auschwitz, Jews." A German voice comes through the loudspeaker. "Welcome to Auschwitz, Jews."

The living crawl out. The dead are pulled out.

"Men to the right! Women to the left! Quickly! Quickly!" The guards push us with their rifles. "Faster! Move! Faster! Move! Left! Right! Left! Right!"

Everything is happening so fast, like in a horrible dream. The people behind me are pushing me forward toward the women's group, but where is

When the American 82nd Airborne Division liberated the Woebbelin concentration camp, they found corpses in the facility's latrines. *(National Archives/USHMM Photo Archives)*

Moishele? Where is Motele? They were near me only a moment ago.

"Moishele! Motele!" I cry out hysterically. "Where are you? Don't leave me. Let's stay together. Don't leave me alone. Motele! Moishele! Motele! Moishele!"

They are lost in the crowd of dazed people. I cannot see them anymore. I keep on calling, "Where are you, my brothers? Where are you, my children? Don't leave me alone. Motele! Moishele!"

I hear names being called out all around me. Children calling their mothers. Mothers calling their children. Husbands calling to wives their last good-byes. And above it all the German commands: "Left! Right! Left! Right!"

A man in a Nazi uniform is pointing with a white baton toward Mrs. Boruchowich. She is pulled out from our group and to the left of us, where a group of older women and mothers with small children are gathered. Her daughter follows her and is

Rows of dead inmates fill the yard of a concentration camp. The bodies of hastily executed victims were left in piles when German troops fled the approaching Allies. (*Photograph by Myers. Reproduced by permission of Corbis.*)

kicked back by a Nazi guard toward our group. I grab Rifkele before she can fall and get trampled by the moving crowd. I hear Mrs. Boruchowich's cries as she, too, disappears from my sight.

"Faster! Faster! Left! Right! Faster! Faster!" I am being carried forward.

"I think I saw my brother, Berl, with Motele and Moishele. They marched by with a group of men." I hear Karola's voice behind me. "They will try to stay together. We must also try to stay together."

Karola is holding her mother's arm. Then we hear "Left!"—and her mother is pulled away from

her. "Hold on, my child. Don't lose your courage. Hold on, my child!" And she, too, is gone.

From all sides I hear people calling: "You must not lose hope! You must not lose hope!"

"You must live!" a woman calls to her daughter as she is pulled toward the group on the left.

My eyes are blurred from burning tears. My head is spinning. And through it all come the voices of strangers calling, commanding: "You must live! You must hope!"

I hope that it is all a horrible nightmare. I'll wake up soon. The nightmare will be gone. My

When Allied troops liberated the camps, they often found few survivors. This four-year-old Polish boy miraculously survived the experience. The boy's father had concealed him in a large sack in order to get the child past the selection process. The Nazis let him live even after he was discovered, although most children his age were not as fortunate. (*National Archives/USHMM Photo Archives*)

brothers will stand beside me. We will be in a free world.

But the nightmare continues. We are pushed forward toward the unknown by whips whistling in the air, their sharp blows landing on the heads and shoulders of the women. Outcries of pain echo all around us.

Karola, Rifkele, and I try desperately to hold on to one another. We are pushed into a long barrack and ordered to undress: "Drop all your clothes and put them in neat piles! Leave all your belongings! Remove your eyeglasses and leave them here! Move forward! Move!"

I move like a zombie. I remove my eyeglasses, which I have worn for the last few years, and feel as if I am suddenly blind, left all alone in the darkness. I am pushed forward, forward.

My head is shaven by a woman in striped prison clothes. "This is to keep the lice out of your hair," she says sarcastically, while cutting into my long, brown

hair with her shaver. I stare at her without really seeing her.

There are mountains of hair all around us: blond, brown, black. Piles of shoes, clothing, eyeglasses surround us, each pile growing bigger and bigger with each passing row of new arrivals.

"Quickly! Quickly! Forward to the showers! Move!" We are pushed into a large room filled with showers. Suddenly the water from the shower head comes at me in full force. The cold spray helps to bring me out of the stupor I have been in. I look at my friends, at their shaven heads, at their horror-filled eyes.

I grab Karola's hand. "Karola, is that you?" I whisper. We stare at each other for a long moment.

"Is that you, Riva? Is that you?" She gasps, transfixed by the sight of my shaven head.

"Out! Out! Quickly! Out!" We are herded outside. The sound of the whip makes us move as fast as

The USHMM
Reports on Genocide

The Holocaust, which literally means "destruction by fire," is commemorated in the United States Holocaust Memorial Museum (USHMM). This museum was established in Washington, D.C., as a testament to Holocaust history and as a memorial to its millions of victims. The USHMM reports that the "stated intention [of the United States and Great Britain] to defeat Germany militarily took precedence over rescue efforts" even after reports of the Nazis' "Final Solution" had been confirmed in 1942. "No specific attempts to stop or slow the genocide were made until [1944, when] mounting pressure eventually forced the United States to undertake limited rescue efforts."

"March into the barrack! Quickly!"

We walk hurriedly into the huge barrack. It is filled with triple-decker bunks. On most decks lie five shriveled bodies with hungry, horror-stricken eyes. Some bunks are not filled yet.

"Where are you from?" parched lips whisper. "Are there still Jews alive outside this hell? Did you see the smoke? Did you see the chimneys? Do you feel the Angel of Death touching you? Can you smell the burning flesh?"

Those eyes, those voices are so unreal, so ghastly. This has to be a nightmare.

"Leave them alone." The voices go on and on. "Leave them alone. They will know soon enough about the smoke, about the smell...."

Why doesn't the nightmare end? It cannot be true. I will not listen to them. I will not look at them. I cover my ears, but the voices are within me now. I am part of them now.

Rifkele grabs hold of a small, skinny woman in her late twenties wearing a dress that is much too big. She looks familiar to her. They stare at each other in disbelief. "Tola? Tola?" Rifkele cries out. "Is that you? I am Rifkele, Rifkele Boruchowich. My God, what did they do to you?"

Tola's eyes fill with tears. "Rifkele? Rifkele? The beautiful, elegant Rifkele without hair, wrapped in rags. This cannot be you."

They fall into each other's arms, sobbing: "What did they make of us? What did they do to us? Dear God, help us remain human. Help us."

"I lost my children, Rifkele," Tola says suddenly through her tears. "They took them from me. I lost them." She buries her head in Rifkele's chest, howling like a wounded animal.

Rikele hugs her close. "I'll stay with you, Tola. We'll stay with you, Riva, Karola, and I."

She is the only one in her bunk. We slide into her bunk and hold one another close. (Sender, pp. 139–155)

we can. We are pushed into the bright sunlight of the warm August air stark naked. With my arms I try to cover my nakedness. My cheeks are hot from embarrassment. I feel so degraded.

Someone is handing out one piece of clothing to each girl to cover our naked bodies. I receive a petticoat big enough to wrap myself in. I look at Rifkele next to me. She is tall, and the blouse she received hardly reaches to the end of her buttocks. I pull off my petticoat and hand it to Rifkele. "I am small, Rifkele. Take this. Your blouse will be big enough to cover me to the knees."

She takes off her blouse and puts it on me lovingly. With tears in her eyes she says, "We are not animals yet. We still have our pride."

Aftermath

Sender spent seven days at Auschwitz in 1944 before being transferred to Camp Mittelsteine and then, near the end of the war, to Camp Grafenort, both forced labor camps in Germany. Soviet soldiers liberated Grafenort on May 7, 1945. Late in 1944, the tide turned decisively against Germany's military forces. As Soviet troops approached Berlin from the east, the SS began to evacuate the concentration camps and death camps of Poland, leaving the bodies of hastily executed victims in heaps. In January 1945 prisoners of Auschwitz who were still able to walk were forced on a death march across the frozen countryside of Poland. Between 15,000-17,000 of the 58,000 marchers died before completing the westward trek to Germany.

Sender managed to survive the war. She married Morris Sender, himself a survivor of the Nazis' brutal reign, in 1945, moved to the United States in 1950, and became a naturalized U.S. citizen. The couple had four children of their own—children, Sender writes, of "the Jewish generation that was not to be, proud human beings, the new link in an old chain." Among Sender's other works are *To Life* (1988) and *The Holocaust Lady* (1992).

Sources

Books

Arad, Yitzhak, *The Pictorial History of the Holocaust,* Macmillan (New York), 1990.

Ayer, Eleanor H., *The United States Holocaust Memorial Museum: America Keeps the Memory Alive,* Dillon Press (New York), 1994.

Boas, Jacob, editor, *We Are Witnesses: Five Diaries of Teenagers Who Died in the Holocaust,* foreword by Patricia C. McKissack, Holt (New York), 1995.

Frank, Anne, *The Diary of a Young Girl,* Doubleday (New York), 1952.

Friedman, Ina, *Escape or Die: True Stories of Young People Who Survived the Holocaust,* Yellow Moon (Cambridge, MA), 1991.

Friedman, Ina, *Flying against the Wind,* Lodgepole Press (Brookline, MA), 1995.

Friedman, Ina, *The Other Victims: First Person Stories of Non-Jews Persecuted by the Nazis,* Houghton (New York), 1990.

Greenfield, Howard, *The Hidden Children,* Ticknor and Fields (New York), 1993.

Lengyel, Olga, *Five Chimneys: The Story of Auschwitz,* Howard Fertig (New York), 1983.

Niewyk, Donald L., *Fresh Wounds: Early Narratives of Holocaust Survival,* University of North Carolina Press (Chapel Hill), 1998.

Perl, Lila, and Marion Blumenthal Lazan, *Four Perfect Pebbles: A Holocaust Story,* Greenwillow (New York), 1996.

Rittner, Carol, and John K. Roth, editors, *Different Voices: Women and the Holocaust,* Paragon House (New York), 1993.

Sender, Ruth Minsky, *The Cage,* originally published in 1986, reprinted, Aladdin Paperbacks (New York), 1997.

Sender, Ruth Minsky, *To Life,* Macmillan (New York), 1988.

Something about the Author, Volume 62, Gale (Detroit), 1990.

Other

Auschwitz: If You Cried, You Died (video), Producers International Corporation, 1991.

A Cybrary of the Holocaust, http://www.remember. org/ (May 16, 2000).

"Genocide, 1941–1945," *World at War Series* (video), A&E Home Video, 1982.

MiamiLINK, http://www.lib.muohio.edu/inet/subj/ history/holoc.html (May 16, 2000).

Shoah (film), Parafrance, 1985.

Triumph of Memory (video), PBS Video, 1972.

United States Holocaust Memorial Museum, http:// www.ushmm.org/ (August 17, 2000).

Witness to the Holocaust (video), National Jewish Resource Center, 1983–1984.

Primo Levi
Excerpt from *Survival in Auschwitz: The Nazi Assault on Humanity*
Translated by Stuart Woolf

First published in 1947; reprinted in 1958

To succeed in conducting their plan for the annihilation of European Jews, German Nazis built a series of camps expressly designed for mass murder. The *Endlösung,* or "Final Solution," to the "Jewish question" required transporting millions of European Jews by train to death camps located in German-occupied Poland. The largest of these camps, Auschwitz-Birkenau, was situated thirty miles west of Kraków, Poland, near the border of Czechoslovakia. Auschwitz first opened in 1940 as a concentration camp, where prisoners were tortured and used as a source of labor for the war effort. The inscription over the main gate of the camp read *"Arbeit macht frei,"* or "Work makes you free." A year later, the Nazis added a larger section called Birkenau, which eventually housed gas chambers and crematoria used in the killing operations.

Most people who arrived at Auschwitz-Birkenau did not survive. As trains pulled up to the railway platform at the camp, the people inside the boxcars were quickly forced to form two lines. Officers of the SS organized the selection process to determine which prisoners would go immediately to the gas chambers and which would be assigned to forced labor. Only about 10 percent of the most able-bodied people were selected for work. These men and women were required to have their heads shaved and to trade in their personal belongings and clothes for striped prison uniforms. They were then tattooed with a registration number and sent to "quarantine" to await work assignment. Selection into the labor force usually only postponed death. Prisoners faced a daily struggle for survival against starvation, contagious diseases, exposure, and the violence of guards. If an inmate escaped from a work site, the remaining laborers often faced execution.

Prisoners who were destined for the gas chamber faced a much more immediate death. Women with small children, children under age fifteen, the elderly, and those who appeared ill or disabled were usually killed the same day they arrived. Believing that they were going to be disinfected for lice, the prisoners entered what looked like large shower rooms. In fact, the shower rooms were specially equipped gas chambers designed to kill thousands of people a day. Poisonous gas released into the air-tight rooms killed victims within fifteen to thirty minutes. Prisoners assigned to a work crew known as the Sonderkommando were given the task of loading bodies from the gas chambers into the crematoria. The corpses of victims were burned either in crematoria or on wooden pyres. Historians generally estimate that between 1.25 to 1.5 million prisoners, mostly Jews, died at Auschwitz-Birkenau. Some scholars believe the number was even higher. When the Soviet army liberated the camp in late January 1945, they found more than 7,000 prisoners alive and warehouses crammed with property stolen from the victims. The storage buildings contained 350,000 men's suits, 837,000 outfits for women, and 7.7 tons of human hair packed in paper bags for shipping.

Before World War II, about 57,000 Jews lived in Italy—more than 10,000 of them were refugees from Germany and Austria. After the German occupation of Italy began in September 1943, thousands of Jews were sent to Italian prisons and concentration camps. More than 8,000 Italian Jews were deported to extermination camps. Among them was Primo Levi, whose ancestors had settled in the Piedmont region of Italy in 1500. Levi had been born in Turin in 1919, and he was a chemistry student when anti-Jewish laws were introduced in 1938. He completed his doctorate in 1943. When Germany took over northern Italy, Levi joined the antifascist resistance, but after being arrested by a fascist militia in December 1943, he was deported to Auschwitz in February 1944. In the following excerpt from *Survival in Auschwitz: The Nazi Assault on Humanity,* Levi describes some of his experiences in the camp.

Survival in Auschwitz:
The Nazi Assault on Humanity

Haftling [prisoner]: I have learnt that I am Haftling. My number is 174517; we have been baptized, we will carry the tattoo on our left arm until we die.

The operation was slightly painful and extraordinarily rapid: they placed us all in a row, and one by one, according to the alphabetical order of our names, we filed past a skilful [skillful] official, armed with a sort of pointed tool with a very short needle. It seems that this is the real, true initiation: only by 'showing one's number' can one get bread and soup. Several days passed, and not a few cuffs and punches, before we became used to showing our number promptly enough not to disorder the daily operation of food-distribution: weeks and months were needed to learn its sound in the German language. And for many days, while the habits of freedom still led me to look for the time on my wristwatch, my new name ironically appeared instead, a number tattooed in bluish characters under the skin.

Only much later, and slowly, a few of us learnt something of the funereal science of the numbers of Auschwitz, which epitomize the stages of destruction of European Judaism. To the old hands of the camp, the numbers told everything: the period of entry into the camp, the convoy of which one formed a part, and consequently the nationality. Everyone will treat with respect the numbers from 30,000 to 80,000: there are only a few hundred left and they represented the few survivals from the Polish ghettos. It is as well to watch out in commercial dealings with a 116,000 or a 117,000: they now number only about forty, but they represent the Greeks of Salonica, so take care they do not pull the wool over your eyes. As for the high numbers they carry an essentially comic air about them, like the words 'freshman' or 'conscript' in ordinary life. The typical high number is a corpulent, docile and stupid fellow: he can be convinced that leather shoes are distributed at the infirmary to all those with delicate feet, and can be persuaded to run there and leave his bowl of soup 'in your custody'; you can sell him a spoon for three rations of bread; you can send him to the most ferocious of the Kapos to ask him (as happened to me!) if it is true that his is the Kartoffelschalenkommando, the 'Potato Peeling Command,' and if one can be enrolled in it.

In fact, the whole process of introduction to what was for us a new order took place in a grotesque and sarcastic manner. When the tattooing operation was finished, they shut us in a vacant hut. The bunks are made, but we are severely forbidden to touch or sit on them: so we wander around aimlessly for half the day in the limited space available, still tormented by the parching thirst of the journey. Then the door opens and a boy in a striped suit comes in, with a fairly civilized air, small, thin and blond. He speaks French and we throng around him with a flood of questions which till now we had asked each other in vain.

But he does not speak willingly; no one here speaks willingly. We are new, we have nothing and we know nothing; why waste time on us? He reluctantly explains to us that all the others are out at work and will come back in the evening. He has come out of the infirmary this morning and is exempt from work for today. I asked him (with an ingenuousness that only a few days later already seemed incredible to me) if at least they would give us back our toothbrushes. He did not laugh, but with his face animated by fierce contempt, he threw at me 'Vous n'êtes pas à la maison.' And it is this refrain that we hear repeated by everyone: you are not at home, this is not a sanatorium, the only exit is by way of the Chimney. (What did it mean? Soon we were all to learn what it meant.)

And it was in fact so. Driven by thirst, I eyed a fine icicle outside the window, within hand's reach. I opened the window and broke off the icicle but at once a large, heavy guard prowling outside brutally snatched it away from me. 'Warum?' [Why?] I asked him in my poor German. 'Hier ist kein warum' (there is no why here), he replied, pushing me inside with a shove.

The explanation is repugnant but simple: in this place everything is forbidden, not for hidden reasons, but because the camp has been created for that purpose. If one wants to live one must learn this quickly and well:

'No Sacred Face will help thee here! It's not a Serchio [a river flowing from the Tuscany region of Italy to the Mediterranean Sea] bathing-party ...'

Hour after hour, this first long day of limbo draws to its end. While the sun sets in a tumult of

A pile of artificial limbs taken from prisoners killed in the Auschwitz gas chambers. *(State Museum of Auschwitz-Birkenau/USHMM Photo Archives)*

fierce, blood-red clouds, they finally make us come out of the hut. Will they give us something to drink? No, they place us in line again, they lead us to a huge square which takes up the centre [center] of the camp and they arrange us meticulously in squads. Then nothing happens for another hour: it seems that we are waiting for someone.

A band begins to play, next to the entrance of the camp: it plays <u>Rosamunda,</u> the well known sentimental song, and this seems so strange to us that we look sniggering at each other; we feel a shadow of

relief, perhaps all these ceremonies are nothing but a colossal farce in Teutonic taste. But the band, on finishing <u>Rosamunda,</u> continues to play other marches, one after the other, and suddenly the squads of our comrades appear, returning from work. They walk in columns of five with a strange, unnatural hard gait, like stiff puppets made of jointless bones; but they walk scrupulously in time to the band.

They also arrange themselves like us in the huge square, according to a precise order; when the last squad has returned, they count and recount us for

Under SS guard, Auschwitz-Birkenau prisoners unload the property of deported Jews. (*Yad Vashem Photo Archives/USHMM Photo Archives*)

over an hour. Long checks are made which all seem to go to a man dressed in stripes, who accounts for them to a group of SS men in full battle dress.

Finally (it is dark by now, but the camp is brightly lit by headlamps and reflectors) one hears the shout 'Absperre!' at which all the squads break up in a confused and turbulent movement. They no longer walk stiffly and erectly as before: each one drags himself along with obvious effort. I see that all of them carry in their hand or attached to their belt a steel bowl as large as a basin.

We new arrivals also wander among the crowd, searching for a voice, a friendly face or a guide. Against the wooden wall of a hut two boys are seated on the ground: they seem very young, sixteen years old at the outside, both with their face and hands dirty with soot. One of the two, as we are passing by, calls me and asks me in German some questions which I do not understand; then he asks where we come from. 'Italien,' I reply; I want to ask him many things, but my German vocabulary is very limited.

'Are you a Jew?' I asked him.

'Yes, a Polish Jew.'

'How long have you been in the Lager [camp]?'

'Three years,' and he lifts up three fingers. He must have been a child when he entered, I think with horror; on the other hand this means that at least some manage to live here.

'What is your work?'

'Schlosser,' he replies. I do not understand. 'Eisen, Feuer' (iron, fire), he insists, and makes a play with his hands of someone beating with a hammer on an anvil. So he is an ironsmith.

'Ich Chemiker,' [I am a chemist] I state; and he nods earnestly with his head, 'Chemiker gut.' But all this has to do with the distant future: what torments me at the moment is my thirst.

'Drink water. We no water,' I tell him.

He looks at me with a serious face, almost severe, and states clearly: 'Do not drink water, comrade,' and then other words that I do not understand.

'Warum?'

'Geschwollen,' he replies cryptically. I shake my head, I have not understood. 'Swollen,' he makes me understand, blowing out his cheeks and sketching with his hands a monstrous tumefaction of the face and belly. 'Warten bis heute Abend.' 'Wait until this evening,' I translate word by word.

Then he says: 'Ich Schlome. Du?' I tell him my name, and he asks me: 'Where [is] your mother?'

'In Italy.' Schlome is amazed: a Jew in Italy? 'Yes,' I explain as best I can, 'hidden, no one knows, run away, does not speak, no one sees her.' He has understood: he now gets up, approaches me and timidly embraces me. The adventure is over, and I feel filled with a serene sadness that is almost joy. I have never seen Schlome since, but I have not forgotten his serious and gentle face of a child, which welcomed me on the threshold of the house of the dead....

Such will be our life. Every day, according to the established rhythm, Ausrücken and Einrücken, go out and come in; work, sleep and eat; fall ill, get better or die....

And for how long? But the old ones laugh at this question: they recognize the new arrivals by this question. They laugh and they do not reply. For months and years, the problem of the remote future has grown pale to them and has lost all intensity in face of the far more urgent and concrete problem of the near future: how much one will eat today, if it will snow, if there will be coal to unload.

If we were logical, we would resign ourselves to the evidence that our fate is beyond knowledge, that every conjecture is arbitrary and demonstrably devoid of foundation. But men are rarely logical when their own fate is at stake; on every occasion, they prefer the extreme positions. According to our character, some of us are immediately convinced that all is lost, that one cannot live here, that the end is near and sure; others are convinced that however hard the present life may be, salvation is probable and not far off, and if we have faith and strength, we will see our houses and our dear ones again. The two classes of pessimists and optimists are not so clearly defined, however, not because there are many agnostics, but because the majority, without memory or coherence, drift between the two extremes according to the moment and the mood of the person they happen to meet.

Here I am, then, on the bottom. One learns quickly enough to wipe out the past and the future when one is forced to. A fortnight after my arrival I already had the prescribed hunger, that chronic hunger unknown to free men, which makes one dream at night, and settles in all the limbs of one's body. I have already learnt not to let myself be robbed, and in fact if I find a spoon lying around, a piece of string, a button which I can acquire without danger of punishment, I pocket them and consider them mine by full right. On the back of my feet I already have those numb sores that will not heal. I push wagons, I work with a shovel, I turn rotten in the rain, I shiver in the wind; already my own body is no longer mine: my belly is swollen, my limbs emaciated, my face is thick in the morning, hollow in the evening; some of us have yellow skin, others grey. When we do not meet for a few days we hardly recognize each other.

We Italians had decided to meet every Sunday evening in a corner of the Lager, but we stopped it at once, because it was too sad to count our numbers and find fewer each time, and to see each other ever more deformed and more squalid. And it was so tiring to walk those few steps and then, meeting each other, to remember and to think. It was better not to think. (Levi, pp. 27–37)

Aftermath

During his ten months as a prisoner in Auschwitz, Levi was fortunate to be given a labor assignment as a chemist at a nearby rubber factory. He also received extra food from an Italian civilian who worked at the camp. Shortly before the Soviet liberation of Auschwitz in late January 1945, Levi fell ill and was placed in the infirmary. Hospitalization saved his life by preventing him from joining other prisoners on the mass camp evacuation or death march ordered by Nazi officials. Levi became one of the few who lived to tell the story of his experiences in the death camp. He attributes his survival to luck, as well as "entering the camp in good health and knowing German." Another element of Levi's fate involved fortunate timing—he arrived at Auschwitz in 1944, after the Germans decided to lengthen the average life span of prisoners in order to increase their labor supply. Due to the dates of his arrival and liberation, Levi was also spared a full winter season at Auschwitz.

After being liberated from Auschwitz, Levi traveled throughout Eastern Europe for nine months. He then returned to Turin to live the remainder of his life in the same apartment in which he had been born. There, he worked as an industrial chemist and raised a family. In an interview with author Philip Roth in 1986, Levi discussed his "rootedness," commenting that he had been away from Turin a total of only two years in his entire life. Haunted by his camp experiences, Levi wrote *Survival in Auschwitz* in 1947. In his next book, *The Reawakening*, Levi describes

the colorful adventures and warm encounters of his travels following liberation. For most of his life, he worked as a chemist and manager at a local paint factory while writing his books. Levi felt that working at the factory kept him "in touch with the world of real things." He retired in 1977, though, to devote all his time to writing. Without leaving behind any explanation, Levi committed suicide in 1987.

SOURCES

Books

Levi, Primo, *Survival in Auschwitz: The Nazi Assault on Humanity,* translated by Stuart Woolf, Simon and Schuster (New York), 1996.

Sender, Ruth Minsky, *The Cage,* Macmillan (New York), 1986.

PRIMARY SOURCE

Rudolph Höss
Excerpt from *Death Dealer:*
The Memoirs of the SS Kommandant at Auschwitz
Edited by Steven Paskuly
Translated by Andrew Pollinger

Nazi Germany was at the height of its power in 1941. The German army invaded the Soviet Union on June 22 and with lightning speed advanced closer and closer toward the capital city of Moscow. With the Soviet invasion, the Nazis succeeded in occupying or dominating almost the entire European continent. In preparing for the Soviet invasion, German leader Adolf Hitler ordered the mobile killing units known as the Einsatzgruppen, or Special Action Squads, to perform "special tasks," which consisted of killing Jews found in the conquered territory. No longer content with forced emigration and imprisonment of Jews, with these actions, the Nazis initiated a systematic plan to murder every European Jew, in the *Endlösung,* or the "Final Solution," to the "Jewish question."

Four separate Einsatzgruppen, ranging in size from 800 to 1,200 men each, accompanied the

German army into Soviet territory and easily carried out their tasks. The roving squads of killers acted swiftly as they raided towns and cities throughout the Nazi-occupied Soviet Union. They ordered Jews to assemble in a central area for the purpose of "resettlement." Once gathered, the Jews were forced to surrender their valuables and remove their outer clothing, which would be sent back and used in Germany. Members of the Einsatzgruppen would then march the men, women, and children to a remote location for execution. Nazis lined their victims up in front of antitank ditches, ravines, or newly dug mass graves and shot them to death one by one. In the small town of Ejszyski, in what is now Lithuania, the Einsatzgruppen killed nearly 4,000 Jews over two days. At Babi Yar, near the city of Kiev, 33,000 Jews were killed in only two days of shooting. By the time the Germans began their retreat from Soviet territory in 1943, the Einsatzgruppen had killed more than 1 million Jews and hundreds of thousands of other Soviet nationals, including Communist party leaders and Roma (Gypsies).

Killing by gunfire, however, placed an enormous psychological burden on the members of the Einsatzgruppen. The men complained of mental anguish caused by having to shoot women, children, and ill people. In August 1941 Nazi leaders ordered the development of alternative methods for mass execution. By fall, they began to use specially equipped trucks, piping poisonous exhaust fumes into airtight sections of the trucks where the victims were held. All four squads involved in the Soviet initiative operated these mobile killing vans. However, carbon monoxide poisoning was difficult at times as the victims might die at different rates from one another. On occasion not all prisoners would be killed, so the poisoning would have to continue until all were dead. Such poisoning was also costly because of the fuel needed to create the fumes. Since gas was needed for the war, the Nazis looked for more efficient methods of killing.

Heinrich Himmler, head of the SS and overseer of the Nazi concentration camp system, visited the notorious camp of Auschwitz in 1941. He ordered its commandant, Rudolph (more commonly known as Rudolf) Höss, to add a much larger section to the existing concentration camp. The new section, known as Auschwitz II or Birkenau, was to be set up for the extermination of masses of people. The first gassing experiment using the poison known as Zyklon B took place in Auschwitz on September 3, 1941, with the initial victims being 600 Soviet prisoners of war and 250 hospital patients.

While awaiting trial and then execution after the war, Höss wrote a detailed account of all aspects of death camp operations, including the gas chambers. The following excerpt is from *Death Dealer: The Memoirs of the SS Kommandant at Auschwitz*, a complete edition of his memoirs and other Nazi documents. In the excerpt, Höss describes the first experiments using Zyklon B, and also reports on the routine gassings at Auschwitz, which became the largest death camp where Jews were exterminated. The success of the experiments pleased Höss, who was relieved not to resort to firing squads. By his own admission, execution by shooting made him squeamish. He preferred the relative efficiency of gas chambers and the use of nearby crematoria to burn the bodies. Höss's manuscript reflects his views after the war, when the executions had stopped: The excerpt should be read with the understanding that he did not know if expressions of compassion would reduce his sentence.

Death Dealer:
The Memoirs of the SS Kommandant at Auschwitz

Before the mass destruction of the Jews began, all the Russian politruks [members of the Communist party] and political commissars [officials of the Communist party] were killed in almost every camp during 1941 and 1942. According to the secret order given by Hitler, the Einsatzgruppen searched for and picked up the Russian politruks and commissars from all the POW camps. They transferred all they found to the nearest concentration camp for liquidation. The reason for this action was given as follows: the Russians were murdering any German soldier who was a member of the Nazi Party, especially SS members. Also, the political section of the Red Army [military forces of communist Russia] had a standing order to cause unrest in every way in any POW

camp or places where the POWs worked. If they were caught or imprisoned, they were instructed to perform acts of sabotage. This is why these political officials of the Red Army were sent to Auschwitz for liquidation. The first small transports were shot by firing squads of SS soldiers.

While I was on an official trip, my second in command, Camp Commander Fritzsch, experimented with gas for these killings. He used a gas called Cyclon B [Zyklon B], prussic acid, which was often used as an insecticide in the camp to exterminate lice and vermin. There was always a supply on hand. When I returned Fritzsch reported to me about how he had used the gas. We used it again to kill the next transport.

The gassing was carried out in the basement of Block 11. I viewed the killings wearing a gas mask for protection. Death occurred in the crammed-full cells immediately after the gas was thrown in. Only a brief choking outcry and it was all over. This first gassing of people did not really sink into my mind. Perhaps I was much too impressed by the whole procedure.

I remember well and was much more impressed by the gassing of nine hundred Russians which occurred soon afterwards in the old crematory because the use of Block 11 caused too many problems. While the unloading took place, several holes were simply punched from above through the earth and concrete ceiling of the mortuary. The Russians had to undress in the antechamber, then everyone calmly walked into the mortuary because they were told they were to be deloused in there. The entire transport fit exactly in the room. The doors were closed and the gas poured in through the openings in the roof. How long the process lasted, I don't know, but for quite some time sounds could be heard. As the gas was thrown in some of them yelled "Gas!" and a tremendous screaming and shoving started toward both doors, but the doors were able to withstand all the force. It was not until several hours later that the doors were opened and the room aired out. There for the first time I saw gassed bodies in mass. Even though I imagined death by gas to be much worse, I still was overcome by a sick feeling, a horror. I always imagined death by gas a terrible choking suffocation, but the bodies showed no signs of convulsions. The doctors explained to me that prussic acid paralyzes the lungs. The effect is so sudden and so powerful that symptoms of suffocation never appear as in cases of death by coal gas or by lack of oxygen.

At the time I really didn't waste any thoughts about the killing of the Russian POWs. It was ordered; I had to carry it out. But I must admit openly that the gassings had a calming effect on me, since in the near future the mass annihilation of the Jews was to begin. Up to this point it was not clear to me, nor to Eichmann [the SS officer responsible for organizing deportations of Jews to death camps], how the killing of the expected masses was to be done. Perhaps by gas? But how, and what kind of gas? Now we had discovered the gas and the procedure. I was always horrified of death by firing squads, especially when I thought of the huge numbers of women and children who would have to be killed. I had enough of hostage executions, and the mass killings by firing squad ordered by Himmler [senior leader of the SS] and Heydrich [deputy head of the SS and director of the Einsatzgruppen].

Now I was at ease. We were all saved from these bloodbaths, and the victims would be spared until the last moment. That is what I worried about the most when I thought of Eichmann's accounts of the mowing down of the Jews with machine guns and pistols by the Einsatzgruppe. Horrible scenes were supposed to have occurred: people running away even after being shot, the killing of those who were only wounded, especially the women and children. Another thing on my mind was the many suicides among the ranks of the SS Special Action Squads who could no longer mentally endure wading in the bloodbath. Some of them went mad. Most ... members ... drank a great deal to help get through this horrible work....

In the spring of 1942 [January] the first transports of Jews arrived from Upper Silesia [a section of southwestern Poland bordering Germany]. All of them were to be exterminated. They were led from the ramp across the meadow, later named section B-II of Birkenau, to the farmhouse called Bunker I. [Camp Commander] Aumeier, Palitzsch, and a few other block leaders led them and spoke to them as one would in casual conversation, asking them about their occupations and their schooling in order to fool them. After arriving at the farmhouse they were told to undress. At first they went very quietly into the rooms where they were supposed to be disinfected. At that point some of them became suspicious and started talking about suffocation and extermination. Immediately a panic started. Those still standing outside were quickly driven into the chambers, and the doors were bolted shut. In the next transport those who were nervous or upset were identified and watched closely at all times. As soon as unrest was noticed these troublemakers were inconspicuously led behind the farmhouse and killed with a small-caliber pistol, which could not be heard by the others. The presence of the Sonderkommando [a group of prisoners assigned to assist in the loading and unloading of the gas chambers, crematoria, and burial pits] and their soothing behavior also helped calm the restless and suspicious. Some of the Sonderkommando even went with them into the rooms and stayed until the last moment to keep them calm while an SS soldier stood in the doorway. The most important thing, of course, was to maintain as much peace and quiet as possible during the process of arriving and undressing. If some did not want to undress, some of those already undressed as well as the Sonderkommando had to help undress them.

With quiet talk and persuasion even those who resisted were soothed and undressed. The Son-

An Allied soldier holds two handfuls of rings that were taken from concentration camp victims by the Nazis at Buchenwald. The box beneath contains more of the rings that were found in a cave near the camp. *(National Archives/USHMM Photo Archives)*

derkommando, which was composed of prisoners, took great pains that the process of undressing took place very quickly so that the victims had no time to think about what was happening. Actually the eager assistance of the Sonderkommando during the undressing and the procession into the gas chambers was very peculiar. Never did I see or ever hear even a syllable breathed to those who were going to be gassed as to what their fate was. On the contrary, they tried everything to fool them. Most of all, they tried to calm those who seemed to guess what was ahead. Even though they might not believe the SS soldiers, they would have complete trust in those of their own race. For this reason the Sonderkommando was always composed of Jews from the same country as those who were being sent to the gas chamber.

The new arrivals asked about life in the camp and most of them asked about their relatives and friends from earlier transports. It was interesting to see how the Sonderkommando lied to them and how they emphasized these lies with convincing words and gestures. Many women hid their babies under piles of clothing. Some of the Sonderkommando watched carefully for this and would talk and talk to the woman until they persuaded her to take her baby along. The women tried to hide the babies because they thought the disinfection process would harm

their infants. The little children cried mostly because of the unusual setting in which they were being undressed. But after their mothers or the Sonderkommando encouraged them, they calmed down and continued playing, teasing each other, clutching a toy as they went into the gas chamber.

I also watched how some women who suspected or knew what was happening, even with the fear of death all over their faces, still managed enough strength to play with their children and to talk to them lovingly. Once a woman with four children, all holding each other by the hand to help the smallest ones over the rough ground, passed by me very slowly. She stepped very close to me and whispered, pointing to her four children, "How can you murder these beautiful, darling children? Don't you have any heart?"…

Occasionally some women would suddenly start screaming in a terrible way while undressing. They pulled out their hair and acted as if they had gone crazy. Quickly they were led behind the farmhouse and killed by a bullet in the back of the neck from a small-caliber pistol. Sometimes, as the Sonderkommando were leaving the room, the women realized their fate and began hurling all kinds of curses at us. As the doors were being shut, I saw a woman trying to shove her children out of the chamber, crying out, "Why don't you at least let my precious children live?" There were many heartbreaking scenes like this....

In the spring of 1942 hundreds of people in the full bloom of life walked beneath the budding fruit trees of the farm into the gas chamber to their death, most of them without a hint of what was going to happen to them. To this day, I can still see these pictures of the arrivals, the selections, and the procession to their death.

As the selection process continued at the unloading ramps, there were an increasing number of incidences. Tearing apart families, separating the men from the women and children, caused great unrest.... Separating those who were able to work only increased the seriousness of the situation. No matter what, the families wanted to stay together. So it happened that even those selected to work ran back to the other members of their family, or the mothers with their children tried to get back to their husbands, or to the older children. Often there was such chaos and confusion that the selection process had to be started all over again. The limited amount of standing room did not permit better ways to separate them. There was no way to calm down these overly excited masses. Oftentimes order was restored by sheer force.

As I have said repeatedly, the Jews have a very strong sense of family. They cling to each other like leeches, but from what I observed, they lack a feeling of solidarity. In their situation you would assume that they would protect each other. But no, it was just the opposite. I heard about, and also experienced, Jews who gave the addresses of fellow Jews who were in hiding....

This incident I witnessed myself: As the bodies were being pulled out of one of the gas chambers, one member of the Sonderkommando suddenly stopped and stood for a moment as if thunderstruck. He then pulled the body along, helping his comrades. I asked the Kapo what was wrong with him. He found out that the startled Jew had discovered his wife among the bodies. I watched him for a while after this without noticing anything different about him. He just kept dragging his share of bodies. After a while I again happened on this work party. He was sitting with the others and eating as if nothing had happened. Was he really able to hide his feelings so completely, or had he become so hardened that something like this really didn't bother him?

Where did the Jews of the Sonderkommando get the strength to perform this horrible job day and night? Did they hope for some special luck that would save them from the jaws of death? Or had they become too hardened by all the horror, or too weak to commit suicide to escape their existence? I really have watched this closely, but could never get to the bottom of their behavior. The ways the Jews lived and died was a puzzle I could never solve.

I could relate countless more of these experiences and occurrences.... These are only excerpts from the total process of the annihilation. They are only glimpses.

The mass annihilation with all the accompanying circumstances did not fail to affect those who had to carry it out. They just did not watch what was happening. With very few exceptions all who performed this monstrous "work" had been ordered to this detail. All of us, including myself, were given enough to think about which left a deep impression. Many of the men often approached me during my inspection trips through the killing areas and poured out their depression and anxieties to me, hoping that I could give them some reassurance. During these conversations the question arose again and again, "Is what we have to do here necessary? Is it necessary that hundreds of thousands of women and children have to be annihilated?" And I, who countless times deep inside myself had asked the same question, had to put them off by reminding them that it was Hitler's order. I had to tell them that it was necessary to destroy all the Jews in order to forever free Germany and the future generations from our toughest enemy.

It goes without saying that the Hitler order was a firm fact for all of us, and also that it was the duty of the SS to carry it out. However, secret doubts tormented all of us. Under no circumstances could I reveal my secret doubts to anyone. I had to convince myself to be a rock when faced with the necessity of carrying out this horribly severe order, and I had to show this in every way, in order to force all those under me to hang on mentally and emotionally.

Everyone watched me. They all wanted to see what kind of impression this made on me, and how I reacted.... Everything I said was thoroughly discussed. I had to make a tremendous effort to pull myself together in order not to show, not even once, in all the excitement after an incident, or to allow my inner doubts and depressions to come out in the open. I had to appear cold and heartless during these events which tear the heart apart in anyone who had any kind of human feelings.... Coldly, I had to stand and watch as the mothers went into the gas chambers with their laughing or crying children.

On one occasion two little children were involved in a game they were playing and their mother just couldn't tear them away from it. Even the Jews of the Sonderkommando didn't want to pick up the children. I will never forget the pleading look on the face of the mother, who certainly knew what was happening. The people in the gas chamber were becoming restless. Everyone was looking at me. I had to act. I gave the sergeant in charge a wave, and he picked up the screaming, kicking children in his arms and brought them into the gas chamber along with the mother, who was weeping in the most heart-breaking fashion. Believe me, I felt like shrinking into the ground out of pity, but I was not allowed to show the slightest emotion.

Hour upon hour I had to witness all that happened. I had to watch day and night, whether it was the dragging and burning of the bodies, the teeth being ripped out, the cutting of the hair; I had to watch all this horror. For hours I had to stand in the horrible, haunting stench while the mass graves were dug open, and the bodies dragged out and burned. I also had to watch the process of death itself through

the peephole of the gas chamber because the doctors called my attention to it. I had to do all of this because I was the one to whom everyone looked, and because I had to show everybody that I was not only the one who gave the orders and issued the directives, but that I was also willing to be present at whatever task I ordered my men to perform....

I had to watch it all with cold indifference. Even minor incidents, which others probably would not have noticed or been affected by, stayed on my mind for a long time.

And yet, I really had no reason to complain about being bored at Auschwitz.

When something upset me very much and it was impossible for me to go home to my family, I would climb onto my horse and ride until I chased the horrible pictures away. I often went into the horse stables during the night, and there found peace among my darlings.

Often at home my mind would suddenly recall some incident at the killing sites. That's when I had to get out because I couldn't stand being in the loving surroundings of my family.... (Höss, pp. 155–163)

Aftermath

Höss served as commandant of Auschwitz from 1940 until late 1943, when he was appointed chief of the SS Economic and Administrative Main Office. He was sent back to Auschwitz in June 1944 on a temporary assignment to manage the extermination of the Jews of Hungary. Senior SS leaders relied on Höss, a perfectionist and loyal bureaucrat, to accomplish the difficult task of murdering 430,000 Hungarian Jews brought to Auschwitz over the course of fifty-six days. The operation was named in his honor—Aktion (Operation) Höss. During his tenure at Auschwitz, Höss was responsible for liquidating some 1.25 to 1.5 million people, most of them Jews. Thousands of non-Jews were also victims of Auschwitz, including 15,000-16,500 Roma from Germany and Austria and 16,000 Soviet prisoners of war. For his "outstanding" service in carrying out his duties at Auschwitz, Höss received praise from his superiors. An SS report in 1944 commended him for his accomplishments as "a true pioneer in this area because of his new ideas and educational methods."

When Germany fell in 1945, Höss took an assumed name, Franz Lang. (His father's first name was Franz.) After being released from a prisoner of war collection point, Höss managed to find work in agriculture. He was recognized and arrested in March 1946 near Flensburg in what was then West Germany. Two months later, he was extradited to Poland. While awaiting trial (and, subsequently, execution), Höss wrote his autobiography and a series of profiles of SS commanders. In March 1947 the supreme court in Warsaw, Poland, sentenced him to death. He felt hanging was somehow shameful and instead requested execution by firing squad, but the Polish tribunal declined his request. On April 16, 1947, Höss was taken to Auschwitz and hanged on gallows placed within yards of the first gas chamber.

SOURCES

Books

Höss, Rudolph, *Death Dealer: The Memoirs of the SS Kommandant at Auschwitz,* edited by Steven Paskuly, translated by Andrew Pollinger, Da Capo Press (New York), 1996.

Korschunow, Irina, *Night in Distant Motion: A Novel,* translated by Leigh Hafrey, David R. Godine (Boston), 1983.

Sender, Ruth Minsky, *The Cage,* Macmillan (New York), 1986.

Life and Death in Nazi-Occupied Denmark and the Netherlands

Jews in every country conquered by Germany during World War II became targets in the Nazi campaign to "cleanse" the population of Europe. In order to launch the *Endlösung,* or "Final Solution," however, the Nazis had to implement a different strategy in each region. For instance, the Jewish population in some countries, mainly those of eastern Europe, was already isolated from the non-Jewish majority. Especially in small towns, Jewish life centered on synagogues and religious study. Many eastern European Jews were further set apart from the main population by their clothing, jobs, and language (Yiddish). Conversely, in western Europe most Jews lived among non-Jews and participated in mainstream culture. Having become assimilated into the general population, this generation of Jews consisted of people generally less staunch in their religious ideals than their grandparents. They had married non-Jews much more often than did Jews in eastern Europe. In some European countries, such as Poland, Jews constituted a large minority, while in others, Italy and Denmark among them, Jews comprised only a small proportion of the population.

While it is true that European Jews faced widespread anti-Semitism, the intensity of the prejudice varied from country to country. Although the citizens of all German-occupied territories endured great suffering, some were treated with much more brutality than others, especially at the beginning of the war. In some hard-hit areas, the process of murdering Jews began earlier and resulted in far more victims. The Nazi party's deeply entrenched sense of racism also affected the treatment of both Jews and non-Jews. The Nazis believed that many eastern Europeans—such as the Russians—were greatly inferior to Germans. Therefore, the mass murder of Jews in Soviet areas began immediately, even though it often caused economic problems for the Germans. In contrast, western Europeans were treated less harshly by the Nazis, at least at first. For example, many historians believe that Denmark initially received special treatment because the Nazis thought of the Danes as "racial cousins."

The SS, the organization in charge of executing Nazi plans for the destruction of Jews, wanted to carry out racial-cleansing measures in every country under German occupation as soon as possible. Although the SS was gaining power within the German government, it still encountered obstacles. The German army did not want to have to fight against resistance groups throughout Europe, so believed it impractical to create a furor among the peoples of conquered countries. German officials were also afraid of disrupting the economy of these countries, as they wanted to use local resources for the benefit of Germany and the war effort. Nazi officials who quarreled with the SS over their plans to destroy the Jewish population

A group portrait of a Jewish resistance group in Poland in 1940. *(Government Press Office, Jerusalem/USHMM Photo Archives)*

were not trying to protect Jews—they simply had other priorities. Nevertheless, the bickering between government agencies usually led to a slowdown in actions against Jews.

The amount of power wielded by the SS in any given country was closely related to the strength of that country's government. In Poland and the conquered parts of the Soviet Union, the Nazis completely abolished the existing national governments and took direct control of all administrative activity. The SS was therefore strongest in these two countries. In other occupied countries, such as Denmark and France, however, the Germans allowed a government to remain in place. In other countries, the approach fell somewhere between the two extremes, with Germans officially eliminating the national government but allowing citizens to carry out the day-to-day administration of the country. The Germans had neither the time nor the manpower to run the local police, the courts, the railroads, or many other operations in each country they conquered. This gave governments and administrators some bargaining power

in occupied countries. German allies, such as Italy and Hungary, were also given considerable leeway in political and economic affairs because the Nazis needed the cooperation of their governments to keep their forces fighting alongside the German army. The Nazis also needed citizens in conquered countries to help kill Jews. It would have been difficult, for example, to provide enough German police forces to control a large country like France, so the Nazis sought the cooperation of the French police in rounding up Jews. In this way, the lives of the Jews themselves became bargaining chips. The government of an occupied country might agree to let the Nazis deport some or all of that country's Jews in return for Nazi cooperation on other issues or a government that was determined to protect Jews could refuse to cooperate in making arrests. Such actions were chancy, though, since occupied countries risked retaliatory action from the Nazis.

Bargaining and negotiating with the Germans changed as the war continued. At first, Germany appeared to be winning the war, and Nazi control of Europe seemed inevitable. Because of the Germans' massive military strength, both their allies and the countries they occupied had limited power to resist German demands. If necessary, the Nazis could simply wipe out a government and impose direct military rule over the land. The tide turned, however, when the Allied armies began to push the Germans back. The occupied countries acquired more bargaining power. Yet the Nazis were still determined to wipe out the Jews, even if Germany lost the war. In the final stages of World War II, the survival of the Jews became a question of time—every delay in the Nazi plan meant that more Jews would be alive when Germany was finally defeated. Still, hundreds of thousands of Jews died because the Nazis succeeded in deporting them only a few weeks, or even days, before the arrival of Allied troops.

The survival of millions of Jews, therefore, depended on factors beyond their control. Jews were more likely to survive in countries that maintained some independence from the Germans, and especially from the SS. Similarly, Jews had a greater chance for survival in countries whose government and people did not share the Nazis' intense anti-Semitism. Even geography was significant in the struggle. Some found safety by escaping to nearby countries not involved in the war, while others survived because Allied armies arrived on the scene before the Nazis could kill them.

The Danes Resist the Germans

When Germany invaded Denmark in 1940, the country had a population of only 4 million people, over half of whom resided in the capital city of Copenhagen. The rest, many of whom were fishermen, lived mostly in small towns and on farms (generally dairy farms). Consisting largely of islands, Denmark—at the closest point—is less than three miles across a strait from neighboring Sweden.

In 1940 there were about 6,500 Danish Jews who, like other Jews in western Europe, were more assimilated into society than the Jews of eastern Europe. Many were doctors, lawyers, and scientists, while others held government jobs or were involved in banking. Danish Jews also had one of the highest rates of intermarriage with non-Jews in the world. In addition to native Jews, there were about 1,500 Jewish refugees in Denmark, who had fled from Germany, Austria, and Czechoslovakia. (Austria and Czechoslovakia had recently been taken over by Germany.) Many thousands of Jews from all over Europe had passed through Denmark on their way to other countries since 1933, when

A Danish World War II Legend

The Danish view toward the Jews has been immortalized in a legend that grew out of the war era. According to the story, the Germans planned to order all Danish Jews to wear the six-pointed Star of David as a form of identification—an order they had enforced in other occupied countries. Learning of the plan, King Christian X, a non-Jew, is said to have put a Jewish star on his

uniform, wearing it on his daily horseback ride through the streets of Copenhagen. He was said to wear the star in defiance of the Nazis, showing his support to Jewish Danes.

(Reproduced by permission of © Hulton Getty/ Liaison Agency)

the movement to escape from the Nazis was in its infancy. The Danish government was willing to accept them temporarily, but, like most countries, was opposed to permitting large numbers of refugees to settle within its borders.

The small Danish army, faced with hopeless odds, offered almost no resistance to the invading Germans. As the occupation began relatively peacefully, the Germans maintained this noncombative atmosphere by allowing the Danish government to remain in office and to continue administering the country. The regular Danish police force carried on its normal functions, and the Germans did not dissolve the army and the navy. The Germans also agreed that they would not mistreat the Danish Jews. Nevertheless, the presence of German troops meant that Germany would have the final say on any important issue.

Some historians have concluded that the Nazis' relatively mild treatment of Denmark may have resulted from the party's racial philosophy, which

Jewish refugees are ferried out of Denmark aboard Danish fishing boats bound for Sweden. *(Frihedsmuseet/USHMM Photo Archives)*

tended to view Danes as fellow members of the Aryan race. Since Denmark was also the first western European country conquered by Germany, experts speculate that the Nazis wanted to use the nation as a model to show that being defeated by Germany was not as catastrophic as many might think. In addition, the lack of military resistance by the Danish armed forces and the comparatively few acts of sabotage at the beginning of the occupation probably influenced German policy in Denmark's favor. A peaceful and cooperative Denmark meant that large shipments of Danish butter and meat could be shipped to Germany. Besides, German generals did not want to commit combat troops to Denmark because they were needed elsewhere—in neighboring Norway, for instance, the German occupation was met with fierce and violent resistance from the beginning. Many of the German soldiers stationed in Denmark were men in their forties and fifties who had developed their own personal beliefs before the Nazis came to power. Few were enthusiastic Nazis. Many of these troops, including officers, were reluctant to attack or arrest Jews.

While the Danes did not resist the Germans at the beginning of the occupation, they also did not readily accept Nazi ideas and propaganda. The government had agreed to most German demands, even restrictions on the traditional Danish freedom of the press, but refused to pass anti-Jewish laws or to fire Jews from government jobs. Jewish students were not expelled from schools or universities, and Jews were permitted to hold religious services. According to Danish law, it was a crime to incite anti-Semitic acts, and this law remained in effect, even though it could not be enforced. The tiny minority of Danish Nazis were treated with contempt by most of their fellow countrymen. The Danish Nazi newspaper *The Fatherland* was called "*The Traitorland*" by anti-Nazi Danes.

Nazi policy changed drastically in late 1942, when Denmark was slated to become part of Germany. As top German officials in Denmark were replaced by tougher, more committed Nazis, the Danes retaliated with increasing acts of sabotage. A wave of strikes swept the country as workers

Theresienstadt

Theresienstadt (Terezin in the Czech language) was the only concentration camp the Nazis ever opened for inspection by outsiders. They set up a "model ghetto" there that differed significantly from other concentration camps. Inmates of this ghetto supposedly ran their own affairs as a self-governing Jewish community. Among the prisoners were well-known German Jewish artists, writers, and scientists, whose disappearance would have raised questions in foreign countries. The inmates organized several orchestras, a choir, and a library with 60,000 books. They also held religious services on a regular basis. The Nazis used Theresienstadt to try to convince the Danes and the rest of the world that conditions in the camps were humane.

Representatives of the International Red Cross were allowed to visit the camp, but just before the visit, the Nazis spruced up the place considerably, opening a school and kindergartens,

a coffeehouse and other stores, and a bank. They even planted flowers. They also reduced the overcrowding in the camp, but did so at a high cost to the inmates, some of whom were sent to Auschwitz to be killed. What Red Cross representatives saw at Theresienstadt was a deception. Apart from a well-known few, inmates were usually in Theresienstadt only temporarily. Most were quickly sent off to Auschwitz, where they were murdered.

The fact that the Jews arrested in Denmark remained in Theresienstadt shows that the pressure of the Danish government and of Danish public opinion may have had some effect on Nazi policy. Unlike the overwhelming majority of Jews who were sent to Theresienstadt, more than 85 percent of the Danish Jews survived.

---

protested German regulations. Declaring a state of martial law in August 1943, Germany sent troops into Copenhagen, then disarmed the Danish army and dissolved the government.

Their next step was to arrest and deport Danish Jews, with the direct approval of German leader Adolf Hitler. Mass arrests were scheduled for October 1, the second night of Rosh Hashanah, the Jewish New Year, when most Jews would be at home. Word of the Nazis' plan was leaked to the Danes by sympathetic Germans in the occupation administration, and the message was passed along to the Jewish community. One non-Jewish Dane, Jorgen Knudsen, found names in the phone book that he thought sounded Jewish. Driving around Copenhagen in the ambulance he drove for a living, he warned each person about the Germans' plans. He shuttled Jews who had nowhere else to go to the hospital, where they were temporarily hidden. Strangers approached Jews on the street and offered them the keys to their apartments for use as hiding places.

Thousands of other Danish Jews were concealed by their non-Jewish neighbors and friends and smuggled out of Copenhagen to smaller towns on the coast. These actions took place while the Germans continued to search for hidden Jews, although many of the German patrols seemed to look the other way. Refusing to cooperate in the search, the Danish police sometimes helped escort Jews to the coast, where they were ferried by fishing boats across the strait to non-occupied Sweden. The Swedish government announced that it would accept all Danish Jews. The small boats, crowded with refugees, sailed from various Danish towns, avoiding German navy patrols.

The evacuation of Jews from Copenhagen took three weeks. During this time, the university closed for a week so that the students could help in the operation. Many Danish organizations publicly protested the German action, and on Sunday, October 3, 1943, Danish ministers read a letter of protest in their churches. The letter stated that the persecution of the Jews was un-Christian and that the Danish church would obey the laws of God,

A photo of the center of Rotterdam, destroyed by German bombing in May 1940. The bombing of Rotterdam was a sign of things to come. *(Reproduced by permission of AP/Wide World Photos)*

not the laws of Germans. Nearly all Danes knew about the smuggling of Jews out of the country, and a large percentage participated in the effort. None are known to have helped the Germans. About 7,200 Jews, along with 700 of their non-Jewish relatives, were transported safely to Sweden.

The Germans succeeded in arresting between 400 and 500 Danish and foreign-born Jews. The Danish government protested these arrests and demanded assurances that the arrestees would be treated properly. Jews from Denmark were sent to the concentration camp at Theresienstadt, in what had been Czechoslovakia. A delegation of the Danish government was eventually allowed to inspect the camp's conditions. The property of Danish Jews, both those who had escaped to Sweden and those who had been arrested by the Nazis, was carefully preserved. Their homes were not seized, nor was their furniture stolen. Non-Jews removed the Torah scrolls from synagogues for safekeeping, and also sent food packages to the deported Jews. Unlike many others imprisoned at Theresienstadt, Danish Jews as a group were never sent to

Auschwitz to be killed. The death toll of Danish Jews at Theresienstadt was fifty-four, and one died at Auschwitz. Of the 8,000 Jews in Denmark on the day of the German invasion, fewer than 100 died at the hands of the Nazis: fifty-five did not survive deportation, about twenty died during the escape to Sweden, and about twenty others committed suicide rather than be captured by the Germans. No other country controlled by Germany saved so high a proportion of its Jewish population.

The Holocaust in the Netherlands

The people of the Netherlands were among those who made the greatest effort to save Jews, but it was also one of the countries in which the fewest Jews survived. Located northwest of Germany, the Netherlands (which literally means "lowlands") lies mostly below sea level; a network of dikes crisscrosses the land, holding back the waters of the North Sea. In English, the Netherlands is often called Holland (though Holland makes up only one section of the country), and the

A deportation point in Amsterdam, the Netherlands. By October 1942, British radio reported that Jews deported from western Europe were being gassed. *(Reproduced by permission of Bildarchiv Preussischer Kulturbesitz)*

people and the language are called Dutch. Although the Dutch language is closely related to German, the history of the Netherlands differs significantly from that of Germany.

At the outset of World War II, the Netherlands remained neutral, just as it had during World War I (1914–1918), declining to ally itself with either Great Britain and France or with Germany. As a democratic country, however, the Netherlands sympathized with Britain and France and opposed the Nazi dictatorship. Under the influence of Germany, a small Nazi party had been organized in the Netherlands, but it did not have great support. The anti-Semitism of the Dutch Nazis was new to the Netherlands and most Dutch people rejected it.

Jews had lived in the Netherlands for hundreds of years. Some had come from Spain and Portugal in the sixteenth and seventeenth centuries. Most Dutch people thought of Jews as fellow citizens, not as outsiders. The anti-Semitic laws passed in Germany and the harsh treatment of German Jews under Hitler's regime shocked most of the Dutch.

About 30,000 Jewish refugees, mainly from Germany, fled to the Netherlands to escape the Nazis, and by 1940, about 140,000 Jews were living in the Netherlands—about 1.6 percent of a total population of 9 million. About 75,000 Jews, more than half of all Jews in the Netherlands, lived in Amsterdam, which had a larger proportion of Jews than any other city in western Europe. Most Dutch Jews outside Amsterdam were relatively well-off, working in business and in professions like law, medicine, and education. This was also true for many who lived in Amsterdam, the world center of the diamond industry; Jews played an important role in the diamond trade as buyers, sellers, cutters, and polishers of the precious stones. Nonetheless, about 40,000 impoverished Jews lived in the old Jewish neighborhood and other areas near the harbor. Many of the men were sailors, longshoremen, and other dock workers in the port.

Although the Netherlands was politically neutral, Nazi Germany still considered it a prime target. In April 1940 Germany had invaded Denmark and Norway, which were also neutral. Then, without any warning, on the night of May 9-10, the Luftwaffe bombed military targets throughout the Netherlands. German paratroopers then seized bridges near the port of Rotterdam, and tanks and infantry rolled over the border. The Dutch army resisted, but the Germans threatened to bomb Dutch cities. Queen Wilhelmina and the Dutch government escaped to England, and the Netherlands began negotiating a surrender on May 14. While the terms of the surrender were being finalized, the Luftwaffe bombed Rotterdam, completely destroying the center of the city.

The German occupation of the Netherlands was harsher than in any other country in western Europe. The percentage of Jews who died at the hands of the Nazis was much higher in the Netherlands than in neighboring Belgium or France. Only in eastern Europe and in areas that became part of Germany itself did the Nazis succeed in killing a higher ratio of Jews than in the Netherlands. Some historians believe the high death toll stemmed from the basic German theory of race. The Nazis apparently thought of the Dutch as members of a German "tribe" that had been separated from the rest of Germany. The party's main goal in occupying the Netherlands was to "reclaim" the region as quickly as possible, and the immediate elimination of Jews was a prerequisite to this goal. The Nazis appointed Arthur Seyss-Inquart to run the Netherlands with absolute power. An Austrian Nazi, Seyss-Inquart had played an important part in Germany's takeover of Austria in 1938. He had also served for a few months as one of the top German officials in Poland, where Nazi plans to destroy the Jews were already far advanced. Seyss-Inquart immediately announced the exclusion of Jews from the terms of the Dutch surrender, which guaranteed certain civil rights to Dutch citizens. He said the Jews were an enemy with whom it was impossible to make peace.

Soon a series of official orders was levied against Dutch Jews: Jewish-owned businesses were taken over; Jewish government employees were "suspended" from their jobs; and Jewish professors were dismissed from universities. The latter action led to student protests and strikes at the universities in Delft and Leiden, which the Germans then closed. In January 1941 all Dutch citizens with at least one Jewish grandparent had to register with Nazi authorities. In February 1941 a crowd of Dutch Nazis marched into the Jewish section of Amsterdam and began to smash windows, set fire to synagogues, and beat Jews. Just as they did in eastern Europe, the Germans wanted to create the impression that the local population hated Jews as much as the Nazis did, and so they secretly helped organize supposedly spontaneous anti-Jewish riots. This plan failed in Amsterdam, however, when people in the Jewish neighborhood, including non-Jews, began fighting back and succeeded in driving the Dutch Nazis out of the area. The Nazis returned later the same day, only to face a well-prepared force of Jews, including many longshoremen and factory workers. Patrols armed with lead pipes guarded Jewish shops, and the Dutch Nazis were beaten back in a series of street battles. Many non-Jewish Dutch citizens also took part in these actions. Three battalions of German police, armed with automatic weapons and tanks, were sent to restore order in the city. Many Jews were injured, and the Germans sealed off the neighborhood by raising the bridges surrounding it. At this point, the Germans ordered the creation of the *Joodse Raad* (Jewish Council), made up of prominent Jews, whose job was to transmit German orders to the Jewish community. This was somewhat similar to the administrative structure in Poland, where the Nazis had established a *Judenrat* in each community.

A short time later, another violent incident occurred: German police were attacked with acid as they entered a Jewish shop in Amsterdam. In revenge, the Germans arrested more than 400 Jews off the streets of Amsterdam and sent them to a concentration camp in Germany. (Only one of them survived the war.) Led by the longshoremen, both Jewish and non-Jewish Dutch workers went on strike to protest this action. Public services, transportation, and large factories ceased their operations, virtually shutting down Amsterdam for three days. The strike spread to two nearby cities, leaving the Germans dangerously close to losing control of the country. They declared a state of martial law and sent large numbers of troops into the city to force people back to work. Strikers faced arrest and deportation to a German concentration camp, or even being shot on the spot. A heavy fine was imposed on the country as punishment for the strike. In the end, the Germans succeeded in quelling the protests. One factor in their success was that the *Joodse Raad* urged people to go back to work. The SS had threatened severe action against Dutch Jews if the strike continued, and the *Joodse Raad* thought cooperation with the Nazis would ensure its community's safety.

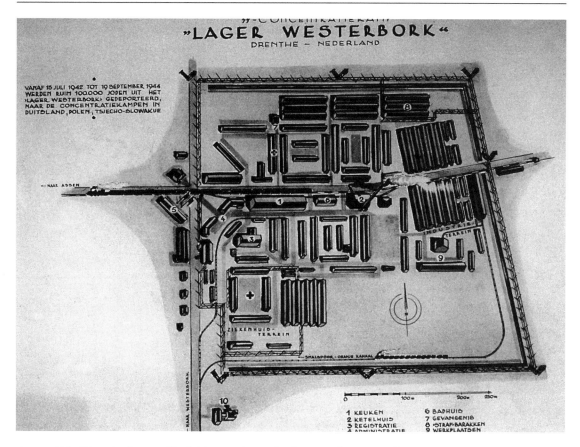

A map of the Westerbork camp. Until July 1942, Westerbork was a refugee camp for Jews who had moved illegally to the Netherlands. *(Toni Heller Collection/USHMM Photo Archives)*

Leading Dutch Jews who opposed the *Joodse Raad*'s policy formed the Jewish Coordinating Council, led by Lodewijk Visser, who had been the presiding judge on the Dutch Supreme Court until he was removed by the Nazis. Visser did not want the Jewish community to deal directly with the Nazis; instead, he contended that the Nazis should transmit their orders for Jews through the regular Dutch authorities, as they did for everyone else. To Visser and his supporters, the formation of a *Joodse Raad* was dangerous because it distinguished Jews from non-Jews.

Separating Jews from the rest of the population was, in fact, Nazi policy in the Netherlands as well as in the rest of German-occupied Europe. One method of achieving this was to require that all Jews wear a Star of David on their clothing at all times. This mandate took effect in the Netherlands in May 1942. Earlier, in summer 1941, other laws had been enacted to prohibit Jews from entering museums or movie theaters, or even walking on certain streets. They were not allowed outside at night, and they could shop only at certain times of

the day. Additional Nazi laws restricted where Jews could live and prevented them from working with non-Jews. Jewish children were not allowed to attend the same schools as their non-Jewish friends and neighbors, and Jewish students were expelled from Dutch preparatory schools in August 1941 and from the universities in 1942. All Jews who were Dutch citizens were ordered to move to Amsterdam by January 1942; non-citizens were supposed to be sent to a camp at Westerbork in the eastern part of the country. Westerbork became a transit camp for sending Jews from the Netherlands to the death camps of eastern Europe. All of these policies were designed to set the Jews apart from the rest of the Dutch citizenry.

The Nazis wanted non-Jews in German-occupied countries to feel that anti-Jewish policies had nothing to do with them, that they strictly related to a "Jewish problem." Convincing non-Jewish Europeans that Jews were not actually part of their nations was a strategy to create indifference and make non-Jews less committed to guarding Jewish interests. The February 1941 strike in Amsterdam

Dutch Jews arrive at the Westerbork camp. *(Trudi Gidan Collection/USHMM Photo Archives)*

was a rejection of this Nazi strategy. By striking to protest the harsh treatment of Jews, the Dutch communicated their belief that an attack on Dutch Jews was an attack on all Dutch people. Dutch workers had many other reasons to hate the Nazis, and the strike was not held solely to protest anti-Jewish actions. However, it produced an atmosphere of rebellion that led to increasing protests against the arrest and deportation of Jews. The strike was the largest single protest staged by non-Jews against the Nazis' anti-Jewish actions in occupied Europe.

Two schools of thought have developed on what might have happened had the *Joodse Raad* urged workers to continue the strike. Some experts theorize that a continuation of the strike would have resulted in a bloodbath. They contend that the Nazis would have killed hundreds of strikers, and Dutch Jews would have been hunted down even sooner. Also, the members of the *Joodse Raad* would have placed themselves in serious danger. Other historians argue that fear of constant reprisals from the Dutch might have caused the Nazis to slow the implementation of their anti-Jewish actions. Laws might have taken longer to enforce, which in turn would have delayed arrests, deportations, and deaths. This delay could have allowed more Jews to survive until the end of the war.

Although there were no other mass protests like the February strike in the Netherlands, the Dutch consistently expressed opposition to Nazi ideas about Jews and continued to resist separating Jews from the rest of the Dutch population. When the Nazis ordered Jews to wear the Star of David, many non-Jewish Dutch people also put the stars on their clothing. (In neighboring Belgium, thousands of non-Jews wore Jewish stars, sometimes in the colors of the Belgian flag.) Others wore a yellow flower on their clothes to show their support of the Jews. Illegal posters urged people to tip their hats in a show of respect when they passed Jews on the street. Protestant and Catholic churches urged Christians to refuse to cooperate with anti-Jewish orders. Eventually, about 20,000 non-Jewish Dutch people were sent to concentration camps for opposing the Nazis' anti-Semitism.

Then the Dutch began to learn about the death camps. Many able-bodied Jewish men, like many non-Jews, had already been sent to labor camps in the Dutch countryside to work for the Germans. At first, the Jews were treated like everyone else in the camps, but in June 1942 the Germans announced that all Jews would be sent to labor camps in Germany. Because the German order also included children, people became suspicious: Why

Inmates at forced labor hauling cartloads of earth at the Mauthausen concentration camp, where many Dutch opponents of the Nazis were sent. *(USHMM Photo Archives)*

A Jewish child (far right) poses with the Dutch family that adopted her. *(Henny Kalkstein Reemy Collection/USHMM Photo Archives)*

would small children be sent to a labor camp? Soon there were rumors that Jews were being sent to their deaths. By October 1942, the Dutch were hearing reports on British radio that Jews deported from western Europe were being gassed.

The Germans began a series of raids to round up Jews, but Dutch police would not cooperate. In fall 1942 German soldiers and Nazi party members, in addition to the police, were given the power to arrest Jews. Jews were seized in their homes late at night and taken to the transit camp at Westerbork. From there, sealed in cattle cars, they were sent by train to Poland to be killed. On October 2 all Jews in the Dutch labor camps were captured and sent to Westerbork. Between July 1942 and September 1944, trains left the Westerbork camp every Tuesday. The trains consisted of ten to fifteen cattle or freight cars, which held 1,000 or more prisoners, and two attached coach cars, in which the Nazi guards rode.

As soon as the arrests began, thousands of non-Jewish Dutch people tried to hide the Jews who refused to report for deportation. This was not easy in the Netherlands, which is a heavily populated country with few remote areas where people might be hidden without attracting attention. There are no mountains or large forests in the

Netherlands, and most Dutch houses did not have cellars because of the danger of flooding. In addition, the Netherlands did not border any neutral country, like Switzerland or Sweden, to which Jews might be smuggled. Ferrying Jews to safety meant a long and dangerous trip through Belgium and France, which were both occupied by Germany as well. Successful escapes involved crossing borders guarded by German patrols, either by sneaking across or by showing false identity papers to border officials. False papers were required to ride on trains, and escaping Jews needed food and safe places to sleep during the trip.

Joachim Simon, known as "Shushu," and his wife, Adina, organized one of the best-known escape routes for Dutch Jews. A German Jew in his early twenties, Simon had traveled to the Netherlands as a refugee in 1938. As the Germans began rounding up Dutch Jews, he managed to obtain false papers and gain entry into France. He then set up a series of contacts along the route to the Pyrenees Mountains, on the border between France and neutral Spain. Returning to the Netherlands, Simon then led three separate groups of Dutch Jews to safety in Spain. After completing his third successful mission, Simon was arrested crossing the Belgian-Dutch border. He was tortured by the Gestapo in an effort to make him reveal the names

The Amsterdam office building where Anne Frank and her family, German refugees from the Third Reich, hid from the Nazis from 1942 to 1944. *(Reproduced by permission of Bildarchiv Preussischer Kulturbesitz)*

of the people who had helped him. Eventually, he became afraid that he would not be strong enough to remain silent throughout the ordeal, and Simon took his own life by slashing his wrists.

One of the Dutch people who worked with Simon was Joop Westerweel, a high school principal in the town of Lundsrecht. Westerweel, who had four children, was not Jewish. In February 1943 he led a group through France to the Pyrenees. Like Simon, he returned to the Netherlands to continue his rescue missions. For more than a year, he hid Jews and ran a network that removed them to safety in Spain or Switzerland, sometimes reminding them not to forget their non-Jewish friends. In March 1944, Westerweel was captured and sent to a concentration camp. He was tortured for five months and finally executed.

Long journeys to Spain or Switzerland were extremely difficult to organize and implement. Trips occurred infrequently and could accommodate only small numbers of people. Because there was no real chance to escape, the majority of the Jews in the Netherlands had to hide until the war was over. In order to do this, they needed the help of many non-Jews who would provide a hiding place in their homes, bring food, and protect them when the Germans asked questions. Thousands of Dutch people came to the aid of Jews. An estimated 25,000 Jews, including about 4,500 children, were hidden in the Netherlands. Well-known diary author Anne Frank and her family were among them. About one-third of Jews hiding in the Netherlands were eventually caught by the Nazis. Even with many people working hard to provide hiding places, informers sometimes revealed hidden Jews to the Nazis.

Most Dutch Jews were unable to hide. Of the 140,000 Jews who had been in the country when the Germans invaded, 107,000 were deported. Around 60,000 (including Anne Frank and her family) were sent to Auschwitz—more than 1,000 survived. About 34,000 were sent to Sobibór, a death camp in eastern Poland (only 19 of these survived). In total, approximately 5,200 Dutch Jews survived deportation—only 4.8 percent of the Dutch Jews who had been deported. By the end of the war, three-quarters of the Jews in the Netherlands had died.

PRIMARY SOURCE

Kim Malthe-Bruun
Excerpt from *Heroic Heart: The Diary and Letters of Kim Malthe-Bruun, 1941-1945*
Edited by Vibeke Malthe-Bruun

Published in 1955

After invading Denmark in 1940, Germany officially declared that it had no intention of seizing any of the country's territory or suppressing its political independence. The country's democratic administration continued—King Christian X retained his sovereignty; the Danish parliament carried out its functions; and the Danish army, navy, and police remained intact. The German accord with Denmark also contained a provision that prohibited Germany from harming Jews living in the country. For the first few years of occupation, this clause remained in effect despite German pressure and the efforts of the small Danish Nazi party that tried to stir up anti-Semitism.

When Germany invaded Denmark, about 8,000 Jews lived in the country—less than 1 percent of the total population of Denmark. The actions taken by the Danish people and government, though, were unique among all European countries under Nazi rule: Nearly all Jews in Denmark survived the war. The situation for Jews in Denmark remained unchanged under German occupation—at first. No anti-Jewish measures were introduced, not even the typical provision requiring Jews to wear yellow badges in the shape of the Star of David. No Jewish property was confiscated, and no Jews were forced from government posts. In fact, the Germans did not even succeed in creating a legal distinction between native Danes of Jewish origin and Jewish refugees. By preventing preparatory measures designed to strip Jews of their rights, Danish leaders delayed the implementation of more drastic measures, such as the creation of ghettos and deportations to extermination camps.

In spring 1943, tensions began to increase between the two governments as Danish resistance operations gathered momentum. The growing strength of the Allied forces encouraged Danish citizens to organize strikes and acts of sabotage against the Germans. In August, a crisis erupted when government officials, including German-appointed Nazi leaders stationed in Denmark, objected to Germany's attempt to tighten its control over Denmark. German military forces entered the capital city of Copenhagen, disarmed the Danish army, imprisoned the king, and dissolved the government. The newly appointed German military leader, General von Hannecken, declared a state of emergency and imposed martial law.

No longer content with postponing the *Endlö-sung*, or the "Final Solution" to the "Jewish problem," the Nazis sent one of their ruthless anti-Semites, Rolf Gunther, to Copenhagen to organize the deportation of all Jews. Rather than send the Jews to concentration and extermination camps, the Germans consented to deport them to the Theresienstadt ghetto in Czechoslovakia. To assist with the deportation operation, Nazi officials arranged for the transfer of German transport vessels and Gestapo police units to Copenhagen. They scheduled the mass arrest and deportation of Jews to begin the night of October 1, 1943, Rosh Hashanah (the Jewish New Year). A few days before the planned seizure, news of the maneuver reached Georg Ferdinand Duckwitz, a German embassy official responsible for all shipping affairs in Copenhagen. Duckwitz decided to reveal his knowledge of the planned attack to local Danish Social Democrats who, in turn, told members of the Jewish clergy. Jewish rabbis warned their congregations, and many people spread the word throughout Copenhagen, where most Danish Jews resided. When the Gestapo raided Jewish residences over the course of several days, they found fewer than 500 people; the rest were safely hidden. Many of those arrested were elderly and apparently did not comprehend the significance of the warning.

Sweden's Immigration Policy

While Sweden remained neutral throughout the war, its immigration policies varied. The country kept a restrictive policy on Jews fleeing Nazi terror, but its citizens harbored some 20,000 Norwegian and Finnish children of Jewish descent. Sweden also formally offered to accept Danish Jews in September 1943.

At first, the Danes acted spontaneously to alert Jews and help them move into hiding. With the assistance of Danish fisherman, many Jews were smuggled across the narrow strait of water separating Denmark and Sweden, which remained neutral during the war. Soon, Danish partisans stepped in and helped organize the massive flight that occurred when the Swedish government publicly declared it was willing to take in all refugees from Denmark. A large-scale rescue operation began, involving many groups of Danish society. King Christian X formally objected to the German actions; church leaders published a strong protest and urged their followers to help the Jews; and universities closed for a week so students and professors could help with the rescue efforts. Over the course of three weeks, some 7,200 Jews were ferried to Sweden, where they remained in safety until the end of the war. Even though the Nazi-planned roundup was considered a failure, the Germans did manage to ship 472 captured Jews to Theresienstadt at the end of October 1943.

As a result of the successful rescue operation, the Danish resistance movement grew in size and strength. For the next two years, until the end of the war, partisans helped maintain a reliable escape route to Sweden. Although the Germans lifted the state of emergency in October 1943, Danish sabotage and resistance efforts intensified. General attacks swept across the country in response to the news of an assassination attempt on Adolf Hitler in July 1944.

Kim Malthe-Bruun was only twenty-one years old when he joined the Danish partisan underground in September 1944. He had spent the previous three years as a merchant seaman traveling throughout Europe. When he docked in various ports, he saw Nazi oppression and mistreatment of Jews firsthand. Like his fellow citizens, Malthe-Bruun was upset by what was going on around him and decided to try to help stop the persecution. His seafaring experience proved useful as he worked with others to transport armaments for resistance efforts.

In December 1944, Malthe-Bruun and several other partisans were arrested by the Gestapo. He spent four months in prison, being harassed and tortured by guards who tried to force him to confess. During his career as a seaman and throughout his captivity, Malthe-Bruun kept a diary and wrote letters to his mother; his girlfriend, Hanne; and his older cousin, Nitte. The portions of his writings that follow reflect the various stages of his life—from his observations while traveling through Germany to impressions of his first resistance activities in fall 1944. As he awaited his trial, Malthe-Bruun reviewed his life and the world events that affected him. In his writings he explains his simple beliefs about life, which remained unshaken in the face of death.

Heroic Heart: The Diary and Letters of Kim Malthe-Bruun, 1941-1945

LUBECK
7 March 1944

... Tonight I've been talking to an Austrian Saloon-keeper. He was burning up with hatred for the Germans. He put his face close to mine and the whites of his eyes showed as he gave vent to all his indignation. He trembled with rage and seemed for once to be able to let himself go. But it was quite a shock to see how humble he became when another guard passed by.

The town is covered with posters—all telling the same story. One depicts a railway station crowded with happy Germans, taken from above. Over the picture lies the heavy shadow of a man in a big coat, and underneath is printed in large letters: "The enemy is listening." Two of the posters preach economy, and I'll never be able to forget the last one. It shows an ugly face reflected in a hand mirror, looking very much like a rat and with a loathsome expression over his features. Almost in relief is an angular, semitic nose and the caption under the poster reads: "Look at yourself in the mirror. Are you a Jew or aren't you?" How rotten all of these people must be in order not to react violently to this. The Germans are like a ripe fruit that has been damaged and now the rottenness has come to the surface.

17 October 1944

How I long for a dash of cold salt water in my face and the sound of sails flapping in the wind, a bicycle ride on a black night, and to arrive at my destination and see a light shining from the top-floor window at Loendal! Now it's always: "Come over right away." "Can't you do this?" "That has to be done right away," etc. It's an exhausting and difficult job, but I wouldn't change it for anything.

HELLERUP
28 November 1944

Dear Nitte,

You must forgive me for having neglected you for so long, but I know you understand that my present life takes all of my time and that my thoughts are filled with everything that comes my way in these crucial days.

This is an extraordinary time we're living in, and it has brought forth many extraordinary people. It's almost beyond my grasp. But I do know that there is no other time in which I would prefer to have lived than the one we are now going through. Everything is trembling and the agony which is part of every birth is everywhere. Never has the world been exposed to such suffering, but never has the feeling of life been as strong or as intense as now. I'm living a fantastic life among fantastic people, and it is through this that I have come close to them. And because true feelings are always exposed when nerves are on edge, I'm getting to know people in a different way than I ever did before.

I used to look at the world through the eyes of a dreamer, and to me it's always had a special glow. Every night I went to sleep with a smile on my lips and a smile in my heart, and every morning I woke up rested and filled with wonder at the life to which I was born.

Now at night I fall into a heavy sleep, taking with me all that is on my mind. But when I wake up, it isn't because I can't sleep any longer, but because something tells me that I have work to do. It is only the present that counts. I feel that I must always follow my inner convictions, always be prepared for the unexpected, always be ready to spring into action. You know what this is like, living for the moment only and with our lives at stake. The group with which I'm working has completely accepted this.

VESTRE PRISON
13 January 1945

Dear ____

As I have the feeling that we will probably be sent south very soon, I'm sending you this message. A hundred and sixty-five left last night.

To begin with, I want as many of you as possible to profit from the experiences I've had since my arrest. I wish that all the clandestine newspapers would publish an urgent appeal to everyone who is working for our country. We don't want to hear anything more about the gruesome methods of the Gestapo and about the unfortunate people who fall into their hands. All this should be kept off the front pages even if the victims happen to be ministers of the gospel. We should print instead all that will serve our best interests, and only this should be put before us in print during the long job that lies ahead.

Many of us do a fine job as long as we ourselves can set the pace, but we fail when we are under duress. Let me give an example. When I was in the toilet the other day a young kid came running in like a scared rabbit, because he was about to undergo questioning. "Will they torture me in there?" He was white as a sheet. "Take it easy and don't betray your friends; nothing is going to happen to you," I said, trying to calm him down. During the questioning he immediately admitted everything and not until later did I realize that I, as well as many others who have been doing a lot of careless thinking and writing, were at fault. I should have talked to him as a man and told him that he would most likely get all hell

beaten out of him, but that it wouldn't be too bad if he didn't let himself go to pieces over something so unimportant.

Everyone goes around picturing these horrors, but no one thinks that it might happen to him, just as no one thinking of death believes that he can also be touched by it himself....

No one should feel that the fight is over the minute he has fallen into the hands of the enemy. That is only the beginning of the struggle to safeguard everything that others as well as you have won by fighting hard. This is the time to show whether you're a man or a coward....

Please remember this. If one day you find yourself in the hands of the traitors or the Germans, brace yourself and look them straight in the eyes. The only difference is that they are now the masters over you physically. Otherwise they are the same low breed of life they were before your arrest. Take a good look at them, and you will see that the only harm they can do you is to give you some blue spots and sore muscles....

You enter a room or a corridor and are told to stand with your face against a wall. Don't stand there in a panic thinking about death. If you're afraid to die, it means that you aren't old enough to take part in the struggle for freedom, or at least not mature enough. If the thought of brute force is enough to frighten you, you are the ideal victim for questioning. Suddenly and without reason they slap you. If you're weak, the physical blow, plus the humiliation of it, will give you such a shock that the Gestapo will immediately gain the upper hand and inoculate you with so much fear that everything will move according to their wishes.

Be calm and show neither hatred nor contempt, since both of these strike out at their easily wounded vanity. Regard them as human beings and make use of this vanity to strike back at them—but very cautiously. It's amazing how easily they fall into the trap....

Still one more thing: The Danes must change their attitude toward the Gestapo. Remember that you belong to a select group while they for the most part are a mob gone wild and therefore without scruples. Remember that this isn't a game and that you can't wave a white flag in the middle of it. This is important for the sake of our country as well as for us personally....

VESTRE PRISON
January 1945
[smuggled out]

Dearest Mother,

You ask if I want anything. There is only one thing: to get out of here. Otherwise I don't need anything. You know that I've always been able to get along on very little.

Thank you for what you said in your letter. It's meant a great deal to me. Your calmness and your wisdom make me very happy. You say that I've fulfilled all your expectations. I'm afraid that all of you see me in some sort of rosy light and forget to look at the facts. You forget that my daily life has prepared me for hardships much worse than the ones I've been exposed to here. Therefore you must realize that none of all the things that are so tough on the others—the food, the bed, the confinement, the questioning, have affected me in the least. I wouldn't have missed this experience for anything. Don't forget either that adventure is in my blood, and at the time of my arrest I was more excited at the thought of the experiences that were ahead of me than anything else. Neither the Gestapo nor anyone else has frightened me in the least. It's the primitive ones who are the most interesting. When they took me ... for questioning I thought that I felt the way an animal trainer must feel when he enters a cage of wild animals. The trainer probably has a sort of affection for the animals, even if he knows that some of them are mangy and have to be destroyed. I've never been afraid of dogs, although I know that you have to proceed with caution when dealing with wild ones.

Until now I haven't been harmed. I had to take my clothes off, but that was all. The man standing beside me looked as if he were about to spring on me, but each time I ignored him without being directly impolite and started to talk to his colleague. Only once did we confront each other, and I realized what would happen if he lost control of himself. I calmly asked him, "Are you afraid?" Never have I seen a more astonished look on anyone's face. Then he flew into a rage but had to check himself because I had turned toward the other fellow, who was apparently his superior. After that he didn't flare up quite so much and did his job with a little less zest....

I learned fast never to say no or answer a question in the negative because it gives them the chance to fly at you and scream that you're a liar, etc. But if you answer their questions in the affirmative, even with the most ridiculous nonsense, they often think that

you've misunderstood the question, that you really don't know anything about it and let it drop....

VESTRE PRISON
21 January 1945
[smuggled out]

Dearest Hanne,

I've just been lying here and thinking about what a marvelous girl you really are. There are so many things in you that I appreciate and love....

A lot of things have happened to me while I've been here which don't happen to everybody. Don't be angry with me, but if I don't manage to get out of here I would like to be sent to Germany, first to Froeslev [a concentration camp in Denmark] to get to know the life there, and then to Germany to see the collapse of the Reich inside its borders. It's going to be enormously interesting. Have faith in me. I don't think that there are many as well-equipped to get through it as I am.

I've always felt that there is a reason for everything and that this chain of events is leading me some place. I feel this more strongly now than ever before. I'd feel cheated if I didn't get out of here either to see the end of the occupation and the people wild with joy here at home or else see the tragedy and breakdown in Germany.

I'm not quite sure how you stand on this, but I think you feel as I do that our lives follow lines which are not accidental and that what happens to us is always for our greatest good....

I must say that up to the present time I've been very lucky to have the chance to live a life so full of change and movement with so many new impressions. It's really wonderful to be alive. I still don't know what death is like, but it would seem to me that it's the high point of our lives. I can't help thinking of this when I see how nervous the Gestapo and the collaborators are when they go into town. But I'm a bit different from them just the same.

VESTRE PRISON
GERMAN SECTION, CELL 411
4 April 1945

Dearest Mother,

Today I went before the military tribunal together with Joergen, Niels and Ludwig. We were condemned to die. I know that you're strong and that you will be *able to take this. But listen to me, Mother. It isn't enough that you are able to take it. You must also understand it. I'm not of importance and will soon be forgotten, but the ideas, the life, the inspiration which filled me will live on. You will find them everywhere—in the new green of spring, in people you will meet on your way, in a loving smile. Perhaps you will also find what was of value to me, you will love it and you won't forget me. I would have liked to grow and mature, but I will still live in your hearts and you will live on because you know that I am in front of you on the road and not behind, as you had perhaps thought at first. You know what has always been my greatest wish and what I thought I would become. Mother dear, come with me on my journey. Don't stop at the last stage of my life, but instead stop at some of the preceding ones and you may find something which will be of value to the girl I love and to you, Mother.*

I have followed a certain path and I don't regret it. I've never betrayed what is in my heart, and now I seem to see the unbroken line which has run through my life. I'm not old, I ought not to die, and still, it seems so simple and natural to me. It's only the brutal way which at first terrifies us. I have so little time left; I don't quite know how to explain it, but my mind is completely at peace. I have always wanted to be like Socrates [the ancient Greek philosopher], but although I have no one to talk to as he had, I feel the same tranquility of spirit and very much want you, Hanne and Nitte to understand this....

How strange it seems to be writing this testament! Each word will stand; it can never be amend-ed, never revoked, never changed. I'm thinking of so many things. Joergen is sitting here in front of me writing a letter to his daughter for her Confirmation—a document for life. We have lived together as friends and now we're going to die together....

Finally there are the children who have recently come to mean so much to me. I had so been looking forward to seeing them and being with them again. Just to think of them makes me happy and I hope they will grow up to be men who will be able to get more out of life than what lies on the surface. I hope that their character will develop freely and never be subjected to prejudice.

Give them my love, my godson and his brother.

I see what the situation in our country is leading up to and I know that Grandfather is right. But remember all of you that the aim shouldn't be to return to the period before the war, but that it is up to you, young and old, to create a broad, human ideal which everyone can recognize. This is the thing that our country needs; something that even a simple peasant boy can look up to and be happy in the thought that he is working and fighting for.

Then, finally, there is my Hanne. Make her see that the pilot stars are still shining and that I was only a beacon on her route. Help her to keep going. She can now become very happy.

In haste—your oldest and only son. (Malthe-Bruun, pp. 107–169)

Aftermath

The Danish public and government refused to abandon the several hundred Jews who were transported to the Czechoslovakian ghetto of Theresienstadt in October 1943. They sent a steady flow of food parcels to the ghetto (sent requiring a signed receipt, which ensured that most of the packages reached the deportees) and warnings to the German government. The Danish ministry also demanded that a delegation be allowed to inspect the ghetto. In June 1944 the Germans finally granted permission for representatives of the Danish and International Red Cross to gain entry into Theresienstadt. Unfortunately, delegates were shown a fake "model ghetto," complete with cafés and stores, which had been built expressly for their visit. Due to persistent Danish interest in the fate of their deported countrymen, however, no Danish Jews were sent en masse to Auschwitz for extermination—only one died there. Some fifty Danish Jews of the original group of 477 died in Theresienstadt, a death rate that reflects the higher standard of care they received compared to other prisoners.

In April 1945, Danish prisoners were transferred by bus from Theresienstadt to Swedish custody. During their trip to Sweden, the buses passed through Denmark, where hundreds of thousands of Danes filled the streets to greet the return of their fellow citizens. A month later, the British army entered Copenhagen and accepted the Ger-

The Danish public and government refused to abandon the several hundred Danish Jews sent to the Czechoslovakian ghetto of Theresienstadt, pictured here. *(Reproduced by permission of YIVO Institute for Jewish Research/USHMM Photo Archives)*

man surrender. Shortly thereafter, Jewish refugees began returning from Sweden. The returning Jews found that their homes, belongings, and even their pets had been cared for by neighbors. Some even came home to newly painted houses and rooms full of fresh flowers.

After liberation, one of the partisans clearing out the Vestre Prison found a letter Malthe-Bruun had received from his cousin Nitte. The back of the sheet of paper was covered with tiny writing by Malthe-Bruun. Written after he had been tortured, the letter had been hidden within the walls of his cell. His mother, Vibeke Malthe-Bruun, collected and edited his diaries and letters, publishing them in 1955, a decade after his death.

SOURCES

Books

Flender, Harold, *Rescue in Denmark,* Simon and Schuster (New York), 1963.

Holliday, Laurel, *Children in the Holocaust and World War II: Their Secret Diaries,* Simon and Schuster (New York), 1995.

Malthe-Bruun, Kim, *Heroic Heart: The Diary and Letters of Kim Malthe-Bruun, 1941–1945,* edited by Vibeke Malthe-Bruun, translated by Gerry Bothmer, Random House (New York), 1955.

Anne Frank
Excerpt from *The Diary of a Young Girl,* written between 1942 and 1944
Edited by Otto H. Frank and Mirjam Pressler

This version published in 1997

Beginning with the annexation of Austria in 1938 and the invasion of Poland in 1939, Nazi Germany set out to seize control of Europe. By 1940, it had conquered France, Belgium, Luxembourg, the Netherlands, Denmark, and Norway, and with each military success, the Germans increased the number of Jews under their rule. Many Jews who had fled Germany in the 1930s to settle in neighboring countries found themselves again under the brutal repression of anti-Semitic policies.

One such family was that of Otto and Edith Frank, who escaped Germany in 1933 with their two young daughters, Margot and Anne, and sought refuge in the Netherlands. They settled in Amsterdam, where Otto started two small food-production businesses, specializing in materials for jams and jellies, and spices. Margot and Anne attended local schools (where Anne was reported to be an average student with a strong interest in reading and writing), learned the Dutch language, and made many friends in their new home. But seven years of stable family life ended abruptly when the Nazis invaded Holland in May 1940.

As in other conquered nations, the Nazis quickly abolished the rights of Jews. They passed a law ordering Jews to surrender their businesses to non-Jews in a process known as "Aryanization." With the help of friends, Otto Frank completed the paperwork required by the decree yet retained control of his businesses. Another law mandated that Jewish children could not attend school with non-Jewish students, thus forcing Anne and Margot to switch schools and attend a Jewish Lyceum established by the Nazis.

By the middle of 1942, the Nazis had opened several camps throughout Poland specifically designed for the deliberate destruction of all European Jews. To conceal their intentions, they used

Otto Frank with his two daughters, Anne (in front) and Margot. *(Reproduced by permission of the Disney Channel, courtesy of AP/World Wide Photos)*

the code name *Endlösung,* or the "Final Solution," to refer to this plan. With the cooperation of numerous local and national bureaucracies, the Germans undertook the complex task of transporting Jews from occupied countries to various death camps. The Nazis created transit camps as a way to control and organize the flow of victims to the gas chambers and crematoria. Often, Jews boarded trains supposedly bound for "resettlement in the East" or relocation to forced labor assignments. Some Jews managed to escape after witnessing death camp operations and returned to inform others of the fate awaiting those ordered to relocate. The first massive deportation to death camps targeted the Jews imprisoned in the ghettos of Poland, and the mass deportation of Jews living in France, Belgium, and Holland began in July 1942.

On July 5, 1942, Margot received orders from a Nazi bureau to register for "labor expansion measures." This ominous letter prompted the Franks to go into hiding immediately. For more than a year, they had planned for such an eventuality. Piece by piece, Otto had moved the family's belongings into a shelter he constructed in the unused upper floors of his office building. At the top of a staircase he built a bookcase that, when slid aside, revealed a secret entrance to this annex. For two years, the Franks and four friends—Mr. and Mrs. van Daan; their teenage son, Peter; and Albert Dussel, an elderly dentist—lived as *onderduikers* ("ones who dive under"), unable to go outside or even make noise during the day, when people were working in the rest of the building. Otto Frank confided in four employees, who helped the hideaways by bringing them food, clothing, and other items during their twenty-five months of seclusion. The four helpers—Victor Kugler, Johannes Kleiman, Elli Voskuijl, and Miep Gies—risked their own lives to try to save their Jewish friends.

Anne Frank had been born Annelies Marie Frank in 1929 in Frankfurt, Germany. Shortly before going into hiding, she received a diary from her father for her thirteenth birthday, June 12, 1942. Over the next two years, she poured her heart into this red and orange checkered book, which she called "Kitty." She described both her darkest moments and her brightest hopes for the future. In 1944 she heard a radio report urging people to collect diaries and letters about their war experiences for possible future publication. Encouraged by her family and friends, she began to edit her earlier diary entries. *The Diary of a Young Girl* is one of the best-known personal accounts of the Nazi era. With insight and clarity, Frank wrote about the troubles of adolescence and the hardships caused by Nazi terror. In preparation for possible publication, Anne used pseudonyms for most of the persons in the diary. The present edition retains the pseudonyms Anne assigned to the people in hiding, while using the real names of the four helpers. The diary reveals that her relationships with other family members were typical of any teenager, despite the very unusual circumstances under which they lived—she competed relentlessly with her sister, adored her father, and felt that nobody—especially her mother—understood her. Perhaps the most remarkable aspect of Frank's life was her ability to hold onto her ideals. Amidst the destruction and killing inflicted by the Nazis, she remained hopeful that one day peace and freedom would return.

The Diary of a Young Girl

SATURDAY, JANUARY 30, 1943

Dearest Kitty,

I'm seething with rage, yet I can't show it. I'd like to scream, stamp my foot, give Mother a good shaking, cry and I don't know what else because of the nasty words, mocking looks and accusations that she hurls at me day after day, piercing me like arrows from a tightly strung bow, which are nearly impossible to pull from my body. I'd like to scream at Mother, Margot, the van Daans, Dussel and Father too: "Leave me alone, let me have at least one night when I don't cry myself to sleep with my eyes burning and my head pounding. Let me get away, away from everything, away from this world!" But I can't do

that. I can't let them see my doubts, or the wounds they've inflicted on me. I couldn't bear their sympathy or their good-humored derision. It would only make me want to scream even more.

Everyone thinks I'm showing off when I talk, ridiculous when I'm silent, insolent when I answer, cunning when I have a good idea, lazy when I'm tired, selfish when I eat one bite more than I should, stupid, cowardly, calculating, etc., etc. All day long I hear nothing but what an exasperating child I am, and although I laugh it off and pretend not to mind, I do mind. I wish I could ask God to give me another personality, one that doesn't antagonize everyone.

But that's impossible. I'm stuck with the character I was born with, and yet I'm sure I'm not a bad person. I do my best to please everyone, more than they'd ever suspect in a million years. When I'm upstairs, I try to laugh it off because I don't want them to see my troubles....

Yours, Anne

MONDAY, JULY 26, 1943

Dear Kitty,

Yesterday was a very tumultuous day, and we're still all wound up. Actually, you may wonder if there's ever a day that passes without some kind of excitement.

The first warning siren went off in the morning while we were at breakfast, but we paid no attention, because it only meant that the planes were crossing the coast. I had a terrible headache, so I lay down for an hour after breakfast and then went to the office at around two. At two-thirty Margot had finished her office work and was just gathering her things together when the sirens began wailing again. So she and I trooped back upstairs. None too soon, it seems, for less than five minutes later the guns were booming so loudly that we went and stood in the hall. The house shook and the bombs kept falling. I was clutching my "escape bag," more because I wanted to have something to hold on to than because I wanted to run away. I know we can't leave here, but if we had to, being seen on the streets would be just as dangerous as getting caught in an air raid. After half an hour the drone of engines faded and the house began to hum with activity again. Peter emerged from his lookout post in the front attic, Dussel remained in the front office, Mrs. van D. felt safest in the private office, Mr. van Daan had been watching from the loft, and those of us on the landing spread out to watch the columns of smoke rising from the harbor. Before long the smell of fire was everywhere, and outside it looked as if the city were enveloped in a thick fog.

A big fire like that is not a pleasant sight, but fortunately for us it was all over, and we went back to our various chores. Just as we were starting dinner: another air-raid alarm. The food was good, but I lost my appetite the moment I heard the siren. Nothing happened, however, and forty-five minutes later the all clear was sounded. After the dishes had been washed: another air-raid warning, gunfire and swarms of planes. "Oh, gosh, twice in one day," we thought, "that's twice too many." Little good that did us, because once again the bombs rained down, this time on the other side of the city. According to British reports, Schiphol Airport was bombed. The planes dived and climbed, the air was abuzz with the drone

Five-year-old Anne's identification card. (*Reproduced by permission of Archive Photos*)

of engines. It was very scary, and the whole time I kept thinking, "Here it comes, this is it."

I can assure you that when I went to bed at nine, my legs were still shaking. At the stroke of midnight I woke up again: more planes! Dussel was undressing, but I took no notice and leapt up, wide awake, at the sound of the first shot. I stayed in Father's bed until one, in my own bed until one-thirty, and was back in Father's bed at two. But the planes kept on coming. At last they stopped firing and I was able to go back "home" again. I finally fell asleep at half past two.

Seven o'clock. I awoke with a start and sat up in bed. Mr. van Daan was with Father. My first thought *was: burglars. "Everything," I heard Mr. van Daan say, and I thought everything had been stolen. But no, this time it was wonderful news, the best we've had in months, maybe even since the war began. Mussolini has resigned and the King of Italy has taken over the government [of Italy].*

We jumped for joy. After the awful events of yesterday, finally something good happens and brings us … hope! Hope for an end to the war, hope for peace.

Mr. Kugler dropped by and told us that the Fokker aircraft factory had been hit hard. Meanwhile, there was another air-raid alarm this morning, with planes flying over, and another warning siren. I've had it up to here with alarms. I've hardly slept, and the last thing I want to do is work. But now the suspense about Italy and the hope that the war will be over by the end of the year are keeping us awake…

Yours, Anne

SATURDAY, JULY 15, 1944

Dearest Kitty,

…. "Deep down, the young are lonelier than the old." I read this in a book somewhere and it's stuck in my mind. As far as I can tell, it's true.

So if you're wondering whether it's harder for the adults here than for the children, the answer is no, it's certainly not. Older people have an opinion about everything and are sure of themselves and their

actions. It's twice as hard for us young people to hold on to our opinions at a time when ideals are being shattered and destroyed, when the worst side of human nature predominates, when everyone has come to doubt truth, justice and God.

Anyone who claims that the older folks have a more difficult time in the Annex doesn't realize that the problems have a far greater impact on us. We're much too young to deal with these problems, but they keep thrusting themselves on us until, finally, we're forced to think up a solution, though most of the time our solutions crumble when faced with the facts. It's difficult in times like these: ideals, dreams, and cherished hopes rise within us, only to be crushed by grim reality. It's a wonder I haven't abandoned all my ideals, they seem so absurd and impractical. Yet I cling to them because I still believe, in spite of everything, that people are truly good at heart.

It's utterly impossible for me to build my life on a foundation of chaos, suffering and death. I see the world being slowly transformed into wilderness, I hear the approaching thunder that, one day, will destroy us too, I feel the suffering of millions. And yet, when I look up at the sky, I somehow feel that everything will change for the better, that this cruelty too will end, that peace and tranquility will return once more. In the meantime, I must hold on to my ideals. Perhaps the day will come when I'll be able to realize them!

Yours, Anne M. Frank (Frank, pp. 60–327)

Aftermath

Frank wrote her last diary entry on Tuesday, August 1, 1944. A few days later, on August 4, the Gestapo received an anonymous tip about the hideaway Jews in the annex and immediately raided the building. Several of the non-Jews who had helped the Franks were arrested and sent to labor camps. The Frank family and the other four occupants of the annex were transported to the Westerbork transit camp on August 8, 1944. They were detained in Westerbork for a month before being transported to the Auschwitz-Birkenau extermination camp. Records indicate they were among the last trainload of prisoners to be transported from Westerbork to Auschwitz-Birkenau. Since most of them were able to work, they were not murdered immediately. In

fall 1944, faced with the prospect of losing the war, the Nazis rushed to finish their goal of racial cleansing and to destroy the evidence of mass murder at the death camps. They stopped deportations from transit camps, accelerated exterminations, and forced remaining able-bodied prisoners to relocate away from advancing Allied forces. As part of the effort to close the death camps, Anne and Margot Frank were sent to the Bergen-Belsen labor camp in October 1944. Their mother, Edith, died of exhaustion and starvation at Auschwitz-Birkenau in January 1945, and Margot died of typhus at Bergen-Belsen in late February or early March. Believing she was the only remaining family member alive, Anne died of the same disease a few days later. Witnesses report she was buried in one of the mass graves at Bergen-Belsen. Otto Frank remained in

Auschwitz until its liberation by the Soviet army on January 27, 1945. He was the only one of the eight hideaways to survive the Holocaust.

Miep Gies, one of the people who helped conceal the Franks, managed to save Anne's diary and other writings. After liberation, Otto Frank returned to Amsterdam knowing he was a widower but still hopeful that his daughters were alive. The same day that the deaths of Anne and Margot were confirmed, Gies returned Anne's diary to Otto. In keeping with Anne's wishes to be a writer, Otto published several portions of the diary in 1947 as *The Annex.* By 1952, a more complete version, *The Diary of a Young Girl,* received worldwide critical acclaim. A stage version of Anne's diary won the 1955 Pulitzer Prize for best play of the year, and a film version followed in 1959. In 1986 the Netherlands State Institute for War Documentation, which retained the original diary following the death of Otto Frank, released a complete unedited version. Proceeds of the publication of *The Diary of a Young Girl* help fund the Anne Frank Foundation, dedicated to fighting anti-Semitism and racism throughout the world. The foundation maintains the annex building, where Anne's original diary is displayed, in Amsterdam,

and operates offices in Basel, Switzerland, and New York, New York.

On May 11, 1944, Anne Frank wrote, "My greatest wish is to become a journalist some day and later a famous writer." Today some 24 million copies of her diary are in circulation in more than fifty editions. Miep Gies, who held on to Anne's original diary, also saved some of her other writings: *Stories and Adventures from the Annex* and *Book of Beautiful Phrases.* Gies herself wrote about her experiences in *Anne Frank Remembered* (1987), which became the basis of an Academy Award–winning documentary film.

Sources

Books

Frank, Anne, *The Diary of a Young Girl,* edited by Otto H. Frank and Mirjam Pressler, translated by Susan Massotty, Bantam (New York), 1997.

Gies, Miep, with Alison Gold, *Anne Frank Remembered,* Simon and Schuster (New York), 1987.

Lindwer, Willy, *The Last Seven Months of Anne Frank,* translated by Alison Meersschaert, Random House (New York), 1991.

P R I M A R Y   S O U R C E

Etty Hillesum
Excerpt from *An Interrupted Life–The Diaries, 1941–1943; and, Letters from Westerbork*
This version published in 1996

From its inception in 1920, the German Nazi party promoted anti-Semitism. After rising to power in 1933, it instituted repressive measures that affected all aspects of the social, political, and economic life of German Jews. When Germany invaded Poland in 1939, tactics to suppress Jews became increasingly more drastic. With each country they conquered, the Nazis brought additional Jews under their domination. Nazi leader Adolf Hitler made repeated threats against the Jews, and as early as 1939 began to imply that he intended to annihilate all European Jewry. In 1941 Hitler and other Nazi leaders approved a

secret plan for the mass murder code-named the *Endlösung,* or the "Final Solution." To accomplish its goals, the Nazi government coordinated the resources of a far-reaching bureaucracy. Millions of Jews were removed from German-occupied countries and transported by train to a network of specially built camps. The Nazis created several different types of camps, including "extermination" camps, which were specifically designed for mass murder.

The path taken by Jewish prisoners of the Nazis varied according to their geographic

An elderly Jewish couple on their way to the Westerbork transit camp. *(USHMM Photo Archives)*

location. Immediately after arrest, Jews in western Europe were retained in transit camps. Situated near populated areas and adjacent to major train lines, transit camps served as waiting stations; Jews were then sent on trains to labor camps or directly to death camps in Poland. In contrast, Jews and other Nazi victims in eastern Europe, were kept first in ghettos before their deportation to death camps or labor camps. In Nazi-occupied areas of the Soviet Union, however, most Jews faced immediate execution by mobile killing squads.

The transit camps gave Jews a taste of life under Nazi control—a life that included constant hunger, systemized humiliation, disease, and death. To keep order within the camps, the Nazis carefully hid their intentions by referring to the inevitable deportation as "resettlement" to the East. Prisoners were allowed to keep whatever possessions they brought with them, although most assets had been confiscated before their arrests. Camp administrators also opened schools for Jewish children and allowed inmates to wear civilian clothes.

In May 1940 the Nazis invaded and conquered the Netherlands. After quickly moving to suspend

the Dutch parliament, the Germans set up their own government and appointed Dutch Nazis to key positions. A series of anti-Jewish decrees stripped Dutch Jews of their political and economic rights. Amid a series of violent struggles with the Jews, the Nazis formed a *Joodse Raad* (Jewish Council) composed of Dutch Jewish leaders, who were held responsible for executing Nazi orders. In February 1941 a strike broke out in reaction to Nazi-organized, anti-Jewish violence in Amsterdam, the Dutch capital. The Nazis intensified their pressure against Jews and resisters, launching their first major roundup of Jews in April 1942. Jews were required to wear a yellow Star of David and relocate to Amsterdam, thereby making the provinces *judenrein* ("free of Jews").

In July 1942 the Nazis began sequestering Jews in Westerbork, a camp originally set up a decade earlier by the Dutch government to house Jewish refugees from Germany. Also in July, a young Jewish woman, Etty Hillesum, secured a job as a typist for the Jewish Council. She was born Esther Hillesum in Middelburg, Holland, in 1914. When Hillesum was ten years old, her family settled in Deventer, a city in the eastern part of the country by the Ijssel River. Her father, Dr. Louis Hillesum, taught classical languages and served as headmaster in the town gymnasium, or academic high school. Her mother was Russian by birth, having fled to the Netherlands after a pogrom. Hillesum and her two brothers, Mischa and Jaap, were intelligent and creative. Hillesum received a law degree and studied Slavonic languages and psychology. Mischa was one of the most promising pianists in Europe, while Jaap discovered several new vitamins at the age of seventeen and went on to become a doctor.

When Hillesum began to work for the *Joodse Raad,* she was twenty-eight years old, well educated, and active in the cultural life of Amsterdam. As part of the *Joodse Raad,* she assisted new arrivals to Westerbork and tended to prisoners during their brief stay. She also comforted Jews and other victims as they boarded trains that would likely take them to their deaths. Train arrivals and departures were the central focus of life in transit camps such as Westerbork, so the Nazis used Jewish workers to assure stability. Knowing that chaos and disorder would jeopardize the orderly progression of inmates to the death camps, the Nazis attempted to trick victims into believing that they were simply being relocated to eastern Europe for forced labor. While Hillesum's association with the influential *Joodse Raad* spared her life for a period of time, she knew her survival depended on the deaths of others, a situation she found increasingly difficult to accept.

Some see the writings of Etty Hillesum as the adult counterpart to the work of young Jewish diarist Anne Frank. Hillesum began her job with the *Joodse Raad* around the time Frank started her diary and went into hiding. In fact, for a while, Hillesum lived just a few miles away from the annex in Amsterdam where the Frank family hid.

In this excerpt, Hillesum discusses her parents and brother, Mischa. Since Mischa was a gifted pianist known throughout Europe, the Nazis considered him to be a "cultural Jew," and offered to allow him to stay with other Jewish artists and intellectuals in a castle in the small town of Barneveld. He pleaded for his parents to be given the same protection, but as Hillesum notes in one of her letters, the Nazis refused his request.

An Interrupted Life—The Diaries, 1941–1943; and, Letters from Westerbork

[18] December, 1942

One summer evening I sat eating red cabbage at the edge of the yellow lupin field that stretched from our dining hut to the delousing station, and with sudden inspiration I said, "One ought to write a chronicle of Westerbork." An older man to my left—also eating red cabbage—answered, "Yes, but to do that you'd have to be a great poet."

He is right, it would take a great poet. Little journalistic pieces won't do. The whole of Europe is gradually being turned into one great prison camp. The whole of Europe will undergo this same bitter experience. To simply record the bare facts of families torn apart, of possessions plundered and liberties forfeited, would soon become monotonous. Nor is it possible to pen picturesque accounts of barbed wire and vegetable swill to show outsiders what it's like. Besides, I wonder how many outsiders will be left if history continues along the paths it has taken....

Finding something to say about Westerbork is also difficult because of its ambiguous character. On the one hand it is a stable community in the making, a forced one to be sure, yet with all the characteristics of a human society. And on the other hand, it is a camp for a people in transit, great waves of human beings constantly washed in from the cities and provinces, from rest homes, prisons, and other prison camps, from all the nooks and crannies of the Netherlands—only to be deported a few days later to meet their unknown destiny.

You can imagine how dreadfully crowded it is in half a square kilometer. Naturally, few follow the

example of the man who packed his rucksack and went on transport of his own accord. When asked why, he said that he wanted the freedom to decide to go when he *wanted to go. It reminds me of the Roman judge who said to a martyr, "Do you know that I have the power to have you killed?" And the martyr answered, "Yes, but I have the power of letting myself be killed."*

Anyway, it is terribly crowded in Westerbork, as when too many drowning people cling to the last bit of flotsam after a ship has sunk. People would rather spend the winter behind barbed wire in Holland's poorest province than be dragged away to unknown parts and unknown destinies deep within Europe, from where only a few indistinct sounds have come back to the rest of us. But the quota must be filled; so must the train, which comes to fetch its load with mathematical regularity. You cannot keep everyone back as being indispensable to the camp, or too sick for transport, although you try it with a great many. You sometimes think it would be simpler to put yourself on transport than have to witness the fear and despair of the thousands upon thousands of men, women, children, infants, invalids, the feebleminded, the sick, and the aged who pass through our helping hands in an almost uninterrupted flow.

My fountain pen cannot form words strong enough to convey even the remotest picture of these transports. From the outside the impression is of bleak monotony, yet every transport is different and has its own atmosphere.

When the first transport passed through our hands, there was a moment when I thought I would

Members of the Jewish police supervise the deportation of Jews from the Westerbork transit camp. *(Trudi Gidan Collection/USHMM Photo Archives)*

never again laugh and be happy, that I had changed suddenly into another, older person cut off from all former friends. But on walking through the crowded camp, I realized again that where there are people, there is life. Life in all its thousands of nuances—"with a smile and a tear," to put it in popular terms.

It made a great difference whether people arrived prepared, with well-filled rucksacks, or had been suddenly dragged out of their houses or swept up from the streets. In the end we saw only the last.

After the first of the police roundups, when people arrived in slippers and underclothes, the whole of Westerbork, in a single horrified and heroic gesture, stripped to the skin. And we have tried, with the close cooperation of people on the outside, to make sure that those who leave are equipped as well as possible. But if we remember all those who went to face the winter in Eastern Europe without any clothes, if we remember the single thin blanket that was sometimes all we were able to dole out in the night, a few hours before departure....

The slum-dwellers arrived from the cities, displaying their poverty and neglect in the bare bar-

racks. Aghast, many of us asked ourselves: what sort of democracy did we really have?

The people from Rotterdam were in a class by themselves, hardened by the bombing raids. "We don't frighten easily anymore," you often heard them say. "If we survived all that, we'll survive this, too." And a few days later they marched singing to the train. But it was midsummer then, and there were no old people yet, or invalids on stretchers bringing up the rear....

The Jews from Heerlen and Maastricht and thereabouts came telling stories that reverberated with the great send-off the province of Limburg had given them. One felt that morally they could live on it for a long time. "The Catholics have promised to pray for us, and they're better at that than we are!" said one of them.

People came with all their rivalries. The Jews from Haarlem said somewhat loftily and acidly: "Those Amsterdammers have a grim sense of humor."

There were children who would not accept a sandwich before their parents had had one. There was a remarkable day when the Jewish Catholics or Catholic Jews—whichever you want to call them—arrived, nuns and priests wearing the yellow star on their habits. I remember two young novices, twins, with identical beautiful, dark ghetto faces and serene, childish eyes peering out from under their skullcaps. They said with mild surprise that they had been fetched at half past four from morning mass, and that they had eaten red cabbage in Amersfoort.

There was a priest, still fairly young, who had not left his monastery for fifteen years. He was out in the "world" for the first time, and I stood next to him for a while, following his eyes as they wandered peacefully around the barracks where the newcomers were being received.

The others—shaven, beaten, maltreated—who poured in along with the Catholics that day stumbled about the wooden hut with movements that were still unsteady and stretched out their hands toward the bread, of which there was not enough.

A young Jew stood very still next to us. His jacket was much too loose, but a grin broke through his stubbly black beard when he said, "They tried to smash the wall of the prison with my head, but my head was harder than the wall!"

Among all the shaved heads, it was strange to see the white-turbaned women who had just been treated in the delousing barracks, and who went about now looking distressed and humiliated.

Children dozed off on the dusty plank floor; others played tag among the adults. Two little ones floundered helplessly around the heavy body of a woman lying unconscious in a corner. They didn't understand why their mother just lay there without answering them. A grey-haired old gentleman, straight as an arrow and with a clear-cut, aristocratic profile, stared at the whole infernal canvas and repeated over and over to himself: "A terrible day! A terrible day!"

And among all this, the unremitting clatter of a battery of typewriters: the machine-gun fire of bureaucracy.

Through the many little windowpanes one can see other wooden barracks, barbed wire, and a blasted heath.

I looked at the priest who was now back in the world again. "And what do you think of the world now?" I asked. But his gaze remained unwavering

and friendly above the brown habit, as if everything he saw was known, familiar from long ago. That same evening, a man later told me, he saw some priests walking one behind the other in the dusk between two dark barracks. They were saying their rosaries as imperturbably as if they had just finished vespers at the monastery. And isn't it true that one can pray anywhere, in a wooden barracks just as well as in a stone monastery, or indeed, anywhere on this earth where God, in these troubled times, feels like casting his likeness?

10 July 1943

Maria, hello,

Ten thousand have passed through this place, the clothed and the naked, the old and the young, the sick and the healthy—and I am left to live and work and stay cheerful. It will be my parents' turn to leave soon, if by some miracle not this week, then certainly one of the next. And I must learn to accept this as well. Mischa insists on going along with them, and it seems to me that he probably should; if he has to watch our parents leave this place, it will totally unhinge him. I shan't go, I just can't. It is easier to pray for someone from a distance than to see him suffer by your side. It is not fear of Poland that keeps me from going along with my parents, but fear of seeing them suffer. And that, too, is cowardice.

This is something people refuse to admit to themselves: at a given point you can no longer <u>do</u>, but can only <u>be</u> and accept. And although that is something I learned a long time ago, I also know that one can only accept for oneself and not for others. And that's what is so desperately difficult for me here. Mother and Mischa still want to "do," to turn the whole world upside down, but I know we can't do anything about it. I have never been able to "do" anything; I can only let things take their course and if need be, suffer. This is where my strength lies, and it is great strength indeed. But for myself, not for others.

Mother and Father have definitely been turned down for Barneveld [a small town containing a castle where influential Jews were temporarily held or detained]; we heard the news yesterday. They were also told to be ready to leave here on next Tuesday's transport. Mischa wanted to rush straight to the commandant and call him a murderer. We'll have to watch him carefully. Outwardly, Father appears very calm. But he would have gone to pieces in a matter of days in these vast barracks if I hadn't been able to have him taken to the hospital—which he is gradually coming to find just as intolerable. He is really at his wits' end, though he tries not to show it. My prayers, too, aren't going quite right. I know: you can pray God to give people the strength to bear whatever comes. But I keep repeating the same prayer: "Lord, make it as short as possible." And as a result I am paralyzed. I would like to pack their cases with the best things I can lay my hands on, but I know perfectly well that they will be stripped of everything; about that we have been left no doubt. So why bother?

I have a good friend here. Last week he was told to keep himself in readiness for transport. When I went to see him, he stood straight as an arrow, face calm, rucksack packed beside his bed. We didn't mention his leaving, but he did read me various things he had written, and we talked a little philosophy. We didn't make things hard for each other with grief about having to say good-bye. We laughed and said we would see each other soon. We were both able to bear our lot. And that's what is so desperate about this place: most people are not able to bear their lot, and they load it onto the shoulders of others. And that burden is more likely to break one than one's own.

Yes, I feel perfectly able to bear my lot, but not that of my parents. This is the last letter I'll be allowed to write for a while. This afternoon our identity cards were taken away, and we became official camp inmates. So you'll have to have a little patience waiting for news of me.

Perhaps I will be able to smuggle a letter out now and then.

*Have received your two letters.
'Bye, Maria—dear friend,
Etty*

[postmarked 15 September 1943]

Christine,

Opening the Bible at random I find this: "The Lord is my high tower." I am sitting on my rucksack in the middle of a full freight car. Father, Mother, and Mischa are a few cars away. In the end, the departure came without warning. On sudden special orders from The Hague. We left the camp singing, Father and Mother firmly and calmly, Mischa, too. We shall be traveling for three days. Thank you for all your kindness and care. Friends left behind will still be writing to Amsterdam; perhaps you will hear something from them. Or from my last letter from camp.

*Good-bye for now from the four of us.
Etty* (Hillesum, pp. 243–360)

Aftermath

Etty Hillesum and her family arrived at Auschwitz-Birkenau from Westerbork on September 10, 1943. The Nazis gassed her mother and father the same day. The Red Cross reported Etty Hillesum's death on November 30, 1943, and her brother Mischa's death on March 31, 1944. After being sent to the Bergen-Belsen labor camp, Etty's other brother, Jaap, survived the war but died shortly afterward, while returning to Holland. While still at Westerbork, Hillesum sensed she would not return from Auschwitz and gave her diaries to a friend with instructions to pass them on to Dutch writer Klass Smelik. Hillesum wanted the diaries published after her death as a way to share with future generations all that she had witnessed. The surviving diary consisted of eight tattered notebooks—Hillesum took the last one with her on the train to Auschwitz-Birkenau. Smelik could not find a publisher and passed the diaries to his son. In 1980, nearly forty years after Hillesum's death, her diaries were redis-covered and finally published. They have been translated into twelve languages and printed in fourteen countries. The entries, along with many letters written from Westerbork, encapsulate Hillesum's life from 1941 until her death in 1943.

Etty Hillesum wrote her final postcard from inside a transport headed to the Auschwitz-Birkenau death camp. She threw the card, addressed to a friend, out of the train car. Farmers found the card and posted it, enabling Hillesum's last thoughts to be heard.

SOURCES

Books

Adler, David, *We Remember the Holocaust,* Henry Holt (New York), 1989.

Hillesum, Etty, *An Interrupted Life—The Diaries, 1941–1943; and, Letters from Westerbork,* Henry Holt (New York), 1996.

14

Life and Death in Nazi-Occupied France

The German occupation of France intensified conflicts that had been growing for more than a century in the country. Some of these conflicts involved whether France should be a monarchy or a republic; the separation of church and state (particularly the role of the Catholic church in the educational system); and the power of the army. As quarreling increased and divisions deepened, the issue of Jewish rights became entangled in this web of clashing opinions. Anti-Semitism grew sharply in the 1930s as groups similar to the Nazis sprang up in France, though they never became so large or well organized as the German party. More and more European countries were adopting dictatorships, many of which were openly anti-Semitic, and some French politicians looked to them as models for their own government. Still, France had been the first country in Europe to give Jews full civil rights, which was one of the reasons that German leader Adolf Hitler despised France.

During the worldwide economic depression of the 1930s, France had a Jewish prime minister, Léon Blum, who was the leader of the French Socialist party. Blum headed a coalition of parties called the Popular Front, or People's Front, that included the French Communists. Much of its support came from French workers. When the Popular Front was elected into office, a wave of factory takeovers and labor strikes swept French

Léon Blum, leader of the French socialist party, was Jewish, and served as prime minister of France from 1936 to 1938. *(Hessiches Hauptstaatsarchiv/USHMM Photo Archives)*

industry. The new government sided with the strikers, who desired higher wages and other improvements for workers.

The Dreyfus Affair

Even though foreign-born Jews viewed France as a safe haven from German leader Adolf Hitler and his Nazi party, the country had its own history of anti-Semitism. In 1894 Captain Alfred Dreyfus, the first Jewish officer to be appointed to the General Staff of the French Army, was falsely accused of treason and sentenced to life in prison. Long buried anti-Jewish sentiments surfaced, and in some places, Jews were attacked on the streets. Although Dreyfus was eventually found innocent and released from prison, the Dreyfus Affair had long-lasting effects in France. Austrian journalist Theodor Herzl, long a proponent of a Jewish homeland, believed that the Jews would never be accepted in modern Europe and would always be victims of prejudice. He further stated that the Dreyfus case showed the French willingness to condemn all Jews. Herzl's words seemed accurate during the Holocaust when the French handed thousands of Jews over to the Nazis.

The Dreyfuss Affair showed that anti-Semitism did exist in France. (Library of Congress)

For many French people, the Popular Front represented the promise of a better life for average citizens. Yet opponents of the coalition contended that Blum and the Popular Front were symbols of the very problems facing France. These critics feared social unrest, warned against the Communists, and called for greater respect for the church and the army. To many of his enemies, Blum was not a "real Frenchman" because he was a Jew. Even after the Popular Front was no longer in power, the anti-Blum faction feared the party might again run France. When war with Germany approached, they coined a slogan: "Better Hitler than Blum."

The Jews of France

To most European Jews, however, France remained a safe haven. Thousands moved to the country from eastern Europe in the 1920s and 1930s. By 1933, when Hitler rose to power in Germany, more than 100,000 foreign-born Jews were living in France, some of whom were citizens. By 1939, two separate Jewish communities had been established. About 150,000 people made up the "old" Jewish population, who did not call themselves *Juifs* (Jews); instead, they usually used the word "Israelite" to describe themselves. They were generally prosperous, working in business, law, medicine, and other professions. Except for their religion, which many did not strictly observe, they were similar to the non-Jewish French people among whom they lived and worked.

The other Jewish community—eastern European Jews who had settled in France—were generally not so well off as the old Jewish elite. Most were workers or ran small businesses, especially in the clothing industry. Many conversed with each other

A French anti-Semitic propaganda poster asking the French people to expose the Jews' plan to take over the world. *(Photograph by R. Peron, courtesy of Snark/Art Resource)*

The Man Who Saved 10,000 Jews

As refugees from northern France headed south, many tried to escape the country altogether. To leave legally, they needed a visa issued by the country where they planned to resettle. In Bordeaux, a French port on the Atlantic coast, thousands of refugees were desperate to obtain these documents so they could board ships leaving the country. They tried to get them from the foreign consulates in the city. The counsel-general of Portugal was Aristides de Sousa Mendes, a lawyer by profession and a deeply religious Catholic (though some of his ancestors were Portuguese Jews who had been forced to convert to Catholicism in 1497). He began to issue large numbers of Portuguese transit visas to French refugees, including Jews. Although Portugal was neutral in the war, it was friendly to Germany, and Portuguese officials told Sousa Mendes to cease issuing the documents. He ignored the order. From June 17 to June 19, 1940, Sousa Mendes granted 30,000 transit visas, 10,000 of them to Jews.

For these actions, he was arrested and sent back to Portugal, where he lost his job and pension and was barred from practicing law. Sousa Mendes said he had disobeyed his government's mandate in order to act as a Christian. He died in poverty in 1954. More than ten years after Sousa Mendes' death, he was honored by Israel as "Righteous Among the Nations," an award given to non-Jews who acted to save Jews. In 1987 the Portuguese government officially named him a hero. Sousa Mendes probably saved more Jews from the Holocaust than any single individual except Raoul Wallenberg.

in Yiddish rather than in French. They were often members of the political organizations they had supported before arriving in France. Eastern European Jews in France were more likely to live in a neighborhood with other Jews than were Jews who had been born in France. During the 1930s, much of the French anti-Semitism was aimed at these so-called foreign Jews rather than at the Israelites.

From 1933 until the beginning of World War II in 1939, some 50,000 more Jews fled to France from Nazi-occupied countries such as Germany, Austria, and what is now the Czech Republic. Very few of these Jews were French citizens; since the Nazis had taken away their right to citizenship, they were considered stateless, with no legal citizenship anywhere. In the late 1930s, Poland and other eastern European countries also passed laws that stripped citizenship from Jews, so some of these refugees who migrated to France were also stateless. In addition, between 25,000 and 50,000 Jewish refugees from the Netherlands and especially from Belgium poured into France in spring 1940 as the German army overran their countries.

Most Jews in France, both French-born and foreign-born, lived in the northern and eastern parts of the country, especially in the city of Paris. Large Jewish communities also formed in Alsace and Lorraine, the eastern French provinces that had been part of the German empire from 1871 to 1918.

Vichy France and the Resistance

When World War II broke out, France was considered the greatest military power in Europe. Although Germany had quickly conquered Poland, Denmark, the Netherlands, and Belgium, no one thought France could be easily defeated. Yet the French army and its ally, Britain, were badly beaten by the German armored divisions that invaded France in May 1940. During six weeks of heavy fighting, the Germans smashed the French army, forced the British to evacuate their army to England, and closed in on Paris. Chaos ensued as the French government fled from Paris and 4 million civilians clogged the roads heading south to escape the advancing Germans. Among them were thousands of Jews, including approximately 50,000

A shocking sight to the French, Adolf Hitler and Nazi generals confer near the Eiffel Tower in Paris. *(Reproduced by permission of © Hulton Getty/Liaison Agency)*

Charles de Gaulle and the Free French

Some French citizens opposed Vichy from the beginning. Charles de Gaulle, a little-known army general, fled to London and declared that France should continue to fight Germany. With British support, he organized French forces that had escaped the country to continue the war alongside the British. Called the Free French, they eventually fought in Africa, Italy, France, and Germany. De Gaulle's goal (which he largely achieved) was for Britain, and later the other Allies (the United States and the Soviet Union), to treat the Free French as the real government of France. De Gaulle had some difficulty getting Allied support. U.S. President Franklin D. Roosevelt disliked de Gaulle and feared that the French leader was an old-fashioned military man who did not believe in democracy. Ultimately, Roosevelt and British Prime Minister Winston Churchill came to recognize de Gaulle as the French leader.

Little-known army general Charles de Gaulle maintained that France should continue to fight Germany. He declared the Free French as the real government of France. *(Library of Congress)*

foreign Jews. Marshal Philippe Pétain, a hero of World War I (1914–1918), was chosen to head the new government. Pétain had helped defeat the Germans in 1918, but in 1940 he was eighty-four and more sympathetic to the Nazis than to the Popular Front.

Pétain quickly agreed to an armistice with Germany to stop the fighting. Under the terms of the agreement, France was divided into two sections: The northern half and all of the Atlantic coast were occupied by the German army; the southern part of the country was controlled by Pétain's regime. The new French government's laws also applied to the German-occupied zone, but only if they did not interfere with German orders. France would also have to pay for the huge cost of the German occupation, millions of dollars per day, and Germany refused to release French soldiers taken pris-

oner in the battle. Pétain's government made its new capital in Vichy, a small city in central France famous for its mineral water and baths. Vichy was chosen because it had many hotels that could be used as government offices. The unoccupied zone become known as Vichy France, and the government was also referred to as Vichy. The town was soon swarming with politicians who had opposed the Popular Front. The French constitution was changed to abolish democracy, and Pétain was given dictatorial powers as the head of the new French state that replaced the French republic. Even the famous slogan of the republic, dating back to the French Revolution, was changed: Instead of "Liberty, Equality, Fraternity," the Vichy motto was "Work, Family, Country."

Networks of resistance groups began to surface in both the German-occupied zone and Vichy

This German gasoline supply train was derailed and burned by explosives placed on the tracks by French resistance fighters. *(Reproduced by permission of AP/Wide World Photos.)*

France. They published illegal newspapers; hid people sought by the Nazis; and attempted to organize opposition to Vichy. At first small and loosely organized, these groups eventually gained more members and engaged in a wide variety of actions. They forged identity papers and other documents needed for Jews to survive in occupied France; used secret radios to send reports on German military forces to England; hid British and American airmen whose planes were shot down over France; attacked German troops; blew up railroad lines; and committed other acts of sabotage, obstructing German military actions and destroying equipment. Jews played an important part in many of these organizations. It is estimated that 15 to 20 percent of active resistance members were Jews, even though they made up less than 1 percent of the population. In addition, several all-Jewish resistance groups were formed.

Most French people, however, were not active in the resistance, at least at the beginning. The few pro-Nazi French were happy that France had been defeated by Germany. Many more agreed with Vichy government policies, supporting cooperation with Germany. The majority, however, were cautiously hopeful, respecting Pétain and believing he would work for the benefit of France in a difficult situation. These citizens did not support the Germans who had conquered their country, nor did they share the Nazis' ideas. They were simply trying to continue to earn a living and send their children to school. They hoped Vichy would be able to arrange for the release of the 2 million French prisoners of war held in Germany. They also hoped Pétain could ease the harsh conditions that the Germans were imposing on their country. Perhaps most of all, however, they hoped the war was over for France.

Collaboration with the Nazis

At the beginning of the occupation, when it appeared that Germany would win the war, some French leaders thought the future of France—and their own personal power—depended on cultivating a close relationship with the Germans. They

World War I hero Marshal Philippe Pétain was chosen to lead the French Vichy government when he was eighty-four years old. He was more sympathetic to the Nazis than the French Communists. *(French Embassy Press and Information Division)*

Pierre Laval, head of the Vichy government beginning in April 1942, claimed he only pretended to cooperate with the Germans, though his actions, and those of some of the other Vichy leaders, suggest otherwise. *(Reproduced by permission of Archive Photos/Popperfoto)*

wanted collaboration, but this union soon took on a meaning beyond simply working together toward a common goal. With 3 million German soldiers occupying the country, many citizens understood that France often had no choice except to obey the Nazis. However, the idea of voluntary collaboration was difficult to accept by the French populace. They were outraged by the publication of news photographs showing Pétain greeting Hitler as a friend. Pierre Laval, the most powerful Vichy leader, openly stated that he hoped Germany would win the war. As time went on, French citizens began to believe that Laval and his fellow collaborators were traitors.

In fact, the Vichy regime cooperated with Germany more than the governments of other occupied countries, even though it had more bargaining power. France controlled most of North Africa, including regions important in the war between Great Britain and Germany, and French troops and administrators in North Africa and in other French colonies were still obeying the orders of the Vichy government. Vichy also controlled the powerful French fleet, which the Germans wanted to keep separate from the British navy, in order to

prevent a formidable union between these forces. The Vichy government never used these powerful advantages to bargain with the Germans.

Most of Germany's goals clashed with the economic interests of the people of France. The Germans wanted to secure money from the French government, to take over many French companies, and to buy French products cheaply. They also wanted access to crops grown on French farms. Before long, they were demanding that French people be sent to Germany to work.

Vichy Passes Anti-Jewish Laws

As was the policy everywhere in German-occupied Europe, the Nazis also wanted to rid France of Jews. Some Vichy leaders believed that by helping attack Jews, they could gain the favor of the German government without becoming unpopular with the rest of their own people. For these leaders, it seemed easier to help the Nazis by being anti-Jewish than by giving in to Germany's other demands. The Vichy regime began targeting Jews even before the Germans issued any orders. Only two months after the armistice, Vichy repealed the law that made

Four female prisoners stand outside a barrack behind a barbed-wire fence at the Gurs transit camp in France, 1942. *(Photograph by Alice Resch-Synnestvedt, courtesy of USHMM Photo Archives)*

it a crime to attack a group because of race or religion. In October 1940 the first specifically anti-Jewish law was passed. It banned Jews from all government jobs, teaching positions, and the armed forces. Also, the number of Jews in many other professions was restricted. The law defined a Jew according to Nazi theory—the number of that person's Jewish grandparents. This meant that a person of Jewish ancestry whose parents had become Catholics—and who had been raised Catholic—was still considered a Jew. In other words, the law treated the Jews as members of a different race, not simply a different religion. This was the first time a racially based law had been put into effect in modern France. The harshest aspects of the law applied to the stateless Jewish refugees, for it took away their legal rights and made them subject to arrest. Soon, 25,000 refugees from Germany, Austria, and the Czech lands were placed in detention camps by French police. Forced to live under terrible conditions with little protection from the cold, people starved to death in some of the camps. There were cases of brutal treatment by the French guards. Other Jews were later put into forced-labor groups.

In March 1941 Vichy created a special government department in charge of Jewish affairs, which was first headed by a notorious anti-Semite, and later by a man who had an even more virulent hatred of Jews. In June, the government ordered that property (such as businesses) owned by Jews be "Aryanized," or taken over and transferred to non-Jews. At the same time, Jews were required to register with the government; the registration lists were used to seek out and arrest Jews.

The Germans had been taking similar measures in their French zone of control. In September 1940, Jews who had fled to southern France were barred by a German order from returning to their homes. Like most of the 4 million French people who had tried to escape to the south during the fighting, most of the Jews wanted to return home after the armistice. The German order forced them to stay in Vichy France and, strictly by chance, saved the lives of many Jews. In April 1941, six months after Vichy placed work restrictions on Jews, the Germans forbade Jews from making a living with certain specified occupations. A month later, all Jews, both French-born and foreign, in occupied France were required to wear the Star of David at all times. The order was extremely unpopular with most non-Jews, just as it was in Belgium and the Netherlands. Jewish war veterans wore the star alongside their military medals and paraded through the streets of Paris as crowds cheered them on. Vichy officials, even leading anti-Semites, refused to extend the order to the Vichy zone. That spring and summer, the Germans arrested almost 7,500 Jews; most were foreigners, but 1,300 were native-born French Jews.

In December 1941, when the resistance tried to kill a German air force officer, the Germans arrested and later deported 1,000 French Jews, most of whom were doctors and lawyers. In addition to imposing an enormous fine of 1 billion francs on the Jewish community, the Germans shot ninety-five hostages, fifty-nine of them Jews. Throughout the occupation, the Germans took civilian hostages and executed them in large numbers whenever the resistance attacked German troops. A high proportion of Jews were always included among the hostages.

Jews Deported to Death Camps

As time passed, the Germans arrested more and more Jews. At first the prisoners were sent to various camps, one of which was at Drancy. In this suburb of Paris, an unfinished low-income housing project had been turned into a detention camp. Administered and guarded by French police (not by the Germans), Drancy eventually became the transit camp for Jews from all of France. They usually stayed until transportation became available, then the Germans packed them into trains of locked cattle cars, about 1,000 people on each train, and sent them to "the east" for "resettlement." This transport cycle was essential to the realization of the *Endlösung*, or "Final Solution," the Nazi name for the plan to eliminate European Jews. From March 1942 until July 1944, almost 78,000 Jews—thousands of them children—left Drancy on the trains; fewer than 3,000 of them returned to France. The main destination was Auschwitz, where almost all captives were killed in gas chambers.

The organization in charge of deporting and killing Jews was the SS, the black-uniformed security force of the Nazi party that was composed of the most dedicated Nazis. The SS intended to arrest and deport all the Jews of France, one trainload at a time and 15,000 people per month. They planned to begin with the occupied zone, but in order to arrest such a large number of people, they needed the cooperation of the French. The SS had only 3,000 police in France, and the German army refused to allow soldiers to take part in the roundup of Jews. (The army was involved, however, in the seemingly random shooting of civilian hostages.) At first Vichy officials would not agree to the use of French police for the Jewish arrests, but the SS threatened to arrest and deport all Jews, including French citizens, if the French did not help. If Vichy ordered its police to cooperate, however, the SS promised to arrest only foreign Jews. Laval, who was running the Vichy government at that point, agreed to the terms. The SS moved quickly to round up the foreign Jews of Paris for deportation. On July 16, 1942, they arrested 12,500 people, only half the number they had planned to capture that day. Single men without families were taken directly to Drancy and from there were sent to Auschwitz.

Since the Germans had not yet authorized the deportation of small children from France, families with children were taken to the Vélodrome d'Hiver (called the Vel' d'Hiv' for short), a glass-enclosed sports arena in Paris used for indoor bicycle races. The French authorities had made no preparations for these prisoners. Guarded by French police, more than 8,000 people (including 4,000 children), slept on the ground or on the bleacher-type seats. They had almost no food, little water, and inadequate sanitation; the heat and the smell were said to be unbearable. Some people went crazy, and several even committed suicide. Childhood diseases like measles spread quickly, but the only medical care was provided by volunteers. Several women gave birth to babies under these terrible conditions. Some prisoners remained at the Vel' d'Hiv' for nearly a week. A few escaped when French policemen looked the other way.

Buses then took the Jews to two detention camps about fifty miles south of Paris, where they remained for two or three more weeks. At that time, adults and older children were marched to the railroad station in a nearby town. The French gendarmes who guarded the camps used clubs and water hoses to separate parents from their younger children, who were left behind. The adults and teenagers were packed onto a train. From the end of July through the first week of August 1942, four of these trains left the camps bound for Auschwitz. At the end of the war, out of the more than 4,000 people who had journeyed on these transports, only thirty-five were still alive. The 3,500 smaller

Some older Jewish children did survive Auschwitz. Here some of them stand in concentration camp uniforms between two rows of barbed wire awaiting their liberators. *(USHMM Photo Archives)*

children, some too young to know their own names, remained at the camps and were cared for by a small group of Red Cross volunteers and mothers who had not been deported. When the children were finally taken to the train station and sent to Drancy, they were told they would be reunited with their parents. Adult prisoners at Drancy took care of them as well as they could until the second half of August, when the children were transported from Drancy to Auschwitz on seven different trains; none survived.

The SS never intended to limit the "Final Solution" in France to foreign Jews, and they soon put pressure on Vichy to arrest Jews who were French citizens. Vichy refused to cooperate. Having fallen behind schedule in deporting Jews from France, the SS tried to convince Vichy to revoke the citizenship of Jews who had not been born in France. If successful, this action would have turned thousands more Jews into foreigners who were subject to deportation. Vichy kept stalling, however. At one point, for instance, Laval agreed to a version of a law that would strip some Jews of their citizenship,

and the SS prepared to arrest and deport more Jews. A month later, however, Laval told the Germans he had changed his mind, that he had not understood that the Jews would be deported. On another occasion, Laval even claimed he had lost his copy of the German proposals and would need a new one. Although the Germans sometimes arrested and deported Jews who were French citizens, including those born in France, they were never able to obtain Vichy's cooperation in the task. Without the assistance of the French government, the SS had a much more difficult time tracking down Jews, so the great majority of the Jews who were deported from France and killed in the Holocaust were foreign-born.

Vichy's Role Changes

The first arrests and deportations of the Jews of France had occurred in the German-occupied zone. But around the time that the children from the Vel' d'Hiv' were being sent to Auschwitz, the first Jews from the Vichy zone—those refugees who had been

What Did Vichy Know?

While the French may not have known the exact details of the fate of deported Jews, especially at first, this was true only for a short time. Unlike ordinary people in Europe, including the Jews, Vichy officials had many ways of finding out what was really happening in other countries. Soon, rumors, and then hard facts, about the death camps reached the Vichy government through various sources, but Vichy continued to collaborate. Historians agree that by then, if any of the leaders of Vichy did not know what was happening, it was because they did not want to know the fate of those being deported.

arrested by Vichy and held in detention camps for more than a year—were also being shuttled to the death camps. In August and September 1942, some 10,000 Jewish refugees were turned over to the Nazis with the aid of French officials. The French further assisted the Germans by arranging for the children of stateless Jews to be deported along with their parents. Jules-Gérard Saliège, the Catholic archbishop of the southern French city of Toulouse, wrote a letter of protest and ordered all his priests to read it during Sunday Mass on August 23, 1942. The letter stated, among other things, that all people, including both Jews and foreigners, were part of the human race and should be treated accordingly.

This situation in Vichy intensified in November 1942 when British and American troops landed in French North Africa to fight the Germans. Control of North Africa had been one of Vichy's most important bargaining weapons, and now it was gone. Within days, the German army crossed into the Vichy zone of France and occupied the whole country except for the southeastern corner. For the next one and one-half years, until the Germans were driven from France, they had direct control of most of the country. The Vichy government still existed, but it became more and more of a puppet government whose actions were controlled by Ger-

many. During this time, the Germans intensified their efforts to capture Jews, but they were usually unsuccessful. More Jews were hiding, and a growing number of non-Jewish French people were protecting them. As the resistance increased in strength and the Allied armies won more and more battles against Germany, many French collaborators became increasingly cautious. In some cases, officials who had cooperated with the Nazis earlier in the occupation were now working secretly with the resistance. At the same time, special pro-Nazi units of French volunteers, called the Milice (Militia), sided with the SS. Before long, the Milice and the resistance were essentially fighting a civil war.

Desperate to fulfill their quotas of French Jews destined for Auschwitz, the SS raided homes that had been set up to care for children of deported Jews and homes for the aged. They swept through detention camps looking for Jews without warning the Vichy authorities, whom they no longer trusted.

The Germans also put tremendous pressure on Italy to allow the arrest of Jews in the Italian-occupied zone of France. When Italy surrendered to the Allies in mid-1943, the SS swept into the area to try to capture thousands of Jews who had sought Italian protection. The main SS target was Nice, the southern French resort city in the Italian zone. The roundup should have been easy—Jews in Nice had not been in hiding and had not needed false identity papers. In addition, among them were many foreigners, who dressed differently or spoke French with an obvious accent. This time, however, the SS did not have the lists of names and addresses that Vichy had prepared for earlier roundups. They also lacked the assistance of the French police. The SS cruised the city in unmarked cars, grabbing pedestrians off the streets to check their identity papers. There were nightly raids on hotels and boardinghouses. The Germans searched every train and bus that left the city and offered large rewards to informers who told them where to find Jews. Still, despite all these measures, the SS was able to capture fewer than 2,000 Jews of the 25,000 to 30,000 known to be in the area of Italian-controlled France.

On June 6, 1944, D-Day, British and American armies landed on the beaches of Normandy in northern France. After heavy fighting, they began to drive the Germans back. As resistance groups throughout France attacked the German forces, the Allies landed a second army in southern France. In late August the tanks of de Gaulle's Free French forces, part of the Allied army that had fought its

This young woman, a member of the French resistance, welcomes British troops liberating a town. *(Reproduced by permission of AP/Wide World Photos)*

American troops landing on the beaches of Normandy, France, on June 6, 1944, D-Day. *(Reproduced by permission of Corbis-Bettmann)*

way eastward from Normandy, entered Paris, where resistance forces had launched a full-scale uprising. By winter, the German troops had been pushed back to their own border. France was free.

Throughout the final months of the war, however, the SS never gave up its plan to eliminate the Jews. Trains left Drancy, bound for Auschwitz, until the Allied bombing of French railroads and sabotage by the resistance made rail travel impossible. The SS tried frantically to deport Jews from France even when the German army needed the deportation trains for military purposes. When the Allied troops reached Paris and Drancy, the Nazis scrambled to send captives directly to the death camps from other places. More hostages, including many Jews, were executed, and people who had been in prisons for months were shot.

In total, about 78,000 Jews who had been in France died in the Holocaust. Approximately 55,000 of these victims were foreigners. The other 23,000 were French citizens, including about 8,000 immigrants who had become citizens and another 8,000 children born in France to foreign parents. (Vichy treated these French-born children as for-

eigners.) But Vichy could claim it had succeeded in saving all but 6,500 "Israelites," the old Jewish community of France.

The Role of French Citizens and Vichy

After the war, Laval tried to justify his actions in the Vichy government by claiming he had to sacrifice foreign Jews in order to save those who were French citizens. He admitted this policy had violated France's duty to those people who had sought its protection. Many of the deportees had lived and worked legally in France for many years and had raised their families there. Thousands of "foreign" Jewish men had volunteered to fight for the French army against Nazi Germany when the war began. Laval claimed that in German-occupied France, there was no other alternative. Laval and other Vichy leaders claimed they had played a double game against the Germans, pretending to cooperate with the Nazis while always trying to yield as little as possible.

Many French collaborators also maintained that they did not realize Jews were being sent to

In an effort to disgrace a woman who collaborated with the Nazis, French resistance fighters placed a large swastika across her chest. *(National Archives/USHMM Photo Archives)*

their deaths. But Vichy leaders could not escape the fact that they had passed anti-Jewish laws on their own, without pressure from the Germans. They had helped the Nazis deport tens of thousands of people, including children, knowing at the very least that the Nazis were treating the Jews with terrible brutality and thousands were dying. Vichy officials were the first to suggest that children of foreign Jews should also be deported. They had organized special pro-Nazi units to hunt down members of the French resistance. In contrast, the Danish and Dutch governments, though far weaker, had refused to take any of these measures. As a result, the Danes were able to offer more protection to Jews living in Denmark.

In part, Vichy officials had collaborated with the Nazis simply to retain their own power. Determined to destroy the democratic tradition of France, they wanted to restructure the country permanently into an authoritative regime. To achieve these goals, they had been willing to cooperate with the German government. Yet Laval and his Vichy colleagues did not help kill Jews they considered to be French. According to historians, Laval was a clever, devious man who, throughout his long political career, was always seeking to get ahead and making deals. In his version of the truth, the deal he made with the Germans saved the lives of thousands of French Jews; the price he paid was to cooperate in the murder of thousands of others. Nearly all experts on the Holocaust reject Laval's argument. They believe that if Vichy had tried to protect all Jews and if the French government had refused to cooperate in the arrests and deportations, fewer Jews would have been sent to death camps.

To many French people, including de Gaulle and the resistance fighters, Vichy was never the real government of France—it was merely a gang of criminals that had taken over the country with the

French women who collaborated with the Germans are driven through Cherbourg, France, on the back of a truck in July 1944. Their heads were shaved as a form of punishment. *(National Archives/USHMM Photo Archives)*

help of the Germans. Opponents of Vichy felt they alone represented the real France: The Vichy regime, not France, had helped the Nazis deport and murder Jews. Yet everyone knew and readily admitted that many French individuals had helped the Germans. Immediately after the German retreat, several thousand collaborators were tried by special resistance-run courts and executed. Members of the Milice were shot by firing squads with little legal formality. Laval was executed after a trial. Pétain was sentenced to death, but his sentence was changed to life imprisonment because of his age and his service to France during World War I. Pétain later died in 1951.

As things settled down in post-war Europe, a myth began to develop in France, characterizing the majority of French citizens as supporters of the resistance and portraying only a small minority as Vichy supporters. People came to believe the majority of the very small number of collaborators had already been punished by the resistance. This

helped to restore pride in France after defeat and occupation by the Germans, and was also an attempt at ending the civil war between Vichy supporters and the resistance. Yet records reveal that some French citizens had helped deport Jews; others had informed the Milice that Jews were hiding in their villages. Many of these people hid their pasts for years after the war.

Although these people comprised only a small minority, many more had supported Vichy, especially at the beginning. For instance, even François Mitterrand, the president of France from 1981 to 1995 and a young man during the war, held low-level jobs in the Vichy government and supported Pétain before becoming a member of the resistance. A large number of French people had approved of the anti-Jewish laws enacted by the Vichy regime, and millions of others who thought the laws were unjust had kept silent.

For Jews especially, the official attitude of France was unacceptable. They believed that the

The French Police

For many years after World War II, the role of the French police in the Holocaust was rarely discussed in France. One reason why concerns the events of August 1944 when the police played a major role in the armed uprising of the French resistance against the Germans in Paris. For many people, those few days of fighting changed the image of the police. Instead of being perceived as an organization that had always collaborated with the Germans, the police were later viewed as fellow resistance fighters. During the late twentieth century, however, more and more people recognized the involvement of the police in the brutal reality of the Holocaust. In 1997 the French police union issued an apology for these actions.

The massive raids to find Jews for deportation in Paris were conducted mainly by the French police under German supervision. This pattern continued throughout the occupation, but the role of the French police during the German occupation is complex. First, they followed orders and participated in rounding up the Jews, supplying the needed manpower. Their cooperation was essential because they knew the neighborhoods and towns. Sometimes the police were extremely efficient, searching carefully for hidden Jews; at times, they were as brutal as the Germans.

However, French police officers often warned Jews before a raid or purposely failed to find them. For instance, during the Paris raid of July 16, 1942, half the Jews targeted for arrest could not be located, almost certainly because word of the operation had been leaked by the French police. Sometimes officers would be sent to arrest a Jewish family and would instead tell them that they should pack a suitcase. Then the officers would leave, saying they would be back in an hour, and no one was surprised if the family was gone when the police returned. Other times, the police simply accepted the word of neighbors that the family had already left town.

country itself, not simply a few Frenchmen, shared some responsibility for the deaths of almost 80,000 people. In 1995, a half-century after the end of the Holocaust, President Jacques Chirac of France officially acknowledged the role France had played in Nazi-organized attacks on the Jews.

15

The Jews and Germany's Allies: Italy and Hungary

Italy was Germany's most important European ally. Dictator Benito Mussolini, who had ruled the country since 1922, and his Fascist party had been models for Adolf Hitler before his rise to power in Germany. The Italian Black Shirts had provided the idea for the German brownshirts, or Nazi Storm Troopers. Still, despite the similarities between Fascist Italy and Nazi Germany, Italian Fascists differed significantly from German Nazis. The Italian Fascists rarely mentioned racial issues and never portrayed the Jews as the main enemy of Italy. Anti-Semitism was relatively rare in Italy, where Jews constituted only one-tenth of one percent of the population. A few Jews even held important positions in the Fascist government during its early years.

After Hitler and the Nazis gained control of Germany, Italy and Germany became close allies. Both sent resources (Italian troops; German airmen and planes) to assist Fascist rebels in Spain during the Spanish Civil War (1936–1939). It soon became clear, however, that Italy and Germany were not equal partners in their endeavors—Germany's much greater economic and military power made it the senior partner and Hitler the leader of the Fascist movement in Europe.

Just before World War II began, Italy passed severe anti-Semitic laws modeled after those in Germany. Although Mussolini had passed these laws in order to win favor with Hitler, he is said to have believed that racial theories were nonsense. With Mussolini's knowledge, his own sister protected Jews, a fact he felt would demonstrate that Italy's anti-Semitic laws were meant to be flexible. Mussolini was unconcerned that the Italian government did not always enforce the new laws strictly, or that Italian officials were known to have accepted bribes from Jews. Few Italians were anti-Semitic, and even some supporters of Mussolini were embarrassed by the laws, and did their best to make them less harsh.

The laws nevertheless affected many Italian Jews, who lost their jobs and were driven into poverty. Jews in the Italian army, even generals, were forced to retire. Jews who had recently settled in Italy, including refugees from the Nazis, were especially hard hit. Many, even those who had become Italian citizens, were forced to leave the country. Some were sent to prison camps where they endured a miserable existence; others were moved to small towns where they were forced to live under police supervision.

While life was difficult for the Jews under Italian jurisdiction, the government refused to deport them from Italian-controlled areas to death camps. Of all the countries occupied or strongly influenced by the Germans, only Italy protected not only native Jews, but also foreign Jews within its own borders and even Jews in Italian-occupied

HOLOCAUST AND WORLD WAR II ALMANAC • *Volume 1*

Jews wait in long lines as part of the deportation process. *(Reproduced by permission of Snark/Art Resource)*

areas of other countries. In the Italian-occupied section of southeastern France, for instance, the government allowed Jews to move about freely, even as they were being rounded up by the Germans only a few miles away. Jews from the remainder of France tried desperately to flee to safety in the Italian zone. The Germans were furious, deploying high-ranking Nazi officials to Rome, Italy's capital, to demand that Mussolini rectify the situation. Mussolini promised to take care of the problem, but in fact did nothing to change the policy. In several cases, Italian troops threatened to use force to prevent the French police, who were working for the Germans, from arresting Jews.

The Italian situation changed in summer 1943. As British and American armies invaded Italy, Mussolini's regime was overthrown and the new government surrendered to the Allied powers. The German army rushed in to occupy the northern half of the country, and it continued to fight against the Allies. Until the end of the war in Europe in May 1945, the Germans directly controlled much of Italy. In the north, they established a puppet state with Mussolini at the helm. Mussolini and his remaining Fascist supporters had little real power and cooperated with the Germans in every way, including arresting Jews. For twenty months, thousands of Jews were arrested and

deported by the Germans with the assistance of Italian Fascists. Many Jews went into hiding and were protected by non-Jewish Italians. A large percentage hid in Catholic monasteries and convents.

The SS searched throughout Italy for Jews; citizens who hid them were taking a great risk. Some historians attribute the willingness of Italians to hide Jews to the fact that it had become clear that Germany was going to lose the war. Still, the actions of the Italians, even at the beginning of the war, demonstrate that most of the nation's people were genuinely concerned with the welfare of the Jews. Of the approximately 45,000 Jews who were still in Italy in 1943, about 8,000 died. With the exception of Denmark, this was a lower percentage than in any other area controlled by Germany.

Hungary

Before World War I (1914–1918), Hungary was part of the Austrian Empire, which controlled much of Central Europe. The empire was often referred to as Austria-Hungary, and its Hungarian portion included many areas that had not been part of the country of Hungary historically. Like Austria and Germany, Hungary suffered massive territorial losses after World War I. In some of the areas of the country it was forced to relinquish,

Hungarian-speaking people constituted either a large minority or a majority of the population, and the desire to regain these territories became a major force in Hungarian politics. Hungarians resented the Treaty of Versailles—the peace treaty that ended World War I and took away various territories. In these ways, Hungarian sentiment mirrored that of Germany. Hungary, like Germany, experienced an attempted communist revolution immediately after World War I, with both the revolutionary government and the forces that defeated it launching extremely violent campaigns. Anti-Semitism was common in Hungary, and many Hungarians blamed the Jews for both the peace treaty and the attempted communist coup. In the early 1920s a wave of bloody pogroms washed over the country.

The government that came to power at this time continued to rule Hungary until almost the end of World War II. Miklós (Nicholas) Horthy, who had been an admiral in the old Austro-Hungarian navy, became regent of Hungary. Regents generally ruled in place of kings (often when the king was a child); since Hungary had no king, Horthy essentially acted as a dictator (although all opposing political parties and the parliament continued to exist). Horthy's government was extremely hostile to Jews. Most Jews were dismissed from government jobs. Jewish admittance to universities was restricted. Violence against Jews began to decrease after the pogroms, but Hungarian citizens remembered how recently the mobs had attacked the Jews.

In 1930, approximately 450,000 Jews lived in Hungary (about 5 percent of the population). Half of them lived in the capital city, Budapest, where they comprised 20 percent of the local population. Budapest's Jews were prominent in the arts, theater, and literary life. Many more were involved in business and commercial activities, where they played an important role in the Hungarian economy, in part, because there were relatively few other members of the middle class. Most Hungarians were still peasants who lived on the land but rarely owned it. They worked on the farms of great landowners, who were the richest and most powerful people in the country. As in other parts of eastern Europe, Jews represented the social class between the peasants and the landowners. The landowners usually did not want to get involved in business activities. The importance of Jews in the economy made them more noticeable, and probably contributed to the strength of anti-Semitism in

Miklós Horthy, regent of Hungary, allied with Hitler to regain Hungarian territory lost after World War I. *(Library of Congress)*

Hungary. The noticeable differences between Hungarian Jews and other Hungarians were also factors in anti-Jewish sentiment. Many Jews in Budapest, like Jews in western and northern Europe, were completely assimilated into Hungarian society. They lived, dressed, and spoke like their non-Jewish neighbors, and a significant number had even become Christians (partially because of anti-Semitism). In the rest of the country, however, Hungarian Jews were often traditional in dress, speech, and the strict observance of Jewish religious laws and customs.

While Hungarian Jews would have faced institutionalized persecution anyway due to widespread anti-Semitism in the country and the attitude of the government, their troubles increased because of Hungary's desire for an alliance with Germany. The mutual quest to regain territory lost after World War I joined the nations philosophically, but only Germany had the power to accomplish this goal. After the Nazis came to power in Germany in 1933, Hungary attempted to strengthen its ties with Germany by attacking Jews. German influence on Hungarian life increased: Violent Nazi-style organizations, such as the Arrow Cross, sometimes supported the government but also pressured it to increase the Hungarian connection to Nazi Germany and to step up anti-Jewish measures. The Nazi government helped finance these groups and spread anti-Semitic propaganda in Hungary.

In 1938 the first Hungarian anti-Jewish law was passed, limiting the number of Jewish employees in private companies to 20 percent of the total. In 1939 a more drastic law restricted Jewish participation in newspaper and radio work, and prohibited Jews from entering professions such as law and medicine unless the number of Jews in those professions fell below 6 percent. Jews born outside Hungary could no longer become citizens, and even Jews born in Hungary lost the right to vote unless their families had lived in the country since 1868. The laws also defined Jews as a race rather than as members of a religion, thus affecting Jews who had converted to Christianity. Hungarian churches opposed this aspect of the laws, but did not oppose discrimination against unconverted Jews.

At the time these laws were passed, Hungary's alliance with Nazi Germany began to pay off in terms of territory. In 1938, after Hitler threatened to go to war, Britain and France watched Germany take a section of Czechoslovakia, despite that country's protests. Hungary was also awarded part of the country as a reward for its friendship with Hitler. The following year, when Germany destroyed Czechoslovakia, Hungary was again awarded a sector. Hungary later received Transylvania, a very large section of Romania, and part of Yugoslavia. All of these areas had large Hungarian-speaking populations and contained almost one-third of a million Jews. By 1941, more than 700,000 Jews were now under Hungarian rule, comprising the largest Jewish population in Europe after Poland and the Soviet Union.

The return of lost territories appeared to be a victory for Hungary, which became Hitler's ally. German troops were allowed to cross through Hungary when Germany invaded Yugoslavia, despite the fact that Hungary had signed a friendship treaty with Yugoslavia. Soon after, Hungary joined Germany in its invasion of the Soviet Union in June 1941. Hungary would ultimately pay a heavy price for its alliance with Germany. Hundreds of thousands of Hungarian soldiers died while fighting in Russia; Hungary was devastated by Allied bombs and invasions; and it lost all of its new territory by the end of World War II. The price paid by the Jews of Hungary for their country's alliance with Hitler was steep.

In the first years of the war, many able-bodied Jewish men (130,000, eventually) were put into forced-labor brigades in the Hungarian army, though they were not allowed to be regular soldiers. When Hungary invaded the Soviet Union, 40,000 Jews in forced-labor brigades were sent to the front lines to accompany Hungarian troops. They were brutally treated by the Hungarian army, given inadequate food and clothing, and subjected to random shootings. About 75 percent of these brigade workers died from the cold, malnutrition, and execution. In 1941 the Hungarian government rounded up and deported more than 20,000 stateless Jews, sending several thousand to be slave laborers for the Hungarian army fighting in the Ukraine and Russia. The rest were transported to a part of the Ukraine then controlled by Germany, where they were massacred by the Einsatzgruppen. Hungarian troops that took part in the Nazi invasion of Yugoslavia murdered 4,000 Jews there, as well as 6,000 non-Jewish Serbs. During these massacres, some Hungarian officers ordered Jews to be buried alive.

Despite these events and the general anti-Semitism of the Hungarian government, most Hungarian Jews were still alive in 1944. German pressure notwithstanding, there had been no more deportations, so Hungarian Jews, unlike Jews in almost every other country, had not been sent to the death camps in occupied Poland. The Hungarian prime minister, Miklós Kállay, publicly declared that he favored resettlement as the long-term solution to Hungary's "Jewish problem," but made it clear that resettlement would not take place until Germany explained where the Jews were being taken. Kállay probably understood that the Nazis would not tell him because the "resettled" Jews were actually being murdered.

As long as Hungarian Jews remained in Hungary, they were far better off than Jews in the rest of Europe. The Soviet army, beating back Germany and its allies, was approaching the old Hungarian border, ready to drive toward Budapest. It appeared at that point that the great majority of Hungarian Jews would survive the war.

Hungarian Jews in Danger

The fortunes of the Hungarian Jews changed in March 1944. Germany correctly suspected that the Hungarian government was attempting to get out of the war in order to avoid a Soviet invasion. In addition, Hitler was furious that the Hungarian government refused to deport the Jews, and demanded that Horthy come to Germany for a meeting. When Horthy arrived, he was taken prisoner by the Germans and was forbidden to communicate with his government. When he was allowed to return to Budapest twenty-four hours later, the Germans controlled Hungary. Carrying out a carefully prepared plan, the Nazis had rushed troops into the country. German officials watched over every department of the Hungarian government. Kállay escaped to Turkey as other political leaders who opposed Hungary's pro-German policies were arrested and opposition political parties and newspapers were banned. The new government was comprised of strong supporters of Germany, including many members of the Arrow Cross movement, the Hungarian Nazis. Instead of an ally of Germany, Hungary was now its puppet.

Suddenly the Jews of Hungary were in immediate danger. German occupation forces and German officials were joined in Budapest by "Jewish experts" from the SS. These SS members were under the leadership of Adolf Eichmann, head of the Jewish Affairs Section of the RHSA, the German Main Office for Reich Security. Eichmann and his men, with the help of their Hungarian supporters, acted much more quickly than they had in other countries. The Nazis were aware that the Soviet army would arrive within months, and within one month, Jews outside of Budapest were being forced to move into ghettos. Once the Jews were concentrated into relatively few ghettos, deportation procedures could begin with greater ease and efficiency, as in Poland. Eichmann divided Hungary into six zones. The plan was to clear Jews from one zone at a time, leaving Budapest for last. The first trains, carrying Jews who had been arrested for changing their addresses without permission (in other words, trying to go into hiding), left for the Auschwitz death camp by the end of April. The organized deportations from the first of Eichmann's zones began in the middle of May. Train after train carried thousands of Jews to Auschwitz, where almost all were immediately gassed. By June 7, nearly 300,000 Jews had been deported; by July 7, less than four months after the Germans took over Hungary, the total was almost 440,000.

A Million Jews for Sale

As in other parts of German-controlled Europe, the approach of the Allied armies and the growing certainty that Germany would lose the war seemed to make the Nazis intensify their efforts to kill Jews. Even if Germany lost the war against the Allies, it would try to win the war against the Jews. The desperate military situation, however, caused certain top Nazi leaders to devise methods to use the Jews to help prevent defeat and to preserve their own lives and positions. Some hoped to make peace with the two major Western Allies, Great Britain and the United States, while continuing to fight the Soviet Union. Some even believed that the British and Americans might join Germany in a war against the communist Soviet Union. These Nazi leaders realized that a deal would only be possible if Hitler was out of the picture. They also realized that continuing the murder of Jews would prevent a deal, but they hoped an offer to end the deportations and gassings would overshadow the prior execution of millions of people. Although the hope for a Nazi alliance with Great Britain and America was unrealistic, the idea provides the background to one of the stranger episodes of the Holocaust.

At the same time Eichmann was preparing for the deportations of hundreds of thousands of Jews, he was also offering some a reprieve from extermination. On April 25, 1944, Eichmann met with Joel Brand, a leader of the Council for Assistance and Rescue. It was an organization of Hungarian Jews known as the Va'ada, the Hebrew word for "council." The Va'ada had operated for two years, helping to smuggle Jews from Poland and Slovakia into Hungary, providing them with false papers, and collecting information on German activities in Poland and elsewhere. The Va'ada also had connections with the American Jewish Joint Distribution Committee, which helped finance rescue efforts in Europe. Alex Weissberg recounts details of the meeting between Eichmann and Brand in *Desperate Mission: Joel Brand's Story as Told by Alex Weissberg* (1958). "I suppose you know who I am," Eichmann told Brand. "I was in charge of the *aktions* in Germany, Poland, and Czechoslovakia. Now it is Hungary's turn." But Eichmann proposed a deal in place of deportations: "I am prepared to sell you one million Jews." Brand was free to take the million people from anywhere in Europe, even Auschwitz. "Who do you want to save?" Eichmann asked. "Young men, young women, old people, children? Sit down and talk."

Eichmann's request included such goods as soap, coffee, tea, and chocolate, but his main desire was 10,000 trucks, which he promised would be used only against the Soviet army, not the British and Americans. "Goods for blood, blood for goods,"

The Allied Priority

By the time Eichmann's offer to Joel Brand was rejected, the British knew that the Nazis had already murdered millions of Jews. They knew about the gas chambers at Auschwitz, and they knew that Hungarian Jews, the largest remaining Jewish population in Europe, were being deported to Auschwitz. While Brand was on his mission to meet with the British, Jewish leaders were urging the British and Americans to bomb the railroad lines from Hungary to Auschwitz, and to bomb the death camp itself. Despite warnings from Jewish leaders that every day was crucial, these ideas were not regarded as high priorities, and the British and American air forces eventually rejected the proposals, saying they involved too many technical difficulties. Many historians have argued that bombing Auschwitz and the rail lines leading to it would have been possible, pointing out that air raids were in fact being conducted near Auschwitz around this time, though they were aimed at other targets nearby. Other historians defend the Allied decision, claiming that it would not have been possible to bomb Auschwitz without killing thousands of prisoners. Bombing railroads, they say, would have had little effect because the lines could have been repaired quickly and alternate routes could have been used in the meantime. It is clear that the Allied leaders had decided that winning the war against Germany as quickly as possible was the most important priority, and they were unwilling to use their air forces for a mission that might delay their military objectives. They refused to give serious consideration to any plan aimed at rescuing the Jews rather than defeating Germany militarily and believed the best way to stop the Nazi murder of the Jews was to defeat Germany. The Allied victory, however, would come too late to save most of the Jews of Hungary.

he told Brand, who would go to Istanbul, Turkey, to make the arrangements. "If you come back from Istanbul and tell me the offer has been accepted, I will close Auschwitz." Then, Eichmann said, he would bring 100,000 Jews to a safe border. Upon receiving the first 1,000 trucks, he would release another 100,000 Jews. "We'll go on like that. A thousand trucks for every hundred thousand Jews."

In Istanbul, Brand met with British government officials and representatives of Jewish organizations, but it soon became clear that the British and Americans would never allow trucks to be sent to the German army for use against the Soviets. Brand hoped he would be able to convince Eichmann to accept money instead. Discussions and negotiations between Brand and the British dragged on, even though Eichmann had extended his offer for only a brief period of time. The mass deportations from Hungary to Auschwitz were soon under way. When Brand tried to travel to Syria to meet with other officials, he was arrested by the British and placed in custody. In mid-July

Eichmann's secret offer was publicly rejected, and called a mixture of blackmail and threats. By then, more than half the Jews of Hungary were dead.

The rejection of Eichmann's deal has been a subject of intense controversy. The British regarded the offer as an attempt to create a split between the Soviet Union and the Western Allies—almost certainly one reason for the offer. Nazi leaders were trying to establish secret contacts with British and American representatives, hoping that a split among the Allies would save Germany from defeat. Until the end of the war, the Nazis remained convinced that the Allies would not stick together. Aware of this Nazi strategy, the Allies were determined to maintain unity until Germany had surrendered unconditionally. Yet this does not entirely explain the way the British treated Joel Brand.

Raoul Wallenberg

By early July 1944, more than 400,000 Jews from all the zones of Hungary, except Budapest, had been deported to Auschwitz on the transport trains. A complicated set of factors, however, temporarily stopped the deportations. Heinrich Himmler tried to negotiate an end to the war with the Americans and British without Hitler's knowledge, and the Hungarian government also maneuvered to get out of the war as the Soviet army invaded. The secrecy that had surrounded the Holocaust was now almost completely stripped away, and the leaders of every country knew about the Nazis' mass extermination campaign. At this time, Raoul Wallenberg set out to save the Jews remaining in Budapest.

Raoul Wallenberg was a Swedish diplomat, a member of one of the richest families in Sweden, a relative of the royal family, and a graduate of the University of Michigan in the United States. He went to Budapest in July, ostensibly as a representative of neutral Sweden, but his true mission was to try to save the Jews. Wallenberg began his efforts by issuing Swedish passports to any Hungarian Jews who had relatives or business contacts in Sweden. Next he began distributing "protective passports" to other Jews that placed them under the protection of the Swedish government. Soon, diplomats from other neutral countries such as Switzerland, Portugal, and Spain also issued protective documents, as did the representative of Catholic leader Pope Pius XII. Wallenberg eventually rented thirty-one buildings and placed Swedish flags on them. He declared them to be Swedish territory, protected in the same manner as a foreign embassy. He then used the buildings to house 15,000 people in what became known as the "international ghetto."

Nevertheless, 200,000 Jews still remained in the Hungarian capital. Despite Himmler's wish to end the deportations, Eichmann was determined to send Budapest's Jews to their deaths. No longer having the option to deport Jews to Auschwitz, which the Nazis were planning to dismantle, Eichmann ordered that they be rounded up and sent on forced marches. In November 1944 the first of a series of death marches began, with around 30,000 people walking through rain and snow for seven days without food, heading for the Austrian border. Guards shot anyone who could not keep up. Wallenberg and his staff attempted to free people from these marches, claiming they were under Swedish protection. He threatened, lied, pleaded, and bribed the Germans and Hungarians, sometimes successfully. When the marches were called off, 160,000 Jews were still alive in Budapest.

That winter, as Soviet artillery and Allied planes bombarded the starving city, the Arrow

Raoul Wallenberg saved the lives of tens of thousands of Hungarian Jews. *(USHMM Photo Archives)*

Cross continued to murder Jews in Budapest. These Hungarian Nazis killed 20,000 Jews, often torturing them first, and throwing their bodies into the River Danube. Even after the Soviet army entered Budapest in January 1945, the killings continued in areas of the city controlled by the Arrow Cross. Finally, after almost a month of heavy fighting, the Soviet army captured the city.

On January 17, 1945, Wallenberg was on his way to a meeting with the Soviet military commander when he disappeared. The Soviet government initially claimed he was under "Soviet protection," and then denied any knowledge of his whereabouts. An official Soviet newspaper declared that he must have been killed by either the Germans or the Arrow Cross. In 1952 several released Soviet prisoners claimed they had seen Wallenberg in prison. In 1956 the Soviet government announced that Wallenberg had died of a heart attack in a Soviet prison in 1947, but reports that he was still alive in Soviet custody continued for many years. No one is sure what really happened to Wallenberg, or why. There is some evidence to suggest that Soviet authorities did not trust the Swedish diplomats in Budapest, apparently suspecting them of being German spies. Some claim the Soviet government may have been suspicious of Wallenberg because of his ties to the United States.

PRIMARY SOURCE

Raoul Wallenberg
Excerpt from *Letters and Dispatches, 1924-1944*
Translated by Kjersti Board

Originally published in 1987
This version published in 1995

On March 19, 1944, Nazi Germany took control of Hungary. Immediately after seizing power, the Nazis banned all opposition political parties and trade unions and placed restrictions on the press. Anti-Jewish laws forced Jews to surrender their jobs and their assets, and Jews were quickly rounded up and crowded into ghettos in preparation for deportation to death camps. By July 7, some 438,000 Hungarian Jews had been transported to Auschwitz for extermination. After King Gustav V of Sweden personally appealed to the Hungarian regent, Miklós Horthy, the Germans yielded to international protests and abruptly halted deportations.

Countries around the world, including the United States, began to reevaluate their policies regarding aid to the displaced Jews of Europe. Established in January 1944, the American War Refugee Board (WRB) made rescuing those in imminent danger of death its goal. While the board never received adequate funding, members decided to focus the resources they did have on the plight of Hungarian Jews. The WRB, along with the World Jewish Congress, consulted with the Swedish government about possible rescue efforts. All three agencies agreed to send young Swedish businessman Raoul Wallenberg to Hungary in an attempt to rescue more than 200,000 Jews remaining in Budapest, the capital of Hungary.

Wallenberg was a member of a distinguished family of bankers and diplomats with close relations to the Swedish royal family. His father, an officer in the Swedish navy, died of cancer before Wallenberg was born, but Wallenberg developed a close relationship with his paternal grandfather, Gustof Wallenberg. He studied architecture abroad at the University of Michigan, an experience that expanded his imaginativeness and self-reliance, two traits that would serve him well during World War II. As an international banker and trader, Wallenberg traveled throughout Europe, including Hungary, before the war.

Since Wallenberg knew Budapest from business trips, he was ideally suited to serve as a diplomat during the German occupation. His status as a citizen of neutral Sweden allowed him to travel unhindered through the city, and secret funding from both the WRB and the World Jewish Congress helped him organize an enormous rescue effort outside the bounds of normal diplomatic constraints. Wallenberg arrived in Hungary in July 1944, just as major deportations ceased. Immediately after arriving in Budapest, Wallenberg concentrated on printing and distributing a new type of "protective passport" that would ensure holders against deportation. These identification papers, marked with a blue and yellow three crown emblem representing Sweden, ultimately saved tens of thousands of Jews. Wallenberg gained agreement from Hungarian authorities that those with protective passports could live in certain buildings called "Swedish houses."

During summer 1944, a degree of stability returned to Budapest as deportations ceased and some Jews were released from internment camps. The calm was short-lived, however, and Wallenberg quickly abandoned plans of returning to Sweden. On October 15 a radical pro-Nazi group, the Arrow Cross party, seized control of Hungary. Armed Arrow Cross gangs roamed the streets of Budapest, robbing and killing Jewish people. Several thousand Jews were murdered, some by submachine gun, and their bodies, stripped of all valuables and even clothing, were thrown into the Danube River. Immediately after the Arrow Cross party gained control of the Hungarian government, Wallenberg began issuing thousands of protective passports. He successfully negotiated with both the Arrow Cross regime and the Nazi occupiers to honor not only the 5,000 Swedish passports, but also similar

This letter of protection, or *Schutzpass,* was issued to Hungarian Jew Lili Katz on August 24, 1944. Raoul Wallenberg's initials are in the bottom left corner. *(Lena Kurtz Deutsch/USHMM Photo Archives)*

Raoul Wallenberg is credited with saving the lives of thousands of Jews. *(Reproduced by permission of UPI/Corbis-Bettmann)*

documents arranged by other neutral parties. To prevent Jews from being killed by anti-Semites, Wallenberg increased the number of protective "foreign houses" for Jews holding diplomatic documents issued by Sweden, the International Red Cross, and other foreign missions. This life-saving operation yielded the establishment of thirty-one safe houses, which were referred to collectively as the "international ghetto." Wallenberg employed 600 Jewish workers to maintain the buildings and manage food distribution, sanitation, and health services. The endeavor required large sums of money, most of it coming from the War Refugee

Board, which received funds from Jewish organizations in the United States. Wallenberg was responsible for sheltering approximately 15,000 Jews residing in this protective area.

Wallenberg also personally intervened to save hundreds of individual Jews, rescued as the Nazis led them on death marches from Budapest to the Austrian border. Wallenberg drove his car along the line of prisoners and ordered Nazi guards to release those with protective passports. The German guards, who could not read Hungarian, were unable to check the papers Wallenberg waved in their faces and did not realize he was simply saving as many people as he could. He frequently performed similar rescue operations on the trains deporting Jews to extermination camps. His accomplishments reflect the motto on the Wallenberg family crest: "To Be—Not To Be Seen."

Prior to his mission in Hungary, Raoul Wallenberg did not have experience as a statesman. His unique background, however, prepared him for the complex challenges involved in serving as a volunteer diplomat. His brief career in banking helped him organize financial transactions. Even his architecture degree came in handy. During college, Wallenberg had completed an assignment to design affordable housing; in Budapest he found ways to house 35,000 people in buildings designed for fewer than 5,000.

Wallenberg sent memorandums back to the Foreign Ministry in Sweden. Excerpted here are two of these memos, containing information about the actions of Nazi and Hungarian officials. The reports provide readers with a glimpse into the mind of Wallenberg, whose straightforward writing style reveals a deep devotion to and compassion for those he committed his life to saving.

Letters and Dispatches, 1924–1944

Memorandum Concerning the Persecution of Jews in Hungary

Enclosed please find a summary of the current situation compiled by a well-informed source. For reasons of safety, the identity of our informant will not be revealed until later....

Conditions in Collection Centers

The parents of one of my informants were sent away in the direction of Poland on July 1. For some reason, the train was returned to the infamous camp at Békásmegyer—as the result, it was thought, of Archbishop Serédi's intervention at the time. My

informant received a message smuggled from his parents, which indicated that they were lacking food and water. He then went there and managed to receive permission, through bribes, to hand over a parcel with food and water. According to his statement, his parents and the other prisoners were then half-dead. They were later taken to Poland.

Another informant visited the departure point at Kassa on May 25 and was shown around by the person in charge, a Baron Fiedler, to whom he had been introduced by a friend that very same day. According to Baron Fiedler, the camp, which covered an area of about 1.5 acres, had originally housed 16,000–17,000 individuals. The camp had been filled on or around May 12. On May 15, the inmates were taken to the newly created ghetto in Kassa. After three days, they were returned to the camp, and the deportations began sometime around May 19. When my informant visited the camp, about 8,000 persons in weakened condition remained. The temperature was about 50 degrees Fahrenheit and the weather rainy and windy. The prisoners were housed beneath narrow covers held up by wooden supports. As their names were called, they were loaded aboard the trains following an extremely invasive body search by the SS, for which both men and women were forced to disrobe. One woman tried surreptitiously to hide her infant under the railroad car, whereupon the child was seized by the leg and hurled headlong into the car. The car was packed so full that the passengers were forced to stand.

According to my informant, Baron Fiedler reported that following an escape by several Jews he had ordered their relatives hung by their feet and beaten around the crotch as a warning to those following behind.

The Deportations

A civil servant in a position to provide an overall view of the transports describes them as horrible and unspeakably brutal. Food often consists of one loaf of bread per car, sometimes of a pound of bread and 8 ounces of marmalade. One bucket of water is allotted to each car. The journey generally takes five days. There are many deaths.

Treatment in
Auschwitz, Birkenau, and Waldsee

The enclosed reports, which state that everybody, with the exception of able-bodied men and young women, has been put to death, is confirmed by the fact that postcards have been received here from these two categories of deportees, but none from older peo-

ple. A journalist assigned to the Hungarian air force is alleged to have returned recently from the Katowice area with information confirming this. I have, however, not yet managed to speak to him.

The Reaction of the Hungarians

Most people you speak to are ashamed of what is happening and maintain that these brutalities are not being committed by Hungarians but only by Germans. However this is not true. Hungarian anti-Semitism is deeply rooted. Positive intervention is usually limited to helping friends by providing food and hiding places. Many deplore the persecution of the Jews, pointing out that it is costing the Hungarians sympathy abroad, and that they risk being treated more harshly than Romania in the event of peace, since Romania's policy toward its Jewish population is known to have become more lenient of late. It would appear, however, that this awareness is limited to the leaders of industry. There is a certain amount of speculation regarding the punishment awaiting those who have taken an active part in these criminal actions.

I might mention, in this connection, that the presence of Jews is sometimes thought to constitute protection against bombing raids. Those who hold this view appear to believe that the scattering of the Jews into about 2,600 Jewish houses all over Budapest, instead of concentrating them in ghettos, is a deliberate act, and that is also the reason why the Jewish workforce has been forbidden to seek shelter during air raids.

Escape Possibilities

The need for ration cards, baptismal certificates, identity papers; the requirement to wear the Star of David; the curfew for Jews during most of the day; the strict control of the streets at night; the lack of cash among Jews; the lukewarm sympathy of the Christian population; and the open and easily surveyable topography of the countryside all combine to make it difficult for the Jews to elude their fate by escaping.

Somewhere in the vicinity of 20,000 to 50,000 Jews are thought to have been hidden in Budapest by Christian friends. Of those who remain in the Jewish houses, it is likely that most are children, women, and old people. The men have been conscripted for work. During the week ending on July 7, a large number of baptisms were performed by Catholic priests. Greater restrictiveness now prevails, however, and three months' instruction is now required for baptism. Many priests have been arrested. By being *baptized, Jews hope to take advantage of the rumored new regulations exempting those baptized from having to wear the Star of David. The number of baptized Jews in Hungary is reported not to exceed 70,000.*

Some slight possibility evidently exists of acquiring Aryan papers belonging to people who have either been bombed out or killed. These command a very high price. I do not know of any cases of false identity papers, however, and the printing establishments are under such strict control that it is, at this point, virtually impossible to escape by this method.

The Jews of Budapest are completely apathetic and do virtually nothing to save themselves.

The Social Democratic Party is in theory pro-Jewish, but is virtually paralyzed and in all likelihood prevented from helping.

I am not familiar with the position and activities of the Communist Party.

Bribes and Corruption

A train with 1,200 Jews destined for Spain en route to Palestine departed quite some time ago, but is presently being held in Hanover. An agreement was allegedly reached between the Jewish Council and the Gestapo, unbeknownst to the Hungarian government, which was told by the Gestapo that the Jews in question would be deported as usual, i.e., put to death....

I am not aware of a single case in which someone has managed to escape from a detention camp, except for the one mentioned in a previous report. The embassy has also received an anonymous report of an alleged escape from the camp at Békásmegyer. Bribes are apparently much less frequent than one might assume, partly because the entire rounding-up and deportation process is so mechanized, swift, and impersonal that outsiders wishing to intervene have not been able to get in touch with the camp commander in question....

Budapest, July 18, 1944
[signed] Raoul Wallenberg

Memorandum Concerning the Jews in Hungary

Situation

Since my last report there has been virtually no change. Some small-scale deportations have taken place, but these are said to have comprised smaller

numbers rather than whole railroad cars. This has made it difficult to verify my information.

Soldiers have continued to surround individual houses in Budapest this week, and Jews have been taken away without warning to labor service or to register for labor service. In some instances, they have then been permitted to return home.

On August 5, SS soldiers staged a coup against the camp at Sarvar during which the commander was forced to turn over 1,500 Jewish prisoners under threat of armored vehicles. As today is Sunday, I have been unable to verify whether they have passed Hegyeshalom. I refer to the enclosed eyewitness report, entitled "[Report of the Royal Swedish Legation]."

For the past two days Budapest has been full of rumors, circulated by the Gestapo, that the great action against the Jews of Budapest is about to begin. I have not yet been able to confirm these rumors.

On the first of this month I had a conversation with His Excellency Miklós Horthy, in the course of which he asked me to provide him with some anonymous written suggestions for actions that might be taken. I submitted one that ended in the demand that individuals with collective passports should be exempted from wearing the Star of David, and that the clergy be given greater freedom to speak their mind. On the third of this month, I had a talk with the minister of the interior. He told me that he would welcome an even greater number of Jews leaving for Sweden and confirmed that they might be allowed to stay in special houses under Swedish protection before their departure. The general decision to deport the Jewish population of Budapest was unresolved, but they were now in the process of securing reassurances from Germany that no harm would befall them.

Both meetings were the result of private initiatives.

The Organization of the Rescue Operation

The staff of the B section now consists of forty individuals, organized into reception, registration, treasury, archives, and departments for correspondence, transportation, and housing, each under separate and competent leadership.

Another six-room apartment has been rented in an adjoining building.

About four thousand applications have been received. No more are being accepted until we have had time to go through and process these. Newly printed protective documents and passport affidavits will be sent out as soon as the applications have been approved.

Results Achieved

A number of individuals have avoided detention. Exact numbers will follow in a subsequent report.

Establishment of a Camp

This coming Wednesday or Thursday we will probably be able to empty the rental property Pozsony-utca 3, a Jewish house, of its present occupants and replace them with the same number of Jews under the embassy's protection. It would be most desirable if we could pay the moving costs and a small compensation to those Jews who are now suddenly vacating their homes in this way. The adjoining houses in the same street will eventually be transformed into Swedish collection centers. They should be able to hold an average of about a hundred people per house.

Budapest, August 6, 1944
[signed] Raoul Wallenberg
Secretary to the Legation

ROYAL SWEDISH EMBASSY
BUDAPEST
DECEMBER 8, 1944

Dearest Mother,

I really don't know when I'll be able to make it up to you for my silence. Another diplomatic pouch leaves today, and once again all you get from me are a few lines written in haste.

The situation is risky and tense, and my workload almost superhuman. Thugs are roaming around the city, beating, torturing, and shooting people. Among my staff alone there have been forty cases of kidnaping and beatings. On the whole we are in good spirits, however, and enjoying the fight....

We can hear the gunfire of the approaching Russians here day and night. Since Szálasi [leader of the Arrow Cross party] came to power, diplomatic activity has become very lively. I myself am almost the sole representative of our embassy in all government departments. So far, I've been to see the foreign minister about ten times, the deputy premier twice, the minister for the interior twice, the minister of supply once, the minister of finance once, etc.

The wife of the foreign minister was a pretty close acquaintance of mine. Unfortunately, she has now left for Merano.

Food is very scarce in Budapest. We managed to stockpile a fair amount ahead of time, however. I have a feeling that it will be difficult to leave after the [Russian] occupation, so I doubt I will get to Stockholm until around Easter. But all this is idle speculation. No one knows what the occupation will be like. At any rate, I will try to return home as soon as possible.

It is simply not possible to make plans at the moment. I really thought I would be with you for Christmas. Now I must send you my best wishes for Christmas by this means, along with my wishes for the New Year. I hope the peace so longed for is no longer so far away....

The enormous amount of work makes the time pass quickly, and I am often invited to late-night feasts of roast suckling pig and other Hungarian specialties.

Dearest Mother, I will say good-bye for today. The pouch must be readied. Greetings, tender and heartfelt kisses to you and the whole family....

Affectionately,
R. Wallenberg (Wallenberg, pp. 168–277)

Aftermath

As the Soviet armies began to occupy Budapest, Wallenberg learned of a joint SS and Arrow Cross plan to blow up both the "international ghetto" and the main ghetto where 70,000 Jews were detained. He brazenly confronted the local German commander, General Schmidthuber, threatening to ensure that the commander would hang if the liquidation occurred. Wallenberg's bold tactic saved the lives of more than 100,000 Hungarian Jews.

When the Soviets were on the verge of capturing Budapest, Wallenberg attempted to negotiate with them for the proper care of the Jews after liberation. He remained in Budapest despite repeated death threats from local fascists who objected to his protection of Jews. Although the Swedish embassy had acted as a diplomatic liaison between

Germany and the Soviet Union during the war, the Soviets distrusted Wallenberg. Responding to their request for a meeting, Wallenberg visited the Soviet army headquarters on January 17, 1945, and disappeared. After the war, the Soviets claimed they had no knowledge of any person named Wallenberg. However, German prisoners of war returning from Soviet camps testified that they had met Wallenberg at various prisons throughout Russia. The Swedish government and Wallenberg's family demanded that the Soviets provide information about Wallenberg's fate. In 1956, amidst worldwide protest, the Soviet Union claimed to have recovered records indicating Wallenberg died in a prison camp of natural causes in 1947.

Of the estimated 725,000 Jews in Hungary in 1941, about 200,000 survived. Nearly half the survivors, 100,000 people, were saved by the efforts of Raoul Wallenberg. In recognition of his actions, the U.S. Congress awarded Wallenberg honorary American citizenship, and Yad Vashem in Jerusalem gave him the "Righteous Among the Nations" medal. Around the world, many schools, streets, and institutions are named in his honor; the U.S. Holocaust Memorial Museum is located at 100 Raoul Wallenberg Plaza in Washington, D.C.

SOURCES

Books

Linneas, Sharon, *Raoul Wallenberg: The Man Who Stopped Death,* Jewish Publication Society (Philadelphia), 1993.

Meltzer, Milton, *Rescue: The Story of How Gentiles Saved Jews in the Holocaust,* Harper and Row (New York), 1988.

Wallenberg, Raoul, *Letters and Dispatches, 1924–1944: Raoul Wallenberg,* originally published in 1987, English translation by Kjersti Board, Arcade Publishing (New York), 1995.

Further Reading

The following list of resources focuses on material appropriate for high school or college students. The list is divided into two major sections: Holocaust Bibliography and World War II Bibliography. The main sections are further subdivided into more specific topics. Please note that although some titles are applicable to more than one topic, they are listed only once. Please also note that web site addresses, though verified prior to publication, are subject to change.

Holocaust Bibliography

General Histories and Overviews of the Holocaust:

Adler, David A., *We Remember the Holocaust*, Henry Holt (New York), 1995.

Altman, Linda Jacobs, *Forever Outsiders: Jews and History from Ancient Times to August 1935*, Blackbirch Press (Woodbridge, CT), 1998.

Arad, Yithak, *The Pictorial History of the Holocaust*, Macmillan (New York), 1992.

Ayer, Eleanor H., *A Firestorm Unleashed: January 1942 to June 1943*, Blackbirch Press (Woodbridge, CT), 1998.

Ayer, Eleanor H., *Inferno: July 1943 to April 1945*, Blackbirch Press (Woodbridge, CT), 1998.

Ayer, Eleanor H., and Stephen D. Chicoine, *From the Ashes: May 1945 and After*, Blackbirch Press (Woodbridge, CT), 1998.

Bachrach, Susan D., *Tell Them We Remember: The Story of the Holocaust*, Little, Brown (Boston), 1994.

Bauer, Yehuda, and Nili Keren, *A History of the Holocaust*, Franklin Watts (New York), 1982.

Chaikin, Miriam, *A Nightmare in History: The Holocaust, 1933–1945*, Clarion Books (New York), 1987.

Cornwell, John, *Hitler's Pope: The Secret History of Pius XII*, Viking (New York), 1999.

Dawidowicz, Lucy S., *The War against the Jews, 1933–1945*, Bantam Books (New York), 1986.

Epstein, Eric Joseph, and Philip Rosen, *Dictionary of the Holocaust: Biography, Geography, and Terminology*, Greenwood Press (Westport, CT), 1997.

Feingold, Henry L., *The Politics of Rescue: The Roosevelt Administration and the Holocaust, 1938–1945*, Rutgers University Press (New Brunswick, NJ), 1970.

Friedman, Saul S., *No Haven for the Oppressed: United States Policy Toward Jewish Refugees, 1933–1945*, Wayne State University Press (Detroit), 1973.

Gilbert, Martin, *Auschwitz and the Allies*, Holt, Rinehart, and Winston (New York), 1981.

Gilbert, Martin, *The Holocaust: The History of the Jews of Europe during the Second World War,* Henry Holt (New York), 1986.

Gutman, Israel, editor, *The Encyclopedia of the Holocaust,* Macmillan (New York), 1990.

Herzstein, Robert E., *The Nazis,* Time-Life Books (Alexandria, VA), 1980.

Hilberg, Raoul, *The Destruction of the European Jews,* Holmes & Meier (New York), 1985.

Lanzmann, Claude, *Shoah: The Complete Text of the Acclaimed Holocaust Film,* Da Capo Press (New York), 1995.

Levin, Nora, *The Holocaust: The Nazi Destruction of European Jewry, 1933–1945,* Schocken (New York), 1973.

Lipstadt, Deborah E., *Beyond Belief: The American Press and the Coming of the Holocaust 1933–1945,* The Free Press (New York), 1986.

Lipstadt, Deborah E., *Denying the Holocaust: The Growing Assault on Truth and Memory,* Penguin (New York), 1993.

Mauldin, Bill, *Up Front,* Henry Holt (New York), 1945.

Meltzer, Milton, *Never to Forget,* Harper and Row (New York), 1976.

Morse, Arthur D., *While Six Million Died: A Chronicle of American Apathy,* Hart (New York), 1967.

Resnick, Abraham, *The Holocaust,* Lucent Books (San Diego), 1991.

Rogasky, Barbara, *Smoke and Ashes,* Holiday House (New York), 1988.

Rossel, Seymour, *The Holocaust: The Fire That Raged,* Franklin Watts (New York), 1989.

Sherrow, Victoria, *The Blaze Engulfs: January 1939 to December 1941,* Blackbirch Press (Woodbridge, CT), 1998.

Sherrow, Victoria, *Smoke to Flame: September 1935 to December 1938,* Blackbirch Press (Woodbridge, CT), 1998.

Shoenberner, Gerhard, *The Yellow Star: The Persecution of the Jews in Europe, 1933–1945,* Bantam Books (New York), 1979.

Shulman, William L., compiler, *Voices and Visions: A Collection of Primary Sources,* Blackbirch Press (Woodbridge, CT), 1998.

Snyder, Louis L., *Encyclopedia of the Third Reich,* McGraw-Hill, 1976.

Strahinich, Helen, *The Holocaust: Understanding and Remembering,* Enslow (Springfield, NJ), 1996.

Trunk, Isaiah, *Judenrat: The Jewish Councils in Eastern Europe Under Nazi Occupation,* Macmillan (New York), 1972.

Weinberg, Jeshajahu, and Rina Elieli, *The Holocaust Museum in Washington,* Rizzoli (New York), 1995.

Wigoder, Geoffrey, editor, *The Holocaust: A Grolier Student Library,* 4 volumes, Grolier Educational (Danbury, CT), 1997.

Yahil, Leni, *The Holocaust: The Fate of European Jewry, 1932–1945,* Oxford University Press (New York), 1991.

Zentner, Christian, Friedemann Bedürftig, and Amy Hackett, editors, *Encyclopedia of the Third Reich,* Collier Macmillan (New York), 1991.

Atlases:

Gilbert, Martin, *Atlas of the Holocaust,* Macmillan (New York), 1982.

United States Holocaust Memorial Museum, *Historical Atlas of the Holocaust,* Macmillan (New York), 1996.

German History, the Early Nazi Movement, the Nazi Government, and Policy toward the Jews before the Holocaust:

Allen, William Sheridan, *The Nazi Seizure of Power: The Experience of a Single German Town, 1930–1935,* Franklin Watts (New York), 1973.

Arendt, Hannah, *The Origins of Totalitarianism,* Harcourt, Brace (New York), 1966.

Auerbacher, Inge, *I Am a Star: Child of the Holocaust,* Prentice-Hall (Paramus, NJ), 1986.

Ayer, Eleanor, *Adolf Hitler,* Lucent (San Diego), 1996.

Bauer, Yehuda, *Jews for Sale?: Nazi-Jewish Negotiations, 1933–1945,* Yale University Press (New Haven, CT), 1994.

Berman, Russell A., *Paul von Hindenburg,* Chelsea House (New York), 1987.

Bullock, Alan, *Hitler: A Study in Tyranny,* Harper and Row (New York), 1964.

Cohn, Norman, *Warrant for Genocide: The Myth of the Jewish World Conspiracy and the Protocols of the Elders of Zion,* Harper & Row Publishers (New York), 1969.

Eimerl, Sarel, *Hitler over Europe: The Road to World War II,* Little, Brown (Boston), 1972.

Friedlander, Saul, *Pius XII and the Third Reich,* Knopf (New York), 1966.

Fuller, Barbara, *Germany,* Marshall Cavendish (New York), 1996.

Gallo, Max, *The Night of the Long Knives,* Harper and Row (New York), 1972.

Goldston, Robert C., *The Life and Death of Nazi Germany,* Bobbs-Merrill (New York), 1967.

Graff, Stewart, *The Story of World War II,* E. P. Dutton (New York), 1978.

Halperin, S. William, *Germany Tried Democracy: A Political History of the Reich from 1918 to 1933,* Norton (New York), 1965.

Josephson, Judith P., *Jesse Owens: Track and Field Legend,* Enslow Press (Springfield, NJ), 1997.

Kluger, Ruth Peggy Mann, *Secret Ship,* Doubleday (New York), 1978.

Marrin, Albert, *Hitler,* Viking (New York), 1987.

Mayer, Milton Sanford, *They Thought They Were Free: The Germans, 1933-35,* University of Chicago Press (Chicago), 1966.

The New Order, Time-Life Books (Alexandria, VA), 1989.

Niemark, Anne E., *Leo Baeck and the Holocaust,* E. P. Dutton (New York), 1986.

Patterson, Charles, *Anti-Semitism: The Road to the Holocaust and Beyond,* Walker (New York), 1989.

Read, Anthony, *Kristallnacht: The Nazi Night of Terror,* Times Books/Random House (New York), 1989.

Rubinstein, William D., *The Myth of Rescue,* Routledge (New York), 1997.

Schleunes, Karl A., *The Twisted Road to Auschwitz: Nazi Policy toward German Jews, 1933–1939,* University of Illinois Press (Urbana), 1970.

Shirer, William L., *The Rise and Fall of Adolf Hitler,* Random House (New York), 1961.

Shirer, William L., *The Rise and Fall of the Third Reich,* Simon and Schuster (New York), 1960.

Snyder, Louis L., *Hitler's Elite,* Hippocrene Books (New York), 1989.

Spence, William, *Germany Then and Now,* Franklin Watts (New York), 1994.

Start, Clarissa, *God's Man: The Story of Pastor Niemoeller,* Washburn (New York), 1959.

Stein, R. Conrad, *Hitler Youth,* Children's Press (Danbury, CT), 1985.

Stewart, Gail, *Hitler's Reich,* Lucent Books (San Diego), 1994.

Thalmann, Rita, and Emmanuel Feinermann, *Crystal Night, 9–10 November, 1938,* Holocaust Library (New York), 1974.

Thomas, Gordon, and Max M. Witts, *Voyage of the Damned,* Stein and Day (New York), 1974.

Toland, John, *Adolf Hitler,* Doubleday (New York), 1976.

Wepman, Dennis, *Adolf Hitler,* Chelsea House (New York), 1989.

Zurndorfer, Hannele, *The Ninth of November,* Quartet Books (Berrien Springs, MI), 1983.

The "Final Solution":

Aly, Gotz, *Final Solution: Nazi Population Policy and the Murder of the European Jews,* Oxford University Press (New York), 1999.

Bower, Tom, *Klaus Barbie, the "Butcher of Lyons,"* Pantheon Books (New York), 1984.

Breitman, Richard, *The Architect of Genocide: Himmler and the Final Solution,* Knopf (New York), 1991.

Browning, Christopher R., *Nazi Policy, Jewish Workers, German Killers,* Cambridge University Press (New York), 2000.

Browning, Christopher R., *Ordinary Men: Reserve Police Battalion 101 and the Final Solution in Poland,* HarperPerennial (New York), 1992.

Des Pres, Terrence, *The Survivor: An Anatomy of Life in the Death Camps,* Washington Square Press (New York), 1976.

Dobroszycki, Lucjan, editor, *The Chronicle of the Lódz Ghetto, 1941–1944,* Yale University Press (New York), 1984.

Friedlander, Henry, *The Origins of Nazi Genocide: From Euthanasia to the Final Solution,* University of North Carolina Press (Chapel Hill, NC), 1995.

Friedrich, Otto, *The Kingdom of Auschwitz,* Harper Perennial (New York), 1994.

Gilbert, Martin, *Auschwitz and the Allies,* Henry Holt (New York), 1990.

Goldhagen, Daniel J., *Hitler's Willing Executioners: Ordinary Germans and the Holocaust,* Knopf (New York), 1996.

Graf, Malvina, *The Kraków Ghetto and the Plaszów Camp Remembered,* Florida State University Press (Tallahassee, FL), 1989.

Gutman, Israel, *Anatomy of the Auschwitz Death Camp,* Indiana University Press (Bloomington, IN), 1998.

Gutman, Israel, *The Jews of Warsaw, 1939–1943,* Indiana University Press (Bloomington, IN), 1982.

Hellman, Peter, *The Auschwitz Album: A Book Based upon an Album Discovered by a Concentration Camp Survivor, Lili Meier,* Random House (New York), 1981.

Höss, Rudolf, *Death Dealer: The Memoirs of the SS Kommandant at Auschwitz,* edited by Steven Paskuly, translated by Andrew Pollinger, Prometheus Books (Buffalo, NY), 1992.

Kogon, Eugen, *The Theory and Practice of Hell: The German Concentration Camps and the System behind Them,* Octagon (Los Angeles), 1973.

Leitner, Isabella, *The Big Lie: A True Story,* Scholastic (New York), 1992.

Levi, Primo, *Survival in Auschwitz,* Macmillan (New York), 1987.

Lifton, Robert Jay, *The Nazi Doctors: Medical Killing and the Psychology of Genocide,* Basic Books (New York), 1988.

Millu, Liana, *Smoke over Birkenau,* Jewish Publication Society (Philadelphia), 1991.

Nomberg-Przuytyk, Sara, *Auschwitz: True Tales from a Grotesque Land,* University of North Carolina Press (Chapel Hill, NC), 1986.

Posner, Gerald L., *Mengele: The Complete Story,* McGraw-Hill (New York), 1986.

Reitlinger, Gerald, *The SS: Alibi of a Nation, 1922–1945,* Viking (New York), 1957.

Rubinstein, William D., *The Myth of Rescue,* Routledge (New York), 1997.

Steiner, Jean Francis, *Treblinka,* Simon and Schuster (New York), 1967.

Stern, Ellen Norman, *Elie Wiesel: Witness for Life,* Ktav Publishing House (New York), 1982.

Swiebocka, Teresa, compiler and editor, *Auschwitz: A History in Photographs,* Indiana University Press (Bloomington, IN), 1993.

Whiting, Charles, *Heydrich: Henchman of Death,* Leo Cooper (S. Yorkshire, England), 1999.

Wiesel, Elie, *The Night Trilogy: Night, Dawn, The Accident,* Hill and Wang (New York), 1960.

Willenberg, Samuel, *Surviving Treblinka,* Basil Blackwell (Maldin, MA), 1989.

Wyman, David S., *The Abandonment of the Jews: America and the Holocaust, 1941–1945,* Pantheon (New York), 1984.

Zyskind, Sara, *Struggle,* Lerner (Minneapolis, MN), 1989.

Poland:

Adelson, Alan, and Robert Lapides, editors, *Lódz Ghetto: Inside a Community Under Siege,* Viking (New York), 1989.

Bernheim, Mark, *Father of the Orphans: The Story of Janusz Korczak,* E. P. Dutton (New York), 1989.

Davies, Norman, *God's Playground,* Columbia University Press (New York), 1982.

Drucker, Malka, and Michael Halperin, *Jacob's Rescue: A Holocaust Story,* Bantam Skylark (New York), 1993.

Eichengreen, Lucille, *Rumkowski and the Orphans of Lódz,* Mercury House (San Francisco, CA), 1999.

Frister, Roman, *The Cap: The Price of a Life,* translated by Hillel Halkin, Grove Press (New York), 1999.

George, Willy, *In the Warsaw Ghetto, Summer 1941,* Aperture Foundation (New York), 1993.

Heller, Celia S., *On the Edge of Destruction: Jews of Poland between the Two World Wars,* Columbia University Press (New York), 1977.

Hoffman, Eva, *Shtetl: The Life and Death of a Small Town and the World of Polish Jews,* Houghton Mifflin Company (Boston), 1998.

Hyams, Joe, *A Field of Buttercups,* Prentice-Hall (Paramus, NJ), 1968.

Kaplan, Chaim A., *Scroll of Agony: The Warsaw Diary of Chaim A. Kaplan,* Indiana University Press (Bloomington, IN), 1999.

Keller, Ulrich, editor, *The Warsaw Ghetto in Photographs,* Dover (Mineola, NY), 1984.

the Elders of Zion, Harper & Row Publishers (New York), 1969.

Eimerl, Sarel, Hitler over Europe: The Road to World War II, Little, Brown (Boston), 1972.

Friedlander, Saul, Pius XII and the Third Reich, Knopf (New York), 1966.

Fuller, Barbara, Germany, Marshall Cavendish (New York), 1996.

Gallo, Max, The Night of the Long Knives, Harper and Row (New York), 1972.

Goldston, Robert C., The Life and Death of Nazi Germany, Bobbs-Merrill (New York), 1967.

Graff, Stewart, The Story of World War II, E. P. Dutton (New York), 1978.

Halperin, S. William, Germany Tried Democracy: A Political History of the Reich from 1918 to 1933, Norton (New York), 1965.

Josephson, Judith P., Jesse Owens: Track and Field Legend, Enslow Press (Springfield, NJ), 1997.

Kluger, Ruth Peggy Mann, Secret Ship, Doubleday (New York), 1978.

Marrin, Albert, Hitler, Viking (New York), 1987.

Mayer, Milton Sanford, They Thought They Were Free: The Germans, 1933-35, University of Chicago Press (Chicago), 1966.

The New Order, Time-Life Books (Alexandria, VA), 1989.

Niemark, Anne E., Leo Baeck and the Holocaust, E. P. Dutton (New York), 1986.

Patterson, Charles, Anti-Semitism: The Road to the Holocaust and Beyond, Walker (New York), 1989.

Read, Anthony, Kristallnacht: The Nazi Night of Terror, Times Books/Random House (New York), 1989.

Rubinstein, William D., The Myth of Rescue, Routledge (New York), 1997.

Schleunes, Karl A., The Twisted Road to Auschwitz: Nazi Policy toward German Jews, 1933–1939, University of Illinois Press (Urbana), 1970.

Shirer, William L., The Rise and Fall of Adolf Hitler, Random House (New York), 1961.

Shirer, William L., The Rise and Fall of the Third Reich, Simon and Schuster (New York), 1960.

Snyder, Louis L., Hitler's Elite, Hippocrene Books (New York), 1989.

Spence, William, Germany Then and Now, Franklin Watts (New York), 1994.

Start, Clarissa, God's Man: The Story of Pastor Niemoeller, Washburn (New York), 1959.

Stein, R. Conrad, Hitler Youth, Children's Press (Danbury, CT), 1985.

Stewart, Gail, Hitler's Reich, Lucent Books (San Diego), 1994.

Thalmann, Rita, and Emmanuel Feinermann, Crystal Night, 9–10 November, 1938, Holocaust Library (New York), 1974.

Thomas, Gordon, and Max M. Witts, Voyage of the Damned, Stein and Day (New York), 1974.

Toland, John, Adolf Hitler, Doubleday (New York), 1976.

Wepman, Dennis, Adolf Hitler, Chelsea House (New York), 1989.

Zurndorfer, Hannele, The Ninth of November, Quartet Books (Berrien Springs, MI), 1983.

The "Final Solution":

Aly, Gotz, Final Solution: Nazi Population Policy and the Murder of the European Jews, Oxford University Press (New York), 1999.

Bower, Tom, Klaus Barbie, the "Butcher of Lyons," Pantheon Books (New York), 1984.

Breitman, Richard, The Architect of Genocide: Himmler and the Final Solution, Knopf (New York), 1991.

Browning, Christopher R., Nazi Policy, Jewish Workers, German Killers, Cambridge University Press (New York), 2000.

Browning, Christopher R., Ordinary Men: Reserve Police Battalion 101 and the Final Solution in Poland, HarperPerennial (New York), 1992.

Des Pres, Terrence, The Survivor: An Anatomy of Life in the Death Camps, Washington Square Press (New York), 1976.

Dobroszycki, Lucjan, editor, The Chronicle of the Lódz Ghetto, 1941–1944, Yale University Press (New York), 1984.

Friedlander, Henry, The Origins of Nazi Genocide: From Euthanasia to the Final Solution, University of North Carolina Press (Chapel Hill, NC), 1995.

Friedrich, Otto, The Kingdom of Auschwitz, Harper Perennial (New York), 1994.

Gilbert, Martin, *Auschwitz and the Allies,* Henry Holt (New York), 1990.

Goldhagen, Daniel J., *Hitler's Willing Executioners: Ordinary Germans and the Holocaust,* Knopf (New York), 1996.

Graf, Malvina, *The Kraków Ghetto and the Plaszów Camp Remembered,* Florida State University Press (Tallahassee, FL), 1989.

Gutman, Israel, *Anatomy of the Auschwitz Death Camp,* Indiana University Press (Bloomington, IN), 1998.

Gutman, Israel, *The Jews of Warsaw, 1939–1943,* Indiana University Press (Bloomington, IN), 1982.

Hellman, Peter, *The Auschwitz Album: A Book Based upon an Album Discovered by a Concentration Camp Survivor, Lili Meier,* Random House (New York), 1981.

Höss, Rudolf, *Death Dealer: The Memoirs of the SS Kommandant at Auschwitz,* edited by Steven Paskuly, translated by Andrew Pollinger, Prometheus Books (Buffalo, NY), 1992.

Kogon, Eugen, *The Theory and Practice of Hell: The German Concentration Camps and the System behind Them,* Octagon (Los Angeles), 1973.

Leitner, Isabella, *The Big Lie: A True Story,* Scholastic (New York), 1992.

Levi, Primo, *Survival in Auschwitz,* Macmillan (New York), 1987.

Lifton, Robert Jay, *The Nazi Doctors: Medical Killing and the Psychology of Genocide,* Basic Books (New York), 1988.

Millu, Liana, *Smoke over Birkenau,* Jewish Publication Society (Philadelphia), 1991.

Nomberg-Przuytyk, Sara, *Auschwitz: True Tales from a Grotesque Land,* University of North Carolina Press (Chapel Hill, NC), 1986.

Posner, Gerald L., *Mengele: The Complete Story,* McGraw-Hill (New York), 1986.

Reitlinger, Gerald, *The SS: Alibi of a Nation, 1922–1945,* Viking (New York), 1957.

Rubinstein, William D., *The Myth of Rescue,* Routledge (New York), 1997.

Steiner, Jean Francis, *Treblinka,* Simon and Schuster (New York), 1967.

Stern, Ellen Norman, *Elie Wiesel: Witness for Life,* Ktav Publishing House (New York), 1982.

Swiebocka, Teresa, compiler and editor, *Auschwitz: A History in Photographs,* Indiana University Press (Bloomington, IN), 1993.

Whiting, Charles, *Heydrich: Henchman of Death,* Leo Cooper (S. Yorkshire, England), 1999.

Wiesel, Elie, *The Night Trilogy: Night, Dawn, The Accident,* Hill and Wang (New York), 1960.

Willenberg, Samuel, *Surviving Treblinka,* Basil Blackwell (Maldin, MA), 1989.

Wyman, David S., *The Abandonment of the Jews: America and the Holocaust, 1941–1945,* Pantheon (New York), 1984.

Zyskind, Sara, *Struggle,* Lerner (Minneapolis, MN), 1989.

Poland:

Adelson, Alan, and Robert Lapides, editors, *Lódz Ghetto: Inside a Community Under Siege,* Viking (New York), 1989.

Bernheim, Mark, *Father of the Orphans: The Story of Janusz Korczak,* E. P. Dutton (New York), 1989.

Davies, Norman, *God's Playground,* Columbia University Press (New York), 1982.

Drucker, Malka, and Michael Halperin, *Jacob's Rescue: A Holocaust Story,* Bantam Skylark (New York), 1993.

Eichengreen, Lucille, *Rumkowski and the Orphans of Lódz,* Mercury House (San Francisco, CA), 1999.

Frister, Roman, *The Cap: The Price of a Life,* translated by Hillel Halkin, Grove Press (New York), 1999.

George, Willy, *In the Warsaw Ghetto, Summer 1941,* Aperture Foundation (New York), 1993.

Heller, Celia S., *On the Edge of Destruction: Jews of Poland between the Two World Wars,* Columbia University Press (New York), 1977.

Hoffman, Eva, *Shtetl: The Life and Death of a Small Town and the World of Polish Jews,* Houghton Mifflin Company (Boston), 1998.

Hyams, Joe, *A Field of Buttercups,* Prentice-Hall (Paramus, NJ), 1968.

Kaplan, Chaim A., *Scroll of Agony: The Warsaw Diary of Chaim A. Kaplan,* Indiana University Press (Bloomington, IN), 1999.

Keller, Ulrich, editor, *The Warsaw Ghetto in Photographs,* Dover (Mineola, NY), 1984.

Klein, Gerda Weissmann, *All but My Life,* Hill & Wang Publishers (New York), 1995.

Landau, Elaine, *The Warsaw Ghetto Uprising,* Macmillan (New York), 1992.

Lewis, Mark, and Jacob Frank, *Himmler's Jewish Tailor: The Story of Holocaust Survivor Jacob Frank,* Syracuse University Press (Syracuse, NY), 2000.

Lifton, Betty Jean, *The King of Children: The Life and Death of Janusz Korczak,* St. Martin's Griffin (New York), 1997.

Lukas, Richard C., and Norman Davies, *The Forgotten Holocaust: The Poles Under German Occupation 1939–1944,* Hippocrene Books (New York), 1997.

Nelken, Halina, *And Yet, Here I Am!* University of Massachusetts Press (Amherst, MA), 1999.

Sender, Ruth Minsky, *The Cage,* Macmillan (New York), 1986.

Sender, Ruth Minsky, *To Life,* Macmillan (New York), 1988.

Spiegelman, Art, *Maus: A Survivor's Tale: And Here My Troubles Began,* Pantheon Books (New York), 1992.

Spiegelman, Art, *Maus: A Survivor's Tale: My Father Bleeds History,* Pantheon Books (New York), 1997.

Stewart, Gail B., *Life in the Warsaw Ghetto,* Lucent Books (San Diego), 1995.

Szner, Zvi, and Alexander Sened, editors, *With a Camera in the Ghetto: Mendel Grossman,* Schocken Books (New York), 1977.

Szpilman, Wladyslaw, *The Pianist,* Picador USA (New York), 1999.

Vishniac, Roman, *A Vanished World,* Farrar, Straus, and Giroux (New York), 1983.

Watt, Richard M., *Bitter Glory: Poland & Its Fate 1918–1993,* Hippocrene Books (New York), 1998.

Ziemian, Joseph, *The Cigarette Seller of Three Crosses Square,* Lerner (Minneapolis, MN), 1975.

Other Countries:

Asscher-Pinkoff, Clara, *Star Children,* Wayne State University Press (Detroit), 1986.

Bitton-Jackson, Livia, *I Have Lived a Thousand Years: Growing up in the Holocaust,* Simon and Schuster (New York), 1997.

Denes, Magda, *Castles Burning: A Child's Life in War,* W. W. Norton (New York), 1997.

Frank, Anne, *The Diary of a Young Girl: The Definitive Edition,* edited by Otto Frank and Mirjam Pressler, Doubleday (New York), 1995.

Gies, Miep, and Alison L. Gold, *Anne Frank Remembered: The Story of the Woman Who Helped to Hide the Frank Family* Simon and Schuster (New York), 1987.

Gold, Alison L., *Memories of Anne Frank: Reflections of a Childhood Friend,* Scholastic (New York), 1997.

Handler, Andrew, and Susan Meschel, editors, *Young People Speak,* Franklin Watts (New York), 1993.

Hutok, J. B., *With Blood and with Iron: The Lidice Story,* R. Hale (London), 1957.

Isaacman, Clara, *Clara's Story,* Jewish Publication Society (Philadelphia), 1984.

Klarsfeld, Serge, *The Children of Izieu: A Human Tragedy,* Abrams (New York), 1985.

Lewy, Guenter, *The Nazi Persecution of the Gypsies,* Oxford University Press (New York), 2000.

Lindwe, Willy, *The Last Seven Months of Anne Frank,* Pantheon (New York), 1991.

Marrus, Michael R., *Vichy France and the Jews,* Basic Books (New York), 1981.

Perl, Lila, and Marian Blumenthal Lazar, *Four Perfect Pebbles: A Holocaust Story,* Greenwillow Books (New York), 1996.

Rol, Ruud van der, and Rian Verhoeven, *Anne Frank: Beyond the Diary,* Viking (New York), 1993.

Roth-Hano, Renée, *Touch Wood: A Girlhood in Occupied France,* Four Winds Press (Portland, OR), 1988.

Siegal, Avanka, *Grace in the Wilderness: After the Liberation, 1945–1948,* Farrar, Straus, Giroux (New York), 1985.

Siegal, Avanka, *Upon the Head of the Goat: A Childhood in Hungary, 1939–1944,* Farrar, Straus, Giroux (New York), 1981.

Velmans, Edith, *Edith's Story,* Soho Press (New York), 1998.

Zuccotti, Susan, *The Italians and the Holocaust: Persecution, Rescue and Survival,* Basic Books (New York), 1987.

Resistance, Survival, and Rescue:

Ainszstein, Reuben, *Jewish Resistance in Nazi-Occupied Eastern Europe: With a Historical Survey of the Jew as a Fighter and Soldier in the Diaspora,* Barnes & Noble (New York), 1975.

Aliav, Ruth, *The Last Escape: The Launching of the Largest Secret Rescue Movement of All Time,* Doubleday (Garden City, NY), 1973.

Atkinson, Linda, *In Kindling Flame: The Story of Hannah Senesh,* Lee & Shepard (New York), 1985.

Ayer, Eleanor A., *The United States Holocaust Memorial Museum,* Silver Burdett Press (Parsipanny, NJ), 1995.

Bauer, Yehuda, *They Chose Life: Jewish Resistance in the Holocaust,* American Jewish Committee (New York), 1973.

Berenbaum, Michael, *The World Must Know,* Little, Brown (Boston), 1993.

Bierman, John, *Righteous Gentile: The Story of Raoul Wallenberg,* Viking (New York), 1981.

Blatt, Thomas Toivi, *From the Ashes of Sobibor: A Story of Survival,* Northwestern University Press (Evanston, IL), 1997.

Block, Gay, and Malka Drucker, *Rescuers,* Holmes and Meier (New York), 1992.

Bosanquest, Mary, *The Life and Death of Dietrich Bonhoeffer,* Harper and Row (New York), 1968.

Chevrillon, Claire, *Code Name Christiane Clouet: A Woman in the French Resistance,* Texas A & M University (College Station, TX), 1995.

Elkins, Michael, *Forged in Fury,* Ballantine Books (New York), 1971.

Flender, Harold, *Rescue in Denmark,* Simon and Schuster (New York), 1963.

Friedman, Ina R., *Flying against the Wind: The Story of a Young Woman Who Defied the Nazis,* Lodge Pole Press (Brookline, MA), 1995.

Gelman, Charles, *Do Not Go Gentle: A Memoir of Jewish Resistance in Poland, 1941–1945,* Archon Books, (North Haven, CT), 1989.

Gilbert, Martin, *The Boys: The Untold Story of 732 Young Concentration Camp Survivors,* Henry Holt & Company (New York), 1997.

Greenfield, Howard, *The Hidden Children,* Ticknor and Fields (New York), 1993.

Gutman, Israel, *Resistance: The Warsaw Ghetto Uprising,* Houghton Mifflin (Boston), 1994.

Haas, Gerda, *These I Do Remember: Fragments from the Holocaust,* Cumberland (Brooklyn, NY), 1982.

Hallie, Philip, *Lest Innocent Blood Be Shed,* Harper & Row (New York), 1980.

Healey, Tim, *Secret Armies; Resistance Groups in World War II,* Macdonald (London), 1981.

Helmreich, William B., *Against All Odds: Holocaust Survivors and the Successful Lives They Made in America,* Simon & Schuster (New York), 1992.

Hewins, Ralph, *Count Folke Bernadotte: His Life and Work,* Hutchinson (New York), 1950.

Holocaust Education—Women of Valor, http://www.interlog.com/~mighty/valor/kath_f.htm (September 12, 2000).

Jewish Partisans, http://www.ushmm.org/outreach/jpart.htm (September 12, 2000).

Keneally, Thomas, *Schindler's List,* Simon and Schuster (New York), 1982.

Kertyesz, Imre, *Fateless,* Northwestern University Press (Evanston, IL), 1992.

Kurzman, Dan, *The Bravest Battle: The Twenty-Eight Days of the Warsaw Ghetto Uprising,* Da Capo Press (New York), 1993.

Landau, Elaine, *The Warsaw Ghetto Uprising,* Macmillan (New York), 1992.

Landau, Elaine, *We Survived the Holocaust,* Franklin Watts (New York), 1991.

Laska, Vera, editor, *Women in the Resistance and in the Holocaust: The Voices of Eyewitnesses,* Greenwood Press (Westport, CT), 1983.

Linnea, Sharon, *Raoul Wallenberg: The Man Who Stopped Death,* Jewish Publication Society (Philadelphia), 1993.

Marton, Kati, *Wallenberg,* Random House (New York), 1982.

Meltzer, Milton, *Rescue: The Story of How Gentiles Saved Jews in the Holocaust,* Harper and Row (New York), 1988.

Mochizuki, Ken, *Passage to Freedom: The Sugihara Story,* Lee and Low Books (New York), 1997.

Pettit, Jayne, *A Time to Fight Back: True Stories of Wartime Resistance,* Houghton Mifflin (Boston), 1996.

Rashke, Richard, *Escape from Sobibor,* University of Illinois Press (Urbana, IL), 1995.

Rittner, Carol, *The Courage to Care,* New York University Press (New York), 1986.

Roberts, Jack L., *Oskar Schindler,* Lucent Books (San Diego), 1996.

Rosenberg, Maxine B., *Hiding to Survive: Stories of Jewish Children Rescued from the Holocaust,* Clarion (New York), 1994.

Schul, Yuri, *They Fought Back: The Story of Jewish Resistance in Nazi Europe,* Schocken Books (New York), 1967.

Stadtler, Bea, *The Holocaust: A History of Courage and Resistance,* Behrman House (West Orange, NJ), 1994.

Stein, R. Conrad, *Resistance Movements,* Children's Press (Chicago), 1982.

Sutin, Lawrence, editor, *Jack and Rochelle: A Holocaust Story of Love and Resistance,* Graywolf Press (Saint Paul, MN), 1996.

Vinke, Hermann, *The Short Life of Sophie Scholl,* Harper and Row (New York), 1984.

Vogel, Ilse-Margaret, *Bad Times, Good Friends,* Harcourt Brace Jovanovich (New York), 1992.

Weinstein, Irving, *That Denmark Might Live; The Saga of Danish Resistance in World War II,* Macrae Smith (Philadelphia), 1967.

Werner, Harold, *Fighting Back,* Columbia University Press (New York), 1994.

Wind, Renate, *Dietrich Bonhoeffer: A Spoke in the Wheel,* Eerdmans (Grand Rapids, MI), 1992.

Wood, E. Thomas, *Karski: How One Man Tried to Stop the Holocaust,* John Wiley & Sons (New York), 1994.

Wygoda, Hermann, *In the Shadow of the Swastika,* University of Illinois Press (Urbana, IL), 1998.

Zahn, Gordon, *In Solitary Witness: The Life and Death of Franz Jaggerstatter,* Holt, Rinehart, and Winston (New York), 1964.

Zassenhaus, Hiltgunt, *Walls: Resisting the Third Reich, One Woman's Story,* Beacon Press (Boston), 1974.

Zeinert, Karen, *The Warsaw Ghetto Uprising,* Millbrook Press (Brookfield, CT), 1993.

Zuccotti, Susan, *The Italians and the Holocaust: Persecution, Rescue, and Survival,* University of Nebraska Press (Lincoln, NE), 1996.

Justice:

Arendt, Hannah, *Eichmann in Jerusalem: A Report on the Banality of Evil,* Penguin (New York), 1977.

Gilbert, G. M., *Nuremberg Diary,* New American Library (New York), 1947.

Hausner, Gideon, *Justice in Jerusalem,* Harper and Row (New York), 1966.

Jackson, Robert H., *The Nürnberg Case, As Presented by Robert H. Jackson, Chief Counsel for the United States, Together with Other Documents,* Cooper Square Publishers (New York), 1971.

Landau, Elaine, *Nazi War Criminals,* Franklin Watts (New York), 1990.

Morin, Isobel V., *Days of Judgment: The World War II War Crimes Trials,* Millbrook Press (Brookfield, CT), 1995.

Noble, Iris, *Nazi Hunter: Simon Wiesenthal,* J. Messner (New York), 1979.

Persico, Joseph E., *Nuremberg: Infamy on Trial,* Viking (New York), 1994.

Ryan, Allan A., *Quiet Neighbors: Prosecuting Nazi War Criminals in America,* Harcourt Brace Jovanovich (San Diego), 1984.

Taylor, Telford, *The Anatomy of the Nuremberg Trials: A Personal Memoir,* Knopf (New York), 1992.

Wiesenthal, Simon, *Justice Not Vengeance,* translated from German by Edward Osers, Grove Weidenfeld (London), 1989.

Wiesenthal, Simon, *The Murderers Among Us: The Simon Wiesenthal Memoirs,* edited, with a profile of the author, by Joseph Wechsberg, McGraw-Hill (New York), 1967.

Displaced Persons:

Blumenson, Martin, *Liberation,* Time-Life Books (Alexandria VA), 1983.

Botting, Douglas, *The Aftermath: Europe,* Time-Life Books (Alexandria, VA), 1983.

Gilbert, Martin *The Holocaust: A History of the Jews of Europe during the Second World War,* Holt, Rinehart and Winston (New York), 1998.

Gilbert, Martin, *Israel: A History,* William Morrow (New York), 1998.

Levi, Primo, *The Reawakening,* Collier Books (New York), 1996.

Nesaule, Agate, *A Woman in Amber: Healing the Trauma of War and Exile,* Soho Press (New York), 1995.

O'Brien, Conor Cruise, *The Siege: The Saga of Israel and Zionism,* Simon and Schuster (New York), 1986.

Sykes, Christopher, *Crossroads to Israel,* Indiana University Press (Bloomington, IN), 1973.

Yahil, Leni, *The Holocaust: The Fate of European Jewry,* Oxford University Press (Oxford), 1987.

World War II Bibliography

General Sources:

Allen, Peter, *The Origins of World War II,* Bookwright Press (New York), 1992.

The Avalon Project at the Yale Law School—World War II: Documents, http://www.yale.edu/law web/avalon/wwii/wwii.htm (September 8, 2000).

Bradley, Omar N., *A Soldier's Story,* Holt, Rinehart & Winston (New York), 1951.

Calvocoressi, Peter, Guy Wint, and John Pritchard, *Total War: Causes and Courses of the Second World War,* Pantheon (New York), 1987.

Churchill, Winston, *The Second World War,* Houghton (New York), 1948–1954, reprinted, 1986.

Collier, Basil, *The Second World War: A Military History,* William Morrow (New York), 1967.

Eisenhower, General Dwight D., *Crusade in Europe,* Doubleday (New York), 1948.

Ethell, Jeffrey L., and Robert T. Sand, *Air Command: Fighters and Bombers of World War II,* Motorbooks International (Osceola, WI), 1998.

Fleming, Peter, *Operation Sea Lion,* Simon and Schuster (New York), 1957.

Graff, Stewart, *The Story of World War II,* E. P. Dutton (New York), 1978.

Hills, Ken, *Wars That Changed the World: World War II,* Marshall Cavendish (New York), 1988.

Keegan, John, *The Battle for History: Re-Fighting World War II,* Vintage Books (New York), 1996.

Keegan, John, *The Second World War,* Penguin (New York), 1990.

Krull, Kathleen, *V Is for Victory,* Knopf (New York), 1995.

Lawson, Don, *Great Air Battles: World War I and II,* Lothrop, Lee & Shepard (New York), 1968.

Leckie, Robert, *Delivered from Evil: The Saga of World War II,* HarperPerennial (New York), 1987.

Leckie, Robert, *The Story of World War II,* Random House (New York), 1964.

Leutze, James R., *Bargaining for Supremacy: Anglo-American Naval Collaboration, 1937–1941,* University of North Carolina Press (Chapel Hill, NC), 1977.

MacArthur, Douglas, *Reminiscences,* Da Capo Press (New York), 1985.

MacDonald, Charles B., *Company Commander,* Burford Books (Springfield, NJ), 1999.

Marrin, Albert, *The Airmen's War: World War II in the Sky,* Atheneum (New York), 1982.

Michel, Henri, *The Second World War,* translated by Douglas Parmee, Deutsch (London), 1975.

Military History: World War II (1939–1945), http://www.cfcsc.dnd.ca/links/milhist/wwii.html (September 8, 2000).

A People at War, http://www.nara.gov/exhall/people/people.html (September 8, 2000).

Reynolds, Quentin J., *Only the Stars Are Neutral,* Random House (New York), 1942.

Roskill, Stephen W., *The Navy at War, 1939–1945,* Collins (London), 1960.

Ross, Stewart, *Propaganda,* Thomson Learning (New York), 1993.

Ross, Stewart, *World Leaders,* Thomson Learning (New York), 1993.

Snyder, Louis L., *World War II,* Franklin Watts (New York), 1981.

Wilmot, Chester, *The Struggle for Europe,* Harper & Row Publishers (New York), 1952.

World War II, http://www.awesomelibrary.org/Classroom/Social_Studies/History/World_War_II.html (September 8, 2000).

Atlases:

Freeman, Michael, and Tim Mason, editors, *Atlas of Nazi Germany,* Macmillan (New York), 1987.

Young, Peter, *Atlas of the Second World War,* Berkley Windhover (New York), 1974.

Asia and the Pacific:

Alexander, Joseph H., *Utmost Savagery: The Three Days of Tarawa,* Naval Institute Press (Annapolis, MD), 1995.

Astor, Gerald, *Operation Iceberg: The Invasion and Conquest of Okinawa in World War II,* D. I. Fine (New York), 1995.

Battling Bastards of Bataan, http://home.pacbell. net/fbaldie/Battling_Bastards_of_Bataan.html (September 26, 2000).

Blassingame, Wyatt, *The U.S. Frogmen of World War II,* Random House (New York), 1964.

Bradley, James, and Ron Powers, *Flags of Our Fathers,* Bantam (New York), 2000.

Castello, Edmund L., *Midway: Battle for the Pacific,* Random House (New York), 1968.

Chang, Iris, *The Rape of Nanking: The Forgotten Holocaust of World War II,* Basic Books (New York), 1997.

Conroy, Robert, *The Battle of Bataan: America's Greatest Defeat,* Macmillan (New York), 1969.

Daws, Gavan, *Prisoners of the Japanese: POWs of World War II in the Pacific,* W. Morrow (New York), 1994.

Dull, Paul S., *A Battle History of the Japanese Navy (1941–1945),* United States Naval Institute Press (Annapolis, MD), 1978.

Fahey, James, *Pacific War Diary: 1942–1945,* Houghton Mifflin (Boston), 1992.

Frank, Richard B., *Guadalcanal: The Definitive Account of the Landmark Battle,* Penguin (New York), 1992.

Fuchida, Mitsuo, and Masatake Okumiya, *Midway: The Battle that Doomed Japan: The Japanese Navy's Story,* Naval Institute Press (Annapolis, MD), 1992.

Gayle, Gordon D., *Bloody Beaches: The Marines at Peleliu,* U.S. Marine Corps (Washington, DC), 1996.

Grant, R. G., *Hiroshima and Nagasaki,* Raintree, Steck-Vaughn (Austin, TX), 1988.

Griffith, Samuel B., *The Battle for Guadalcanal,* University of Illinois Press (Urbana, IL), 2000.

Hallas, James H., *The Devil's Anvil: The Assault on Peleliu,* Praeger (Westport, CT), 1994.

Harris, Nathaniel, *Pearl Harbor,* Dryad Press (North Pomfret, VT), 1986.

Hirschfeld, Wolfgang, *Hirschfeld: The Story of a U-Boat NCO, 1940–1946,* as told to Geoffrey Brooks, U.S. Naval Institute (Annapolis, MD), 1996.

Hoehling, A. A., *The Lexington Goes Down: A Fighting Carrier's Last Hours in the Coral Sea,* Stackpole Books (Mechanicsburg, PA), 1993.

Hubbard, Preston John, *Apocalypse Undone: My Survival of Japanese Imprisonment during WWII,* Vanderbilt University Press (Nashville, TN), 1990.

Kessler, Lynn, editor, *Never in Doubt: Remembering Iwo Jima,* Naval Institute Press (Annapolis, MD), 1999.

Linzey, Stanford E., *God Was at Midway: The Sinking of the USS Yorktown (CV-5) and the Battles of the Coral Sea and Midway,* Black Forest Press (San Diego, CA), 1996.

Manchester, William, *American Caesar: Douglas MacArthur, 1880–1964,* Little, Brown (Boston) 1978.

Manchester, William, *Goodbye, Darkness: A Memoir of the Pacific War,* Little, Brown (Boston), 1979.

Marrin, Albert, *Victory in the Pacific,* Atheneum (New York), 1983.

Mishler, Clayton, *Sampan Sailor: A Navy Man's Adventures in WWII China,* Brassey's (Washington, DC), 1994.

Morin, Isobel V., *Days of Judgment,* Millbrook Press (Brookfield, CT), 1995.

Morison, Samuel Eliot, *History of United States Naval Operations in World War II: Coral Sea, Midway and Submarine Actions, May 1942–August 1942,* Vol. 4, Little, Brown (Boston), 1950.

Petillo, Carol Morris, *Douglas MacArthur: The Philippine Years,* Indiana University Press (Bloomington, IN), 1981.

Prange, Gordon W., Donald M. Goldstein, and Katherine V. Dillon, *At Dawn We Slept: The Untold Story of Pearl Harbor,* Viking (New York), 1991.

Prange, Gordon W., Donald M. Goldstein, and Katherine V. Dillon, *God's Samurai: Lead Pilot at Pearl Harbor,* Brassey's (Washington, DC), 1990.

Raymer, Edward C., *Descent into Darkness: Pearl Harbor, 1941: A Navy Diver's Memoir,* Presidio Press (Novato, CA), 1996.

Rice, Earle, Jr., *The Attack on Pearl Harbor,* Lucent (San Diego), 1997.

Ross, Bill D., *Iwo Jima: Legacy of Valor,* Vanguard Press (New York), 1986.

Ruhe, William J., *War in the Boats: My World War II Submarine Battles,* Brassey's (Washington, DC), 1994.

Sauvrain, Philip, *Midway,* New Discovery Books (New York), 1993.

Schaller, Michael, *Douglas MacArthur: The Far Eastern General,* Oxford University Press (New York), 1989.

Schlesinger, Arthur, Jr., and Richard H. Rovere, *The MacArthur Controversy and American Foreign Policy,* Farrar, Straus and Giroux (New York), 1965.

Shapiro, William E., *Pearl Harbor,* F. Watts (New York), 1984.

Sherrow, Victoria, *Hiroshima,* New Discovery Books (New York), 1994.

Skipper, G. C., *Battle of Leyte Gulf,* Children's Press (Chicago), 1981.

Skipper, G. C., *Submarines in the Pacific,* Children's Press (Chicago), 1980.

Sledge, Eugene B., *With the Old Breed: At Peleliu and Okinawa,* Naval Institute Press (Annapolis, MD), 1996.

Smith, Myron J., Jr., *The Battles of the Coral Sea and Midway, 1942,* Greenwood Publishing (New York), 1991.

Smith, William Ward, *Midway: Turning Point of the Pacific,* Thomas Y. Crowell Company (New York), 1966.

Smurthwaite, David, *The Pacific War Atlas: 1941–1945,* Facts on File (New York), 1995.

Spector, Ronald H., *Eagle against the Sun: The American War with Japan,* Free Press (New York), 1985.

Stafford, Edward P., *The Big E: The Story of the U.S.S. Enterprise,* Random House (New York), 1962.

Stein, R. Conrad, *The Battle of Guadalcanal,* Children's Press (Chicago), 1983.

Stein, R. Conrad, *The Battle of Okinawa,* Children's Press (Chicago), 1985.

Stein, R. Conrad, *Fall of Singapore,* Children's Press (Chicago), 1982.

Stein, R. Conrad, *Hiroshima,* Children's Press (Chicago), 1982.

Stinnett, Robert B., *Day of Deceit: The Truth about FDR and Pearl Harbor,* Free Press (New York), 2000.

Sullivan, George, *The Day Pearl Harbor Was Bombed: A Photo History of World War II,* Scholastic (New York), 1991.

Takaki, Ronald, *Hiroshima: Why America Dropped the Atomic Bomb,* Little, Brown (Boston), 1995.

Taylor, Theodore, *The Battle off Midway Island,* Avon (New York), 1981.

Thomas, Gerald W, and Roger D. Walker, editors, *Victory in World War II: The New Mexico Story,* University of New Mexico Press (Las Cruces, NM), 1994.

Tregaskis, Richard, *Guadalcanal Diary,* Modern Library (New York), 2000.

Tuleja, Thaddeus V., *Climax at Midway,* W. W. Norton (New York), 1960.

Ward, Harold, *Don't Go Island Hopping during a War!,* Harold Ward, 1999.

Webber, Bert, *Silent Siege-III: Japanese Attacks on North America in World War II: Ships Sunk, Air Raids, Bombs Dropped, Civilians Killed: Documentary,* Webb Research Group (Medford, OR), 1992.

Yahara, Hiromichi, *The Battle for Okinawa,* John Wiley and Sons (New York), 1997.

Zhigeng, Xu, *Lest We Forget: Nanjing Massacre, 1937,* Chinese Literature Press (Beijing), 1995.

Zich, Arthur, and the editors of Time-Life Books, *The Rising Sun,* Time-Life Books (Alexandria, VA), 1977.

Europe, the Atlantic, Africa, and the Soviet Union, 1939–1943:

Allen, Kenneth, *Battle of the Atlantic,* Wayland (London), 1973.

Barnett, Correlli, *The Battle of El Alamein: Decision in the Desert,* Macmillan (New York), 1964.

Blanco, Richard L., *Rommel, the Desert Warrior: The Afrika Korps in World War II,* J. Mesmer (New York), 1982.

Brook-Shepherd, Gordon, *Anschluss: The Rape of Austria,* Macmillan & Company (London), 1963.

Churchill, Winston S., *The Second World War: The Gathering Storm, Vol. 1,* Cassell (London), 1948.

Ciano, Galeazzo, conte, *The Ciano Diaries, 1939–1943,* edited by H. Gibson, Doubleday (Garden City, NY), 1946.

Collier, Basil, *The Battle of Britain,* B.T. Batsford (London), 1962.

Collier, Richard, *The Sands of Dunkirk,* E. P. Dutton (New York), 1961.

Cook, Don, *Charles de Gaulle: A Biography,* Putnam (New York), 1983.

Corti, Eugenio, *Few Returned: Twenty-Eight Days on the Russian Front, Winter 1942–1943,* University of Missouri Press (Columbia, MO), 1997.

De Gaulle, Charles, *Memoirs of Hope, 1958–62,* Simon & Schuster (New York), 1971.

Drieman, J. E., editor, *Winston Churchill: An Unbreakable Spirit,* Dillon Press (Minneapolis, MN), 1990.

FitzGibbon, Constantine, *London's Burning,* Ballantine Books (New York), 1970.

Gehl, Jürgen, *Austria, Germany, and the Anschluss, 1931–1938,* Oxford University Press (New York), 1963.

Hoobler, Dorothy, and Thomas Hoobler, *World Leaders Past and Present: Joseph Stalin,* Chelsea House (New York), 1985.

Humble, Richard, *U-Boat,* Franklin Watts (New York), 1990.

James, Robert Rhodes, editor, *Winston S. Churchill: His Complete Speeches 1897–1963,* Chelsea House (New York), 1974.

Keller, Mollie, *Winston Churchill,* F. Watts (New York), 1984.

Kronenwetter, Michael, *Cities at War: London,* New Discovery Books (New York), 1992.

Lane, Tony, *The Merchant Seamen's War,* Manchester University Press (Manchester, England), 1990.

Lewis, Jonathon, and Phillip Whitehead, *Stalin: A Time for Judgment,* Pantheon (New York), 1990.

Macintyre, Donald G. F. W., *Narvik,* W.W. Norton & Company (New York), 1960.

Manchester, William, *The Last Lion: Winston Spencer Churchill* Little, Brown (Boston), 1983–88.

Marrin, Albert, *Stalin,* Viking Kestrel (New York), 1988.

McNeal, Robert, *Stalin: Man and Ruler,* New York University Press (New York), 1988.

Medvedev, Roy, *Let History Judge: The Origins and Consequences of Stalinism,* Columbia University Press (New York), 1989.

Mellor, John, *Forgotten Heroes: The Canadians at Dieppe,* Methuen (Toronto), 1975.

Payne, Robert, *The Great Man: A Portrait of Winston Churchill,* Coward, McCann and Geoghegan (New York), 1974.

Pitt, Barrie, and the editors of Time-Life Books, *The Battle of the Atlantic,* Time-Life Books (Alexandria, VA), 1977.

Reynaud, Paul, *In the Thick of the Fight,* translated by J. D. Lambert, Simon and Schuster (New York), 1955.

Reynolds, Quentin James, *The Battle of Britain,* Random House (New York), 1953.

Rose, Norman, *Churchill: The Unruly Giant,* Free Press (New York), 1994.

Ross, Stewart, *World Leaders,* Thomson Learning (New York), 1993.

Ryan, Cornelius, *A Bridge Too Far,* Simon and Schuster (New York), 1995.

Schoenfeld, Maxwell P., *Sir Winston Churchill: His Life and Times,* second edition, R.E. Krieger (Malabar, FL), 1986.

Severance, John B., *Winston Churchill: Soldier, Statesman, Artist,* Clarion Books (New York), 1996.

Shirer, William L., *The Collapse of the Third Republic,* Simon and Schuster (New York), 1969.

Shirer, William L., *The Sinking of the Bismarck,* Random House (New York), 1962.

Simon, Yves, *The Road to Vichy, 1918–1938,* translated by James A. Corbett and George J. McMorrow, Sheed and Ward (New York), 1942.

Skipper, G. C., *The Battle of Britain,* Children's Press (Chicago), 1980.

Skipper, G. C., *Battle of Stalingrad,* Children's Press (Chicago), 1981.

Skipper, G. C., *The Battle of the Atlantic,* Children's Press (Chicago), 1981.

Skipper, G. C., *Fall of the Fox, Rommel,* Children's Press (Chicago), 1980.

Skipper, G. C., *Goering and the Luftwaffe,* Children's Press (Chicago), 1980.

Skipper, G. C., *Invasion of Sicily,* Children's Press (Chicago), 1981.

Sloan, Frank, *Bismarck!,* Franklin Watts (New York), 1991.

Snell, John L., *Illusion and Necessity,* Houghton Mifflin (Boston), 1963.

Souster, Raymond, *Jubilee of Death: The Raid on Dieppe,* Oberon Press (Ottawa, Ontario, Canada), 1984.

Stein, R. Conrad, *Dunkirk,* Children's Press (Chicago), 1982.

Stein, R. Conrad, *Invasion of Russia,* Children's Press (Chicago), 1985.

Stein, R. Conrad, *Siege of Leningrad,* Children's Press (Chicago), 1983.

Taylor, Theodore, *Battle of the Arctic Seas: The Story of Convoy PQ 17,* Crowell (New York), 1976.

Topp, Erich, *The Odyssey of a U-Boat Commander: Recollections of Erich Topp,* translated by Eric C. Rust, Praeger (Westport, CT), 1992.

Ulam, Adam, *Stalin, the Man and His Era,* Beacon Press (Boston), 1989.

Vause, Jordan, and Jurgen Oesten, *Wolf: U-Boat Commanders in World War II,* Airlife (Osceola, WI), 1997.

Warth, Robert D., *Joseph Stalin,* Twayne (New York), 1969.

Weygand, Maxime, *Recalled to Service,* William Heinemann (London), 1952.

Whitelaw, Nancy, *Joseph Stalin: From Peasant to Premier,* Dillon Press (New York), 1992.

Woodrooffe, T., *The Battle of the Atlantic,* Faber (New York), 1965.

Germany:

Allen, William Sheridan, *The Nazi Seizure of Power: The Experience of a Single German Town, 1922–1945,* Franklin Watts (New York), 1984.

Ayer, Eleanor, *Adolf Hitler,* Lucent (San Diego), 1996.

Ayer, Eleanor, *Cities at War: Berlin,* New Discovery Books (New York), 1992.

Baynes, Norman H., editor, *The Speeches of Adolf Hitler, April 1922–August 1939: An English Translation of Representative Passages,* Gordon Press (New York), 1981.

Berman, Russell A., *Paul von Hindenburg,* Chelsea House (New York), 1987.

Binion, Rudolph, *Hitler among the Germans,* Elsevier (Amsterdam), 1976.

Bracher, Karl Dietrich, *The German Dictatorship: The Origins, Structure, and Effects of National Socialism,* Praeger (New York), 1970.

Bullock, Alan, *Hitler: A Study in Tyranny,* Harper and Row (New York), 1971.

Clark, Alan, *Barbarossa: The Russian-German Conflict, 1941–1945,* William Morrow (New York), 1965.

Eimerl, Sarel, *Hitler over Europe; The Road to World War II,* Little, Brown (Boston), 1972.

Fest, Joachim C., *The Face of the Third Reich: Portraits of the Nazi Leadership,* Pantheon (New York), 1970.

Friedman, Ina R., *The Other Victims: First-Person Stories of Non-Jews Persecuted by the Nazis,* Houghton Mifflin (Boston), 1990.

Gallagher, Hugh Gregory, *By Trust Betrayed: Patients, Physicians, and the License to Kill in the Third Reich,* Holt (New York), 1990.

Gilbert, Felix, editor, *Hitler Directs His War: The Secret Records of His Daily Military Conferences,* Octagon Books (New York), 1982.

Goldston, Robert C., *The Life and Death of Nazi Germany,* Bobbs-Merrill (Indianapolis), 1967.

Gordon, Harold J., *Hitler and the Beer Hall Putsch,* Princeton University Press (Princeton, NJ), 1972.

Harris, Nathaniel, *Hitler,* Trafalgar (North Pomfret, VT), 1989.

Hauner, Milan, *Hitler: A Chronology of His Life and Time,* St. Martin's Press (New York), 1983.

Heyes, Eileen, *Adolf Hitler,* Millbrook Press (Brookfield, CT), 1993.

Hitler, Adolf, *Mein Kampf,* translated by Ralph Manheim, Houghton Mifflin (Boston), 1971.

Johnson, Eric A., *Nazi Terror: The Gestapo, Jews, and Ordinary Germans,* Basic Books (New York), 2000.

Kershaw, Ian, *The "Hitler Myth": Image and Reality in the Third Reich,* Oxford University Press (New York), 1987.

Klemperer, Victor, *I Will Bear Witness 1941–1945: A Diary of the Nazi Years,* Volume 2, Random House (New York), 1998.

Langer, Walter C., *The Mind of Adolf Hitler: The Secret Wartime Report,* Basic Books (New York), 1972.

Manvell, Roger, *SS and the Gestapo,* Ballantine Books (New York), 1969.

Massaquoi, Hans J., *Destined to Witness: Growing Up Black in Nazi Germany,* W. Morrow (New York), 1999.

Merkl, Peter H., *The Making of a Stormtrooper,* Princeton University Press (Princeton, NJ), 1980.

Nevelle, Peter, *Life in the Third Reich: World War II,* Batsford (North Pomfret, VT), 1992.

Pulzer, Peter G., *The Rise of Political Anti-Semitism in Germany and Austria: 1867–1918,* John Wiley (New York), 1964.

Rich, Norman, *Hitler's War Aims,* W. W. Norton (New York), 1973.

Seaton, Albert, *The Russo-German War, 1941–1945,* Frederick A. Praeger (New York), 1970.

Shirer, William L., *Berlin Diary,* Knopf (New York), 1941.

Shirer, William L., *Twentieth Century Journey: A Memoir of a Life and the Times,* Volume 2, *The Nightmare Years, 1930–1940,* Bantam Books (New York), 1984.

Speer, Albert, *Inside the Third Reich,* Galahad Books (New York), 1995.

Spence, William, *Germany Then and Now,* Franklin Watts (New York), 1994.

Stein, R. Conrad, *Hitler Youth,* Children's Press (Chicago), 1985.

Stern, Fritz, *Dreams and Delusions: The Drama of German History,* Yale University Press (New Haven, CT), 1999.

Steward, Gail B., *Hitler's Reich,* Lucent Books (San Diego), 1994.

Tames, Richard, *Nazi Germany,* Batsford (North Pomfret, VT), 1992.

Toland, John, *Adolf Hitler,* Anchor Books (New York), 1992.

Wepman, Dennis, *Adolf Hitler,* Chelsea House (New York), 1989.

Williamson, David, *The Third Reich,* Bookwright Press (New York), 1989.

Italy and Fascism:

Chrisp, Peter, *The Rise of Fascism,* Bookwright Press (New York), 1991.

Hartenian, Lawrence R., *Benito Mussolini,* Chelsea House (New York), 1988.

Knox, MacGregor, *Mussolini Unleashed, 1939–1941: Politics and Strategy in Fascist Italy's Last War,* Cambridge University Press (New York), 1986.

Leeds, Christopher, *Italy under Mussolini,* Putnam (New York), 1972.

Lyttle, Richard, *Il Duce: The Rise and Fall of Benito Mussolini,* Atheneum (New York), 1987.

Moseley, Ray, *Mussolini's Shadow: The Double Life of Count Galeazzo Ciano,* Yale University Press, (New Haven, CT) 2000.

Stille, Alexander, *Benevolence and Betrayal: Five Italian Jewish Families Under Fascism,* Summit Books (New York), 1991.

Wiskemann, Elizabeth, *The Rome-Berlin Axis: A History of the Relations Between Hitler and Mussolini,* Oxford University Press (London), 1949.

Japan:

Barker, Rodney, *The Hiroshima Maidens: A Story of Courage, Compassion, and Survival,* Penguin Books (New York), 1985.

Behr, Edward, *Hirohito: Beyond the Myth,* Villard Books (New York), 1989.

Black, Wallace B., and Jean F. Blashfield, *Hiroshima and the Atomic Bomb,* Crestwood House (New York), 1993.

Butow, Robert J. C., *Tojo and the Coming of the War,* Stanford University Press (Stanford, CA), 1969.

Grant, R. G., *Hiroshima and Nagasaki,* Raintree, Steck-Vaughn (Austin, TX), 1988.

Hersey, John, *Hiroshima,* Vintage Books (New York), 1989.

Hogan, Michael J., editor, *Hiroshima in History and Memory,* Cambridge University Press (New York), 1996.

Hoobler, Dorothy, and Thomas Hoobler, *Showa: The Age of Hirohito,* Walker (New York), 1990.

Maruki, Toshi, *Hiroshima No Pika*, Lothrop, Lee & Shepard (New York), 1982.

Oe, Kenzaburo, *Hiroshima Notes*, Grove Press (New York), 1996.

Sekimori, Gaynor, *Hibakusha: Survivors of Hiroshima and Nagasaki*, Kosei (Tokyo), 1986.

Selden, Kyoko, and Mark Selden, editors, *The Atomic Bomb: Voices from Hiroshima and Nagasaki*, M.E. Sharpe (Armonk, NJ), 1989.

Severns, Karen, *Hirohito*, Chelsea House (New York), 1988.

Sherrow, Victoria, *Hiroshima*, New Discovery Books (New York), 1994.

Sherwin, Martin J., *A World Destroyed: Hiroshima and the Origins of the Arms Race*, Stanford University Press (Stanford, CA), 2000.

Stein, R. Conrad, *Hiroshima*, Children's Press (Chicago), 1982.

Japanese War Crimes:

Askin, Kelly Dawn, *War Crimes Against Women: Prosecution in International War Crimes Tribunals*, Martinus Nijhoff (The Hague), 1997.

Brackman, Arnold C., *The Other Nuremberg: The Untold Story of the Tokyo War Crimes Trials*, Morrow (New York), 1987.

Ginn, John L., *Sugamo Prison, Tokyo: An Account of the Trial and Sentencing of Japanese War Criminals in 1948, by a U.S. Participant*, McFarland (Jefferson, NC), 1992.

Hosoya, Chihiro, et. al., *The Tokyo War Crimes Trial: An International Symposium*, Kodansha (Tokyo), 1986.

International Military Tribunal for the Far East, *The Tokyo Major War Crimes Trial: The Records of the International Military Tribunal for the Far East: With an Authoritative Commentary and Comprehensive Guide*, edited by R. John Pritchard, published for the Robert M.W. Kempner Collegium by Edwin Mellen Press (Lewiston, NY), 1998.

Minear, Richard H., *Victor's Justice: The Tokyo War Crimes Trial*, Princeton University Press (Princeton, NJ), 1971.

Piccigallo, Philip, *The Japanese on Trial: Allied War Crimes Operations in the East, 1945–1951*, University of Texas Press (Austin, TX), 1979.

Röling, Bernard Victor Aloysius, *The Tokyo Trial and Beyond: Reflections of a Peacemonger*, Polity Press (Cambridge, England), 1993.

Tanaka, Toshiyuki, *Hidden Horrors: Japanese War Crimes in World War II*, Westview Press (Boulder, CO), 1996.

The United States:

Ambrose, Stephen E., *Band of Brothers: E Company, 506th Regiment, 101st Airborne from Normandy to Hitler's Eagle Nest*, Simon and Schuster (New York), 1992.

Ambrose, Stephen E., *The Victors: Eisenhower and His Boys: The Men of World War II*, Simon and Schuster (New York), 1998.

Bernstein, Alison R., *American Indians and World War II: Toward a New Era in Indian Affairs*, University of Oklahoma Press (Norman, OK), 1999.

Brimner, Larry Dane, *Voices from the Camps*, Franklin Watts (New York), 1994.

Brokaw, Tom, *The Greatest Generation*, Random House (New York), 1998.

Brokaw, Tom, *The Greatest Generation Speaks: Letters and Reflections*, Random House (New York), 1999.

Burns, James M., *Roosevelt: The Soldier of Freedom*, Harvest/Harcourt (New York), 1973.

Cannon, Marian, *Dwight David Eisenhower: War Hero and President*, Franklin Watts (New York), 1990.

Cohen, Stan, *V for Victory: America's Home Front During World War II*, Pictorial Histories Publishing (Missoula, MT), 1991.

Darby, Jean, *Douglas MacArthur*, Lerner (Minneapolis, MN), 1989.

Davis, Kenneth S., *FDR: The New Deal Years, 1933–1937*, Random House (New York), 1979.

Davis, Kenneth S., *FDR: The New York Years, 1928–1933*, Random House (New York), 1979.

Devaney, John, *Franklin Delano Roosevelt, President*, Walker (New York), 1987.

Divine, Robert A., *The Reluctant Belligerent: American Entry into World War II*, John Wiley and Sons (New York), 1965.

Dolan, Edward F., *America in World War II: 1942*, Millbrook Press (Brookfield, CT), 1991.

Dolan, Edward F., *America in World War II: 1943*, Millbrook Press (Brookfield, CT), 1992.

Donovan, Robert J., *PT 109: John F. Kennedy in World War II*, McGraw-Hill (New York), 1961.

Duden, Jane, *1940s*, Crestwood (New York), 1989.

Francis, Charles E., *The Tuskegee Airmen: The Men Who Changed a Nation*, Branden Publishing (Boston), 1993.

Freedman, Russell, *Franklin Delano Roosevelt*, Franklin Watts (New York), 1983.

Fremon, David K., *Japanese American Internment in American History*, Enslow Publishers (Springfield, NJ), 1966.

Gilbo, Patrick F., *The American Red Cross: The First Century*, Harper and Row, Publishers (New York), 1981.

Goodwin, Doris Kearns, *No Ordinary Time, Franklin and Eleanor Roosevelt: The Home Front in World War II*, Simon and Schuster (New York), 1994.

Graham, Otis L., Jr., and Meghan Robinson Wander, editors, *Franklin D. Roosevelt, His Life and Times: An Encyclopedic View*, G. K. Hall (Boston), 1985.

Hacker, Jeffrey H., *Franklin D. Roosevelt*, Franklin Watts (New York), 1983.

Harris, Jacqueline L., *The Tuskegee Airmen: Black Heroes of World War II*, Dillon Press (Parsippany, NJ), 1995.

Harris, Mark Jonathan, Franklin Mitchell, and Steven Schechter, editors, *The Homefront: America during World War II*, G. P. Putnam's Sons (New York), 1984.

Holway, John B., *Red Tail Black Wings: The Men of America's Black Air Force*, Yucca Tree (Las Cruces, NM), 1997.

Homan, Lynn M., and Thomas Reilly, *Tuskegee Airmen*, Arcadia Tempus Publishing Group (Charleston, SC), 1998.

Langer, William L., and S. Everett Gleason, *The Undeclared War, 1940–1941*, P. Smith (Gloucester, MA), 1968.

Lawson, Ted W., *Thirty Seconds Over Tokyo*, Buccaneer Books, 1999.

Levine, Ellen, *A Fence Away from Freedom*, G. P. Putnam (New York), 1995.

Mauldin, Bill, *Back Home*, William Sloane Associates (New York), 1947.

Mauldin, Bill, *The Brass Ring*, W. W. Norton (New York), 1971.

McKissack, Patricia, and Frederick McKissack, *Red-Tail Angels: The Story of the Tuskegee Airmen of World War II*, Walker (New York), 1995.

Miller, Nathan, *FDR: An Intimate History*, originally published in 1983, reprinted, Madison Books/University Press of America (Lanham, MD), 1991.

Morgan, Ted, *FDR: A Biography*, Simon and Schuster (New York), 1985.

Murphy, Audie, *To Hell and Back*, Holt (New York), 1949.

O'Connor, Barbara, *The Soldiers' Voice: The Story of Ernie Pyle*, Carolrhoda Books (Minneapolis, MN), 1996.

Olesky, Walter, *Military Leaders of World War II*, Facts on File (New York), 1994.

Perkins, Frances, *The Roosevelt I Knew*, Viking (New York), 1946.

Pfeifer, Kathryn Browne, *The 761st Tank Battalion*, Henry Holt (New York), 1994.

Pyle, Ernie, *Brave Men*, Henry Holt (New York), 1944.

Rubenstein, Harry R., and William L. Bird, *Design for Victory: World War II Posters on the American Home Front*, Princeton Architectural Press (New York), 1998.

Spies, Karen Bornemann, *Franklin D. Roosevelt*, Enslow (Springfield, NJ), 1999.

Stanley, Jerry, *I Am an American: A True Story of Japanese Internment*, Crown (New York), 1994.

Stein, R. Conrad, *The Home Front*, Children's Press (Chicago), 1986.

Stein, R. Conrad, *Nisei Regiment*, Children's Press (Chicago), 1985.

Sweeney, James B., *Famous Aviators of World War II*, Franklin Watts (New York), 1987.

Uchida, Yoshika, *Desert Exile: The Uprooting of a Japanese-American Family*, University of Washington Press (Seattle), 1982.

Whitman, Sylvia, *Uncle Sam Wants You: Military Men and Women in World War II*, Lerner (Minneapolis, MN), 1993.

Whitman, Sylvia, *V Is for Victory*, Lerner (Minneapolis, MN), 1993.

Woodrow, Martin, *The World War II GI,* Franklin Watts (New York), 1986.

Wrynn, V. Dennis, *Detroit Goes to War: The American Automobile Industry in World War II,* Motorbooks International (Osceola, WI), 1993.

Women and the War:

Bowman, Constance, *Slacks and Calluses: Our Summer in a Bomber Factory,* illustrated by Clara Marie Allen, Smithsonian Institution Press (Washington, DC), 1999.

Carl, Ann B., *A Wasp Among Eagles: A Woman Military Test Pilot in World War II,* Smithsonian Institution Press (Washington, DC), 1999.

Cole, Jean Hascall, *Women Pilots of World War II,* University of Utah Press (Salt Lake City, UT), 1992.

Colijn, Helen, *Song of Survival: Women Interned,* White Cloud Press (Ashland, OR), 1995.

Colman, Penny, *Rosie the Riveter: Women Working on the Home Front in World War II,* Crown (New York), 1995.

Danner, Dorothy Still, *What a Way to Spend a War: Navy Nurse POWs in the Philippines,* Naval Institute Press (Annapolis, MD), 1995.

Fessler, Diane Burke, *No Time for Fear: Voices of American Military Nurses in World War II,* Michigan State University Press (East Lansing, MI), 1996.

Frank, Miriam, Marilyn Ziebarth, and Connie Field, *The Life and Times of Rosie the Riveter: The Story of Three Million Working Women during World War II,* Clarity Educational Productions (Emeryville, CA), 1982.

Green, Anne Bosanko, and D'Ann Campbell, *One Woman's War: Letters Home from the Women's Army Corps, 1944–1946,* Minnesota Historical Society (St. Paul, MN), 1989.

Gruhzit-Hoyt, Olga, *They Also Served: American Women in World War II,* Birch Lane Press (Secaucus, NJ), 1995.

Gunter, Helen Clifford, *Navy WAVE: Memories of World War II,* Cypress House (Fort Bragg, CA), 1994.

Hicks, George L., *The Comfort Women: Japan's Brutal Regime of Enforced Prostitution in the Second World War,* W.W. Norton & Company (New York), 1995.

Holm, Jeanne, and Judith Bellafaire, editors, *In Defense of a Nation: Servicewomen in World War II,* Vandamere Press (Arlington, VA), 1998.

Honey, Maureen, editor, *Bitter Fruit: African American Women in World War II,* University of Missouri Press (Columbia, MO), 1999.

Howard, Keith, editor, *True Stories of the Korean Comfort Women,* Cassell (London), 1995.

Jopling, Lucy Wilson, *Warrior in White,* Watercress Press (San Antonio, TX), 1990.

Kaminski, Theresa, *Prisoners in Paradise: American Women in the Wartime South Pacific,* University Press of Kansas (Lawrence, KS), 2000.

Keith, Agnes Newton, *Three Came Home,* Little, Brown (Boston, MA), 1947.

Kelsey, Marion, *Victory Harvest: Diary of a Canadian in the Women's Land Army, 1940–1944,* McGill-Queens University Press (Toronto), 1997.

Lucas, Celia, *Prisoners of Santo Tomas: A True Account of Women POWs Under Japanese Control,* Cooper (London), 1975.

Monahan, Evelyn M., and Rosemary Neidel-Greenlee, *All This Hell: U.S. Nurses Imprisoned by the Japanese,* University of Kentucky Press (Lexington, KY), 2000.

Noggle, Anne, and Dora Dougherty Strother, *For God, Country, and the Thrill of It: Women Airforce Pilots in World War II,* Texas A&M University Press (College Station, TX), 1990.

Norman, Elizabeth M., *We Band of Angels: The Untold Story of American Nurses Trapped on Bataan by the Japanese,* Random House (New York), 1999.

Nova, Lily, and Iven Lourie, editors, *Interrupted Lives: Four Women's Stories of Internment During World War II in the Philippines,* Artemis Books (Nevada City, CA), 1995.

Reynoldson, Floria, *Women and War,* Thomson Learning (New York), 1993.

Scharr, Adela Riek, *Sisters in the Sky, Volume 1: The WAFS,* Patrice Press (St. Louis, MO), 1986.

Scharr, Adela Riek, *Sisters in the Sky, Volume 2: The WASP,* Patrice Press (St. Louis, MO), 1988.

Sinott, Susan, *Doing Our Part: American Women on the Home Front during World War II,* Franklin Watts (New York), 1995.

Tomblin, Barbara Brooks, *G. I. Nightingales: The Army Nurse Corps in World War II*, University Press of Kentucky (Lexington, KY), 1996.

Treadwell, Mattie E., *United States Army in World War II: Special Studies: The Women's Army Corps*, Office of the Chief of Military History, Department of the Army (Washington, DC), 1954.

Weatherford, Doris, *American Women and World War II*, Facts on File (New York), 1992.

Weitz, Margaret Collins, *Sisters in the Resistance: How Women Fought to Free France, 1940–1945*, John Wiley and Sons (New York), 1998.

Williams, Vera S., *WACs: Women's Army Corps*, Motorbooks International Publishers, 1997.

Williams, Vera S., *Women Airforce Service Pilots of World War II*, Motorbooks International Publishers (Osceola, WI), 1994.

Wise, Nancy Baker, and Christy Wise, *A Mouthful of Rivets: Women at Work in World War II*, Jossey-Bass (San Francisco, CA), 1994.

Zeinert, Karen, *Those Incredible Women of World War II*, Millbrook Press (Brookfield, CT), 1994.

Children in the War:

Bertini, Tullio Bruno, *Trapped in Tuscany, Liberated by the Buffalo Soldiers: The True World War II Story of Tullio Bruno Bertini*, Dante University Press (Boston), 1998.

Besson, Jean-Louis, *October 45: Childhood Memories of the War*, Creative Editions (Mankato, MN), 1995.

Butterworth, Emma Macalik, *As the Waltz Was Ending*, Four Winds (New York), 1982.

Chapman, Fern Schumer, *Motherland: A Daughter's Journey to Reclaim the Past*, Viking (New York), 2000.

Cross, Robin, *Children and War*, Thomson Learning (New York), 1994.

Drucker, Olga Levy, *Kindertransport*, Henry Holt (New York), 1992.

Emmerich, Elsbeth, *My Childhood in Nazi Germany*, Bookwright Press (New York), 1991.

Foreman, Michael, *War Boy: A Country Childhood*, Arcade (New York), 1990.

Heyes, Eileen, *Children of the Swastika: The Hitler Youth*, Millbrook Press (Brookfield, CT), 1993.

Holliday, Laurel, *Children in the Holocaust and World War II*, Pocket Books (New York), 1995.

Isaacman, Clara, *Clara's Story*, Jewish Publication Society (Philadelphia), 1984.

Kuper, Jack, *Child of the Holocaust*, Berkley Books (New York), 1993.

Loy, Rosetta, *First Words: A Childhood in Fascist Italy*, Metropolitan Books/Henry Holt (New York) 2000.

Lukas, Richard C., *Did the Children Cry?: Hitler's War Against Jewish and Polish Children, 1939–1945*, Hippocrene Books (New York), 1994.

Marx, Trish, *Echoes of World War II*, Lerner (Minneapolis, MN), 1994.

Nicholson, Dorinda Makanaonalani Stagner, *Pearl Harbor Child: A Child's View of Pearl Harbor—From Attack to Peace*, Arizona Memorial Museum Association (Honolulu), 1993.

Silwowska, Wiktoria, editor, *The Last Eyewitnesses: Children of the Holocaust Speak*, Northwestern University Press (Evanston, IL), 1998.

Stalcup, Ann, *On the Home Front: Growing up in Wartime England*, Linnet Books (North Haven, CT), 1998.

Toll, Nelly S., *Behind the Secret Window: A Memoir of a Hidden Childhood During World War II*, Dial Books (New York), 1993.

Tunnell, Michael O., and George W. Chilcoat, *The Children of Topaz*, Holiday House (New York), 1996.

Ungerer, Tomi, *A Childhood under the Nazis*, Tomic (Niwot, CO), 1998.

Wassiljewa, Tatjana, *Hostage to War*, Scholastic Press (New York), 1997.

Wilkomirski, Binjamin, *Fragments: Memories of a Wartime Childhood*, Schocken Books (New York), 1997.

Wojciechowska, Maia, *Till the Break of Day*, Harcourt, Brace, Jovanovich (New York), 1972.

Events in Europe, 1944 and Later:

Alperovitz, Gar, *Atomic Diplomacy: Hiroshima and Potsdam*, Simon and Schuster (New York), 1965.

Ambrose, Stephen E., *Citizen Soldiers: The U.S. Army from the Normandy Beaches to the Bulge to the Surrender of Germany*, Simon & Schuster (New York), 1997.

Balkoski, Joseph, *Beyond the Beachhead: The 29th Infantry Division in Normandy*, Stackpole Books (Mechanicsburg, PA), 1999.

Banfield, Susan, *Charles de Gaulle*, Chelsea House (New York), 1985.

Black, Wallace B., *Battle of the Bulge*, Crestwood House (New York), 1993.

Bliven, Bruce, *The Story of D-Day: June 6, 1944*, Random House (New York), 1956.

Bourke-White, Margaret, *"Dear Fatherland, Rest Quietly": A Report on the Collapse of Hitler's "Thousand Years,"* Simon and Schuster (New York), 1946.

Collins, Larry, and Dominique Lapierre, *Is Paris Burning?*, Castle, 2000.

Conot, Robert E., *Justice at Nuremberg*, Harper (New York), 1983.

Dolan, Edward F., *The Fall of Hitler's Germany*, Franklin Watts (New York), 1988.

Evans, Richard J., *In Hitler's Shadow: West German Historians and the Attempt to Escape from the Nazi Past*, Pantheon (New York), 1989.

Feis, Herbert, *Between War and Peace: The Potsdam Conference*, Princeton University Press (Princeton, NJ), 1960.

Goldstein, Donald M., Katherine V. Dillon, and J. Michael Wenger, *Nuts! The Battle of the Bulge: The Story and Photographs*, Brassey's (Washington, DC), 1994.

Hine, Al, *D-Day: The Invasion of Europe*, American Heritage Publishing Company (New York), 1962.

Keegan, John, *Six Armies in Normandy: From D-Day to the Liberation of Paris*, Penguin (New York), 1994.

Lamb, Richard, *War in Italy 1943–1945: A Brutal Story*, Da Capo Press (New York), 1996.

MacDonald, Charles B., *The Mighty Endeavor: American Armed Forces in the European Theater in World War II*, Da Capo Press (New York), 1992.

MacDonald, Charles B., *A Time for Trumpets: The Untold Story of the Battle of the Bulge*, Bantam Books (New York), 1985.

Marrin, Albert, *Overlord: D-Day and the Invasion of Europe*, Atheneum (New York), 1982.

Morin, Isobel V., *Days of Judgment*, Millbrook Press (Brookfield, CT), 1995.

Posner, Gerald L., *Hitler's Children: Sons and Daughters of the Third Reich Talk about Their Fathers and Themselves*, Random House (New York), 1991.

Rice, Earl, *The Nuremberg Trials*, Lucent Books (San Diego), 1997.

Ryan, Cornelius, *The Last Battle*, Simon & Schuster (New York), 1966.

Ryan, Cornelius, *The Longest Day: June 6, 1944*, Simon and Schuster (New York), 1994.

Sheehan, Fred, and Martin Blumenson, *Anzio, Epic of Bravery*, University of Oklahoma Press (Norman, OK), 1994.

Skipper, G. C., *Death of Hitler*, Children's Press (Chicago), 1980.

Skipper, G. C., *Mussolini: A Dictator Dies*, Children's Press (Chicago), 1981.

Stein, R. Conrad, *World War II in Europe: America Goes to War*, Enslow Press (Hillside, NJ), 1984.

Toland, John, *The Last 100 Days*, Random House (New York), 1966.

United States Department of State, *The Conferences at Malta and Yalta, 1945*, Greenwood Press (Westport, CT), 1976.

Whitelaw, Nancy, *A Biography of General Charles de Gaulle*, Dillon Press (New York), 1991.

Secret Codes and Weapons, Spies, and Sabotage:

Aldrich, Richard J., *Intelligence and the War Against Japan: Britain, America and the Politics of Secret Service*, Cambridge University Press (New York), 2000.

Alvarez, David J., editor, *Allied and Axis Signals Intelligence in World War II*, Frank Cass (Portland, OR), 1999.

Alvarez, David J., *Secret Messages: Codebreaking and American Diplomacy, 1930–1945*, University of Kansas Press (Lawrence, KS), 2000.

Ambrose, Stephen E., and Richard H. Immerman, *Ike's Spies: Eisenhower and the Espionage Establishment*, University Press of Mississippi (Jackson, MS), 1999.

Andryszewski, Tricia, *The Amazing Life of Moe Berg: Catcher, Scholar, Spy*, Millbrook Press (Brookfield, CT), 1996.

Bixler, Margaret T., *Winds of Freedom: The Story of the Navajo Code Talkers of World War II*, Two Bytes (Darien, CT), 1992.

Breuer, William B., *MacArthur's Undercover War: Spies, Saboteurs, Guerillas, and Secret Missions,* John Wiley and Sons (New York), 1995.

Daily, Robert, *The Code Talkers,* Franklin Watts (New York), 1995.

Durrett, Deanne, *Unsung Heroes of World War II: The Story of the Navajo Code Talkers,* Facts on File (New York), 1998.

Gardner, W. J. R., *Decoding History: The Battle of the Atlantic and Ultra,* United States Naval Institute (Annapolis, MD), 2000.

Goldston, Robert C., *Sinister Touches: The Secret War Against Hitler,* Dial Press (New York), 1992.

Halter, Jon C., *Top Secret Projects of World War II,* J. Messner (New York), 1978.

Harper, Stephen, *Capturing Enigma: How HMS Petard Seized the German Naval Codes,* Sutton Publishing, 2000.

Hinsley, Francis H., *British Intelligence in the Second World War,* Cambridge University Press (New York), 1993.

Hodgson, Lynn-Philip, *Inside—Camp X,* Blake Books, 1999.

Hohne, Heinz, *Canaris: Hitler's Master Spy,* Cooper Square Press (New York), 1999.

Holmes, W. J., *Double-Edged Secrets: U.S. Naval Intelligence Operations in the Pacific During World War II,* United States Naval Institute (Annapolis, MD), 1998.

Jakub, Jay, *Spies and Saboteurs: Anglo-American Collaboration and Rivalry in Human Intelligence Collection and Special Operations,* St. Martin's Press (New York), 1999.

Johnson, David Allen, *Germany's Spies and Saboteurs,* Motorbooks International (Osceola, WI), 1998.

Jones, Catherine, *Navajo Code Talkers: Native American Heroes,* Tudor Publications (Greensboro, NC), 1997.

Kahn, David A., *Hitler's Spies: German Military Intelligence in World War II,* Da Capo Press (Cambridge, MA), 2000.

Kilzer, Louis, *Hitler's Traitor: Martin Bormann and the Defeat of the Reich,* Presidio Press (Novato, CA), 2000.

Kiyosaki, Wayne S., and Daniel K. Akaka, *A Spy in Their Midst: The World War II Struggle of a Japanese-American Hero,* Madison Books (Lanham, MD), 1995.

Lawson, Don, *The Secret World War II,* Franklin Watts (New York), 1978.

MacDonnell, Francis, *Insidious Foes: The Axis Fifth Column and the American Home Front,* Oxford University Press (New York), 1995.

Marks, Leo, *Between Silk and Cyanide: A Codemaker's War 1941–1945,* Free Press (New York), 1999.

Marrin, Albert, *The Secret Armies,* Atheneum (New York), 1985.

McIntosh, Elizabeth P., *Sisterhood of Spies: The Women of the OSS,* GK Hall (Thorndike, ME), 2000.

Moon, Tom, *This Grim and Savage Game: The OSS and the Beginning of U.S. Covert Operations in World War II,* Da Capo Press (Cambridge, MA), 2000.

Paul, Doris A., *The Navajo Code Talkers,* Dorrance (Philadelphia, PA), 1973.

Paz Salinas, Maria Emilia, *Strategy, Security, and Spies: Mexico and the U.S. as Allies in World War II,* Pennsylvania State University Press (University Park, PA), 1997.

Rogers, James T., *The Secret War: Espionage in World War II,* Facts on File (New York), 1991.

Showell, Jak P. Mallman, *Enigma U-Boats: Breaking the Code—The True Story,* Naval Institute Press (Annapolis, MD), 2000.

Stevenson, William, *A Man Called Intrepid: The Secret War,* Harcourt, Brace (New York), 1976.

Sutherland, David, *He Who Dares: Recollections of Service in the SAS, SBS, and MI5,* United States Naval Institute (Annapolis, MD), 1999.

Tarrant, V. E., *The Red Orchestra,* John Wiley and Sons (New York), 1996.

Tickell, Jerrard, *Odette: The Story of a British Agent,* Chapman & Hall (London), 1949.

Warriors: Navajo Code Talkers, photographs by Kenji Kawano, Northland (Flagstaff, AZ), 1990.

Wires, Richard, *The Cicero Spy Affair: German Access to British Secrets in World War II,* Praeger (Westport, CT), 1999.

Holocaust and World War II Fiction:

Aaron, David, *Crossing by Night,* Thorndike Press (Thorndike, ME), 1993.

Abbott, Margot, *The Last Innocent Hour: A Novel,* St. Martin's Press (New York), 1991.

Allbeury, Ted, *A Time Without Shadows,* Mysterious Press (New York), 1991.

Allington, Maynard, *The Fox in the Field: A WWII Novel of India,* Brassey's (Washington, DC), 1994.

Amis, Martin, *Time's Arrow,* Harmony Books (New York), 1991.

Appelfeld, Aharon, *The Age of Wonders,* D. R. Godine (Boston), 1981.

Appelfeld, Aharon, *Badenheim 1939,* D. R. Godine (Boston), 1980.

Appelfeld, Aharon, *For Every Sin,* Weidenfeld & Nicolson (New York), 1989.

Appelfeld, Aharon, *Immortal Bartfuss,* Weidenfeld & Nicolson (New York), 1988.

Ballard, J. G., *Empire of the Sun,* V. Gollancz (London), 1984.

Bassani, Giorgio, *The Garden of the Finzi-Continis,* MJF Books (New York), 1996.

Bassett, James, *Cmdr. Prince, USN: A Novel of the Pacific War,* Simon and Schuster (New York), 1971.

Beach, Edward, *Run Silent, Run Deep,* Holt (New York), 1955.

Begley, Louis, *Wartime Lies,* Knopf (New York), 1991.

Bellow, Saul, *The Bellarosa Connection,* Penguin (New York), 1989.

Benchley, Nathaniel, *Bright Candles: A Novel of the Danish Resistance,* Harper and Row (New York), 1974.

Benchley, Nathaniel, *A Necessary End: A Novel of World War II,* Harper and Row (New York), 1976.

Boll, Heinrich, *Billiards at Half-Past Nine,* Weidenfeld and Nicholson (London), 1961.

Booth, Martin, *Hiroshima Joe,* Penguin (New York), 1987.

Boraks-Nemetz, Lillian, *The Old Brown Suitcase: A Teenager's Story of War and Peace,* Ben-Simon Publications (Port Angeles, WA), 1994.

Borowski, Tadeusz, *This Way For the Gas, Ladies and Gentlemen,* Penguin (New York), 1976.

Boulle, Pierre, *The Bridge over the River Kwai,* translated by Xan Fielding, Gramercy Books (New York), 2000.

Boyne, Walter J., *Eagles at War,* Crown (New York), 1991.

Callison, Brian, *A Flock of Ships,* Putnam (New York), 1970.

Clavell, James, *King Rat,* Little, Brown (Boston), 1962.

Dailey, Janet, *Silver Wings, Santiago Blue,* G. K. Hall (Boston), 1984.

De Hartog, Jan, *The Captain,* Atheneum (New York), 1966.

Deighton, Len, *City of Gold,* Thorndike Press (Thorndike, ME), 1992.

Deighton, Len, *Goodbye, Mickey Mouse,* Knopf (New York), 1982.

Deighton, Len, *XPD,* Thorndike Press, Thorndike, ME, 1981.

Demetz, Hanna, *The House on Prague Street,* St. Martin's Press (New York), 1980.

Dickey, James, *To the White Sea,* Houghton Mifflin (Boston), 1993.

Drucker, Malka, and Michael Halperin, *Jacob's Rescue,* Delacorte Press, (New York), 1996.

Drury, Allen, *Toward What Bright Glory?: A Novel,* Morrow (New York), 1990.

Earl, Maureen, *Boat of Stone,* Permanent Press (Sag Harbor, NY), 1993.

Epstein, Leslie, *King of the Jews,* Coward, McCann & Geoghegan (New York), 1979.

Fink, Ida, *The Journey,* Plume (New York), 1993.

Fleming, Thomas, *Loyalties: A Novel of World War II,* HarperCollins (New York), 1994.

Follett, Ken, *Churchill's Gold,* Houghton Mifflin (Boston), 1981.

Follett, Ken, *Eye of the Needle,* G. K. Hall (Boston), 1978.

Follett, Ken, *Night over Water,* Morrow (New York), 1991.

Forester, C. S., *The Good Shepherd,* Little, Brown (Boston), 1955.

Forsyth, Frederick, *The Odessa File,* Viking (New York), 1972.

Garfield, Brian, *The Paladin: A Novel Based on Fact,* Simon and Schuster (New York), 1979.

Gifford, Thomas, *Praetorian,* Bantam (New York), 1993.

Green, Gerald, *Holocaust,* Bantam (New York), 1978.

Greene, Graham, *The Tenth Man,* Simon and Schuster (New York), 1985.

Griffin, W. E. B., *The Corps,* Putnam (New York), 1990.

Griffin, W. E. B., *Honor Bound,* Putnam (New York), 1993.

Griffin, W. E. B., *Line of Fire,* Putnam (New York), 1992.

Harel, Isser, *The House on Garibaldi Street,* Viking Press (New York), 1975.

Harris, Robert, *Enigma,* Random House (New York), 1995.

Harris, Robert, *Fatherland,* Random House (New York), 1992.

Heller, Joseph, *Catch-22,* Dell (New York), 1961.

Hersey, John, *A Bell for Adano,* Knopf (New York), 1944.

Hersey, John, *The Wall,* Knopf (New York), 1950.

Hersey, John, *War Lover,* Knopf (New York), 1959.

Higgins, Jack, *Cold Harbour,* Simon and Schuster (New York), 1990.

Higgins, Jack, *The Eagle Has Flown,* Simon and Schuster (New York), 1991.

Higgins, Jack, *The Eagle Has Landed,* Holt (New York), 1975.

Hill, Grace Livingston, *All Through the Night,* J. B. Lippincott (New York), 1945.

Hunter, Stephen, *The Master Sniper,* Morrow (New York), 1980.

Iles, Greg, *Black Cross,* Dutton (New York), 1995.

Iles, Greg, *Spandau Phoenix,* Dutton (New York), 1993.

Isaacs, Susan, *Shining Through,* G. K. Hall (Boston), 1990.

Jones, James, *From Here to Eternity,* Scribner (New York), 1951.

Jones, James *The Thin Red Line,* Scribner (New York), 1962.

Katkov, Norman, *The Judas Kiss,* Dutton (New York), 1991.

Keneally, Thomas, *Schindler's List,* Simon and Schuster (New York), 1982.

Kerr, M. E., *Gentlehands,* Harper & Row (New York), 1978.

Kis, Danilo, *Hourglass,* translated by Ralph Manheim, Farrar, Straus (New York), 1990.

Klein, Edward, *The Parachutists,* Doubleday (Garden City, NY), 1981.

Korda, Michael, *Worldly Goods,* Random House (New York), 1982.

Kosinski, Jerzy, *The Painted Bird,* Modern Library (New York), 1970.

Kuznetsov, Anatoly, *Babi Yar,* Farrar, Straus and Giroux (New York), 1970.

Lanham, Edwin, *The Clock at 8:16,* Doubleday (Garden City, NY), 1970.

Lay, Beirne, Jr., and Sy Bartlett, *Twelve O'Clock High,* Harper (New York), 1948.

Leboucher, Fernande, *Incredible Mission,* Doubleday (New York), 1969.

Levitin, Sonia, *Annie's Promise,* Atheneum (New York), 1993.

Litewka, Albert, *Warsaw: A Novel of Resistance,* Sheridan Square Press (New York), 1989.

Lowry, Lois, *Number the Stars,* Houghton Mifflin (New York), 1989.

Ludlum, Robert, *The Holcroft Covenant,* R. Marek Publishers (New York), 1978.

MacInnes, Helen, *Above Suspicion,* Little, Brown (Boston), 1941.

MacInnes, Helen, *Assignment in Brittany,* Little, Brown (Boston), 1942.

MacInnes, Helen, *While Still We Live,* Harcourt Brace (New York), 1989.

MacLean, Alistair, *Force 10 from Navarone,* Doubleday (Garden City, NY), 1968.

MacLean, Alistair, *The Guns of Navarone,* Doubleday (Garden City, NY), 1957.

MacLean, Alistair, *H.M.S. Ulysses,* Collins (London), 1955.

MacLean, Alistair, *Where Eagles Dare,* Collins (London), 1967.

Mailer, Norman, *The Naked and the Dead,* Rinehart (New York), 1948.

Marvin, Isabel R., *Bridge to Freedom,* Jewish Publication Society (Philadelphia), 1991.

Matas, Carol, *After the War,* Simon & Schuster (New York), 1996.

Matas, Carol, *Daniel's Story,* Scholastic (New York), 1993.

Matas, Carol, *Lisa's War,* Scholastic (New York), 1987.

Michener, James, *Tales of the South Pacific,* Macmillan (New York), 1947.

Monsarrat, Nicholas, *The Cruel Sea,* Burford Books (Short Hills, NJ), 2000.

Morris, M. E., *The Last Kamikaze,* Random House (New York), 1990.

Nathanson, E. M., *The Dirty Dozen,* Random House (New York), 1955.

Ondaatje, Michael, *The English Patient,* Knopf (New York), 1992.

Orlev, Uri, *The Man from the Other Side,* translated from the Hebrew by Hillel Halkin, Houghton Mifflin (New York), 1989.

Ozick, Cynthia, *The Messiah of Stockholm: A Novel,* Knopf (New York), 1987.

Ozick, Cynthia, *The Shawl,* Knopf (New York), 1989.

Piercy, Marge, *Gone to Soldiers,* Summit Books (New York), 1987.

Provost, Gary, and Gail Levine-Provost, *David and Max,* Jewish Publication Society (Philadelphia), 1988.

Reeman, Douglas, *The Destroyers,* Putnam (New York), 1974.

Remarque, Erich Maria, *Arch of Triumph,* translated by Walter Sorrell and Denver Lindley, Ballantine (New York), 1998.

Remarque, Erich Maria, *The Night in Lisbon,* Harcourt, Brace & World (New York), 1964.

Remarque, Erich Maria, *A Time to Love and a Time to Die,* Harcourt Brace (New York), 1954.

Shaw, Irvin, *Young Lions,* Random House (New York), 1948.

Silman, Roberta, *Beginning the World Again,* Viking (New York), 1990.

Singer, Isaac Bashevis, *Enemies, a Love Story,* Noonday Press (New York), 1989.

Starbird, Kaye, *The Lion in the Lei Shop,* Harcourt, Brace (New York), 1970.

Steinbeck, John, *The Moon Is Down,* Viking (New York), 1942.

Struther, Jan, *Mrs. Miniver,* Harcourt, Brace (New York), 1940.

Taylor, Theodore, *To Kill the Leopard,* Harcourt Brace (New York), 1993.

Thayer, James, *S-Day: A Memoir of the Invasion of England,* St. Martin's Press (New York), 1990.

Thomas, Harlan, *A Yank in the RAF,* Random House (New York), 1941.

Trotter, William R., *Winter Fire,* Dutton (New York), 1993.

Tuccille, Jerome, and Philip Sayetta, *The Mission: A Novel about the Flight of Rudolf Hess,* D. I. Fine (New York), 1991.

Uris, Leon, *Battle Cry,* Putnam (New York), 1953.

Uris, Leon, *Exodus,* Doubleday (Garden City, NY), 1958.

Uris, Leon, *Mila 18,* Doubleday (Garden City, NY), 1961.

Uris, Leon, *QB VII,* Doubleday (Garden City, NY), 1970.

Vonnegut, Kurt, Jr., *Mother Night,* Delacorte Press (New York), 1966.

Vonnegut, Kurt, Jr., *Slaughterhouse-Five, or, The Children's Crusade: A Duty-Dance with Death,* Dell (New York), 1968.

Vos, Ida, *Anna Is Still Here,* Houghton Mifflin (Boston), 1993.

Vos, Ida, *Hide and Seek,* translated by Terese Edelstein and Inez Smidt, Houghton Mifflin (New York), 1981.

Welt, Elly, *Berlin Wild: A Novel,* Viking (New York), 1986.

Westheimer, David, *Von Ryan's Express,* Doubleday (Garden City, NY), 1964.

Westheimer, David, *Von Ryan's Return,* Coward McCann & Geoghegan (New York), 1980.

White, Theodore, *Mountain Road,* W. Sloan (New York), 1958.

Wiesel, Elie, *The Forgotten,* Summit Books (New York), 1992.

Wiesel, Elie, *Night,* Bantam (New York), 1960.

Wiesel, Elie, *The Town Beyond the Wall: A Novel,* Schocken Books (New York), 1995.

Wilder, Billy, *Stalag 17,* University of California Press (Berkeley, CA), 1999.

Wolff, Virginia Euwer, *The Mozart Season,* Henry Holt (New York), 1991.

Wouk, Herman, *The Caine Mutiny,* Doubleday (Garden City, NY), 1951.

Wouk, Herman, *War and Remembrance,* Little, Brown (Boston), 1978.

Wouk, Herman, *The Winds of War,* Little, Brown (Boston), 1971.

Yolen, Jane, *Devil's Arithmetic,* Viking Penguin (New York), 1988.

Index

Note: This is a cumulative index for volumes 1, 2 and 3. Volumes are paginated individually. Each volume number appears in boldface italics, followed by a colon. Page numbers appearing in italic type refer to pages containing illustrations: *m* indicates a map; *c* indicates a chart; and *t* indicates a table.

Murrow, Edward R., *2:* 229-238; *3:* 323, 323-327
   See also: War correspondents
Mussolini, Benito, *1:* 32; *2:* 134-135; *3: 236, 328,* 328-332, *330, 331*
   Childhood and education, *3:* 328-329
   Declaration of war, *1:* 130
   Disgrace and death, *1: 310; 2:* 134-135; *3:* 332
   Fascism, *1:* 32; *3:* 329-330
   and Hitler, *1: 226, 313; 3:* 330-332
   Munich Conference, *1:* 109
Mutiny, 2: 468
Muto, Akira, *2:* 450
My Struggle. See: Mein Kampf
Myth of the Twentieth Century, The, 1: 50

N

Nagano, Kamechiro, *1:* 276
Nagano, Osarni, *2:* 450
Nagasaki, *2: 93, 294, 295; 3:* 485
Nagumo, Chuichi, *3: 435*
   See also: Pearl Harbor
Nakasone, Yasukiro, *2:* 447
Nanking, *1:* 113-118, *114, 115*
Nasty Girl, The, 2: 470
National Socialist German Workers' party. *See:* Nazi party
Native Americans and World War II, *2: 79, 3: 333,* 333-338, *334, 336*
NATO (North Atlantic Treaty Organization), *2:* 393
Naumann, Erich, *2:* 439
Navajo Code Talker Alphabet, *3: 335t*
Navajo Code Talker Order, *3:* 336
Navajo Code Talkers, *2: 79; 3: 333,* 333-338, *337*
   See also: Intelligence in World War II; Pacific War
Nazi doctors, *1:* 163-167, 366-367, 368, 369; *3:* 43-48, 304-308, 461
Nazi hunters, *3:* 35, 259-263, 513-517
Nazi party
   Early rally, *1: 33*
   Euthanasia, *1:* 147-149
   Evolution from German Workers' party, *1:* 21-23
   First appearance, *1: 9,* 14, *23, 27*
   Flag, *1: 25*
   Forced labor policy, *1: 85, 106, 156; 2:* 3-4, 120
   Goose-step, *1: 53*

"Kinder, Küche, Kirche", 2: 120
Leadership Corps and war crimes guilt, *2:* 320
Military training, *1: 216*
"Nazi Party Day," *1: 79*
Noninterference with industry and business, *1:* 56
Persecution of homosexuals, *3:* 228, 230-231
Program, *1:* 34, *118m, 119m, 121m, 125m*
Religion, *1:* 49, 50-52
Sterilization program, *1:* 147, 163-167
Symbols, *1: 25, 48, 79; 3:* 182
Waffen-SS, 1: 152
War crimes trials in other countries, *2:* 323-324
Wartime priority, *1:* 332
   See also: Germany; Gestapo; Hitler, Adolf; Nuremberg Trials; Schutzstaffel; Sicherheitsdienst; Sturmabteilung
Nazi-Soviet Pact, *1:* 118-120, *120,* 287
Nazional Sozialistische Deutsche Arbeiterpartei. *See:* Nazi party
Nebelung, Günther, *2:* 435
Nehru, Jawaharlal, *2:* 401
Nemeth, Lajos, *2:* 426
Neo-Nazis, *2:* 350; *3:* 213
Nesaule, Agate, *2:* 384-385
Netherlands
   Anne Frank Foundation, *1:* 423
   Bombing of Rotterdam, *1:* 404
   Deportation point, *1:* 405
   Diary of a Young Girl, The, 1: 419-423
   Frank, Anne, *1: 412, 419,* 419-423, *421*
   German invasion, *1:* 125-126, 138-139
   Gies, Miep, *1:* 423; *3: 171,* 171-174
   Hillesum, Etty, *1:* 423-428
   History, *1:* 405-406
   Joodse Raad, 1: 406-408
   Protection of Jews, *1:* 404-405, *410, 411*
   Rejection of Nazi anti-Semitism, *1:* 405
   Westerbork transit camp, *1: 408,* 410, *414, 422, 424, 426*
Neurath, Konstantin von, *2:* 319, 433
New Guinea, *1:* 284; *2:* 259-260, *260m*

Newfoundland Conference, *1:* 208, 223
Niemöller, Martin, *1: 52,* 91
Night, 2: 358; *3:* 510
Night and Fog (film), 2: 359, 467
"Night and Fog"/*Nacht und Nebel, 2:* 6
Night of Broken Glass. *See Kristallnacht*
Night of the Long Knives, *1:* 52-56
Night Train to Munich, 2: 459
Nimitz, Chester, *2: 254m,* 255; *3: 339,* 339-344, *343,* 437
92nd Division (U.S.), *2:* 134
Nisei, *2:* 109, 137; *3:* 276
   See also: Japanese Americans; Korematsu, Fred T.; Toguri, Iva; Weglyn, Michiko
No Time for Fear: Voices of American Military Nurses, 2: 149-155
Norman, Max, *2:* 80
Normandy (battle), *2: 56,* 56-59, *59*
Normandy landing. *See:* Allied invasion of Europe
North Africa, *1: 211m,* 212, *213,* 231, 305-308, *307m*
North Atlantic Treaty Organization (NATO), *2:* 393
Northeroft, Erima Harvey, *2:* 445
Norway, *1:* 124-125, *125m; 3:* 374, 375
Nosske, Gustav, *2:* 439
Noth, Werner, *2:* 444
Notorious, 2: 459
Nuclear weapons. *See:* Atom bombs
Number of Jews killed in the Holocaust, *2:* 403-405, *405c*
Number of people killed in World War II, *2: 152c,* 381-383
Numbered prisoners, *1:* 362, 378
Nuremberg, *1: 53; 2:* 349, 417
Nuremberg Laws, *1:* 57-60, *58,* 75-82, *81,* 163
Nuremberg (television film), 2: 455
Nuremberg Trials, *2:* 314-345, 407-444
   Allied Control Council, *2:* 417, 420-421
   Attitude of German people regarding, *2:* 419-420
   Chart of Defendants and Outcomes, *2: 433c-444c*
   Classification of Nazi frameworks as criminal organizations, *2:* 410-411
   Defendants and trial personnel, *2:* 417; *3:* 460, 480
   Defendants of main trial, *2: 316,* 316-321, *317, 409*

Definition of crimes, *2:* 408-409; *3:* 47, 211
Definition of war of aggression, *2:* 410
Early trials, *2:* 313-316
Effect of Cold War, *2:* 421
Einsatzgruppen Trial, *2:* 323, *439c*
Federal Republic of Germany and legal jurisdiction, *2:* 420
Flick Trial, *2:* 323, *436c*
Göring testimony, *3:* 188
High Command Trial, *2:* 323, *441c*
Hostage Trial, *2:* 323, *437c-438c*
I.G. Farben Trial, *2: 322,* 323, *436c-437c*
Involvement of all affected nations and groups, *2:* 410
Judges' bench, *2:* 320
Justice Trial, *2:* 322, *435c*
Krupp Trial, *2:* 323, *439c-440c; 3: 281*
Later trials and trials summaries, *2:* 321-323
Legal wars v. illegal wars, *2:* 411
List of leading defendants, *2:* 408
Main Trial, *2: 316,* 316-321, *317, 433c*
Major defendant sentences, *2:* 409-410
Medical Trial, *2: 321,* 322, *434c*
Milch Trial, *2:* 322, *434c*
Ministries Trial, *2: 323, 324, 440c-441c*
Nazi leader defendants, *2: 409*
Office of the United States Government for Germany (OMGUS), *2:* 417
Paris Agreements, *2:* 420
Pohl Trial, *2:* 322, *435c-436c*
Press gallery, *2: 330, 337*
Related trials held elsewhere, *2:* 324-329, *326, 328,* 407-408
RuSHA Trial, *2:* 323, *438c*
Spandau prison, *2: 319,* 334
Stages of Jewish persecution established, *2:* 418
Statute of limitations, *2:* 411, 421-422
Transition Agreement, *2:* 420
See also: British war crimes trials; War crimes trials in Japan; war crimes trials in various European countries by name
Nuremberg Tribunal, *3:* 47

Nurses, *1: 280, 281; 2: 132,* 149-155, *149, 150, 151, 153, 154*
"Nuts!," *2:* 224
    See also: Battle of the Bulge; McAuliffe, Anthony

O

O the Chimneys (book), *2:* 358
Oberhauser, Herta, *2:* 434
Objective, Burma, 2: 459
Occupation. *See under:* Japan; West Germany
    See also: Cold War; German Democratic Republic; German Occupation; Occupation of Germany by the Allies
Occupation of Germany by the Allies, *2:* 230, 392-393
Odyssey of a U-Boat Commander, 1: 239
Oeschey, Rudolf, *2:* 435
Office of Civilian Defense, *2:* 100-101
Office of Production Management, *2:* 95-96
Office of Scientific Research and Development (OSRD), *3:* 197
Office of Strategic Services (OSS), *2:* 10-11, *77,* 78
    See also: Intelligence in World War II
Ohlendorf, Otto, *1: 247,* 250, 251; *2: 439*
Ohrdruf, *2: 233*
Oka, Takasumi, *2:* 451
Okawa, Shumei, *2:* 451
Okinawa (battle), *2: 180,* 272, *280m,* 281-283, *284, 285m,*
Oklahoma (USS), *1:* 270, 298
"Old Blood and Guts." *See:* Patton, George Smith, Jr.
Olympic Games (1936), *1: 55, 57,* 59-60, *59,* 82
Omaha Beach. *See under:* Allied invasion of Europe
On the Town, 2: 460
One Against the Wind, 2: 468
101st Airborne Division, *2:* 53
"One-Two-Three," *2:* 32
Oneg Shabbat Archives, *1:* 174
Onodera, Kaun, *2: 142*
OPA (Office of Price Administration and Civilian Supply), *2:* 97
Operation Anvil, *2:* 59, *60m*
Operation Barbarossa, *1:* 217-218, *230*
Operation Cobra, *2:* 62

Operation Daybreak, *3:* 218
Operation Fortitude, *2:* 74-75
Operation Overlord. *See:* Allied invasion of Europe
Operation Petticoat, 2: 459
Operation Reinhard, *1:* 327
Operation T-4. *See:* T-4 program
Operation Torch, *1:* 289-290, *290m*
Ophuls, Marcel, *2:* 359
Opitz, Klara, *2:* 442
Oppenheimer, J. Robert, *2:* 85, *86, 87,* 90; *3: 345,* 345-350, *348*
    See also: Atom bombs
Oregon attacked by Japanese, *2:* 104
Orphans' March, *1:* 177; *2:* 273
Oshima, Hiroshi, *2:* 451
OSRD (Office of Scientific Research and Development), *3:* 197
OSS (Office of Strategic Services), *2:* 10-11, *77,* 78
    See also: Intelligence in World War II
Oster, Heinrich, *2:* 437
Ostindustrie GBMH (Osti), 2: 419
Ostrowoski, Vladislav, *2:* 442
Ott, Adolf, *2:* 439
Otto, Walter, *2:* 442
Outcast: A Jewish Girl in Wartime Berlin, 1: 70-75
Owens, Jesse, *1:* 59
    See also: Olympic Games

P

Pacific War
    Aleutian Islands, *2: 254m,* 258, 259
    Allied bombing of Japan, *2: 291*
    Allied strategy, *2:* 249-255, *251m, 253, 254m,* 256
    Battle of the Coral Sea, *1:* 285; *2: 254m,* 259, *260m*
    Internment camps in Southeast Asia, *2:* 261-266, *262, 264, 265*
    Morale in U.S., *2: 251,* 253
    Rivalry between U.S. navy and army, *2:* 253-255, *254m, 255*
    U.S. industrial advantage, *1: 210; 2:* 252
    U.S. strategy to invade Kyushu, *2:* 283-288, *285m*
    Western Pacific from Hawaii to Japan, *1: 217m*
    See also: Pearl Harbor
Pacific War Diary, 2: 258
Pacifism. *See:* Jaggerstatter, Franz; Rankin, Jeannette

The Design of Life

The
Design of
Life

Renato Dulbecco

Yale University Press
New Haven and London

Copyright © 1987 by Yale University.
All rights reserved.
This book may not be reproduced, in whole
or in part, in any form (beyond that
copying permitted by Sections 107 and 108
of the U.S. Copyright Law and except by
reviewers for the public press), without
written permission from the publishers.

Designed by James J. Johnson
and set in Aster Roman by
The Composing Room of Michigan.
Printed in the United States of America by Vail-Ballou Press,
Binghamton, N.Y.

Library of Congress Cataloging-in-Publication Data

Dulbecco, Renato, 1914–
  The design of life.

  Includes index.
  1. Biology. 2. Life (Biology) I. Title.
QH309.D85 1987   574   87–2104
ISBN 0–300–03791–0 (alk. paper)

*The paper in this book meets the guidelines for permanence
and durability of the Committee on Production Guidelines
for Book Longevity of the Council on Library Resources.*

10 9 8 7 6 5 4 3 2 1

Contents

Preface

The purpose of this book is to present to the unprepared reader the exciting developments that have taken place in biology, with accelerated rhythm, since the fifties. In the first two chapters I have provided the background for reading this book, avoiding most technical terminology, which is one of the main barriers for the unprepared reader, and replacing it with plain English terms; technical terms that had to be retained are explained. I have often given technical names in parentheses to allow interested readers to pursue subjects in more technical publications.

The basic concept of this book is that life is the expression of coded instructions contained in a chemical present in all living organisms: DNA. These instructions cause the manufacture of other chemicals, the main class of which are proteins, and these make the cells grow and work. The characteristics of organisms—their shapes and what they do—depend upon the proteins they contain. The proteins carry on the duties of life, for which DNA is not needed, but without DNA there are no proteins. DNA is thus the hidden ruler of life.

Life on earth has advanced in many different directions since its inception billions of years ago. This evolution was determined by DNA, which through the eons has caused the manufacture of proteins with new, astonishing characteristics. DNA, therefore, is also the intelligence of life, determining what life will be and guiding its evolution.

Given the fundamental role of DNA, several chapters in this book (4, 5, and 6) explore its characteristics: how it is constructed, how it reproduces, what instructions it contains, how these instructions are executed. One of the crucial points in the evolution of DNA was the appearance of sexuality. The main characteristics and meaning of that complex function are the subjects of chapters 9, 10, and 11.

DNA and proteins alone are not, however, sufficient to produce and maintain life. It requires energy, which comes from the sun. Chapter 3 examines how the sun's energy is utilized. Life requires communication between the parts of each organism and between organisms. How this communication is carried out within an organism to make it a harmonious whole is examined in chapters 8, 17, and 18, and communication between creatures in a common environment is examined in chapter 16.

Because life is a struggle in which organisms try to overcome each other, the organisms need defenses. One such defense protects animals against germs, using extraordinary DNA acrobatics. The fascinating organization of this defense is described in chapters 13 and 14.

The organisms that exist on earth vary from the extremely simple to the enormously complicated: in all cases, however, a living organism derives from a simple unit that generates complexity. In many organisms evolution toward complexity takes place as they develop from fertilized eggs; chapter 12 is devoted to this process. Another sort of evolution, which causes the formation of complex creatures from simple molecules, has occurred as long as life has existed. This evolution is taken up in chapter 20.

The study of life shows that in advanced creatures DNA is not the sole ruler. In them the autocracy of DNA, almost absolute in simple creatures, is mitigated. Instead DNA acts as a benevolent dictator that has relinquished some of its power to the organisms themselves, allowing them to determine their own fate within some rigidly determined boundaries. Not surprisingly, in these organisms the complexity of life and its democratization occasionally generate some confusion. We see the results of such confusion in the ambiguity of sex (chapters 10, 11) and in the simulation and perturbation of communication by drugs acting on the brain (chapter 19).

I have tried to present a balanced, well-informed account of all the many facets of life. What I report is the result of the work of a large army of scientists, whom I wish to acknowledge. I have not identified most individual contributions because to do so is impossible. Occasional names are cited to show that there are people behind the discoveries, examples of those many who spent their lives in the effort, often but not always successful, to clear up some facet of the mystery of life. I also wish to express my gratitude to colleagues who had the kindness and patience to discuss with me some sections of this book and to contribute invaluable suggestions. They are Floyd Bloom, Max Cowan, Walter Eckhart, Ed Lewis, Fritz Melchers, Wylie Vale, and Larry Swanson.

I wish also to acknowledge the dedicated help of my secretary, Betty Lang, not only for her unfailing help in the many typings of successive versions but also for her many useful suggestions.

The Design of Life

CHAPTER 1

DNA: The Thread of Life

Difficult Questions

Tremendous public interest has been generated by the now frequent announcements in the daily press and television media concerning discoveries and developments in the fields of biology and biotechnology. This response is indicative of the hope and faith engendered by the rapid progress these fields have made in recent years. We seem close to manipulating organisms at will, for the purpose either of changing their nature or of producing desired chemicals. No longer must we wait for nature to take its course before we can reap its bounty. Substances previously made in the secrecy of the cell can now be made in test tubes by genetically engineered bacteria.

Many new companies have been formed to exploit advances in biotechnology. A United States Supreme Court decision has given strength to such enterprise by ruling that a genetically engineered bacteria or plant can be patented like any other unique and useful invention. There seem to be powerful financial incentives for exploring the practical potential of the new technologies, and the high share prices these new companies command testify to the faith people have in their success.

The newly found confidence in the good to be produced by our increased power over the mechanism of life is tempered by questions about what impact these new technologies will have on life as we know it. Will there be drastic changes as a result? Will the changes be good or bad for the human race? Should we continue developing artificial hearts or conceiving babies in test tubes? When does human life begin, and how does this affect policies about abortion? And the debate rages between evolutionists and creationists about the origin of life on earth. The kinds of questions being asked show how little is really understood about the nature of that seemingly familiar concept, *life.*

The world contains many living creatures, which display such an enormous variety of characteristics that we may wonder whether they share any common property. Some common properties are easy to see—for instance, the ability of creatures to grow and multiply. Plants make seeds that generate plants of the same type; animals mate and generate similar animals; bacteria or molds grow into very large numbers if the conditions are favorable. Having recognized growth and multiplication as attributes of living things, we may ask how such processes are carried out.

These observations, however, do not allow us to comprehend what life is and what its intimate mechanisms are. We have approached an understanding in recent years by analyzing the properties of living creatures in minute detail. The process is not yet completed, for new intriguing aspects are continually being discovered. Our present understanding has been reached over many decades of study, during which the objects of biological investigations have been scaled down to ever smaller creatures. At first studies centered on large organisms such as the larger plants or animals; then they shifted to focus on flies and some simple marine creatures. Next came forms of life invisible to the naked eye, such as molds or bacteria, and finally the smallest forms, the viruses. We will trace the course of this inquiry and the wonderful discoveries that punctuated it.

The Cells

The first contributions to an understanding of life were made by anatomists, who opened up bodies of animals and cadavers and found that they contain well-defined internal parts, or *organs*, such as the brain, the liver, and the kidneys. The body of an animal or a plant, made up of all its constituent organs, is called an *organism*—though this term is used also for the simplest living things such as bacteria or viruses. Then the question was asked: how are the various organs different? Anatomists could see different patterns on the cut surface of a liver or a brain, which hinted at a different fabric in the two organs, but observations made with the naked eye could go no further.

In the seventeenth century important advances were made in the grinding of lenses; they allowed the construction of fairly powerful single-lens *microscopes*. One of the pioneers was Robert Hooke, an English physicist, who cast his gaze both on the immense, studying the stars, and on the minute, using a simple microscope. In 1665 he described the little honeycomb holes he saw in examining a thin slice of cork. He thought of them as the cells of a monastery (a common image in his time) and therefore called them *cells*. What he had seen were really only the remnants of the living plant, the dried-up wooden partitions that had separated the living cells. But with this observation Hooke had identified the simplest living units that can exist.

Around the same time, Anton van Leeuwenhoek, a Dutch cloth merchant in the city of Delft, made the most powerful microscope of its time. When he put his eye to it, he saw a new world: the marsh water was teeming with small creatures, running in every direction. He had discovered the simplest organisms, such as protozoa, algae, yeasts, or bacteria.

From then on progress was rapid. Scientists recognized that each organ is made up of a large number of living cells, and that the cells of different organs look different and do different things. Thus the cells of the brain transmit signals, those of muscles become shorter when a signal reaches them through a nerve, liver cells are chemical factories, and so on. In animals, cells are not separated by the partitions typical of plant cells that Hooke saw; cells of animals touch each other.

These and other such findings eventually showed that living creatures vary greatly in number of cells, from the single cell of a bacterium to the ten thousand billion of a human. A single-celled organism can have only the complexity of that cell and do only what that cell does. An organism made of millions or billions of cells has much greater complexity and does many things that a cell alone cannot do. Activities of large organisms typically result from the joint efforts of many cells of different kinds.

The phenomenon of cooperation among cells shows why it is useful for an organism to have a very large number of small cells: the cells' large number allows for many specializations, and their small size, because of the mechanics of cell function and multiplication, presents an advantage for the growth and activity of an organism. A cell must pick up many substances from the environment and return the waste to it. The amount required by a cell is proportional to its volume, but the supply is proportional to its surface, through which the substances are received. When the size of the cell increases, the demand increases much more than the supply: if cell size increases tenfold, demand increases a thousandfold but supply only a hundredfold. Larger cells, then, are difficult to feed, and they do their job in a sluggish, inefficient way.

The most direct reason for the subdivision of organisms into cells must be evolutionary. During the earliest, primitive stages of life the first units must have been, of necessity, small, very simple cells, living independently. In subsequent evolution, transient aggregates of cells occurred, probably similar to those formed today by some bacteria (see chapter 12). This stage was the prelude for the formation of the large organisms that exist today, in which cells are permanently aggregated. The cell was the initial unit of life, and it remained so as life evolved. Analysis of cell composition and function must therefore precede any serious attempt to define life.

What Is a Cell?

To understand what a cell is, we can begin by looking into it, discovering all its intimate details. A good tool for this purpose is the modern light microscope, very much improved from the one built by van Leeuwenhoek. This instrument, which works by deflecting light waves, cannot reveal details smaller than about one-thousandth of a millimeter, similar to the length of light waves. Though this may seem a tolerably small dimension, it is in fact very coarse when looking at cells, where the important dimensions are comparable to the size of atoms—on the order of one-millionth of a millimeter. The *electron microscope,* by deflecting beams of electrons, can reveal details of that size. In a container from which the air has been evacuated, electrons—infinitesimal electrically charged particles—travel at a speed close to that of light. They are accompanied by waves that are comparable to light waves but of several thousand times shorter wavelength. In the electron microscope the deflection of these waves is used to produce an image that is not visible to the eye but can be recorded on photographic film.

Membranes

Membranes serve both to define a cell externally and to partition it internally. Seen through a light microscope cells taken from an animal show a sharp outline (fig. 1.1) that is produced by a baglike envelope enclosing each cell. The envelope is very pliable and adapts to changes of shape as the cell moves. The largest object within the envelope, about half the size of the cell and centrally located, is the round or oval *nucleus,* and everything outside the nucleus forms the *cytoplasm,* the

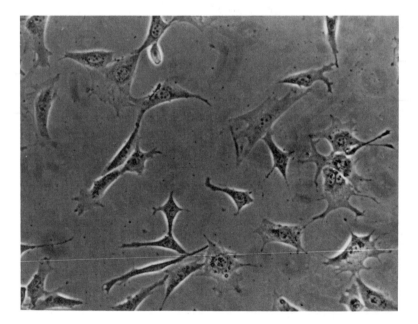

Figure 1.1. Several living cells seen in the light microscope. They are rat cells kept in a glass dish in the laboratory. They are surrounded by a sharp edge, a membrane that separates them from the environment around them. Each cell has fingerlike extensions that move constantly. Through them the cell propels itself on the glass. Inside the cell we can see the nucleus. Magnified 1,000 times.

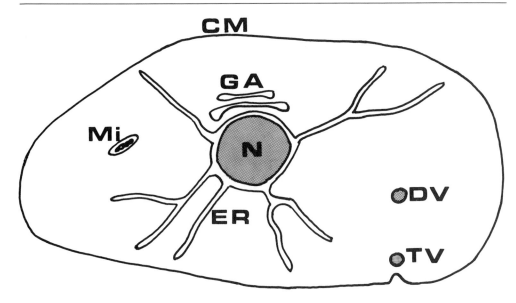

Figure 1.2. A diagram of the main compartments separated by membranes in an animal cell. Some plant cells would have, in addition, chloroplasts. Each line is a double-layered membrane such as those shown in Figure 1.3. N = nucleus, CM = cellular membrane, ER = endoplasmic reticulum, Mi = mitochondrion, GA = Golgi apparatus, TV = transport vesicle, DV = digestion vesicle.

cell matrix (fig. 1.2). The electron microscope shows that the envelope is made up of two extremely thin sheets closely adhering to each other, which together form the cell *membrane* surrounding the whole cell (fig. 1.3). The electron microscope also shows that the nucleus itself is surrounded by an inner and an outer membrane, separated by a thin space. The two membranes have many holes—*pores*—which are kept aligned by special grommetlike structures. Substances move from the cytoplasm to the nucleus, and vice versa, through the pores.

The outer nuclear membrane continues into a network of membranes that crisscross the cytoplasm (see fig. 1.2). A system of membranes forms tubes—the *endoplasmic reticulum* (fig. 1.4)—which are very important for the manufacture of cell products. Also important for this manufacture are certain flat, membrane-bound discs with hollow interiors, called the *Golgi apparatus* for the Italian physician who discovered them in 1883 (see fig. 1.2). The largest of the other identifiable bodies in the cytoplasm are *mitochondria:* roughly egg-shaped, they are surrounded by two membranes and are filled by characteristic folds of the inner membrane. The mitochondria generate the energy for the cell's activities (see chapter 3). Further bodies take the form of small droplets of various sizes, each surrounded by a membrane. Some of these carry food into the cells from the outside; others digest it, changing it to simple substances the cell can use. Different droplets export materials produced by the cell to the outside world. Plant cells

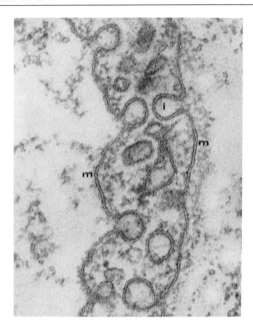

Figure 1.3. The membrane surrounding a cell seen in the electron microscope. This is an extremely thin section of cells present in the lining of a fine blood vessel in the tongue of a rat. The cell is flat and thin and can be imagined to extend both above and below the page. On both sides the cell is bounded by a double line, which is the membrane (m). The membrane forms several loops and rings that are produced by invagination (i) in the act of engulfing droplets of liquid into the cell. Magnified 325,000 times. Courtesy of George Palade.

have, in addition, *chloroplasts*, green granules whose organization is similar to that of mitochondria. They contain a green substance called *chlorophyll* ("green leaf") that utilizes sunlight to build cellular products (see chapter 3).

The Nucleus

Seen in the light microscope, the nucleus contains many irregular specks and threads not characteristic enough in appearance to tell us what they are for. The role of the nucleus is revealed by the dramatic events that take place when a cell divides to form two cells. In preparing for division, the cell accumulates materials and increases in size until, upon reaching a certain size, it develops a furrow in the middle. This furrow, deepening more and more, finally splits the cell into two equal parts, which are the "daughter" cells. In time each of these cells will divide again and then again, as the cells increase in number. Divisions may succeed each other within ten or fifteen minutes in embryos at the beginning of their development, or every day or so in cells of adult animals. The embryo can divide rapidly because it merely partitions preformed materials (see chapter 12); cells of adult

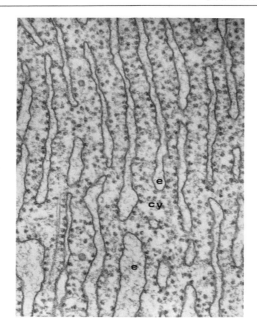

Figure 1.4. The endoplasmic reticulum in a thin slice of a cell of the rat pancreas seen in the electron microscope. The endoplasmic reticulum is a system of hollow tubes similar to flattened hoses, the wall of which is made by a membrane. In the section, membranes appear as double lines, corresponding to the two sheets that make up the membrane (see chapter 2). The tubes of the endoplasmic reticulum (e) are embedded in the cytoplasm (cy); between them are many small dark round bodies, sometimes ill defined. They are the ribosomes, which manufacture the proteins of the cell (see chapter 2). Some of the proteins end up in the cavities of the endoplasmic reticulum. Magnified 140,000 times. Courtesy of George Palade.

animals divide less frequently because they must double all their materials before dividing. Many cells divide only rarely, after periods of weeks and months. The timing of division is controlled by a number of variables, such as temperature, availability of nutrients, and special chemicals produced within the organism.

Every daughter cell emerging from a division must contain all the parts present in the mother cell. For mitochondria and the various bodies found in the cytoplasm, this is easily accomplished: new ones are formed all the time in the period between divisions and are then distributed more or less equally to the two daughter cells. The nucleus presents a special case because it remains single throughout. Finer observations, however, show that events similar to those that go on in the rest of the cell also go on within the nucleus (fig. 1.5). The essential components of the nucleus are extremely long, very thin, and uniform threads, visible only in the electron microscope (fig. 1.5: 1). They double in the interval between the two cell divisions (fig. 1.5: 2) and, when the cell divides, are distributed equally to the daughter cells. In cells ready to divide, these threads become recognizable as rods in the light microscope, for they coil tightly, becom-

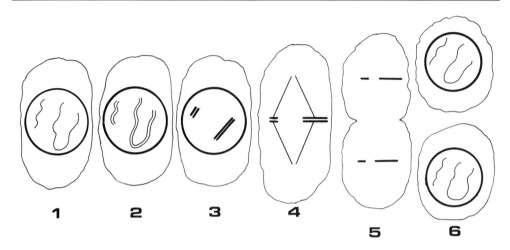

Figure 1.5. The events going on in the nucleus of a cell during the division cycle: (1) The cell emerging from the previous division has a single copy of each thread; two, of different length, are shown here. (2) Then each thread doubles. The two sister threads remain associated. (3) Before the cell divides, each thread coils into a chromatid. The two sister chromatids stay together and appear as a single unit, the chromosome. Two chromosomes are shown. (4) The lines represent microtubules (see chapter 2), which connect the chromosomes to the two poles of the cell. (5) The two chromatids of each chromosome migrate to opposite poles; the division furrow appears between them. (6) Finally the cell divides, the nuclei re-form and the threads unwind, causing the chromatids to disappear.

ing much shorter and thicker (fig. 1.5: 3 and 4). The rods become more distinct and align themselves in a characteristic way in the middle of the cell. Each coiled nuclear thread is called a *chromatid.* The two chromatids resulting from the doubling of a nuclear thread, called *sister chromatids,* remain associated side by side forming a *chromosome* ("colored bodies," so called because they stain intensely with some dyes, fig. 1.6). The number of chromosomes is characteristic of the species to which the cell belongs. Humans have forty-six chromosomes; fruitflies have eight. The various chromosomes have distinguishing features by which they can be identified (see fig. 1.6). Soon the membranes that surround the nucleus break up and dissolve. The chromosomes align themselves in a characteristic way in the middle of the cells; at the same time, thin lines appear, connecting the two chromatids of each to opposite poles of the cell (see fig. 1.5: 4). The chromatids start separating, usually in the middle of the chromosome, and are slowly pulled to each side (see fig. 1.5: 5). When this process is completed, the chromatids are in two equal groups at the two poles of the cell. The furrow that divides the cell forms between them, and as the cell completes division, membranes are rebuilt around the chromatids, forming two nuclei, one for each daughter cell. Each daughter cell gets one copy of each nuclear thread: the two cells are equal. Finally the chromatids regain their threadlike appearance and become invisible to observation with the light microscope (see fig. 1.5: 6). This complex process is called *mitosis.*

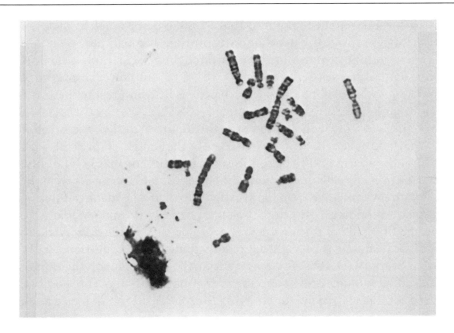

Figure 1.6. The chromosomes of a dividing cell of a Chinese hamster. The chromosomes were obtained at stage 4 of the previous figure. Each contains two chromatids (a line between the chromatids of a chromosome is distinguishable at the ends of some chromosomes). The chromosomes were stained by a method that causes the appearance of a system of bands, different in each chromosome. Magnified 2,000 times. Courtesy of Geoff Wahl.

The subdivision of chromatids between daughter cells is absolutely precise: *each cell gets a complete set*. This differs from the *approximately* equal splitting of all other cell components. The process has to be exact because each pair of chromatids is different from all others and performs essential functions that cannot be supplied by any other chromatid. All the members of each class of other cellular components (for example, mitochondria) are equal and perform the same roles: having one more or less does not have any marked consequence for the cell.

The Role of Chromosomes

The chromosome were a mysterious oddity until the early part of this century. Their nature and role became clear only after the study of heredity, *genetics*, began. At the beginning of this century students of heredity recognized that certain variable features of parent organisms, such as color of eyes, hair, feathers, or flowers, are inherited in a regular way in descendants. This represented the rediscovery of the basic laws of inheritance established during many years of observations, initiated in 1856, by the Czech monk Gregor Mendel. While tending a monastery garden in Brno, Mendel studied the inheritance of colors in pea flowers. He formulated the hypothesis that a color is determined by factors—later called *genes*—present in the plant and transmitted through the seeds. Although Mendel knew nothing of genes, he demonstrated their regular inheritance pattern by making careful crosses between plants with different flower colors (fig. 1.7). At the time of his path-breaking discovery, there was little interest in these aspects of inheritance, and his results went unnoticed.

The rediscovery of Mendel's laws brought about a great interest in the study of genes. What and where were they? Evidently they must be present within the germ cells—the sperm and the egg—in some constituent that is infallibly transmitted to the progeny cells at division. The chromosomes were a good candidate. A quirk of nature was of great help in investigating their role in inheritance. Among the organisms used in genetic studies a small fruitfly, *Drosophila*, gained prominence in the first part of this century. It could be easily grown in bottles, with a fruit mash as food, and it reproduced readily under these conditions, with a new generation every two weeks. It was easy to make crosses involving hundreds or thousands of individuals and to observe individuals with new, rare combinations of features. A property crucial for studying *Drosophila* chromosomes was found in

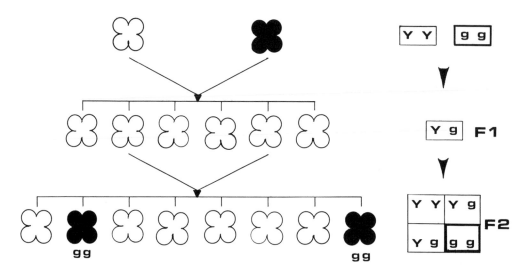

Figure 1.7. A cross with peas carried out by Mendel. The scheme on the left shows the crosses. He crossed plants by transferring pollen from one to the other. One kind had yellow flowers, the other kind, green flowers. All plants produced by the seeds (F1) had yellow flowers. Cross-pollination among these plants produced F2 plants, of which one-fourth had green flowers. The scheme on the right shows the interpretation of the crosses. It assumes two factors: g for green and Y for yellow, two of each per pea plant. F1 plants inherit Y from one parent, g from the other; so they all are Yg. In F2 plants there are four possible combinations. They can derive either g or Y from both parents, or Y from one parent and g from the other. When a plant is Yg, its flowers are yellow, and yellow is said to be dominant. The reason is that the Y causes the production of the yellow substance, whereas g produces no substance. Only when Y is absent can flowers be green.

the salivary glands, which have enormous cells with very large nuclei. These cells never divide, and surprisingly, their chromosomes are evident all the time. If the salivary glands are squashed on a glass slide, the nuclei burst and the chromosomes stick, distended, to the glass, where they can easily be studied by light microscopy (fig. 1.8). Unlike the chromosomes seen in cells during mitosis, they are not coiled, but extended, and are much longer and thicker (*giant chromosomes*).

All these unusual features derive from a peculiarity of the cells. They start like any other cells, with a single thread for each chromosome. Each thread duplicates as if the cell were to divide, but the cell does not, and the two threads stick together. Then the threads duplicate again, and the new copies again stick to the old ones, forming a bundle of four. Again, no cell division: instead, the cells become larger. This process is repeated many times, generating exceptionally large cells that contain bundles of several hundred identical threads. These are large enough to be easily seen in the light microscope and recognized as giant chromosomes.

Stained with the proper dyes, these chromosomes look like stacks of clear and dark cross-bands (fig. 1.8). The bands reflect features of the individual threads,

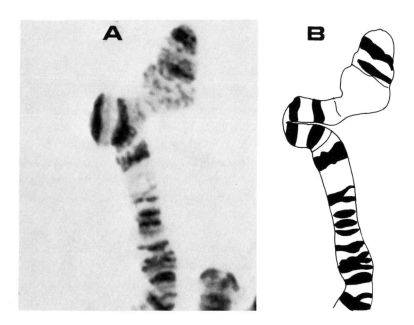

Figure 1.8 (A) A giant chromosome of the salivary gland of the fly *Drosophila*. The chromosome has been stained in such a way as to reveal cross-bands that are all different from one another in shape and staining intensity. The bands are related to specific genes. (B) The chromosome is Y-shaped because a segment is duplicated in such a way that it bends between the two repeated segments. These then tend to stick to each other. This duplication causes a change in the color of the eyes of the fly. Magnified 1,500 times. Courtesy of E. B. Lewis.

which are aligned exactly side by side. The lengths and the appearance of the cross-bands along the chromosome vary from one point to another in a characteristic way, so that the bands can be individually recognized and numbered.

Geneticists started suspecting that the bands had something to do with the genes. An important clue was given by flies with malformed eyes, which, instead of being large and round, are small and bar-like. The "bar-eye" feature is transmitted hereditarily, implicating a gene. The chromosomes of the salivary gland cells of such flies have a characteristic abnormality: two identical, and adjacent, groups of three bands are present in one of the chromosomes, owing to duplication of a short chromosome segment. All flies with bar eyes have the duplication, which is absent in normal flies. Evidently a gene controlling the shape of the eye is located in the duplicated region of the chromosome. Figure 1.8 shows a different duplication, which causes color changes in the eyes of the fly.

Since this discovery was made, extensive work with organisms of many different kinds has confirmed and greatly extended these conclusions. Genes, identified by the hereditary characteristics they control, can be located at precise places on chromosomes. The arrangement of genes on each chromosome constitutes the *genetic map* of that chromosome. Chromosomes, because they contain genes, which determine what an organism is and does, are among the most important constituents of living creatures.

Simpler Organisms

Does the role of chromosomes apply to single-celled organisms such as bacteria? At first sight, bacteria seem unlike animal or plant cells. They are much smaller—less than one-tenth the size of an animal or plant cell—and show many other striking differences. For example, bacteria lack internal bodies like the nucleus or the mitochondria, as well as internal membranes. In addition, there is greater complexity to the cell membrane in bacteria, which in some bacteria is reinforced by a rather rigid cell wall and in others is double. These differences set bacteria apart as *prokaryotic* cells (that is, preceding the nucleated cells), distinct from the *eukaryotic* cells of animals and plants.

Bacteria, however, are much more similar to eukaryotic cells than these differences suggest. For instance, they have components that perform the essential function of nuclei and of mitochondria. Although, as seen through the light microscope, they lack visible chromosomes, they do have inheritance and genes just like animal or plant cells. Electron microscopy shows that bacteria, in fact, have threads like those that form the chromosomes of animal cells, but these are characteristically uncoiled instead of coiled. The activity of mitochondria is performed in bacteria by extensions of the surface membrane inside the cytoplasm; their efficiency as energy producers is so great that bacteria can multiply much more rapidly than eukaryotic cells.

The presence of chromosomal threads containing genes in bacteria shows that these threads are important throughout the living world. To understand life, we must understand how these threads are made, which means entering the world of chemistry.

Two Essential Kinds of Chemicals

If, using a blender, we gently break up a piece of liver in a mild detergent solution, we can see the piece forming a turbid suspension. The detergent dissolves the cell membrane, leaving the cell nuclei intact. After removing the nuclei and a certain amount of debris from the rest, we have a clear liquid that looks like water. But the liquid is not plain water, for if we heat it, it becomes turbid. This happens because it contains the chemicals that are the main constituents of the cytoplasm: the proteins. When heated, the proteins become altered and tend to stick together. Exactly the same process happens when raw egg whites touch the surface of a hot frying pan.

If we now collect the nuclei left over from this experiment and add them to a strong detergent solution, we see a different effect. Examining a droplet of the mixture under the microscope, we see that the nuclei break up rapidly. At the same time the solution becomes gelatinous. A simple experiment that tells why the solution is so viscous can be made by putting the solution into a cup and suspending a razor blade by a thin string so that it is immersed in the liquid. If we turn the blade by, say, half a turn and let it go, the blade will slowly creep back about a quarter of a turn. Apparently the solution contains long invisible springs. These springs are made up of the chemical that has the greatest importance in life: deoxyribonucleic acid, known as DNA. DNA is made up of very long, thin filaments, which in solution stick to each other, making flexible, elastic ropes.

The presence of DNA in the solution can be demonstrated by a chemical reaction that generates a deep red dye. If we expose cells to that reaction, the DNA-containing nucleus will stain red. If we treat cells in division, the chromosomes will stain intensely because they contain DNA. But they also contain other substances, including much protein. As a result of all these experiments, we are able to conclude that the most basic properties of life, the properties that specify the characteristics of the individual and are transmitted hereditarily, probably reside in either the protein or the DNA of the chromosomes. In order to define which of these chemicals forms the genes, we must enlist the help of a special kind of life, the *viruses*.

The Chemical in the Genes

Diseases produced by viruses have been known since the dawn of mankind. Small-pox was one of the scourges of this earth until very recently; virus-induced diseases of plants have always been noticed because of the discoloration or spots they produce. Because they are even smaller than bacteria, viruses are invisible by light microscopy, but they display hereditary characteristics and have genes just as cells do. For a long time viruses were known only by their effects on cells. Some viruses kill the cells outright; others change them into cancer cells. With the advent of the electron microscope it became possible to see viruses, in solutions with viral effects on cells, which regularly display very small crystal-like bodies, called *viral particles.*

Such observations did not reveal the constituents of the viral particles. This knowledge was first obtained when in 1935 Wendell Stanley produced a plant virus, the *tobacco mosaic virus,* in pure form. The virus came from juices squeezed from diseased tobacco plants. Stanley showed that the rodlike particles of this virus are made up of only two chemical constituents, *RNA (ribonucleic acid)* and *protein.* RNA is very closely related to DNA; both are generally referred to as *nucleic acids.* This was a beginning, but the results did not tell us what the genes were, particularly because tobacco mosaic virus did not lend itself to studies of heredity.

A decisive step forward was made when a physicist turned biologist, Max Delbrück, began working with a kind of virus called a *bacteriophage,* whose name (from the Greek) means "eater of bacteria." The virus was so named for the effects that follow its addition to a culture of bacteria. The culture, turbid from the masses of bacteria it contains, rapidly becomes clear, as if the virus had eaten the bacteria. The virus infects the bacteria, multiplies within them, producing a vast number of progeny particles, and then dissolves the bacteria, leaving the clarified broth with billions of bacteriophage particles per cubic centimeter.

Bacteriophages (*phages* for short) soon became a popular object of investigation. Relatively simple and rapidly growing (their population can increase a thousandfold in half an hour), they were recognized as being extremely useful for studies of both chemistry and heredity. Like tobacco mosaic virus, they are also made up of two constituents: one is protein, the other is DNA (instead of RNA).

The question whether the genes are made up of proteins or DNA (or RNA in tobacco mosaic virus) could finally be answered by using phages in conjunction with a technological advance: the newly introduced *tracer technology.* This technology employs radioactive atoms in order to trace the course of a chemical compound given to cells. Radioactive atoms with the same chemical properties as those of the corresponding regular atoms are prepared by nuclear bombardment in an atomic pile. Because they produce radiation, they can be detected and measured by using proper radiation counters. Substances of various kinds containing the radioactive atoms are made in the laboratory; when they are fed to living cells, they become parts of the components of the cells.

The crucial test of the chemical nature of the phage genes was carried out in 1952 by Alfred D. Hershey and Martha Chase, using bacteriophage T4. A T4 phage particle looks like a tadpole: it has a big head—which contains the DNA—attached to a rodlike tail that acts like a spring-loaded syringe (see fig. 1.9). The T4

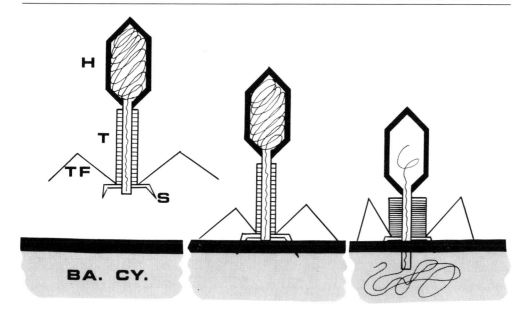

Figure 1.9. Infection of a bacterium by bacteriophage T4. At left the phage is seen approaching the bacterium. The membrane of the bacterium is dark gray; the cytoplasm (BA, CY) is light gray. In the phage we distinguish the head (H) containing the DNA, a tail with a central tube (T) surrounded by a sheath, spikes (S), and tail fibers (TF). In the middle the phage has contacted the bacterial membrane with the tail fibers and grabbed it with its spikes. At right the shortening of the sheath has caused the tube to penetrate into the bacterial cytoplasm, releasing the phage DNA into the cell.

tail has a tube (equivalent to the needle of a syringe) that can penetrate the wall of a bacterium. The tube is surrounded by the injection mechanism: a powerful extended coil spring connecting a system of spikes to the phage head. The syringe injects the T4 DNA into the bacterium in which the phage multiplies. When the spikes grab the bacterial surface, they release the spring: its contraction pushes the head and the attached tube against the bacterial wall. The tube goes through the wall and injects the phage DNA into the cell. This initiates the production of new T4 phages. Hershey and Chase grew two cultures of bacteriophage T4, one in a broth containing radioactive sulfur, which ends up in protein, the other in broth containing radioactive phosphorus, which ends up in DNA. The two kinds of bacteriophage particles, one marked in protein, the other in DNA, were added to bacteria; they rapidly became attached to the bacteria and within minutes began to multiply within them. In less than half an hour thousands of new bacteriophage particles were released by each infected bacterium.

A special step was added in the experiment: the bacteria were blended at high speed in an electric blender a few minutes after mixing with the bacteriophage— after most bacteriophage particles had become attached to the bacteria. The effect of the violent blending was to tear the bacteriophages off the bacteria. Astonishingly, the agitation did not interfere with the multiplication of the bacterio-phages inside the bacteria: new phage was produced as before. Evidently a component of the virus essential for its reproduction—either the DNA or the protein—had already gone into the bacteria when they were blended. The radioactive markers showed that the DNA had gone into the bacteria and remained with them after the blending; most of the protein had stayed outside and had been ripped off. Clearly, the DNA contained the genes controlling the multiplication of the bacteriophage.

This result had great repercussions, because it confirmed a striking result obtained with bacteria in 1944 by O. T. Avery, C. McCloud, and M. McCarty. Their experiment involved a strain of bacteria highly virulent for mice (which it kills in a short time) and a derivative of that strain that had lost virulence and was unable to kill. The nonvirulent bacteria were exposed to an extract of the virulent bacteria and then inoculated into mice: unexpectedly, the mice died. It turned out that the extract contained DNA. This result conveyed the message—astonishing at that time—that DNA was able to transfer the property of virulence, a hereditary characteristic, from one bacterium to another. At the time this fact was not properly appreciated, because very little was known about DNA. Considered together with the bacteriophage experiment, however, the results gave irrefutable proof of the role of DNA, the carrier of information for the hereditary characteristics of viruses and bacteria. (In some viruses RNA performs this role.) This addition to our knowledge was combined with the information that in eukaryotic cells both DNA and the genes are in the chromosomes, and the conclusion was reached that DNA carries the information for hereditary characteristics in all living creatures and that genes are made of DNA (or of RNA in some viruses). Later these conclusions were fully validated by direct analysis of the genes.

What Is Life?

We can now begin to approach the question: what is life? It is evident that there can be no life without nucleic acids, but neither are nucleic acids sufficient for life. All chemical laboratories have bottles filled with DNA or RNA, which stand there for years, unchanged, small grains of dust, totally immutable, certainly not life. But the nucleic acid of a virus becomes alive after it enters the cells: there it multiplies, and causes profound changes in the cells. Both effects derive from the actuation of the instructions contained in the DNA of the virus. So, for a virus, life is expression of the instructions contained in its genes. By examining a large variety of creatures we see that their DNAs, too, act in the same way. Multiplication of the DNA, and of a whole cell or a whole organism, is a constant feature of life, although it may employ different means. The other basic feature of life is the carrying out of the many and varied genetic instructions encoded in DNA, from burrowing in the sand to flying, from the buzzing of bees to the singing of birds, from the instinctive reactions of worms to the consciousness of humans. But why are the activities of different creatures so varied?

We can say with assurance that different creatures display different activities because their genes are different, and that therefore something in their DNA (or RNA) is different. We can condense our findings about life by saying that life is *the actuation of the instructions encoded in the genes.*

This statement is just the beginning of the answer. The rest of the answer lies in the examination of all the complex and extremely varied functions of the genes of living creatures, in the different ways the problems related to living have been solved by individual species, and of how the interactions of diverse creatures shape the living world. The book of life is immense, and no one can read it all. We can, however, investigate some themes—because they are well understood, or because they are basic to most forms of life, or because they shape our thinking.

CHAPTER 2

The Machinery of the Cell

The Chemistry of Life

Living organisms, like all matter, are made of atoms. The most common in living things are carbon (C), hydrogen (H), oxygen (O), nitrogen (N), and phosphorus (P). Many other atoms, also important, occur in smaller amounts.

An atom can be compared roughly to the sun and its planets: it comprises a nucleus surrounded by electrons moving around it at different distances. Because the nucleus is positively charged, it holds the negatively charged electrons by electric attraction. The closer the electrons to the nucleus the more strongly they are held. For this reason peripheral electrons can be exchanged between atoms. If two atoms become entangled so that they equally share two electrons, they are held strongly together and form a *chemical bond* (fig. 2.1). Some chemical bonds are formed by as many as four or six electrons shared by two atoms.

Atoms joined by chemical bonds are called *molecules*, which are the basis of the chemistry of life. A molecule, then, contains at least two atoms. For instance, a molecule of oxygen, O_2, is made up of two oxygen atoms bound to each other, and a molecule of water, H_2O, two atoms of hydrogen bound to one of oxygen. Biological molecules may be made up of many atoms, even thousands. The largest are called *macromolecules*, and their special properties are essential for life.

Ions

Because an atom contains both positive and negative electric charges that exactly balance each other, it is electrically neutral. But when an atom loses one or more of its peripheral electrons to another atom, it becomes positively charged, or when it acquires electrons, it becomes negatively charged. Both kinds of electrically

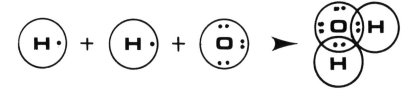

Figure 2.1. Chemical bonds connect one atom of oxygen (O) with two of hydrogen (H) to form a molecule of water (H_2O). Dots represent electrons. The chemical bonds are formed by pairs of electrons shared by the two atoms.

charged atoms are called *ions*. By flowing in and out of cells they accumulate or dissipate electric charges that play important roles in the cells' activities. Molecules, too, can gain or lose electrons, acquiring electric charges that are essential for the interactions between molecules that carry out life's functions; they are also ions.

Some molecules, when dissolved in water, readily become ions: *acidic* molecules generate negative ions; *basic* molecules generate positive ions. An acidic molecule can be represented as AH, electrically neutral, where A represents an atom or a combination of atoms. In water it splits into a negative ion (A^-) and a positive *hydrogen ion* (H^+). Figure 2.2, for example, shows the behavior of muriatic acid (HCl) in water. H gives away an electron, becoming H^+, a hydrogen ion; the electron is picked up by Cl, which becomes Cl^-, a chloride ion. The two ions (H^+ and Cl^-) with opposite charges are attracted to each other but are kept apart by molecules of water. Water itself can split into two ions, OH^- and H^+, but very few molecules do so. Although rare, such splitting allows a basic molecule, B, to acquire a positive electric charge by picking up a hydrogen ion, becoming BH^+. B again stands for an atom or a group of atoms. Thus NH_3 (ammonia) becomes NH_4^+, an ammonium ion.

The addition of either an acidic or a basic substance to water changes the amounts of free hydrogen ions in the water: acidic substances increase the amount, and basic substances decrease it. It is the increased concentration of hydrogen ions that we perceive when we taste water containing an acidic substance such as vinegar; the more hydrogen ions in the water, the more acidic the solution.

Figure 2.2. Formation of ions. Muriatic acid (HCl, shown in the center) is made up of one atom of hydrogen (H) and one of chlorine (Cl). In water, the muriatic acid molecule splits into two ions, as shown on the right: the positively charged hydrogen ion (H^+) and the negatively charged chloride ion (Cl^-).

Plasticity

The characteristics of living creatures depend on the properties of their macromolecules. One such feature is *plasticity*, or the ability to change shape, as in the contraction of muscles or the crawling motions of single cells. A change of shape requires a rearrangement of the molecules. Macromolecules can do this easily because they are held together by many weak bonds, different from the chemical bonds that hold the atoms within a molecule.

These weaker bonds are usually of three types. One, called the *ionic bond*, is generated by the attraction of opposite charges of two molecules, both of which are ions. Another type, the *hydrogen bond*, is formed by a hydrogen atom shared between two molecules, almost as electrons are shared between atoms in chemical bonds. A third type connects fatty or fat-seeking substances (called hydrophobic, meaning that they hate water) in a watery environment; this is known as a *hydrophobic bond*.

Each of these bonds can be easily broken and re-formed. The macromolecules of a cell can change partners by shifting such bonds from one molecule to another without altering the integrity of the cell, and this is the basis of cell plasticity. Extreme examples are fluid substances. Water molecules are held together by hydrogen bonds between oxygen atoms (fig. 2.3). A hydrogen atom connecting molecule A to molecule B can readily abandon B and exchange it for C; thus water

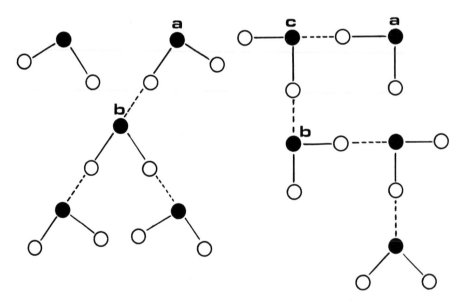

Figure 2.3. Partner shifting in water. Solid circles are oxygen atoms, empty circles hydrogen atoms. Solid lines indicate the chemical bonds that hold the atoms in the water molecules; the dashed lines denote the hydrogen bonds that connect molecules of water to each other. At the left, molecule a is connected to molecule b, but at the right, molecule a has left b to become associated with c.

has no shape. The opposite situation is found in solids such as crystals, in which atoms keep their relative position under enormous stress because they are connected by large numbers of rigid, essentially unbreakable bonds.

Cells are neither liquid nor solid; they fall somewhere between the two extremes. The macromolecules that make up cells can exchange partners like the molecules of a liquid, but in a more limited way. Constituents of cells that are essentially liquid are the membranes that surround the cells and partition them inside. They are made up of arrays of long fatty molecules kept aligned side by side by hydrophobic bonds (M in fig. 2.4). These molecules readily slide with respect to each other, like water molecules, but they remain aligned inside the membrane. The fatty molecules of the membrane can be compared to dancers performing a writhing dance on a crowded floor and continually changing partners. This ability of fatty molecules to slide past each other makes membranes very elastic.

Building macromolecules and breaking and re-forming their bonds require

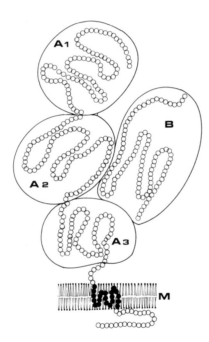

Figure 2.4. A protein present at the surface of many animal cells (see major histocompatibility antigens in chapter 14). The small circles represent amino acids. They form a continuous chain, which is folded to produce three balls, also called domains: A1, A2, and A3. Where the loops of the chain run near each other, they establish weak bonds (not shown). This protein is associated with a second protein, B, to which it is connected by weak bonds between amino acids. Protein A is held in the cell membrane (M), which is made up of two layers of fatty molecules. Fatty molecules are shown as lines, each of which is connected to a black dot, the water-seeking end. The protein is held in the membrane by a string of fat-seeking amino acids (black).

energy, as do many other activities of the cell. This energy is derived from a molecule called *ATP* (for adenosine triphosphate), which is a readily expendable chemical *energy currency*. ATP contains three groups of phosphates, which lock the energy in their chemical bonds. The energy is released when ATP splits and loses one of the phosphates. By using external energy, the cells reconstitute ATP. We will see in chapter 3 how ATP is generated.

Proteins

Important macromolecules for the activities of the cells are *proteins*. They are formed by long chains of *amino acids* connected by strong chemical bonds. In a given protein, amino acids follow each other in a characteristic order, or *sequence*: different proteins have different sequences. The number of possible sequences, even within a short chain, is staggering because at every position in the chain there can be any of twenty different amino acids. Thus a chain of ten amino acids could be made, theoretically, in ten trillion different ways. Each amino acid gives the protein a special property: some make it capable of associating with water or water-soluble substances, whereas others make it seek fatty substances. Some amino acids contribute to the protein a positive charge, others a negative charge, and still others no charge at all. These properties determine the interactions of a protein with other molecules.

Altering the sequence of amino acids in the chain often changes the properties of the protein for another reason as well: the chain is folded onto itself, and the sequence determines how it folds. Some proteins take the shape of little balls, some become a string of balls (*domains*) connected to one another like A1, A2, and A3 in figure 2.4, and some form sheets or thick filaments. Folding is maintained by weak bonds of the amino acids among themselves and with their environment. For instance, fat-seeking amino acids of the same chain tend to stick together, whereas water-seeking ones tend to reach into the watery juice of the cell. Hydrogen bonds form between many of the amino acids, and ionic bonds connect others. Numerous weak bonds hold chains of amino acids in contorted configurations, like irregular balls of yarn. A protein, therefore, has a well-defined three-dimensional shape determined by the sequence of its amino acids.

A protein can be likened to a network of fairly soft springs, corresponding to the internal bonds. They allow the protein to take several shapes that vary significantly from one another. Transitions from one shape to another occur easily because the lengthening of some connections is compensated by the shortening of others. Because the overall energy needed is small, it can often be provided by the heat of the environment. These changes are essential for the dynamic functions of the protein, as will be explained below. Also crucial is the proteins' ability to form multiple weak bonds with other macromolecules. The multiplicity of the bonds ensures the stability of the connections; their individual weakness allows plasticity.

Assembly of Structures

In organisms, protein molecules assemble into large complex structures that perform highly specific, sophisticated functions. As an example, consider the assembly of a complicated viral particle, that of the bacteriophage T4 (see chapter 1). The T4 particles consist mainly of nucleic acid and fifty different kinds of protein, each one in many copies. The particles are assembled inside bacteria after the necessary proteins are made in each cell. Although it seems incredible, out of this great mishmash thousands of T4 particles assemble without a hitch because of the precise program built into the proteins' amino acid sequences. That the assembly is split into three subassemblies—one for the head, another for the tail, and the third for the tail fibers (fig. 2.5)—simplifies the process somewhat. Two devices ensure that the proteins are added one at a time in proper order in each subassembly. First, each protein has two locking sites, one for the protein that precedes it in the assembly, the other for the protein that follows it. Thus, they can lock onto each other in only one orientation. Second, each unassembled protein hides the locking site for the next protein; only after it joins the structure does a rearrangement of the protein's internal bonds make the site accessible. As a result the proteins cannot assemble piecemeal, but only in the proper order.

To see how assembly proceeds, let's indicate the proteins as A', B, C, D, ... The prime sign of the initial protein, A', indicates that the locking site for the next protein is exposed and accessible, ready to bind the next protein. The steps of assembly will be, in succession:

$$A' + B \quad = \quad A'B \qquad \rightarrow \qquad A'B'$$
$$A'B' + C \quad = \quad A'B'C \qquad \rightarrow \qquad A'B'C'$$
$$A'B'C' + D \quad = \quad A'B'C'D \ldots, \qquad \rightarrow \qquad A'B'C'D' \ldots$$

and so on. Arrows indicate that the binding site for the next protein is unmasked after a protein is assembled. As the structure grows, some of the assembled proteins may undergo additional changes of shape or bits may be chopped off to stabilize the assembly. When the three subassemblies are finished (including the DNA in the head subassembly), they join to form a complete viral particle. The process, in spite of its complexity, is almost foolproof: misassembled particles are very rare.

No Life without Structures

Among the structures fundamental to life are filaments that determine the shapes and motion of all cells. The entire cytoplasm is pervaded by a very thin three-dimensional network, recognizable by electron microscopy, that holds everything together. A network of somewhat coarser but still *thin filaments* (two to three millionths of a millimeter) is the cell's muscle: their shrinkage causes the cell to change shape. Other, somewhat thicker, *intermediate filaments* differ in the two

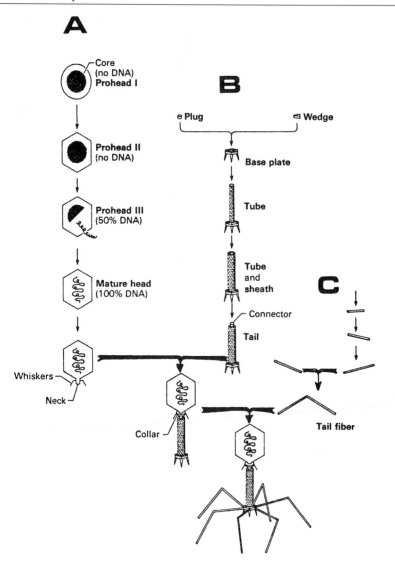

Figure 2.5. The pathways for the assembly of a particle of phage T4. The head subassembly (A) is at left, that for the tail (B) in the center, and that for the tail fibers (C) at right. At every step (indicated by an arrow) new proteins are added. The head shell is first built around a protein core, which is then broken down and replaced by DNA, made separately. The finished phage particle is at the bottom. (Modified from B. D. Davis, R. Dulbecco, H. N. Eisen, and H. S. Ginsberg, *Microbiology*, 3d ed. [Hagerstown, Md: Harper & Row, 1980], p. 904.)

main types of body cells, the *fibroblasts* and the *epithelia*. Fibroblasts are located in the deeper layer of the skin, around blood vessels, and so on. Epithelia are polygonal cells that make up the superficial layer of the skin, the liver, and many other internal organs. In fibroblasts the intermediate filaments hold the nucleus in the center of the cells and help cell movement (fig. 2.6); in epithelia, they make the cell

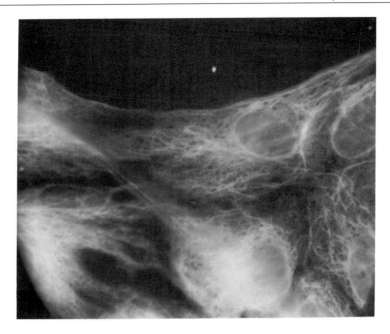

Figure 2.6. Intermediate filaments of fibroblastic cells grown in a plastic dish. The filaments are made recognizable by the binding of specific antibodies (see chapter 13) to the protein of the filaments. The antibodies carry a fluorescent tag, which emits green light when illuminated with blue light. The photograph records the emitted light. This technique is called *immunofluorescence*. In order to allow the antibodies to reach the filaments, the cells were treated with acetone which destroys the cellular membrane. The filaments penetrate all parts of the cells and are especially concentrated around the nucleus. Magnified 2,000 times.

rigid and reinforce connections with other cells (fig. 2.7), helping them make sheets. Even thicker filaments (about one one-hundred-thousandth of a millimeter in diameter), the *microtubules* (fig. 2.8), constitute the skeleton of the cells and coordinate their movements.

The Composition and Role of Microtubules

Disruption of any of the filamentous structures has severe consequences for the cells. As an example, we will see what happens when microtubules are disrupted by drugs. Microtubules are bundles of fibers made up of two kinds of protein molecules and arranged with great regularity (fig. 2.9). Because pairs of molecules are continuously added to the end of each fiber, using energy indirectly provided by ATP, while other pairs are removed, microtubules are in a perpetual state of flux. But during mitosis those connecting the chromosomes to the poles of the cell become stabilized because the removal of constituent molecules is reduced. By associating with special proteins, they promote the migration of chromosomes to the poles; the microtubules are the tracks and the other proteins, the engine.

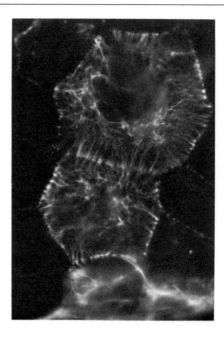

Figure 2.7. Intermediate filaments of epithelial cells grown in a plastic dish. The filaments are demonstrated by the technique of immunofluorescence described in the legend to figure 2.6. These filaments are made up of proteins called *keratins* that are different from those of the intermediate filaments of fibroplastic cells. The filaments, arranged radially, become thicker where they reach the cell surface. Where two cells touch, their respective thickenings are aligned, forming a structure called a *desmosome* that holds the cells tightly together. The dark gap between the two thickenings contains proteins different from keratins. Magnified 2,000 times.

Bundles of microtubules also bend—or slide in respect to each other—to propel sperm or single-celled organisms.

The role of microtubules has been clarified by using drugs to disrupt them. Among these drugs is *colchicine,* derived from the meadow saffron (*Colchicum autumnale*). It has been known for more than two centuries that this drug is useful for relieving the pains of gout. At the end of the last century, after the drug became available in pure form, investigators studied its effects on dogs. They noticed a marked increase in the number of mitoses (cell divisions) in actively growing tissues, suggesting that the drug accelerated cell growth. In reality, however, the number of cell divisions is not increased. Rather, colchicine *stops* mitoses at the easily recognizable stage in which the chromosomes line up in the center of the cell (fig. 1.5), so that a tissue exposed to the drug has many such cells. Colchicine stops cell division by binding to the protein molecules that make up the microtubules, hiding their locking sites, so they can no longer assemble. The microtubules become progressively shorter and finally disappear, destroyed by the normal process of dissolution. Because their disappearance prevents cell division,

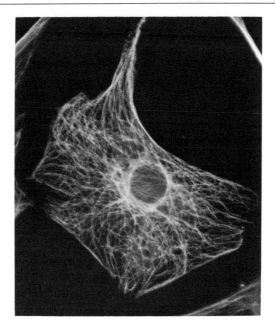

Figure 2.8. Microtubules in a cell growing in a plastic dish. The microtubules are made recognizable by immunofluorescence, as described in the legend to figure 2.6, using antibodies to a microtubule protein. Magnified 2,000 times. (From S. H. Cox, P. N. Rao, and B. R. Brinkley, in H. Bush, S. T. Crooke, and I. Daskal, eds., *Effects of Drugs on the Cell Nucleus* [New York: Academic Press, 1979].)

drugs related to colchicine are used in the treatment of cancer to block cell multiplication.

This effect of colchicine seems at first sight remote from its effect on gout. But in fact the drug relieves the pain of the disease by interfering with another function of microtubules. In gout, white blood cells eat up small crystals of uric acid that accumulate in the joints. Cells, damaged by the crystals, then release irritating substances into the joint, causing intense pain. The cells need the activity of microtubules to engulf the crystals. Colchicine, by dissolving the microtubules, prevents the engulfment and the process that generates pain.

Structures in Muscles and in the Brain

The movement of muscle cells is based on two types of protein filaments that are parallel to each other: one thin, the other thick, pointing in opposite directions. They are connected by cross-links of other proteins, thus forming ladderlike structures in which the cross-links are the rungs (fig. 2.10). All the thick filaments are attached to a transverse bar at one end forming a sort of comb; the thin filaments are connected to another transverse bar at the opposite end, forming another comb. The two combs interdigitate. When a suitable signal arrives (see chapter

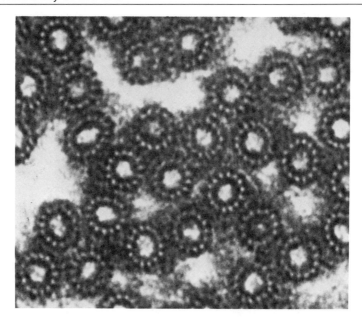

Figure 2.9. Microtubules present during cell division in a single-celled eukaryote. The microtubules are seen in cross section. Each is a bundle of thirteen or so filaments, forming a long cylinder. Magnified 470,000 times. Courtesy of U. Eichenlaub-Ritter.

17), the cross-links, using ATP energy, cause the two kinds of filaments to slide past each other, bringing the transverse bars closer together and shortening the muscle. This is the basis of muscle contractions. The thin filaments mentioned previously, which are in all cells, are simplified muscles.

Structure is important not only for movement but also for the operation of the brain. Signals in the brain are transmitted from one nerve cell to another by chemical substances (chapter 17). Chemicals released by one cell bind to special structures, the *receptors*, present at the surface of another cell. The association of the chemical modifies the shape of the receptor, which then changes some property of the receiving cell. This change is the signal, which the cell then transmits to other cells. All cells have receptors that respond to chemical signals emanating from other cells, either neighboring or distant.

Go-between Molecules: Enzymes

The ability to change shape is essential for the action of certain protein molecules, called *enzymes,* which promote many chemical reactions that involve displacements of electrons. There are strong barriers to these displacements, but enzymes can circumvent them, allowing the reactions to progress a billion times faster than they otherwise would. The trick is that enzymes temporarily incorporate the

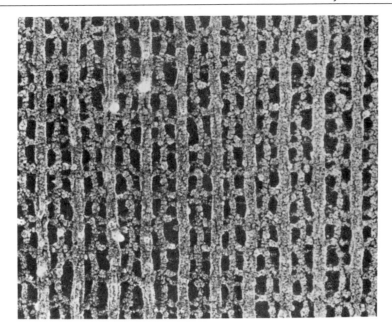

Figure 2.10. Electron micrograph of a thin section of an insect flight muscle. The two kinds of filaments, thick and thin, run vertically. All the thick filaments are connected to one type of cross-band above the figure, the thin filaments to another type of cross-band below the figure. The filaments are connected at regular intervals by cross-bridges, which, by using ATP, cause the two types of filaments to slide past each other. Magnified 200,000 times. (From J. E. Heuser and R. Cooke, *J. Mol. Biol.* 169:97–122 [1983]. Reproduced with permission.)

reacting molecules into their own structure. A particular enzyme can achieve this union, however, with only one type of molecule, the *substrate;* bonds are formed between the substrate and the enzyme, generating a new structure, the *enzyme-substrate complex.* The internal bonds of both the enzyme and the substrate are modified, and the electrons of the substrate acquire a position more favorable for the reaction. If, for instance, the substrate has to be split, the movement of the electrons weakens the chemical bonds that hold its two parts together and the bonds then easily break under the impact of environmental heat. The two parts of the substrate are released, and the enzyme returns to its original shape. As an analogy we might think of two rings connected by a padlock; their separation while the padlock is closed is extremely unlikely. If the padlock were shaken violently for a long time, it might open, but with a key (the enzyme) it can be opened in a flash.

The various steps in a reaction mediated by an enzyme can often go either way. An enzyme that splits molecule AB into A and B may also join A and B to form AB, because A and B fit equally well within the enzyme as AB, and within the enzyme the changes to the network can occur in opposite directions. One of the two reactions, however, occurs much more easily because it requires less energy. For instance, it is easier to separate two amino acids connected by a chemical bond than it is to join them in order to form the bond. The bond can be formed only if the enzyme gets the energy it needs from ATP, the energy currency of the cell.

To perform such precise roles, enzymes are greatly specialized, each acting on only one substrate, or perhaps on several substrates of extremely similar chemical constitution, and repeating the same chemical reaction over and over. Thus, a cell has many different enzymes, one type for each of its chemical reactions.

To appreciate how useful enzymes are, consider what happens when an animal eats. The food, either plant or animal products, contains among other things proteins. To utilize the proteins, the animal splits them in the gut into separate amino acids. These are taken up and distributed to the cells of the body, which utilize them to build the proteins they need. The stomach and intestine produce enzymes that break the chemical bonds between amino acids without damage to the animal's digestive organs. A chemist bent on obtaining the same effect without enzymes would have to employ harsh conditions that would destroy the animal itself. But the chemist's tools are crude compared to the delicate, extremely selective enzymes: thousands side by side in the same cell perform their reactions without interfering with one another.

In the very early period of the history of life, no enzymes existed. Some life reactions nevertheless occurred with the help of metals, rocks, or primitive life molecules, although at an extremely slow pace. It must have taken thousands of years to accomplish what a living cell can do today in a matter of seconds or minutes.

Membranes

Membranes are other structures essential for the cells, isolating them from the external environment and compartmentalizing them internally (see chapter 1). Membranes regulate the exchange of substances between a cell and its environment and are crucial for energy transformation (chapter 3).

The properties of membranes are very different from those of the structures examined so far. An electron microscope shows that a membrane is a double layer formed by two sheets, or leaflets, attached to each other (see fig. 1.2). Each sheet is a continuous layer of long and thin fatty molecules, called *phospholipids* (fig. 2.11), held parallel to each other by hydrophobic bonds. Each sheet, or leaflet, of the membrane is like an enormously wide bundle of pickets. The thickness of the sheet is equal to the length of the pickets—the fatty molecules. Their reciprocal attraction holds the sheets together.

In water such a membrane would tend to roll into itself, forming a drop like oil. This is prevented, however, by water-seeking or *hydrophylic* groups at the ends of the fatty molecules, which are in contact with water. These groups form a continuous thin layer. If we imagine passing through the membrane starting from

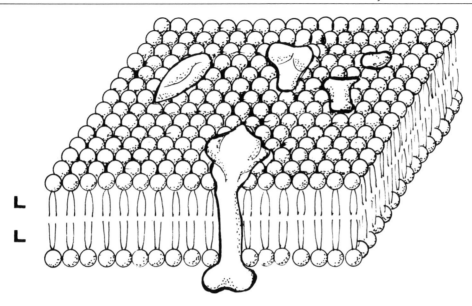

Figure 2.11. A patch of membrane showing the two leaflets (L) made up of fat-seeking molecules which are terminated by water-seeking groups, shown as spheres, at the two outer surfaces. Proteins are seen sticking out above the membrane or crossing its entire thickness.

the watery environment outside the cell, we first meet the water-seeking ends of the fatty molecules and then the rest of the fatty molecules of the first leaflet. Then we encounter the fatty molecules of the other leaflet and finally their water-seeking ends, which are in contact with the watery juices of the cell's interior. The two outer layers make the membrane perfectly stable in a watery environment. Many protein molecules are attached to membranes, some on one side and some on the other. Other molecules, like the one represented in figure 2.4, pass through the membrane, sticking out on both sides. Protein molecules carry out many essential functions that will be described later.

Why should the cell go to all the trouble of making a fatty membrane and then coating it with two water-seeking surfaces? The main reason is that the fatty membrane is needed to insulate the interior of the cell from the environment or one cell compartment from another. A membrane with a fatty core performs this function perfectly because it cannot be crossed by the water-soluble substances present inside and outside the cell.

Many substances, however, do cross membranes. Proteins made inside cells must cross the cell membrane to go out. Among these are the digestive enzymes produced by cells of the salivary glands, which enter the mouth, and those of the pancreas, which are deposited in the intestine. Proteins that coat the cell's exterior as a slimy layer or that act as glue between cells also must cross the cell membrane; so must the proteins of receptors that feel for or attach to substances present in the environment. Other proteins must enter the cells from the outside:

for instance, the defensive antibodies (chapter 13) in mother's milk must cross the cells of the baby's intestine in order to reach the blood and defend the infant against viruses or bacteria.

All this traffic of protein molecules would seem to be incompatible with the impermeability of the cell membrane. But in fact there is no contradiction because these molecules do not move freely through the cell membrane; they have to use special devices. Proteins can enter cells from the outside only if they stick to the special receptors each cell has on its surface. Each kind of receptor binds only one kind of protein and brings it into the cell.

Lessons from a Virus in Transporting Proteins

Getting In

Much has been learned about how certain proteins are transported in or out of cells by observing through an electron microscope such viruses as those that cause flu or measles. The particles of these viruses have a characteristic shape. Each has a molecule of nucleic acid (RNA) surrounded by two coats (fig. 2.12)—an inner coat made up of protein molecules and an outer coat comprising a membrane studded with proteins.

Before it is transported into the cell, a viral particle must touch a suitable receptor and stick to it (fig. 2.13: A). The cell membrane with the attached particle is then drawn inside the cell and pinched off, forming a transport vesicle, or *endosome*, containing a viral particle and freely suspended in the cytoplasm (fig. 2.13: B and C). The contents of the endosome vesicle are made acidic by an influx of hydrogen ions—H^+, also called *protons*. The acidity causes the fusion of the membrane of the viral particle with the membrane of the vesicle (fig. 2.13: D). The viral RNA with its inner coat is set free in the cytoplasm (fig. 2.13: E). The released viral RNA finds its way to the part of the cell where it will replicate, and the endosome then splits. One part, carrying the viral membrane, fuses with a vesicle of another kind, a *lysosome*, where the membrane is broken down by powerful enzymes. The other part of the endosome, containing the receptor, returns to the cell surface to display its receptor again.

Many kinds of proteins enter cells in a similar way. For instance, the antibody molecules in mother's milk mentioned earlier are picked up by cells of the baby's intestine. They become enclosed in vesicles that migrate through the cytoplasm and fuse with the cell membrane on the opposite side of the cell. There they are released into the blood to perform their function.

The endosome is only one of many types of *transport vesicles* that carry proteins attached to membranes from one membrane to another. When a vesicle derived from membrane A moves through the cytoplasm and reaches membrane B, it fuses with it. The protein is now part of membrane B. The pinching off,

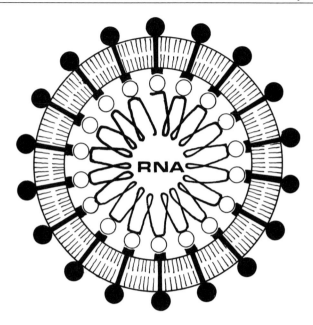

Figure 2.12. A cross section of the Semliki Forest virus, named for the area of Africa in which it was discovered. Viruses of this type, called togaviruses, are common in tropical rain forests; they are propagated by mosquitoes and induce a variety of diseases in animals and humans. The virus is surrounded by a membrane, which holds the protein molecules of the outer layer (black). These molecules are connected internally to those of the inner layer (shown as round and clear), which in turn are connected to the centrally located RNA.

internalization, and separation of vesicles from membrane A, and the fusion with membrane B, takes place without leaving any holes in the membranes. This is possible because the membranes are essentially liquid, and at points of contact two membranes become a single one. A protein can be transported by this mechanism through several membranes, where it is modified in various ways. The vesicles have a way of knowing where they must go: *how* they do it we do not understand.

Getting Out

Viruses are also useful for understanding how proteins exit from cells. Viral proteins are made close to the tubes of the endoplasmic reticulum, which, as we saw in chapter 1, form a network within cells (fig. 2.14). The newly made protein molecules cross the membrane of the endoplasmic reticulum and enter its cavities.

The crossing is engineered in a complex way, not completely understood, which separates the molecules that are destined for the cavity of the endoplasmic

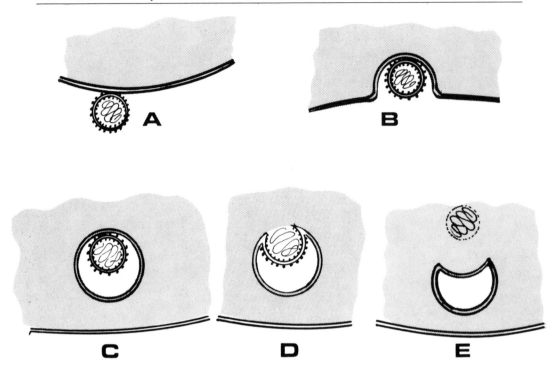

Figure 2.13. Entry of a togavirus particle into a cell. The gray cytoplasm is lined by the cell membrane, shown as a double line. (A) The virus makes contact with the external surface of the cell. The proteins of the viral surface establish a connection with receptors of the cell membrane. (B) The membrane is pulled in. (C) It is then pinched off, releasing into the cytoplasm a membrane vesicle containing the viral particle. (D) Within the vesicle the membrane of the viral particle fuses with the membrane of the vesicle. (E) The viral RNA surrounded by a single layer of protein molecules is released free in the cytoplasm.

reticulum from those that are not. In outline, this is what happens. The protein molecules cross the membrane while they are made on special particles, the ribosomes (fig. 2.15: 1). These proteins are marked by a special feature: a sequence of several fat-seeking amino acids at the beginning of the chain, known as a *signal sequence* (fig. 2.15: 2). This sequence binds to a small particle containing several proteins and a small piece of RNA (fig. 2.15: 3). The particle directs the signal sequence to a docking protein at the outer surface of the endoplasmic reticulum, where it can enter the membrane (fig. 2.15: 5). Many other amino acids, not necessarily fat-seeking, follow the leader and enter the membrane (fig. 2.15: 6), where the signal sequence is trapped. The rest of the chain emerges into the cavity of the endoplasmic reticulum and folds into its final shape. An enzyme then cuts off the signal sequence from the rest of the chain (fig. 2.15: 7). Now the protein sticks out into the cavity of the tube, still attached to the membrane at the other end by another series of fat-seeking amino acids (the *anchor sequence*) or by other special molecules at the end of the chain. If the protein lacks an anchor sequence, it

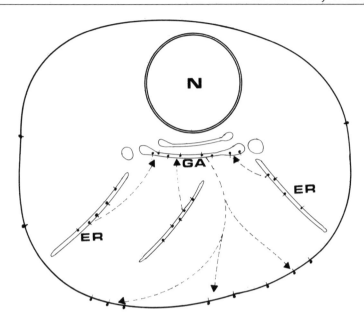

Figure 2.14. The path followed by the protein of the other layer of the virus in order to reach the cell surface. The protein enters the endoplasmic reticulum (ER) and then reaches the Golgi apparatus (GA) where it is completed by the addition of sugars. From there it travels to the cell membrane in membrane-bound vesicles. At the membrane it is oriented so that most of it sticks outside; only the tail end protrudes into the cytoplasm. (N = cell nucleus.)

is released free into the cavity (fig. 2.15: 8) and will be later exported. There are many variations of this process: some very long amino acid chains have several signal sequences and enter the membrane at several points. They remain interwoven with the membrane, making as many as ten passes through it. Proteins that make channels (see below) follow this plan.

The molecules anchored to the membrane reach the cell surface via a complex route. They are first transferred to the membrane-bound spaces known as the Golgi apparatus (see again fig. 2.14), where their synthesis is completed by the stepwise addition of sugars. These water-seeking sugars make the proteins compatible with the watery environment in which the virus spreads. Finally the proteins reach the cell membrane. The part of the amino acid chains containing the sugars sticks outside of the cell, while a shorter segment reaches into the cytoplasm. These sugar-containing surface proteins are called *glycoproteins*.

The proteins of the inner coat of the virus particles are destined to stay in the cytoplasm. Because they lack a signal sequence, they cannot cross the membrane of the endoplasmic reticulum, and they become associated with the viral nucleic acid after it has replicated. The inner-coat protein and the nucleic acid form particles, which reach the inner side of the cell membrane. There they associate with the cytoplasmic ends of the glycoproteins of the outer coat, gathering them

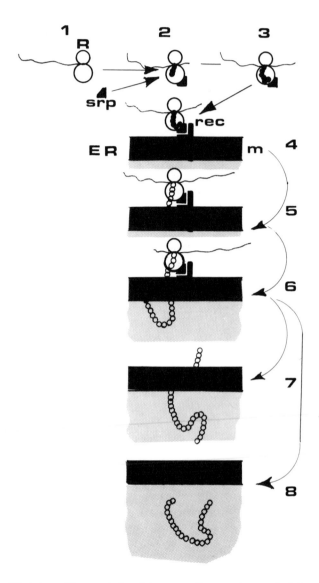

Figure 2.15. A simplified view of how a viral protein crosses the membrane of a tube of the endoplasmic reticulum. (1) The protein is made when a particle on which it is made, a ribosome (R), joins an appropriate RNA messenger (thin line) (see chapter 4). The association takes place in several steps which are not shown. (2 and 3) As the amino acid chain begins to grow, the signal sequence (black) is made first, causing the ribosome to bind a signal recognition particle (srp). (4) The signal recognition particle binds to a receptor protein (rec) attached to the membrane (m) of a tube of the endoplasmic reticulum. The membrane, in cross section, is dark gray and the cavity of the tube, light gray. (5) The signal sequence (s) enters the membrane. (6) Other amino acids follow and enter the cavity of the tube. (7) The connection between the signal sequence and the amino acid chains are cut. If the protein has an anchor sequence (a), it is held by the membrane, but most of it sticks out in the cavity. (8) If the protein does not have an anchor sequence, it is released free into the cavity and from there will be exported out of the cell later.

together into patches. The patches curl outward and become spheres that detach from the cell surface as viral particles.

In cells not infected by viruses many proteins reach the cell membrane using the same path. They also remain anchored to the cell membrane and have sugars attached—that is, they are glycoproteins. Among these are the proteins that make up receptors—molecules that are able to bind and relay chemical signals from outside the cell. An example was shown in figure 2.4.

Exported Proteins

Proteins that are exported from the cell—such as the saliva enzymes—follow the same path as glycoproteins, with one difference: they lack the anchor sequence. Therefore, they do not remain associated with the membrane of the endoplasmic reticulum but become free in its tubes (see fig. 2.15: 8). From there they reach the outside of the cell in a somewhat different way (fig. 2.16). After going through the

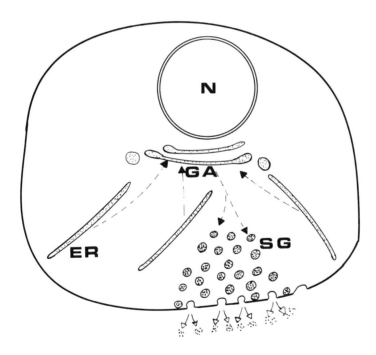

Figure 2.16. How a protein is exported out of a cell. The protein is released free into the tubes of the endoplasmic reticulum (ER). From there it proceeds to the Golgi apparatus (GA) and then to vesicles called secretory granules (SG), which are free in the cytoplasm. These vesicles are probably made by pinching off pieces of the membrane of the Golgi apparatus, enclosing the protein molecules. The secretory vesicles reach the cytoplasmic side of the cell membrane, adhering to it. When they fuse with the cell membrane, they release the protein into the cell's environment. (N = cell nucleus.)

Golgi apparatus and receiving their sugars, they become enclosed in special vesicles known as *secretory granules* (fig. 2.16: SG) and stay in the cytoplasm for days. When a special chemical signal reaches the cell, they adhere to the cytoplasmic side of the cell membrane, fuse with it, and discharge their contents out of the cell. We will examine this process in greater detail in considering the function of nerve cells in chapter 17.

Special Markers

Proteins are made in the cytoplasm, and from there they can travel to various destinations: the cell surface, the nucleus, the mitochondria, or the lysosomes. The destinations are determined by special amino acid sequences analogous to the signal sequence, but with different targets. Proteins that go to the nucleus have sequences that bind to the nuclear pores, through which they reach the nuclear contents. Among these proteins are enzymes for DNA replication and for transferring information from DNA to proteins (see chapter 4), and the proteins of viruses that replicate in the nucleus.

Proteins destined for lysosomes, on the other hand, have a special sugar, a mannose derivative, as a recognition marker. Among them are enzymes that break down the complex sugars of glycoproteins that enter the cells—an important function of lysosomes, especially in liver cells. If these proteins lack the sugar, they are shunted to the cell membrane and there are excreted. In some humans affected by a hereditary "storage disease," an enzyme of this kind is made without the recognition marker. The lysosomes, lacking the enzyme, then fill up with the unbroken sugar chains, which greatly impair their functions.

Specific Channels

Many water-soluble substances that go into and out of cells all the time do not cross the fatty leaflets, nor are they transported within vesicles. Instead they cross the membrane using special structures known as *channels*—rings of protein molecules embedded in the membrane. Channels are used by ions, by substances needed for manufacturing cellular macromolecules (such as the amino acids used for making proteins), and by sugars needed for energy. There are many kinds of channels, each letting through a single substance or a class of related substances; their selectivity allows the cytoplasm to maintain a composition different from that of the cell's external environment.

A main distinction among channels is the manner in which they allow substances through. In a *passive channel* a substance moves from the side where it is more concentrated (more abundant) to the side where it is less concentrated. Because this movement is like that of water flowing downhill, it requires no energy. In an *active channel*—also called a *pump*—a substance always moves in a given direction, even if it must go from a place of low concentration to one of high concentration. Like water flowing uphill, this flow requires energy, which is supplied by ATP.

Ion Flows

Ions that go through channels may be either positively charged, such as sodium (Na^+), potassium (K^+), and calcium (Ca^{++}), or negatively charged, such as chloride (Cl^-). Their flow through the cell membrane affects many of a cell's properties because they regulate the operation of almost every component of the cell machinery. As we will see below, they also determine the electrical properties of the plasma membrane and control the flow of other substances in and out of a cell.

The passive ion channels are pores that select ions according to their charge and size: some allow the passage of Na^+ ions, others of K^+ ions, and so on. The selectivity of the pores allows us to consider the various ions within or outside a cell as forming separate reservoirs, although they are mixed together.

Of the active ion channels the most important is the *Na-K pump*, which transports Na^+ ions out of the cell and K^+ ions into it. Basically the pump is a shuttle activated by ATP energy; we can visualize its operation as a cyclic series of structural rearrangements as shown in figure 2.17. At a certain point in each cycle, a protein of the channel extracts energy from ATP, causing the changes of shape that determine the operation of the shuttle.

Many Na-K pumps are scattered in the membranes of the cells. They keep the

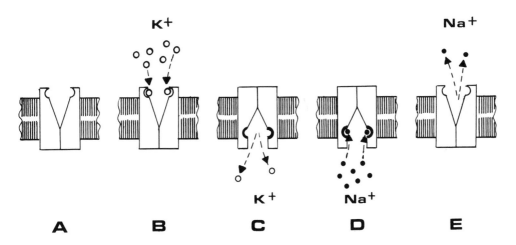

Figure 2.17. The cyclic operation of the Na-K pump. The pump is shown imbedded in a piece of membrane. The cytoplasm is below, the cell's environment above. (A) The channel is open to the outside and closed inside. (B) K^+ ions (empty circles) from the outside bind to the accessible sites. (C) The channel changes shape and ejects the K^+ ions into the cytoplasm of the cells. It exposes sites for Na^+ ions. (D) Na^+ ions from the cytoplasm bind to the sites. (E) The channel again changes shape, ejecting Na^+ ions to the outside environment and returning to its initial shape. The cycle can now start again.

interior of the cell poor in Na$^+$ ions and rich in K$^+$ ions, compared to the environment. The concentration of either ion inside the cell remains steady because for each of them the amount moved by the pumps is equal to that flowing in the opposite direction through passive channels. Moreover, if the internal Na$^+$ rises beyond a certain level, it stimulates the pump, which increases the export of Na$^+$.

Electric Voltage across Cell Membranes

The cell is an electrical battery with a voltage difference between inside and outside maintained by the asymmetric flow of ions through passive channels. The Na-K pump does not contribute directly to this voltage because in a given time it moves equal numbers of electrical charges in opposite directions. The voltage is maintained mainly by the passive outflow of K$^+$ ions, which depletes the interior of the cell of positive charges (fig. 2.18). As a result the inner side of the cell membrane becomes negatively charged. The voltage difference between inside and outside, known as the *membrane potential*, is of the order of twenty to eighty thousandths of a volt (millivolts), depending on the cells. (In comparison, a penlight battery has a voltage of fifteen hundred millivolts.) The membrane potential is indirectly maintained by the Na-K pump, which keeps the ion concentrations different on the two sides of the cell membrane.

In spite of its low value, the membrane potential has an essential influence on

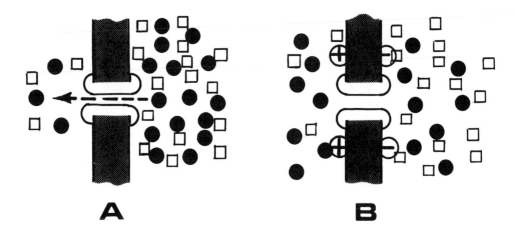

Figure 2.18. Origin of membrane potential. (A) The operation of the Na-K pump (not shown) enriches the cytoplasm (to the right of the membrane) of K$^+$ ions (solid circles). They are counterbalanced by negative ions (white squares), so that there is no charge excess on either side of the membrane. K$^+$ ions flow passively through a channel that is impermeable to other ions (arrow). (B) The outflow of K$^+$ ions leaves an excess of negative charges on the cytoplasmic side of the membrane; the excess of positive charges at the outer side generated by the outflow is rapidly dissipated. The imbalance on the cytoplasmic side confers a negative voltage on the inner side of the membrane compared to the outer side.

proteins embedded in the cell membrane, such as receptors, enzymes, and the ion channels themselves. These proteins have both positively and negatively charged atoms and tend to orient themselves with the positive parts toward the interior of the cell which is negative (opposite charges attract each other). The strength of the force that keeps a protein in that position depends on the membrane potential; the force is strong because the distance between opposite charges is minute. As we shall see in chapter 17, this force is the key to the operation of the nerve cells and of the brain computer.

Although the passive flow of Na^+ ions into the cells contributes little to the membrane potential, it has other important consequences. For instance, it provides the energy for carrying into the cells other substances such as amino acids and sugars. These substances are more concentrated in the cells than outside, so their transport is uphill and requires energy. Ultimately the Na-K pump produces the energy for these transports by maintaining the Na^+ concentration within the cells lower than that outside.

Given that the imbalance of Na^+ and K^+ ions on the two sides of the cell membrane is so important, it is not surprising that cells invest about 30 percent of their total energy to run the Na-K pumps, which maintain the imbalance. How significant this may be is seen in a strain of genetically defective mice that are obese and have an especially efficient Na-K pump. Perhaps these mice use the energy left over for building excessive quantities of body components. This, however, is not true of obese humans: they do not have especially efficient Na-K pumps.

Artificial Channels

Passive ion channels do not exist solely for the benefit of the cells; they are also made by some organisms to kill others. Some of the antibacterial agents (antibiotics) manufactured by bacteria or molds and used in the warfare among these organisms are passive ion channels—*ionophores,* or carriers of ions. These are rings formed by a small number of amino acids, which can settle in a bacterial cell membrane. Each ionophore permits the free flow of certain ions. For instance, one type lets through K^+ ions; another allows the passage of several ions with a single positive charge. One ionophore exchanges K^+ for H^+ and another exchanges Na^+ for H^+. The specificities of the various ionophores depend on the features of the channel, especially the ability of the channel proteins to make transient connections with certain substances. The effect of these ionophores is to abolish the differences of ion concentrations between the inside and outside of the cells, with considerable impairment or destruction of cellular activities. *Monensin,* an ionophore that exchanges Na^+ for H^+, is used in veterinary medicine to combat parasites that invade animals.

CHAPTER 3

Energy from the Sun

Life may be thought of as the expression of DNA instructions, which determine the formation and activity of the cells. From this concept we might form the image of life as a totally self-contained, earthly phenomenon. But this image neglects a fundamental point: life is generated by energy. Energy is needed for arranging atoms into molecules and molecules into structures. The electronic changes that determine enzyme activity also require energy, as do ion flows and movements of cells. Earthly life, then, is an expression of the energy of the universe. Conversely, the existence of energy has perhaps made the existence of life inevitable because it provides the means for achieving order and organization.

The energy for earthly life comes from the sun. In this respect, the whole biological world can be divided into two subworlds. One, made up of green plants and certain microorganisms, is self-sufficient: it absorbs energy from sunlight and transforms it into chemicals that can be utilized by all creatures. The other subworld is parasitic: composed of all organisms of the animal kingdom and many microorganisms, it exists by using as food the energy-rich chemicals produced by the first subworld.

Thus, if the sun's light were to fail, most life would be annihilated, an event that apparently almost occurred sixty million years ago when dinosaurs roamed the earth. Although powerful, seemingly invincible creatures, they became extinct quite rapidly, at least in terms of geological time. During the same period another mysterious phenomenon occurred, traces of which were discovered by geologists working in Italy. They found, deep in the ground, a layer rich in iridium, a metal very rare on earth; subsequently similar layers were found elsewhere on land and at the bottom of the ocean and lakes. Because the position of the layer, which was of extraterrestrial origin, indicates it was deposited at the time of the dinosaurs' disappearance, the two events have been linked.

A Long Night

Although, of course, no one can know for certain what occurred, some scientists have hypothesized that a celestial body, such as a large meteorite or asteroid, collided with the earth. The impact, carrying the force of many hydrogen bombs, destroyed the body itself as well as the portion of the earth where it hit. Great masses of rock, dirt, and water were carried into the atmosphere as fine dust, augmented by smoke from ignited forests. This immense cloud, thick and almost impenetrable to light, then rose into the highest limits of the atmosphere, shrouding the earth for months, perhaps even years. During the long night that ensued, no vegetation could grow, nor could many species of microscopic green plants survive. Their dying out, in turn, meant a decrease in the conversion of carbon dioxide to oxygen (see below). The accumulation of carbon dioxide in the atmosphere made the earth much too warm for the larger creatures who were already suffering from lack of food. Only smaller species could find enough to eat and adapt to the changing environment. The cloud very slowly settled as celestial dust on the surface of the earth, accounting for the layer of iridium found by geologists. When the sun shone again, it was upon a different earth, with a biological world largely recast. A similar but lesser catastrophe, also accompanied by the deposition of an iridium-rich layer, occurred about thirty million years ago and was also associated with extinction of some species of microscopic marine animals.

The explanation of these extinctions as the consequence of a long night is hypothetical and may not be entirely correct. But such an event would probably have been the last straw for the dinosaurs, whose numbers already had been decimated by major climatic changes. And the scenario serves to dramatize the essential role of sunlight for the life we know on earth.

Conversion of the Sun's Energy

The process by which the sun's energy is captured by plants to produce energy for cells is called *photosynthesis*. This transformation is difficult. Every object exposed to sunlight captures some of its energy as heat, but this is not what living creatures need. They need energy that can be translated into chemical reactions, and for this purpose, plants and some bacteria possess highly specialized structures.

In plants, the structures are enclosed in small green bodies, the *chloroplasts*, which fill the cells of the leaves. They use the energy of sunlight to build a sugar from water and carbon dioxide, releasing oxygen in the process. The sugar, which stores the energy, is then distributed to all cells, where the energy is converted into ATP, the energy currency. In most cells the conversion, much of which consumes oxygen, is carried out in small bodies of another type, the *mitochondria*.

Chloroplasts and mitochondria are similar: barely visible with the light microscope, they are shown by the electron microscope to be made up of folded membranes. The process by which they carry out the energetics of life can be summarized as follows: sunlight + water + carbon dioxide generates oxygen + sugar, and in turn oxygen + sugar generates water + carbon dioxide + energy. This fundamental chemistry of life produces the oxygen needed by the biological world from carbon dioxide, which existed in the atmosphere on earth before life began. In turn, most carbon dioxide now is produced from oxygen and sugar by the biological world as it performs its activities. We will see now how these energy transformations take place.

Photosynthesis

The first inkling of the existence of photosynthesis came from the observations of Joseph Priestley, an English clergyman with a keen interest in science. In 1774 he demonstrated in a two-part experiment that plants produce oxygen. First he showed that a candle burning in a closed vessel depletes its oxygen, making the air unsuitable for the life of a mouse. Then he slowly restored the life-supporting ability of the air by introducing a living sprig of mint into the vessel. Priestley, however, did not recognize that sunlight was also needed for the restoration. That need was discovered five years later by the Dutch physician Jan Ingenhousz.

Energized Electrons

The energy that drives life is carried by the electrons of molecules present in living cells. Light comes from the sun in packets called *photons,* which are of different colors ranging from red to violet; mixed together they produce the familiar white sunlight. Each photon carries considerable energy, the amount of which depends on its color: highest in violet photons, lowest in red. When a photon hits a molecule, it fuses with one of its electrons, giving it its energy. Sometimes the acquired energy causes the electron to leave the molecule, which then becomes an ion. In other cases it promotes a rearrangement of the electrons in a chemical reaction.

In photosynthesis the energy of the photons is captured and used to elevate electrons derived from water from a lower to a higher energy level (fig. 3.1). These high-energy electrons, temporarily stored in special molecules, ultimately are used to manufacture sugar, a process in which the electrons progressively release their energy until they return to water where they started. The chloroplasts, in which photosynthesis takes place, are like microscopic balloons with a double wall made up of membranes and filled with flat bags stacked on top of each other (fig. 3.2). The bags also have membranes and these are the most crucial for photosynthesis. There is within the chloroplast an inner space within the bags and an outer space called the matrix between the bags and the inner chloroplast membrane. Both the bag membrane and the chloroplast membrane are mostly impermeable, but they have channels for some ions and other substances. The outer

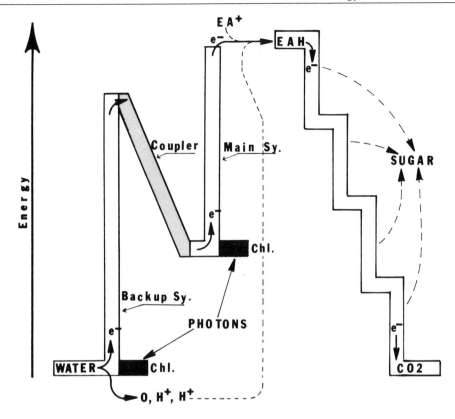

Figure 3.1. General view of photosynthesis. Electrons flow from water through the backup system to the main system and from there to the electron acceptor EA$^+$. The energy for this flow comes from the sun's photons impinging on chlorophyll molecules (Chl). The two systems are connected by coupling proteins. Removal of electrons from water is followed by release of oxygen (O) and free hydrogen ions (H$^+$). Some of these are utilized for producing EAH, the hydrogenated electron acceptor. In a subsequent reaction involving a series of steps the electrons lose energy and become bound to CO_2 to produce a sugar.

membrane of the chloroplast, permeable to many substances, plays almost no part in photosynthesis.

The photosynthetic apparatus is made up of proteins associated with the bag membranes. Molecules of *chlorophyll* trap the sun's red photons, letting all other colors through and thus appearing green. Some yellowish substances related to vitamin A are also used in photosynthesis: because they are abundant in carrots they are called *carotenoids*. Bacteria capable of photosynthesis use different light-absorbing substances, also in association with membranes.

Each light-absorbing molecule is attached to proteins forming the structure that utilizes the trapped energy. Without the proteins the light-absorbing molecules would absorb the photons but would transform their energy into heat, so that no photosynthesis would take place. In each structure the protein molecules are arrayed in an *electron transfer chain*, a sort of ladder along which the electrons

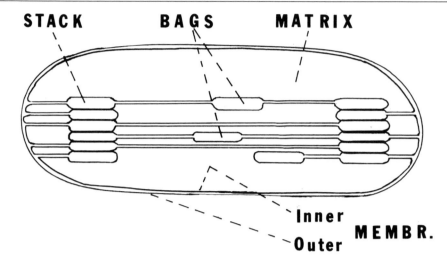

Figure 3.2. Cross section of a chloroplast, showing the various membranes and the compartments they separate.

run when they acquire energy from photons (see fig. 3.1). Each ladder has a chlorophyll molecule at one end. Chloroplasts have two ladders joined to each other, one lower, the other higher. The electrons first climb the lower ladder, called the *backup system,* and then, after receiving additional energy from another photon, they climb the second ladder, the *main system.* Here they attain the highest energy. These high-energy electrons are temporarily stored in molecules known as *electron acceptors,* positively charged molecules that we will indicate as EA^+; each of them upon receiving two electrons (which are negatively charged) is changed into EA^-.

To understand the subsequent step in this chain of events, we must look again at the first step: the extraction of electrons from water (figs. 3.3 and 3.4: L). The removal of the electrons causes water molecules to split, generating oxygen and hydrogen ions (H^+). Of these three products, the electrons end up in EA^-, and oxygen is released as gas in the chloroplast matrix. What remain are the hydrogen ions, which perform two important functions. Some combine with EA^-, changing it into EAH, uncharged. This is a high-energy molecule known as the *hydrogenated electron acceptor,* which stores part of the energy of the sun's photons as chemical energy. Other hydrogen ions are pumped into the space within the stacked bags, using energy provided by the electron transport chains (see also fig. 3.7). Their accumulation produces a high pressure because they cannot cross the bag membrane except through sparsely scattered channels connected to special enzymes. The pressurized outflow of H^+ ions through these channels causes the enzymes to produce ATP, the energy currency—another way the energy of sunlight is stored. The bag membrane plays an essential role in this process by segregating the

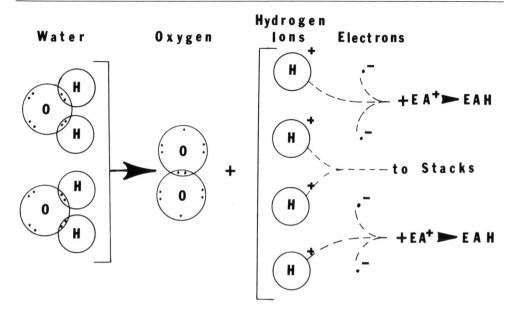

Figure 3.3. The decomposition of water in photosynthesis. Two water molecules generate one molecule of oxygen gas, four electrons, and four hydrogen ions. The four electrons together with two H+ ions are used to hydrogenate two electron acceptors (EA+) which become EAH. The remaining two electrons are accumulated in the stacks.

hydrogen ions and the oxygen resulting from the decomposition of water by the backup system. If these products were not separated, they would reunite, generating heat for which cells usually have little use. (We will see an exception below.)

Using a Single Ladder

Primitive organisms capable of photosynthesis have only the upper ladder, the main system, and cannot extract electrons from water. Rather, they extract them from molecules, such as certain sulfur derivatives, that are present only in special environments, using them to convert EA into EAH. The lower ladder, the backup system, is needed for obtaining electrons from water. The widespread availability of water explains the development of the backup system in evolution, and the adoption of the two-ladder system in almost all organisms capable of photosynthesis.

The double system, of course, is more complex than a system with a single ladder, but it works smoothly because the flow of electrons from the lower to the upper ladder is well regulated. Regulation is carried out by proteins that couple the two ladders (fig. 3.1). The regulation is destroyed by certain *herbicides*, which bind to the coupling proteins, blocking the electrons' flow from one system to the other. The block stops photosynthesis and kills the plant.

PHOTOSYNTHESIS IN CHLOROPLASTS

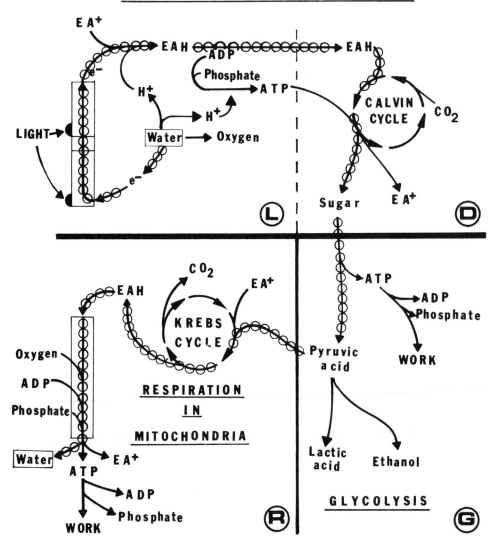

Figure 3.4. Energy flow sheet. Energy flows from sunlight to the different kinds of work to be performed: mechanical, as in muscles; chemical, to build cell constituents; electrical, for the operation of the brain and other organs. The substances required at each step are surrounded by squares; the outputs by circles. This flow sheet reflects the evolution of life on earth. It begins with the light-dependent events of photosynthesis (L), which generate oxygen and then a sugar in the dark (D); it continues with the utilization of sugar without oxygen in glycolysis (G) and terminates with the utilization of the product of glycolysis—pyruvic acid—using oxygen in respiration (R). The path of the electrons from water in L to water in R is emphasized by rows of circles.

The Electrons Lose Energy

ATP and the hydrogenated electron acceptor EAH made in the chloroplasts are utilized to make the sugar in which the energy of sunlight is permanently stored (fig. 3.4: D). The sugar, made by an ingenious, highly efficient mechanism, is a chain of *six* groups of atoms, each of which can be manufactured from carbon dioxide and water with the use of energy. The sugar is not made, however, by forming six separate groups and joining them together. Instead, one group of atoms is added to a preexisting smaller sugar made up of *five* such groups. This addition, although simple in principle, is complicated in practice: it requires fifteen steps, each one involving specialized enzymes. The energy is supplied by the hydrogenated electron acceptors (EAH) and the ATP generated in photosynthesis. The crucial step is the flow of high-energy electrons from EAH to molecules of carbon dioxide (CO_2) that are present in the atmosphere, making them suitable to become part of the sugar. The end result is that the six-group sugar is made, and the starting five-group sugar is regenerated.

The manufacture of the six-group sugar is a *cyclic process* (that is, a process that repeats itself) because the starting component, the five-group sugar, is changed by additions or manipulations to yield the six-group sugar plus itself. So the process can go on and on as long as energy and CO_2 are available. The series of reactions is known as the *Calvin cycle*, from its discoverer, Melvin Calvin. As we will see, cycles operating on the same general principle are extensively used in cells in the manufacture of many compounds. They have become widely adopted through evolution because they are economical. The starting compound is recycled and is needed only in small amounts; no waste is produced.

Distributing the Sugar's Energy

The sugar produced by photosynthesis is the main immediate source of energy for the living world. In plants the sugar produced in the leaves is distributed to the whole plant: part of it is used by the cells for energy (see below), and another part is transformed into a variety of permanent plant components, such as wood, and into food stores, such as starch; both are complex sugar derivatives. When animals eat plant products they break down these derivatives into sugars in their digestive tracts. The sugars then enter the bloodstream and go to all cells of the body.

All cells of plants or animals, as well as bacteria, use sugars as a source of energy which they transfer to ATP in order to make the energy readily utilizable. This occurs in a stepwise process that is broadly the reverse of that by which the sugar was formed from sunlight energy, water, and carbon dioxide. Using oxygen, the sugar is transformed into carbon dioxide and water while ATP is formed. The end products generated in this transformation are the same as would be obtained if the sugar were burned. The difference is that in the cells the chemical energy of the sugar is retained, whereas burning wastes the sugar's energy as heat.

The utilization of the sugar to generate ATP occurs in two main phases. The first, called *glycolysis* (that is, splitting of the sugar), does not require oxygen (fig. 3.4: G) and extracts only a small fraction of the sugar's energy. The second phase, *respiration* (fig. 3.4: R), requires oxygen and extracts from the sugar the full amount of energy available.

Glycolysis

Glycolysis is a process that occurs in all cells. In cells that live without air it is the only method by which sugars are utilized. This is the case, for instance, of certain bacteria that live in the water of deep marshes from which oxygen has been removed by other organisms. Glycolysis is also the process by which yeast thrive in the brewers' vats without air or oxygen. In eukaryotic cells glycolysis takes place in the cell's cytoplasm, although oxygen is present. The essence of glycolysis is the splitting of the six-group sugar into two halves; some energy is released in the process and is transferred to ATP. The final product of glycolysis is *pyruvic acid*, which still retains a great deal of the sugar's energy and is a central compound in energy utilization in cells.

In life without oxygen, pyruvic acid undergoes limited changes; one of the final products is *ethyl alcohol* (ethanol). For instance, yeast growing under oxygen-free conditions produces large amounts of alcohol, which is distilled to produce fine alcohol or alcoholic beverages. Another product derived from pyruvic acid in the absence of oxygen is *lactic acid*, which accumulates in muscles during intense physical work, when oxygen supply cannot keep pace with sugar consumption, and causes muscle cramps.

A New Cycle

In life with oxygen the energy left in pyruvic acid is fully extracted. The acid is injected into a cyclic enzyme pathway (fig. 3.4: R), the first such cycle ever recognized. Called the *Krebs cycle* because it was discovered in 1937 by Hans Krebs, this cycle and other reactions connected with it take place in mitochondria (see chapter 1 and figs. 3.5 and 3.6). Like chloroplasts, mitochondria have two main spaces—one within the folds of the inner mitochondrial membrane, which correspond to the bags of chloroplasts, and the other, the matrix between the folds and the mitochondrial membrane. The nine enzymatic steps of the Krebs cycle occur within the matrix, generating from sugar both ATP and EAH similar to those of photosynthesis. The hydrogenated electron acceptors in turn inject their electrons into an electron transport chain similar to those present in the chloroplasts (fig. 3.7). The difference is that in the mitochondria the electrons *release* their energy, (which they obtained from the breakdown of the sugar), whereas in the chloroplasts they *acquire* energy from the absorbed photons. The energy released by the electrons in the mitochondria is spent in pumping hydrogen ions into the

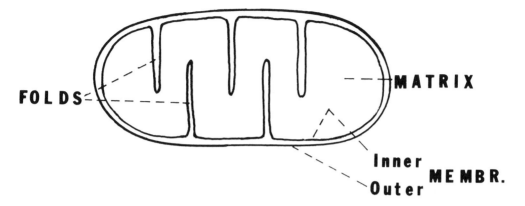

Figure 3.5. Cross section of a mitochondrion showing the membranes, the folds of the inner membrane, and the various spaces.

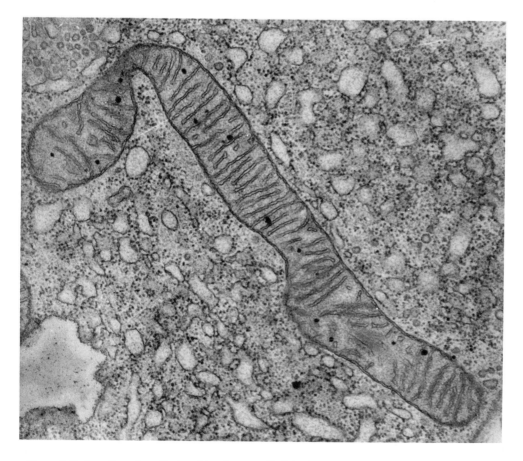

Figure 3.6. A section of a mitochondrion from a cell of the human pancreas. Courtesy of G. Palade.

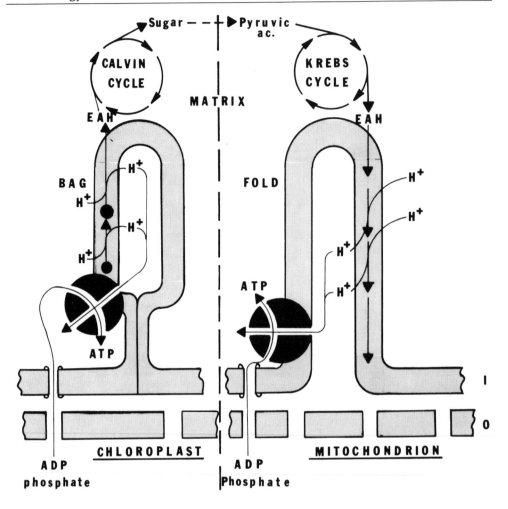

Figure 3.7. Chloroplasts and mitochondria are similar. The stacks of the chloroplasts correspond to the folds of mitochondira; both enclose spaces where H+ ions accumulate. The outflow of these ions through the ATP-making enzyme causes the conversion of ADP + phosphate to ATP. The chemical cycles unfurl in both cases in the matrix. The flow of electrons, however, proceed in opposite directions to EA+ in chloroplasts to form EAH, and from EAH in mitochondria to form ATP and regenerate EA+.

space within the membrane folds. As in chloroplasts, the pressure of the accumulated ions is then used for ATP production. The electrons, having released their energy, are finally returned to oxygen, which is dissolved in the watery liquid of the matrix. As oxygen atoms receive electrons, they combine with some of the accumulated hydrogen ions and form water. The overall process is the reversal of photosynthesis.

ATP produced in the Krebs cycle accumulates within the mitochondrial matrix and is then exported to the surrounding cytoplasm through channels that cross the inner mitochondrial membrane, as do several other substances that are part of the Krebs cycle. Their transport is helped by the imbalance of hydrogen ions on the two sides of the membrane. The intense traffic through the membrane channels is coordinated in such a way that it causes no imbalance of substances or of electric charges between the two sides of the membrane.

Respiration as the Inverse of Photosynthesis

The relatedness between photosynthesis and respiration can be recognized in many details (fig. 3.7). For instance, some proteins of the electron transfer chain are identical in mitochondria and in chloroplasts. In both particles the electron transport chains are associated with membranes that are equivalent: the folds of the mitochondrial membrane correspond to the bags of chloroplasts. Hydrogen ions accumulate in the space within the folds in mitochondria, as they accumulate in the space within the bags in chloroplasts. In both particles hydrogen ions leave that space by interacting with enzymes that produce ATP, and in both cases the enzymes are located on the matrix side of the membrane. The crucial difference is the direction of the electron flow. In photosynthesis, electrons energized by the sun's photons flow up from water to the final electron acceptors to which they yield their energy. In mitochondria high-energy electrons derived from the hydrogenated electron acceptors flow downward to oxygen, which is converted into water and the released energy transferred to ATP. The possibility of inverting the electron flow is not surprising because each step of electron transfer can go in either direction depending on which side has more energy.

The complete utilization of a sugar (such as glucose) in the presence of oxygen is extremely efficient: it produces eighteen times as much ATP as glycolysis alone in the absence of oxygen. The overall yield obtained with oxygen corresponds to nearly 40 percent of the chemical energy present in the sugar. This is a very high yield indeed, unmatchable by manmade devices. The high efficiency of respiration explains why in evolution life turned from a form able to exist without oxygen to one utilizing oxygen. This could happen, however, only after photosynthesis produced enough oxygen to build up a sufficient concentration in the atmosphere.

Coupling and Uncoupling

In both chloroplasts and mitochondria the flow of electrons through the electron transport chain provides the energy for the accumulation of hydrogen ions in the membrane-bound space of the bags or the folds (fig. 3.7). Electron transport and accumulation of hydrogen ions are coupled. If the accumulation of hydrogen ions is impossible, no ATP is formed, although all needed enzymes may be present and ready to work. For instance, broken mitochondria do not make ATP. Its production is also prevented by poisons (such as 2,4-dinitrophenol) that make the inner membrane freely permeable to hydrogen ions, and the energy of the electrons is transformed into heat.

Conversion of chemical energy into heat brought about by uncoupling is useless under most conditions. An exception is found in animals during hibernation, when they produce heat in a special kind of fat tissue, the brown fat. In winter, these animals do not use their muscles, which normally produce heat from ATP. Rather, heat is produced directly in specialized mitochondria when a protein with the properties of an ionophore enters the fold membranes, making them leaky for hydrogen ions. A similar device is used by cold-water fish for keeping the brain warm and active (see chapter 16).

Chloroplasts and Mitochondria: What Are They?

Chloroplasts and mitochondria have properties so different from those of the other constituents of a cell that the question arises: what are they really? The answer is surprising: although so essential to eukaryotic cells, they are actually fairly independent of them. Their shapes and compositions strongly suggest that they are related to bacteria. Presumably they derive from bacterialike cells that sometime during evolution colonized a primitive eukaryotic cell. These bodies are cells within cells: each is enclosed in its own membrane; each contains a circular DNA molecule, similar to those of bacteria, which replicates independently of the DNA of the cell nucleus; each contains the entire machinery for making proteins.

Most proteins found in mitochondria or chloroplasts, however, are made in the cell's cytoplasm on instructions of nuclear genes and then reach the bodies. These proteins have as addresses special amino acid sequences that bind to receptors present on the membranes of the chloroplasts or mitochondria. The receptors are the gates through which the cytoplasmic proteins enter the body. The address tells not only the destination of a protein but also whether it should reach into the matrix or remain connected to the membrane. Only a few proteins are made within these small bodies upon instruction of their own genes; and these genes are controlled by nuclear genes. These bodies, therefore, although of independent origin, are subservient to the needs of the cells in which they reside.

The Trapped Chloroplast

Eukaryotic cells must have become associated with the prokaryotic precursors of chloroplasts and mitochondria at a very early stage in their evolution (fig. 3.8). In fact, the genes of chloroplasts and mitochondria are very similar in all eukaryotic cells. The chloroplasts of today's plant cells are remnants of the earliest living cells, those that existed before there was oxygen in the atmosphere. At that time the energy of sunlight was utilized in a crude way to modify molecules present on the early earth (see chapter 20). Sugarlike substances generated in this way could

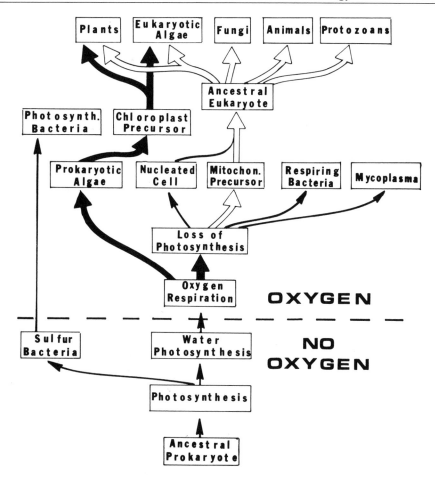

Figure 3.8. Origin of chloroplasts and mitochondria. The path of respiration is shown by double lines, that of photosynthesis by heavy black lines.

be utilized by the early prokaryotes, but were extremely scarce. The development of life received a great boost from photosynthesis, which allowed cells to make sugars with much greater efficiency.

We can deduce the properties of the primitive photosynthetic cells by examining the prokaryotic cells that are today capable of photosynthesis. These cells comprise two main groups: single-celled (prokaryotic) algae and photosynthetic bacteria. The single-celled algae carry out photosynthesis more or less like plant cells: they use chlorophyll, and their photosynthetic apparatus is contained in foldings of the cell membrane, which correspond to the bags of chloroplasts. Present-day photosynthetic bacteria, in contrast, are quite different, the most surprising difference being that far from producing oxygen, they are killed by it. They possess the main photosynthetic system, that is, the upper ladder of the chloroplasts, but no backup system, or lower ladder, so they cannot split water.

Instead they extract electrons from molecules with chemical properties similar to those of water, such as sulfur derivatives. Some bacteria, for instance, use hydrogen sulfide, the stink gas. In hydrogen sulfide (H_2S) sulfur replaces the oxygen present in water (H_2O). Because sulfur is chemically related to oxygen and can replace it in many compounds, H_2S and H_2O have similar properties. Photosynthetic bacteria that use H_2S instead of water produce sulfur instead of oxygen, and sulfur, which is not a gas, accumulates within the cells. Some of these bacteria exist in exceptional environments, such as volcanic hot pools, which bubble from deep reservoirs lacking oxygen but rich in H_2S. These bacteria have also developed the ability to live at very high temperatures, which would kill all other living cells.

Because modern photosynthetic bacteria are so different, we may conclude that today's chloroplasts derived from a photosynthetic prokaryote related to modern unicellular prokaryotic algae.

Mitochondrial Precursors

The mitochondria of today's eukaryotic cells derived from a different kind of primitive prokaryotic cell: a respiring prokaryote. During the evolution of life, such creatures probably arose after the photosynthetic cells had become abundant. Sugars, or sugarlike compounds, as well as oxygen, were then available in the environment. Cells that could utilize efficiently these ready-made substances did not need photosynthesis and therefore could safely lose their capability for it. Perhaps it was even advantageous because making unnecessary proteins is a burden for cells. So the photosynthetic machine progressively turned into a respiration machine. The change gave these cells the ability to utilize an abundant source of food, allowing them to spread enormously in most environments.

Joining Efforts

Because eukaryotic cells have a glycolytic system, it is thought that their precursors existed when sugars were avilable but there was very little oxygen. These early eukaryotes may have gained access to food by engulfing and digesting prokaryotic cells, as amoebas (single-celled eukaryotes) do today. This feeding method, made possible by the flexibility of the cell membrane (see chapter 2), is very efficient and may account for the spread of these cells on earth.

When enough oxygen had accumulated in the atmosphere, it became highly advantageous for the primitive eukaryotic cells to use it in order to utilize sugar energy fully. This ability was acquired the easy way, by incorporating a prokaryote already able to do so. We can only guess how this happened. Perhaps a respiring prokaryote engulfed as food survived by chance, colonized the eukaryotic cell, and became a mitochondrion. The acquisition of a respiring prokaryote probably occurred only once or perhaps a few times in the history of life, for all mitochondria present today in animal cells seem to descend from the same progenitor. They have common properties, the most striking of which are the special features of the genetic code (see chapter 4). Mitochondria of fungi and plants might have been acquired in a separate event because they are somewhat different from those of animals in the general organization of their DNA, although they have similar genes.

Mitochondria differ from most present-day bacteria, which suggests that the prokaryotic precursor of mitochondria was an ancestor of the present-day prokaryotes or belonged to a branch that did not undergo great development. Bacteria with unusual properties that might be related to such a precursor exist today— the *archaebacteria*. The lineage derived from the lucky eukaryotic cell that was colonized became predominant over all others, generating all current eukaryotes. Its success is explained by its ability to utilize available food energy much more completely through respiration.

Plants probably acquired the photosynthetic prokaryotes that became their chloroplasts in a similar manner. It is likely that the acquisition of the chloroplast followed the acquisition of the mitochondrion because all eukaryotic cells have mitochondria, whereas only some have chloroplasts (fig. 3.8). The considerable similarity of present-day chloroplasts to some present-day prokaryotes suggests that the prokaryote was already fully evolved when it was captured as a chloroplast and has not changed much since then. But again this is only a guess.

The Value of Togetherness

The hypothesis that one or two prokaryotic cells were incorporated into a eukaryotic cell may seem farfetched. That the hypothesis is not implausible, however, is shown by frequent examples in which a prokaryote, or even a eukaryote, becomes a guest inside a eukaryotic cell to the benefit of both—a situation called *symbiosis*, which means living together. For instance, corals, which are primitive marine animals, contain within their bodies free-living photosynthetic prokaryotes inherited at birth. The association is beneficial because the prokaryote supplies the coral with carbohydrates and oxygen through photosynthesis, while in turn the coral supplies the prokaryote with other nutrients, a suitable environment, and protection.

Another kind of association between a photosynthesizing and a nonphotosynthesizing organism has enormous significance for the living world. It is the association of leguminous plants, such as alfalfa or beans, with soil bacteria capable of converting atmospheric nitrogen into foodstuff—*nitrogen fixation*. The association is initiated by the bacteria, which actively invade the roots of the plants. The plant in turn reacts by producing special root nodules in which the bacteria settle. Both partners benefit because the bacteria make available to the plant nitrogenous compounds essential for making proteins and are in turn supplied with the sugars manufactured by the plant through photosynthesis. The association has had important consequences for agriculture and food production.

Saving for a Rainy Day

During the long history of life on earth the balance between consumption of carbon dioxide + water and production of oxygen + sugars has always shifted in the direction of production. Only a fraction of the sugars produced was returned to carbon dioxide and water. A large part remained as sugar and its derivatives in the form of—among other things—wood buried in the soil that became almost pure carbon (coal) and enormous numbers of microorganisms buried in the bottom of seas that became crude oil. The buried sugars left free an equivalent amount of oxygen (with which they would otherwise have reacted, producing carbon dioxide and water). The free oxygen accumulated in the atmosphere, building a substantial layer over the earth's crust. The coal, the oil, and the oxygen were, so to speak, stores set aside by nature for a rainy day.

The emergence of the human species has drastically changed the situation. Human beings have burned wood, coal, and oil, producing large amounts of carbon dioxide and water and using oxygen at a high rate. The rainy day arrived. This consumption is not only frenzied but wasteful: it uses great quantities of the accumulated energy stores not to build living creatures but to produce heat. There are fears that carbon dioxide production by human activities will far exceed utilization by plants. If so, carbon dioxide would accumulate in the atmosphere, creating a "greenhouse effect": light from the sun would reach the earth unhindered, but loss of heat from the earth would be reduced. As a result the earth would warm up and the polar ice caps would melt, causing an ecological disaster.

It is not clear whether we have yet reached the point of imbalance. The amount of carbon dioxide in the atmosphere is continuously monitored on the mountain Mauna Loa in Hawaii, as well as in the Antarctic. A slow increase has been observed in the last twenty years at Mauna Loa, amounting to about 20 parts per million (fig. 3.9); the increase in the Antarctic has been smaller, reflecting lesser industrial development in the Southern Hemisphere. The observed increase is about half what would be expected from the amount of carbon dioxide released into the atmosphere; the other half becomes dissolved in the oceans. The increase corresponds to a small fraction of the total carbon dioxide present in the atmosphere (about 340 parts per million), but its accumulation may be viewed as a threatening trend.

The amount of carbon dioxide released annually is staggering—about 20 trillion kilograms. It is unclear what consequences it will have, however, because the amount of carbon dioxide in the atmosphere can be altered by many factors. The present amount is probably fairly low in terms of the earth's history: much

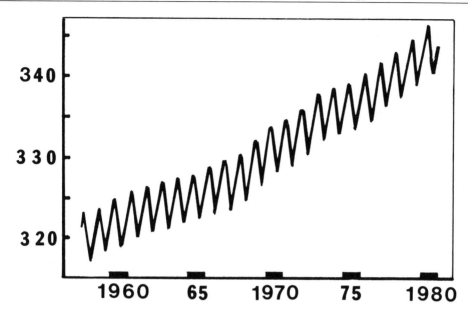

Figure 3.9. Changes in CO_2 concentration in the atmosphere measured at Mauna Loa in Hawaii. A continuously increasing trend is superimposed on an annual variation. (From M. J. Rycroft, *Nature* 295:190–91 [1982].)

was present in the early atmosphere and large quantities were released by volcanic activity. Both life-dependent and life-independent mechanisms continuously change the amount of carbon dioxide. If it increases, for instance, the subsequent increase in the temperature of the earth has compensating effects: carbon dioxide is removed more rapidly because photosynthesis becomes more active and also because more carbon dioxide disappears by reaction with rocks. Fixation of carbon dioxide to rocks, in turn, increases photosynthesis by increasing the nutrients in the oceans. This favors the multiplication of the microscopic ocean plants which carry out about half of the earth's photosynthesis. Without these regulatory events, life on earth might be very different from what it is now, because the intensity of the sun's radiation has probably increased since life began by as much as 25 percent. Without some form of compensation, the earth's temperature might today be in the 50° centigrade range. But in fact, the average temperature of the earth appears to have remained fairly constant.

The changes induced by human activity are superimposed on these complex natural changes, and like them, the manmade changes will be resisted by the regulatory mechanisms. Nevertheless, a concern remains: these mechanisms operate very slowly in comparison to the rate at which carbon dioxide is presently generated by human activity. Regulation, therefore, may not be able to keep up with overproduction. Everything considered, it is difficult to predict what the overall consequences of enhanced carbon dioxide production will be. And although they may not be of concern to us today, they may acquire great significance in the future.

Another important consequence of high energy consumption is apparent—the enormous increase in the human population. This is a vicious circle: the increased consumption of stored energy has allowed an increase in the number of humans on earth; in turn the demand for new energy has increased. The process may continue for a while, increasing both the size of the human population and the consumption of energy resources, but eventually the energy stores will inevitably dwindle. Then the process will *have* to reverse itself—a painful prospect if it is left to the forces of nature and the ravages of starvation and exposure.

Two other extreme scenarios remain. One, scientists may succeed in harnessing the energy of the atoms, achieving sustained nuclear fusion, a possibly cleaner source than that based on fission and practically inexhaustible. This energy would serve as a replacement for the exhausted stores originally provided by photosynthesis. Or second, a nuclear war will break out, perhaps over competition for remaining energy sources. This would make the availability of energy stores irrelevant: few people would be left to utilize them, and the balance of nature would be reestablished. Of course, what the conditions of life would be for the remaining humans is another question.

CHAPTER 4

The Language of DNA

We learned in Chapter 1 that DNA is the source and master of all heredity. How it is able to rule all forms of life is directly dependent on its composition and structure. To understand fully the nature of heredity, then, we must first examine the chemistry of DNA.

DNA as a Chemical

The gigantic molecules of DNA must form only from the association of great numbers of smaller molecules. This fact was borne out by the studies of DNA's constitution that were carried out in the 1940s and 1950s, before its biological significance was recognized. At that time DNA seemed just another natural product, rather messy to work with and therefore a challenge to biochemists. These studies established that DNA is made up of four *bases* designated as A, G, T, and C (for *adenine, guanine, thymine,* and *cytosine*), a sugar (*deoxyribose*), and phosphate, all connected by chemical bonds. The simplicity of the chemical composition is astonishing in view of the incredible variety and complexity of information it encodes, determining and orchestrating the features of all living organisms from viruses to humans.

Many early attempts to explain how the chemical constituents are arranged in DNA were unsuccessful. A striking regularity, however, was discovered in DNAs from many sources: there are always equal parts of A and T, and of G and C. Although this constancy was a strong hint that DNA has a regular organization, its nature was not revealed until studies were made of the effects of X rays on strings of dried crystalline DNA. In these strings the DNA molecules are aligned side by side, parallel to each other. The X rays, upon hitting a string, scatter in many directions. A mathematical analysis of the pattern of scattering demonstrated that a DNA molecule is a spiral and gave information about its dimensions and its pitch. On the basis of this information, James Watson and Francis Crick, working at the University of Cambridge in 1953, solved the enigma of the structure of DNA. They showed that a molecule of DNA is constructed like a zipper: it has two *strands*, each made up of a string of hooks (the bases) attached to a ribbon of alternating molecules of sugar and phosphate; the two strands are coiled around each other in a *double helix*. Usually the helix is right-handed, or twisted like a right-handed screw (an important exception will be discussed later). A direction can be assigned to each DNA strand, based upon the orientation of the sugar-phosphate linkages that make up the strand's "spine." Thus any strand of DNA can be represented by an arrow. In the two strands that make up the double helix, the directions of the two spines are always opposite, so that the double helix can be represented as two parallel lines pointing in opposite directions. This directionality is important because it is recognized by enzymes crucial for DNA's role as master of heredity. As we will see below, all these enzymes interact with a strand and follow it in only one direction.

The strands are held together by weak associations (mainly hydrogen bonds) between the bases, as the strands of a zipper are held together by its opposing hooks. A on one strand always associates with T on the other strand, and G with C (fig. 4.1), forming the two *base pairs*, A-T and G-C. As a result, the amounts of A and T and those of G and C are always equal. The strands coil around each other because of the shapes of their constituents. The two strands make a complete turn in a length of DNA containing ten base pairs. We will see that this coiling has important consequences.

Because connections that hold the two bases of a pair—and thus the two strands—together, are weak, the pairs can readily be dissolved and re-formed. This is another property important to the functions of DNA. A long double helix nevertheless is very stable because the bonds between the two strands are so numerous. Similarly, in a zipper the connection between any two hooks is weak, but all the hooks together make a strong association. The stability of the double helix protects the bases from damage by many enzymes and chemical agents. The DNA helix thus combines the advantages of both stability and plasticity.

The regular association of the bases in pairs suggests that the bases are signals in a code in much the same way that dots and dashes are used in the Morse code. The biological properties of DNA do in fact reside in the *sequence* of the four bases, that is, how they follow each other on a strand, in the same way as the meaning of the Morse code resides in the sequence of dots and dashes. The DNA sequence represents genetic instructions that are precisely maintained from one generation to another through replication in which new DNA molecules are formed from existing ones. In the DNA double helix the bases are not accessible; rather, they are bound to each other in pairs and are buried in the center of the helix. The sequence of the bases cannot be read until the strands are separated. This is what happens when DNA's genetic instructions are utilized by cells.

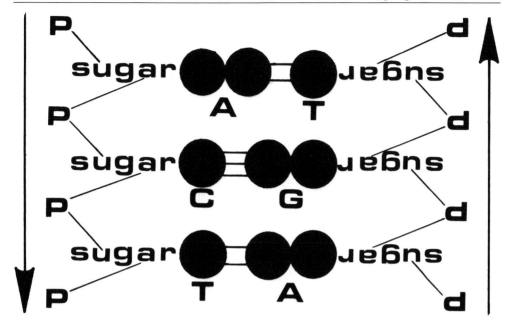

Figure 4.1. The DNA double helix is made up of two base pairs, AT and GC. Each pair has a member with a double ring (A or G) and a member with a single ring (T or C), so the overall length of the two pairs is constant. Hydrogen bonds, shown as lines, connect the bases in each pair; the GC pair has three bonds and is more strongly connected. Each base is connected to a sugar (deoxyribose), forming a nucleoside. The sugars are connected by phosphate groups (P), forming a continuous strand. The group made up of a base, a sugar, and a phosphate is called a nucleotide. Each phosphate is connected in different ways to the sugar above or below it. This inequality gives a direction to the strand (arrow). The two strands have opposite directions.

Replication and Complementarity

A DNA double helix must replicate—it must produce copies identical to itself in order to pass on the genetic information it contains. The mechanism of replication, a process exclusive to DNA and to some RNAs, is based on the unique association of the bases to make pairs: A-T and G-C. This association determines a one-to-one relation between the two strands: given the sequence of the bases on one strand, the sequence on the other strand is completely determined. Because these strands are not identical—where one has A the other has T, and where one has G, the other has C—they are said to be *complementary* to each other.

Complementarity is the basis of replication; a strand generates a complementary strand and remains associated with it in a new double helix (fig. 4.2). If the original helix is ↑S-↓S′ where ↓S′ is the strand complementary to strand ↑S, replication generates two new strands, ↑s and ↓s′, thus producing two new double helixes, ↑S-↓s′ and ↑s-↓S′, in which ↓s′ is complementary to ↑S and

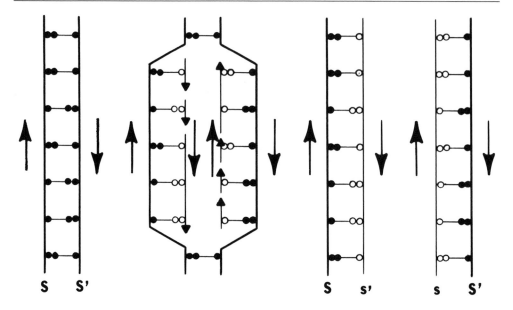

Figure 4.2. Replication of a DNA helix. For the sake of simplicity, the double helix is shown as two straight complementary strands—S and S' (left). They have opposite directions (arrows) and are connected by the base pairs. In replication (center) each strand builds a new complementary strand (thin lines, open circles) beginning at some point along the double helix. One half of the strand grows away from the point of origin and is continuous; the other half grows toward the point of origin and is in pieces. At the end of replication two new strands have been made (s', s, thin lines, open circles), which remain connected to the preexisting ones, generating two identical helixes (Ss', sS'), each with one old and one new strand.

↑s to ↓S'. In each helix the old and the new strands are associated as in the original helix. The overall replication of DNA results in the formation of two "daughter" double helixes, identical to each other and to the preexisting "parental" double helix. The principle of complementarity for reproducing information is familiar from an everyday example: to produce a photographic copy of a document we first make a negative (the complementary copy) and then a positive, which, being a negative of the first negative, is identical to the original document. The positive copy is twice complementary to the original.

The mechanics of replication is fairly simple: it is initiated by proteins that bind to the paired bases, at special sequences at the *origin of replication,* loosening their association. Then the replication enzyme comes into play. It is called *polymerase* (the ending *-ase* always indicates an enzyme) because it assembles a structure from many elementary constituents. The polymerase matches bases to the first available base of one strand. When a complementary base is presented, it is held in place, whereas noncomplementary bases are rejected. Then new bases are matched to the second base of the strand, and a complementary one is joined to the previous one using ATP energy. Bases are not presented alone: each is attached to a sugar (deoxyribose) and a phosphate group. The entire complex is called a *nucleotide*. Connecting the sugar of one complex to the phosphate of the next automatically forms the ribbon which is the backbone of the new strand. The process goes on serially until it reaches the end of the strand to be replicated. The same process occurs independently on the other strand, but proceeding in the opposite direction. An interesting aspect of replication is that a new DNA strand is always initiated by a short piece of RNA, which is later removed and replaced by DNA. As we will see later, this characteristic has important implications for the evolution of DNA.

In order to keep the genetic instructions unaltered through replication, it is important that the base sequences of the daughter helixes be exactly like those of the original, parental helix. If a wrong base is inserted in one of the new strands, the mistake, called a *mutation*, is perpetuated at subsequent replications. There is, however, an effective device for minimizing errors, the *proofreading function* of the enzyme that carries out replication. Each time a new base is added the enzyme tests whether it fits correctly. Only the proper base fits well; any others cause a noticeable mismatch and are removed by the enzyme. This automatic testing and correcting mechanism ensures that replication is extremely accurate. The error rate is very low: among a hundred million bases forming a new strand there is, on the average, only one incorrect base.

It must be emphasized that errors do occur and moreover have an important role: they are essential for evolution. Without these mistakes the type of life we know on earth would not exist (see chapter 20). The error rate can be considered a compromise between the need to keep the DNA sequence constant from one generation to the next and the opposite need to create enough innovation and variation for the purpose of evolution.

Not all DNA found in nature is in the form of a double helix. Some viruses have DNA molecules made up of only one strand (*single-stranded DNA*). This DNA replicates basically like double helical DNA: first, a new strand ($\downarrow$ s') complementary to the original one ($\uparrow$ S) is made, generating a double helix ($\uparrow$ S- $\downarrow$ s'). This double-stranded DNA is used like a stamping machine and generates many single strands as complements of the new strand. Thus they are like the original strand— $\uparrow$ S. This is an important consequence of the beautiful complementarity of DNA: twice complementary = identical. The new strands are assembled into new viral particles as they are made.

Repair of Damaged DNA

Another important consequence of the presence of two strands in DNA is that it allows repairs. DNA of cells is frequently damaged by any of a variety of injurious agents—some that permeate our environment, such as the cosmic radiation that comes from outer space or the ultraviolet radiation from the sun, and others that are produced by human activity, such as radiation and chemicals. The damages inflicted are of different kinds: a strand may be cut, a base may be altered, or two bases may be joined. Because any one of these damages can impair the survival or function of the cell in which it occurs, it is fortunate that DNA has developed the means for making repairs.

The double helix is as essential for this process as it is for replication. Viruses that contain a single-stranded DNA are very easily killed by chemicals or radiation to which double-stranded DNA is resistant. When a virus's DNA strand is cut, the two pieces remain separated for good; the virus is dead. But when a strand is cut in double helical DNA, the intact complementary strand holds the two pieces together (fig. 4.3: A). In one type of repair, a process is set in motion that reconnects the cut strand, reestablishing its continuity. Other types of repair may do just the opposite: they may start by demolishing a piece of one strand. For instance, when ultraviolet light alters a base or fuses two bases together on the same strand, the damaged segment is first demolished and then rebuilt as a complement of the intact strand, as in replication (fig. 4.3: B).

In only one case are damaged bases directly repaired, and it involves an elegant mechanism. An enzyme captures photons of blue light from the sun and uses their energy to undo abnormal bonds made between adjacent bases by the sun's ultraviolet light. This type of repair can take place equally well in double-stranded or single-stranded DNA.

Because organisms have been bathed in ultraviolet light from the sun through the long history of their evolution, the repair of its damage has become extremely effective. Only one in two thousand damages in bacterial or phage DNA persists unrepaired; the others disappear. The importance of this repair is best demonstrated in some people in whom it fails. They are affected by the disease *xeroderma pigmentosum* (meaning pigmented dry skin), which is the consequence of a hereditary defect. The areas of the skin ordinarily exposed to sunlight, such as the face, become very thick, dark, and scaly, and in time develop multiple cancers. The ultraviolet light causes alteration of the DNA bases, and they are not corrected. The accumulation of unrepaired damage alters the genes of the skin cells, and the altered genes change some into cancer cells (see chapter 15).

DNA's Tight-Packed Quality

Molecules of DNA are very long, as could be inferred from the great viscosity of DNA solutions. The extent of their length, however, was appreciated only in the sixties, when it was first measured directly. One method used radioactive tracer technology. Bacteria are grown in a broth containing radioactive substances that become incorporated into their DNA when it replicates. After the bacteria have multiplied several times, their DNA is extracted and isolated in pure form. A thin solution of the DNA is then run over a glass slide, so that its molecules become stretched and oriented lengthwise in the direction of flow. After the slide is dried, it is covered with a thin layer of photographic emulsion and kept in the darkness

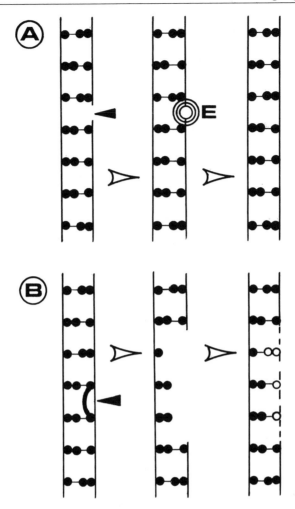

Figure 4.3. Examples of repair of DNA damages. In A, a strand is broken between two bases (pointer); repair enzymes (E) fill the gap and rebuild an intact strand. In B, ultraviolet light has caused two adjacent single-ring bases to fuse (pointer). Repair enzymes demolish a length of the damaged strand including the fused bases; then they refill it with a new piece (dashed), which is made as the complement of the intact strand. In this way the damaged strand is reconstituted exactly as it was before being damaged.

for several months. During this time radiation emitted by the radioactive atoms generates silver grains in the emulsion, producing what is called an *autoradiograph*. When the emulsion is developed one sees arrays of black dots along the entire length of the DNA molecules, which can then be measured.

With this technique it was found that the DNA of a virus or a bacterium is about a thousand times as long as the viral particle or the cell in which it is enclosed. The same is true of the DNA of other living organisms. For instance, the DNA of a human chromosome is two to three centimeters long, whereas the nucleus of the cells in which it is enclosed has the diameter of only a thousandth of a centimeter.

The DNA of an organism is so long because its information is contained in a linear, one-dimensional form—the sequence of the bases. The products generated by this information, the proteins, contain the information in three-dimensional form, however, and are therefore much more compact. Owing to its great length, DNA is tightly packed in all organisms. In viruses it is coiled like a ball of yarn. In the chromosomes of plants or animals it is packed in a series of coils in association with special proteins, the *histones*. These DNA-protein complexes are called *chromatin* because in tissue sections they take up dyes. They form microscopic beads regularly connected to each other by the DNA itself, giving the appearance of a string of pearls (fig. 4.4). Each bead contains a core of histones with the DNA wound around it. In bacteria also the DNA has a comparable regular arrangement around different protein cores.

DNA Rings

The studies of bacterial DNA dried on slides provided a surprising result: it is a double helix closed into a ring. Each strand has no beginning and no end; the two strands are regularly intertwined, as in other DNAs. Subsequently many other small DNAs, such as those of some viruses and mitochondria, were also found to be ring-shaped. The existence of DNA in the shape of a ring is not merely a curiosity. It reveals an important aspect of DNA biology that was discovered when investi-

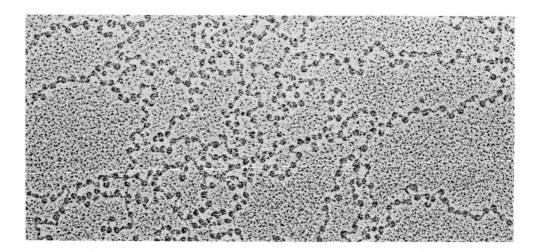

Figure 4.4. Chromatin from a fly. It is made up of beads of equal size regularly spaced on a DNA helix, which is the thread connecting the beads. Magnified 100,000 times. Courtesy of S. L. McNight and O. L. Miller.

gators tried to explain how these molecules replicate while retaining their ring shape.

The ability of these molecules to replicate regularly seems surprising because during replication the strands of the double helix must separate while new strands are built alongside them. At the end of replication the two original strands are completely separated, each with a different daughter molecule. In ring-shaped molecules such a separation should not happen: the strands should remain intertwined because there is no weak spot where they could open. This can be easily demonstrated by twisting two strings around each other and then tying the ends of each string.

In a DNA ring, the two strands can separate only if one is cut, but there is no evidence that a permanent cut is made during replication. The paradox was solved when special *swivel enzymes* were discovered: they cut one strand, allow it to unwind a little, and then reseal it, making many temporary cuts instead of a permanent one. When a cut is made, the intact strand slips through it, removing one turn of the double helix; thus the two parental strands become less and less intertwined as replication proceeds. Each new strand winds around one of the separated parental strands. When replication is completed the two daughter rings are released free. These enzymes work without spending energy: they use the energy of the cut bond to restore it.

Because its replication would appear to be so difficult, it seems surprising that circular DNA is common in simple organisms. But in fact the circular shape is favorable because it avoids a major problem associated with the replication of linear DNA: how both ends can be replicated completely. The problem arises from the fact that in a DNA double helix the two strands have opposite directions and replication can proceed in only one direction on each strand. If replication starts in the middle of a DNA molecule, as is usual, it will completely copy the right-hand part of one strand and the left-hand part of the other. Both new strands will grow *away* from the starting point. But in the other halves the new strand must grow *toward* the starting point; these halves are made as short pieces which begin at various places along the parental strands and then are joined (see fig. 4.2, center diagram). For *complete* replication of these two halves a piece of each new strand would have to start at the very end of the strand it copies. But apparently this is impossible, so replication would be incomplete at the two ends of the DNA molecules. Circular DNA avoids this problem because it has no ends. In linear DNAs the problem has been solved by a variety of devices that add to the complexity of replication.

Once the swivel enzymes were identified, it was unexpectedly recognized that they are also needed in the replication of cellular linear DNAs. Because these DNAs are so long, they become tightly entangled, forming knots and loops. In eukaryotic cells these loops are not free, but are tightly connected to the nuclear envelope. Each loop, then, is equivalent to a ring and requires swivel enzymes for its replication.

It was also discovered that the DNA helix not only must be loosened during replication but at times must be tightened, using a second kind of swivel enzyme present in cells. If at the end of replication some part of a daughter double helix is too loose, the enzyme brings it to the normal state of winding. This eliminates a problem of underwound helixes: the strain of the bonds between bases makes them accessible to cutting enzymes or damaging chemicals.

DNA as the Carrier of Information

DNA, whether of a virus, a bacterium, or the cellular chromosomes of larger organisms, contains the *genetic information* that specifies the hereditary characteristics of the creature of which it is a part. This information is contained in *genes*, which are segments of DNA, or in some viruses, RNA. All DNA molecules contain more than one gene, and often hundreds or thousands of them. Not recognizable by looking at DNA, even in the electron microscope, genes classically have been identified by studying the changes produced in the organism when its DNA is altered. More recently it became possible to identify them by determining the sequence of the bases, which have special arrangements around genes. Each gene contains the information for the amino acid sequence of a protein molecule which is said to be *specified* by the gene. Through the proteins the genes determine the characteristics of the cells—they are the units of heredity.

The DNA of a virus, a bacterium, or a cell is the total of the genes of the organism and constitutes its *genome*, the characteristics of which are clarified by the study of inheritance. Viruses or bacteria which have a single copy of the genome, are said to be *haploid*, and eukaryotic cells, with two copies, are called *diploid*. The two copies of a gene in a cell are identical except for occasional limited differences. When the copies show differences, the gene is said to be present in two *forms*, also called *alleles*. Individuals of the same species may differ extensively in DNA sequences, a phenomenon known as *polymorphism*.

Since the genome of every creature is equal to its DNA, we should be able to equate the genetic information to the composition of DNA. In order to do so, however, we must first examine the molecular bases of the genetic information and of its function.

Transferring Information to RNA

The problem of how the instructions for making a protein are coded in a gene was not resolved until the 1960s, when the code was deciphered following many advances in our understanding of the function and chemistry of nucleic acids. The instructions of the genes, it was learned, are utilized in two steps: first, the instructions are transferred from DNA to a different type of nucleic acid, RNA, and, second, the instructions are transferred from RNA to protein.

The cells' RNA is made up, like DNA, of chains of bases, but it differs from DNA in three important features. One is that RNA is composed of single strands (except in some viruses, in which it is, like DNA, double helical). In cells RNA does not need a two-stranded structure because it does not replicate. An RNA strand, however, may contain stretches of complementary bases and may fold onto itself, forming double helical segments distributed without apparent order over the strand. As a result, RNA strands are usually folded in irregular and complex ways (fig. 4.5). Folding is important because it controls the interaction of the RNA with proteins, such as enzymes that break down single-stranded RNA. It is also impor-

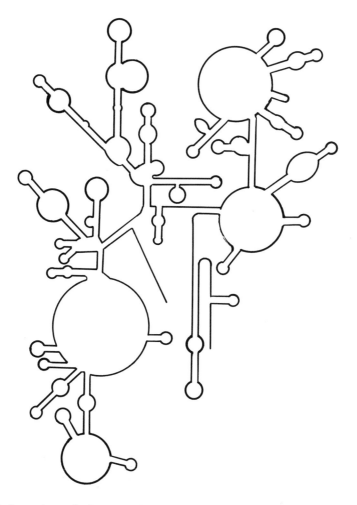

Figure 4.5. This figure shows the bizarre and complicated shape taken by an RNA by folding onto itself. Made up of 1,543 bases, it is one of the ribosomal RNAs that will be considered later. The straight parallel lines represent complementary segments; the circles are segments without complements. The figure is drawn to maximize the proportion of paired segments; we don't know, however, what shapes the RNA takes in the cells. The organization is probably significant because the ribosome contains about fifty proteins, which probably bind to the various unpaired stretches. (From H. F. Noller and L. R. Woese, *Science* 212:403–10 [1981].)

tant for the function of many RNAs that require changes of shape: some RNAs act as enzymes. Its complex folding gives it many of the properties of proteins. The second special feature of RNA—which is responsible for its name, *ribonucleic acid*—is that the ribbon holding the bases contains the sugar *ribose* rather than the slightly different deoxyribose present in DNA. This difference enables the two nucleic acids to interact with different proteins and enzymes, keeping their roles separate. The third difference is that in RNA there is no T (thymine) in its base sequence; it is replaced by the closely related U (uridine). The reason for the difference, probably, is that T is much less vulnerable to chemical damage than is U. The presence of the stable T is important for DNA, which perpetuates itself and must faithfully transmit its information to the progeny. Its adoption to replace U can be viewed as an evolutionary step because RNA probably preceded DNA. The replacement was needed, together with other devices such as the proofreading function of DNA polymerase, to markedly reduce the error rate, which is very high in RNA. This is seen in some viruses with a genome made up of RNA: they have a high propensity for mistakes, but they use them to their own advantage in adapting to growth in different kinds of cells. Because cellular RNA is made by copying DNA, because it is short-lived, and because it has no progeny, errors are much less serious.

Transcription

The handing over of the instructions of the genes to RNA is called *transcription* because RNA uses the language of DNA—that is, the nucleic acid bases are the code elements. Transcription has some features in common with DNA replication, but it differs in other respects. It also begins with a loosening of the DNA helix, but the enzymes involved are different; the main enzyme is a *transcriptase*. This enzyme builds an RNA strand complementary to one of the DNA strands, which is therefore called the *template* strand. The RNA produced is the *transcript* of that DNA segment. Its base sequence (with U replacing T) is identical to that of the other DNA strand, the *coding* strand, which contains the genetic instructions. The transcript is the complement of the complement of the coding strand and therefore identical to it (fig. 4.6).

   Transcription is initiated when appropriate proteins bind to the template strand of DNA. The transcription machinery insinuates between the two DNA strands, pushing them apart over a short stretch. The sequence of the DNA bases can thus be read. RNA nucleotides (bases connected to the sugar [ribose] and phosphate) are presented to the first base of the template strand of DNA; a nucleotide with the complementary base is retained. Then another nucleotide is selected and joined to the first one. At every step the transcription machinery moves one base ahead, building the RNA strand. This strand remains associated with the DNA template only through the last few newly joined nucleotides; the rest hangs freely. The DNA that has been transcribed closes behind the moving

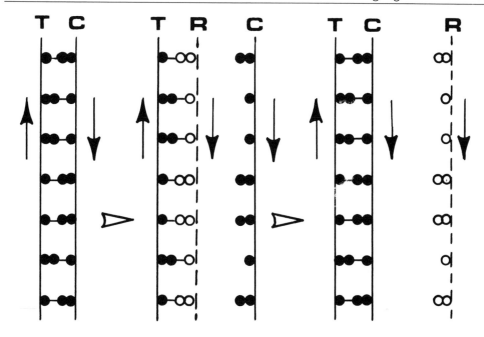

Figure 4.6. Transcription of a DNA helix. The DNA helix, shown on the left, contains a template strand (T) and a coding strand (C). As shown in the middle diagram, the new RNA strand (dashed) is complementary to the template strand; this RNA has the same sequence and direction as the coding strand. As a result of transcription, as shown on the right, the original DNA helix is reconstituted as a new RNA strand, the transcript, is made.

transcription site, re-forming the double helix. As transcription proceeds, the opening in the double helix filled with the transcription machinery moves from one end to the other of the gene (fig. 4.7): at the end it detaches completely from the DNA. The RNA strand is released free, and the transcription machinery becomes available for transcribing the same or another segment. New RNAs can start while other RNAs are in progress on the same gene. In the electron microscope the DNA of a gene with all the RNA transcripts at various states of completion looks like a Christmas tree (fig. 4.8). At the end of transcription the DNA is exactly as it was before transcription began.

In any given gene only one strand acts as template, but different genes on the same DNA molecule may use different strands. The direction of transcription is related to the direction of the DNA strand and is therefore opposite on the two strands. The direction of transcription is unambiguously defined: we can use it as a reference and talk of segments that are "upstream" or "downstream" to any transcribed sequence.

Transcription is the first step in the *expression* of a gene—that is, the series of events by which the gene influences the state of the cell. Any given gene is expressed only under well-defined circumstances, which differ for the various genes

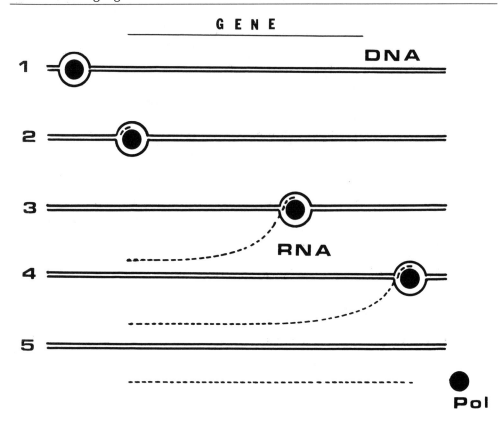

Figure 4.7. Transcription of a gene, which is shown as two parallel strands. Diagrams 1 through 5 depict three successive moments of the transcription of the gene, beginning at the control end (left) and ending at the other end. (1) The transcribing enzyme (RNA polymerese: Pol), indicated as a black disc, first binds to DNA outside the gene to be transcribed, which is indicated by the thin line. (2) The enzyme reaches the beginning of the sequence to be transcribed and starts making RNA (dashed line). (3) Transcription has reached the middle of the gene. (4) Transcription reaches the end of the gene. (5) Transcription has ended, and both the enzyme and the RNA fall off the DNA. At any one moment during transcription the DNA helix is opened in a short loop; in the loop the growing RNA is associated with the template strand of the DNA by base pairs. The RNA made (the transcript) is usually longer than the gene.

of the same genome. At any one time a cell makes only the proteins that are needed by activating the expression of the corresponding genes. Other genes are kept silent because making an unnecessary protein is wasteful of energy. In animals no more than 10 to 20 percent of all genes are expressed in any given cell. The expression of a gene is accordingly *regulated,* most of the regulation taking place at the level of transcription. Regulation is entrusted to a special signal—that is, a short DNA sequence close to the gene. By interacting with regulatory proteins, a signal determines whether a gene is transcribed, how frequently, and where precisely transcription begins or ends. The sequence of the gene determines what

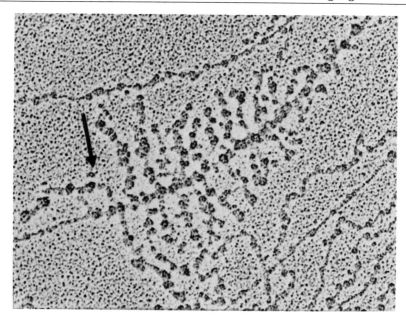

Figure 4.8. Gene DNA from a fly together with its RNA transcripts at various stages of completion, in the shape of a Christmas tree. The tip of the tree is where transcription begins; the base of the tree (arrow) is where it ends. The trunk of the tree is the DNA. As soon as a transcript clears the start point, another one begins; they all proceed equally toward the stop point, growing in length but remaining attached to the DNA. At the stop point they are complete and fall off. Magnified 100,000 times. (From an electron micrograph by S. L. McNight and O. L. Miller, in B. D. Davis, R. Dulbecco, H. N. Eisen, and H. S. Ginsberg, *Microbiology*, 3d ed. [Hagerstown, Md.: Harper & Row, 1980], p. 956.)

product it specifies; the controls determine how and when. The coding sequences are like the keys of a piano; the controls are the fingers of the pianist. Both are essential for the performance.

The signals that control transcription of different genes are designed according to the same general plan, but they differ greatly in details. Several signals are in a *control region* located upstream of the gene in the direction of transcription (fig. 4.9). The dissection of this region in eukaryotic cells by the use of DNA cloning (see chapter 7) offers the following picture: closest to the gene is a short *locating* segment (with the sequence TATA or similar), which determines precisely where transcription begins; if that is removed, transcription still occurs but each transcript begins at a different place. A short distance upstream is another signal, probably where the transcriptase binds to DNA. If that site is removed, there is no transcription. These two sequences together are also known as the *promoter*. Finally, still farther upstream is a segment of great importance: it either stimulates transcription—the *enhancer*—or inhibits it—the *silencer*— in response to special proteins made in the cells.

Enhancers, which are the best known, have extraordinary properties which were revealed by scientists making artificial genes, using the technology of genetic engineering (see chapter 7). An amazing property of many enhancers is their ability to enhance transcription after they are moved one to two thousand bases away from their usual location, either upstream or downstream. (In fact, sometimes the enhancer is located within the gene or downstream.) Moreover, an enhancer retains its activity if it is inverted back to front. In brief, an enhancer controls transcription on either side of its location and at a considerable distance. How it accomplishes this, however, is not clear. Apparently, after binding the special proteins, the enhancer alters the structure of the chromatin, facilitating or inhibiting interaction of the transcriptase with the promoter. The presence of underwound segments of the double helix, sometimes with unusual left-handed coiling, may contribute to the enhancers. Both arrangements favor the separation of the strands, making it easier for the transcriptase to bind to the template strand.

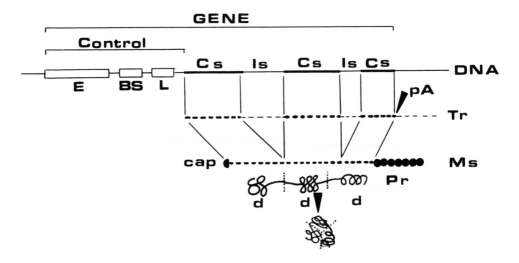

Figure 4.9. Transcription of an eukaryotic gene and formation of an RNA messenger. The gene includes the control region, the coding sequences (Cs) and the intervening sequences (Is) (not in scale). The control region is made up of the locating sequences, L (also called TATA box because they frequently contain that sequence), the enzyme-binding sequences (BS), and the enhancing sequences (E). The transcript (Tr) reproduces both coding and intervening sequences and extends beyond the end of the gene. The transcript is then processed into the messenger (Ms). A cap is positioned at the upstream end of the transcript and a chain of As (poly A) at a place marked by a special signal containing the sequence (AAUAA) that marks the downstream end of the messenger. The rest is cut off. The messenger is thus delineated. Within these limits the intervening sequences are excised, completing the processing. Within the messenger a start triplet (AUG) follows the cap: there translation begins. It stops at a stop triplet. The resulting protein (Pr) is often made up of domains (d), each corresponding to a coding sequence. The domains remain relatively distinct after the protein has folded into its final shape (shown at bottom).

Except for short stretches that are relatively constant, the base sequences of enhancers vary from one gene to another. Different enhancers interact with regulatory proteins present only in certain cell types. These interactions determine in which cells a certain gene is transcribed and with what efficiency. The most efficient enhancers are present in viral DNAs, which need a high rate of transcription for replicating rapidly.

Multiple Controls of Transcription

The enhancer is an important device for controlling the transcription of genes, but it is not by any means the only one. Transcription is under multiple controls that interact in ways we do not fully understand. Some seem to work in an absolute way and start transcription by overruling any other control, whereas others merely have a reinforcing action. This complex organization probably reflects the need for strict regulation of when and how a gene is transcribed; it is also needed because multiple signals, both from outside and within the cell, may call for activation of a gene. The intricacy of controls probably also depends on how they developed in evolution, as new controls were added to preexisting ones. Evolution does not follow a plan: it is opportunistic, using what is already available and adding to it as more is needed. The only test of a certain device is whether it works, not whether it is well designed.

One regulation of transcription involves chemical changes of the DNA. A frequent change occurs at the sequence:

$$-C-C^*-G-G-$$
$$|\ \ |\ \ |\ \ |$$
$$-G-G-C^*-C-.$$

A *methyl group* (m-group) may be added by special enzymes to the two central Cs (indicated by asterisks). With few exceptions, m-groups are present in the control region of genes that are not transcribed. The significance of these groups is convincingly demonstrated by introducing genes into cells: a gene carrying m-groups will remain inactive, whereas one without m-groups will be transcribed. Amazingly, the presence or absence of m-groups will persist in these genes through many replications: it is a self-perpetuating feature. The number of m-groups can be reduced by growing cells in the presence of a modified C (azacytidine), which is incorporated in DNA, instead of regular C, and prevents the attachment of m-groups. After this treatment some silent genes become fully active. Not all genes that have the modified C become active, however, so other factors must be implicated, too.

Doctors have tried to use the effect of the modified C for medical purposes in the case of a patient who carried a defective gene for a globin, one of the proteins that make up hemoglobin, the oxygen carrier of the blood. As we will see in the next chapter, there are several globin genes, of which some are active in fetal life, others in adult life. In this patient, it was an adult gene that was defective. It could be compensated, in principle, if the corresponding fetal gene could be revived. The patient was treated with the modified C and within weeks showed a marked improvement: a considerable amount of fetal hemoblobin appeared in the blood. The success, however, was not obtained through the anticipated route. Rather, the modified C reactivated the fetal gene by interfering with DNA replication, revealing what seemed to be a previously unknown regulatory mechanism.

Another controlling factor in transcription is the state of the chromatin. A segment containing the control region is very compact in inactive genes, but loose in active genes. The tightness of chromatin can be judged from the effect of DNA-cutting enzymes, which cut the DNA much more easily in loose than in tight chromatin. Studying the state of chromatin revealed another important principle: a gene, although inactive, may be ready to become activated when specific signals reach the cell. These *ready genes* have loose chromatin. For instance, genes for globin have a loose chromatin in immature—not fully developed—red blood cells. Although they are not continuously transcribed, transcription will start as soon as certain signal substances bind to the cells.

The many devices regulating transcription are used especially in development. An organism begins with a single cell, the fertilized egg, and then undergoes many changes of shapes and functions. Different cell types appear and disappear in succession, according to changes in the activity of their genes. Regulation of transcription is central to this evolution, which will be considered in chapter 12.

In bacteria the transcription of genes controlling utilization of nutrient types that are only occasionally available is strictly regulated. In the absence of a particular nutrient the activity of the genes essential for utilizing that nutrient is blocked by proteins, specified by regulator genes, that bind very tightly to the control regions. These proteins are called *repressors*. A well-understood example is the mechanism controlling the utilization of lactose, the sugar present in milk. It involves several genes all connected to the same control regions, which are normally repressed. When lactose is added to the bacteria's environment, it combines with the repressor within the cells, blocking its action. The genes are then transcribed and their proteins are made, causing the utilization of the sugar. The active state lasts only as long as the sugar is available. This control saves the bacteria much energy that would otherwise be wasted if the proteins for utilizing lactose were made all the time.

The repressor molecules have evolved a highly specialized interaction with the DNA. They bind to DNA segments called *palindromes*, which consist of two identical base sequences pointing in opposite directions. The repressor itself is made up of two identical protein molecules, and each binds to one of the sequences of the palindrome, which is essentially embraced by the repressor. The double interaction allows a very effective repression.

Instructions to Proteins: A Translation Code

After transcription has transferred the genetic instructions from the DNA template to the RNA transcript, the instructions are then transferred in turn from the transcript to protein. Here the "language" changes because proteins are sequences of amino acids. If we keep to the language analogy, we can call this transfer a *translation*.

Proteins use twenty structural code elements (the amino acids), whereas nucleic acids use four (the bases): a language with four letters is translated into one with twenty letters. Information must be transferred using a *translation code*, in which several bases define an amino acid. If the number of bases per amino acid has to be constant, its minimum number would be three: if it were two, the four bases could specify only sixteen amino acids. This arithmetical fact was appreciated early in the study of the translation code and guided the research. It turned out that three is the right number. Before the translation code could be broken, however, it was essential to unravel the molecular mechanism of translation and to develop a system for translating RNAs of known sequences into proteins in the test tube, independent of the cell.

The code was first deciphered by building in the laboratory short RNAs with known simple base sequences, mostly repetitions of a single base or of groups of three bases. When these RNAs were added to the machinery that makes proteins, they caused the formation of simple proteins, usually made up of repetitions of a single or a few amino acids. These experiments showed that an amino acid is specified by a sequence of three bases—a *triplet* or *codon*—and made it possible to determine which amino acid corresponds to each triplet. They also clarified an important characteristic of the translation code: there are no signals showing where a triplet ends and the next begins. For this reason the code is said to be comma-free.

The validity of the *genetic code* determined in this way has since been extensively verified by comparing the base sequences of genes with the amino acid sequences of the corresponding proteins. The codes used by many viruses, bacteria, animals or plants were found to be the same. The fundamental result is that, with some minor exceptions—for instance, in mitochondria (see below)—the same code is used by all creatures. *The code is universal.*

Setting the Reading Frame

The number of possible combinations of bases, sixty-four, is much larger than the number of the amino acids, which is twenty. What does nature do with the extra triplets? The answer is that it depends on the triplets (fig. 4.10). Some do not correspond to any amino acid, but perform the essential function of specifying where translation begins or ends.

The *start triplet* (AUG) ensures the proper setting of the reading frame. At the

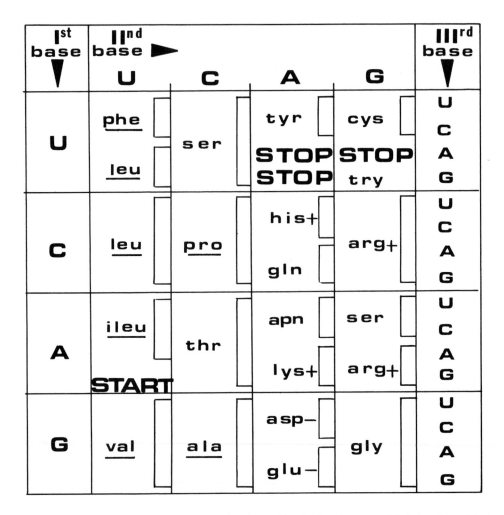

Figure 4.10. Translation code. All possible triplets formed by the four bases are listed, together with the amino acids or signals they specify. Four triplets (heavy characters) are signals: one (AUG) is the start codon, which specifies where translation starts. At other positions the same triplet specifies an amino acid (MET). Three stop triplets (UAA, UAG, and UGA) specify where translation ends; only one is used in each instance. Eight amino acids are entirely defined by the first two bases, the third base being irrelevant; eleven others can have either of two bases at the third position, and only two (MET, TYR) require a specific third base. Two amino acids (LEU, ARG) can even accept two different first or second bases. Underlined are the fat-seeking amino acids; + denotes that the amino acid has a positive charge in the protein, and − that it has a negative charge. Notice that amino acids sharing these features are grouped together in such a way that the substitution of one base often changes an amino acid into another with the same characteristics.

other end of the gene, one or two *stop triplets* (of which there are three kinds) define the end of the amino acid chain and also ensure its detachment from the translation machinery on which it is assembled. Stop triplets are required because the messenger continues beyond the end of the gene but must not be translated. The beginning of translation must be absolutely precise because the triplets are translated by fixing the correct *reading frame* of the first triplet and then continuing one triplet after another to the end. How crucial this is can be seen by what would happen if translation skipped just one base and the reading frame was shifted by one position in the whole gene. The effect would be disastrous. Consider, for instance, the short sequence given below together with the corresponding amino acids:

UUU.GCC.GUC. ACA.UGG.UAC (bases)
Phe-Ala-Val-Thr-Try-Tyr (abbreviated names of amino acids)

If the reading frame were shifted by only one position, the amino acid sequence would change as follows:

U.UUG.CCG.UCA.CAU.GGU. AC (bases)
Leu-Pro-Ser-Glm-Gly (amino acids)

The sequences of the two amino acid chains would be completely different, and the protein formed after the frame shift would be useless for the cell.

The remaining extra triplets have an optional use: they are *alternate triplets*. Several triplets, therefore, can code for the same amino acid. *One triplet, however, never codes for more than one amino acid.* In many triplets the third base (in the direction of reading) plays almost no role—any base will do. So the code is, in effect, a doublet-plus code. Different organisms tend to use one of the bases in the third position in preference to the others. Thus the facultative third base contributes flexibility to the use of DNA sequences.

More important differences in the code are observed in mitochondria, the intracellular particles devoted to energy conversion. As we have seen, mitochondria are like cells-within-a-cell and have their own DNA transcription and translation system. The main difference is that a sequence that is elsewhere a stop triplet codes for an amino acid in the mitochondria of animal cells. In addition, two amino acids are determined by triplets different from those in common usage. These differences point to the separate origin of the prokaryotic cell that became a mitochondrion.

Redefining the Gene

Potentially a base sequence could be read in three ways, depending on whether the reading frame began with the first, the second, or the third base. The same DNA segment, therefore, could contain three genetic instructions for three proteins with different amino acid sequences and different properties. Does nature ever take advantage of this opportunity? Yes, especially in viruses in which, rather frequently, two frames of the same DNA segment contain information for two distinct proteins. Which of the possible proteins is actually built depends not only on the DNA sequence but also on which part of the transcript is utilized in translation. We will return to this point below.

The observations on overlapping genes show that nature makes use of every device that is available and possible. Its use of overlapping genes in viruses is probably related to the need for economy because their genomes are so small. The observations also show that our concept of the gene must now be redefined. It is not a sequence of bases, but a *coding sequence*. A sequence of bases, then, contains three coding sequences and, in principle, three genes.

How the Code Is Used

Translation is carried out in a complex machinery made up of both proteins and RNAs, using ATP energy. The RNA transcript becomes associated with the machinery as the *messenger* (usually known as an mRNA) that carries the information from the gene. In bacteria the transcript is directly used as messenger; in eukaryotic cells it must first be modified—or *processed* (see fig. 4.9). The processed messenger has at its beginning an especially modified G—a *cap*—, a chain of As— a *poly A tail*—at its end, and had some segments removed (see the discussion of split genes below). The processed messenger is then transported to the cytoplasm, where the proteins are assembled. An RNA messenger has a limited life during which it is translated many times and is finally destroyed by degrading enzymes. Its short life allows a cell to shift promptly from the expression of one set of genes to another.

The machinery for making proteins is made up of *ribosomal particles*, or ribosomes (fig. 4.11), *transfer RNAs*, and enzymes. The ribosomal particles (so called because they contain RNA) form the framework on which the amino acid chain is assembled. They were discovered in the early 1950s by workers at the Rockefeller Institute in New York City. Ribosomes have a core made up of three RNAs (*ribosomal RNAs*) surrounded by some fifty different proteins. Transfer RNAs, or tRNAs for short, are the most crucial components of the translation machinery. They function as adaptors: each receives an amino acid from a donor molecule and transfers it to the amino acid chain being synthesized. There are many tRNAs, at least one for each amino acid. Each tRNA carries an amino acid at one end and has three exposed bases at the other end: they are the *anticodon*, which is complementary to the triplet, or codon, corresponding to the carried amino acid in the translation code. The anticodon of the tRNA binds to the triplet of the messenger RNA, positioning the amino acid for incorporation into the amino acid chain as it is being assembled.

During translation an amino acid chain is made by the cooperation of messenger RNA, ribosomes, tRNAs, and enzymes. Ribosomes become associated one at a time with the messenger RNA and run along its length as the chain is built.

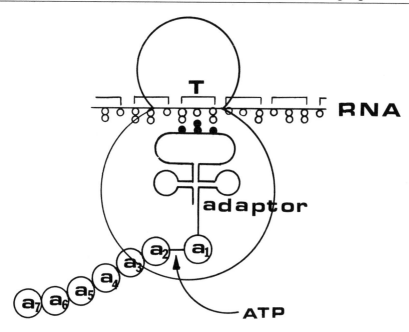

Figure 4.11.   The mechanics of translation. The ribosome is made up of two parts, each consisting of ribosomal RNAs encased in proteins. The smaller part binds the RNA messenger, shown here as a series of triplets (coding units). The larger part binds the tRNA adaptor. Three bases of the tRNA match a triplet, T, of the messenger; the adaptor carries the amino acid corresponding to that triplet (shown as a_1). Using ATP energy, this amino acid will be joined to the amino acid chain already formed (here consisting of six amino acids). a_1 is the amino acid added last.

The amino acid chain is built by the addition of new amino acids one at a time in a series of repetitive steps. At each step the ribosome moves to a new triplet on the messenger, carrying the tRNA corresponding to the previous triplet, which holds the growing amino acid chain. The tRNA corresponding to the new triplet joins the ribosome and connects the amino acid it carries to the growing chain; the tRNA of the previous triplet falls off. The ribosome moves to the next triplet. When a ribosome reaches the stop triplet, it leaves the messenger and releases both the old tRNA and the amino acid chain. The same messenger is translated many times, each time generating the same amino acid chain. As soon as a ribosome has cleared the start site on the RNA, another can become attached. Many ribosomes with the attached amino acid chains hang on a messenger, which thus resembles some futuristic necklace (fig. 4.12).

Split Genes

Among the changes eukaryotic transcripts undergo during processing to become messengers, the most dramatic is the removal of internal pieces. Most genes of eukaryotes and of viruses that grow in their cells are made up of pieces with

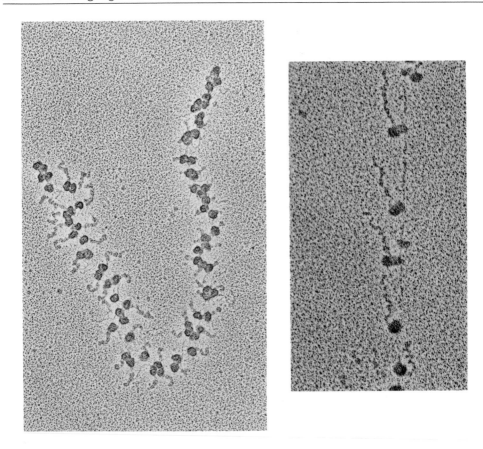

Figure 4.12. RNA messenger and associated ribosomes as seen in the electron microscope. (A) A whole messenger, magnified 50,000 times. Translation begins at 1 and ends at 2, where the amino acid chains are released. (B) A stretched preparation, magnified 100,000 times, showing the RNA messenger as a thin thread and several ribosomes with the attached amino acid chains. (From C. Franke, J. E. Edstrom, A. W. McDowall, and O. L. Miller, *EMBO Journal* 1:59–62 [1982].)

different roles. Some pieces contain *coding sequences* (called *exons* because they exit from the nucleus going to the cytoplasm), which are responsible for specifying the amino acid sequences of the corresponding proteins. Other pieces inserted between the coding sequences do not specify amino acids. They are known as *intervening sequences* (called *introns* because the majority remain in the nucleus).

Almost all genes of eukaryotes contain intervening sequences, as can be easily established by electron microscopy. The approach is to examine double helixes formed artificially by a strand of messenger RNA and the corresponding template strand of DNA. (We will see in chapter 5 how these helixes are made.) Intervening sequences appear as unpaired DNA loops because they lack corresponding segments in the RNA (fig. 4.13). Their numbers vary widely, from one to fifty or so in a gene; their lengths also vary enormously, from about fifty bases to twenty-thousand. As a result the DNA of a gene may be twenty times as long as its messenger

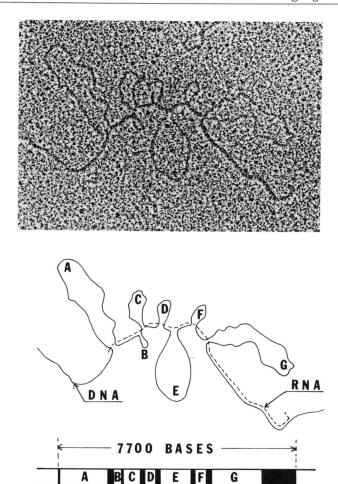

Figure 4.13. Intervening sequences of a gene that specifies egg albumin in chicken seen by electron microscopy (enlarged 180,000 times). Partial helixes were formed by annealing the gene DNA to its RNA messenger. The electron microscopic photograph is above, and its interpretation below. Seven loops of the template strand of DNA (A to G) corresponding to intervening sequences do not form helixes because complementary sequences do not exist in the RNA. The map of the gene with coding sequences (solid) and intervening sequences (open) is shown at the bottom. (From P. Chambon, *Scient. Am.* 244:60–71 [1981].)

RNA. The intervening sequences are removed when the transcript is processed by *splicing* the coding sequences together (fig. 4.9). Therefore, intervening sequences are absent in the messenger RNA.

Precision of Splicing

The splices that generate the messengers must be made with absolute precision in order to maintain the correct reading frame. Two bases that are hundreds, even thousands, of bases apart must be brought together without error. This can occur only through recognition of specific base sequences as splicing signals.

In animal cells characteristic sequences do indeed exist both at the borders between an intervening sequence and the adjacent coding sequence and within the intervening sequence itself. The upstream boundary contains the doublet GU, and the downstream boundary the doublet AG. These doublets are surrounded by other bases that are also rather constant and, together with them, form what is known as *consensus sequences*. A relatively constant internal sequence exists twenty to forty bases away from the downstream border. If any of these sequences is altered, splicing either does not take place or is defective. In most cases the rest of the intervening sequence plays no role in splicing: it can be changed or even removed without problems.

The effectiveness of the splicing signals is shown by the consequences of an abnormal signal in a special form of chronic anemia known as *beta thalassemia*, a genetic disorder found especially among people of Mediterranean ancestry. The affected individuals have an alteration in one of the genes for beta globin, a component of hemoglobin. Surprisingly, in one form of the disease, no normal protein is made, although the gene has normal coding sequences. The defect lies in an intervening sequence (fig. 4.14): a UG doublet is changed into AG, which is the downstream splicing signal. This abnormal signal is located nineteen bases before the regular one. The intervening sequence is usually spliced at this abnormal signal, leaving the nineteen extra bases in the messenger RNA—one base more than needed for maintaining the correct reading frame. The new frame has a stop triplet within the gene so that a much shorter, useless protein is made. The splicing signal, however, is not always used: from time to time it is skipped and splicing occurs at the normal signal, allowing the production of small amounts of normal beta globin.

Even given the presence of these signals, the extreme accuracy of splicing remains puzzling. For instance, how is it possible that genes with many intervening sequences are correctly spliced? It would seem that sometimes the upstream end of the first intervening sequence might become connected by accident with the downstream end of the last intervening sequence, eliminating all the coding sequences in between. This and other problems are avoided for the most part because splicing of transcripts of the complex genes of higher organisms is carried out by large *splicing complexes* containing the transcript, splicing enzymes, and other cellular proteins. The complex is associated with small RNAs that are usually found associated with proteins in small particles called *snurps* (for "small nuclear ribonucleoprotein particles"). We understand how this complex takes care of the alignment of the reading frame and avoids accidental skipping of sequences. The alignment is maintained by the small RNAs. One of them, U1, has a sequence complementary to the consensus sequence found at the upstream end of an intervening sequence. This small RNA can form double helixes with this end and may also hold another part of the intervening sequence toward the down-

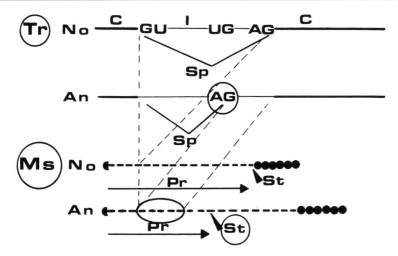

Figure 4.14. A splicing defect leads to hereditary chronic anemia. Above, the diagram shows the transcript (Tr) of the beta-globin gene of normal individuals (No) and of their anemic counterparts (An). Below are the corresponding messengers (Ms) and proteins (Pr). C = coding sequences (heavy lines), I = intervening sequences (thin lines). GU, AG are the normal splicing signals. In the anemic individual, a mutation replaces the normal doublet UG with AG (circled). When messengers are made, the replacement creates an extra splicing signal (Sp). Most transcripts of the anemic individual are processed using this abnormal signal, so that a short segment of the intervening sequence (oval) becomes incorporated into the RNA messenger. This insertion causes a shift of the reading frame when translation reaches the normal coding sequence. In this abnormal frame there is a premature stop (St) signal (circled): the protein made is much shorter than the normal and is highly abnormal, owing to the frame shift.

stream end, causing the formation of a closed loop. The second cut then follows. Other snurp RNAs help in other steps of RNA processing, such as in locating the precise site of poly A addition to the messenger. Skipping from one intervening sequence to another is probably prevented because splicing is regulated; as we have seen, the same transcript is processed in different ways in different cells. Some of the proteins of the splicing complex are apparently able to direct the splicing to the appropriate intervening sequence in a way that depends on the cell type in which splicing takes place.

The segments removed by splicing are in the form of RNA circles, with or without a short tail, depending on the organism. The formation of closed loops means that as a bond between an intervening and a coding sequence is broken, it is re-formed with another nucleotide of the intervening sequence, probably with no need for an energy source. In the simplest cases, not even proteins are needed: in a single-celled eukaryote the RNA, acting as an enzyme, splices itself. This is not the only case in which RNA performs the function of an enzyme: certain enzymes, although predominantly of protein, contain RNA as an essential component. It is not surprising that RNA can perform enzymatic activity because, by folding, it forms complex three-dimensional structures similar to proteins and is capable of many rearrangements (see fig. 4.5). The enzymatic activity of proteins is based on similar properties (see chapter 2). The finding of enzymatic activity in RNA is important because it shows that in the evolution of life enzymatic activities could be performed by RNA before proteins made their appearance.

Whatever their origin, the presence of many separate coding sequences confers great flexibility on a gene because they can be assembled in various ways by splicing, enabling the gene to specify many different proteins. For instance, a gene for a muscle protein, which has eighteen separate coding sequences, generates at least ten different messengers and the corresponding proteins. Six coding sequences, responsible for the basic characteristics of the protein, are present in all messengers, whereas the others, needed for optional properties, vary. Messengers of different compositions are made in different cell types and at different stages of development of the same organism.

The Fate of the Excised Sequences

A question of considerable interest concerns the intervening sequences. Do they perform any specific function? We have no general answer to this question. Some people feel that nature would not have retained them unless they did something useful, but we cannot be too dogmatic. Perhaps intervening sequences were important in evolution, but have no special utility today.

One approach to this question has been to try to find their specific functions. In these attempts, different results have been obtained in different systems. Many intervening sequences evidently lack specific functions because in the course of evolution they have accumulated too many base changes, which would severely impair any function they might have. Such evolutionary changes can be recognized by comparing the same intervening sequence in different species. On the other hand, specific functions have been recognized in a few cases, especially in lower eukaryotes. In yeast mitochondria, an intervening sequence together with a coding sequence specify a protein needed for splicing. Some introns contain enhancers for the transcription of the gene. In some organisms the splicing event itself appears to be essential for the formation of a functional messenger RNA. If splicing is prevented by altering an intervening sequence, the messenger RNA is not made and unprocessed transcripts accumulate in the nucleus. Perhaps the splicing enzymes, which are associated with the nuclear membrane, have the additional function of transporting the processed messenger RNA to the cytoplasm. Some genes function well, however, without intervening sequences at all.

The varied roles of different intervening sequences and splicing events should come as no surprise. Nature does not abide by hard and fast rules—it follows opportunity.

Were the Early Genes Split?

In bacteria, in contrast to eukaryotic cells, intervening sequences are exceptional, although they are found in a virus that grows in bacteria, in mitochondria (which as we saw in the last chapter have a bacterial origin), and in a special class of bacteria of ancient origin, the archaebacteria. The presence of split genes in such primitive organisms suggests that they were formed early in the development of life and are a window opened over the past history of the biological world. Life forms lacking split genes must have lost them in evolution. Most split genes cannot have been formed by the accidental insertion of pieces of DNA—a phenomenon of frequent occurrence—because genes with similar functions and therefore of similar origin in animals and plants have often similar intervening sequences. An interesting possibility is that split genes arose during the evolutionary assembly of larger genes from smaller ones. One reason for this hypothesis is that in some genes the coding sequences correspond to semiautonomous parts of the corresponding proteins known as *domains*. It is likely that the smaller genes evolved separately and were then joined in a phenomenon known as *exon shuffling*. This possibility is supported by looking at the composition of genes coding for related proteins. They share some coding sequences, presumably responsible for the common properties, and differ in other coding sequences devoted to the special properties of the proteins. Intervening sequences may therefore be remnants of the DNA surrounding the primordial genes, retained because it was difficult to join the genes precisely; it was easier to join the DNA roughly and then trim the transcript.

This approach is still used in the organisms living today: genes for immunoglobulins, which play an important role in the fight against infections, are assembled in animals from separate pieces located at distant locations in the genome. After assembly, the coding sequences of the various pieces remain separated by intervening sequences, which are then removed when the transcript is processed. During evolution there seems to have been a tendency to lose intervening sequences, as can be seen by studying some glycolytic enzymes that have persisted throughout evolution. Rarity of intervening sequences in bacteria would be an extreme expression of this trend.

Why Are Bacteria Different?

This characteristic of bacteria may be attributed to the conditions under which translation occurs in these organisms. Because they do not have a nuclear membrane, their DNA is not separated from the translation apparatus, and transcripts are translated before they are finished. This arrangement maximizes the speed of protein manufacture and therefore cell multiplication. This is essential for most bacteria which compete with each other mainly through the speed at which they utilize the limited resources present in the environment. Under these circumstances there is no time for splicing.

In contrast, speed of multiplication is not essential for mitochondria, which are regulated by the cell, and perhaps not even for archaebacteria, which live in very special environments where freedom for evolution may be limited. Nor do animals and plants compete with each other through speed of multiplication. Their competition is played out in terms of their perfection of adaptation to the environment. The large genes assembled from pieces increase enormously the range of molecular tools useful for this adaptation.

From all this, we may deduce that splicing is a rather ancient process in evolutionary terms. It is probably a leftover from a time when genomes were made up of RNA (see chapter 20). RNA molecules probably acted then both as genes and as messengers, as they do today in some viruses. The transition to DNA genomes may be represented by other viruses that have RNA genes but during replication copy them into DNA by a process of *reverse transcription* (see chapter 15).

The primordial use of RNA as genetic material and its subsequent transition to DNA may explain why the replication of any DNA begins with RNA. The interpretation is that, after the switch to DNA, it was easier to leave the delicate function of beginning a strand as it was and then replace the RNA segment with DNA, rather than forge an entirely new mechanism. The preexistence of RNA genomes may even explain the need for the transcription step. After the switch to DNA, the genetic information still had to be returned to RNA for translation because RNA had the primordial ability to interact with the translating machinery.

CHAPTER 5

Organization of Sequences in the Genome

Reading the language of the genes by determining the sequences of their bases is an important approach to the understanding of life. But because the genomes of plants or animals are so very large, the task is immense. Thus, complete DNA sequences have been determined so far only for the smallest organisms, such as viruses. Although the time is approaching when we will be able to describe the whole genome of a plant or animal, for the moment we can describe larger genomes only in general terms, highlighting their overall features and explicating small parts of the whole.

A variety of technologies has revealed many important properties of the organization of the DNA sequences. Although one might think that these studies would have revealed DNA's immutability, the most striking observation has been the opposite: DNA is highly changeable. But because DNA is the master of life and life itself is change, this should come as no surprise.

Hybridization: Breaking and Re-forming Helixes

Before considering the studies' findings, we will examine how they were obtained. The first technology to provide insight into the organization of base sequences in nucleic acids—*nucleic acid hybridization*—was developed in the 1950s. This technology is based on the reversibility of the double helix. The helix can melt—that is, separate into its two complementary strands—at a high temperature close to the boiling point of water. The heat breaks all the hydrogen bonds between complementary base pairs simultaneously. If the temperature is then progressively lowered, the complementary strands reunite to re-form double helixes. This process, like that used to remove internal stresses in newly heated glass, is called *annealing*. At the lower temperature the strands try repeatedly to form double helixes, but for the most part they can form only short unstable helical stretches between accidentally complementary segments. When complementary strands meet in register, however, all the hydrogen bonds between complementary bases are rapidly formed, proceeding in a zipperlike fashion from the point of first adhesion down the length of the strand. This double helix then persists because the temperature is not high enough to melt it. Helixes thus formed are often *hybrid*—their two strands come from two different helixes. At the end of the annealing period, remaining single strands are selectively destroyed by appropriate enzymes, and the intact helixes are separated from the debris.

This technology is applicable to both DNA and RNA: although RNA in cells is usually single stranded, it can form double helixes with complementary strands of either RNA or DNA. In fact the first hint of the existence of messenger RNA was derived from its ability to hybridize with the gene DNA.

Hybridization is a sensitive method for determining whether two DNAs have similar sequences, or are *homologous:* they can form hybrid helixes only if almost all their bases are complementary. DNAs that differ in a small proportion of bases also form helixes, but they are less stable and melt at a lower temperature. Thus, temperature measures how well matched the base sequences are: the greater the homology, the higher the melting temperature.

An important use of nucleic acid hybridization is to identify a given gene in the DNA of a cell or organism by using *radioactive probes*, prepared by making the gene DNA from building blocks containing radioactive atoms (see chapter 1). To identify the gene, a small amount of the probe is mixed with a large amount of the target DNA, and the mixture is melted and then annealed (fig. 5.1). It is unlikely that the strands of the probe will re-form double helixes among themselves, because they are very few; rather, they are more likely to make double helixes with homologous sequences contained in the DNA, because they are more abundant. At the end of the experiment more radioactivity will be found in helical DNA than if the probe were annealed alone. This method is sufficiently sensitive to detect one gene among a million or more unrelated ones, or a single gene in a human cell.

Identifying Genes

As an example of this process, we will see how radioactive probes were used to show that cells of a mouse cancer caused by a virus harbored the virus's genes. In the 1960s it was not clear how a virus changed regular cells to cancer cells; it seemed to alter them in a hit-and-run attack and then disappear. To learn what happens to the viral DNA, the virus was grown in a nutrient liquid containing a radioactive T (thymine) derivative, which is incorporated in DNA. Highly radioactive DNA extracted from this virus was used as the probe. After annealing it with the DNA of the cancer cells, the radioactivity found in hybrid helixes showed that the cancer cells contained about one copy of the viral DNA. Moreover, the viral DNA to which the probe hybridized was found to be linked by chemical bonds to

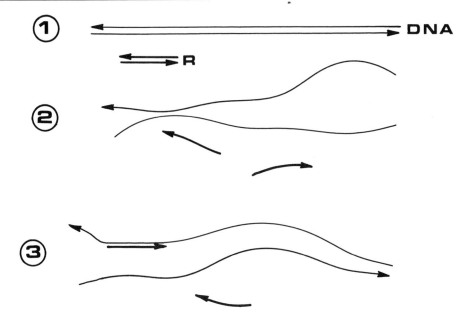

Figure 5.1. Identifying a gene with a radioactive probe for that gene (R, heavy lines). The probe is mixed with the DNA (1) and then melted (2). During annealing (3), some strands of the probe form hybrid helixes with the gene DNA.

the cellular DNA, as if it were a cellular gene: the viral DNA was *integrated* in the cellular DNA. Thus the cancer under study was caused by the continued presence of viral genes, which explained why the descendants of a cell that has been made cancerous by a virus are all cancerous: they inherit the integrated viral DNA. The result also showed that in eukaryotic cells two separate DNAs (that of the virus and that of the cell) can easily link to form a single molecule. As we will see later, this property of DNA has enormous biological significance.

The radioactive viral DNA was also used as a probe to study the transcription of the viral genes in the cancer cells. The DNA was annealed with RNA messengers obtained from the cells. Again radioactive helixes were generated, but fewer than would be expected if all the viral genes had been transcribed. The results showed that cancer is caused by special genes present in the virus, a conclusion later generalized to other viruses (see chapter 15).

Enzymes: Specific Scissors

Radioactive probes similar to those just described can be prepared for only some DNAs—for instance, genes whose messengers are abundant in cells. The RNA messenger is copied into DNA by the enzyme *reverse transcriptase*, obtained from some cancer viruses (see chapter 15). For most genes suitable probes cannot be made by isolating the DNA of the gene or its transcript because there is no suffi-ciently pure and abundant source. This difficulty has been overcome by tools developed in the 1970s. In these newer technologies an essential role is played by special enzymes, called *site-specific endonucleases*, that cut DNA at specific places, or sites. (Endonucleases are enzymes that cut a nucleic acid strand by breaking the chemical bonds between consecutive bases.)

These enzymes were discovered by scientists trying to understand the strange behavior of bacteriophages in certain bacteria (fig. 5.2). It was observed that a phage, which can be readily grown in cultures of bacterium A (1 and 2 in fig. 5.2) would produce almost no progeny in cultures of bacterium B (3). The rare phage particles that were produced (4) were unusual because they were then capable of growing normally in bacteria of type B (5, 7) as well as in those of type A (6). Even more unusual was the reversibility of the change: the phage produced by these rare particles of bacteria of type A (6) again grew minimally in B cells.

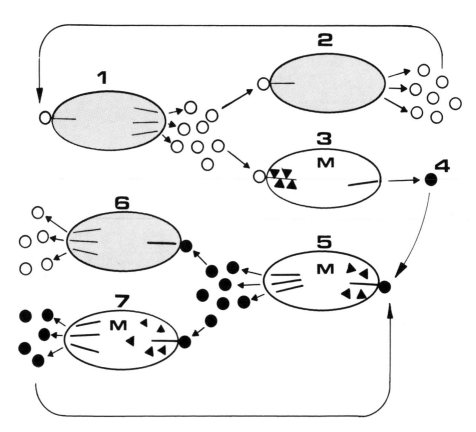

Figure 5.2. Effects of site-specific endonucleases and modifying enzymes (M) on phage DNA. Bacteria of type A is shown as gray; bacteria of type B is clear. DNA protected by m-groups is shown as heavy lines, unprotected DNA as thin lines. Phage particles with protected DNA are shown as solid circles, those with unprotected DNA as empty circles. For further explanation, see text.

Enzymes of one class break down the DNA of the infecting phage; those of the other class change the DNA, making it resistant to breakdown. The enzymes that break down DNA were called *restriction endonuclease* to signify the fact that the phage was restricted to growth in certain bacteria. In the reported observations bacteria of type B had both enzymes, but bacteria of type A had neither. DNA of phage grown in A bacteria was vulnerable in B cells because its DNA was not modified. A few DNA molecules escaped obstruction because they were modified by the enzymes of the B cells and continued to grow in them. When returned to A cells their progeny was made without modification and was therefore vulnerable in B cells. The enzymes that altered the DNA were called *modifying enzymes;* they made the DNA resistant to the endonuclease by changing some bases chemically, usually through addition of m-groups (see chapter 4).

These observations were interesting in that they revealed the existence of a new class of tremendously useful endonucleases, although they were discovered by scientists trying only to solve a biological riddle with no practical purpose in mind. Moreover, they revealed the importance of the attachment of m-groups to DNA. Later it was shown that this alteration has much broader significance in the functional processes of DNA, as we saw in chapter 4.

It was soon recognized that the endonucleases responsible for the phage behavior had an astonishing specificity. In contrast to previously known endonucleases which cut DNA between any two bases, these enzymes cut it only at particular sequences of bases, the *target sequences*. These sequences are short palindromes—they vary in length between three and eight bases and are the same when read from either strand direction (fig. 5.3). The enzyme cuts the DNA within the target by making two cuts that are symmetrical in respect to the center of the palindrome. Most enzymes make staggered cuts so that the two strands remain connected by one or a few base pairs. The connection, however, is too weak to hold

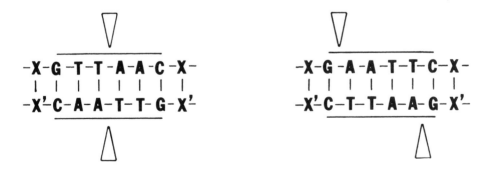

Figure 5.3. Target sequences for two site-specific endonucleases. Bases outside the target are indicated as x and x'. The triangles indicate where the two strands are cut. The enzyme at the left is produced by the bacterium *Haemophilus parainfluenzae;* the one at the right by the bacterium *Escherichia coli*. The enzymes are referred to by the abbreviated name of the bacterium: Hpa1 and EcoR1. R stands for a plasmid that specifies the enzyme, and 1 refers to a particular enzyme when the bacterium produces several.

the strands together, and they fall apart. The result is a complete cut of the helix, which cannot be repaired. The symmetry of the target sequence is related to the symmetry of the cutting enzyme, which is made up of two equal protein molecules. The two recognize identical sequences on each strand and cut at exactly the same place. We have seen an analogous situation with repressors and the sequences they recognize (chapter 4).

Enzymes isolated from different bacteria recognize different targets: about a hundred are known. In each bacterial species the modifying enzymes act on the target of the cutting enzymes, adding m-groups to protect the DNA of the bacterial cell from the cutting enzyme present in the same cells. It may seem surprising that a cell should make a cutting enzyme and then a modifying enzyme to protect itself against the first one. Why such a complex system? A possible answer is that the enzymes provide a method for preventing the invasion of cells of one bacterial species by DNA from another species, or from phage or other invading DNAs (see chapter 6). We can think of the invading DNA as a long snake trying to sneak into new territory, where it is met by defending soldiers with powerful claws, which cut it to pieces. Legal DNA—that which belongs to the territory—is defended by suitable armor; it is attacked by the defenders but suffers no harm. These enzymatic systems are important weapons in the warfare between DNAs in bacteria.

Specific Fragments

The site-specific cutting enzymes have become an essential tool in the study of the base sequences of DNA. Their applications are as diverse as the identification of viruses and the prenatal diagnosis of congenital diseases. A DNA exposed to one of the many cutting enzymes is broken into fragments that are characteristic of that particular DNA because they depend on its base sequence: they form its *fingerprint*. Different enzymes produce different fingerprints that can be individually purified. Although the DNA of an animal cell produces hundreds of thousands of fragments that cannot be isolated individually, that of a small virus can be cut into, say, ten characteristic fragments that can be differentiated from each other by their lengths. When the fragments are few, they can be ordered according to their position in the DNA, which then constitutes the DNA's *map*. Genes or even their parts can be located on the map as the basis for studying their activities. Radioactive copies of the fragments can be used as probes for the corresponding genes in nucleic acid hybridization. A probe will detect whether a certain gene is present in cells, and if so, in what amounts and whether it is transcribed.

The fingerprint yielded by each virus is different from those of even closely related viruses. This is important for diagnosis of viral diseases and for tracing viral strains during an epidemic. Altered genes may yield an abnormal fingerprint if the change is in a target sequence for an endonuclease. When this happens, the enzyme does not cut the target, and the two segments, instead of being separated at that point, remain joined. A gene altered in this way by hereditary defects is identified by the fingerprint of DNA obtained from cells present in a small sample of the fluid that surrounds the early embryo. This principle is applied to the diagnosis of some hereditary diseases—for instance, a form of thalassemia, in which a globin gene is altered.

In other hereditary diseases there is no change in any of the targets. These diseases can be recognized by taking advantage of the normal polymorphism— that is, the presence of small variations of base sequences in the same segment of DNA of different individuals. These differences originating in evolution may eliminate some endonuclease target or create new ones. In either case the fingerprint is altered. If a segment of DNA very close to the altered gene has a special fingerprint, its recognition is tantamount to recognizing the altered gene itself. This principle is applied to the diagnosis of phenylketonuria, a disease that causes mental retardation by preventing the formation of an amino acid needed by the brain cells. In both thalassemia and phenylketonuria, as in many other cases, the prenatal diagnosis gives the patient the option of terminating the pregnancy at an early stage. Or in the case of phenylketonuria, a diet may be prescribed to control the defect immediately after birth.

An enormous boost to the study of DNA sequences was given by two other technological advances. One was DNA cloning, described in chapter 7, which allows the production of a large amount of any fragment. The other was the development of efficient methods for determining the sequence of the bases of cloned DNA. These important developments were made possible by the newly acquired knowledge and understanding of the chemistry of DNA and of the action of many enzymes. Thanks to these technologies, it is now possible to determine both the general arrangement of the bases on long pieces of DNA and the detailed sequences of especially interesting segments. We will review below some of the most significant findings obtained by these methods.

Genes in Many Copies

That complex creatures have large numbers of genes has long been recognized. At first it was thought that each gene was present in a single copy per genome, or in Beadle and Tatum's slogan: "one gene, one enzyme." Now we would express the same concept as "one gene, one protein," because many enzymes made up by more than one kind of protein contain the information of more than one gene. The one gene–one protein concept satisfies our innate need for simplicity. Nature, however, does not work so simplistically, as the methods for studying genes soon showed. It is now recognized that unique genes are limited to the simplest creatures, such as viruses and bacteria; eukaryotic cells contain *families* of from a few to several hundred related genes, which are similar in sequences and specify proteins performing the same function. In some families all the genes are essentially identical.

The gene families present in eukaryotes satisfy various requirements related to the increased functional and developmental complexity of the organisms. Some families provide similar proteins at various stages of development; others satisfy the need for large amounts of a certain product. Families of a third class provide a spectrum of related but somewhat different proteins for the performance of special functions. We will consider specific examples of each group.

Genes Functioning at Various Periods in Development

One might think that a gene whose protein is needed only at various stages during the development of an individual could be turned on and off repeatedly according to the need, but this is not what happens. Instead, a gene that has been active at a certain stage of development will then be turned off for good; if the protein is needed again at a subsequent stage, a new gene is activated. An example are the genes for *globins*, the proteins that make up hemoglobin in red blood cells. Hemoglobin comprises two molecules of alpha globin and two of beta globin, which together bind the *heme*, an iron-containing molecule. Oxygen bound to the iron is transported through the body. Mammals have a family of alpha-globin genes and one of beta-globin genes in different chromosomes. Humans have five alpha genes and seven beta genes. In each family some genes are active in early embryonic life, others later in fetal life, and still others in the adult.

In this and other cases the successive appearance of similar proteins at different stages of development makes sense in view of what we know of gene control. At any stage of development a set of genes is activated by specific regulatory substances that bind to the control regions of the genes. These substances and control regions, which operate at various stages, must be different; otherwise all the genes would be activated at the same time. The situation can be likened to our showing a set of slides with a projector that does not reverse: if we wish to show the same slide several times, we must put several copies in the carousel, each with a different number. Each slide is equivalent to a different gene of the same family and the number on the slide corresponds to the control region of the gene.

The similarity of the genes of each family suggests that they are slightly modified copies of the same primordial gene. In the case of the globin genes these evolutionary changes seem to be going on even now, as judged from differences between man and monkeys. Adult humans have two active beta genes—one supplying most of the beta globin, the other only 2.5 percent of it. In some monkeys the weak gene makes no protein at all, suggesting that even in humans it is losing ground and possibly is on its way out. The reduction of activity in man and the inactivity in monkeys suggests alterations of the transcription of the gene or its control. If genes can go out of business, then it is essential to have more than one performing the same function.

Genes for Quantity

A different role for gene families is that of producing large amounts of the product; this is the case of the genes for ribosomal RNAs. They determine the sequences of the three kinds of RNAs present in the ribosomal particles that are essential components of the protein-making machinery (chapter 4). These RNAs are needed in large quantities in cells of all organisms, which are packed with ribosomal particles. Eukaryotes, from yeast to humans, have families comprising hundreds of ribosomal RNA genes. They are arranged in repeats in which the genes for the three RNAs are always in the same order (*tandem repeats*). This arrangement can be seen by cutting the DNA of the cells with a site-specific endonuclease that cuts a single target in each repeat. A large number of identical fragments are generated because the distance between successive cuts is constant (fig. 5.4); they can be easily recognized because of their abundance. Another family of genes present in many copies (presumably, again, because the products are needed in large amounts) is that specifying histones, the small proteins that accompany the DNA in chromatin. In some species the genes for five different histones form tandem quintets—that is, groups of genes always in the same order.

Genes for Diversity

The genes for immunoglobulins form a family of different significance; their function is to provide diversity. Vertebrates and especially mammals have a considerable number of such genes. They differ from each other in some sequence detail; no two of them are identical. The differences ensure a large diversity of immunoglobulins, which is biologically very important. These molecules will be considered in detail in chapter 13. We see, then, the contrasting use of repeated genes: some (those for ribosomal RNAs) are highly uniform to produce a uniform product in abundance, whereas others (those for immunoglobulins) differ to ensure the diversity of the proteins.

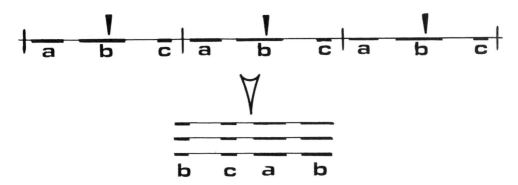

Figure 5.4. Hypothetical tandem repeats containing three genes, a, b, and c. When the DNA is cut by a site-specific endonuclease with a target within gene b (arrow), it generates identical fragments from all repeats.

Endless Repeats

The DNA sequences we have considered so far correspond to genes with known functions. Surprisingly, however, *most DNA sequences have no apparent function whatever.* The study of such sequences explains some puzzling observations, such as the stunning differences of DNA amounts in cells of even closely related organisms. If the DNA contained only the genes needed for the life of the organism, the amount of DNA should depend on the genetic complexity of the species. It would be easy to understand, for example, why animal cells should contain thousands of times more DNA than bacteria, as animals require a vast amount of genetic information for embryological development and the formation of the immune system and the nervous system. But genetic complexity does not explain why the cells of lizards, say, have twenty times more DNA than human cells.

A first step in the solution of this enigma is the recognition that in all higher organisms a large proportion of DNA—as much as 98 percent in humans—does not code for proteins. Part of the noncoding DNA is in the intervening sequences, but a much larger part is between genes, scattered throughout the genome. Much of this DNA is made up of repeated sequences, with units of various length from a dozen or so bases to several thousands. Like repeated genes, these sequences form families whose members have very similar lengths and sequences. The human genome (3 billion base pairs altogether) contains many extensive families. One, for instance, is made up of about 500,000 equal segments, interspersed with regular genes, each about 300 base pairs long, taking up a total of 150 million base pairs altogether.

In many species some highly repetitive sequences are present in big blocks in tandem arrangement. They are concentrated at the points where the two sister chromatids are pulled apart at cell division (chapter 1) and at the ends of the chromosomes. They may be important in the movement and replication of the chromosomes. A striking finding is that both their base sequences and the number of segments differ enormously between one species and another. Some species have 20,000 times as many segments as other, even related, species.

The flooding of the genome with all these repeated sequences of various kinds is dramatic and puzzling. Even more puzzling are the strange properties they sometimes display. For instance, in some plants the DNA bordering on some repeated sequences shows unusual exchanges of parts and loss of segments and gene activity. Usually these sequences are segregated to special chromosomes—the B chromosomes, which are highly variable in related species. These and other extraordinary properties of repeated sequences are related to the ability of DNA to move around in the genome; we will return to them in the next chapter.

No specific function can be ascribed to the many repetitive sequences of animals or plants. They do not specify proteins, and some of them are not even transcribed. It has been proposed that some repeats may regulate the functions of genes or the replication of segments of DNA, but these roles have not been demonstrated. It is the great variability of the numbers of segments and of their base sequences from species to species that raises the suspicion that these sequences have no function at all.

The highly repetitive sequences, however, may have consequences. It has been suggested that they maintain the separation between species by preventing two individuals of different species from producing fertile progeny—a suggestion based on their constancy within a species and the differences between species. Perhaps these sequences play a part in the formation of germ cells. In organisms with sexual reproduction (see chapter 9), identity of repetitive sequences may be essential for the pairing of chromosomes and therefore for the formation of germ cells. An individual born to two parents from different species with different repetitive sequences would not form germ cells and would be infertile.

We have left open many questions about the distribution of sequences over the genome. For instance, how do large gene families arise? What causes the dramatic differences between related species? Why are members of some families all similar to one another while those of other families are different? We will consider these and other questions in the next chapter, after having examined how DNA changes.

CHAPTER 6

The Changing DNA

Mutation

A major discovery during the early part of this century was the fact that genes change. It was found that populations of the fruitfly *Drosophila* produce from time to time individuals with eyes colored apricot, cinnabar, vermilion, or white instead of the usual red. In some, such as bar-eyed flies, the shape of their eyes change. More recently, studies of DNA sequences have shown that such changes, called mutations, are alterations in the sequence of genes, such as replacements of bases, loss of DNA segments, or insertion of new segments. A mutation frequently abolishes the function of a gene, which may be reflected in the loss of activity of an enzyme. Different mutations that make the same enzyme inactive are localized in the gene(s) that specify the enzyme. The study of these mutations led to the first definition of the gene.

Although mutations occur spontaneously, they can also be promoted by artificial means. This important discovery, made in 1926 by the geneticist Hermann Muller, made it possible to understand how mutations occur. Muller showed that *Drosophila* flies mutate more often if they are exposed to X rays. Since then many other agents have been shown to cause mutations: radiations, such as those generated in the detonation of atomic bombs, ultraviolet light from the sun, and many chemicals, mostly produced in the laboratory or by industry. More recently it has become possible to introduce mutations in small, completely known genomes, at any location and essentially at will, using the technology of genetic engineering. One approach is to make in the laboratory a DNA segment of fifteen or twenty bases equal to the sequence of a segment of a gene but with one different base. This segment is then hybridized to the genome DNA, generating hybrid molecules with one complete strand of the gene and the other limited to the artificial segment. The segment is elongated, using a polymerase, to complete the gene DNA. After replication the hybrid produces a complete double-helical mutant genome. This procedure is known as *site-directed mutagenesis.*

As a result of these and other discoveries, we now understand the different ways in which mutations arise. Some are formed during DNA replication, when a wrong base is positioned in place of the right one; the testing and correcting mechanism of normal replication, however, makes this mistake very rare. More frequently, mutations occur because of errors of repair when the DNA is damaged by radiations or chemicals. The enzymes that rebuild the damaged strand after the damage is removed are not those that make new DNA during replication, and they make many more mistakes. An extremely high number of mutations is produced when a special repair system, called the *SOS system*, comes into action. As its name implies, this repair is the last chance for salvaging a severely damaged genome. The system, which has been studied especially in bacteria, becomes active when a great deal of DNA has been demolished. The SOS enzymes work against time: they must fill the DNA gaps before DNA-cutting enzymes attack the intact strand, causing irreparable damage. Because the first order of business is simply to fill the gaps, how they are filled is less important. Wrong bases positioned at many places result in mutations that often lead to severe gene defects in the surviving cells. The SOS enzymes are not made in normal cells because their genes are repressed. They become active only when there is extensive DNA damage—which is fortunate, given the nature of these enzymes.

Change in the coding sequence of a gene can have different effects. On the one hand, a change of the last base of a triplet often has no consequence because the amino acid specified remains the same (chapter 4); this is a *silent mutation.* In contrast, a base change in one of the first two positions of a triplet usually causes replacement of one of the amino acids, although the consequence for the protein will vary, depending on the triplet. The astute organization of the translation code tends to minimize the consequences of the replacement: the original amino acid is often replaced by another with similar properties, such as that of being fat-seeking or water-seeking or possessing a positive or negative electric charge. If this is the case, the function of the protein may remain unaltered, keeping the mutation silent. Its function is usually lost, however, when the mutation interchanges amino acids with different properties or generates a termination signal, which stops the growth of the amino acid chain prematurely, producing an incomplete protein. Especially serious is the addition or removal of a base, for this causes a shift of the reading frame and jumbles the part of the protein beyond the mutation, making it useless.

Recombination

An important outcome of the study of mutations as markers for specific genes was the discovery that genes move around. This is the phenomenon of *genetic recom-*

bination, which changes the relative position of genes or of pieces within a gene. Recombination can be detected, for instance, when one chromosome of a cell has two mutations, and the homologous chromosome has none (fig. 6.1). If recombination occurs, the two mutations may be redistributed in such a way that each chromosome ends up with one mutation. If both mutations affect a gene for the same enzyme, the cell ends up with no enzyme at all, whereas before it had been adequately supplied by the gene with no mutation.

Recombination was recognized by students of heredity in plants and animals long before they knew about DNA because it occasionally separates characteristics that are usually inherited together. One type, *homologous recombination,* identified first because it produces regular predictable consequences, occurs between any pair of long homologous DNA segments (about fifty or more bases). It is the consequence of events that are reminiscent of those occurring during replication and repair. Here is approximately what happens (fig. 6.2): a recombination enzyme cuts a strand in one of the DNA helixes, causing it to unwind and partially separate from the complementary intact strand. The loose end of the strand then invades the other double helix, establishing base pairs with the complementary strand in the homologous segment. If the two strands form a stable helix, other events follow: cuts are produced by enzymes in various strands and are followed by local repair. Finally the two helixes are rebuilt with some parts exchanged.

Mutation and homologous recombinations are powerful causes of DNA changes. By a succession of mutations the base sequences can slowly change; by recombination the changed sequences can be joined. In time, the accumulated DNA changes can become very extensive, providing a basis for evolution.

A Special Recombination

Mutations and homologous recombination, however, do not explain completely DNA's mobility. For instance, they do not explain how an immunoglobulin gene is formed during the life of an individual by the assembly of several distant pieces

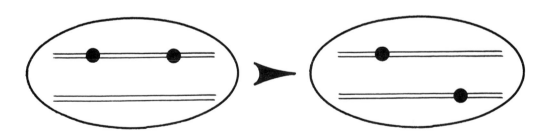

Figure 6.1. Recombination between two homologous genomes present in the same cell. At first (left) one genome has two mutations, whereas the other has none. After recombination each genome has one mutation.

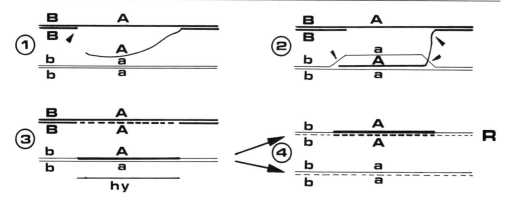

Figure 6.2. Steps in homologous recombination. (1) Two homologous helixes are near each other. One carries a B gene and an A gene. The other genome has variant genes (indicated as b and a). A cut of a strand (at pointer) in one of the helixes causes it to unwind. (2) The unwound strand pairs with the homologous complementary strand of the other helix. Strands are cut at various places (at pointers), and a piece of strand of the lower helix is cut off. (3) The upper helix rebuilds the lost strand (dotted line); in the lower helix the invading strand is incorporated, producing a hybrid helix in which one strand has gene A, and the other, gene a. (4) As the hybrid helix replicates, it produces a recombinant helix carrying the new gene combination bA (shown as R), and a replica of the original lower helix.

(chapter 13), nor do they account for the formation of genes in pieces during evolution. These events are produced by exchanges between DNA sequences with limited or no homology; thus they cannot be produced by the enzymes of homologous recombination.

The mechanisms of these exchanges were first clarified by interesting observations with certain bacteriophages, the DNA of which can become integrated into cellular DNA. Integration is the result of a recombination between two spots, or sites, one in viral DNA, the other in cellular DNA. The two sites are homologous, but over a sequence that is too short for homologous recombination. Because it is carried out by enzymes that recognize the two DNA sites where the exchange occurs, this recombination is called *site-specific*.

DNA That Jumps Around

In contrast to the requirements of site-specific recombination, which are very strict, some other forms have much looser sequence requirements—or possibly no requirements at all. An example is the integration of the DNA of a cancer virus (mentioned in chapter 5) in cellular DNA. A similar form of recombination is used by certain DNA sequences known as *movable elements*, which are present in cells of all kinds. In the 1930s Barbara McClintock, while studying the genetics of corn, observed mutations that changed the color of the kernels. These mutations were erratic: they would occur in a gene for a number of generations; then the gene would return to a stable form while another gene became highly unstable. She suggested that these mutations were due to movable genetic elements that altered the activity of genes by settling near them.

The molecular basis of her observations was demonstrated only recently through work with bacteria. The cells contain movable elements that are known as *insertion sequences* because they move easily from place to place, settling almost anywhere in the host genome. Like McClintock's movable elements, they inactivate the genes in which they settle, generating what looks like a mutation. The insertion of the movable element within a gene profoundly alters the coding sequence or introduces a termination signal that stops the progress of translation.

The anatomy of a bacterial insertion sequence is simple and characteristic. A DNA segment of several hundred to a thousand or so base pairs is flanked by two *terminal repeats*—short identical sequences pointing in the same or opposite directions (fig. 6.3). The presence of inverted repeats, those pointing in opposite directions, can be recognized by electron microscopy after the DNA is heated to separate the strands and then annealed. The inverted segments of the same strand form a helix, generating a "lollipop." The existence of the two repeats shows that

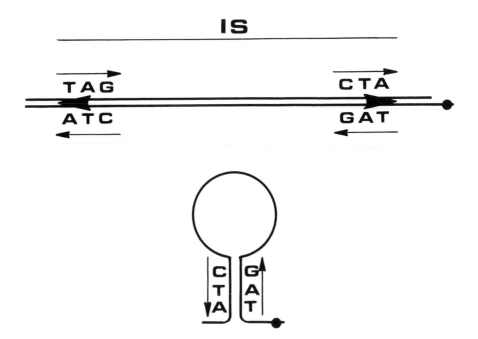

Figure 6.3. Diagram of an insertion sequence, the length of which is indicated by the upper line (IS). It is flanked by two double helical segments that are identical but point in opposite directions (heavy arrows). Three bases are shown in the repeats, but there are always more. When the DNA is melted and annealed, the inverted repeats of the strand marked by a black dot may pair together, generating the "lollipop" figure shown below. The other strand can do the same.

both ends of an insertion sequence independently recombine with the bacterial DNA. The enzyme causing this type of replication is specified by a gene of the insertion sequence itself. Recombination is part of the mechanism of replication of an insertion sequence: one of the daughter copies remains at the old site, and the other is inserted at a new site. Insertion sequences, therefore, tend to increase in number, spreading in the host's genome. The enzyme causing this type of replication is specified by a gene of the insertion sequence itself.

Movable elements exist in all living creatures. They have been recognized in yeast and in the fly *Drosophila*, where they produce dramatic effects, such as unstable mutations or infertility. In higher animals some viruses that regularly integrate in the cellular genome are comparable to movable elements (see chapter 15), as are some repetitive sequences of the mammalian genome, which will be considered later.

Some bacterial insertion sequences have especially interesting effects: they control neighboring cellular genes by switching them on or off. These insertion sequences change orientation reversibly—for instance, from AB to BA, and vice versa—but remain in the same place in the DNA. The change is caused by recombination between the inverted repeats that flank the sequence—those in the stalk of the "lollipop." Some of these *invertible elements* present a signal that initiates transcription of a neighboring gene in one orientation and a signal that terminates it in the other (fig. 6.4). The back-and-forth switching of these elements is controlled by special genes, which probably specify the enzymes carrying out the recombination. In some bacteria and bacteriophages the controlling genes are responsive to environmental conditions. The switching allows these organisms to invade new hosts by changing surface molecules, one of the many mechanisms used by parasites in the continuous struggle against a host's defenses.

Mobile Genes

Insertion sequences are the simplest types of a series of movable elements of escalating complexity. The next type—bacterial elements that carry genes for resistance to bacteria-killing drugs (antibiotics)—is called *transposons* because they shift from one place to another. Each has resistance genes bracketed by two identical insertion sequences which contribute the functions needed for moving around. The resistance genes allow the host bacteria to grow in an environment containing antibiotics, consequently promoting the spread of the transposon itself. Transposons pick up the resistance genes from the bacterial genome in which the genes are not very active because of regulatory constraints. Lacking constraints, they become fully active in the transposons.

Movable bacterial elements of a third type are small DNA rings called *plasmids*. They differ from the elements previously described in that they are disconnected from the main DNA of the cell and multiply independently. A bacterium may contain from one to a hundred or more copies of the same plasmid, depending

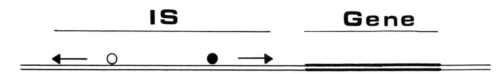

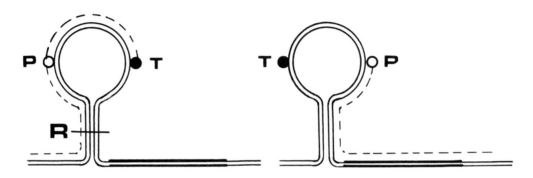

Figure 6.4. An insertion sequence acting as a switch for an adjacent gene. The sequence (IS) is flanked by inverted repeats (arrows) and contains a promoter, where transcription begins (open circle), and a terminator, where it ends (solid circle). In the configuration shown at left below, the terminator stops any transcription (dotted line) before it reaches the gene. The gene is inactive. In the configuration shown at right below, the promoter initiates transcription, which extends into the gene. The gene is active. One configuration can change into the other by recombination (R) between the inverted repeats.

on the kind. Plasmids, which can become inserted in the host cell's DNA, alternate between a free and an integrated state. Some promote the formation of bridges between bacteria, moving through them from one cell to another which increases their tendency to spread. They are equivalent to the viral genomes that are capable of peaceful coexistence with cells.

More complex still are certain plasmids known as *resistance transfer factors*, which also carry genes for resistance to antibiotics. They differ from transposons in that they not only pick resistance genes from bacteria but carry them into other bacteria, spreading resistance. Many of them carry several resistance genes which they obtain by accumulating transposons (fig. 6.5). Factors for multiple resistance and their transmissibility from one cell to another severely handicap the antibacterial therapy used in clinical and veterinary medicine. Their spread is promoted by the unnecessary use of antibiotics in medical practice, which confers an advantage on bacteria resistant to many drugs. This is an example of the harmful effects of using powerful biological agents without adequate appreciation of their consequences.

The most movable among all these elements are viruses, which replicate in cells as free autonomous genomes, some made up of DNA, some of RNA. Their

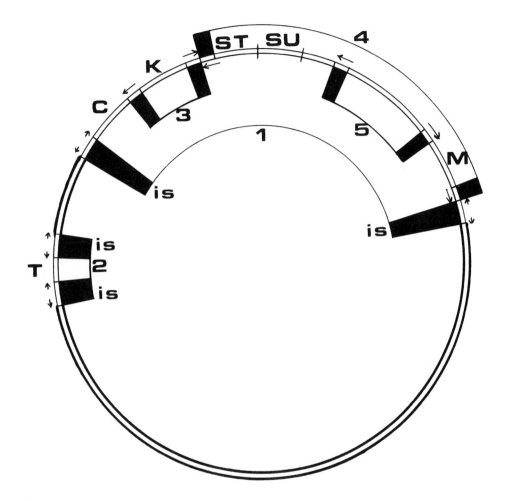

Figure 6.5. The anatomy of a bacterial resistance transfer factor. The factor is a ring-shaped DNA helix. Part of it (heavy lines) represents the original plasmid and contains genes devoted to its replication and to its transfer from one bacterium to another. Another part is made up of transposons, which have entered the original plasmid separately. Transposons 1 and 2 entered the plasmid at independent sites; transposons 3 and 4 entered within transposon 1; and transposon 5 entered within transposon 4. The sequence in which the various inserts took place is unknown. Any transposon can readily move in and out of the factor. The arrows indicate the inverted repeat sequences that flank transposons 3, 4, and 5. Transposons 1 and 2 are flanked by insertion sequences (is) that are different for the two transposons. Each insertion sequence, in turn, is flanked by two short inverted repeats. The resistance transfer factor contains genes that confer resistance to the following antibiotics: chloramphenicol (C) within 1, tetracyclin (T) within 2, kanamycin (K) within 3, streptomycin (ST), sulfonamide (SU), and mercury (M) within 4, and ampicillin (A) within 5. (Modified from S. N. Cohen and J. A. Shapiro, *Scientific American* 242:60 [1980].)

relatedness to transposable elements is clear in the case of retroviruses (see chapter 15), which have a genome bracketed by two rather long repeats. Viruses, like plasmids, move from cell to cell, but in a more efficient way: they wrap their genomes in a shell of protein molecules or in a membrane to form viral particles. The particles are released, often after the cells die, and invade other cells. Like plasmids, some viral genomes can become integrated in the cellular DNA or can pick up cellular genes, an event that sometimes creates a cancer virus (see chapter 15).

The Increase of Genes in Number

DNA's mobility is not limited to the specialized sequences or genomes we have considered so far. Every DNA sequence can jump around, although not as frequently and efficiently. This ability explains the formation of the gene families considered in the previous chapter. Having examined the various mechanisms by which genes can change or move around, we can now investigate how the families arose. Two conditions are necessary for a gene family to be created: a gene must generate copies of itself and insert them into the genome as extra genes, and their sequences must be prevented from drifting apart without restraint under the drive of mutational events.

There is much evidence that genes can double: a DNA containing genes A, B, C, D, E, F . . . evolves into one with genes A, B, *C, C,* D, E, F . . . . Gene C has doubled. This event is commonplace. It is the mechanism, for instance, by which flies cope with extremely high demands for certain proteins when they make eggs. The developing egg is surrounded by feeder cells that supply needed components, such as proteins for its shell. The number of genes for proteins in the feeder cells increases hundreds of times—a phenomenon called *gene amplification.* The new copies of the genes are present as free DNA. A similar gene amplification can be recognized in some flies by observing the salivary gland chromosomes in the microscope. It will be recalled from chapter 1 that these giant chromosomes are made up of bundles of DNA molecules connected side by side with their sequences in perfect register. The chromosomes are characterized by cross-bands that bear a fixed relation to genes. Amplification of genes in some bands causes them to swell, forming puffs (fig. 6.6). That DNA replicates in the puff can be shown by exposing the cells to a radioactive molecule suitable for making DNA; autoradiography then detects the radioactivity.

Gene amplification can also be observed when cancer cells are treated with the anticancer drug methotrexate. This drug antagonizes a factor essential for manufacturing the T nucleotides needed for making DNA, thereby killing the cancer cells. The effectiveness of methotrexate, however, declines after its initial success because the cells become resistant to it by manufacturing increased amounts of the factor it antagonizes. The amplification of the corresponding gene is demonstrated in these cells by using radioactive probes. In cell cultures exposed

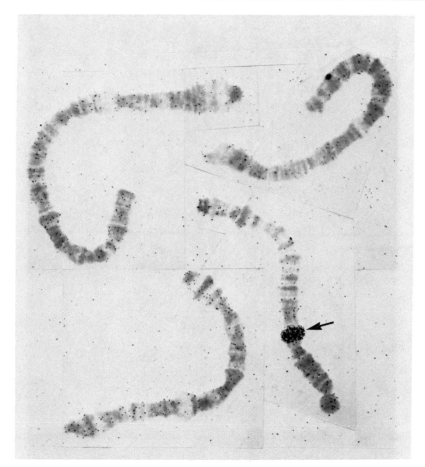

Figure 6.6. A puff in one of the four salivary gland chromosomes of a fly. The puff (at arrow) is revealed by autoradiography after hybridizing the whole chromosome with a probe for a gene contained in the puff. The puff has a high concentration of silver grains because it contains sixteen copies of the gene DNA. This gene is active at only one stage of development. Magnified 1,500 times. (From D. M. Glover et al., *PNAS* 79:2947 [1982].)

to extremely high concentrations of methotrexate the number of genes can reach a hundred or more. The repeated segment is quite large, containing much extra DNA besides the gene; when the repeated segments are numerous, they are easily recognizable in the chromosomes as a region with special staining properties (fig. 6.7).

These observations raise two questions: how does amplification occur, and is it caused by methotrexate? Concerning the first question, it seems that amplification takes place in two steps. First, a piece of the chromosome is doubled by local

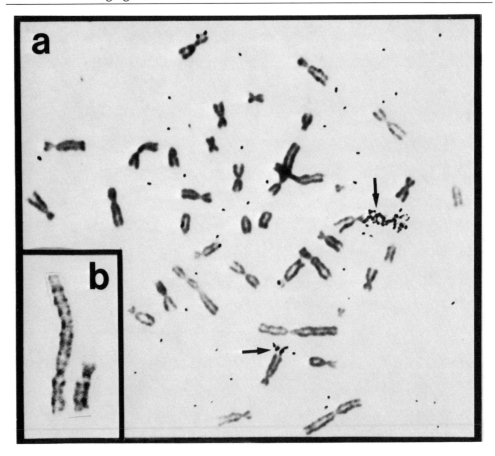

Figure 6.7. Accumulation of copies of an amplified gene in a chromosome of a cell resistant to a cell-killing drug, PALA. Panel a shows the chromosomes of a cell in mitosis. The chromosomes were hybridized to a radioactive probe for the gene responsible for resistance to PALA; a radioautograph was then made. The silver grains show that two chromosomes contain copies of the gene (at arrows). This is the result of DNA exchanges. Insert b shows the chromosome with the longest number of copies of the gene together with the normal chromosome of the same pair. The long chromosome contains 150 repeats of the gene with flanking sequences. Magnified 1,000 times. Courtesy of G. Wahl.

DNA replication and recombination (figs. 6.8, 6.9). Then further doublings occur by a different mechanism, unequal recombination (to be discussed below), which comes into play when each homologous chromosome has at least two copies of a gene. Concerning the second question, however, the role of methotrexate in amplification is not clear. It seems that the gene can be amplified in cells not exposed to methotrexate, although the drug can induce amplification by preventing the incorporation of Ts in newly made DNA. The gap left by the absence of a T either becomes the starting point of new local replication or activates error-prone repair similar to the bacterial SOS system.

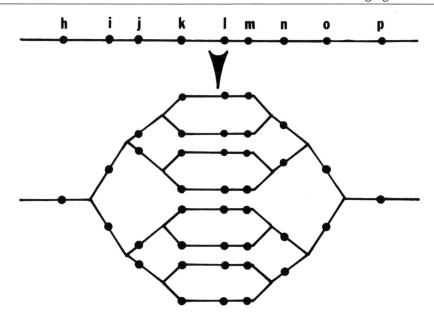

Figure 6.8. Mechanism of gene amplification by local replication. The initial DNA double helix (shown as a single line) is seen at top. It carries markers h to p. Repeated local replication is assumed to begin around marker l and to proceed in both directions. The result is shown at bottom. This model predicts that the markers will not be equally represented: there should be a gradient, central markers (k, l, m) being most frequent and markers at either side less frequent. Such gradients are in fact observed. The complex structure can then be resolved by a series of recombinations to generate a linear structure with repetitions.

In some cases amplified genes form distinct small chromosomes, called *double minute chromosomes* (fig. 6.10). Containing exclusively the amplified segment, they are not connected to the apparatus that regularly distributes each chromosome of a pair to the two daughter cells at division. Rather, they are distributed at random, so that some cells get more, and some get less. Thus the extent of amplification varies from cell to cell. Double minute chromosomes are found not only in cancer cells treated with cell-killing drugs but also in some congenital human diseases characterized by high incidence of cancer. Thus, gene amplification, or the mechanism that causes it, has many different biological effects.

Genes in Any Number

Genes present in more than one copy in a chromosome can be easily amplified to great numbers. An example is the formation of families of genes for ribosomal RNAs in the fly *Drosophila*. The number of these genes varies slightly among different flies, but an extreme variation occasionally occurs: a fly may have many fewer genes than the average and be severely crippled because it cannot make sufficient amounts of proteins. What is surprising is that such a crippled fly can

Figure 6.9. Electron micrograph of DNA obtained from the feeder cells of the fly *Drosophila*, showing the effect of local replication according to the scheme of figure 6.8. The unreplicated DNA is below; the amplified DNA is at the top. Several bifurcations are indicated by arrows. Magnified 50,000 times. (From Y. N. Osheim and O. L. Miller, Jr., *Cell* 33:543–53 [1983].)

generate as offspring normal flies with a regular number of ribosomal RNA genes. The normal flies are generated by a process known as *unequal recombination*.

We saw in chapter 1 that when a DNA helix, a chromatid, replicates it produces two daughter helixes, the sister chromatids. Because they have identical sequences, the two sister chromatids can undergo homologous recombination and generate exchanges detectable by staining techniques (fig. 6.11). Normally these *sister chromatid exchanges* have no noticeable consequences because the parts exchanged are identical (fig. 6.12). But in the case of repeated genes, recombina-

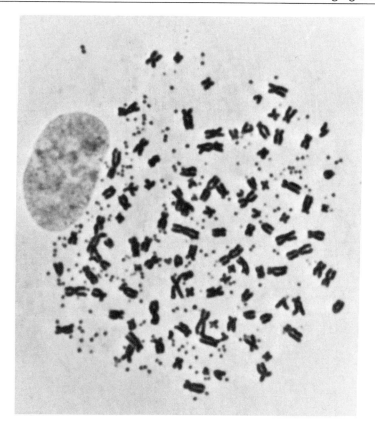

Figure 6.10. Double minute chromosomes in a cell resistant to methotrexate as they appear during mitosis. The regular chromosomes are X-shaped because their chromatids are still connected together at the centromere (the structure through which they are pulled apart at a later stage of mitosis). Double minute chromosomes, which are present in great numbers, look like dots, often paired. Magnified 1,000 times. (From J. Masters, B. Keely, H. Gay, and G. Attardi, *Molecular and Cellular Biol.* 2:498–507 [1982].)

tion can occur between noncorresponding repeats. For instance, repeat number 2 of a helix may recombine with repeat number 55 of the other helix. The result of this unequal recombination is that one helix gains all the repeats between the two recombination points, whereas the other helix loses them. After the chromatids move to the two daughter cells, one cell will have gained 53 genes, which are lost by the other.

Direct evidence that sister chromatid exchanges can modify the number of repeated genes in a family was obtained through experiments with a strain of yeast unable to make a certain amino acid and therefore unable to grow. By genetic engineering, the gene for the synthesis of the amino acid was fused to a ribosomal RNA gene, and the complex was then introduced into the deficient yeast, enabling it to grow. In its progeny many cells lacked the amino acid gene, whereas others had several copies—a result to be expected from unequal recom-

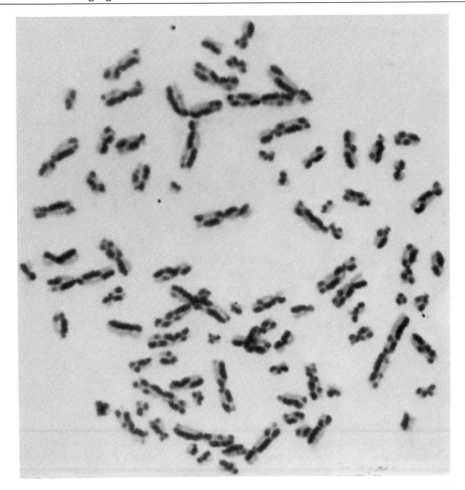

Figure 6.11. The effect of double chromatid exchanges seen in chromosomes during mitosis. Each chromosome contains the two sister chromatids, which have not yet separated. Before entering mitosis, the cells were treated in such a way as to make the two chromatids distinguishable by staining, one being dark, the other light. Many chromatid exchanges occurred after the treatment. As a result, each chromatid contains alternating light and dark segments derived from the two original chromatids. Magnified 1,000 times. (From S. Wolff et al., *Nature* 265:347 [1977].)

bination between the ribosomal RNA gene attached to the amino acid gene and the other ribosomal RNA genes of the cells.

Correction

The mechanisms by which genes move around and are amplified explain the formation of gene families, but they do not explain a puzzling characteristic of

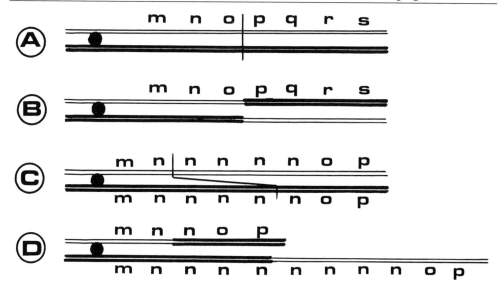

Figure 6.12. (A) Exchange between two sister chromatids. (B) The exchange has no functional consequence because the genetic constitution of the chromatids remains unchanged. (C) Unequal exchange between chromatids in which gene n is repeated. (D) This exchange has functional consequences because the lower chromatid has gained three n genes while the upper one has lost them. The centromere (black circle) holds the chromatids together while the exchanges take place.

some families, in particular that of ribosomal RNA genes that are made of *almost identical* members. How is this uniformity maintained in spite of the occurrence of mutations and other genetic changes? A possible mechanism is *sequence correction*, which occurs whenever there is recombination, as, for instance, during sister chromatid exchange. Correction occurs when recombining DNA helixes exchange strands, generating *hybrid segments* (refer again to fig. 6.2).

As an example, let's consider the case in which a GC base pair, produced by mutation, replaces the regular AT pair in one of two homologous genes undergoing recombination (fig. 6.13). In the hybrid segment G would pair with T or C with A; in either case the two bases would not be complementary. They do not form the regular hydrogen bonds, and they stay at a greater than normal distance from each other, distorting the helix. Where the helix bulges, a repair mechanism comes into play: repair enzymes remove a string of bases on one strand and fill the gap by copying the other strand. In this way one of the genes acquires the sequences of the other gene over a certain length. This process is also known as *gene conversion*. During unequal recombination, gene conversion causes the replacement of part of a gene with the corresponding part of another gene of the same family. It is a mechanism for reshuffling the genes' information and is used by many organisms; we will see several examples in this book. Frequent repetitions

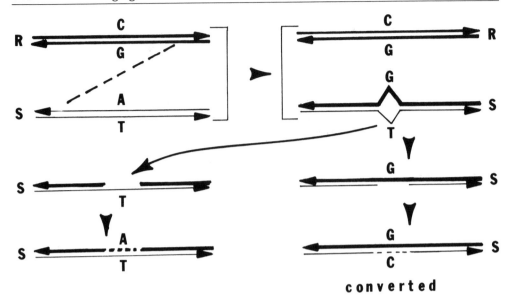

converted

Figure 6.13. Error correction in a hybrid double helix formed between two genes of a pair. The two chromosomes R and S (upper left), differing at a base pair, undergo recombination, generating a hybrid segment in chromosome S (right). Two bases do not form regular bonds. The bulge is eliminated by enzymes that remove one of the two bases and rebuild the strand by copying the other strand. The result at left is the same as the original S chromosome, whereas that at right has been corrected, becoming like the R chromosome.

of gene conversion can maintain the uniformity of the sequences in a family of genes.

Genes Jumping Around

Multiple copies of a gene may be formed by jumping DNA such as transposons. Some animals have families of repetitive sequences in which each member is bracketed by two equal short repeats. It is inferred that these repetitive sequences are transposons because the repeats are their hallmark. Some repetitive sequences are found inserted within other repetitive sequences, or even in the intervening sequences of some genes, suggesting they are invaders. In plants, transposing elements are suspected to form the B chromosomes, which, as we saw in chapter 4, alter the activity of neighboring genes like movable elements.

Jumping elements of another kind, viruses, may also cause DNA movement. In fact, the constitution of some of the largest families of relatively short repeats (eighty to three hundred base pairs), which exist in many animals, suggest that they are produced by the same process of reverse transcription of RNA into DNA that causes the replication of retroviruses. Like RNA messengers, the sequences have a string of As at what would be the downstream end, and, like the integrated retroviral genomes, they are flanked by two short inverted repeats. The sequences are somewhat homologous to various cellular RNAs. Some are similar to the RNA present in the particles that recognize the signal sequence during the manufacture of proteins in cells; others are related to various kinds of transfer RNAs, which are part of the protein-making machinery. That these sequences are in rapid evolution is clear from the fact that they differ markedly even in related species. New members seem to be continuously produced, using internal signals for transcription by the special transcriptase that produces transfer RNAs. The inference is that after being transcribed into RNAs, they are then retranscribed back into DNA and integrated at a different place. Thus these sequences seem to be in a highly dynamic state.

The question arises: which kind of enzyme carried out the reverse transcription of these sequences? It might be the enzyme used by retroviruses; if so, these viruses play an important role in generating new gene copies and in the evolution of cells. Or the cells themselves might contain a gene for a reverse transcriptase, perhaps as part of a transposable element that was the precursor of retroviruses. The answer is not yet known.

Impotent Genes

The amplification of sequences by reverse transcription explains the existence of certain genes that are closely related in sequences to active genes, but have mutations that prevent function. These *pseudogenes* are usually located far from the genes to which they are related and have features characteristic of reverse transcription: they are terminated by a series of AT pairs, they lack intervening sequences, and they are flanked by two short inverted repeats. These features clearly show that these are *invading genes* which were made by reverse transcription of messages and were then integrated at random in the genome.

Another class of pseudogenes has a different origin. They are present in all families of repeated genes, such as those for globin, for immunoglobulin, and for ribosomal RNAs. These pseudogenes, although they have the same organization of regular genes, have altered sequences and are therefore unable to cause the synthesis of functional protein—they are *dead genes*. The primary alteration causing the formation of pseudogenes may be failure of transcription; mutations would then accumulate because they are inconsequential. This interpretation is based on a study of a globin pseudogene that is not transcribed. After the gene was isolated and connected to the control region of an active globin gene, it was transcribed again. Evidently in the chromosome the pseudogene had a faulty control region. A globin gene with minimal or no transcription (mentioned in chapter 5) is probably in the process of becoming a pseudogene through this mechanism.

Although pseudogenes are inactive, they are not inconsequential because they can donate some of their sequences to active genes by gene conversion (see below). For this reason they are important in evolution.

DNA Jumping from One Cell to Another

DNA movements are not confined to a cell. DNA can also move from one cell to another through plasmids or viruses and from one individual to another during sexual intercourse (see chapter 9). All these movements may appear to be special cases, but in fact they reflect a general property of DNA. DNA from many sources (cells, bacteria, or viruses) can colonize animal cells grown in the laboratory, provided the right method is used. When DNA is presented to a cell in fine clumps, it is swallowed and some of it finds its way to the cell's genome, where it becomes integrated. The foreign genes, then an integral part of the cell's DNA, are often able to express their activity from their new location. The same result can be obtained by injecting the DNA into the cell, using a microsyringe. If, for example, the DNA is injected into the nucleus of a mouse's fertilized egg, the genes will be found in many cells of the adult animal and sometimes even in its germ cells.

The success of these laboratory experiments shows that cells have mechanisms for unrestrained transfer of DNA and that they sometimes use them. They raise the question whether DNA is ever transferred naturally from one species to another. Although there is no evidence for transfer of naked DNA from one cell to another, transfer does occur across membranes within the same cells—between nucleus and mitochondria or chloroplasts, and between mitochondria and chloroplasts. Exchanges between cells of different species are promoted by viruses: cancer viruses transfer cancer genes from one animal species to another with obvious consequences, and the same viruses may well transfer, unnoticed, other kinds of genes.

Cancer genes are also transferred to plants by a bacterium that carries a cancer-inducing plasmid that becomes integrated in the plant DNA. Cancer is produced by the activity of the plasmid's genes. Transfer of genes from animal to plant cells, and vice versa, might also be mediated in similar ways by bacteria or viruses acting as intermediate vectors.

Some Unanswered Questions

All the information available about repeat sequences and their origin leaves unanswered the question, why are they so abundant in eukaryotes but absent in prokaryotes? Although bacteria are also capable of recombination and transposition, most of them have no families of repeat sequences, nor do mitochondria in animal cells, which are modified prokaryotes.

Just why this is so is not certain. In bacteria, repeat sequences might be detrimental: these organisms compete with each other in speed of growth, and they would be slowed down if the size of the genome were increased by irrelevant DNA. In the case of animal mitochondria another reason may be inferred: all their DNA is packed with genes essential for the cells, and any transposition would be lethal. Another possible reason is the lack of intervening sequences in bacteria and animal mitochondria; these genomes therefore lack places where new DNA could be inserted without inactivating genes. It would be impossible for mobile DNA to colonize the genome successfully, settling in a safe place and from there making forays to other relatively vulnerable spots. These, however, are all speculations; we don't know the real reasons for this difference between eukaryotes and pro-karyotes.

Also unanswered is the question raised at the beginning of this chapter: why do lizards have twenty times more DNA than humans? We know only that the difference is in the highly repetitive sequences. An intriguing possibility concerns the internal temperatures of the animals: mammals maintain their temperature at a level usually higher than that of cold-blooded animals, such as lizards. The amount of DNA tends to be higher in organisms that live at a lower temperature. This effect is strong in plants: for instance, wheat that is adapted to cold climates has considerably more DNA than regular wheat. But even if the temperature difference accounts for lizards' having more DNA, we do not understand the reasons for it. The increased DNA may be useful at the lower temperature or, conversely, living at a low temperature may make a higher DNA content more tolerable.

DNA Movement and Life

We have so far described the sequences of genomes and the changes they undergo, but we have neglected the most important aspect (except in isolated cases): what is the effect of these changes on the life of the organism?

A general answer is that DNA changes have important repercussions for the cells in which they take place and for DNA itself because they affect the activity of the cells and their interaction with the environment. These interactions ultimately determine which kinds of DNA variation are acceptable. An adventurous DNA, with many movable elements, tandem repeats, and sites for effective site-specific recombination, will change and move around a lot. This mobility will often interfere with the orderly function of the genes, effecting the cell unfavorably. If the cell cannot compete favorably in its environment, the DNA it contains will disappear. By this mechanism of *cell selection* DNA's intrinsic tendency to change and move around is kept in check. The mechanism does not *directly* prevent the DNA from changing or moving around excessively, but it eliminates those cells in which excessive movement has happened; it exerts, in other words, an after-the-fact control on DNA's characteristics.

Adventurous DNA, however, is not all bad. Useful effects, for instance, are the intermingling of sequences and the duplication of genes, which have played an immense role in shaping today's life. DNA's adventurousness, then, is a double-edged sword. Whether certain consequences are good or bad for life depends on the conditions in which the cells live. More specific answers can be had by considering a few examples.

Many parasites that lead a precarious existence in the body of their animal host are under continuous attack by the host's defenses, yet they manage to survive. In several cases, DNA mobility provides the mechanism.

Important among these are trypanosomes, the small eukaryotic parasites that in Africa cause sleeping sickness in humans and some animals. They are stubbornly resistant to the defenses of the organisms they infect because they continuously change their coats. These small creatures are carried by tsetse flies, which inject them into the bloodstream of the animals they feed on. The animal responds by producing special protein molecules—antibodies that bind to the coat of the parasite and stop its growth. The coat on any given parasite is made up of numerous molecules all of the same kind. But when the antibodies have almost gained control, parasites with a different coat make their appearance. The existing antibodies do not bind to the new coat, the parasites multiply again unhindered, and the animal has to produce a new kind of antibody to cope with the changed coat. This requires a week or two, during which time the parasites with the new coat increase to large numbers. The cycle repeats itself: when the new antibodies are produced, the second wave of parasites disappear, but yet another kind emerges with coat molecules different from the first two. If the animal survives, it becomes permanently infected, harboring a continuously changing population of parasites.

The study of this phenomenon has uncovered an amazing organization in the parasite's DNA. Radioactive probes specific for the genes that specify coat proteins have revealed that a hundred or more genes are devoted to coat variation, each gene specifying one kind of coat molecule. These genes are grouped together in the genome, forming a large family. Very similar to each other, they vary in details; the proteins they specify are sufficiently different to recognize different antibodies. Only one is active at a given time—that is, only one is transcribed and generates coat molecules. The coat variation is obtained by activating only one in turn in various ways. In one mechanism, the active gene is found at a special location, an *expression box* at the end of a chromosome, some distance from the other inactive genes. The DNA upstream to the expression box has sequences that promote transcription. One of the inactive genes, located far from the end of the chromosome, can become active later by inserting a copy into the expression box to replace the preexisting gene; but the original copy of the activated gene still remains at the old site, keeping the repertoire of the genes unchanged (fig. 6.14). The replacement of the genes probably occurs by gene conversion; some sequences of the old gene responsible for the interaction with antibodies are replaced by those of the new gene. Another mechanism of variation involves untranscribed genes located at the ends of some chromosomes, which are moved by

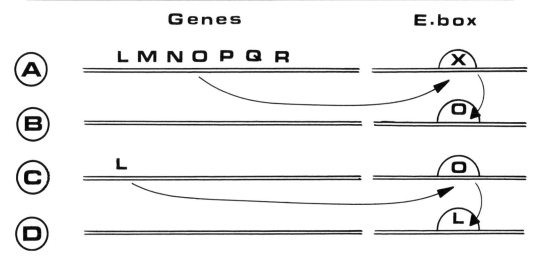

Figure 6.14. The mechanism of coat change in trypanosomes by gene transposition. (A) It shows some genes (indicated as L to R) for the coat proteins and the expression box occupied by gene X. Gene O is being moved to the expression box. (B) Gene O is now in the expression box and specifies the coat protein. (C) While gene O is in the expression box, gene L is being moved. (D) Gene L has replaced gene O and specifies the new coat protein. The silent copies of all genes remain unchanged at their location.

recombination to the end of an active chromosome, where they are transcribed; the gene that was formerly active persists but becomes inactive. And finally, in a third mechanism we do not understand, a gene may become active even without changing position. It is not clear why there are three mechanisms of gene activation. Presumably it has to do with the life cycle of the parasite, which switches between two hosts: flies and humans. The various mechanisms may operate at different phases of the cycle.

This fascinating genetic mechanism is employed, although with some changes, by other parasites. The agent of relapsing fever, a spirochete (a bacterium), encounters similar problems and solves them by a similar gene exchange. Another bacterium, the agent of gonorrhea, uses a somewhat different method in which part of the gene for the hairlike appendages by which it sticks to the cells of the urinary canal is changed. Again this change permits it to elude the defense of the host. The mechanism is surprisingly similar to that by which genes for immunoglobulin are generated in animals (see chapter 13). All these devices are extremely effective for promoting the survival of the parasites.

Another important consequence of DNA mobility and variation appears to be related to the formation of new species (see chapter 20). We have already seen that the highly repetitive sequences might maintain the separation of species by affecting the pairing of the chromosomes during the formation of germ cells. They may also cause the formation of new species in the following way: a mutation appears in one of the repeats of a creature and in successive generations spreads within the family of repeats by gene conversion. At first the mutated repeats are in a small proportion and do not interfere with the pairing of chromosomes. If, however, they become predominant or replace the whole family, the chromosomes that contain them can no longer pair with the chromosomes of a normal individual. This event divides the creatures into two distinct groups: one with most repeats mutated, the other without mutations. Fertile matings will occur within one or the other group, but not between them. The creatures with the mutated genes become isolated from the rest of the population and form a new species. Although this is an attractive model for the generation of new species, it is hypothetical.

DNA: What Is Its Role after All?

The first impression of DNA is that of a conservative element of the cells, which stores almost immutable genetic information, essentially equal for all the individuals of a species—not only for now but for all the foreseeable future as well. This view, however, does not hold in the face of many of DNA's characteristics, such as split genes, gene amplification, reverse transcription, movable sequences, repeated sequences, plasmids, and viruses. These features shed a new, unexpected light on DNA. The conservative, stodgy old gentleman is not what he looks like: he is a revolutionary, moving around a lot and constantly threatening the orderly regularity of the genome.

This is not surprising, after all. DNA is the only constituent of the cells that has the ability to reproduce itself. This ability must originally have been an attribute of even small DNA segments, and unlimited replication must have been the goal of life from the beginning. But limitations soon arose. We can see this by trying to imagine how the most primitive cell might have behaved. This cell, which already represented an advanced step in the evolution of life, probably contained a small piece of DNA capable of replication. The DNA in turn must have contained genes of various kinds: those specifying proteins needed for its replication, transcription, and translation; genes for the machinery needed for making such proteins; genes for making the membranes to hold all these ingredients together; and genes for energy transformation—already an impressive array of mechanisms. In these cells the DNA probably tended to replicate in an uncontrolled way at the fastest possible speed. The speed, however, depended on factors extraneous to the DNA, such as the supply of food and sources of energy, which are derived from the environment. So, in fact, the speed of DNA replication came to depend on environmental factors.

Once a population of such cells built up in a certain localized environment, they would compete for food, and a DNA that developed more efficient methods for food utilization could outgrow the others. Specialization of the DNA in this direction occurred through mechanisms already built into DNA, such as mutation, recombination, and joining of segments. Using these devices, the DNA of some cells learned how to control its growth, avoiding excessive bursts of replication followed by starvation. A progressive improvement of the regulatory controls slowly led to the organization that is today characteristic for a large part of DNA. This is the *responsible DNA,* whose functions are attuned to the needs of the cell.

A major step in this process of DNA domestication was the formation of long DNA molecules by the joining of shorter molecules. Bacterial cells ended up with a single long DNA molecule that replicated by starting at a single point. This strategy avoided competition among independent molecules in the same cell. Eukaryotic cells, on the other hand, came to be composed of several long DNA molecules, but they continued to replicate as if they were made up of small independent segments. Thus mammalian DNA today contains as many as fifty thousand such segments among its few tens of chromosomes. They probably represent previously separate molecules. The replication of all these segments in a cell is now coordinated and responsive to the availability of food supplies or growth-controlling substances. The many controls of transcription, influenced by a variety of environmental substances, are probably parts of this scheme.

Not all DNA, however, become responsible. Some molecules retained their innate tendency to more or less unrestrained replication. These molecules of *irresponsible DNA* became specialized as insertion sequences, transposons, movable elements, plasmids, and viruses, all coexisting with responsible DNA in the same cell. Whereas the responsible DNA governed the competition of the cell with other cells, the irresponsible DNA continued to take care only of itself. It perfected its mechanisms for parasitizing the responsible DNA by becoming integrated into it; like an invading, anarchic guest, it altered the function of the responsible DNA. These effects were mostly damaging for the cell because they inactivated genes, but occasionally they were useful—when, for instance, by chance they caused the doubling of needed genes. One can envision a tug of war: responsible DNA bent on increasing the cell's fitness for its environment versus irresponsible DNA tending only to increase its own amount regardless of its relationship to the cell's needs.

We can think of the situation existing today in animal and plant cells as a state (or stalemate) in this drawn-out battle. Irresponsible DNA today pervades responsible DNA in the form of many kinds of repeated sequences and pseudogenes. These invasions may have claimed as victims the cells that lost essential genes and disappeared. Organisms existing today may be those in which the invasion occurred, but their genes withstood disruption. That most repeated sequences are not transcribed, so that they do not soak up energy or upset the working of the cell, may represent a useful compromise.

In the advanced organisms living today, then, a sort of equilibrium may have been reached in which irresponsible DNA is largely under control of responsible DNA for its replication. The widespread presence of irresponsible DNA may even protect the genome: new integrations of moving DNA tend to occur mostly in the repeated sequences that already exist without affecting essential genes, because the recombination sites that were instrumental in the integration of these sequences allow new wandering DNA to settle in. Moreover, although many forms of irresponsible DNA, all bent on their own perpetuation, still persist as autonomous elements, they sometimes help responsible DNA. For instance, resistance transfer factors protect bacteria from attack by antibiotics by mobilizing genes for resistance.

There is no way to judge a priori the value of a certain DNA. In the large variety of cells that exist in the biological world, the fate of all DNAs, including irresponsible ones, is tightly tied to the performance of the cells to which they belong. Irresponsible DNA carrying antibiotic-resistance genes is beneficial to bacteria, but not to animals, in which it is a parasite. Salvation for some DNAs is for others ruin.

DNA against DNA: this is the war of life. The selfishness of DNA reflects on the cells, and from the cells on the organisms, and from the organisms on the social complexes they construct. Existing at every level is competition for food and other requirements of special value to each type of organization, a competition that may not end until one of the competitors is destroyed. On the other hand, necessity has imposed cooperation: between DNAs within the same cell, between cells in organisms, and between organisms that form societies. Cooperation and competition go hand in hand at every level as a biological necessity; their precarious balance varies with the evolutionary stage, the state of genes, and the interactions of cells, individuals, and social groups. The balance may shift in unpredictable ways to generate new genomes, new cells, new species, new social organizations. In the living world everything flows: we can be certain of what exists today but not of the shape of tomorrow.

CHAPTER 7

Slave DNA

For a long period in the history of life, DNA was confined to cells, determining their characteristics during the development of individuals or the evolution of species. DNA also learned how to move from one cell to another as a plasmid or a virus, sometimes crossing species barriers. By using its many techniques of recombination, DNA gave rise to an immense number of combinations of genes.

In the late seventies a new episode began in the saga of DNA mobility. Scientists learned how to join at will genes from cells of widely different origins and to introduce the combined molecules into yet another set of different cells. Human's ability to produce new gene combinations freed DNA from the constraints imposed by nature and placed it in the hands of scientists. DNA the master had been made slave—an awesome event that the human imagination could hardly cope with. Like any event of possibly enormous significance, it has generated anxiety and profound emotional reactions, ranging from exhilaration to fear. Is this the beginning of a new stage of life?

Cloning and Amplifying DNA

Scientists obtained these sensational results by their persistent efforts to learn how genes are made and how they work. To acquire this knowledge they needed a way to determine the sequences of the bases of any given gene. The first step in this direction was to develop methods for isolating genes cleanly from the rest of the DNA and for producing them in large amounts.

The main tools in this technology are the site-specific DNA-cutting enzymes we have already met in chapter 5. But although these enzymes allow scientists to

127

isolate genes present in small viral genomes, they are ineffective with large genomes, in which each gene is a very small proportion of the total DNA. This difficulty was overcome by the brilliant approach of DNA cloning. The term *clone* identifies a population of DNA molecules which, having been derived from the same ancestor, are identical (except for rare mutations).

The general principle of DNA cloning is to isolate a gene and replicate it many times, generating a very large number of copies. This is accomplished by inserting the gene into a small self-replicating DNA—for instance, that of a bacteriophage or a plasmid—which acts as *cloning vector*. The cloning vector with the inserted gene, called the *hybrid vector*, is then introduced into bacteria where it replicates, generating a large number of copies of itself and, consequently, of the inserted gene.

The construction of the hybrid vector relies on the use of site-specific cutting enzymes that make two closely staggered cuts in the target sequence (fig. 7.1). A typical procedure employs an enzyme that cuts the vector at a single target, producing two fragments if the vector is linear (such as phage DNA) or a single linear molecule if the vector is a ring (such as plasmid DNA). The cut ends have short protruding tails complementary to each other (see chapter 5). The same enzyme is used to separate the gene from the rest of the DNA, ensuring that the tails of the gene and the vector are the same. Complementary tails join, forming helixes that hold the pieces together. The joints are then stabilized by a tying enzyme, *ligase*, which connects the two ends of the strands by chemical bonds. The target for the cutting enzyme, needed for the next step, is thus reconstituted.

Certain conditions must be met for making a hybrid vector. The gene must be isolated without altering its essential properties and must be inserted at a place where it does not impair the multiplication of the vector. To satisfy these conditions for a variety of genes, different cloning vectors were developed containing targets for different cutting enzymes.

After multiplication in bacteria, the hybrid vector is separated from bacterial DNA and is cut with the same enzyme used to prepare the vector. The enzyme cuts at the exact boundary between gene and vector, releasing the gene DNA in its original form and in large amounts. This DNA can be cut with other site-specific enzymes, as described in chapter 5, providing segments suitable for sequence analysis and for manipulations.

The progress of the cloning technology has been such that it is now possible to subdivide the whole genome of an organism into many segments, each contained in a vector. A collection of such hybrid vectors constitutes a "library." Libraries have been made for the entire genome of viruses, of bacteria, of the fruitfly *Drosophila*, and of human chromosomes. These libraries are used for isolating specific genes, provided DNA or RNA probes are available. Fragments of the cloned DNA can be fused together in any order and orientation to build new DNA sequences. The totality of these manipulations is called "genetic engineering."

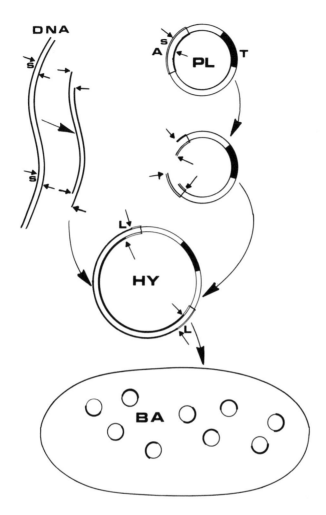

Figure 7.1. Preparation of a hybrid vector. The vector at the right is a plasmid (PL) carrying two genes for resistance to antibiotics: A (ampicillin) and T (tetracycline). When the plasmid is introduced into a bacterium, it makes it resistant to these antibiotics. The plasmid contains, among others, a target for a site-specific cutting enzyme, s, identified by two arrows within the A gene. When the plasmid is cut by the enzyme, the A gene is inactivated. At left is shown the cellular DNA containing the gene of interest and targets for the same site-specific cutting enzyme. After the DNA is cut, the gene is isolated. The tails left by the enzyme in the gene and in the open plasmid are complementary. Using these tails the two DNAs are annealed together and permanently joined by the linking enzyme (L) to form the hybrid vector (HY). The hybrid plasmid is introduced into bacteria (BA) in which it replicates, producing many identical copies of itself. Bacteria containing the hybrid plasmid can be identified because they are resistant to antibiotic T but not to antibiotic A.

Consequences of Cloning

Rare Drugs

The achievements of the technology of DNA cloning for learning about genes and DNA sequences have been remarkable. Many of the results obtained and their impact on our understanding of DNA and of life are described in various parts of this book. The possible applications of this technology, however, go well beyond the knowledge they provide. It might be useful for producing new drugs, improving crops, and possibly for treating humans affected by hereditary diseases. Many of these applications have already been realized in the laboratory and by industry and others are on the drawing board. Still others are at the dream stage.

Recombinant DNA offers a new approach for manufacturing drugs that are produced naturally in the body. Among them are small proteins, the polypeptide hormones (see chapter 8), and viral proteins that could be used as vaccines for protecting people from infection. There are difficulties, however.

Cloning a human gene and making it work in bacteria is by no means simple. A general difficulty is that eukaryotic genes are not correctly expressed in many prokaryotes. These organisms do not recognize eukaryotic transcription signals and do not remove intervening sequences (see chapter 4), nor do they finish the proteins by splitting off pieces or by adding sugars as done by eukaryotic cells (see chapter 2). The finishing changes are crucial: splitting off parts allows an amino acid chain to fold into the proper shape; sugars keep the protein dissolved in a watery medium and mediate many interactions with other body constituents.

In the short history of the industrial use of DNA technology, all these difficulties have been met and solved in various ways. The problems of transcription signals have been solved by attaching the eukaryotic genes to efficient bacterial signals, and the problems arising from intervening signals have been met by cloning a DNA obtained by reverse transcription of cellular messengers, which lack the sequences. Some of the problems can be avoided in certain cases. One of the first targets of DNA cloning was the human gene for *growth hormone*, which is produced by the pituitary (a small gland at the base of the brain) and is required for growth of the body (see chapter 8). This hormone has a special property: each kind of mammal makes a different kind that acts only on individuals of the same species. Growth of human beings, for example, is promoted only by human growth hormone. In contrast, animal insulin is active in humans; bovine insulin is commonly used for treating people with diabetes. Human growth hormone needed for treating dwarfs is extracted from pituitary glands removed from cadavers. Not only is it very scarce and expensive, but it carries the danger of infection with agents of certain poorly understood chronic brain diseases. The gene for growth hormone does not contain intervening sequences and can be cloned directly.

But how could one clone this gene? Because it is just one of the hundred thousand or so genes present in human DNA, it was like finding a needle in a haystack. The isolation was made possible by the knowledge of the amino acid sequence of the hormone, which indicated the approximate size of the RNA messenger. Messengers of that size were obtained from tumors of the pituitary gland that produce the hormone; a fraction containing the messenger for growth hormone was identified for its ability to promote synthesis of the hormone in an artificial translation system. For final purification, DNA copies of these messengers, made by using the reverse transcriptase (see chapter 6), were cloned in bacteria (fig. 7.2). Pure clones were finally isolated from some colonies produced by the bacteria. The crucial question remained as to whether the growth hormone produced by the clones would be active—that is, capable of compensating for the hormonal deficiency in humans. But none of the possible obstacles materialized. The hormone produced in bacteria (called *recombinant growth hormone*) is fully active.

Another example of a substance of considerable interest produced through DNA cloning is *interferon*, a small protein. It is an extremely powerful substance made by many cells in response to viral infection, which prevents viral multiplication in cells. It also controls the cells' growth. It was thought that interferon might be useful for fighting viral diseases such as the common cold or flu, and possibly cancer, too. Like growth hormone, only interferon produced by human cells is active in humans. Because of these properties, it became an early candidate for manufacture by cloning.

The approach used for growth hormone could not be used for interferon, however: it is produced by cells in too small amounts to permit determination of the amino acid sequence. The strategy for cloning was based on the ability of the interferon messenger to make cells resistant against cell-killing viruses. Various fractions of RNA messengers from interferon-producing cells were deposited in spots on cultures of cells, which were later exposed to the virus. Only cells receiving the interferon messenger survived. Once the RNA fraction containing the interferon messenger was identified, it was transcribed into DNA and cloned. As in the case of growth hormone, it was not certain that the interferon produced in bacteria would be biologically active. Satisfactory yields were obtained by splicing the interferon genes to a bacterial control. The antiviral activity of the recombinant interferon proved to be similar to that of interferon made by animal cells. Moreover, the bacterial product lacks the impurities present in preparations from animal cells and is less toxic.

The work with interferon genes led to an important discovery—that there are three different kinds of interferons and many interferon genes. The multiplicity of genes would have gone undetected without DNA cloning. A practical consequence is that there are many interferons which may have different effects. Moreover, hybrid interferons produced by joining parts of the various genes in vitro have new and possibly useful characteristics.

The final example to be considered is more complicated. The desired product was a protein of large size, called factor VIII, which is essential for blood clotting

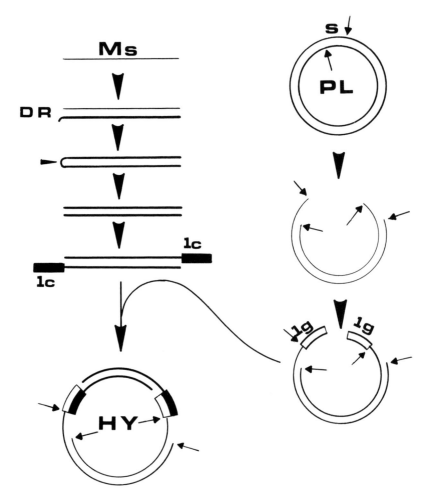

Figure 7.2. Cloning a gene starting from its RNA messenger. The messenger (Ms) is copied into DNA, using the reverse transcriptase, to generate a mixed double helix (DR) in which one strand is DNA (heavy line), the other RNA (thin line). After removing the RNA strand with an appropriate enzyme, a complementary DNA strand is built, using the same reverse transcriptase; the new DNA strand remains connected to the preexisting one. Cutting the connection (arrow) generates a regular double helical DNA. Then strings of Cs to serve as linkers (solid boxes, lc) are connected at the corresponding ends of each strand (the corresponding ends are at opposite ends of the helix because the strands point in opposite directions). As in figure 7.1, the vector plasmid (PL) has a target for a site-specific cutting enzyme (s), delineated by two arrows, and is cut by the enzyme. Strings of Gs to serve as linkers (empty boxes, lg) are added at the two corresponding ends of the cut plasmid. The cut plasmid is then annealed with the product of reverse transcription. The strings of Gs on one DNA make base pairs with the strings of Cs on the other generating the hybrid vector (HY). Small segments of the hybrid vector have only one strand: once the plasmid is introduced into bacteria, the gaps are filled by the repair enzymes of the cells. There are many variations and improvements of this basic method.

when blood vessels are cut or wounded. Platelets adhering to the damaged cells of the blood vessels release factors that start the clotting process. A series of enzymes present in the blood is activated one after another in a chain of events that culminates in the conversion of a blood protein, fibrinogen, into insoluble fibrin. Fibrin enmeshes the platelets, forming the clot. Clotting is deficient in individuals with defects in the gene for factor VIII, which is one of the enzymes. The condition—hemophilia A—exposes the patients to lethal bleeding from minor wounds. Factor VIII is a very rare commodity; it is present only in extremely small amounts in normal blood. Hemophiliacs are given a blood concentrate that restores clotting, but its use has great drawbacks. The concentrate is in very scarce supply and demand is high: there are more than ten thousand hemophiliacs in the United States. The recipients are at great risk of infection with certain blood-borne viruses: blood concentrates are one of the major sources of contamination with AIDS and hepatitis. Hence there is great need for an independent source of factor VIII through DNA cloning. But factor VIII could not be made in bacteria: it is a large protein and has lots of sugars added to it. To make the factor, new cloning vectors had to be developed that would be able to grow and make their products in animal cells.

Very efficient suitable vectors were developed from certain cancer viruses—retroviruses (see chapter 15). When a retrovirus infects an animal or human cell, its genome becomes integrated in the cell's DNA, flanked by sequences that allow a high expression of its genes. The normal viral genes are removed and replaced by the gene to be cloned, together with a gene for drug resistance, which allows the selection of the cells carrying the engineered genome.

Using a retroviral vector the factor VIII gene was cloned and expressed in cells growing in cultures; active protein is released in the culture medium. The gene could be identified using another novel development in biological technology: the monoclonal antibodies to be described in chapter 13. These antibodies are extremely selective reagents for identifying and isolating individual proteins. Factor VIII obtained from human plasma was first enriched and purified as much as possible by conventional means. It was then purified to a much greater degree using a monoclonal antibody. The amino acid sequence of part of the factor was determined, and from it the corresponding sequence of bases in DNA was deduced, using the translation code (see chapter 4). Segments of DNA with this sequence were made in the laboratory and used as probes for identifying the gene in libraries of human DNA. The gene was isolated and cloned.

Yeast and Plant Vectors

An interesting direction in the construction of eukaryotic vectors was taken when scientists based them on plasmids that grow in yeast cells. These eukaryotic cells grow much more rapidly than animal cells in simple media, almost like bacteria. An interferon gene attached to a yeast transcription signal cloned in yeast gave a higher yield than the bacterial vectors. But yeast vectors do not always splice correctly the intervening sequences of animal genes. This was not a problem with the interferon gene, however, for it does not contain intervening sequences.

Another thorny problem has been how to introduce foreign genes into plant cells, which would be useful for improving the yields of valuable products or making crop plants resistant to diseases. Neither bacterial nor animal virus vectors can carry genes into plant cells. A promising system uses a plasmid carried by certain soil bacteria that invade plant cells, causing them to become tumor cells. The plasmid is responsible for the tumor-causing activity. When the bacterium enters a plant cell, the plasmid is released and becomes integrated in the DNA of the cell, expressing its cancer-inducing genes. Genes introduced in this plasmid close to its control region become integrated in the DNA of plant cells and persist in the cells of the tumor that develops.

New Vaccines

Another field in which DNA cloning is expected to have a great impact is that of the production of vaccines for protecting humans or animals against viruses. Traditionally viral vaccines have been made by using either a genetically altered virus able to confer immunity but unable to cause disease (*live vaccines*) or a regular virus killed by agents that do not impair its ability to generate immunity (*killed vaccines*). In either case, because the virus must be grown in adequate amounts in cultures of animal cells, vaccines cannot be made if suitable cells are not available.

This problem has limited production of vaccines to some viruses that produce severe diseases, such as infantile diarrhea, often fatal, or hepatitis B, which causes liver cancer in many tropical or subtropical countries. An effective vaccine for hepatitis B is made up of viral proteins from the blood of chronically infected humans, but it is in scarce supply. Vaccines of the killed type can conceivably be prepared by cloning the genes for the proteins of the viral coat, which confer immunity to the virus. This approach has been successful with hepatitis B: the gene was cloned in bacteria as well as in yeast and in cultures of animal cells. A viral protein produced by all three cell types has proved effective in protecting chimpanzees against infection by the virus. Because the vaccine lacks nucleic acid the possibility of causing infection rather than immunization is excluded.

Even for viruses that can be easily grown in cell cultures, DNA cloning in bacteria or eukaryotic cells offers new opportunities. For instance, it may reduce the danger inherent in making the vaccine or in the vaccine itself. An example is the virus of foot-and-mouth disease, which produces catastrophic epidemics in cattle. This virus is so dangerous that its study in the United States is confined to a laboratory isolated on a small island. The foot-and-mouth disease protein can be produced in bacteria. Success has also been obtained with flu virus, which from time to time gives rise to human epidemics marked by high mortality rates and pronounced economic losses.

DNA cloning may even allow a more direct approach to viral vaccines. Once a gene is cloned in a bacterial vector, it is easy to determine the sequence of its bases, from which the sequence of amino acids in the protein can be inferred using the translation code (see chapter 4). Small segments of the protein, which are adequate for conferring immunity, can be made chemically in the laboratory without cells of any kind. They have been found useful as vaccines in experimental systems. This technology would have the advantage of yielding a pure product, free of cellular constituents that might generate side effects. A drawback is that the small protein fragments, in order to be effective as vaccines, must be coupled to big proteins and mixed with adjuvants. Although this creates some problems, they can be surmounted.

These results are very promising, but they do not necessarily imply that cheap and effective viral vaccines made in bacteria or yeast are just around the corner. The results are extremely important because they show that through the use of appropriate vectors, eukaryotic genes can be expressed in various kinds of cells. There is a difference, however, between showing that the genes can be expressed and expressing them at a level that can be industrially useful. The latter problem is still a very difficult one to solve in most cases.

Can We Undo Altered Genes?

An important question of a different kind is whether genetic engineering can contribute to alleviating genetic defects in humans. Hundreds of thousands of persons are affected by inborn defects of many kinds, such as thalassemia, deficiency of growth hormone, and hemophilia. Presently anyone born with such a disease is condemned for life to the existence of a sick person, with no hope of improvement.

An inborn defect is caused by a mutation, which alters the function of a gene. We should remember that humans, animals, and most plants are diploid—they have pairs of homologous genes. A person in whom only one gene of a pair is altered is normal nevertheless because the other gene supplies the function. Such a person usually is unaware of the defect and is likely to transmit it to the progeny. Anyone with defects in both genes may require replacement therapy for life—for instance, periodic transfusions. Naturally there is strong pressure to find the means to replace the altered genes. Is it possible to introduce a normal gene into the cells of these individuals? Would the gene then be able to function and supply enough of the product?

The possibility of treating gene defects has increased markedly since the advent of DNA cloning. One approach is to introduce a good gene into some cells of an adult individual so that they may provide the normal product. We will call this approach *somatic therapy* (somatic cells are cells of the body, excluding the germ cells). Another approach is to introduce the gene into a fertilized egg cell. If it becomes integrated in the host DNA and ends up in most cells of the adult, including the germ cells, both the individual and his or her progeny may be normal. We will call this approach *germ cell therapy*. Somatic therapy of human patients may be realized in the near future; germ cell therapy is still a matter of academic pursuit with foreseeable applications in animals.

Among the human diseases that might be susceptible to gene therapy is thalassemia, which is caused by the alteration of a globin gene. The condition occurs quite frequently in certain parts of the world, especially around the Mediterranean basin and in Asia. In patients with the severe form, in which both homologous genes are altered, too little hemoglobin is made, and transport of oxygen from the lungs to the rest of the body is inadequate. Death often follows at a young age. The deficiency can be compensated with blood transfusion from a healthy donor, but has to be repeated regularly because the transfused red cells have a limited life. The procedure also entails many risks. Somatic therapy is possible in principle because the disease affects only one kind of cell in the body, those that generate red blood cells. These cells can be easily obtained from the bone marrow, treated, and reintroduced into the body. In contrast, genetic defects causing alterations in many kinds of cells, or in cells that are not accessible—for instance, those of the brain—would be much less amenable to treatment.

In the treatment of thalassemia the strategy is to introduce a normal globin gene into the bone marrow cells, which include the precursors of red blood cells. Attempts were first made in mice. A retroviral vector containing the globin gene was introduced into cells taken from the bone marrow; they became established in 10 to 20 percent of them. The cells were then reinoculated into the animal, and some returned to the bone marrow. Very few of the cells carrying the inserted gene were precursors of red blood cells, however, so their contribution was small, probably negligible. To obtain a significant effect, what remains of the bone marrow after removing the cells for treatment must be destroyed by X rays and toxic chemicals. When the cells are reintroduced they then have the opportunity to repopulate the whole bone marrow. The procedure—bone marrow transplantation—is dangerous because the treated individual is left without defenses against viruses and bacteria for several weeks until the bone marrow is repopulated. But if the treatment succeeds, there is a good chance that the genetic defect will be compensated.

This protocol is suitable in principle for patients who, however, must face the dangers of bone marrow transplantation. But for some, this approach trades a dangerous treatment for certain death. Most likely candidates are children with deficiency in ADA (adenosine deaminase) enzyme, which is required for the development of the immune system. These children, who are in constant danger of being overcome by infections that are trivial for normal people, always die at a young age.

A Matter of Risk

The main problem in the treatment of genetic defects by gene therapy is the evaluation and acceptance of risk, inevitably carried by any new therapeutic process. The possibility cannot be excluded that it will have unknown, even harmful, consequences, for the severity of the risk cannot be evaluated in a scientific and impartial way.

Clearly this undefined risk must be acceptable to the person undergoing the therapy. This is likely if the perceived possible gain is greater than the perceived possible risk. A person who is dying of a disease will accept almost any risk in exchange for a hope of recovery. In practice, however, the risk assessment and its acceptability are determined not by the patient but by committees who use different standards. The perception of risk by the members of the committee is completely different: for them the risk is ultimately to their own reputation among their peers. Because they do not stand to gain anything personally from the experiment, but stand only to lose if something goes wrong, they cannot accept any risk. When the risks are undefinable, only the patient is capable of making a judgment valid for himself.

Acceptance of a risk balanced by a possible gain is common in medicine: for instance, many acts of surgery, transplantation to replace diseased organs, or transplantation of bone marrow in leukemia therapy. These interventions carry both a high mortality risk and a full recovery potential. The difference between these interventions and the attempts of gene therapy is that in the former case both risk and gain are defined, but in the latter both are undefined. It is clear that the problem of risk will have to be realistically faced before substantial progress is possible in this field. We will come back to this point later.

Germ Cell Therapy

In this approach a gene is introduced into a fertilized egg in the hope that the gene will become integrated in the embryo's genome and that it will then persist and function in most cells of the adult organism. Recombinant DNA containing a gene attached to a suitable control region is injected into the nucleus of a fertilized mouse egg, using a microinjection apparatus (fig. 7.3). The embryo is then transferred to the uterus of a surrogate mother. In a fraction of cases the injected embryo develops, generating a normal adult. Integration of the injected gene occurs in a fraction of treated mice, and in some of them the gene is present in the germ cells and is thus transmitted to the progeny. But even when integration occurs, it is often delayed until after the DNA has replicated several times; in that case only some of the cells of the adult animal contain the foreign gene.

Striking results have been obtained by injecting a gene for growth hormone of rat or human origin into a mouse embryo. The gene was attached to the control region of a gene that is activated by certain metals, such as zinc, probably as part

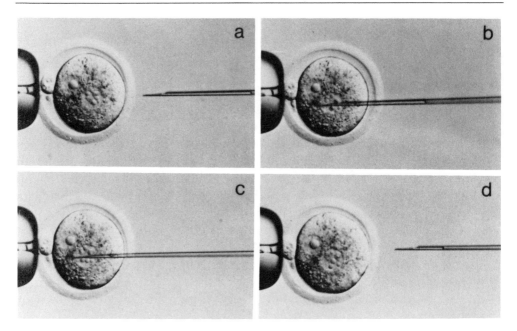

Figure 7.3. DNA injection into a fertilized mouse egg cell. (a) The fine glass injection needle approaches the egg, which is held by suction at the end of a glass pipette (at left). The two nuclei—one from the egg, the other from the sperm—can be recognized as round areas containing prominent spheres (the nucleoli), one in one nucleus, and several in the other. The injection needle contains a small amount of DNA solution. (b) The needle has penetrated the egg cell; its opening is within the nucleus with several nucleoli. (c) Most of the DNA has been injected into the nucleus. (d) The needle has been withdrawn; it is possible to estimate how much DNA was injected by comparing it with a. Courtesy of R. Evans.

of a system of detoxification. When the engineered mice were weaned, they were put on a zinc-rich diet in order to activate the gene. These *transgenic* mice produced large amounts of growth hormone, especially in the liver (which does not produce it normally), and grew almost twice as big as normal. This result, although striking, shows a weakness of the approach: the foreign growth hormone gene is regulated not as the normal growth hormone gene of the pituitary gland but as the zinc-sensitive gene of the liver, because it has the control region of that gene, which is very active in the liver. Regulation depends not on the gene itself but on the control region. The regular growth hormone gene in the pituitary gland was certainly shut off by the high concentration of the hormone in the blood (see chapter 8).

This technology is very important for the study of the regulation of a specific gene within a variety of normal cells in the environment of an intact animal. Its possible practical application, at least for some time, may be to farm animals. It may be economically advantageous to generate strains of cattle or other animals endowed with faster growth and larger size without worrying how and where the inserted gene is expressed. Nevertheless, a worry of another kind remains: the possible unfavorable effects of a high concentration of growth hormone in the blood (a thousand times the normal amount in the giant mice). One possibility is that excessively stimulated cells might become cancerous.

Is this the way to go for remedying genetic defects in human beings? Conceivably, this approach might be used when both partners in a couple are healthy carriers of the same defective gene. An egg from the woman, fertilized in a test tube with sperm from the man, would be injected with a healthy gene and placed back into the uterus of the woman. The egg would develop into a normal fetus and, eventually, adult. If the gene had become immediately integrated in the DNA of the egg, it would be present in all cells, keeping the individual free of the targeted disease. But, in reality, this is only fantasy. Many practical reasons militate against such an experiment. For one, as shown in the case of the mouse, the chances of immediate integration of the gene are very small. And the integrated genes are located randomly in the genome, often inactivating essential genes and producing new hereditary defects. Given the current state of technology, the chances of generating a gene defect would be much higher than that of curing one.

The Opportunity of a Choice

The most valuable contribution of DNA cloning to the control of genetic defects in humans may turn out to be different from the approaches discussed so far. It may be the development of methods for identifying healthy carriers of altered genes, as well as fetuses in which both genes of a pair are altered. As we discussed in chapter 6, both goals can already be accomplished in some cases; in the future, identification is likely to become more general. The affected persons would then have choices based on sound information. A couple of healthy carriers of the same defective gene might decide not to have children, or they might accept the 25 percent chance of having an abnormal child. If they conceive a fetus altered in both genes and the defect is ascertained early enough in pregnancy, they may accept termination of pregnancy, or they may decide to let it go to completion, knowing what the consequences will be. This sort of informed choice may be the only course available for some time; and it may still be the best one in the future, even if realistic possibilities of somatic or germ cell gene therapy become reality.

Protecting Workers?

The possibility of using DNA recombination together with other chemical or molecular techniques for identifying genetic differences among individuals opens the possibility of screening applicants for their genetic suitability to a job. This would apply to jobs that involve exposure to conditions that are well tolerated by some individuals but not by others, depending on their genetic constitution. An example would be jobs involving exposure to chemicals that increase the chance of cancer developing. Many substances are themselves harmless, but in the body they are changed by enzymes present in cells into cancer-inducing agents. It is possible that, owing to genetic differences, some individuals generate the cancer-inducing derivatives in especially large amounts. Because these individuals would be at a high risk of cancer, they could well be denied such jobs. Another example is the deficiency of the enzyme G6PD. This deficiency occurs especially in male American blacks and Mediterranean Jews, in whom exposure to certain chemicals may cause extensive breakage of red blood cells, leading to extreme anemia. Again it could be concluded that these people should be denied jobs where exposure to such chemicals is possible.

One may debate the preventive and economic value of such screenings, but from a social standpoint, they are fraught with dangerous consequences. Such testing would certainly lead to abuses. One consequence could be discrimination, because the tests could be used for rejecting workers who are undesirable to an employer for other reasons. Because relatively hazardous conditions exist in many jobs, the tests would create a class of individuals with inheritable and permanent handicaps.

At the present time few such tests carry scientific validity, but the number may increase in the future. If so, genetic evaluation may become a major social issue, capable of creating a deep split in our society.

Producing Better Crops

Applications of genetic engineering to agriculture are under active consideration. Results are not imminent, however, because our knowledge of the inner workings of plant cells is rather limited. But the goals in this area are of considerable economic importance. Among them are increasing the yield of photosynthesis (see chapter 3); changing the composition of the proteins stored in seed (wheat, for example) to make them more suitable for human nutritional requirements; increasing the resistance of crop plants to parasites, drought, or high salinity of the soil; and preventing frost damage to plants.

A highly cherished goal is that of transferring to economically important plants, such as wheat, the machinery of nitrogen fixation, which transfers electrons to atmospheric nitrogen, converting it, with the addition of hydrogen, into ammonia and then into proteins. Presently only the leguminous plants, such as beans or alfalfa, have this machinery. Nitrogen exists in unlimited amounts in the atmosphere, but it is useless to the living world. And nitrogen fixation is the only source of the new nitrogen needed for all the proteins existing in the biological world. Thus extension of this process to other plants would have enormous economic significance.

In legumes, nitrogen fixation is carried out not by the plants themselves but by special soil bacteria that become associated with the plants in the so-called root nodules. It is a cooperative interaction of the plant and the bacteria in the nodules that leads to nitrogen fixation. Because the transfer of the process to other plants is presently hampered by a scanty knowledge of the genes that carry it out, the main effort in this field has been to clone the genes in order to study how they work. These studies show that the process involves some seventeen genes, which appear to have special requirements such as rare metals (molybdenum). Even when the operation of the genes is fully understood, however, it may still be difficult to transfer the whole machinery to plant cells and make it work. Attempts have been made to transfer the genes to yeast—as the simplest eukaryotic host—without obvious success.

In another approach, the genes that enable the leguminous plants to enter into partnership with the nitrogen-fixing soil bacteria are transferred to non-leguminous plants. Among these genes are those for leghemoglobin, a substance very similar to the hemoglobin present in the blood of animals, and those for proteins that allow the bacteria to bind to the nodule cells. This approach, which is probably more likely to succeed, requires cloning the genes in a vector suitable for transfer to plant cells, such as the T_1 plasmid discussed above or vectors based on viruses capable of invading plant cells.

A separate problem is the protection of plants from frost damage. In fields the leaves are covered by bacteria that promote formation of ice crystals at low temperatures. A derivative lacking this property was produced in the laboratory, with the intention of spreading it onto fields to protect the plants. Greenhouse experiments suggest that it may work. This attempt has been very controversial because many fear that the abnormal organisms may alter the delicate ecological balance between microorganisms in nature, with possible bad effects. Arguments pro or con on such intervention have left many on either side unconvinced.

Biotechnology

Genetic engineering is part of a centuries-old effort to bend life processes to industrial purposes. Some fermentation processes, for instance, are as old as human civilization. Among these are the leavening of bread and the production of alcohol from sugars by using yeast, and the manufacture of cheese by using a variety of molds and bacteria. In more recent times the industrial use of microbiology has progressively increased with the growth in knowledge of biochemistry and genetics.

The range of useful reactions catalyzed by bacteria or molds is immense. It includes the leaching of low-grade ore of copper or uranium in order to extract the metals in pure form, the detoxification and degradation of sewage and other waste products, the conversion of methane present in natural gas to cheap and nutritious animal feeds. These feeds, known as *single-cell protein*, are made up of the bodies of protein-rich bacteria or yeasts that can grow on methane. Steroid hormones—such as female sex hormones and cortisone, which have wide medical uses—are produced by bacteria from agricultural wastes. And, of course, we are all familiar with antibiotics, which are produced in large variety by molds and bacteria and are used medically to combat bacterial infections.

The use of microorganisms in these and many other applications is not surprising: microorganisms carry out an immense variety of chemical reactions by using their enzymes. As we saw in chapter 2, enzymes are catalysts of enormous specificity, able to produce chemical reactions under the mildest conditions. This is very different from chemical synthesis, which has much lower specificity and requires harsher conditions and large expenditures of energy.

Patentable Microorganisms

All applications of biotechnology started with empirical observations. The microorganisms originally used were those naturally available. Yeast naturally growing on grapes was used to carry out the alcohol fermentations; molds and bacteria naturally infecting milk were exploited for producing cheese. But as knowledge of microbiology and genetics grew, it became possible to understand and influence these processes. Progress in genetics, microbiology, and biochemistry went hand in hand with the industrial applications of these sciences: the brewing and chemical industries were among the strongest sponsors of research. The result is that now wine and cheese are made with special pure strains of microorganisms, and so is the purification of sewage or the leaching of metal ores. The introduction of mutations in existing strains has led to the development of new strains that generate desirable products in quantities many times greater than those originally possible.

Industry supported the microbiological research for improving the products and reducing the costs. In time it became questionable whether an industry had exclusive rights to the specially selected or altered strain it had developed. The U.S. Supreme Court had to consider this problem, determining whether microbial strains developed in the laboratory could be patented; its judgment was that they could. The case examined concerned a bacterial strain developed for the conversion of crude oil into nontoxic water-soluble products. Such a strain is of obvious value for many applications, including the cleaning up of oil spills. More recently the same judgment has been extended to plants.

Quantum Jumps

The present efforts must be considered against this broader background: genetic engineering contributes new ways for doing what industrial microbiologists have done all along. Instead of generating new strains by the long and haphazard process of generating mutations and selecting the most suitable ones, scientists can now produce variant genes by manipulating the cloned gene DNA or, in some cases, by making DNA in the laboratory. The range of new applications will increase as the structure of genes and its effects on their functions become more fully known.

Several quantum jumps, however, have been made possible by the new technologies. One has been the manipulation of not just microbial genes but also eukaryotic genes derived from plants, animals, or humans. Another has been the combining of genes derived from different species, no matter how distant they are; plant and animal genes can be spliced either with each other or with microbial genes. Finally, genes can be made from scratch in the laboratory, usually with base sequences able to encode the amino acid sequence of existing proteins—for instance, interferon. But this is not a necessary condition: any sequence can be made, cloned, and amplified in a bacterial or eukaryotic vector. Whether the product will be a copy of an existing gene, or a nonfunctioning piece of DNA, or a functional gene entirely new under the sun, depends in part on the ability of the scientists and in part on the many restraints controlling gene structure and functions.

The Problem of Risk

As we have seen in the field of genetic therapy, an element of risk is implicit in any procedure that is entirely new. Lack of precise information prevents an accurate assessment of the risk and can make it appear intolerable, especially to some. Experimentation in genetic engineering raised fears that it might lead to dire consequences. Now that these fears have abated it is interesting to examine how the events unfolded because the history is a good example of how the problem of risk can be tackled.

The new technology of genetic engineering reminded many of the recent history of atomic energy, which started with fundamental discoveries about the structure of matter, developed into the unleashing of the awesome energy locked in the atomic nuclei, and ended in the detonation of the most destructive weapons ever conceived. Could genetic engineering follow a similarly frightening evolution? Fear was inspired by the quantum jumps already mentioned. It was felt that scientists might reorient the evolution of life; by creating new genes, they might even create new life. Were scientists playing God?

The most frightening accomplishment seemed to be the splicing of genes held separate by nature in different parts of a genome or, much worse, in the genomes of different species. It was feared that splicing violated the careful separation maintained by nature to keep the genes under control. The genes would be "unleashed"—inevitably with harmful consequences. What these might be was left to one's imagination.

A relatively simple example of these fearful outcomes was built on the observation that normal cells may be transformed into cancer cells by altering the relations between some normal cellular genes. As will be discussed in chapter 15, normal animal cells contain "cancer genes," which are normally held in check; they express their functions only at appropriate times and places. But when they are incorporated into the genome of viruses, the genes lose their restraints and become cancer genes; the viruses that carry them become cancer viruses. This is a case of natural genetic engineering entailing harmful consequences.

More generally, many feared that the very foundation of genetic engineering—that of using irresponsible DNA to amplify segments of responsible DNA—might have the consequence of recruiting responsible DNA into the irresponsible kind, turning upside down the process of evolution, which has built up responsible DNA at the expense of irresponsible DNA. Moreover, the technology would make it possible for the newly formed irresponsible DNA to be enormously amplified, possibly offsetting the balance of nature, which is extremely sensitive to shifts in the amounts of gene products within cells.

The use of bacteria originally isolated from the human gut to propagate this DNA added another frightful dimension. It was thought that some cells carrying cloned cancer genes might reenter the gut by accident, repopulating it. Unleashed cancer genes present in the bacteria would find their way to the cells of the infected individual, inducing cancer, and the bacteria would spread from one individual to others, generating a cancer epidemic.

A Moratorium and a Debate

Scientists agreed that these possibilities should be seriously considered. They stopped the burgeoning experiments and started thinking and debating about what should be done. The debate spilled into the lay world and in time involved every layer of society, from workers and unions to heads of state. There was an outcry: the genie must not be let out of the bottle!

The debate polarized on two points. One side insisted that genetic engineering is a tremendous boost for mankind and will solve all problems from cancer to famine; the other looked upon genetic engineering as a scourge, fraught with unbearable risks. Scientists and others who lined up on the two fronts were mostly following intuition: there was no reasoned ground on which to base the predictions.

One argument that was raised in the course of the debate and that became more and more accepted over the years was that nature is flexible, that evolution has tested many (perhaps all) possible gene combinations, and that whatever a scientist makes in the test tube has already been made by nature at one time or another and perhaps exists, unnoticed, in our world. This concept was strengthened by the ongoing discoveries of irresponsible DNA, its widespread presence throughout all forms of life, its ability to jump around from one cell to another and from one species to another, constantly creating and dissolving new combinations of genes. This process, taking place through the millennia in vast populations of organisms of many kinds, must indeed have tested an enormously large number of gene combinations. There is no question, then, about the scientist playing God: he can either copy what has already been done or create useless junk.

Arguments of this type contributed to defining the issues, convincing many that the possibility of a catastrophe was unrealistic. Of course, nobody could categorically rule it out. But the weakening of this argument reinforced the counterargument about the good aspects of genetic engineering. As fears of catastrophe abated, the debate started concentrating on realities: how to use genetic engineering with minimal danger. Perhaps the genie could be let out of the bottle by moving it to another bottle where it could be observed and studied.

Physical Containment

The possibility of creating a new cancer virus consciously or unconsciously became the paradigm against which the defenses against the risks of the new technology were measured. The concept of confinement emerged: experiments must be carried out under conditions capable of categorically preventing the escape into the world of an unwanted recombinant. It was recognized that the risk might come not from recombinants containing well-characterized genes of known properties but from recombinants of unknown characteristics produced accidentally. With the available technology, they might sometimes be produced together with desired ones. The manipulations had to be carried out under strict confinement until the desired recombinant could be characterized and isolated; then it would be extracted from the confined area, and everything else would be destroyed.

It was accepted that the risk of making accidental recombinants entailing possible harm varied according to the type of experiment; what was needed was a system of classification according to risk. Four types of confinement were defined—P1 to P4, with P4 the strictest. In fact, P4 was so strict that suitable facilities were not available anywhere in the world, except in a few installations devoted to the development of agents of bacteriological warfare. These principles were embodied in a set of rules called guidelines, which were enforced by the agencies supplying grants for research. These developments occurred initially in the United States, Britain, and a few other nations. No debate ensued in many countries for some time: scientists were free to do as they pleased, and some were busy carrying out in the open experiments that were elsewhere forbidden. In time, however, the guidelines were almost universally accepted.

Biological Containment

But almost as it emerged, the concept of physical containment was criticized. Even if it were true that nothing could escape from a P4 facility—what about an accident? If a piece of equipment blew up within a facility, breaking its seals and scattering its contents, the safety of confinement would vanish. Physical containment was a fallacy.

A new concept emerged, that of biological containment. Because the vectors used initially in genetic engineering were plasmids or phages, which must propagate in bacteria, it was decided to manipulate both the vectors and their host bacteria in such a way that they could exist and multiply only under extremely demanding conditions. If they escaped from the laboratory or if they contaminated a worker, they could not survive. Strains like this were built with several strict safety features. A bacterium with one such feature escaping its laboratory environment would have a one-in-a-million to one-in-a-hundred-million chance of infecting a worker. In the case of bacteria with several such features, the chances would be essentially nil. Because biological containment is infinitely more efficient than physical confinement, it was adopted and sanctioned in the guidelines, and physical requirements were greatly relaxed.

After these rules were adopted, thousands of experiments were performed in laboratories throughout the world, without the slightest incident. Even experiments carried out in some countries with no containment before the adoption of the guidelines proved harmless. Moreover, large-scale experiments testing the possibility of a cancer epidemic occurring in mice turned out negative. The mice were fed bacteria carrying a cloned DNA obtained from a cancer virus. The exposed animals developed no cancer and showed no signs of infection from the virus. It was much safer, in fact, for the mice to swallow the cloned DNA than the virus itself. These practical demonstrations of safety led to a progressive relaxation of the guidelines, reducing the risk assessment of individual experiments. It became clear that the genie of genetic engineering was not so menacing. Or perhaps there was no genie at all.

A New Debate

Genetic engineering is not without dangers, but they are not the kind that was debated. They may come in part from the enormous range of interventions in living creatures made possible by the new technology and in part from the acquisition of extensive detailed knowledge about genes, individuals, and races. The danger of interventions is that they may be carried out prematurely without adequate consideration of possible consequences. They may not produce the catastrophe envisioned in the earlier debate, but they may bring in their train other ills: damage to individuals, invasion of privacy, ethical blunders. We have discussed a few such consequences, and many more can be envisioned. Acquisition of intimate knowledge about people is dangerous not in itself but in its possible consequences: knowledge can be misinterpreted and, especially, misused, turning it into an instrument of discrimination and oppression.

The possibility of dangers like these has begun to be widely recognized. No doubt we will witness another debate on these issues—more significant than the first one and probably more difficult to resolve.

CHAPTER 8

Communications among Cells

Every cell contains all the genes of an organism, regardless of its size and complexity, but not all the genes are active at any given time. Rather, they are regulated according to the needs of the cell and the organism. In previous chapters we have seen how regulation takes place within a cell. Now we will consider how it takes into account what is happening in other cells of the same organism. This regulation is based on the transmission of signals between cells through either contacts or special communicator substances.

Communication by Touch

Contacts between cells have important consequences. The first step in the invasion of cells by viruses or bacteria is their sticking to the cells; contacts stimulate the defensive cells of the animal body to swallow the invaders. Contacts cause the formation of cell aggregates that are important in the reproduction of some bacteria, molds, and simple organisms (see chapter 12), and in higher animals they initiate the association of cells during the formation of organs in development. Red blood cells leave the bone marrow and enter the blood when they lose a surface molecule that holds them to an adhesive network; they stay in the blood until other surface molecules become modified by age, and then they are captured and destroyed by special cells. All these interactions are mediated by molecules of the cell surface and involve a great deal of selectivity.

That animal cells exchange small molecules and ions through connecting channels when they are in contact was at first hard to accept: cells observed in the light microscope seemed to be completely separated by the membranes that surrounded them. And when researchers studied the flow of electric current applied to cells in cultures through microscopic syringe needles, they found, as had been expected, that current injected into a cell does not flow into the surrounding liquid: the cells are indeed well insulated from the outside. Unexpectedly, however, they found that current flows easily from a cell to its neighbors, thus learning also that cells, though insulated, are in communication with each other. The same was true of young embryos; but as the embryo develops and distinct organs appear a separation occurs: cells of the same organ remain connected, whereas those of different organs become insulated from each other.

The channels of communication, revealed by these experiments, are localized to special junctions visible in the electron microscope and called, because of their appearance, *gap junctions* (fig. 8.1). They are formed by patches in which the membranes of two cells are extremely close to each other, leaving only a thin gap. Plugs made up of protein molecules with a central hole straddle the two membranes, allowing the flow of ions and therefore the passage of electrical current through the central hole.

Molecules can also pass through these channels: a dye injected into a cell slowly spreads to adjacent cells, creeping through the holes of the gap junctions. The holes, although large enough to allow the passage of many small molecules such as amino acids or the bases needed for nucleic acid synthesis, do not allow the passage of large molecules such as enzymes or nucleic acids. They maintain a uniform distribution of ions and small molecules in neighboring cells, avoiding differences of electrical potential which would generate undesirable effects. Neighboring cells can undergo diversification during the development of an organism by making and keeping different proteins that cannot go through the channels. The pancreas, for instance, has cell types each producing a different communicator protein (hormone), yet they are connected by junctions through which ions flow freely.

Communicator Substances

Communicator substances, released by certain cells into the surrounding fluid or into the blood, act on target cells in close proximity or far away. At the target cell

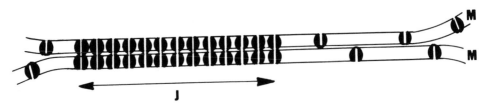

Figure 8.1. Diagram of a gap junction seen in cross section. The membranes (M) of the two cells in contact—one above, the other below—are very close to each other. The junction (J) is the area where the particles contained within the two membranes are closely packed and form the channels between the two cytoplasms. Similar particles outside the junction are not paired and do not form channels.

communicators interact with surface receptors (see chapter 2), which then send signals to the interior of the cell instructing it to perform some new function. A communicator recognizes one or a few kinds of receptor, a specificity that is possible because there are at least as many kinds of receptors as there are communicators. Communicators can be amino acids, small proteins, or fatty substances. The proteins vary greatly in size, from three to a few hundred amino acids; the small ones are usually called *peptides*. Receptor proteins are more complex and contain hundreds or thousands of amino acids. Some are made up of a single protein molecule; others are complexes of several molecules.

Traditionally, communicators were distinguished as several separate groups before their basic similarity was recognized. The first group to be identified was that of *hormones*, which carry out distant communication by spreading through the blood. Related to hormones in their effects are growth factors, which control the multiplication of cells, and differentiation factors, which control cell diversification. Another group of communicators, found mainly in the nervous system where they transmit signals between nerve cells at very short distances, is that of *neurotransmitters*. They are mostly amino acids or their derivatives. Communicator peptides are widely distributed throughout the body. Some—*neuropeptides* (so called because they were discovered first in the nervous system)—may perform the roles of either hormones or neurotransmitters. There are apparently no clear distinctions among the various classes of communicators, so that it is best to consider them as a single group composed of specialized subgroups.

We will discuss here those communicators that are traditionally known as hormones and growth or differentiation factors. The special roles neurotransmitters and neuropeptides play in the nervous system will be considered in chapter 17.

Ubiquitous Regulators

Communicators are produced by specialized cells in creatures of all kinds, from the very simple to the highly complex. In the most primitive animals they are mostly produced by isolated cells and spread to others by diffusion; they have a local and graded action. For instance, in hydra (a primitive marine animal) a hormone causing formation of the head is produced by cells scattered in the body of the animal. Different concentrations of the communicator along the length of the animal determine where the head is formed (see chapter 12).

In higher animals, hormones are usually produced by cells of special organs, called *endocrine glands*, which pour their product into the blood. These organs were formed in the course of evolution by the grouping together of originally isolated cells. For instance, the insulin-producing cells of the islets of the pancreas, as they are present in today's mammals, were preceded by isolated cells in the gut in very primitive mollusks. In primitive fishes (which are more advanced) such cells are already gathered in small nests. Today's mammals, however, still have cells producing other hormones scattered among the cells of the gut epithelium. Hormone production evolved hand in hand with the development of nervous activity, which is based on the use of communicators.

About a hundred known hormones control the many body activities of animals. They determine the proper development of the body and its size; they control sex development, the maintenance of blood sugar and blood pressure, the operation of the digestive and urinary system. They are the key to subjective feelings and changes of blood chemistry associated with stress, as well as the changes in skin color observed in certain animals. In brief, through a vast number of chemical reactions, hormones participate in the control of essentially all body functions.

Hierarchical Hormones

In some cases a hormone controls a cell producing another hormone and determines when it will produce it and how much. Hormones with these properties form hierarchical organizations. Such an organization of tremendous importance in more advanced animals is the three-tier system controlled by the brain. The main control area—called, in mammals, the *hypothalamus*—is situated in the most ancient part of the brain (in evolutionary terms). Experimental damage of the area in rats or other animals causes a dramatic decrease in the production of several hormones; conversely, electrical stimulation enhances their production. Here is where the nervous system and the hormonal system converge (fig. 8.2).

The hypothalamus is a very special endocrine organ: it produces the *hormones of the first tier*, known as brain hormones, which are made by specialized nerve cells. It should come as no surprise that nerve cells produce hormones because all nerve cells produce communicators as part of their normal operation. What is special about the hypothalamic hormones compared to other brain communicators is that they, like other hormones, reach their target cells through the blood. As we will see, however, some of them do it in an unusual way, which directly connects nerve function and hormone production. The hormones controlled by the hypothalamus have to do with activities in which the brain plays a great part, such as sexual acts, emotions, and stress.

The discovery that hypothalamic nerve cells produce special controlling hormones was revolutionary. It was first hinted at by anatomists' observation that some hypothalamic cells contain substances capable of taking up dyes in a way different from other cell constituents. It was then shown that these substances are suddenly released from the cells when certain nerve fibers are stimulated. Other studies showed that the substances are released in close proximity to specialized veins, so that they rapidly enter the blood flow. These special small veins terminate in the important hormone-producing organ at the base of the brain, the *pituitary*, thus connecting the two areas.

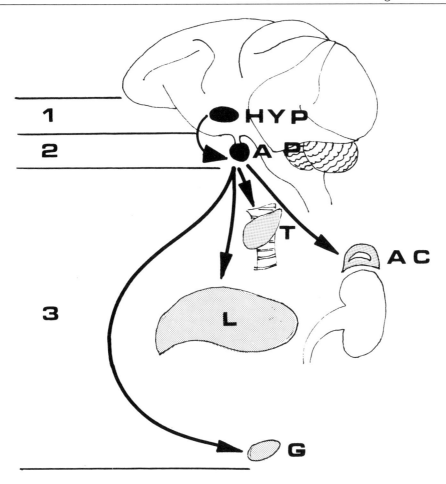

Figure 8.2. The hierarchical system of hormone. The first tier (1) is the hypothalamus (HYP), which controls the organ of the second tier (2), the anterior pituitary (AP). The pituitary in turn controls several glands of the third tier (3)—the thyroid (T), adrenal cortex (AC), liver (L), and gonads (G).

These studies were completed when investigators identified and purified hypothalamic hormones. The presence of the hormones in juices squeezed from pieces of hypothalamus was first revealed by their effect on pituitary cells cultivated in test tubes: the response was similar to that seen in the pituitary of an animal. These effects were used to isolate the hormones and characterize them chemically. Because the hormones were present in only minute amounts in the juices, purification was extremely difficult. The laboratories of R. Guillemin at Baylor University and the Salk Institute and of Andrew Shally at Tulane University required hundreds of thousands of sheep hypothalami to isolate just one of the hormones, TRH (thyrotropin-releasing hormone; see below). Fortunately, these hormones have a very simple constitution and therefore resist the harsh chemical treatment employed in purification. Once their constitution was known, the hormones could be made in the laboratory.

Two Types of Hypothalamic Hormones

Extensive research in many laboratories over many years showed that hypothalamic hormones are made by two types of nerve cells (fig. 8.3). Only those produced by one of the types belong to the hierarchical system as first-tier hormones. Fibers (axons) extending from these nerve cells end in the proximity of the private veins that reach the *anterior part of the pituitary*. This is a key endocrine gland, which, under control of the hypothalamic hormones, produces several highly important

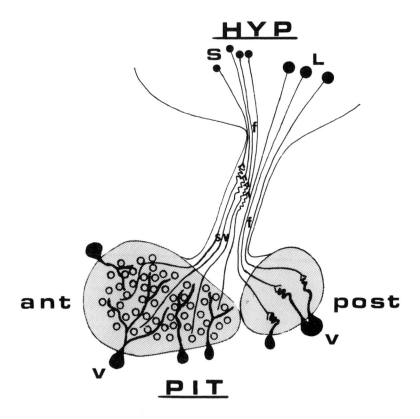

Figure 8.3. Production of hormones by the hypothalamus (HYP). Hormones are produced by two groups of nerve cells. Cells with small bodies (S) produce hormones that control the anterior pituitary (PIT). The hormones are released at the end of the long fibers (f) emanating from these nerve cells (the axons), where they contact special veins (SV). From these veins the blood flows to the anterior pituitary. Cells with large bodies (L) release the hormones they produce, also through fibers, to veins of the general circulation in the posterior pituitary (post). Veins (v) coming from the pituitary contain both these hormones and those produced by the anterior pituitary.

second-tier hormones. These hormones in turn flow through the blood to reach several endocrine glands situated in different parts of the body, where they control the production of hormones of the third tier.

Each *second-tier hormone* is made in the anterior pituitary under control of one or two first-tier hormones of the hypothalamus (see table 8.1). These hormones control the growth of the body, many aspects of cell chemistry and development, the stress response, sexual activity, pregnancy, and lactation. Production of each pituitary hormone is controlled by two opposite hypothalamic signals—one stimulatory (indicated as +), the other inhibitory (indicated as −). In some cases hormones render both signals; in others, a hormone stimulates and nerve signals inhibit. The hypothalamic hormones themselves are also regulated in a similar way by hormones of the third tier and by nerve signals.

Negative Feedback

These regulatory mechanisms accurately control the amount of a given hormone that is released at a given time. Consider, for instance, the release of the pituitary hormone (ACTH) that stimulates hormone production by the adrenal, a small

Table 8.1   The Hormones of the Hierarchical System

Hypothalamic Hormones (First Tier)	*Pituitary Hormones (Second Tier)*	*Peripheral Hormones (Third Tier)*	*Peripheral Organs*
TRH+ (Thyrotropin releasing Ho)	TRS (Thyrotropin releasing Ho)	Thyroid Hormones (T3, T4)	Thyroid
CRH+ (Corticotropin releasing Ho)	ACTH (Adrenal corticotropic Ho)	Corticosteroids	Adrenal medulla
GoRH+ (Gonadotropin releasing Ho)	FSH (Follicle stimulating Ho) LH (Luteinizing Ho)	Estrogen Progesterone Androgens	Gonads
GHRH+ (Growth hormone releasing Ho) Somatostatin− (Growth hormone inhibiting Ho)	GH (Growth Ho)	Somatomedin	Liver
PRH+ (Prolactin releasing Ho) PIH− (Prolactin inhibiting Ho)	PRO (Prolactin)		

gland near the kidney. If the concentration of the hormones produced by the adrenal cortex increases in the blood, less ACTH is made, the production of the adrenal hormones decreases, and their level in the blood returns to normal. Similarly, abundance of thyroid hormones in the blood causes a decrease in the production of the stimulating pituitary hormone. In these and other cases, a negative feedback from the third-tier hormone keeps the production of the controlling pituitary hormone on an even balance. The negative feedback affects also the production of hypothalamic hormones: gonadal hormones restrain production of the hypothalamic hormone that increases gonadal activity through the pituitary (see chapter 9).

The regulation of hormone production can be altered by changing the control of the genes involved. Production of ACTH, for instance, may escape its normal control when the negative feedback on the hypothalamus fails because of stress, depression, or anorexia nervosa: then the adrenal hormones reach high concentrations in the blood. An extreme example is the case of a growth hormone gene that was coupled to the control region of a zinc-sensitive gene and then introduced into a fertilized mouse egg cell (see chapter 7). In the adult animal produced by that egg the foreign gene escaped the normal regulation because it was not governed by its regular control region. Instead, it followed the regulation of the zinc-sensitive gene. When zinc was fed to the mouse, continuously stimulating the control region, the concentration of growth hormone in the blood rose nearly a thousandfold over that of normal mice. Remarkably, the effect of this tremendous increase was only a near doubling of the size of the animal. The limited effect may be attributed to the control mechanisms reducing the production of the third-tier hormones in the liver or the response of the body cells to them. We will see below how these reductions might take place.

Independent Hormones

Many kinds of hormone-producing cells are outside the hierarchical system just described. Certain hypothalamic nerve cells produce hormones in an unusual way: they channel them through fibers that extend all the way to the *posterior part of the pituitary*. These nerve cells make two hormones—one, vasopressin, controlling urine production and blood pressure, the other, oxytocin, determining contraction of the uterus at delivery and milk flow during lactation. It was formerly believed that these two hormones were made in the posterior pituitary itself; but in time it was determined that they enter the main blood circulation in the pituitary but are made in the hypothalamus. The posterior pituitary is made up of a vast number of fibers coming from these hypothalamic nerve cells associated with a network of minute blood vessels. The hormones travel along the fibers and in the posterior pituitary leave them and enter the fine blood vessels. The process is similar to that by which neurotransmitters reach the end of nerve fibers and from there are transferred to other nerve cells (see chapter 17).

Many other hormones are made at many places in the body. Adrenalin is produced in special cells of the adrenal that derive from the nervous system; it increases pulse rate and blood pressure. The hormone is also produced by cells of the nervous system, where it acts as a neurotransmitter. Small glands near the thyroid—parathyroids—produce a hormone that controls the chemistry of bone formation. The islets of the pancreas produce several hormones including insulin, which mainly controls the production and utilization of sugars by cells of the body and the concentration of sugar in the blood. Insufficient production of insulin by the islet cells causes diabetes. Food digestion is controlled by hormone-producing cells present in the lining of the stomach and intestine. The heart atrial hormone controls blood pressure and Na^+ excretion by the kidney. Other independent hormone-producing cells are found in the bronchi.

In mammals, hormone-producing cells are present in the placenta, which in pregnancy establishes the connection between the mother and the fetus. The placenta produces hormones similar to those made by the anterior pituitary and the ovary. During pregnancy the placental hormones ensure the progress of gestation and the development of the breasts for lactation. At parturition prolactin from the pituitary and hormones of the adrenal cortex take over, inducing lactation in the prepared breast.

An interesting hormone, melatonin, is produced by a small gland resembling a pine cone—the pineal gland—hidden among parts of the brain. This hormone responds to the alternation of day and night: it is made mostly at night and induces sleep. It also acts on the gonads to reduce sexual activity. The effect in many animals is that reproduction can take place only during the season in which the days are longer and food most abundant. This control of activity by the alternation of light and darkness is called photoperiodism and is especially pronounced in plants. Through hormonal changes it controls the alternation of dormancy and growth and the time of flowering; thus long-day and short-day plants produce flowers only during the appropriate periods.

Hormones for Differentiation

Many of the hormones mentioned so far are essential for the normal development of animals' organs. Their development, however, is also influenced by many other substances, most of them small proteins that are not traditionally considered hormones, although they share with them many characteristics. They recognize target cells interacting with specialized receptors, and they have hormonelike effects. Of these substances, one is needed for proper development of the skin (epidermal growth factor) and one for the nervous system (nerve growth factor) (see chapter 18). Many similar factors control the growth and development of blood cells and of cells of the immune system (see chapter 14). Among these is erythropoietin, which is required for making red blood cells (hence its name). It is produced in large amounts in animals or humans exposed for prolonged periods to reduced oxygen concentrations (for instance, at high altitudes), increasing the production of red blood cells to compensate for the deficiency. Examples from lower animals also show that many aspects of differentiation are determined by chemical substances produced by the body's cells. There are probably hundreds of substances involved in the control of differentiation, as many as there are different cell types in an organism. Most, however, have still to be discovered.

What Hormones Are and How They Are Made

Most of the hormones produced in animals—including those made in the hypothalamus and in the anterior pituitary—belong to the class of *peptide hormones*—that is, they are made up of chains of amino acids. A related group of hormones includes those produced by the thyroid gland, called T4 and T3, and the adrenalin produced by the adrenal medulla: they are *modified amino acids*. Hormones produced by the adrenal cortex and by the gonads form another group: they are fat-seeking substances related to cholesterol, a normal component of cellular membranes. Because of their chemical structure, they are called *steroid hormones*.

These three classes of hormones are manufactured in different ways. Amino acids are made by special enzymes. Peptide hormones, being proteins, are directly specified by genes and are made in cells by translating their RNA messengers. Steroid hormones are made by chemical reactions mediated by enzymes that determine the detailed chemical structure on which the specificity of the hormone depends. Steroid hormones with the same function are identical or similar in different species. Peptide hormones made in different species, although generally similar, differ in details. As a result some peptide hormones, like growth hormones, act only on cells of the species in which they are made.

Some peptide hormones are made when a much longer chain of amino acids—itself devoid of hormonal activity—splits. This phenomenon has important consequences: the fragments obtained when the chain splits are distinct hormones with different but coordinated properties. For instance, the hormone controlling stress (ACTH) is produced in the anterior pituitary by the splitting of a much longer amino acid chain; this may also generate endorphin (a substance with pain-killer activity acting on nerve cells) and three hormones controlling the color of the skin (fig. 8.4). The formation of these pigment-controlling hormones in the pituitary explains the old observation that tadpoles become permanently pale after the pituitary is surgically removed. The precursor splits in various ways in response to a novel situation that induces stress, and the products cause different effects. ACTH elicits the stress response of the adrenal; the pigmentation hormones camouflage the animal; and the endorphin helps it endure pain if the worst happens (see chapter 17).

The pigmentation hormones control the color of the skin through an interesting mechanism. They affect large cells present in the skin, the melanophores, which contain granules of a dark substance—the pigment. In the absence of pig-

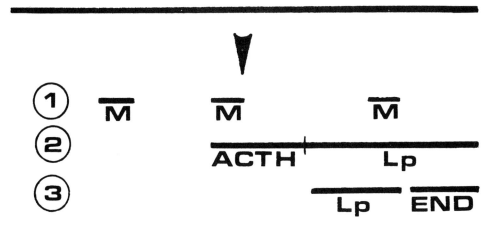

Figure 8.4 Splitting of a long amino acid chain to produce different hormones in the pituitary. Three cleavage patterns (1, 2, and 3) are possible; they generate three different combinations of hormones. The different types of cleavage take place in different cells of the pituitary. Cleavage 1 generates three pigmentation hormones (M); cleavage 2 generates the corticotropin (ACTH); cleavage 3 generates endorphin (END). The Lp fragments are known as lipotropins; their function is unknown.

mentation hormones, the granules clump together near the nucleus; they cannot trap much light, so the skin has a light color (see fig. 8.5). When the hormones are present, they induce the granules to spread throughout the melanophores, stopping most of the light and making the skin uniformly dark. In some animals melanophores containing colored pigments are responsible for the color changes the animals undergo either through hormonal or nervous stimulation. This device allows many of them to maintain a color matching that of their background.

How Hormones Tell the Cells What To Do

Peptide Hormones

Hormones can fulfill their many critical functions because they are "intelligent" substances; each selects only special cells on which to act. Even when many hormones are mixed together, each homes in on its target cells without interfering with the action of the others. A striking example of this discrimination, for instance, involves the sex hormones. Male and female animals contain both male and female hormones; yet the development of sexual characteristics of the individual proceeds appropriately in the large majority of cases.

The precise aiming of hormones is based exclusively on the first step of their interaction with cells: they bind to highly discriminating receptors. A receptor for hormone A will bind A very strongly but will not bind hormone B (or sometimes will bind it only weakly), and vice versa. Each class of hormone uses a different

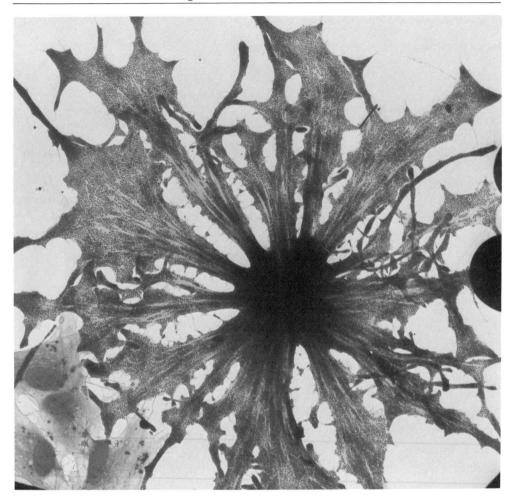

Figure 8.5. A fish pigment cell with dispersed pigment granules seen in the electron microscope. The cell is in the form of a star with many arms densely packed with round dark grains of pigment. Magnified 3,000 times. (From M. McNiven, M. Wang, and K. R. Porter, *Cell* 37:753–65 [1984]. Published with permission.)

type of receptor: those for peptide hormones are located at the surface of the target cells, those for steroids in the cells' cytoplasm and nucleus, and those for the thyroid hormone T3 in the nucleus. Steroids and T3 can reach intracellular receptors because they are largely fat-seeking molecules. They can easily cross the lipid bilayer of the cell membrane, whereas peptides, being water-seeking, cannot.

Intracellular Messengers

Peptide hormones effect cells only if they bind to the surface receptors; injected into the cells, they have no effect. After binding the hormone, the receptor causes the production of molecules that act as a second messenger within the cell, the first messenger being the hormone itself. The receptors act as bridges spanning the cell membrane; they connect the external hormones to the internal cell machinery.

A small molecule, *cyclic AMP* (cAMP), is used as second messenger by many peptide hormones (fig. 8.6). It is produced from ATP by an enzyme associated with hormone receptors. Cyclic AMP binds to enzymes and activates them. Key enzymes are protein kinases, which attach phosphate groups to other proteins. The chemical group changes profoundly the properties of the proteins because it is rather bulky and negatively charged. Some among the changed proteins have regulatory activities. Through these changes cAMP modifies many cell activities, activating the release of products already made or the transcription of previously inactive genes.

Some peptide hormones use, instead of cAMP as second messenger, calcium ions, causing changes of its concentration within the cells. Ca^{++} ions affect the state of the cell by binding to a small protein, calmodulin, which has the shape of a four-leaf clover (fig. 8.7). After binding four Ca^{++} ions the protein exposes a surface that sticks to other proteins (fig. 8.8), such as protein kinases or other enzymes, activating them to perform their function. Having done this, calmodulin releases the bound Ca^{++} and again becomes inactive until it combines with four new Ca^{++} ions.

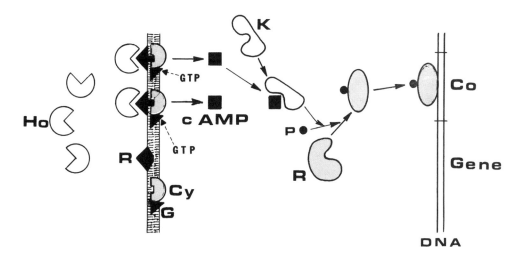

Figure 8.6. Production of the intermediate messenger cAMP by peptide hormone. The hormone (Ho) binds to receptors (R, black) present in the cell membrane, causing them to change shape. The hormone-receptor complex becomes associated with cyclase (Cy, gray) and a protein (G) which degrades GTP. Cy is activated to produce cAMP. The cAMP then combines with a protein kinase (K) and activates it. The activated kinase in turn transfer phosphate groups (P) to regulatory proteins (R, gray), which change shape and act on the control region (Co) of a gene.

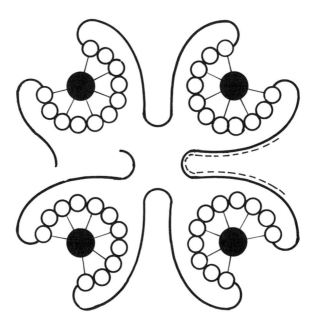

Figure 8.7. Calmodulin. The amino acid chain is represented by a line except in the four places where it binds Ca++ (black). There it is shown as a series of open circles. The overall shape is that of a four-leaf clover. In this conformation some parts of the protein (dashed line) can bind to appropriate target proteins.

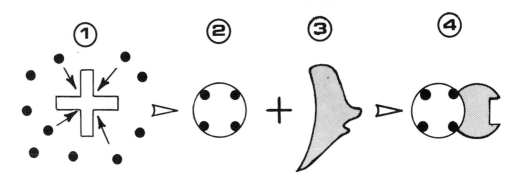

Figure 8.8. Calmodulin can mediate the effect of Ca++ ions acting as second messenger. (1) When Ca++ ions (black dots) become abundant in the cells, they bind to inactive calmodulin (shown as a cross). (2) The calmodulin changes shape and becomes active (shown as a circle). (3) The target for calmodulin is an enzyme or regulatory protein (gray). (4) Calmodulin and its target protein make a complex that directly or indirectly acts on genes. Then calmodulin releases its four Ca++ ions and returns to its original, inactive shape.

Calmodulin and cAMP produce similar end results by different means. Whereas cAMP is normally absent—having been spent in the activation of the target enzyme—and is made when needed, calmodulin is present all the time but in an inactive state. It becomes active by binding Ca^{++} and loses activity after releasing it.

The ability of a cell to respond to a hormone in a characteristic way is determined by the cell receptors recognizing the hormone and by the second messenger being able to activate the genes that produce the response. Addition of cAMP to cells that use it as second messenger elicits the changes that are normally induced by the hormone itself. The differences among cAMP-induced changes in cells of different types reflect the varying states of readiness in the cells' genes, and this is built into the cells as they are formed during the development of the organism.

The role of the interaction of the hormone with its receptors and of the second messenger with certain prepared genes can be illustrated through a comparison. The many houses of a town correspond to cells of different types; entry to each is gained by introducing a key (a hormone) into a lock (the receptor). In some houses the key opens the entry door, in others it activates the garage door opener, in others it neutralizes an alarm system, and in others it calls a guard. The differences depend on the relation of the lock (the receptor) to the devices that control access (the genes). The activated lock may cause electricity (the second messenger) to flow through wires that control the other devices (the genes); in other houses the lock may release compressed air (another second messenger) that runs through tubes and activates the devices (the genes). The effect of introducing a key into a lock depends first on the compatibility between the two and then on how the lock is connected to the devices. These connections were made when the houses were built.

What the readiness of a cell to respond to a hormone means in molecular terms is not always clear. Often genes capable of responding to a second messenger can be recognized because their chromatin has an open structure and the DNA does not have m-groups (see chapter 4). Presumably these changes make the DNA accessible to proteins that regulate gene expression after they have interacted with the second messenger.

An example of the complex role of the second messenger in the action of a peptide hormone is the regulation of the release of the hormone that stimulates milk production, prolactin, from pituitary cells. This example also shows that hormones often work together with signals from the nervous system in telling the cells what to do. A hypothalamic hormone stimulating prolactin production binds to receptors of a class of pituitary cells that are programmed to make prolactin. The binding promotes the synthesis of cAMP as second messenger; cAMP then stimulates transcription of the prolactin gene. This effect is counteracted by a hypothalamic hormone that inhibits cAMP production by binding to other receptors of the same pituitary cells. The prolactin-producing cells are also controlled by a third substance, dopamine, a neurotransmitter released by nerve fibers (see chapter 17). Dopamine also inhibits cAMP production by acting on a third type of receptor on the prolactin-producing cells. In these effects the production of the second messenger (cAMP) integrates the action of three different signals. The concentration of cAMP in the cells reflects their balance; the prolactin gene recognizes only this balance.

Steroid and Thyroid Hormones

Steroid hormones bind to receptor proteins present in the cytoplasm or the nucleus of hormone-susceptible cells. In the absence of hormone, molecules of the receptor protein form pairs, which are maintained by weak bonds between fat-seeking surfaces of the two molecules. Hormone molecules that are themselves fat-seeking can bind to these surfaces and break the pairs, whereupon each hormone molecule remains attached to one receptor molecule. Such hormone-receptor complexes can move from the cytoplasm to the nucleus and bind to chromatin, activating transcription of certain genes. The thyroid hormone reaches the nucleus directly and binds to a nuclear receptor, another protein. The hormone-receptor complex again interacts with chromatin and activates the transcription of genes. For steroid hormones and thyroid hormone, the hormone-receptor complex is the second messenger. As in the case of peptide hormones, genes that are transcribed upon binding a hormone-receptor complex are prepared during development. The chromatin of these genes also has a loose structure, and its DNA has fewer m-groups.

Stopping the Effect of the Hormone

Autoregulation

Once a hormone has become bound to a receptor and has performed its function, its action must terminate to enable the cells to adjust their response rapidly to changes in the amount of a hormone that reaches them. Termination occurs quickly because peptide hormones, after they have acted, are destroyed in a series of steps. After the second messenger is released, the cell begins by swallowing the receptor with the attached hormone in the same way it swallows a viral particle attached to its receptor (see chapter 2). The receptors with the bound hormones detach from the cell membrane as vesicles free in the cytoplasm (endosomes). The hormone molecules are handed over to lysosomes where they are destroyed. In some cases the receptors too are destroyed; in others they are recycled to the cell surface. Destroyed receptors are replaced by new ones.

The invagination and subsequent destruction of the receptors after the attachment of the hormone are important steps in controlling the action of a hormone on a cell. Cells that are continuously bombarded by molecules of a hormone end up losing most of the receptors for that hormone because its manufacture cannot keep up with destruction. As a result the ability of the cells to respond to the hormone is reduced—a phenomenon known as *down-regulation,* or *subsensitivity.* Conversely, cells that are not exposed to a hormone for some time accumulate an excess of receptors, which are continuously manufactured. These cells are more sensitive to the hormone than are normal cells—*supersensitivity.* These opposing responses of cells have the same regulatory meaning: they tend to minimize the consequences of exposure to too much or too little hormone. These mechanisms may participate in reducing the effects of excessive amounts of growth hormone in mice carrying a cloned growth hormone gene.

Certain substances used in medicine bind to the receptors for a hormone but do not cause their disappearance. They bind to the receptors because they resemble the hormone, but the resemblance is insufficient to cause release of the second messenger; thus they do not elicit the hormone's normal action. Substances of this kind—known as *antagonists*—prevent the binding of the regular hormone, blocking its activity. They are made in some organisms to disable enemy organisms or are prepared by the pharmaceutical industry for treating diseases. The effect of antagonists shows that a substance can cause changes in the cells only if it interacts with the receptors in a meaningful way; mere binding is not enough. Down-regulation of the receptors apparently is determined only by meaningful interactions. This is a wise arrangement: substances that lack hormone activity must play no role in regulating the number of receptors.

The cells of an animal maintain an appropriate level of receptors in the presence of the hormones to which they are exposed. Down-regulation is prevented by a suitable adjustment of many variables: the concentration of the hormone, the number of its receptors, the strength with which they bind the hormone, and the rate of disappearance of the receptor-hormone complexes. In each cell the rate of receptor loss equals the ability of the cell to regenerate them.

Possibly related to this problem is the *pulsating release* of some hormones. In sexually mature mammals the hypothalamic hormone that controls the gonads through the pituitary is released in pulses every hour or so. Pulsation is essential for the normal action of this hormone: when it is steadily produced, it has little effect. Pulsation begins at puberty and leads to the strong sexual development that occurs at that time. If the hormone is maintained at a high level in mature animals by continuous artificial administration, the pituitary cells rapidly become unable to respond: they stop production of the hormones stimulating the ovary, and the animal becomes sterile. The converse is occasionally seen in some infant girls who, for unknown reasons, have a pulsating production of the hormone: their genital system reaches maturity and they start menstruating. How pulsation works is not clear. It may be a device for preventing down-regulation of receptors, but this concept has not been substantiated through experiments.

External Regulation of Receptors

The autoregulation of receptors, in which the hormone itself adjusts the number of its receptors, is only one form of regulation. The number can also be changed by other hormones and other factors, with dramatic consequences. An example is the change in the number of oxytocin receptors in the muscle of the rat uterus during pregnancy. Oxytocin, one of the two hypothalamic hormones released into the blood in the posterior pituitary, causes contraction of the uterus. The number of receptors for the hormone increases considerably in the muscles of the uterus just before labor. Consequently the uterus contracts, although the amount of oxytocin produced does not change. A less dramatic increase of oxytocin receptors takes place also in the breasts where the hormone promotes the extrusion of milk. In both uterus and mammary gland the changes of receptor numbers are perfectly attuned to the functional requirements.

A much more complex regulation of receptors controls the cyclic release of a mature egg from the ovary in female animals (see chapter 9). Studies in rats show that the egg surrounded by feeder cells matures in a follicle (fig. 8.9). When the egg is still immature, the feeder cells have receptors for the pituitary follicle-stimulating hormone (FHS), and under its action they multiply and produce a female steroid hormone, estrogen (fig. 8.9: 1). They also start making receptors for another pituitary hormone, the luteinizing hormone (LH) (fig. 8.9: 2), enabling them to respond to a surge of LH production in the pituitary by secreting fluid into the follicle. The follicle bursts and the egg is released into the tubes (ovulation), where it can be fertilized (fig. 8.9: 3). After the egg is released, receptors of a new kind appear at the surface of the feeder cells: prolactin receptors (fig. 8.9: 4). Prolactin and LH working together convert the feeder cells into yellow luteal cells which produce a new female hormone, progesterone, and the next ovulatory cycle starts.

But the scenario changes if ovulation is followed by pregnancy. Production of prolactin then steps up markedly in the pituitary, while prolactinlike and progesteronelike hormones are made in the embryo. The greatly increased concentration of these hormones in the blood blocks the ovulatory cycle. The block persists during lactation and suckling, when prolactin production is maintained at a high level by nerve signals emanating from the stimulated nipple. Only after suckling ceases does the prolactin production decrease and a new ovulatory cycle begin. This natural method of contraception, which allows the mother to concentrate her resources on the newborn, is lost if the infant is bottle-fed.

An interesting variation of this method of contraception is seen in an Australian marsupial, the Tamar wallaby. At the end of January (the middle of summer) the female gives birth and the young wallaby enters the pouch and begins to suckle. The following day the female mates: in this species pregnancy does not block the cycle. An egg is fertilized and grows for a few days, but then stops and becomes dormant as a high level of prolactin inhibits progesterone production. The young suckling in the pouch keeps the level high throughout the winter. In the

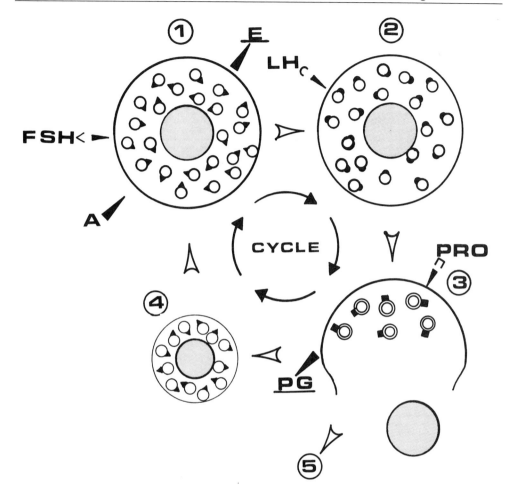

Figure 8.9. Hormonal regulation of the follicular cycle in the ovary. (1) The follicle is represented by the large egg cell (gray) surrounded by small feeder cells and enclosed by a membrane (heavy line). FSH receptors (solid triangles). A = androgen (produced by other cells) which is converted into estrogen (E) by the feeder cells. (2) LH receptors (solid semicircles). (3) Prolactin receptors (solid squares). The cells become converted into luteal cells (double outline), which produce progesterone (PG). (4) The beginning of a new cycle: both the egg and the follicle are small. (5) If the egg is fertilized, the cells persist as lutheal cells.

spring the baby is weaned, but the embryo remains dormant: a hormone of the pineal gland now keeps prolactin production high. The gland's effect decreases after the summer solstice in December; as the days become shorter, the embryo resumes its growth, and birth takes place again at the end of January. (It should be kept in mind that marsupials have a short gestation time because most of the fetal development occurs in the pouch.) There is an evident meaning in this complex regulation: the young must emerge from the pouch at the most favorable time, at the beginning of the growing season.

Occasional Unwanted Effects from Hormones

Because hormones are such powerful agents, it is not surprising that in excessive concentrations they may be damaging. An example is thyroid hormone, which in excess produces characteristic toxic phenomena, such as hyperactivity, heavy perspiration, tremor, and rapid pulse. Another example is DES (diethylstilbestrol), a substance produced by the chemical industry which has the same action as estrogen, although it is chemically different. It binds very strongly to the estrogen receptors, causing appropriate cellular changes. For some time DES was used on the farm to improve the weight of calves, with considerable economic success. Serious complications, however, appeared when DES was administered in large doses to pregnant women to stave off a threat of spontaneous abortion. Female fetuses showed abnormal development of the vagina which degenerated into cancer in adolescence. The excessive administration of the hormone during the development of the organ altered the course of development, and cancer was the eventual consequence. Once this effect was recognized, the medical use of DES was abandoned and its use on the farm was banned in most countries.

Hormonal deficiencies on the other hand, result in many human diseases through either of two mechanisms: a reduced production of hormone or an insufficiency of its receptors. Diabetes, for instance, can be incurred both ways, and recognizing which mechanism is at work is important because treatment is different. Deficiency of insulin production can be compensated by the administration of insulin, but deficiency of receptors cannot. In the latter case administration of high doses of insulin would actually further increase the deficiency by reducing the number of receptors through down-regulation. The right approach then would be to stimulate receptor formation using other hormones or drugs.

Insulin receptors are often attacked in adults by defensive proteins produced by the body—antibodies—which have an unusual specificity; this is called autoimmune disease (see chapter 14). These antibodies block or damage the receptors at the surface of cells throughout the body. In some cases antibodies have the opposite effect, that of stimulating the receptors, as in an autoimmune disease in which antibodies are made to the TSH receptors present at the surface of thyroid cells. TSH is the pituitary hormone that drives the thyroid cells to produce thyroid hormone. The antibodies bind to the receptors in a way that mimics the action of TSH itself and instruct the cells to make more thyroid hormone. The excessive production causes toxic effects. Occasionally, antibodies to insulin receptors also have a transient insulinlike activity, but it soon stops through down-regulation of the receptors. Antibodies' ability to mimic the hormone, however, is not common: more often they act as antagonists, blocking its effect. The results depend on where precisely an antibody binds to the receptor. Most often it binds to a part that does not directly interact with the hormone. These antibodies do not mimic the hormone's action, but block its access to the receptor.

CHAPTER 9

Sex: ♀ and ♂

Self-replication is frequently found in nature. Viral particles, bacterial cells, and cells of higher organisms can all multiply autonomously, without interacting with other cells or organisms. But the multiplication of the higher organism itself, whether an animal or a plant, requires the collaboration of two individuals in a sexual act. Why did DNA relinquish the autonomy of the single genome, submitting to the need for intercourse between two genomes? It is not because in higher organisms a single germ cell is always incapable of replication: in certain lower species, such as bees or aphids or even lizards, a germ cell can generate a whole organism without fertilization (*parthenogenesis*). Moreover, many organisms have a choice of either sexual or asexual reproduction. But sexual reproduction from time to time is essential even for these organisms, and it prevails overwhelmingly throughout the living world. Its widespread use must result from some critical advantages to the creatures that employ it. We will presently see what these advantages are.

But sexuality has also created many problems. Sexual reproduction is highly complex and requires the functions of many genes; so it is costly in information and energy. The complicated development of the many organs and structures needed for sexual reproduction may be easily altered by gene malfunctions or misreading of signals among cells. As a result the roles of the sexes are not so well defined, and sometimes they are even clearly ambiguous. We will see many examples in this in the following chapters. Ambiguity may create problems, but it can also possess a positive value, especially for creatures living in highly variable environments. It enables them to choose between sexual or asexual reproduction or to change sex, depending on the circumstances. Ambiguity, however, is not frequently useful. It is likely that it was not built purposefully into sexuality but was a consequence of the complexity of the mechanisms involved.

Various Forms of Sexuality

The Sexy DNA

In human terms, we think of sex as a distinction between males and females and as a process by which new individuals are generated through intercourse. But biologically, sex is a basic property of DNA: it is the ability of DNA molecules to exchange parts and to move from one cell to another. The sexual performances of complex organisms are the means of mixing their DNAs.

How can we visualize sexuality in single molecules of DNA, such as the genomes of viruses or bacteria? In these creatures sexuality is expressed only occasionally. A virus can replicate for many generations without a sexual act, but when two viruses of the same species invade the same cell, their DNAs may exchange parts by recombination. This constitutes the viruses' intercourse, although it lacks the characteristics we usually associate with sexuality, such as the meeting of male and female. Though the two viruses have sex, they do not have gender; they look exactly alike and perform identical roles in the intercourse. Yet their sexuality is basically similar to that of plants or animals.

Bacteria, again, do not regularly employ sexuality. In most cases a bacterial cell derives from a single parent. The monotony of asexual reproduction, however, is broken by uninvited guests, the plasmids, the small DNA molecules that live within bacteria (see chapter 4). Plasmids are restless and frequently move from one bacterium to another across bridges they have formed and through which the contents of the two bacteria communicate *(conjugation)*. Later the two bacteria separate again. But if bacterial conjugation stopped here, it would not be a sexual act. It becomes sexual when the plasmid carries with it the DNA of the bacterium in which it lives. The carried DNA recombines with the DNA of the host bacterium, generating a new assortment of genes. Thus conjugation between bacteria becomes mating.

DNA has used sex to build the organisms that exist today. Sex is the basis of the evolution of responsible DNA and of the organisms it generated. During evolution pieces of DNA were joined, others were distributed to various organisms, and the sequences were continuously reshuffled (see chapter 20).

Enters Gender

In the mating of bacteria the two partners perform different roles because one donates its genetic material to the other: the donor bacterium (containing the plasmid) acts as male, the recipient bacterium as female. In this primitive differentiation of genders, the sex difference is not inherent in the bacteria but is created by the presence or absence of the plasmid and can be inverted in a subsequent mating. The next step toward classical sex is the adoption of a regular mating scheme between individuals. Many unicellular creatures practice mating, at least at certain stages of their life cycle. Among them are molds—for instance, the baker's yeast used to make bread.

A cell of budding yeast usually produces progeny cells asexually: a small bud forms on its surface, grows, and develops into a new cell, which then breaks free. But from time to time two cells mate, which in the case of yeast means that the cells fuse and form a new cell, combining their genes. The mating cells are visually indistinguishable from each other, but they differ chemically. In yeast, only cells with different chemistries *can* mate. By dictating this chemistry genes determine to which of two mating types a cell will belong. Cells of each mating type produce a small protein that induces cells of the opposite type to mate. The two mating cells come, in most cases, from different parents, which ensures the mixing of genes. In the case of some other molds not all cells mate, but only special ones, the *gametes*. These creatures display a clear sex differentiation into male and female genders.

Diploid Cells and Gametes

When in sexual reproduction two cells fuse, their product has twice as much DNA, twice as many genes and chromosomes than the original cells. This doubling, however, cannot go on indefinitely, for individuals of a species maintain a constant amount of DNA and number of chromosomes per cell. Organisms utilizing sexual reproduction avoid this complication through a mechanism that is easily recognized in budding yeast. Yeast that reproduces asexually often has a single copy of each gene and each chromosome in any of its cells—it is haploid—whereas the yeast generated by fusion has two copies of each gene and chromosome—it is diploid. From time to time diploid yeast generates haploid cells by a complex process known as *meiosis*, or reduction, in which the chromosomes of the diploid cell replicate once while the cell divides twice. Each resulting cell, then, is haploid. During reduction the homologous chromosomes pair—that is, they align exactly side by side—and undergo recombination (fig. 9.1).

Yeast oscillates this way between the haploid and the diploid state, as do all creatures of equal or greater complexity. In animals and most plants the body is formed by the diploid cells; the gametes are haploid. Some lower plants—for example, mosses—are exceptional: haploid cells form the main plant on which diploid cells grow in small appendages. In animals the gametes form the egg and the sperm; in plants they are associated with other haploid cells to form the egg sac and pollen. Many fungi—mushrooms, for example—are prevalently haploid: when a diploid cell arises by fusion of two haploid cells, it segregates immediately into two haploid cells.

Significance of Sexual Reproduction

What is fundamental in sexual reproduction is not the building up of a population of diploid cells but the scrambling of the genes. This happens in the reduction step,

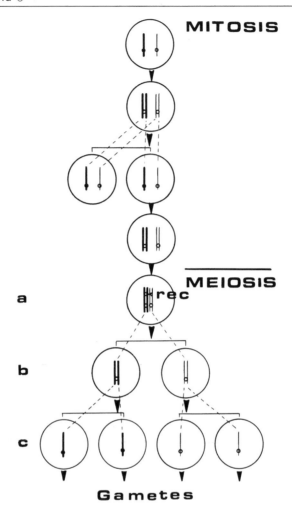

Figure 9.1. A comparison of mitosis and meiosis. Mitosis (cell division) goes on repeatedly in all cells during the life of an organism and always follows DNA replication; meiosis (reduction) takes place only in the formation of gametes. In mitosis the homologous chromosomes remain separate. In contrast meiosis begins with the pairing of the two homologous chromosomes, between which recombination (rec) takes place. Then in two successive cell divisions without DNA replication, the four chromatids are distributed to four different gametes.

when haploid cells (usually as gametes) are formed again from diploid cells. In the latter, each of two homologous chromosomes, and therefore of genes, derives from a different parent. This cell, therefore, is like a cell infected by two viruses or like a bacterium into which a plasmid has carried the DNA of another bacterium. In the reduction step one chromosome of each pair is distributed at random to the two daughter cells, which are haploid. The chromosomes themselves exchange parts by recombination. So the genes of the haploid daughter cells are a new combination of genes.

Reduction may take place immediately after a diploid cell is formed or a long time later after it has repeatedly multiplied. In humans, for instance, it takes place months or years after the formation of the initial diploid cell—the fertilized egg.

Guarding against Self-sufficiency

The females of some animals—ants, bees, aphids—are self-sufficient: they can reproduce without mating (parthenogenesis). When the haploid egg cells begin their development they double their chromosome number, so the resulting animals are diploid like other animals. Any two homologous genes, however, are identical, which explains why parthenogenesis does not occur more frequently. Because of its simplicity, it would seem to be desirable, but evidently it has unfavorable consequences.

Also self-sufficient at least potentially are creatures that produce both eggs and sperm, *hermaphrodites*. Many primitive animals that live attached to some kind of fixed support (like oysters or sea urchins) or that move about very little (like earthworms) are hermaphroditic. Clearly this is a potentially useful condition because it makes it possible for these isolated individuals to reproduce by self-fertilization. Many plants too are hermaphroditic, probably for the same reason. Elaborate devices, however, make it difficult for them to fertilize their eggs with their own sperm. These devices vary. Oysters, for instance, change periodically from male to female, so that an individual produces at any one time either eggs or sperm, but usually not both. Starfish and sea urchins, which live in tightly packed groups, use a different strategy. Each animal accumulates its eggs and sperm internally in separate compartments and releases them at the same time. But the animal releases with its gametes a substance that acts as a chemical signal to neighboring animals, inducing them to release their gametes as well. In this way gametes produced by many individuals are released almost simultaneously, and because they are mixed together by water currents, self-fertilization is very unlikely.

Hermaphroditic plants also have elaborate devices to guard against self-fertilization. In some species male and female gametes reach maturity at different times, so that gametes of the two sexes are never present simultaneously on the same plant. In other species the male organs are very prominent in some plants and the female organs in others, so that a fertilizing insect will pick up pollen from one plant and deposit it into the female organ of another. Another device is chemical self-incompatibility (similar to the mating-type incompatibility of yeast): the pollen of a plant cannot penetrate the female organ of the same plant. It can do so only in plants with different self-incompatibility genes.

All these devices to prevent self-sufficiency, either as parthenogenesis or as self-fertilization, share the same goal: to prevent the formation of diploid cells with pairs of identical genes. The fusion of two gametes of different origins to ensure the mixing of genes is all-important. The value of sexual exchanges in nature is also emphasized by the importance attached to the product of fertilization, the fertilized egg. Many animals or plants that can reproduce asexually produce fertilized eggs when conditions become difficult and survival of the individual is problematic. For instance, the water flea, a small insect that reproduces asexually throughout the summer, produces fertilized eggs as winter approaches. The eggs will survive during the cold months when the water fleas themselves cannot. Similarly, plant seeds, which are slightly developed embryos, can survive drought, long storage, and extreme weather conditions. In both these cases, the fertilized eggs (particularly the seeds) have protective layers and other features that give them a high survival potential. The absence of such features in other cells of the body makes the product of fertilization especially valuable.

Influence of Detrimental Genes

Discrimination against self-sufficiency may be related to the presence of altered genes. If in a diploid organism one of the genes of a pair is altered, the consequences are not necessarily bad because the other gene of the same pair can supply the needed product. But in a self-sufficient organism an altered gene is detrimental for its progeny. A defect owing to an altered gene in a parthenogenetic organism is immediately revealed in the progeny: both copies of the gene are altered. In a self-fertilizing organism two copies of an altered gene come together in 25 percent of the progeny because half of the gametes contain the altered gene and each altered gamete has a 50 percent chance of fusing with another altered gamete. In both cases of self-sufficiency an altered gene causes a high proportion of sick progeny, and this, of course, is unfavorable to the species. In contrast, organisms that reproduce by cross-fertilization can tolerate altered genes perfectly well because the same gene is rarely altered in both mating organisms.

Nothing, however, is straightforward or universally valid in the biological world. We can see this by applying our conclusions above to crop plants. We would expect cross-fertilization to be preferred over self-fertilization, but this is not always the case.

On the one hand, an example of the value of cross-fertilization is corn. If these plants are produced by self-fertilization over many generations, their vigor declines markedly because pairs of altered genes tend to accumulate. Subtle advantages might also accrue to this plant if it has two different forms of a gene in all or most pairs. Thus corn used in commercial production is hybrid—it is generated by cross-fertilization, resulting in what is called hybrid vigor.

On the other hand, many plant species—wheat, for one—can be regularly propagated by self-fertilization. Is this possible because they lack altered genes? In considering this question we must recognize that a connection between cross-fertilization and altered genes can arise in two ways. One possibility is that cross-fertilization developed in the course of evolution in response to the presence of altered genes in order to prevent their deleterious effects. Self-fertilization would then be possible only in plants that lack such genes. But it is not clear why deleterious genes would not accumulate in these plants, since gene changes are inevitable. The other possibility is that some species encourage, whereas others discourage, self-fertilization for reasons unrelated to the load of deleterious genes. Altered genes can then accumulate in plants that discourage self-fertilization but not in those that encourage it. In self-fertilizing plants the appearance of an altered gene would cause the extinction of the lineage. We cannot know for sure, but this explanation seems more likely to be correct. We must also realize that crop plants, which are selected and maintained by human activity, do not have to follow the same rules as wild plants, which are exposed to different selective pressures. The behavior of wheat, then, does not *necessarily* contradict what we have said about the drawbacks of self-fertilization.

Genetic Control of Sex

Many Genes for Sex

The basic act of sex—the exchange of parts between DNAs—requires the participation of many genes, sometimes in large numbers. In its simplest form, it needs only special enzymes and other proteins to carry out recombination, but in advanced organisms the investment is much greater: many genes are needed for the formation of the gametes, which are very different from the organism's other cells. Unlike them, the gametes are generated through the complicated process of reduction, and they must fuse with each other.

Gametes have special properties connected to the mechanics of fertilization and to the roles they perform. Because the egg accumulates lots of nourishment and the special molecules needed initially by the embryo—for instance, the translation machinery—it is large and stationary (see chapter 12). In many creatures the fertilized egg develops in a protected environment within the body of the mother, such as the uterus in mammals. To achieve this result the egg sits at or near the site where the embryo will develop, and the sperm, which contributes only its genes, must search for it. The animal sperm is a swimmer because it must travel through water in the case of primitive creatures or through body fluids in the case of vertebrates. Its penetration is favored by a small aerodynamically shaped head and strong whipping tail. In some cases it is guided by chemical attractants produced by the egg. In plants, the male gamete—contained in the pollen—is transported to the egg by an insect, by air currents, or, in the case of aquatic plants, by water currents.

The differences between the sexes involve the whole organism. In order to bring the animal sperm near the egg, animals employ some form of copulation between mature individuals of opposite sexes. Simple creatures (amphibia, fishes) have little specialization for this function: both the male and the female have a simple canal through which the sperm or the eggs exit from the body. During copulation the orifices of the two canals are brought close to each other: either the sperm enters the female canal (as in birds) or both sperm and eggs are ejaculated together (as in most fish). The sexual apparatus of many animal species, however, are more highly specialized. The male is provided with a penis which he inserts into the vagina of the female, leading to the deposition of the sperm cells close to the egg. Many genes are devoted to the development of these structures.

The necessary nerve circuits that control the mechanics of copulation require still more genes, which adds to the differences between the sexes. Other, probably numerous, genes are devoted to ensuring that individuals of different sexes seek each other out and that they want to copulate, one in a masculine, the other in a feminine way.

Many genes are involved in the expression of either the female or the male personality, and they are fundamental to the differentiation between the sexes. In generating differentiation, genes work together with sex hormones (see chapter 8). But because hormone production is also under the control of the genes, the problem of sex differentiation can be reduced, in the first approximation, to that of the function of the sex-control genes.

Sexual Determination

The genetic control of sex is complex and varies according to species. There is, however, an underlying regularity. Sex determination must fulfill the biological requirement of generating individuals of opposite sexes in suitable proportions. Many species in which the proportions are equal (flies, birds, mammals) have a common mechanism, which is basically to identify one of the sexes with a special chromosome. Every fertilized egg has an equal chance of inheriting or not inheriting this chromosome, and the number of males in a population equals that of females, ensuring the maximum possible number of matings.

The mechanism of sex determination could not be understood until the bases of genetics were discovered in the first part of this century. Before then, back to the time of Aristotle, philosophers offered a variety of curious explanations. One was that, in humans, sperm from the right testicle cause the product of conception to be male, and those from the left testicle, to be female. Because the right side of the body was considered to be "better" than the left side, this theory implied male superiority. Another explanation was that the higher of the two testicles produced the male—again asserting male superiority, at least physically. Perhaps a feminist trend can be discerned, however, in still another explanation that eggs from one of the ovaries give rise to males, and those from the other ovary become females.

The first hint of the importance of chromosomal differences came from microscopic studies of the formation of the sperm in certain insects. The cells that ultimately become sperm cells divide very frequently, and many could be seen in the act of division. In dividing cells the chromosomes can be easily recognized (see chapter 1). While looking at them, investigators noticed that in some individuals one chromosome could always be distinguished from the others by its different shape, and that this chromosome behaved strangely. At the stage when the homologous chromosomes pair off in the reduction step it did not, thus leaving one of the regular chromosomes also unpaired. It was inferred that this special chromosome might be relevant to sex differentiation, and the inference was later supported by more extensive studies. The odd chromosome and its nonpairing counterpart were called *sex chromosomes*. For lack of better identification, they were designated X and Y—a terminology that survives today.

Further analysis showed that in every species in which sex chromosomes can be recognized, one of the sexes has two equal sex chromosomes (XX), whereas the other sex has two different ones (XY): the Y chromosome distinguishes the sexes. Which sex has one or the other arrangement depends on the species. In mammals and in the fruitfly *Drosophila*, which is widely used for genetic studies, the female sex is XX, the male XY. In birds it is the opposite: the male is XX, the female XY. When haploid gametes are formed in the XX sex, both gametes will receive one X chromosome and are all alike in this respect. When gametes are formed in the XY sex, some gametes will receive X as sex chromosome, and others will receive Y: they are, therefore, of two kinds. At fertilization a Y gamete of the XY sex, fusing with an X gamete of the XX sex produces an XY embryo; an X gamete of the XY sex produces an XX embryo. The gametes of the XY sex, whether male or female, determine the sex of the offspring.

There are many interesting variations of the XY method of sex determination, especially in insects. Thus, in honeybees, the queen is fertilized by the male once in her lifetime in the nuptial flight; from then on she uses the sperm store for fertilizing her eggs. Whether or not an egg is fertilized depends on the availability of sperm. Immediately after the mating, sperm is abundant and the eggs are all fertilized and develop as females. These may become queens or workers, depending on the food they receive; the majority become workers. Late in the season, when the supply of sperm runs low, more and more eggs remain unfertilized. They develop into male drones, which are haploid, and will take to the air in search of a queen. It is interesting how the chromosomal control and the environmental control (food) affect the expression of sexuality and the proportions of individuals of different kinds in the population. These factors have profound effects on the economy and sociology of the hive. But what is the connection between genetics of sex determination and the sociology of the hive? Evidently there are two possibilities: either genetics determines the sociology, or sociology causes the selection of genetic types especially suitable to it. It is likely that both mechanisms played a role in evolution and that genetics and sociology developed hand in hand.

Gender as the Balance of Genes

The X-Y system of sex determination operates basically through a balance of the number of copies of the X chromosomes with the number of copies of the other, regularly pairing, chromosomes—the *autosomes*—which we will indicate collectively as A. Diploid creatures have two copies of autosomes, that is, they are 2A. The existence of the balance has been shown very clearly by studies with the fruitfly *Drosophila*, in which the female sex is 2X, that is, XX. A ratio of unity between autosomes and X chromosomes (2A/2X) determines the female sex, whereas a ratio of 2 (2A/X) determines the male sex. The role of the balance is shown by other chromosome constitutions that are exceptionally observed: 4A/4X and 3A/3X are normal females, as would be expected from a unity ratio between A and X. 4A/3X and 3A/2X have a ratio between 1 and 2; they are intermediate between male and female—*intersexes*. Both externally and internally these flies are mixtures of some female-looking and some male-looking parts. Obviously the intermediate ratio has allowed in some parts the predominance of male genes and in others, of female genes, apparently with no fixed rule. Ratios smaller than unity (3A/4X) and larger than 2 (3A/1X) have been observed and dubbed superfemales and supermales, respectively. The flies that carry them are sickly, however, and their supersexuality lies exclusively in the eyes of the beholder.

The Y chromosome, which in the flies identifies masculinity, essentially plays no role in the balance of sex chromosomes in this creature. Its accidental presence in a fly that also has two X chromosomes does not decrease her femaleness. In *Drosophila* the Y chromosome is important only because it contains genes that are required for the motility of the sperm; a male fly without a Y chromosome, therefore, develops like a normal male but is sterile. The Y chromosome, in contrast, plays an essential role in sex differentiation of many other species. In humans, for instance, the sex balance is determined by the (A+Y)/X ratio. Normal males are (2A+Y)/X; normal females, 2A/2X. As in *Drosophila*, changes of this ratio lead to abnormalities of sexual characteristics. Thus individuals with (2A+Y)/2X are males (owing to the presence of the Y chromosome), but they have small testes and are sterile. Those with (2A/X) (no Y) are sterile females, who do not achieve sexual maturity and have many abnormalities. Larger changes in the ratio, such as (2A+Y)/4X or (2A+2Y)/2X, cause mental defects. Some rare individuals with 2X and no Y are nevertheless normal males: one of the X chromosomes contains a piece of the regular Y chromosome, which it acquired in a previous genetic exchange. They, therefore, conform to the basic rule, but show that most of the Y chromosome is irrelevant for sex determination.

The crucial role of the balance of sex chromosomes implies that in both the sex chromosomes and the autosomes there are sex-determining genes, some for maleness, others for femaleness. There must also be control genes to direct the expression of the sex-determining genes. In humans, sex-determining genes are in various chromosomes; genes for maleness are, surprisingly, in the X chromosomes. Certain mutations in the X chromosome can cause an XY individual to develop as a female. Evidently they inactivate maleness-determining genes. And inversely, certain autosomal mutations cause an XX individual to develop characteristics of both sexes by inactivating femaleness-determining genes.

The presence of genes for opposite sexes in many chromosomes, including X, explains why XX determines femaleness in some animals, but maleness in others. The outcome depends on the location of the various genes. In different species, the genes have become distributed in a variety of ways among the chromosomes during the course of evolution.

Many observations have shown that the interplay of these genes takes place during development of the organism. Every organism starts with the potential of being of either sex; which one will finally emerge depends on the sex chromosomes through the control they exert on other genes. In fruitflies or mice, two autosomal genes—a control gene and a switch gene—are known to be important for this control. Their interplay is thought to proceed as shown in figure 9.2. The switch gene can take either a male or a female state. When it is in the male state it promotes the development of male traits and inhibits that of female traits. In the female state the two effects are reversed. The state of the switch gene is determined by the control gene. When the control gene is inactive, the switch gene is in the male state; when it is active, the switch gene is in the female state. The control gene, in turn, is controlled by other genes in the sex chromosomes. Malfunction of either gene in fruitflies or mice gives rise to a sex that does not agree with that of the chromosomes. For instance, if the control gene does not work, a chromosom-

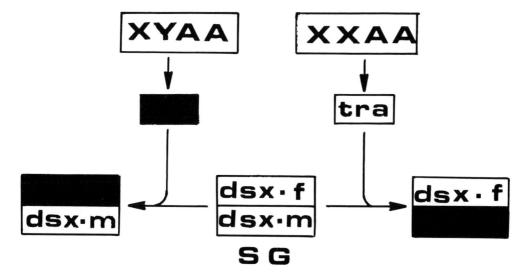

Figure 9.2. Model for the interplay of a switch gene and a control gene in the fly *Drosophila*. The final result depends on the chromosome constitution, whether XYAA (where X and Y are the sex chromosomes and AA the autosomes) or XXAA. If it is XYAA (left) the control gene tra (transformer) is inactive (blocked out), causing the switch gene SG to enter the male mode (dsx-m). The switch gene can be in either the male (m) or female (f) mode. It is called dsx (double sex) because its abnormality causes double-sexed flies. If the chromosome constitution is XXAA (right), the control gene tra is active and as a result the switch gene enters the female mode. (Modified from J. M. Belote and B. S. Baker, *Proc. Natl. Acad. Sci USA* 79:1568–72 [1982].)

ally female animal (XX) will develop as a male; but a chromosomally male animal will develop as a normal but sterile male.

What Is a Switch Gene?

The conclusions outlined above were reached by studying the effects of mutations, but they tell us nothing about how the genes work. Especially interesting in this respect is the operation of the switch gene. Deep insight into the operation of this gene has been gained from the study of the creature, yeast. We know that haploid yeast cells have one of two possible mating types which for brewer's yeast are called *a* and *alpha*. The mating types are equivalent to the sexes of higher organisms: only cells of different types mate, generating diploid cells. Some strains of yeast are predominantly of one type and rarely generate progeny of the other type. Other strains, in contrast, are always a mixture of cells of the two types: a control gene makes the cells switch back and forth from one mating type to the other. This apparently is a device to ensure the persistence of the strains when the cells are widely dispersed: a single cell can generate a whole new population of both haploid and diploid cells, an important characteristic for yeast, as we will see. For the moment, however, we are concerned with the mechanism of switching.

Modern advances in genetics and genetic engineering have given us the following picture. The switch gene responsible for switching from one mating type to the other is made up of three parts located on the same chromosome, but distant from one another (fig. 9.3). There are two storage sites, one for the *a* gene, the other for the *alpha* gene, and an expression box in between. Only the gene in the expression box is active; those in the storage sites are not. In the switching strains the gene in the expression box is frequently replaced with the other gene from the storage site while the storage site keeps a copy of the gene. Replacement probably occurs by gene conversion (see chapter 6) after an enzyme cuts the double helix. Switching is probably controlled by the gene that specifies the cutting enzyme. The operation is similar to that controlling the switching of coats in trypanosomes (see chapter 6).

An Inactive X Chromosome

The occurrence of mental deficiencies and other abnormalities in humans with an aberrant ratio of X chromosomes to autosomes shows that the X chromosomes contain other important genes in addition to those controlling sex. In fact, genetic studies in many species have identified in these chromosomes many genes with other functions. A question naturally arises: are these genes expressed more strongly in XX than in XY individuals? The answer is no; in many species there is no such difference between the two sexes. This arises from the fact that one of the two X chromosomes is inactivated in the XX sex; that is, most of its genes do not function, making males and females functionally equal for most X chromosome

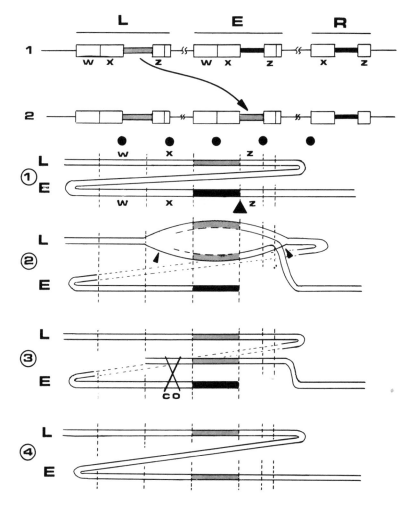

Figure 9.3. The operation of the sex switch gene of yeast. L and R are the left and right storage sites, E the expression box. The left gene (gray) is *alpha*. The right gene (black) is *a*. Each gene is bracketed by sequences w, x, and z, which are identical for each gene. (1, at top) Gene *a* is in the expression box. (2) Gene *alpha* replaces *a* in the expression box. The probable mechanism of the switch is shown in the four steps following. (1) w and x of the left gene pair with the same sequences of the gene in the expression box. A cutting enzyme (triangle) binds to DNA at the right end of the expressed gene (black). (2) The enzyme makes a complete cut of the double helix (which remains held together by protein). The piece to the right of the cut pairs with the homologous part (z) of the left gene and is then extended to the left, making a new copy of the left gene. (3) The lower area of the loop with the new copy of the left gene is isolated (black triangles in step 2) and its x region undergoes crossing over (CO) with the x region to the left of the expressed gene. (4) The formerly expressed gene is eliminated and is replaced by the left gene. (Modified from J. N. Strathern et al., *Cell* 31:183–92 [1982].)

genes. It is as if every individual had just one X chromosome (for most genes). One might expect that an X chromosome is inactivated to ensure the same gene balance in both sexes. If such a balance were crucial, however, it should take place in all diploid creatures with an XY type of sex determination, but, as in the case of birds, it does not. The reasons for this species difference are unknown.

A possible explanation is that X inactivation is another device for sex determination. X and Y chromosomes, although differing in most sequences, share genes; some might be important for sex determination. X inactivation would have the role of reducing the contribution of these genes in XX individuals, thus allowing the Y chromosome to play the controlling role. The equalization of the sexes in respect to expression of other X chromosome genes would be a secondary windfall. In birds the different arrangement of sex-determining genes would make X inactivation irrelevant or even undesirable. Other compensatory mechanisms would balance the expression of other X chromosomal genes in the two sexes. This interpretation of X inactivation follows the principle that nature does not work from general blueprints, but uses whatever arrangement can be generated in evolution, provided it works.

Many aspects of X inactivation are mysterious. In species in which the female is XX, the X chromosome coming from the father is inactivated when an egg is fertilized. The egg therefore starts with a single active X chromosome (from the mother). At the first division of the egg, the paternal X chromosome is reactivated, and both X chromosomes are active. As the embryo develops, inactivation of one of the Xs occurs in groups of cells at different times. In all cases inactivation coincides with a major developmental change of the cells. What this means is unknown. Adding to the complexity is the fact that not *all* genes of an X chromosome are inactivated. Several of those that escape inactivation do not play any special role in the determination of sex.

After birth either of the two X chromosomes of an XX individual can be inactive in different cells essentially at random. The effect is seen in some humans who have two different forms (alleles) of the same gene in the two X chromosomes, giving rise to distinguishable enzymes. If clones are grown from individual cells of such a person, none yields both types of enzyme. Various clones will contain one or the other enzyme.

As to the mechanism of inactivation, the most consistent observation is that the inactive X chromosome has two DNA features characteristic of inactive genes: condensed chromatin and abundance of m-groups (see chapter 5). The condensation is such that in mammalian cells the whole inactive X chromosome shrinks to a little blob, easily recognizable by light microscopy. This blob is so characteristic that its presence in a cell is sufficient to identify it as female. The importance of m-groups is readily seen by transferring the DNA of cells with a recognizable gene in the inactive X chromosome to other cells. The gene remains inactive in the receiving cells. But if the donor cells are grown for some generations in the presence of the drug azacytidine, which prevents the formation of m-groups (see chapter 5), the gene is active after transfer. This reactivation affects only a few genes, not the whole chromosome. What makes most of the genes in an X chromosome lose or gain activity together in the normal process of inactivation and reactivation is still a mystery.

A Peculiar Inheritance

Most inherited characteristics are transmitted equally from the parents to their progeny regardless of the sex of the progeny, but characteristics that are due to genes on X chromosomes are an exception. An example is the disease known as hemophilia (see chapter 7), in which profuse bleeding occurs after minor wounds, such as circumcision or tooth extraction, because blood clotting is defective. The disease is due to a deficiency of substances involved in blood clotting which are specified by genes in the X chromosome. It affects only males when the single X chromosome carries a defective gene. Females with one altered gene do not have the disease if the other gene of the same pair is normal. The good gene is active in half of their cells, causing the production of an adequate amount of clotting substance.

The pattern of inheritance of hemophilia became publicized because it affected several former European princes, all descendants of Great Britain's Queen Victoria. That no princess was affected is explained by the inheritance of the X chromosomes (fig. 9.4). The disease is transmitted by normal-appearing females (such as the queen) who have one altered and one normal X chromosome and manifests itself in male descendants (for instance, Prince Alexis of Russia) who inherit the altered chromosome through the seemingly normal mother. Other altered genes of the X chromosomes follow the same pattern of inheritance.

Genes of autosomes are inherited and express their defects in a different way. When a single autosomal gene is altered in one parent, regardless of sex, each progeny has a 50 percent chance of receiving it. The presence of the altered gene goes unnoticed in either sex because the product supplied in all cells by the normal gene of the same pair is usually sufficient for maintaining the function. If two individuals with the hidden defective gene mate, each progeny—whether male or female—has a 25 percent chance of having two defective genes and therefore of being affected by disease (fig. 9.5).

Hormonal Control of Sex

The direct effect of the sex differentiation genes is to orient the differentiation of the germ cells into sperm or eggs and that of the gonads into testes or ovaries. In vertebrates, both differentiations occur when the primitive germ cells, which are formed in another part of the embryo, migrate to two masses of cells inside the abdomen, from which the gonads will develop. In the genetic male the germ cells settle in the center of the cell mass, which then develops into a network of tubes

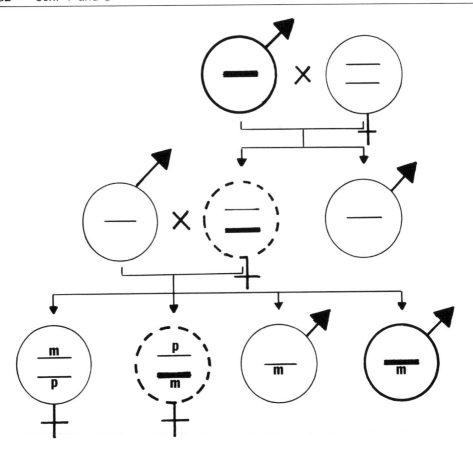

Figure 9.4. The special inheritance of the X chromosome. (Only the X chromosomes are indicated.) Abnormal chromosomes are thick lines, normal ones thin. Thick circles: individuals expressing the abnormality; thin circles: normal individuals; dashed thick circle: individual with an abnormal sex chromosome, who carries the abnormality but does not express it. ♂ = male, ♀ = female. The cross of an affected male with a normal female (above) generates carrier females and normal males. The cross of a carrier female with a normal male produces normal males and females, carrier females, and affected males. m = X chromosome inherited from the mother; p = chromosome inherited from the father (paternal).

and starts manufacturing sperm cells. In the genetic female the germ cells settle in the outer layer of the cell mass, which then grows in thickness to become the ovary, and the germ cells develop into egg cells.

The sex chromosomes determine how the primitive germ cells and the undifferentiated gonads will develop, a process called primary sex determination. Secondary differences between the male and the female body (genitalia, hair, muscular development, size and shape of the body, and so on) are produced later by the combined effect of the sex differentiation genes and the sex hormones.

In vertebrates, another important difference between males and females is

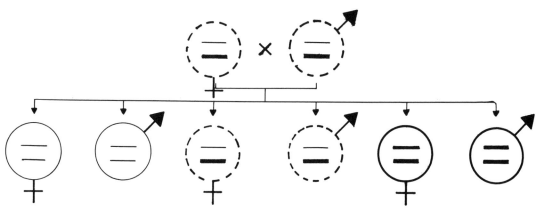

Figure 9.5. Inheritance of an autosomal gene. Only one pair of autosomes is indicated. Symbols are the same as in figure 9.4. A cross between two carriers produces the chromosome combinations shown at bottom, which all have one paternal and one maternal chromosome. Affected individuals or carriers can be of either sex.

the regimen of hormone production. Whereas the female produces sex hormones and mature eggs according to a cycle, the male produces male hormones and mature sperm continuously throughout the period of sexual maturity. This difference has a functional role, because the purpose of the male in reproduction is to fertilize females at the time they are ready—at ovulation. Evidently, since there is a time restriction on the availability of one of the partners, the other partner must be unrestricted for optimum success. As we have seen in the previous chapter, the cyclic variation in females is caused by a complex interaction among the hormones of the hypothalamus, the pituitary, and the ovary.

An Important Switch

Sex hormones are primarily manufactured in the gonads. They belong to the class of steroid hormones which are very similar, differing only in chemical details. Many of these hormones are interconvertible by enzymes present in cells. Male hormones, or androgens, are made in the testes by cells situated between the sperm-producing tubules. Female hormones are produced in the ovary by cells present in the follicles, the small vesicles in which the eggs develop (see chapter 8). Follicles generate estrogens and progesterone in alternating waves. Estrogens are so called because in many species they induce estrus, that is, sexual receptivity in the female. Estrogens are female hormones in most vertebrates; they are also made in very simple animals, such as lobsters, as a step in the manufacture of other hormones. Progesterone is made only in viviparous animals, which keep the fertilized eggs in their bodies.

Progesterone works only on cells prepared by previous exposure to estrogen.

For instance, under the influence of estrogen, the glandular lining of the mammalian uterus grows in thickness, but remains qualitatively unchanged. After the switch to progesterone, the lining starts secreting specific products. If the egg is fertilized, it finds in the progesterone-modified endometrium the environment required for nesting in and for proceeding with the formation of the embryo. An endometrium stimulated by estrogen alone is not suitable.

In viviparous animals the switch from estrogen to progesterone during the ovarian cycle is fundamental to the function of the female reproductive system. It is part of a cycle of hormones and attitudes (to be discussed further below) that reflect the dual nature of the female as mate and as mother: she must first mate with a male in order to achieve fertilization of the egg, and then she must take care of the product of fertilization. Estrogens prepare the female for mating; progesterone builds up conditions favorable to the development of the egg if it is fertilized. After fertilization, progesterone production continues, preventing further ovulation. The hormone is later replaced by those produced by the embryo itself, which have the same effect. If the egg is not fertilized, progesterone production stops. In women and other primates this causes the proliferated endometrium to slough off with the loss of much blood (menstruation). Immediately a new follicle starts maturing and the cycle begins again.

An animal produces not only the hormones of its own sex but also those of the other sex because of the chemical relatedness of steroid hormones. Estrogens are made by chemically changing androgens: the ovary first makes androgen and then converts it into estrogen. In the testes, too, a proportion of the androgen produced is converted to estrogen. In both sexes androgen is also produced by the adrenal gland. In females this androgen is converted into estrogen by the cells that make up the body fat—an important source of estrogen. The role of fat explains why women dancers, who are very thin, are deficient in estrogen and often do not cycle, and why obese women have a higher than normal incidence of cancers that are promoted by estrogen, such as that of the breast. The presence of the opposite hormones within the same body may lead to imbalances that have important consequences.

Hormone and Gene Balance

Both genes and hormones contribute to determining sexual characters: in different species one or the other prevails. In the fly *Drosophila*, for instance, the prevalent control is genetic. This is seen in some females in which one of the X chromosomes is lost at the first division of the fertilized egg: of the two cells generated then, one is XX, the other X. One cell will give rise to the right half of the body, the other to the left half. Of these, one (X) is a full male (because the Y chromosome plays no sex-determining role in this species), the other (XX) is a full female. Hormones circulating through the body could not cause such a sharp demarcation, which is strictly consonant with the genetic constitution of the cells.

In the majority of animals, however, the control of sexual characteristics is due mainly to sex hormones, but the influence of the genes is still felt. In vertebrates, the development of the XY sex requires hormones, regardless of whether it is male or female. In mammals a castrated male (XY) embryo will develop as a female, whereas a castrated female embryo will not change; but in the case of birds or lizards, in which the female is XY, a castrated female embryo will develop as a male, whereas a castrated male embryo will not change. This effect explains a human disease—testicular feminization syndrome—in which genetically male individuals, although possessing testes, develop a feminine body. As a consequence of a genetic defect they lack receptors for the male hormones they produce, which are therefore ineffective.

An abnormal supply of a hormone can also overrule the genetic sex determination, leading to development as males. A striking example is the cattle freemartin: in a multiple pregnancy a female fetus becomes masculinized if its blood circulation communicates with that of a male fetus and the male hormones circulate through its body. The male fetus, however, is not affected by the female hormones. A similar and even more extreme result is obtained when two newts of opposite sexes are connected like Siamese twins, so that the two circulations intermix. If they are connected early enough in development, the ovary of the female partner is transformed into a functional testis, which produces sperm and manufactures male sex hormones.

Developmental disturbances of those types do not occur in multiple pregnancies in primates. They have never been observed in human pregnancies with twins of different sexes, nor in marmoset monkeys, in which pregnancies are regularly double. Why do these disturbances occur only in some species? We don't know the answer. The differences nevertheless show the absence of fixed blueprints in the organization and function of creatures of different species.

A Critical Period

The sex hormones produced by the gonads of the embryo act at certain critical periods to determine whether the internal and external genitalia, the general characteristics of the body, and the network of certain parts of the brain will be of male or female type. These effects afford an important insight on how an animal develops.

The genitalia are determined early during embryonic life. In the still neutral early embryo, two canals form equally in males and females. One of these canals has the potential for generating a uterus, the oviducts that connect the uterus to the ovaries, and the upper part of the vagina (the lower part comes from the skin). The other canal can generate the ducts carrying the sperm from the testes to the urinary canal. At some point in development the sex hormones produced in the embryo direct the appropriate canal to develop and the other to disappear. In the male the testes and the connecting ducts will later descend from the abdomen into the scrotum. The sex hormones also determine the alternative differentiation of the skin into the external genitalia. An excessive amount of hormones of the opposite sex during the critical period may perturb these events. Estrogens produced in excess in the testes of some male human fetuses during the critical period misdirects sex development, causing the feminization of some traits.

In advanced species such as mammals, the sex organs, once formed during the critical period, cannot be changed: beyond that time no hormonal manipulation can redirect the established sexual anatomy. The main reason is that there is no reservoir of cells able to take the alternative course of differentiation. In lower vertebrates (for example, certain birds, fish, or amphibia) a reservoir of uncommitted cells persists, and true sex reversal is possible, even in the adult. In some of these species an extreme situation prevails: the gonads die at the end of each mating season and are rebuilt (from cells that can go in either the male or female direction) before the new season. The outcome depends on environmental variables, such as the diet. If a young male toad is castrated and given an appropriate diet, it will change into a full-fledged female with an egg-containing ovary.

In humans, the sex hormones are continuously produced at a low level after birth until puberty, when their production increases and becomes pulsating (see chapter 8). These changes are responsible for the marked enlargement of the sex organs and for the appearance of other sex-related characteristics that persist in the adult body. In both sexes an increased muscular development occurs at puberty, resulting from a greater production of male hormones; in females, these hormones are supplied by the adrenal. This change is especially strong in males, possibly so that they may fight for the female's attention. In humans, puberty is also a period of intense personality change caused by the profound effects of sex hormones on the brain (see chapter 10). Sexual awareness also produces problems of adjustment that will be considered in subsequent chapters.

Ambiguities

The mechanism of genetic and chemical balance by which the sex of an individual is determined is inherently ambiguous. Relatively small shifts in the interaction between the control genes and the sex-determining genes or in the rate of hormone production or disposal can change the expressed sex. They may cause the development of intersexes or may even lead to a sex reversal—the expression of a sex not consonant with the XY constitution of the individual. Everything depends on the organization of the control mechanism.

Simpler creatures are endowed with extraordinary plasticity of sex determination, as shown by two examples. One is that of a small fish: each male swims around near the bottom surveying a small harem of females, which live in individual burrows where they raise their young. The male fertilizes each female in turn. This routine continues undisturbed until the male dies or disappears. When that happens, one of the females emerges from her burrow, becomes a male, and performs the role of fertilizing the remaining females. This arrangement is essential to ensure the reproductive activity of the group—one of the goals of nature. Another striking example is found in a marine worm: neutral—that is, sexually undifferentiated—larvae settle on the ocean floor, where they develop as females. If, however, a larva lands on the mouth appendages of a female that was already there, it develops as a male. It enters the female body where it takes on the life of a parasite, providing her with sperm to fertilize her eggs.

The flexibility of sex determination in these two examples is probably caused by specialized influences on the control of the sex-determining genes. In the fish the control may derive from hormones that accumulate in the body of unfertilized females and cause masculinization when they reach a sufficient concentration. In the marine worm, the control may derive from contacts of the larva with signal molecules on the surface of the female body.

One of the environmental variables affecting sex differentiation of creatures that do not maintain a constant temperature is the ambient temperature. The effect can go in either direction. Among some oysters, which alternate between the male and the female sex, females become rarer and rarer as the temperature of the water decreases. But the larvae of a small fish in colder water tend to develop mostly into females. There is apparently no generally uniform response.

In many reptile species, whether an egg will develop as male or female depends on the temperature at which it is kept during a critical period—around the middle of the incubation time. Again the effect varies in different species. Many turtles and alligators produce males at high temperatures (around 34° C), females at lower temperatures. Lizards behave in the opposite way. The snapping turtle follows neither pattern: it produces males at intermediate temperatures, females at either extreme.

The strong dependence of the sex of a reptile on the temperature at which the egg is incubated may be the source of serious complications. If the temperature of the environment should become sufficiently abnormal, the eggs would all develop into animals of the same sex and the species would become extinct. Did this complication ever arise? It may have played a role in the extinction of dinosaurs, which we discussed earlier. It is likely that the eggs of those reptiles were sensitive to temperature changes like those of today's reptiles. If the temperature of the atmosphere rose owing to an accumulation of carbon dioxide (as outlined in chapter 3), and if the change lasted long enough, it might have generated a world of all-male dinosaurs, dooming them to extinction.

The reasons for the effects of temperature on reptiles' sex determination are not understood. But some speculations have centered on the biology of the animals. One reason proposed for the response of alligator eggs is that at the lower temperatures at which they develop, females use less of the egg's food reserves; after hatching, they mature more rapidly. The result is advantageous for reproduction in a population where a male usually fertilizes several females. Another reason given is that the females of the alligators prefer to inhabit the cooler marshes where they hatch, whereas the males prefer the warmer canals beside the levees where they hatch. The production of each sex in its own habitat would avoid long voyages immediately after hatching, when the animals would be exposed to predators.

These explanations, however, do not take into account the genetic bases for these adaptations. It is possible, in fact, that the adaptations are caused by special mutations well known in microorganisms which make the gene product ineffective at a higher temperature. Depending on which gene has the mutation, the male or the female characteristics would be affected. The significance of such a change does not necessarily have to be "adaptive," that is, capable of conferring an advantage on the affected individuals. It may be merely "tolerable" for a certain species in a certain environment if it does not create problems.

In mammals and birds chromosomal control of sex determination is very efficient because their embryos evolve in an environment that is constant for both nourishment and temperature, eliminating the effect of environmental variables during development. Species that develop in a variable environment must necessarily be affected by its variations. Different species are intrinsically more sensitive than others to such environmental influences in relation to their genetic constitution.

The Evolution of Sex

Equalization of Sexual Roles

We have seen, then, that differentiation between sexes, although so basic to life and universal in its expression, is brought about in different species by mechanisms of extreme diversity. This great variability depends on the ability of nature to adapt to circumstances, such as the background from which a species evolved, its other characteristics, and the environment in which it lives. Underlying this variability is a basic evolutionary trend toward equalizing the roles of the two sexes in reproduction.

The role of the female is much more dominant in lower forms of life. The reason is that eggs are more adequate than sperm to produce a whole new individual. Indeed, exclusively female lineages can be maintained over a number of generations by many lower species up to the level of lizards. In contrast, there are no exclusive male lineages in any species. As we have seen in the case of water fleas, however, existence of exclusively female lineages is limited by their inability to persist under difficult conditions, through which the product of fertilization can survive: hence the need for the male sex.

Despite this limitation, the role of the female may still predominate in lower species in other ways. An example is the angler fish, which lives in the depths of the ocean where encounters between individuals of opposite sex are rare. When a young male (which is quite small) encounters a female (which is much larger), he attaches to her by sinking his teeth into her skin. From then on he stays there, leading a parasitic life, nourished by juices from the female, and supplying her with sperm for fertilizing her eggs. This and other examples suggest a picture of the male as little more than a test tube for growing sperm for the female. Beyond that the burden of perpetuating the species rests on the female.

In more advanced creatures the situation is changed by the marked development of the brain, which introduces new rules for the interaction of the sexes. Although the female still has the biologically immense responsibility of bearing and rearing the young, this responsibility is alleviated by the role of the male as provider of food or as paternal protector of the young.

The Origin of Sex

As is true of all evolutionary questions, when we speculate on the evolution of sex, we can discuss only possibilities and alternatives on the basis of what we know. Nobody witnessed the events when they occurred, nor can we reproduce them in the laboratory. Our point of departure in considering this question is the recognition that the basic attribute of sexuality—the ability of DNA molecules to exchange parts—exists in all forms of life, from viruses and bacteria to higher organisms. These exchanges are possible because of the presence in every cell of enzymes that can perform the events of recombination. They must have developed at a very early period in the evolution of life, perhaps as part of mechanisms for repairing DNA damages wrought by the ultraviolet light of the sun. These enzymes presumably caused primitive DNA molecules to join, generating the longer molecules that are at the basis of life as we know it today.

Given the fact that basic sexuality, at the DNA level, is a general attribute of living creatures, we can ask: how and why did it generate sexual differentiation? Was it because sexual reproduction promotes the multiplication of creatures more effectively than does asexual reproduction? This may be true in part. Although no clear advantage of sexuality can be recognized in the reproduction of viruses and bacteria, it can be seen in the case of yeast: diploid yeast, the product of sexual reproduction, is more vigorous than haploid yeast. Also important for yeast and similar creatures is the ability to switch reversibly from the diploid to the haploid state, a property that is intimately connected to sexuality. In the haploid state yeast can more readily adapt to changes in the environment by expressing useful changes of the genes immediately after they occur (because there is only a single copy of each gene). In the diploid state this type of adaptation is not so easy, because a change in a gene may be masked by the unaltered gene of the same pair. But the diploid state has the advantage that an unfavorable gene is masked by a normal homologous gene. So yeast can overcome both the problem of environmental change and that of the accumulation of unfavorable genes by dwelling in one or the other form. Higher creatures are usually diploid with pairs of genes that may be different; this common trait can be attributed to the slow growth of these creatures, which do not need to adapt rapidly to fast changes in the environment. The ability of diploidy to cover up unfavorable genes becomes the most desirable characteristic.

In spite of the clear advantages of sexual reproduction in many species, we cannot say that these advantages were responsible for the evolution and regular use of sexual reproduction. In fact, there might be another important reason for sexuality: that it plays a fundamental role in the formation of new species. The formation of complex organisms during evolution would have been impossible, or would have occurred in a very different way, if the primitive short DNA molecules had not been able to fuse by recombination. Without fusion the big genomes with large gene repertoires present in the world today would not exist. These, of course, are hypotheses. But they do account in a logical way for the observations, on the basis of events that are experimentally observable. It is difficult to imagine other hypotheses that could account equally well for what we know.

We can conclude, then, that there is no simple answer to the question: how did sex evolve? We can draw a tentative picture, however. As in other areas of biology, a phenomenon that was possible (exchange of parts of DNA) participated in various evolutionary events, such as the fusion of DNA molecules, duplication, insertion or deletion of DNA segments, joining of preexisting sets of integrated genes, and so on. This caused the evolution of living creatures and in turn was directed by evolution into the form of sex we are familiar with. Along the evolutionary path the sexual phenomena and the evolutionary events continually influenced each other. As a consequence, sex as present in higher organisms would be inconceivable if many of these organisms' properties were absent, and conversely, the properties of the organisms would be inconceivable without sex. Like other biological processes, sex must have evolved through a highly integrated series of events; it progressed, as it were, "by pulling itself up by the bootstraps."

At the beginning of this chapter we raised the question of why DNA relinquished the autonomy of the single genome. The answer is: because mixing genomes gave DNA a tremendous boost. But as this goal was pursued, sex achieved a development perhaps far beyond the needs of DNA. Once the process was started it became irresistible: it proceeded in every possible direction, reaching the limits of what is feasible. In biology, once a door is opened, the space behind it is quickly filled.

CHAPTER 10

Sex: ♂ and ♀

Getting Together

It would be futile for creatures to be differentiated into males and females if individuals of both sexes did not recognize each other as potential partners, if they did not find each other, if they did not want to mate, or if they did not know how to do it. Because self-fertilization is either impossible or strongly discouraged, all these steps are essential for generating progeny, and they must take place efficiently.

The problems of attraction and recognition between members of opposite sexes have been solved by nature in a bewildering variety of ways. This variety is not surprising: the goal of nature is to ensure the mixing of the genes; how that goal is reached is irrelevant, provided it happens with a good chance of success. The details are left to the inventiveness of the genes of the species. The penalty for failure is extinction.

Many clues are used in courtship for identifying an individual seeking a partner and for enticing members of the opposite sex. Among the clues are color displays, movements, sounds, smells, and offers of reward. Color displays are frequently used by male birds (the peacock, for example) in order to interest the female, who selects her suitor on this basis. Among the birds of paradise of New Guinea and Australia the showy tail plumage of the male is so large the bird can hardly fly, but this is what the female likes: the longer the tail, the more desirable the mate. Conversely the color of the female butterfly in flight, or the luminous body of some female beetles, attract the males. Specific movements are probably important in sexual approaches in any species, and they reach a spectacular development in certain butterflies and grasshoppers: whole formations of winged males perform dances and hovering exercises for the excitement of the females. Birds use the most extravagant performances of gestures and dances in courtship, which differ markedly from one species to another, even among related ones. Rhythm is a crucial signal for fireflies: males fly around at night flashing their lights at a rhythm that is characteristic of the species. The females sitting on the ground recognize the proper signal and flash in return.

Sounds are important to birds, which are highly vocal creatures who have a large repertoire of songs to ensure communication of a variety of messages. The songs performed by the male are characteristic of each species, with minor dialectal differences related to geographical location. The females readily identify their partners. Male crickets also produce species-characteristic songs (by scratching the wings one against the other). Crickets of some species, however, mate without a song. Subsonic vibrations generated by rapid movements of the legs are used for communication between males and females of certain spiders that live on banana leaves; the signaling by the female leads the male unerringly to her. And, of course, the tone of voice is a signal of sex differentiation and maturity in humans, subtle nuances signifying interest, invitation, or rejection.

Highly specific chemicals—*pheromones*—are frequently used as sex attractants by insects. They are mostly employed by females, although in some species it is the male that is perfumed (fig. 10.1). Male moths can recognize the smell of the females of their species even when it is extremely diluted, having been released some several kilometers away. One molecule of the pheromone of the silkworm moth is sufficient to stimulate a male. And the proper pheromone can be recognized by males even if it is mixed with more than twenty smells produced by females of other species. In different insect species the sex smells are produced by chemicals that are very similar to each other. The animals easily detect differences so slight they are hard to detect in sophisticated chemical laboratories. Many pheromones have been chemically identified and produced in the laboratory. Because of their high effectiveness and specificity, insect pheromones are very promising as weapons in the control of insect pests, luring them to their doom. Each would attract insects of only one species, without disturbing those of others.

Substances of the same general constitution as insect pheromones are used, too, by some marine algae and other lower plants. The sperm recognizes the pheromone released by unfertilized eggs and homes in on it, a phenomenon that shows how widely pheromones are used to promote fertilization in the living world.

Among other creatures, male snakes recognize and follow the smell left by the females of the species in their tracks. Some wandering spiders are attracted by the odor of the silken line of the female, and male cockroaches have on their antennas very sensitive sensors for female smells. Fish also possess smell. This may seem strange to us because we are used to thinking of odors as wafting through the air. We may not be able to recognize smells in the water, but fish do: they have a very fine nose. Mammals also use smells as sex signals. The male mouse excites the

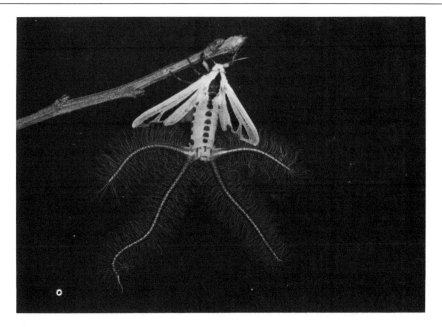

Figure 10.1. A spectacular display of the scent organs by a male of a species of moths. The organs are normally retracted. (From D. Schneider et al., *Science* 215:1264–65 [1982].)

female of the same species with its smell, but the smell of a foreign male frightens her and, through complex nerve mechanisms, may even block her pregnancy. Monkeys or cattle will not mate with their nostrils plugged up. Odors are also part of the sexual behavior of humans. Males and females develop characteristic sweat glands in the armpits and around the anus at puberty; their products contribute to the atmosphere of sexual arousal. Humans also use their brain and their technology to produce erotic odors: artificial perfumes act as sex attractants, perhaps paraphrasing natural odors or enhancing them in subtle ways.

All these signals—songs for birds, smells or pheromones for insects and other animals—serve as more than simply sex attractants, however. They are used for many messages. For instance, among social insects, the queen bee produces pheromones that not only attract male drones in the nuptial flight but also, through obscure mechanisms, block maturation of the ovaries of other potential queens and activate colonies for swarming. The specific meaning of a signal depends on its context.

Certain creatures express their sexual drive by becoming architects and builders. Male bowerbirds of New Guinea, for instance, make complex constructions out of sticks to entice the females (fig. 10.2). The size and design of the constructions vary with the species; some are one or two meters high. They are surrounded by a round garden, or platform, covered with moss, which is in turn surrounded by a wall. The bird places piles of objects of different colors in the

Figure 10.2. Bower of a bowerbird living in the mountains of New Guinea. The male bird arranged the sticks around a small tree, built a platform at its base, and decorated it with three mounds of blue, yellow, and green fruit. He stands on a branch offering a blue fruit to the female, who perches on a branch above. (From J. M. Diamond, *Science* 216:431–34 [1982].)

garden; then it sits near its building waiting for the female. From time to time he takes positive action and tries to dismantle the bowers of other males. The larger and more ornate the bower, the more likely it is to entice a female. Merely a symbol of power, however, the bower is not used as a nuptial chamber or as a nest. The female will make the nest herself in a secluded spot. There is wisdom in this: her subdued plumage is not easily noticed by predators intent on eating her eggs, whereas the male's showy plumage would certainly attract predators, as would such a conspicuous nest.

Frequently, food is offered by the male in order to interest the female; the offer is sometimes real, sometimes symbolic. An authentic food offer is made by the male of the black-tipped hangingfly. (The name derives from the fly's manner of resting by hanging from a twig.) The male captures a housefly or a daddy longlegs and, after feeding briefly, offers the carcass to a waiting female. Whether she will

take it depends on the size of the offering. If the carcass is big enough, she will **accept** it and will mate unromantically while feeding. The male bowerbird offers **fruit** to females, but male penguins present only pebbles. The pebble seems to be a **symbolic** offering, perhaps representing a token for nest building rather than food. **The** males of certain kinds of birds make yet another offer: each builds a nest and sits in it, advertising itself as a partner of serious substance.

How a mate is selected is not at all clear, but certainly there are definite rules. In fact, even in promiscuous species (such as dogs or certain monkeys) females show clear-cut preferences or exclusions. But the rules differ from species to species. Females of many species choose their mate on the basis of the male's display, but the displays vary enormously among different species. In some cases mate selection is determined by previous learning. Thus a colored snow goose tends to mate with another whose color is that of the snow geese the bird associated with in early life, when its own plumage developed. Male ducks raised exclusively with other male ducks tend to try to mate with males as adults. Early imprinting, at least in some cases, is important, then, in the mate selection process.

Deception

Because sex signals are powerful motors of animal behavior, it is not surprising that, in nature's cussedness, they are used fraudulently by some creatures for their own advantage. One approach is mimicry. The flowers of some orchids produce the characteristic sex smells of bees or wasps in order to lure these insects into fertilizing them. Male bees that respond to the odorous signals are further misled by visual displays: the flowers look like female bees in many details—eyes, body spots, even genitalia. The poor male is totally confused. Under the impression he has found a suitable partner, he attempts copulation with the flower. In doing so he charges his skin with pollen, which is located in the flower at a strategic spot. When finally the male becomes aware that he has been taken in and moves to what seems to be another attractive female (of course, another flower), he is duped again into depositing the pollen onto the stamen, effecting fertilization.

Another example of mimicry is that used by males of the black-tipped hangingfly. Instead of hunting for the flies he needs as offerings for his courtship, he tries to steal them from other males. Approaching a male that is holding prey, he lowers his wings, a gesture characteristic of females when they are ready to mate. The waiting male offers the prey to the mimicking male, who will feed and resist copulation as a female would do in the initial stage. Then the mimicking male will try to run off with the prey, often successfully. Mimicry is also used by female fireflies to attract and eat the males of smaller species. The mimicking female responds to the flashing rhythm of the flying male as if it were of the same species; when the male homes in, it is attacked and killed.

Another type of deception is cuckoldry. Thus in some species of singing frogs, nonsinging males position themselves close to a singing male and mate with a female attracted by the song. Males of a species of sunfish tend to build nests in which they fertilize the eggs spawned by the females they attract and then care for the eggs and the larvae. Males that do not make nests may imitate female behavior: they enter the nests of other males, together with the spawning females, and release their sperm. The hard-working nest builder thus cares for the offspring of the interlopers. Cuckoldry is really a genetic fraud: in both cases the genes of legitimate males are replaced by those of the cuckolders under the guise of legitimacy.

Variety in Mating Practices

ACROBATIC MATING. Just as varied as the devices for mutual attraction are the circumstances of mating, which may be very strenuous (for instance, in flight by bee queens and male drones) or very trying (under the threat of death by the female mantis or the black widow spider, which eat mates that cannot make a quick escape). But perhaps the most fascinating mating is that of the grunion, a small fish that lives near the shores of California. This fish has the peculiar habit of mating on sandy shores rather than in the water. It accomplishes this feat by taking advantage of the highest tides. The fact that on the shores of California these tides occur around midnight has given rise to the legend of the fish that dance on the beach by moonlight. This nocturnal mating is not readily observed. In the northernmost reaches of the Gulf of California, however, the highest tide is delayed many hours, because from the mouth of the Gulf it must travel about a thousand miles to the northern end. There the highest tide occurs in the early afternoon, so the mass mating of the grunions can be observed in full sunshine.

The sight is unforgettable: a big wave sweeps over the empty beach, and as it retreats it leaves the sand covered with thousands of fish. Each female stands up with her tail in the sand, digging a hole with frantic twisting motions of her body, and with several males wrapped around her. In a wink the eggs are ejected and sperm ejaculated into the sandy hole. Within a few seconds everything is covered again by a successive wave. After it retreats, the beach is again smooth and empty. Sand washed over the holes has buried the fertilized eggs, which will undergo partial development there. The process will be completed with the next high tide, when the emerging fish will be washed back to the ocean by the highest wave.

How do the fish know where to go and when? What impels them to be washed up in unison onto the sand? And how do the sea gulls, who line the beach during the last half hour before the big wave, know that their dinner is coming? These are still mysteries.

MATING TO DEATH. Certain animals have a strange life cycle: they do not mate for most of their lifetime but finally engage in an orgy of mating and die shortly afterward. Salmon are well-known examples of this life cycle: they leave the stream where they are born, swim to the ocean, and later return, attracted by the characteristic smell of the water. After the males have fought fiercely, they mate and then rapidly wither and die. A similar life cycle is observed in some marsupial mice in Australia. Many plants too undergo this cycle. Well known is the century plant; as a last effort it produces such a dramatic inflorescence that it looks more like a tree than a flower.

The reasons for these peculiar cycles are not known, and although we like to think there are reasons for everything, there may be none. Analyzing the circumstances under which these life cycles take place, we can see that they fit very well the characteristics of the environment in which the organisms live. Although we can say that this is how they survive, that does not explain why such organisms exist at all. The reason may be buried in the history of their DNAs and may have nothing to do with their environment. We will come back to this point in chapter 20.

The rapid aging of the males—for instance, the salmon—after they have performed their reproductive function is another puzzle. But the aging phenomenon is poorly understood in any case: in all creatures it seems to follow a mysterious program. Because we do not understand the program in general, we certainly cannot explain the peculiarities of any given program.

SEXUALITY AND AESTHETICS. The mating signals used by animals could be considered, in human terms, as artistic expressions. We recognize beauty of the mate as a prime factor in sexual attraction. The beauty of a spider or an orangutan may not be perceptible to us, but beauty is in the eyes of the beholder. (Probably a male orangutan would not care very much for the beauty of a woman.) Music is the sexual attractant in bird songs; rhythm, in the flashing of fireflies; architecture, in the bowerbirds' constructions; colors, in birds' displays; and perfumes, for moths and many animals.

Humans use all these methods for sexual attraction: the beauty, the songs, the well-furnished bedroom, the enhanced colors of the lips and face, the rhythm of movements in dancing, the perfumed body. Humans, however, have moved one step beyond other animals: they have abstracted the meaning of these attractants beyond their immediate values and have developed them into aesthetic experiences to a large extent disconnected from sexuality.

Sexual Behavior

All these fascinating phenomena of communication and interactions between individuals, aimed at achieving the procreation of their progeny, show how important a part the brain plays in the performance of the sexual functions. In the animals that perform these feats, DNA has delegated the functions of reproduction to many parts of the body formed during the development of the organism. Of course, DNA has shaped these complexes by building up an appropriate system of genes and continually perfecting them during evolution. But in terms of the performance of the sexual function, DNA must passively wait until fertilization occurs. Having relinquished direct control of reproduction, DNA can only introduce changes in the genes in the chance of making the process more efficient. The brain seems to be remote from DNA, but it is itself, of course, a creation of DNA.

In different species the genes directly control some components of the pattern of behavior that is already inscribed in the brain of the newborn. These patterns are the direct consequence of the primary organization of the neural network. It is clear that they are not learned: in fact, they develop in individuals reared alone; they are inherited traits characteristic of the species. These components of behavior must be considered as automatic reactions released, in suitably prepared individuals, by various forms of sex-oriented communication. Each of these behavioral patterns involves a series of actions that occur one after another in a highly reproducible sequence. They are *fixed action patterns.*

In the more complex organisms sexual behavior contains components that are fixed and others that are modifiable by learning and therefore vary from one individual to another or according to circumstances. Introducing the element of learning into the vital process of reproduction is DNA's riskiest venture. It removes much of the genetic control from the unfolding events. Adoption of this scheme may have been dictated by the advantage it offers, or it may have been accepted as a compromise. It is possible that once learning entered the scene, DNA had to make do with it and to bend it to its own purpose of reproduction. DNA has been successful because learning has become a tool of reproduction. The compromise—if there was one—works well, but offers problems.

Even in animals displaying learned behavior, the fixed components may still be extensive. They may also be so elaborate that it is difficult to know whether they are learned or automatic. Take, for instance, nest building by birds. Female birds of a given species select specific building materials, such as twigs (often only of a certain tree) or a certain type of grass, and assemble them into structures of rather complex architecture. All this seems very well thought out. But the plan is not the result of "thinking" on the part of the bird: if a female is kept in a cage without suitable materials, she will attempt to use her long feathers as sticks, although they are attached to her body and she cannot detach them. In a similar vein, an inexperienced female rat given inadequate building materials will try to build a nest of air, and she will go through the motions of shaping a nonexistent roof and smoothing down nonexistent walls.

The important influence of learning on inborn behavioral patterns is evident in birds. Young males reared in a soundless environment (for instance, a sound-proof chamber) develop a rudimentary repertoire of songs. But in the company of adult birds of the species, the young enrich their repertoire by learning. What they learn, however, are mostly songs characteristic of the species. The song, therefore, is basically inscribed in a genetically determined brain network. Learning either allows the full expression of the inscribed program or adds phrases compatible with it. Also genetically imprinted is the responsiveness of female birds, which is maximal for songs of the same species.

How is sexual behavior inscribed in the neural network? It should be possible to trace at least the genetically determined organization, which is likely to be part of the network of the brain. We will examine the observations made in the female rat.

The Sexy Brain

The brain is usually considered to be the organ responsible for perception, for analyzing complex information, and for producing out of it instructions for action. This is the logical function of the brain computer. But as we have seen in chapter 8, the brain also has another facet, which is especially important in sex: it is a chemical laboratory producing hormones. The hypothalamus contains the hormone-producing nerve cells as well as nerve cells that respond to sex hormones produced in the gonads. On reaching the brain through the blood, these hormones alter the reaction of the nerve cells to the signals they receive.

The hypothalamus and neighboring nerve centers are the main regulators of sexuality. They control the production of sex hormones in the gonads and coordinate sexual behavior. The coordination is based on information about mate recognition as well as one more general information relevant to sexual behavior, such as the length of daylight, the availability of food, the season, and so on. The sex hormones reaching the nerve centers influence both this coordination and its effects.

The Sex Clock

In mammals the cyclic fall and rise of the two female sex hormones, estrogen and progesterone, is controlled by a sex clock situated in the hypothalamus, which, as we saw in chapter 8, acts on the body through the pituitary. In both males and females this control of sexual functions is ultimately carried out by two pituitary hormones that affect the gonads: the follicle-stimulating hormone (FSH) and the luteinizing hormone (LH). These hormones act on the ovaries in females and on the testes in males. We also saw in chapter 8 that in the female, FSH, after reaching the ovary through the blood, stimulates the maturation of a follicle and the synthesis of estrogens. In contrast, LH causes the rupture of the follicle and the release of the egg cell—ovulation. After ovulation the follicle is transformed into the corpus luteum, which synthesizes progesterone. In the male, FSH promotes the development of the testes and sperm production; LH, the production of the male hormones, androgens. To maintain the cyclicity of the ovary, FSH and LH must not act on it simultaneously. But this is excluded because production of the two hormones by the pituitary is also cyclic.

Cyclicity is maintained by a network of interactions that generates both stimulatory and inhibitory signals. Stimulatory, for instance, is the effect of pituitary

FSH on estrogen production by the ovary, or of pituitary LH on progesterone production by the ovary. Inhibitory is the effect of estrogens on the release of FSH from the pituitary and of progesterone on that of LH. Thus the periodicity of ovulation is generated by these interactions. The hypothalamic hormone causes production of FSH in the pituitary, which in turn stimulates production of estrogen in the ovary. As estrogen inhibits further FSH production, the pituitary switches to LH, which causes ovulation and progesterone production in the ovary. But progesterone inhibits LH production; so the pituitary, under the influence of the hypothalamic hormones, switches back to producing FHS. This cycle continues for life, as long as there are immature eggs in the ovary. One or more eggs mature at each cycle, building active follicles which produce the ovarian hormones. When all immature eggs are used up, the formation of follicles ceases and the hormones are no longer produced by the ovary.

In addition to these regulatory loops connecting the gonads to the hypothalamus and the pituitary, additional feedback loops connecting the hypothalamus to other parts of the brain are essential in cyclic sexual behavior. The sex clock involves many parts of the brain, which perform both secretory and information-processing functions. How well the system of feedback operates in an animal can be checked by injecting estrogen: a regularly cycling female reacts with production of LH (the feedback response).

The operation of the hormonal sex clock is very delicately adjusted; in humans any new FSH surge causes the maturation usually of only one egg. In contrast, FSH administration to women to combat sterility frequently results in the maturation of several eggs, causing multiple pregnancies of as many as six or seven fetuses. The natural release of the hormone differs from its artificial administration in the rate at which it reaches the target organs—the ovary, pituitary, and brain. The difference points up the fine adjustment of the sex clock.

In females of certain species, such as cats and rabbits, the sex clock stops running just before ovulation: the mature egg is not released but remains in the follicle. The LH surge takes place as a consequence of stimuli reaching the brain during mating and is rapidly followed by ovulation. This system of control is important for animals living alone, for which meetings between members of the opposite sex are rare: an occasional encounter has a much higher chance of resulting in fertilization. Moreover, the egg reaches the uterus at about the same time as the sperm from the vagina, thus contributing to the same goal. So it seems that this type of control developed during evolution in response to the solitary life of these animals. But the opposite may be true also—that the special control of the sex clock developed first and allowed the animals to take up a solitary form of life.

In the male the release of pituitary hormones is also under control of the hypothalamic hormone (GnRH), but FSH, LH, and the sex hormones are released from the pituitary without cycling. There is no feedback response to an injection of estrogen. In males the control system involves different hypothalamic nerve

centers. Nevertheless the controlling hypothalamic hormone still plays an important role in males, as shown by its ability to increase the sexual activity of men
who are defective in the production of pituitary hormones.

The regimen of sex hormone production (cyclic or continuous) determined by
these controls is not affected by the amounts of hormone produced, which are low
in childhood and much higher after puberty. Puberty itself is a phenomenon of the
brain: it is a progressive change of the response of hypothalamic nerve cells to the
controlling influences of hormones.

The production of sex hormones is also controlled through the brain by external variables that have an important influence on breeding. One is the length of
the day, which acts through the pineal gland located in the center of the brain (see
chapter 8). The importance of the influence of day length on reproduction is clear
because of the seasonal variation: young cannot be born when the season is unfavorable. The suitable season may be signaled by other changes as well: for a
mountain rodent the signals are plant products that show whether the growing
season is beginning or ending. In this animal a product of growing seedlings
stimulates production of sex hormones and therefore reproduction, whereas a
product of mature grass inhibits it. In the unpredictable environment in which the
animal lives it is essential that the growing season be clearly identified.

Control of Sexual Behavior

The different operation of the hypothalamic-gonadal system in males and females
shows that their brains differ. The question of what the differences are can be only
partly answered because the brain is so complex. It contains an extremely large
number of nerve cells distributed among many different centers, all connected by
thick bundles of fibers through which the cells communicate. Each center is connected to most of the others, and when a decision must be made, there is extensive
consultation among them.

Sexual behavior is no exception. The decision of whether or not it should be
activated is based on an analysis of information from many sources. Among these
are perceptions coming from the outside, which show whether conditions are
right for raising a family. Is there enough light, food, water? Is the season right?
Other perceptions give information about the male: is he sending signals indicating that he wants to mate? Is he palpating the female body in the right sequence at
the suitable places? Are there threatening conditions, such as a foreign male
around? The inquiry includes the state of the female: has the body been exposed to
estrogen long enough to expect that there is a mature egg in the follicle? Or has
progesterone been elevated in the last several hours, showing that ovulation has
taken place and an egg is ready to be fertilized?

All this involves a great deal of cross-talk among the various nerve centers.
The outcome is then channeled to the hypothalamus which coordinates the infor-

mation received. If the balance shows that mating is advisable, the hypothalamus allows the transmission of action signals to the muscles. A fixed pattern of activity is released and inevitably leads to mating and the fertilization of the egg.

Sexual Behavior of the Female Rat

Because many aspects of its behavior are well understood, the female rat is much-studied in investigations of sexual behavior. Hormonal conditions can be easily manipulated. The ovaries are removed to cut off the main production of estrogens and progesterone, and then the hormones are administered in controlled amounts and at times suitable for experiments.

As a result of the hormonal manipulations, the castrated animals are first unreceptive to mating. They become receptive again after they have been given estrogen for several days and then progesterone for several hours. These hormones act on the hypothalamus and neighboring parts of the brain; they enter the nerve cells and bind to receptor molecules in the cell nucleus. The hormone receptor complex causes some inactive genes to become active or, conversely, some active genes to be shut off. As a result some nerve cells become more receptive, others less so, to the signals they receive. In this way the chemical signal provided by the sex hormones is translated into a change of the function of the neural network. The hormones greatly increase the chance that sexual behavior will be displayed in the presence of a male.

The integration of multiple information through the estrogen-primed hypo-thalamus initiates the mating behavior, and the treated female rat goes through the sexual ritual, which is similar to that displayed by normal females at the proper phase of the hormonal cycle. She shakes her head violently so that her ears wiggle, a performance that must be irresistible to the male. It is probably the equivalent of a sexy dance. The movements of the head stimulate the movement-detecting apparatus in the female's ears, generating a self-exciting effect. This information too is channeled to the hypothalamus, where it further increases the effectiveness of signals that promote mating. As a result, the female makes rapid to and fro movements, backing against the male and stopping suddenly, clearly suggesting that she should be mounted. In response, the male clutches the back of her body with his paws and palpates up and down; he thrusts his penis against her skin around the vagina and the anus, signaling his own intention to mate.

Presently the main obstacle resides in the female's normal posture: her vagina is against the ground, so that intromission of the penis is impossible. The extensive skin stimulation by the male paws and penis provokes an automatic reflex by which the female crouches with her belly against the ground, bringing the back of her body upward so as to make the vagina accessible. After that, intromission and fertilization occur automatically.

The Neural Network in Rat Mating Behavior

The crouching reflex just described is characteristic of the sexual behavior of the female rat and is essential for mating. Much has been learned by studying this reflex. Laboratory observations show that necessary for eliciting the reflex is pressure on a large area of the skin from the lowest nipple to the vagina. The more this area is stimulated by the paws or the penis of the male, the more promptly the crouching reflex appears. Studies of the brain show that the signals from the stimulated area are received by nerve cells of the spinal cord, which are connected directly to the nerve cells responsible for activating the crouching muscles. The signals, therefore, could be transmitted to the muscles through this short route within the spinal cord, causing a crouching reflex without the intervention of the brain. But this short route is normally blocked by local inhibitory circuits.

The control of the crouching reflex conforms to the general hierarchy of centers within the central nervous system (see chapter 18). Although it could be executed over the very short spinal route, this does not happen: the reflex is held in abeyance until cleared by the brain. The information from the stimulated skin is transmitted to the brain, where it spreads through many of its centers. There the information is mixed with a great deal of information from other sources and is then channeled back to the hypothalamic clearing centers. These, after evaluating all the information, finally give the go-ahead to the reflex. They promote the performance of the reflex through the spinal route by relieving the block that normally prevents it.

The control of the crouching reflex is similar, therefore, to that of the safety brakes on a train. The brakes are kept open by air pressure acting against powerful springs; they are closed by the springs when the engineer opens a valve, causing the air pressure to drop. The springs are equivalent to the influences blocking the short spinal route. The hypothalamus supplies the equivalent of the air pressure needed for releasing the brakes when it allows the reflex to proceed. If the spinal cord is severed in such a way as to prevent the arrival of the brain signals, crouching becomes impossible. This operation is like cutting the air lines between the cars and the engine of the train: the result is an immediate clamping of the brakes.

The brain centers that act as a clearing station for crouching behavior can be identified by taking advantage of what is known of this behavior. The electrical stimulation of the centers must induce the behavior, their destruction must abolish it, and injection of estrogen into the centers must facilitate it. These three approaches concur in identifying two hypothalamic centers as crucial to the crouching behavior. These centers are connected essentially to the whole brain and therefore integrate information coming from a wide variety of sources as well as from memory related to past experience. In these centers, estrogen binds to a special class of nerve cells, which probably combine the information received from the hormones and the nerve signals.

The control of sex behavior in the male rat appears substantially similar in its general features to that in the female. The clearing neurons, however, although they are in the same general area of the brain, are in different centers and bind androgens.

A Critical Period in Brain Sex Determination

The hypothalamus and neighboring centers, then, are the major coordinators of sexual activities in either female or male animals—but how does the hypothalamus become female or male oriented? In both sexes the hypothalamus is at first uncommitted and is capable of eliciting either male or female behavior. This can be shown in amphibians by performing cuts at various levels of the brain: some cuts cause female animals to respond to mating stimuli in a male fashion. How is it then that an animal usually behaves in only one fashion, as a full-fledged male or female? At some stage of development, the hypothalamus becomes sexually committed, so that it is bound to perform the functions characteristic of one sex. Commitment is based on the arrangement of connections between nerve cells, which is different in males and females.

In the rat the answer to the question of how the hypothalamus becomes sexually differentiated is clear and quite astonishing: differentiation is determined not by genetic differences but by the sex hormones acting at a critical period of brain development. This critical period is distinct from that for the differentiation of the gonads discussed in the previous chapter. In mammals it occurs later, either late in fetal life or immediately after birth. The time can be determined by manipulating the hormonal influences that determine commitment. At the beginning of the critical period, small crystals of androgen are implanted in the hypothalamic centers that determine sexual behavior in a female rat. The implantation shifts the balance of hormones reaching the hypothalamic nerve cells in the male direction. The result is that the animal, when adult, will display male mating behavior, will lack the cycling of the pituitary hormones FSH and LH, and will not give a feedback LH response to estrogen. In this genetically female animal the pattern of connections between nerve cells in the hypothalamus and other brain systems will be that of a male. The rat will lose its femininity and gain masculinity. The results are permanent and cannot be reversed by subsequent hormonal manipulations. Experiments have shown that in the rat the critical period spans over two weeks after birth.

Comparable behavioral changes can be elicited in the male. Thus a male rat castrated during the critical period reveals the underlying femaleness that exists in species in which the female sex is XX. It will acquire female behavior, which will persist even if later the animal receives a graft of testes. If, instead, the animal is grafted with an ovary, it will develop a cycling pattern of hormone release.

If the implantation of androgen in females or the castration of males is delayed until after the end of the critical period, they have no effect: the sexual behavior of the animal has become immutable. Animals whose behavioral sex is changed by the hormonal treatment do not change their gonads (which are determined at an earlier period). In spite of the changed behavior the testes remain testes and the ovary remains an ovary; the type of germ cells the individual can produce also remains unchanged.

The consequences of the hormones are so significant during the critical period because the hypothalamic nerve cells develop the neural connections then. Which connections are made depends on the type of hormone the cells are exposed to. This modulating effect of sex hormones is an interesting case of external factors influencing the development of the brain. We will see in chapter 18 that the brain is very plastic during development and adapts to many environmental conditions. Nerve signals and hormones reaching the brain have an important influence in forging the ultimate pattern of the brain network.

Variations on the Theme

The intricate way in which sex hormones influence brain cells during the critical period varies widely between species. For instance, it has been found, paradoxically, that in rats implanted with androgen, the affected nerve cells actually respond to estrogen, which they make from the androgen. So in the male rat the cells receive the male sex signal as androgen, but in order for it to be effective, they must convert it into estrogen. Why, then, doesn't estrogen produced in the female have a masculinizing effect? The answer is strange: at the time of the critical period estrogen produced by the gonads does not reach the brain cells but is trapped in the blood by a special protein that binds estrogen but not androgen. Thus the mechanism for determining sexual behavior involves a protein that has nothing to do directly with either sex or behavior.

Estrogen produced from androgen seems to be the masculinizing signal also in humans, whereas in many species androgen acts directly. In different species, moreover, the male commitment of the brain may be caused by different androgens; and in some species the type of androgen directing the brain may even be different from that directing the development of the genitalia. Nevertheless, in spite of these variations and peculiarities, the result is similar among species. Reaching the same objective through very different pathways is characteristic of nature, an observation that applies to other phenomena as well. When a certain result can be obtained by many routes, the route adopted in a given species depends on many, often imponderable, characteristics of that species. Any route is acceptable to nature, provided it reaches the goal.

Another interesting aspect of hormonal changes during the critical period is that they may affect to a different extent the several characteristics that together constitute sexual behavior. In the males of some species characteristics other than mating behavior were studied—feedback response of LH to estrogen, aggression, posture of urination, territorial marking, vocalization—and the responses to the implantation of androgens in the hypothalamus often varied. These observations suggested that features of behavior are controlled independently, presumably by different groups of nerve cells, and that the various groups may be affected in different ways by uncontrolled variables of the experiments—for example, the precise site of implantation of androgen, the extent of the hormone's spread, or the stage of development of the brain at the time. These observations perhaps explain why human males who lack androgen receptors in target cells, although feminized in all other characteristics, nevertheless maintain the normal male non-cyclic pattern of LH release.

Sex Hormones in Adults

In adults of either sex the brain centers depend on the continued presence of the appropriate sex hormone for performing their functions. If the hormone supply is stopped by castration, for instance, the performance of sexual behavior is suspended. In castrated females the change tends to occur quickly, especially in some species such as the rat, whereas in males the change takes place more slowly. In the case of castrated male dogs, it may be a matter of years before the change is completed. The effect is reversible: proper sexual behavior is restored when the hormone supply is renewed. An adult female rat defeminized by castration is refeminized by the administration of estrogen and progesterone in the proper sequence.

The effect of sex hormones is also dramatic in song birds. Normally the male sings, not the female, for the several brain centers that control singing are more highly developed in males than in females. The centers' size, on which the extent of its song repertoire depends, waxes and wanes with the bird's supply of male hormone. The centers, which are small in newly hatched males, increase greatly during puberty and the birds begin to sing. Their maximum size is attained in the spring when singing activity is high, and their size declines in the summer when both the production of male hormone and the amount of singing decline. If an adult female canary is castrated and then given androgens, they cause a malelike development of the song brain centers and she acquires the ability to sing almost like a male. The enlargement of the centers results from an increase in the size and number of neurons (caused by the multiplication of reserve cells) and an increase in the number of connections.

The action of hormones, however, is subordinated in the adult to brain control. For instance, androgen will stimulate mounting behavior in an adult male ring dove only if the animal has lived for some time with females and has developed interest in mating; otherwise it will have no effect. A comparable brain influence can be seen in male monkeys. Androgen production increases in these animals when they are together with females, but only when they are living under social conditions that allow mating. The increase does not occur in subordinate males who do not normally mate. The brain, then, exerts a crucial control both on the response to sex hormones and on their production.

Evolution of Sexual Behavior

In the invertebrates and lower vertebrates sexual behavior seems completely controlled by the genes: it is stereotyped, characteristic of a given species, and exhibited normally even by animals raised in isolation. In the female rat, as we have seen, the control is more complex, however. Although it includes a genetically programmed reflex—that of crouching—the reflex is controlled by information collected from a wide variety of sources and elaborated in the brain center.

The differences in the control of sexual behavior among species are correlated to the differences in their brain development. As new brain stations become available in the course of evolution, preexisting centers retain their old role, but the new centers now participate in determining sexual behavior. For instance, mammals have, in common with lower vertebrates, centers at the base of the brain, such as the hypothalamus, that are exclusively involved in automatic reflexes, but they also have additional centers. Much of their basic control still resides in the older centers, but it has come to be modified by a vast amount of information emanating from the higher brain centers. Thus, their responses are less automatic and have acquired new safeguards. Their brain has slowed down their sexuality, which conflicts with DNA's concern with reproduction.

By extrapolation, it seems likely that sexual behavior in humans is controlled by a complex mixture of automatic reflexes and elaborate brain analysis. Erection of the male penis and ejaculation of the sperm are reflex phenomena, but their control must be highly complex: the human repertoire of controlling information and its elaboration by brain centers is much greater than in any other species. We know little, however, about the determination of human sexual behavior. We cannot directly extrapolate from what we know about the rat, for instance, because no two species are alike, and the diversity between fairly distant species may be considerable. In the case of humans, we will never be able to ascertain experimentally whether the concept of the critical period for sexual behavior and its hormonal control applies. There is no direct evidence even for monkeys.

Indirect support for the concept, however, comes from abnormalities observed in some human males, who, owing to a defect in the manufacture of androgens in the testes, experience an androgen deficiency during fetal life. These individuals, who are born with intersexed or female genitalia, probably because the female XX sex prevails when androgens are deficient, are usually raised as girls, and may display female sexual behavior as adults. The opposite effect occurs in female embryos when there is excessive production of androgens in the adrenal cortex. In childhood these genetically female individuals display behavior more typical of boys than of girls. It is clear that androgens cause these changes. If estrogens are administered to the mother during pregnancy, they prevent the behavioral alterations by counterbalancing the effect of androgens. Humans, therefore, appear as sensitive as rats to hormonal imbalances during fetal life. In the known cases, the imbalances modify the development of both the sexual organs and sexual behavior, presumably because they are present during both critical periods. The time at which these periods occur, however, remains undetermined.

Yet Another Critical Period?

There are suggestions that in humans another critical period for sexual brain development occurs during the first two years of life. The behavioral variable that might be molded during this period cannot be studied in animals: it is gender identity—that is, whether a person feels like a male or a female. It seems that the awareness of being male or female is strongly influenced by the intimate and extensive interactions the child has with the environment from the moment of birth. How the parents consider the child in that period—whether as a boy or a girl or whether clothes or toys characteristic of the male or female sex are provided—gives the child the first gender identification, or the *sex of rearing*. This initial orientation will have considerable influence on the identity of the individual at least throughout childhood. The influence, however, may not stretch into adult life.

The sex of rearing frequently clashes with the genetic sex when the external genitalia are not well developed at birth, as in the case of children who experience defects in the manufacture of androgens during the fetal period. These genetically male children may be raised as females and, before puberty, behave as females. Often, however, the androgen deficiency corrects itself at puberty because androgen production picks up strongly at that time. The recognition of the true sex comes as a surprise when the voice of the "girl" changes and testes are discovered hidden in the abdomen (they fail to descend to the scrotum when fetal androgen is insufficient). Many of these children rapidly adopt the male gender identification and retain it through life, with no apparent problem.

In contrast, individuals who are insensitive to androgens owing to a defect of the androgen receptors in the target cells maintain both female development and female gender identity in adulthood. In these individuls the effects of androgens are essentially eliminated, whereas in those of the former group they are simply reduced. Sex hormones, therefore, seem to play an important role also for gender identification.

Pair Bonding

Sex is the most powerful factor dominating the interaction between individuals throughout the biological world. The complexity of the interactions depends on the species. In species with the simplest brain organization, individuals of opposite sex seek each other for the sole purpose of mating, or they establish permanent relationships of a parasitic nature; some examples have already been given. In the more highly developed species, social patterns, based on sex, develop and assume greater complexity as the complexity of the brain increases. The force driving the most advanced interactions is pair bonding, which in human terms is the individual's need to have a long-term affiliation with another individual, both as sex partner and as companion. In the human species pair bonding is based on the most exquisite brain functions—those expressing love and affection, and generating artistic expression.

Presence or absence of pair bonding in animal species does not follow any recognizable rule. Many mammals display pair bondings, but others do not. Pair bonding is very frequent in less advanced species, such as birds, though some bird species are promiscuous. Their pair bonding may take different forms, such as pairing for a breeding season or for life, and is usually maintained by the performance of rituals from time to time, probably directed at reviving mutual interest. For instance, as a ritual certain ducks tread water side by side, in almost upright position, with the outer wings raised. The rituals differ from species to species and are probably inscribed in the genes.

Pair bonding often takes place within a family. Typical families contain a mating pair and nonmating members, whose roles within the family vary enormously. At one extreme are the families of marmoset monkeys, which are quite similar to those of humans. At the other extreme are the large families of certain mole rats, which live underground in regions of Africa. In these families the size of the animal determines its role. The largest animals, including several males and a single female, are the breeders. The breeding female apparently produces a pheromone that prevents the other females from breeding. The larger animals spend most of their time sleeping, huddled together to keep warm, while the smaller animals work.

There are interesting specializations. In the families of some wolves the nonmating members, who are sibs or relatives of the mating pair, care attentively for the young and feed the mother when the puppies are small. The organization of these families is hierarchical: although all members hunt together, when they catch prey the mating male feeds first, showing his dominance. The pattern of mating dominant male together with nonmating subordinates exists also in the families of certain monkeys. Dominance or subordination of a given male, however, applies only to the family in which he lives. If he is subordinate, he displays no interest at the sight of the females of the family, but outside the family, he promptly mates when paired with a female. This behavior is perhaps comparable to the incest taboo in humans, whereby males do not feel sexual attraction to female members of their family. In primates, therefore, there are close connections among mating behavior, bonding behavior, and group influence: relationships between individuals are at least as important as the sexual drive. These findings strengthen the notion already derived from other examples that in primates sexual behavior is fundamentally dominated by the brain.

The pattern of interrelations between sexes in human society is related to some of the patterns observed in animals, but, of course, it is also highly distinctive, not only because the species is different, but especially because the brain is so much more developed. Variation also exists in different human societies, depending on the culture, the circumstances, and the individuals. Although some people often seek mating as an exciting adventure and an end unto itself, or may need it to relieve tension created by abstinence, a certain degree of bonding always develops. This will vary markedly depending on the programming of the brain both genetically and through past experience. In most cases, bonding comes to dominate the male-female relationship, leading to the establishment of long-lasting pairs. The long duration is perhaps related to the long time required for raising progeny to the level of independence.

CHAPTER 11

Human Brain over Sex

The Brain versus DNA

DNA invented sex as a means of achieving a more efficient method of reproduction—one based on the redistribution of genes in new combinations. But in doing so DNA became the slave of sexuality in an unstoppable progression. In the simplest creatures sexuality was limited to DNA recombination. In more advanced creatures sexuality came to involve additional features in order to promote the fusion of the genomes. These features had the effect of improving the reproductive ability of the DNA and were still fully controlled by it. In the most advanced creatures the brain became part of the control of sex: simple brains acted as passive relays, receiving signals from appropriate peripheral stations and transmitting orders to suitable muscles, and more complex brains acted in a more independent way. They took over the decision of whether or not to mate after analyzing the relevant information.

As we saw in the previous chapter, the role of the brain has reached a peak in humans: their mating is to a large extent controlled by the brain and follows its goals. Gamete fertilization, which is the goal of DNA, has become essentially incidental. The brain has dissociated mating from fertilization by inventing many forms of birth control; it even tends to eliminate the meaning of sexual differentiation by allowing matings between individuals of the same sex. Biologically, these are momentous developments, which frustrate the main goal of DNA—reproduction. Also, many humans think their cooperation is not needed to perpetuate the species, and so, for economic or other reasons, they may choose not to mate.

Thus the brain is pitted against DNA, and the individual, against the species—a worrisome situation. Could this trend persist to the point that it will imperil the existence of the human species?

Ambiguities

Many ambiguities built into the mechanism of sexual reproduction contribute to this state of affairs. We have seen that the sexual profile of an individual of any species evolves throughout life, with a succession of critical steps that mold its characteristics. If the outcomes of all the steps point in the same direction, the result is clear-cut: the individual will be either a male or a female in all characteristics. Not all the steps, however, may be consonant. Then we are faced with the question: what is the individual's sex?

We can define sex in various ways according to different criteria: the external genitalia at birth—the *legal sex;* the constitution of the chromosomes and the genes—the *genetic sex;* the hormones produced—the *hormonal sex;* the behavior displayed—the *behavioral sex;* the self-identity—the *gender sex.* If these definitions are not in agreement with one another, which is the individual's real sex? The answer depends on the vantage point. From a legal point of view the decision seems simple enough; it is a matter of inspection of the external genitalia, but in reality this is the least significant and the least sensitive definition. For an athlete competing in the Olympics, the hormonal sex during the development of the body is the most important because it determines body development and muscular strength. From the point of view of the outside world, which is concerned with the behavior of the individual, the behavioral sex is the most relevant. From the point of view of self-identification in the proper gender role, the gender sex is the important one.

Of these various characterizations the behavioral and the gender sex are the most difficult to define. They are most vulnerable to ambiguity, because they depend on a delicate balance among many genes and their products, hormones, stimulatory and inhibitory brain circuits, and interactions between individuals. The balance involves the brain, as well as many chemical events. Given this complexity, it is surprising that the expression of sexual characteristics so frequently falls neatly into one or the other of two precisely defined classes: males and females.

But is it really true that the two classes are so well defined? Anatomically, the differentiation is sharp in the largest majority of cases, but can one say the same of behavior and gender identity? A close analysis reveals that, on the contrary, the demarcation of sexual behavior and gender identity into separate male and female compartments is not at all clear. In fact, we have seen that many simple creatures can interchange male or female roles as well as gonads, depending on needs, and many are even bisexual—male and female at the same time. But in these cases the sexual ambiguity is transient, and it ends up, practically speaking, in the expression of one or the other sex in a clear way. The ambiguity is really important in the case of sexual behavior and gender identity in mammals, and especially in humans, because often it is not resolvable and can lead to a dissociation of the sexual personality.

The possibility of ambiguity is so pronounced in humans because the brain, the dominant force in sexual behavior, can assign so many different solutions to the problem of sex identity, depending on circuitry and previous programming. When we come to consider how each individual sees himself or herself in the sexual role, the many possible solutions form a kind of continuum. Each solution does not encompass just the individual, but the individual in relation to others and to the world. This relation will vary depending on which other individuals are considered to be the paradigm—the whole of mankind? the whole of male humans? of female humans? certain other groups of humans? perhaps specific human individuals?

A Continuum of Interactions

No human, perhaps, feels sexually indifferent to all other humans, male or female. A person of either sex will have a spectrum of sexual reactions toward either females or males. For a given individual the two spectra may overlap to a certain extent, so that, for instance, any male will find a class of females to whom he can relate less well, sexually, than to a certain class of males. The attraction spectra vary widely among different individuals of the same sex: that of certain males may reach far into what is on the average the range of females, and vice versa.

In the history of mankind these differences between sexual attitudes have long been recognized, although usually not understood. For purposes of simplification, humans are traditionally divided into a small number of well-defined classes. *Heterosexuals* make up one class: they are what people are supposed to be—interested exclusively in individuals of the opposite sex. They are contrasted to *homosexuals*, whose sexual interest and attraction is toward people of the same sex.

Homosexuality

Why are homosexuals segregated in a special class? They are genetically males or females whose own gender identification agrees with the legal and genetic sex; they have no abnormality of sexual anatomy and in general are normal in the production of sex hormones and in the hypothalamic control of hormone production. But they are put in a special class because they are not completely heterosexual in their sexual practices. Is this a valid reason?

The separation is rather arbitrary because many homosexuals are also attracted to the opposite sex. Most homosexuals are as heterogeneous a group in their preferences as are heterosexuals, and they range from a nearly heterosexual to an extreme homosexual spectrum. The many differences in behavior that traditionally distinguish homosexuals are not noticeably more profound than the differences observed in a sample of heterosexuals with similar cultural backgrounds and education. For instance, many people think that male homosexuals are less masculine and more feminine than heterosexuals. But there seems to be no substance to this belief: comparable populations of heterosexuals and homosexuals contain the same numbers of effeminate males. Many homosexuals, in fact, do not admire the effeminate male at all, but hold him in contempt. Another point to be considered is that people who have had some homosexual experience are not a tiny minority: in 1948 Kinsey estimated they constituted 37 percent of U.S. males.

The bonding relations between homosexuals are similar to those between individuals in a heterosexual pair; the sexual acts in which they can participate, however, are limited, of course, by their similar sexual anatomy. Homosexuals must resort to other than vaginal techniques for intercourse, such as anal, oral, or masturbatory practices.

Homosexuals seem to be different because they tend to be promiscuous. Some male homosexuals have hundreds of different partners in a year. This promiscuity of male homosexuals is a factor in the spread of viral diseases such as AIDS or hepatitis B, which are efficiently transferred in male homosexual contacts. Sexual promiscuity, however, is a feature of society rather than of a subgroup. The incidence of venereal diseases propagated by heterosexual contacts, for instance, is high in the general population. Moreover, many heterosexuals increasingly use the sexual techniques employed by homosexuals, as shown by the rising incidence of oral infections with herpes virus 2, which mainly infects male or female genitalia. The fact is that sexual mores are highly variable in the human race; they depend on the culture and therefore on the place and the historical period. Males may also tend to be promiscuous even in heterosexual contacts, probably because the male has traditionally been the hunter always looking for a mate. In heterosexual contacts this tendency is generally restrained by the female, who may seek continuity more than adventure and may fear unwanted pregnancies, although this is also changing. In male homosexual contacts neither of these restraints exists.

A MATTER OF CIRCUMSTANCES. Human homosexuality is universal and has always existed. In some societies males are regularly homosexual for a period of their life. Homosexuality was accepted, too, by the ancient Greeks, especially in some cities. The modern term *lesbian* refers to the poet Sappho, who lived on the island of Lesbos where she was rumored to engage in sexual activities with young women. Homosexuality was rejected, however, by the Judaic tradition just before Christ, and this rejection has persisted throughout the Christian period.

In this tradition, homosexuals are deviants. Some advocates of law and order believe that they must be banned from society; some liberals believe they must be treated as sick people. Biologically neither of these positions may be correct: animals who know nothing about morality or law and order display widespread evidence of homosexuality. Young monkeys, for example, in a favorite game frequently mount each other, regardless of sex. And among adult monkeys the submissive males relieve their tensions by homosexual matings, although this practice exists only in the presence of dominant males. Away from them, the submissive males become heterosexuals. Homosexuality in these animals, then, is merely a phase of life, dictated by group relationships.

WHY HOMOSEXUALITY? Many attempts have been made to find special reasons for homosexuality, and hormonal alterations in the expected direction have sometimes been detected. For instance, some female homosexuals may have more androgens than normal and may lack the feedback response of LH to an estrogen injection. No children with clear hormonal disturbances, however, grow up homosexual. Studies suggest that homosexuality is fostered by influences of the family environment during childhood. It seems that homosexuals tend to come from homes in which they could not identify well with one of the parents (for example, an overbearing mother or an absent or punitive father). In contrast, children raised by homosexuals do not have an increased tendency toward homosexuality. It is also possible that homosexuality is fostered by accidental opportunities in childhood and adolescence. Children who grow up together and sleep in the same bed frequently indulge in homosexual pastimes.

The degree of conformity to the gender role during childhood and adolescence seems most significant for the development of sexual preferences. Individuals well adjusted to their role during that period have little chance of being homosexuals in adult life. Homosexual preferences, therefore, seem to have their roots during the early development of the individual. But how early? Are prenatal influences of hormonal or genetic nature involved? There is no clear evidence that they play a determining role, but neither is there evidence to the contrary. The analysis needed to establish or reject the role of prenatal influences is not possible to make.

Homosexuality is a stable condition: no form of treatment (including psychoanalysis) has had much success in converting homosexuals to heterosexuality. In fact, among homosexuals who voluntarily go to psychiatrists (a special group, probably with unusual personal problems), 70 to 80 percent remain homosexual. What about the 20 to 30 percent who shift? Don't they indicate that therapy can be successful? The best reply to this question is another question: what proportion of heterosexuals with personal problems would be persuaded by psychiatrists to become homosexuals in a hypothetical society in which heterosexuality was considered deviant?

Transsexuality

A sexual attitude whose origin may lie, at least in part, in early influences during the critical period for gender identification is transsexuality. *Transsexuals* are individuals of either sex, but more frequently males, who firmly consider themselves members of the opposite sex and feel an intense hatred for their own sex. The males hate their genitalia, especially their erections or ejaculations, and they reject sexual activity. The women hate their breasts and especially menstruation.

They, however, have a high interest in sexual activities. Transsexuals are rather rare; their numbers are estimated at one in a hundred thousand people.

These persons have grown up with a gender identity in opposition to their legal-genetic sex. In contrast to some intersexes with well-defined hormonal disturbances, transsexuals can never resolve the clash between gender identity and genetic sex. At puberty, when some of the intersexes resolve their ambiguity, the transsexuals' aversion to their own sex becomes even more acute because they become more strongly aware of the sexual traits they reject. They cannot accept life as it is given to them but live in a world of fantasy in which their sexual role is reversed.

Transsexuals, like homosexuals, want to have sexual relations with individuals of their own genetic sex. There is, however, a profound difference between the two groups. Homosexuals use their genitalia for this purpose in a way appropriate to their genetic sex, whereas transsexuals do not. For them the gender sex is opposite to the genetic sex, whereas for homosexuals it is the same. In fact, transsexuals, especially men, usually reject homosexuality.

In order to resolve the deep conflict in which they are caught, transsexuals frequently want to change their sex through surgery. This is a desperate resort, because few derive any real benefit from it. Transsexuals can be very determined to achieve this goal, however, pursuing the option vigorously. The purpose of the surgery is to remove the anatomical evidence of their genetic sex and to construct a semblance of their subjective sex. Surgery is usually performed only after a long period of observation (up to two years) to determine whether it has a chance of being useful. First, massive doses of hormones appropriate for the new sex are administered. They have the welcome result of suppressing the expression of the old sex: they reduce sexual arousal in men and menstruation in women. Androgens, when given to women, induce the development of a beard, a big penis-like clitoris, and a high sexual appetite. After the hormonal treatment the gonads are removed, as well as the women's breasts or the man's penis; the larynx is altered to change the voice, and the man's beard is epilated. Men are provided with a fake vagina; women, sometimes, with a skin appendage to simulate a nonexcitable penis. Altogether the intervention achieves a pitiful travesty of the sex that is so strongly felt. The result is of practical use in only a small proportion of individuals (probably about 10 percent) in whom it successfully relieves the inner conflict. Indeed some transsexual men after surgery have changed legal sex and have married heterosexual men. They claim to obtain sexual satisfaction in intercourse.

The sex-reassignment intervention benefits only people who were already socially well adjusted, and it benefits women more than men. It is tragic if the transsexual comes to regret the operation because it cannot be undone: the surgery is irreversible. There has been at least one known case of suicide among the failures. Many long-term studies of people who have changed sex are needed to see what the actual long-term benefits may be. Unfortunately, no other form of treatment seems to help these unhappy people, although, as an alternative to surgery, some transsexual women take up a lesbian life-style, sometimes with useful results.

The reasons for transsexuality are enveloped in mystery: the relatively small number of cases has precluded any real study. The effect of the hypothalamic implantation of hormones in rats during the critical period for development of sexual behavior suggests that in transsexuals something might have gone wrong hormonally at the comparable time. Like the implanted rats, female transsexuals are female in both anatomy and hormones, but some parts of the brain appear to be male. Transsexuality, then, may result from disturbances in the brain centers involved in gender identification.

Transvestites

Another abnormal form of sexual behavior is found in *transvestites*. They are males who, without rejecting their own sex, nevertheless derive intense sexual pleasure from dressing like women, sometimes wearing just one or two garments of female attire. The erotic arousal distinguishes them from some male homosexuals who like to cross-dress but do not derive sexual excitement from it. The mere sight of female garments, in shops, for instance, may arouse intense sexual desire in a transvestite, which he will relieve by masturbation. These persons are heterosexuals; they do not have homosexual connections, and they usually marry heterosexual women.

There is no known anatomic, genetic, or hormonal basis for their attitude. Abnormalities during childhood have sometimes been blamed for their behavior; but it is much too easy to attribute peculiarity of behavior to vague events in a distant past. It is likely that there may be a disease basis. No psychiatric or drug treatment alters the behavior, suggesting that it has been irreversibly determined at some early stage of development. Some transvestites have tried sex-reassignment surgery but without benefit.

CHAPTER 12

From A to Z

If organisms are to perform their great number of diverse activities efficiently, they must possess many specialized apparatuses. In the simplest organisms, such as bacteria, many activities are carried out by the same cell using different structures: energy transformation takes place in association with membranes; food utilization is carried out by enzymes free within the cells; movement is the function of special appendages such as flagella. But in larger and more complex organisms a variety of functions is carried out by specialized cell types situated in different organs. The taking in of food is the function of the digestive system in animals and of the roots in plants. The taking in of oxygen is the function of the lungs in terrestrial animals, the gills in aquatic creatures, and the leaves in plants, which also pick up carbon dioxide. In animals the elaboration of food is carried out to a great extent in the liver, and the disposal of wastes, in the lungs, the liver, and the kidneys.

Regulated Multiplication

Two basic processes participate in the development of an organism: it increases in size and it acquires shape. These two processes go on concurrently but are independent; each can take place without the other. We will first consider how an organism increases in size by increasing the number of cells. To generate a harmonious organism, the multiplication of the cells must occur according to a precise plan, so that the balance among the organism's parts is maintained. This coordination is achieved by signals, some of which are relayed by the communicator substances discussed in chapter 8. Most of the signals, however, are still unknown.

Cells multiply by going through a *cycle* (fig. 12.1). During part of the cycle the DNA replicates, making a new copy of the whole genome; this is the *S phase* (S for

218

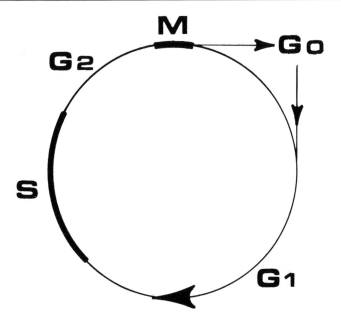

Figure 12.1. The cell division cycle. See discussion in text. M = mitosis (cell division); S = period of DNA synthesis and doubling.

"synthesis of DNA"). At the end of the S phase a diploid cell temporarily has four copies of the genome—it is tetraploid. In the next period new proteins required for the division of the cell are made; this is the *G2 phase* (G for "gap"). Then the cell divides, generating two regular diploid daughter cells (that is, with two sets of chromosomes); this is the *M phase* (M for "mitosis"; see chapter 1). In the daughter cells the DNA does not begin to replicate immediately. The end of the M phase is followed by a long interval during which the cell doubles all its constituents except the DNA. This is the *G1 phase;* then a new S phase takes place. Actively multiplying cells go cyclically through a succession of G1, S, G2, and M phases within a period varying from ten minutes (in some early embryos) to many days. Many measurable characteristics of the cells change in a reproducible way during the cycle. Certain proteins appear and disappear at various phases, some of them driving the cycle. Little is known, however, of what controls the cycle, although external substances, such as growth factors, are certainly part of it.

The length of the cycle is controlled mainly at the G1 phase. If the appropriate growth factor is present, the cell will proceed to the end of G1 and then on to S and so on. If the factor is not present, the cell enters a *resting phase*, called G0. It can stay in that phase, in a dormant state, for hours, days, or even years. The arrival of the growth factor at any time is like the prince's kiss to Sleeping Beauty: the cell returns to life in G1, and the cycle restarts. The shifts from G1 to G0 and vice versa may involve ion movements across the cell membrane, which by changing the internal ion concentrations and the membrane potential (see chapter 2) affect the functions of many proteins.

Embryos from Eggs

Organisms made up of many cells can begin their separate existence in a variety of ways. For instance, in the hydra, a very simple creature that lives in water, new individuals can be generated from pieces cut from an adult. In more advanced organisms, new creatures derive from a fertilized egg.

In vertebrates the egg is large because it contains food, often in the form of yolk. The amount of food is abundant in the eggs of birds and reptiles, but sparse in fish and mammals. The eggs of fish do not need ample reserves because they rapidly reach a stage where they can find food by themselves in the water; the eggs of mammals do not need reserves because they are nourished by the mother. In contrast the eggs of birds and reptiles develop while enclosed in a hard shell, and they must be self-sufficient for a long time. The relative abundance of yolk in an egg is important also for another reason: as we will see later, it influences the early stages of development.

After the egg is fertilized, the female and male nuclei (which are haploid— that is, each has a single set of chromosomes) fuse, generating a diploid nucleus. This nucleus repeatedly divides, partitioning the egg cell into separate cells. At each division the two daughter cells remain together, so that externally the embryo may have the same size and appearance of the original egg cell. In spite of this apparent lack of events, however, important changes have taken place in the embryo. For instance, in a snail embryo the direction of the plane that separates the first two daughter cells determines whether the snail will develop a left-handed or right-handed shell.

In the early period of development the size of the embryo remains unchanged because the cells become progressively smaller as they increase in number. (The fertilized egg is much larger than the cells of an adult organism.) These early divisions lack both G1 and G2 phases and take place at a tremendous rate—one every ten minutes in embryos of the fruitfly *Drosophila*, one every half hour in some frogs. The egg cell does not manufacture new constituents because it has an endowment from the mother. The initial development of the embryo is determined by the mother's genes—for instance, the handedness in snails. The period of frantic cell division comes abruptly to an end when the cells finally reach the size of those of the adult organism. Then new cell constituents must be made at each cycle, and the G1 and G2 phases appear. From then on, as the number of cells increases, the embryo will increase in size.

At the end of the period of rapid cell multiplication the embryos of different kinds of organisms vary in shape. In mammals the embryo looks like a raspberry (*morula*); in fishes it is like a small balloon (*blastula*) made up of a layer of cells surrounding a liquid-filled space; in birds or amphibians it is like a disc floating on the yolk underneath (*blastoderm*).

In embryos of all kinds the next step is the rearrangement of the cells to generate a stack of three layers consisting of an outer layer, the *ectoderm*, a middle layer, the *mesoderm*, and an inner layer, the *endoderm*. The stack is generated in various ways by migration of cells. One process, long studied by embryologists, is *gastrulation*, in which the middle layer is generated by cells that leave the inner layer, positioning themselves between it and the outer layer (fig. 12.2).

Once the three layers are formed in the vertebrate embryo, an extremely

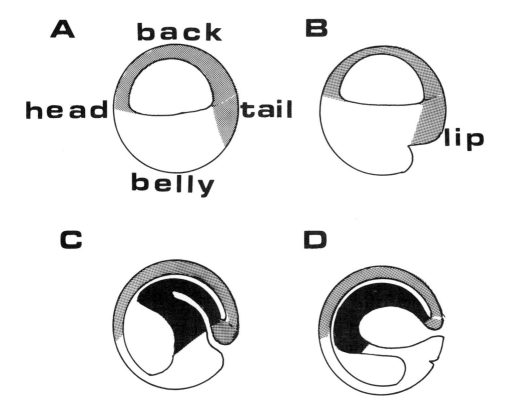

Figure 12.2. Gastrulation in an amphibian embryo, depicting four phases. The embryo is shown as cut through the middle. The anatomical designations in A refer to those of the future organism. (A) The embryo before gastrulation: in the gray area are the cells that will give rise to the outer layer (ectoderm); the lower part is made up of yolk-containing cells; and in the center is a liquid-filled space. (B) The beginning of gastrulation: cells start to move in at a place called the blastopore, of which the back (dorsal) lip is indicated. (C) A large number of cells have moved inside the embryo from its surface, displacing the liquid; the invaginated part in dark gray will generate the inner layer (entoderm) which will later give rise to the middle layer (mesoderm). (D) The completion of gastrulation: the dark gray and light gray parts actually are in contact; the blastopore becomes the anus.

important event takes place: the head-to-tail axis of the embryo becomes defined by migration and reassociation of cells. A rod of cells, the *notochord*, forms in the middle layer. Immediately above the length of this rod the upper layer thickens, forming two long lips which then join above, generating the *neural tube* (fig. 12.3). At the sides of the notochord, cells of the middle layer gather into masses, the *somites*, which are equally arranged at both sides.

During the subsequent development of the embryo these structures will give rise to the organs and tissues. The neural tube will generate the central nervous system. The peripheral nerves and their ganglia will develop from cells that migrate out of the neural lips before they join together. These wandering cells form first two ridges at the sides of the neural tube, the *neural crests*, from which they will move on to their destinations. The somites generate the muscles and bones of the vertebrae. The ectoderm will develop into the skin, and the endoderm will form the digestive tract, including the organs associated with it, like the liver or pancreas. The kidney, the circulatory apparatus (heart, blood vessels), and the bones will develop mostly from the mesoderm.

In very simple animals the early embryo is made up of a series of *segments* connected to each other in a chain. This reflects the progressive increase in length that occurred during evolution by the repeated addition of replicas of preexisting segments. In insects and in many primitive creatures the segments remain recog-

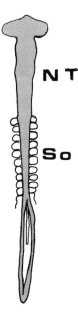

Figure 12.3. The neural tube (NT) of a chicken embryo. At its sides are two rows of somites (SO). In front (top of figure) the brain is developing from the tube; the two lateral bulges will become the retinas of the eyes. Toward the tail end (bottom of figure) the neural fold is still open and below it can be seen the notochord.

nizable throughout life, although they may undergo extensive diversification. In vertebrates the segmentation is revealed by the equal spacing of the somites. In adult vertebrates remnants of the segments are the vertebrae of the spinal column, the ribs, and the segmental nerves and their ganglia.

As a consequence of various foldings the early embryo develops three sacs filled with liquid (fig. 12.4). A shock-absorbing sac—the *amniotic sac,* enclosed in a membrane—surrounds the body of the embryo; a urinary sac—the *allantoic sac* (so called because it is sausage-shaped)—accumulates the refuses continuously generated by the cells of the embryo; and a food sac—the *yolk sac*—contains the food reserve. In the embryos of mammals the urinary sac, together with what remains of the outer layer after the various foldings, develops into a life-sustaining organ—the *placenta*—embedded in the uterus of the mother. Through the placenta the embryo absorbs food and oxygen from the mother and returns to her the urine it produces.

Development outside the Mother's Body

The development of a new creature takes place only in part within the body of the mother, and in some organisms it occurs entirely outside. Fish eggs are fertilized in the water soon after they are released, and in amphibians, birds, and

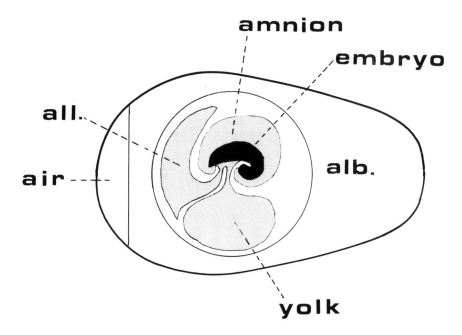

Figure 12.4. A section through the middle of a chicken egg to show the three sacs: the amnion, the allantois (all), and the yolk sac. The embryo floats in the liquid albumen (alb) and is enclosed in the shell. At left is the air bubble.

reptiles, the mother ejects eggs that contain very primitive embryos. The embryos of birds and reptiles are enclosed in a hard shell that protects them from mechanical insults and, because it does not let water through, keeps them from drying. Oxygen, however, can enter through the shell, and carbon dioxide can exit. Wastes are stored as uric acid which, being insoluble, takes little space and is nontoxic. These creatures hatch by breaking the shell, the birds with the beak, the reptiles with a hard nose. A mammal ejects her embryo at parturition when it has reached an advanced stage of development. Very immature is the embryo released by a marsupial, but there is a remedy: the embryo crawls into the mother's pouch, grabs one of her teats in its mouth, and there continues its development.

The hatching of an egg or the ejection of a newborn from the mother's body at parturition do not mark the end of development—it continues through life. Many organs are completed postnatally. The persistence of development is demonstrated when a part of the body is amputated by accident or surgery and is reconstructed in varying degrees (*regeneration*), depending on the species and the site of damage. In amphibians an amputated limb regenerates completely, whereas in mammals it does not. But a broken bone or wounded skin is rebuilt even in mammals. Moreover, a kind of regeneration goes on all the time in the organs or tissues of all animals because a proportion of the cells dies continuously and is replaced by new cells, with no change of characteristics. Thus the laws of development continue to apply even after birth.

Death and Resurrection: Metamorphosis

In many organisms the newborn may be a creature with characteristics remote from those of the adult: dramatic changes take place after birth. In the case of flies or butterflies the newborns are caterpillars, called larvae (because they mask the potential adult within). Newborn frogs are tadpoles, which have gills like fish and live in water. Larvae or tadpoles are transformed into adult animals through the process of *metamorphosis*. Under the influence of thyroid hormone, the tail muscles of the tadpole die off and the gills disappear while the lungs develop. The change, although profound, is progressive and not too dramatic. But the changing of a caterpillar into a butterfly is highly dramatic: it is like death and resurrection. Under hormonal influence, the larva, called now a pupa, ceases any outward life activity, simply hanging from a twig as if it were dead. Within the thick skin of the chrysalis or cocoon all the organs of the larva die off and are replaced with new ones, formed from persisting groups of embryonic cells. A completely new creature develops under the protective coat and finally emerges equipped with wings. Metamorphosis is crucial in insects that are encased in a rigid armor. In order to develop and grow they must shed the old armor, or molt, and make a new one. They may do this many times, always under hormonal control.

Some species tend to spend all their time in the larval stage. They carry on all the business of life, including reproduction, without bothering to undergo metamorphosis. An example is the axolotl, the tadpole of a South American sala-mander. The reason, probably, is a lack of thyroid hormone, for if the hormone is injected into an axolotl, it undergoes metamorphosis into a salamander. Sala-manders of other species do, however, metamorphose spontaneously.

In animals, such as mammals, that do not undergo metamorphosis profound changes occur nevertheless at some stages of development, although they are less recognizable. For instance, during the development of a mammalian embryo, the primitive kidney dies and is replaced by an entirely new organ in a partial meta-morphosis. Important changes also occur at the time of sexual maturation in the sexual organs and the brain. Like metamorphosis, they too are induced by hor-mones. At puberty a new individual emerges under the old skin.

The larval and the adult stages represent two completely different kinds of life. Aquatic larvae may generate adult animals that live on dry land; crawling larvae may change into flying adults; and parasitic larvae may change into free-living adults or vice versa. This alternation of modes of life has evolutionary implications. For instance, the transition of tadpoles to frogs reflects the emer-gence of land animals from fish. Presumably an amphibious life cycle, starting in water and ending on land, was one of the ways the transition could be accom-plished with minimal trauma. The newborn could continue to develop in the water in which its ancestors had lived and the fully developed, much more endur-ing adult was sent off to land.

Specialization

As the fertilized ovum develops, it generates cells that become progressively more specialized and more restricted in the repertoire of cells they in turn can generate. Thus, in the early embryo, each cell can generate a complete adult animal: the repertoire of cell types these early cells can generate is unlimited. At a subsequent stage of development, however, the ectoderm becomes restricted to generating the precursors of the skin and the nervous system—the neural tube. Later, some cells of the neural tube will generate precursors of nerve cells, while other cells—those of the neural crest—will generate cells of two types of peripheral ganglia, pig-mented cells of the skin, and cells of the adrenal medulla (the inner part of the gland). Subsequently the range of these cell types become further restricted. Nerve cell precursors will generate various kinds of nerve cells, but other cell types will produce descendants of only one or a few kinds.

Specialization occurs at varying rates in different organisms. In insects or in simpler organisms, such as nematodes (small wormlike creatures) or leeches, it begins early in development according to a rigid plan. These embryos are said to be mosaics; they are made up of separate parts, each of which will later be ampli-fied into a different organ. In vertebrates, specialization develops more slowly, and many cells remain capable of progressing in various directions for a long time. This type of development is said to be *regulated:* the developmental destiny of a cell depends not so much on where it comes from as on where it is located in the body. Its destiny is largely determined by its environment according to a program specified by the genes. We will return to these differences below.

Lineages

Sooner or later the range of progenies a cell can produce is restricted to a well-defined lineage, even in regulated embryos. The role of the environment then is mainly to determine when a certain kind of differentiation will take place. Even at this stage a lineage may develop into a small tree containing various cell types. The replacement of cells that goes on all the time in the adult body is based on the presence of cells that generate defined lineages. They are called *stem cells*, and they can reproduce themselves as they are or generate cells of a small number of types. An organism contains many kinds of stem cells. For instance, some generate the cell types in the epidermis (the epithelial layer of the skin), whereas others generate all the various types of blood cells. Stem cells always exist in small numbers in an animal because they can undergo extensive, although not indefinite, multiplication without changing characteristics. They are practically immortal—during the lifetime of the individual—whereas the more specialized cells they generate have a short life span and must be continuously replaced by the stem cells.

Stem cells can be identified at a very early stage in creatures that form mosaic embryos. For instance, in a minuscule nematode, which contains less than nine hundred cells in all, it is possible to catalog each cell and follow its destiny. In normal development all the cells of these organisms derive from a relatively small number of stem cells. Each cell undergoes exactly the same evolution in each nematode; the number of divisions each cell undergoes is fixed, as well as the destiny of each daughter cell resulting at each division. So all individuals of the species are identical.

The regularity of lineages in nematodes or leeches can be interpreted in two ways. Either a cell knows what to do at each stage, independently of its own environment, or it is told what to do by its neighbors. In the latter case the environment of each cell must continuously change. This is the case indeed because the neighboring cells change through repeated cell divisions. In a creature with a small number of cells, the environment of corresponding cells of different animals would undergo identical changes, generating identical lineages. Lineages then could be produced by following either internal or external instructions.

Whether development occurs one or the other way can be determined either by destroying some of the cells—thus changing the external instructions—or by altering the genome through mutations—thus altering the internal instructions. In nematodes or leeches, both changes alter the precise pattern of development. If a cell is destroyed, the behavior of neighboring cells often changes: so evidently cells do influence their neighbors. Mutations may cause a cell to follow the developmental pattern of its mother or grandmother, an effect that is difficult to interpret.

In embryos of all kinds a cell expresses its normal destiny as long as it is surrounded by normal neighbors, but if these are changed, it can generate different cell types. Changing the neighbors shows what a cell can do—that is, it exposes its *developmental potential*, which is broader than according to its normal destiny. The difference varies greatly depending on the species and the stage of development. In regulated embryos the developmental potential is very broad in the earlier stages: a single cell taken from a mouse embryo at the eight-cell stage can generate a complete normal animal. Even later the potential remains broad: cells whose normal developmental destiny is to make an ear can be induced to make the lens of the eye if they are transplanted to the site where the lens normally develops. But as development proceeds, the developmental potential becomes progressively more restricted until each cell becomes *committed* to produce just one lineage or one kind of structure. In mosaic embryos the developmental potential is more restricted, but it is difficult to say how much, for in these embryos it is technically more difficult to change the cells' environment by transplanting fragments from one place to another in the embryo.

The Specialty of Plants

In flowering plants new organisms are produced from haploid spores, which are generated in the flowers through the process of chromosome reduction, or meiosis (see chapter 9). The male spores—*microspores*—are made in the anthers, and the much larger female spores—*macrospores*—in the pistils (fig. 12.5). Spores of the two types do not directly fuse, but each multiplies to form a small structure that carries the gametes—a *gametophyte*. In contrast, the mature plant, which carries the spores, is called a *sporophyte*.

The male gamete-bearing structure is a grain of pollen, which is attached to the surface of the anther. The corresponding female structure is the egg sac, which is contained within the pistil. In these gamete-bearing structures the nuclei behave in characteristic ways. The pollen grain contains three haploid nuclei. Two of them will become sperm nuclei. The egg sac contains a small number of haploid nuclei, usually seven. Fertilization occurs after a pollen grain sticks to the pistil. The pollen grain sends a tiny tube containing the sperm nuclei into it. If the pollen comes from a compatible plant (see chapter 10), the tube reaches the egg sac and penetrates it. One of the sperm nuclei fertilizes one of the cells of the egg sac, which is equivalent to an animal egg cell, and will develop into the embryo. The other sperm nucleus fertilizes a cell with two nuclei, which therefore ends up with three copies of the genome—thus, it is triploid. Its function is to build a unique triploid tissue, *endosperm*, which accumulates reserve materials useful for the growth of the embryo (proteins, fatty substances, sugars). The fertilized egg generates the

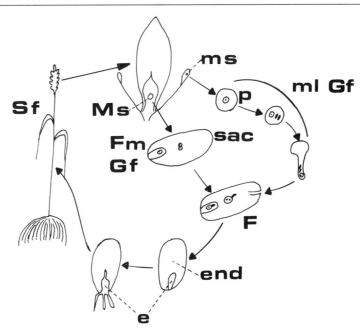

Figure 12.5. The life cycle of a flowering plant. The flower (at top) has anthers which contain the male microspores (ms) and pistils containing the female macrospores (Ms). The microspore forms the male gametophyte (ml Gf), that is, the pollen grain, which has two sperm nuclei (black). The macrospore forms the female gametophyte (Fm Gf), which consists of the embryo sac. At fertilization (F) the pollen tube penetrates the sac. Fertilization is double because one sperm nucleus fertilizes the egg cell, and the other fertilizes a cell with two nuclei, which generates the endosperm (end). The embryo (e) develops, forming the sporophyte (Sf) which is the adult plant.

new diploid plant, the sporophyte, which later produces the haploid spores by a process of chromosome reduction. The growth of the plant goes therefore through a cycle in which gamete-bearing structures, usually microscopic, alternate with spore-bearing structures, the plants with which we are familiar.

The first event following fertilization is the formation of a seed. The fertilized egg undergoes many cell divisions, which give rise to the rudiments of the root, the shoot, and the cotyledons (the structures that store food). Envelopes develop around the embryo, transforming it into a dormant seed, suitable for dispersal over great distances.

Germination of the seed starts the main phase of the life of the diploid plant. Initial development is supported by food reserves in the endosperm and the cotyledons. Important in determining the directions of initial growth are earth's gravity, which directs the shoot upward and the root downward and light, which attracts the shoot. The postnatal life unfolds with considerable variations depending on the species. In plants postnatal development continues throughout life. In fact plants grow in size and continuously or seasonally produce new organs, such as leaves or channels for the transport of water or food, until death.

Fundamental Steps of Development

In all higher plants and animals the varied and complicated steps of development have several basic events in common, which can be summarized as follows: (1) a diploid nucleus is formed at fertilization; (2) this nucleus replicates and the egg is partitioned; by repeated nuclear replications and cell divisions, a small mass of cells is formed; (3) the main axis becomes defined in the small embryo—head-to-tail in animals, shoot-to-root in plants; (4) the basic embryo is constructed around this axis through the suitable positioning of preexisting or newly made cells; and (5) organs are formed by characteristic movements and assembly of cells. We will now inquire into the mechanisms that bring about these events.

The Control of Shapes

How a single cell can develop into an organism with a large number of different cells according to a fixed plan is a fascinating problem, and one that is far from solved. Development is brought about by the action of genes, a conclusion supported by many facts. For instance, organisms with identical genes—such as identical twins or mice of inbred strains—develop essentially identical shapes. But animals of the same species, on the other hand, can develop very different features as a consequence of mutations. We see this variability in dogs, in which mutations have determined the many differences in shape of the various breeds. In insects, as in the fruitfly *Drosophila*, single mutations can cause drastic shape changes: as will be discussed below, a part of the abdomen can become the thorax (the chest) or a leg can grow out of the head.

That the genes should determine the features of organisms is not surprising because the genes determine the characteristics of all the molecules of the body. In turn, every event that unfolds in the organism must depend on the properties of these molecules, in cooperation with such environmental factors as temperature, humidity, light, or the pull of gravity. The real problem is *how* shape is attained, how *morphogenesis* (the generation of form) occurs under the concerted action of the genes and the outside factors. This is the most mysterious chapter of biology, for although we have some idea of the process, we know almost nothing of the details. Our ignorance hides events the knowledge of which is essential for understanding the basic aspects of life and crucial for applications in many fields from medicine to agriculture.

The interplay of events that ultimately lead to the complete specialization of the cells starts at the very beginning of development. The first step is to generate polarity—the head-to-tail or back-to-front axis in the essentially spherical embryo. Polarity is recognizable after the first division of an amphibian egg because the two daughter cells contain different amounts of yolk. One of the factors causing polarity is gravity: droplets containing the dense yolk tend to settle in the lower part of the egg cell. After the first division, then, the lower cell has more yolk. Another early difference is caused by the entry of the sperm into the egg. At the point of entry it wounds, as it were, the membrane of the egg, causing a rearrangement of its internal filaments. If the entry point is obliterated, eggs do not develop polarity and do not form a notochord or neural tube.

A general mechanism that creates new shapes is the sinking in of cells from the surface of the embryo to its interior, as when a gastrula is formed (see fig. 12.2). A similar event takes place at many other stages of development. For instance, it happens during the formation of the eye, which develops from a stalk coming from the brain (fig. 12.6). When the bulbous end of the stalk comes in contact with the skin, its tip sinks in toward the brain and changes into a cup. At the same time the

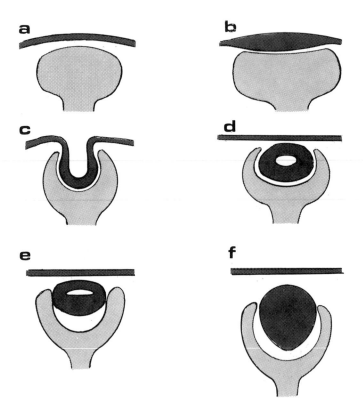

Figure 12.6. The formation of the eye cup. (a) The brain stalk (light gray) reaches the skin (dark gray). (b) The skin becomes thicker. (c) Both the stalk and the skin start forming a cup. (d) The skin cup separates from the skin, forming a hollow sphere. (e) The part of the sphere in contact with the brain stalk (dark gray) becomes thicker. (f) The sphere becomes large and solid, forming the lens of the eye.

skin touching the end of the stalk becomes thicker and also sinks forming a cup. The skin cup then closes, becoming a vesicle, while the skin reseals above it. The vesicle will give rise to the lens of the eye.

Why do the cells sink in? In the formation of the eye cup this phenomenon is due to a rearrangement of the inner filaments of the cells. The thin filaments, similar to those present in muscle, become shorter, changing the shape of the cell from that of a brick to a wedge. One might think of the stones cut in the shape of wedges that were used by the Romans to build archways and domes. In this case, the skin cells build a reverse dome. As in muscle, the filaments become shorter in response to a signal that increases the abundance of free Ca^{++} ions in the cells. The effect is mediated by the Ca^{++}-binding protein, calmodulin (see chapter 8).

These findings explain the mechanics of cup formation. We don't know, however, why the filaments contract; presumably some gene is activated to permit release of Ca^{++} ions or their entry into the cells. This activation of genes is referred to as differentiation. But this is still not the whole story. Even if we understood how the filaments contract, we would still have to explain why all the cells in a certain area of the skin differentiate and change shape, whereas those of neighboring areas do not. In other words, we need to learn how the *pattern* of differentiation is controlled.

The delineation of the disc of sinking cells on the skin of the embryo, forming a pattern element, and the differentiation of the cells are two fundamental processes of development, which occur many times at different locations and with different characteristics. We will deal with these two phenomena separately because their mechanisms seem very different.

Induction of a Structure

We have seen that development of an embryo is directed by external influences from the very beginning. In frog eggs the sperm entry point and the force of gravity identify a special area of the egg, the so-called gray crescent, before any cell division takes place. This area will later develop into the future backside of the body, while the rest of the egg will provide the belly side. The opening of the gastrula, called the *blastopore* (see fig. 12.2), coincides with one edge of the gray crescent. In turn the position of the blastopore will determine the position and orientation of the future body within the egg.

Among the first structures that develop in the frog embryo is the notochord, which appears as a string of cells of the middle layer stretching from the lip of the blastopore onward. Soon afterward the *neural fold* appears as a thickening of the outer layer above the notochord. The formation of the neural fold has been a favorite object of study by embryologists because it is a clear-cut event, easily observed in readily available material, such as frog eggs. These studies reached a climax in 1924, when Hans Spemann and M. Mangold, working in Friburg, Germany, showed that cells close to the lip of the blastopore determine the formation of the fold. They took a piece of the lip from an embryo and grafted it to a similar embryo, some distance away from the existing blastopore. The grafted embryo developed two neural folds: one connected to its own blastopore, the other connected to the graft. In this experiment cells whose normal developmental destiny was to become skin of the belly became nervous system instead; they apparently were not yet determined to become skin. This phenomenon, in which the destiny of embryonic cells is controlled by grafted cells, was called *induction;* the group of cells capable of causing induction was called the *organizer.*

The result of this experiment conveyed the important message that signals are transmitted from the organizer to the receptive cells. In this case the signal directs the formation of the main axis of the embryo. There are numerous other examples of induction, leading to the conclusion that it is a basic phenomenon in normal development.

What is the signal of induction? It was widely assumed that it would prove to be a chemical released by the organizer, but the substance could not be identified for a long time. No one was surprised by this failure because it was thought that the inducer might be a very labile substance, produced in minute amounts and present in only a few of the thirty thousand cells composing the embryo when the neural fold develops. Only recently a small protein capable of inducing neural tube formation has been isolated from chicken embryos. The long delay in identifying the inducer had important consequences. Studies on the mechanism of development, because they were denied a chemical solution, took a theoretical direction, and efforts were directed at explaining development according to physical principles. This approach turned out to be very useful: it yielded the basic concept that morphogenesis is preceded by the formation of a pattern determined by the different concentrations of a hypothetical substance designated as the *morphogen.*

Help from Slime Molds

This field has been more recently revitalized by progress in what would seem to be a distant field: the study of the behavior of certain single-celled eukaryotes that undergo development. They associate with one another, forming multicellular complexes with characteristic shapes. In these cases the chemical nature of the morphogens could be determined; it was then possible to investigate their mode of action. These creatures are *slime molds,* which are simple eukaryotes present in soil.

Slime molds were so named because they lead a double life similar to that of real molds. For long periods real molds exist as long thin cells connected to each other to form an intricate network called *mycelium* (the substrate of a mushroom), which spreads in the top layer of the soil. From time to time the filaments join to form mushrooms. The mushroom is a real multicellular organism, in which the cells assemble and differentiate to produce defined organs, like the cap and the stem. Development and differentiation, therefore, can be observed even in organisms that for most of their life cycle are essentially made up of single cells.

Slime molds, however, are unrelated to real molds. Their cells are like amoebas, which can be grown in cultures on plastic dishes containing jelled agar loaded with bacteria. The amoebas eat the bacteria, attaining very high numbers. When a culture of slime mold exhausts its food supply, it undergoes dramatic changes. Within a matter of hours the cells begin to aggregate, forming thick streamers, whorls, and circles (fig. 12.7). Progressively the cells move toward the center of the culture, merging into an elongated mass, or slug (fig. 12.8). In the case of some slime molds the slug crawls slowly toward a source of light; in others, it is stationary; in all cases it finally erects itself on the agar, forming a thick stalk with a swelling at the top, the fruiting body. The whole process takes about twenty-four hours. The top swelling contains special cells, the spores, embedded in a slimy goo. The spores are modified cells with thick coats, capable of resisting dryness and heat and suitable for dispersal and survival under unfavorable circumstances. In this respect they are comparable to the spores formed by many kinds of bacteria. If the spores are transferred to a fresh agar plate, they give rise again to growing cells.

The development of the fruiting body goes on through displacement and

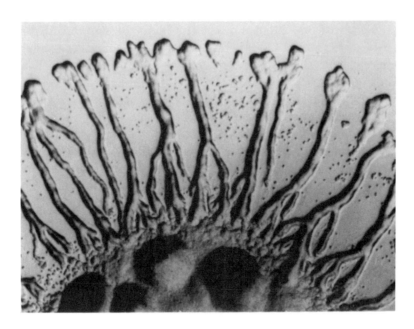

Figure 12.7. Streamers forming in a culture of slime mold after the food is exhausted. (From O. Shimomura, H. L. B. Suthers, and J. T. Bonner, *Proc. Natl. Acad. Sci. USA* 79:7376–79 [1982]. Reproduced with permission.)

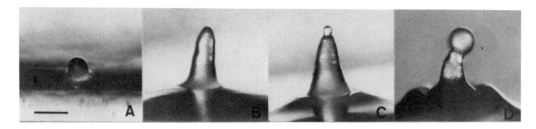

Figure 12.8. The formation of the fruiting body in a culture of slime mold. (A) A mass of amoebas surrounded by mucous material (line at bottom = 0.1 mm). (B) Formation of the neck of the stalk by amoebas rising upward from the mass shown in A. (C) Through an opening at the top of the stalk spores begin to flow out. (D) The spores accumulate at the top of the stalk embedded in a mucous matrix. (From M. D. Deasey and L. S. Olive, *Science* 213:561–62 [1981].)

aggregation of cells, not through an increase in their numbers. The process involves morphogenesis as well as differentiation (changes of gene expression).

How a population of identical amoebas can generate a complex structure containing different cell types is a fascinating question. An important step in its solution was the discovery of the chemical signals that cause the formation of the structure. In the case of one species of slime mold (*Dictiostelium discoideum*) the signal is a molecule we have met before: cyclic AMP. Other slime molds use other molecules, also fairly simple, for the same purpose. In the culture, cyclic AMP transmits signals from one cell to another. The chemical is produced by some cells and binds to surface receptors of others. The role of cyclic AMP, acting outside the cells, is different from that which it performs as second messengers in cells affected by hormones (see chapter 8). In the slime molds cyclic AMP is the hormone—that is, the first messenger—but it is the second messenger as well, because it also controls gene expression within the cells. The slime mold cells are very simple and need a simple control system.

Before the discovery of the role of cyclic AMP it was thought that several signal molecules were involved in the development of the slime mold, because it is made up of several events. Now we know that cyclic AMP at different concentrations activates different programs that are built in the genes of the cells and produce a variety of consequences. Some of the effects are mediated, however, by other substances—by communicator molecules acting upon cell contact and by other molecules released by the cells.

One instruction given to the cells by cyclic AMP is for movement and aggregation. When cyclic AMP binds to their surface receptors, the cells start moving toward the cyclic AMP source, and in so doing, they stick to each other. Movement occurs at a narrow range of cyclic AMP concentrations. Another instruction given is for relaying. This means that within seconds after a cell binds cyclic AMP, it will itself start to produce cyclic AMP. This production lasts for a minute or so.

Through relaying, the signals for movement and aggregation spread throughout the culture.

A characteristic feature of cyclic AMP production is its pulsation, which is caused by several factors. One is the short duration of cyclic AMP release by a relaying cell. Another is the rapid onset of refractoriness—the temporary inability of the cell (for two or three minutes) to respond to a new stimulation by cyclic AMP, so that it cannot respond to the cyclic AMP that it itself produces. A third factor is the production of an enzyme that breaks down cyclic AMP throughout the culture, ensuring that the substance produced by a cell will reach only neighboring cells. The signal can travel to distant cells only through a series of relays.

Production of cyclic AMP begins, probably at random, in rare cells in the middle of the culture where cell density is highest. These cells begin to aggregate and to transmit the signal to nearby cells. They in turn relay the signal, which progressively spreads out from the center. So the cells continue to move toward the center where they accumulate. The pulsating nature of the signal generates waves of motion and aggregation. They culminate in the formation of whorls and rings that move toward the center.

While these morphogenetic events unfold, the cells acquire new properties. All the effects we have described—movement, relaying, cell elongation—are the result of the activation of formerly silent genes. Many of these changes are in response to changes of cAMP concentration outside the cells. Cells aggregate because new proteins, some containing sugars, others able to bind sugars, make their appearance at their surfaces. Molecules of the two proteins on different cells bind to each other, forming bridges between the cells. Special sugars that appear only at this stage seem crucial for aggregation. More than a thousand genes, corresponding to about a third of the whole genome, begin transcription, after the food is exhausted, in groups that are activated one after the other. The need of so many genes for this simple differentiation shows how demanding the differentiation of complex organisms must be. This process culminates in the formation of the slug, which is produced by the differentiation of the cells into two types: those that will become spores and those that will become stalk cells. The latter cells appear early throughout the culture and accumulate in the forward or elevated part of the slug where they become foamy and die, providing support to the spore cells. These cells, originating in the densest part of the culture, occupy at first the rear or lower part of the slug, but finally move to its top. The various steps of differentiation are caused in part directly by cyclic AMP, in part by other cell products, and in part by contacts between cells.

Pattern Formation

The main lesson derived from the study of slime molds is that a single morphogenetic substance—cyclic AMP—can elicit a series of morphogenetic events, depending upon its concentration in different parts of the culture. We can say that the concentration of the morphogen in the culture forms a *pattern* that determines the subsequent development of the culture.

These results are highly relevant to embryonic development in animals. They suggest that a single signal substance may be adequate to define the pattern that underlies the development of a complex organ. The pattern's formation may involve critical factors, such as the precise concentration of the morphogen, the abundance of its receptors on the cells, the distances between the cells, and their ability to relay a signal. In embryos the first pattern may develop as the consequence of initial differences (such as yolk distribution or sperm entry point) that affect the production or distribution of a morphogen. The pattern of distribution then determines subsequent development by inducing differentiation of cells (that is, by directing different groups of cells to express different genes). Initial small differences in the local amounts of morphogen can in the end generate large differences in the final pattern through self-reinforcement. The final pattern is similar in different individuals because it is determined by the modalities of self-reinforcement and the distribution of the cells. The initial triggering differences, though essential for starting the process, are irrelevant to the final outcome.

The slime mold studies fail, however, to explain important aspects of animal morphogenesis. For instance, they do not explain how the pattern for the eye lens remains confined to a disc of cells without invading surrounding areas. How is the boundary of the disc formed? This is a tough question. Much effort has been directed at solving this problem, using both experimental approaches and the building of theoretical models. Especially useful for such experiments are amphibian or chicken embryos, or simple animals like hydras or leeches. The main manipulation used is changing the relation of parts of the embryo during development. In some creatures (such as hydras and amphibia) the manipulations can also be carried out during regeneration, that is, during the reconstruction of parts of the adult body (for instance, limbs) that have been cut off. Regeneration is possible in these species because immature cells, with broad developmental potential, persist in the adult. The absence of such cells makes regeneration essentially impossible in birds or mammals.

Manipulations of Development

The results of these studies have demonstrated once more how plastic development is in many creatures. Plasticity is possible because the self-regulation of pattern formation allows the formation of organs in a reproducible way independently of local variations. Marked deviations appear only when the morphogenetic pattern is seriously disrupted.

Very interesting observations can be made in amphibians, birds, and some insects by interfering with limb development. Formation of a limb is initiated by the appearance of a swelling, the *limb bud*, which is made up of cells of the mesoderm of the embryo, covered by cells of the ectoderm. In one type of experiment the buds of, say, the left anterior limbs are surgically removed from two embryos; each limb bud is then grafted onto the stump left by the amputation in the other embryo. If the orientation of the grafted bud in respect to the embryo is exactly maintained, the limb develops in a normal way. If the bud is rotated so that the part normally facing the head now faces the tail, a strange thing happens: the grafted bud generates not one but two limbs, and sometimes even three. In all cases an additional limb is the mirror image of the adjacent one. This symmetry is easily recognized from the features of wrist and finger bones. If the fingers are 1-2-3-4 in the normal orientation, a double limb may be 1-2-3-4-3-2-1, and a triple limb may be 2-3-4-3-2-3-4 (not all fingers are always formed) (see figs. 12.9 and 12.10).

Similar observations can be made in adult amphibians or insects in which a limb is amputated. In amphibians, after the amputation, the stump becomes covered by a layer of cells with embryonal characteristics, which regenerate the limb. If the layer of embryonal cells is surgically removed and grafted to a stump, the results again depend upon the relative orientation of the two, as in an embryo. In adult insects such as cockroaches, similar results are obtained by exchanging parts of a limb between two individuals. The outcome again depends upon the relative orientation of the parts after the exchange.

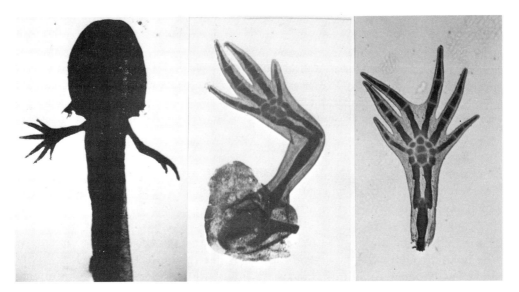

Figure 12.9. Effect of organizer transplantation on limb development in axolotl. Left photograph shows the result of transplantation in which at the limb bud stage, a fragment of the limb organizer was inserted at the anterior edge of the limb bud. The resulting limb is a composite of the two back halves of a normal limb, one that mirrors the other. The right limb is normal. The central photograph shows the bone structure of the normal limb, with the posterior side to the right. The right photograph shows the bone structure of the operated limb that is made up of two posterior parts symmetrically arranged. Courtesy of J. M. W. Slack.

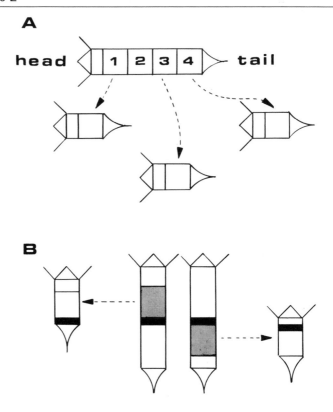

Figure 12.10. Experiments on hydra development. (A) The salami experiment: each of four slices (1 through 4) produces a complete hydra with both head and tail. (B) Importance of the relative position of cells within the slice rather than in the original hydra. Slices are taken from two hydras in such a way that they share a section coming from the same level (black). This section will in one case generate a tail (left), in the other a head (right). The outcome depends on the position of the section in the slice (gray).

The similarity of these results in different species suggests that they reveal a general property of limb bud development. Before trying to interpret the results, however, we must consider results of experiments with much simpler species which can be interpreted similarly.

Among these other species is the hydra, a primitive creature made up of a tube terminated at one end by the head and at the other by the tail, who normally propagate through buds that sprout from the rear end of the body. A whole hydra can be easily regenerated from pieces. An interesting result is obtained by slicing the body of the hydra like a salami. Each slice re-forms a complete individual. The significant fact is that in each slice the head develops at what was the head end of the slice, and the tail at its tail end (fig. 12.11: A). Each slice, therefore, remembers the head-tail orientation it had in the original hydra, regardless of whether it was close to the head or to the tail. What is crucial is the *relative position* of the cells in the slice; the actual position is irrelevant. This principle is confirmed in a dramatic way by cutting two slices from two individuals in such a way that the tail end of

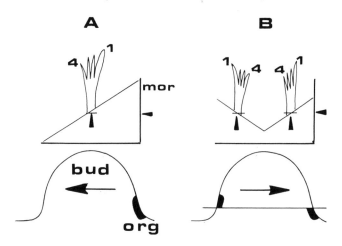

Figure 12.11. Interpretation of limb rotation experiments. (A) In normal development an organizer (org) is present at the rear part of the limb bud. The organizer produces a morphogen (mor) which becomes distributed in a gradient (shown above) with highest concentration at the organizer. The limb develops where the concentration of the morphogen has a certain value (arrow). (B) The bud has been cut and rotated by 180°, splitting the organizer (black). A part of it is now at the front of the bud. Morphogen is now produced at both ends of the bud, as shown above, forming a double gradient. The concentration of the morphogen is adequate for limb development at two points (arrows), so two limbs develop. They are mirror images of each other because they are on opposite slopes of the gradient. Fingers 1 and 4 are identified.

one is at the same position as the head end of the other (fig. 12.11: B). After each of the two slices rebuilds a whole individual, the thin layer that derived from the same level of the hydras gives rise to a head in one case and a tail in the other.

How do the cells remember their relative position? There must be signals either within the cells or between them. These two possibilities are tested by dissociating a hydra into individual cells. After the cells are reaggregated, they reconstitute a complete hydra, with characteristic head and tail. How this happens we don't know. Very informative, however, is a variation of this experiment. Segments of hydras, obtained at known locations, are dissociated and are then allowed to reassociate separately, forming stable aggregates. When aggregates of this kind are pressed together into intimate contact, they develop into a complete hydra. Let's assume that aggregates of different origin are pressed together in different sequences. What would happen? The aggregates again rebuild a hydra, the shape of which depends on two factors: the origin of the segments before they were dissociated, whether they were close to the head (H) or to the tail (T), and the order in which the cell aggregates are placed together. If the order is HTH, heads are formed at the two ends; if the order is THT, a head is formed in the middle. This shows that the cells keep, even after dissociation, the information of their relative position in the creature from which they were taken. The information must be carried by the amounts of some substance present within the cells or attached to them. It cannot be due to substances separate from the cells and present around them. Nor can it be due to a directional signal contained in the cells, pointing to the head or the tail in the whole individual, because its orientation would not be maintained after the cells are separated and reaggregated.

A possible explanation for the nature of the positional information comes from yet another experiment. A headless anterior piece of hydra is connected to a posterior piece from another hydra. A head forms at the junction. If, however, the transplanted anterior piece contains the head, no new head is formed: the transplanted head inhibits formation of a new head. In another experiment, a small fragment of head is transplanted to a hydra far from the existing head: it will induce formation of a new head. The two experiments show that a head fragment can either induce or inhibit formation of another head, depending on its size.

An important additional finding in this experiment is that the same effects can be produced using *extracts of hydra heads*. In the hydra, therefore, the positional information results from the interplay of two substances: an inducer and an inhibitor of head formation. The inducer is a small protein (a peptide) made up of eleven amino acids, which at extremely low concentrations stimulates multiplication of hydra stem cells and their differentiation into nerve cells, causing head development. The inhibitor is an even smaller, fat-seeking molecule. These morphogenetic substances belong to the class of communicators, such as the growth and differentiation factors we already encountered in chapter 8. How these substances control development we do not know. Presumably they act by binding to receptors on the cells, but ultimately they must alter the expression of genes. Inducer and inhibitor may act on different receptors, producing their opposite effects by influencing in different ways the production of second messengers, as hormones do (see chapter 8). Their effects do not merely cancel each other, because the two molecules have different properties: the activator is bound to a large carrier molecule and hence does not move too far and has a short life, whereas the inhibitor, being small, is more mobile and lasts a longer time. The interplay between inducers and inhibitors may be the basis for all phenomena of morphogenesis.

Gradients

The results of the experiments reviewed above suggest that the development of an organ is preceded by the formation of a pattern of morphogenetic substances—which probably are growth or differentiation factors—associated with the cells. The pattern then determines the shape of the future organ. This would be like forming a pattern with different shades of gray on a sheet of paper and then translating the different shades into different colors or relief. The pattern is generated by different concentrations of the morphogenetic substances, which are generated by some of the cells and then spread by diffusion. Within a certain area, or field, their concentration varies gradually in a certain direction, forming what is called a *gradient*. For instance, it is likely that along the body of the hydra there is a gradient of both the inducer and the inhibitor of head formation; both substances are most abundant close to the head and least abundant close to the tail. The two gradients are, however, different, that of the inducer being concentrated near the head and that of the inhibitor more spread out. The morphogenetic substances act on the cells, affecting their genes: where a substance is more abundant its effect on the genes is more pronounced than where it is sparse. In this way a gradient of diffusible substance is transformed into a gradient of expression of some genes, in a way that we do not understand. When we slice a hydra the cells that were closest to the head in each slice have more of some substance made in the cells under control of the head inducer than those at the opposite end. They, therefore, give rise to a head, while the other end becomes a tail. The persistence or continued production of the substances within the cells accounts for the results of the experiments.

A further conclusion can be drawn from a comparison of the distribution of the substance made under instruction of the head inducer in two slices, one close to the original head, the other close to the tail (see fig. 12.11: A). The amount of the substance present in cells of the back surface of the forward slice (no. 1) is much higher than that present in cells of the forward surface of the back slice (no. 4). Yet the former cells, although containing more of the substance, generate a tail, whereas the latter ones, which contain less of the substance, generate a head. What counts is the different concentration *within the slice.* Similarly there must also be a gradient of the inhibitor of head formation, which is also more abundant close to the head. We will see below how the two factors are thought to interplay.

The concept of a morphogenetic gradient is entirely theoretical because in almost all cases the substances have not been identified. Yet it is a useful concept because it offers a plausible explanation of complex findings. For instance, the observations with the limb buds can be explained by the presence of an organizer region at the posterior edge of a limb, which produces a limb inducer. The concentration of the inducer has its highest value at that place and the lowest at the opposite edge. We assume that the limb develops at a point in the gradient where the concentration of the inducer has a certain intermediate value between the two edges. The polarity of the limb (that is, whether finger 1 is toward one edge or the other) is related to the downhill direction of the gradient, the direction in which the concentration of the inducer decreases. When the bud is rotated on its stump, part of the organizer is moved to the anterior edge (fig. 12.9). This generates two gradients, sloping in opposite directions. A concentration of the inducer suitable for limb development is now present at two points. As a result two limbs develop. Because the slopes of the two gradients point in opposite directions, the polarities of the two limbs are also opposite: they are mirror images of each other.

The fact that when multiple limbs are formed two adjacent limbs are always of opposite polarity is a natural consequence of the gradual variation of the concentration of the inducer. This condition requires that two consecutive equal values are on gradients with slopes pointing in opposite directions. This interpretation is strongly supported by the production of double symmetric limbs by transplanting a segment of the posterior edge to the anterior edge of a limb (fig. 12.10).

Models of Development

These ideas do not specify the characteristics of the morphogen. It could be many things: it could be a growth or differentiation factor, or a substance with a catalytic action such as an enzyme, or a substance that connects cells to each other. Regardless of the nature of the morphogen, however, its effects can be mathematically predicted. Different mathematical models can be made depending on a number of assumptions.

One popular model assumes that the pattern results from the interplay of inducing and inhibitory substances, as found in hydra, with two conditions: (1) that the activator promotes its own formation, and (2) that the range of action of the activator is shorter than that of the inhibitor. These conditions are fulfilled for the activator in cultures of slime molds: the activator promotes its own synthesis through relaying, but it is continuously destroyed by an enzyme distributed uniformly through the culture; hence the activator has a localized action. The second condition is fulfilled in the hydra. This model can explain many complexities of development, such as the formation of regularly spaced bristles or scales on the skin of insects, the complex geometrical patterns observed in butterflies, the regular spacing of leaves on a stem, and their alternation on opposite sides of the stem.

Following this model we can produce a more complete, although still hypothetical, picture of the development of an embryo. The initial homogeneity of the egg is broken by the entry of the sperm and by gravity. These two factors determine the direction of the initial morphogenetic gradient and polarity. As the cells increase in number they recognize different values of the gradient and undergo differentiation—they express different genes depending on these values. This primary differentiation generates secondary gradients at left and right of the primary axis, each the mirror image of the other. These gradients in turn cause secondary differentiation and morphogenesis. The organs formed (for instance, the limbs) are similar at the left and right sides, but one is the mirror image of the other in respect to the middle plane of the embryo, because the gradients of the morphogens slope toward the middle line. Development proceeds in a series of successive steps, each occurring in a similar way. These steps are all different from each other, however, because at each step the morphogens are different and the cells responding to them are different, too. As a consequence, the differentiation they induce is different at each step. For instance, the disc that will sink in to form the eye is the result of previous morphogenesis and is delineated by it. The cells of the disc produce a new morphogen, generating a new gradient within the disc. This morphogen causes the expression of genes for the contractible filaments. Neighboring cells are insensitive to this gradient because they are the result of a different development and do not have the receptors for the morphogen active in the disc. As a result the cells of the disc, but not the surrounding cells, are induced to express the new genes, whose effect is to make the cells wedge-shaped.

According to this model, the genes influence development in two ways. They specify the morphogenetic substances appropriate for each stage of development. They also specify receptors that make it possible for a certain group of cells to respond to certain morphogenetic substances. In response to the morphogens, the cells express a certain set of genes (that is, undergo a certain differentiation). Evidently these steps must be accurately coordinated in space and time. The genes are the key to this coordination. Development, therefore, is a most complex and sophisticated expression of gene activity. It is no wonder that it is so difficult to decipher.

Genes Controlling Development

Much progress is nevertheless being made in learning about genes that affect development. This happens especially by studying mutations that affect development, which are known in many animal species. These mutations do not simply hinder development; they cause a wrong development. For instance, in the fruitfly *Drosophila* one mutation causes a leg to develop on top of the head, at the place normally occupied by a feeler; another mutation causes the fly to have four wings instead of two.

Mutations affecting development in this fly have been studied a great deal because both the genetics and the development of the fly are well known. With the advent of genetic engineering the nature of the mutations and the organization of the genes in which they occur were defined at the molecular level.

Segmentation

Let's first briefly see how a fly develops. The fertilized egg has a central nucleus, which, after fertilization, divides rapidly while the egg itself remains undivided. After nine nuclear divisions the five hundred or so nuclei migrate to the surface. The partitioning of the egg cytoplasm begins four or five divisions later, and each nucleus becomes associated with a cell. At this stage the embryo is a layer of cells surrounding the central yolk. The subdivision into three layers occurs later, at gastrulation. A wormlike larva is finally produced, and the mature insect is formed after metamorphosis. All the organs of the adult insect develop from reservoirs of embryonic cells (each committed to form a certain organ) called *imaginal discs* because they give rise to the completed fly, also called imago, or image.

For understanding the significance of the mutations, we must look at the segmentation of the *Drosophila* body. Almost two hours after the beginning of development, when it has almost six thousand nuclei and the cytoplasma is not yet partitioned, a very young larva appears completely smooth and uniform on the outside, even through the electron microscope; yet its nuclei are organized in twenty-eight circular bands that envelop the body like the skin of a zebra. The bands are recognized because their cells have different destinies, as can be seen by marking them and determining where they go. Cells of different bands will produce different parts of the future body. Later fourteen visible rings, or segments, each including two primitive bands, appear at the surface layer of the larva (the outside) and are separated from each other by circular furrows. The segments are identified by the distribution of hard plaques, hair, and so on, on their skin. Three segments make up the head; behind them three segments make up the thorax (chest); and further behind eight segments make up the abdomen. The adult fly has the same number of segments, but they are much more specialized. Each of the three thoracic segments has a pair of legs, which differ somewhat from one segment to another; in addition the second segment has a pair of wings, and the third segment, a pair of rudimentary wings (the halteres).

Mutations affecting segmentation fall into three groups: (1) those affecting the polarity of the egg, both head to tail and back to front, (2) mutations reducing the number of segments, and (3) those altering the organization of some segments, but not their numbers.

Mutations affecting polarity are numerous. They have a special characteristic: they are caused by changes in genes of the mother, not of the embryo. The substances specified by these genes are produced by the mother and are introduced into the developing egg. Some mutations affect anterior-posterior polarity, others the abdominal-dorsal polarity. Embryos produced by some mutants do not produce any belly cells; the larvae have only a back and soon die. In some cases injecting into the cytoplasm of a mutant larva a small amount of cytoplasm from a regular egg corrects the defect. The amount needed may be as little as 1 percent of the entire larva, showing that in normal eggs the substance is present in excess, for reasons we do not understand. A safety device?

Sorting Out of Cells

Mutations in some twenty different genes reduce the number of segments by suppressing some of the primitive bands. Embryos carrying one kind of mutation (*hairy*) make the series 1, 4–5, 8–9, and so on, up to 28, whereas the other (*fushi tarazu*, which is Japanese, meaning too few segments) makes the complementary series 2–3, 6–7, 10–11, and so on, up to 26–27. The pairs do not correspond to those that later generate segments: in each pair one band corresponds to the posterior half of a future segment, the other to the anterior half of the next one. The genes in which these mutations occur have been cloned, and probes to identify the mRNAs in the cells and antibodies to identify the proteins have been prepared. In normal larvae both mRNAs and proteins are found in the cells of the bands that are abolished in the mutants, although the agreement is not perfect at certain periods of development. The proteins are in nuclei, where they probably affect the expression of genes. Clearly, the expression of special genes is required for the development of the bands.

When the embryo is about two hours old the mRNA of these two genes are recognizable in cells throughout the body; progressively they become localized to the pairs of primitive bands. The changes show that the cells containing one or the other active gene are progressively sorted out into their final distribution. We do not know why the cells are subdivided into two separate but interlocked groups of band pairs. Perhaps earlier in evolution the flies had one gene and fourteen bands: a duplication of the gene may have caused the addition of a pair of new bands to each preexisting pair, doubling their number.

The expression of these two genes is transient; after about two hours their mRNAs are replaced by new mRNAs which transcribe a new gene: *engrailed*. These new mRNAs become progressively localized to *alternate* primitive bands, which later will give rise to the posterior part of each final segment. These mRNAs persist into later development, suggesting that the gene *engrailed* is responsible for maintaining the differentiation between the anterior and posterior part of each final segment. Mutations in this gene cause the apparent fusion of segments because the segments fail to differentiate.

The three genes (*hairy, fushi tarazu,* and *engrailed*) operate in a hierarchical way. This is shown by studying the expression of the RNA messenger of each gene in flies that are mutant for one of the other two genes. The regular appearance of *fushi tarazu* messenger takes place only if the *hairy* gene is normal; and the appearance of the *engrailed* pattern of expression over the embryo requires that both *fushi tarazu* and *hairy* be normal. There is therefore this hierarchy: *hairy* → *fushi tarazu* → *engrailed*. Each gene product allows the regular expression of the next gene; the first and second genes act transiently to establish the periodicity of segments, which is finally maintained by the expression of *engrailed*.

How the periodicity is obtained we do not know, but we can think of it in this way. It is probably initiated by the expression of the anterior-posterior polarity genes of maternal origin which lay down the primitive segmentation. This allows *hairy* to be expressed in a periodic way in half of the segments. Its gene product suppresses the expression of *fushi tarazu* in the same segments, allowing it to be successively expressed in the other set of segments. The combination of the two genes activates *engrailed*, the product of which ends up shutting off the two earlier acting genes.

Monsters

Mutations altering the shape of the final segments have been known for many years for the extraordinary effects they produce. The most striking is the appearance of a leg in the head in place of a normal feeler (fig. 12.12), a mutation

Figure 12.12. Photograph obtained with a scanning electron microscope of a fly with the *Antennapedia* mutation. The two large almost spherical surfaces with a grid pattern in the lower part of the photograph are the eyes. The two hornlike structures just above the eyes are two legs, which replace two normal feelers (antennae). (From *Science* 224:1224 [1984]. Courtesy of R. Turner.)

called *Antennapedia*. Another striking mutation—the *bithorax*—causes the fly to have four wings instead of two (fig. 12.13). Many mutations have effects related to these, although they are less startling. They are said to belong to the *Antennapedia or bithorax system.*

The *bithorax* mutations have the same general property of causing a segment to look like the one ahead: they *anteriorize* a segment. In the four-winged fly the forward part of the third thoracic (3T) segment (farthest away from the head) resembles the second thoracic (2T) segment. Part of the 3T segment has normally rudimentary wings (halteres), but the mutant has true wings, like those of the normal 2T segment: the 2T segment seems to be doubled. Another mutation (*postbithorax*) makes the back part of 3T look like 2T. Other mutations make the first abdominal (1A) segment, normally without legs, resemble the 3T segment, which has legs; these flies have seven or eight legs instead of six. The most extreme mutation, *Ultrabithorax*, makes all segments behind 2T—that is, 3T and all abdominal segments—look like 2T. Many *bithorax* mutations alter preferentially either the anterior or the posterior part of a segment. Evidently the primitive bands from which the segments derive retain some of their individuality.

The genes in which the *bithorax* and the *Antennapedia* mutations occur are responsible for producing substances needed for the normal development of the segment changed by the mutation. It is not known whether they are morphogens

Figure 12.13. A strong anteriorization of the third thoracic segment causes a fly to develop four regular wings. In normal flies only in the anterior (2T) segments are the wings fully formed; in the posterior (3T) segment they are rudimentary (called halteres). The change shown here is produced by the simultaneous presence in the fly of three different mutations of the *bithorax* group. (From W. Bender et al., *Science* 221:23–29 [1983].)

or substances produced under the control of morphogens. They are especially interesting genes.

The Genes

The genes that when altered cause such extraordinary effects have been cloned. They reside in a very long segment of DNA (more than 300,000 base pairs long) in which the changes responsible for all the *Antennapedia* and *bithorax* mutations are localized. This segment is subdivided into three transcription units, which from left to right (arbitrary) are the *Antennapedia* unit, the *bithorax* thoracic unit, and the *bithorax* abdominal unit. Within each unit different mutations affect individual segments; the spatial order of these units is the same as that of the segments they alter. This similarity is very striking: it suggests an evolutionary relationship between the elongation of the body of the larvae and of the addition of new genes, but we do not understand how they are connected.

The mutations of the *bithorax* and *Antennapedia* systems of genes have unusual features that hint at the properties of their products. The genes are extremely long, compared to *Drosophila* genes that specify enzymes or other products, and have many long intervening sequences. They generate multiple messengers, probably by splicing the transcript in various ways: the mRNAs may have different coding and control sequences (see chapter 4), allowing the genes to be controlled in their own ways in different cells or at various stages of development. Another peculiarity is that none of the known mutations is caused by a change of a single base, as is the case for most other mutations in the fruitfly. The *bithorax* mutations are mostly caused by insertions either of mobile elements, which are abundant in *Drosophila*, or of other pieces of DNA. The most drastic mutation, *Ultrabithorax* (which makes all segments behind 2T look like 2T), consists of the complete absence of the two *bithorax* units. A possible reason for the absence of point mutation is the abundance of intervening sequences: most single base substitutions would occur in them and would not affect the function of the genes. In contrast, insertions anywhere in a gene would make it inactive by stopping the progress of transcription or by introducing frame shifts (see chapter 4).

Almost all the *bithorax* mutations produce the observable effect only when they alter both homologous genes. Such mutations are *recessive*. They are caused by DNA changes that inactivate the functions of genes that are still adequate when one of the pair is left active. Special are the *Ultrabithorax* and the *Contrabithorax* (*Cbx*) mutations, which produce an observable effect even when they affect only one of the genes—they are *dominant* (hence, by convention, their capitalization). Whereas *Ultrabithorax* completely abolishes the function of the gene complex, *Contrabithorax* has a localized effect, but opposite to that of the other *bithorax* mutations, because it posteriorizes the 2T segment, making it similar to a 3T segment. This mutation is special also in its origin: it is caused by the insertion of a DNA fragment containing the gene for the 3T segment into the gene responsible for the 2T segment. Its effect is dominant because it expresses a new function: the 3T gene at the 2T location takes control of the 2T segment, which then looks like 3T.

This result shows that in each gene of the *bithorax* complex we can distinguish two sequences, responsible for "how" and "where" a gene works. The "how" sequence causes the body segment on which it acts, regardless of where it is, to develop the characteristics of a certain *segment*—say, what is normally 3T. The "where" sequence is the *address*, which determines on which one of the fourteen segments the gene will act. Normally the "how" and "where" coincide so that, for instance, the 3T segment has 3T characteristics. In the *Cbx* mutation, segment number and address do not coincide because the sequence for 3T characteristics has been moved to the address 2T.

How does the address work? How does a gene know how to act on a certain segment? Any gene is present in the cells of every segment; only its expression may depend on the segment. The localized expression of a "how" gene requires the interaction of special proteins with the address sequence of that gene, making it active at the proper place. We know very little about these proteins, except that they seem to be specified by genes outside the *bithorax* complex. We don't know what the address sequences are either.

The existence of the address sequences is suggested by an interesting feature of the *bithorax* and other developmental genes. Many of them share a sequence corresponding to a sixty-amino-acid protein, referred to as *homeobox* (because the developmental genes, such as *bithorax*, are called homeotic). This sequence is not present in other types of *Drosophila* genes; it is the hallmark of developmental genes. It is highly conserved in evolution, being present with little change from yeast to worms, amphibians, and humans. Clearly, this sequence plays an important role. It specifies a protein capable of binding to DNA, suggesting that developmental genes of this type act by regulating the transcription of other genes, called *realizator genes*, which are responsible for building the structures characteristic for each segment. Each "how" sequence would interact with a specific set of realizator genes. If, as seems likely, the homeobox is transcribed together with the rest of the gene, its protein may open up the DNA of the control area of the realizator genes, recognized by the "how" sequence. The realizator genes would be like safety boxes that recognize two keys: a general key (the homeobox protein common to all segments) and a special key (the specific "how" sequences). We can envisage therefore a hierarchical system of controls acting in a cascade that ultimately activates the realizator genes that make all the components of a certain segment.

A Model

Following is a possible hypothetical scheme for understanding in a very simplified way the development of the fly. In the course of evolution the fly evolved from a creature made up mostly of identical segments, all developed under the control of the same gene and the same morphogenetic substance which we will call *1Tm* (meaning 1T morphogen) (fig. 12.14). Then, progressively, evolution diversified the segments in a head-to-tail direction. First all segments from the 2T segment backward developed a common new 2T morphogen (*2Tm*) as the basis for a more complex development. The production or action of the original 1Tm was blocked by the new morphogen in all segments; the 2Tm remained active only in the 1T sequence. In the next step all segments beginning with the 3T segment underwent an additional change, developing a new *3Tm* which overruled the preexisting ones. Then a morphogen for the 1A segment and all those posterior to it made its appearance. In these segments the new morphogen again overruled the preexisting ones. The process continued in the remaining posterior segments. The result is that a gene for a single morphogen remains active in each segment while those for morphogens of the previous stages remain inactive, although they may play a role in intermediate stages of morphogenesis. Under this model recessive mutations inactivating both genes for the morphogen expressed, say, in the 3T segment would permit the activity of the gene for the morphogen of the previous stage, which is the normal morphogen for the 2T segment. This model explains why these mutations always anteriorize a segment—that is, why they make it look like the one ahead. In a refinement of this model, it is suggested that a morphogen, and

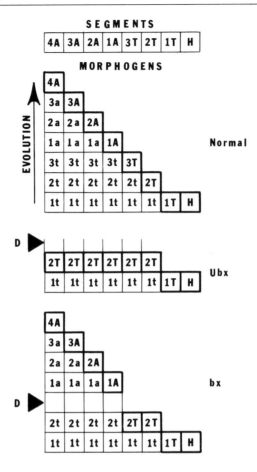

Figure 12.14. A model for the effects of the *bithorax* mutations. At top are the segments of the fly from the head (H) to the 4A segment. Subsequent segments are omitted. Below is the hypothetical distribution of morphogens. Each morphogen is indicated by the designation of the segment of which it is characteristic. It is assumed that during evolution the diversification of originally identical segments (excluding the head), having the 1T morphogen, took place by the successive appearance of new morphogens (arrow), owing to the formation of new genes. As a new morphogen appeared in a segment it suppressed the previous ones. The morphogens expressed in each segment are capitalized and surrounded by heavy boxes. The disappearance of one or more morphogens by alterations in the corresponding genes causes a suppressed morphogen to be expressed, in a hierarchical order. *Ubx* = *Ultrabithorax*; the defect (D, black triangle) affects all morphogens that appeared after 2Tm. *bx* = *bithorax*; the defect eliminates 3Tm.

therefore a gene, controls the anterior half of one segment and the posterior half of the one ahead of it.

This model can explain the puzzling result observed in flies carrying both the exceptional *Cbx* mutation—which, as we have seen, posteriorizes the 2T segment, making it similar to 3T—and a pair of recessive *pbx* mutations—which by themselves would anteriorize the 3T segment, making it similar to 2T. These flies have two almost normal 3T segments. The conversion of the 2T segment into a 3T segment is readily explained as the consequence of the *Cbx* mutation. What seems surprising is that the 3T segment itself remains unchanged, in spite of the *pbx* mutations, which by eliminating the normal 3Tm should reveal the underlying 2Tm. But in these flies, owing to the *Cbx* mutation, the gene for the 2Tm carries the 3T address, explaining the result.

In this model the T2 segment does not normally express the 3Tm and other morphogens, although it contains their genes (all genes are present in all cells). What prevents the gene from working? Other mutations, different from those considered so far, suggest that in each segment another gene blocks the expression of *bithorax* genes with a higher segment number. Clearly a device like this is required for preventing all segments from becoming like the one added last in evolution. Mutations that cause the failure of this mechanism make all segments look like 13, the penultimate segment; all segments from 12 on are posteriorized. Under the model, in order to maintain the individuality of each segment, the expression of genes with either lower or higher numbers must be prevented. Apparently this is achieved by two different mechanisms.

In summary we can visualize the fly development occurring by a succession of steps. The *first step* is carried out by maternal morphogens or morphogen-producing substances that are introduced into the egg during its development and determine its head-to-tail and back-to-front polarity. These morphogens are distributed evenly in the egg, but they can establish a gradient as the result of local asymmetries, such as the slight curvature of the egg. These initial gradients then determine the distribution of the two first gene products made in the embryo (*fushi tarazu* and *hairy*, probably two morphogens), which together carry out the *second step*, causing the identification of twenty-four primitive bands. In a *third step* the bands are subsequently differentiated between anterior and posterior halves of the future segment by the product of the third gene (*engrailed*) and probably additional unknown genes. A *fourth step* is the further differentiation of the segment by the action of developmental genes of two main groups: *Antennapedia* for the head and *bithorax* for thorax and abdomen. Their products control the genes that build the various segments and are in turn controlled by regulatory genes, probably related to the gradients established in the second step. The developmental genes of the fourth step in turn direct the expression of many realizator genes that specify the proteins needed for building the various structures of the individual segments. It is likely that the morphogenetic substances responsible for these steps are also produced in the imaginal discs, which rebuild the various structures at metamorphosis, probably repeating a related developmental sequence.

We conclude that the study of mutants affecting development provides general support for the idea that early development is regulated by a succession of morphogens acting one after another in fields that become more and more restricted as development proceeds. The molecular analysis of the fly mutants brings us a step closer to defining what these morphogens are and how they operate.

Program of Gene Expression

We must now inquire into the mechanisms by which cells achieve their specialization in development. We have seen that in a multicellular organism, development is characterized by the successive evolution of cell types forming a tree, which from the trunk (the fertilized egg) opens up into an increasing number of branches, corresponding to the final cell types.

The specialization of the cells is brought about by proteins that appear and disappear during the unfolding of development following changes in the expression of genes. Development reflects the program according to which genes change activity. In chapter 5 we have seen an example of such a program in the globin gene family, where different genes are expressed in succession in the embryo, the fetus, and the adult. The expression in various organs also changes: embryonic globin genes are expressed in the yolk sac, fetal genes in the liver and spleen, adult genes in the bone marrow. The globin genes that are not expressed are usually not transcribed and have the hallmarks of inactivity such as a dense chromatin and many m-groups (see chapter 4).

Important for controlling the transcription of the genes are the enhancers discussed in chapter 4, which are active in different cells at different stages of differentiation. The enhancer controlling the transcription of immunoglobulin genes (see chapter 13) works only in lymphocytes, which normally produce immunoglobulins. If an immunoglobulin gene is transferred from a lymphocyte into a cell of another type, its transcription ceases.

Gene expression may be caused by different processing of the same transcript. This probably happens in the bithorax system; it seems that each type of messenger is made only in certain parts of the embryo and at certain phases of development, following different controls. A model for this type of regulation is the gene for the enzyme amylase, which breaks down starch into sugars. Liver and salivary glands contain two different forms of the enzyme, which are specified by the same gene through two different RNA messengers.

The regulatory changes of the genes we have just discussed do not involve irreversible changes of the base sequences. In animals, however, the differentiation of lymphocytes (which will be discussed in chapter 13) is accompanied by structural rearrangements of the genes. Is it possible that other developmental steps also involve similar rearrangements?

An answer to this question has been sought by studying the developmental potential of whole nuclei derived from cells at various stages of development. The experiment was carried out in frog eggs: the nucleus of a fertilized egg cell was removed by microsurgery and was then replaced by a nucleus obtained from a tissue of another frog. The result was clear: if the grafted nucleus comes from a cell of a relatively young embryo, the egg will develop into a tadpole, which will then evolve into an adult frog through metamorphosis. Evidently in the young embryo the nucleus has not undergone any irreversible change. If, however, the nucleus is obtained from an adult frog, the reconstituted egg will develop only as far as a tadpole. It seems, therefore, that in frogs irreversible changes occur in later development. Similar experiments in the mouse have shown that irreversible changes occur much earlier, in the initial stages of development. We do not know the nature or the significance of these changes, however.

The Importance of Environment

The local environment has a profound influence on cell differentiation, probably by providing suitable signals either as cell contacts or differentiation factors. The role of the local environment is shown, for instance, by the fact that blood cells of various lineages can differentiate only at characteristic sites, such as the liver in fetal mice and the bone marrow in the adult. If an immature cell taken from an animal is injected into another mouse of the same inbred strain, it will proliferate and differentiate only if it reaches these same sites. Mice of some mutant strains do not supply the needed environment, and the cells injected into them fail to differentiate.

The development of many epithelial organs, such as the mammary and salivary glands, depends on substances supplied by cells derived from the middle layer of the embryo (mesoderm), which are generally known as mesenchyme (because they sneak between other cells). The mesenchyme determines the final destiny of the epithelial structure. For instance, epithelium of the mammary gland grafted to the mesenchyme of the salivary gland will develop a salivary gland architecture, and vice versa. The mesenchyme also determines the development of hair, feathers, or teeth. The reverse influence is also observed. For instance, if the embryonic mesenchyme destined to give rise to a tooth is covered by the epithelium of the skin of a limb bud, the tooth mesenchyme forms cartilage as if it were part of a limb. So the influence between mesenchyme and epithelium is reciprocal.

The importance of the local environment for cell differentiation is dramatically demonstrated by the extensive migrations of cells from the places where they are produced to those where they will differentiate. Most cells must move to the proper place to reach maturity; they know exactly when and where to go, following a well-determined path.

The migration of germ cell precursors—those cells destined to give rise to germ cells—has been studied for a long time because they can be easily recognized: they are much larger than other cells and have characteristic granules or pigments. In the early embryos (blastulas) of some amphibia they emerge from the lower part of the embryo, which is called the *vegetative pole*. (The upper part of the embryo, the *animal pole,* generates most of the body.) At gastrulation these cells move inside the embryo together with the inner layer (endoderm). Subsequently the germ cell precursors migrate to two ridges from which the gonads will develop, located between the ectoderm and the lining of an inner cavity (this lining is the future peritoneum). As they migrate, the germ cell precursors transiently adhere to the cells they encounter on their way, and move from one to the next. These contacts seem to direct their migration.

Another characteristic migration is that of cells of the neural crest, which is part of the neural fold (fig. 12.15). As they emerge from the neural lips the cells divide into two groups. Some follow the inner face of the outer layer of the embryo (ectoderm) in a lateral direction, away from the neural tube; they will become pigment cells (p in fig. 12.15) and will remain associated with the skin. Another group of cells penetrates deeply into the body of the embryo, crawling between the neural tube and the somites. Of these cells some stay close to the outer layer of the embryo and form the *sensory ganglia* (se in fig. 12.15); others proceed farther, reaching the notochord, and form the chain of the so-called *sympathetic ganglia* (sy in fig. 12.15). Other cells of this group proceed more deeply (ad in fig. 12.15) to

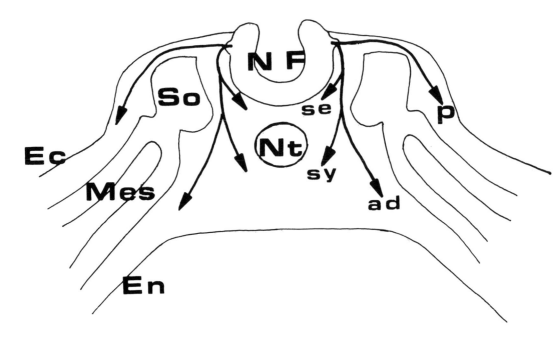

Figure 12.15. Migration of neural crest cells to various destinations in the vertebrate embryo. The migration pathways are shown by the thick lines and arrows. The cells give rise to pigmented cells (p), sensory ganglia (se), sympathetic ganglia (sy), and part of the adrenal gland (ad). NF = neural fold; Nt = notochord; So = somite; Mes = mesenchyme (middle layer) split into two sheets that enclose what will become the spaces surrounding the gut and the lung. Ec = ectoderm (outer layer), which will give rise to the skin, and En = inner layer, which will give rise to lung and gut.

form the central part, or *medulla,* of the adrenal gland. Cell migration is also extensive during the development of the brain, as will be discussed in chapter 18.

The significance of cell migration in development is obscure. The goal of some migrations may be to reunite cell types that were close to each other at a preceding stage of evolution, but later separated. Perhaps in their migration they retrace the steps followed during separation.

Migration is essential for differentiation because it leads the cells to places with a suitable local environment. Germ cell precursors or neural crest cells that stray out of their way and do not reach the proper target organ do not differentiate. In a strain of mice called black-eyed white, the neural crest cells do not migrate to the skin, so pigment-producing cells are not made, although their black eyes indicate that the mice have the machinery for making pigment.

Death as a Developmental Process

Although we are familiar with the fact that organisms die, we are not generally aware that individual cells may die in a healthy organism through a mechanism programmed by the genes. We observed earlier programmed death in the simple developmental system of the slime molds: the stalk of the fruiting body is formed by the bodies of dead cells. The precise programming of cell death is especially evident in the development of small nematodes, where the fate of all individual cells can be determined. That one of the daughter cells emerging from the division of certain cells always dies is not a matter of chance.

In many organisms entire organs develop and then die and disappear, dissolved by enzymes present in the cells themselves. Such massive cell deaths occur during metamorphosis; during the development of limbs, blood cells, and the nervous system in animals; and in the formation of compound leaves in plants. The mammalian kidneys pass through three successive stages, of which the first two are in large part eliminated by cell death.

Programmed cell death often occurs when a growth factor specific for the cells ceases to be made. Growth factors and certain hormones are in the first place survival factors; they are required for keeping the cells alive. An example is the mammary gland of female mammals, which shrinks considerably after lactation is ended. A great reduction of the amount of prolactin reaching the gland causes death of milk cells. At metamorphosis massive cell death is also caused by the disappearance or, in some cases, the new appearance of certain hormones.

Massive cell death may have evolutionary significance. In the development of the kidneys it characterizes the transition from one type of structure to another, reproducing the evolutionary transition from one form of kidney to another. In these cases the development of the individual recapitulates crucial stages in the evolution of the species. The death of organs in metamorphosing animals may have a similar meaning. The death of the primitive kidney is a kind of metamorphosis restricted to a single organ.

A Terminal Event

A special developmental step takes place in lineages that give rise to large numbers of cells performing the same function, such as red blood cells, muscle cells, or epithelial cells of the skin. In these lineages, the pattern of differentiation unfolds up to the penultimate step, generating reserve cells that can go only one step further. The reserve cells persist unchanged until upon demand of the organism a special signal makes them take the terminal step. For instance, a small protein, hemopoietin, signals the need for red cell production when red cells in the blood are insufficient to transport needed oxygen; this happens regularly at high altitudes. Hemopoietin causes the terminal differentiation of the reserve cells, the erythroblasts, to red blood cells. In many animals the red blood cells are produced by an unequal division of the erythroblasts. One of the daughter cells inherits most of the cytoplasm—including the hemoglobin but not the nucleus—and becomes a red blood cell. These cells remain in circulation until they become too old and are destroyed—again a programmed death.

In muscle tissue, terminal differentiation also involves a dramatic event: the reserve cells, the elongated myoblasts, fuse end-to-end, forming a long rod, a muscle fiber with a single cell membrane and many nuclei. Proteins needed for muscle contraction make their appearance within the muscle fiber and generate the complex structure characteristic of striated muscle (see chapter 17).

Terminal differentiation of reserve cells in cultures is well suited for studying changes of gene regulation. Cultures of these cells undergo terminal differentiation if they are exposed to certain chemical inducers, such as DMSO (dimethylsulfoxide). These substances have no obvious relationship to those that induce terminal differentiation in the animal. It is not clear how they work, but they cause terminal differentiation of essentially all the cells in the culture in a relatively short time and are therefore an important research tool. Much has been learned by using these substances. For instance, when precursors of red cells, erythroblasts, are induced by DMSO to differentiate into red cells, the production of several proteins is discontinued while that of others is started or enhanced. In the differentiation of muscle precursor cells to muscle fibers the amount of muscle proteins increases several hundredfold in each cell. In both cases the protein changes are due to changes in the transcription of the genes.

CHAPTER 13

Genes for Defense

In the previous chapter we saw, in a general way, how the genes control the regular, progressive unfolding of the developmental pattern of complex organisms. In this chapter we will consider the development of a single cellular system in detail: that of the immune system. This system, which plays a crucial role in the survival of animals in a competitive environment, develops in a fascinating way. Its operation involves complex interactions between cells and the most bewildering genetic mechanism encountered in the whole of biology.

Organisms of every kind are exposed to the attack of infectious agents, such as bacteria, viruses, or parasites, which try to invade and kill them. An unrelenting fight goes on all the time between the organism and its invaders, and in most cases one or the other must succumb. In the course of evolution animals developed very elaborate systems of defense against infectious agents—the immune system among them. Many types of cells take part in this defense, and many genes are devoted to it.

The immune system received its name from the long recognized fact that animals become immune, or resistant, to a virus or bacterium after they survive a first infection. The study of this phenomenon has revealed the system's marvelous properties: it can render an animal immune to a large number of invading germs; it has amazing specificity in its recognition of these agents; and it remembers previous encounters with an infectious agent for a long period of time. All these properties result from finely tuned interplays of various kinds of cells and from amazing genetic acrobatics.

Elements of the Immune System

The cells of the immune system are part of the larger system of the cells of the blood: the *hemopoietic* (blood-making) *system*. These cells are generated by stem cells that arise in the membranes surrounding the embryo; in the adult they are localized in the bone marrow or other specialized organs. The stem cells differentiate into various lineages. Among their descendants are the cells that ultimately generate both the red and the white cells of the blood. Two kinds of hemopoietic cells are essential for immunity: the *macrophages*, which have the ability to engulf germs and other small particles, and the *lymphocytes*, which perform the main function of immunity.

Macrophages

Central to the functioning of the entire immune system are macrophages. It is possible that they were the first type of defensive cells to appear in the course of evolution. Macrophages have extremely sticky surfaces, suitable for trapping infectious agents. The trapped material is swallowed by the cell, where it is killed by toxic molecules and dissolved by powerful enzymes. Macrophages play a further essential role in immunity because, as we will see below, bits of a disintegrated parasite are returned to their surface where they can interact with lymphocytes. Macrophages, moreover, release powerful substances that affect other cells, enhancing their ability to fight against infection.

The effectiveness of macrophages alone as defensive elements is limited by their inability to confer lasting resistance to recurring invasions by an agent. They have no memory of a previous encounter with an agent, and therefore they do not learn how to cope better with a renewed invasion.

Lymphocytes

Lymphocytes, which are known in great detail, derive their name from their abundance in the lymph, the liquid that bathes the cells of the body. After leaving the fine blood vessels and crawling among surrounding cells in the search for germs, they return to the main blood circulation through a special network of channels called the lymphatic vessels.

Lymphocytes are divided into two main groups, the B and the T lymphocytes, each made up of several subgroups. These two cell types play very different but equally important roles in immunity. The designations of B lymphocytes derive from studies in birds, in which these cells mature—acquire their final features—in the bursa, a kind of pouch connected to the intestine. In mammals, which do not have a bursa, the B lymphocytes mature in the bone marrow, but bones are unsuitable in birds because they are very slim and contain air sacs (see chapter 16). In birds as well as in mammals, T lymphocytes mature in the thymus, an organ in the chest.

In adult animals both types of lymphocytes are found throughout the body—in the blood, the lymph, the bone marrow, the spleen, along the intestine, and in the lymph nodes, which are stations along the lymphatic vessels. The thymus contains only T lymphocytes, but their production stops when this organ, which is very large at birth, essentially disappears in the adult. Different classes of lymphocytes reach various organs, their destination determined by the cells that line the walls of the organs' finest blood vessels. Lymphocytes of different groups recognize the surface molecules of these cells and use them for homing in on the organs. They adhere to the lining of the blood vessels and then cross their thin walls.

Antibodies

The immune system provides another form of defense against infectious agents—*antibodies*, special protein molecules made by B lymphocytes and present in the blood. Antibodies stick to molecules collectively called *antigens*, which are widely distributed; they are exposed at the surface of germs. The term *antigen* does not denote any special chemical constitution, only that the molecules are the targets of antibodies. When an infectious agent invades an animal, it elicits the formation of antibodies, which then bind to the antigens of its surface. This binding initiates a series of events that lead to the death of the agent. Many chemicals injected into an animal can also elicit the formation of antibodies and therefore are also antigens. All proteins, many complex sugars, and other substances have this property.

Each antibody molecule is made up of two equal parts, associated in the form of the letter Y (fig. 13.1: 1). They are held together in the stem, each part forming one of the arms. Antibodies have special patterns of amino acids at the tips of the two branches of the Y. They are the antigen-binding sites, also called *idiotypes* (meaning special sites). The two sites are identical in an individual molecule, but usually differ among molecules (fig. 13.1: 2). They are made in such a way as to fit exactly some chemical detail of the antigen, which we will call the antigenic spot, also known as the epitope (meaning the marker). The antigenic spot and the binding site fit into each other like a hand and its glove. Owing to this very close fit, an antibody binds strongly to the appropriate antigens. The close fit makes antibodies very selective: one that binds to, say, protein A does not usually bind to protein B, and vice versa. An antigen often has several antigenic spots and therefore can bind several different antibodies. An antibody molecule, in contrast, binds only one kind of antigenic spot because its two binding sites are identical. All the antibodies that can be produced in the body of an animal can bind to an enormous variety of antigenic spots of different chemical constitutions.

Some B lymphocytes release into the blood the antibody molecules they manufacture, but others hold onto them and display them on their surfaces with the binding sites sticking out. All the antibodies a lymphocyte presents at its surface or releases into the blood are identical: a lymphocyte makes only one kind. The antibodies stuck at the cell surface act as receptors for the antigen. This terminology is equivalent to that of hormone-responsive cells, which have receptors for the hormone. When antigen molecules bind to surface antibodies, a lymphocyte changes in important ways, which will be discussed later.

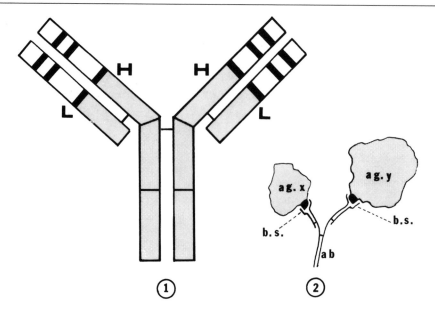

Figure 13.1. (1) General characteristics of an antibody molecule. The antibody is made up of four protein molecules, two identical heavy chains (H), and two identical light chains (L). Each chain is made up of a variable region (light) and constant region (gray). The light chain has a single constant domain; the heavy chain has three, which form the stem of the Y. In the variable regions are three highly variable complementarity-determining regions (black), separated by constant framework regions. (2) With its two identical binding sites (b.s.), an antibody binds two identical antigenic spots (black), which may be part of different antigens (ag. x and ag. y).

A Triple Cooperation

T lymphocytes, we suspect, were the second group of immune cells to appear in the course of evolution after macrophages. Especially important among them is a class called T helper lymphocytes, which are provided with receptors for antigens. In humans they are identified by a special glycoprotein known as T4. These T lymphocytes cannot be stimulated by an antigen directly, but only by an antigen that is attached to macrophages or other antigen-presenting cells. As we will see below, the cooperation between these two immune cells has profound implications. When stimulated by an antigen, T lymphocytes release powerful substances with defensive activity (see chapter 14).

The defensive system based on antibody production by B lymphocytes was probably the last to evolve. B lymphocytes respond to infectious agents in two ways. One response, which is of limited value, is based on the recognition of the repetitive molecular patterns that exist at the surface of many infectious agents. B lymphocytes are stimulated by the multiple contacts to both multiply and release antibodies. When a population of lymphocytes is activated in this manner by a certain agent, the released antibodies are a heterogeneous mixture of molecules with different binding sites, not necessarily related to the agent, which accounts for the response's limited defensive value.

The antibody-producing system reached its maximal development when it learned how to produce a highly specific response through the cooperation of a B lymphocyte with an antigen-presenting cell and a T helper lymphocyte (fig. 13.2). The triple cooperation occurs in two steps. First, the antigen-presenting cell captures the antigen, modifies it, and displays it on its surface. If the antigen is a

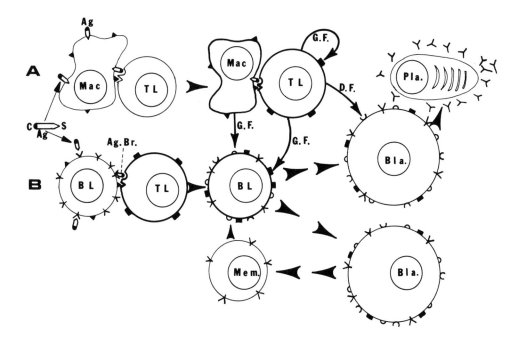

Figure 13.2. The triple interaction between macrophage (Mac), T. lymphocyte (TL) and B lymphocyte (BL). The interaction is initiated by antigen (Ag), in which we distinguish an antigenic spot (S) and a carrier region (C). (A) Antigen binds to a macrophage, with the carrier region sticking out. A T lymphocyte binds to it and to a surface molecule of the macrophages, which is a protein determined by major histocompatibility (MHC) loci (black triangles) (see chapter 14). The association activates the cells (shown by a thick outline). As a result they start producing growth factors (G.F.) and differentiation factors (D.F.), mostly for B lymphocytes. A growth factor acts on the T cells that produce it, causing their multiplication. (B) The activated T lymphocyte binds to the carrier region of an antigen bound to an antibody molecule on a B lymphocyte. The antigen is the bridge (Ag. Br.) between the two cells, in conjunction with the MHC protein. The B lymphocyte becomes activated (thick outline), and develops receptors for the growth and differentiation factors released by the activated macrophage and T cell. Under their influence the B cell becomes a blast cell (Bla.), which multiplies, forming a clone. Finally under the influence of differentiation factors, most blast cells differentiate into plasma cells (Pla.), whereas some become quiescent memory cells (Mem.). The plasma cells are characterized by an abundant endoplasmic reticulum (the thin elongated spaces) and release antibody molecules into the surrounding medium.

protein, it is presumably engulfed in vesicles and directed to lysosomes where it is broken down by enzymes. Surviving fragments are channeled back to the surface, where they are displayed. The details of this process, however, are not known. This step is essential because the T helper cells do not bind free antigen. Important among the antigen-presenting cells are macrophages. T helper lymphocytes with receptors suitable for the presented antigen become activated (fig. 13.2: A). In the meantime the antigen is also captured by B lymphocytes through their external immunoglobulins. The activated T helper lymphocyte interacts with the antigen-carrying B lymphocyte (fig. 13.2: B) and stimulates it to produce antibodies. The T helper lymphocyte is therefore the mediator between the antigen-presenting cell and the B lymphocyte for the purpose of antibody production.

The crucial role of the T helper cells explains the severe consequence of their destruction in the AIDS disease (acquired immunodeficiency syndrome). The virus is very selective for these cells, which it invades by using the T4 glycoprotein as the point of attack. Lacking T helper lymphocytes, these individuals cannot mount an immune response and will succumb to infectious agents, such as viruses, bacteria, or molds, that are common in the human environment but are ordinarily harmless for individuals protected by an efficient immune response.

The T and the B lymphocytes participating in such an interaction bind to the same antigen but not to the same part. For instance, if the antigen is a protein with a sugar attached, the T helper lymphocyte may recognize a piece of the protein itself, and the B lymphocyte, the sugar. This difference is described by saying that the receptors (antibodies) of the B lymphocyte bind to the antigenic spot of the antigen, whereas the receptors of the T lymphocyte bind to the carrier of the antigenic spot (fig. 13.2). The same carrier may be associated with several different antigenic spots; and through that carrier the same activated T cell may interact with different B lymphocytes bearing antibodies for different antigenic spots. The recognition of different parts of the antigen by the two types of lymphocytes is crucial in the generation of an immune response, because it allows the antigen to bridge, ideally, the two cell types during their interaction: the antigenic spot is bound to the receptors of the B lymphocyte and the carrier to the receptors of the T lymphocyte. The two parts of the antigen need not be connected, however; B lymphocytes can alter the antigen and present its carrier portion to the T lymphocytes just as macrophages do. The carrier portion then establishes the crucial connection between the B and the T lymphocytes, whereas the antigenic spot is bound only to the former.

The effects of the triple interaction are momentous. All three participating cells become activated, meaning that they acquire new properties. Both the macrophage and the T lymphocyte start producing many factors that are essential for the production of antibodies. The activated B lymphocytes respond to interaction with the antigen by proliferating. They become larger (blast cells) because they make lots of new RNA, protein, and DNA. Their proliferation leads to the formation of large clones of equal cells, all displaying the same antibodies. Most of the B lymphocytes of these clones undergo terminal differentiation into antibody-producing plasma cells (*plasma* meaning a fraction of the blood), which, instead of holding the antibody, release it into the blood in large amounts. The production of this antibody is called the *primary response* of the organism to the antigen.

MEMORY. The formation of the clones is responsible for another important aspect of immunity—the establishment of *immunological memory*. This event allows an animal to respond to a second infection with a prompter and more effective antibody response than to the first infection (*secondary response*). Immunological memory is the consequence of the formation of clones of both T and B cells with receptors for the antigen. A fraction of these cells avoid terminal differentiation and persist as memory cells for a long time (ten to twenty years in humans). If there is a new infection by the same agent, or an exposure to the same antigen, these cells are reactivated to multiply by a repetition of the same process that elicited the primary response. Because the memory cells are more numerous than are lymphocytes carrying the same receptors in individuals never infected, the secondary response is stronger and much more rapid than the primary response.

In an animal that has not experienced a certain infection, or that has never encountered a certain antigen, T and B lymphocytes with receptors for that antigen are present in very small numbers. We will see below how they are generated. The immune response is based on the selective proliferation of these cells under the influence of the antigen, which is called clonal selection. This concept—that the antigen causes the amplification of a preexisting clone of an antibody-producing lymphocyte—was revolutionary when McFarland Burnet introduced it to replace theories proposing that the antigen instructs the formation of specific antibodies. Selection of cells already containing the appropriate gene is the only possible mechanism: the antigen cannot remodel the genes.

EXCEPTIONAL ANTIGENS. The collaboration between the cells in the triple complex is crucial for an immune response to most antigens. Only some very large antigens, with many repeating groups, can bypass it and activate B lymphocytes directly, without T-cell help. Small antigens do not. The large repetitive antigens are probably effective because they can convey to B lymphocytes two kinds of signals similar to those they normally receive in the triple interaction (fig. 13.3). One signal is generated by the ability of repetitive antigens to bind to many receptors on the same B lymphocyte, presumably mimicking the activating effect of the T lymphocyte, which also establishes many connections with the B cell through antigen bridges. The other signal is produced by the repetitive antigen interacting with special receptors that stimulate the growth of the B lymphocyte; these cells can thus dispense with the growth factors normally provided by the macrophage and the T cell. Some types of repetitive molecules activate T lymphocytes instead of B lymphocytes.

We have said above that this method for activating B lymphocytes probably

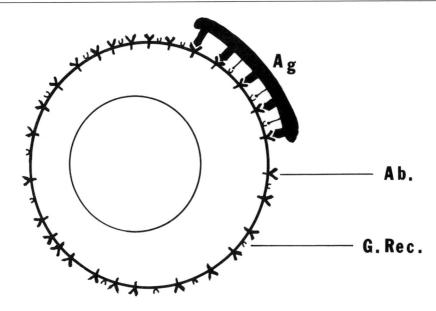

Figure 13.3. Activation of a B lymphocyte by an antigen with multiple identical antigenic spots. The lymphocyte has at its surface antibody molecules (Ab.) that serve as receptors for the antigen (thick black prongs). It has also other receptors that control the growth of the cell (growth receptors: G. Rec.). The antigen has chemical groups that can bind to these receptors as well. The repetitive antigen performs therefore two functions normally performed by T cells in conjunction with macrophages: it binds several surface antibody molecules at the same time, activating the lymphocyte, and causes it to grow by stimulating the growth receptors.

preceded, in evolution, the method based on the triple interaction. It is conceivable that the latter method developed subsequently in order to allow the production of antibodies in response to small antigens. Such a response is very important because many infectious agents produce extremely potent toxic substances, toxins, which are small molecules. Examples are the toxins produced by the bacteria responsible for diphtheria or tetanus. Antibodies to the toxins are essential for the survival of the animal: they bind to the toxins and neutralize them, rendering them ineffective. Moreover, during the invasion of an organism by a germ or a virus, small molecules of the surface of the infecting agent are released into the blood or between the cells in the tissues and organs. Utilizing these molecules as a signal for activating antibody production can greatly accelerate the defense of the organism.

SPECIFIC KILLER CELLS. Important for the defense provided by the immune system are other lymphocytes of the T class, the T killer lymphocytes, which differ from T helper lymphocytes in that they have a different marker glycoprotein, T8, instead of T4 (in humans). These lymphocytes kill parasites and even normal body cells if they are invaded by a germ or a virus. Like B lymphocytes, each T killer lymphocyte has many identical surface receptors capable of binding an antigen. Although they are not antibodies, they recognize antigens with a comparable discrimination. Like B lymphocytes, all the T lymphocytes of an organism have a vast repertoire; together they recognize many antigens and many germs.

A triple cooperation is also involved in the activation of the T killer lymphocytes. Their action is especially important in the case of invasion by viruses. When a virus invades an animal for the first time, it can rapidly infect a number of cells, which then become capable of releasing large amounts of new virus into the body. If these cells are allowed to release the viral progeny, the infection would become very serious, possibly unstoppable. The organism must kill the cells before new virus is released, a job performed by T killer lymphocytes. No disadvantage is incurred by killing these cells because they would be lost anyhow.

Like T helper cells and B lymphocytes, killer lymphocytes have special surface receptors through which each lymphocyte recognizes a certain antigen. Killer lymphocytes that recognize antigens of the invading virus bind to the viral molecules that stick out of the surface of the virus-invaded cells. For maturing and displaying the killing activity, killer lymphocytes must interact with T helper lymphocytes that recognize the same antigen, producing the needed growth-stimulating substances. As a result, clones of cells able to differentiate into T killer lymphocytes are formed. As in the case of B lymphocytes, some of the activated cells become memory cells, which persist for a long time. Upon a subsequent invasion by the same virus, these cells multiply and generate large numbers of killer cells ready to destroy the virus-infected cells.

In all the cell interaction discussed so far, certain special molecules present at the surface of cells are necessary partners. They will be considered in the next chapter.

The Problem of Recognition

We can now turn to one of the major problems concerning our understanding of the immune system: how do the antibodies recognize antigens? The problem is twofold. First, how does an antibody molecule recognize a certain antigenic spot and no others? Second, how is the large variety of antibodies necessary to recognize different spots generated? Modern biology's success in solving these two problems is one of its major accomplishments.

To understand the magnitude of these problems, we must realize that the number of different antigenic spots recognized by an animal's antibodies is immense—it is at least a million. They include not only spots on molecules naturally present in the living world but also those on many manmade molecules that never occur in nature.

To gain a deeper insight in both problems, we must consider the structure of antibodies. These molecules are among the most studied and best known in the whole of biology because they are very important and readily available: they constitute a substantial proportion of all protein molecules of the blood.

Antibodies were recognized chemically during studies of the composition of the blood before their function was known. They were identified as members of a group of proteins called globulins, and for this reason they are designated *immunoglobulins* (Igs). Further studies showed that they are made up of several classes which can be distinguished from one another on the basis of size and other properties. The various classes are identified by letters of the English alphabet, such as IgG—immunoglobulin G—or IgM—immunoglobulin M. We will see later their significance. Many attempts made to obtain immunoglobulins in pure form from the blood were frustrated, however, because even the best preparations seemed never to be quite pure; they would include heterogeneous molecules with somewhat different properties. This was surprising, because biological molecules, when available in sufficient amounts, can usually be readily obtained in pure form.

Help from Cancer

Help for unraveling this puzzle came from an unexpected source: a cancer of immune cells. Patients with an infrequent type of tumor of the bone marrow, multiple myeloma (the ending *-oma* designates a cancer), were found to have considerable amounts of an unusual protein in their blood. It turned out to be an immunoglobulin: the myelomas are cancers of antibody-producing cells.

A striking observation is that the immunoglobulin molecules produced by a myeloma and found in the patient's blood, in contrast to those present in the blood of normal individuals, are homogeneous and therefore can be obtained in pure form. However, myeloma immunoglobulins produced in different patients usually differ. A mixture of immunoglobulins of a certain class from different myeloma patients has the same heterogeneity as the immunoglobulin of the same class obtained from a normal individual.

These findings explained why the immunoglobulins of normal individuals are never identical. The key factor was the recognition that each cancer derives from a single cell—it is a clone. All the cells of a myeloma, being identical, make the same immunoglobulin. It was concluded that each cell of the normal immune system produces one immunoglobulin, and that different cells produce immunoglobulins that, even when similar in general features, differ in details, such as binding sites. The inference is that immunoglobulin molecules of the same class present in the blood of an animal are heterogeneous because they have different binding sites. The structural variety corresponds to the variety of antigenic spots they recognize.

These results, first obtained in humans, apply to all animals. For instance, myelomas of laboratory mice also produce pure immunoglobulins. These myelomas became an essential tool for studying the immunoglobulins in detail because they can be easily induced in some strains of mice by an injection of paraffin oil.

Immortalizing Immune Cells

Even more direct evidence for the inference that immunoglobulins recognizing different antigenic spots have slightly different structures was obtained by immortalizing individual immunoglobulin-producing lymphocytes. Normal lymphocytes have a very limited life span in cultures. Immortalization was accomplished in 1975 by George Kohler and Cesar Milstein, who fused B lymphocytes from the spleen of normal mice with cells of a mouse myeloma that does not produce an antibody (fig. 13.4). Fusion is accomplished by chemicals that join their membranes into a single membrane. In the fusion product, the hybrid cell, the two nuclei are at first separate, but then they also fuse. This cell inherits the

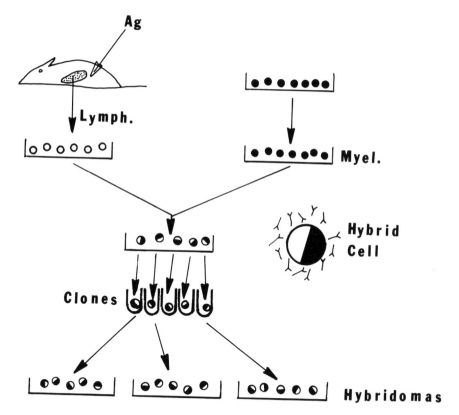

Figure 13.4. Production of monoclonal antibodies. A mouse is immunized by repeated injections of an antigen (Ag). Its spleen is then removed and the lymphocytes (lymph.) it contains are dispersed in a liquid culture medium. At the same time a culture of myeloma (Myel.) cells is prepared. The lymphocytes and the myeloma cells are fused together to yield hybrid cells. These cells have the genes of both cells involved in the fusion (shown as clear or black parts). They continually produce the antibody that was produced by the lymphocyte. Individual hybrid cells are separated into small containers filled with culture medium, where they grow, producing clones of hybrid cells: the hybridomas. Each hybridoma culture produces a homogeneous monoclonal antibody.

genes and the essential properties of both original cells. Like the myeloma cell, it is immortal and can multiply indefinitely; like the B lymphocyte, it produces a single type of antibody. Clones of the hybrid cells grown in the laboratory are known as *hybridomas*. They produce large amounts of the antibody that was originally produced by the fused B lymphocyte; the immunoglobulin is highly homogeneous, like those produced by myelomas. Hybridomas made with different lymphocytes from the same spleen produce immunoglobulins with different characteristics, which display the range of differences already observed with different myelomas.

If the spleen cells are obtained from an animal previously infected with a virus, each hybridoma produces an immunoglobulin known as a *monoclonal antibody* that recognizes just one antigenic spot of the virus. Different hybridomas obtained from the same spleen produce immunoglobulins that, even if they are of the same class, are slightly different and recognize different antigenic spots of the virus. This result confirms the correlation of the physical properties of the immunoglobulins with their ability to bind antigens.

Details of Organization

Using immunoglobulins produced by myelomas or hybridomas, it has been possible to learn precisely how they are made. We have already seen that each is made up of two identical arms, joined in the shape of a Y (fig. 13.1). Each arm in turn is made up of two chains of amino acids: a heavy chain with 440 amino acids (for most antibody classes) and a light chain with half that number. Each chain is made up of distinct domains of 110 amino acids, four for the heavy and two for the light chain, presumably generated in evolution from duplications and divergence of a primordial gene. In each arm the tips of the heavy and light chains together form the binding site. To which antigenic spot the antibody will bind depends on the amino acids constituting the two chains. Presence of positive or negative charges at various positions and various degrees of curvature and flexibility in either chain will determine the specificity.

Only one domain of each chain is important for antigen recognition: it is the *variable region* of each chain, which is appreciably different in immunoglobulins of the same class produced by different lymphocytes. The variable region of the heavy chain and that of the light chain together form the binding site. The rest of each chain constitutes the *constant regions*, which do not contribute to the specificity of the antibody. They are important for holding the four chains of an immunoglobulin together and for determining the class of the immunoglobulin and its role in immunity. These points will be discussed later.

Not the whole variable region is important for antigen discrimination, but only a small part of it. Studies of the sequences of amino acids showed that the binding site is made up of three short sequences (called *complementarity-determining regions*), which are highly variable in different immunoglobulins; they are separated by rather constant stretches (the *framework regions*) of amino acids, which are buried inside the molecule. The basis for antigen discrimination must be found in these small highly variable regions.

These findings raise important questions. How is the large number of specificities and of different amino acid sequences generated? Why are they confined to the three short regions?

The origin of the large number of different sequences is a problem for the genes, which specify the amino acid chains. Each immunoglobulin must be determined by at least two genes, one for the heavy, the other for the light chain. In order to account for the large number of different sequences, there should be many genes for each chain. The number would depend on how antigen discrimination is generated; if it is generated mainly by one chain, there should be a million or so genes for that type of chain in the mouse genome. If both chains contribute more or less equally—as one would expect to be the case, for reasons of economy—at least a thousand genes would be needed for each chain. These estimates would apply to one class of immunoglobulins, but there are several classes, differing in the heavy chain. Hence the estimate of the genes needed for specifying all the heavy chains must be increased accordingly, into the ten thousand range. To see whether this picture is correct, we must count the number of genes.

As we have seen in chapter 5, the number of genes can be counted using radioactive DNA probes. For immunoglobulin genes these are readily prepared from myeloma cells or hybridomas. When the genes are counted, however, the results are extremely surprising. In the DNA of mouse embryos or adult mouse liver, a probe corresponding to the variable region of a light chain detects about three hundred genes, whereas a probe corresponding to the constant region of the same chain detects just one. Even more startling is the finding that the DNA segments corresponding to the constant and the variable regions of the same chain are at distant places on the same chromosome. We reach the astonishing conclusion that in these DNAs there is no gene for a complete immunoglobulin chain, either light or heavy; there are separate genes for fragments of these chains. In contrast, a complete gene for each chain is regularly detected in the DNA of myelomas. The base sequence of this gene corresponds to the amino acid sequence of the immunoglobulin produced by the myeloma; undoubtedly it is the right gene.

Generating Diversity

These observations demonstrate that events never previously observed in any other biological system determine the great range of antibody specificities. The genome of germ cells does not contain any gene for a complete chain of an immunoglobulin, but only separate gene segments for each chain. When a cell differentiates to become a B lymphocyte, the various gene segments are brought together and assembled into the complete genes for the two chains.

The fascinating events that create the two genes in mice were pieced together by Susumu Tonegawa and collaborators working at the Basel Institute of Immunology in Switzerland. By cloning the genes or their segments from myelomas or embryos and comparing their sequences, they obtained the following results (fig. 13.5). In myeloma cells a light chain gene is made up of three separate segments present in the embryo at distant places on the same chromosome. The three pieces are a light chain *variable region segment* (V), corresponding to 95 amino acids; a *joining segment* (J), corresponding to 15 amino acids; and a *constant region segment* (C), corresponding to 110 amino acids. A light chain gene, therefore, is assembled as VJC. This is accomplished by excising considerable lengths of DNA between the segments or removing them to other parts of the genome. After assembly, the segments of the coding sequences continue to be separated by noncoding se-

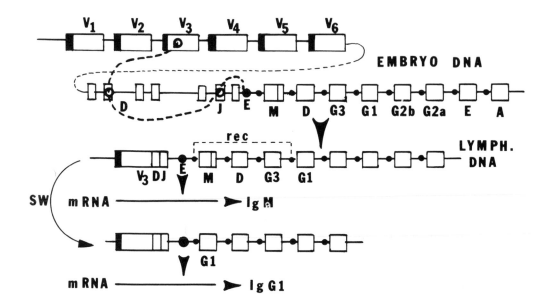

Figure 13.5. Rearrangement of the heavy chain genes. In the DNA of the mouse embryo there is a family of variable region segments (V), each with its own signal for initiation of transcription (black), a family of D segments, one of J segments, and eight constant region segments from M to A. Only six V genes are shown, but there are hundreds. In the lymphocytes, the first rearrangement selects one V segment (V₃ here), one D, and one J (as shown by the heavy dashed line), which are joined to the series of constant region segments. Between the J and the M segments is the enhancer (E) for the transcription of the gene. The assembled gene usually expresses an immunoglobulin of the M class because the transcription from the V segment reaches only as far as the end of the first constant region segment. The events leading to the assembly of a light chain gene are similar, except that there are no D regions. In the heavy chain gene a second rearrangement then causes a switch (SW) to another class, by removing the DNA in between. In the figure the recombination (rec), indicated by a dashed line, generates a gene that expresses immunoglobulin G1. The switch recombination occurs between special sequences—known as switch regions—that precede each constant region segment and are indicated by black dots.

quences which are reproduced in the transcript and are removed as intervening sequences when the RNA messenger is made.

The assembly of heavy chain genes occurs on another chromosome and is even more complicated: *joining segment* (J) links up with a *diversity segment* (D), which is not present in the light chain assembly; then this group links up with a heavy chain *variable region segment* (V) and finally a *constant region segment* (C). A heavy chain, therefore, is assembled as the complex VDJC. Although each D segment specifies only a small number of amino acids, the segments, nevertheless, are very important for the diversity of antibody specificities. In the assembled genes the D segments specify one of the highly variable complementarity-determining regions, which, as we have seen, are crucial for antigen discrimination.

The DNA rearrangements of the immunoglobulin genes are reminiscent of those of the coat genes of the trypanosomes that were discussed in chapter 6 and of the switch gene for the yeast mating type discussed in chapter 9; they are much more complex, however. They are probably produced by site-specific recombinations. The recombination sites are characteristic segments of seven or nine bases with nearly constant sequences, separated by spacers of characteristic length. The lengths of the sequences and of the spacers are probably related to the characteristics of the enzymes that carry out the exchanges.

The number of different immunoglobulins generated in this way is adequate to explain the large number of antigenic spots they recognize. We can easily see this in the mouse. This species has two gene systems for the light chain on two different chromosomes. One is the lambda gene system, which contains two V region segments and four J and four C segments; the other is the kappa gene system, which contains perhaps three hundred V segments, five J segments, and one C segment. There is a single gene system for the heavy chain on another chromosome. It contains perhaps two hundred V, over twelve D, four J, and eight C segments. The random assembly of V and J segments on the kappa chain can produce twelve hundred combinations, whereas the VDJ assembly on the heavy chain can give more than ten thousand different combinations. (The eight C segments do not count because they do not contribute to antigen recognition.) If an antibody molecule is formed by assembling a light and a heavy chain at random, some 10 million different antibody molecules can be generated in a mouse. This is more than enough to account for the large number of antigenic spots recognized by immunoglobulins.

The variability of the multiple V and D segments was generated in evolution. The characteristics of the base sequences show that the V segments were generated by duplications and subsequent diversification of a primordial gene. In this process the mechanism known as gene conversion seems to have played an important role, because many V segments contain short sequences identical to those of other segments.

The generation of diversity of antibodies does not end with the joining of the gene segments, however. This is shown by comparing the base sequences of the gene segments present in cells of mouse embryos with the amino acid sequences of the immunoglobulins produced by mouse myelomas. Some amino acids of the immunoglobulins are not in accord with the base sequences of the embryonic gene segments. These differences arise by various mechanisms. One is the imperfect joining of the various gene segments during recombination. Another is the occurrence of mutations during lymphocyte maturation. Mutations occurring in the cells of the body (or soma) are defined as *somatic;* they must be distinguished from *germinal mutations* which are already present in the germ cells. Most of the somatic mutations of immunoglobulin genes occur in the highly variable complementarity-determining regions and contribute to their variability. Some of these mutations are due to the insertion or deletion of a few bases at the V-D or V-J junction. Somatic mutations make an important contribution to antibody diversity. This is especially true in species such as humans in which the number of variable region genes is relatively small.

Evidently there is a special mechanism causing these somatic mutations, because they occur only at certain places. Moreover they are produced at a specific time—during the last stage of the maturation of antibody-forming cells. The mechanism is unknown: its unraveling is an important challenge to molecular biologists.

In summary, the fantastically useful antibody diversity is generated by several mechanisms. One is evolutionary diversification of the many gene segments present in the germ cells. Another is the joining of V segments with J and D segments at random. A third is imprecise joining of these segments. Finally, the fourth mechanism consists of somatic mutations. These variation-producing mechanisms affect mostly the highly variable regions and, consequently, the binding sites. The variation does not affect the general shape and stability of the molecules, which depend on the essentially invariable framework and constant regions.

These sources of variability can easily account for the formation of an enormous number of different immunoglobulins, which is probably much larger even than the number actually existing. In fact, some may never be expressed (see chapter 14). The variability of the highly variable regions, which are exposed at the surface of the binding sites, produces the diversity of antibodies and their great power of antigen discrimination.

It is interesting that several of these mechanisms, like the imperfect joining at recombination and the formation of mutations, are based on mistakes of DNA dynamics. As we saw in chapter 4, organisms have elaborate methods for controlling errors in DNA, but in the immune system these methods are abrogated in favor of generating diversity. Nature can use even errors to its advantage. In the present case errors are confined to well-defined segments of the genome and are produced only in somatic cells, sparing the hereditarily transmitted genes. But, as we will see in chapter 20, errors occurring in germ cells and transmitted hereditarily are also exploited by nature in the course of evolution.

The Gene Is Expressed

In the germ-line configuration the V and C segments are transcribed, but at a low rate. After a complete gene is assembled, it is transcribed at a high rate. Some transcription-promoting mechanism must become activated during the assembly of the gene. It turns out that the enhanced transcription is due to sequences known as enhancers (see chapter 4), one of which has been identified adjacent to C segments of the light and heavy chains (fig. 13.5). When the gene is assembled this sequence becomes incorporated in one of the intervening sequences of the complete gene, and does not therefore contribute to the amino acid sequence of the protein. From that central position the enhancer causes a rapid transcription of the gene, which begins at a start signal associated with the V segment.

An assembled immunoglobulin gene is transcribed only in lymphocytes: if it is introduced in a cell of a different kind, it is not transcribed. Several sequences are responsible for the cell-specific transcription: the enhancer, the start signals, and sequences within the gene. All these sequences, in turn, are controlled by proteins specified by other differentiation-specific genes which are active in B cells but not in other cells. This control explains why in the formation of hybridomas it is essential to fuse a lymphocyte to a myeloma cell rather to cells of other types. Myelomas are cancers of lymphocytes, and their genes permit the transcription of the immunoglobulin genes. Numerous previous attempts to generate hybridomas using as fusion partners cells not derived from lymphocytes regularly failed.

A crucial consequence of these findings is that when an organism is invaded by an infectious agent it already has cells capable of making antibodies against that agent. How did the organism know of the impending infection? The answer is that the organism did not know, but nevertheless had machinery ready to make antibodies against a large variety of agents. The organism did not create this machinery; it was created by the genes during the long process of evolution. The machinery, acting in a vast number of lymphocytes through an enormous number of combinations of the available gene fragments, builds an immense number of immunoglobulin genes, each able to produce a different antibody. This gigantic repertoire ensures that no matter what infectious agents or other foreign substance enters the body, some lymphocyte will make an antibody capable of binding to it. This particular lymphocyte is then picked out of the whole gamut of lymphocytes in the triple complex and is induced to multiply and to produce a large clone. In the meantime all other lymphocytes remain quiescent. The majority of them may never be called upon to perform their service during the life of the animal.

Thus when an organism mounts its defense in response to attack, the defenses have been planned long before, not only in their general characteristics, but also in the details of the defensive tools, the antibodies. The great variety of gene fragments required for making the vast repertoire of antibody genes was developed in evolution by the usual mechanisms that create gene families, such as the repeated doubling of genes, and their divergence through mutation, gene conversion, and recombination. Through the eons this process was probably influenced by the exposure of the organisms to a continually renewing variety of infectious agents coming from the outside. The need to cope with them directed, by selection, the spontaneous process of gene divergence, amplifying the useful genes and weeding out the useless ones. Selection continues to operate at a different level in the individual by the amplification of the cells with useful genes. But this process is essential only for the individual; it does not leave a trace in evolution.

A Single Binding Site

Surprisingly, in a clone of immunoglobulin-producing lymphocytes, all cells make immunoglobulins with only one kind of binding site. A lymphocyte with two homologous sets of chromosomes, each with its complete set of immunoglobulin gene segments, should be able to assemble two different immunoglobulins, one for each chromosome set. But, in fact, *a cell never assembles two functional genes* of either heavy or light chains with different binding sites. Only when the first assembly is abnormal, and does not end up in the synthesis of a functional chain, does a second assembly take place in the other chromosome. This is fairly common: mistakes during assembly are rather frequent because the DNA exchanges are complex.

Failure to assemble a second complete gene for either a light or a heavy chain reveals the operation of a regulatory mechanism aimed at the control of the immune response. Clear evidence was obtained by introducing a complete gene for a heavy or light chain of an immunoglobulin of the M class, the first assembled, into a fertilized mouse egg (see chapter 7): in many of the B lymphocytes of the host in which the injected gene was expressed, there was no D-J joining, which is the first step in heavy chain gene assembly. The presence of an assembled gene blocks a new assembly at the very beginning. The mechanism of this control is unknown, but its objective is clear: the manufacture of two heavy and two light chains, with different variable regions in the same cells would be very unfavorable. Each of the two heavy chains would bind one of the two light chains at random, producing four different binding sites: the cell clone formed under stimulation by an antigen recognized by one of the four immunoglobulins would produce 75 percent of useless protein. Moreover, many antibodies would have two different binding sites, decreasing their efficiency.

Another regulatory mechanism ensures that the rearrangement of the heavy chain gene takes place before that of the light chain gene. This regularity may reflect the evolution of immunoglobulins. It seems likely that the heavy chain developed first because some can recognize the surface of certain bacteria by themselves. Moreover, in many antibodies the heavy chain carries most of the specificity for antigen recognition.

Differentiation of B Lymphocytes

These molecular events are part of the developmental program through which B lymphocytes reach maturity (see fig. 13.6). Part of this program unfolds in the absence of a foreign antigen. The first gene assembly, involving the heavy chain gene, takes place in *pre-B cells,* and causes the assembly of the IgM heavy chain gene (as VDJC). This gene is always of the M class. Heavy chains accumulate in the cytoplasm. Then pre-B cells give rise to *immature B cells,* in which light chain genes also become assembled; complete antibodies of the M class are made (called IgM) and remain attached to the surface membrane with the binding sites sticking out. Finally *mature B lymphocytes* appear; they are small cells with the antibodies at their surfaces. Each cell contains antibody molecules of one specificity, but now they are of two classes, IgM and IgD. These cells are in the G0 phase of the growth cycle (see chapter 12); they persist as small lymphocytes until the antigen they recognize enters the body. They become activated in the triple complex, moving to the G1 phase.

In the process of manufacturing all the proteins needed for multiplication and further differentiation, these cells become blast cells, multiply, and, as we have already seen, form B cell clones. After the cells cease multiplying, some persist as small memory cells for future use; the majority differentiate into plasma cells, which represent the terminal state of B lymphocyte differentiation. Each plasma cell releases large amounts of immunoglobulins which have the same binding site as was expressed in the original immature B cell; the heavy chain, however, and therefore the class of the antibodies may differ in various groups of plasma cells derived from the same original B cell. We will see below how this happens.

Throughout the life of the individual new pre-B cells are produced all the time. In them new heavy and light chain genes are assembled, giving rise to new and different immunoglobulins. The repertoire of available antibodies, therefore, is continuously renewed. Memory cells, which recognize antigens to which the organism has been exposed, persist unchanged. The result is that new opportunities for recognizing antigens continually arise, but the specificities that have already proved useful persist. It is a very efficient way to utilize the potential built into the system that generates antibody diversity.

If an antigen is repeatedly administered, the antibody produced evolves, becoming more effective and binding the antigen more strongly. The shift is due to the replacement of the early clones of antibody-forming B lymphocytes with new ones. The shift probably occurs because the newly injected antigen is rapidly bound by antibodies in the blood, which prevent it from reaching the memory

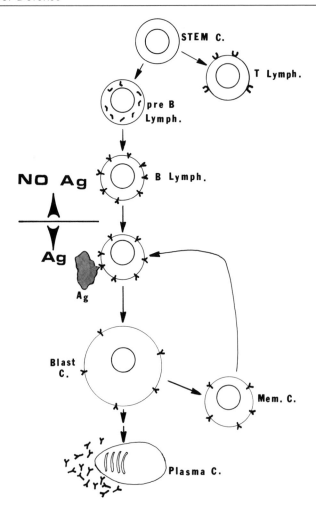

Figure 13.6. Evolution of cellular types in the immune response. In the absence of antigen, stem cells differentiate into both B and T lymphocytes. The assembly of antibody genes begins in pre-B lymphocytes. They produce only the heavy chain of an immunoglobulin, which accumulates in the cytoplasm. This cell then develops into a quiescent B lymphocyte, which has genes for both chains, and produces complete antibody molecules and displays them at its surface. It does not release them into the blood. When antigen (Ag) arrives, one of its antigenic spots binds to the immunoglobulin displayed by a lymphocyte and stimulates it to form a clone, as was outlined in figure 13.2. Most of the clones differentiate into plasma cells. Some of the lymphocytes become memory cells.

lymphocytes displaying the same antibody. They are not stimulated to multiply and produce more antibody. B lymphocytes displaying better antibodies can capture the antigen by displacing the already bound antibodies; the cells are activated and multiply, and produce the new efficient antibodies. These more efficient clones are in part formed from preexisting clones by somatic mutations, and in part are new clones generated by new gene rearrangements. In the mouse they tend to have K light chains, which are more variable because they have a larger number of V segments to choose from.

Switching from One Chain to Another

We have seen that in the mouse the heavy chains (of the M class) made in immature B cells remain bound to the cell membrane. After the antibody binds to the appropriate antigen, the cells multiply, and instead of holding onto their IgMs, they start releasing them into the blood. Then other changes happen: most cells switch to producing immunoglobulins with the same binding site but with different heavy chains. The molecular mechanisms underlying these puzzling changes have been ascertained, and they turn out to be fairly simple (fig. 13.7).

The switch from membrane-bound to released IgM is caused by changes in the processing of the transcript. The IgM is first held in the lymphocyte membrane because like many other membrane proteins, the M heavy chain possesses an anchor sequence (fig. 13.7: 2). Release of IgM occurs after a different processing of the RNA transcript for the heavy chain removes the anchor sequence. The protein goes clear through the membrane (fig. 13.7: 1). The change in processing may be due to a change of the enzymes that carry it out or of substances that control it.

The switch to new immunoglobulin classes is revealed by the *appearance of both IgM and IgD* (with the same binding site) in the same lymphocyte. This shift is also caused by a different processing of the RNA transcripts. The mouse contains eight constant region segments of the heavy chain called M, D, G3, G1, G2b, G2a, E, and A close to each other in that order. We will indicate them as C_M, C_D, and so on. In other animals there are equivalent segments, but the nomenclature is different. The class of each immunoglobulin is determined by the constant region segment that is joined to J. In mature B lymphocytes not exposed to antigen, J is joined to C_M. The RNA transcripts made in these cells include, however, the C_D sequences—that is, they are $VDJC_MC_D$ (fig. 13.7). In lymphocytes that produce both IgM and IgD, transcripts are processed to generate sometimes $VDJC_M$, sometimes $VDIC_D$ in the same cell (fig. 13.7: 3). By a similar mechanism some rare cells may even make three antibodies of the same specificity with different heavy chains, when the transcript extends further into the series of constant region segments.

The switch from the production of IgM to that of IgG or other kinds of immunoglobulins is usually the result of a *second DNA rearrangement* of the heavy chain gene (see fig. 13.5). This is again produced by a site-specific recombination between characteristic switch sequences that precede each constant region segment. Most frequently the new rearrangement connects J to one of the four C_G constant region segments, usually C_{G1}, eliminating the intervening C_M and C_D segments. Then IgG1 is made. Switching to production of IgE or IgA occurs by removing a longer DNA segment, which includes C_M, C_D, and all the C_G genes. How a certain

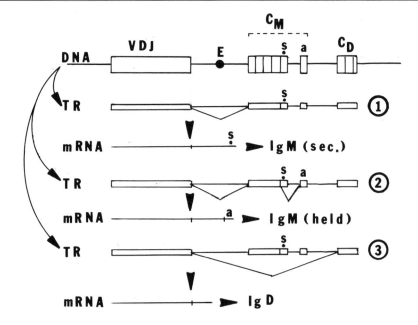

Figure 13.7. Mechanism of the change from retained to secreted immunoglobulin. The gene resulting from the first rearrangement is shown at the top (most of the constant region segments are left out). The M and the D constant segments (indicated as C_M and C_D) have several coding sequences separated by intervening sequences shown as lines. One of the C_M coding sequences contains a triplet that generates a stop signal (s) for translation; another contains an anchor sequence (a). The DNA is translated into a transcript (TR) that is identical in all cases. What differs is the splicing of the transcript. (1) VDJ segment is spliced to C_M. The RNA messenger (mRNA) contains the stop signal s; the protein made, IgM, does not contain the anchor sequence and is secreted. (2) An additional splicing removes the stop signal and incorporates the anchor sequence (a). The IgM is made and retained in the cell membrane. (3) The splicing entirely removes the M gene, connecting VDJ to C_D. The protein made is IgD.

constant region is selected in individual cells is unknown. The choice reflects the state of differentiation of the cells, which is controlled by many external factors, including interaction with other cells and antigens. After the rearrangement, the RNA transcripts retain the same initial part, but terminate at the end of the first constant region segment connected to J. Different rearrangements may take place in lymphocytes of the same clone, which then yields immunoglobulins of a single specificity but of different classes.

Immunoglobulins: Jacks of All Trades

Why are there so many different classes of immunoglobulins? This has to do with their many functions. The simplest function is to recognize the antigen and bind to it, as antibodies recognizing viruses or bacterial toxins do. The toxin or the virus are neutralized—they are made harmless by the antibody itself. To protect humans against tetanus, for instance, antibodies that recognize the toxin (produced in horses) are injected immediately after an infection has occurred, affording short-term protection. Long-term protection requires vaccination—the injection of chemically altered toxin, which is nontoxic but capable of conferring immunity. Within a few weeks, specific antibodies and memory cells capable of long life are produced.

In other infections the antibodies act by more indirect mechanisms that involve other molecules or cells. The class of the heavy chain determines which one of these functions the antibody will perform, confirming the great functional and evolutionary significance of this chain. We will now look at some specific examples.

IgG: Lethal Signal

The binding of antibodies to bacteria infecting an animal has little effect in itself, but it leaves the bacteria prey to macrophages, which gobble them up. Macrophages have surface receptors for the constant regions of some immunoglobulin heavy chains, especially of the G2a class, regardless of the specificity of their binding sites. These receptors can also recognize other immunoglobulins, but only if they form bundles by binding to adjacent antigenic spots on a bacterial surface. When antibodies bridge a bacterium to a macrophage, the macrophage swallows the bacterium and destroys it by using its enzymes.

Certain bacteria, such as those causing tuberculosis or leprosy, present a special problem. Like other bacteria, they are engulfed by macrophages, but because they are protected by a tough waxy coat, they resist the dissolving enzymes. Animals, however, have a remedy for this complication. A special class of T helper lymphocytes, stimulated by bacterial antigens displayed by the infected macrophages, release powerful substances that activate the macrophages to become much more potent bacterial killers; they also activate other defensive mechanisms. These special T helper cells are responsible for a test commonly employed by physicians to detect a current or past tubercular infection. Tuberculin, an extract of tubercle bacilli, is injected into the skin. An individual who has been previously infected has tuberculin-specific T helper cells; they become activated by the injection to produce a secondary response within ten to twelve hours. The substances released by the T cells cause reddening and swelling of the skin at the injected site; with time these changes become more pronounced, reaching a peak in two to three days and then slowly subsiding. This phenomenon is known as *delayed hypersensitivity* because of the long time it takes for the changes to develop; the special T helper cells are called *T cells of the delayed hypersensitivity type.*

IgM and IgG: Activating Complement

Another consequence of the binding of antibodies to a bacterial surface is the activation of the *complement system*—a system of proteins that are capable of assembling into small rings, which penetrate the cell membrane and act as ionophores. The insertion of the rings causes cell death by eliminating the ionic difference between inside and outside that is crucial for cells' survival.

The rings are assembled according to the general principles already discussed for the assembly of a phage (see chapter 2). The complement system is made up of more than twenty distinct proteins dissolved in the blood, which are normally inactive because each has a safety plug, a short amino acid sequence that blocks its activity. The system is activated by antibody molecules of the proper class bound to an antigen. Unbound antibodies are ineffective; otherwise they would activate the complement system in the blood. Binding to the antigen evidently produces a considerable distortion of the structure of the whole antibody molecule, which reaches as far as the stem of the Y. Proteins of the complement system recognize the distorted constant region of the heavy chain, starting a chain reaction with complicated ramifications. Each protein of the system is in turn activated to cleave the safety plug of the next protein. Many molecules of the last activated protein become bound together in the cell membrane and form the ring, which spans the fatty layer of the membrane. This penetration occurs because fat-seeking parts of the proteins are unmasked while they are assembled. The activation of complement has also other effects, such as activating macrophages and attracting other defensive cells. Altogether these effects conjure up a powerful defensive action.

Only antibodies of some classes (IgM, IgG1 or IgG3 in mice) are able to activate the complement system. IgM molecules can act individually, but IgG molecules must be present in clusters. The need for clustering shows that the complement system is specifically designed for attacking infectious agents that have many identical antigenic spots on their surface. IgM molecules, when bound to an antigen, can act individually because each is a cluster of five immunoglobulins held together by a joining protein. The requirement for clustering is also a safety feature preventing accidental activation of the complement systems on unbound antibodies which are normally single.

IgA: Immunoglobulins in Body Secretions

Immunoglobulins are not found only in the blood or the lymph; they are also present in essentially all secretions such as those of the nose, stomach, gut, and mammary and salivary glands, and in the bile produced by the liver. The antibodies are secreted by the epithelial cells of the various glands. All secreted immunoglobulins are of the same class, IgA, and are produced by lymphocytes present near the secreting epithelium. Before being released from the lymphocytes, the same joining protein used by IgM connects these immunoglobulins into pairs. The pairs, through the joining protein, bind to receptors present at the surface of the epithelial cells (fig. 13.8): single immunoglobulins lacking the joining protein do not bind. A receptor with the attached antibody is internalized into the cell within a membrane-bound vesicle that travels to the other part of the cell. There the

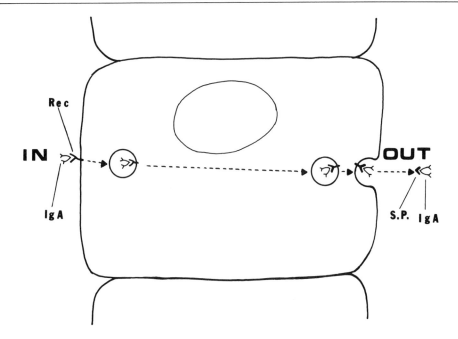

Figure 13.8. Transepithelial transport of IgA. The figure represents a section through an epithelium running up and down. The various cells are sealed to each other, preventing the passage of molecules from inside the body (IN) to the outside (OUT). OUT could be the lumen of an alveolus producing milk in the breast, or the lumen of the gut. IgA molecules produced as pairs connected by a joining segment at the IN side of the epithelium bind to receptors (Rec). Then the membrane holding the receptor-antibody complex is internalized as a vesicle, which travels to the opposite side of the cell. There it fuses with the cell membrane, and the receptor-antibody complex is exposed to the outside. An enzyme cuts the receptors into two parts, of which one remains with the cell membrane, and the other goes free with the IgA double molecule. The latter part of the receptor is known as a secretory piece (S.P.).

vesicle fuses with the cell membrane, and the receptor with the attached antibody is externalized. Finally an enzyme cuts off the receptor, releasing the antibody, with a piece of receptor attached, from the membrane. The piece of receptor is known as the secretory piece.

The main role of IgA, which is secreted when antigen reaches the secreting cells, is to bind to bacteria, preventing them from reaching and damaging the epithelium. IgA, therefore, *is the first line of defense against infectious agents* reaching the organism through the mouth, nose, and so on. IgA can also clear the blood of bacteria that have invaded the body. The bacteria, together with the bound antibody, are taken up by liver cells and secreted into the bile, using the same pathway followed by the antibodies themselves. IgA antibodies in the breast secretion (colostrum) at the beginning of lactation have the important role of protecting the newborn from gut infections. This is essential in many animal species, such as the human, in which the newborn is immunologically immature and for some time cannot mount an immune reaction of its own. The newborn is also protected by antibodies, mostly of the IgG class, which were transferred to the blood of the fetus by the mother during pregnancy.

IgE: Allergy

The well-known phenomena of allergy are caused by special blood cells, the most important of which are the *basophyls* (so called because they are stained by basic dyes). These cells have receptors that capture IgE antibodies after they are released by the producing lymphocytes (fig. 13.9). The basophyls strongly hold the antibody molecules through the stem of the Y, leaving the arms and the binding sites free. Immunoglobulins of other classes are not captured and do not contribute to allergic phenomena.

An antigen entering the body for the first time may elicit production of IgE antibodies, without other immediate consequences. The antibodies, however, are captured by basophyls and other cells, which then lie in wait. When at some later time there is a new influx of the same antigen, it finds basophyls with the appropriate IgEs on their surface and binds to them. The binding causes an instantaneous and very strong reaction. Vesicles stored in the basophyl's cytoplasm immediately release their contents, which include several very active substances, such as histamine. These substances cause fluid leakage from the fine blood vessels and contraction of smooth muscles in the small air ducts of the lungs.

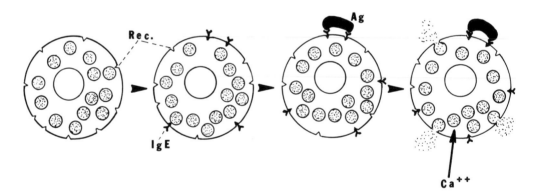

Figure 13.9. The basis of allergy. At left we see an unarmed basophyl; it has surface receptors (Rec.) for IgE, and contains many vesicles loaded with histamine and other substances. When IgE is produced, it sticks to the receptors through the stem of the Y. The basophyl is now armed, but causes no effect. When an antigen (Ag) recognized by the IgE molecules reaches the cell, it cross-links two IgE molecules already bound to receptors. This is the signal for the release of the contents of the granules. The release is mediated by the entry of calcium ions (Ca^{++}) into the cell, which causes the vesicles to fuse with the inner side of the cell membrane, releasing their contents to the outside. If Ca^{++} entry is prevented by blocking their channels through the cell membrane, the release of the vesicle contents does not occur. This is the mechanism of action of some anti-asthmatic drugs.

IgE bound to basophyls and other cells is the key to the allergic phenomena of anaphylactic shock, hay fever, or formation of hives on the skin. After a first exposure to the antigen, basophyls with IgE antibodies at their surfaces are present in all tissues of the body. The form taken by the reaction upon a new exposure to the antigen depends on how the antigen enters the body, because only basophyls encountering the antigen are activated. If the antigen is injected, especially intravenously, it activates basophyls throughout the body, causing within a few minutes an anaphylactic shock through massive loss of fluid from capillaries altered by histamine. Guinea pigs, which are especially sensitive to this reaction, can be killed within minutes. By the same mechanism, a bee sting can cause severe anaphylactic shock in a sensitized human. Hay fever is most frequently produced by pollen, which reaches the bronchi and the lung through the air, and reacts locally with basophyls laden with antibodies. The result is the contraction of the muscles of small air ducts (asthma) and an alteration of capillaries along the respiratory tract, with enhanced fluid secretion. Hives follow the local injection of antigen into the skin and are caused by the rapid but localized flow of liquid out of the small blood vessels. This phenomenon is the basis of a test for identifying the substances to which a person may be allergic.

The strength of the IgE production in response to an antigen varies greatly from one antigen to another and also depends on the method of immunization. It is greater if the antigen is in very small amounts: thus a person may become allergic to pollen after being exposed to no more than one-millionth of a gram in a whole year. These extremely low doses induce allergy because they elicit very little production of IgG antibodies. If IgG were present when the antigen was re-introduced, it would bind to it, blocking it before it reached the IGE-producing lymphocytes; the allergic reaction would then be prevented. The balance between production of IgG and IgE is maintained, presumably, by suitable regulatory T cells (see chapter 14).

The production of IgE varies also in intensity in different species and in different individuals of the same species, owing to genetic differences. Individuals with a high IgE production are more prone to develop allergic responses. Guinea pigs are among the highest IgE producers. These differences depend on the pattern of the second switching in the formation of the immunoglobulin heavy chains.

It seems strange that animals should produce an immunoglobulin with such damaging effects. IgE, however, is produced for very good reasons. A clue is that IgE is very high in the blood of individuals harboring certain parasites, such as intestinal roundworm. This correlation reveals another property of basophyls and other cells that bind IgE: after they bind the antigen, they release, together with the factors already mentioned, substances that attract parasite-attacking cells. Thus the production of IgE, like that of all other immunoglobulins, has a defensive value. Individuals who, under the present conditions of good hygiene, bear the burden of annoying or debilitating allergies would be privileged under more natural conditions of extensive infestation with parasites.

CHAPTER 14

Essential Signals

During the course of evolution the genes invented the marvelous devices described in the last chapter for defending organisms from invading infectious agents. But the devices by themselves are not enough: they must operate without upsetting the balanced performance of the organism. We will now see how the many constraints introduced by the genes achieve this purpose. The controls, based on a system of signals between cells, can be used as a paradigm for the probable operation of other complex cellular systems.

Several kinds of interactions between cells control the performance of the immune system. Some are *contacts* between cells; others are *substances* produced by cells of one type and acting on another type. We have seen in the previous chapter that contacts between antigen-presenting cells, such as macrophages carrying antigen molecules, and T helper lymphocytes select T lymphocytes with receptors for the antigen. In the contact both cell types are activated to produce substances which, although not made before, are needed for the further unfolding of the immune defense. In another stage, interaction between T helper lymphocytes and B cells, both recognizing the same antigen, selects the proper B lymphocyte. At this stage substances produced by activated T helper cells and macrophages act on the B lymphocytes, stimulating them to multiply and differentiate. Other interactions, again involving T helper cells, generate T killer lymphocytes. These lymphocytes, in turn, kill their target cells after establishing extensive contacts with them. The killer cells then inject proteins that assemble into rings in the membrane of the target cells. These rings, similar to those formed by complement (see chapter 13), act as indiscriminate ion channels; the loss of the ion gradient kills the cells. So both contacts and chemical communicators control the operation of the immune system.

Mediator Molecules

All the interactions between cells of the immune system involve a great deal of selectivity. They occur not between just any two cells, but only between cells identified by *pairs of surface structures,* which form bridges between the interacting cells. In the interaction between a T lymphocyte and an antigen-presenting cell (such as a macrophage), one of the structures is the antigen presented by the macrophage, which binds to the antigen-recognizing receptors on the T helper cell. The second structure, which we have not yet described, is made up of molecules belonging to the so-called *major histocompatibility complex (MHC);* they are present at the surface of the macrophage and also bind to the receptors on T lymphocytes (see chap. 13, fig. 13.2). The interaction of these two surface structures with the receptors has a different significance. Recognition of the antigen selects the T lymphocytes capable of recognizing the antigen and causes their clonal expansion. The recognition of the MHC molecules by the T cell receptors is an absolute requirement for the success of the previous interaction. MHC molecules and their receptors are like a lock and key: if they fit the lock, the interaction involving the antigen can take place; otherwise it cannot.

The existence of the MHC surface proteins was discovered by studying how skin can be grafted from one animal to another. It was found that if the donor and the recipient are two animals taken at random from a natural population, the graft is usually rejected. Within a few weeks the transplanted skin sloughs off and is replaced by a scar and by host skin growing in from the edges of the wound. Skin rejection is an immunological phenomenon mediated by T killer lymphocytes. If a new transplant is later made, it is rejected even faster, showing the establishment of immunological memory.

The basis of graft rejection was understood using inbred mouse strains, prepared by strict brother-sister matings over a large number of generations. Animals of an inbred strain are genetically identical; different inbred strains differ in a number of genes. These strains are important for studying and mapping mouse genes. Animals of one strain are interbred with those of another strain different in recognizable genetic characteristics; the distribution of these characteristics in the progeny defines the arrangement of the genes.

An important outcome of these studies was that skin can be successfully grafted between two animals that have identical forms of genes located in a well-defined chromosome region. This region was called the major histocompatibility locus (*locus* means that it contains several genes with related functions; *histocompatibility* means compatibility of tissues). Some of the genes of this region specify the MHC proteins of the cell surface. The proteins themselves were first identified with the help of antibodies produced by mice of one strain immunized with cells of another strain differing at a single MHC gene. Later many of the genes present in the locus were fully characterized using the technology of genetic engineering. As a result of this work we know that the MHC locus contains several families of genes, each performing a different function.

Diversity of Mediators

The use of inbred mouse strains for studying MHC proteins and their role in the interactions between immune cells was based on the fact that each MHC gene exists in a large number of slightly different forms (alleles) in any animal species. This diversity, known as *polymorphism*, is the result of evolutionary modification of an ancestral gene by mutation or by recombination or gene conversion between genes of the same family. A slightly different protein corresponds to each form (or allele) of the same gene. Within a given animal as well as within different animals of the same inbred strain, the MHC proteins are identical. But within a natural population the chance that two animals taken at random have the same form of the gene, and therefore the same MHC proteins, is very small. By taking advantage of these relationships, investigators have shown that all the interactions that take place in the immune system are critically dependent on the types of MHC protein present on the interacting cells. This dependence gives rise to two main phenomena in which the role of MHC proteins is apparently opposite. One is that killer lymphocytes of one mouse strain will kill cells of another strain with *different MHC protein*, as in skin grafts. The other phenomenon is that the killer lymphocytes specific for the antigen of a virus will kill cells with *the same MHC protein* infected by that virus, but will not touch cells infected by the same virus if they have a different MHC class I protein. These killer cells are said to be MHC restricted.

These results obtained with mice can be generalized to all vertebrates. Proteins corresponding to two families of MHC genes are needed for the interactions involving cells of the immune system. They are designated as class I and class II MHC genes. The interaction of T helper lymphocytes with macrophages involves mainly the products of class II genes; that of T killer lymphocytes with their target cells involves the products of class I genes.

Further refinements of these experiments showed that in the killing of virus-infected cells what is required is not *identity* of MHC proteins on the interacting cells, but *compatibility* between the MHC protein of the target cell with receptors of T killer lymphocytes whose role is to recognize that protein.

T Lymphocytes "Learn"

T lymphocytes derive from stem cells present in the bone marrow, from which B lymphocytes also derive. Immature T cells migrate in small numbers to the thymus, which provides the environment appropriate for their full development. There they multiply extensively and reach maturation into the various forms of T lymphocytes, such as helper or killer cells. During the process of maturation they "learn" to display receptors compatible with the MHC proteins present on cells of the thymus (the "self" MHC proteins, meaning those of the same individual). This phenomenon of learning has interesting consequences. For instance, the cells of a mouse derived from two parents of which one has the form A of a class I MHC gene, and the other the form B have both proteins: they are AB. Their T killer lymphocytes end up with receptors compatible with both proteins, A and B. Another interesting consequence is that T lymphocytes can be induced to display abnormal receptors when bone marrow cells—containing the immature lymphocytes—of an animal with the form A of a class I protein are transferred into an animal expressing a protein of form B (fig. 14.1). The immature T cells will migrate to the

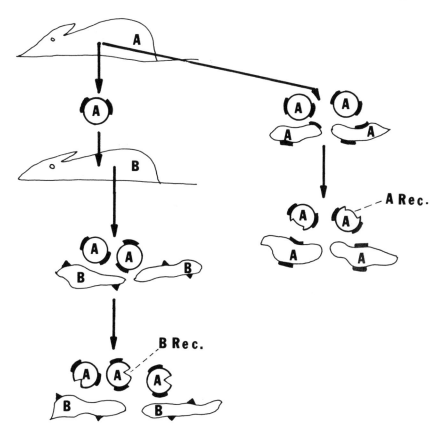

Figure 14.1. Influence of the cellular environment on MHC receptors displayed by immune cells. Immature cells of the immune system (shown as round) taken from a mouse with the A form of a gene for the mHC locus express A-type proteins on their surfaces (black rectangles). They have no receptors for the proteins. If they are left in the same mouse (right-hand branch), where they are surrounded by cells (shown as elongated) also displaying the A protein, they mature developing receptors for A protein (A Rec., shown as rectangular indentations). If on the contrary they are transplanted to a mouse with the B form (left-hand branch), they develop among cells displaying B protein (shown as triangles) and will mature developing receptors for B protein (B Rec., shown as triangular indentations); but they continue to display the A protein on their own surfaces.

host's thymus where they will develop into T killer cells with receptors for form B MHC protein. They will kill virus-infected cells expressing a class I protein of form B, but not A, as they would have done had they stayed in the animal in which they originated. These confused killer lymphocytes, although recognizing B molecules as "self," continue to express their original A molecules at their surfaces. Normally this complexity does not occur because lymphocytes carry receptors for the MHC proteins of their own body, which are the only ones they see during maturation.

The adaptation of T lymphocytes, regardless of their origin, to become compatible with molecules present on cells of the same individual is fundamental for the operation of the immune system. It allows the various cell types of the same individual to interact, producing an immune response, ridding the organism of germ-infected cells, and respecting the normal cells of the body.

This compatibility is evidently of great biological significance; how it develops, however, we don't know. While the compatibility develops in the thymus, the presence of antigen-presenting cells is obligatory, suggesting that the mechanism is related to that by which T or B lymphocytes are stimulated to multiply in the triple complex—that is, a clonal selection. Perhaps cells recognizing through their receptors the self form of MHC proteins are stimulated to multiply, whereas T cells with other receptors are destroyed. We will come back to this point later.

No matter how T lymphocytes learn, the result is that, when interacting with cells of the same organism, they must recognize *both* the foreign antigen and the appropriate MHC molecule: they must have a double recognition. Two types of MHC molecules are the obligatory recognition signals: class II proteins in the interactions between immune cells, and class I proteins in that of immune cells with other cells (in most cases).

T Lymphocytes Recognize Antigen

It is of great interest to know how this double recognition takes place, but this goal has been elusive for many years. In spite of strong efforts the T lymphocyte structures that recognize the antigen could not be identified. The goal, however, was finally reached in two steps. The first was to demonstrate that T lymphocytes have structures with properties expected of receptors for the antigen. Like the immunoglobulins for B lymphocytes, these receptors should be different in different T lymphocytes. Monoclonal antibodies (see chapter 13) were prepared after immunizing mice with T lymphocytes of several clones grown in cultures. Some of the antibodies were indeed specific for a single clone and recognized characteristic surface molecules, probably the receptors. The second step was to isolate the genes for the receptors. RNA messengers were extracted from T lymphocytes and copied into DNA; molecules specific for T lymphocytes (because they did not hybridize to messengers extracted from B lymphocytes) were cloned. Among these T lymphocyte–specific sequences were those corresponding to the genes for the antigen receptors.

This and other approaches showed that T lymphocyte receptors are, like immunoglobulins, made up of two chains; like the gene for the heavy chain of immunoglobulins, the corresponding genes are assembled during development from separate V, D, J, and C fragments. The diversity of V and D segments, variable joining, and somatic mutations provide variability, but less than in the case of immunoglobulin genes. These genes are evidently related to those for immunoglobulins. They specify two amino acid chains of the receptors, alpha and beta. A third gamma gene, related to the other two, is much less variable and may be part of a different receptor. The genes are rearranged and transcribed during maturation of T lymphocytes in the thymus. The gamma gene does this very early, and is later followed by the other two.

Because the T lymphocytes have a single type of receptor, made up of both alpha and beta chains, it seems likely that both the antigen and the MHC protein present on the interacting cell are recognized together by the receptor; they must be associated together at the cell surface. Conclusive evidence for such an association has indeed been obtained. The single receptor probably sees the general outline of a complex formed by the antigen associated with the MHC protein, without recognizing either component separately. This explains the behavior of some T lymphocytes that recognize antigen A with MHC protein A, but can also recognize a different combination in which both partners are changed, such as antigen B with MHC protein C. The second combination, although made with different components, "looks" to the receptors like the first one. The MHC proteins may have characteristics that enable them to bind to the antigenic proteins in the cell membrane, but probably not to any protein. Selection by the MHC proteins explains the special repertoire of antigens recognized by T cells, which differs from that of B cells. Because the latter lymphocytes bind antigen directly, they tend to recognize surface characteristics of the antigen, whereas T lymphocytes, especially of the helper type, often recognize internal parts, which are less water-seeking and more likely to bind to MHC protein in the membrane of antigen-presenting cells.

That a foreign antigen must become associated with an MHC protein before eliciting an immune response explains why mice of certain inbred strains mount poor antibody responses to some foreign antigens. The effect is usually caused by a particular form of a gene for class II proteins, which do not readily associate with some antigens or form complexes that are poorly recognized by the available T lymphocyte receptors. Similar differences occur also in humans in whom the equivalent of the mice MHC locus is the *HLA locus* (from human leukocyte antigen, for historical reasons). As in the case of mouse MHC genes, there are many, slightly different forms of HLA genes, and some of them decrease the response to certain antigens. The MHC genes responsible for the effect are called immune response genes.

This control may explain why there are so many different forms (alleles) of MHC genes: each form would favor the recognition of a certain group of antigens. New forms may become established when an infectious agent with novel properties makes its appearance: the new forms are those that allow the organism to cope with the new agent. Moreover, a multiplicity of forms of MHC genes is also advantageous because in normal interbreeding populations an individual usually expresses two different forms of the same gene (one per chromosome set) and can, therefore, recognize two sets of antigens. The result is that the repertoire of foreign antigens against which the organism can mount a successful defense is increased. This advantage would favor the diversification of the MHC genes in evolution.

The Meaning of the MHC Protein

Why do MHC proteins play such an important role in the immune response? An answer to this question has begun to emerge from studies of the genes of the MHC locus and the proteins they specify. First, these proteins are present in all vertebrates, implying that they have considerable importance for the organisms. Even lower creatures, like sponges, have proteins with related functions in cell-cell recognition. Another relevant point is that the MHC locus contains, in addition to genes for class I and for class II proteins, many genes for other surface proteins, as well as genes for the components of the complement system. So, except for the complement genes, the locus specifies proteins of the cell surface involved in cell recognition. The inclusion of complement genes may not be fortuitous, because B lymphocytes have receptors for certain components of the complement system; the binding of complement to these receptors regulates the growth of the cells. It is possible that the complement system originated from genes for proteins with regulatory functions acting through the cell surface. The fact that all these genes form a locus—that is, an evolutionarily stable association—is probably also significant, although its meaning is not clear. Perhaps the genes are kept together by a need for some common regulation, yet unknown.

Another interesting point is the similarity of class I and class II proteins to immunoglobulins, suggesting a common origin in evolution. This would make sense because they are both key elements of the defense system against infectious agents. Given the possible evolution of the immune system as discussed in chapter 13, it is likely that genes of the MHC locus were the first to appear and were essential for the action of T cells before B cells made their appearance. As B cells and immunoglobulin genes developed, their functions remained intimately enmeshed with those of the MHC proteins. This is a hypothesis, but it helps in thinking about the organization, function, and regulation of the immune system as we know it today.

The binding of the MHC protein—together with antigen—to the receptors on T lymphocytes has important functional consequences. This can be deduced from the effect of monoclonal antibodies that bind the T cell receptors. If the antibody molecules are connected by a solid support, so that many of them can bind to receptors on the same T lymphocyte, they induce the lymphocyte to produce the growth factors required for its own proliferation and to display the corresponding receptors on its own surface. The T cells then proliferate by stimulating themselves. This stimulation leads to the formation of clones of helper T cells specific for the antigen recognized by the receptor. This observation, together with similar observations with multivalent antigens on B cells, suggests that in the interaction between immune cells the presentation of multiple groups rigidly connected and with the proper geometry maximizes the activating effect. The result perhaps explains why molecules in solution cannot in general activate an immune response and why interactions between cells are needed.

How Are Foreign Cells Recognized?

One of the questions related to skin rejection is why some T killer lymphocytes kill cells carrying a class I protein of another mouse strain, without foreign antigen. A possible answer is that killer cells with receptors recognizing self MHC protein A associated with a foreign antigen can recognize non–self MHC protein B as if it were AZ, where Z is a hypothetical foreign antigen that may or may not exist (fig. 14.2). So when a killer lymphocyte binds to and kills a normal cell of another inbred mouse strain, which has a different MHC protein, it may recognize it as a cell of its own strain modified by a foreign antigen. The difficulty is, however, that T lymphocytes able to kill cells with foreign MHC proteins form a special subset and are more common than T lymphocytes recognizing any given foreign antigen in conjunction with self MHC protein. Evidently much remains to be learned.

The Problem of Self-Tolerance

So far we have considered the various ways in which T lymphocytes recognize antigens. We will now consider the complementary problem: how they *fail* to recognize self antigens. This problem is twofold: no killer lymphocyte kills cells

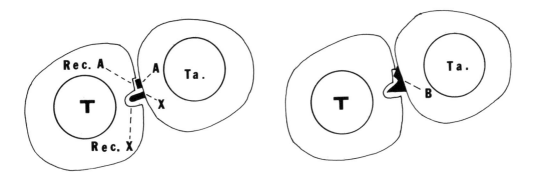

Figure 14.2. Possible interpretation of the ability of certain T killer lymphocytes to kill cells with a foreign MHC protein. At left, the T killer lymphocyte (T) has receptors that recognize MHC protein A (Rec. A), as well as for a foreign (e.g., viral) antigen X (Rec. X) on the target cell (Ta.). At right the same killer cell recognizes a target cell displaying MHC protein B, because it resembles the combination of MHC protein A plus the foreign antigen X.

with self MHC protein unless it is associated with a foreign antigen, and no other self antigen is recognized as foreign.

How these effects are obtained is not obvious, considering how the repertoire of T cell receptors develops. Like antibodies at the surface of B cells, these receptors are displayed at the surface of T cells that have not yet interacted with antigen. The lack of receptors recognizing self MHC proteins and the inability to develop an immune response to the myriad of proteins present at the surface of the body cells or in the blood is surprising. The general answer to these questions is that in neither case is lack of response due to an intrinsic inability of the immune system to respond to these antigens. It is the result of the exposure of the immune system to them early in life, as an expression of a regulatory network that controls the operation of the immune system. Lymphocytes capable of such unwanted recognitions are kept in abeyance.

One possibility is that lymphocytes with the capability of performing these forbidden functions die (clonal deletion), presumably during their maturation in the thymus. This possibility is supported by the high mortality of lymphocytes in the thymus: of those born there only 3 percent survive. Another explanation involves a special type of T lymphocytes, the T suppressor cell.

Clonal deletion cannot be the only mechanism of self exclusion, because an immune reaction against self antigens can be regularly elicited in adult organisms using suitable means. For instance, a mouse injected with a product of thyroid cells, thyroglobulin, mixed with a special adjuvant (some examples will be given below) readily develops an immune response against the thyroid gland. The response is due to the growth of clones of preexisting lymphocytes carrying antibodies for that protein. Such lymphocytes can be actually identified in normal adult animals. Yet mice do not normally produce significant amounts of antibodies against their own thyroglobulin. Obviously, the lymphocytes are not normally stimulated to multiply and mature.

The counterpart of this observation is that a mouse capable of producing antibodies or T killer lymphocytes to a foreign antigen will fail to do so if the antigen is administered in a suitable way (see below). Then the antigen induces a state of induced tolerance to itself; and, most important, the state of tolerance is transferred to normal mice by T lymphocytes taken from the tolerant animal.

The lymphocytes responsible for transferring tolerance, called *T suppressor cells*, are not well known. They differ in surface characteristics from those we have encountered so far: they share the T8 molecules with killer lymphocytes but have other exclusive molecules, called I-J. These special lymphocytes seem to abolish the response of the organism to the antigen by blocking T helper lymphocytes that recognize certain antigens or MHC proteins. Then neither antibodies nor killer lymphocytes that recognize these molecules are produced. Suppression is especially effective during the primary immune response; reactivation of memory cells is much less affected. Impairment of T suppressor cells may explain why treatment of embryos with antibodies to the I-J determinants causes breakdown of self-tolerance when the animal reaches adulthood, resulting in autoimmune disease (see below). T suppressor cells may also suppress their own production, ensuring that their effects are controlled.

Suppressor cells seem also to control the course of an immune response. Antibodies or killer cells to a foreign antigen are not produced in ever increasing amounts when antigen is continuously administered. Suppressor cells may participate in this control because their formation is induced by complexes of a foreign antigen with antibodies, which signal that antibodies specific for that antigen are abundant in the body. This is part of the network of interactions that regulates the immune response. The normal role of T suppressor cells would then be to limit the excessive production of any given antibody.

Tolerance, like an immune response, is MHC-restricted: it is not produced unless a foreign antigen is recognized in conjunction with a self MHC protein. An animal tolerant to antigen X in conjunction with its own MHC protein A is not tolerant to X presented in conjunction with MHC protein B. So the two pathways, of response or suppression, diverge after a common first step.

Importance of How Antigen Is Presented

The phenomenon of induced tolerance suggests that injection of a foreign antigen can either induce or suppress an immune response. One of the factors is whether T helper lymphocytes or T suppressor lymphocytes are activated. It seems that both cell types are always elicited, but one predominates.

An important factor controlling the balance between the response and suppression is how the antigen is administered. Suppression predominates when antigen is supplied at a low concentration and as single, unaggregated molecules. This mode of presentation may be important for determining the natural tolerance to self antigens, which are continuously released or shed from the body cells in very small amounts and are not aggregated. Suppression is also favored by the opposite condition—that is, when an antigen is administered in very large quantities. An immune response is more likely to arise when antigen is injected at medium concentrations and in aggregated form, especially in conjunction with an adjuvant, such as a bacterial extract containing components of the bacterial surface, or repetitive chemicals. These substances act by stimulating macrophages, which then become more effective in producing growth and differentiation factors and in presenting the antigen to T helper lymphocytes.

Normal Immunity against Self

Among the components of the regulatory network that are especially important seems to be a special type of antibody, which regularly accompanies the immune response to a foreign antigen. It is elicited by the antibody generated in this response—which we will call the *primary antibody*—acting as antigen. The organism, although immunologically tolerant to the constant regions of antibodies, which are always present in the blood, is not tolerant to the binding site of the new antibody. *Secondary antibodies* recognizing the binding site of the primary antibody are therefore formed, and are known as *antiidiotypic* because the variable region including the binding site is also known as the idiotype. The binding site of the secondary antibody is similar in shape to the antigenic spot of the antigen that elicited the immune response: both recognize the binding site of the primary antibody (fig. 14.3). The secondary antibody is therefore a pseudo-antigenic spot, or the internal image of the antigen. That secondary antibodies have a regulatory role is suggested by their appearance at the time when the production of the primary antibody reaches a maximum and before it declines. A secondary antibody may have a regulatory role because it looks like the antigenic spot but is attached to a different carrier, the antibody molecule. As a carrier, the antibody has special properties: through the stem of the Y it can interact with immune cells involved in the regulation of the production of the primary antibody. It may also activate the production of T suppressor lymphocytes.

The regulatory role of secondary antibodies can be seen in another context: when the immunizing antigen is a communicator molecule which interacts with highly selective receptors in the body. As shown in figure 14.4, the secondary antibody has the same shape as the communicator molecule itself: twice comple-

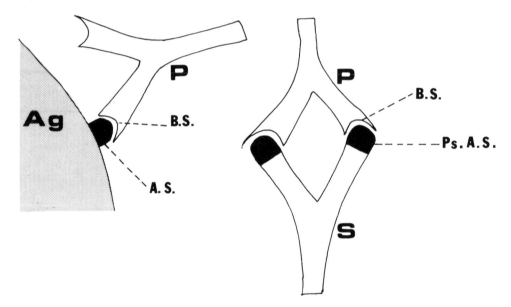

Figure 14.3. Primary and secondary antibodies. At left the binding site (B.S.) of the primary antibody (P) recognizes an antigenic spot (A.S., black) of an antigen (Ag). At right is the secondary antibody (S), which recognizes as an antigenic spot the binding site (B.S.) of the primary antibody (P). The binding site of the secondary antibody is a pseudo–antigenic spot (Ps.A.S.) and resembles the true antigenic spot in its external surface.

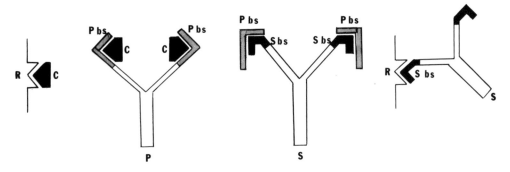

Figure 14.4. Secondary antibodies to a communicator molecule bind to its receptor: C = communicator; R = receptor; P = primary antibody; P bs = binding site of the primary antibody; S = secondary antibody; S bs = binding site of the secondary antibody.

mentary means equal. The secondary antibody can often interact with the receptor like the communicator itself. It may block access of the communicator to its receptors, preventing the function of the communicator, or it may mimic the communicator, causing an excessive stimulation of the cells. As discussed below, both consequences can cause disease.

The internal-image property of secondary antibodies makes them useful as vaccines to control viral infections in cases in which the viral antigen is not available in sufficient amounts to produce ordinary vaccines. Usually the antigen is sufficient to generate monoclonal antibodies, which are then used to prepare the vaccine. Antibodies induced by injecting the monoclonal antibody into an animal constitute the vaccine; these are secondary antibodies to the antigen. In the organism the vaccine elicits the formation of antibodies to the internal image: they are *tertiary antibodies* to the antigen.

Immunity as Disease

Breakdown of self-tolerance, with immune response to self antigens, sometimes causes disease both in animals and in humans. These *autoimmune diseases* may be caused by antibodies to self components (autoantibodies) or T killer lymphocytes that recognize cells of the same organism. An example is a special form of diabetes that appears in young people. In some cases it is the consequence of antibodies to the cells of the pancreatic islets, which produce insulin. The islet cells are then killed by special killer cells that recognize the stem of the antibody bound to the cells. In other cases antibodies are directed at the receptors that bind insulin in all cells of the body. The receptors with the bound antibodies disappear, owing to down-regulation. In either cases the cells of the body are deprived of the important regulatory influence of insulin. Other autoimmune diseases have as targets the thyroid, the muscles, or the nervous system.

The production of autoantibodies, if abundant, may also be damaging by an indirect mechanism: the formation of large amounts of antigen-antibody complexes. Because they are not readily excreted into the urine, they accumulate in the kidneys choking them and preventing the elimination of wastes. The result is kidney failure, often leading to death.

The mechanism that breaks down the immunological tolerance to the self antigens in these diseases is not always clear. In some cases the disease may be caused by secondary antibodies (see fig. 14.4), as in Grave's disease, for instance, in which the cells of the thyroid gland overproduce their hormones, creating generalized toxic effects. An antibody behaving like the pituitary hormone controlling the thryoid, thyrotropin, causes the excessive secretion. Another mechanism involved in autoimmune disease may be the presentation of an antigenic spot in an unusual way—on a different carrier, for instance. This may occur when bacteria or viruses infecting an organism have antigenic spots equal to those of some normal body component. This mechanism may be responsible for diverse diseases such as multiple sclerosis, some forms of diabetes, and arthritis. Injection of self antigen together with an adjuvant may also cause autoantibodies. Viruses appear as important causes of autoimmune diseases because they either mimic a self antigen or damage the body cells, releasing into the blood cellular components that are normally hidden within the cells, or opening up areas of the body normally forbidden to the immune system, such as the brain. Usually there is no tolerance to molecules confined to the interior of cells or present in excluded sanctuaries, but when they are released from their confinement and introduced into the blood, they can elicit an immune response. Viruses may also induce an immune response by acting as adjuvants. The viral particles, or their nucleic acids, may bind molecules that are usually dispersed, and therefore elicit tolerance, converting them into particulate, reiterated antigens, which are more likely to elicit an immune response.

Autoimmune diseases are prevalent in individuals with certain forms of class II genes of the MHC locus (in mice) or of the HLA locus (in humans). Some forms of the genes promote autoimmunity to only single self antigens, one at a time; others promote autoimmunity to many such antigens. An example of the latter class is found in the human disease lupus erythematosus. The affected individuals may develop, among others, antibodies to their own DNA, to their mitochondria, and to components of the filamentous structures of their own cells. The information for making these antibodies is in the normal antibody repertoire, but it is not usually expressed.

The Fetus: A Protected Graft

In all mammals a pregnant female can be thought of as bearing a foreign graft, the fetus. The cells of the fetus have MHC proteins determined by genes derived from both the mother and the father; the paternal proteins usually differ from the maternal ones. This should create a serious problem: the immune system of the mother should react to the foreign paternal MHC antigens, destroying the cells of the fetus. We know well that this does not happen, but we don't know precisely why. Many mechanisms are probably involved. Thus fetal MHC proteins are expressed poorly in those cells of the placenta that are in contact with the maternal blood, thus reducing the mother's reaction. The immune response of the mother is also depressed by hormones that are produced during pregnancy. Proteins made only in pregnancy inhibit early steps of the immune response. Fetal antigens exposed to the mother's blood may be covered by protecting antibodies. Finally, T suppressor lymphocytes may be induced in the mother by the slow buildup of fetal antigens within her body.

Communicators Galore

We saw in the last chapter that hormonelike substances released by some cells and acting on other cells play an important role in the activation of cells leading to an immune reaction. Many of them are known. They were identified after it became possible to grow cells of the immune system, such as various kinds of lymphocytes or macrophages, in laboratory cultures. Many of these cultures steadily produce communicators, making them available for investigation. In turn, long-term growth of immune cells in culture became possible after their biology was understood. For instance, cultures of T helper cells responding to a certain antigen could be established by growing populations of T cells on layers of macrophages displaying that antigen on their surfaces. Substances produced by some of these cultures could be used to establish cultures of other cells.

This slow but very useful work led to the recognition of factors promoting growth or differentiation of many kinds of cells of the hemopoietic system. The factors that are most important for the immune system are generated by macrophages and T helper lymphocytes. They are collectively known as *lymphokines*, that is, stimulators of lymphocytes or other immune cells. These communicators are extremely varied and sophisticated. Each one performs a highly specific role, but they all act in concert to promote the buildup of immune defenses.

As an example of the interplay of these factors we can look at those involved in the triple interaction. Activated macrophages produce a factor that stimulates the multiplication of T helper lymphocytes. The factor is called *interleukin-1*, meaning that it carries signals between two leukocytes (white blood cells). Under its influence T helper lymphocytes produce another factor called *interleukin-2* and display at their surface receptors for this factor. Interleukin-2, acting on the receptors, stimulates the multiplication of the T helper cells themselves. This is an example of a positive feedback by which *a cell stimulates its own growth*. Under the influence of interleukin-2, T lymphocytes also produce factors that, together with other factors produced by macrophages, stimulate B lymphocyte growth. In addition, the activated T lymphocytes produce another important substance—*gamma in-*

terferon. Interferons are small proteins that have important effects on many kinds of cells: they make them resistant to viruses, inhibit their growth, and alter the expression of some of their genes. Gamma interferon has the special property of increasing the expression of class II MHC genes at the surface of macrophages, boosting by as much as tenfold the effectiveness of these cells as partners in the triple complex.

This complex system of interactions comes into play after both macrophages and T helper cells are activated by reciprocal contacts or (for helper cells) by contact with a large repetitive molecule. The ability of B lymphocytes to respond to the factors likewise appears after their activation by contact with antigen or with a large repetitive molecule. In this way all the influences that activate the immune response are brought together and reinforce each other.

We have seen in this chapter how complex the regulation of development is in the well-studied immune system. Other developmental systems not yet as well known can be expected to be equally complex and may use comparable devices for achieving harmonious development. The actual mechanisms may, however, turn out to be quite different, because other systems operate under different circumstances. In each system the genes have developed appropriate means for reaching their purposes, using in a pragmatic way what works best. They have many tricks at their disposal, and they use them as is expedient. They rarely use the same approach in different situations: they are very inventive. This versatility of nature poses a strong challenge to scientists who try to penetrate its secrets.

CHAPTER 15

Unruly Genes

The normal process of development is brought about by the unfolding of the activity of the genes according to a precise program. When some crucial genes start functioning at the wrong time or place, however, the program is upset, and the anomaly generates cancer cells, whose characteristics differ profoundly from the norm. Because they have escaped the regulatory influences that usually govern the expression of the cellular genes, cancer cells express genes that should not be expressed in the normal adult body.

Cancer cells are said to be malignant because their behavior violates two basic rules of the organization of the body. One is that normal cells respect normal tissue boundaries. For instance, the cells of the epithelial layer of the skin, the *epidermis*, are usually contained within a continuous membrane, the *basement membrane*, which separates them from the underlying support layer, the *derma*. When cells of the epidermis become malignant, they cross the basement membrane and infiltrate the derma. From there they may invade fat tissue, muscles, and other organs. The second basic rule is that normally cells are confined to certain organs. But cancer cells colonize distant organs, a process called *metastasis* (meaning migration). For instance, cells of breast cancers may be found in the brain, the liver, or the bone.

These are the violations that make cancer cells so dangerous. Metastases, by their sheer mass, alter the normal operation of essential organs. Cancer cells may invade the blood vessels, causing blood loss and destruction of the surrounding tissue. They also produce substances that upset the working of the body and withdraw from the organism essential nutrients in inordinate amounts. For these reasons cancer is ruinous for the body and ultimately lethal.

Cancer occurs in all higher organisms, both plants and animals, but its evolution varies greatly in different species. Our most extensive description of cancer is of that occurring in human beings, owing to its great medical importance.

Progression: Steps in the Development of Cancer

Both in humans and experimental animals a long interval of months or years, depending on the species, elapses between the beginning of the process and the appearance of cells with the deviant characteristics described above. The length of the lag can be measured in people after a single exposure to a cancer agent, such as X rays and other forms of radiation. For instance, human beings were exposed to a large dose of radiation when atomic bombs were exploded over Japanese cities during the Second World War. Among the survivors a high incidence of leukemias (cancers of white blood cells) began appearing about two years after the explosion and peaked seven years later. New cases continued to appear along after that. Breast cancers were detected after several years and peaked eighteen years after the explosion. The period between the onset of exposure and the appearance of cancer is even longer when people are continuously exposed to small doses of a cancer-causing agent. In the case of cigarette smokers, the delay between the beginning of smoking and the detection of lung cancer is about thirty years. Intervals of comparable length have also been observed in workers who were chronically exposed to chemicals that were later found to cause cancer.

What happens during the long silent period of cancer development can be inferred from studies with animals and with cells in cultures. In these systems the changes that characterize a clinically recognizable cancer occur one at a time in a series of steps. The first is enhanced cell multiplication, provided the growth factors required by the cells are present. In the second step the cells can multiply without growth factors, and they subsequently acquire a property that normal cells do not have: the ability to grow in gelled agar (normal cells in culture grow attached to a solid surface, such as special plastic or glass). In a later step the cells become able to form a localized tumor in animals, provided there are no immunological barriers. In yet another step they can invade surrounding tissues, and finally they acquire the property of producing metastases. This succession of steps on the road to malignancy is called *progression*.

Both the cellular changes occurring during progression and their mechanisms are ill defined. It is clear, however, that changes of the cell surface are important and that they are due to alterations of the expression of the cell's genes. Beyond that we know very little.

Initial Events

The initial events of cancer in experimental animals are also complex, which was first demonstrated experimentally in the 1940s by Isaac Berenblum and Peyton

Rous. They produced tumors in mice by repeated applications of tar. The tumors were not malignant—they remained localized and their cells had normal characteristics—but they could evolve to malignancy in additional steps. The crucial observation was that no cancers were produced if too little tar was used, but they would appear later if the mice's skin was exposed to croton oil or was wounded. Croton oil was originally selected as an irritant, but it turned out to contain powerful substances that activate cell multiplication and affect the course of differentiation. These observations were the basis for the concept that at least two steps are involved in cancer formation: *initiation* (by tar) and *promotion* (by croton oil). Initiation is permanent: the skin cancers appear if the promoting substance is applied many months after the tar; it seems to involve some gene change, probably a mutation. In contrast, the effect of promotion is transient. If the skin is exposed to the promoter first and the initiator later, no cancer is produced.

The concept that initiation consists of damage to DNA is supported by the ability of many of the known cancer-producing substances to alter DNA. Some do it directly; others, after being modified by cellular enzymes. It seems strange that these enzymes should generate cancer, for it is a distortion of normal events. The cells' enzymes neutralize and dispose of noxious chemicals coming from the outside and even internal substances, such as certain steroid hormones. This process of detoxification goes through many chemical steps. The compounds that can damage DNA are generated as transient intermediates, and during their brief life they may attack the DNA, causing mutations.

Their ability to induce mutations can be demonstrated in the laboratory, using cultures of bacteria or animal cells in which a mutation produces some easily noticeable change. The bacteria or the cells are grown in a nutrient medium containing the cancer-producing substance together with a mixture of detoxifying enzymes extracted from rat liver. The enzymes generate the DNA-damaging compounds, which then cross the cell membranes and reach the DNA. By this approach many cancer-producing substances have been shown to induce mutations, findings that support the notion that initiation is the result of a mutation. Promotion may be necessary then to permit the expression of the mutated gene.

Mutational Origin Questioned in Some Cases

Not all cancers are caused by mutations, however. Some can be induced by substances that do not damage DNA, such as asbestos, hormones, or sheets of plastic inserted under the skin of a mouse or a rat. These observations throw doubt on the generality of the mutational origin of cancer. An additional element of doubt derives from the fact that agents that cause DNA damage also damage other constituents of the cells, such as RNA and proteins. Can we be certain that it is the DNA damage, and not the other damage, that causes cancer?

The mutation model seemed strongly supported by the irreversibility of cancer. But this argument is weakened by the recognition that not only mutations but also developmental changes are irreversible, at least in mammals, and they are caused not by mutations but by changes in the state of activity of the genes. The crucial argument against the idea that all cancers are caused by mutations, however, is the occurrence of cancers that are clearly reversible.

The cells of an embryonic cancer called teratocarcinoma (meaning cancer derived from an altered embryo) can revert to the normal state. It can be easily produced in certain mouse strains by injecting either immature germ cells or a young embryo into the testis of an adult mouse. The cancer that frequently develops at the site of injection is unusual. It contains cancer cells mixed with adult mouse tissues, such as skin, nervous system, muscle, or even teeth. If cells of this cancer are transferred from mouse to mouse, it can be shown that the cancer is made up of two kinds of cells—unrestricted cells, which resemble the cells of the early mouse embryo, and differentiated cells. The first are malignant: a single unrestricted cell injected into a mouse is capable of growing into a cancer containing both unrestricted and differentiated cells. The differentiated cells, on the other hand, are not malignant, showing that as unrestricted cells differentiate, they lose malignancy.

Loss of malignancy can also be realized by injecting one or a few unrestricted cells into an early mouse embryo. The cells then participate in the normal development of the embryo and in the formation of the adult animal. If the injected cell carries distinguishing genetic markers, such as a special coat color, the mouse developing from that embryo will display the markers on its body. The reversion of these cancer cells to normality is therefore influenced by the cell environment and is coupled to differentiation.

The conclusion that normal embryonic cells become malignant when they are moved to an adult environment, and revert to normality when placed back into their normal environment, the mouse embryo, is remarkable. It suggests that the cancer state may be induced and maintained in the embryonic cells by exposure to differentiation factors that are present in the adult mouse. These factors are abnormal for the embryonic cells and cause them to behave abnormally. Once the cells are returned to the influence of the differentiation factors present in the embryo, they return to normality.

The teratocarcinoma cells seem not to have any permanent alteration in their DNA, because they participate normally in the construction of the adult mouse body. This cancer, therefore, may not result from genetic damage. It may derive from reversible gene changes similar to those that give rise to differentiation. Instead of a *genetic* mechanism, then, it would be an *epigenetic* mechanism (that is, beyond the genes), occurring at the level of transcription, of messenger formation, of translation, or of protein activity.

An epigenetic mechanism can also be involved in the origin of cancers caused by hormones. We saw in chapter 8 that many hormone-producing glands belong to a hierarchical system in which production of one hormone is controlled by another. For instance, ovarian steroids are controlled by hormones of the pituitary gland. The pituitary is, in turn, controlled by feedback from the ovarian hormones acting on the hypothalamus. If the ovary is transplanted to the spleen, its hormones no longer reach the brain: they are poured into a vein that ends up in the liver, where they are destroyed by the detoxification enzymes. The feedback is abolished and the pituitary keeps producing an excess of the hormones that stimulate the ovary. This strong and persistent stimulus causes the multiplication of the hormone-producing cells of the ovary because the pituitary hormone stimulates not only hormone production but also growth in these cells. In the long run, the persisting growth stimulus causes the formation of a cancer of ovarian cells. Many other factors that, like hormones, control growth or development may play a similar role in the formation of other cancers. The teratocarcinoma is a good model.

Chromosomal Changes

Cancer cells do not merely grow, however, but differ in many ways from the normal cells of the organ in which they arise. Some of the differences are not directly cancer-related. They exist because the cancer cells arise not from the terminally differentiated cells that make up the organs of adult animals but from less differentiated reserve cells. This has been detected most readily in leukemias, the cancers of blood cells, because the developmental pathway leading to mature blood cells is well known, and various leukemias are made up of cells at different stages of development. There is more uncertainty concerning many other organs because their normal developmental pathways are not known.

Owing to these uncertainties, it is difficult to assess the origin of cancers that appear to be made up of abnormal cells—for instance, cancers that produce hormones not made by the normal mature cells of the organ in which they appear. Thus peptide hormones and neuropeptides are made by cancers of the bronchus; other unusual hormones are made by cancers of the pancreas. Are these anomalies the result of the profound abnormality of the cancer cells? Perhaps, but an alternative explanation is that these cancers derive from rare cells that normally produce the same hormones in the organ in which the cancer arose or during its development. In fact, cells producing neuropeptides are present in the normal bronchus. A more likely interpretation, then, is that the cancer cells have some fetal characteristics.

Other anomalies are more strictly characteristic of the cancer state—for instance, an abnormal number of chromosomes. Such cells are said to be *aneuploid*—they do not have the regular, or euploid, number of chromosomes. They may have less or more; in some cancers the regular number almost doubles. These anomalies originate through an unknown mechanism from irregularities during cell division, when the chromatids of the mother cells are distributed to the two daughter cells. The aneuploid state has severe consequences for the cells because it upsets the balance of genes and their state of regulation. It is as if the cells had many mutations. The abnormality progressively increases as the cancer grows because some of the aneuploid cells overgrow the other cells, forming the main mass of the cancer.

Cancer from Viruses

Our understanding of the nature of cancer, and of the mechanisms that produce it, is based mostly on what has been learned by studying viruses that cause cancer. Because viruses have a small number of genes, it is possible to determine which viral genes are responsible for a cancer. Considerable insight into the nature of cancer has come from the study of such viral cancer genes, or oncogenes.

DNA Viruses

In the late 1950s, a small virus with a DNA genome was found to induce cancers in mice and other rodents. Because it produced several kinds of cancer, it was called *polyoma virus*. Later a different virus with similar properties was isolated from cultures of monkey cells and was called *simian virus 40* (from the order of isolation), abbreviated as SV40.

The study of these viruses explained why the change of a normal cell into a cancer cell by a virus is an irreversible process. Both the cell and its progeny continue to be cancer cells because viral genes capable of maintaining the state become inserted into the DNA of the cells and then stay there permanently—a phenomenon called *integration*. (We have seen in chapter 5 how these facts were established using radioactive DNA probes.) The integrated viral DNA is referred to as *provirus* because under certain conditions it gives rise to production of new virus. Viral genes active in the provirus maintain the cancer state in the cells.

In polyoma virus these genes cause the manufacture of three proteins, all of which cooperate in changing the cells. Two of the proteins have well-defined functions: one interacts with the cellular DNA, and the other becomes inserted in the membrane of the cell. This dual effect accords with the need for more than one step in the production of cancer by chemicals, as discussed above.

RNA Viruses

Another class of viruses contributed even more to our understanding of cancer. They have an RNA genome, which in the cells is transcribed into DNA. This phenomenon is known as *reverse transcription* because it reverses the normal flow of genetic information; the viruses themselves have become known as *retroviruses*. Within the cells, the form of the viral genome that is important in the cancer-causing process is made up of DNA and, again, becomes integrated in the cellular DNA as provirus. Its transcription generates new RNA genomes, and they end up in new virus particles that continuously trickle out of the cells.

Many retroviruses infect animals without causing cancer. Their genomes contain three genes that perform functions essential for the replication of the virus. The retroviruses that induce cancer have an additional gene—the oncogene—which is not useful for the virus. It is, in fact, harmful because it is normally inserted among the viral genes, replacing pieces of them and making them inactive. These viruses are crippled and cannot multiply by themselves, although they can do so in cells that are also infected by a complete retrovirus. The genes of the normal virus supply the proteins the cancer-inducing virus cannot make.

The position of the oncogene shows that it is foreign to the viral genome and has been inserted by some transposition or recombination. It could come from some other virus or perhaps from some normal cellular gene. That the latter alternative is possible was ascertained by making radioactive probes to the oncogene of a chicken virus called the Rous sarcoma virus from its discoverer, Peyton Rous. These probes detected homologous sequences in the DNA of normal chicken cells that contained no retrovirus genome, showing that the oncogene came from a cellular gene. Subsequently it was found that the DNAs of other organisms, from yeast to humans, also contain sequences homologous to that oncogene. The sequences are similar in different species: the degree of variation is comparable to that of genes that perform essential functions, such as the globin genes. The virus presumably captures the oncogene from the cells in which it replicates, as a result of a rare recombination event. The sequences present in normal cells were called *proto-oncogenes*.

The shattering conclusion was thus reached that the oncogene is closely related to a normal gene that performs some essential function in the animal; otherwise, it would not have remained so constant in evolution. Because of these interesting results, the oncogene became an urgent subject of research. Many other oncogenes were rapidly discovered in other retroviruses; it is likely that there are fifty to a hundred in the animal genome.

These discoveries raised many new questions. What is the normal function of proto-oncogenes? How do normal cells escape the cancer-causing action of these genes present in their own genomes? How do oncogenes change normal cells into cancer cells? Are oncogenes responsible for the origin of all cancers or only some? What is their relation to the multiple steps of cancer?

Oncogenes and Proto-Oncogenes

The first question concerned whether the proto-oncogenes present in normal cells are identical to the oncogenes in viruses. The answer, obtained by cloning the genes, is that they differ in two ways: the viral oncogenes are somewhat altered, either shorter or differing in some bases, and they are transcribed at a much higher rate owing to the strong viral enhancers that control them. The alterations are important for the cancer-inducing activity of many oncogenes. Their function is released from the regulatory controls that restrain the activity of normal proto-oncogenes, and they are said to be activated.

Some unaltered proto-oncogenes may start the cells on the road to malignancy if their rate of transcription is markedly increased and a large amount of the protein is made in the cells. This effect can be obtained by introducing into the cells a cloned proto-oncogene coupled to an efficient control region obtained from a retrovirus. A proto-oncogene can also be activated at its normal location by the integration of a retroviral genome in its proximity, which increases its transcription and often alters its sequences.

Proto-oncogenes are thought to be developmental genes, for they are active at certain stages of normal development. In fact some of them have sequences related to the developmental genes of *Drosophila*. They may be involved in specific steps of differentiation, which vary for different proto-oncogenes. It seems that they become cancer agents when they are expressed in cells in which they are not normally expressed. For instance, the proto-oncogene corresponding to an oncogene that causes bone cancer in mice is active in normal mice both during early embryonic development and during adulthood, when it is expressed in the blood-forming cells of the bone marrow. Yet this oncogene induces a cancer of bone-forming cells. Expression in abnormal cells may allow the oncogene to escape the regulatory influences, generating an unstoppable stimulus toward growth or differentiation. The situation may be comparable to that encountered by embryonic cells transferred to an adult environment in the formation of teratocarcinomas.

Oncogenes in Spontaneous Cancers

The oncogenes we have described are present in viruses and affect experimental animals. Some activated oncogenes are also associated with spontaneous cancers in humans. They are detected by extracting DNA from the cancer cells and introducing it into normal test cells on which they confer malignant characteristics. DNA extracted from a variety of human cancers has this property. Activated oncogenes, however, are detected in only about 15 percent of all cancers of a given type; we will discuss the significance of this finding below. Several of the oncogenes obtained from human cancers are related to those present in viruses, but some are different.

As is the case for oncogenes present in viruses, those in human cancers are not identical to the normal proto-oncogenes. In some cases the difference affects only a single base, but at a strategic position: the single amino acid replacement in the protein considerably alters its three-dimensional structure, making it suitable for altering the cells.

The mode of action of oncogenes has been intensively studied in the hope of understanding what cancer is and how it comes about. The efforts were directed at identifying the proteins specified by oncogenes and finding out what they do in cells.

The results have indicated that the proteins of a majority of oncogenes can be distinguished in four groups which outline a fundamental regulatory pathway of the cells. The proteins of one class have a nuclear location and may bind to DNA; those of another class are enzymes (called protein kinases) that add phosphate groups to other proteins; those of a third group are related to growth factors or their receptors; and those of a fourth group are related to a membrane protein involved in the action of some hormones that use cAMP as second messenger. It seems surprising that proteins with such different characteristics should produce the same result. Possibly they do so because they all belong to a system of communication that carries growth and differentiation signals from external factors to the genes according to the sequence: factor → receptor → second messenger → nucleus → genes. Once the pathway is activated at any point, the signal will proceed from there to the end. Many such pathways exist, probably converging on different genes: which one is used by each cell type depends on its state of differentiation. This scheme is in accord with the observation that different oncogenes act as cancer agents on cells at different stages of differentiation.

We can see how an oncogene works by examining as a paradigm the protein of the Rous sarcoma virus oncogene (called *src*, abbreviated from sarcoma). This protein is an enzyme, a protein kinase. Many protein kinases exist in normal cells and have powerful regulatory effects by activating or inactivating enzymes. Because a kinase recognizes only a short amino acid sequence in proteins, it can alter many kinds of proteins if they share that sequence. The protein kinase corresponding to the viral oncogene differs from these normal kinases in that it attaches the phosphate residue to a different amino acid in the proteins (tyrosine instead of threonine or serine). Owing to its different target, the oncogene kinase may affect gene-regulating proteins with effects as powerful as those of the usual kinases.

The proteins changed by the oncogene kinase in cells have been intensely studied. Some are proteins of the cell membrane; others are enzymes of glycolysis (the process, outlined in chapter 3, that extracts energy from sugars without oxygen). It happens that cancer cells are altered both in their surfaces and in the regulation of glycolysis, but it is not known whether the altered proteins are responsible for these changes. It is likely that alterations produced by the oncogene will also cause activation of genes that should be silent or inactivation of others that should be active.

These observations may help explain how other oncogenes work. The proteins that go into the nucleus may directly affect the expression of cellular genes. Oncogenes that specify molecules related to growth factors or their receptor may also work through the kinase pathway because many receptors are kinases acting on tyrosine. So an oncogene-controlled receptor may have effects equivalent to those of the Rous sarcoma virus oncogene; and a normal receptor may do the same when an oncogene-controlled growth factor binds to it. Not all oncogenes need affect this same pathway; in fact, there is evidence for effects on other pathways.

The activation of growth by some oncogenes ties in directly with the findings with teratocarcinomas and other cancers that do not appear to be generated by mutations. It supports the idea that an inappropriate production of a factor either from within or from without the cells can be the cause of cancer. In the formation of teratocarcinoma, inappropriate factors are produced, as far as we know, not by activated oncogenes but by normal genes. The factors are inappropriate simply because they are directed at adult cells but act on embryonic cells. In the embryonic cells the factors produce an imbalance of cellular genes, which then persist as long as the abnormal factors are present. The normal balance is restored when the cells are exposed to the factors produced by the early embryo.

The findings also tie in with the ability of many cells to produce growth factors that stimulate their own growth. We have seen an example in the proliferation of activated T helper lymphocytes (chapter 13). Deregulation of such an autocrine (that is, feedback) pathway is another mechanism for unrestrained cell multiplication and cancer initiation.

In many cases, as we have seen, a proto-oncogene becomes changed into an active oncogene by changes introduced in its base sequence when it is captured by virus. In proto-oncogenes not captured by viruses, similar changes may be produced by cancer-causing chemicals. These DNA-damaging substances may cause cancer by converting proto-oncogenes into oncogenes.

An interesting method of conversion is recombination between two nonhomologous chromosomes, an infrequent event known as translocation. A relationship between chromosome translocation and cancer has been recognized for a long time: characteristic translocations occur in many cancers. They are especially well known in some cancers of lymphocytes. Among them are the Burkitt's lymphoma (from the man who first described it), which is especially frequent in children in certain areas of Africa, and cancers occurring in mice injected with paraffin oil, called plasmocytomas because their cells are similar to plasma cells. In either cancer, one of the chromosomes involved in the translocation contains immunoglobulin genes, whereas the other chromosome contains a proto-oncogene known as *myc* (from the name of a chicken virus in which it was discovered).

Both mice and humans have immunoglobulin genes on three chromosomes: one for the heavy chain, one for the kappa light chain, and the third for the lambda light chain. Three kinds of translocations affecting immunoglobulin genes are therefore possible and are found in the lymphomas. In all cases the effect of the translocation is to bring the proto-oncogene very close to one of the immunoglobulin genes. The translocation seems to be important for the origin of these cancers because it is always present. The molecular mechanisms by which the translocation deregulates the proto-oncogene, however, are poorly known.

Oncogenes and Cancer Progression

The possibility that activation of new oncogenes is the cause of the stepwise increase of cancer malignancy (progression) must be considered because oncogenes in suitable combinations can reinforce each other in cell cultures. Some oncogenes (including *myc*) have the main effect of stimulating cell multiplication. Cells containing one of these oncogenes in an active state are immortalized—they continue to multiply indefinitely—in contrast to normal cells, which undergo a limited number of replications and then die. Other oncogenes change the properties of the cells into those of cancer cells—they transform them—without immortalizing them. Among them are oncogenes of the *ras* family (from the name of a mouse virus) which are detected in many human cancers. Cells containing both kinds of oncogenes have the complete characteristics of tumor cells—they are both transformed and immortal. This explains why, as already mentioned, polyoma virus causes transformation using at least two proteins: their functions correspond to those of the two classes of oncogenes.

Other evidence suggests, however, that there is more to progression than cooperation of oncogenes. In a large fraction (about 85 percent) of advanced human cancers, active oncogenes are not found, although it is not known whether they are truly absent or impossible to detect with available approaches; and in experimental systems in mice, cancer cells containing an active oncogene can lose it altogether on progressing to higher malignancy. It seems that oncogenes may be important in the early stages of cancer progression, but not in the advanced stages. This conclusion is supported by the characteristics of advanced cancers: they are made up of cells with very different properties, suggesting that they have undergone widespread genetic changes, including alterations of the chromosomes.

Among these changes there is loss or inactivation of genes with anticancer activity. Evidence for the role of these genes comes from studies of a hereditary human cancer of the eye: retinoblastoma. Children who inherit a chromosome with a defect in a certain gene develop this rare cancer when an unrelated event inactivates the other gene of the same pair. The disappearance of the anticancer genes allows oncogenes present in the cell to take over, causing cancer. The presence of anticancer genes is the expression of the organism's defense against cancer—defenses that must be especially strong in long-lived organisms, such as humans, to prevent cancer development at a young age in a large proportion of individuals.

A possible, although hypothetical picture of cancer and progression is the following. Oncogenes start the process by conferring on cells unlimited growth capability, together with some changes in properties. Progression is determined secondarily by other genetic changes produced by the permanent state of growth of the cells or by other unknown effects of oncogenes. Permanent growth may cause gene changes because in cells that replicate continuously errors may occur more frequently or may be repaired less readily than in normal cells. Unknown effects of activated oncogenes may derive from unusual DNA exchanges or activation of transposing elements. The overall result, perhaps through a combination of effects, would produce many alterations in the cellular genome, with random distribution. Cells with changes promoting infiltration or metastasis would replace the others in successive waves, giving rise to the stepwise progression of malignant cancers. These changes occur unequally in different cell lineages present within the same cancer, generating the marked heterogeneity that is characteristic of cancers.

Agents of Human Cancer

We have mentioned so far several agents causing cancer in animals: X rays, chemicals that damange DNA, hormones, growth factors, bits of plastic. One may ask which agents are responsible for the seemingly spontaneous cancers that occur in humans. Only a small proportion of these can be attributed to some of the agents listed above. The causes of the others are hidden in the type of life individuals lead.

Cigarette Smoking

The great success story of investigations into the causes of human cancers is the demonstration that perhaps 90 percent of cancers of the lung are connected with cigarette smoking. The connection was difficult to recognize without special studies because the time interval between the beginning of smoking and the appearance of cancer is very long. The curve showing the increase over the years of the average number of cigarettes consumed in a country is essentially the same as that for the incidence of lung cancer in that country. But the two curves are displaced by thirty years: that is how long it takes for the cancer process to unfold.

These findings are strengthened by other observations. One is that the incidence of cancer varies proportionally to the number of cigarettes smoked daily. Another comes from the study of groups that decided to quit smoking, as many British physicians did when the role of smoking in cancer became known. Whereas in the smoking population lung cancers continued to appear at an increasing rate over the years, among these physicians the rate stopped increasing and then declined.

That cigarette smoking can induce cancer is not surprising. An analysis of the smoke shows that it contains a large number of cancer-inducing chemicals, both initiators and promoters. These substances are concentrated in the so-called tar formed by the smoke as it cools. Because cigarette smoke so effectively induces cancer, it is natural that it should cause cancer in the lung, which it hits in a direct way. Smoking contributes to other cancers as well, especially of the mouth and of the digestive apparatus. It also dramatically enhances the ability of asbestos to induce lung cancers. Heavy smokers exposed to asbestos may incur up to thirty times as many cancers as nonsmokers.

Since cigarette smoke has been identified as a cause of cancer, the question arises: why do people continue to smoke? But any campaign to induce them to stop has only limited effects, owing perhaps to human nature. One important factor is that smoking is addictive. As we will discuss at greater length in chapter

19, many substances create a state of dependence, so that individuals used to consuming them cannot readily stop or, if they do, can easily return to using them. The nicotine present in cigarette smoke is one of the most powerfully addictive substances known.

If quitting is so difficult, then it should be possible to decrease through education the number of people who take up the smoking habit in the first place, but again there are difficulties. Smoking supports a vast industry; the economies of several states depend on growing tobacco. Moreover, the industry engages in incessant and effective propaganda. One result can be seen in the progressive increase of both cigarette consumption and, many years later, of lung cancer among women, at whom the propaganda of the tobacco industry is especially directed.

Education, however, has begun to bear fruit. A decided decline in the incidence of lung cancer has begun to take place among men, as their consumption of cigarettes has declined. Another result has been the production and relative popularity of cigarettes with a reduced tar content. Their consumption may have contributed to the decrease in lung cancer, although they are just as harmful in other respects (for instance, in contributing to coronary disease).

Cancer from Food?

Cancer incidence shows marked differences among the countries of the world. Breast cancer, for instance, occurs much more frequently in the Western world than in Japan; conversely, Japan has a higher incidence of stomach cancer. These differences are not due to genetic differences between Westerners and Japanese: Japanese who migrated two generations ago to the United States slowly acquired the cancer rates characteristic of Americans. So something in people's life-style determines cancer risks.

This seemed to be a useful lead for identifying factors that cause cancer, and investigations concentrated on comparing national diets. It was possible to correlate the high gastric cancer in Japan with a high consumption of dried or salted fish, which contains the potent cancer agents nitrosoamines. Other striking regularities were observed: there is an almost perfect correlation between consumption of fat and incidence of cancer of the breast, and a similar correlation between consumption of meat and cancer of the large intestine, the colon. At first, these correlations were thought to indicate a cause-and-effect relationship: fat produces breast cancer; meat produces colon cancer. There are confusing factors, however, because it turns out that the incidence of breast cancer correlates even better with gross national product. Moreover, subsequent enquiries on the diets of individuals with cancer compared to those of healthy individuals of similar background did not confirm the role of diet. So it seems that any comparison between countries is confused by some hidden variable like the consumption of a certain food. There may be several variables, in fact, making it very difficult to identify them.

These investigations were started in the hope of providing an easy formula for decreasing the risk of cancer. Although these hopes were frustrated, a useful lesson emerged: a life lived without excess and without taking unnecessary risks, such as smoking, reduces the incidence of cancer. The Seventh-Day Adventists of California follow such a life-style, and their cancer incidence is half that of other Californians. The natural causes of cancer seem to reside in excess: in excessive eating, with consequent increase in weight, which promotes cancer of the breast; in smoking, which increases the risk of lung cancer; in excessive drinking of alcoholic beverages, which increases the risk of cancer of the mouth and esophagus; in sexual promiscuity, which enhances the risk of cancer of the cervix of the uterus. The mechanisms appear to be varied. An increased body weight increases the production of estrogen by enhancing the conversion of androgens (chapter 9); smoke and alcohol damage the cells they touch; sexual promiscuity promotes the spreading of viruses that predispose to cancer.

There are also substances in food that *decrease* the risk of cancer. The most important sources are vegetables such as carrots, which contain substances related to vitamin A, and those of the cabbage family. Selenium, a rare element present in soils and foods, also seems important: people living in areas depleted of selenium have a higher cancer incidence.

Viruses in Human Cancers?

Viruses offered some of the most important clues about the nature of cancer. They are important agents of cancer in such species as chicken, mice, and cats, but their role in human cancer has been much more difficult to establish. The main reason is that the role of a virus can be directly verified in animals by inoculating them with the virus; in humans indirect criteria must be used, such as the presence of viral genes in cancer cells. But that does not mean that they *cause* cancer.

These difficulties can be seen by considering the role of a virus implicated in human cancer and studied intensively over several decades—the EB virus (from the names of its discoverers, Epstein and Barr). This virus is distantly related to the herpes virus, which produces cold sores. EB virus is almost always present in the cells of Burkitt's lymphoma which, as already mentioned, carry a translocation involving the *myc* oncogene. The EB virus is also associated with certain cancers of the nose in adults, especially in China. In young people it causes glandular fever (infectious mononucleosis), a serious and protracted disease, but not a cancer. The virus is widespread throughout the world and is involved in at least three diseases, two of which are cancers; but in the vast majority of people, it causes no disease at all. It has been proposed that the EB virus generates cancer only in association with favoring circumstances, such as malaria: in Africa the distribution of malaria overlaps well with that of Burkitt's lymphoma.

Since the discovery of the characteristic translocation activating the *myc* proto oncogene, the role of the EB virus in Burkitt's lymphoma has become questionable. Which is the primary event in this cancer: the virus or the translocation? It seems likely that it is the translocation because it is constantly present, whereas the virus is not. Outside Africa most Burkitt's lymphomas do not contain the virus. A possible solution to this enigma may be found in the cooperation of oncogenes: the EB oncogene and the *myc* oncogene can cooperate to produce the lymphoma. But the EB oncogene may be replaced by other (unknown) oncogenes or undefined cellular changes. Malaria would provide a favoring background by modifying the growth of lymphocytes.

Viruses may participate in the causation of other cancers. Among them are liver cancer in Africa and Asia, in which the virus of hepatitis B is strongly implicated; a lymphoma of T lymphocytes observed especially in Japan and the Caribbean, in which a new retrovirus has been discovered (human T-lymphotropic virus, or HTLV); and cancer of the cervix of the uterus, which is related to infection with a virus that causes warts in the genitals (papilloma virus). In no case is there a unique association of the virus with the cancer because most individuals infected by the virus do not have the cancer. Evidently cancer induction requires additional circumstances besides viral infection, perhaps the inactivation of anticancer genes. The precise role of viruses in cancers remains to be established.

The Body's Defenses

The question of whether the body defends itself against the cancer cells is an old one. It has long been proposed that the immune system carries out this defense by recognizing the cancer cells as non-self and destroying them with the help of T killer lymphocytes and other killer cells. Support for this view derives especially from studies of virus-caused cancers in experimental animals. The cells of these cancers usually contain viral proteins at their surfaces; they are recognized as foreign by the immune system, which causes destruction of the cells. But in the case of spontaneous human cancers in an advanced state, there is little evidence for an immune response. Apparently the immune system does not see the cancer cells as foreign, either because they lack foreign antigens or because the immune system has become tolerant to them.

A popular concept—that the immune system defends the body from incipient cancers by destroying most of them before they reach detection—is embodied in the elegant phrase *immune surveillance*. But it is not clear whether the phrase corresponds to reality. An argument against the effectiveness of immune surveillance is the lack of an excess of cancers in mice of a special strain with severely impaired development of T lymphocytes (the nude mice, so called because they are also hairless). But the surveillance might be carried out by cells other than T lymphocytes. Humans with a defective immune system do show an increased frequency of certain cancers, but the effect is modest and the mechanism controversial. The failure of immune defenses in humans may be due to the absence of foreign antigens on the cancer cells, except for those of viral origin. In fact, the proteins of the cancer cells are specified by normal cellular genes; even active oncogenes fundamentally express normal proteins. Extensive studies using monoclonal antibodies, which have exquisite specificity, have failed to identify antigens that are solely present in cancer cells. An alternate possibility is that the immune system recognizes the cancer cells as foreign but has become tolerant of them and does not try to reject them. New therapeutic attempts based on this concept try to boost rejection by decreasing the tolerance.

Yet that the body must possess defenses against cancer is attested to by differences in rates of cancer among species. For instance, cancer incidence in humans is by far lower, per unit of time, than in mice. In general, species with a longer life span have a lower cancer incidence per year. Thus, long-lived animals must have special genetic mechanisms that defend against cancer. The anticancer genes are part of these mechanisms. Other possible important variables are the balance and control of the growth and differentiation factors, the stability of the genome, the efficiency of the detoxifying enzymes and of the DNA repair mechanisms, the gene balance that keeps oncogenes in check, the susceptibility to promoting agents or to cancer-inducing viruses, and the spreading and activity of mobile DNA sequences.

It is a highly complex situation, which is difficult to unravel, especially in the case of humans, where experimentation is impossible. A complete understanding of human cancer may require a complete knowledge of the human genome, a classification of the genes expressed in cells of various types, and knowledge of the various changes present in cancer cells. It is a gargantuan task, but it may be crucial if we are fully to understand and conquer human cancer.

CHAPTER 16

Exploring the World

The Many Adaptations of Life

Living creatures have invaded all corners of the world, from the tops of mountains to the bottoms of oceans, from polar regions to deserts. Some birds can fly at altitudes of seven thousand to eight thousand meters. Other creatures live in the vents at the bottom of the oceans, where extremely hot fumes from deep in the earth leak through cracks of the earth's mantle. In any of these environments creatures must eat (often somebody else); they must not be eaten; and they must reproduce. These requirements are essential for the survival of the species. The genes, therefore, had to develop the necessary tools for the required adaptations—both in terms of body chemistry suitable for performing under extreme conditions and in terms of ability to communicate in order to recognize other creatures as aggressor, prey, or mate.

An overview of these adaptations shows how varied they are. Nature is inventive. The structures and the chemical mechanisms responsible for these adaptations are highly sophisticated. One might not expect that creatures would have at their disposal tools comparable to those produced by the most sophisticated human technology. But when we examine these adaptations we enter a world as amazing as that of science fiction—except that it is real creatures, not fantasies, performing the functions: they have radar and sonar, use magnetic navigation, detect pressure and vibration. We gain the impression that our imagination creates in fiction only what nature has already created in reality. There may be a good reason for this similarity. Nature, probably, has utilized all possible avenues for adaptation offered by physics and chemistry; the human mind has followed the same path and may be approaching the same limit, although with more cumbersome machinery.

315

Surviving Extreme Temperatures

Life in a Hot Environment

Most of life exists at the moderate temperatures with which we are familiar. But creatures have adapted to both very hot and very cold environments. It has been known for some time, for instance, that some bacteria, called *thermophilic* (heat loving), can grow in volcanic hot pools at temperatures reaching 80°C. Nevertheless, it was rather a shock when a bacterium capable of growth at 105°C (above the boiling point of water) was isolated from a hot water spring in the ocean. That, however, is still below the temperature used for sterilization (that is, for killing all bacteria and other microorganisms), which is carried out in the autoclave at about 120°C. It has even been claimed that bacteria grow in vents in the ocean floor, the so-called black smokers twenty-five hundred meters below the surface through which very hot water (350°C or more) emerges from the depths of the earth. In spite of the high temperature, however, the water does not boil because the pressure is so high: it would boil at 460°C.

But growth even at 105°C is amazing. For if bacteria are to grow, membranes must not melt, DNA must replicate and be transcribed, proteins must be made, enzymes must work. Common bacteria would not pass any of these tests. To understand how it is possible for bacteria to live at this high temperature, we must recognize that organisms display a continuum of temperature tolerance that ranges from the freezing to the boiling point of water and beyond. A considerable resistance to high temperatures, then, is not altogether unusual for bacteria. In fact, spores of many ordinary bacteria survive, although they do not multiply, at the temperature of boiling water, and some proteins of the animal body also can withstand boiling.

Thus, there is a range of adaptations to increasing temperatures, and we don't know its upper limit. Very high temperatures, however, have a destabilizing effect on biological structures—an effect that must be compensated in order to maintain life. Protein molecules are probably stabilized by special arrangements of the internal bonds and by extra bonds. DNA could be stabilized by molecules that make additional links between the two chains. Membranes could be reinforced by fatty molecules that span the two leaflets; more stable membranes could be made up of a single, thicker leaflet.

Some other creatures facing the problem of high temperatures are those living in the desert. Here the problem of heat is compounded by dryness; both conditions must be surmounted.

Desert animals defeat heat in three ways: they avoid it, they fight it, or they live with it. Most small animals avoid heat by living underground during the day and emerging from their burrows only at night when temperatures are more tolerable. Other animals fight heat by evaporating water, either through the skin or through the lungs. This defense, however, uses up water, which is scarce in the desert, so it is of limited value. Only one animal is wise enough to live with heat: the camel. The camel's strategy is to start the day with a cool body, at about 34°C (compared with 37°C or more for other warm-blooded animals). During the day the camel absorbs heat, letting the temperature rise to about 41°C. Above that temperature the animal must fight heat by using evaporation, but its body is so well insulated by thick fur that usually this is not necessary.

Some desert animals, like the kangaroo rat, survive without ever drinking water at all—which is especially amazing because they live on dried seeds. Although these animals minimize the loss of water through the lungs or the skin, they cannot avoid the need for water altogether. For instance, some water is necessary for eliminating wastes through the kidney as urine. Desert rodents get this small amount of water in part from the seeds they eat (which are never totally dry) but mostly from an internal source: as a by-product of food utilization. We saw in chapter 3 that when sugars react with oxygen in the mitochondria, one of the end products is water. The rodents utilize this water for their essential needs. It is a parsimonious way of life, but obviously a successful one.

Life in a Cold Climate

Some organisms must cope with the other temperature extreme—that of cold. And here again, mammals face cold the same way they face heat: either by fighting it or by living with it. The third strategy is not an alternative in this case, because cold cannot be avoided: mammals cannot hide from it. To fight cold means that more sugars and fats must be burned and the heat retained under the protection of a thick fur and a layer of fat. This is the strategy employed by most mammals. Others that live with cold do it by hibernating. They replenish their fat reserves, protect themselves from heat loss as best they can, and enter a long sleep. While they sleep they produce the small amount of heat they require by burning sugars directly in special mitochondria, which are a kind of very efficient internal furnace. Some animals while hibernating reach a state of near-death: they are very cold and have a very slow heartbeat. But as their environment warms, they return slowly to their normal state. The most popular hibernator, the bear, is a bit of a fraud: it goes into a prolonged sleep, but it can be easily interrupted even by a light stimulus like a gentle kick. Still other organisms merely become inactive in the cold. And finally, many species survive the cold season by producing dormant embryos, which they may do in elaborate ways, some of which were described in chapter 9.

But whatever their strategy, animals must make sure their blood does not freeze and their brain continues to work. In the case of some polar fish, the first condition is assured by the presence in their blood of large amounts of a peptide (a small protein), which acts as antifreeze. The problem of keeping the brain working is a serious one for fish, however, because the heat produced inside their body is rapidly lost to the surrounding water. Some fish, therefore, have developed special mechanisms for keeping the brain warm. An example is swordfish. They stay near the surface of the water at night where they stalk their prey, but during the day they descend to considerable depths (five hundred meters or more) where the water is cold. To keep their brain warm, they utilize a mass of brown cells that resemble in properties the brown fat of hibernating animals. The brown color comes from an enzyme of mitochondria, which is abundant in the cells and is the source of heat. Veins coming from the brown cells run very close and parallel to the arteries that carry blood to the brain, but the directions of the two flows are opposite. Thus, the blood going to the brain is kept warm at a temperature 10°C to 14°C higher than that of sea water. To perform the function of heater the mass of brown cells is much larger than the brain: it weighs 50 grams, whereas the brain weighs only 2 (in a 130-Kg animal). It is fortunate that the brain is so small: it can easily be kept warm.

Life in the Deep Seas

Marine animals have an obvious need for special adaptations. Because they swim, they must maintain the right buoyancy, which is often accomplished through the use of an appropriate gas-filled bladder. But their main problem is to control the level of salt in the blood, which must be maintained at a critical concentration in order to keep all the various ion pumps (see chapter 2) working at the right pace. Terrestrial animals drink water that has less salt than their blood, so they must accumulate salt, a relatively easy task. Marine animals, in contrast, live in water that has more salt than their blood; if they drink it, they face the more difficult task of getting rid of the excess.

A variety of solutions to this problem has evolved among species. Many fish eliminate excess salt by actively pumping its ions out of their gills. Some marine mammals, like seals or some whales, bypass the problem altogether by feeding on fish. Most whales, however, feed on small sea creatures and in the process ingest a large quantity of sea water. They get rid of the extra salt through their kidneys, which are much more efficient at this task than are those of terrestrial animals. Sea birds and sea turtles have found yet another solution: they pump the ions out of the body in special salt glands located either in the nose or in the eye. The secretion of these glands contains salt at twice the concentration of sea water. The pumping is carried out at the expense of ATP energy.

Another adaptation required by sea mammals is that of deep divers who must avoid the problems connected with dissolution of air nitrogen into the blood. This occurs when the lungs are exposed to high pressure at great depths. Dissolved nitrogen would make these animals sleepy, and when they returned to the surface, the nitrogen would be released in the form of gas bubbles, causing the bends. The sea mammals have solved the problem by collapsing their lungs so completely when they dive that they contain no air at all.

Making the Most of Oxygen

The problem of assuring that enough oxygen is breathed is also solved in a variety of ways by creatures living in different environments. Low-altitude organisms, of which humans are an example, find plenty of oxygen in the air, so they get into trouble only when they move into high altitudes. Then they encounter two problems: oxygen is scarce, and the blood retains much less of the carbon dioxide produced by their cells. This waste substance controls the acidity of the blood: if there is too little carbon dioxide, the blood becomes less acid. The lower acidity, in turn, slows down the brain centers that control breathing. So, paradoxically, at high altitudes people breathe less efficiently, compounding the problem of scarce oxygen.

Adaptations in creatures living at high altitudes, like high-flying birds, have solved these problems. They extract much more oxygen from the air by using especially efficient lungs and extra air sacs in the bones. Moreover, their brain works properly even when the blood's acidity is low. In fact, the low acidity is advantageous for these birds because it increases the capacity of hemoglobin for oxygen; so the transport of scarce oxygen is more efficient.

Marine diving mammals, such as seals or whales, face a different problem concerning oxygen. They must go without access to air for quite long periods. Countering this is the unusually large amount of hemoglobin in their blood that stores the oxygen they need. They do not store air in the lungs as we would do. Another device entails the shutting off of the blood supply to the muscles during a long dive, so that it is diverted almost exclusively to the heart and brain, which need the oxygen most. During the dive the body muscles extract energy from sugars through glycolysis, which, as will be recalled from chapter 3, requires no oxygen. Lactic acid accumulates in the muscles, but it is then utilized as a source of energy at the end of the dive when oxygen becomes available again.

Methods of Communication in Various Species

No creature lives alone on earth; each is part of the whole complex of life. A creature must find others of the same species in order to mate for perpetuating that species; it must identify creatures on which it can feed and others that would use it as food. Many creatures, moreover, live in societies in which they must help one another in a variety of ways. For all these reasons creatures must exchange information. Many kinds of signaling, based on chemical or physical phenomena, can be used; and which one a given creature utilizes varies according to the environment in which it lives.

We are familiar with signaling among animals, but we are less aware that plants are capable of communication, too. Yet there are striking examples of this. For instance, when the leaves of poplars or sugar maples are stripped, the plants react defensively by producing noxious chemicals that make their remaining leaves less appetizing. This personal defense, however, extends to other plants in close proximity. These neighbors also start producing the noxious chemicals, apparently under the influence of some airborne substance released by the stripped plant.

Communication through Light

Light is a most important source of information. Besides its obvious utility for indicating day and night, and the length of the day—two variables of enormous importance for living creatures—it is also useful for determining the direction of objects or of other creatures. Detectors of this sort are easily built because light photons contain large amounts of energy and can easily change the configuration of electrons in many kinds of molecules. We saw in chapter 3 how this ability of photons has been utilized in photosynthesis since very early in evolution; light has also been used as a communicator at least as long.

Plants, which depend entirely on sunlight for generating the ATP they need, have methods for detecting light. We recognize the facts, but know little about the mechanisms. Some plants want to absorb as much sunlight as possible, and to this end they keep their leaves always perpendicular to the direction of the light. Others, wanting to minimize the amount of heat that comes with sunlight, keep their leaves parallel to the direction of the light. Finally, some plants orient their leaves in a fixed way along the meridian—for instance, always facing east-west. The advantage of that orientation may be high light utilization in the morning and evening when it is cool and less heat reception during mid-day. Thus plants strike their own balances between capturing light and overheating.

How the leaves maintain their orientation in the various cases is not known. Many sun-following plants have cells in the form of lenses at their upper surfaces; each cell concentrates the light in one spot. The movement of the leaves is caused by specialized cells at their bases, which change their degree of swelling and therefore their size depending on the direction of light. But how the lens cells and the swelling cells are connected—if indeed they are—we don't know.

Even single-celled organisms use light to explore the environment. Some of them have an *eye spot*, which is a light detector associated with structures for propulsion. The detector directs the motion of the organism toward the light. The mechanism may be similar to that used by bacteria for moving toward a source of food, which will be discussed below. Moving toward the light is especially important in the case of photosynthetic organisms.

All animals of greater complexity have specialized devices for light detection, which we will call *eyes*, even if they look very different from the eyes of mammals. Eyes are built according to three designs. One type is exemplified by eye spots, which are present, for instance, in some worms. These eyes do not make an image of the world; they only detect the direction from which light (or shadow) comes.

They are important for catching prey or for defense against predators. Another design is exemplified by the *mammalian eye*, which is made like a camera. It has a lens, which focuses an image of the world on the light-sensitive layer, the *retina*. It also has a diaphragm, the *iris*, which controls how much light is allowed to enter. This type of eye became extremely refined in the course of evolution. The protein molecules that pack the lens have been selected in such a way that at the concentration ideal for giving a good image they make a completely clear lens. This is not a simple matter because a concentrated protein solution tends to be turbid. Optically, the lens is very advanced. The concentration of protein, and therefore its ability to deflect the light, varies in different layers of the lens—an arrangement that confers on the lens extremely good optical qualities: the lens focuses the image without distortion over a large range of distances. The retina is packed with sensors, which send their signals to the brain. The eye developed the ability to discriminate colors, using a combination of sensors. From impulses generated by the various kinds of sensors the brain reconstructs both the shape and the color of the objects viewed by the eye. We will see how this is done in chapter 18.

A third design for eye construction is the *composite eye*, which is present in a large number of advanced invertebrates, such as insects (fig. 16.1). This eye is made up of a hundred or so small independent eyes, *ommatidia* (meaning small eyes), all close to each other and radially oriented, each one with its own photosensors (fig. 16.2). This arrangement allows the eye to scan an almost spherical field, wider than that of the vertebrate eye; various parts of the eye can concentrate on different parts of the scene in ways that are useful for the specific goals the various creatures pursue.

There is an enormous number of variations of each one of these basic eye designs. The variety is correlated with the specific adaptations of the various species and their precise requirements for survival.

SIGNALS TO THE BRAIN. Essential for the development of the eye was the availability of light sensors, which detect small light differences and convert them into signals that the brain can analyze. The essential function of the eye, in fact, is to allow the brain to generate an image of what is seen.

Light is detected by specialized nerve cells, the *photosensors* (also known as photoreceptors), which generate a nerve signal as a result of a light change. In all photosensors an intermediate step between detecting light and sending the signal is a change in the flux of ions through the cell membrane. We know that in all cells the Na-K pump removes Na^+ ions from the interior of the cells and pumps in K^+ ions. As a result the interior of the cells is rich in K^+ ions and poor in Na^+ ions. N^+ ions tend to flow back into the cell through passive channels, whereas K^+ ions flow out (see chapter 2). Normally the balance of these flows determines the polarization of the cell membrane, making it negative inside. If the entry of Na^+ decreases, or the exit of K^+ increases, the inside surface of the membrane becomes more negative—that is, its polarization is increased. The reverse changes have the

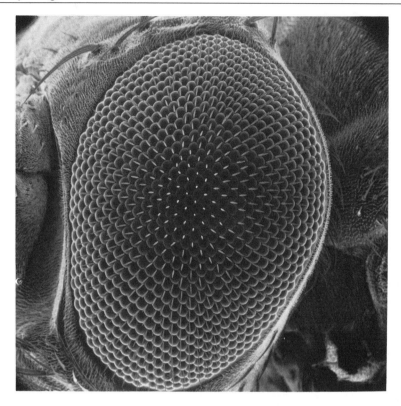

Figure 16.1. The composite eye of the fruitfly *Drosophila*. Each of the small curved surface of an elementary eye, an ommatidium, of which there are about eight hundred, pointing in all directions. The bright lines between ommatida are hairs. Scanning electron microscope photograph: magnified about 300 times. (From D. F. Ready, T. E. Hanson, and S. Benzer, *Developm. Biol.* 53:217–40 [1976].)

opposite result. The effect of light on the photosensors is to change the opening of the ion channels, in some cases increasing it, in others decreasing it. In the horseshoe crab *limulus* and many other invertebrates, an increased illumination reduces outflow of K^+ ions, causing decreased polarization of the membrane and generating a nerve impulse. In contrast, in mammals increased illumination decreases the inflow of Na^+ ions, increasing the polarization of the membrane. The increased polarization does not generate a nerve impulse but works by modulating impulses initiated elsewhere (see chapter 18). Still other arrangements are attuned to the characteristics of the neural network that analyzes the signals.

Our knowledge of the conversion of light to flow of ions is based especially on the study of *rods,* one of the two types of sensors of the mammalian retina, but the mechanism is similar in the other type of sensors, the *cones.* Rods are very sensitive photosensors, a hundred times more so than cones. A single light photon can generate a signal in a dark-adapted rod. But in order to generate a signal many

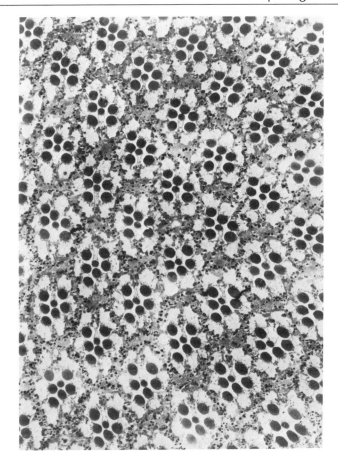

Figure 16.2. The retina of the composite eye shown in figure 16.1. A section through the base of the eye shows that each elementary eye has eight photosensors, of which seven are very prominent, with a characteristic arrangement. Electron microscope photograph; magnified 2,600 times. (From Ready, Hanson, and Benzer).

Na^+ channels must be closed; the rod, therefore, must have an *amplification mechanism*. The study of the chemical events that follow exposure to light explains how this amplification works.

The other segments of rods are full of stacks of hollow membrane-bound *discs*, which contain molecules of rhodopsin. A molecule of rhodopsin is made up of a protein molecule (opsin) and a light-absorbing molecule related to vitamin A, retinal. Rhodopsin is related to a protein that converts light into ATP energy in certain photosynthetic bacteria. The amino acid chains of rhodopsin weave back and forth through the membrane of the discs in such a way that part of the protein is in the interior of the disc and part outside in the cytoplasm of the rod. The retinal is associated with the protein within the disc. The absorption of a photon by retinal causes a rearrangement of bonds in the protein, which transmits the signal across the disc membrane, and the separation of the retinal from the protein.

Considering how the activation of a rhodopsin molecule affects Na^+ channels in the membrane of the rod, we are confronted with two problems. One is that many Na^+ channels are affected: there is amplification of the signal. The other is that the discs are separated from the rod membrane by a narrow gap the signal must cross. Both problems are solved at once by a mechanism involving two proteins of the external surface of the disc membrane, which we will call G (transducin) and P (phosphodiesterase).

Rhodopsin, G, and P act one after another. Rhodopsin activated by light activates G. Activated G, in turn, activates P, which then breaks down cyclic GMP (a substance similar to cyclic AMP, but with G instead of A). Cyclic GMP molecules keep open the Na^+ channels; their breakdown causes the closure of the channels. A single activated rhodopsin molecule activates a few hundred G molecules; each activated G activates one P, but one activated P breaks down many molecules of cyclic GMP. Through this amplification mechanism, a light photon causes the breakdown of a large number of molecules of cyclic GMP and the closure of many Na^+ channels, sufficient to generate an electric signal. This mechanism also explains how the signal is transmitted from the disc to the rod membrane.

An activated rhodopsin is incapable of detecting new photons because it has lost retinal. The association is slowly reestablished by enzymatic reactions without intervention of light. If the eye is illuminated with intense light, many rhodopsin molecules lose retinal and become incapable of detecting photons. The ability of the eye to detect light is accordingly decreased. This loss of sensitivity constitutes the *adaptation* of the eye to light. If darkness follows, the regeneration of rhodopsin progressively restores the sensitivity to the maximum level: the eye becomes dark adapted again.

Many fish and amphibians have another light-sensitive protein in addition to rhodopsin. It is porphyropsin, which is more sensitive to red light. Porphyropsin may be especially suitable for seeing in murky water, where red light predominates. An especially ingenious use of the two proteins is found in the bullfrog, which usually is in the water with only its nose and half of each eye above the surface. The retina of the eye is made up of two parts: the one receiving light from the air contains rhodopsin, whereas the one receiving light from the water contains porphyropsin. So the animal can see equally well the two halves of its split world.

INFORMATION FROM LIGHT. Light plays a major role in the developmental processes of animals and plants. One reason is that the length of daylight is related to the season, which is very important in plant or animal reproduction. Both animals and plants have means for detecting the length of day. In most animals information coming through the eyes influences the operation of the pineal gland. The hormone produced by the gland regulates many body functions. In some creatures with very thin skulls such as birds, fish, and amphibians, the pineal gland itself detects the light changes. Others like lizards or frogs use for this purpose a special eye, situated close to the midline of the head, and called, therefore, the parietal eye (parietal is the name of a bone stretching from the middle line to the side of the skull).

In the case of plants the length of the day determines whether or not flowers will be produced; some plants produce them when days are long, others when they are short. The day length is perceived by the leaves, which then alter the balance of hormones. When the appropriate hormone balance is obtained, the apical shoots will become flowers. This phenomenon is known as *photoperiodism.*

There are other subtle ways in which creatures utilize light for obtaining information. For instance, bees and many other homing animals use the direction of vibration (polarization) of the light waves coming from the sky as a directional reference. That light polarization can be useful for orientation can be seen by a person wearing a pair of sunglasses with polarizing lenses that let through light with only one direction of polarization. These glasses cut off light reflected from a wet pavement because it is polarized in a wrong way. They also show different attenuation of sky light, depending on where it comes from, because sky light is polarized. Many animals, especially those with compound eyes, have devices for detecting polarization. Squid, for instance, have two sets of light receptors, which detect light polarized in two perpendicular directions. Presumably they have two representations of the world, the comparison of which provides enhanced contrast for underwater vision.

Another device enables some creatures to detect the infrared light emitted by warm objects so that they can be "seen" in the dark (infrared light is invisible to the eye). Many snakes use infrared light sensors for identifying the direction of a small animal, like a mouse, for instance. On that clue alone they can strike at the moving animal with deadly accuracy. The snakes' infrared detectors are pits situated in front of the head. Each has a narrow opening and a large cavity, across which is stretched a very thin membrane surrounded by air on both sides and richly penetrated by nerve endings. If a source of infrared light is placed in front of the pit, a narrow beam enters through the opening and strikes a small region of the membrane. The area it strikes depends on the location of the source in respect to the pit's opening. Because the membrane is so thin, it is rapidly warmed by the beam. The extremely sensitive nerve endings in the membrane can detect an increase in temperature of only $0.003°C$, so they readily localize the area hit by the infrared light. From information from various pits the brain computes the position of the source both in direction and distance.

GENERATING LIGHT. Many creatures active under conditions of low or no ambient light generate their own light. Among these are insects that are active at night or aquatic creatures that live at depths of a thousand meters or more where sunlight barely reaches. Light is also made by the microscopic creatures that generate the "red tide" at the ocean surface and make the breakers luminous.

Creatures use the light they produce for several purposes. Fireflies use it as a sexual signal, and fish and other marine animals use it to attract mates or prey, to illuminate the surroundings, or to defend themselves. For instance, some squid, when threatened by predators, eject light-emitting substances instead of ink in order to confuse them.

Light is generated in elaborate structures, which may involve lenses and colored filters, depending on the desired effect. The basic mechanism for generating such bioluminescence is similar in all cases, but different in details. The basic reaction is between a substance with mobile electrons (luciferin—a substance that brings light), an appropriate enzyme (luciferase), oxygen, and ATP. Using ATP energy, the luciferase causes a reaction of luciferin with oxygen, generating a compound with high-energy electrons. As they fall to a lower energy state, they emit light.

Seeking the Poles

It was thought for a long time that living creatures have nothing to do with magnetism, except in a figurative or symbolic way. But in fact nature has not ignored the existence of the magnetic field that envelops the earth.

The clearest example of the use of magnetism is the bacteria that live in the mud of marshes. They have at their surfaces several long thin appendages called flagella, which stick together and whip around in a circular motion (fig. 16.3). The rotation of the flagella propels a bacterium through the liquid. If one observes a small drop of marsh water containing several bacteria, one will see that, curiously, they all swim in the same direction. This behavior is caused by an internal compass, which orients the cells in the direction of the terrestrial magnetic field. The compass is made up of a row of crystals of the iron compound magnetite, which is naturally magnetic. The bacteria make the magnetite from iron dissolved in the water. In the Northern Hemisphere the orientation of the magnets in respect to the flagella is such that the bacteria move toward the North Pole. If they are exposed to a powerful magnet, they likewise move toward its North Pole.

Why should the bacteria care about the North Pole? There is a good reason. These organisms live in the depth of marshes where there is no oxygen. If they swim to the surface, the oxygen there poisons them. By seeking the North Pole in the Northern Hemisphere, the bacteria go not only north but also down—because of the direction of the attractive force of the earth's magnetic field.

But what do these bacteria do in the Southern Hemisphere where the North Pole points up rather than down? As would be expected, most of them swim to the surface of the water and die. The few that survive have changed allegiance. They move toward the South Pole and thus descend to the bottom of the marsh. These bacteria, then, can have a compass pointing in either direction: those with the right orientation survive, and the others do not. When a bacterium divides, the magnetite is distributed, more or less equally, between the two daughter cells. The new magnets manufactured by the daughter cells keep the same orientation be-

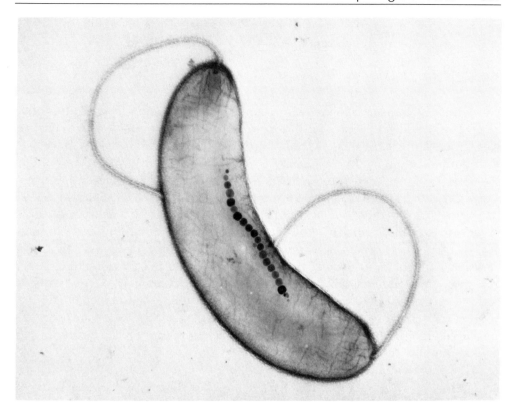

Figure 16.3. A magnetic bacterium seen in the electron microscope. At the two ends the bacterium has two long appendages, the flagella, which, by whipping around, propel it through the ligand medium. Inside the cell is a string of small crystals of magnetite, which orient the bacterium in the electric field of the earth. Magnified 56,000 times. (From R. P. Blakemore and R. D. Frankel, *Scient. Amer.* 245:58–65 [1981].)

cause as they grow they are oriented by the preexisting ones. The orientation is hereditarily—but not genetically—controlled. Cells with an orientation opposite to that prevailing in the population are produced from time to time, presumably when a daughter cell inherits no magnets. When such a cell makes new ones, they can be oriented either way.

These findings with bacteria raise the possibility that many other organisms may be able to detect the earth's magnetic field and use it as a directional reference. Such a property would be important during migrations, for instance (see below). Many animals have been searched for magnetite, and small amounts have been found in bees, pigeons, dolphins, many kinds of fish, sea turtles, and even humans. In humans, as in other primates and rodents, magnetite is found in the bones of the skull that surround the nose. What these findings mean is not clear. Attempts have been made to see whether homing species, like pigeons, salmon, and bees, can orient themselves in the earth's magnetic field. The results suggest that some species do. Magnetite may be formed, however, as a means of getting rid of excess iron. It is suitable for this purpose because it is insoluble: the iron is trapped forever. But much remains to be learned in this field.

Electrical Signals

Electrical phenomena, as we saw in chapter 2, control important features of all cells. They are also the basis for the operation of the nervous system (see chapter 17). It is not surprising, then, that some organisms have used electricity as a means of communication.

Certain African fish and electric eels have an organ that generates electrical discharges several hundred times a second. These fish also have eletrical sensors along the sides of their bodies, related to those that detect mechanical waves, which are extremely sensitive: they can detect even one-hundredth of a millionth of a volt. The pulses produced by the electrical organ propagate through the water, forming a kind of cloud around the fish. If an object enters the cloud, it creates a distortion that is detected by the electric sensors. The characteristics of the distortion give information about the obstacle: Is it a living organism? What is its motion? Is it predator or prey? A kind of radar is at work, although one operating on a different principle. The information is precious because it can be obtained in darkness and without contact.

The electrical pulses emitted by a fish are detected by other fish, which can determine from their characteristics the sender's species and even its sex. So electricity is used as a mating signal.

All creatures in water emit electrical signals, although they are much weaker than those emitted by electric organs. They are created by the many electrical activities that go on in the body. These signals can be picked up at the surface of human beings, too, as an expression of the heart's or brain's activity. In the water these activities give rise to weak electrical currents, and the corresponding signals are picked up by predators, like sharks, which have extremely sensitive electrical sensors. It is a highly efficient and astute way to detect prey, even when it is hidden in turbid water or in the mud.

Another possible use of electrical signals by fish is for establishing direction. Because ocean currents flowing through the magnetic field of the earth produce electrical currents, as in a dynamo, they can be used by fish as directional references. Moreover, the swimming of a fish through the earth's magnetic field also produces electric currents. Their characteristics depend on the direction of the motion relative to the magnetic field, so that they may give the fish information about its own direction.

Communication through Taste and Smell

The senses of taste and smell play multiple roles in species communication. They are the means by which organisms identify suitable food. Many species also use the sense smell for mate recognition (see chapter 10). Others generate unpleasant tastes or smells in order to deter other animals from attacking and preying upon them.

All these forms of communication are based on sensors—present in all living creatures—that recognize special chemical substances. In terrestrial animals, the sensors for taste are different from those for smell. They are epithelial cells that send signals to the brain through connecting nerve fibers; smell sensors, in contrast, are nerve cells that send signals directly to the brain. The ability to smell is not exclusive to terrestrial animals; fish also have noses, that is, cavities lined with cells similar to those present in the nose of air-breathing animals. Fish also have taste sensors, which can be located at many points on the surface of the body.

In all creatures taste and smell are used to detect two diverse groups of substances: taste detects water-soluble substances, which are fairly abundant; smell detects substances that are present in diluted concentrations and are not very soluble in water. Among the substances that some animals taste or smell is water itself, which some animals seek and others avoid.

THE TASTE BUDS OF BACTERIA. Bacteria can recognize specific chemical molecules. Sensing differences in the concentration of a substance in the medium in which they swim, they move toward a source of food, such as some sugars or amino acids, or move away from a repellent, such as nickel or cobalt ions. This phenomenon is called *chemotaxis*, meaning the movement of the cell under a chemical influence. For the purpose of the following discussion, high or low concentrations of an attractant and low or high concentrations of a repellent will be considered interchangeable.

Chemotactic bacteria have long thin appendages, flagella, which by their rotation propel them through a watery medium. In a medium providing an attraction stimulus, the flagella rotate in a counterclockwise direction. From time to time the direction of the motion is temporarily inverted to clockwise, causing the bacterium to tumble and change direction. In a liquid without attractants or repellents the bacterium makes short runs, then changes direction, runs again, and changes direction again, all in a random fashion; thus it does not go anywhere. If, however, a source of attractant is present in the medium, the changes of direction become less random: its runs toward the source last longer than those in the opposite direction, and it moves in jumps toward the source.

The movement of the flagella is controlled by a system of *transducers* of which four kinds are known, each with different specificities. They are protein molecules similar to receptors and made up of several domains inserted in the cell membrane. One domain reaches outside the membrane and acts as receptor for the attractant; a second domain anchors the protein to the membrane; and a third sticks out in the cytoplasm. The cytoplasmic domains have sites for attachment of m-groups (methyl groups), which have variable occupancy: the transducers are highly methylated in the presence of high concentrations of the attractant they recognize. M-groups are attached to the transducer by an enzyme and removed by another enzyme; their number on the transducer results from the interplay of these two enzymes.

The transducers control the rotation of the flagella by comparing in the following manner the concentration of the attractant at a certain point in time with what it was at a previous point. The measurement of the concentration *at a given point in time* is based on the binding of molecules of attractant to the outer domain of the transducers. Each molecule binds to the transducers for a brief time and then leaves it. As a result, if the concentration of attractant is high, the proportion of occupied transducers is high, and vice versa. The concentration has an opposite effect on the *sensitivity* of the transducers, which decreases under conditions of high occupancy with an attractant. The system adapts to these concentrations in much the same way that the eye adapts to light of various intensities. Because the sensitivity level persists for some time (as it does in the eye), it measures the attractant concentration at a *previous point in time*. The mechanism of adaptation is some structural change of the transducer after binding attractant.

The relationship of attractant occupancy (corresponding to the present attractant concentration) to sensitivity (the past concentration) determines the response of the bacterium. If the ratio continues to increase—that is, present concentration higher than past concentration—no or little tumbling takes place, and the cell moves on though increasing concentrations of attractants. If the ratio decreases, tumbling occurs. Instructions for tumbling are conveyed to the flagellar motor by a small protein present in the cytoplasm, but the details are not known.

A second adaptive mechanism is provided by the m-groups attached to the cytoplasmic domain of the transducer: they adjust the basic sensitivity of the transducers so that the cell can have effective chemotaxis over a large range of concentrations of attractants or repellents. It is interesting that the enzyme that removes the m-groups when attractant is low is related to the protein that controls the flagellar motor, suggesting that a common control achieves the two objectives of tumbling and lowering the basic sensitivity to the attractant. As a result when the concentration of attractant decreases, the cell not only tumbles but also increases its basic sensitivity: it moves to a different space and at the same time adjusts to the lower availability of attractant. A simple and efficient system.

Not many animals are, like these bacteria, covered by taste sensors all over the body, but some are. For instance, the starfish or the sea cucumber are literally covered by chemical sensors. These animals probably need them because they form intimate associations, based on chemical signals, with other members of their communities. Among the important signals are those that cause all the animals to spawn at the same time (see chapter 10). In contrast, most other animals have taste sensors only in the mouth. Insects have separate sensors for different groups of substances, such as salt, water, sugars, and acids.

DISCRIMINATION. Most discriminating of all is the sense of smell, which can identify a very large number of chemicals. This is reflected, for instance, in the ability of insects to discriminate among many closely related pheromones (see chapter 10). The sensitivity of the sense of smell is remarkable: only nine molecules of the odorous substance emitted by skunks, for instance, are needed for human beings to recognize the smell.

Recognition of smells takes place in the *olfactory epithelium*, the lining that covers the upper part of the nose. This lining is penetrated by a large number of nerve cells and is covered by mucus arranged in several layers of different viscosity. Each nerve cell has a bundle of long hairlike appendages (cilia) traversing the mucus layer from the bottom to the top. At the opposite end of these cells is a nerve fiber that goes to the brain. A remarkable and unusual characteristic of these nerve cells is that they are replenished all the time from a reservoir of undifferentiated cells.

Smell results from the interaction of odorous substances with receptors present in the hairs of the nerve cells. The spectrum of receptors determines the spectrum of odors that can be perceived. The chemical machinery that generates a nerve impulse from the interaction of an odorous molecule with a receptor is similar to that used in hormone-sensitive cells (see chapter 8). It causes release into the cytoplasm of a second messenger, cyclic AMP; this molecule, in turn, seems to be responsible for changing the opening of ion channels to generate a nerve impulse.

Altogether we understand very little of how smells are characterized, although we can formulate hypotheses. One possibility is that the receptor proteins are extremely varied, almost like antibodies or T lymphocyte receptors (see chapters 13 and 14): the brain would know which cell has which protein and, on this basis, identify the smell. Another possibility is that the lining of the nose is a chemical machine that separates molecules according to their properties, such as solubility in the mucus or the ability to diffuse through it. The various substances would stimulate different groups of cells, and the brain would identify the substances from the location of the responding nerve cells. The most puzzling finding is the continuous formation of new nerve cells; it is likely to be important, but we don't know the reason for it.

Using Sound Waves

Most animals have some kind of hearing, which is the perception of sound waves. As we have seen in chapter 10, insects or spiders produce and receive sounds as part of communication between mates, but sound communication is especially developed in vertebrates.

Sound signals are received by special organs that in invertebrates may be located in various parts of the body but in vertebrates are present only in the head.

The key constituent of these organs is the *hair cell*, which is made like a shaving brush (fig. 16.4). It has a round, elongated body covered at one end by a clump of long fine hairs, evenly spaced where they emerge from the cell but clumped together at the top. At the other end the cell body is connected to nerves through which it sends signals to the brain.

The hair cell emits a signal if the hair tuft is pushed sideways even by a minimal amount—something corresponding to the width of a few atoms. This happens because the movement disturbs the reciprocal position of the hairs in the tuft. The displacement, in turn, mechanically opens passive ion channels located at the tips of the hairs; through them positively charged ions rush into the cell. The ion influx lowers the membrane potential of the cell, sending a signal to the brain through the connecting nerve fibers.

How sound waves cause movements of these hair tufts differs among various animals, but the basic principle is similar. In mammals the sound waves traveling

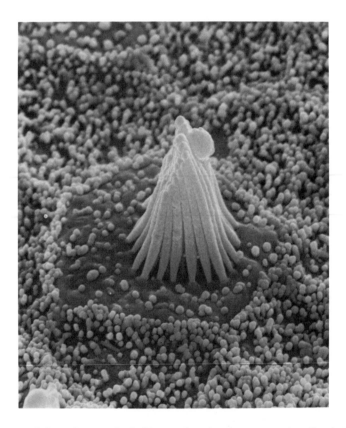

Figure 16.4. A hair cell from the ear of a bullfrog. It has the characteristic bundle of about fifty hairs, clumped at the top. One of the hairs is different: it is thicker and more rigid, and has a swelling at the top. Although very prominent, it is not required for activity: it is absent in human ears. Scanning electron photograph; magnified 20,000 times. (From A. J. Hudspeth, *Scient. Amer.* 248:54–64 [1983].)

through the air hit the outer ear and are funneled by its folds into the ear canal, which ends against the flexible membrane of the eardrum. The sound waves cause pressure changes against the membrane, which then oscillates back and forth. The displacements of the membrane are transmitted through a chain of three small bones to an opening in the bone of the skull. This opening is the end of a canal of complicated shape called the labyrinth, which is dug in the thickness of the bone. The labyrinth is full of liquid that transmits the vibration generated by the sound.

FUNCTIONS OF THE LABYRINTH. The labyrinth has several sections. The part devoted to sound detection is a long tube, which in mammals is curled almost like a snail and therefore is called the *cochlea*. The tube is divided into three compartments separated by two membranes that run the length of the tube (fig. 16.5). The upper and lower compartments are in communication and are filled with the vibrating fluid, which, like all body fluids, is poor in K^+ ions. The middle compartment is filled with static liquid rich in K^+ ions. The hair cells are stuck in the lower membrane, with the hairs sticking out in the middle compartment and connected to a membrane secured at the side, which forms a kind of roof over them. Positive ions continuously flow from the K^+-rich fluid of the middle com-

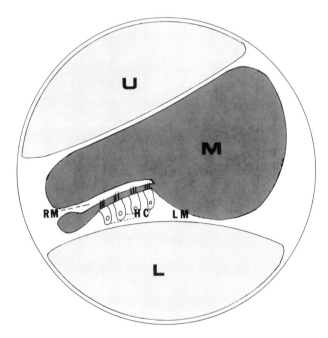

Figure 16.5. A cross section through the cochlear tube. The tube contains three compartments, upper (U), middle (M), and lower (L). Upper and lower compartments (light gray) containing fluid with low K^+ content receive sound waves, whereas the middle compartment (dark gray), rich in K^+, does not. Vibrations through the lower compartment are transmitted to the lower membrane (LM) and hair cells (HC), the hairs of which are stuck to the stationary roof membrane (RM).

partment into the hair cells, which are in contact with the K^+-poor liquid of the lower compartment. The vibrations caused by the sound waves are transmitted through the lower compartment to the hair cells, displacing the tips of the hairs stuck in the roof membrane. The ion channels open and close in synchrony with the sound, causing pulsations in the ion flow and generating signals that reach the brain through the nerve fibers associated with the cells.

Different hair cells respond to different pitches (frequencies) of sound. This tuning is generated by several mechanisms. Depending on the pitch, the vibration of the membranes causes different excursions at different places, the location of which depends on the acoustic properties of the canals and the membrane itself. Additional factors are tuning of the hair tufts and electrical tuning of the hair cell membranes. Low-frequency sounds are detected at the tip of the cochlea, and high-frequency sounds at its base. The brain identifies the pitch of the sound from the location of the hair cells from which it receives signals.

The other two sections of the labyrinth are devoted to the detection of movement rather than sound recognition. One section has three fluid-filled circular canals at right angles to each other. Each canal has a bulge containing a flexible membrane in the form of a dome and filled with jelly. At the base of the dome is a clump of hair cells, anchored to the bone, with the hairs sticking into the jelly. If the head spins, the liquid tends to lag behind in one or more of the canals, owing to its own inertia. The liquid pushes the membrane of the dome, distorting it; the hairs of the hair cells are bent, and a signal goes to the brain.

The other section is made up of two fluid-filled sacs that detect changes of speed—that is, acceleration. They operate on the same principle used by instruments that detect earthquakes. Each contains a clump of hair cells anchored to the bone and touches a membrane loaded with dense crystals. If the head makes a sudden movement, the hair cells move with it, but the crystal-loaded membrane lags behind. The hair tufts bend, and a signal reaches the brain. These sacs allow us to feel the starting and stopping of an elevator, for instance, although we do not see it moving. The three canals and the two sacs are essential for determining the equilibrium of the body and controlling its movements.

The hair cells are versatile sensors and can be adapted to a variety of purposes. In the ear they detect sound and acceleration. As we will see below, they are also suitable for detecting changes of pressure.

DETECTING WHERE A SOUND COMES FROM. We can readily locate the direction of a noise in a horizontal plane. The brain computes the direction from the differences of the pressure waves reaching the two ears. They are hit at slightly different times by a sudden sound, and the changes in pressure they perceive while the sound goes on are not quite synchronous.

The direction in a vertical plane is estimated from the reflections caused by the ridges and folds of the outer ears. Our ears are not well designed for this task, however, and we are not good at it. The creature that performs this sort of detection best is the barn owl (fig. 16.6), which eats small animals, especially mice. Because it hunts at night, the owl must locate the position of its prey very precisely without seeing it. To this end, the owl has special ears. Its outer ears, which are enormous, include the two yellow haloes around the eyes, the *facial ruff*. Despite appearances, the ruff has nothing to do with the eyes. Rather, it is made up of stiff feathers that channel the sound into two grooves extending from the beak to the ears. Another special feature is that the opening of the right ear points upward, and that of the left ear downward. In this way the balance of the sound reaching the two ears is affected by the vertical position of the source. Owls identify the horizontal direction of a sound the same way humans do, and equally well, but because of the facial ruff, they are greatly superior in locating a vertical direction. In fact, if the ruff is shaved, the animal loses its vertical discrimination, while retaining the horizontal one.

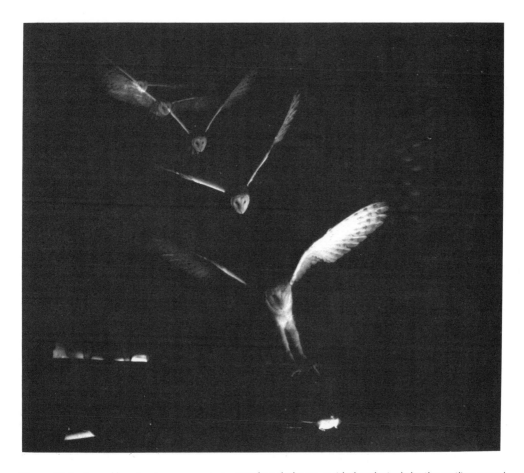

Figure 16.6. An owl homing in on a mouse in complete darkness, guided exclusively by the rustling sound of its prey. Courtesy of M. Konishi.

Creatures without outer ears (like tree frogs) detect the horizontal direction of a sound by lateral movements of the head which scan the various directions. They can estimate the vertical direction by scanning with their head pointing up or down. Fish have a much tougher problem in detecting the origin of a sound, because sound travels much faster in water than in air and reaches the two ears almost at the same time. Yet fish can locate a sound's origin quite well and can also estimate its distance fairly accurately. Apparently they do this by analyzing two features of the sound waves: the changes in pressure (like terrestrial animals) and the oscillating displacement of the water molecules. The pressure changes are detected by gas-filled channels that touch the ear but are actually part of the swim bladder, which imparts buoyancy to the fish. The movements of the water are measured by acceleration detectors similar to those in the mammalian ear that detect head movement.

ANIMAL SONAR. Animals that must hunt, navigate, or mate in the darkness do not simply rely on sound generated by the object of their searches. Some of them use sonar—*echolocation*. They generate rapid sound clicks and determine the direction of the object from the echoes they receive back. Sonar is used by both terrestrial and marine mammals: insect-eating bats use it in the air, and dolphins, whales, and seals, in the water. The sound used is in the ultrasonic range (inaudible to the human ear) because it is more effective.

Information about the location and other characteristics of the object is obtained from the delay of the echo, the spectrum of its frequencies, and their intensities. The direction of the returning sound is determined by the ears as described above. This type of sonar can be very precise. The bat, for instance, can locate objects in both the horizontal and the vertical planes as efficiently as the owl, and it effectively pursues a rapidly moving target.

Touch at a Distance

We know that organisms detect objects that touch their skin. (We will discuss this further in chapter 18.) But as a means of sensing the environment another kind of touch may be even more important—touch at a distance. This is possible in water where movement causes local pressures to build up. Fish and tadpoles (but not frogs because they live in air) have exquisitely sensitive devices to detect these pressures. They look like small capsules with a very thin wall cut in half, with their bases at the skin and the dome in the water. At the bottom each capsule has a hair cell, similar to those used in sound detection. The wall of the capsule can easily bend when the water pressure changes locally. Then the liquid that fills the capsule moves the hairs of the hair cells, and their movement generates a nerve signal. The pressure detectors are arranged along a line at the side of the fish—the *lateral line* which stretches from head to tail.

Fish make use of these detectors to recognize moving creatures in their close surroundings and to detect obstacles they encounter on their paths; the obstacles perturb the normal pattern of pressure around the moving fish. Information from the lateral line is especially useful for fish that live in schools: it continually tells them about the location of other fish in the school.

Restless Dwellers

The sophisticated methods animals use for exploring the environment are essential tools for those that migrate regularly from one place to another on the earth. In fact, members of a large number of species are not content to live their lives at the place where they were born but are spurred to migrate far afield, usually returning to the place of origin before the end of their lives. This behavior is observed in creatures of all kinds: small marine invertebrates, sandworms, crabs, insects— like locusts or monarch butterflies—ladybugs, many kinds of fish, reptiles, birds, and even mammals, both flying (bats) and nonflying (caribou, deer, and others). The migratory instinct characteristic of the human species is found throughout the biological world.

Each species has its own pattern of migration, which is correlated with either feeding or reproductive habits. The distance traveled may be very long, in many cases ranging in the thousands of miles. Much of this may be over water: some birds migrate from the Aleutian Islands to Hawaii, more than two thousand miles away.

Not only do creatures travel long distances; they locate their destinations with great precision. The salmon leaves the stream in which it is born, reaches the ocean, travels hundreds or thousands of miles, and then returns home, usually to its stream of origin. Eel eggs hatch in the Sargasso Sea; the transparent larvae are transported by ocean currents to the North American or European continental shelves. When they reach the coastal waters they take to rivers and streams, swimming upstream in large numbers as they grow to full size. After some years of sedentary life they swim back to the sea and follow the current to the Sargasso Sea, where they mate and die. Several years of travel through varied environments are involved in their odyssey.

How these spectacular feats are accomplished is a matter of considerable interest. How do the animals know when and where to go? And how do they manage to get there?

The urge to go is generated by a complex of environmental and hormonal factors. Desert locusts migrate when food becomes insufficient, mostly because the population has grown too large. Then they form swarms of up to ten thousand million insects and fly to a more favorable feeding area. Many other species migrate at a precise time of the year; the urge, probably, is supplied by hormonal changes controlled by the pattern of daylight. The main control of these changes appears to be in the pineal gland, hormones of the thyroid gland, and the gonads.

Migratory animals find their way by following a variety of clues. Marine animals, as in the case of eels, often follow the current. What is more difficult to understand is how salmon find their streams of origin or how birds navigate over great distances, sometimes over water.

Some of the clues followed by birds are apparently innate, for birds reared alone develop the urge to migrate. Most migrate at night and use several kinds of information: the position of the sun at sunset, the polarization of the sky light, or the position of the stars. The clues they follow have been learned by studying the birds in a planetarium, where they are shown skies of various types. Under the appropriate sky they try to take off in the direction followed during the regular migration of the species. Thus, they follow genetically determined instructions. They must be quite complicated not only because of the many variables involved but also because the position of the sun or the stars varies with the time of day. The birds, then, must inherit a time-adjusted map of the sky. That this is the case can be shown by adapting birds to longer or shorter days. After a while their own clock is shifted in respect to the normal clock, and they take off in a direction that is false, but that is correct for their subjective time. How these intricate instructions are encoded in the genes and how the genes mold the brain of the creature so that it will be able to find its way are mysteries, and difficult ones to solve.

Another possible clue followed by migratory animals is magnetism, used sometimes by homing pigeons. When pigeons return to their loft from a distant place, they mostly use as reference the position of the sun, correcting for the time of day. They can orient themselves pretty well, however, even under covered skies, and some experiments suggest that magnetism is used under these conditions. Pockets of magnetite crystals are indeed present in pigeons at the base of the head and are possibly connected to the stretch sensors of the muscles. Depending on their orientation the crystals may induce signals in the sensors which then influence the strength of contraction of certain muscles and therefore the direction of flight.

Important orientation clues are also offered by smells. Many experiments show conclusively that pigeons recognize familiar smells in the wind and are guided by them. Smells in the water are the main clue for salmon when they home in on their stream of origin. When they are at a distance, they may use the sun or magnetism as reference.

Familiar landmarks, also used by homing pigeons when they approach their loft, are used by bees when they return to a food source. Bees, and ants as well, use both the sun and the direction of polarization of sky light for guidance. A bee that has found food instructs other bees on how to reach it through a dance, or a series of revolutions, that identify the position of the food in respect to that of the sun.

We see that nature, through built-in instruments, uses most of the systems of navigation that we have invented. Not much is new under the sun.

CHAPTER 17

The Machinery of the Brain

The Brain and DNA

In the evolution of life DNA created the brain because devices were needed for sensing the environment: prey had to be identified, predators avoided, a mate located. The primitive brain was capable only of automatic reactions, but as evolution continued, it acquired greater prominence. It evolved to the point of being the arbiter of essential decisions—for instance, whether to mate or not. In the human species the brain has still greater power; it can even decide whether to live or not to live.

DNA had to keep control of these developments. Early in the evolution of life it was easy: DNA could specify each single brain cell. As it became useful to increase vastly the number of brain cells, direct control became impossible, so DNA's control became indirect. The DNA role was limited to specifying the general rules for the brain's organization, allowing the environment to determine its fine details. This was a smart move for DNA, because living creatures must primarily fit their environment. As we will see in chapter 18, during the development of the individual its environment selects after the fact the details of organization that allow the organism to perform best. DNA makes the brain and the environment tests its details, and either approves or rejects them. The brains of advanced creatures can adapt especially well to the environment because they are flexible; the same basic organization can adapt to many different environments. Even in them DNA has retained some control of the final organization in an indirect way because it specifies the rules by which the brain adapts to the environment. The brain's decisions, however, do not have to comply with DNA's goals; they can even countermand them. But these decisions ultimately test the inventiveness of DNA because they affect the ability of the species to survive.

The partial independence of the brain from DNA developed progressively in evolution. At first the rules of DNA were simple and ruthless: organism was pitted against organism in a fight for supremacy, in which the loser disappeared. The brain was merely a tool in this fight. But in the most advanced species, especially humans, the rules are less simple because the brain intervenes. It introduces not only constraints but also equivocation in the fight for supremacy. On one hand, it generates destructive weapons for the all-out fight; on the other, it generates awareness that the fight can lead to the destruction of individuals, and possibly of the species, and of DNA itself. So the push for supremacy, which is the goal of DNA, is dampened by the brain. Will this precarious balance last? If it ends, which way will humanity go? These are questions that cannot be answered because, as we will see in chapter 20, the course of evolution is not straightforward: it is full of hidden unforeseeable events.

The brain is part of the *nervous system*, which senses the environment, controls the motion of muscles, and reaches decisions for action. The first hint of how this system operates was given by the discovery that a muscle contracts—becomes shorter—if an electrical current is applied to the nerve connected to it. Later, electrical activity was observed in nerves and in the brain, suggesting that the system is an electrical machine. The brain, then, is both a chemical and an electrical machine. Electrical phenomena are responsible for transmitting signals within nerve cells, but the transmission from one cell to another, which is fundamental to the decision-making function of the brain, depends largely on chemical events.

The brain contains a vast number of special cells called *neurons*, decision-making elements distantly comparable to the transistors used in computers. A kind of computer, the brain in advanced species, like humans, is highly sophisticated. Each neuron is able to respond to a large number of signals from other neurons—some positive, some negative—summing them up. Each neuron, therefore, is much more than a transistor; it is itself a computer. The use of chemicals for transmitting the signals contributes to the brain's sophistication.

Neurons

The neurons are cells with very special properties (fig. 17.1). They have a central *body*, which looks more or less like any other cell, roundish or somewhat elongated. But attached to the body are appendages of two kinds that are absent in other kinds of cells: the *dendrites* and the *axon*. The dendrites are like the branches of a tree, whose trunk is the cell body. They are thick near the body and become thinner as they repeatedly branch. In structure and function the dendrites are very much like the body of the neuron. Some dendrites are smooth, and others are covered with bumps, which, as we shall see, have an important functional meaning. The axon, in contrast, is always single at the start, but may branch off later.

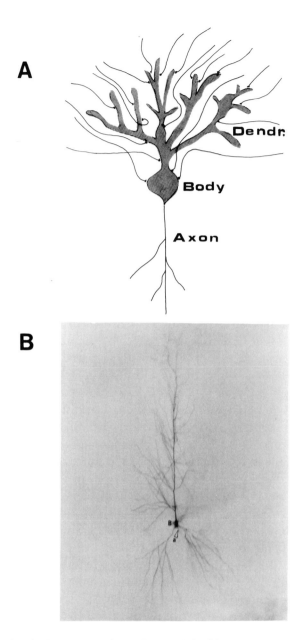

A

Dendr.

Body

Axon

B

Figure 17.1. (A) Sketch of a neuron. It shows the rounded cell body, with the dendrites coming out at one end and the axon at the other. The axon is much thinner and longer, and branches repeatedly. The body and the dendrites of the neuron are connected to a large number of axon branches coming from other, usually distant, neurons. These axon branches have buttons at their ends, the synapses. (B) Photograph of a neuron of the cerebral cortex of a rat. In order to visualize the neuron, it was impaled by an extremely thin needle through which a small quantity of an enzyme (peroxidase) was injected. The enzyme slowly became distributed throughout the neuron and a chemical reaction it catalyzed generated a brown substance, which makes it visible. The neuron body (b) is at its lower part. All the appendages are dendrites; some of them are faint because they stretch toward the back and are masked by unstained brain matter. The point of emergence of the axon (a) is shown by the arrow. Only its very beginning is visible because it curves away. Magnified 170 times. Courtesy of W. Maxwell Cowan.

Comparing it to a tree, it would be a very long tap root. Whereas the dendrites reach only a short distance away, something like ten to twenty times the size of the body of the neuron, the axon may be extremely long; in large animals it may be a meter long or more. Bundles of long axons constitute the nerves, which stretch from the brain or the spinal cord to the muscles, sensors, and glands throughout the body. Axons are very thin, but they display a range of sizes. When an axon branches, its diameter usually remains constant.

The tip of each branch of the axon has a tiny button that touches the dendrite of another neuron, forming a *synapse*, or junction. Some axons form synapses with muscle fibers or with cells of glands. Synapses are specialized structures that transfer signals from the axon to the neuron. Each neuron is surrounded by a maze of axons coming from many other neurons. It looks like a tree infested by vines that envelop it with tiny branches and have numerous suckers, the synapses, that stick to various parts of the tree. A neuron may have 100,000 synapses or more on its body and dendrites.

The neurons contain several kinds of filamentous proteins, such as microtubules (see chapter 2), that maintain the shape of the neuron and are important for its function. Neurons also contain many mitochondria (see chapter 3) which convert sugar into ATP. Because neurons need much ATP to run the various ion pumps that are essential for their functions, they use lots of sugar.

The neuron body—which contains the nucleus—and the dendrites manufacture the substances needed for the activities of the neuron. They pick up amino acids from the surrounding fluid and convert them into proteins. They make membranes and many molecules important for their functions. The finished products flow down the axons toward the synapses in groups that travel at different speeds—some move quickly (400mm a day) and others very slowly (0.3mm a day). The axon is a two-way road, because it also transports molecules from the synapses to the body of the neuron. The transport is probably carried out by microtubules, abundant in axons, in conjunction with other proteins. Some of the proteins made in the body (for instance, the receptors, which we will discuss below) go to the synapses where they perform their functions and then are returned to the body for reutilization. Other molecules going from the synapse to the body are foreign to the neuron; they are picked up by the synapse from the environment surrounding it. As we will see in the next chapter, researchers take advantage of this feature for mapping the course of the axons. Proteins picked up at a synapse, after reaching the body of a neuron, may be picked up by the axon of another neuron. Using this route, poisons or viruses can damage the organism by spreading throughout the nervous system.

Ions through the Neuronal Membrane

The operation of a neuron as a decision-making device is based on two properties: one is the generation of electrical currents, which carry signals from the cell body to the synapses through the axon and its branches; the other is the conversion of these electrical signals into chemical signals in the synapses (fig. 17.2). The receiving neuron then converts the chemical signals back into electrical signals.

We will examine first the generation of electrical signals in axons. This property is based on the characteristics of the membrane that surrounds the axon. Like the membranes of all cells, the neuron's membrane is basically made up of a double layer of fatty molecules, which separates the interior of the neuron from its environment. And as in other cells, the two compartments are connected to each other only by channels made up of protein molecules. Different channels admit different substances, such as electrically charged ions, sugars, or amino acids.

The operation of neurons depends on the movements of ions through their membranes (fig. 17.3). Three kinds of ions are positively charged: sodium (Na^+), potassium (K^+), and calcium (Ca^{++}), whereas one, chloride (Cl^-), is negatively charged. Most of the channels for these ions are passive; that is, they allow the passage of ions downhill from the compartment of higher concentration to that of lower concentration. Neurons, in addition, like other cells, contain sodium-potassium pumps, which pump sodium ions out of the cell and potassium ions into the cell. As a result, the inside of neurons, like that of all other cells, is rich in

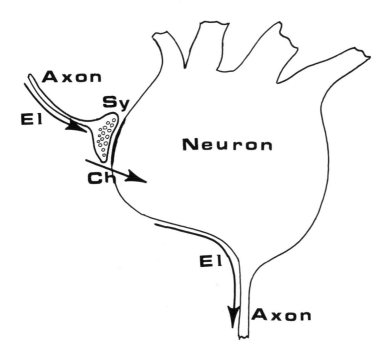

Figure 17.2. Propagation of signals from one neuron to another. The axon of a distant neuron carries an electrical signal (El). At the synapse (Sy) the electrical signal is converted into a chemical signal (Ch). In the neuron the signal is converted back into an electrical signal that is channeled into the axon at the bottom.

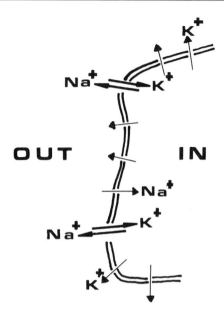

Figure 17.3. A segment of neuronal membrane (shown as a double line) is crossed by several ion channels which are essential for the function of the neuron. They include the active channels that pump Na⁺ ions out and at the same time K⁺ into the cell; there are passive channels that allow the passage of ions from the compartment where the concentration is higher to that where it is lower. Shown are passive K⁺ channels, through which K⁺ continuously exits from the neuron, and passive Na⁺ channels, through which Na⁺ enters the neuron. The membrane potential is determined by the passive flows.

potassium and poor in sodium. The operation of the pump consumes the largest part of the ATP generated in neurons, and the ion imbalances it creates are the main motor for their operation. Again as in other cells, passive ion flows are the main cause of the electrical phenomena of neurons (see chapter 2). The downhill flow of K⁺ ions out of the neuron polarizes the neuronal membrane, generating a resting membrane potential, which usually has the value of about seventy millivolts (negative inside).

The membrane surrounding the axon has an additional property: it is *excitable*. This means that a small voltage applied to a patch of membrane causes a much greater voltage surge, which then propagates as a signal down the axon. Excitability is caused by the presence of special passive ion channels in the membrane—the *voltage-sensitive channels*, which are controlled by the membrane potential. These channels are closed when the membrane potential is at its resting value and open when it becomes less negative. The importance of these channels is shown by their presence in the neurons of all creatures throughout the animal kingdom, from worms to mammals.

We can visualize voltage-sensitive ion channels as deformable tubes crossing

the membrane. They are made up of several protein molecules containing electrically charged chemical groups (fig. 17.4). The positive groups will be attracted
toward the inner side of the membrane, which is negatively charged, and the
negative groups toward the outside, creating a stress within the walls of the tube.
When the membrane has its normal resting potential, the tension is high and
collapses the channel. If, however, the membrane is *depolarized*—that is, its potential changes from -70 mV to, say, -50 mV—the tension declines and the channel
opens.

Neurons have three main types of voltage-sensitive channels: for Na^+ ions

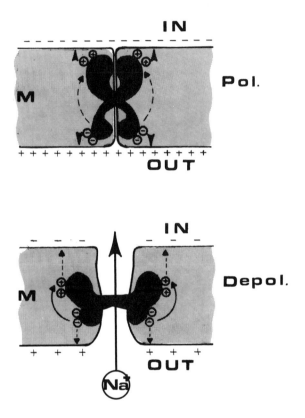

Figure 17.4. A model for the voltage-dependent Na^+ channel. It is formed by two (or more) protein
structures with opposite electric charges at their ends, embedded in the neuronal membrane (M). When
the membrane is normally polarized, with many negative charges at its inner surface (Pol., above), the
strong attraction (arrows) of opposite charges between molecules of the channel and the membrane
overcomes the weaker internal attractions (dashed arrows). The structures are stretched and the channel is
closed. When the membrane is partly depolarized, with fewer negative charges at its inner surface (Depol.,
below), the attractions between channel and membrane decrease (dashed arrows), allowing the internal
attraction to predominate (continuous arrows). The structures collapse and the channel opens, allowing the
flow of Na^+ from the liquid outside the cell (where it is abundant) to the space within the cell (where it is
scarce).

and for K$^+$ ions in the axons, and for Ca^{++} ions in the synapses. The voltage-sensitive Na$^+$ channels make the axonal membrane excitable (fig. 17.5). When these are open, Na$^+$ ions (which are much more abundant outside than inside the axon) rush into the axon, pushed in, as it were, by the outside crowding. They are also attracted by the internal negative voltage. The channels are rather sparse; they are separated by distances comparable to the diameter of the axon. Yet they generate a very strong signal because when they are open, each of them lets in fifty times as many Na$^+$ ions as a sodium-potassium pump carries out, within the same time. The inflow of Na$^+$ ions depolarizes the membrane. In contrast, the opening of the voltage-sensitive K$^+$ channels increases the polarization of the membrane (making it more negative) because when they are open, K$^+$ ions are pushed out of the neuron by the high concentration they have inside it (although they are held back somewhat by the internal negative potential).

The opening of the voltage-sensitive Na$^+$ channels is triggered when the

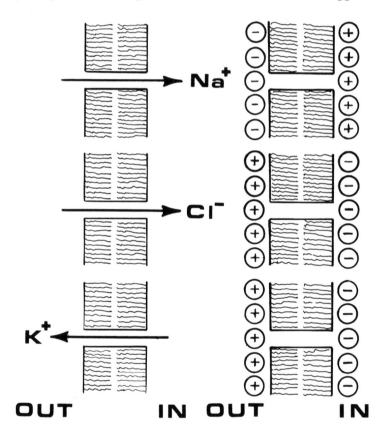

Figure 17.5. Different roles of passive ion channels. The channels for Na$^+$, K$^+$, and Cl$^-$ are shown at the left. At the right are shown the consequences they have for the membrane potential. The Na$^+$ channel tends to depolarize the membrane (making it more positive inside) by bringing in positive charges; the Cl$^-$ channel tends to polarize it (making it more negative inside) by bringing in negative charges; and the K$^+$ tends also to polarize it, but by the opposite mechanism—by letting positive charges out of the cell.

membrane potential reaches the critical value of -55 mV. When that voltage is reached, the membrane becomes *excited*. This means that there is a massive inflow of Na^+ ions, which in a millisecond or two reverses the membrane potential to a value of $+40$ mV, 100 mV more than the resting potential. This dramatic change has profound effects on the ion channels themselves: the voltage-sensitive Na^+ channels reclose (*inactivation*), while the K^+ channels open. These changes cause an inversion of the flow of positive ions across the membrane, which within a few milliseconds brings the membrane potential back to its original value of -70 mV.

For a brief period after they close, the voltage-sensitive Na^+ channels cannot reopen. The membrane cannot be excited—it has become *refractory*—but within a short time the action of the sodium-potassium pump restores the normal Na^+ and K^+ concentrations inside the axon, and everything returns to the initial state. The whole process can then start again.

These rapid changes of membrane potential take place in a small patch of the axonal membrane, while the rest of the membrane remains at its usual resting potential. The voltage difference between the excited patch and the rest of the axon causes the flow of electrical currents. They do not go far: they rapidly lose strength by leaking to the surrounding fluid through the imperfectly insulating axonal membrane. The currents succeed, however, in depolarizing an adjacent patch of membrane to the critical potential. A whole new cycle takes place in this patch: the voltage-dependent Na^+ channels open, the membrane potential reverses for a brief time to a positive value, and then it returns to normality. From there the depolarization spreads to the next patch, and so on. In this way, a wave travels from the point initially excited to the synapse at the end of the axon by jumping from one patch to another. At any point along its path, this wave is recognized by an instrument recording the voltage within the axon as a sudden, transient shift of electrical potential. In the tracing of the instrument it appears as a spike. The wave of depolarization does not become attenuated because it is continuously re-created during its propagation. This self-regenerating wave is called an *action potential*.

The speed of propagation of an action potential depends on the diameter of the axon. In larger axons a larger fraction of the current generated at one point moves down the axon, compared to what is lost through the membrane. The voltage changes it produces can trigger a new action potential at greater distance: the action potential makes longer jumps. The length of the jumps determines the speed of propagation because the current spreads instantaneously from one patch to another, whereas regeneration of the action potential at each patch takes time. Differences in the speed of propagation are useful for the operation of the brain. A signal channeled through multiple pathways, with axons of different diameters, will reach the ends of the axons at different times. These differences may be used to compensate for different delays in the various pathways or to ensure simultaneous arrival of signals through axons of different lengths converging onto a common target.

Spikes of action potential are yes-or-no signals because they always have the same strength. A spike does not give any information about the strength or the duration of the signal that elicited it; this information is obtained in a different way. Under the influence of a continuous triggering potential, a neuron will fire, will become refractory, will recover and fire again, and so on, generating a persistent train of spikes. The interval between the spikes depends on the value of the triggering voltage and on many characteristics of the neuron. The information concerning the strength of the triggering signal is therefore coded in the frequency of firing.

The membrane covering the dendrites and the body of a neuron usually lacks voltage-dependent sodium channels and is not excitable. In these segments, signals are propagated by the passive spreading of electrical currents, which do not go far and rapidly disappear by leaking through the membrane to the outside. Passive spreading of currents is the only method of signal propagation in some invertebrate and vertebrate neurons. Although some of these neurons have voltage-sensitive Na channels, they do not generate action potentials because the depolarization produced by inflow of Na^+ ions is attenuated by a strong K^+ outflow that prevents the buildup of the critical potential needed for firing. The current flowing in these neurons depends on the summation of all the voltage changes generated in them by arriving signals. These neurons are suitable for local computation but not for sending signals to distant stations.

Fast Transmission

The speed of propagation of the action potential is markedly increased in axons that have a thick insulating layer called *myelin*. This layer is a thin cytoplasmic extension that is wrapped several times around the axon by specialized cells. The myelin markedly increases the electrical resistance of the membrane, decreasing the leakage of current; a voltage change propagates much farther without regeneration. The myelin-covered segments of the axon do not have voltage sensitive Na^+ channels and are not excitable. The myelin sheath is interrupted, at regular intervals, by short rings (*nodes*) of naked excitable membrane, in which action potentials can be generated. The distance between the rings is a millimeter or so, about a thousand times the distance between voltage-sensitive channels in naked axons. Action potentials are generated in the rings when, as already described, their membrane is depolarized. They are extra strong because the membrane of the rings is packed with voltage-sensitive Na^+ channels. When all these channels open at once, they produce a very strong current. The resulting action potential propagates very far in the myelinated segments between the rings, where the loss of current to the surrounding tissue is minimized. So the depolarization originated in a ring reaches the next ring. The action potential propagates along the axon by jumping from one ring to the next. The overall propagation is much more rapid than that in naked axons because there are many fewer regenerations with attending delays.

In myelinated axons the intactness of the myelin layer is essential for the propagation of the action potential. Destruction of myelin in certain demyelinating diseases, such as multiple sclerosis, decreases the insulation of the axon and stops propagation. After some time new voltage-sensitive Na$^+$ channels appear in the demyelinated membrane, restoring signal transmission. The myelin sheet is finally regenerated, with almost complete functional recovery, which contributes to the course of the disease. Probably of autoimmune origin (see chapter 14), it is characterized by steps of deterioration followed by improvement.

Drugs in the Channel

The generation of action potentials is blocked by some biological poisons. An example is tetradotoxin found in the puffer fish, which is abundant in tropical and subtropical areas of the oceans. A similar toxin—saxitoxin—is produced by the microscopic sea animals that give rise to the red tide. Shellfish, like clams or mussels, that eat the red tide animals become very poisonous. Both poisons bind to the voltage-sensitive Na$^+$ channels, blocking them so that no action potential can develop. Because the operation of the body of an animal continuously depends on the propagation of action potentials through an innumerable number of nerve axons, these poisons are lethal even at a very low dose. In fact, molecule per molecule, tetradotoxin is one of the most powerful poisons known.

This poison is certainly an effective protective weapon for the puffer fish as a species. The sacrifice of a number of puffer fish will rid the water of predators that tend to use it as a dinner. Yet puffer fish are eaten by humans, who take advantage of the uneven distribution of the poison in the body of the fish. The poison is abundant in the internal organs, especially the liver and the ovary, but it is absent in the muscles. The fish is eaten in Japan (where it is called *fugu*) mainly as a bravado. Especially licensed cooks remove the internal organs without rupturing them so that the poison will not contaminate the muscles, which are the portion eaten. Nevertheless, several deaths every year are witness to the danger of this practice, especially in the hands of amateurs.

Local anesthetics, such as novocaine, used to prevent pain during surgery also block the action potential but in a strange way: the more active the axon, the more effective the block (use-dependent block). These substances act on the voltage-sensitive Na$^+$ channels when they are open, but not when they are closed. They are most effective on channels that become repeatedly active within a short time. This mechanism of action is the basis for the activity of chemically related drugs (such as lidocaine) that block life-threatening fast firing in the heart muscle (fibrillation) without interfering with the normal slow action potentials of the heartbeat.

Poisons of another group, either from plants (like veratridine) or from animals (like batrachotoxin, from Central American frogs, which is used to poison arrow tips), have the opposite effect. They make the Na$^+$ channels liable to open at the resting membrane potential in the absence of a triggering depolarization; and when a channel is normally opened by depolarization, they make it stay open longer than it should. The result is excessive excitability of the neuronal membrane and formation of action potentials in the absence of input signals. Some insecticides (DDT, pyrethroids) act in a similar way.

Other poisons that increase excitability are found in the venom of African scorpions or in sea anemone. They keep the channels open by blocking the inactivation step. The result is excessive excitation throughout the nervous system with generalized muscle contractions that may prevent breathing and cause death. Another toxin from a Central American scorpion changes the critical potential for firing, thus increasing excitability.

The different effects of the various poisons on the Na$^+$ channel show that its various states (voltage-dependent opening, the open state, the inactivation step) are due to the activity of different parts of the channel proteins. The effect of each poison depends on the role played by the site to which it binds. These poisons have allowed greater understanding of the composition of the channel. They are useful for identifying its components because each poison continues to bind to the same component even after it is dissociated from the channel. Scientists using this approach have identified three different proteins that perform different functions in the channel. If the three proteins are incorporated together in an artificial membrane, they reconstitute a channel that allows the passage of Na$^+$ ions.

Synapses, Neurotransmitters, Receptors

An action potential is started in an axon by a triggering depolarization. Now we must consider how the triggering voltage is generated. The voltage can be provided by touching a nerve (which is a bundle of axons) with an electrode connected to a battery. It will generate a spike of action potential, which will run along the nerve. If the nerve is connected to a muscle, the muscle will twitch.

Normally the action potential is initiated by chemical signals coming from synapses (fig. 17.6). Most synapses are chemical transducers; only some are electrical shunts between neurons. A chemical synapse is made by the close apposition of the membrane of the axon carrying the signal with that of the neuron receiving the signal. The axonal membrane forms the transmitting end (often called presynaptic), and the neuronal membrane forms the receiving end (also called postsynaptic (fig. 17.6: 1). As seen in the electron microscope, the two membranes are separated by a very thin crevice, the *synaptic cleft* (fig. 17.6: 2). The transmitting end is like a bag full of tiny *vesicles;* the receiving end is a simple membrane, usually of increased thickness. In an unknown synapse observed in the electron microscope the direction in which signals are transmitted can be deduced from these features. The two members are held rigidly together by connecting strands and are electrically insulated from each other.

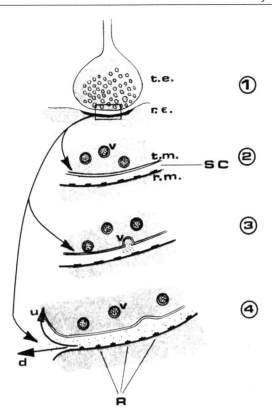

Figure 17.6. A synapse and its operation. (1) General shape of a synapse, with a transmitting end (t.e.) full of vesicles, and a receiving end (r.e.) characterized by a thick membrane. (2) A small part of the synapse shown at greater magnification. The transmitting end bounded by the transmitting membrane (t.m.) contains membrane-bound vesicles full of a chemical transmitter (dots), whereas the receiving membrane (r.m.) is covered with receptors, shown as thickenings. (3) A vesicle (v) fuses with the transmitting membrane and opens into the synaptic cleft (SC) where it pours its contents. (4) The transmitter released from the vesicle reaches the receptor (R) on the receiving membrane. Excess transmitter is removed either by uptake (u) at the transmitting end or by breakdown and diffusion (d).

Each of the tiny vesicles present in the transmitting end contains a droplet of a neurotransmitter substance. The neurotransmitter is the chemical carrier of the nerve signal from the axon to the receiving neuron. It is poured into the synaptic cleft when a spike of action potential running down the axon reaches the synapse. Several steps are involved in this transmission. The action potential opens voltage-sensitive Ca^{++} channels: calcium ions flow into the transmitting end of the synapse. The arrival of the ions causes some vesicles to move closer to the inner side of the membrane of the transmitting end following a network of microtubules and then to fuse with the inner face of the membrane (fig. 17.6: 3). The vesicles open to the outside, pouring their contents into the synaptic cleft. The fusion of vesicles with the membrane is a complex and generally not understood process involving several proteins, such as synapsin I, which is bound to the outside of the vesicles and tends to associate with microtubules. Ca^{++} ions, via calmodulin (see chapter 8), activate enzymes that add phosphate groups to proteins. Synapsin I after receiving phosphates is released from the vesicles, initiating the fusions.

The neurotransmitter molecules thus released into the cleft rapidly reach *receptors*, which in large numbers cover the membrane at the receiving end of the synapse and bind to them (fig. 17.6: 4). Each receptor controls a passive ion channel. The binding of the neurotransmitter changes the shape of the receptor and opens the channel. The inflow of the ions changes the membrane potential of the receiving neurons, with various consequences described below. These events differ in two major ways from those involved in the propagation of an action potential: the passive ion channels are activated *chemically rather than electrically*, and they allow inflow of *different kinds of ions with a variety of consequences*.

Excitation and Inhibition

The effects of the inflow of ions on the receiving neuron depend on the nature of the ion channel and on the kind of ion it admits. In this respect there are two main kinds of synapses, which are also distinguished by structural details recognizable in the electron microscope. In *excitatory synapses* (fig. 17.7) the released neuro-transmitter opens Na^+ channels, depolarizing the receiving membrane. In *inhibitory synapses* (fig. 17.8), it opens either Cl^- channels or K^+ channels. When Cl^- channels are open, chloride ions (more abundant outside the cell) rush in. Because they carry a negative charge, their effect is opposite to that of Na^+ ions: they hyperpolarize the neuronal membrane; that is, they make its inner side even more negative than the resting potential (refer again to fig. 17.5). The opening of K^+ channels has a similar result because K^+ ions flow out of the cells, reducing the internal positive charge. In either case the increased polarization of the membrane makes it less likely that it will initiate an action potential under the effect of a depolarization caused by a nearby synapse. This effect is called *inhibition*. Whether a synapse is excitatory or inhibitory depends mainly on the nature of the neurotransmitter and its receptors.

In an excitatory synapse the inflow of ions generates an electric current in the receiving end, changing its membrane potential. These events are very fast: the change of potential occurs about half a thousandth of a second after the arrival of the action potential at the transmitting end of the synapse. Most of this time is spent in the opening of the Ca^{++} channels at the transmitting end. Although the time interval is very short, it represents an important delay in the propagation of the signal. As we will see in the next chapter, this delay has important consequences for the working of the brain.

Also important for the operation of a synapse is the amount of neurotransmitter released and the length of time it remains in the synaptic cleft. If much is released or if it remains for a long time, the signal relayed will be stronger. In order

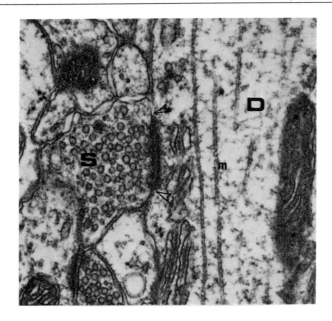

Figure 17.7. Electron micrograph of a small extremely thin section of a human brain showing an excitatory synapse (S) on a dendrite (D). The synapse is characterized by the numerous vesicles and by the thickening of the membrane at the point of contact with the dendrite (two arrows). The membrane at the receiving end of the synapse shows a strong thickening, whereas that at the transmitting end does not. On this basis the synapse can be classified as excitatory. Numerous microtubules (m), sectioned longitudinally, can be seen in the dendrite. The dendrite also contains a mitochondrion (M). Photograph courtesy of W. Maxwell Cowan.

to control the strength of the signal both variables are delicately regulated. The length of neurotransmitter action is controlled by eliminating any excess; neurotransmitter that has not stuck to receptors in the receiving end may be broken down by enzymes or may be taken back by receptors present on the transmitting end of the synapse (fig. 17.6: 4). The differences in the life of the neurotransmitter in synapses of various kinds contribute to their diversity.

Molecular Events

Studies with very sensitive instruments show that the response of the ion channels to the binding of the neurotransmitter to receptors is extremely rapid: it takes the time needed for a group of protein molecules to change shape. This is one of the few opportunities to follow the molecules at work! The response of the ion channels is studied by recording the voltage changes near the receiving end of a synapse. Especially useful are the large synapses between nerve and muscle, which we will consider below. If the recording is made at low amplification, the voltage changes generated by the activation of the synapse follow a smooth wave. If the amplification is increased, the recorded signal becomes noisy; the line trembles a lot.

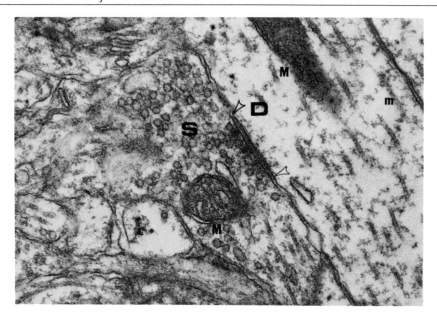

Figure 17.8. Electron micrograph showing an inhibitory synapse. The photograph is similar to that in figure 17.7. The inhibitory character of the synapse, which is outlined by arrows, is shown by the almost equal thickening of the membranes at the receiving and transmitting ends. (Symbols are as in figure 17.7.) Photograph courtesy of W. Maxwell Cowan.

Increasing the amplification further reveals that the noise is due to many minisignals, which sum up to give the overall change recorded at low amplification. Each minisignal corresponds to the discharge of a vesicle containing several hundred molecules of neurotransmitter into the synaptic cleft.

Recording the electrical pulse generated by the opening of a single ion channel gives striking results. A channel may open within a few millionths of a second after the neurotransmitter binds to the receptor; it may open completely or partially; and once open it may briefly close and open again. A channel stays open, with some flickering, for a few thousandths of a second; then it recloses spontaneously and becomes refractory for a second or so until finally it spontaneously recovers responsiveness. These recordings give us a glimpse of the intimate working of life: a response that achieves its purpose but is full of uncertainties deriving from many microscopic chance events, such as opening and closing of bonds in response to local fluctuations in energy supply, ion concentrations, and many other variables.

Transmitters, Modulators, and Their Receptors

The chemical transmission of signals, which is characteristic of synapses, is an example of chemical communication and employs functions that have a wide use in many kinds of cells. The release of neurotransmitter into the synaptic cleft is an act of secretion and is performed as in other cells; like them, it requires Ca^{++} ions. The neurotransmitters behave similarly to polypeptide hormones, both in the way they are released and in the way they act. The inflow of ions they induce in neurons is sometimes brought about by second messengers similar to those that mediate the action of hormones. Some neurotransmitter receptors even share with hormone receptors the ability to generate cyclic AMP within the neuron and to cause the addition of phosphate groups to proteins.

The whole nervous system of an animal employs a great variety of chemical communicators. Chemically, they belong to two classes. Neurotransmitters, which were recognized first, are small molecules, such as amino acids or similar molecules. Neuropeptides, which were recognized more recently, are short chains containing from a few to about forty amino acids.

The communicators of the nervous system perform two main functions. Neurotransmitters and some neuropeptides carry signals through the short distance of the synaptic cleft from one neuron to another. Most neuropeptides act as modulators, which modify the transmission of signals by transmitters, either reducing or enhancing it. They may act also as brain hormones by acting at a distance through the blood. Neuropeptides and brain hormones, considered in chapter 8, are very similar in chemical constitution and in distribution within the nervous system; we will consider them here together.

Both neurotransmitters and modulators act by binding to specific receptors in the receiving end of synapses. Each neurotransmitter or modulator recognizes more than one class of receptors. Different receptors are identified because they bind the neurotransmitter or modulator, as well as substances chemically related to them, with different and characteristic strengths. Some receptors activate the production of cyclic AMP. The properties of the receptor activated by a neurotransmitter in a certain neuron will determine the consequence for that neuron, not the nature of the neurotransmitter itself.

Some neurons produce only one communicator, either a neurotransmitter or a neuropeptide. Others produce both a simple neurotransmitter and a neuropeptide; the neuropeptide appears to act as modulator because it is mixed together with the neurotransmitter in the same vesicles. By virtue of the variety of communicators, many different classes of neurons can be identified, each manufacturing a certain transmitter or a certain modulator. This individuality parallels the functional individuality of the neuron: the bodies of neurons making a certain communicator are found together in localized regions of the nervous system devoted to a separate function (fig. 17.9). This distribution explains the characteristics of certain brain diseases. The malfunction of an enzyme needed for the manufacture of a neurotransmitter or a defect in a gene for its receptor generates Parkinson's disease and possibly schizophrenia, in which only some functions of the nervous system are altered. This is possible because the affected transmitter is manufactured in groups of neurons that perform certain functions.

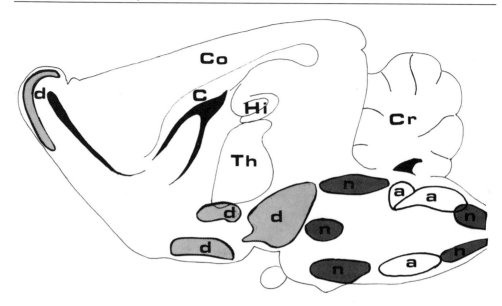

Figure 17.9. Idealized section through a rat brain showing the localization of some simple transmitters. a = adrenaline, d = dopamine, n = noradrenaline. Inner cavities are in solid black. Indicated are also some of the main brain structures: cortex (Co); the crossconnections between the two brain hemispheres (C); the thalamus (Th), a structure important for the reception of sensory signals; the hippocampus (Hi; so called because it has the shape of a horse ring), important for memory; and the cerebellum (Cr), important for equilibrium. (Adapted from T. Hökfelt, O. Johansson, and N. Goldstein, *Science* 225:1326 [1984].)

Neurotransmitters

Some transmitters (glutamate, aspartate, glycine, B-alanine) are amino acids, which are the building blocks needed by every cell for making proteins (table 17.1). Others (adrenaline, noradrenaline, dopamine, serotonin, GABA—short for gamma-aminobutyric acid) are derivatives of amino acids. Some neurotransmitters are derived from other compounds regularly present in cells, such as adenosine and its derivatives, which are used for making nucleic acids, and acetylcholine derived from choline, which is a constituent of cellular membranes. The properties of neurotransmitters are appropriate to their function. They can cross cellular membranes only through specific transport systems; hence they cannot leave the synaptic vesicles. Once released, they cannot reenter the cells randomly.

Each single neurotransmitter tends to have a prevalent function, either excitatory or inhibitory, although with some exceptions. For instance, in vertebrates the neurotransmitters of the catecholamine group (adrenaline, noradrenaline, dopamine) and the two amino acids, glutamate and aspartate, are usually excitatory. We recognize the effect of glutamate in the "Chinese restaurant syndrome": monosodium glutamate, added to the food as flavor enhancer, stimulates neurons that control blood vessels, causing warming and reddening of the skin. Cate-

Table 17.1   The Simple Neurotransmitters and Their Relations to the Main Classes of Cellular Macromolecules

Nonneural Functions	*Neurotransmitters*
Proteins ← { Tyrosine	Dopamine → Noradrenaline → Adrenaline
Tryptophan ⟶	Serotonin
Histidine ⟶	Histamine
Glycine	Glycine
Glutamic Acid	Glutamic Acid → GABA
Aspartic Acid	Aspartic Acid
Beta-alanine	Beta-alanine
Membranes ← Choline ⟶	Acetylcholine
Nucleic Acids ← { Adenosine	Adenosine
ADP	ADP
ATP	ATP

cholamines are, however, inhibitory in some brain neurons. GABA and glycine are usually inhibitory. Some other neurotransmitters show no clear trend, being either inhibitory or excitatory, depending on the receptors they interact with. Some transmitters—for instance, dopamine or adenosine—may also have a modulatory action on certain neurons.

The adoption by nature of the rather complicated mechanism for transmitting signals from one neuron to another, based on neurotransmitters, must have good reasons because it is universal; in fact, chemical transmission is present in the nervous system of all animals, even the most simple. One reason is that transmitters work using the same machinery as hormones, but are used for a local, very fast action. Another reason, perhaps, is that specific systems for the selective transport of amino acids into cells were developed early in the evolution of life and were coupled with ion transports that provide the required energy. It would be a short step from there to using the amino acids for *eliciting* ion transport.

Another reason for neurotransmitters is that, as we have already seen, they confer great flexibility on the nervous system. By their use, the action potential of an axon can be converted into either an excitatory or an inhibitory signal with a large variety of quantitative differences. This duality is fundamental to the operation of the neural network. The multiplicity of neurotransmitters of either kind, and of modulators, greatly enhances the subtlety of performance of the nervous system. Each neurotransmitter or modulator acts in a quantitatively different way; each can be regulated independently of others; each may have different effects by binding to different receptors; each can be restricted to a certain class of neurons, conferring on that class a functional individuality. New classes of neurons can be easily added in evolution using different transmitters. The study of neuroactive drugs (see chapter 19) gives dramatic demonstration of the subtleties of nervous system functions made possible by the variety of transmitters and modulators.

Neuropeptides

Neuropeptides, a subset of peptide hormones, are communicator substances present throughout the biological world, even in plants and single-celled organisms. For instance, a peptide determining one of the mating types in yeast is very similar to the hypothalamic hormone controlling the gonads through the pituitary, which acts also as a neuropeptide in the brain. The yeast peptide binds to the receptors for the hormone. Neuropeptides are produced both in the brain and in other organs, many of them in the gut, others in the bronchi, the pancreas, or the kidney. Neuropeptides are made by the heart and by cells in the skin of frogs. Conversely, some classical peptide hormones act as neuropeptides in brain cells.

That neuropeptides play a role in the operation of the brain was first revealed by studying the action of morphine, the drug present in opium, which has been used for a very long time to kill pain and create euphoria. It was discovered that the brain contains receptors for morphine. This was surprising because morphine is a plant product: what business has the brain with it? As a possible explanation, it was thought that perhaps the morphine receptors normally recognize a substance produced in the brain. An activity able to block the binding of morphine to its receptors was found in brain extracts. The activity could be assigned to two classes of peptides called *enkephalins* and *endorphins*. Endorphin has a longer amino acid sequence, which includes the sequence for enkephalins, which have only five amino acids.

This success stimulated more work, and as a result we now know of many neuropeptides belonging to about thirty families. The total number of individual neuropeptides is likely to be two hundred or so because each family contains several members with closely related structures. For instance, there are four endorphins and two enkephalins. The multiple forms of neuropeptides are generated by various mechanisms: by different processing of the RNA transcripts, by different cleavages of longer precursor proteins, and by chemical modification of the component amino acids. Different cells producing neuropeptides of the same family (for instance, in the brain or the gut) usually produce slightly different molecules, assuring the individuality of the various cell types.

Most neuropeptides appear to act as modulators. Only some have been definitely shown to act like transmitters—that is, to cause either excitation or inhibition of a synapse when they are applied near it through a microscopic pipette. Even when they act as transmitters, they do so in a peculiar way: for instance, the potential changes they induce in the receiving neuron are much slower than those induced by regular neurotransmitters. As modulators, neuropeptides can have dramatic effects. For instance the vasointestinal peptide (VIP) markedly increases the effectiveness of the neurotransmitter acetylcholine in binding to its receptors. Other neuropeptides modulate the amount of a neurotransmitter released or its life in the synaptic cleft by binding to the regulatory receptors at the transmitting end of a synapse. The modulatory action of neuropeptides is slow and fairly long lasting because it involves chemical changes of neuronal proteins, such as attachment of phosphate groups. The effects are not well localized: synapses close to the site of release are also affected. This broad effect may be related to the functional specialization of small groups of neurons. For these characteristics the effect of modulators confers plasticity on the operation of the nervous system.

How do we know that a neuropeptide or any other substance performs the functions of a neurotransmitter? This conclusion is reached in various stages. The presence of the substance in neurons, especially in the synapses, is indicative. Some neurotransmitters are recognizable because they are fluorescent—when illuminated with a light of suitable color, they emit light of a different color, which can be detected by microscopic examination. Neuropeptides can be recognized by using appropriate antibodies labeled with a fluorescent dye that becomes localized only in neurons containing the peptide. The presence of enzymes involved in the manufacture of the substance in neurons shows that the substance plays an important role; it may be a transmitter. More conclusive evidence is obtained if the application of the substance to a synapse using a very fine pipette causes either depolarization or hyperpolarization of the receiving membrane. The significance of this finding is further enhanced if the same substance is released when the transmitting end of the synapse is depolarized in the presence of Ca^{++} ions (which are needed for transmitter release). Additional supporting evidence is the presence in the neurons of mechanisms removing any excess of the substance, such as receptors in the transmitting end of synapses, or enzymes that destroy the substance around the neurons. In spite of all these criteria, however, it is sometimes difficult to establish conclusively that a substance is a transmitter: some, in fact, are identified only tentatively. The difficulties are especially great for neuropeptides.

The same or similar neuropeptides are often produced both in the brain and in other organs. It would seem that this dual production might generate problems. Release of one of these powerful substances into the blood might upset the function of the brain, which is so delicately balanced. But neuropeptides released into the blood do not interfere with the function of most of the central nervous system. Between the blood and the brain there is an insurmountable barrier, the so-called *blood-brain barrier*. Substances circulating in the blood reach all cells through the fine blood vessels. In most parts of the body, they can readily cross their walls: some substances exit through gaps between the cells lining the vessels; others are transported across these cells in vesicles. In the central nervous system, however, the fine blood vessels lack these features. Their lining represents an effective barrier between the blood and the nerve cells, except for oxygen or nutrients, such as sugars and amino acids, that the brain uses in large amounts. An additional barrier is provided by the sheaths of glial cells that surround the blood vessels. Neuropeptides do not cross these barriers and cannot reach the brain from the blood.

The blood-brain barrier protects most of the brain except a small part near the pituitary. Several groups of neurons in that area of the brain are, as it were, windows on the blood, monitoring its composition and informing the rest of the brain of their findings. For instance, one of these groups of neurons is known as the vomiting center: it recognizes abnormal chemical substances picked up by the blood in the gastrointestinal tract. Substances that seep from the capillaries in this part of the brain, however, are soon stopped and do not reach the rest of the brain.

By and large, the blood-brain barrier divides the body into two compartments: the central nervous system (which includes the brain and the spinal cord) and the rest of the body. Outside the blood-brain barrier is that part of the nervous system that controls the heartbeat, contraction of smooth muscles, glandular secretion, blood circulation, kidney function, and so on. This part of the nervous system is accessible to substances present in the blood as well as substances produced within the neurons themselves. The local substances participate in the local transmission of signals, whereas substances arriving via the blood produce generalized effects such as increased blood pressure, diarrhea, vomiting, and so on.

The blood-brain barrier is reinforced by sheets of *glial cells* (fig. 17.10). These cells, which do not transmit signals, are interposed between the neurons and the fine blood vessels; they also fill the spaces between neurons and surround myelinated axons, producing the myelin sheath. All substances, such as oxygen, sugars, and amino acids, destined for neurons must traverse a thin sheath of glial cell cytoplasm that tightly surround them. Thus these cells control the influx of substances to neurons. Glial cells also have other roles related to the transmission of signals within the brain. They scavenge excess amounts of some transmitters and maintain a constant extracellular ionic environment, which is essential for the operation of neurons. Especially critical is the extracellular concentration of K^+ ions, which affects the K^+ outflow and the resting potential of the neuronal membrane. K^+ ions exit from active axons during the recovery phase of the action potential, as well as from channels present in inhibitory synapses. The all-pervading glial cells correct the increased K^+ concentration outside neurons by acting as K^+ sponges: they absorb the ions through passive channels. The long-term constancy of the extracellular ion concentrations is maintained by the endothelia that line the walls of the fine blood vessels: they limit the efflux of K^+ to the brain and transport excessive K^+ into the blood using a sodium-potassium pump.

Specific Functions of Neuropeptides

Brain neuropeptides seem to be responsible for basic feelings such as hunger, thirst, pain, fear, and pleasure, whereas neurotransmitters are responsible for

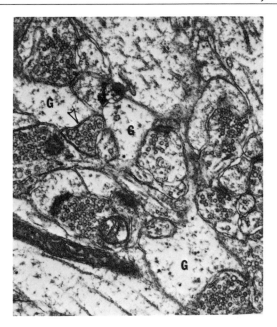

Figure 17.10. Electron micrograph of an extremely thin slice of human brain showing appendages of glial cells (G) among neurons, many of which contain synapses. The glial cells are recognizable for the small dense spots. A very thin crevice of constant width separates the two types of cells (arrows). Photograph courtesy of W. Maxwell Cowan.

sensations and movements. We can see the special role of neuropeptides in a few typical cases.

THIRST AND HUNGER. Thirst can be caused by loss of water from the cells (dehydration) or by loss of blood. Loss of water is detected by brain neurons, which respond to the accompanying changes in sodium concentration. An abundant loss of blood is probably detected by nerve endings in the large veins and arteries associated with the heart, which become less stretched.

The feeling of thirst and the drinking response after loss of blood involve the neuropeptide angiotensin, which normally is present in very low concentrations in the kidney and the brain. Blood and brain contain much larger amounts of a longer peptide, angiotensinogen, which, as the name indicates, can generate angiotensin, but is itself inactive. Nerve signals induced by loss of blood and fall of blood pressure cause the release into the blood or the brain of the enzyme renin, which cleaves off some amino acids from angiotensinogen, converting it into active angiotensin. So angiotensin, which cannot cross the blood-brain barrier, is generated on both sides of it. Angiotensin in the blood acts on neurons not protected by the blood-brain barrier; angiotensin made in the brain acts on other neurons. Angiotensin from both sources induces the feeling of thirst. Thirst can be induced experimentally in rats by injecting renin at a suitable place in the brain, which is therefore known as the thirst center. The local formation of angiotensin causes the animal to drink avidly even if previously satiated. If the thirst center is destroyed, the rat stops drinking even under conditions of strong dehydration.

Angiotension also has other effects that minimize the consequences of blood loss: it increases blood pressure by exciting those parts of the peripheral nervous system that control the contraction of the muscles of small blood vessels, and by stimulating the release of the hormone vasopressin from the posterior pituitary. Both effects decrease the volume of the fine blood vessels, increasing the efficiency of the available blood.

Angiotensin also increases the appetite for sodium, which tends to compensate for its loss. Injection of renin in the rat hypothalamus causes the animal to drink a concentrated solution of salt (sodium chloride) that normal rats would never touch. Blood angiotensin has parallel peripheral effects that complement the central effect: it increases adsorption of sodium from the gut and decreases its loss from the kidney. Overproduction of an adrenal steroid hormone, aldosterne, under angiotensin stimulation is responsible for sodium retention. These and other effects of angiotensin, working on the two sides of the blood-brain barrier, defend blood volume and pressure, retain water and sodium, and stimulate the individual to replace them.

The effects of blood angiotensin are counteracted by a hormone produced in the atria, the cavities of the heart that receive the blood from the body. The atrial hormone inhibits events leading to increased blood pressure, such as angiotensin and vasopressin production and the constriction of blood vessels. The antagonistic action of the atrial hormone to angiotensin is also shown by studies of genetically hypertensive rats, which have fewer receptors for atrial hormone and more for angiotensin in the part of the brain accessible to these hormones.

Two neuropeptides are known to control appetite. Neuropeptide Y injected into the hypothalamus of a satiated rat causes the animal to eat; it will devour in a few hours an amount of extra food corresponding to what it would normally eat in a day. The other neuropeptide is colecystokinin (CCK), which is a fragment of a larger peptide present in the stomach (gastrin). When injected into the blood it inhibits food intake, perhaps by increasing oxytocin in the blood. CCK is an excitatory peptide abundant in the brain in neurons that use either dopamine or serotonin as neurotransmitter and is released together with them at the synapses. CCK is also found in the gut, where it causes contractions of the gallbladder.

PAIN. Another all-pervading sensation in which neuropeptides play an important role is pain, which is produced by strong stimulation of specialized nerve fibers present in the skin and various organs. The signals are transmitted to the brain by a chain of neurons recognizable for their thin axons, which contain the neuropeptide substance P. It seems likely that substance P acts as transmitter in the pain pathway, not only because it is abundant in the pain neurons, but also because it is released from the axons when they are experimentally excited, and its release requires the presence of Ca^{++} ions in the extracellular fluid. In mice the application of substance P excites the neurons involved in the sensation of pain. The animals respond as if they were affected by chronic pain, with intense biting and scratching of the skin. A substance present in red pepper, capsaicin, which depletes substance P from the neurons, causes loss of pain sensation (analgesia).

Not only the transmission of pain signals but also their control involve neuropeptides. It has been known for thousands of years that pain can be suppressed by opium, which contains morphine. This substance binds to the same neuronal receptors as a group of neuropeptides, including endorphins and enkephalins, which are collectively known as opioid peptides. Morphine and brain opioids are unrelated chemically, but they bind to the same receptors because of an accidental similarity of binding sites, producing similar effects. Endorphin is produced also in the pituitary and the adrenal cortex. At all sites the neuropeptide is generated by cleavage of a larger precursor peptide that also produces ACTH (see chapter 8). The brain appears also to contain genuine morphine of undefined origin.

Opioid peptides are present in neurons of many species, from earthworms to humans. The three known kinds of brain opioids—enkephalins, beta-endorphins, and dynorphins—have in common four or five amino acids; they are present in different neurons. Opioid peptides and morphine utilize three kinds of receptors designated by the Greek letters delta, kappa, and mu. The opioid peptides act mainly on delta receptors, and morphine on mu receptors, reducing excitability: both receptors hyperpolarize neurons, inhibit action potentials by increasing K^+ outflow, and decrease the release of excitatory transmitters. Kappa receptors, in contrast, when acted upon by certain opioids, appear to increase excitability, suggesting that the opioid system is balanced, capable of contrasting effects.

An important function of the opioid peptides, especially enkephalin and endorphin, is to control the sensation of pain. They do this by transmitting signals from neurons of an area in the central part of the brain—a kind of analgesia center—which when electrically stimulated generates a striking pain-killing effect. The effect is so powerful that the stimulation through permanently implanted electrodes is used in medicine to alleviate intolerable pain in patients afflicted by chronic diseases. Several lines of evidence show that these brain neurons control pain by using opioid neuropeptides, which then suppress the release of substance P from the neurons of the pain pathway.

Excitation of the analgesia centers may be the cause of the analgesic effect of the traditional Chinese practice of acupuncture. This practice, which itself induces pain, appears to cause the release of brain opioids because its effect is abolished by naloxone, a specific antagonist of these peptides. Insertion of a needle in a part of the body seems to cause the activation of part of the pain-control pathway, which then produces analgesia at other sites. The detailed acupuncture maps of Chinese medicine may reflect the organization of the connections between the pain axons and the control neurons. This inference is supported by the observation that in rats analgesia of the tail can be induced by a mild electric shock to a front paw. The "nose twitch" used for controlling horses may also act through a similar mechanism.

How useful acupuncture is for alleviating pain in humans is not clear. Clinical studies on its effect on chronic pain have given contradictory results, and claims concerning its effect on acute pain (as in surgery) seem to have been overstated. The effects are good in some exceptional individuals, but in the majority of people they seem mediocre or poor, especially in Western countries.

STRESS. Stress is generated in rats exposed to inescapable punishment, such as periodic electric shocks. The response to stressful conditions is mainly dependent on corticotropin-releasing factor (CRF), which not only releases ACTH from the anterior pituitary but also coordinates the endocrinal and neuronal mechanisms of stress. Under conditions of stress both opioid peptides and ACTH are released both in the brain and into the blood. Brain and blood opioids are kept separate by the blood-brain barrier; those in the blood act on neurons of the peripheral nervous system. Acting at both sites, the peptides induce considerable analgesia during stressful conditions. At the same time excessive release of the hormone ACTH, which controls the adrenal, stimulates overproduction of cortisone, a steroid hormone that kills lymphocytes—a phenomenon of uncertain biological significance. The consequence of the loss of lymphocytes is seen in mice of certain strains kept for prolonged periods under mildly stressful conditions (such as a noisy environment with frequent changes of illumination). They have an increased incidence of virus-induced cancer of the breast, which is fairly common in these strains.

Signals to Muscle

We have examined how neurons transmit and elaborate signals, using many methods of communication. Other cells, such as those producing hormones, also transmit signals, but neurons are much more specialized. They are part of a system of communication that transmits sensory signals from the outside world to the brain, and action signals from the brain to the peripheral organs. This line of communication begins with some form of energy (such as light waves, pressure, chemical energy) impinging on suitable sensor cells. Each kind of sensor detects one form of energy and transforms it into a change of membrane potential, which in turn generates an action potential in an axon that enters the brain. At synapses the action potential is converted into chemical signals of various kinds. New action potentials are generated at the synapses, which spread the signals to many other neurons in the brain. The brain computer analyzes all these input signals and sends output signals through other neurons, using again alternating electrical and chemical impulses. Finally action potentials reach the muscles or secretory glands (like the tear glands or the salivary glands) or, in certain animals, the pigment cells of the skin. At all these places the action potentials are again converted into chemical signals. As a result muscles contract, glands secrete their products, or pigment granules are redistributed. Electrical and chemical signals conveyed by neurons continuously pervade the animal body and mediate every activity.

The results of action potentials reaching peripheral organs are highly varied, depending on the anatomical and functional characteristics of each organ. As an example of such results, we will examine the effects on muscles.

The signals for the skeletal muscles (which move the limbs and other parts of the body) originate in *motor neurons*, situated in the spinal cord. They travel through myelinated axons that gather in thick bundles to form *peripheral nerves* and then separate to go to their various destinations. The axons terminate on *muscle fibers*, very long thin contractile tubes formed during development by the fusion of strings of special precursor cells. The fibers are surrounded by an excitable membrane—that is, one containing voltage-dependent ion channels. The muscles are big bundles of muscle fibers. Each axon terminating on a muscle fiber branches into a small tree and forms a *neuromuscular junction*, a very large synapse that performs the same function as synapses on neurons.

At the junction, the action potential causes the release of a neurotransmitter: acetylcholine in vertebrates, GABA or glutamate in invertebrates. The receiving end of the junction in vertebrates has a large number of receptors for acetylcholine, which are made recognizable by the binding of an animal poison, bungarotoxin (figs. 17.11 and 17.12). Acetylcholine causes depolarization of the membrane of the synapse, generating a triggering potential. An action potential caused by the opening of Na^+ channels spreads to the membrane of the muscle fiber and to membranous tubes that crisscross it (fig. 17.13). Through these tubes the action potential rapidly pervades the whole fiber, quickly releasing free calcium ions from a store of ions bound to proteins of the membranes. The buildup of the concentration of free Ca^{++} ions causes the concentration—the shortening—of the fiber. Relaxed muscle fibers contain very little free Ca^{++}: what is generated is immediately extruded through special channels using energy released by the simultaneous inflow of Na^+ ions through passive channels.

Contraction is the result of a molecular rearrangement. Muscle fibers contain protein molecules that form two kinds of filaments, thin and thick, which are like two combs (see chapter 2). Under the influence of Ca^{++} ions, filaments of the two kinds slide past each other (in the process burning chemical energy as ATP previously stored in the fiber) and bring the two combs closer together. The coordinated sliding of the filaments in many similar combs causes a twitch, or a rapid shortening of the muscle, followed by relaxation. Sustained contraction occurs when the nerve fires persistently and twitches follow each other at great speed.

Pacemakers

Signals generated and transmitted without neurons are regularly used in several muscular organs such as the heart or the intestine. In the heart, the signals that control the beat are generated in specialized muscle cells; a group of them, the

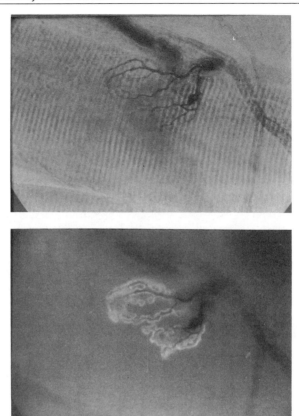

Figure 17.11. A neuromuscular junction seen in the light microscope. Top of the picture: the axon coming from above, left, branches repeatedly in contact with the muscle fiber, which is recognizable for its striation, in contact with the axon terminals. Bottom: the same junction is revealed by the fluorescent labeling of bungarotoxin bound to the acetylcholine receptors, which surround the axon terminals. Photograph courtesy of J. Patrick.

node, is located in the right atrium, the cavity into which the blood flows from the general circulation. The node is the *pacemaker* of the heart: it produces rhythmic action potentials that then spread through the whole organ.

These signals, like those of neurons, are generated by an ionic mechanism with important distinctive features. When the heart is relaxed and blood flows into it, enlarging its cavities, a steady influx of Ca^{++} ions depolarizes the membrane of the node cells. As the critical potential is reached, voltage-dependent Na^+ channels open, causing an influx of Na^+ ions and an action potential. In contrast to neurons or skeletal muscles, the action potential persists for a fairly long time (*slow potential*) mainly because the outflow of K^+ ions, which should terminate it, is delayed. The action potential spreads slowly from the node to all parts of the heart through bundles of node cells, causing contraction of the heart muscle.

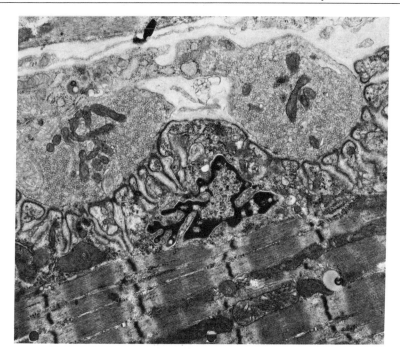

Figure 17.12. Electron micrograph of a thin section through a neuromuscular junction, in which the acetylcholine receptors have been saturated with bungarotoxin. At the top are two axon terminals, full of vesicles containing acetylcholine, with many mitochondria. Below them is the receiving membrane which is folded in a complicated way and is covered with receptors. The thick, dark gray line outlining the membrane is due to deposits of bungarotoxin on the receptors. At the bottom is the muscle fiber containing the contractile elements, which appear as longitudinal lines interrupted by two types of alternating crossbands, one very dark on a light background, and one light and faint. The two types of cross-bands are connected to the two types of filaments that slide past each other. Photograph courtesy of J. Patrick.

These two characteristics have important consequences for the operation of the heart. The slow propagation of the depolarization through the node cells causes a delay between the contraction of the atrium, which receives blood from the veins, and the ventricle, which pushes the blood into the arteries. The delay allows the blood to fill the ventricle before its contraction begins. The long duration of the action potential allows contraction of the muscle to persist until each cavity empties its contents. Thus nature takes advantage of the many special characteristics of the excitability of the node cells for optimizing the function of the heart pump. The action potentials generated in succession in different parts of the heart produce electric currents that spread throughout the body and can be picked up by electrodes applied to the skin. The recorded electrical changes are

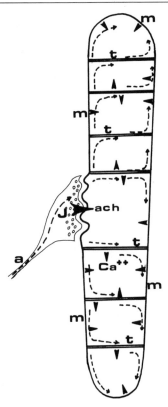

Figure 17.13. Propagation of the action potential through a muscle fiber. The muscle action potential (dashed lines) originates at the junction (J) after a nerve action potential has arrived through the axon (a), causing release of acetylcholine (ach). The potential spreads through the membrane of the muscle fiber (m) and the cross-tubes (t). As a result Ca^{++} ions are mobilized from all the membranes (arrows), causing contraction.

the *electrocardiogram* (ECG), which in medicine gives important information on the state of the heart muscle.

The heart receives nerve fibers from two sources outside the central nervous system. Some fibers, called *parasympathetic*, that use acetylcholine as neurotransmitter slow down the heart beats by hyperpolarizing the membrane of the node cells; other fibers, called *sympathetic*, using adrenaline as neurotransmitter, depolarize the cells and increase the rate. The sympathetic nerves are excited by emotive states or physical exertion, accounting for the increased heart rate under these conditions. Their excitation after the heart has been damaged by coronary thrombosis is very injurious and often lethal; in medicine this effect is alleviated by drugs that block the receptors through which these nerves act. The basic function of the heart, however, does not require any nervous input: a heart severed from all its connections will continue to beat. A heart transplanted into a new host does not form connections to the nerves, so its rate is determined solely by its own pacemaker and remains unchanged, regardless of emotions or efforts. Thus absence of nervous connections makes the heart imperturbable: but imperturbability is not in the best interest of the individual, who cannot adjust blood flow to the changing situations of life.

Smooth Muscle

Muscles that cause contraction of canals of the body, such as the gut, are smooth: they do not have cross-striations because they lack well-organized combs. They contract, however, by a mechanism similar to that of striated muscles. These muscles promote the flow of the contents of the canal (feces, urine, sperm) by the orchestrated contraction of several kinds of bundles of fibers. An example is the contraction of ringlike muscles surrounding the lumen of the gut. This contraction, which proceeds in one direction, is not determined by nerve signals; it is initiated locally.

Smooth muscle is made up of very long, thin, separate cells rather than fibers. As in the heart muscle, the cells have special contacts through which a triggering potential can propagate, generating an action potential within each cell. In this way, thousands of cells may contract at the same time. The triggering potential, of the slow type, is generated within some of the cells, which act as pacemakers. The cells that start the contraction are not specialized, any cell can do it.

Like the heart, the smooth muscles of some organs (such as the gut) receive axons from the two types of nerve cells that control the heart. The effects of the two types of nerves, however, are opposite to those seen in the heart because the distribution of receptors for the two neurotransmitters is different.

A unique type of smooth muscle is the *catch muscle* of animals with two shells, like clams or oysters; its contraction causes the shells to stay shut for long periods of time. Contraction is caused by nerve-induced bursts of action potential, which act as in other muscles; what is unique is the persistence of the contraction after the membrane potential has returned to the resting value. The sliding filaments contain a protein that changes shape irreversibly, causing the unusual behavior. Once they are shut, the shells are opened by a special nerve signal that induces hyperpolarization of the membrane and relaxation of the muscle. The shells then open by a spring action at their hinge.

High-Voltage Batteries

The excitable membranes of neurons and muscle fibers are electrical batteries that develop an electrical current as a result of ion flow. We have seen that in neurons the sudden opening of the voltage-sensitive channels can change the potential difference between the two sides of the membrane by about 0.1 volt.

Conceivably, a battery made by many thousands of such membranes would produce discharges of hundreds or thousands of volts. And if the surface of the membranes were large enough, the discharge could also have considerable intensity.

Since such a high-voltage battery is possible, it is no wonder that nature has actually constructed it. These batteries are found in some aquatic animals, which use them for signaling and for stunning their prey or aggressors. An example is the electric organ of the electric eel. This battery is made up of many thousands of elements, each a simplified, flattened muscle fiber comprising a neuromuscular junction that, as in muscle, works through acetylcholine release. The elements are connected in serial stacks to accumulate voltage, and the stacks are connected in parallel to increase current. For this battery to fire, a nerve-induced depolarization must occur simultaneously at all the junctions. Such a perfect coordination is achieved by many neurons firing simultaneously; and the different distances the signals have to travel to reach the different parts of the electric organ (which is many centimeters long) are compensated by using axons of different diameters in which the action potentials travel at different speeds. A perfect design!

CHAPTER 18

The Design of the Brain

The organization of connections between neurons is the basis for the operation of the brain. This organization is made up of two parts: the network of axons, which determines how neurons are interconnected, and the synapses, which give meaning to the action potentials relayed by axons, by converting them into signals that are meaningful for the receiving neuron. We will see in this chapter that the organization of connections is built by utilizing two kinds of instructions: those given by the genes and those given by the environment in which the animal lives. The genes acting both in evolution and in development specify the general organization of connections by directing many crucial events, such as the expansion of certain brain parts, the differentiation of new types of neurons within them, the death of certain neurons, the migration of precursors destined to become neurons to appropriate places, and the establishment of a large number of connections between neurons of the various classes. These instructions cause the formation of many more connections than are needed. The environment acts at this point by stabilizing the connections that are useful for the operation of the brain; those that are not useful disappear. The final and the only significant state of the brain organization, therefore, is strongly influenced by the functions it performs.

Adding and Subtracting

We will begin by examining how the organization of synapses affects the function of the nervous system. The release of transmitters at synapses generates electric currents in the body or dendrites of neurons. The membranes covering these parts of neurons usually do not generate action potentials; hence the currents spread passively, without self-regeneration. As they spread they lose strength by leaking out through the neuronal membrane. The loss of current is less rapid than in axons, because the dendrites have a much larger diameter. As a result, the current generated at a synapse will tend to spread through a large proportion of the dendritic tree and the body of the neuron itself.

Whether or not the neuron will fire, sending an action potential through its axon, depends on the characteristics of the synapse, such as the kind of ion channels it controls, the strength and duration of the signal, and where it is located in the neuron. The stimulation of an excitatory synapse will not necessarily cause the neuron to fire: the result depends on events that go on at many other synapses and in many parts of the neuron. One factor is the amount of transmitter that is released. Whereas a strong release may cause the neuron to fire, the release of a small amount of transmitter will cause only a slight depolarization, below the critical value for initiating an action potential. But the signal is not lost: the neuron may still fire if the weak depolarization collaborates with other depolarizations induced by neighboring synapses. If inhibitory synapses are activated together with an excitatory synapse, the two effects sum up, one with a positive, the other with a negative sign, and the excitation is decreased.

Topography

An important variable affecting the response of a neuron is how synapses are distributed on its surface. A lonely synapse, situated at considerable distance from other synapses, usually elicits only a local response: if its activation does not cause the neuron to fire, it will have no other effect. Interactions easily occur between synapses close to each other and are dominated by their relative positions. For instance, an inhibitory synapse can most effectively counteract an excitatory synapse if it is between it and the beginning of the axon, where action potentials are usually initiated. In fact, inhibitory synapses are usually found on the neuron body (often close to where the axon begins) or on adjacent parts of dendrites; excitatory synapses are commonly found further out in the dendrites.

The importance of the relative position of synapses is borne out by electron microscopy of the central nervous system, which reveals many special arrangements with possible functional meanings. One such arrangement is that of *piggyback*, or *serial synapses* (fig. 18.1: A), in which an axon is connected to another axon, and the latter to a dendrite; the position of the vesicles and other structural details show that signals flow from the outer to the central axon and then to the dendrite. The outer synapse is inhibitory and modulates the function of the inner synapse. Another frequent arrangement is that of *side-by-side reciprocal synapses* (fig. 18.1: B): a pair of synapses between two dendrites, close to each other, with opposite directions. Electron microscopy identifies one synapse as excitatory, and the other as inhibitory. When a signal goes through the excitatory synapse it activates the inhibitory synapse, and this, in turn, inhibits the neuron itself. In this way the neuron that first fired becomes inhibited. A reciprocal synapse, therefore, is a device for causing self-inhibition of a neuron.

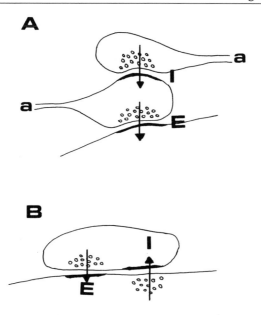

Figure 18.1. Two special arrangements of synapses frequently found in the brain. (A) Two piggyback synapses, one inhibitory (I), the other excitatory (E). Inhibition by the outer synapse modulates the excitation caused by the inner synapse. (B) Two side-by-side synapses, one inhibitory (I), the other excitatory (E). This arrangement causes self-inhibition of the firing neuron. a = axon.

The shape of the dendrite that receives synapses may also be very significant. Many dendrites are covered by short *spines,* each receiving a synapse (figs. 18.2 and 18.3). The narrow neck of the spine damps the spreading of electrical currents generated by synaptic activity within the spine. The width and length of the neck determine the severity of the damping. For most spines the current flowing into the neuron is largely independent of the strength of the synaptic signal, being controlled almost exclusively by the characteristics of the neck.

The spines may play important roles in the function of the brain. A neuron with many synapses connected to spines can count, as it were, how many synapses are activated at the same time. Whether the neuron will fire or not will depend essentially on that number and very little on the strength of the individual signals because each contributes a constant and limited depolarization. This property may be utilized by the large neurons of the cerebral cortex which, from the shapes of their body, are called pyramidal. These neurons send signals to distant parts of the brain and to motor neurons in the spinal cord. The dendrites of the pyramidal neurons are covered by a multitude of synaptic spines. The pyramidal cells may take a tally of how many connecting neurons vote yes for action, and fire if there are enough yesses (that is, if they altogether lower the membrane potential to the critical value), without considering whether they are enthusiastic or halfhearted.

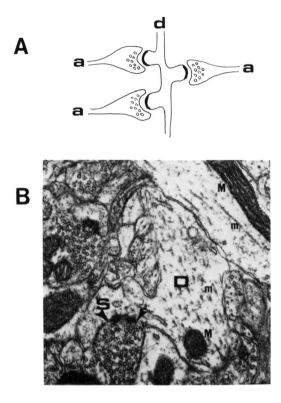

Figure 18.2. Synapses on dendritic spines. (A) A drawing showing a small dendrite (d) with three spines, each having a synapse. (B) Electron micrograph of an extremely thin section of human brain showing a dendritic spine (S) connected to a dendrite (D). The dendrite contains many microtubules (m) and a mitochondrion (M). The synapse connected to the spine (arrows) is excitatory. Photograph courtesy of W. Maxwell Cowan.

Synapses connected to spines may also play a role in memory. Many observations in a variety of animals show that the width of the neck is modified by the flow of signals through the synapses. In experimental systems, repeated electrical stimulations of a pathway induce a long-lasting, perhaps permanent enlargement of the necks of the spines. The synapses connected to such spines have an increased influence on the activity of the neuron. This is the essence of memory—that is, the facilitation of signal transmission through a frequently used pathway. The enlargement of the necks requires the manufacture of new proteins, presumably as building blocks. Conversely, the spines become narrower if the pathway is under-utilized, as is found in the pathways connected to the eyes in blindfolded newborn animals.

One gains the impression of an extreme but orderly complexity in the ar-

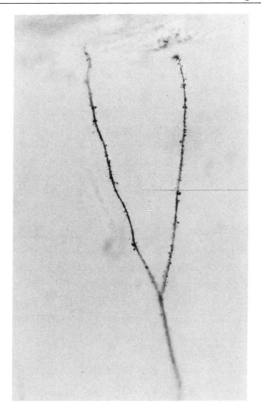

Figure 18.3. An enlarged detail of figure 17.1: B in chapter 17, showing three dendrites. Each is covered along its entire length with spines, which are just visible at this magnification. Magnified 1,700 times. Courtesy of W. Maxwell Cowan.

rangement of synapses, which has the effect of allowing a vast range of graded interactions. This large range contributes in an important way to the computing capability of the nervous system.

Excitation by Inhibition

The pain-killing effect of opioid neuropeptides discussed in the previous chapter demonstrates in a vivid way how excitation and inhibition cooperate in the brain. Opioids inhibit signal transmission when applied directly to neurons of the pain pathway. The same effect is obtained by the electrical stimulation of a part of the brain that might be called the analgesia area, causing the release of opioid peptides along the pain pathway. The same result is reached either by directly inhibiting the pathway or by stimulating neurons that inhibit the pathway.

Similarly, excitation can be obtained either directly, or by inhibition of an inhibitory neuron—*disinhibition*. The decrease of an inhibitory signal increases the contribution of concurrent excitatory signals to the overall output of a neuron, which responds to a balance of signals. An example of disinhibition is the induction of widespread excitation of neurons, with generalized muscular contractions (convulsions), by enkephalins and beta-endorphins injected in the part of the brain called the hippocampus (fig. 17.9 in chapter 17). The opioids act by inhibiting inhibitory neurons. Another opioid, dynorphin, does not produce the same effect because it acts on different receptors and inhibits different neurons.

General Organization

The performance of the nervous system depends not only on what each synapse does but also on how neurons are connected to each other. These connections form the network of the nervous system. For understanding the operation of the nervous system, it is essential to understand the organization of the network in every detail. This is impossible in higher organisms, such as mammals, because the network is too complex, but it can be done to a certain extent in simple animals, such as leeches, which have a far simpler network. We will begin by considering the main features of the organization.

The bodies of simpler animals are formed by a series of similar segments attached to each other (see chapter 12). The nervous system is made up of *neuron centers*, or *ganglia*, located in each segment and mostly forming a double series along the long axis of the animal. The neurons of the various ganglia are interconnected in a regular way: some axons connect to identifiable neurons of the same ganglion or of the other ganglion of the same pair; other axons connect to neurons of the ganglion that precedes or follows along the axis of the animal. Neurons of all ganglia form a single network, although there is also local specialization. This dual nature of the nervous system—as a generalized, holistic network and localized, specialized centers—exists throughout the animal world. It is essential for the operation of the system. The specialization is important if the animal has to recognize certain sensations, such as a contact or pain on a certain part of its skin, and the holistic network is needed for coordinating the global response of the animal to that local recognition. It would be no use for an animal to respond to a sting by frantically moving only the closest leg; it must move all legs, on both sides of the body, in a coordinated way in order to get away from what caused the sting.

Similar principles of organization are followed in higher animals, including humans. They have a more complex nervous system which includes the brain and the spinal cord (the central nervous system) and segmental ganglia, which are comparable to those of more primitive creatures. The segmental organization of the central nervous system in vertebrates is recognized, for instance, by considering the connections of the ganglia. Each vertebra of the spine is associated with a pair of *autonomic ganglia* and a pair of *sensory ganglia*. The autonomic ganglia control the operation of internal organs and are also connected to the spinal cord. They are so named because they may continue to operate regularly if their connections to the central nervous system are cut. They can maintain, for instance, the regular movements of the intestinal wall, which push the food and the stool through the digestive tract.

Sensory ganglia receive sensations from the skin and other organs and channel them to the spinal cord and to the brain. Each neuron in these ganglia has a long thin extension, functionally equivalent to a dendrite (although resembling an axon in structure), which reaches to peripheral sensory organs in the skin, muscles, and internal organs; it also has a true axon that terminates in the spinal cord. Through its connections, each sensory ganglion connects a well-defined area of the skin to a segment of the spinal cord. In the trunk these skin segments are circular bands with segmental organization; the skin areas covering the arms and the legs are extensions of some of these bands. In the spinal cord the sensory ganglia are connected to neuron centers that are segmentally arranged. The centers corresponding to different segments are not, however, independent: each is connected to other centers in a complex network. The brain can be considered as formed by several segments of the nervous system that have undergone enormous development and specialization.

Many Levels of Computing

Each segment of the spinal cord also contains neurons that send axons to muscle—*motor neurons*. At each segment the motor neurons receive signals from the sensory neurons of the same segment through interconnecting neurons—*interneurons*. Interneurons regulate the output signals of the motor neurons on the basis of the input signals; they are also connected to the global network. Each segment of the spinal cord is therefore a sophisticated computer that controls the contraction of a group of muscles. The extensive connections between the various segments increase the complexity and the sophistication of the spinal cord computer.

The connections between sensory and motor neurons have important consequences. For instance, they control the strength of muscular contractions. The signals relevant for this control come from the muscles themselves. *Stretch sensors* in a muscle and the connecting tendon may warn that the contraction is getting too strong or too weak; then the motor neurons alter their firing rate, correcting the excess. Another effect of the connections are certain automatic responses called *reflexes*. For instance, if a painful stimulus comes from the skin of a leg, the leg is precipitously withdrawn by contraction of the appropriate muscles. Reflexes are generated entirely by the direct interaction of sensory and motor neurons contained in the spinal cord. The withdrawal reflex involves many muscles, which are stimulated by motor neurons present in several segments of the spinal cord. The coordination of their contractions is possible because the neurons of the various segments are all connected to each other.

Two Interconnected Halves

The spinal cord is made up of two halves, one the mirror image of the other. Each half receives signals and sends orders related to its side of the body. The brain is similarly made of two halves that are richly interconnected at every level. Besides these short connections, the two halves are also tied by important distant connections. We can recognize them by examining how each segment of the spinal cord informs the higher part of the nervous system, the brain, of the information it receives from its sensors and of the signals it sends to the muscles. The information is transmitted by long axons that reach the brain from spinal neurons of many kinds. These axons are collected in bundles that become progressively thicker as they approach the brain where they terminate in a large number of neuron centers. It is striking that the majority of these axons cross the midline and reach the opposite side of the brain; only a small proportion stay on the side of the animal where their neuron bodies are located. It is not clear why so much crossing is needed. The practical result is that although both sides of the brain are informed of what happens in any point of the animal, the left side is principally connected with the right side of the body, and vice versa.

The presence of two interconnected halves in the nervous system, one the mirror image of the other, is the consequence of the principles of development (see chapter 12). The nervous system, being located along the axis of the body, must have mirror symmetry within itself. Each neuron center of each kind is therefore double, with one part at the left, and the other at the right side. The many interconnections between the two parts are needed to cope with this fact. Owing to these interconnections, the nervous system, including both brain and spinal cord, is a single supercomputer.

The two halves of the nervous system perform essentially equal functions, each one relating to one half of the body (which, as mentioned above, can be at the same or the opposite side of the neuron). An important exception is the human brain, in which the two *hemispheres* are not quite mirror images of each other. Each is covered by a deeply folded layer full of neurons, the *cortex*, but the specialization of certain areas of the cortex is different in the two sides. For instance, in most people the speech centers are on the left hemisphere. Under normal conditions this lack of symmetry has no consequence because the two hemispheres are richly interconnected by thick bundles of neurons that cross from one to the other side, so whatever is experienced by one side of the brain is immediately relayed to the other side. However, if these connections are cut (as is sometimes done surgically in the treatment of epilepsy), many brain functions become confined to just one hemisphere. Thus, information from all sensors (touch, visual, auditory) connected to one hemisphere is processed in that hemisphere; the other hemisphere knows very little, only what transpires from some remaining connections deep in the base of the brain. In the responses of the individual, this disconnection gives rise to characteristic defects which are detectable by proper tests. The individual is then said to have a "split brain."

The neuron centers of the brain, besides receiving information from essentially every part of the body, also act in reverse by sending signals to the spinal cord. These signals modify the result of the local computations carried out in the spinal cord. The brain signals are the result of much additional information and usually put a brake on the locally determined action. A reflex called for by the spinal cord may be stopped by signals from the brain: an example is the control of lordosis in the female rat (see chapter 9). We see the result of the brain control when a physician tests the knee reflex of a patient by hitting the tendon below the kneecap: the normal response is a light kicking of the foot. But if the patient pays too much attention to what is going on, the influence of the brain may block the reflex. If the physician asks the patient to look elsewhere and to grasp one hand with the other and pull, the brain is distracted and the reflex can take place.

Immense Complexity

The brain contains hundreds of brain centers on each side, many of them richly connected to each other and to the spinal cord. The immense number of interconnections makes it difficult to unravel the role of each center. Because interconnections are very extensive, a simple stimulus, like touching a part of the skin or hearing a snapping sound, sends action potentials running through the neurons of many brain centers. In spite of the enormous extent of interconnections, however, the specialization of many neurons centers can be recognized. The brain is an assembly of both specialized and highly interconnected neuron centers.

The basic principles of the interconnections is that input signals from the spinal cord usually reach the brain centers, indirectly, through a series of intermediate stations, each a neuron center. At every station, axons from lower neurons make synapses with neurons that send their axons to higher centers, with local interneurons, and often with neurons that send axons back to the lower centers. Each intermediate center also receives axons from many other centers higher up. Each station is therefore not merely a relay; it is a powerful computer which, through a rich network of interneurons, analyzes the input signals in reference to a vast amount of information coming from other brain centers.

A consequence of the organization of the network is that a signal originating at a sensor progressively spreads to many neurons throughout the nervous system (*divergence*). In each neuron the information received is utilized for different purposes, such as transmission to a next stage, comparison with information coming from other stations, or inhibition of the flow of information in another pathway. Conversely, a central neuron receives signals from many peripheral stations (*convergence*) and compares them with one another. A certain proportion of the information reaching the brain is stored in it as memory, which can be later retrieved and used in the processing of new signals.

In this great complexity many centers merely refine the computations carried out at lower levels. These centers are not absolutely necessary for the performance of the function in which they are involved. If they are destroyed the function may still be performed but in a less precise and coordinated way. For instance, hamsters deprived of the cortex from birth perform reasonably well and display play behavior as well as maternal behavior. These functions are performed by evolutionarily older centers at the base of the brain. The higher centers are not equally dispensable in humans, who usually suffer many substantial deficits even when quite small parts of the brain are destroyed, as by a stroke. For example, they may lose the ability to speak, to move the opposite side of the body, or to perform the higher intellectual functions.

These effects are understandable from the point of view of evolution. The simplest vertebrates had a well-developed spinal cord but only an extremely rudimentary brain. This nervous system was simple, but was adequate for elaborating all the signals needed for moving, eating, recognizing the environment, and mating. Later in evolution new neuron centers were added in succession. Each new addition left the preexisting network largely unchanged, adding to it more advanced machinery. In the more advanced organisms the removal (by the surgeon or by disease) of some higher center returns the system to a more primitive state, which in some cases may be quite adequate for function. This is not true, however, if the addition of new machinery has created completely new functions (like speech) and has caused secondary changes in the lower centers.

Methods

These conclusions about the organization of the nervous system are based on the identification of neuron centers and their connections. How is this done? The answer is: in many ways. Large neuron centers can be readily recognized by cutting the brain because they have a grayish color—the *gray matter*—which stands out against the *white matter* made up of myelinated axon bundles. More than half of the human brain is made up of gray matter. A large proportion is in the cortex, which contains about 100 billion neurons. The neuron centers can be identified more completely by cutting thin slices from a certain part of the brain and then staining them with dyes that selectively enhance the bodies of neurons. And because neurons have very distinct shapes, they are also easily recognized by examination in the light microscope. These simple techniques give a coarse idea of the centers and their connections, but do not reveal the details. Individual axons cannot be followed by these approaches: they are very thin and very long and do not follow straight lines, so that a brain slice contains only small pieces of them.

The first general method used for detecting connections was based on the defects left by the destruction of small areas of the brain through trauma or disease. When the body of a neuron is destroyed, the axon dies, too, and if it had myelin, it loses it. In slices of brain tissue treated with dyes that stain myelin, bundles of such dead axons remain unstained, revealing the main connections between neuron centers. More recent methods allow the detection of the individual axons connected to a given neuron body in experimental animals. In one method the enzyme peroxidase is injected at a determined spot in the brain; the enzyme is taken up by synapses (which normally take up proteins) and is carried through the axons to the respective neuron bodies, even at a considerable distance. Thus localization of the enzyme, detected by the production of a dye visible in the microscope, shows the location of the bodies of neurons that send their axons to the injected place. In the reverse approach an amino acid containing a radioactive atom is injected, and the amino acid is taken up by the bodies of neurons present in the area. The radioactive proteins made in the neuron bodies travel along the axons to the synapses, where they can be demonstrated by the technique of radioautography. This method locates the ends of the axons that originate in the injected areas.

Other approaches are functional rather than anatomical. Electrodes are placed inside individual neuron bodies, recording the electrical activity after a stimulus, such as a touch of the skin, a light flash, or a clicking noise. Neurons showing electrical changes must be connected, directly or indirectly, to the stimulated sensor. Conversely, one can determine which muscles contract when a specific neuron is electrically stimulated. Additional information is obtained by determining the distribution of transmitters and their receptors, or by studying synapses under electron microscopes.

The neuron centers that are active during the performance of some task can be identified because they consume sugar. An abnormal sugar (2-deoxyglucose) that can enter the cells but is not utilized by them as a source of energy is radioactively labeled and injected in the blood of an animal during the performance of the task. The active neurons accumulate the radioactivity and can be identified again by autoradiography. The active areas can also be recognized by a conservative approach, suitable for humans; xenon, a radioactive element that releases positive electrons (positrons), is injected into the bloodstream. Because centers engaged in functional activity have an increased blood flow, they will contain more xenon and can be recognized by the positron emission, which can be precisely localized by scanning the head from the outside.

The combination of all these approaches has led to the discovery of many connections among brain centers and between centers and sensors or muscles. These results have revealed the enormous complexity of the brain network.

Detailed Organization

This great complexity prevents us from learning the details of the network in complex animals. But some insight into this problem has been gained by studying the nervous systems of primitive creatures that have a small number of neurons. For completely understanding the operation of a network, one would have to identify all neurons and all the connections and learn how each neuron is affected by impulses coming from every other neuron. Unfortunately, this goal has not been achieved in any animal. Each, however, has yielded some part of the needed information.

The *anatomy of the network*—the identification of all the neurons and their connections—has been completely worked out in a small nematode, a soil worm, which is only 1 mm long. Each has exactly 302 neurons, which are formed during development by a precise pattern of cell division, migration, and cell death (see chapter 12). The connections between neurons have been studied by sectioning the whole nervous system into a large number of very thin, contiguous slices and examining them in the electron microscope. This immense work has shown that in different animals the basic pattern of connections is constant but the fine branches are variable. Presumably the connections of these branches are influenced by local factors that are not completely reproducible from one animal to another. An exact description of the network, valid for all animals, is therefore impossible. But the results tell a great deal about how the network is made. We will return to this point later.

The nematode is not suitable for exploring the *functional characteristics of the network*, how each neuron affects other neurons. The neurons are too small to permit the safe insertion of electrodes needed for injecting currents or for recording polarization changes. Moreover, even in this small animal, there are too many neurons—more than ninety thousand pairs.

For functional studies even simpler systems are needed. They can be found in small parts of simple nervous systems, such as small ganglia of invertebrates (for instance, some mollusks, leeches, lobster, sea snails, or small crabs). They have a very small number of large cells that perform some well-identifiable function without much input from other parts of the nervous system. As a first approximation they can be considered independent.

These systems also have limitations. Even in these small ganglia the connections and signaling between neurons can be studied experimentally only by concentrating on the most essential responses. The operation of the whole network is then inferred from these partial observations, using theoretical models with computer simulations. In several systems the models generated appear to be quite close to reality because they predict in considerable detail the electrical activities recorded during function from the various neurons or the muscles they control.

Especially useful are neuronal circuits that generate rhythmic behavior in the animal, such as the swimming of the leech. Leeches swim by a series of muscular contractions that take place in succession from head to tail in each segment of the body. All segments have the same organization: each has two sets of muscles and a ganglion, formed by two symmetric groups of about a hundred neurons. In each segment ten motor neurons control the muscles and four interneurons control the motor neurons. Attention has been concentrated on these four control neurons. They are connected to each other by inhibitory synapses (in addition to an electrical synapse), forming a circular chain. If the first neuron is excited, it inhibits the second neuron in the chain, which thus removes its inhibition on the third neuron (disinhibition). This neuron then becomes maximally sensitive to excitation. If it fires, it inhibits the fourth one which thus stops inhibiting the first neuron. The second neuron, however, also inhibits the fourth, and this in turn will disinhibit the first, causing the third neuron to fire. The sequence of inhibition and disinhibition occurs in a cycle. The model, based on all the connections ascertained experimentally, predicts that the four neurons should fire in succession from the first to fourth and back to the first, as they do in the animal.

A control neuron of a certain segment is also connected to neurons of other segments, both anterior and posterior to it. It is striking that in all segments it is connected to equivalent neurons. For instance, the first neuron of segment six makes inhibitory synapses on the second neuron of segment six as well as on the second neurons of segments one to ten. This regularity is probably the result of genetic instructions, which address the axon branches of any neuron numbered one to any neuron numbered two, regardless of the segment. We will see below that in other systems, too, a neuron addresses a certain type of neuron but not any individual neuron. The connections between the ganglia of different segments maintain the proper time difference between the contraction of the muscles of the various segments. There are also unidirectional connections between ganglia of adjacent segments; they make the contraction wave unidirectional, from head to tail.

Circuits for Recognizing Movement

In many animals, from insects to mammals, the operation of the visual system has been a favorite area of investigation because the neuron centers to which the eyes are connected are well known. How the visual networks of invertebrates detect moving objects is fairly well understood. An example is the movement detector of the locust, which responds to a sudden localized movement in any place in the visual field, causing the insect to jump. This is a defense-related circuit that detects the approach of a predator. The circuit must be activated by light changes occurring in a small part of the visual field; otherwise it would be activated by eye movements or by rapid changes from a brightly lit place to the shade or vice versa.

The network is characterized by a large interneuron, called the *giant movement detector* (fig. 18.4). Recording the changes of electrical potential in this detector shows that a moving spot of light striking the eye causes strong signals. If, however, the eye also sees moving stripes a certain distance away from the spot, the signal is reduced or abolished. The reduction is attributed to a network that responds to changes of illumination on a large part of the visual field by inhibiting the neurons stimulated by the light spot. Although the inhibitory network is not entirely known, it seems likely that it acts according to the following model. Light impinging on the eye sensors excites ON neurons when it is turned on and different OFF neurons when it is turned off. Axons from the ON and OFF neurons directly reach excitatory neurons called type I. Axons from these neurons have excitatory synapses on the giant movement detector neuron, as well as on inhibitory interneurons called type II. These interneurons inhibit the excitatory neurons of type I, except those that were directly stimulated by the ON and OFF neurons. As a result,

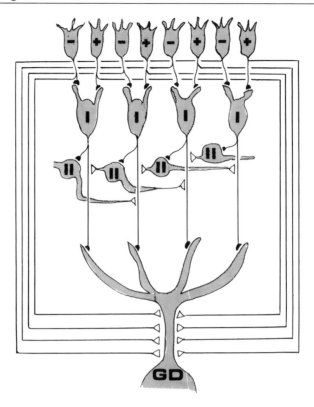

Figure 18.4. A model of the organization of the network of the movement detector of the locust. Signals reach the ON (+) or OFF (−) neurons. Axons of these neurons make excitatory synapses (round, black) with type I neurons, and more distant inhibitory synapses (triangular, open), with a dendrite of the giant detector (GD). Axons from type I neurons make excitatory synapses with the giant detector as well as with interneurons of type II. Each of the latter interneurons make inhibitory synapses with neurons of type I, except the one from which it receives signals. How this network operates is shown in figure 18.5. (Modified from C. H. F. Rowell, M. Oshea, and J. L. D. Williams, *J. Exp. Biol.* 68:157–85 [1977].)

the neuron of type I excited by the light spot sends its signal unimpeded to the movement detector, while surrounding neurons of type I send no signal, being inhibited by neurons of type II. This *lateral inhibition* (fig. 18.5: A) explains how the network identifies a light spot, provided the light striking the rest of the visual field does not change.

This system would not compensate for sudden changes of illumination on a large part of the visual field, such as those occurring when an animal comes out of a hole into bright daylight. The light would excite many neurons of type I, which would then transmit their excitation to the movement detector before the slower lateral inhibition sets in. Lateral inhibition is slower because it has to go through an additional interneuron, with attending time delay at the synapse.

This possible complication is eliminated by another characteristic of the

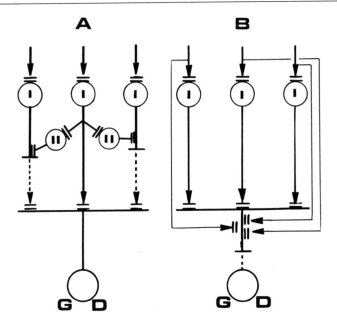

Figure 18.5. Two characteristics of the operation of the model for the movement detector of figure 18.4. (A) Lateral inhibition. A signal received by the central type I neuron reaches the giant detector (GD) as well as two interneurons of type II. The interneurons inhibit the two lateral type I neurons, which cannot send signals to the giant detector (dotted lines). Pairs of parallel lines indicate where there are synaptic delays in the transmission of the signals. (B) Feed forward inhibition. Branches of the three axons (coming from ON or OFF neurons; see fig. 18.4) form inhibitory synapses with the giant detector, reaching it before the excitatory signals going through neurons of type I, which have one extra synaptic delay.

network (fig. 18.5: B): branches of the ON and OFF axons that activate neurons of type I form inhibitory synapses with the movement detector. They inhibit the detector before it receives excitations through the neurons of type I, which have to go through one additional synapse. This model is called *feed forward inhibition.* In this system each ON or OFF neuron can produce only a small inhibitory signal in the movement detector, but many of them together can totally inhibit it. In this way a stimulus coming from a few ON or OFF neurons can activate the detector through type I neurons, but simultaneous signals from many ON or OFF neurons cannot—they inhibit it.

The Major Pathways of Complex Organisms

The Spreading of a Touch Sensation

We will now consider the general characteristics of some of the major pathways present in complex organisms, beginning with those transmitting touch sensations. We have seen that when the skin of an animal is touched, signals are transmitted to the spinal cord through a sensory ganglion. The signals are analyzed in the spinal cord to see whether they require immediate action through a reflex and are then forwarded to the brain, most to the opposite side of the body. The signals reach the brain through various paths: some go directly, whereas others are interrupted in a neuron center at the border between spinal cord and brain, from which new axons go to the brain. All these signals finally converge into a major brain center, the thalamus (see fig. 17.9 in chapter 17), which also receives inputs from many other kinds of sensors. From the thalamus, axons reach the cerebral cortex. All the touch signals converge onto a small area of the cortex, the *sensory area*, where they generate a conscious sensation. This is not, however, the only pathway through which the signals go: the various brain centers intercalated in the pathway also send axons to other parts of the brain that do not contribute to the touch sensation but use the information for other purposes. For instance, when we go up or down a staircase, the main pathway informs us that a foot has touched a step, but other pathways use the same information to maintain the equilibrium of the body and to control the leg movements so that they do not overstep or understep.

The area of the cortex where the touch pathway terminates has been electrically stimulated in humans during surgery performed under local anesthesia for medical purposes. The stimulation generates the sensation that a part of the body has been touched. The localization of the sensation depends on where the sensory cortex has been stimulated. By stimulating many different points it has been established that the sensory cortex contains a *map* of the body in which each point corresponds to a defined area of the skin. It is not a regular map because the areas of the cortex corresponding to the fingers are much larger than those corresponding to the abdomen. The signals coming from the fingers are analyzed in a much more detailed way, explaining why their skin is so sensitive.

Another pathway connecting the skin to the cortex is that of pain sensation, which is activated when the skin is pricked by a needle, say, or touched by a hot object. The pain signals do not arise in the touch sensors; they are generated by different specialized sensors and go through a different pathway. Transmission of the pain signals is influenced by centers in the lower part of the brain. We have seen that electrical stimulation of these centers causes pain to disappear (see chapter 17). The axons of neurons located in these midbrain centers descend to the spinal cord, where they make synapses with neurons of the pain pathway, conveying inhibitory signals.

Converging Signals to Muscles

Stimulation of an area of the cortex that is adjacent to the sensory area and is called the *motor area* causes muscle contractions. This area also contains a map of the body, which, like that of the sensory area, is distorted: in humans the fingers and lips have a disproportionately large representation in the cortex. This explains why both fingers and lips are so versatile and can perform such accurate movements with total control. The neurons of the motor cortex are also richly connected to many other areas of the brain. They receive axons from the adjacent sensory cortex, the parts of the brain elaborating visual signals, and those related to equilibrium. The motor cortex sends orders to the muscles through axons that descend to the spinal cord and terminate onto the motor neurons, which are directly responsible for muscle contractions. The descending axons have many branches that terminate on a variety of other brain centers, especially the so-called basal ganglia (gray masses at the base of the brain), and also the thalamus and centers determining the equilibrium of the body during walking or standing, such as the cerebellum. These connections inform the various neuron centers of the instructions to muscles. The neuron centers react by sending signals to the cortex, which can modify the instructions as they are continuously generated.

Visual Perception

The best studied network in the complex brain of mammals is that dedicated to the analysis of *visual signals*. Signals from the eye sensors (such as the rods discussed in chapter 16) are analyzed first by a network present in the retina. The retina contains neurons because it is a part of the brain that during development moved to the eye but still remained connected to the brain through the optic nerve (fig. 18.6). The first step in the analysis carried out by the retina is the conversion of the hyperpolarizing signals of the sensors (see chapter 16) into regular depolarizing signals. This step is carried out by *relay cells* connected to neurons that, through a number of stations, send signals to the brain.

The information going to the brain is quite different from that received by the sensors. If a round spot of uniform light shines in an eye, all sensors hit by the light respond equally, regardless of the size of the spot. In contrast, axons going from the retina toward the brain fire briskly only if the spot is small; they do not fire if it is large. As in the movement detector of the locust, this localization is the result of lateral inhibition. The model of the locust movement detector is applicable to the network of the retina of all animals, including humans.

The axons from the retina converge in the middle of the brain onto a part of the thalamus called the lateral geniculate body because it is bent like a knee. In this center the axons make synapses with neurons that send their axons to the visual area of the cerebral cortex, the highest brain station in the elaboration of visual signals.

An important characteristic of this pathway is the extensive use of inhibition. In fact, the visual cortex not only receives axons from the geniculate body but sends some to it. These descending axons terminate on inhibitory interneurons that interconnect the cells of the geniculate body. The descending axons and those ascending to the cortex from the geniculate body form a closed loop with negative feedback, which puts a brake on the strength of the signals. Inhibition is widely

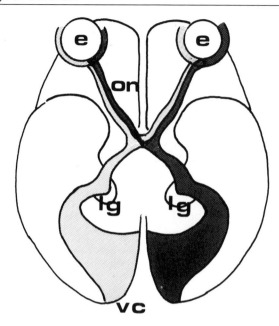

Figure 18.6. Diagram of the pathway of connections from the eye to the visual cortex (VC). The left parts of the retinas from both eyes send axons to the right lateral geniculate center (lg), whereas the right parts of the retinas send them to the left geniculate center. From the geniculate centers axons go to the cortex at the same side. e = eye; on = optic nerve.

used in the network of the visual system, as it is in other brain networks. In the brain about one-third of all neurons are inhibitory.

The elaboration of the visual signals takes place first in an area of the cerebral cortex that receives the axons from the lateral geniculate body. This is called area 17, from a catalog of parts of the cortex based on neuron types, density, and distribution. In this area a very extensive analysis is carried out by neurons connected in ascending chains and bridged by interneurons. The analysis is important for the determination of shapes. This is based on the ability of neurons present in area 17 to display orientation specificity. These neurons respond not to round spots of light presented to the eye but to bars of light that make certain angles with the horizontal; different neurons respond to bars of different inclinations. Most neurons respond best to moving lines and to movement in a particular direction. They send signals to neurons of a second group, which respond to lines with suitable orientation contained within a certain rectangle. Neurons of a third group respond to lines again of certain orientations but also of a certain length: if a line is too long, they respond less. Within each group different neurons respond to a bright line on a dark background, or to a dark line on an illuminated background, or to an edge between a dark and a lighted field. In all cases, the orientation and length requirement remain the same.

From these characteristics we surmise that the eye analyzes an object by splitting it into a number of independent features, such as the orientation of a line, its length and brightness, and whether it moves and how fast. Analysis in other areas of the cortex receiving signals from area 17 identifies other features, such as thickness and length of lines, color, direction of movement, and so on. As the analysis proceeds, individual neurons react to more and more complex patterns. Certain neurons in monkeys react to a picture of a monkey face but not to its dispersed elements.

What we perceive as a picture results from the resynthesis of all these features detected in the brain. The process is very different from the point-to-point equivalence of a photograph; it is a digital analysis of the type one might expect from a highly sophisticated computer. The various features are separated from each other by a kind of filtering system, in which the information from a group of eye sensors is allowed to proceed if it possesses a certain feature, but is stopped if it does not. Other parallel filters let through information possessing different features. In the end, all the information is utilized and cataloged; the catalog constitutes the basis of the perceived visual picture.

But how can the catalog yield an image? How are the various features connected to each other? This reconstruction is possible because of another characteristic of the system: there is a one-to-one correspondence between points of the retina and of the cortex. In other words, the area 17 of the visual cortex is a map of the retina.

To understand how the map is made up, we should remember that the cortex is a sheet 2 to 3mm thick, folded in a complex way and containing several layers of neurons. Neurons of a given layer are all of the same shape; those of different layers are different. Studies of the visual cortex of the cat show that in area 17 the information concerning a certain location on the retina is contained in a vertical prismatic column—that is, a box full of neurons that extends through the thickness of the cortex at a precisely determined point (fig. 18.7). The cross section of each column is about 2 by 2mm. In area 17 of the cortex there are about a thousand vertical columns, each made up of a series of vertical flat slabs. In each slab all neurons have the same orientation requirement. Neurons of different slabs respond to different orientations; all possible orientations are taken care of in the different slabs of each column. Proceeding beyond the end of a column, one finds another column, which refers to an adjacent area of the retina. This column again is made up of a set of vertical slabs that take care of all orientations in succession. Each slab contains many interconnected neurons arranged in several layers, which carry out the orientation analysis. Presumably in different columns the slabs responding to a given orientation have identical networks; they may be analogous to the printed circuit boards that are used in the construction of computers.

In this way the eye is covered by an ideal grid, which is reproduced in the cortex: in each square the orientation feature is given by the number of the slab

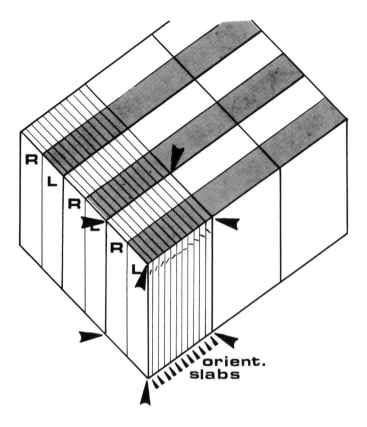

Figure 18.7. Diagram of area 17 of the visual cortex showing nine vertical prismatic columns, of which one is indicated by heavy arrows. Each column consists of many orientation slabs; the orientation of lines recognized by neurons in each slab are indicated. Each column also consists of two eye-dominance half-columns, one predominantly for the right eye (R) and one for the left eye (L). The half-columns form rows, indicated by the gray bands. (Modifed from D. H. Hubel and T. N. Wiesel, *Proc. Royal Soc. London B*. 198:1 [1977].)

where the responding cells are contained. The grid is somewhat distorted: the grid squares corresponding to the center of vision—the fovea, the part of the retina where acuity is greatest—are the most numerous. The grid of the cortex, therefore, does not represent equal surfaces of the retina, but surfaces *corrected for acuity of vision*. We find in the map of the visual field what we have already found in the sensory and motor maps: they are distorted according to the needs of the functions they perform, which, after all, is the reason for their existence.

Another important characteristic of visual perception is the sense of depth, which results from cooperation of the two eyes. The generation of the sense of depth requires binocular neurons, which respond to light impinging on both eyes. Up to the level of the geniculate body all neurons are monocular; they respond to stimulation of only one eye and so are the first neurons of the cortex. Cortical neurons more distant from the retina have a binocular response.

In order to allow binocular vision, signals from corresponding points of both eyes converge onto the same vertical column, in the following way (refer again to fig. 18.6). The retina of either eye can be considered as made up of two parts, left and right; the left part of each retina sends axons to the lateral geniculate body of the left side of the body, and the right part to the right geniculate body. Because the optical image in the eye is inverted, the left geniculate body corresponds to the right field of vision of both eyes, and the right body to the left field. Axons coming from the two eyes don't mix in the geniculate body: they terminate in neurons that are in alternating layers, three for the eye at the same side and three for the eye at the opposite side (fig. 18.8). The signals from the two eyes reach the cortex separately: for each location on the retina, two sets of axons reach the cortex, one for each eye. The result, at least in cats, is that each column in area 17 is split into two half-columns (refer again to fig. 18.7). In each half-column the first neurons receiving signals directly from the geniculate neurons respond to signals coming from one eye; so there is one half-column for the right eye and the other for the left eye. Successive neurons respond to signals coming from both eyes, but not equally. Neurons of the half-column corresponding to the right eye still show a dominant influence of the right eye; they respond more intensely to illumination of that eye. The converse is true for the left eye. The cortical columns are therefore split into two eye-dominance columns, each containing the same number of orientation slabs.

The left and the right half-columns of adjacent columns are aligned, because their position is determined by the path of the bundle of axons coming from the geniculate body. This is shown clearly if a radioactive amino acid is injected into one eye. After some time, radioactive proteins will accumulate in the terminals of axons connected to that eye in all stations up to the cortex; their distribution is demonstrated by autoradiography. Slices of cortex cut tangentially to its surface are glued to glass slides and covered with photographic emulsion; after keeping the slides in the dark for several weeks, radiation emitted by the radioactive proteins generates silver grains in the emulsion. Photographic development and fixation then reveals in these slides a series of stripes of the width corresponding to the columns (fig. 18.9). The stripes are formed by rows of half-columns; as they reach parts of the map where acuity is greater, the stripes branch. The relationship between eye-dominance columns and orientation preference are not as regular as represented in figure 18.7; there are places where orientation preference is almost absent, and other places where it changes abruptly over a short distance. The two sets of eye-dominance columns and the neurons they contain are parts of the mechanism that permits stereoscopic vision, but do not explain it. Stereoscopic vision results from further elaboration of the signals in other cortical areas.

When an eye looks at a long line, signals travel to many columns of the visual cortex. The cortical slabs involved in the analysis are disconnected and do not form a line at all. The whole line is coded by pairs of numbers, one giving the coordinates, and the other the orientation. How can this code yield the perception of a continuous line? The continuity is probably established at a separate stage of

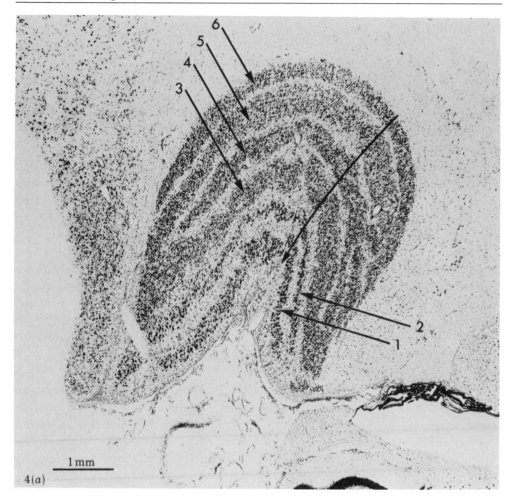

1 mm

4(*a*)

Figure 18.8. Cross section through the right lateral geniculate center of an adult macaque monkey in which the body of the neurons are stained. The center contains six layers of neurons (dark gray) separated by layers of axons (light gray). Neuron layers 1, 4, and 6 receive signals from the opposite, left, eye; layers 2, 3, and 5 receive them from the right eye, at the same side. Each layer is a map of the retina. All maps are in register, so that all points on the central arrow correspond to the same point on the retina. (From D. H. Hubel and T. N. Wiesel, *Proc. Royal Soc. London B.* 198:1 [1977]. Reprinted with permission.)

analysis, using information from various sources. The area involved would be expected to have a map of the retina. Perhaps a dozen areas of the brain in addition to area 17 of the visual cortex fulfill this requirement. For instance, each lateral geniculate body has such a map, but it is broken up in pieces. Other visual maps are found in several areas of the cerebral cortex, and one in a neuron cluster called the *visual claustrum*, whose neurons are connected both to the geniculate body and the cortex without being on the direct pathway. The neurons of the claustrum have characteristics that might make them suitable as continuity neurons be-

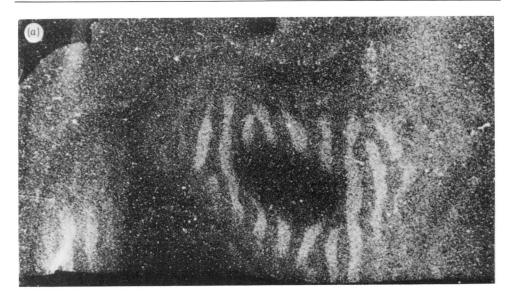

Figure 18.9. Ocular-dominance bands of an adult macaque. The bands are formed by the apposition of ocular-dominance half-columns, as shown in figure 18.7. A radioactive amino acid has been injected in one eye. Tangential sections were cut from the visual cortex, and autoradiographs were made from them. The bright lines contain the silver grains, revealed by lateral illumination against a dark background. The photograph is a composite of several sections because the cortex is curved. Magnified 12 times. (From D. H. Hubel and T. N. Wiesel, *Proc. Royal Soc. London B.* 198:1–59 [1977]. Reproduced with permission.)

cause they respond when the eye sees long continuous lines of proper orientations regardless of brightness or movement.

How Is the Brain Made?

We will now move to a more general problem. We recognize that the brain is a fantastic machine with a large number of neurons and intricate interconnections. How could it possibly be made starting from a single cell, the fertilized egg? This is a question that cannot be answered completely; we have some information about the basic mechanisms, but we are ignorant about many important steps.

The first point worth considering is how the organization of the completed brain of any animal or human relates to the genes of that individual. Is it possible that the whole network is specified, in every detail, by the genes? The answer is clearly no. There are as many as several thousand billion neurons in a human being, and something like ten to a hundred trillion synapses compared to perhaps 100,000 functional genes in all. The brain is also much too complex for genetic control of the type used for immunoglobulins (chapter 13). The genes, therefore, which must do lots of other things as well, can specify only some general aspects of the network.

Help from Mutations

This basic concept is supported by the study of development and by what we know of the effect of mutations that alter the nervous system in humans or animals. All the known mutations have broad effects on the nervous system: each affects a whole class of neurons or some functional process that is common to a large number of neurons.

Among the mouse mutations, several cause changes in the cerebellum, the part of the brain devoted to coordination of movement and equilibrium, altering its performance; one of the mutants is called *reeler* and another *staggerer*. The reeler mutation causes changes in a whole class of cerebellar neurons called *Purkinje cells*. These neurons receive the results of the analysis carried out in the cerebellum and send related signals to other parts of the brain.

To understand the consequence of the reeler mutation we must see how the Purkinje cells are formed during development. The cerebellum, like other parts of the brain, develops from the inner side of the neural tube. Cells destined to give rise to various types of brain cells line the wall of the tube where they multiply. After completing the last cell division and attaining terminal differentiation, some of the cells start migrating toward the outer surface of the tube wall. They are guided by the surfaces of glial cells, which stretch radially from the inner to the outer surface. In their migration, certain cells go far, almost to the outer surface, whereas others stop at various points in between. In this movement some cells pass others. For instance, in the cerebral cortex the cells that go farthest migrate last, so they must pass all those that migrated before them. Because each cell knows where to stop, together they give rise to cell *layers*, which are characteristic of the structure of many parts of the brain, including the cerebral cortex and the cortex of the cerebellum. Dendrites and axons, as well as the connections to other neurons and all the characteristics that distinguish various classes of neurons, are made after the precursor cells have reached their final destination. In layered parts of the central nervous system all cells of a certain morphological class belong to the same layer.

In the cerebellar cortex, cells destined to generate Purkinje cells normally stop at an intermediate layer between an outer thick layer of axons and an inner layer of small cells called *granules*. In reeler mice they do not migrate far enough; they stop at a position inside the granule layer rather than outside it.

These observations localize the defect to the migration of the precursors of Purkinje cells; but they do not tell us why the migration is altered. Is it because there is a defect in the Purkinje cells or in the mechanism that guides their progression? This question has been answered by the ingenious approach of making mice, called *chimeric mice*, that have cells of two mouse strains. (Chimera is a mythical monster with a lion's head, a goat's body, and a serpent's tail.) These mice are produced by mixing together the dissociated cells of two early embryos of the two strains, which form a single embryo. If this mixed embryo is implanted into the uterus of a hormonally prepared female mouse, it will develop into an adult chimeric mouse. Suppose we make the initial cell fusion using cells of a reeler embryo and that of a normal embryo carrying some identifying marker: what will be the behavior of the Purkinje cells in the chimeric adult mouse? In all these chimeric mice the cells of the two parents are intermixed, but not completely: they form small patches in which the cells are all of one kind. Patches of the two types are mixed together at random. In the cerebellum, small patches of Purkinje cells are at the normal position, outside the granule cells; others are at a wrong place, inside the layer of granule cells. If we examine the markers that distinguish the reeler from the normal cells, a surprising result can be seen: many cells at the normal position come from the reeler parent, and many at the abnormal position came from the normal parent. We conclude that it is not their fault if the Purkinje cells do not migrate to the right place: it must be the fault of some other cells. The guess is that they are the glial cells; although they normally guide migrating neurons to the proper location, in the reeler mice they guide them to a wrong location.

The effect of the reeler mutation is not visible only in the cerebellar cortex: the layering of the cerebral cortex is also altered, essentially inverted, in the reeler mice. This shows that the migration disturbance is generalized, implying that the mechanisms that determine and guide the migration of all different neuronal precursors have something in common: probably the glial cells.

Two main lessons are derived from this observation: a mutation affects whole classes of neuronal precursors, altering their migration. The mutation acts through some cell-to-cell interaction essential for proper migration. These results show that a process important in the development of the nervous system (as well as of other systems [see chapter 12]) is the coordinated migration of precursor cells under the control of some other types of cells.

Axonal Guidance

The reeler mice have disturbances of coordination and movement that can be explained by the disorder of cerebellar organization. But what about the upside-down organization of the cerebral cortex: does it have any consequence? In order to find out about this point we may concentrate on the visual cortex, and ask whether the analysis of visual signals is perturbed. Again the answer is astonishing: the visual function is perfectly normal. This result provides another lesson: that the level at which a neuron is located in the cortex is not critical for the connections it makes with axons. In the cortex, as in other parts of the nervous system, axons travel long distances, guided by a highly specialized tip with hair-like appendices, the *growth cone;* it is like a hand with many fingers, which are continuously extended and retracted. Some finger always finds a cell or an axon it can adhere to, probably because it has compatible surface molecules. This contact then determines the direction the axon will take. In the cortex, axons often reach the target neurons with which they make synapses by following first a certain layer; but before reaching their destination they may abandon that layer and aim onto the appropriate neurons in another layer. The layer is not the main reference for making connections; the axon seeks and recognizes the appropriate type of neuron independently of the layer in which it is contained. This principle is followed in the reeler mice. The axons, after following the right layer, bend in a direction opposite to that of normal axons in order to reach the misplaced target neurons. The result shows that the misplaced neurons still guide the right axons to them. So the layering is not important for the connections. Interchanging a whole layer with another is of little consequence, because the connections are made following specific attractions without regard to the layer.

Thus it is evident that axons have a remarkable ability to find their target neurons even under unusual circumstances. This principle is also illustrated in a striking way by an observation made in frogs. If the skin of a frog is stimulated by touch or electrically, the animal responds with a wiping movement directed at the part of the skin that was stimulated. Animals in which parts of the skin from the belly and from the back are interchanged will make a misplaced wiping movement—one that is not directed at the stimulated skin. If the belly skin, now on the back, is stimulated, the animal will scratch the belly, not the piece of skin to which the stimulus was applied. To explain this result, one first thinks that after the transplantation the nerves from the sensory ganglia in the center of the body regenerate outward, reaching the same skin to which they were originally connected, although it is now remote. They would then direct the response to the proper muscles, which know nothing of the transplantation. But this is not true: the transplanted skin is re-innervated by the closest nerve. Belly skin transplanted to the back is innervated by nerves from the back of the frog, not from its belly. We must conclude that fibers from nerves coming from the back do what they are not supposed to do: through an abnormal route they become connected to neurons that normally receive information from the nerve coming from the belly. It is the connection between nerve and central neurons that is changed. Although the mechanism of this phenomenon is not known, it clearly shows that the peripheral organ determines the central connections.

The central connections are made in a precise way, as shown by the one-to-one relationship between the retina and the brain centers. The establishment of these connections has been studied—especially at the first station reached by axons from the retina, a center called *tectum* (because it is in the roof of a central canal that extends through the central nervous system). The tectum is a map of the retina. The overall correspondence between points on the retina and points on the tectum must arise when the axons grow from the retina. As they grow, the axons must retain the relative positions of the sensors to which they are connected. How do they do it? Observations made during normal development and the study of alterations imposed experimentally during development or regeneration show that axons from the retina go to the tectum following local clues. First, they go there in preference to other places, whereas axons from other origins do not go to the tectum. Second, each axon has a strong preference for connecting to neurons in a certain part of the tectum. The axons know precisely where to go, because if two parts of the tectum are surgically exchanged, the axons, going through a devious route, reach the appropriate part, although it is misplaced.

What is the *guidance mechanism* that guides the growth cones of the axons? There seem to be several. Guidance by glia channels is one of them, but perhaps not the most important. Chemical guidance is another possibility: certain parts of the tectum seem to attract certain axons by producing specific attracting substances. Guidance by other cells and neighboring axons through specific adhesion molecules also plays a role: the growing axons maintain their reciprocal position during growth but undergo characteristic changes of route when they touch certain cells. The final destination of an axon depends also in part on its starting position within the bundle coming from the eye. Axons maintain their relationship by actively interacting with each other. Various guidance mechanisms probably operate in different places, even for the same axons; the simultaneous cooperation of several mechanisms seems to be used to ensure the right connections.

All these various mechanisms work in a reproducible way. During embryonic development axons growing out of neurons of a certain center have been observed to proceed always along a stereotyped path; and even if the neurons are artificially displaced, the axons rapidly find the way to their proper targets. To proceed with such reproducibility and compensatory ability, the axon may perhaps follow a morphogenetic gradient, such as those discussed in chapter 12: at any point such a gradient would have a slope of definite direction pointing toward a given spot. The concentration of adhesive molecules identified by a growth cone may form such a gradient: in the developing retina a protein that is required for synapse formation is distributed in a gradient. The thin hairlike extensions of the growth cone may detect the gradient, using the principle used by bacteria for recognizing a food gradient (see chapter 16).

All the guidance mechanisms can only direct the neurons in the right direction: they cannot determine the map because the *precise* final destination of the axons is not predetermined. This is shown, for instance, by removing part of the retina: the remaining axons will spread to the whole tectum, still leaving the map unaltered as much as possible. In the inverse operation, in which the retina is untouched and the tectum is reduced, all retinal axons find a neuron, often displacing legitimate axons. There is much competition between axons, even under normal conditions.

Functioning Is Surviving

Many observations show that the ultimate organization of the network is determined by function. This is not surprising. Neurons themselves are affected by function: they continue to exist only if they are active. This principle also applies outside the nervous system: each cell is stimulated by the performance of its function to produce more of its specific products and sometimes to replicate. The reverse is also true: think of the muscles of an athlete and those of a person immobilized by paralysis.

The principle that function causes a cell to develop maximally the attributes needed for its performance explains many observations—for instance, what happens to a monkey when a finger is cut. We have seen that through many stations, axons related to skin sensors finally reach the frontal cortex, which contains maps of the surface of the body. Each finger is represented in the map. Soon after the finger is cut and the corresponding neurons become inactive, the areas of the cortex corresponding to the neighboring fingers start enlarging. In time these neurons completely fill the territory of the cut finger. The old synapses are dismantled and replaced by new ones formed by the invading axons. Evidently axons corresponding to a certain finger are normally restrained from expanding by axons related to the other fingers. This example shows that the network is modeled by a *synaptic competition* by which synapses tend to replace each other and that function determines the outcome of the competition.

Also interesting is the consequence of visual deprivation on the formation of ocular-dominance columns in area 17 of the cerebral cortex in monkeys. Newborn monkeys lack ocular-dominance columns: most neurons respond to stimulation of both eyes. The columns are formed during the first six weeks of life even if both eyes are kept closed all the time so that there is no visual stimulation. In normal animals most of the axons connecting the half-column in which one eye is dominant to the other eye are withdrawn during these six weeks, perhaps because they are displaced by those relating to the dominant eye. In monkeys made monocular at birth by sealing one eye closed, the axons from the functional eye persist even where they would be normally withdrawn. Then all columns end up being entirely colonized by the axons from the active eye, without contribution from the inactive eye. Only functional axons, evidently, can successfully compete during the modeling process.

An even more dramatic observation on the role of function in organizing the connection has been made in the tectum of the barn owl, which is very proficient at localizing a source of sound in space. In the tectum neurons that receive signals from the ears or from the eyes are interspersed; the visual and the auditory maps are in an amazing concordance. The same area of the tectum corresponds to the same point in space for both auditory and visual localization. This coincidence makes sense because it allows the two types of information to help each other and to substitute for each other if necessary. That the extraordinary concordance is brought about by function is shown by comparing the organization of the two maps in owls in which the ear is plugged at birth in order to distort the perception of auditory signals. In these birds the visual map is aligned with the auditory map altered by the plugged ear. The concordance lasts as long as the ear is plugged. But if the plug is removed, the two maps shift in the way expected from the normalization of hearing. Evidently the sets of migrating axons do not form the two maps solely by following local clues: function is the most important factor. Moreover, the axons can rearrange their connections even after the network has been finalized in accord with the environment. The observations with the owl reveal another point: the recovery of map position after unplugging the ear is guided by the eye, because it fails if the eyes are closed. The two types of function evidently work together, and both are needed for the correct arrangement of connections.

Maintenance by Specific Growth Factors?

It is possible that the connections established by the growth of bundles of axons from the neurons of a given center to those of another distant target center are maintained by another mechanism: the production of specific growth factors by the target neurons. The factors would be responsible for the survival and activity of the neurons that make the connections. This concept has evolved from observations with the well-studied *nerve growth factor*. This factor, a small protein, was discovered by a remarkable accidental observation. A cancer originated in a rat was implanted into a chick embryo in order to study the behavior of the cancer cells. While conducting the study, researchers noticed that the neurons of the peripheral ganglia of the embryo went awry: their axons, instead of growing into the organs of the embryos, grew into the cancer. Moreover, the ganglia were several times as large as in normal embryos. It turned out that the cells of the implanted tumor made large amounts of the growth factor, which stimulated the multiplication of neuronal precursor cells and attracted their axons. This observation permitted the subsequent isolation and characterization of the factor. The nerve growth factor (NGF) is a differentiation hormone (see chapter 8), which is required for the normal development and maintenance of peripheral neurons of the sympathetic and the sensory systems. Injection of an antiserum to NGF into a newborn animal blocks its activity and prevents the development of the sympathetic system. The NGF that normally acts on these peripheral neurons is manufactured by cells of the target tissues innervated by the neurons; the neurons require the factor for survival. The factor is taken up by receptors in the axon endings and is transported back to the neuron's body, where presumably it performs its activity.

Although NGF acts also on brain cells, it was difficult to find this out. The sympathetic neurons on which NGF primarily acts use catecholamine as neurotransmitters. But many efforts for detecting similar activity of NGF on catecholamine-using neurons in the brain failed. Finally it was observed that in cultures NGF acts on a different class of brain neurons: they use acetylcholine as transmitter. In them the factor markedly increases the manufacture of an enzyme needed for making acetylcholine. In mammals the bodies of acetylcholine neurons are concentrated mainly in several basal centers at the lower anterior part of the brain and send bundles of axons to the hypocampus and the cortex. NGF seems to play an essential survival role for these neurons: the target neurons in the hippocampus and the cortex manufacture the factor, which is picked up by the axon terminals of the basal neurons and conveyed to the neuron bodies in the basal centers. That NGF is important for these neurons is shown by the adverse effect of antibodies to the factor. And it is suspected that diseases affecting these neurons, of which Alzheimer's disease is one, may be produced by a breakdown of the survival-inducing function of the factor.

One is tempted to generalize, suggesting that connections between neuron centers are maintained by the production of specific factors by the target neurons that are needed for the survival and activity of the neurons connected to them. The NGF would be one of these factors, but there would be many others still unknown. This hypothesis is supported by the observation that cutting the axons often leads to the death of the neurons, perhaps because they are deprived of the survival factor. This would imply that the biochemical diversity of groups of neurons, reflected in the variety of transmitter they use and the growth factors to which they are sensitive, is essential for the organization of connections.

Mechanism of Plasticity

We conclude that the formation of a map is based on several mechanisms. The genes, unable to ensure directly a perfect correspondence between two centers, have built mechanisms that allow the formation and establishment of overall connections. These connections are laid down in great excess, using many local clues and chemical signals; then the connections are rearranged on the basis of their functional roles, possibly through the use of specific growth and mainte-nance factors made in larger amounts in active neurons. The general mechanisms by which function determines the rearrangements in this last step are also, of course, determined by the genes. By affecting the development of the nervous system, the genes can have important effects on all brain processes.

The examples reported above do not reveal the mechanism or the structural basis of plasticity of neuronal connections. Information on this point is afforded by, among others, the extraordinary phenomenon of *long-term potentiation:* if a pathway is intensely stimulated, the neurons to which it is connected respond to stimulation with stronger and longer-lasting activity. The change persists for many days. Associated with the increased response is a structural change in the dendritic spines to which synapses are connected; the size of the neck of the spines increases. In many other circumstances as well, strong stimulation of neurons causes the dendritic spines to increase in size. The very arrangement of synapses on spines on adult neurons may be the result of functional stimulation going on over a long period of time.

Long-term potentiation involves changes in the receiving neurons in the stim-ulated pathway. The changes are produced when two different synapses attached to the same neuron are stimulated, especially if in a repetitive way. The mechanisms involve the entry of Ca^{++} ions into the neurons: injection of Ca^{++} blockers into the neurons abolishes potentiation. A crucial part of the mechanism seems to be the activation of enzymes (protein kinases) that add phosphate groups to proteins. The modification of special proteins at strategic sites in the neuron seems therefore to be the basis of long-term potentiation; there may also be synthesis of new proteins. Long-term potentiation is believed to be an intimate part of the mechanisms that cause learning and the establishment of memory.

Another powerful mechanism by which function can alter the network is *axon sprouting*. If a peripheral nerve is wounded, cutting many axons, the nerve can regenerate because the axons sprout at the cut ends. The sprouts retrace the path of the former axons and reestablish the normal synapses. Similar sprouting occurs in the central nervous systems after damage to a pathway, although the sprouting axons usually do not extend very far. Sprouting seems to be caused by the release of growth factors from the damaged neurons. When damages in the central nervous system cause some pathways to degenerate, with loss of synapses, sprouting may occur either from the damaged pathways or even from connected pathways that were themselves undamaged. In either case new axons reestablish synapses with the neurons that lost synapses as a consequence of the damage. Even without degeneration, sprouting can occur as a consequence of functional deprivation, when sequels of degeneration and sprouting give rise to a reorganization of the network.

Sprouting is much more pronounced in very young animals; it occurs extensively at the age at which important circuits are laid down in the nervous system, such as those related to behavioral sex determination and establishment of gender identity. For the development of visual connections the first six weeks in the life of a monkey represent a sensitive period comparable to that for sexual differentiation in the hypothalamus. Both periods are characterized by extensive remodeling of interneuronal connections, which is directed by variables related to function. In the sensitive period for sexual behavior, the function-related variable is the type of sex hormone available; in the sensitive period for ocular dominance, it is something related to the performance of the visual function. Perhaps the required stimuli are certain kinds of neuronal signals, either electrical or chemical, connected with functions. Sprouting can even be exploited for medical purposes: it may allow the surgical repair of brain damage, because it is promoted at will by using growth factors released by the damaged tissue. A brain fragment transplanted to a damaged area shows extensive sprouting, forming synapses with neurons of the old brain if an extract of damaged brain is added to it.

The Peripheral Nervous System Is Plastic, Too

The peripheral nervous system is formed by cells migrating from a part of the neural tube known as the neural crest (see chapter 12, fig. 12.15); they form the sensory ganglia and the ganglia of the autonomic system. The autonomic system includes the *sympathetic system*, made up of ganglia located at the sides of the spinal column, and the *parasympathetic system*, which has ganglia in many internal organs. Both sympathetic and parasympathetic ganglia receive inputs from the central nervous system. As we have already seen in chapter 17, the axons they send to the internal organs regulate many essential functions, such as the heartbeat and the movements of the gut. In each function the sympathetic and parasympathetic signals have opposite effects.

Many steps involved in the development of the autonomic system are controlled by clues deriving from the cell's environment. For instance, environmental influences control the type of transmitter a neuron makes. Normally, sympathetic neurons make adrenaline as transmitter, whereas parasympathetic neurons make acetylcholine. When the cells start migrating from the neural crest, they all make acetylcholine. Production of adrenaline is induced by other cells at the sites where the migrating cells settle. After the cells have met these inducers, they are committed to producing adrenaline, and they do so even if they are removed from their normal environment and kept in cultures. But if the cultures also contain cells of other types, the cells from the neural crest go back to making acetylcholine. This change does not occur if the cells are kept active in a depolarized state; then the cells will continue to produce adrenaline. It is possible that in the animal, sympathetic neurons continue to produce adrenaline even if they are surrounded by cells that would make them shift to acetylcholine, because they receive nerve signals from central neurons. We conclude that the differentiation to sympathetic cells is reversible and under both environmental and functional control.

Once the migrating neural crest cells have gathered together in ganglia, they send axons to the internal organs, often a considerable distance away. The progress of these axons also occurs under control of environmental clues. In some instances, the navigation of the axon is aided by pathways already laid down by other types of cells—for instance, muscles or blood vessels. But these channels are often altogether absent and are replaced by chemical signals. One of the signal substances is the nerve growth factor that, as we have seen, is required for the growth and maintenance of sympathetic and sensory neurons.

Neurons not only receive differentiation signals from other cells but also deliver such signals to cells. This can be seen in the muscle. Cutting the nerve to a muscle causes progressive disappearance of the acetylcholine receptors present in the neuromuscular junctions (see chapter 17) and the appearance of receptors outside the junctions, where the receptors are normally absent. These new receptors have different properties: for instance, they have a slower response to acetylcholine; some are even associated with tetradotoxin-resistant Na^+ channels. If the axon of the cut nerve regenerates and the muscle becomes active again, the new receptors disappear and are replaced by the regular receptors. What is essential for maintaining the normal receptor distribution in muscle fibers is the generation of action potentials.

The differentiation of receptors in muscles during embryonic development follows the same pattern: in the embryo they appear first throughout the surface of the muscle fibers, but after axons reach the fibers, the receptors become progressively concentrated in the neuromuscular junctions. The reasons for these changes are not clear.

These observations demonstrate that two-way interactions between neurons and the cells to which they are connected affect the manufacture of specific gene products, the differentiation of the cells, and the establishment of connections. All these effects are an expression of the enormous plasticity of the nervous system.

The Laws of the Network

The observations reported above (and many others) suggest that the conclusions reached for the formation of maps in the brain can be generalized. In the whole nervous system the final formation of the neural network takes place according to the following principles. At first the genetic blueprint determines the differentiation of undifferentiated cells into many classes of neurons, depending on the time of development and location. An important mechanism of differentiation is the migration of the precursor cells to suitable positions, followed by morphologic and functional differentiation. A second step is extension of dendrites and axons, which takes place in an equal way for all neurons of a certain class. A third step is the formation of connections. The genetic blueprint determines which kind of target cell, but not precisely which one, an axon will seek. This process is mediated by attracting or orienting factors produced by the target cells or other cells and by contacts of the growing axons with cells of many kinds. The general mode of action of these directional signals on the axons are also genetically specified. When the third step is accomplished, each class of neurons will have established the maximum possible number of synapses with the target neurons in competition with axons of the same type. The network formed is extremely extensive, but not very selective. At this step a neuron does not yet play an individual role; each one acts only as a member of its class.

The final step is the remodeling of the synaptic connections, which confers on each neuron its individuality. This step takes place mostly after birth according to instructions derived from function. Synapses that are kept active persist; nonfunctional ones disappear. Function is measured in relative terms; the degree of functionality of different synapses determines the result of their competition. This may be the most crucial step for shaping the neuronal network and the one most sensitive to environmental influences. This process goes on through most of the life of the individual, allowing it to learn newer and newer tricks and to become fully adapted, in a functional sense, to the environment in which it lives. This process makes each individual different from all others.

Brain versus Computers

It is common to compare the brain to a computer. But if we follow the brain of an animal through its development, we see how different it is from a computer. The brain is a self-made network, of which the genes determine the basic features. Ultimately the network is made to suit the needs of the individual in which it resides. A very large number of instructions, which in computers would be called software and restricted to discs or tapes, are built by progressive improvement into the hardware, the neuronal network of the brain. Later the same process continues in a more localized, microscopic way to account for lifelong learning and establishment of memory traces. Are these in the hardware or in the software of the brain computer? Perhaps the question has no meaning because the network has both functions and is continuously evolving by synaptic adaptation.

The brain, then, is an extremely efficient and sophisticated (although slow) computer that performs feats no manmade computer can do in spite of its much greater speed. A simple everyday achievement of the brain, for instance, is to recognize a person in a crowd by his face. This is an impossible task for a computer. The secret of the brain is that it processes information through many parallel but different pathways at the same time, continuously comparing the successive stages of evaluation through the various pathways and building from them a progressively more defined mental image. In this way the brain reaches a holistic result such as that of recognizing a face. The computer follows a single pathway. Its power lies in its ability to analyze.

CHAPTER 19

Understanding from Drugs

Drugs or poisons that act on synapses allow us to explore the functional significance of the organization of the network determined by connections between
neurons. Drugs give a deep insight into the way the brain determines the personality of the individual, both in animals and in humans. We will examine the action
of a number of drugs in some detail.

Many drugs act on synapses; their effects are much more subtle than those of
substances acting on axons, because synapses offer many more and varied targets.
In the axon the targets are mainly limited to the two voltage-dependent ion channels (for Na^+ and for K^+) (see chapter 17). In synapses, both at the neuromuscular
junction and between neurons, drugs can interfere with the manufacture of neurotransmitters, the mechanism of their release, the receptors on which they act, and
the devices that dispose of excessive neurotransmitters after their release. The
multiplicity of neurotransmitters, and of the receptors that each of them recognizes, also contributes to the multiplicity of targets. Many drugs are selective,
affecting only a class of synapses with a certain neurotransmitter-receptor combination, and they tend to affect sections or centers of the nervous system where
such a combination is prevalent. Because of this selectivity, drugs that affect
synapses are useful for identifying the neuronal complexes that form functional
units in the nervous system, complementing the results provided by anatomical
and functional observations.

Of the many drugs affecting the function of synapses, some are natural, and
others are made in the laboratory. Natural substances were discovered by observing the effects of plant extracts or animal poisons: an example is morphine. The
others were made artificially in the search for agents capable of influencing pain
or sleep or of controlling nervous or mental disorders in humans.

Muscle Paralysis

Several poisons affect the synapse between axon and muscle fiber at the neuromuscular junction. Among the best known is curare, the extract of a vine used by South American Indians to poison the tips of their arrows for hunting or warfare. The active ingredient, tubo-curarine, binds very strongly to the acetylcholine receptors, blocking signal transmission. The substance causes paralysis of all muscles, but not at the same time: it begins in the muscles of the toes and ends in those for respiration. The poison does not interfere with sensory processes, such as sight, touch, or pain.

Surprisingly, this powerful poison has no effect on other synapses in which acetylcholine is the neurotransmitter. For instance, it does not affect the nerves of the autonomic system that control the heartbeat. The reason is that acetylcholine interacts with different receptors in the two organs. The receptors of the heart nerves have the special property of binding a mushroom poison, muscarine, which mimics the action of acetylcholine, slowing down the heart rate to dangerous levels and even stopping it. Accordingly, the receptors are known as muscarinic. Those of the neuromuscular junction are called nicotinic, because they bind nicotine, a component of tobacco smoke, which also acts on them like acetylcholine, promoting muscle contraction. But muscarine does not act on the neuromuscular junction nor nicotine on the heart nerves. This was the first evidence for the ability of neurotransmitters to interact with different receptors, producing various effects.

Other poisons interacting with the neuromuscular junctions are bungaratoxin, from a rattlesnake, and latratoxin, from the black widow spider, and also toxins produced by the botulin and tetanus bacteria.

Enhancing Motor Activities and Behavioral Arousal

Many drugs affect synapses between neurons with different effects depending on the neurotransmitter used by the synapse. Several drugs affect transmission of signals mediated by the catecholamines which include dopamine (DA), noradrenaline (NA), and adrenaline (A). The drugs that enhance the performance of these neurotransmitters increase motor activity, producing hyperactivity and excitement, whereas those that inhibit their performance decrease motor activity and are generally calming. Important differences among drugs of each class depend on features of the synapses and the neurons on which they act.

Catecholamine transmission is enhanced by amphetamines and cocaine; both drugs easily cross the blood-brain barrier. They act by slowing down the removal of a neurotransmitter after it is released into the synapse, thus increasing its life in the synapse and prolonging its effect. Amphetamines, in addition, increase the release of DA and activate the DA receptors, essentially like DA itself. The potent stimulatory action of these substances is reflected in the nickname "speed" given to one of the amphetamines.

The stimulatory effect can be demonstrated in rats that are kept in large cages with several side arms containing interesting objects. Normal rats tend to spend much time exploring the side arms, but after amphetamine administration, they tend to run around most of the time in the larger compartment, neglecting the side arms. They need action and lose interest in the details of the environment that surrounds them. In animals trained to perform a certain task (such as pressing a level in order to avoid an electric shock), low doses of amphetamines enhance the speed and effectiveness of the response. In this case the hyperactivity benefits the performance of the task. Amphetamines also accelerate learning.

The stimulatory effect of amphetamine is also revealed by a special experimental technique: intracranial self-stimulation. Animals with electrodes permanently implanted in areas of the brain in which electrical stimulation is pleasurable are trained to stimulate their brain by frequently pressing a lever to close the circuit. They can be trained even to increase the current until the pleasurable effect reaches a maximum. After taking amphetamine, the animals adjust the current to a lower value, suggesting that the electrical stimulation has become more effective.

These effects of amphetamine in animals are mediated by the neurotransmitter DA. DA antagonists given with the drug decrease its effect, and if the DA neurons are selectively damaged by a toxin, the effect of amphetamine disappears.

Other experiments on animals have clarified the localization of the excitatory effects of amphetamines and cocaine. An animal has a fine tube implanted in a selected area of the brain; the tube is connected to a minute syringe that allows the delivery of very small amounts of the drug when the animal presses a lever. Usually the animal is presented with two levers, one of which has no effect. When the syringe contains amphetamines or cocaine, the animal very rapidly learns to select and press the lever that causes the injection. The brain sites in which the effect is produced seem different for amphetamines and cocaine. This effect is decreased considerably if a DA antagonist is mixed with the drug, pointing again to DA as the main neurotransmitter used by the neurons affected by these drugs.

The result shows that the effect of the drugs is pleasurable. The surprising result of further experimental refinements, however, is that the pleasure may not derive from the hyperstimulation of DA receptors. In these experiments the animals are trained to use amphetamine by a procedure known as conditioning. They are first given an injection of the drug in their cages and then are placed for half an hour in a special box. Animals of a control group are first placed in the special box and are given the drug after returning them to their cages. After a certain period of training, the animals are given an injection of saline, containing no drug, as a placebo and are then placed in the special box. Animals trained to receive amphetamine before being placed in the box display augmented motor behavior as if they had been injected with the drug. Animals of the control group do not.

This experiment shows that during training the animals learn the association between injection and the compulsion to display enhanced motor activity once they are placed in the special box. The learned association makes them respond to the placebo. Strikingly, the learned response is not caused by DA neurons. The stimulation of the DA receptors is necessary during training, because the animals do not learn the association if a DA antagonist is mixed with the injected drug. Once the animals have learned, however, the antagonist is without effect: its presence in the placebo injection does not decrease the hyperactivity of the animals after they are placed in the box.

This result suggests that after some time the repeated stimulation of the DA receptors produces lasting consequences in other neuronal systems that do not depend on DA for their activity. This is a recurring theme in the action of drugs on the brain.

Combating Fatigue

The euphoria-producing effects of cocaine have been known to South American Indians for centuries. Pre-Columbian clay statues often model the face with one cheek bulging, because it is full of a quid of chewed coca leaves, and one of the most common artifacts of the period is a little bottle that was made to contain lye. Once the leaf was thoroughly chewed, a little of the lye was added in order to extract cocaine in active form. The Spanish invaders soon recognized the value of this practice: it enabled the Indians to put in a long day of hard work, for the cocaine induced euphoria and hyperactivity, and reduced fatigue.

Today cocaine is usually sniffed through a small tube (a rolled-up $100 bill is not unusual, according to newspaper reports); the substance is rapidly absorbed through the lining of the nose and reaches the blood vessels with almost immediate effect. As a side effect, cocaine causes constriction of the small blood vessels of the nose, damaging its lining. With continued use, the lining may be totally destroyed. The effects of cocaine are even more rapid—and more dangerous—when the drug is administered by intravenous injection. If the arousal is excessive, the user damps it by taking sedatives, such as methaqualone (Quaalude).

In addition to these effects, amphetamines have other consequences, because they act on all parts of the brain that use catecholamines as neurotransmitter. For instance, they cause loss of appetite, apparently through an increase of NA-based transmission in the hypothalamus. At high doses amphetamines disturb the operation of neuronal centers at the base of the brain, producing a stereotyped behavior. Its characteristics vary from species to species, depending on other brain activities: rats sniff, make neck movements, gnaw; cats may take fixed grotesque postures, in which the movements of different parts of the body appear totally disconnected; monkeys move their head rapidly from side to side, pick their skin, stare. Two neuron centers at the base of the brain cause this effect: they are rich in neurons that use DA as neurotransmitter. Prolonged use of amphetamines results in other behavioral changes that will be considered later on.

Fighting Depression

The existence of another class of drugs affecting the transmission of signals by catecholamines was discovered by following up an accidental observation that a drug used to treat tuberculosis patients improved their mood. It turned out that this drug inhibits an enzyme that breaks down catecholamines in the synapses. The released neurotransmitter then persists for a longer time, generating a stronger signal. These observations ultimately led to the synthesis of the tricyclic antidepressants (a name derived from their chemical structure), which cause marked improvement in patients with one type of depression. These drugs reinforce transmission of signals by the catecholamine noradrenaline (NA) and adrenaline (A), and by serotonin (SE), a neurotransmitter derived from the amino acid trypotophane (see chapter 17). The drugs increase the life of neurotransmitters in the synapse and prolong their action by blocking their re-uptake by the emitting end. Other antidepressant drugs act through different and more complex mechanisms. The involvement of catecholamines and SE in depression is also shown by the *induction* of depression by reserpine, a drug once used against hypertension, but later discontinued because of this complication. Reserpine decreases the release of NA and SE by depleting their stores in the synaptic vesicles.

These observations show that there is an intimate relationship between the state of catecholamine-mediated transmission and depression. The effect of antidepressants on mood, however, seems not to be the direct consequence of the increased strength of signals carried by catecholamines. The main reason is that the effect appears one to three weeks after a patient has begun treatment, whereas the strength of the nerve signals carried by catecholamines are immediately increased by the treatment. It was first thought that the therapeutic effect resulted from the disappearance of catecholamine receptors after prolonged exposure to high concentrations of neurotransmitter; this would explain the delay. As in the case of hormones, prolonged exposure to a neurotransmitter causes the disappearance of many receptors, decreasing the response of the neurons to the neurotransmitter (*subsensitivity*). Conversely, if the normal exposure to neurotransmitter is decreased, the neurons become more responsive (*supersensitivity*). This intrepretation was in agreement with the induction of depression by reserpine, which increases the response of the receptors.

It was subsequently found, however, that some antidepressants that have the direct effect of reinforcing transmission by SE alter receptors for SE in such a way that they continue to bind the neurotransmitter, although they no longer respond to it. These drugs produce their clinical effect by acting on some substance that modulates the activity of the receptors after the neurotransmitter is bound. Such a substance could be a neuropeptide. If this result applies to all antidepressants, their clinical effects would not be caused by reinforcing catecholamine signals. This possibility is supported by the profound differences between the effects of antidepressants and those of amphetamines and cocaine. All three kinds of drugs enhance signal transmission by catecholamines, but differ completely in their long-term consequences. Amphetamines and cocaine markedly increase motor activity but have only a marginally beneficial effect on depressed patients; in contrast the antidepressants do not increase motor activity. Amphetamines and antidepressants may even act on different neurons, because they bind to different receptors. So the type of depression that responds to the antidepressant drugs seems to be a phenomenon involving the malfunction of a special class of neurons, not necessarily those using catecholamines as neurotransmitters.

The possibility that patients *learn* to respond to antidepressants is reinforced by behavioral experiments in humans, of the type performed with amphetamines in animals. If, after a period of training in which antidepressants are administered, the patient feels improved, he will respond to the administration of placebo in the same way as to the drug itself. This result again suggests that the mechanism of depression and the mode of action of the drugs may be beyond the catecholamine or serotonin receptors on which the drugs directly act. The blockade of the receptors might be the first step, causing secondary changes in other brain centers more directly responsible for the disease. These changes would take place slowly, as these brain centers learn to recognize the blockade. This would explain why the antidepressants do not act immediately but only after a few weeks, which would be required for the learning process. We must recognize, however, that these phenomena are very poorly understood and that key elements of the picture may be still unknown.

Dopamine and Psychoses

Another aspect of the biology of catecholamine, especially DA, is revealed by the affects of a class of drugs called neuroleptics; these drugs are antipsychotic. They are effective in the treatment of schizophrenia, a human disease characterized by strange thought disorders, withdrawal, decreased feeling of affect, hallucination, and paranoid ideation. Some of these drugs (for example, chlorpromazine) contain a tricyclic ring reminiscent of the tricyclic antidepressants. Neuroleptics block a class of DA receptors (called D_2) that when activated by DA cause the intracellular release of cyclic AMP. The release is suppressed by the drugs, reducing locomotor activity and decreasing the performance of learned tasks. A trained animal will perform the learned task after receiving the drug only if the stimulus is greatly increased—for instance, if an electric shock replaces a visual warning signal. Such a decreased responsiveness is a regular effect of the reduction of DA-based transmission.

The therapeutic effect of neuroleptics has given rise to the "dopamine hypothesis" of schizophrenia, according to which the disease is generated by an enhancement of the transmission of signals by DA. This view is supported by the increased binding of DA to certain parts of the brain of schizophrenic patients. It is also in accord with a dramatic accentuation of the symptoms of schizophrenia by amphetamines, which also increase transmission by the same neurotransmitter, and by the drug L-dopa, which is converted into DA in the brain. A difficulty with this hypothesis, however, is the slow therapeutic effect of neuroleptics, which contrasts with the immediate block of DA signals they produce.

As with antidepressant drugs, it is possible that learning also plays a role in the response of schizophrenia to drugs. It may be that schizophrenia, like depression, is the direct result not of excessive DA transmission in the neuron system affected by the drugs but of alteration of some other center connected with the DA-controlled neurons. And as with antidepressive drugs, the blockade of the DA receptors may secondarily affect the operation of these other systems on which the disease more directly depends. This view is supported by the observation that in animals neuroleptics slowly cause effects on various neuron systems in the gray masses at the base of the brain (the basal ganglia) as well as in the cortex. Changes in the equivalent centers in the human brain might be responsible for schizophrenia. The uncertainties concerning the mode of action of these drugs make it impossible to understand which alterations are directly responsible for the disease.

Further uncertainty is created by another observation: patients treated for a long time with some neuroleptic drugs develop characteristic symptoms such as making involuntary movements of their mouth and tongue, as if they were chewing. These effects are attributed to alterations in the function of a center at the base of the brain that is very rich in DA neurons, the striatum. This suggests that this center is implicated in the genesis of schizophrenia. The neuroleptics that do not produce this complication inactivate DA receptors in the cortex, rather than in the striatum, supporting a different hypothesis: that schizophrenia arises from changes in the cortex rather than in the striatum. It may well be that the symptoms are produced as a complication by drugs that, as a side effect, damage the striatum. The picture is further confused by the observation that some schizophrenics who were never treated with neuroleptics develop the symptoms anyway.

Inducing Inhibition

We will now move to an entirely different class of drugs—those that enhance the effectiveness of GABA as transmitter in inhibitory synapses (see chapter 17). These drugs afford important insights into the significance of GABA signals in the overall balance of the nervous system. They are known as minor tranquilizers to distinguish them from drugs with much more profound effects, known as major tranquilizers. The observation that a chemical compound administered to aggressive monkeys made them easier to handle in the laboratory led to the drugs' discovery.

The most important class of minor tranquilizers are benzodiazepines, which include several well-known drugs, like Valium and Librium. Being fat-seeking, they easily cross the blood-brain barrier. In humans, as well as in animals, these substances resolve anxiety. Their effect can be studied in rats trained to respond to a sound by pressing a lever, after which they are rewarded with food. When the animals are well trained the regimen is changed: after pressing the lever they receive an electric shock to the feet instead of food. The shock is made progressively more intense in successive trials. In normal rats the shock, conflicting with previous training, rapidly abolishes the lever-pressing response. But animals fed Librium continue to respond according to training, ignoring the electric shocks. In general, benzodiazepines relieve the effect of punishment in learned behavior in animals, not by changing the recognition of the signal, but by increasing tolerance to the punishment.

Librium also resolves conflicts between animals in a social situation—for instance, between two male rats in a cage in which neither has established a territory. The animals are curious and worried by each other's presence; they examine each other carefully by sniffing, crawling over and under each other, or grooming. This interaction is decreased by novel features, such as a sudden bright light, that may introduce anxiety into the tense situation. Librium decreases the effect of the novel feature and keeps the interaction at a high level, apparently by reducing anxiety. Benzodiazepines also have other effects: they are sedative, prevent seizures (that is, they are anticonvulsant), and relax muscular spasms. Some benzodiazepines are specialized for some of these effects.

Our understanding of the mechanism of the action of benzodiazepines is only partial, but what we know throws considerable light on the biological effects of the interaction of GABA with its receptors. We have seen in chapter 17 that this neurotransmitter causes the opening of Cl^- (chloride) channels. The increased Cl^- inflow increases the polarization of the receiving neuron (its membrane potential becomes more negative inside) and decreases its propensity to fire in response to signals from excitatory synapses. The neuron is quieted. Benzodiazepines enhance this effect. They do not merely duplicate the role of GABA because they work only when the neurotransmitter is released; they cannot replace it. They bind not to the GABA receptors but to receptors of their own that are associated with the GABA receptors and the chloride channels. The connection between benzodiazepine receptors, the GABA receptors, and the channel is so intimate that they are all isolated and purified as a unit from neuronal membranes.

The presence in the brain of receptors for benzodiazepines, of which there are several kinds, raises an important question: what is their normal function? The most likely explanation is that they recognize some normal body substance, probably a regulator of neuronal activity with a calming effect on the brain. This explanation is supported by the reduced number of receptors in the brains of animals prone to seizures. Several body substances interacting with the benzodiazepine receptors have been extracted from animal brains. One is a small protein, and another, a molecule of a group called beta-carbolines. Both substances bind strongly to benzodiazepine receptors, especially the special beta-carboline. Whereas the protein causes anxiety when injected into the rat brain, the beta-carboline has a tranquilizing effect; other beta-carbolines, however, are anxiety-inducing. The significance of these brain substances is unknown.

Receptors for benzodiazepines, somewhat different from those of neurons, are present in a variety of nonneuronal cells; their role is unknown but hints at a wide use of endogenous benzodiazepine-like substances in the body.

Related to the action of benzodiazepines are those of barbiturates and ethanol. Like benzodiazepines, they resolve anxiety and have a sedative effect. They also interact, although in different ways, with the GABA receptor–chloride channel complex, increasing Cl^- uptake into neurons; the effect is blocked by antagonists binding to the GABA receptor or to the Cl^- channel.

Blocking Inhibition

Whereas drugs that enhance the activity of the GABA receptor–chloride channel complex have a sedative action, drugs that inhibit this activity have strong excitatory effects. This is the case of picrotoxin, which comes from the seeds of a tropical plant and can bind to and block the chloride channels. Another substance with similar effect is strychnine, which blocks the inhibitory activity of neurotransmitter glycine (see chapter 17), especially on neurons of the spinal cord. These drugs cause generalized muscular contractions that may culminate in convulsions and possible death by asphyxiation.

Convulsions result from positive feedback between two brain centers: center A excites center B, which in turn excites A. This feedback normally is kept in check by inhibition. If inhibition is reduced, reverberation escalates to a climax of generalized muscular contractions with loss of consciousness until it is interrupted by insufficient supply of oxygen and sugar to neurons. In the nervous system, blocking inhibition has far more dramatic effects than promoting excitation. Drugs, such as amphetamines or cocaine, that enhance the action of excitatory neurotransmitters produce far more moderate phenomena than do picrotoxin or strychnine.

Hallucinations

Some drugs have the extraordinary effect of creating an "insight," a perception that appears to be an alternative to the usual perception and is equally credible. The reality of these drug-created perceptions—called hallucinations—is absolute for the individual who experiences them and persists in memory after the action of the drug ceases. The perceptions can be visual, consisting of complex and plastic images not necessarily in recognizable forms, or auditory, such as sounds or words.

Hallucinogens, the substances that cause hallucinations, have been known for a long time; their insights sometimes have been considered to be religious experiences. South American Indians elicited them using psilocyn, from a sacred mushroom, and mescaline, from the dried peyote cactus. These substances bear chemical similarities to catecholamines and amphetamines; some derivatives of amphetamines in fact cause hallucinations. Presently other hallucinogens have more widespread use. One is LSD (d-Lysergic acid diethylamide), the most potent, which is derived from an alkaloid contained in the highly poisonous ergot fungus of rye and wheat and induces mostly visual images. Another is phencyclidine, known as PCP or angel dust, which was developed in the fifties as an anesthetic agent, but was never used because its hallucinogenic activity was soon recognized. The use of the drug has varied consequences, including convulsions and a long-lasting psychosis similar to schizophrenia. Phencyclidine is frequently lethal.

The mode of action of hallucinogens is little understood, because it can be studied only in animals, in which the occurrence of hallucinations is hard to detect. Limited progress has been made by comparing the reactions of animals to drugs that produce hallucinations in humans with those of chemically related drugs that do not. These studies suggest that hallucinogens alter in various ways the analysis of incoming sensory stimuli and change the interaction between the cortex and lower brain centers.

LSD and mescaline bind to receptors in several parts of the brain, which are probably also receptors for the neurotransmitter SE (serotonin). This conclusion is based on the fact that by the comparative test mentioned above LSD is recognized in animals as a SE-like substance, whereas related substances that do not cause hallucinations are not recognized as SE-like. A derivative of amphetamines, which causes hallucination, destroys the ends of axons using SE as transmitter, but this may be a special effect. It is not clear how the interaction of LSD with its receptors causes hallucinations. The visual hallucinations may be attributed to a changed response of neurons of the visual pathway, altering the elaboration of visual information. These conclusions are only tentative because LSD acts also on neurons of other brain centers.

Phencyclidine (PCP), which also binds to special receptors, has two consequences. One is inhibition of signal transmission through nicotinic acetylcholine receptors. The other is blockage of K^+ channels in the transmitting end of a variety of synapses. The K blockage prolongs the duration of the action potential, causing an increase of Ca^{++} influx in the transmitting end of synapses, and enhances the release of neurotransmitter. In the already mentioned behavioral tests in animals, PCP is recognized as a substance interacting with receptors for adenosine (which may be a neurotransmitter or a modifier of a neurotransmitter). Adenosine-like substances act as sedative agents, suggesting that perhaps PCP causes hallucinations by antagonizing their action. Known adenosine antagonists, however, do not have consequences similar to those of PCP. Other evidence links PCP to one of the receptors for opiates. Evidently the mechanism of action of PCP is poorly known.

Hallucinogens also have nonneuronal effects. They cause the contraction of blood vessels, increasing the blood pressure. Contraction of brain arteries and lack of oxygen to neurons may contribute to the hallucinogenic activity.

Addiction

Other drugs active on the central nervous system share with those we have discussed the ability to induce both rapid and slow changes that alter the responsiveness of the nervous system. As a paradigm we will consider opiates, such as morphine or heroin. These substances bind to receptors for endogenous opioids, such as enkephalin and endorphin (see chapter 17). There are several classes of opiate receptors, with different characteristics.

The persistent use of opiate drugs elicits a characteristic series of events in humans or animals. Rapidly they become tolerant (less sensitive) to the drugs; an ever higher dose is needed to produce the same effect. In time these individuals become dependent; if they interrupt the drug they face a complex of highly unpleasant withdrawal symptoms, consisting of restlessness, vomiting, diarrhea, insomnia, and craving for the drug. Administration of the drug immediately relieves the symptoms. Withdrawal symptoms are also elicited by the morphine antagonist naloxone, which binds to the same receptors, blocking them, but without producing opiate-like effects. After several months of drug use, the individuals become addicted; even if they succeed in discontinuing the use of the drug, they tend to return to it later. Addiction is a long-term, often lifelong, commitment to the drug.

Many other neuroactive drugs—such as barbiturates, cocaine, amphetamines, nicotine, alcohol—have similar consequences. These various substances have different immediate effects but have as a common denominator the ability to induce dependence. Dependence is specific for a certain drug: heroin use does not induce dependence to cocaine or nicotine, and vice versa. Within the same group, some drugs induce dependence more readily than others, without correlation with their effectiveness in producing the effects for which they are taken. Among opiates, dependence is readily established by morphine and heroin, which are chemically very similar, but less so by the chemically different methadone. Dependence is not necessarily associated with tolerance: LSD induces rapid tolerance but no dependence.

Two types of mechanisms are available for explaining habituation to opiates. One consists of changes of the neurons carrying the opiate receptors; another involves complex brain functions.

Addiction in the Cell

Prolonged exposure of neurons to opiates (morphine or heroin) causes disappearance of a fraction of opiate receptors. Hence, higher doses of the drug are required for producing the same effect. This phenomenon, equivalent to tolerance, is prevented by the morphine antagonist, naloxone. Among different opiates the ability to induce loss of receptors is correlated with the addictive potency, suggesting that the loss plays a role in addiction.

This possibility is supported by observations on smooth muscle cells of the guinea pig intestine, which contract when the nerves are stimulated. Local application of opiates decreases the contraction, but their effect decreases upon repeated application; to restore the response the dose must be increased. This is a clear case of tolerance. The cells can also be made dependent by opiates: exposure to the antagonist naloxone to block the receptors after prolonged treatment with an opiate induces the equivalent of withdrawal symptoms: the muscle cells undergo excessive contractions.

Addiction in the Mind

These cellular phenomena based on loss of receptors probably explain the development of tolerance and dependence and the rapid appearance of withdrawal symptoms when the opiate is discontinued or the antagonist naloxone is administered. They do not explain chronic addiction, however, because they occur too rapidly. They reach their maximum expression in about two days, whereas addiction sets in progressively over a period of months.

The long-term phenomena connected with the use of addictive drugs are not fully explained. They probably depend on complex interactions among brain centers, of which we have little understanding. A glimpse into this complexity is afforded by observations made in rats, using the technique of intracranial self-stimulation described earlier. They show that the pleasurable effect of morphine and the development of dependence arise in different brain centers. Minute quantities of morphine are injected directly into selected parts of a rat brain. The animal likes the effects of injection into one area—let's call it area A—as deduced from the fact that it proceeds to self-administer the substance in that area, whereas it does not like the effect in area B because it does not reinforce it by self-administration. But prolonged continuous administration in area B, although not pleasurable, produces dependence, which is detected by the onset of withdrawal symptoms after administration of the antagonist naloxone; on the other hand, administration in area A, which is pleasurable, causes no dependence.

Many brain centers are probably involved in generating a withdrawal reaction. One of these centers is implicated by the observation that addicts to opiates or nicotine can be spared somewhat the craving symptoms during withdrawal if they are given a substance—clonidine—that acts like the neurotransmitter NA. This finding correlates with the observation that in animals NA decreases electrical activity in a brain center that becomes hyperactive during withdrawal. So it seems that NA-dependent neurons of known localization are directly involved in the expression of withdrawal symptoms, regardless of the drug.

Again, a Question of Learning

The fact that a drug, even when delivered directly into the suitable brain center, elicits dependence only after prolonged administration raises difficulties similar to those already encountered with the slow therapeutic effects of antidepressants and neuroleptics. Are some of the effects the result of learning? We do not have a good model to explain these slow effects, and we can only speculate that an indirect mechanism may be at work.

The establishment of chronic addiction raises similar questions. Why does an addict who discontinues the use of a drug and suffers the withdrawal symptoms later return to the drug, seemingly forgetful of the previous sufferings? The relapse may occur many months after quitting. Evidence shows that the mechanism of relapse has an important learned component. For instance, addicted monkeys trained to receive an injection of morphine at the flash of a red light will be equally satisfied by an injection of saline when the light is flashed. And they do not show the withdrawal symptoms they would show without injection. What prevents withdrawal is not the drug itself but the perception of having received it. Similarly a pusher can dilute his heroin without risk if the environment and the circumstances are right: the perception of the addict is that the drug is effective. A striking example of the effect of expectation was observed during attempts at rehabilitating heroin addicts by injecting them with endogenous opiates such as B-endorphin. Injections of a saline placebo (unknown to the patient) had considerable beneficial effect. Evidently training and expectation dominate the response, both in humans and in animals.

Even experiencing withdrawal symptoms depends very much on the circumstances. For instance, when heroin addicts, who often commit crimes, are imprisoned, they readily recover from withdrawal and can live without drugs as long as they stay in prison. But when they are released and go back to the environment where they have experienced withdrawal in the past, they invariably feel the withdrawal sickness and the craving for the drug. Similar effects can be seen in animals: addicted monkeys trained to periods of deprivation after the sound of a buzzer have withdrawal symptoms after the buzzer goes on even if they are not deprived.

The fact that addiction builds up slowly after repeated exposures to the drug suggests that it involves the buildup of some kind of memory. But the memory of what? In all likelihood it is the memory of the strong pleasurable effect of the high produced by an addictive drug. The experienced pleasure probably varies for different drugs, but it has the same consequence: it is remembered as an experience worth repeating. In fact, the drugs that are most strongly addictive (morphine, nicotine, cocaine) are those that generate the most profound effect of well-being. The subjective value of the various addictive drugs may depend on the drug as well as on the personality of the individual and on circumstances. If addiction is maintained by the remembrance of that pleasurable effect, its memory must be much more effective than the remembrance of the pains of withdrawal.

Returning to the drug is strongly facilitated by circumstances that more vividly remind the individual of those blissful periods—a certain locality, a certain music, certain friends, or the sight of the paraphernalia (syringe for the injection of morphine, a package of cigarettes, little tubes for inhaling cocaine). The effect of circumstances is not surprising because associations have a powerful effect on behavior. The classical procedure of conditioning in animals gives an example. A dog salivates and secretes stomach juices upon the sight of food. If the food is regularly presented in association with another signal, such as a special light or sound, the animal will learn to salivate and produce stomach juices when the signal is presented without food. We can easily recognize the importance of association for other effects. Circumstances that make us remember pleasurable experiences can make us desire to relive those experiences. That special circumstances may also promote withdrawal symptoms can probably be explained in the same way.

What initiates the chain of events leading to addiction? The propensity to take up an addictive drug seems to be a special characteristic of human society. The young may turn to drugs in imitation of others, or they may succumb to group influences in the school or on the street. Being able to obtain drugs easily seems not to be too important, although it may encourage experimentation. Another mechanism of addiction is exposure to a drug such as morphine for medical purposes.

A person who experiments with a drug will not necessarily become addicted to it. This has been shown by several studies, one of which dealt with American soldiers in Vietnam. Of the many there who experimented with heroin, relatively few became addicted. The determining factors are undefined; they probably have to do with the personality of the individual and a host of life circumstances. The drug that most effectively induces addiction is probably nicotine. Most of the people who start smoking cigarettes become addicted to it. The degree of addiction varies: some people can shed the habit more or less readily, but others cannot. Again, what determines the difference is undefined.

Why some people get hooked to one drug and not to another is also not clear. The opportunity to obtain the drug does not seem to be responsible for the choice: most addicts have experimented with many drugs and often use more than one at the same time. This selection, too, may involve the personality of the individual, who values the pleasurable experience provided by one drug over that of others.

The complex nature of drug addiction explains why it is so difficult to treat and why the outcome is so unpredictable. The treatment used most widely reflects a surrender of medicine to reality: heroin addicts are given the smallest possible maintenance doses of opiates (methadone in this country, heroin in England), until the personal conditions change and heroin becomes unnecessary. Such a change, of course, may or may not occur. That it quite frequently does happen, however, even without treatment is shown by extensive surveys of former addicts: in time many of them drop out of the drug scene. Perhaps the circumstances under which the individual lives and, again, his or her personality determine how persistent addiction is.

Drugs in Disease

Certain types of disease affect the nervous system, causing destruction of neurons in well-localized areas. The reasons for the death of the cells and the localization are in most cases unknown. One prominent example is Parkinson's disease, which afflicts a large number of people, starting in adult life and progressing slowly. Patients' movements become slow and their faces inexpressive; they develop tremors. It has been known for a long time that the disease is associated with destruction of neurons in a small brain area called the substantia nigra (because the neurons contain granules of black pigment that accumulate through life). The axons of cell bodies present in the S. nigra terminate in the striatum, which we have already encountered. These neurons use DA (dopamine) as neurotransmitter, which accumulates in the axon terminals in the striatum. It has also been known that these patients have reduced amounts of DA in the striatum. All this information implicates a reduction of DA production in the S. nigra neurons as the origin of the disease, a concept reinforced by the usefulness of treatment with L-dopa, a substance that is converted into DA in the body.

These findings, although interesting and useful in practice, do not explain what causes the disease and why the neuronal damage is localized to one brain center. A clue was provided from an unexpected source, an accident in a laboratory. In the late seventies an amateur chemist tried to make a compound similar to heroin in a makeshift laboratory. He took some of the substance he made and, a short time afterward, developed symptoms of severe Parkinson's disease. For several reasons it was possible to connect the onset of the disease with the chemical he had made: he was too young for normal Parkinson's, the onset of the disease was much too sudden, and his sister also became ill. By testing with animals, investigators traced the disease to a substance, MPTP, that had been generated as a by-product when the heroin-like compound was made. This substance is extremely powerful: it does not have to be ingested in order to affect people; in this case, the amounts the patient inhaled while working in the laboratory were sufficient. In the brain it binds to an enzyme present in neurons that use the neurotransmitter dopamine. The enzyme mistakes MPTP for DA and works on it, converting it into a powerful toxin, which bears considerable chemical similarity to the herbicide paraquat. The toxin is especially powerful for neurons of the S. nigra because it binds to their black pigment, by which it is trapped and progressively released within the cells. Blocking the enzyme with an inhibitor prevents the toxic effect of MPTP.

These findings have raised the possibility that Parkinson's disease may be produced by chronic exposure to very small amounts of substances related to the one made by accident, perhaps in rare individuals who cannot properly detoxify it. This possibility is only hypothetical, however.

Lessons from Drugs

Several conclusions can be derived from our knowledge about the action of drugs on synapses. One is that although each drug acts on neurons with a well-defined type of receptor, the clinical effects may be produced through the intervention of other neurons that do not use that receptor. The specificity of the receptors permits the dissociation of the two effects. Another conclusion is that the indirect effect probably involves a learning step, in which some neurons learn to respond to changes in the neurons directly affected by the drug. In humans this process of learning does not reach the level of consciousness, suggesting that the subconscious learning by brain centers of what other parts of the brain do may be an important mechanism not only of drug action but also of personality development and of disease. There is finally the conclusion that recognizing the receptors affected by a drug is only the first step for understanding how the drug works. There are complications: in addition to the indirect effects, there is the fact that any type of receptor is never localized to just one brain center. This incomplete localization complicates the identification of the neuron center responsible for the consequences of a drug.

In the broader context of life the effects of drugs show that the complex nervous system built by DNA in the most advanced creatures exposes them to many poisons and diseases. This seems an inseparable characteristic of life; as it develops into more complicated forms, it becomes more and more vulnerable to damage—the complexity itself creates the vulnerability. Yet the complexity is useful because it allows creatures to live in varied environments, to obtain every possible means of livelihood, and to form societies that enhance their ability to survive. On the other hand, evolution has probably minimized the vulnerability of creatures with complex brains; part of its very complexity might be due to safeguards against that vulnerability.

CHAPTER 20

A Life Odyssey

DNA has pervaded earth with an enormous variety of creatures. About a million different species exist, many of them lowly, like bacteria or single-celled eukaryotes, and others, of varying degrees of complexity, like plants and animals. Among the creatures more familiar to us are about twenty-five thousand species of birds, six thousand of reptiles, and fifteen thousand of mammals. But underlying this tremendous variety is a common thread—DNA. All living organisms are made up of cells that perform many similar chemical reactions. All organisms have genes made up of DNA (or RNA in some viruses), and they express the functions of these genes in identical ways through the processes of transcription and translation. And all organisms carry out these processes using the same machinery and the same translation code, with very minor exceptions. How did DNA produce such a great variety of living creatures out of this basic uniformity?

Through the centuries people were impressed by the variety; the underlying regularity has been recognized only recently. In thinking about the past, people have taken themselves as the frame of reference, recognizing that humans come from humans in an uninterrupted series. But how far back did life's history extend? All cultures of the world have developed answers to this question, and all have postulated a finite time, although a time that is long in terms of human experience—several thousands of years, for instance. How the human species and others appeared on earth in the first place was left to the imagination; the different cultures have offered a variety of explanations. It has been thought, for instance, that living creatures were made by an all-powerful creator who has always existed. Others have said that humans came from two parents, symbolized by earth and sky. Still others thought that living creatures emerged from within the earth or from a miraculous egg. All these explanations were usually shrouded in poetic and philosophical veils. The Judeo-Christian tradition, which permeated the

Western world, is contained in the Book of Genesis, according to which earth and all creatures were created some six thousand years ago.

Every Cell from a Cell

In time other points of view also developed. Naturalists observed that certain creatures regularly emerge from some environments; for instance, slugs or flies seem to grow out of muddy spots and maggots out of putrid meat. These observations led to the idea of *spontaneous generation*—creatures form spontaneously in certain characteristic environments. It was only in the seventeenth century that Francesco Redi, an Italian physician, proved that maggots do not come from meat. He performed what was, perhaps, the first scientific experiment ever made in biology. He left two freshly cut pieces of meat exposed to the air. One was covered with gauze to keep away the flies that he always saw buzzing around the meat; the other was left uncovered. In time, both pieces of meat became putrid, but only the uncovered one developed maggots, demonstrating that the maggots came from the flies.

Other similarly basic discoveries were also made in relatively recent times. It may seem surprising that not until the eighteenth century was it recognized that sperm is essential for the reproduction of animals. A final discovery was that made by the French scientist Louis Pasteur, who in the nineteenth century showed that alcoholic fermentation is caused by self-reproducing organisms. He placed a fermentable mash in flasks that were in communication with the environment through tubes whose thin curved necks precluded the access of dust from the air. He boiled some of the flasks to destroy all life. The mash in those that were not boiled fermented, but the mash in the boiled flasks remained unfermented until it was returned to the open air. Thus, Pasteur demonstrated there is life in the air, in organisms too small to be seen with the naked eye. These were the organisms the Dutch cloth merchant van Leeuwenhoek had seen, using his primitive microscope (see chapter 1).

These discoveries established the general principle that all living beings derive from other living beings in an uninterrupted chain from the earliest time to the present. Each species forms a continuous lineage. It was not only this concept, however, that contradicted the creationist account of Genesis, according to which each species existed independently from the moment of creation. Difficulties for that idea had started to appear long before with early geological investigations that clearly suggested that various layers of rocks had been deposited at different and probably ancient times. Moreover, from the rate of formation of contemporary layers of sediment it could be inferred that some of the layers had been deposited much earlier than the time claimed by Genesis for the origin of earth. Even greater difficulties emerged when fossil remains of animals and plants were discovered in the earth layers. Most of them did not correspond to any known living creature, and they appeared to be extremely old. The finding of flint tools deep within the earth suggested that even the human species had a much more antique origin than that accorded to it by the religious tradition.

Attempts then were made to update the idea of creationism. The French naturalist George Cuvier suggested a series of creations to explain the new evidence. In his view, the past was punctuated by a series of catastrophic events, about thirty of them, over a period of about eighty thousand years. Each event had wiped out the existing life; then a new act of creation restored life, but in a new form.

The new discoveries, however, produced a great ferment of thinking, and the idea arose that the various forms of life revealed by the fossil record were connected to present-day life. These ideas culminated in the writings of Charles Darwin and Alfred Russel Wallace, who in the middle of the nineteenth century put forward the theory of evolution. This theory stated that life evolved by a continuous variation from simple to more complex species. It also proposed that the path of evolution was determined by competition between individuals for food and other resources. The individuals that were better adapted to their environment would have more progeny. Evolution, therefore, was based on the dual processes of *adaptation* and *natural selection*—processes that determined the characterization of the species and their changes through evolution.

Species

The many forms of life on earth today can be distinguished in separate groups. Dogs are different from cats, pine trees from sycamores, and so on. Each distinct group is a *species*, and every creature belongs to one or another. The bases for this separation are quite obvious in many cases but less clear in others. For instance, does a Saint Bernard dog belong to the same species as a dachshund? Although the features of these two animals are so different, nevertheless, they are both dogs.

Scientists have devised criteria that define species. One criterion is based on many measurements of the features of organisms, such as the shapes of its parts—like bones or hair or leaves or flowers—and how they are built. Differences in body chemistry are also considered as distinctive features. The comparison of these measurements among a large number of organisms differentiates them into species. Some features may be shared by several groups, but others are distinctive. Within a species, however, not all measurements give the same result: *they span a certain range.* Thus, these measurements show that the Saint Bernard and the dachshund, although so different, belong to the same species.

Another criterion for assigning organisms to species is their ability to breed with one another and produce viable and fertile progeny. Animals of the same species can do so; those of different species usually cannot. The Saint Bernard and the dachshund do interbreed; their progeny is rather strange but entirely viable. So, according to this criterion as well, they belong to the same species. There are exceptions to this rule, however. Many plants that according to the previous criterion should be of different species do interbreed, and some animals of different species, like horses and asses, interbreed also. But their progeny is abnormal: either it is incapable of living to adulthood or it grows up infertile (like the mule).

The concept of species is based on the properties of DNA. All the measured quantities, as well as the ability to interbreed, reflect the activities of the genes. Organisms of the same species are similar because they have the same genetic organization. They may differ, however, and rather decidedly, in the state of some genes, which is the phenomenon of polymorphism (see chapter 6). Dogs are highly polymorphic, for instance, which accounts for our dachshund and Saint Bernard. Mutations in many genes cause great differences in body size and weight, without changing the basic plan according to which the animal is built. Several mutations change the color of the coat. Other mutations control the tail (straight or up-curled), the legs (long or short), the shape of the muzzle (pointed or flat, as in bulldogs), and the carriage of the ears (lop or erect). Selective breeding has concentrated the various polymorphic characteristics in different groups. Polymorphism is very pronounced also in humans as shown by the marked differences in height, weight, and the color of skin, hair, and eyes.

An Atomic Clock

How long have the present species been in existence? What do we know about the past? A record exists in fossilized remnants of living things, which are occasionally excavated from deep in the ground. These remnants are rarely of organisms living today; the majority are unknown to us. The analysis of their features from what remains tells us that they belonged to many different species. The age at which each of these creatures was alive can be inferred with good accuracy from the characteristics of the rock in which they are embedded. An important approach to determining a rock's age is *radioactive dating*, based on the transformation of one atom into another with release of radioactivity—a process known as radioactive decay. With time the amount of the original atom decreases, whereas that of the derived atom increases; the age of the rock can be determined by the extent of decay.

A method of radioactive dating is based on the existence of uranium in some crystals. Uranium comes in two main forms, both radioactive, 235_U and 238_U. They decay, generating two different forms of lead, 207_{Pb} and 206_{Pb}. Radioactive decay of these and other atoms goes on at a constant rate, unchangeable by wetness or heat or pressure and characteristic for each atom. It takes a precisely defined period of time for the radioactive conversion of a certain proportion of each atom. Because the various atomic forms can be measured with extreme precision, the decay is a clock of extreme accuracy, which can determine exactly when a crystal was formed. Fossils embedded in the rock are assumed to have been laid down at the same time.

Studies of fossils and of the rocks in which they have been found have shown that living creatures have existed for a great length of time. We can say with assurance that microscopic organisms existed three billion years, perhaps even three and half billion years ago. Fossils of the first vertebrates go back 500 million years, those of the first primates 60 million years, and those of humans about 100,000 years. The period over which fossils of a given species were laid down, however, varies greatly. Some species existed for a few tens of thousand years, others for many million years.

The Molecular Record

The science of evolution describes the whole of life as a tree. Every species present today is at the tip of one of the thinnest branches, which eventually is connected to the main trunk and earth, where life began. All the branches, except the thinnest, represent species now extinct, some of which have left traces in the fossil record. Because all species belong to the same tree, they have in common certain basic molecular properties, such as the translation code. But differences in other properties appear along the branching—*divergence*. Species at the tip of two branches that derive from a common branch are similar in most properties, and species separated by many branchings show many differences. Such differences in the degree of relatedness between species were noticed by Darwin and were among the evidence that first supported the idea of evolution.

Although the degree of relatedness of certain species can be recognized from the many features of the organisms, such as their shapes and sizes, or the anatomy of their parts, these features are not immediately related to what evolves—that is, to the genes. The properties of organisms are connected to the genes through the complicated process of development, and its complexities may make it difficult to establish the true degree of relatedness between two organisms; they may either obscure it or make it appear closer than it is. The degree of relatedness can be recognized much more easily in the genes, by examining their base sequences. This comparison must be carried out on a large scale: it is a job of such magnitude that it can proceed only very slowly. A certain amount of information about relatedness of DNA sequences is presently available but not as much as we would like to have.

As second best material for determining relatedness we can use proteins, because a sequence of amino acids is the direct translation of a sequence of DNA bases. The protein record is not equivalent, however, to the DNA record because many DNA changes are not reflected in amino acid changes. One reason is that in the translation code more than one triplet of bases usually corresponds to an amino acid (see chapter 4). Another reason is that the DNA contains important sequences that are not expressed in the sequence of amino acid; they include controlling sequences, enhancers, and intervening sequences.

The data that can be derived from the studies of base sequences in DNA or of amino acid sequences in proteins constitute the *molecular record*. The concept of life as an evolutionary tree and our understanding of DNA lead to some predictions about the characteristics of this record. One is that the base sequences present in different species should be related to each other in ways compatible with the methods of DNA variation, which we have examined in chapter 6. Another is that the degree of relatedness should vary for different genes, depending on how basic their functions are to life. Genes that perform essential functions should show little variation; most changes would cause the death of the organism and would be lost. Such genes are said to be *conserved*. For instance, genes specifying enzymes involved in the basic processes of respiration should maintain considerable similarities among all respiring species. Genes involved in the specification of the brain should be similar only among animals that have a brain. Within the same gene some bases or sequences should be more conserved than others, depending on their functional meaning. For instance, in each triplet the first and second bases should be more conserved than the third base, which has a limited role for determining the amino acid (see chapter 4). And parts of a gene specifying amino acids crucial for the function of a protein should be more conserved than those specifying amino acids with a lesser functional role. In all cases conservation means that organisms without changes are more likely to survive and reproduce than those with changes.

The study of sequences confirms these expectations. Genes that perform essential functions in very distant species, such as bacteria and mammals, are highly conserved. Among these genes is that for cytochrome C, which is one of the proteins of the electron transport chains active in respiration (see chapter 3). Highly conserved also are enzymes that break down proteins. These enzymes enable the most diverse organisms to utilize proteins derived from other living organisms as a source of food. The pancreas of animals makes five such enzymes, which are very similar in different animal species. Bacteria also contain enzymes with activities similar to those of the mammalian enzymes, and the mammalian and bacterial enzymes show great similarities in their central cores.

A very detailed comparison can be made among the globin genes of different species. We have already seen in chapter 5 that globins are constituents of hemoglobin, the protein that transports oxygen in the blood. We have seen that hemoglobin contains two molecules of alpha globin and two of beta globin. In humans there are two families of globin genes, one of the alpha and one of the beta genes. We know that the various members of a family are expressed at various phases of development. The arrangement of the human genes of the beta family can be compared with that found in several other primates that, on the basis of the fossil evidence, have various degrees of relatedness to humans. The genes have identical arrangements in the three species that are most related to one another (humans, gorillas, and baboons); the arrangement is different in owl monkeys, which are further removed, and even more so in the lemur, a more distant prosimian. In the rabbit and mouse, which are much further away from humans, the difference is the largest. The relatedness of the sequences closely parallels the relatedness of the species deduced from the fossil record, as predicted by the concept of evolution.

The concept of evolution predicts that DNA sequences without functional meaning should change considerably—*diverge*—with time. The expectation is confirmed by the observations on different bases within a triplet. In different species changes of the third base of a triplet, which in most cases do not cause an amino acid change (*silent replacement*; see chapter 4), are much more frequent than changes of the other two bases. The third base changes can be considered, as a first approximation, irrelevant for the organism; their proportion in animals of two diverging species therefore should not be affected by differential survival of organisms with or without changes. It would depend mainly on the time since divergence and the rate at which the changes occur—how frequently per unit of time. Comparison of pairs of species deriving from a common ancestor show that third base differences occur at the rate of approximately 1 percent per each million years since the separation of the two species, as deduced from the fossil record.

Base changes that cause the replacement of amino acids are less frequently observed. The rate at which these replacements accumulate depends strongly upon the type of protein affected and on the position of the changed amino acid in the protein; many organisms with such replacements die without transmitting them to their progeny. Even replacement of amino acids less crucial for the function of a protein occur at one-tenth the rate of silent base replacement. In all cases the differences in the rates do not mean that replacements at the first and second bases of triplets *occur* less frequently than those at the third base: the interpretation is that they *persist* less frequently. The actual rate of occurrence may be the same, but functional disadvantage cuts down the proportion of genes in which some replacements took place.

Because the third base replacements are almost inconsequential, it is believed that they reflect the true rate of occurrence and are a valid *molecular clock*. The clock is not absolutely precise because the rate at which the changes occur depends on the characteristics of the enzymes involved in DNA replication and repair—the rate is itself subject to evolution. For instance, the changes occur more frequently in rodents than in primates. Nevertheless, the time of divergence of two species calculated from the molecular clock agrees reasonably well with that derived from the fossil record.

One might expect that the highly repetitive sequences, which constitute the majority of DNA, would also show high variability, but this is not always the case. Some of these sequences, present as "spacers" between the globin genes, do not show a high variation among species. They must perform some function related to the control of the expression of the genes. One possibility is that they control the state of the chromatin, which changes with the state of gene expression (see chapter 4). Another kind of DNA that would be expected to show high divergence is that of intervening sequences, which separate the coding sequences of genes. We know that only the "consensus sequences" of each intervening sequence are essential. What is found is partly in agreement with expectation: intervening sequences show high divergence, except for the consensus sequences. What was not expected, however, is that their length remains highly constant. If there were no constraints, the length of the intervening sequences should vary as a result of insertions and deletions; but such a variation is rarely observed. The result suggests that the length of intervening sequences is more important than their sequences for some aspect of RNA processing.

The observed evolutionary changes of DNA can be attributed to the various mechanisms of variation that we have already discussed (see chapter 6). For instance, the evolution of the globin gene families can be explained as follows. The primordial gene underwent a first duplication, and then one of the products was transposed to a different place in the genome. The two genes diverged by mutations and small deletions to become the alpha and the beta genes, and then each gene duplicated again and their products diverged further. Another mechanism was probably also very important in evolution: gene conversion with sequence correction during sister chromatid exchange. Its occurrence may explain why the two contiguous beta genes of any individual are much more similar than the average of all similar genes in the whole population. In the globin genes there is also evidence for unequal recombination during sister chromatid exchange. We know that unequal recombination between two chromatids containing two very similar genes can generate chromatids with either one or three genes. Indeed, some individuals have one or three alpha globin genes instead of the customary two.

In conclusion, the molecular record is in almost complete accord with the evolutionary expectations. A few discrepancies do exist; if further investigations clarify them, the accord will be perfect.

The Fossil Record

The evidence of the molecular record concerns the species that exist now. An overall view of the course of evolution is given by the fossil record. The fossils represent a book about the history of life on earth from a very early stage. It is a fascinating book to read, but also an incomplete one; many pages are missing owing to insufficient fossils. For most classes of organisms we have only one significant fossil remnant every hundred thousand years—in some cases even every million years. Moreover, most fossils contain only the hard parts of organisms, like skeletons and shells; soft parts have been preserved only rarely, as when circumstances were favorable to their impregnation with minerals. Fossil records, nevertheless, provide clear information concerning the time at which various organisms existed.

If we look at the periods during which the various species represented in the fossil record were alive, a peculiar feature emerges; evolution seems to have occurred in leaps and bounds. Certain species persisted with no appreciable change for periods of many millions of years. This long period of persistence is called *stasis*. A few species of ancient origin exist even today—for instance, the horseshoe crab, which is common on the eastern seaboard of the United States. It has existed unchanged for 200 million years. Most species, however, have suddenly disappeared while new species appeared.

The disappearance of a species is not sudden by our perception of time. "Sudden" events lasted from five thousand to fifty thousand years—a brief period in the time scale of evolution, which stretches over billions of years, but long with reference to the life span of the individuals. Five thousand years are sufficient for the appearance of a new species. This has been observed in recent times: new species of fish have already appeared in some lagoons that became separated from Lake Victoria in Africa about four thousand years ago. The most important thing in the disappearance of species is not the time but the circumstances, as we will see below. Another striking feature of the fossil record is that there are no intermediate forms between successive species; the record seems to have gaps.

The periods of stasis, the gaps in the record, the sudden disappearance of old species and appearance of new ones raise important questions on how evolution occurred. But recent explorations have shed new light on these points. Some of these explorations led to the discovery of previously unknown fossils that filled some big gaps, indicating that the gaps may be due simply to insufficient exploration. There are, however, other explanations for the gaps, and as we will see below, they may illuminate the process of evolution.

Especially interesting are the results obtained on the evolution of rather primitive creatures on the shores of Turkana Lake in Africa. The earth layers of the shores which were inhabited by many species of mollusks similar to present-day snails, were laid down during a period of 5 million years. During this time the level of the lake underwent several important changes, either rising or retreating. During the retreats (which were due presumably to drought and strong evaporation) the salinity and alkalinity of the water increased, generating a stress on the snail species. These changes were associated with a marked decrease of the proportion of individuals of certain species. We know from many other examples, some observed even in recent times, that a change in water salinity and alkalinity can cause the extinction of species of aquatic animals. Measurements of a large number of shells of the Turkana snails led to the interpretation that while some prevalent species became extinct during the changes of the lake, new species appeared that persisted as long as the abnormal conditions lasted. When conditions returned to normality, the area was reinvaded by the species originally present; presumably they had been marooned in other basins by the lake's retreat. With the return of the old species, the new species in turn disappeared, suggesting that they were not well fit for the normal conditions. No evidence of intermediate links between the old and the new species was found, supporting the view that the absence of links was also genuine. Although an approach that takes into account only the size and shape of the shell is inherently incomplete, these results show the fluctuating response of animal populations to the changing environment, and the emergence of new populations, possibly new species, not as a continuous transition from the preexisting ones but as a jump. A theory of evolution must explain these findings.

The Mechanism of Evolution

Darwin thought that evolution occurred by the gradual accretion of many small gradual changes. But he lacked the knowledge of genetics needed for substantiating this view. Subsequently, the discovery of periods of stasis and the sudden disappearance of species and appearance of new ones suggested that evolution did not occur gradually but by sudden leaps. The expression "punctuated equilibrium" was used to indicate this succession of events. Gradual changes can be attributed to a succession of small genetic changes such as mutations, but the sudden changes are more difficult to explain. It was proposed that they are caused by a genetic revolution brought about by some drastic DNA variation, such as the invasion of the genome by transposing elements that could produce many changes in a short time. Such large hypothetical variations are referred to as *macroevents*, in contrast to the usual small changes, *microevents*.

Just as difficult to understand as the occurrence of large jumps is the absence of changes during the periods of stasis, which for some species lasted millions of years. Genetic changes must have continued to occur because they are unstoppable, but they did not leave their mark. Evidently stasis must have involved more than just DNA: a genome is not an isolated entity; it must be taken in the context of its environment. The lack of change in a species in a period of stasis can then be explained in two ways. One, the changes occurred but were neutral—they did not affect the performance of the organism. The other possibility is that the changes were bad for individuals in which they occurred and caused their disappearance.

Neutral Changes?

The idea that neutral changes can drive evolution is supported by mathematical models that show that in an interbreeding population certain gene forms (alleles) can drift, becoming greatly enriched or depleted in a random way without the intervention of selection for or against them; this is called *genetic drift*. We can see a similar tendency in the ribosomal RNA genes, although its mechanism is different. A mutation in one of the genes of the family either will be eliminated or, after considerable fluctuation, will spread to the whole family. The phenomenon of gene conversion is responsible for these changes.

The great evolutionary power of neutral changes is seen in a simplified system: a viral RNA is replicated in the test tube by the viral replicating enzyme in a mixture where both the enzyme and the precursor molecules needed for replication are introduced by the experimenter. The RNA molecules resulting from replication are themselves replicated and the process is repeated over a large number of generations, during which their characteristics are continuously monitored. In this system genetic changes occur at a very high rate because RNA is very mutable. A rapid accumulation of changes causes the original molecular type to be replaced by other molecular types not at random but with predominance of certain types. But molecules of one type in subsequent replication can drift into new types. The number of molecules of the various types is not uniform: the distribution of the genetic types is like a mountain landscape, with high peaks (the predominant types) separated by valleys. But the landscape is fluid: from time to time a peak can flow into a valley and then join another peak. The changes causing this evolution are neutral. Selection, however, can cause important additional modifications of the distribution, as can be seen by introducing into the replicating mixture an unusual precursor. Then some molecular types increase in abundance, whereas others disappear. In a similar way the occurrence of neutral (or almost neutral) changes is at the basis of this molecular polymorphism observed in all species—that is, the variety of types of proteins or DNA sequences without obvious consequences.

Neutral changes, however, are not sufficiently frequent to explain the whole of evolution. This can be deduced from the limited extent of polymorphism (about 20 percent of the genes) in species in which it has been thoroughly studied. If all changes were neutral, one would expect 100 percent. Moreover, a change that is neutral under certain circumstances may be subject to selection under other circumstances. Examples are changes in the immune response gene of the major histocompatibility locus (see chapter 14). An individual carrying a changed form of one of these genes, which responds poorly to a certain infectious agent (a virus or a bacterium), may find itself greatly handicapped if the agent appears in its environment. Without the agent, the mutation would be neutral.

Two Environments

Genetic changes have a selective value—they are good or bad—because evolution operates on the genes through the individuals. The genes are thus exposed to two environments: an inner and an outer environment. The inner environment is formed by the state of all the other genes, which must operate in balance. We have seen how significant this balance is for sex determination (see chapter 9). The balance of the genes gives rise to the adult body through the complicated process of development. Genetic changes that upset the regular development of the organism are not permissible. So the internal environment creates serious constraints on the accumulation of genetic changes. Many unacceptable changes do occur in the genes but are not seen because they doom the organism. The outer environment is the world in which the individual lives. The genes are exposed to that environment through the organism in which they reside. Many gene changes make an individual less suitable to survive in the external environment and are lost together with the individual. The external environment, therefore, also creates constraints on the accumulation of genetic changes.

The influence of these constraints is certainly a cause of stasis. Species that have developed an excellent adaptation to the two environments tend to remain constant because any genetic change is unfavorable; the changes occur but are weeded out. Stasis generated in this way persists as long as the internal and external environments remain constant.

But a sudden collapse of the equilibrium between the genome and its environments, either internal or external, has dramatic effects on the population, and many individuals are eliminated. The species may disappear and be replaced by a new one. Such events appear to have taken place in the Turkana basin through a drastic change of the external environment. Existing species went through a crisis, and several of them became almost extinct. Not all individuals disappeared, however; the species went through a bottleneck. The individuals that survived were genetically different—as an expression of the normal polymorphism—and more suitable for the crisis situation. During the stasis, individuals with these phenotypes were not especially well adapted, but could persist and were revealed by the crisis and the near extinction of the species. During the crisis they initiated new lineages endowed with greater survival value. What precisely constituted the advantage of these individuals we cannot say, because only the shells remain.

A contemporary example of a similar phenomenon is the presence of genes for thalassemia in humans (see chapter 4). The genes are unfavorable to individuals, who nevertheless manage to survive and reproduce. Some of these genes confer resistance to malaria. In an area without malaria, the affected individuals represent a very small fraction of the population, but if there were a sudden extensive spread of malaria, they would be the best fit and the thalassemia gene would spread.

The general conclusion is that a new population emerging from a bottleneck is already contained, although not recognizably so, in a preexisting one. Whether or not individuals of this population will constitute a new species depends on additional factors that determine their ability to interbreed with individuals of the population from which they derived.

Many other examples suggest that environmental changes can have profound consequences and cause the disappearance of species. Among these are catastrophic events such as the collision of the earth with asteroids (see chapter 3) and extreme lowerings of the surface temperature, as in the Ice Ages. Crisis and extinction severe enough to put a species through a bottleneck may also result from changes of the internal environment. For instance, transposable elements may invade the genome, upsetting the gene balance or disrupting the regular developmental process.

Isolation

A bottleneck in which rare individuals with unusual properties emerge out of the genetic reservoir of the old species appears to be important for the emergence of a new species. A bottleneck may develop even if there is no crisis. One mechanism is the migration of a small group of individuals to a segregated environment, for instance, a remote island. The genetic reservoir of the small migrant population is very restricted, but it may include individuals with unusual genes that can become established either by random drift or by selection under the new circumstances. If so, these individuals may generate a new population with special genetic characteristics, possibly a new species; this situation is known as the *founder effect*. Similar events take place during the domestication of wild animals. The few animals captured by humans are a small sample of their species. They may be enriched with hidden domestication genes, which are made evident by selective inbreeding. The domesticated species deriving from these animals was already contained in hidden form in the wild species. Domestication is impossible, however, if these hidden genes do not exist in the wild species. For instance, attempts to domesticate fur animals have shown that it is possible to domesticate foxes but not minks.

Theoretically, isolation of a small population may also result from changes of the genome. One possible mechanism, based on mutations in highly repetitive DNA sequences, has been described in chapter 6. Another mechanism might be the occurrence of changes that alter sexual behavior, such as the appearance of an altered pheromone in an insect species or a changed song in a species of birds. The individuals that recognize that changed pheromone or song form an isolated inbreeding population; from it a new species may develop.

In plants, isolation often occurs when special rare hybrids are formed between two species. These hybrids contain the complete genomes of the two parental species; they are *polyploid*. The hybrids are isolated from either parent by a chromosomal mechanism. If we indicate the two sets of homologous chromosomes of the parental species as AA and BB, the hybrid is ABAB. When gametes are formed in the hybrid, the homologous chromosomes pair with each other during reduction as AB/AB. Pairing is perfect because chromosomes A pair with A and B with B, and regular gametes can be formed. But crosses between the hybrid and either parent are not fertile because at reduction, pairing occurs as A/AB or B/AB, and chromosome pairing is incomplete, preventing the production of gametes. In this case the polyploid plant forms a new species. The formation of such hybrids is a powerful mechanism of plant evolution, which allows very efficient adaptation by combining two genomes with different characteristics. This explains why one-fourth of flowering plants are polyploid.

Breeding incompatibility between the individuals of the old and the new species can be the cause of the formation of a new species in some cases, as in the last examples given, or its consequence in others. Secondary breeding incompatibility develops when the new population has different constraints to genetic variation compared to the old one. Now sexual characteristics may make interbreeding impossible; the species is then launched on its lonely voyage, past the point of no return. The possible outcomes are success or doom.

These mechanisms of speciation—the formation of a new species—explain why new species appear suddenly and why there are no intermediate links between the new and the old. The type of organism that emerges, although not new, was previously in a minority and is brought to the fore without delay by the new conditions. It may have been unrecognizable because its special properties, suitable for the new conditions, were not recognizable externally. Starting from that background, new gene arrangements can be made in a relatively short evolutionary time, for instance, hundreds or thousands of generations. An important role may be played by mutations that affect development. As discussed in chapter 12, a single developmental mutation of this kind may produce a large body change. They can rapidly alter the external anatomy, which determines such important adaptive factors as the ability to feed, fight, mate, or avoid predators.

Which Genetic Changes?

We can now return to the concepts of microevent and macroevent. Macroevents were proposed for explaining the sudden changeover of species observed in the fossil record. Many of these changes, however, can be explained by the hypothesis that genetic diversity, which occurs gradually during stasis by the mechanisms of DNA variation considered in chapter 5, is suddenly revealed by changed circumstances. The observations reported above support this explanation.

Molecular considerations also suggest that the genetic changes cannot occur too suddenly nor can they be produced by drastic mechanisms such as widespread transpositions. Transposition is mainly a mechanism for inactivating genes and for moving around DNA sequences. Its negative effects on organisms would greatly outweigh the positive effect of creating new combinations of sequences. Point mutations are much more suitable for the latter purpose. Genetic macroevents are also unsuitable for another reason: life is based on a vast number of interactions of protein molecules among themselves and with other molecules. For instance, many enzymes are made up of two or more different protein molecules that act in concert. If one is changed, the other must also change in a concordant way, and this can happen only gradually. In an enzyme made up of two molecules, A and B, the following series of events can be visualized. Protein A changes slightly by mutation, weakening somewhat its interaction with protein B, but still within the range of survival. Then another mutation changes protein B, making it more compatible to the already changed protein A. More small steps of the same kind follow. In the end the diversification can become such that the new protein A, although capable of interacting with the new protein B, can no longer interact with the old protein B. The probability of maintaining such concordance through a cataclysmic genetic event is remote. The most likely outcome of such of an event would be a profound perturbation of the interactions of many molecules, causing the death of the individual.

Many evolutionary changes must also occur in a concordant way in different individuals. Among these are the specializations leading to mate recognition in animals. A change in the chemistry of a pheromone must be accompanied by suitable changes in the smell receptors of the mate that recognizes it. A change in plumage color of a male bird must be accompanied by a change of the brain network of the female so that she continues to find him fascinating. All these changes can easily proceed by small additive steps.

A problem with the role of small genetic changes in evolution is their low frequency. The genomes that exist today could not have been built in the available time by the accumulation of randomly occurring point mutations at the rate they occur today. The problem is similar to that of writing the *Divine Comedy* by assembling letters at random. But in fact that was not the way Dante wrote it. The assembly of letters into phonemes and words and the way words must be arranged into sentences were worked out before him. Similarly, no present genome was made by arranging bases at random. That approach was probably used in the very early period of evolution; subsequently, the mechanisms of gene duplication, recombination, transposition, and conversion allowed a rapid exchange of rather complex units of information, generating a vast number of different combinations.

In early evolutionary times, however, the formation of the different base sequences that were later amplified or interchanged by these mechanisms must have taken place by mutation. At this level there is still a problem with the extremely low rates of mutations in DNA, such as those that calibrate the molecular clock of evolution. This difficulty may be circumvented by the role of RNA in evolution. As discussed below, it is likely that RNA preceded DNA. The mutation frequency of RNA replication, as measured with viruses, is ten to a hundred thousand times higher than with DNA, because RNA is intrinsically more unstable and does not use any editing function in replication (see chapter 4). It is possible that a great deal of the sequence variation existing today arose in RNA before the switch to DNA. DNA would have contributed mostly the ability to exchange parts. Another related point is that a good proportion of DNA is today made up of sequences produced by reverse transcription (see chapter 5). Reverse transcription also has a high error rate; much recent variation may be generated by this mechanism. Sequences generated by reverse transcription are not parts of active genes, but can contribute to the formation of new genes by gene conversion. These two mechanisms can account for an enormous amount of mutation during evolution.

Are Viruses Motors of Evolution?

The role of reverse transcription in molding the genome and its important contribution to the generation of mutations raise the question whether retroviruses, or some ancient precursors of them, have played an especially important role in evolution. In a speculative way one may conceive of a retrovirus widely infecting a species and establishing a sort of coexistence with its members. Most individuals would be invaded by replicating virus but would retain their own capacity to reproduce. The continued viral replication would flood the infected cells with reverse transcriptase, causing a marked increase in the frequency of mutations. Infection of germ cells, which is common in retrovirus infection, would cause mutations in germ cell precursors or in oocytes; some of them would be transmitted to the progeny. At the same time the insertion of proviruses in the cellular genes and other effects would be detrimental for the growth and development of the organism. This species would be under accelerated evolution both for the greatly increased mutation frequency and for the general weakening of the species, which would create a bottleneck. The great number of mutations, occurring over a period of many generations, would cause progressive but rapid (in geological time) changes of the genome, possibly still compatible with harmonious changes of the proteins of the organism, as is required. Among the genetic changes induced by the virus some would in time cause resistance to the virus itself. Individuals with this characteristic would form a new stable population, in which both the high mutagenesis and the deleterious effects of the infection had subsided. This population would then constitute a new species.

An example approaching this hypothetical model is provided by infection of human populations with the AIDS retrovirus: the virus spreads rapidly, generating a protracted infection that sometimes culminates in a wasting disease. In the disease phase the virus is actively multiplying in some cell types; the infection does not impair sexuality, and the virus is sexually transmitted. The viral reverse transcriptase appears to be highly mutagenic because of the great variability among different isolates of the virus. We don't know, however, whether the virus can infect germ cells and induce germinal mutations. This hypothetical model offers a plausible mechanism for "rapid" appearance of new species independently of important environmental changes and without the intervention of catastrophic genetic events.

The Meaning of Adaptation

A basic concept of evolution is that of natural selection: a species expands or shrinks depending on how well it fits the environment. The process that generates fitness—called adaptation—involves both the acquisition of useful characteristics and the loss of those that are useless.

The mechanism by which new characteristics are acquired is illustrated by an observation on the Darwin finches that inhabit the Galapagos Islands. These animals feed on small seeds which they crack with their beaks. In 1977 a period of drought greatly reduced the crop of these seeds, although the production of bigger seeds was much less affected. The population of finches dwindled because their normal staple was no longer available, and they could not crack the bigger seeds with their small beaks. A new population of finches emerged: they had larger beaks and were capable of feeding on the large seeds. These individuals were present but rare and therefore unnoticed in the original population. This example shows that *adaptation is a population shift;* it is not the individual that acquires the new character, but the species, by changing its composition.

The loss of useless characteristics occurs according to the same principle, although in a more subtle way. It is not immediately obvious why animals of an underground species are blind or why birds become unable to fly after they are confined to a remote island. The mere fact that the function is unnecessary is not sufficient for its disappearance; there is nothing wrong with having a useless function. The disappearance may be caused by random genetic drift or by a negative selective value. The latter is the case if the persistence of the function reduces the fitness of the individual. For birds that settle in distant islands where there are no predators, ability to fly may be damaging. Although flying is essential for escaping predators, the birds may consume unnecessarily a great deal of energy if they continue to fly in their absence. Genetic variants that cannot fly save that energy, which they can expend in the production of a larger progeny. Under these circumstances, loss of flying has a positive adaptive value. Again the population shifts, amplifying what formerly were rare variants. The predisposition to generate such variants is itself a genetic characteristic: only birds of some species easily become flightless. These are birds in which the bone structures and muscles for flight develop after birth; limited genetic changes can cause loss of flight. The potential for flightlessness is in the species.

The case of the underground blind animals is less clear. For instance, we don't know whether underground life or blindness was the first event. It is conceivable, in fact, that animals made blind by a genetic change could survive only by living underground where they would be protected from predators. There they would be isolated from the original species and would diverge, generating a new species.

The last examples show that it is often difficult to decide what brought about a certain adaptation. This is clearly shown by some classical mistakes in interpreting population changes, such as the appearance of large numbers of dark moths in English cities after the Industrial Revolution. The dark moths were thought to be better adapted to the smoky environment: they would more easily escape the attention of predatory birds because they were better camouflaged. Subsequent studies, however, showed that the dark moths are eaten by birds just as readily as light-colored moths. It seems that the dark moths are better adapted because their dark color traps more of the sun's heat through the smoky haze. Another example is the presence of feathers on birds: we may think they are an adaptation to flight, but in fact, feathers appeared first in reptiles, where they were useful as thermal insulation. When birds developed from reptiles, they presumably kept the feathers for the same reason: lightweight insulation. Subsequent evolution specialized the feathers for flight.

Some adaptations have to do with a special situation: the selection of the mating partner. In some species of birds a female selects her mate on the basis of his plumage display—the showier the display, the greater his success. A showy display, therefore, is an adaptive characteristic. But in some cases the display is so showy the bird can hardly fly. It must, therefore, decrease the fitness of the bird by requiring lots of energy and reducing its protection from predators. In the end, then, the adaptation becomes counterproductive: it is a runaway selection. The adaptation must reach a balance between increased sexual success and decreased life expectancy. The showy plumage is probably maintained at a maximum beyond which the overall fitness of the species would decrease.

Large adaptive changes must have gone on a little at a time, pushed by circumstances. Let's consider, for instance, the emergence of land animals from fish. We certainly cannot think that one day a fish leader collected its acolytes and shouted "Let's march on to land!" The transition probably occurred through thousands of bottlenecks. It took place in shallow lakes or streams during dry periods when the water shrank to small pools and marshes, causing many fish to die. We can imagine this sequence of events. It just happened that some among those fish, for no reason in the world, developed a little pouch out of the back of their mouth, surrounded by a network of blood vessels. This little appendage was only a nuisance when water was high, but became useful during the drought when the fish had to swallow lots of air rather than water. Then many modifications caused by mutations increased its efficiency, so that the fish could live either under water or in air. Fish with these characteristics—lungfish—still exist today in the marshes of the Congo River and of other rivers in Africa and South America.

We can visualize further steps as follows: once adaptation to the use of air became fairly advanced, the fish spent more time on land, using their fins to propel themselves. The fins became more like legs, because they were useful to explore land farther and farther away. At the beginning, life on land was easy: no predators threatened, so slow locomotion was acceptable and there was no incentive to return to water. The gills then became unnecessary and actually a drawback since they lost lots of inner water by evaporation. But they could not be completely abandoned: some sections had become the beds of useful bones or of endocrine glands. These sections were retained, and the others lost.

Progressively, the transition from water to land took place in an immense number of small coordinated steps. Some steps may have occurred by random drift, but it is likely that many were promoted by crises that brought to the fore new creatures with more favorable characteristics under the circumstances. The overall transition, like every evolutionary change, was not a triumphal march: it was an odyssey.

Selection for the Genes

Natural selection acts on the individuals of a species, but through the individual, selection acts on its genes. What is the goal of selection: the protection of the individuals or the protection of the genes?

That selection is for the genes is made clear by adaptations that actually endanger the individual. A typical case is altruism, which is displayed by some animal species, such as ground squirrels. If a predator approaches a colony, any individual seeing it gives a special noise to alert the others, who then escape to their burrows. The animal giving the alarm performs an altruistic act: it attracts the attention of the predator to itself and wastes precious time before hiding. Thus the altruistic act is damaging for the individual itself, but useful for the whole colony, which otherwise might easily fall prey to the predator. If the colony represents an inbreeding group in which most genes are shared, altruism is a useful method of selection for the genes.

Altruism must be maintained by special genes determining the necessary brain network. Some genes must also lower competition within the group. If the individual giving the alarm were exposed to serious competition by those it saves, altruism would be damaging. Then it would be better for the individual to escape and let the predator kill its competitors.

Evolution in the Laboratory

The account of evolution given above is based on molecular and historical evidence and on our knowledge of the living world as it is today. Many events were postulated without direct evidence. Because of the lack of hard evidence, it might be said that the concept of evolution is abstract, theoretical, possibly a figment of the imagination. The question therefore arises: can we reproduce evolution in the laboratory? Obviously, we cannot do so using long-extinct creatures or large present-day animals. Because evolutionary events take place over many generations, it would take centuries to experiment with mice, say. But we *can* design an experiment using fast-reproducing organisms like bacteria or fruitflies.

For such an experiment, we use bacteria, which grow rapidly in flasks in a liquid broth as long as the food is abundant. If the conditions of their environment are kept constant and they are regularly transferred to fresh flasks containing the same kind of broth when their food is exhausted, they retain their characteristics unchanged: they are in stasis. But we can introduce an evolutionary bottleneck by, for instance, adding penicillin to the culture, whereupon most of the bacteria disappear: the culture becomes almost extinct. We find, however, that a few bacteria survive in the penicillin-containing broth and form a new culture. The adaptation of the culture is due to the presence of penicillin-resistant bacteria in the original population. These rare constituents of the genetic reservoir of the species have saved the day. Now, however, if the bacteria adapted to penicillin are returned to the normal broth, the population shifts progressively in the reverse direction. Variants have emerged that are more fit to grow in regular broth than are the bacteria adapted to penicillin.

But as long as bacteria adapted to growth in penicillin-containing broth are kept in that medium, the culture remains in stasis. Now, once again, we introduce a new crisis: streptomycin is added to the medium, and the culture will be saved only if streptomycin-resistant bacteria are present in the population.

We cannot say in this case whether the three kinds of cultures—the normal population, the bacteria growing with penicillin, and those growing with strep-tomycin—are three different species, for there is no good way of defining species in bacteria. To ask this question, we may experiment with the fruitfly *Drosophila*, where the definition of species is straightforward. When these flies are placed in bottles containing a fruit mash as food, they multiply and a new generation emerges every two weeks. Our experiment with them must last for months or years—much longer than in the case of the bacteria.

In one such experiment, a population of flies in stasis was exposed to a drastic environmental change: the temperature was raised to the point of intolerance, and the fly population dwindled under the stress. Gradually, however, the bottles became repopulated: some flies were resistant to the higher temperature. These flies also looked different than those of the previous population. Their ability to grow at high temperature and their new appearance were due in part to gene forms already present in the old population and in part to new mutations. These flies did not interbreed with those of the old population: they were a new species.

In another experiment, the selection of a new species was obtained without exposing the fruitflies to stress. Instead, at each generation flies were selected for increased length of the bristles that cover their body. The other flies with shorter bristles were discarded, creating a bottleneck. Again the characteristics of the population progressively changed, shifting to bristles of extreme length. And when the new flies were mixed with those of the old population, again they did not interbreed: a new species had been selected. In this case the selection was carried out by changing the internal environment. Selecting for a certain bristle length had meant selecting for certain genes, and apparently with them other genes were also selected—genes that had nothing to do directly with bristle formation. They were responsible for the breeding incompatibility with regular flies.

From these experiments, we conclude that evolution can indeed be re-produced in the laboratory. The changes observed in the experimental popula-tions and the way they occurred corresponded exactly to the prediction of the theory of evolution.

How Did It All Begin?

We can trace the evolution of today's life from some very simple creatures present billions of years ago. But one fundamental question still remains: where did these simple creatures come from? How did life begin? The answers to these questions are buried in the cosmic mysteries of the universe. We can only explore possibilities.

We start by speculating whether life began on earth or started elsewhere in the cosmos and came to earth. These alternatives, of course, are untestable, so we can reach no firm conclusion. But the idea of extraterrestrial origin must be accepted as a possibility, simply because there is no way to rule it out. A terrestrial origin would mean that life arose on earth from what was available on the planet during its first billion years—the period before the organisms present now as fossils made their appearance. Unlike the first possibility, this one can be examined more closely. Some information is available. and evidence may be obtained in the laboratory.

During these early times, the earth had rocks, oceans, and an atmosphere containing no oxygen. The atmosphere, probably, was similar to that of Titan, the Jovian planet, which is known from space explorations. It contained hydrogen, carbon dioxide, water, some ammonia, methane, hydrogen cyanide, and a few other gases. The ingredients from which life could have arisen, then, are these gases, water, salts, and rocks of various kinds.

The initial problem is to determine whether it was possible for these ingredients to generate the molecules that make up today's life, such as amino acids or nucleic acid bases. We know that the manufacture of these substances requires energy: where would that come from? The only possible sources were light from the sun, both visible and invisible, especially ultraviolet, and electrical discharges from storms. An attempt was made in the laboratory to see whether electrical discharges would produce amino acids in the mixture of gases and water described above. The results were astonishing: many amino acids were formed, in amounts far greater than could be expected. The experiment showed clearly that one of the first steps in the generation of life was possible on the early earth.

The next step, also reproduced in the laboratory, was to see whether these amino acids could form chains corresponding to today's proteins. This step would require a considerable concentration of the amino acids, but it was found that, although they were produced at an extremely low rate, they could accumulate. With no creatures to eat them or enzymes to destroy them, and unlimited time at hand, the amino acids could indeed reach the needed concentrations. Over many millions of years a soup of amino acids and other molecules was formed, and the amino acids could join to form short chains.

There is some question about the handedness of the amino acids. Their chemical structure is such that they can exist in two forms, in each of which the arrangement of the atoms is the mirror image of the other. Like screws, amino acids can be either left-handed or right-handed. Screws are usually right-handed; the amino acids that compose today's life are left-handed. How could left-handed amino acids be selected in the soup, excluding the others? The answer may be found in the tendency of amino acids of the same handedness to assemble. It can be shown in the laboratory that as soon as a few amino acids of the same handedness form a chain, they select similar ones for new additions. Thus the use of one kind of amino acid to make proteins seems to have come about naturally in the early stages of life. The selection of left-handed amino acids may be related to the basic electronic mechanisms that determine handedness. The laws of physics show that these mechanisms have a slight bias toward left-handedness. Other reasons may be biological: for instance, the necessity of proteins to interact with nucleic acids, which also have a handedness.

By these mechanisms small proteins were made; they probably facilitated the formation of more proteins. The next question is how nucleic acids got into the scene. The primordial soup, as it is reproduced in the laboratory, contains, besides amino acids, molecules that can act as building blocks for nucleic acids. These molecules too may have become organized in short chains comparable to those of present-day nucleic acids, but we lack direct evidence for this possibility. They might have gathered around some of the primitive proteins; the preferential association of certain amino acids with these simplified nucleic acids or their building blocks may have determined the characteristics of the translation code.

Before more complex molecules could be assembled, a better source of energy had to be provided. Membranes, crucial in this process, could be formed by spontaneous association of molecules that were partly water-seeking, partly fat-seeking, like those of present-day membranes. These membranes could have been instrumental in the partitioning of ions, creating differences in concentration, which, as we saw in chapter 3, are the basic source of energy for today's cells. Sugars needed for making nucleic acids might have been produced in the primordial soup; they became abundant, however, only after photosynthesis began, about 2.8 billion years ago.

The first type of nucleic acid to appear on earth was probably RNA. We have many hints of this order of appearance in today's life. One is that DNA replication begins with RNA, and another is that some viruses have a genome made of RNA that replicates as RNA. Viruses of another class may represent the transition between RNA and DNA genomes; they have a genome made of RNA that during replication is copied into DNA. As discussed in chapter 4, the existence of DNA transcription and of RNA splicing as basic life processes also support the existence of RNA before DNA. The initial presence of RNA may have been crucial for producing a large amount of different sequences, given its high propensity for mistakes. But because of this propensity, RNA is not suitable as a genome containing many genes; its use is limited to small viruses with very few genes. For more complex organisms a much more stable and reliable molecule was needed: the double helical DNA.

Thus, it is possible to reconstruct in broad outline the origin and development of life on earth from components present on earth. The same components, however, are present in the gas clouds of the interstellar spaces. We know this because the light that has traversed these interstellar clouds is "colored" as if it went through a colored glass, and its "color," analyzed by very sensitive instruments, is the same as that of light that has gone through a mixture of substances like those of the primordial soup. Moreover, a meteorite of distant cosmic origin, the Murchison meteorite that fell in Australia in 1969, was found to be loaded with amino acids; many were identical to those of today's living creatures. So we return to our first possibility: that the primordial life molecules are generated in space in the same way they could have been on earth and that they may have reached earth from space.

If the primitive constituents of life are everywhere in the universe, life may exist in many other places. No one knows whether this is true or not; there are too many imponderables. One problem, for instance, is how much carbon dioxide (CO_2) there is in the primitive atmosphere of a planet. The amount must be just right because CO_2 is the heat insulator of the atmosphere. If there is too much, it will produce a strong greenhouse effect and the temperature will rise greatly, producing an inferno. This is what happened on the planet Venus. Conversely, if there is too little CO_2, the temperature will be too low and the planet will become a world of ice, which is what happened on Mars. Thus, there is a narrow range of the level of CO_2 that allows the development of life. On the early earth the CO_2 concentration fell within this range; later on, life took control of CO_2 and established a balance between its production by respiring organisms and its elimination by plants, which convert it into oxygen. Who knows in how many other worlds such a precise range existed?

If planets with the characteristics of earth do exist, it is likely there is life on them. Given the size of the universe, it seems inevitable that there should be life elsewhere. That life, however, would not necessarily be similar to ours because evolution is full of chance events—it is a network of branching points. At each branching a certain number of paths are possible, depending on the characteristics of the organisms present at that point. Which path is chosen depends on the vagaries of genetic changes and on the environment. The internal environment also imposes severe constraints that reflect the past history of the species. So the path of life can proceed in many—even opposing—directions from the same start. The enormous variety of possible outcomes can be seen on earth, which hosts creatures as diverse as bacteria, insects, birds, mammals, and plants. And this is probably only a small sample of all the possible outcomes.

If there is life elsewhere in the universe, the questions arise: is it intelligent by human standards? Is it technological? Investigators are attempting to detect intelligent life in the universe by listening to radiowaves with highly sophisticated apparatuses. The idea is that waves emitted by a civilization comparable to ours could be received on earth and recognized for their rhythm or other distinguishing features. So far we have heard nothing, but this does not mean very much: it shows only that we are not closely surrounded by technological civilizations. In the meantime, we are improving our listening ability and continuing to monitor the skies.

A Role for Creation?

The traditional concept that life resulted from an act of creation is still accepted by some groups. They have tried to have this concept recognized in law as a valid alternative to the science of evolution. The creationist trend finds its strength in religious, ethical, and moral considerations. During the last hundred years its popularity has waxed and waned, depending on the strength of these feelings.

One reason for the persistence of the creationist idea has been the difficulty for the nonspecialist to evaluate the technical validity of the arguments on which the concept of evolution is based. Recently the creationist movement has entered the technical arena, attacking the scientific bases of evolution. One of the creationist arguments has been that the concept of evolution is invalid because it cannot be reproduced in the laboratory and it cannot be tested experimentally. If true, this argument would be serious, because a scientific theory is valid only if it can be tested by experiments that might show it to be wrong. If the experiments are carried out and do not contradict it, the theory remains acceptable. But it is not true that the occurrence of evolution cannot be tested in the laboratory. We have just described some experiments with bacteria and fruitflies that have clearly demonstrated the occurrence of natural selection, adaptation, and speciation. Of course, the evolutionary events that took place over a period of many thousands of years cannot be reproduced in the laboratory.

The observation that in certain periods of the earth's history, like the Cambrian, many complex organisms appeared at once is taken by creationists as an argument for the sudden creation of those species, and another argument concerns the absence of connecting forms in the fossil record. This would seem to contradict the continuity implicit in evolution, but as we have already discussed, neither of these findings actually contradicts the concept of evolution.

Creationist thinking is encouraged by the discussions, often acrimonious, among evolutionists on how exactly evolution should be interpreted. These discussions suggest that the theory of evolution is arbitrary. This view, however, does not recognize the nature of scientific inquiry, which is based on the continuous reevaluation of theories as new observations are made. The disagreements show only that the present models of evolution are approximate. Anybody who understands the scientific process recognizes that this uncertainty does not invalidate the basic concept of evolution. In science no theory is ever final: each continues to evolve as new data become available and new refinements are possible.

Some creationist theories try also to take into account present scientific knowledge. One approach is to interpret Genesis' days of creation as ages; for some this is a negotiable point. Another approach postulates two creations—one at the beginning millions of years ago and the other six thousand years ago, as Genesis describes. A nonnegotiable point concerns fossils. They are supposed to have resulted from the worldwide flood as recounted in Genesis. The ebb and flow of its waters would also have generated the layering of the earth's crust.

Even with these modifications the creationist view can be maintained only if one accepts a great deal of absurdity. For instance, one must reject the dating of rocks by radioactive decay methods, which reveal an enormously long time scale. But this dating is on very solid scientific bases and simply cannot be denied. Doubting it is like doubting the existence of sunlight, of atomic weapons, or of nuclear plants, all of which depend on the same atomic reactions that are at the basis of radioactive dating. One may well doubt atomic bombs, but the doubt is of little value if the mushroom cloud appears on the horizon. Another absurdity has to do with the flood. More water than is contained in all the oceans would be needed to cover the whole world at the depth specified by Genesis. Where did it come from? And where did it finally go? And what about Noah's ark? How large a vessel would be needed to accommodate the million or so species present on earth—not to mention the food needed to keep them alive? And how would one prevent the cat from eating the mouse or any other predator from eating its prey? It is obvious that this story can have only a symbolic meaning, not a literal one.

The only point where there may be room for creationism is at the origin of life, which we must recognize is still mysterious. As we have discussed, life could have originated entirely on earth from earth's components; but there is the equally plausible model according to which the first molecules incorporated into living matter originated in the interstellar spaces. If so, what materials rained down on earth to initiate our life? These could have been simple molecules produced by the action of radiation on the gases that fill the interstellar spaces. But they could also have been microscopic living things similar, for instance, to present-day bacteria. If these microscopic creatures reached earth from space, were they the result of evolution or creation? One can certainly maintain that such living micro-organisms were made by a creator and then dispersed throughout the universe, a view considered plausible by some physical scientists. They point out that the probability of making even the simplest possible living cell by assembling atoms at random is essentially nil. But this difficulty, as already discussed, is only apparent.

A dispassionate evaluation of all the available facts leads to the conclusion that the creationist arguments have little to contribute to understanding how present-day life came about. Only at the beginning, more than three billion years ago, might creation have occurred, but there is nothing to prove or disprove it. Whether or not one accepts its role is finally a matter of personal philosophy. The personal preferences that are part of the arguments of both evolutionists and creationists are tainted with a doctrinaire tinge. The hard-core evolutionist will categorically exclude any role of creation at any time; the hard-core creationist will not hesitate to deny well-established facts. Both feel a moral duty to uphold

CHAPTER 21

Epilogue: What is Life?

In this book we have looked into many facets of life: the molecules of living organisms, their functions, how they are connected by regulatory circuits, how they evolve. Now perhaps we can answer the question we asked at the beginning: what is life?

Some Answers to Our Question

Life as Change

A traveler through the prairie states often sees the mounds of the prairie dog with one of the animals standing on top, frozen like a statue, the immobile sentinel of its compound. Its instructions, coming probably from its genes, tell it that as long as it stands unflinching and stonelike, even with a predator approaching, nobody, including the predator, will recognize it as a living creature. For in the biological world, life is movement.

But life is more than movement, it is change. A cell changes shape, muscles contract, flagella whip around, blood circulates through blood vessels, ions move through channels, and currents traverse axons, muscle, the heart, and the brain. In living creatures everything changes. If a radioactive molecule capable of ending up in a protein is injected into a living organism, it will make most proteins radioactive. If we measure the radioactivity in the proteins at subsequent times, we will find that it progressively decreases. The proteins present at the time of injection are gradually destroyed and replaced by identical ones, which keep the function going.

Even a radioactive label introduced into DNA will be lost with time: DNA, the chemical, is not forever. Although it is conserved in replication, parts of it are continuously removed and replaced in the various processes of repair, recombination, and transposition that go on through life. The replacements do not change the genetic information because they reproduce the original.

These continuous unstoppable changes of living organisms are carried out by proteins. They make up the structures that contract, the ion channels, the enzymes. There cannot be life, of the type we know, without proteins.

Life as Reproduction

Reproduction is a necessity of life, for life is an expansive force that tends to penetrate every corner of the physical world, from the depths of the oceans to the higher reaches of the atmosphere, from the deserts to the mountains, from the Arctic to the equator. Reproduction is the basis of evolution, which establishes the continuity of life from its beginning, more than 3 billion years ago, to now. The ability to reproduce is characteristic of all creatures, from the simplest, such as viruses, to the most complex.

In the present world reproduction is an attribute of DNA; in an earlier evolutionary period it was in all likelihood an attribute of RNA. Every form of reproduction is in the end the doubling of DNA or RNA molecules by a process of self-complementarity. Because all cells, at least in certain stages of their development, reproduce, reproduction and the ability to change go hand in hand in all living organisms and the cells that make them up.

Life as Structure and Order

Proteins can mediate the changes that are characteristic of life because they form structures—that is, three-dimensional solids with well-defined shapes. The structures of life are made in such a way that they can change: many weak bonds connect the different parts. Some of these bonds connect parts of the same protein molecule; others connect different molecules within the same complex. The reversible shifting of these bonds allows the structures to undergo reversible changes. A cell, the unit of living organisms, can be considered to a certain extent as a superstructure in which each molecule is related to all others. Some groups of molecules are related to each other rather strongly to form complexes; these complexes in turn are related to each other more weakly, and so on, in a hierarchical organization of decreasing interactive strength. Almost everything that happens in a cell involves every molecule it contains, but to a different degree, depending on how strongly it interacts with the original event.

The main components of the structures of life, the proteins, are made up of chains of amino acids arranged in a certain order that differs for each protein. The order of the amino acids determines the structure. The structure is directly responsible for the function of the protein, and the order of amino acids is indirectly responsible. The order of amino acids reflects, in turn, the order of bases in the DNA of the gene. Signals travel through these structures to reach their targets.

For many functions it is the structure that is essential, not the order. The most extreme case is that of membranes, which are made up of fatty molecules arranged side by side, forming leaflets. Within a leaflet the molecules move constantly around: there is no order. But the structure is maintained by the association of the fatty molecules and by their arrangement in two leaflets, with the fat-seeking ends touching each other and water seeking ends exposed to the watery environment. If two membranes touch, the fatty molecules of each can mix together, forming a unique membrane and causing the two membranes to fuse. Membranes are very plastic structures because the bonds holding the molecules are of a special nature and very weak.

Variable structure and order are the basic attributes of life, which distinguish it from the physical world in which molecules tend to maximum disorder, as in gases and liquids, or to rigid association, as in crystals. The order of life results from the selection of random events. In the course of evolution short nucleic acid chains were presumably formed at random with no prearranged order of the bases, except for physical constraints. Some of these chains were capable of performing functions useful for life, and the order of these sequences was selected by their functions and was preserved. New chains were added again by chance, and again selection chose some and rejected others. Order, then, is intimately connected with function. For the progressive increase of order during evolution, reproduction was also needed as a means to test newer and newer orders of bases. Reproduction needs energy in the form of ATP; thus order requires energy. Energy alone could not give the order of life because order is related to a functional goal; energy plus selection can.

There cannot be life without energy, because there cannot be life order without it. Life treads a thin line between order and chaos, related to its use of energy. Energy can be used to build strong chemical bonds between atoms. But life is based mainly on the plasticity of weak bonds that can be continuously broken and re-formed. Life exists in a world of weak bonds. In a world of strong bonds life is impossible because the bonds are essentially unbreakable. That is the realm of rocks and crystals, not of life.

The Connections of Life

The weak bonds involved in life's interactions increase the probability of errors, and life and errors are intimately connected. Errors generate the mutations that are at the base not only of evolution but also of disease. Weakness of connections allows enzymes to interact with substrates, and antibody molecules to change shape when bound to antigen, initiating special reactions such as that leading to complement release. But the weakness of interactions allows also a growth control gene to become a cancer gene, when its base sequence undergoes small changes that allow it to escape its normal controls. Weak interactions are responsible for the numerous ambiguities of life, such as those perturbing the regular differentiation of the sexes and their expression.

The connections of life, however, cannot all be weak; for certain goals great strength is required. Nature achieves strength by *redundancy*—by making multiple connections. Redundancy is built into the structure of antibody molecules, which have two identical binding sites. By binding to two antigenic spots at the surface of a virus, they establish a firm connection with it. The strong connection is needed for the biological effect. It is also a safety feature: occasional encounters with antigenic spots that look like those of the virus do not distract the antibody or cause damage to body components. Also redundant are the complex regulatory pathways that regulate essential functions. Very often nerve signals, hormonal signals, and ionic signals work together: if one fails, regulation can still be maintained, although within a reduced range.

Sometimes life needs irreversible processes; then irreversibility is brought about by some irreversible event such as the cutting off of a piece of protein. We see an application in the assembly of the coat of bacteriophage T4. A special program built into the components allows their orderly assembly. The resulting structure is still weakly connected, however, and is reinforced by the cutting off of bits of various proteins, creating new binding possibilities. These changes make the process irreversible, but there is no harm done because making the phage coat is a one-way process. The coat is a box that, once made with the DNA inside, does not have to open any more. To allow the phage DNA to get out and infect a new bacterium, the coat has a spigot, the tail, which reacts to contacts and opens the box. After the DNA has come out, the now-useless box is discarded.

The same principle is applied in other life processes, such as the assembly of the complement system or the clotting of blood. Both phenomena take place through chain reactions involving many proteins that change shape and interact with each other in a sequential way. Each protein affected by the previous one is an enzyme that cuts a piece off the next protein in the chain, revealing its enzymatic acvitity. Once the final change is made, the product performs its task and is then discarded. All these irreversible processes are not central to life but are specialized tools for obtaining specific results.

Life as a Hodgepodge

It may seem that life aims at specific goals. The coordination of its different functions is amazing, as can be seen in the operation of control systems, from the brain to the chemical communicators. But when we analyze in detail how this coordination is achieved, we gain a different impression. Take, for instance, the growth of an axon, which is fundamental for making the brain network. It is clear that the axon follows many clues, possibly shifting from one to another as it advances and changing direction several times. The signals used, probably different for different axons, seem to be those that became available one after another in evolution, perhaps by accident, and happened to work. Because they worked they were retained. Finally the axons reach a certain kind of neuron, although not a specific one. Many more axons than are needed aim at the same type of neuron and then fight it out among themselves. Those that make it establish a connection with the target neuron; those that fail are withdrawn.

This approach obtains the remarkable result of establishing meaningful functional connections between neurons, and we admire it. But we can see that there is no grand plan; the result is obtained by trial and error. The only beauty of this approach is that it works. This is a fundamental aspect of life: associations are established however possible through the use of a great hodgepodge of clues, signals, molecules. Associations that work are retained, and the others are thrown away. Life is pragmatic; it recognizes only success.

We can recognize also that building and destroying is the fate of life. The bowerbird builds its castle, but goes about demolishing the unguarded castles of its competitors. A growth factor produced by many animal cells stimulates growth of one kind of cells, fibroblasts, but blocks that of another kind, epithelia. These contradictions are possible because life depends on a finely tuned balance of interactions with opposite meanings. Small differences in the complex regulatory circuits can lead to building or destroying. Think of the brain processes involved in the ideation and construction of a bowerbird castle: they probably go on in the bowerbird's brain whether it is contemplating its own or another bird's castle. But then there is a switching point: it is mine; it is yours. One branch leads to preservation; the other, to destruction. The growth factor also confronts in either cell type a certain pathway of enzymes. In one cell it may stimulate the pathway moderately, and in the other, excessively; or perhaps one of the pathways has a branching point that the other does not have. In any case a small difference may again determine the opposing outcome.

In the complex regulation of life, which is dominated by interactions of very low energy, a small detail is often crucial for the end result. A cancer-inducing oncogene (for instance, *myc*) can emerge from the normal proto-oncogene with a variety of changes. We cannot offer a clear rationale for the effects they have, nor can we understand their meaning because we do not understand the complexity of the genetic systems in which the gene operates in different cell types. Any one of the structural rearrangements can disarrange the balance of one system but not of the other.

A House of Cards

Life is an amazing process by which blind matter, using energy, organized itself and formed ordered structures that work on the environment, extracting energy and modifying it in an enormous number of ways. It pulled itself up, as it were, by the bootstraps in a pragmatic way. It used every arrangement that worked, without preconceived plans, and ruthlessly threw away what did not work. Thus it built a house of cards made up of many species and based on the earthly environment. It is a house of cards because it could be blown down by any drastic change of the environment. Yet the construction is so well adapted it seems indestructible. Its strength lies in the fact that it changes all the time: as some cards blow away, they are replaced by others that make the house more stable.

Its stability, however, is always temporary, and its precariousness must be recognized by us humans, who have the power to effect tremendous environmental changes. We must remember that life is more than the human species and that the human species needs the whole of life.

In the most recent step of evolution, the brain—present in some form in all animals—has become the predominant force, reaching its maximum in the human species. The brain offers new solutions to the problems of life, in part reinforcing the tactics adopted by nature, but also offering new ones. In the human species the brain introduces new values, different from those adopted by nature; it creates the new environment of ideas, which become a powerful motor of many aspects of life.

The brain tends to invert the process of the development of life by following plans based on concepts it considers comprehensible rather than following the trial-and-error approach. The significance of this difference can be seen, for instance, in the different ways brain and nature tend to solve the problem of providing edible crops for human consumption. Nature has generated a vast number of species of crop plants, none of them very efficient, but with a great variety of properties. The brain has developed a few of these crops to a very high level of efficiency, discarding and often destroying all the others. A new card has been added to the house, and temporarily it works very well. But what will happen if an important enviromental change—uncontrollable pests, a climatic shift—blows that card away? Nature would react by drawing on the vast resources of plant genes to develop substitutes. The brain is making that impossible by eliminating this immense background: if the card goes, a section of the house will collapse.

To a certain extent the brain can understand the problems it generates. But can it understand them all? Can the brain's approach of planning be combined with nature's of trial and error? Can the brain survive an evolutionary bottleneck? The present state of evolution is perhaps the test of the advanced brain. The next bottleneck may tell whether it has the long-term survival value that is needed for life.

Index